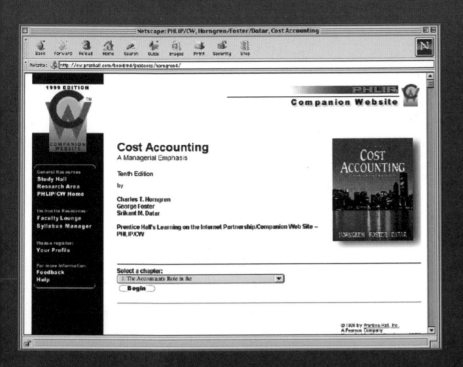

■ SYLLABUS MANAGER:

- ◆ Allows instructors to construct online syllabi tailored to assignments and events for their classes and linked to specific modules on the website and other online content
- ◆ Provides students with quick access to course materials by using a calendar feature found on the navigation bar.

■ FACULTY RESOURCES/LOUNGE:

- ◆ Password protected site
- ◆ Downloads of online supplements
- ◆ Archive of teaching resources created by faculty at other schools using this text
- ◆ Chat room for faculty use only
- ◆ Teaching tools for the "Current Events" and "Internet Exercises"

■ STUDY GUIDE:

- ◆ Separate true/false, multiple-choice, fill-in-the-blank, and essay practice tests for each chapter
- ◆ "Hints" for each problem
- ◆ Immediate feedback on tests with total score, and an explanation provided for each incorrect answer
- ◆ Ability to e-mail results to faculty members or other designated individual
- ◆ All questions created specifically for the web site; no duplication of questions taken from test, text bank, or print study guide

PHLIP/CW is provided free upon adoption
www.prenhall.com/horngren

All Internet Resources are updated every two weeks by PhD-granted professors around the world, as well as a team of full-time technical support staff.

You can always rely on PHLIP/CW to provide you and your students with the services you need!

Remember! Only Prentice Hall offers you a toll-free number for technical support with accounting products.

Simply call **1-800-875-4118** for assistance.

PRENTICE HALL SERIES IN ACCOUNTING

Charles T. Horngren, Consulting Editor

TENTH EDITION

Cost Accounting

A MANAGERIAL EMPHASIS

Charles T. Horngren
Stanford University

George Foster
Stanford University

Srikant M. Datar
Harvard University

with Annotations by
Robert Capettini
San Diego State University

PRENTICE HALL
Upper Saddle River, NJ 07458

Library of Congress Cataloging-in-Publication Data

Horngren, Charles T.
  Cost accounting: a managerial emphasis / Charles T. Horngren,
George Foster, Srikant M. Datar ; annotations by Robert J.
Cappetini.— 10th ed.; annotated instructor's ed.
    928 pp.
  Includes bibliographical references and index.
  ISBN 0-13-760554-4
  1. Cost accounting. 2. Costs, Industrial. I. Foster, George,
1948–   .   II. Datar, Srikant M.   III. Title.
HF5686.C8H59 1999
  658.15'4—dc21   99-27568
                                                     CIP

Executive Editor: *Annie Todd*
Associate Editors: *Kathryn Sheehan;*
            Natacha St. Hill Moore
Editorial Assistant: *Fran Toepfer*
Editor-in-Chief: *P. J. Boardman*
Development Editor: *Dave Cohen*
Director of Development: *Steve Deitmer*
Executive Marketing Manager: *Beth Toland*
Marketing Assistant: *Bob Prokop*
Senior Production Editor: *Anne Graydon*
Associate Managing Editor: *Sondra Greenfield*
Permissions Coordinator: *Monica Stipanov*
Senior Manufacturing Supervisor: *Paul Smolenski*
Senior Manager, Manufacturing
and Prepress: *Vincent Scelta*
Design Director: *Pat Smythe*
Interior Design: *Mary McDonnell*
Photo Researcher: *Teri Stratford*
Image Permissions Supervisor: *Kay Dellosa*
Cover Design: *Lorraine Castellano*
Cover Photo: *Segal/Index Stock Imagery, Inc.*
Composition and Full-service: *Progressive Information
Technologies/Progressive Publishing Alternatives*

To Our Families

Joan, Scott, Mary, Susie, Cathy (CH)
The Foster Family (GF)
Swati, Radhika, Gayatri, Sidharth (SD)

Brief **Contents**

Contents

3
COST-VOLUME-PROFIT ANALYSIS   59

4
JOB COSTING   95

5
ACTIVITY-BASED COSTING AND ACTIVITY-BASED MANAGEMENT   135

PART TWO

Tools for Planning and Control

6

MASTER BUDGET AND RESPONSIBILITY ACCOUNTING 177

7

FLEXIBLE BUDGETS, VARIANCES, AND MANAGEMENT CONTROL: I 219

8

FLEXIBLE BUDGETS, VARIANCES, AND MANAGEMENT CONTROL: II 253

9

INVENTORY COSTING AND CAPACITY ANALYSIS   289

PART THREE
Cost Information for Decisions

10

DETERMINING HOW COSTS BEHAVE   327

11
DECISION MAKING AND RELEVANT
INFORMATION   377

12
PRICING DECISIONS AND COST
MANAGEMENT   421

PART FOUR
Cost Allocation and Revenues

PART FIVE
Quality and JIT

18
SPOILAGE, REWORK, AND SCRAP 647

19
QUALITY, TIME, AND THE THEORY OF CONSTRAINTS 675

20
INVENTORY MANAGEMENT, JUST-IN-TIME, AND BACKFLUSH COSTING 711

PART SIX

Investment Decisions and Management Control Systems

21

CAPITAL BUDGETING AND COST ANALYSIS   747

22

MANAGEMENT CONTROL SYSTEMS, TRANSFER PRICING, AND MULTINATIONAL CONSIDERATIONS   787

23

PERFORMANCE MEASUREMENT, COMPENSATION, AND MULTINATIONAL CONSIDERATIONS   821

Preface

Studying cost accounting is one of the best business investments a student can make. Why? Because success in any organization—from the smallest cornerstore to the largest multinational corporation—requires the use of cost accounting concepts and practices. Cost accounting provides key data to managers for planning and controlling, as well as costing products, services, and customers. Topics covered in this book also are of great value in personal financial management. For example, gaining an understanding of budgeting yields lifelong returns.

The central focus of this book is how cost accounting helps managers make better decisions. Cost accountants are increasingly becoming integral members of decision-making teams instead of just data providers. To link to this decision-making emphasis, the "different costs for different purposes" theme is used throughout this book. By focusing on basic concepts, analyses, uses, and procedures instead of procedures alone, we recognize cost accounting as a managerial tool for business strategy and implementation. We also prepare students for the rewards and challenges facing them in the professional cost accounting world both today and tomorrow.

STRENGTHS OF THE NINTH EDITION RETAINED AND ENHANCED

Reviewers of the ninth edition praised the following features, which have been retained and strengthened in the tenth edition:

- ◆ Exceptionally strong emphasis on managerial uses of cost information
- ◆ Clarity and understandability of the text
- ◆ Excellent balance in integrating modern topics with existing content
- ◆ Emphasis on human behavior aspects
- ◆ Extensive use of real-world examples
- ◆ Ability to teach chapters in difference sequences
- ◆ Excellent quantity, quality and range of assignment material

The first thirteen chapters provide the essence of a one-term (quarter or semester) course. There is ample text and assignment material in the book's twenty-three chapters for a two-term course. This book can be used immediately after the student has had an introductory course in financial accounting. Alternatively, this book can build on an introductory course in managerial accounting.

Deciding on the sequence of chapters in a textbook is a challenge. Every instructor has a favorite way of organizing his or her course. Hence, we present a modular, flexible organization that permits a course to be custom-tailored. *This organization facilitates diverse approaches to teaching and learning.*

As an example of the book's flexibility, consider our treatment of process costing. Process costing is described in Chapters 17 and 18. Instructors interested in filling out a student's perspective of costing systems can move directly from job-order costing described in Chapter 4 to Chapter 17 without interruption in the flow of material. Other instructors may want their students to delve into activity-based costing and budgeting and more decision-oriented topics early in the course. These instructors may prefer to postpone discussion of process costing.

CHANGES IN CONTENT AND PEDAGOGY OF THE TENTH EDITION

The pace of change in organizations continues to be rapid. The tenth edition of *Cost Accounting* reflects changes occurring in the role of cost accounting in organizations and in research on cost accounting. Examples of key additions and changes in the topic areas of the tenth edition are:

1. *Increased coverage of strategic uses of cost information.* A new chapter (13) on Strategy, Balanced Scorecard, and Strategic Profitability Analysis discusses the applications of management to strategy, implementation of strategy, and the balanced scorecard to evaluate strategy, reengineering and downsizing, strategic profitability analysis, and productivity measurement.

2. *Activity-based costing (ABC) introduced in a single chapter* (Chapter 5) with explicit linkages to simpler job-costing systems (presented in Chapter 4). New ABC-related material on budgeting (Chapter 6), variance analysis (Chapters 7 and 8), overhead allocation (Chapter 14), and customer-profitability analysis (Chapter 16) has been added.

3. *Increased attention to decision uses of cost accounting information.* This increase occurs in many topic areas, such as activity-based costing (Chapter 5), variance analysis (Chapters 7 and 8), capacity analysis (Chapter 9), relevant costs and prices (Chapters 11 and 12), and cost allocation (Chapter 14).

4. *Systematic incorporation of new and evolving management thinking* including supply chain analysis (Chapters 1 and 20), theory of constraints (Chapter 19), intangible asset valuation (Chapter 21), and EVA (Chapter 23).

5. *Incorporating advances in technology* into coverage of topics. This addition includes the use of web-technology to fast-track the budgeting process (Chapter 6), use of "push" technology in airline pricing decisions (Chapter 11), and use of the internet in corporate purchasing/supply-chain analysis (Chapter 20).

Major Changes in Content and Sequence

The overwhelming feedback from instructors and students was for a reduction in length. We have reduced the number of chapters in the tenth edition to 23 (from 26 in the ninth edition). This was achieved by consolidating the coverage in three topic areas (cost allocation, inventory management and JIT, and capital budgeting) from two chapters in each case in the ninth edition to a single chapter in the tenth edition. One chapter in the ninth edition (Chapter 24) was eliminated and much of its content incorporated into other chapters. In addition, special attention has been given to streamlining presentations in every chapter of the book as well as providing better and clearer explanations. Each chapter was scrutinized by knowledgeable critics before a final draft was completed. The result is a shorter and more student-friendly book.

Specific major changes in content and-in the sequence of individual chapters are:

1. Chapter 4 now covers the basics of job costing methods, using manufacturing as the detailed example followed by examples from the service and merchandising sectors. Chapter 5 is a new chapter on activity-based costing that uses a new illustrative example and draws on material in both Chapters 4 and 5 of the ninth edition. The same seven-step approach to job costing used in Chapter 4 of the tenth edition is contained in Chapter 5. Chapter 5 focuses on how ABC modifies the implementation of the basic steps. The cost hierarchy is discussed as an integral part of Chapter 5. These two chapters explain product costing using a single cost-pool system, a departmental costing system, and an ABC system. Chapter 5 also presents activity-based management (ABM), using ABC information for management decisions.

2. Chapter 13 is a new chapter that describes the applications of management accounting to strategy. This chapter covers topics on the implementation of strategy using the balanced scorecard, a new method by which accounting information can be used to evaluate strategy, reengineering, and downsizing.

3. Chapters 14 through 23 of the tenth edition have been restructured to consolidate material in the ninth edition:

◆ Chapter 14 on "Cost Allocation" consolidates Chapters 13 and 14 of the ninth edition.

◆ Chapter 20 on "Inventory Management, Just-in-Time, and Backflush Costing" consolidates Chapters 20 and 21 of the ninth edition.

OVERTURE

"Cost Accounting is music to your ears!"

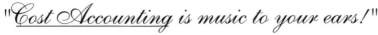

COST ACCOUNTING, *Tenth Edition*
Charles T. Horngren, George Foster, and Srikant M. Datar

"It is obvious why this is . . . the leading text in the field. The writing is excellent, the organization of the chapters is excellent. The material is accurate and timely."
– Leslie Kren, *University of Wisconsin, Milwaukee*
"The rewrite of Chapter 1 is especially good. Decision making is definitely the focus of Cost Accounting.*"*
–Jan Pitera, *Broome Community College*

◆ Activity-based-costing (ABC) is now consolidated into a single new Chapter 5.

"The authors have done a superb job on the revision and enhancement of what for years has been the leading text in the field."
–Russell A. Taussig,
University of Hawaii

◆ Streamlining of material has decreased the number of chapters from 26 to 23 chapters.

◆ The quality of writing has been enhanced, especially in the topics of cost-volume-profit analysis, job costing methods, activity-based costing, variance analysis, and process costing.

"The manuscript seems much more readable and crisp in approach. I eagerly await my copy of the tenth edition. I trust I will be able to teach from it this coming fall semester."
–Jean Hawkins,
William Jewell College

◆ An innovative Chapter 13 describes the applications of management accounting to strategy.

"The authors have done an outstanding job in relating the role of the accountant to the formulation and control of top-level corporate strategy."
–Russell Taussig

◆ An extensive technology support program–video, software, and multiple Internet solutions–is available to adopters.

◆ Extensive links to actual company practice appear throughout the book.

"Concepts in Action and the Surveys of Company Practice pieces convey the perception of cutting edge and an air of freshness to the chapters."
–Gim Seow, *University of Connecticut*

◆ Chapter 21 on "Capital Budgeting" consolidates Chapters 22 and 23 of the ninth edition.

◆ Chapter 13 Appendix ("Productivity Measurement") of the tenth edition draws on material from Chapter 24 of the ninth edition.

◆ Chapter 16 Appendix ("Mix and Yield Variances for Substitutable Inputs") of the tenth edition draws on material from Chapter 24 of the ninth edition.

◆ Chapter 17 Appendix (Operation Costing) draws on material from Chapter 20 of the ninth edition.

4. Chapter 17 (Process Costing) has been rewritten, using the five-step approach of the eighth edition, in place of the four-step approach used in the ninth edition. The concept of equivalent units and the steps in the various methods of process costing (weighted-average, FIFO, and standard costing) are explained in more detail. Chapter 18 (Spoilage, Rework, and Scrap) uses the same five-step approach in Chapter 17 of the tenth edition.

5. Numerical company examples in key chapters have been updated or revised to streamline the exposition and provide better explanations. Chapter 6 has a new budgeting example of budgeting for a furniture manufacturer. Chapter 9 has a single coordinating example to illustrate year-by-year differences among absorption, variable, and throughput costing. Chapter 11 has a new example of relevant revenues/relevant costs for sales office closings. Chapter 16 has a new example to illustrate sales variance analysis in multi-product settings.

The Solutions Manual for instructors includes a chapter-by-chapter listing of the major changes in the text of the tenth edition.

Assignment Material

The tenth edition continues the widely applauded tight link between text and assignment material formed in previous editions. We have also significantly expanded the assignment material, provided more structure, and added greater variety.

End-of-chapter assignment material is divided into four groups: Questions, Exercises, Problems, and a Collaborative Learning Problem. Questions require students to understand basic concepts and the meaning of key terms. Exercises are short, structured assignments that test basic issues presented in the chapter. Problems are longer and more difficult assignments. Each chapter has an ethics-related problem. The Collaborative Learning Problem is the last assignment in each chapter. These problems are group assignments that require students to think critically about a particular problem or specific business situation.

ILLUSTRATIONS OF ACTUAL BUSINESSES

Students become highly motivated to learn cost accounting if they can relate the subject matter to the real world. We have spent considerable time interacting with the business community, investigating new uses of cost accounting information and gaining insight into how changes in technology are affecting the roles of cost accounting information. Real-world illustrations are found in many parts of the text.

Concepts in Action Boxes. Found in many chapters, these boxes discuss how cost accounting concepts are applied by individual companies. Examples are drawn from many different countries, including the *United States* (Cummins Engine on p. 9, Colorscope on p. 108, Wells Fargo Bank on p. 154, Commonwealth Edison on p. 309, American Airlines on p. 391, and Cincinnati Bengals on p. 758, *Brazil* (Volkswagen on p. 386), *Canada* (Toronto Dominion Bank on p. 190), *Germany* (Mueller Lehmkuhl on p. 72), *Indonesia* (Asia-Pacific Rayon on p. 269), and the *United Kingdom* (Cooperative Bank on p. 342 and Allied-Signal Skelmersdale on p. 694).

New boxes covering the use by managers of the internet have been added. These include budgeting (p. 190), pricing decisions (p. 391), and procurement/selling (p. 722).

These Concepts in Action boxes cover a diverse series of industries including airline transportation, automobiles, banking, ceramics, computers, electronics, electric utilities, internet equipment, manufacturing, leasing, and sporting teams.

Surveys of Company Practice Boxes. Results from surveys in more than 15 countries are cited in the many Surveys of Company Practice boxes found throughout the book. Examples include:

◆ Activities of a management accountant (p. 14)—cites evidence from the United States and Canada.

◆ Management purposes for classifying costs (p. 34)—cites evidence from Australia, Japan and the United Kingdom

◆ Activity-based cost information (p. 151)—cites evidence from United States, Canada, Ireland, New Zealand and the United Kingdom

◆ Standard costs (p. 226)—cites evidence from United States, Ireland, Japan, Sweden and the United Kingdom.

◆ Variable costing (p. 302)—cites evidence from the United States, Canada, Ireland, Japan, Sweden, and the United Kingdom.

◆ Pricing practices (p. 438)—cites evidence from the United States, Australia, Ireland, Japan and the United Kingdom.

◆ Purposes of cost allocation (p. 499)—cites evidence from the United States, Australia, Canada, and the United Kingdom.

◆ Customer profitability analysis (p. 585)—cites evidence from the United States, Australia and the United Kingdom.

◆ Capital budgeting practices (p. 761)—cites evidence from the United States, Australia, Canada, Ireland, Japan, Scotland, South Korea, and the United Kingdom.

◆ Transfer pricing practices (p. 802)—cites evidence from the United States, Australia, Canada, India, Japan, New Zealand, and the United Kingdom.

◆ Performance measures (p. 831)—cites evidence from the United States, Australia, Germany, Italy, Japan, Sweden, and the United Kingdom.

This extensive survey evidence enables students to see that many of the concepts they are learning are widely used around the globe.

Photos from Actual Companies. All chapters open with a photo that illustrates an important concept discussed in that chapter. These photos feature many different companies including Boeing (p. 327), Carlton Hotel (p. 821), The Gap (p. 377), General Motors (p. 135), John Deere (p. 95), PepsiCo (p. 27), Symantec (p. 59), Tabasco (p. 607), Xerox (p. 675), and Yahoo! (p. 1).

Each Concepts in Action box also has an accompanying photo.

SUPPLEMENTS TO THE TENTH EDITION

A complete package of supplements is available to assist students and instructors in using this book. Supplements available to students include the following:

◆ **Student Guide and Review Manual** by John K. Harris.

◆ **Student Solutions Manual** by Charles T. Horngren, George Foster, and Srikant M. Datar.

◆ **Computerized Applications in Cost Accounting** by David M. Buehlmann and Dennis P. Curtin.

◆ **ABC CD-ROM** EasyABC Quick™ helps you create a model of a business and identify and analyze the real costs associated with activities, processes, and products. EasyABC Quick includes extensive on-line help and is an important tool to help accelerate learning and understanding of activity-based costing.

- ◆ **PHLIP/CW** (Prentice Hall's Learning on the Internet Partnership/Companion Web site at **www.prenhall.com/horngren**) offers the most expansive Internet-based support available. Our Web site provides a wealth of resources for students and faculty.
- ◆ **Spreadsheet Templates** by Albert Fisher, Community College of Southern Nevada.

Supplements available to instructors include the following:

- ◆ **Annotated Instructor's Edition** with annotations by Robert J. Capettini, San Diego State University.
- ◆ **Instructor's Manual and Media Guide** by Jean L. Hawkins, William Jewell College.
- ◆ **Test Item File** by Marvin L. Bouillon, Iowa State University, and Thomas Hoar, Houston Community College.
- ◆ **Prentice Hall Custom Test** by ESA, Inc.
- ◆ **Solutions Manual** by Charles T. Horngren, George Foster, and Srikant M. Datar.
- ◆ **Solutions Transparencies** by Horngren, Foster, and Datar.
- ◆ **Solutions Manual for Computerized Applications in Cost Accounting** by David M. Buehlmann and Dennis P. Curtin.
- ◆ **Solutions to Spreadsheet Templates** by Albert Fisher
- ◆ **Videos:** Beverly Amer, Northern Arizona University
- ◆ **Powerpoint Presentation:** Olga Quintana, University of Miami
- ◆ **WebCT** Customize your own on-line accounting course with WebCT. You can create full-length on-line courses or simply produce on-line materials to supplement existing courses. Even if you have no technical experience or technical knowledge, WebCT is easy to use.
- ◆ **PHLIP/CW** (Prentice Hall's Learning on the Internet Partnership/Companion Web site at **www.prenhall.com/horngren**) offers the most expansive Internet-based support available. Our Web site provides a wealth of resources for students and faculty.

ACKNOWLEDGMENTS

We are indebted to many for their ideas and assistance. Our primary thanks go to the many academics and practitioners who have advanced our knowledge of cost accounting.

The package of teaching material we present is the work of many skillful and valued team members. John K. Harris aided us immensely at all stages in the development and production of this book. He critiqued the ninth edition and gave a detailed review of the manuscript for the tenth edition. Robert J. Capettini reviewed the manuscript and gave suggestions for improvement in addition to working on the *Annotated Instructor's Edition.* Sheryl Powers and Emanuel Schwarz gave much valued input on both the text and solutions manual. Beverly Amer proved to be an invaluable resource in researching and writing the photo essays and video cases.

Professors providing detailed written reviews of the previous edition or comments on our drafts of this edition include:

Kenneth M. Boze,
University of Alaska, Anchorage

Leslie G. Eldenburg,
University of Arizona

Amin A. Elmalllah,
California State University, Sacramento

Martin G. Fennema,
Florida State University

Rosalie C. Hallbauer,
Florida International University

Jean L. Hawkins,
William Jewell College

Jiunn C. Huang,
San Francisco State University

Larry N. Killough,
Virginia Polytechnic Institute and State University

Leslie Kren,
University of Wisconsin, Madison

Gary J. Mann,
University of Texas at El Paso

Arijit Mukherji,
University of Minnesota

Janice Pitera,
Broome Community College

Gim S. Seow,
University of Connecticut

Bin N. Srinidhi,
Rutgers University

Russell A. Taussig,
University of Hawaii

Audrey G. Taylor,
Wayne State University

Carolyn A. Streuly

Peter D. Woodlock,
Youngstown State University

Thomas L. Zeller,
Loyola University, Chicago

Technical Reviewers

Robert H. Bauman, Allan Hancock College; Alice Sineath, Forsyth Technical Community College; Peter D. Woodlock, Youngstown State University

The faculty participating in the many focus groups on the ninth edition provided highly valued feedback. Many students provided input on this and the previous edition including Sudhatar Balachandran, Susan Cohen, Elizabeth Demers, Philip Joos, Patricia Joseph, Kazbi Kothaval, Mee Sook Lee, Erik Steiner, and Kenton Yee. The assistance of Kathy Chiu, Richard Corcoran, Marko Curavic, Ignacio Mijares, Guy Nachtomi, Aradhana Sarin, Jason Thomas, Oltac Unsal, and David Yoon in checking the Solutions Manual was much appreciated. In addition we have received helpful suggestions from many users, unfortunately too numerous to be mentioned here. The tenth edition is much improved by the feedback and interest of all these people. We are very appreciative of this support.

Our association with CAM-I has been a source of much stimulation as well as enjoyment. CAM-I has played a pivotal role in extending the frontiers of knowledge on cost management. We appreciate our extended and continued interaction with Jim Brimson, Callie Berliner, Charles Marx, R. Steven Player, Tom Pryor, Mike Roberts, and Pete Zampino.

We thank the people at Prentice Hall for their hard work and dedication, including Annie Todd, Steve Deitmer, and David Cohen, Anne Graydon, Beth Toland, Paul Smolenski, Natacha St. Hill Moore, Kathryn Sheehan, and Fran Toepfer, Pat Smythe, and Lorraine Castellano. We would also like to thank Sondra Greenfield, Monica Stipanov, Vincent Scelta, Bob Prokop, P. J. Boardman, Jim Boyd, Michael Weinstein, and Brian Kibby for their support and encouragement throughout the process, and Donna King at Progressive Publishing Alternatives.

Jiranee Tongudai managed the production aspects of all the manuscript preparation with superb skill and much grace. We are deeply appreciative of her good spirits, loyalty, and ability to stay calm in the most hectic of times. The constant support of Niesha Bryant, Katie Haskin, Chris Lion, Carla West, and Debbie Wheeler is greatly appreciated.

Appreciation also goes to the American Institute of Certified Public Accountants, the Institute of Management Accountants, the Society of Management Accountants of Canada, the Certified General Accountants Association of Canada, the Financial Executive Institute of America, and many other publishers and companies for their generous permission to quote from their publications. Problems from the Uniform CPA examinations are designated (CPA); problems from the Certified Management Accountant examination are designated (CMA); problems from the Canadian examinations administered by the Society of Management Accountants are designated (SMA); problems from the Certified General Accountants Association are designated (CGA). Many of these problems are adapted to highlight particular points.

We are grateful to the professors who contributed assignment material for this edition. Their names are indicated in parentheses at the start of their specific problems.

Comments from users are welcome.

CHARLES T. HORNGREN, GEORGE FOSTER, SRIKANT M. DATAR

About the Authors

CHARLES T. HORNGREN is the Edmund W. Littlefield Professor Emeritus of Accounting at Stanford University. A graduate of Marquette University, he received his MBA from Harvard University and his Ph.D. from the University of Chicago. He is also the recipient of honorary doctorates from Marquette University and De-Paul University.

A Certified Public Accountant, Horngren served on the Accounting Principles Board for six years, the Financial Accounting Standards Board Advisory Council for five years, and the Council of the American Institute of Certified Public Accountants for three years. In addition, he served as a trustee of the Financial Accounting Foundation, which oversees the Financial Accounting Standards Board and the Government Accounting Standards Board for six years.

A member of the American Accounting Association, Horngren has also served as its President and Director of Research. He received the Outstanding Accounting Educator Award in 1973, when the association initiated an annual series of such awards.

The California Certified Public Accountants Foundation gave Horngren its Faculty Excellence Award in 1975 and its Distinguished Professor Award in 1983. He is the first person to have received both awards. In 1985, the American Institute of Certified Public Accountants presented him with its first Outstanding Educator Award. Five years later, he was elected to the Accounting Hall of Fame.

In 1993, Horngren was named Accountant of the Year, Education, by the national professional accounting fraternity, Beta Alpha Psi.

Professor Horngren is a member of the National Association of Accountants, and served on its research planning committee for three years. He was also a member of the Board of Regents, Institute of Management Accounting, which administers the Certified Management Accountant examinations.

Charles T. Horngren, the Consulting Editor for the Prentice Hall Series in Accounting, is the coauthor of six other books published by Prentice Hall: *Principles of Financial and Management Accounting: A Sole Proprietorship Approach and Principles of Financial and Management Accounting: A Corporate Approach*, 1994 (with Walter T. Harrison, Jr., and Michael A. Robinson); *Introduction to Financial Accounting*, Fifth Edition, 1993 (with Gary L. Sundem and John Elliott), *Introduction to Management Accounting*, Ninth Edition, 1993 (with Gary L. Sundem), *Financial Accounting*, 1992, and *Accounting*, Second Edition, 1993 (with Walter T. Harrison, Jr.).

GEORGE FOSTER is the Paul L. and Phyllis Wattis Professor of Management at Stanford University. He graduated with a university medal from the University of Sydney and has a Ph.D. from Stanford University. He has been awarded honorary doctorates from the University of Ghent, Belgium, and from the University of Vaasa, Finland. He has received the Outstanding Educator Award from the American Accounting Association.

Foster has received the Distinguished Teaching Award at Stanford University and the Faculty Excellence Award from the California Society of Certified Public Accountants. He has been a Visiting Professor to Mexico for the American Accounting Association.

Research awards Foster has received include the Competitive Manuscript Competition Award of the American Accounting Association, the Notable Contribution to Accounting Literature Award of the American Institute of Certified Public Accountants, and the Citation for Meritorious Contribution to Accounting Literature Award of the Australian Society of Accountants.

He is the author of *Financial Statement Analysis*, published by Prentice Hall. He is co-author of *Activity-Based Management Consortium Study (APQC and CAM–I)* and *Marketing, Cost Management and Management Accounting (CAM–I)*. He is also co-author of two monographs published by the American Accounting Association—*Security Analyst Multi-Year Earnings Forecasts and The Capital Market* and *Market Microstructure and Capital Market Information Content Research*. Journals publishing his articles include *Abacus, The Accounting Review, Harvard Business Review, Journal of Accounting and Economics, Journal of Accounting Research, Journal of Cost Management, Journal of Management Accounting Research, Management Accounting*, and *Review of Accounting Studies*.

Foster works actively with many companies, including Apple Computer, ARCO, BHP, Digital Equipment Corp., Exxon, Frito-Lay Corp., Hewlett-Packard, McDonalds Corp., Octel Communications, PepsiCo, Santa Fe Corp., and Wells Fargo. He also has worked closely with Computer Aided Manufacturing-International (CAM-I) in the development of a framework for modern cost management practices. Foster has presented seminars on new developments in cost accounting in North and South America, Asia, Australia, and Europe.

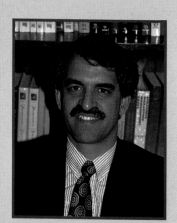

SRIKANT M. DATAR is the Arthur Lowes Dickinson Professor of Business Administration at Harvard University. A graduate with distinction from the University of Bombay, he received gold medals upon graduation from the Indian Institute of Management, Ahmedabad, and the Institute of Cost and Works Accountants of India. A Chartered Accountant, he holds two masters degrees and a Ph.D. from Stanford University.

Cited by his students as a dedicated and innovative teacher, Datar received the George Leland Bach Award for Excellence in the Classroom at Carnegie Mellon University and the Distinguished Teaching Award at Stanford University.

Datar has published his research in various journals, including *The Accounting Review, Contemporary Accounting Research, Journal of Accounting, Auditing and Finance, Journal of Accounting and Economics, Journal of Accounting Research*, and *Management Science*. He has also served on the editorial board of several journals and presented his research to corporate executives and academic audiences in North America, South America, Asia, and Europe.

Datar has worked with many organizations, including Apple Computer, AT&T, Boeing, British Columbia Telecommunications, The Cooperative Bank, Du Pont, Ford, General Motors, Hewlett-Packard, Kodak, Mellon Bank, Novartis, Solectron, Store 24, TRW, VISA, and the World Bank. He is a member of the American Accounting Association and the Institute of Management Accountants.

1

The Accountant's Role in the Organization

When you have finished studying this chapter, you should be able to

1. Identify three major purposes of accounting systems
2. Describe cost accounting and its relation to management accounting and financial accounting
3. Distinguish between the planning and control decisions of managers
4. Distinguish among the problem-solving, scorekeeping, and attention-directing roles of a management accountant
5. Describe the set of business functions in the value chain
6. Identify four key themes that are important to managers attaining success in their planning and control decisions
7. Describe three guidelines that help management accountants increase their value to managers
8. Understand how cost accounting fits into an organization's structure
9. Understand the importance of professional ethics to management accountants

Successful companies, such as Yahoo!, are built on a foundation of creative and hard-working teams and an attention to the management of revenues and costs.

M odern cost accounting provides key information to managers for their decision making. Modern cost accounting cuts across all facets of the organization. The study of modern cost accounting yields insights into both the manager's role and the accountant's role in an organization. The number of large companies with senior executives who have accounting backgrounds—Coca-Cola, Fidelity Investments, Loral Aerospace, and Nike, to name but a few—illustrates the superb training that accounting provides managers.

This book has management decision making as its dominant focus. The key issue we examine is how accounting can provide financial and nonfinancial information that will help the collective decision making throughout the organization. We start by considering the major purposes of accounting systems.

THE MAJOR PURPOSES OF ACCOUNTING SYSTEMS

Accounting is a major means of helping managers (a) to administer each of the activity or functional areas for which they are responsible, and (b) to coordinate those activities or functions within the framework of the organization as a whole. This book focuses on how accounting does, in fact, assist managers in these tasks. Accounting provides information for three major purposes:

1. *Routine internal reporting* for the decisions of managers. Such information is provided for decisions that occur with some regularity. For example, an oil company such as Texaco makes daily planning decisions on the price they charge retail outlets (such as service stations) for refined oil. Daily reports on the gross margin Texaco earns for refined oil is one input into these pricing decisions. As a second example, Marriott monitors weekly cost reports (covering items such as labor and energy) at each of its hotels as part of its cost control practices.

2. *Nonroutine internal reporting* for the decisions of managers. This information affects decisions that occur irregularly or without precedent. For example, a planning decision by Xerox to have an independent company manage its information technology function (that is, outsourcing this function) included analysis of cost data that were specifically collected for that decision. Xerox had not previously made a decision of this type. As a second example, a consumer products company (such as H. J. Heinz Company) may design a special cost tracking system to manage the costs of implementing a recent product recall due to an unprecedented safety scare.

3. *External reporting* to investors, government authorities, and other outside parties on the organization's financial position, operations, and related activities. This information is used by some regulatory bodies such as the Financial Accounting Standards Board or the Internal Revenue Service. In other cases, the information is used by managers in other organizations in their decision making. For example, a company may provide its financial statements to a potential new supplier who is assessing the financial risk of selling on credit instead of cash. A second example would be the financial statements that a movie company, such as Twentieth-Century Fox, provides to screen stars whose compensation includes a percentage of movie revenues or movie profits.

Each major purpose of accounting often requires a different way of presenting or reporting the information in an accounting system. An ideal data base (sometimes called a data warehouse or infobarn) consists of small detailed bits of information that can be used for multiple purposes. Accountants combine or adjust ("slice or dice") these data to answer the questions from particular internal or external users.

MANAGEMENT ACCOUNTING, FINANCIAL ACCOUNTING, AND COST ACCOUNTING

A distinction is often made between management accounting and financial accounting. **Management accounting** measures and reports financial and nonfinancial information that helps managers make decisions to fulfill the goals of an organization.

Management accounting focuses on internal reporting. **Financial accounting** focuses on reporting to external parties. It measures and records business transactions and provides financial statements that are based on generally accepted accounting principles. Managers are responsible for the financial statements issued to investors, government regulators, and other outside parties. Moreover, executive compensation is often directly affected by the numbers in these financial statements. Therefore, managers are interested in both management accounting and financial accounting.

Cost accounting provides information for both management accounting and financial accounting. It measures and reports financial and nonfinancial information that relates to the cost of acquiring or consuming resources by an organization. Cost accounting includes those parts of both *management accounting* and *financial accounting* where cost information is collected or analyzed.

The internal-external distinction just mentioned is only one of several major differences between management accounting and financial accounting. Others include management accounting's emphasis on the future (budgeting) and on influencing the behavior of managers and employees. Noteworthy too is that management accounting is not nearly as restricted by generally accepted accounting principles (GAAP) as is financial accounting. For example, managers may feel free to charge interest on owners' capital to help judge a division's performance even though such a charge is not allowable under GAAP.

Reports such as balance sheets, income statements, and statements of cash flow are common to both management accounting and financial accounting. In short, most companies adhere to, or only mildly depart from, GAAP for their basic internal financial statements. Why? Because accrual accounting provides a uniform way to measure an organization's financial performance for both internal and external purposes. But management accounting is more wide-ranging than financial accounting. It embraces more extensively such topics as the development and implementation of strategies and policies, budgeting, special studies and forecasts, influence on employee behavior, and nonfinancial as well as financial information.

Cost Management and Accounting Systems

The term *cost management* is widely used today. Unfortunately, no uniform definition exists. We use **cost management** to describe the activities of managers in short-run and long-run planning and control of costs. For example, managers make decisions regarding material usage or changes of plant processes and product designs. Information from accounting systems helps managers make such decisions. But the systems and the information by themselves are not cost management.

Cost management has a broad focus. For example, it includes (but is not confined to) the continuous reduction of costs. Indeed, the planning and control of costs is often inextricably linked with revenue and profit planning. For instance, to enhance revenues and profits, managers often deliberately incur additional costs for advertising and product modifications.

Cost management is not practiced in isolation. It is often carried out as a key part of general management strategies and their implementation. Examples include programs that enhance customer satisfaction and quality and programs that promote "blockbuster" new product development.

We now illustrate the important contribution of management accounting to the planning and control decisions of managers.

PLANNING AND CONTROL DECISIONS

Study Exhibit 1-1. It provides an overview of how one management accounting system plays a pivotal role in both *planning* and *control* decisions at the *Daily Sporting News* (DSN). The system is designed to help the collective decisions throughout the organization. Note that:

◆ **Planning** is deciding on organization goals, predicting results under various alternative ways of achieving those goals, and then deciding how to attain the desired goals.

EXHIBIT 1-1

How Accounting Facilitates Planning and Control at *The Daily Sporting News*

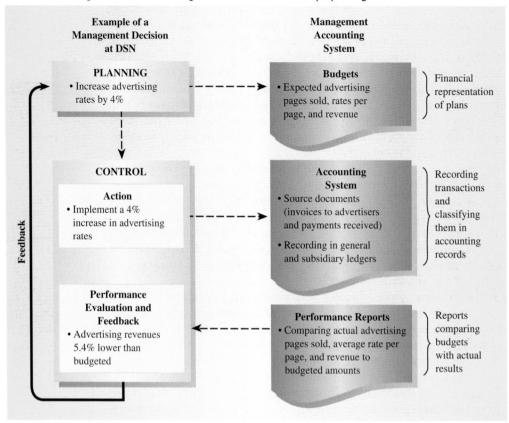

Points to Stress Planning and control are distinct activities, but they go hand in hand. To maximize the benefits from planning (e.g., budgeting), the mgr. should use that plan as a benchmark for controlling (i.e., assessing the effectiveness and efficiency of implementation). Conversely, it is difficult to control activities without a plan or budget.

Curriculum Linkage Many students have learned about *management by exception* in management and production courses. Instructors can reinforce this by asking students to illustrate this concept (and the role acctg. information plays in management by exception) in the context of the students' work experiences.

◆ **Control** is (a) deciding on, and taking, actions that implement the planning decisions, and (b) deciding on performance evaluation and the related feedback that will help future decision making.

The left side of Exhibit 1-1 provides an overview of this process. The right side highlights how the management accounting system facilitates decisions.

Consider first the planning decisions at DSN. A key goal of DSN is to increase operating income. To achieve this goal, three main alternatives were considered:

1. Change the selling price per newspaper,
2. Change the rate per page charged to advertisers, or
3. Reduce labor costs by having fewer workers at DSN's printing facility.

DSN's editor, Naomi Crawford, decided to increase advertising rates by 4% to $5,200 per page for March 2001. She budgeted advertising revenues to be $4,160,000 ($5,200 × 800 pages predicted to be sold in March 2001). A **budget** is the quantitative expression of a proposed plan of action by management for a future time period and is an aid to the coordination and implementation of the plan. Budgets are not only essential to planning, but are also an integral part of control. The information used to project budgeted amounts frequently includes past financial and nonfinancial information routinely recorded in management accounting systems.

Now consider DSN's control decisions. One such decision involves how to communicate the new advertising rate schedule to DSN's sales representatives and advertisers. Control also includes performance evaluation decisions, such as a monthly "attainment of manager objectives" review in which actual results are compared to budgeted amounts. During March 2001, DSN sold advertising, sent out invoices, and received payments. These invoices and receipts were recorded in the

EXHIBIT 1-2
Performance Report of Advertising Revenues at *The Daily Sporting News* for March 2001

(1)	Actual Result (2)	Budgeted Amount (3)	Difference: (Actual Result − Budgeted Amount) (4) = (2) − (3)	Difference as a Percentage of Budgeted Amount (5) = (4) ÷ (3)
◆ Advertising pages sold	760 pages	800 pages	40 pages Unfavorable	5.0% Unfavorable
◆ Average rate per page	$5,080	$5,200	$120 Unfavorable	2.3% Unfavorable
◆ Advertising revenues	$3,860,800	$4,160,000	$299,200 Unfavorable	7.2% Unfavorable

accounting system. Advertising revenues for March 2001 are the aggregate of the advertising done in March 2001 for each individual account. Exhibit 1-2 shows DSN's performance report of advertising revenues for March 2001. This report indicates that 760 pages of advertising (40 pages less than the budgeted 800 pages) were sold in March 2001. The average rate per page was $5,080 compared with the budgeted $5,200 rate, yielding actual advertising revenues in March 2001 of $3,860,800. The actual advertising revenues in March 2001 are $299,200 less than the budgeted $4,160,000.

The performance report in Exhibit 1-2 could spur investigation and further decisions. For example, did the Marketing Department make sufficient efforts to convince advertisers that, even with the new rate of $5,200 per page, advertising in the DSN was a good buy? Why was the actual average rate per page $5,080 instead of the budgeted rate of $5,200? Did some sales representatives offer discounted rates? Did other newspapers experience a comparable decline in advertising revenues? Answers to these questions could prompt Crawford to take subsequent actions, including, for example, motivating marketing to renew efforts to promote advertising by existing and potential advertisers.

A well-conceived plan includes enough flexibility so that managers can seize opportunities unforeseen at the time the plan is formulated. In no case should control mean that managers cling to a preexisting plan when unfolding events indicate that actions not encompassed by the original plan would offer better results for the organization.

Feedback: Linking Planning and Control

The main link between planning and control is provided by feedback—see Exhibit 1-1. **Feedback** involves managers examining past performance and systematically exploring alternative ways to make better informed decisions in the future. Feedback can lead to a diverse set of changes, including changes in goals, in the way decision alternatives are identified, and in the broadness of the information collected when making predictions. Management accountants can play a key role in this link between planning and control. We now consider three specific roles management accountants perform to further illustrate their decision support.

Problem-Solving, Scorekeeping, and Attention-Directing Roles

Management accountants perform three important roles—problem-solving, scorekeeping, and attention directing.

- **Problem solving**—Comparative analysis for decision making. This role asks, of the several alternatives available, which is the best? An example is DSN comparing the expected revenues and expected costs of proposals from three different organizations to develop an Internet version of its *Daily Sporting News*.

- **Scorekeeping**—Accumulating data and reporting reliable results to all levels of management. This role asks how am I doing? Examples at DSN are the recording of revenues, purchases of newsprint paper, and payment of payroll.

Points to Stress When the director of finance reports to the division president, the president is more likely to see the director of finance as a "helper." However, the director of finance's perceived (or actual) independence may be compromised if she reports directly to the executive in charge of the unit for which she is keeping score. This ethical issue arises in Exer. 1-24 and Prob. 1-28.

Points to Stress/Reinforcing Problems The necessity for mgt. accountants to play "helper" (attention-directing/problem-solving) and "watchdog" (scorekeeping) roles simultaneously underscores the importance of interpersonal skills. Exer. 1-18 and 1-19 and Prob. 1-27 cover the scorekeeping, attention-directing, and problem-solving functions.

Example Product-cost information permeates all 3 roles. In the *scorekeeping* role, accountants accumulate product-cost information for both external and internal reporting. Product-cost information can help identify cost mgt. opportunities (i.e., *attention-directing*), and it is used in make–buy decisions where mgrs. compare the cost of making the product or component to the cost of buying it from an external supplier (i.e., *problem solving*).

◆ **Attention directing**—Helping managers properly focus their attention. This role asks which opportunities and problems should I look into? Examples at DSN are (a) the number of unsold copies of the DSN returned per day by its sales outlets, and (b) the daily utility costs of operating the printing presses. Attention directing should focus on all opportunities to add value to an organization, not just cost-reduction opportunities.

Management accountants serve each of these three roles in both planning decisions and control decisions. For planning decisions, the problem-solving role is most marked. Consider DSN's planning decision to increase operating income by increasing advertising rates per page (see Exhibit 1-1). The management accountant could provide information about past increases or decreases in advertising rates at DSN and the subsequent changes in advertising revenues. Information on advertising rates charged by competing media outlets (including other newspapers) could also be collected and analyzed by the management accountant in this problem-solving role. The management challenge at DSN is to increase operating income. The management accountant collects and analyzes information to assist the manager in making a better decision about whether to increase the advertising rate per page, and, if so, the magnitude of the increase.

For control decisions at DSN (which include both actions to implement planning decisions and decisions about performance evaluation), the scorekeeping and attention-directing roles are most important. Information is fed back to managers in these two roles. An example of the scorekeeping role is the accounting system recording details of advertising revenues for the DSN and reporting a summary of them in the monthly income statement. An example of the attention-directing role would be a report that highlights the reduced March 2001 advertising revenues with details of the specific advertising accounts that have reduced or stopped advertising in the DSN after the advertising rate increase was announced. Managers could then decide to target these advertising accounts for intensive follow-up by DSN sales representatives.

Managers are in a continual process of decision making. Information used in the scorekeeping and attention-directing roles often leads to subsequent planning decisions. Information that prompts a planning decision is frequently reanalyzed and supplemented by the management accountant in the problem-solving decision support role. There is ongoing interaction between planning and control decisions. Consequently, management accountants often are simultaneously performing two or all of the problem-solving, scorekeeping, and attention-directing roles.

Managers are best served by the management accounting information that is both relevant and timely. Management accountants increasingly view managers as their customers. For example, a management accounting group at Johnson & Johnson (the manufacturer of many consumer products, such as Band Aids) has a vision statement including the phrases "delight our customers" and "be the best." The success of management accounting depends on whether the planning and control decisions of managers are improved by the accounting information provided to them. Nortel, the global telecommunications company, has its managers evaluate the accounting group when major changes in the accounting systems are made. The support of managers is essential to management accountants being allocated the sizable resources (such as for computer software) required to provide adequate decision support.

THE VALUE CHAIN OF BUSINESS FUNCTIONS

OBJECTIVE 5

Describe the set of business functions in the value chain

Planning and control decisions focus on one or more different business functions in which both managers and management accountants perform important roles. The term **value chain** refers to the sequence of business functions in which usefulness is added to the products or services of an organization. The term *value* is used because as the usefulness of the product or service is increased, so is its value to the customer. Exhibit 1-3 shows six business functions. Here we illustrate how these functions apply to a SONY television set. Management accountants provide decision support for managers in each of these six business functions.

EXHIBIT 1-3
Managers in Different Parts of the Value Chain

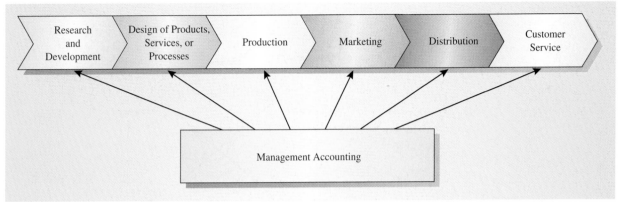

- **Research and development**—the generation of, and experimentation with, ideas related to new products, services, or processes. At SONY, this function includes research on alternative ways of television signal transmission (such as analog or digital) and on the clarity of different shapes of television screens.

- **Design of products, services, or processes**—the detailed planning and engineering of products, services, or processes. Design at Sony includes determining the number of component parts in a television set and the effect of alternative product designs on manufacturing costs.

- **Production**—the acquisition, coordination, and assembly of resources to produce a product or deliver a service. Production of a SONY television set includes the acquisition and assembly of the electronic parts, the cabinet, and the packaging used for shipping.

- **Marketing**—the manner by which companies promote and sell their products or services to customers or prospective customers. SONY markets its television set through trade show presentations at retailers' conventions and through advertisements run in newspapers and magazines.

- **Distribution**—the delivery of products or services to the customer. Distribution for SONY includes shipping to retail outlets, catalog vendors, and other channels through which customers purchase televisions.

- **Customer service**—the after-sale support activities provided to customers. SONY provides customer service on its television sets in the form of customer-help telephone lines and warranty repair work.

Do not interpret Exhibit 1-3 as implying that managers should proceed sequentially through the value chain. There are important gains to organizations (in terms of, say, cost, quality, and the speed with which new products are developed) from having the individual business functions of the value chain work concurrently as a team. However, none of these functions in the value chain can be skipped. Each function is essential to SONY in delivering quality television sets to its customers and having those customers remain satisfied (and even delighted) over time.[1]

Senior managers of an organization (including those from individual business functions of the value chain) are responsible for shaping its overall strategy, as well as how resources are to be obtained and shared, and how rewards are to be given. This responsibility covers the entire value chain.[2]

Teaching Tip/Reinforcing Problems
To reinforce the value-chain concept, ask a student to illustrate activities/costs in each function in the context of his work experience. The Problem for Self-Study and Exer. 1-20 and 1-21 reinforce this section.

Correcting Student Misconceptions
Students are often confused about the difference between R&D and Design. The distinctions are not always clear cut, but R&D is basic research and idea generation, while Design turns those ideas into reality. Design encompasses development of prototype products and the mfg. process by which the products are produced.

Example Acctg. can help mgrs. administer individual functions by, for example, analyzing the effect of changing from fixed salary to commission-based compensation for the sales force (marketing function). Acctg. can also help mgrs. coordinate across functions by, for example, analyzing whether more effort (and money) spent in R&D and Design will reduce subsequent Production and Customer Service costs.

[1]In some cases, companies subcontract one or more of these six business functions. For example, product design may be subcontracted to a company specializing in product design. Even with such subcontracting, however, the challenge of coordinating all the business functions remains.

[2]The *value chain* presented in Exhibit 1-3 could be expanded to separately highlight costs implicitly included in one or more of the individual business functions. Examples include administrative costs and future cash outlays associated with actions of the current period (such as environmental cleanup costs).

EXHIBIT 1-4
Key Themes in Management Decision Making

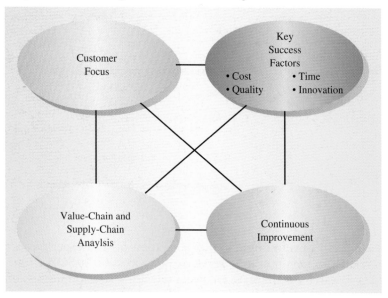

ENHANCING THE VALUE OF MANAGEMENT ACCOUNTING SYSTEMS

The design of a management accounting system should be guided by the challenges facing managers. Exhibit 1-4 presents four key themes that are important to managers attaining success in their planning and control decisions. Management accounting can play a key role in helping managers focus on these four themes.

1. *Customer focus.* Customers are pivotal to the success of an organization. The number of organizations aiming to be "customer-driven" is large and increasing. For example, ABB (Asea Brown Boveri)—a global manufacturer of industrial products—gives high priority to customer focus:

> Customer Focus is a guiding principle to the way we do business. It is an attitude about everything we do that prompts us to constantly ask ourselves: "How can I add value for the customer?" Our commitment to Customer Focus has been reinforced by the measurable impacts it has had on employee morale and the bottom line.

The challenge facing managers is to continue investing sufficient (but not excessive) resources in customer satisfaction such that profitable customers are attracted and retained. We discuss this theme in Chapter 13 where we address customer performance measures. Chapter 16 looks at customer-profitability analysis.

2. *Key success factors.* These operational factors directly affect the economic viability of the organization. Customers are demanding ever-improving levels of performance regarding several (or even all) of the following:

◆ *Cost.* Organizations are under continuous pressure to reduce the cost of their products or the services they sell to their customers.

◆ *Quality.* Customers expect higher levels of quality and are less tolerant of low quality than in the past.

◆ *Time.* Time has many components, including the time taken to develop and bring new products to market, the speed at which an organization responds to customer requests, and the reliability with which promised delivery dates are met. Organizations are under pressure to complete activities faster and to meet promised delivery dates more reliably than in the past in order to increase customer satisfaction.

The Finance Group at Cummins Engine Reinvents Itself

For many years the finance group at Cummins Engine adopted a "we make the rules, you follow them" attitude when dealing with line managers. These managers viewed the finance group as being "preoccupied with transaction processing, not very responsive to user needs . . . and having a command and control" mindset. When Cummins faced increased competition, it undertook dramatic efforts to "do more with less" and to "work smarter as well as harder." These efforts included the finance group. A Finance Leadership Team was formed. Membership included line-manager groups, information systems people, and members of Cummins' worldwide finance organization. The top priority goal of the project was for finance to "make their work more valuable to Cummins Engine." Increased attention was paid to "the [Accounting Department] providing output that its customers deem important." These included:

◆ Budgets and planning
◆ Providing management with readily accessible data for decision support

One initiative adopted was to increase the percentage of resources devoted to decision support and to reduce the resources spent on transaction processing. For example, the finance team visited the finance departments of other companies (such as Ford and Hewlett-Packard) and concluded that "best practice" companies for accounts payable averaged $0.80 per transaction. Cummins estimated its own cost at $3.17. The team concluded that major reorganization was necessary at Cummins to move to "best practice." Its entire procurement process, including accounts payable, was centralized into a single location (Columbus, Indiana). Greater linkage between existing purchasing systems and accounts payable was achieved, both at the employee level and at the information systems level. The result? "Processing costs per invoice rapidly approaching the benchmark of the best-practice companies, error rates are down, and user satisfaction is increasing."

Source: T. Compton, L. Hoshower, and W. Draeger, "Reengineering Transaction Processing Systems at Cummins Engine," *Journal of Cost Management,* Vol. 12, No. 3 and conversations with management.

◆ *Innovation.* There is now heightened recognition that a continuing flow of innovative products or services is a prerequisite for the ongoing success of most organizations.

Managers need to continually track their performance on the chosen key success factors vis-à-vis competitors. This tracking of companies outside their own organization alerts managers to changes in the external environment that their own customers are also observing and evaluating.

We discuss this theme in Chapter 5 on using activity-based costing to guide cost reductions; Chapter 12 on target costing; Chapter 13 on linking innovation and internal process improvements to customer satisfaction; and Chapter 19 on cost of quality reports, bottlenecks, and manufacturing lead time.

3. *Continuous improvement.* Continuous improvement by competitors creates a never-ending search for higher levels of performance within many organizations. Phrases such as the following capture this theme:

◆ A journey with no end.
◆ We are running harder just to stand still.
◆ If you're not going forward, you're going backwards.

Points to Stress These 4 themes can also be applied to functions within a business. For example, mgt. accountants (MA) must satisfy their customers (managers) by satisfying key success factors. MA must provide high-quality information on a timely basis, for a reasonable cost. MA can develop innovative formats and analyses to facilitate mgt. decisions. They should provide information regarding all elements of the value chain and the supply chain. MA should continually strive to provide better-quality information, faster, at a lower cost.

EXHIBIT 1-5
Supply Chain for a Cola Bottling Company

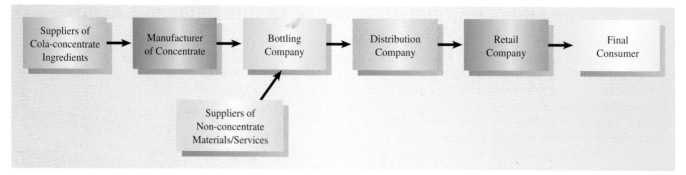

To compete, many companies are concentrating on continually improving different aspects of their own operations. Keep in mind, though, that different industries will focus on improving different operational factors. For example, airlines seek to improve the percentage of their flights that arrive on time. Internet companies seek to improve the percentage of each 24-hour period that customers can access their online systems without delay. Sumitomo Electric Industries, the Japanese manufacturer of electric wire and cable, has daily meetings so that all employees maintain a continuous focus on cost reduction.

We discuss this theme in Chapter 6 on kaizen budgeting, Chapter 7 on continuous improvement and standard costs, and Chapter 10 on learning curves.

4. *Value-chain and supply-chain analysis.* This theme has two related aspects:

◆ Treating each of the business functions in Exhibit 1-3 (p. 7) as an essential and valued contributor, and

◆ Integrating and coordinating the efforts of all business functions in addition to developing the capabilities of each individual business function.

The term **supply chain** describes the flow of goods, services, and information from cradle to grave, regardless of whether those activities occur in the same organization or other organizations. Consider the beverage products of Coca-Cola or Pepsi-Cola. Many companies play a role in bringing these products to the final consumers. Exhibit 1-5 presents an overview of the supply chain. Cost management emphasizes integrating and coordinating activities across all companies in the supply chain as well as across each business function in an individual company's value chain. To illustrate, both Coca-Cola and Pepsi-Cola bottling companies work with their suppliers (such as glass and can companies and sugar manufacturers) to reduce their materials-handling costs.

We discuss this theme in Chapter 7 on variance analysis, Chapter 12 on target-costing, and Chapter 20 on just-in-time (JIT) and supply-chain analysis.

These four themes frequently overlap. For example, customer focus (theme 1) is now a key ingredient in new product development at many companies (theme 2). Product designers are encouraged to search for cost-reduction opportunities at all stages in the value chain and supply chain (themes 3 and 4).

KEY MANAGEMENT ACCOUNTING GUIDELINES

Three important guidelines help management accountants provide the most value in performing their problem-solving, scorekeeping, and attention-directing roles: employ a cost-benefit approach, give full recognition to behavioral as well as technical considerations, and use different costs for different purposes.

Cost-Benefit Approach

Management accountants continually face resource allocation decisions, such as whether to purchase a new software package or whether to employ a new associate. A **cost-benefit approach** should be used in these decisions—resources should be

---

Curriculum Linkage These 4 themes reflect contemporary mgt. practice. Subsequent chaps. consider how these themes affect mgt. acctg. systems. Students will have been exposed to many of these themes in business core courses in mgt., marketing, and production. Instructors can help students integrate knowledge across "functional silos" by reinforcing and asking students to apply these concepts learned in other courses.

New in This Edition This edition has added supply-chain analysis to the value-chain analysis section. This emphasizes the importance of good-quality business relationships between a firm and its suppliers.

Example Toyota often loans its engineers to suppliers in order to help suppliers streamline their production processes. Toyota expects to receive a share of suppliers' cost savings in the form of reduced prices.

OBJECTIVE 7

Describe three guidelines that help management accountants increase their value to managers

spent if they promote decision making that better attains organizational goals in relation to the costs of those resources. The expected benefits from spending those resources should exceed their expected costs. Although the benefits may take many forms, they can be summarized as the collective set of decisions that will better attain the organization's goals.

Consider the installation of a company's first budgeting system. Previously, the company used historical recordkeeping and little formal planning. A major benefit of installing a budgeting system is that it compels managers to plan more formally. They may make a different, more profitable set of decisions than would have been made using only a historical system. Thus, the expected benefits exceed the expected costs of the new budgeting system. These costs include investments in physical assets, in training people, and in ongoing operating costs of the system.

Behavioral and Technical Considerations

The cost-benefit approach is the overarching criterion that assists managers in deciding whether, say, to install a proposed budgeting system instead of continuing to use an existing historical system. Note the human side of why budgeting is used. As was just mentioned, budgets induce a different set of collective decisions because of compelled planning. A management accounting system should have two simultaneous missions for providing information: (a) to help managers make wise economic decisions, and (b) to motivate managers and other employees to aim and strive for goals of the organization.

Do not underestimate the role of individuals and groups in management planning and control systems. Both accountants and managers should always remember that management systems are not confined exclusively to technical matters such as the type of computer software systems used and the frequency with which reports are prepared. Management is primarily a human activity that should focus on how to help individuals do their jobs better. For example, it is often better for managers to personally discuss how to improve performance with underperforming workers rather than just sending those workers a report highlighting their underperformance.

Different Costs for Different Purposes

This book examines alternative ways to compute costs. A major theme is different costs for different purposes. This theme is the management accountant's version of the "one shoe does not fit all sizes" notion. A cost concept used for the external reporting purpose may not be an appropriate concept for internal routine reporting to managers. Consider the advertising costs associated with launching a major new Microsoft product. The product is expected to have a useful life of 2 years or more. For external reporting to shareholders, television advertising costs are fully expensed in the income statement in the year they are incurred. This immediate expensing is a requirement of generally accepted accounting principles governing U.S. external reporting to shareholders. In contrast, for evaluating management performance (an example of the internal routine reporting purpose), the television advertising costs could be capitalized and then written off as expenses over several years. Microsoft could capitalize these advertising costs if it believes this treatment better represents the performance of the managers launching the new product. There are multiple external parties and multiple internal parties for which financial reports are prepared. Any specific accounting method (such as immediate expensing of television advertising costs) is unlikely to be the preferred method for all external parties or all internal parties. Indeed, even an individual manager may prefer accounting method A for one decision and accounting method B for another decision.

A management accountant following these three guidelines operates within a given organizational structure. We now discuss how organizational structure affects the reporting responsibilities of the management accountant.

New in This Edition This new section highlights the importance of (1) assessing the costs and benefits of actions, (2) dealing with the human side of decisions, and (3) recognizing that different costs are needed to solve the wide variety of problems facing management.

Points to Stress Although it is difficult to quantify the costs and benefits of acctg. systems, a decision about the system will be made. The question is whether costs and benefits are considered implicitly (as part of a "gut feeling") or explicitly, where effects of different estimates can be examined.

Reinforcing Problems Exer. 1-23 covers the key management accounting guidelines.

Points to Stress The "best" information system depends on both technical and human aspects of the specific situation. This is a major difference between financial acctg., in which all firms must comply with GAAP, and mgt. acctg., in which choices are based on an explicit or implicit cost-benefit analysis. Mgt. acctg. students must do more than memorize rules. They must evaluate the situation, decide which technique or information system is most appropriate, and implement it.

ORGANIZATIONAL STRUCTURE AND THE MANAGEMENT ACCOUNTANT

Line and Staff Relationships

Most organizations draw a distinction between line and staff management. **Line management** is directly responsible for attaining the objectives of the organization. For example, managers of manufacturing divisions may have particular levels of budgeted operating income targeted as well as certain levels of product quality, safety, and compliance with environmental laws targeted. **Staff management,** such as management accountants, exists to provide advice and assistance to line management. For example, a plant manager (a line function) may be responsible for investing in new equipment. A plant management accountant (a staff function) assists the plant manager by preparing detailed operating cost comparisons of alternative pieces of equipment.

Increasingly, organizations are emphasizing the importance of teams in achieving their objectives. These teams can include both line and staff management with the result that the traditional distinctions between line and staff are less clearcut than they were a decade ago.

The Chief Financial Officer and the Controller

The **chief financial officer (CFO)**—also called the **finance director**—is the senior officer empowered with overseeing the financial operations of an organization. The responsibilities of the CFO vary among organizations, but they usually include the following areas:

◆ Controllership—includes providing financial information for both reports to managers and reports to shareholders.

◆ Treasury—includes banking and short-term and long-term financing.

◆ Risk management—includes managing financial exposure to interest rate and exchange rate changes and derivatives management.

◆ Taxes—includes income taxes, sales taxes, and international tax planning.

◆ Internal audit—includes reviewing and analyzing the financial and other records to attest to the integrity of the organization's financial reports and to adherence to its policies and procedures.

In some organizations, the CFO is also responsible for information systems. In other organizations, an officer of equivalent rank to the CFO—termed chief information officer—is responsible for information systems.

The **controller** (also called the *chief accounting officer*) is the financial executive primarily responsible for both management accounting and financial accounting. This book focuses on the controller as the chief management accounting executive. The modern controller does not do any controlling in terms of line authority except over his or her own department. Yet the modern concept of controllership maintains that the controller does control in a special sense. That is, by reporting and interpreting relevant data (problem-solving and attention-directing roles), the controller exerts a force or influence that impels management toward making better informed decisions.

Exhibit 1-6 presents the organization chart of the CFO and the corporate controller at Nike, the leading footwear and apparel company. The CFO is a staff management function that reports to the most senior line managers (who in turn report to the board of directors). As in most organizations, the corporate controller at Nike reports to the CFO. Organization charts like that in Exhibit 1-6 show formal reporting relationships. In most organizations, informal relationships also exist that must be understood when managers attempt to implement their decisions. Examples of informal relationships are friendships among managers (of a professional or personal kind) and the personal preferences of senior managers as to the type of managers he or she chooses to rely on in decision making.

The CFO at Nike is one of thirteen corporate officers. These include the Chief Executive Officer (CEO), the President and Chief Operating Officer (COO),

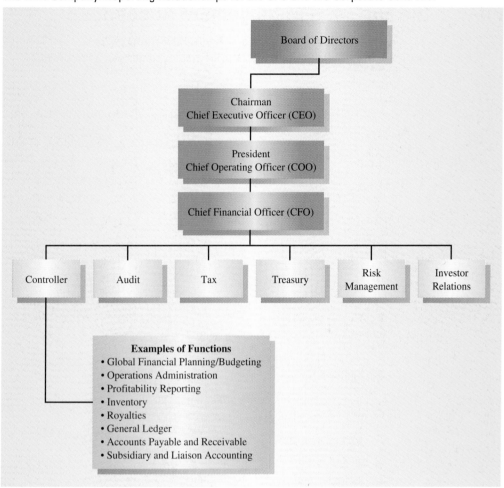

the Treasurer, and ten vice presidents (such as for its geographic regions in the United States, Asia Pacific, and Europe; for its products of apparel and footwear; for its brand management; for its global human resources; and a chief legal counsel). Exhibit 1-6 provides examples of the functions undertaken in the controller group. Each of Nike's major geographic groups (United States, Asia Pacific, and Europe) has its own group controller. Many individual countries within each geographic group also have a country controller.

A key responsibility of all members in an organization, whether in line management or staff management, is ensuring compliance with the organization's ethical standards. We now discuss ethical issues. Accountants have special responsibilities regarding ethics, given their responsibility for the integrity of financial information provided to internal and external parties.

PROFESSIONAL ETHICS

Accountants consistently rank high in public opinion surveys on the ethics exhibited by members of different professions. Professional accounting organizations play an important role in promoting high ethical standards.

Ethical Guidelines

Professional accounting organizations representing management accountants exist in many countries. Appendix D discusses professional organizations in the United States, Canada, Australia, Japan, and the United Kingdom. Each of these organizations provides certification programs. For example, the **Institute of Management**

Points to Stress Students are often unaware of the variety of jobs available to accountants. Exh. 1-6 illustrates the diverse areas that report to the CFO. An understanding of acctg. is essential in many of these areas. Instructors can use the article *1994 Salaries* (by Schroeder and Reichardt) from the June 1995 issue of *Management Accounting* to stimulate students' interest in mgt. acctg. careers, CMA certification, and advanced degrees. Also, direct the students' attention to the Survey of Company Practice box. It describes what a management accountant does and what skills and abilities are necessary to do the job.

OBJECTIVE 9

Understand the importance of professional ethics to management accountants

"A Day in the Life" of a Management Accountant

What activities do management accountants perform? A survey of CMAs[a] found that 10% or more perform the following activities (percentages add across rows):

	Daily	Weekly	Monthly	Quarterly or Annually	Never Perform
Managing the accounting/ finance function	64%	14%	11%	5%	6%
Internal consulting	36	32	19	7	6
Accounting systems and financial reporting	18	28	36	9	9
Human resources and personnel	11	23	25	22	19
Financial and economic analysis	10	15	39	24	12

In terms of importance, managers ranked abilities and skills as follows:

1. Work ethic
2. Analytical/problem-solving skills
3. Interpersonal skills
4. Listening skills

What changes in the future are projected for management accountants? Work activities projected to become more important were:

1. Long-term strategic planning
2. Performance evaluation
3. Customer and product profitability

The increasing use of information technology in the future was seen as helping management accountants spend a lower percentage of their time on "data collection and financial statement preparation" and a higher percentage on "financial analysis."

A survey of U.S. controllers[b] reinforced these findings. The controllers were asked how they anticipate spending their time 5 years hence vis-à-vis how they spend their time today:

> The shift is clearly away from activities we traditionally think of as the core of the controller's responsibilities—managing the function, ensuring business controls, and planning and reporting—and moving toward activities we think of as business partnering—decision support, improvement initiatives, and business leadership.

The controller of Northern Telecom supported this finding, arguing that "you must be seen as a business person first and an accounting person second. I'm considered a part of the business team."

[a]G. Siegel and B. Kulesza, "The Practice Analysis of Management Accounting."

[b]L. Berry and J. Scheumann, "The Controller's Good Intentions."

See Appendix A for full citations.

Accountants (IMA)—the largest association of management accountants in the United States—provides a program leading to the **Certified Management Accountant (CMA)** certificate. This certificate indicates that the holder has met the admission criteria and demonstrated the competency of technical knowledge required by the IMA.

The IMA has issued a *Standards of Ethical Conduct for Management Accountants.* Exhibit 1-7 presents the IMA's guidance on issues relating to competence, confidentiality, integrity, and objectivity. The IMA provides its members with an Ethics Hotline service. Members can call professional counselors at the IMA to discuss their ethical dilemmas. The counselors help identify the key ethical issues and possible alternative ways of resolving them, and confidentiality is guaranteed.[3]

Typical Ethical Challenges

Ethical issues can confront management accountants in many ways. Here are two examples:

◆ **Case A:** A management accountant, knowing that reporting a loss for a software division will result in yet another "rightsizing initiative" (a gentler term than "layoffs"), has concerns about the commercial potential of software for which R&D costs are currently being capitalized for internal reporting purposes. The division manager argues vehemently that the new product will be a "winner" but presents limited evidence to support her opinion. The last two products from this division have been unsuccessful. The management accountant has many friends in the division and wants to avoid a personal confrontation with the division manager.

Reinforcing Problems Exer. 1-24 and Probs. 1-28 through 1-30 reinforce the discussion of the importance of ethics to accountants.

◆ **Case B:** A packaging supplier, bidding for a new contract, offers the management accountant of the purchasing company an all-expenses-paid weekend to the Super Bowl. The supplier does not mention the new contract when giving the invitation. The accountant is not a personal friend of the supplier. He knows cost issues are critical in approving the new contract and is concerned that the supplier will ask for details about bids by competing packaging companies.

In each case the management accountant is faced with an ethical challenge. Case A involves competence, objectivity, and integrity. The management accountant should request that the division manager provide credible evidence that the new product is a commercially viable one. If the manager does not provide such evidence, period expensing of the R&D costs is appropriate. Case B involves confidentiality and integrity. Ethical issues are not always black or white. For example, the supplier in Case B may have no intention of raising issues associated with the bid. However, the appearance of a conflict of interest in Case B is sufficient for many companies to prohibit employees from accepting free "favors" from suppliers. Exhibit 1-8 presents the IMA's guidance on "Resolution of Ethical Conflict." The accountant in Case B should discuss the invitation with his immediate supervisor. If the visit is approved, the supplier should be informed that the invitation has been officially approved subject to his following corporate policy (which includes the confidentiality of information).

Most professional accounting organizations around the globe issue statements about professional ethics. These statements include many of the same issues discussed by the IMA in Exhibits 1-7 and 1-8. For example, the Chartered Institute of Management Accountants (CIMA) in the United Kingdom identifies the same four fundamental principles as in Exhibit 1-7—competency, confidentiality, integrity, and objectivity.

---

[3]Details of the IMA's guidance on ethical issues, including its Ethics Hotline, are on its website (www.imanet.org). See also R. Sweeney, "Ethics on the Line," *New Accountant*, Vol. X, No. L.

EXHIBIT 1-7
Standards of Ethical Conduct for Management Accountants

Practitioners of management accounting and financial management have an obligation to the public, their profession, the organization they serve, and themselves, to maintain the highest standards of ethical conduct. In recognition of this obligation, the Institute of Management Accountants has promulgated the following standards of ethical conduct for practitioners of management accounting and financial management. Adherence to these standards, both domestically and internationally, is integral to achieving the Objectives of Management Accounting. Practitioners of management accounting and financial management shall not commit acts contrary to these standards nor shall they condone the commission of such acts by others within their organizations.

COMPETENCE

Practitioners of management accounting and financial management have a responsibility to:

- ◆ Maintain an appropriate level of professional competence by ongoing development of their knowledge and skills.
- ◆ Perform their professional duties in accordance with relevant laws, regulations, and technical standards.
- ◆ Prepare complete and clear reports and recommendations after appropriate analysis of relevant and reliable information.

CONFIDENTIALITY

Practitioners of management accounting and financial management have a responsibility to:

- ◆ Refrain from disclosing confidential information acquired in the course of their work except when authorized, unless legally obligated to do so.
- ◆ Inform subordinates as appropriate regarding the confidentiality of information acquired in the course of their work and monitor their activities to assure the maintenance of that confidentiality.
- ◆ Refrain from using or appearing to use confidential information acquired in the course of their work for unethical or illegal advantage either personally or through third parties.

INTEGRITY

Practitioners of management accounting and financial management have a responsibility to:

- ◆ Avoid actual or apparent conflicts of interest and advise all appropriate parties of any potential conflict.
- ◆ Refrain from engaging in any activity that would prejudice their ability to carry out their duties ethically.
- ◆ Refuse any gift, favor, or hospitality that would influence or would appear to influence their actions.
- ◆ Refrain from either actively or passively subverting the attainment of the organization's legitimate and ethical objectives.
- ◆ Recognize and communicate professional limitations or other constraints that would preclude responsible judgment or successful performance of an activity.
- ◆ Communicate unfavorable as well as favorable information and professional judgments or opinions.
- ◆ Refrain from engaging in or supporting any activity that would discredit the profession.

OBJECTIVITY

Practitioners of management accounting and financial management have a responsibility to:

- ◆ Communicate information fairly and objectively.
- ◆ Disclose fully all relevant information that could reasonably be expected to influence an intended user's understanding of the reports, comments, and recommendations presented.

Source: Institute of Management Accountants, "Standards of Ethical Conduct for Practitioners of Management Accounting and Financial Management," *Management Accounting*, Vol. LXXIX, No. 1.

EXHIBIT 1-8
Resolution of Ethical Conflict

In applying the standards of ethical conduct, practitioners of management accounting and financial management may encounter problems in identifying unethical behavior or in resolving an ethical conflict. When faced with significant ethical issues, practitioners of management accounting and financial management should follow the established policies of the organization bearing on the resolution of such conflict. If these policies do not resolve the ethical conflict, such practitioners should consider the following courses of action:

◆ Discuss such problems with the immediate superior except when it appears that the superior is involved, in which case the problem should be presented initially to the next higher managerial level. If satisfactory resolution cannot be achieved when the problem is initially presented, submit the issues to the next higher managerial level.

   If the immediate superior is the chief executive officer, or equivalent, the acceptable reviewing authority may be a group such as the audit committee, executive committee, board of directors, board of trustees, or owners. Contact with levels above the immediate superior should be initiated only with the superior's knowledge, assuming the superior is not involved. Except where legally prescribed, communication of such problems to authorities or individuals not employed or engaged by the organization is not considered appropriate.

◆ Clarify relevant ethical issues by confidential discussion with an objective advisor (e.g., IMA Ethics Counseling Service) to obtain a better understanding of possible courses of action.

◆ Consult your own attorney as to legal obligations and rights concerning the ethical conflict.

◆ If the ethical conflict still exists after exhausting all levels of internal review, there may be no other recourse on significant matters than to resign from the organization and to submit an informative memorandum to an appropriate representative of the organization. After resignation, depending on the nature of the ethical conflict, it may also be appropriate to notify other parties.

Source: Institute of Management Accountants, "Standards of Ethical Conduct for Practitioners of Management Accounting and Financial Management," *Management Accounting*, Vol. LXXIX, No. 1.

PROBLEM FOR SELF-STUDY

(Try to solve the following problem before examining the solution that follows.)

PROBLEM
Campbell Soup Company incurs the following costs:

   a. Purchase of tomatoes by a canning plant for Campbell's tomato soup products.

   b. Materials purchased for redesigning Pepperidge Farm biscuit containers to make biscuits stay fresh longer.

   c. Payment to Backer, Spielvogel Bates, the advertising agency, for advertising work on Healthy Request line of soup products.

   d. Salaries of food technologists researching feasibility of a Prego pizza sauce that has minimal calories.

   e. Payment to Safeway for obtaining shelf space to display Campbell's food products.

   f. Cost of a toll-free telephone line used for customer inquiries about possible product defects in Campbell's Soups.

   g. Cost of gloves used by line operators on the Swanson Fiesta breakfast food production line.

   h. Cost of hand-held computers used by Pepperidge Farm delivery staff serving major supermarket accounts.

Required
Classify each cost item (a–h) as one of the business functions in the value chain shown in Exhibit 1-3 (p. 7).

a. Production	**c.** Marketing	**f.** Customer service
b. Design of products, services, or processes	**d.** Research and development	**g.** Production
	e. Marketing	**h.** Distribution

SUMMARY

The following points are linked to the chapter's learning objectives:

1. Accounting systems exist to help decision making that furthers the goals of the organization. This assistance occurs by providing information for three major purposes: (a) routine internal reporting to managers; (b) nonroutine internal reporting to managers; and (c) external reporting to investors, government authorities, and other outside parties.

2. Cost accounting measures and reports financial and other information related to the acquisition or consumption of an organization's resources. Cost accounting provides information to both management accounting and financial accounting.

3. Planning decisions of managers include deciding on organization goals, predicting results under various alternative ways of achieving those goals, and then deciding how to attain the designated goals. Control decisions include taking actions to implement the planning decisions and deciding on performance evaluation and the related feedback that will help future decision making.

4. In most organizations, management accountants perform multiple roles—problem solving (comparative analysis for decision making), scorekeeping (accumulating data and reporting reliable results), and attention directing (helping managers properly focus their attention).

5. Managers in all business functions of the value chain are customers of accounting information. The business functions in the value chain are research and development; design of products, services, or processes; production; marketing; distribution; and customer service.

6. Four key themes that are important to managers attaining success in their planning and control decisions are customer focus, key success factors, continuous improvement, and value-chain and supply-chain analysis.

7. Three guidelines that help management accountants increase their value to managers are (a) employ a cost-benefit approach, (b) give full recognition to behavioral as well as technical considerations, and (c) apply the concept of different costs for different purposes.

8. Cost accounting is an integral part of the controller function in an organization. In most organizations, the controller reports to the chief financial officer, who is a key member of the senior management team.

9. Management accountants have important ethical responsibilities that are related to competence, confidentiality, integrity, and objectivity.

TERMS TO LEARN

Each chapter will include this section. Like all technical terms, accounting terms have precise meanings. Learn the definitions of new terms when you initially encounter them. The meaning of each of the following terms is given in this chapter and also in the Glossary at the end of this book.

attention directing (6)
budget (4)

Certified Management Accountant (CMA) (15)

chief financial officer (CFO) (12)
control (4)
controller (12)
cost accounting (3)
cost-benefit approach (10)
cost management (3)
customer service (7)
design of products, services, or
    processes (7)
distribution (7)
feedback (5)
finance director (12)
financial accounting (3)

Institute of Management Accountants
    (IMA) (13)
line management (12)
management accounting (2)
marketing (7)
planning (3)
problem solving (5)
production (7)
research and development (7)
scorekeeping (5)
staff management (12)
supply chain (10)
value chain (6)

ASSIGNMENT MATERIAL

QUESTIONS

1-1 Describe the major purposes of accounting systems.

1-2 How does management accounting differ from financial accounting?

1-3 Distinguish planning decisions from control decisions.

1-4 What are three important roles that management accountants perform?

1-5 "Management accounting should not fit the straitjacket of financial accounting." Explain and give an example.

1-6 Describe the business functions in the value chain.

1-7 A leading management observer stated that the most successful companies are those that have an obsession for their customers. Is this statement pertinent to management accountants? Explain.

1-8 Describe four key themes that are important to managers attaining success and in which management accounting can play a key role in decision support.

1-9 Explain the term *supply chain* and its importance to cost management.

1-10 What three guidelines help management accountants provide the most value to managers?

1-11 "Knowledge of technical issues such as computer technology is a necessary but not sufficient condition to becoming a successful accountant." Do you agree? Why?

1-12 As a new controller, reply to this comment by a plant manager: "As I see it, our accountants may be needed to keep records for shareholders and Uncle Sam—but I don't want them sticking their noses in my day-to-day operations. I do the best I know how. No bean-counter knows enough about my responsibilities to be of any use to me."

1-13 As used in accounting, what do IMA and CMA stand for?

1-14 Name the four areas in which standards of ethical conduct exist for management accountants in the United States. What organization sets forth these standards?

1-15 What steps should a management accountant take if established written policies provide insufficient guidance on how to handle an ethical conflict?

EXERCISES

1-16 Management accountants and customer focus. A recent Annual Report of Ford Motor Company included the following comments:

◆ Delivering great value to our customers. That's our passion.

◆ Throughout Ford Motor Company we're focused on improving the quality and value of our products, and speeding delivery to market.

◆ All our efforts are aimed at exceeding customer expectations. That's the best way to reach and keep customers.

Required

1. Who are the customers of the management accounting function?
2. How might the Ford Motor Company credo of "exceeding customer expectations" for their motor vehicles also apply to its management accounting function?

1-17 Major purposes of accounting systems. Barnes and Noble is a book retailing company. The majority of its sales are made at its own stores. These stores are often located in shopping malls or in central business districts. A small but increasing percentage of sales are made via its Internet shopping division, where its major competitor is Amazon.com.

The following five reports were recently prepared by the management accounting group at Barnes and Noble:

1. Annual financial statements included in the Annual Report sent to its shareholders.

2. Weekly report to Vice President of Operations for each Barnes and Nobles store—includes revenues, gross margin, and operating costs.

3. Study for Vice President of New Business Development of the expected revenues and expected costs of the Barnes and Noble Internet division selling music products (CDs, cassettes, etc.) as well as books.

4. Weekly report to book publishers and trade magazines on the sales of the top ten selling fiction and nonfiction books at both its own stores and in the Internet division.

5. Report to insurance company on losses Barnes and Noble suffered at its three San Francisco stores due to an earthquake.

Required
1. What are the three major purposes of accounting systems?
2. Identify the major purpose served by each of the above five reports prepared by Barnes and Noble's management accounting group.
3. For each report, identify both a planning decision and a control decision use by a manager (either at Barnes and Noble or another company).

1-18 Problem solving, scorekeeping, and attention directing. For each of the following activities, identify the main role the accountant is performing—problem solving, scorekeeping, or attention directing.

1. Preparing a monthly statement of Australian sales for the IBM marketing vice president.

2. Interpreting differences between actual results and budgeted amounts on a performance report for the Customer Warranty Department of General Electric.

3. Preparing a schedule of depreciation for forklift trucks in the Receiving Department of a Hewlett-Packard plant in Scotland.

4. Analyzing, for a Mitsubishi international manufacturing manager, the desirability of having some auto parts made in Korea.

5. Interpreting why a Birmingham distribution center did not adhere to its delivery costs budget.

6. Explaining a Xerox Shipping Department's performance report.

7. Preparing, for the manager of production control of a U.S. steel plant, a cost comparison of two computerized manufacturing control systems.

8. Preparing a scrap report for the Finishing Department of a Toyota parts plant.

9. Preparing the budget for the Maintenance Department of Mount Sinai Hospital.

10. Analyzing, for a General Motors product designer, the impact on product costs of some new headlight lamps.

1-19 Problem solving, scorekeeping, and attention directing. For each of the following activities, identify the main role the accountant is performing—problem solving, scorekeeping, or attention directing.

1. Interpreting differences between actual results and budgeted amounts on a shipping manager's performance report at a Daewoo distribution center.

2. Preparing a report showing the benefits from leasing motor vehicles rather than owning them.

3. Preparing journal entries for depreciation on the personnel manager's office equipment at Citibank.

4. Preparing a customer's monthly statement for a Sears store.

5. Processing the weekly payroll for the Harvard University Maintenance Department.

6. Explaining the product-design manager's performance report at a Chrysler division.

7. Analyzing the costs of several different ways to blend materials in the foundry of a General Electric plant.

8. Tallying sales, by branches, for the sales vice president of Unilever.

9. Analyzing, for the president of Microsoft, the impact of a contemplated new product on net income.

10. Interpreting why an IBM sales district did not meet its sales quota.

1-20 Value chain and classification of costs, computer company. Compaq Computer incurs the following costs:

a. Electricity costs for the plant assembling the Presario computer line of products.

b. Transportation costs for shipping the Presario line of products to a retail chain.

c. Payment to David Kelley Designs for design of the Armada Notebook.

d. Salary of computer scientist working on the next generation of minicomputers.

e. Cost of Compaq employees visit to a major customer to demonstrate Compaq's ability to interconnect with other computers.

f. Purchase of products of competitors for testing against potential future Compaq products.

g. Payment to television network for running Compaq advertisements.

h. Cost of cables purchased from outside supplier to be used with the Compaq printer.

Required
Classify each of the cost items (a–h) into one of the business functions of the value chain shown in Exhibit 1-3 (p. 7).

1-21 Value chain and classification of costs, pharmaceutical company. Merck, a pharmaceutical company, incurs the following costs:

a. Cost of redesigning blister packs to make drug containers more tamper-proof.

b. Cost of videos sent to doctors to promote sales of a new drug.

c. Cost of a toll-free telephone line used for customer inquiries about usage, side effects of drugs, and so on.

d. Equipment purchased by a scientist to conduct experiments on drugs yet to be approved by the government.

e. Payment to actors on an infomercial to be shown on television promoting a new hair-growing product for balding men.

f. Labor costs of workers in the packaging area of a production facility.

g. Bonus paid to a salesperson for exceeding monthly sales quota.

h. Cost of Federal Express courier service to deliver drugs to hospitals.

Required
Classify each of the cost items (a–h) as one of the business functions of the value chain shown in Exhibit 1-3 (p. 7).

1-22 Management themes and changes in management accounting. A survey on ways organizations are changing their management accounting systems reported the following:

a. Company A now prepares a value-chain income statement for each brand it sells.

b. Company B now presents in a single report all costs related to achieving high quality levels of its products.

c. Company C now presents in its performance reports estimates of the manufacturing costs of its two most important competitors, in addition to its own manufacturing costs.

d. Company D reduces by 1% each month the budgeted labor assembly cost of a product when evaluating the performance of a plant manager.

e. Company E now reports profitability and satisfaction measures (as assessed by a third party) on a customer-by-customer basis.

Required
Link each of the above changes to one of the key themes that are important to managers attaining success (see Exhibit 1-4, p. 8).

1-23 Key management accounting guidelines, integrating management accounting systems. Jeannette Smith is the newly appointed controller of National Foods, a large food and beverage products company with headquarters in St. Helens, England. The company has 53 separate European subsidiaries. The company has grown largely by acquisition. Over 30 different companies in Europe have been acquired by National Foods in the last 5 years. National Foods left each company's management in place with their own internal management structure and accounting systems. Recently, however, several factors have led National Foods to consider adopting a more centralized management style with all subsidiaries using the same management accounting system. One factor is the demands of several major customers of National Foods to link their own information systems to those of National Foods. Currently, this linkage is not possible. A second factor is large unexpected losses at the Polish and Spanish subsidiaries of National Foods.

Smith is hired by National Foods to lead the development of an integrated management accounting system that will be used in each of its subsidiaries. The same recording procedures will be used in each subsidiary, along with the same chart of accounts. The goal is for National Foods to be able to simultaneously access and analyze the data in the management accounting system in each of its subsidiaries.

Required

1. Describe how each of the following guidelines could be important to Smith in her management accounting system challenges at National Foods:
   a. Employ the cost-benefit approach.
   b. Give full recognition to behavioral as well as technical considerations.
   c. Use different costs for different purposes.
2. Smith will report to Alex Murphy, the CFO of National Foods. Discuss key areas of Murphy's responsibility.

1-24 Professional ethics and reporting divisional performance. Marcia Miller is division controller and Tom Maloney is division manager of the Ramses Shoe Company. Miller has line responsibility to Maloney, but she also has staff responsibility to the company controller.

Maloney is under severe pressure to achieve the budgeted division income for the year. He has asked Miller to book $200,000 of revenues on December 31. The customers' orders are firm, but the shoes are still in the production process. They will be shipped on or about January 4. Maloney says to Miller, "The key event is getting the sales order, not shipping of the shoes. You should support me, not obstruct my reaching division goals."

Required

1. Describe Miller's ethical responsibilities.
2. What should Miller do if Maloney gives her a direct order to book the sales?

PROBLEMS

1-25 Planning and control, feedback. Naomi Campbell, editor of *The Daily Sporting News* (DSN), decides in April 2001 to reduce the price per newspaper from $0.70 in April 2001 to $0.50 starting May 1, 2001. Actual paid circulation in April is 7,500,000 (250,000 per day × 30 days). Campbell estimates that the $0.20 price reduction will increase paid circulation in May to 12,400,000 (400,000 × 31 days). The actual May circulation turns out to be 13,640,000 (440,000 × 31 days). Assume one goal of DSN is to increase operating income. The budgeted increase in circulation would enable DSN to charge higher advertising rates in later months of 2001 if those budgeted gains actually occur. The actual selling price in May 2001 is the budgeted price of $0.50 per newspaper.

Required

1. Distinguish between planning and control at DSN, giving an example of each.
2. Prepare a performance report for DSN newspaper revenues for May 2001 showing the actual results, budgeted amounts, and the difference between actual results and budgeted amounts.
3. What two types of action might Campbell take based on feedback from the May 2001 circulation revenues?

1-26 Planning and control decisions; Internet company. WebNews.com is an Internet company. It offers subscribers multiple online services ranging from an annotated TV guide to local-area information on restaurants and movie theaters. It has two main revenue sources:

◆ Monthly fees from subscribers. Recent data are:

Month/Year	Actual Number of Subscribers	Actual Monthly Fee per Subscriber
June 1998	28,642	$14.95
December 1998	54,813	$19.95
June 1999	58,178	$19.95
December 1999	86,437	$19.95
June 2000	146,581	$19.95

◆ Banner advertising fees from companies advertising on WebNews.com page sites. Recent data are:

Month/Year	Advertising Revenues
June 1998	$ 400,988
December 1998	833,158
June 1999	861,034
December 1999	1,478,072
June 2000	2,916,962

The following decisions were made in the June to October 2000 period:

a. June 2000. Decision to raise the monthly subscription fee from $19.95 per month in June 2000 to $24.95 per month in July 2000. The $19.95 fee first applied in December 1998.

b. June 2000. Decision to inform existing subscribers that the July 2000 subscription fee would be $24.95.

c. July 2000. Decision to upgrade the content of its online services and to offer better Internet mail services.

d. October 2000. Demotion of Vice President of Marketing after significant slowing of subscriber growth in accounts and revenues. Results include:

Month/Year	Actual Number of Subscribers	Actual Monthly Fee per Subscriber
July 2000	128,933	$24.95
August 2000	139,419	$24.95
September 2000	143,131	$24.95

Budgeted amounts (set in June 2000) for the number of subscribers were 140,000 for July 2000, 150,000 for August 2000, and 160,000 for September 2000.

e. October 2000. Decision to reduce the monthly subscription fee from $24.95 per month in September 2000 to $21.95 in October 2000.

Required
1. Distinguish between planning decisions and control decisions at WebNews.com.
2. Classify each of the (a) to (e) decisions as a planning or a control decision.

1-27 Problem solving, scorekeeping, and attention directing; Internet company (continuation of 1-26). Management accountants at WebNews.com can play three key roles in each of the five decisions described in Problem 1-26: problem solving, scorekeeping, and attention directing.
Required
1. Distinguish between the problem-solving, scorekeeping, and attention-directing roles of a management accountant at WebNews.com.
2. For each of the five decisions outlined in 1-26, describe a problem-solving, scorekeeping, or attention-directing role. Where possible, provide your own example of an information item that a management accountant could provide for each decision.

1-28 Software procurement decision, ethics. Jorge Michaels is the Chicago-based controller of Fiesta Foods, a rapidly growing manufacturer and marketer of Mexican food products. Michaels is currently considering the purchase of a new cost management package for use by each of its six manufacturing plants and its many marketing personnel. Four major competing products are being considered by Michaels.

Horizon 1-2-3 is an aggressive software developer. It views Fiesta as a target of opportunity. Every 6 months Horizon has a 3-day user's conference in a Caribbean location. Each conference has substantial time allowed for "rest and recreation." Horizon offers Michaels an all-expenses paid visit to the upcoming conference in Cancun, Mexico. Michaels accepts the offer believing it will be very useful to talk to other users of Horizon software. He is especially looking forward to the visit as he has close relatives in the Cancun area.

Prior to leaving, Michaels receives a visit from the president of Fiesta. She shows him an anonymous letter sent to her. It argues that Horizon is receiving unfair favorable treatment in Fiesta's software decision-making process. The letter specifically mentions Michaels' upcoming "all-expense-paid package to Cancun during Chicago's cold winter." Michaels is deeply offended. He says he has made no decision and believes he is very capable of making a software choice on the merits of each product. Fiesta currently does not have a formal written code of ethics.

Required
1. Do you think Michaels faces an ethical problem in regard to his forthcoming visit to the Horizon's user's group meeting? Refer to Exhibit 1-7 (p. 16). Explain.
2. Should Fiesta allow executives to attend user meetings while negotiating with other vendors about a purchase decision? Explain. If yes, what conditions on attending should apply?
3. Would you recommend that Fiesta develop its own code of ethics to handle situations such as that just described? What are the pros and cons of having such a written code?

1-29 Professional ethics and end-of-year games. Janet Taylor is the new division controller of the snack foods division of Gourmet Foods. Gourmet Foods has reported a minimum 15% growth in annual earnings for each of the past 5 years. The snack foods division has reported annual earnings growth of over 20% each year in this same period. During the current year, the economy went into a recession. The corporate controller estimates a 10% annual earnings growth rate for Gourmet Foods this year. One month before the December 31 fiscal year-end of the current year, Taylor estimates the snack foods division will report an annual earnings growth of only 8 percent. Warren Ryan, the snack foods division president, is less than happy, but he says with a wry smile, "Let the end-of-year games begin."

Taylor makes some inquiries and is able to compile the following list of end-of-year games that were more-or-less accepted by the previous division controller:

a. Deferring routine monthly maintenance in December on packaging equipment by an independent contractor until January of next year.

b. Extending the close of the current fiscal year beyond December 31 so that some sales of next year are included in the current year.

c. Altering dates of shipping documents of next January's sales to record them as sales in December of the current year.

d. Giving salespeople a double bonus to exceed December sales targets.

e. Deferring the current period's advertising by reducing the number of television spots run in December and running more than planned in January of next year.

f. Deferring the current period's reported advertising costs by having Gourmet Foods outside advertising agency delay billing December advertisements until January of next year or having the agency alter invoices to conceal the December date.

g. Persuading carriers to accept merchandise for shipment in December of the current year although they normally would not have done so.

Required
1. Why might the snack foods division president want to play the end-of-year games described above?
2. The division controller is deeply troubled and reads the *Standards of Ethical Conduct for Management Accountants* in Exhibit 1-7 (p. 16). Classify each of the end-of-year games (a–g) as (i) acceptable, or (ii) unacceptable according to that document.
3. What should Taylor do if Ryan suggests that end-of-year games are played in every di-

vision of Gourmet Foods and that she would greatly harm the snack foods division if she does not play along and paint the rosiest picture possible of the division's results?

COLLABORATIVE LEARNING PROBLEM

1-30 Global company, ethical challenges with bribery. Shell Oil Company operates in many parts of the globe. These operations include oil exploration, production, transportation, refining, and marketing. One challenge faced by Shell is how to handle requests for "bribes" and "facilitating payments." The chairman of Shell's operations recently gave an address where he claimed that "Shell loses valuable business because it refuses to pay bribes . . . "

One form of bribe is a payment to a private bank account that is portrayed as a charitable donation. Shell makes many payments to charities, so a charitable payment would not be an unusual accounting entry. Shell's chairman noted that "on occasion it has been suggested to me that Shell's cause would be much helped by a donation to a national cultural or humanitarian fund—which just happens to have a bank account in Switzerland." Another form of a bribe is a payment to an "intermediary" in which a company pays a third party for a "go-between" role that could be more efficiently handled without the third party. The "intermediary" (such as a local law firm) handles the bribery payment plus takes an extra facilitating payment. The accounting system would show only a payment to the third party (say, an accounting entry for legal services).

The Shell Chairman concluded the address as follows:

> We do not bribe. We do not sanction any type of illegal payment of any kind anywhere, directly or indirectly and any employee who is found to have done so will be dismissed and, if possible, prosecuted. The principle employees have to follow is simple: "Just say no."

Required

Form groups of two or more students to complete the following requirements.

1. Suppose you are a shareholder of Shell. Would you prefer that Shell pay bribes if it means "gaining valuable business"?

2. Suppose you are the CFO of Shell. You suspect that one of your overseas subsidiaries is making payments to a local law firm for being an "intermediary." This subsidiary also makes payments to several Swiss-based "humanitarian funds" of questionable nature. How would you determine whether bribery is occurring? If you discover it is, what actions would you take?

3. Suppose again you are the CFO of Shell. A major oil discovery by Shell occurs in a country whose political regime is a dictatorship. His extended family has vast business dealings with oil companies. Shell's market capitalization increases by $2 billion when news of the discovery is released. Shell owns the oil leases and is negotiating with the government for construction of an oil refining plant. You are told by the dictator's key advisor that approval of the plant construction is contingent on one of the dictator's sons being given 10% equity in the oil refinery (with no payment). You contact two other oil companies with prior dealings in this country and hear stories about "facilitating payments" and other questionable expenditures. One company calls it an "auditor's nightmare." The board of directors of Shell has asked you (as CFO) to make a presentation on all financial aspects of the oil refinery project. What ethical issues (with proposed solutions) would you raise in your presentation?

2

An Introduction to Cost Terms and Purposes

learning objectives

When you have finished studying this chapter, you should be able to

1. Define and illustrate a cost object
2. Distinguish between direct costs and indirect costs
3. Explain variable costs and fixed costs
4. Interpret unit costs with caution
5. Distinguish among manufacturing-, merchandising-, and service-sector companies
6. Describe the three categories of inventories commonly found in manufacturing companies
7. Differentiate between inventoriable costs and period costs
8. Explain why different ways of computing product costs are appropriate for different purposes

Worker involvement is an essential part of cost management on a Pepsi bottling line.

Different cost concepts and terms are often used in accounting reports. Managers who understand these concepts and terms are able to (a) best use the information provided, and (b) avoid misuse of that information. Communication among managers is greatly facilitated by there being common understanding on the meaning of cost concepts and terms. This chapter discusses cost concepts and terms found in both internal and external uses of accounting information.

COSTS AND COST TERMINOLOGY

Accountants define **cost** as a resource sacrificed or forgone to achieve a specific objective. It is usually measured as the monetary amount that must be paid to acquire goods and services. An **actual cost** is the cost incurred (a historical cost) as distinguished from budgeted or forecasted costs.

To guide their decisions, managers want to know how much a particular thing (such as a product, machine, service, or process) costs. We call this "thing" a **cost object,** which is anything for which a separate measurement of costs is desired. Exhibit 2-1 provides examples of seven different types of cost objects at Procter & Gamble, the consumer products company.

EXHIBIT 2-1
Examples of Cost Objects at Procter & Gamble

Cost Object	Illustration
◆ Product	◆ *Crest Tartar Control:* Original Flavor toothpaste product
◆ Service	◆ Telephone hotline providing information and assistance to users of *Pampers Diapers* products
◆ Project	◆ Research and development project on alternative scent-free formulations of *Tide* detergent products
◆ Customer	◆ Safeway, the retailer, who purchases a broad range of Procter & Gamble products
◆ Brand category	◆ *Vidal Sasson* range of hairstyle products
◆ Activity	◆ Development and updating of Procter & Gamble's website on the Internet
◆ Department	◆ Environmental, Health, and Safety Department of Procter & Gamble

A costing system typically accounts for costs in two basic stages—accumulation and then assignment. **Cost accumulation** is the collection of cost data in some organized way by means of an accounting system. For example, a plant that purchases paper rolls for printing magazines collects (accumulates) the costs of individual rolls purchased in any one month to obtain the total monthly paper purchase costs. Beyond accumulating costs, managers assign costs to designated cost objects to help decision making. **Cost assignment** is a general term that encompasses both (1) tracing accumulated costs to a cost object, and (2) allocating accumulated costs to a cost object. For example, costs may be assigned to a department to facilitate decisions about departmental efficiency. Also, costs may be assigned to a product or a customer to facilitate product or customer-profitability analysis. A key question in cost assignment is whether costs have a direct or an indirect relationship to a particular cost object.

DIRECT COSTS AND INDIRECT COSTS

Cost Tracing and Cost Allocation

◆ **Direct costs of a cost object** are related to the particular cost object and can be traced to it in an economically feasible (cost-effective) way. For example, the cost of the cans or bottles is a direct cost of a Pepsi soft drink. The cost of

EXHIBIT 2-2
Cost Assignment to a Cost Object

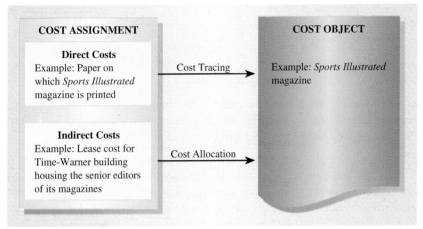

Points to Stress *Cost assignment* is a general term for attaching either direct or indirect costs to cost objects. The distinction between direct and indirect costs is important because direct costs are directly traced to the cost object, while indirect costs are often pooled and then allocated to the cost object with less precision. Mgt. therefore, has more confidence in the accuracy of direct costs. The text uses the term *cost tracing* to refer specifically to assigning direct costs to cost objects. *Cost allocation* is reserved for assigning indirect costs to cost objects.

the cans or bottles can be easily traced to the Pepsi soft drink. The term *cost tracing* is used to describe the assignment of direct costs to the particular cost object.

◆ **Indirect costs of a cost object** are related to the particular cost object but cannot be traced to it in an economically feasible (cost-effective) way. For example, the cost of quality-control personnel who conduct taste and content tests on multiple soft drink products bottled at a Pepsi plant is an indirect cost of a Pepsi soft drink. Unlike cans or bottles, it is difficult to trace quality-control personnel costs to a specific Pepsi soft drink. The term **cost allocation** is used to describe the assignment of indirect costs to the particular cost object.

In Exhibit 2-2 we illustrate direct and indirect costs and both forms of cost assignment, (cost tracing and cost allocation) using the example of *Sports Illustrated*, the magazine published by Time-Warner. The cost object in Exhibit 2-2 is the *Sports Illustrated* magazine. The paper on which the magazine is printed is a direct cost. This paper can be traced to each magazine issue being printed in an economically feasible way. Consider now the cost of leasing the building that houses the senior editorial staff of such Time-Warner magazines as *Time*, *People*, and *Sports Illustrated*. This leasing cost would be an indirect cost of *Sports Illustrated*. It is not possible to trace the lease amount to a specific magazine's editorial staff. It is possible, however, to allocate the lease cost among each magazine product of Time-Warner using the relative percentage of total floor space occupied by the editorial group of each magazine.

Correcting Student Misconceptions Students have trouble with the distinctions between direct/indirect costs and cost tracing/cost allocation. Familiar examples can help. Public accounting firms directly trace direct professional labor costs to each audit engagement (through time sheets). In contrast, rent on the firm's office and depreciation on its computers cannot be traced to individual engagements. These are indirect costs that must be allocated to the different engagements. Allocation of indirect costs is a difficult but important topic that is covered in more detail in Chaps. 5 and 14.

Reinforcing Problems Exer. 2-19 and 2-23 through 2-25 cover direct versus indirect costs.

Factors Affecting Direct/Indirect Cost Classifications

Several factors affect the classification of a cost as direct or indirect:

1. *The materiality of the cost in question.* The greater the cost in question, the more likely that it is economically feasible to trace that cost to a particular cost object. Consider a mail-order catalog company. It would probably be economically feasible to trace the courier charges for delivering each package directly to the individual customer. In contrast, the cost of invoice paper included in the package sent to the customer is likely to be classified as an indirect cost because it is not economically feasible to trace the cost of this paper to each customer. The benefits of knowing the exact number of, say, 0.5 cents worth of paper included in each package do not exceed the costs of money and time in tracing the costs to each package.

2. *Available information-gathering technology.* Improvements in this technology are increasing the percentage of costs classified as direct. Bar codes, for example, allow many manufacturing plants to treat certain materials previously classified as indirect costs as direct costs of products. Many component parts now come with a bar code on them that can be scanned at every point in the production process. Bar codes can be read into a manufacturing cost file by waving a "wand" in the same quick and efficient way supermarkets now enter at their checkout counter the cost of many items purchased by their customers.

3. *Design of operations.* For example, classifying a cost as direct is facilitated if an organization's facility (or part thereof) is used exclusively for a specific cost object, such as a specific product or a particular customer.

4. *Contractual arrangements.* For example, a contract stating that a given component (an Intel Pentium chip) can be used only in a specific product (an IBM PC) makes it easier to classify the component as a direct cost of the product.

This book examines different ways to assign costs to cost objects. For now, be aware that a specific cost may be both direct and indirect. How? *The direct/indirect classification depends on the choice of the cost object.* For example, the salary of an Assembly Department supervisor at Ford would be a direct cost of the Assembly Department but an indirect cost of a product such as the Ford Explorer. We now discuss costs and their behavior.[1]

COST-BEHAVIOR PATTERNS: VARIABLE COSTS AND FIXED COSTS

Costing systems record the cost of resources acquired and track their subsequent use. Recording these costs allows managers to see how these costs behave. Consider two basic types of cost-behavior patterns found in many accounting systems. A **variable cost** changes in total in proportion to changes in the related level of total activity or volume. A **fixed cost** remains unchanged in total for a given time period despite wide changes in the related level of total activity or volume. Costs are defined as variable or fixed with respect to *a specific cost object* and for *a given time*. We illustrate these two basic types of costs with a manufacturing-sector example. Consider costs at the Detroit plant of Ford.

◆ *Variable Costs*: If Ford buys a steering wheel at $60 for each of its Ford Explorer vehicles, then the total cost of steering wheels should be $60 times the number of vehicles assembled. Total steering wheel costs is an example of a variable cost, a cost that changes *in total* in proportion to changes in the number of vehicles assembled (see Exhibit 2-3, Panel A). A second example of a variable cost is a sales commission of 5% of each sales revenue dollar (see Exhibit 2-3, Panel B). In Panels A and B, the costs are represented by a straight line. The phrases "strictly variable" or "proportionately variable" are sometimes used to describe the variable costs represented in Exhibit 2-3. In both Panels A and B, the cost per unit of a variable cost remains the same. For example, the steering wheel costs $60 for each vehicle assembled.

◆ *Fixed Costs*: Ford may incur $20 million in a given year for the leasing and insurance for its Detroit plant. Both these costs are unchanged in total over a designated range of the number of vehicles assembled during a given time span. Fixed costs become progressively smaller on a per unit basis as the number of vehicles assembled increases. For example, if Ford assembles 10,000 vehicles at this plant in a year, the fixed cost for leasing and insurance per vehicle would be $2,000 ($20,000,000 ÷ 10,000). If 50,000 vehicles are assembled, the fixed cost per vehicle would be $400 ($20,000,000 ÷ 50,000).

Do not assume that individual cost items are inherently variable or fixed. Consider labor costs. An example of labor costs being purely variable is when workers

---

[1]Cost-behavior questions appear in professional examinations with regularity. For example, see the supplement to this textbook: J. K. Harris, *Student Guide and Review Manual* (Upper Saddle River, N.J.: Prentice Hall, 2000). The first three chapters of this supplement are available, free of charge, at Prentice Hall's website: (www.prenhall.com/harris).

EXHIBIT 2-3
Examples of Variable Costs

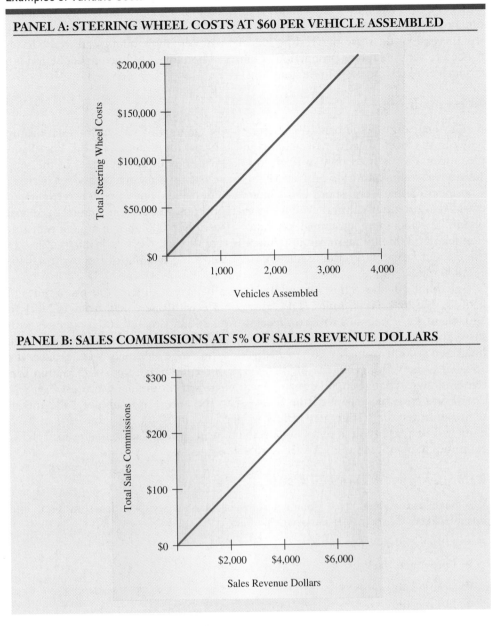

PANEL A: STEERING WHEEL COSTS AT $60 PER VEHICLE ASSEMBLED

PANEL B: SALES COMMISSIONS AT 5% OF SALES REVENUE DOLLARS

are paid on a piece-unit (piece-rate) basis. Some textile workers are paid on a per shirt sewed basis. In contrast, labor costs at a plant in the coming year are appropriately classified as fixed where a labor union agreement has a set annual salary and conditions, contains a no-layoff clause, and severely restricts an organization's flexibility to assign workers to any other plant that has demand for labor.

Cost Drivers

A **cost driver** is a factor, such as the level of activity or volume, that causally affects costs (over a given time span). That is, a cause-and-effect relationship exists between a change in the level of activity or volume and a change in the level of the total costs of that cost object.

The cost driver of variable costs is the level of activity or volume whose change causes the (variable) costs to change proportionately. For example, the number of vehicles assembled is a cost driver of the cost of steering wheels.

Costs that are fixed in the short run have no cost driver in the short run but may have a cost driver in the long run. Consider, for example, the cost of testing personal computers at Compaq. These costs consist of Testing Department equipment and staff costs that are difficult to change and hence fixed in the short run with respect to changes in the volume of production. Thus, volume of production is not a cost driver of testing costs in the short run. In the long run, however, Compaq will increase or decrease the Testing Department's equipment and staff to the levels needed to support future production volumes. Therefore, volume of production is a cost driver of testing costs in the long run.

Relevant Range

A **relevant range** is the band of activity or volume in which a specific relationship between the level of activity or volume and the cost in question is valid. For example, a fixed cost is fixed only in relation to a given range (usually wide) of the total activity or volume and for a given time span (usually a particular budget period). Consider Thomas Transport Company (TTC), which operates two refrigerated trucks that carry agricultural produce to market. Each truck has an annual fixed cost of $40,000 (including an annual insurance cost of $15,000 and an annual registration fee of $8,000). The maximum annual usage of each truck is 120,000 miles. In the current year (2001), the predicted combined total hauling of the two trucks is 170,000 miles.

Exhibit 2-4 shows how annual fixed costs behave at different levels of miles of hauling. Up to 120,000 miles, TTC can operate with one truck; from 120,001 to 240,000 miles, it operates with two trucks; from 240,001 to 360,000 it operates with three trucks. This pattern would continue as TTC adds trucks to its fleet. The bracketed section from 120,001 to 240,000 is the range at which TTC expects the $80,000 to be valid, given the predicted 170,000-mile usage for 2001. Within this relevant range, changes in miles hauled will not affect the annual fixed cost.

Fixed costs may change from one year to the next. For example, if the annual registration fee for refrigerated trucks is increased in 2002, the total level of fixed costs will increase (unless offset by a reduction in other fixed items) even if TTC continues to operate in the 120,001–240,000 range.

Relationships of Types of Costs

We have introduced two major classifications of costs: direct/indirect and variable/fixed. Costs may simultaneously be:

- ◆ Direct and variable
- ◆ Direct and fixed
- ◆ Indirect and variable
- ◆ Indirect and fixed

Correcting Student Misconceptions Fixed costs are only fixed in the short- (or intermediate-) run and within the relevant range. In the long-run, investment in PPE can change, as can lease rates, etc. If production increases dramatically, additional PPE is likely to be necessary. If production is cut drastically, PPE may be sold in a "rightsizing" initiative.

Curriculum Linkage The basic assumption of a relevant range also applies to variable costs. In economics, students should learn that the VC/unit increases at high output levels due to overtime premiums, machine breakdowns, etc. Because it is often expensive to obtain cost data outside the relevant range, managers often confine analysis to output levels within the relevant range. In some cases, data may not even exist outside the relevant range.

EXHIBIT 2-4
Fixed Cost Behavior at Thomas Transport Company

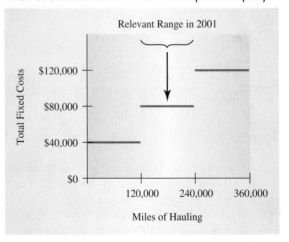

EXHIBIT 2-5
Examples of Costs in Combinations of the Direct/Indirect and
Variable/Fixed Cost Classifications

		Assignment of Costs to Cost Object	
		Direct Cost	**Indirect Cost**
Cost-Behavior Pattern	**Variable Cost**	◆ Cost object: Ford Explorer Example: Tires used in assembly of automobile	◆ Cost object: Ford Explorer Example: Power costs at Detroit plant. Power usage is metered only to the plant where multiple products are assembled.
	Fixed Cost	◆ Cost object: Ford Explorer Example: Salary of supervisor on Ford Explorer assembly line	◆ Cost object: Ford Explorer Example: Annual lease costs at Detroit plant. Lease is for whole plant at which multiple products are assembled.

Exhibit 2-5 presents for the Ford Explorer vehicle examples of costs in each of the four simultaneous cost classifications.

TOTAL COSTS AND UNIT COSTS

Using Averages and Unit Costs

Accounting systems typically report both total cost amounts and average cost-per-unit amounts. A **unit cost** (also called an **average cost**) is computed by dividing some amount of total costs by the related number of units. The "units" might be expressed in various ways. Examples are hours worked, packages delivered, or automobiles assembled. Suppose $40,000,000 of manufacturing costs were incurred in 2001 to produce 500,000 mobile phones at the Memphis plant of Cellular Products. Then the unit cost would be $80:

$$\frac{\text{Total manufacturing costs}}{\text{Number of units manufactured}} = \frac{\$40,000,000}{500,000} = \$80 \text{ per unit}$$

If 480,000 units are sold and 20,000 units remain in ending inventory, the unit-cost concept helps in the assignment of total costs in the income statement and balance sheet:[2]

Cost of goods sold in the income statement, 480,000 units × $80	$38,400,000
Ending inventory of finished goods in the balance sheet, 20,000 units × $80	1,600,000
Total manufacturing costs of 500,000 units	$40,000,000

Unit costs are found in all areas of the value chain—for example, unit cost of product design, of sales calls, and of customer-service calls.

Use Unit Costs Cautiously

Unit costs are frequently used in financial reports. However, for many decisions, managers should take a straightforward analytical approach and think in terms of total costs rather than unit costs. Consider the manager of the Memphis manufac-

[2]This example assumes no beginning inventory and ending work in process.

OBJECTIVE 4
Interpret unit costs with caution

Purposes for Companies Distinguishing between Variable Costs and Fixed Costs

Many chapters in this book illustrate the insights gained from distinguishing between variable costs and fixed costs. One survey of U.S. companies reported the following ranking of purposes for distinguishing between variable and fixed costs (1 = most important purpose).[a]

Rank	Purpose	Chapter(s) in This Book Discussing the Purpose in Detail
1 (equal)	Pricing	4, 5, 11, 12, and 13
1 (equal)	Budgeting	6
3	Profitability analysis—existing products	4, 5, 11, 12, and 13
4	Profitability analysis—new products	11, 12, and 13
5	Cost-volume-profit (CVP) analysis	3
6	Variance analysis	7, 8, and 16

Surveys of Australian, Japanese, and United Kingdom companies provide additional evidence on the ranking by managers of the many purposes for distinguishing between variable costs and fixed costs (1 = most important purpose):[b]

	Ranking by		
Purpose	Australian Companies	Japanese Companies	United Kingdom Companies
Pricing decisions	1	5	1
Budgeting	2	2	3
Making profit plans	3	1	2
Cost reduction	6	3	5 (equal)
CVP analysis	4 (equal)	4	4
Cost-benefit analysis	4 (equal)	6	5 (equal)

These surveys highlight the wide range of decisions for which managers feel an understanding of cost behavior is important.

[a]Adapted from Mowen, *Accounting for Costs as Fixed and Variable*.

[b]Blayney and Yokoyama, "Comparative Analysis of Japanese and Australian Cost Accounting and Management Practices." Full citations are in Appendix A at the end of the book.

turing plant of Cellular Products. Assume the $40,000,000 costs in 2001 comprise $10,000,000 of fixed costs and $30,000,000 of variable costs (at $60 variable cost per phone assembled). Suppose now that the fixed costs and the variable costs per phone in 2002 are expected to be unchanged from 2001. The budgeted costs for 2002 at different production levels are:

Units Produced	Variable Cost Per Unit	Total Variable Costs	Total Fixed Costs	Total Costs	Unit Costs
100,000	$60	$ 6,000,000	$10,000,000	$16,000,000	$160
200,000	$60	$12,000,000	$10,000,000	$22,000,000	$110
500,000	$60	$30,000,000	$10,000,000	$40,000,000	$ 80
800,000	$60	$48,000,000	$10,000,000	$58,000,000	$ 72.50
1,000,000	$60	$60,000,000	$10,000,000	$70,000,000	$ 70

A plant manager who used the 2001 unit cost of $80 per unit would underestimate actual total costs if 2002 output is below the 2001 level of 500,000 units. If actual volume is 200,000 units due to, say, the presence of a new competitor, actual costs would be $22,000,000. Using the unit cost of $80 times 200,000 units predicts $16,000,000, which underestimates the actual total costs by $6,000,000 ($22,000,000 actual cost minus $16,000,000). An overreliance on unit cost in this situation could lead the plant manager to have insufficient cash available to pay costs if volume declines to 200,000 units. For decision making, managers should think in terms of total costs rather than unit costs.

We now discuss cost concepts used in different sectors of the economy. We first define three different sectors and provide examples of companies in these different sectors.

MANUFACTURING, MERCHANDISING, AND SERVICE-SECTOR COMPANIES

Companies in the manufacturing, merchandising, and service sectors of the economy are frequently referenced in this book.

◆ **Manufacturing-sector companies** purchase materials and components and convert them into different finished goods. Examples are automotive companies, food processing companies, and textile companies.

◆ **Merchandising-sector companies** purchase and then sell tangible products without changing their basic form. This sector includes companies engaged in retailing (such as book stores or department stores), distribution, or wholesaling.

◆ **Service-sector companies** provide services or intangible products to their customers—for example, legal advice or audits. Examples are law firms, accounting firms, banks, insurance companies, transportation companies, advertising agencies, radio and television stations, and Internet-based companies.

The distinction between inventoriable costs and period costs is now examined. This distinction is important in both the manufacturing and merchandising sectors of the economy.

FINANCIAL STATEMENTS, INVENTORIABLE COSTS, AND PERIOD COSTS

The distinction between *inventoriable costs* and *period costs* is a key one in the generally accepted accounting principles that govern financial reporting. This section discusses and illustrates this distinction. As background, we first note the different types of inventory that companies hold and some commonly used classifications of manufacturing costs.

Types of Inventory

Manufacturing-sector companies purchase materials and components and convert them into different finished goods. They typically have one or more of the following three types of inventor:

1. **Direct materials inventory.** Direct materials in stock and awaiting use in the manufacturing process.[3]

2. **Work-in-process inventory.** Goods partially worked on but not yet fully completed. Also called **work in progress.**

3. **Finished goods inventory.** Goods fully completed but not yet sold.

Merchandising-sector companies purchase and then sell tangible products without changing their basic form. They hold only one type of inventory, which is the

[3]This chapter assumes that all materials in "Direct Materials Inventory" are direct materials of the telephone systems sold by Cellular Products. Chapter 4 illustrates the more general case where part of the materials costs in "Materials Inventory" are traced to products as direct materials costs of products being manufactured and the other part is allocated to products as part of indirect manufacturing costs.

product in its original purchased form. Service-sector companies provide only services or intangible products to their customers and hence do not hold inventories of tangible products for sale.

Commonly Used Classifications of Manufacturing Costs

OBJECTIVE 6

Describe the three categories of inventories commonly found in manufacturing companies

Three terms with widespread use when describing manufacturing costs are direct materials costs, direct manufacturing labor costs, and indirect manufacturing costs.

1. Direct materials costs are the acquisition costs of all materials that eventually become part of the cost object ("work in process" or "finished goods"), and that can be traced to the cost object in an economically feasible way. Acquisition costs of direct materials include freight-in (inward delivery) charges, sales taxes, and custom duties.

2. Direct manufacturing labor costs include the compensation of all manufacturing labor that can be traced to the cost object in an economically feasible way. Examples include wages and fringe benefits paid to machine operators and assembly-line workers.

3. Indirect manufacturing costs are all manufacturing costs that are considered part of the cost object, units finished or in process, but that cannot be traced to that cost object in an economically feasible way. Examples include power, supplies, indirect materials, indirect manufacturing labor, plant rent, plant insurance, property taxes on plants, plant depreciation, and the compensation of plant managers. Other terms for this cost category include **manufacturing overhead costs** and **factory overhead costs.** We use *indirect manufacturing costs* and *manufacturing overhead costs* interchangeably in this book.

We next describe the important distinction between inventoriable and period costs.

Correcting Student Misconceptions
Students are often confused when labor costs are inventoriable costs (IC) or period costs (PC). In service firms, direct labor is an operating cost that is a PC (expensed in the period incurred because services cannot be inventoried). In merchandising firms, sales salaries are marketing costs, not costs of acquiring goods for resale (i.e., not part of CGS), so they are PC. In mfg. firms, factory workers' wages are IC. These wages are necessary to produce the products (so the wage costs are inventoriable), and products stored as inventory have future value because they will generate revenue (so the inventory is an asset).

Inventoriable Costs

OBJECTIVE 7

Differentiate between inventoriable costs and period costs

Inventoriable costs are all costs of a product that are regarded as an asset when they are incurred and then become cost of goods sold when the product is sold. For manufacturing-sector companies, all manufacturing costs are inventoriable costs. Cost incurred for direct materials, direct manufacturing labor, and indirect manufacturing costs create new assets, first work in process and then finished goods. Hence manufacturing costs are included in work in process and finished goods inventory (they are "inventoried") to accumulate the costs of creating these assets. When finished goods are sold, the cost of the goods sold is recognized as an expense to be matched against the revenues from the sale. Note that the cost of goods sold includes all manufacturing costs (direct materials, direct manufacturing labor, and indirect manufacturing costs) incurred to produce the goods sold. Sales may occur in a different accounting period than the period in which the goods were manufactured. Thus, inventorying manufacturing costs during manufacturing and expensing the manufacturing cost of goods sold later when revenues are recognized achieves better matching of revenues and expenses.[4]

Correcting Student Misconceptions
Students also have difficulty with the notion that some costs are assets (IC are unexpired costs, i.e., assets with value) while others are expensed as incurred (PC are expired costs, i.e., their value has been used). They also need to understand that IC have value as long as the firm owns them. When the inventory is sold, the value expires and is transferred from the balance sheet to the income statement as an expense (CGS).

For merchandising-sector companies, *inventoriable costs* are the costs of purchasing the goods that are resold in their same form. These costs are the costs of the goods themselves and any incoming freight costs for those goods. For service-sector companies, the absence of inventories means there are no inventoriable costs.

Period Costs

Period costs are all costs in the income statement other than cost of goods sold. These costs are treated as expenses of the period in which they are incurred because they are presumed not to benefit future periods (or because there is not sufficient evidence to conclude that such benefit exists). Expensing these costs immediately best matches expenses to revenues.

---

[4]*Inventoriable costs* are frequently referred to as *product costs* in the financial reporting literature and in financial accounting textbooks.

For manufacturing-sector companies, period costs include all nonmanufacturing costs (for example, research and development costs and distribution costs). For merchandising-sector companies, period costs include all costs not related to the cost of goods purchased for resale in their same form (for example, labor cost of sales floor personnel and marketing costs). The absence of inventoriable costs for service-sector companies means that all their costs are period costs.

We now illustrate the inventoriable cost versus period cost distinction using the financial statement of a manufacturing company.

Reinforcing Problems Exer. 2-26 and Prob. 2-36 cover issues of inventoriable costs and period costs.

ILLUSTRATING THE FLOW OF INVENTORIABLE COSTS AND PERIOD COSTS

Manufacturing-Sector Example

The income statement of a manufacturer, Cellular Products, is shown in Exhibit 2-6. Revenues of Cellular are (in thousands) $210,000. **Revenues** are inflows of assets (almost always cash or accounts receivable) received for products or services provided to customers. Cost of goods sold in a manufacturing company is often computed as follows:

Correcting Student Misconceptions Students are often confused about the category of inventory used in a mfg. firm's CGS section. Normally, only FG are sold, so FG is the inventory used to adjust CGM to obtain CGS.

$$\begin{matrix} \text{Beginning} & \text{Cost of} & \text{Ending} & \text{Cost of} \\ \text{finished goods} + & \text{goods} & - \text{finished goods} = & \text{goods} \\ \text{inventory} & \text{manufactured} & \text{inventory} & \text{sold} \end{matrix}$$

For Cellular Products in 2001, the corresponding amounts (in thousands) in Exhibit 2-6 (Panel A) are:

$$\$22{,}000 + \$104{,}000 - \$18{,}000 = \$108{,}000$$

Reinforcing Problems Exer. 2-27 and Probs. 2-28 through 2-31 and 2-34 through 2-37 cover CGM and CGS.

Cost of goods manufactured refers to the cost of goods brought to completion, whether they were started before or during the current accounting period. In 2001, these costs amount to $104,000 for Cellular Products (see the Schedule of Cost of Goods Manufactured in Panel B of Exhibit 2-6). A line item in Panel B is "Manufacturing costs incurred during the period" of $105,000. This item refers to the direct manufacturing costs and the indirect manufacturing costs that were incurred during 2001 for all goods worked on during that year, regardless of whether all those goods were fully completed during 2001.

Cellular Products classifies its manufacturing costs into the three categories described earlier:

1. *Direct materials costs*. These costs are computed in Exhibit 2-6 (Panel B) as follows:

$$\begin{matrix} \text{Beginning} & \text{Purchases of} & \text{Ending} & \text{Direct} \\ \text{direct materials} + & \text{direct materials} - & \text{direct materials} = & \text{materials} \\ \text{inventory} & & \text{inventory} & \text{used} \end{matrix}$$

$$\$11{,}000 \quad + \quad \$73{,}000 \quad - \quad \$8{,}000 \quad = \$76{,}000$$

2. *Direct manufacturing labor costs*. Exhibit 2-6 (Panel B) reports these costs as $9,000.

3. *Indirect manufacturing costs*. Exhibit 2-6 (Panel B) reports these costs as $20,000.

Teaching Tip There is no need for students to memorize the CGM schedule if they understand the intuition. Think of the CGM schedule as summarizing the flow of costs in the plant through 3 buildings, from the DM warehouse (#1) to the factory (#2) to the FG warehouse (#3). Picture each square in Exhibit 2-8, panel A in the balance sheet section as a building. In each building, we calculate a "generic CGS" for the inventory in that building (BI + costs added - EI = costs out). In building #1, we make this calculation for DM inventory: BI of DM + purchases of DM - EI of DM = DM used. In building #2, we make this calculation for WIP inventory: BI of WIP + (DM used + DML + IMC) - EI of WIP = CGM. In building #3, we make this calculation for FG inventory: BI of FG + CGM - EI of FG = CGS.

Correcting Student Misconceptions Because freight-in is necessary to obtain DM, it is treated as part of DM cost. Freight-out is a marketing expense because it arises from delivering FG to customers.

Exhibit 2-7 shows related general-ledger T-accounts for Cellular Products' manufacturing cost flow. Note how the cost of goods manufactured of $104,000 is the cost of all goods completed during the accounting period. These costs are all inventoriable costs. Such goods completed are transferred to finished goods inventory. They become cost of goods sold when sales occur, which depends on the nature of the product, business conditions, and types of customers.

The $70,000 for marketing, distribution, and customer-service costs are the period costs of Cellular Products. They include, for example, salaries to salespeople, depreciation on computers and other equipment used in marketing, and the

PANEL A

Cellular Products
Income Statement
For the Year Ended December 31, 2001 (in thousands)

Revenues		$210,000
Cost of goods sold:		
Beginning finished goods, January 1, 2001	$ 22,000	
Cost of goods manufactured (see Panel B)	104,000 ◄	
Cost of goods available for sale	126,000	
Ending finished goods, December 31, 2001	18,000	108,000
Gross margin (or gross profit)		102,000
Marketing, distribution and customer-service costs		70,000
Operating income		$ 32,000

PANEL B

Cellular Products
Schedule of Cost of Goods Manufactured[a]
For the Year Ended December 31, 2001 (in thousands)

Direct materials:		
Beginning inventory, January 1, 2001	$ 11,000	
Purchases of direct materials	73,000	
Cost of direct materials available for use	84,000	
Ending inventory, December 31, 2001	8,000	
Direct materials used		$ 76,000
Direct manufacturing labor		9,000
Indirect manufacturing costs:		
Indirect manufacturing labor	7,000	
Supplies	2,000	
Heat, light, and power	5,000	
Depreciation—plant building	2,000	
Depreciation—plant equipment	3,000	
Miscellaneous	1,000	20,000
Manufacturing costs incurred during the period		105,000
Add beginning work-in-process inventory, January 1, 2001		6,000
Total manufacturing costs to account for		111,000
Deduct ending work-in-process inventory, December 31, 2001		7,000
Cost of goods manufactured (to Income Statement)		$104,000

[a]Note that the term *cost of goods manufactured* refers to the cost of goods brought to completion (finished) during the year, whether they were started before or during the current year. Some of the manufacturing costs incurred during the year are held back as costs of the ending work-in-process inventory; similarly, the costs of the beginning work-in-process inventory become part of the cost of goods manufactured for the year. Note too that this schedule can become a Schedule of Cost of Goods Manufactured and Sold simply by including the beginning and ending finished goods inventory figures in the supporting schedule rather than in the body of the income statement.

cost of leasing warehouse space for distribution. Operating income of Cellular Products is $32,000. **Operating income** is total revenues from operations minus cost of goods sold and operating costs (excluding income taxes).

Newcomers to cost accounting frequently assume that indirect costs such as rent, telephone, and depreciation are always costs of the period in which they are incurred and are not associated with inventories. However, if these costs are related to manufacturing per se, they are indirect manufacturing costs and are inventoriable.

EXHIBIT 2-7
General-Ledger T-Accounts for Cellular Products' Manufacturing Cost Flow

Work-in-Process Inventory				Finished Goods Inventory				Cost of Goods Sold	
Bal. Jan. 1, 2001	6,000	Cost of goods manufactured	104,000	Bal. Jan. 1, 2001	22,000	Cost of goods sold	108,000	108,000	
Direct materials used	76,000			104,000					
Direct manuf. labor	9,000								
Indirect manuf. costs	20,000								
Bal. Dec.31, 2001	7,000			Bal. Dec.31, 2001	18,000				

Recap of Inventoriable Costs and Period Costs

Exhibit 2-8 highlights the important differences between inventoriable costs and period costs.

Panel A uses the manufacturing sector to illustrate these differences. The merchandising sector is shown in Panel B. First study Panel A. The manufacturing costs of the finished goods include direct materials, other direct manufacturing costs, and indirect manufacturing costs. All these costs are inventoriable: They are assigned to work-in-process inventory or finished goods inventory until the goods are sold.[5]

Consider now Panel B of Exhibit 2-8. A retailer or wholesaler buys goods for resale without changing their basic form. The *only* inventoriable cost is the cost of merchandise. Unsold goods are held as merchandise inventory whose cost is shown as an asset in the balance sheet. As the goods are sold, their costs are written off in the income statement as cost of goods sold. A retailer or wholesaler also has a variety of other operating, marketing, distribution, and customer-service costs, which are period costs. In the income statement, period costs are deducted from revenues without ever having been regarded as part of inventory.

Prime Costs and Conversion Costs

Two terms used in manufacturing costing systems are prime costs and conversion costs. **Prime costs** are all direct manufacturing costs. For Cellular Products, prime costs are $85,000 ($76,000 direct materials cost + $9,000 direct manufacturing labor cost). As information-gathering technology improves, companies can add additional direct-cost categories. For example, power costs might be metered in specific areas of a plant that are dedicated totally to the assembly of separate products. In this case, prime costs would include direct materials, direct manufacturing labor, and direct metered power (assuming there are already direct materials and direct manufacturing labor categories). Computer software companies often have a "purchased technology" direct manufacturing cost item. This item, which represents payments to third parties who develop software algorithms included in a product, is also included in prime costs. **Conversion costs** are all manufacturing costs other than direct material costs. These costs are incurred to transform direct materials into finished goods. For Cellular Products, conversion costs are $29,000 ($9,000 direct manufacturing labor cost + $20,000 of indirect manufacturing costs).

Some manufacturing companies have only a two-part classification of costs—direct materials costs and conversion costs. For these companies, all conversion costs are indirect manufacturing costs. An example is costing systems in some highly automated plants. These systems often do *not* have a direct manufacturing labor cost category because tracing these costs to products is not perceived to be cost-effective.

---

[5]In this chapter we assume that all manufacturing costs are inventoriable. The term *absorption costing* is used to describe the method in which all manufacturing costs are inventoriable. Chapter 9 discusses this method and two alternative methods—*variable costing* (only variable manufacturing costs are inventoriable) and *throughput costing* (only one variable cost, direct materials, is inventoriable).

EXHIBIT 2-8
Relationships of Inventoriable Costs and Period Costs

PANEL A: MANUFACTURING COMPANY

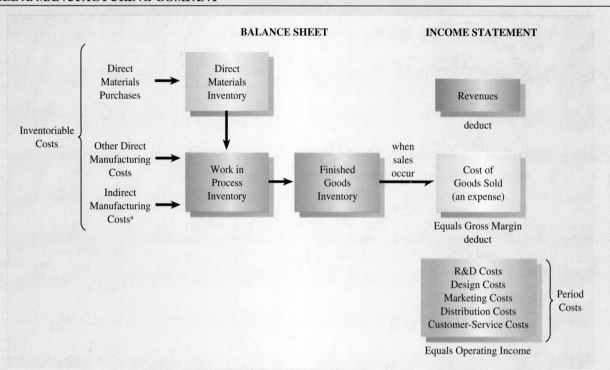

[a]Examples: Indirect manufacturing labor, plant supplies, insurance and depreciation on plant. (Note particularly that where insurance and depreciation relate to the manufacturing function, they are inventoriable, but where they relate to nonmanufacturing business functions (for example, marketing and distribution), they are not inventoriable.

PANEL B: MERCHANDISING COMPANY (RETAILER OR WHOLESALER)

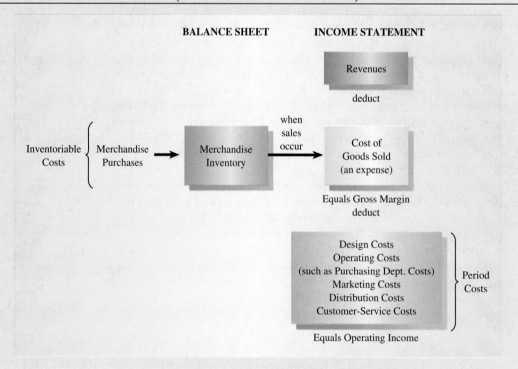

Harley-Davidson Eliminates the Direct Manufacturing Labor Cost Category[a]

Harley-Davidson's Motorcycle Division for many years used a three-part cost classification in its manufacturing facilities—direct materials, direct manufacturing labor, and manufacturing overhead. In the mid-1980s, a task force of Harley-Davidson managers analyzed how its manufacturing product-cost structure compared with the administrative costs required to collect, inspect, and report data in its accounting system, with the following results:

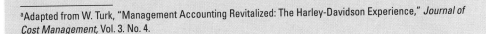

	Manufacturing Product-Cost Structure	Administrative Cost Effort
Direct materials	54%	25%
Manufacturing overhead	36	13
Direct manufacturing labor	10	62

The administrative costs associated with tracking direct manufacturing labor as a separate cost category included:

- Operator's time to fill out labor tickets
- Supervisor's time to review labor tickets
- Timekeeper's time to enter the labor data and review the output reports for errors
- Cost accountant's time to review the direct-labor and variance data

Harley-Davidson concluded that tracing direct manufacturing labor to products did not meet the cost-benefit test. Direct manufacturing labor costs were only 10% of total manufacturing costs but required 62% of the administrative effort used to track all manufacturing costs. The company now includes all manufacturing labor costs as part of manufacturing overhead costs. It uses a two-part classification of direct materials and manufacturing overhead.

[a]Adapted from W. Turk, "Management Accounting Revitalized: The Harley-Davidson Experience," *Journal of Cost Management,* Vol. 3. No. 4.

MEASURING COSTS REQUIRES JUDGMENT

Judgment is frequently required when measuring costs. Differences can exist in the way accounting terms are defined. Care should be taken to define and understand the way costs are measured in any organization or situation in which costs are an issue. We first illustrate this point with respect to labor cost measurement.

Measuring Labor Costs

Manufacturing labor cost classifications vary among companies, but the following distinctions are generally found:

Direct manufacturing labor (defined earlier)
Manufacturing overhead (examples of prominent labor components of this manufacturing overhead follow):
    Indirect labor (compensation)
        Forklift truck operators (internal handling of materials)
        Janitors
        Plant guards
        Rework labor (time spent by direct laborers redoing defective work)
        Overtime premium paid to all plant workers
        Idle time
    Managers' salaries
    Payroll fringe costs (for example, health care premiums, pension costs)

Points to Stress The text uses the term direct manufacturing labor because labor incurred in other elements of the value chain can also be traced directly to cost objects. For example, in some cases, sales labor can be traced directly to specific customers.

All manufacturing labor compensation, other than that for direct labor and managers' salaries, is usually classified as *indirect labor costs*, a major component of manufacturing overhead. The term *indirect labor* is often divided into many subclassifications. The wages of forklift truck operators are generally not commingled with janitors' wages, for example, although both are regarded as indirect labor.

Managers' salaries are usually not classified as indirect labor. Instead, the compensation of supervisors, department heads, and all others who are regarded as manufacturing management is placed in a separate classification of manufacturing overhead.

Overtime Premium

Costs are classified in a detailed fashion primarily to associate an individual cost with its specific cause or reason for incurrence. Two classes of indirect labor need special mention. **Overtime premium** consists of the wage rate paid to all workers (for both direct labor and indirect labor) in *excess* of their straight-time wage rates. Overtime premium is usually considered a part of overhead. Consider an example from the service sector. George Flexner does home repairs for Sears Appliance Services. He is paid $20 per hour for straight-time and $30 (time and a half) for overtime. His *premium* is $10 per overtime hour. If he works 44 hours, including 4 overtime hours, in one week, his gross compensation would be classified as follows:

Direct service labor: 44 hours × $20	$880
Overtime premium: 4 hours × $10	40
Total compensation for 44 hours	$920

Reinforcing Problems Prob. 2-33 covers the issue of overtime premium.

Why is the overtime premium of direct labor usually considered an indirect rather than a direct cost? After all, it can be traced to specific batches of work. Overtime premium is generally not considered a direct charge because the scheduling of repair jobs is generally either random or in accordance with minimizing overall travel time. For example, assume that jobs 1–5 are scheduled for a specific workday of 10 hours, including 2 overtime hours. Each service call (job) requires 2 hours. Should the job scheduled during hours 9 and 10 be assigned the overtime premium? Or should the premium be prorated over all the jobs? The latter approach does not "penalize"—add to the cost of—a particular batch of work solely because it happened to be worked on during the overtime hours. *Instead, the overtime premium is considered to be attributable to the heavy overall volume of work. Its cost is thus regarded as part of service overhead, which is borne by all repair jobs.*

Sometimes overtime is not random. For example, a rush job may clearly be the sole source of the overtime. In such instances, the overtime premium is regarded as a direct cost of the services on that job.

Another subclassification of indirect labor is the **idle time** of both direct and indirect manufacturing or service labor. Idle time typically represents wages paid for unproductive time caused by lack of orders, machine breakdowns, material shortages, poor scheduling, and the like. For example, if the Sears repair truck broke down for 3 hours, earnings would be classified as follows:

Direct service labor: 41 hours × $20	$820
Idle time (service overhead): 3 hours × $20	60
Overtime premium (service overhead): 4 hours × $10	40
Total earnings for 44 hours	$920

Clearly, the idle time is not related to a particular job, as we have already discussed, nor is the overtime premium. Hence both are considered indirect costs.

Benefits of Defining Accounting Terms

We cannot overemphasize the value of a thorough understanding of the classifications and cost terms introduced in this chapter and later in this book. Managers, accountants, suppliers, and other people will avoid many misunderstandings if they agree on the meanings of technical terms.

Consider the classification of manufacturing labor *payroll fringe costs* (for example, employer contributions to employee benefits such as social security, life insurance, health insurance, and pensions). Some companies classify these costs as manufacturing overhead. In other companies, however, the fringe benefits related to direct manufacturing labor are treated as an additional direct manufacturing labor cost. Consider, for example, a direct laborer, such as a lathe operator or an auto mechanic whose gross wages are computed on the basis of a nominal or stated wage rate of $20 an hour, may enjoy fringe benefits totaling, say, $5 per hour. Some companies classify the $20 as direct manufacturing labor cost and the $5 as manufacturing overhead. Other companies classify the entire $25 as direct manufacturing labor cost. The latter approach is conceptually preferable because these costs are a fundamental part of acquiring direct manufacturing labor services.

The warning here is to pinpoint what direct manufacturing labor includes and excludes in a particular situation. Achieving clarity may preclude disputes regarding cost reimbursement contracts, income tax payments, and labor union matters. For example, some countries offer substantial income tax savings to companies such as Intel that locate plants there. To qualify, the "direct manufacturing labor" costs of these companies in that country must equal at least a specified percentage of the total manufacturing costs of their products. Disputes have arisen regarding how to calculate the direct manufacturing labor percentage for qualifying for such tax benefits. For instance, are payroll fringe benefits on direct manufacturing labor part of direct manufacturing labor costs, or are they part of manufacturing overhead? Depending on how companies classify costs, you can readily see how firms may show "direct manufacturing labor" as different percentages of total manufacturing costs. Consider a company with $5 million of payroll fringe costs (figures are assumed, in millions):

Classification A			Classification B		
	Cost	Percentage		Cost	Percentage
Direct materials	$ 40	40%	Direct materials	$ 40	40%
Direct manufacturing labor	20	20	Direct manufacturing labor	25	25
Manufacturing overhead	40	40	Manufacturing overhead	35	35
Total manufacturing costs	$100	100%	Total manufacturing costs	$100	100%

Classification A assumes that payroll fringe costs are part of manufacturing overhead. In contrast, classification B assumes that payroll fringe costs are part of direct manufacturing labor. If a country sets the minimum percentage of direct labor costs at 25%, the company would receive a tax break using classification B, but not using classification A. In addition to fringe benefits, other debated items are compensation for training time, idle time, vacations, sick leave, and overtime premium. To prevent disputes, contracts and laws should be as specific as feasible regarding definitions and measurements.

Many cost terms found in practice are not sufficiently precise to avoid ambiguity as to their meaning. We now show how the purpose facing a manager plays a key role in determining the meaning of cost terms.

The Many Meanings of Product Cost

The term *product cost* is widely used. A **product cost** is the sum of the costs assigned to a product for a specific purpose. Exhibit 2-9 illustrates how three different purposes can result in three different measures of product cost:

1. *Pricing and product emphasis decisions*. For this purpose, the costs included are all areas of the value chain.

2. *Contracting with government agencies*. Government agencies frequently provide detailed guidelines on the allowable and nonallowable items in a product cost. For example, some government agencies explicitly exclude marketing costs from reimbursement to contractors and may reimburse only a part of R&D costs. Hence, the second bracket in Exhibit 2-9 shows how a specific contract may allow for all design and production costs and part of R&D costs.

EXHIBIT 2-9
Different Product Costs for Different Purposes

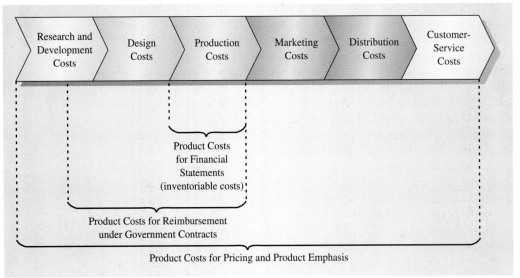

3. *Preparing financial statements for external reporting under generally accepted accounting principles.* The focus here is on inventoriable costs. Under generally accepted accounting principles, only manufacturing costs are assigned to inventories in the financial statements.

Exhibit 2-9 illustrates how a product cost for external reporting can include only inventoriable costs in the financial statements, or a broader set of costs for reimbursement under a government contract, or a still broader set of costs for the pricing and product-emphasis decisions.

This section has focused on costs in the value chain of business functions. The same caution about the need to be precise about cost concepts and their measurement applies to each cost classification introduced in this chapter. Exhibit 2-10 summarizes the key cost classifications.

EXHIBIT 2-10
Alternative Classifications of Costs

1. Business function
   a. Research and development
   b. Design of products, services, and processes
   c. Production
   d. Marketing
   e. Distribution
   f. Customer service
2. Assignment to a cost object
   a. Direct costs
   b. Indirect costs
3. Behavior pattern in relation to changes in the level of a cost driver
   a. Variable costs
   b. Fixed costs
4. Aggregate or average
   a. Total costs
   b. Unit costs
5. Assets or expenses
   a. Inventoriable costs
   b. Period costs

(Try to solve this problem before examining the solution that follows.)

PROBLEM

Campbell Company is a metal and wood cutting manufacturer, selling products to the home construction market. Consider the following data for the year 2001:

Sandpaper	$ 2,000
Materials-handling costs	70,000
Lubricants and coolants	5,000
Miscellaneous indirect manufacturing labor	40,000
Direct manufacturing labor	300,000
Direct materials, Jan. 1, 2001	40,000
Direct materials, Dec. 31, 2001	50,000
Finished goods, Jan. 1, 2001	100,000
Finished goods, Dec. 31, 2001	150,000
Work in process, Jan. 1, 2001	10,000
Work in process, Dec. 31, 2001	14,000
Plant-leasing costs	54,000
Depreciation—plant equipment	36,000
Property taxes on plant equipment	4,000
Fire insurance on plant equipment	3,000
Direct materials purchased	460,000
Revenues	1,360,000
Marketing promotions	60,000
Marketing salaries	100,000
Distribution costs	70,000
Customer-service costs	100,000

Required

1. Prepare an income statement with a separate supporting schedule of cost of goods manufactured. For all manufacturing items, indicate by V or F whether each is basically a variable cost or a fixed cost (where the cost object is a product unit). If in doubt, decide on the basis of whether the total cost will change substantially over a wide range of units produced.
2. Suppose that both the direct materials and plant-leasing costs are tied to the production of 900,000 units. What is the unit cost for the direct materials assigned to each unit produced? What is the unit cost of the plant-leasing costs? Assume that the plant-leasing costs are a fixed cost.
3. Repeat the computation in requirement 2 for direct materials and plant-leasing costs, assuming that the costs are being predicted for the manufacturing of 1,000,000 units next year. Assume that the implied cost-behavior patterns persist.
4. As a management consultant, explain concisely to the president why the unit costs for direct materials did not change in requirements 2 and 3 but the unit costs for plant-leasing costs did change.

SOLUTION

1.
Campbell Company
Income Statement
For the Year Ended December 31, 2001

Revenues		$1,360,000
Cost of goods sold:		
Beginning finished goods, January 1, 2001	$ 100,000	
Cost of goods manufactured (see schedule below)	960,000	
Cost of goods available for sale	1,060,000	
Ending finished goods, December 31, 2001	150,000	910,000
Gross margin (or gross profit)		450,000
Marketing, distribution and customer-service costs		
Marketing promotions	60,000	
Marketing salaries	100,000	
Distribution costs	70,000	
Customer-service costs	100,000	330,000
Operating income		$ 120,000

Campbell Company
Schedule of Cost of Goods Manufactured
For the Year Ended December 31, 2001

Direct materials:		
Beginning inventory, January 1, 2001		$ 40,000
Purchases of direct materials		460,000
Cost of direct materials available for use		500,000
Ending inventory, December 31, 2001		50,000
Direct materials used		450,000 (V)
Direct manufacturing labor		300,000 (V)
Indirect manufacturing costs:		
Sandpaper	$ 2,000 (V)	
Materials-handling costs	70,000 (V)	
Lubricants and coolants	5,000 (V)	
Miscellaneous indirect manufacturing labor	40,000 (V)	
Plant-leasing costs	54,000 (F)	
Depreciation—plant equipment	36,000 (F)	
Property taxes on plant equipment	4,000 (F)	
Fire insurance on plant equipment	3,000 (F)	214,000
Manufacturing costs incurred during 2001		964,000
Add beginning work in process		
January 1, 2001		10,000
Total manufacturing costs to account for		974,000
Deduct ending work in process		
December 31, 2001		14,000
Cost of goods manufactured (to Income Statement)		$960,000

2. Direct material unit cost = Direct materials used ÷ Units produced
    = $450,000 ÷ 900,000 = $0.50
   Plant-leasing unit cost = Plant-leasing costs ÷ Units produced
    = $54,000 ÷ 900,000 = $0.06

3. The direct material costs are variable, so they would increase in total from $450,000 to $500,000 (1,000,000 × $0.50). However, their unit costs would be unaffected: $500,000 ÷ 1,000,000 units = $0.50.

In contrast, the plant-leasing costs of $54,000 are fixed, so they would not increase in total. However, the plant-leasing costs per unit would decline from $0.060 to $0.054: $54,000 ÷ 1,000,000 = $0.054.

4. The explanation would begin with the answer to requirement 3. As a consultant, you should stress that the unitizing (averaging) of costs that have different behavior patterns can be misleading. A common error is to assume that a total unit cost, which is often a sum of variable unit costs and fixed unit costs, is an indicator that total costs change in a wholly variable way as production levels change. The next chapter demonstrates the necessity for distinguishing between cost-behavior patterns. You must be wary especially about average fixed costs per unit. Too often, unit fixed costs are erroneously regarded as being indistinguishable from unit variable costs.

SUMMARY

The following points are linked to the chapter's learning objectives:

1. A cost object is anything for which a separate measurement of costs is desired. Examples include a product, service, project, customer, brand category, activity, and department.

2. A direct cost is any cost that is related to a particular cost object and that can be traced to it in an economically feasible way. Indirect costs are related to the particular cost object but cannot be traced to it in an economically feasible way. A cost can be direct regarding one cost object and indirect regarding other cost objects. This book uses the term *cost tracing* to describe the assignment of direct costs to a cost object and the term *cost allocation* to describe the assignment of indirect costs to a cost object.

3. A variable cost changes in total in proportion to changes in the related level of total activity or volume. A fixed cost remains unchanged in total for a given time period despite wide changes in the related level of total activity or volume.

4. Unit costs of a cost object should be interpreted with caution when they include a fixed-cost component. When making total cost estimates, think of variable costs as an amount per unit and fixed costs as a total amount.

5. Manufacturing-sector companies purchase materials and components and convert them into different finished goods. Merchandising-sector companies purchase and then sell tangible products without changing their basic form. Service-sector companies provide services or intangible products to their customers.

6. Inventoriable costs are all costs of a product that are regarded as an asset when they are incurred and then become cost of goods sold when the product is sold. Period costs are all costs in an income statement other than cost of goods sold.

7. The three categories of inventory found in many manufacturing companies depict stages in the conversion process—materials, work in process, and finished goods.

8. Managers can assign different costs to the same cost object depending on their purpose. For example, for the external reporting purpose the inventoriable costs of a product include only manufacturing costs. In contrast, costs from all areas of the value chain can be assigned to a product for pricing and product-emphasis decisions.

This chapter contains more basic terms than any other in this book. Do not proceed before you check your understanding of the following terms. Both the chapter and the Glossary at the end of the book contain definitions.

actual cost (p. 28)
average cost (33)
conversion costs (39)
cost (28)
cost accumulation (28)
cost allocation (29)
cost assignment (28)
cost driver (31)
cost object (28)
cost of goods manufactured (37)
direct costs of a cost object (28)
direct manufacturing labor costs (36)
direct materials costs (36)
direct materials inventory (35)
factory overhead costs (36)
finished goods inventory (35)
fixed cost (30)
idle time (42)

indirect costs of a cost object (29)
indirect manufacturing costs (36)
inventoriable costs (36)
manufacturing overhead costs (36)
manufacturing-sector company (35)
merchandising-sector company (35)
operating income (38)
overtime premium (42)
period costs (36)
product cost (43)
prime costs (39)
relevant range (32)
revenues (37)
service-sector company (35)
unit cost (33)
variable cost (30)
work-in-process inventory (35)
work in progress (35)

QUESTIONS

2-1 Define *cost object* and give three examples.

2-2 Define *direct costs* and *indirect costs*. How are these terms related?

2-3 Why do managers consider direct costs to be more accurate than indirect costs?

2-4 Name three factors that will affect the classification of a cost as direct or indirect.

2-5 Describe how manufacturing-, merchandising-, and service-sector companies differ from each other.

2-6 What is a *cost driver*? Give one example.

2-7 Define *variable cost* and *fixed cost*. Give an example of each.

2-8 What is the *relevant range?* What role does the relevant range concept play in explaining how costs behave?

2-9 Explain why *unit costs* must often be interpreted with caution.

2-10 What are three different types of inventory that manufacturing companies hold?

2-11 Distinguish between *inventoriable costs* and *period costs.*

2-12 Do service-sector companies have inventoriable costs? Explain.

2-13 Define the following: *direct materials costs, direct manufacturing labor costs, indirect manufacturing costs, prime costs,* and *conversion costs.*

2-14 Describe the *overtime premium* and *idle time* categories of indirect labor.

2-15 Define *product cost.* Describe three different purposes for computing product costs.

EXERCISES

2-16 **Total costs and unit costs.** A student association has hired a musical group for a graduation party. The cost will be a fixed amount of $4,000.
Required
1. Suppose 500 people attend the party. What will be the total cost of the musical group? The unit cost per person?
2. Suppose 2,000 people attend. What will be the total cost of the musical group? The unit cost per person?

3. For prediction of total costs, should the manager of the party use the unit cost in requirement 1? The unit cost in requirement 2? What is the major lesson of this exercise?

2-17 **Total costs and unit costs.** Susan Wang is a well-known software engineer. Her specialty is writing software code used in maintaining the security of credit-card information. Wang is approached by the Electronic Commerce Group (ECG). They offer to pay her $100,000 for the right to use her code under license in their *e.procurement* software package. Wang rejects this offer because it provides her with no upside if the *e.procurement* package is a runaway success. Both parties eventually agree to a contract where ECG pays Wang a flat fee of $100,000 for the right to use her code in up to 10,000 packages. If *e.procurement* sells more than 10,000 packages, Wang receives an additional $8 for each package sold beyond the 10,000 level.

Required
1. What is the unit cost to ECG of Wang's software code included in its *e.procurement* package if it sells (a) 2,000 packages, (b) 6,000 packages, (c) 10,000 packages, and (d) 20,000 packages? Comment on the results.
2. To predict ECG's total cost of using Wang's software code in *e.procurement*, which unit cost (if any) of (a) to (d) in requirement 1 would you recommend ECG use? Explain.

2-18 **Computing and interpreting unit manufacturing costs.** Finish Forest Products (FFP) produces three different paper products at its Vaasa lumber plant—Supreme, Deluxe, and Regular. Each product has its own dedicated production line at the plant. It currently uses the following three-part classification for its manufacturing costs—direct materials, direct manufacturing labor, and indirect manufacturing costs. Total indirect manufacturing costs of the plant are $150 million ($20 million of which is fixed per month). This total amount is allocated to each product line on the basis of direct manufacturing labor costs at each line. Summary data (in millions) for the most recent month (July 2001) are as follows:

	Supreme	**Deluxe**	**Regular**
Direct materials costs	$84.0	$54.0	$62.0
Direct manufacturing labor costs	14.0	28.0	8.0
Indirect manufacturing costs	42.0	84.0	24.0
Pounds produced	80	120	100

Required
1. Compute the unit manufacturing cost per pound for each product produced in July 2001.
2. Suppose that in August 2001, production was 120 pounds of Supreme, 160 pounds of Deluxe, and 180 pounds of Regular. Why might the July 2001 unit manufacturing cost information be misleading when predicting total manufacturing costs in August 2001?

2-19 **Direct and indirect costs, effect of changing the classification of a cost item (continuation of 2-18).** Finish Forest Products (FFP) employs a consultant to help reduce energy costs at its Vaasa plant. Currently, FFP does not trace energy costs to each product line. The energy consultant notes that each production line at the Vaasa plant has multiple energy meters and that tracing of energy costs to each line is possible. Of the $150 million of indirect manufacturing costs in July 2001, $90 million is for energy costs traceable to individual production lines. The remaining $60 million of indirect manufacturing costs of the plant (including the $20 million fixed costs per month) is allocated to each product line on the basis of direct manufacturing labor costs at each line. Using this information, FFP's cost analyst reports the following revised numbers (in millions) for July 2001:

	Supreme	**Deluxe**	**Regular**
Direct materials	$84.0	$54.0	$62.0
Direct manufacturing labor	14.0	28.0	8.0
Direct energy costs	39.8	40.7	9.5
Indirect manufacturing costs	16.8	33.6	9.6
Pounds produced	80	120	100

Required
1. What is the difference between a direct cost and an indirect cost?
2. Why might FFP's managers prefer energy costs to be a direct cost rather than an indirect manufacturing cost?

3. Compute the revised unit manufacturing cost per pound for each product produced in July 2001. Compare these costs with those computed in requirement 1 of Exercise 2-18. Comment on any differences in the unit-cost numbers.

2-20 Cost drivers and the value chain. A Johnson & Johnson analyst is preparing a presentation on cost drivers at its pharmaceutical drug subsidiary. Unfortunately, both the list of its business functions and the accompanying list of representative cost drivers is accidentally randomized. The two lists now on the computer screen are:

Business Function	Representative Cost Driver
A. Production	1. Minutes of T.V. advertising time on "*60 Minutes*"
B. Research and Development	2. Number of calls to toll-free customer phone line
C. Marketing	3. Hours the Tylenol packaging line is in operation
D. Distribution	4. Number of packages shipped
E. Design of Products/Processes	5. Hours spent designing tamper-proof bottles
F. Customer Service	6. Number of patents filed with U.S. Patent Office

Required
1. Match each business function with its representative cost driver.
2. Give a second example of a cost driver for each business function of Johnson & Johnson's pharmaceutical drug subsidiary.

2-21 Cost drivers and the value chain. A Toyota analyst is preparing a presentation on cost drivers. Unfortunately, both the list of its business functions and the accompanying list of representative cost drivers is accidentally randomized. The two lists now on the computer screen are:

Business Function	Representative Cost Driver
1. Design of Products/Processes	1. Number of cars recalled due to defective parts
2. Customer Service	2. Number of machine assembly-hours
3. Marketing	3. Number of research scientists
4. Research and Development	4. Hours of computer-aided design (CAD) work
5. Distribution	5. Number of sales personnel
6. Production	6. Weight of cars shipped

Required
1. Match each business function with its representative cost driver.
2. Give a second example of a cost driver for each business function of Toyota.

2-22 Variable costs and fixed costs. Consolidated Minerals (CM) owns the rights to extract minerals from beach sands on Fraser Island. CM has costs in three areas:

a. Payment to a mining subcontractor who charges $80 per ton of beach sand mined and returned to the beach (after being processed on the mainland to extract three minerals—ilmenite, rutile, and zircon).

b. Payment of a government mining and environmental tax of $50 per ton of beach sand mined.

c. Payment to a barge operator. This operator charges $150,000 per month to transport each batch of beach sand—up to 100 tons per batch per day to the mainland and then return to Fraser Island. (That is, 0–100 tons per day = $150,000 per month; 101–200 tons per day = $300,000 per month, and so on.) Each barge operates 25 days per month. The $150,000 monthly charge must be paid even if less than 100 tons are transported on any day and even if Consolidated Minerals requires fewer than 25 days of barge transportation in that month.

CM is currently mining 180 tons of beach minerals per day for 25 days per month.

Required
1. What is the variable cost per ton of beach sand mined? What is the fixed cost to CM per month?
2. Plot a graph of the variable costs and another graph of the fixed costs of Consolidated Minerals. Your graphs should be similar to Exhibits 2-3 and 2-4. Is the concept of relevant range applicable to your graphs?
3. What is the unit cost per ton of beach sand mined (a) if 180 tons are mined each day, or (b) if 220 tons are mined each day? Explain the difference in the unit-cost figures.

2-23 Classification of costs, service sector. Consumer Focus is a marketing research firm that organizes focus groups for consumer-product companies. Each focus group has eight individuals who are paid $50 per session to provide comments on new products. These focus groups meet in hotels and are led by a trained independent marketing specialist hired by Consumer Focus. Each specialist is paid a fixed retainer to conduct a minimum number of sessions and a per session fee of $2,000. A Consumer Focus staff member attends each session to ensure that all the logistical aspects run smoothly.

Required

Classify each of the following cost items as:

a. Direct or indirect (D or I) costs with respect to each individual focus group.

b. Variable or fixed (V or F) costs with respect to how the total costs of Consumer Focus change as the number of focus groups conducted changes. (If in doubt, select on the basis of whether the total costs will change substantially if there is a large change in the number of groups conducted.)

You will have two answers (D or I; V or F) for each of the following items:

Cost Item	D or I	V or F
A. Payment to individuals in each focus group to provide comments on new products.		
B. Annual subscription of Consumer Focus to *Consumer Reports* magazine.		
C. Phone calls made by Consumer Focus staff member to confirm individuals will attend a focus group session. (Records of individual calls are not kept.)		
D. Retainer paid to focus group leader to conduct 20 focus groups per year on new medical products.		
E. Meals provided to participants in each focus group.		
F. Lease payment by Consumer Focus for corporate office.		
G. Cost of tapes used to record comments made by individuals in a focus group session. (These tapes are sent to the company whose products are being tested.)		
H. Gasoline costs of Consumer Focus staff for company-owned vehicles. (Staff members submit monthly bills with no mileage breakdowns.)		

2-24 Classification of costs, merchandising sector. Home Entertainment Center (HEC) operates a large store in San Francisco. The store has both a video section and a musical (compact disks, records, and tapes) section. HEC reports revenues for the video section separately from the musical section.

Required

Classify each of the following cost items as:

a. Direct or indirect (D or I) costs with respect to the video section.

b. Variable or fixed (V or F) costs with respect to how the total costs of the video section change as the number of videos sold changes. (If in doubt, select on the basis of whether the total costs will change substantially if there is a large change in the number of videos sold.)

You will have two answers (D or I; V or F) for each of the following items:

Cost Item	D or I	V or F
A. Annual retainer paid to a video distributor.		
B. Electricity costs of HEC store (single bill covers entire store).		
C. Costs of videos purchased for sale to customers.		
D. Subscription to *Video Trends* magazine.		
E. Leasing of computer software used for financial budgeting at HEC store.		
F. Cost of popcorn provided free to all customers of HEC.		
G. Earthquake insurance policy for HEC store.		
H. Freight-in costs of videos purchased by HEC.		

2-25 Classification of costs, manufacturing sector. The Fremont, California, plant of New United Motor Manufacturing, Inc. (NUMMI), a joint venture of General Motors and Toyota, assembles two types of cars (Corollas and Geo Prisms). Separate assembly lines are used for each type of car.

Required

Classify each of the following cost items as:

a. Direct or indirect (D or I) costs with respect to the type of car assembled (Corolla or Geo Prism).

b. Variable or fixed (V or F) costs with respect to how the total costs of the plant change as the number of cars assembled changes. (If in doubt, select on the basis of whether the total costs will change substantially if there is a large change in the number of cars assembled.)

You will have two answers (D or I; V or F) for each of the following items:

Cost Item	D or I	V or F
A. Cost of tires used on Geo Prisms.		
B. Salary of public relations manager for NUMMI plant.		
C. Annual awards dinner for Corolla suppliers.		
D. Salary of engineer who monitors design changes on Geo Prism.		
E. Freight costs of Corolla engines shipped from Toyota City, Japan, to Fremont, California.		
F. Electricity costs for NUMMI plant (single bill covers entire plant).		
G. Wages paid to temporary assembly-line workers hired in periods of high production (paid on hourly basis).		
H. Annual fire insurance policy cost for NUMMI plant.		

2-26 Inventoriable costs vs. period costs. Each of the following cost items pertains to one of these companies—General Electric (a manufacturing-sector company), Safeway (a merchandising-sector company), and Excite (a service-sector company):

a. Perrier mineral water purchased by Safeway for sale to its customers.

b. Electricity used to provide lighting for assembly-line workers at a General Electric refrigerator assembly plant.

c. Depreciation on Excite's computer equipment used to update directories of websites.

d. Electricity used to provide lighting for Safeway's store aisles.

e. Depreciation on General Electric's computer equipment used for quality testing of refrigerator components during the assembly process.

f. Salaries of Safeway's marketing personnel planning local-newspaper advertising campaigns.

g. Perrier mineral water purchased by Excite for consumption by its software engineers.

h. Salaries of Excite's marketing personnel selling banner advertising.

Required

1. Distinguish between manufacturing-sector, merchandising-sector, and service-sector companies.
2. Distinguish between inventoriable costs and period costs.
3. Classify each of the cost items (a–h) as an inventoriable cost or a period cost. Explain your answers.

 2-27 Computing cost of goods manufactured and cost of goods sold. Compute cost of goods manufactured and cost of goods sold from the following account balances (in thousands) relating to 2001:

Property tax on plant building	$ 3,000
Marketing, distribution, and customer-service costs	37,000
Finished goods inventory, January 1, 2001	27,000
Plant utilities	17,000
Work-in-process inventory, December 31, 2001	26,000

Depreciation of plant building	9,000
General and administrative costs (nonplant)	43,000
Direct materials used	87,000
Finished goods inventory, December 31, 2001	34,000
Depreciation of plant equipment	11,000
Plant repairs and maintenance	16,000
Work-in-process inventory, January 1, 2001	20,000
Direct manufacturing labor	34,000
Indirect manufacturing labor	23,000
Indirect materials used	11,000
Miscellaneous plant overhead	4,000

PROBLEMS

2-28 Cost of goods manufactured. Consider the following account balances (in thousands) for the Canseco Company:

	Beginning of 2001	End of 2001
Direct materials inventory	$22,000	$26,000
Work-in-process inventory	21,000	20,000
Finished goods inventory	18,000	23,000
Purchases of direct materials		75,000
Direct manufacturing labor		25,000
Indirect manufacturing labor		15,000
Plant insurance		9,000
Depreciation—plant building and equipment		11,000
Repairs and maintenance—plant		4,000
Marketing, distribution, and customer-service costs		93,000
General and administrative costs		29,000

Required
1. Prepare a schedule of cost of goods manufactured for 2001.
2. Revenues in 2001 were $300 million. Prepare the 2001 income statement.

2-29 Income statement and schedule of cost of goods manufactured. The Howell Corporation has the following account balances (in millions):

For Specific Date		For Year 2001	
Direct materials, Jan. 1, 2001	$15	Purchases of direct materials	$325
Work in process, Jan. 1, 2001	10	Direct manufacturing labor	100
Finished goods, Jan. 1, 2001	70	Depreciation—plant building and	
Direct materials, Dec. 31, 2001	20	equipment	80
Work in process, Dec. 31, 2001	5	Plant supervisory salaries	5
Finished goods, Dec. 31, 2001	55	Miscellaneous plant overhead	35
		Revenues	950
		Marketing, distribution, and	
		customer-service costs	240
		Plant supplies used	10
		Plant utilities	30
		Indirect manufacturing labor	60

Required
Prepare an income statement and a supporting schedule of cost of goods manufactured for the year ended December 31, 2001. (For additional questions regarding these facts, see the next problem.)

2-30 Interpretation of statements (continuation of 2-29).

Required

1. How would the answer to Problem 2-29 be modified if you were asked for a "schedule of cost of goods manufactured and sold" instead of a "schedule of cost of goods manufactured"? Be specific.

2. Would the sales manager's salary (included in marketing, distribution, and customer-service costs) be accounted for any differently if the Howell Corporation were a merchandising-sector company instead of a manufacturing-sector company? Using the flow of costs outlined in Exhibit 2-8, describe how the wages of an assembler in the plant would be accounted for in this manufacturing company.

3. Plant supervisory salaries are usually regarded as indirect manufacturing costs. When might some of these costs be regarded as direct manufacturing costs? Give an example.

4. Suppose that both the direct materials used and the plant depreciation are related to the manufacture of 1 million units of product. What is the unit cost for the direct materials assigned to those units? What is the unit cost for plant building and equipment depreciation? Assume that yearly plant depreciation is computed on a straight-line basis.

5. Assume that the implied cost-behavior patterns in requirement 4 persist. That is, direct materials costs behave as a variable cost and depreciation behaves as a fixed cost. Repeat the computations in requirement 4, assuming that the costs are being predicted for the manufacture of 1.2 million units of product. How would the total costs be affected?

6. As a management accountant, explain concisely to the president why the unit costs differed in requirements 4 and 5.

2-31 Income statement and schedule of cost of goods manufactured. The following items (in millions) pertain to Chan Corporation:

For Specific Date		For Year 2001	
Work in process, Jan. 1, 2001	$10	Plant utilities	$ 5
Direct materials, Dec. 31, 2001	5	Indirect manufacturing labor	20
Finished goods, Dec. 31, 2001	12	Depreciation—plant,	
Accounts payable, Dec. 31, 2001	20	building, and equipment	9
Accounts receivable,		Revenues	350
Jan. 1, 2001	50	Miscellaneous manufacturing	
Work in process, Dec. 31, 2001	2	overhead	10
Finished goods, Jan. 1, 2001	40	Marketing, distribution, and	
Accounts receivable,		customer-service costs	90
Dec. 31, 2001	30	Direct materials purchased	80
Accounts payable, Jan. 1, 2001	40	Direct manufacturing labor	40
Direct materials, Jan. 1, 2001	30	Plant supplies used	6
		Property taxes on plant	1

Chan's manufacturing costing system uses a three-part classification of direct materials, direct manufacturing labor, and indirect manufacturing costs.

Required

Prepare an income statement and a supporting schedule of cost of goods manufactured. (For additional questions regarding these facts, see the next problem.)

2-32 Interpretation of statements (continuation of 2-31).

Required

1. How would the answer to Problem 2-31 be modified if you were asked for a schedule of cost of goods manufactured and sold instead of a schedule of cost of goods manufactured? Be specific.

2. Would the sales manager's salary (included in marketing, distribution and customer-service costs) be accounted for any differently if Chan Corporation were a merchandising-sector company instead of a manufacturing-sector company? Using the flow of costs outlined in Exhibit 2-8, describe how the wages of an assembler in the plant would be accounted for in this manufacturing company.

3. Plant supervisory salaries are usually regarded as indirect manufacturing costs. When might some of these costs be regarded as direct manufacturing costs? Give an example.

4. Suppose that both the direct materials used and the plant depreciation are related to the manufacture of 1 million units of product. What is the unit cost for the direct materials assigned to those units? What is the unit cost for plant building and equipment depreciation? Assume that yearly depreciation is computed on a straight-line basis.

5. Assume that the implied cost-behavior patterns in requirement 4 persist. That is, direct materials costs behave as a variable cost and plant depreciation behaves as a fixed cost. Repeat the computations in requirement 4, assuming that the costs are being predicted for the manufacture of 1.5 million units of product. How would the total costs be affected?

6. As a management accountant, explain concisely to the president why the unit costs differed in requirements 4 and 5.

2-33 Overtime premium, defining accounting terms. Gwen Benson, Ian Blacklaw, and Eduardo Cabrera are sales representatives for Electronic Manufacturing, Inc. (EMI). EMI specializes in low-volume production orders for the research groups of major companies. Each sales representative receives a base salary plus a bonus based on 20% of the actual gross margin of each order they sell. Prior to this year, the bonus was 5% of the revenues of each order they sold. Gross margin in the revised system was defined as revenue minus cost of goods sold. EMI uses a three-part classification of manufacturing costs—direct materials, direct manufacturing labor, and indirect manufacturing costs. Indirect manufacturing costs are determined as 200% of direct manufacturing labor cost.

Benson receives a report on an EMI job for BBC, Inc. She is dismayed by the low gross margin on the BBC job. She prided herself on not discounting the price BBC would pay by convincing them of the quality of EMI's work. Benson discussed the issue with Blacklaw and Cabrera. They share with her details of their most recent jobs. Summary data are as follows:

Customer	Westec	La Electricidad	BBC
Sales Representative	Blacklaw	Cabrera	Benson
Revenues $420	$820	$480	
Direct materials	$250	$410	$270
Direct manufacturing labor	$ 40	$100	$ 60
Indirect manufacturing	$ 80	$200	$120
Direct labor-hours	2 hours	5 hours	2 hours

Benson asks Hans Brunner, EMI's manufacturing manager, to explain the different labor costs charged on the Westec and BBC jobs given that both of them used 2 direct-labor hours. She was told the BBC job was done during overtime and that the overtime rate was 50% higher than the $20 per hour straight-time rate. Benson noted that she brought the BBC order to EMI one week ago and that there was no rush to complete the job. In contrast, the Westec order was a "hot-hot" one with a request it be done by noon the day after the order was received. It was done in regular (non-overtime) working time. Brunner said that the "labor cost" he charged to the BBC job was actually the amount paid to the workers on that job.

Required
1. What is the gross margin EMI would report on each of the three jobs?
2. Assume that EMI charges each job for direct labor at the $20 straight-time rate (and that the indirect-manufacturing rate of 200% includes overtime premium). What would be the revised gross margin EMI would report on each of the three jobs? Comment on any differences from requirement 1.
3. Discuss the pros and cons of charging the BBC job the $30 per hour labor rate.
4. Why might EMI adopt the 20% gross margin incentive instead of the prior 5% of revenue incentive? How might EMI define "gross margin" to reduce possible disagreements with its sales representatives?

2-34 Finding unknown balances. An auditor for the Internal Revenue Service is trying to reconstruct some partially destroyed records of two taxpayers. For each of the cases in the accompanying list, find the unknowns designated by capital letters.

	Case 1	Case 2
	(in thousands)	
Accounts receivable, 12/31	$ 6,000	$ 2,100
Cost of goods sold	A	20,000
Accounts payable, 1/1	3,000	1,700
Accounts payable, 12/31	1,800	1,500
Finished goods inventory, 12/31	B	5,300
Gross margin	11,300	C
Work in process, 1/1	0	800
Work in process, 12/31	0	3,000
Finished goods inventory, 1/1	4,000	4,000
Direct material used	8,000	12,000
Direct manufacturing labor	3,000	5,000
Indirect manufacturing costs	7,000	D
Purchases of direct material	9,000	7,000
Revenues	32,000	31,800
Accounts receivable, 1/1	2,000	1,400

2-35 Fire loss, computing inventory costs. A distraught employee, Fang W. Arson, put a torch to a manufacturing plant on a blustery February 26. The resulting blaze completely destroyed the plant and its contents. Fortunately, certain accounting records were kept in another building. They reveal the following for the period from January 1, 2001 to February 26, 2001:

Direct materials purchased	$160,000
Work in process, 1/1/2001	$34,000
Direct materials, 1/1/2001	$16,000
Finished goods, 1/1/2001	$30,000
Indirect manufacturing costs	40% of conversion costs
Revenues	$500,000
Direct manufacturing labor	$180,000
Prime costs	$294,000
Gross margin percentage based on revenues	20%
Cost of goods available for sale	$450,000

The loss is fully covered by insurance. The insurance company wants to know the historical cost of the inventories as a basis for negotiating a settlement, although the settlement is actually to be based on replacement cost, not historical cost.

Required
Calculate the cost of:
1. Finished goods inventory, 2/26/2001.
2. Work-in-process inventory, 2/26/2001.
3. Direct materials inventory, 2/26/2001.

2-36 Comprehensive problem on unit costs, product costs. Tampa Office Equipment manufactures and sells metal shelving. It began operations on January 1, 2001. Costs incurred for 2001 are as follows (V stands for variable; F stands for fixed):

Direct materials costs	$140,000 V
Direct manufacturing labor costs	30,000 V
Plant energy costs	5,000 V
Indirect manufacturing labor costs	10,000 V
Indirect manufacturing labor costs	16,000 F
Other indirect manufacturing costs	8,000 V
Other indirect manufacturing costs	24,000 F
Marketing, distribution, and customer-service costs	122,850 V
Marketing, distribution, and customer-service costs	40,000 F
Administrative costs	50,000 F

Variable manufacturing costs are variable with respect to units produced. Variable marketing, distribution, and customer-service costs are variable with respect to units sold.

Inventory data are:

	Beginning, January 1, 2001	Ending, December 31, 2001
Direct materials	0 lb.	2,000 lb.
Work in process	0 units	0 units
Finished goods	0 units	? units

Production in 2001 was 100,000 units. Two pounds of direct materials are used to make one unit of finished product.

Revenues in 2001 were $436,800. The selling price per unit and the purchase price per pound of direct materials were stable throughout the year. The company's ending inventory of finished goods is carried at the average unit manufacturing costs for 2001. Finished goods inventory at December 31, 2001, was $20,970.

Required
1. Direct materials inventory, total cost, December 31, 2001.
2. Finished goods inventory, total units, December 31, 2001.
3. Selling price per unit, 2001.
4. Operating income, 2001. Show your computations.

2-37 Budgeted income statement (continuation of 2-36). Assume management predicts that the selling price per unit and variable cost per unit each will be the same in 2002 as in 2001. Fixed manufacturing costs and marketing, distribution, and customer-service costs in 2002 are also predicted to be the same as in 2001. Sales in 2002 are forecast to be 122,000 units. The desired ending inventory of finished goods, December 31, 2002, is 12,000 units. Assume zero ending inventories of both direct materials and work in process. The company's ending inventory of finished goods is carried at the average unit manufacturing costs for 2002. The company uses the first-in, first-out inventory method. Management has asked that you prepare a budgeted income statement for 2002.

Required
1. How many units of finished goods should be produced in 2002? Show your computations.
2. Prepare a budgeted income statement for 2002.

2-38 Cost analysis, litigation risk, ethics. Sam Nash is the head of new product development of Forever Young (FY). Nash is currently considering Enhance, which would be FY's next major product in its beauty/cosmetics line. Enhance represents a new direction for FY. All FY's current products are cosmetics applied to the skin by the consumer. In contrast, Enhance is inserted via a needle into the skin by a doctor's nurse after an initial meeting with a doctor. Each treatment is planned to cost patients $300 and will last three months. Enhance is an animal-based product that fills out the skin so that fewer wrinkles are observable.

FY plans to sell Enhance to doctors for $120 a treatment, providing the doctor with a large incentive to promote the product. Nash, however, questions the economics of this product. At present, the costs recognized are research and development, manufacturing by a third party, marketing, distribution, and a small amount (less than $1 million) for customer support. Nash's main concern is with recognizing in the current costing proposal potential future litigation costs (such as the costs of lawyers and expert witnesses in defending lawsuits related to Enhance). He points to the litigation with breast implants and notes that a settlement of over $4 billion is being discussed in the press. He also notes the tobacco company litigation and those proposed billion dollar settlements. Elisabeth Savage, the CEO and president of the company, totally disagrees with Nash. She maintains she has total confidence in her medical research team and directs Nash not to include any dollar amount for potential litigation cost in his upcoming presentation to the board of directors on the economics and pricing of the Enhance product. Nash was previously controller of FY and has a long background in finance. His current job represents his first nonfinance position, and he views himself as potential CEO material.

Required
1. What reasons might Savage have for not wanting Nash to record potential future litigation costs on the product in a presentation on Enhance's economics and pricing?

2. Suppose Savage asks Nash to give her an "off-the-record" presentation on the possible magnitude of the potential litigation costs of Enhance. What information should Nash use to develop such a presentation and to estimate such costs?

3. After hearing Nash's presentation (see requirement 2), Savage directs Nash to drop any further discussion of the litigation issue. He is to focus on making Enhance the blockbuster product that field research has suggested it will be. Nash is uneasy with this directive. He tells Savage it is an "ostrich approach" (head-in-the-sand) to a real problem that could potentially bankrupt the company. Savage tells Nash to go and think about her directive. What should Nash do next?

COLLABORATIVE LEARNING PROBLEM

2-39 Movie profit sharing, defining terms. Brad Fittler, first-time author of *The Sporting Life*, has just had a meeting with Bill Harrigan, a senior executive of Golden Ventures (GV). GV is a major movie studio with many successes. *The Sporting Life* is a best-selling novel about the personal and professional career of Allan Langer, a recently retired football superstar. Harrigan bubbled with excitement during the meeting. He said the book was the "best thing he had seen in many years" and would make "*Titanic* look like a minor movie." Fittler felt great about a luminary such as Harrigan being so full of praise for a film based on a book that many publishers initially rejected as "not meeting their commercial criteria."

After the meeting, Fittler called Penny Carr, a friend for many years. Carr shows Fittler some extracts from an expose on "Accounting, Hollywood-Style"—see Exhibit for Problem 2-39. Fittler is dismayed by the Cumulative Distribution Statement. He thought *Paul Sterling, Superstar* was a box-office success and yet it still is over $60 million "in the red."

Required
You are asked to give advice to Brad Fittler. Specifically, he wants you to:

a. Identify the weaknesses in the Golden Ventures' Cumulative Distribution Statement for an author whose payment is 5% of operating income.

b. Propose ways to reduce (or even eliminate) the weaknesses you identify in (a) for a contract for Fittler.

EXHIBIT FOR PROBLEM 2-39

Golden Ventures' Report on
Paul Sterling, Superstar
Cumulative Distribution Statement (in millions)
From July 1, 2000 to March 31, 2001

1.	Gross receipts[a]	$ 160.295
2.	Less distribution fee[b]	56.103
3.	Gross after distribution fees	104.192
4.	Less distribution expenses[c]	55.063
5.	Balance	49.129
6.	Less gross participation fees of directors, screen stars, etc.[d]	32.059
7.	Balance	17.070
8.	Less negative cost[e]	68.420
9.	Balance	(51.350)
10.	Less interest on negative cost[f]	10.786
11.	Operating income	$ (62.136)

[a]The studio's revenues from the film to date. All U.S. theater and television revenues are included. Only 50% of non-U.S. revenues are included. Only 20% of the gross is included for home video revenues. The film's video distributor, Golden Ventures Home Video (100% owned by GV) kept 80% since it was treated as a separate company. Revenues from non-theater, non-video, and non-television sources are not included.
[b]Distribution fees. Covers overhead costs of running a studio and is a flat percentage (35%) of revenues.
[c]Distribution expenses. The actual costs of putting the movie in theaters, including advertising, printing copies of the film, and transportation.
[d]Gross participation fees of directors, screen stars. The major "talent" in the movie receive 20% of the gross receipts for the first $200 million and 25% thereafter.
[e]Negative cost is the cost of producing everything that is seen on screen, from film, sets, and up-front fees paid to the cast and crew.
[f]Interest on negative cost. The studio views the cost of financing a film as a loan and charges 125% of the prime rate for any negative balance in line 9 as long as the movie "remains in the red."

CLASSIC

"Cost Accounting is music to your ears!"

COST ACCOUNTING, *Tenth Edition*
Charles T. Horngren, George Foster, and Srikant M. Datar

There are many reasons a classic remains a classic. Pure quality, excellent composition, and outstanding acceptance are just a few of them. Like the works of Mozart and Beethoven, **Cost Accounting** has always stood the test of time . . . and been recognized as a masterpiece!

◆ **Composed to set new standards from the very first edition . . . and still leading the market today!**

"Horngren has always been given top marks by students in their evaluations of texts at the ends of semesters. The insertion of questions in the text at various points works well. It focuses the attention of the reader on the discussion that follows."
–Russell A. Taussig,
University of Hawaii

◆ **Over 2 million students are singing the praises of Horngren/Foster/Datar's Cost Accounting!**

"I also liked the 'real world' examples provided in the text . . . students really like them. [And] I like the end-of-chapter problems . . . . These problems give the students an opportunity to test what they need to study before attempting assigned materials."
–Peter Woodlock,
Youngstown State University

3

Cost-Volume-Profit Analysis

learning objectives

After studying this chapter, you should be able to

1. Understand basic cost-volume-profit (CVP) assumptions
2. Explain essential features of CVP analysis
3. Determine the breakeven point and output to achieve target operating income using the equation, contribution margin, and graph methods
4. Incorporate income tax considerations into CVP analysis
5. Explain the use of CVP analysis in decision making and how sensitivity analysis can help managers cope with uncertainty
6. Use CVP analysis to plan costs
7. Apply CVP analysis to a multiproduct company
8. Adapt CVP analysis to multiple cost driver situations
9. Distinguish between contribution margin and gross margin

Companies such as Symantec sell software programs such as Norton Crash Guard at computer conventions. By distinguishing the fixed costs from the variable costs of participating at the convention, Symantec can determine its profit or loss at various levels of sales, including the sales it must achieve to break even.

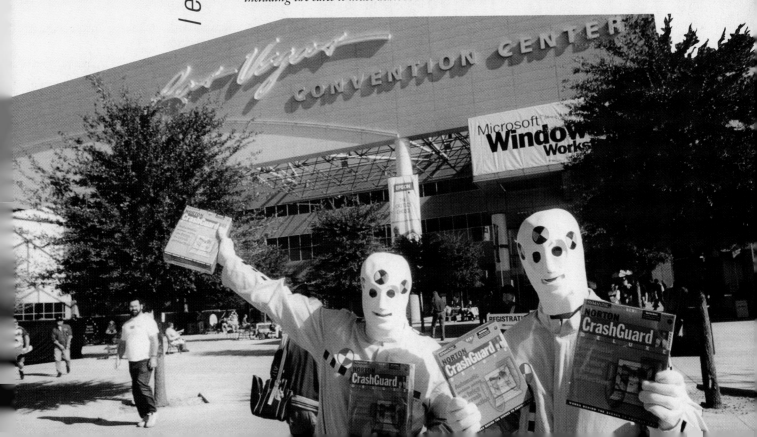

Teaching Tip Motivate students by pointing out that surveys have shown that over 50% of responding companies use some form of CVP analysis.

Points to Stress Mgt. acctg. research has shown that volume, while not the only cost driver, is usually a major cost driver.

OBJECTIVE 1

Understand basic cost-volume-profit (CVP) assumptions.

Points to Stress What if these CVP assumptions aren't met? If **1** is not met, multiple cost and revenue drivers could be used (covered later in this chapter). If **2** or **3** aren't met, economists' curvilinear TR and TC functions could be estimated. Alternatively, TR and TC functions are often approx. linear within a narrow relevant range. If **4** is violated, sensitivity analysis or expected value analysis as described in the Appendix can help managers make CVP decisions when faced with uncertainty. If **5** is violated, CVP can be performed with multiple products, and can be repeated for different product mixes, as explained subsequently. Finally, if the analysis covers a long time period, **6** is violated. The solution is to use discounted cash flow procedures as explained in Chap. 21.

Points to Stress The assumptions are valid only for short-run decisions because (1) total fixed costs are fixed only in the short run, and (2) the time value of money is ignored. If CVP analysis is used in long-run or product life-cycle decisions, fewer costs are fixed, and the analysis is based on discounted cash flows.

This chapter examines one of the most basic planning tools available to managers: cost-volume-profit analysis. **Cost-volume-profit (CVP) analysis** examines the behavior of total revenues, total costs, and operating income as changes occur in the output level, selling price, variable costs per unit, or fixed costs. Managers commonly use CVP analysis as a tool to help them answer such questions as, How will revenues and costs be affected if we sell 1,000 more units? If we raise or lower our selling prices? If we expand business into overseas markets? These questions have a common "what-if" theme. By examining various possibilities and alternatives, CVP analysis illustrates various decision outcomes and thus serves as an invaluable aid in the planning process.

COST-VOLUME-PROFIT ASSUMPTIONS AND TERMINOLOGY

Cost-volume-profit (CVP) analysis is based on several assumptions.

1. Changes in the level of revenues and costs arise only because of changes in the number of product (or service) units produced and sold—for example, the number of television sets produced and sold by Sony Corporation. The number of output units is the only *revenue* and *cost driver*. Just as a cost driver is any factor that affects costs, a **revenue driver** is any factor that affects revenues.

2. Total costs can be divided into a fixed component and a component that is variable with respect to the level of output. Recall from Chapter 2 (Exhibit 2-5, p. 33) that variable costs include both direct variable costs and indirect variable costs of the product. Similarly, fixed costs include both direct fixed costs and indirect fixed costs of the product. We discuss detailed approaches to determining fixed and variable components of costs in Chapter 10.

3. When graphed, the behavior of total revenues and total costs is linear (straight line) in relation to output units within the relevant range (and time period).[1]

4. The unit selling price, unit variable costs, and fixed costs are known and constant. (This assumption is discussed later in the chapter and in the appendix to this chapter.)

5. The analysis either covers a single product or assumes that the sales mix when multiple products are sold will remain constant as the level of total units sold changes. (This assumption is also discussed later in the chapter.)

6. All revenues and costs can be added and compared without taking into account the time value of money. (Chapter 21 relaxes this assumption.)

Many companies (and divisions and plants of companies) in industries such as airlines, automobiles, chemicals, plastics, and semiconductors have found the simple CVP relationships to be helpful in strategic and long-range planning decisions as well as decisions about product features and pricing. In other real-world settings, the simple assumptions described above may not hold. For example, predicting total revenues and total costs may require multiple revenue drivers (such as number of output units, number of sales visits made to customers, and number of advertisements placed), and multiple cost drivers (such as number of output units and number of batches in which units are produced). The basic CVP ideas may still be useful in these situations, but the analysis is more complex. Managers and accountants, however, must always assess whether the simplified CVP relationships generate sufficiently accurate predictions of how total revenues and total costs behave. Managers should consider using a more complex approach that, for example, considers

[1]For example, one set of conditions in which assumption 3 is descriptive includes the following: Selling prices are constant within the relevant range; productivity is constant within the relevant range; and costs of production inputs are constant within the relevant range. Under what conditions would assumption 3 not be descriptive? On the revenue side, reductions in the selling price may be necessary to spur sales at higher levels of output. On the cost side, variable costs per unit may decline when output increases as employees learn to work more efficiently. The learning curve is discussed in Chapter 10.

multiple revenue drivers and multiple cost drivers, and cost functions that are not linear, if doing so will significantly improve their decisions.

Before explaining the basics of CVP analysis, we must first clarify some terms. As described in Chapter 2,

$$\begin{array}{ccc} \text{Operating} \\ \text{income} \end{array} = \begin{array}{ccc} \text{Total revenues} \\ \text{from operations} \end{array} - \begin{array}{ccc} \text{Cost of goods sold and operating costs} \\ \text{(excluding income taxes)} \end{array}$$

Net income is operating income plus nonoperating revenues (such as interest revenue) minus nonoperating costs (such as interest cost) minus income taxes. For simplicity, throughout this chapter we assume nonoperating revenues and nonoperating costs are zero. Thus, net income is computed as:

$$\text{Net income} = \text{Operating income} - \text{Income taxes}$$

ESSENTIALS OF COST-VOLUME-PROFIT ANALYSIS

To see how CVP analysis works, consider the following example.

OBJECTIVE 2

Explain essential features of CVP analysis

> **EXAMPLE:** Mary Frost plans to sell Do-All Software, a home-office software package, at a heavily attended two-day computer convention in Chicago. Mary can purchase this software from a computer software wholesaler at $120 per package with the privilege of returning all unsold units and receiving a full $120 refund per package. The units (packages) will be sold at $200 each. She has already paid $2,000 to Computer Conventions, Inc., for the booth rental for the two-day convention. Assume there are no other costs. What profits will Mary make for different quantities of units sold?

Points to Stress In the Do-All example, the privilege of returning unsold units renders the CGS strictly variable with respect to the # of units sold.

The booth rental costs of $2,000 are fixed costs because they will not change no matter how many units Mary sells. The costs of the package are variable costs because these costs increase in proportion to the number of units sold. For each unit that Mary sells, she incurs a cost of $120 to purchase it. If Mary sells 5 packages, the variable purchase costs are $600 ($120 × 5).

Mary can use CVP analysis to examine changes in operating income as a result of selling different quantities of software packages. If Mary sells 5 packages, she will receive revenues of $1,000 ($200 × 5), incur variable costs of $600 ($120 × 5) and fixed costs of $2,000, and show an operating loss of $1,600 ($1,000 − $600 − $2,000). If Mary sells 40 packages, she will receive revenues of $8,000 ($200 × 40), incur variable costs of $4,800 ($120 × 40) and the same fixed costs of $2,000, and show an operating income of $1,200 ($8,000 − $4,800 − $2,000).

Teaching Tip Link this example back to the CVP assumptions: (1) the number of units drives the TR and TVC, (2) costs are easily divided into variable and fixed, (3) the costs are linear within the relevant range, (4) the unit SP and the unit VC are known and constant, (5) there is just a single product, and (6) the time period is short enough that the time value of money is not relevant.

Note that the only numbers that change from selling different quantities of packages are *total revenues* and *total variable costs*. The difference between total revenues and total variable costs is called **contribution margin.** Contribution margin is an effective summary of the reasons that operating income changes as the number of units sold changes. The contribution margin when Mary sells 5 packages is $400 (total revenues, $1,000 minus total variable costs, $600), and the contribution margin when Mary sells 40 packages is $3,200 (total revenues, $8,000 minus total variable costs, $4,800). Note that contribution margin calculations subtract all variable costs. For instance, if Mary had paid a salesperson a sales commission on each unit sold to sell Do-All Software at the convention, variable costs would include the cost of the package plus the sales commission.

Contribution margin per unit is a useful tool for calculating contribution margins. The **contribution margin per unit** is the difference between the selling price and the variable cost per unit. In the Do-All Software example, the contribution margin per unit = $200 − $120 = $80. Contribution margin can then be calculated as:

$$\text{Contribution margin} = \text{Contribution margin per unit} \times \text{Number of packages sold}$$

For example, when 40 packages are sold, contribution margin = $80 × 40 = $3,200.

Contribution margin is a key concept in CVP analysis. It represents the amount of revenues minus variable costs that contribute to recovering fixed costs. Once fixed costs are fully recovered, contribution margin contributes to operating

EXHIBIT 3-1
Contribution Income Statement for Different Quantities of Do-All Software Packages Sold

	Number of Packages Sold				
	0	1	5	25	40
Revenues at $200 per package	$ 0	$ 200	$ 1,000	$5,000	$8,000
Variable costs at $120 per package	0	120	600	3,000	4,800
Contribution margin at $80 per package	0	80	400	2,000	3,200
Fixed costs	2,000	2,000	2,000	2,000	2,000
Operating income	$(2,000)	$(1,920)	$(1,600)	$ 0	$1,200

Points to Stress Total contribution margin, UCM, and CM% are important concepts in business which will be used often to help mgrs. gauge the relative profitability of a product. The contribution income statement (CI/S) differs from the GAAP I/S (with costs separated into inventoriable and period costs). For the CI/S, costs are separated by how they behave (i.e., fixed or variable) without regard as to whether they are inventoriable or period costs. These issues will be used extensively in Chaps. 9 and 12.

income. Exhibit 3-1 calculates the contribution margins for different quantities of packages sold and shows how contribution margin recovers fixed costs and generates operating income. The income statement presentation in Exhibit 3-1 is called a **contribution income statement** because it groups line items by cost-behavior patterns to highlight the contribution margin. Note how each additional unit sold from 0 to 1 to 5 increases contribution margin by $80 per unit, recovering more of the fixed costs and reducing the operating loss. If Mary sells 25 packages, the contribution margin equals $2,000 ($80 × 25), exactly recovering the fixed costs and resulting in zero operating income. If Mary sells 40 units, the contribution margin increases by another $1,200 ($3,200 − $2,000), all of which becomes operating income. Note that as you move across Exhibit 3-1 from left to right, the increase in contribution margin exactly equals the increase in operating income (or the decrease in operating loss).

Instead of expressing the contribution margin as a per unit amount, we can also express it as a percentage. **Contribution margin percentage** (also called **contribution margin ratio**) is the contribution margin per unit divided by the selling price. In our example,

$$\text{Contribution margin percentage} = \frac{\$80}{\$200} = 40\%$$

The contribution margin percentage is the contribution margin achieved per dollar of revenues. It indicates that 40% of each dollar of revenue (40 cents) goes toward contribution margin.[2]

Mary can calculate the total contribution margin for different sales levels by multiplying the contribution margin percentage by the total revenues shown in Exhibit 3-1. For example, if Mary sells 25 packages, revenues would be $5,000 and contribution margin would equal 40% × $5,000 = $2,000, exactly offsetting fixed costs.[3] Mary breaks even by selling 25 packages worth $5,000.

THE BREAKEVEN POINT

OBJECTIVE 3

Determine the breakeven point and output to achieve target operating income using the equation, contribution margin, and graph methods

The **breakeven point** is that quantity of output where total revenues equal total costs—that is, where the operating income is zero. Why would managers be interested in the breakeven point? Mainly because they want to avoid operating losses,

[2]Contribution margin as a percentage of variable costs is $66\frac{2}{3}\%$ calculated as follows:

Selling price	$200
Deduct contribution margin per unit	80
Variable costs per unit	$120

Contribution margin per unit divided by variable costs per unit = $80 ÷ $120 = $66\frac{2}{3}$ percent.

[3]Note from Exhibit 3-1 that, given a contribution income statement, contribution margin percentage can also be calculated as contribution margin divided by total revenues. For example, if 40 packages are sold, contribution margin percentage = $3,200 ÷ $8,000 = 40 percent.

and the breakeven point tells them what level of sales they must generate to avoid a loss. This section will continue to use the Do-All Software information to examine three methods for determining the breakeven point: the equation method, the contribution margin method, and the graph method.

The following abbreviations are useful in the subsequent analysis.

$$USP = \text{Unit selling price}$$
$$UVC = \text{Unit variable costs}$$
$$UCM = \text{Unit contribution margin (USP} - \text{UVC)}$$
$$CM\% = \text{Contribution margin percentage (UCM} \div \text{USP)}$$
$$FC = \text{Fixed costs}$$
$$Q = \text{Quantity of output units sold (and manufactured)}$$
$$OI = \text{Operating income}$$
$$TOI = \text{Target operating income}$$
$$TNI = \text{Target net income}$$

Equation Method

Under the equation method, the income statement can be expressed using the preceding terminology in the form of the following equation:

$$\text{Revenues} - \text{Variable costs} - \text{Fixed costs} = \text{Operating income}$$

$$(USP \times Q) - (UVC \times Q) - FC = OI \tag{1}$$

This equation provides the most general and easy-to-remember approach to any CVP situation. Using the Do-All Software information from earlier in the chapter and setting operating income in the preceding equation equal to zero, we obtain:

$$\$200Q - \$120Q - \$2{,}000 = \$0$$
$$\$80Q = \$2{,}000$$
$$Q = \$2{,}000 \div \$80 = 25 \text{ units}$$

If Mary sells fewer than 25 units, she will have a loss; if she sells 25 units, she will break even; and if she sells more than 25 units, she will make a profit. This breakeven point is expressed in units. It can also be expressed in revenue dollars: 25 units $\times$ $200 selling price = $5,000.

Contribution Margin Method

The contribution margin method simply uses the concept of the contribution margin to rework the equation method. We start with the preceding equation 1:

$$(USP \times Q) - (UVC \times Q) - FC = OI$$

Rewriting equation 1, we have:

$$(USP - UVC) \times Q = FC + OI$$

That is,

$$UCM \times Q = FC + OI$$

$$Q = \frac{FC + OI}{UCM} \tag{2}$$

At the breakeven point, operating income is, by definition, zero. Setting OI = 0, we obtain:

$$Q = \frac{FC}{UCM} \tag{3}$$

$$\frac{\text{Breakeven}}{\text{number of units}} = \frac{\text{Fixed costs}}{\text{Unit contribution margin}}$$

Teaching Tip The equation method has 2 advantages. First, if students can remember the income statement format, they can reconstruct the equation; memorization is unnecessary. Second, the equation form is more general and so is easier to apply with multiple products (see product mix discussion later in the chapter), with multiple cost and revenue drivers, and with changes in the cost structure.

Correcting Student Misconceptions Some students will try to use this contribution margin (CM) formula for all CVP problems. Emphasize that the CM formula is valid only for (1) a single product, (2) a single output-related cost driver, and (3) only if there are no changes in the cost (and revenue) structure.

The calculations in the equation method and the contribution margin method appear similar because one is merely a restatement of the other. In our example, fixed costs are $2,000, and the unit contribution margin is $80 ($200 − $120). Therefore,

$$\text{Breakeven number of units} = \frac{\$2,000}{\$80 \text{ per unit}} = 25 \text{ units}$$

We can also algebraically manipulate equation 3 to calculate breakeven revenues using the contribution margin percentage. Multiplying both sides of equation 3 by the USP gives:

$$\text{Breakeven in revenue dollars} = \text{Breakeven number of units} \times \text{USP} = \frac{\text{FC} \times \text{USP}}{\text{UCM}}$$

$$= \frac{\text{FC}}{\dfrac{\text{UCM}}{\text{USP}}} \quad \text{(by dividing both numerator and denominator by USP)}$$

$$= \frac{\text{FC}}{\text{CM\%}} \qquad \begin{array}{l}\text{[because contribution margin percentage (CM\%) equals} \\ \text{unit contribution margin (UCM) divided by} \\ \text{unit selling price (USP)]}\end{array} \qquad (4)$$

In the Do-All Software example, $\text{CM\%} = \dfrac{\text{UCM}}{\text{USP}} = \dfrac{\$80}{\$200} = 40\%$

$$\text{Breakeven in revenue dollars} = \frac{\text{FC}}{\text{CM\%}} = \frac{\$2,000}{40\%} = \$5,000$$

Graph Method

In the graph method, we plot a line for total costs and a line for total revenues. Their point of intersection is the breakeven point. Exhibit 3-2 illustrates this method for our Do-All Software example. Because we have assumed that total costs and total revenues behave in a linear fashion, we need only two points to plot each line.

1. *Total costs line.* This line is the sum of the fixed costs and the variable costs. Fixed costs are $2,000 at all output levels within the relevant range. To plot fixed costs, measure $2,000 on the vertical axis (point *A*) and extend a line horizontally. Variable costs are $120 per unit. To plot the total costs line, use as one point the $2,000 fixed costs at 0 units sold (point *A*) because variable costs are $0 when 0 units are sold. Select a second point by choosing any other convenient output level (say, 40 units sold) and determining the corresponding total costs. The total variable costs at this output level are $4,800 (40 × $120). Because fixed costs are $2,000 at all output levels within the relevant range, total costs at 40 units sold are $6,800 ($2,000 + $4,800), which is point *B* in Exhibit 3-2. The total costs line is the straight line from point *A* passing through point *B*.

2. *Total revenues line.* One convenient starting point is $0 revenues at 0 units sold, which is point *C* in Exhibit 3-2. Select a second point by choosing any other convenient output level and determining the corresponding total revenues. At 40 units sold, total revenues are $8,000 (40 × $200), which is point *D* in Exhibit 3-2. The total revenues line is the straight line from point *C* passing through point *D*.

The breakeven point is the quantity of units sold for which the total revenues line and the total costs line intersect. At this point (25 units sold in Exhibit 3-2), total revenues equal total costs. Exhibit 3-2, however, shows the profit or loss outlook for a wide range of output levels besides the breakeven point. For quantities of sales less than 25 units, total costs exceed total revenues, and the purple area indicates regions of operating losses. For quantities of sales greater than 25 units, total revenues exceed total costs, and the green area indicates regions of operating incomes.

Reinforcing Problems Basic CVP analysis is covered in Exer. 3-16 through 3-21, 3-27, 3-29, and 3-30, and Probs. 3-33 through 3-36.

Curriculum Linkage In contrast to the linear model depicted in Exh. 3-2, economists usually specify curvilinear TR and TC functions:

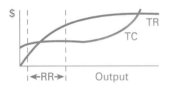

With the relevant range (RR), a linear approximation is OK, but projections outside the RR will be misleading. At higher volumes, the linear approx. overstates TR (since prices must be cut to increase volume) and understates TC (since ever higher output increases costs such as overtime premium). Overstating revenues and understating costs yields a bad combination in which the linear model overestimates profit at high volume levels (beyond the RR).

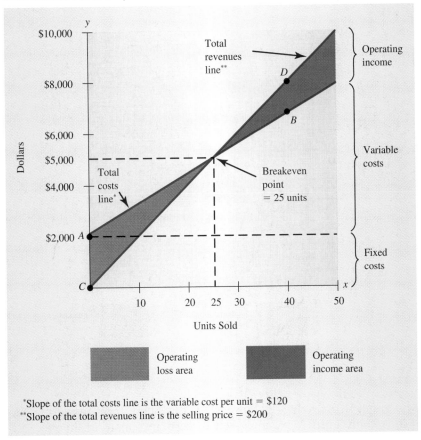

EXHIBIT 3-2
Cost-Volume-Profit Graph for Do-All Software

*Slope of the total costs line is the variable cost per unit = $120
**Slope of the total revenues line is the selling price = $200

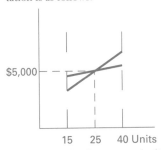

Target Operating Income

We introduce a profit element to our calculations for Do-All Software by asking, How many units must be sold to earn an operating income of $1,200? Using equation 1, we need to find Q for which:

$$\$200Q - \$120Q - \$2,000 = \$1,200$$

$$\$80Q = \$2,000 + \$1,200 = \$3,200$$

$$Q = \$3,200 \div \$80 \text{ per unit} = 40 \text{ units}$$

Alternatively, we could use the contribution margin method and equation 2, in which the numerator now consists of fixed costs plus target operating income:

$$Q = \frac{\text{Fixed costs} + \text{Target operating income}}{\text{Unit contribution margin}} = \frac{\text{FC} + \text{TOI}}{\text{UCM}}$$

$$Q = \frac{\$2,000 + \$1,200}{\$80} = \frac{\$3,200}{\$80 \text{ per unit}} = 40 \text{ units}$$

Proof:

Revenues, $200 per unit × 40 units	$8,000
Variable costs, $120 per unit × 40 units	4,800
Contribution margin, $80 per unit × 40 units	3,200
Fixed costs	2,000
Operating income	$1,200

The revenue in dollars to earn an operating income of $1,200 can also be calculated directly using the approach of equation 4, on page 64,

$$\text{Revenue in dollars} = \frac{\text{FC} + \text{TOI}}{\text{CM\%}} = \frac{\$2,000 + \$1,200}{0.40} = \frac{\$3,200}{0.40} = \$8,000$$

EXHIBIT 3-3
Profit-Volume Graph for Do-All Software

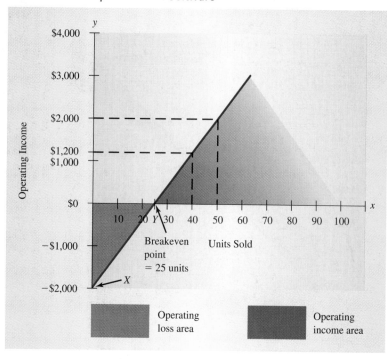

The graph in Exhibit 3-2, however, is not helpful for answering the question of how many units Mary must sell to earn an operating income of $1,200. Why not? Because it is not easy to determine the point at which the difference between the total revenues line and the total costs line is $1,200. Recasting Exhibit 3-2 in the form of a profit-volume (PV) graph is of great help in answering this question.

A **PV graph** shows the impact on operating income of changes in the output level. Exhibit 3-3 presents the PV graph for Do-All Software (fixed costs of $2,000, selling price of $200, and variable costs per unit of $120). The PV line can be drawn using two points. One convenient point (*X*) is the operating loss at zero units sold, which is equal to the fixed costs of $2,000. A second convenient point (*Y*) is the breakeven point—25 units in our example (see p. 63). The PV line is the straight line from point *X* passing through point *Y*. To find the number of units Mary must sell to earn an operating income of $1,200, draw a horizontal line corresponding to $1,200 on the *y*-axis. At the point where this line intersects the PV line, draw a vertical line to the *x*-axis. The vertical line intersects the *x*-axis at 40 units, indicating that by selling 40 units Mary will generate operating income of $1,200.

Target Net Income and Income Taxes

Thus far, we have ignored the effect of income taxes in our CVP analysis. At times, managers want to know the effect of their decisions on income after taxes. Net income is operating income minus income taxes. CVP calculations for target income must then be stated in terms of target net income instead of target operating income. For example, Mary may be interested in knowing the number of units of Do-All Software she must sell to earn a net income of $1,200, assuming an income tax rate of 40 percent. We modify the target operating income calculations of the previous section to allow for income taxes. Using the equation method,

Revenues − Variable costs − Fixed costs = Target operating income

Furthermore,

$$\text{Target net income} = (\text{Target operating income}) - (\text{Target operating income} \times \text{Tax rate})$$
$$\text{Target net income} = (\text{Target operating income})(1 - \text{Tax rate})$$

$$\text{Target operating income} = \frac{\text{Target net income}}{1 - \text{Tax rate}}$$

Substituting for target operating income, we have

$$\text{Revenues} - \text{Variable costs} - \text{Fixed costs} = \frac{\text{Target net income}}{1 - \text{Tax rate}}$$

Substituting numbers from our Do-All Software example, we have

$$\$200Q - \$120Q - \$2,000 = \frac{\$1,200}{1 - 0.40}$$

$$\$200Q - \$120Q - \$2,000 = \$2,000$$

$$\$80Q = \$4,000$$

$$Q = \$4,000 \div \$80 \text{ per unit} = 50 \text{ units}$$

Alternatively, we could use the contribution margin method of equation 2 and substitute:

$$\text{Target operating income} = \frac{\text{Target net income}}{1 - \text{Tax rate}}$$

That is,
$$Q = \frac{\text{Fixed costs} + \dfrac{\text{Target net income}}{1 - \text{Tax rate}}}{\text{Unit contribution margin}} = \frac{FC + \dfrac{TNI}{1 - \text{Tax rate}}}{UCM}$$

$$Q = \frac{\$2,000 + \dfrac{\$1,200}{1 - 0.40}}{\$80} = \frac{\$2,000 + \$2,000}{\$80 \text{ per unit}} = 50 \text{ units}$$

	Proof:		
	Revenues, $200 per unit × 50 units		$10,000
	Variable costs, $120 per unit × 50 units		6,000
	Contribution margin		4,000
	Fixed costs		2,000
	Operating income		2,000
	Income taxes, $2,000 × 0.40		800
	Net income		$ 1,200

Focusing the analysis on target net income instead of on target operating income will not change the breakeven point. Why? Because, by definition, operating income at the breakeven point is $0, and thus no income taxes will arise.

Mary can also use the PV graph in Exhibit 3-3. For a target net income of $1,200,

$$\text{Target operating income} = \frac{\text{Target net income}}{1 - \text{Tax rate}} = \frac{\$1,200}{1 - 0.40} = \$2,000$$

From Exhibit 3-3, to earn target operating income of $2,000, Mary will need to sell 50 units.

USING CVP ANALYSIS FOR MAKING DECISIONS

We have seen how CVP analysis is useful for determining breakeven quantities and the quantities for achieving targeted operating income and targeted net income. Managers also use CVP analysis to guide other decisions.

Points to Stress Because no income tax is paid at the BEP, income taxes don't affect the BEP. However, increases in income tax rates increase the # of units that must be sold to generate a given net income (NI). In the text's Do-All example, when income tax was 0%, sales of 40 units generated $1,200 NI. With a more realistic 40% tax rate, an extra 10 units (50-40) must be sold to generate $1,200 NI.

Reinforcing Problems Exer. 3-22 and 3-23 and Probs. 3-38 and 3-44 cover the role of income taxes in CVP analysis.

Teaching Tip Memorization is unnecessary if students can recall the income statement format. In this example,

Target Op. Inc.	TOI
−Tax (Tax Rate × TOI)	−0.4 TOI
Target N.I.	0.6 TOI = $1,200
	TOI = $2,000

OBJECTIVE 5

Explain the use of CVP analysis in decision making and how sensitivity analysis can help managers cope with uncertainty

Decision to Advertise

Consider again the Do-All Software example. Suppose Mary anticipates selling 40 packages. Exhibit 3-2 indicates that Mary's operating income would be $1,200. Mary is considering placing an advertisement describing the product and its features in the convention brochure. The advertisement will cost $500. This cost will be fixed because it will stay the same regardless of the number of units Mary sells. She anticipates that advertising will increase sales to 45 packages. Should Mary advertise? The following table presents the CVP analysis.

	40 Packages Sold with No Advertising (1)	45 Packages Sold with Advertising (2)	Difference (3) = (2) − (1)
Contribution margin ($80 × 40; $80 × 45)	$3,200	$3,600	$ 400
Fixed costs	2,000	2,500	500
Operating income	$1,200	$1,100	$(100)

Operating income decreases by $100, so Mary should not advertise. Note that Mary could focus only on the difference column and come to the same conclusion: If Mary advertises, contribution margin will increase by $400 ($80 per unit × 5 additional units), and fixed costs will increase by $500, resulting in a $100 decrease in operating income.

Decision to Reduce Selling Price

Having decided not to advertise, Mary is contemplating whether to reduce the selling price of Do-All Software to $175. At this price, she thinks sales will be 50 units. At this quantity, the software wholesaler who supplies Do-All Software will sell the packages to Mary for $115 per package instead of $120. Should Mary reduce the selling price? No, as the following CVP analysis shows.

Contribution margin from lowering price to $175, ($175 − $115) × 50 units	$3,000
Contribution margin from maintaining price at $200, ($200 − $120) × 40 units	3,200
Increase/(Decrease) in contribution margin from lowering price	$ (200)

Because the fixed costs of $2,000 do not change, decreasing the price will lead to a $200 lower contribution margin and a $200 lower operating income.

Mary can examine other alternatives to increase operating income such as simultaneously increasing advertising costs and lowering prices. In each case, Mary will compare the changes in contribution margin (through the effect on selling price, variable costs, and output volume) to the changes in fixed costs and will choose the alternative that gives the highest operating income.

SENSITIVITY ANALYSIS AND UNCERTAINTY

Reinforcing Problems Exer. 3-26 and Probs. 3-37, 3-38, and 3-43 cover CVP analysis and sensitivity analysis.

Before choosing among alternatives, managers frequently undertake sensitivity analysis. **Sensitivity analysis** is a "what-if" technique that managers use to examine how a result will change if the original predicted data are not achieved or if an underlying assumption changes. In the context of CVP analysis, sensitivity analysis answers such questions as, What will operating income be if units sold decreases by 5% from the original prediction? and What will operating income be if variable costs per unit increase by 10 percent? The sensitivity of operating income to various possible outcomes broadens managers' perspectives as to what might actually occur before they make cost commitments.

The widespread use of electronic spreadsheets enables managers to conduct CVP-based sensitivity analyses in a systematic and efficient way. Using spreadsheets, managers can easily conduct this analysis to examine the effect and interaction of changes in selling prices, variable costs per unit, fixed costs, and target oper-

EXHIBIT 3-4
Spreadsheet Analysis of CVP Relationships for Do-All Software

Fixed Costs	Variable Costs Per Unit	Revenues Required at $200 Selling Price to Earn Operating Income of			
		$0	$1,000	$1,500	$2,000
$2,000	$100	$ 4,000	$ 6,000	$ 7,000	$ 8,000
	120	5,000	7,500	8,750	10,000
	140	6,667	10,000	11,667	13,333
2,500	100	5,000	7,000	8,000	9,000
	120	6,250	8,750	10,000	11,250
	140	8,333	11,667	13,333	15,000
3,000	100	6,000	8,000	9,000	10,000
	120	7,500	10,000	11,250	12,500
	140	10,000	13,333	15,000	16,667

ating incomes. Exhibit 3-4 displays a spreadsheet for our Do-All Software example.[4] Mary can immediately see the revenues that need to be generated to reach particular operating income levels, given alternative levels of fixed costs and variable costs per unit. For example, revenues of $6,000 (30 units at $200 per unit) are required to earn an operating income of $1,000 if fixed costs are $2,000 and variable costs per unit are $100. Mary can also use Exhibit 3-4 to assess what revenues she needs to break even (earn operating income of $0) if, for example, the booth rental at the Chicago convention is raised to $3,000 (thus increasing fixed costs to $3,000) or if the software supplier raises its price to $140 per unit (thus increasing variable costs to $140 per unit).

An aspect of sensitivity analysis is **margin of safety**, which is the amount of budgeted revenues over and above breakeven revenues. Expressed in units, margin of safety is the sales quantity minus the breakeven quantity. The margin of safety answers the "what-if" question: If budgeted revenues are above breakeven and drop, how far can they fall below budget before the breakeven point is reached? Such a fall could be due to a competitor having a better product, poorly executed marketing programs, and so on. Assume that Mary has fixed costs of $2,000, a selling price of $200, and variable costs per unit of $120. For 40 units sold, the budgeted revenues are $8,000 and the budgeted operating income is $1,200. The breakeven point for this set of assumptions is 25 units ($2,000 ÷ $80) or $5,000 ($200 × 25). Hence the margin of safety is $3,000 ($8,000 − $5,000) or 15 (40 − 25) units.

Sensitivity analysis is one approach to recognizing **uncertainty**, which is the possibility that an actual amount will deviate from an expected amount. Another approach is to compute expected values using probability distributions. The appendix to this chapter illustrates this approach.

COST PLANNING AND CVP
Alternative Fixed-Cost/Variable-Cost Structures

CVP-based sensitivity analysis highlights the risks and returns that an existing cost structure holds for an organization. This insight may lead managers to consider alternative cost structures. CVP analysis can help managers evaluate various alternatives. Consider again our Do-All Software example. Our original example has Mary paying a $2,000 booth rental fee. Suppose, however, Computer Conventions offers Mary three rental alternatives:

---

[4]A spreadsheet package such as Excel facilitates sensitivity analyses.

Teaching Tip The following linkage helps students integrate several topics in this chapter: The text discusses 2 approaches to dealing with uncertainty in CVP analysis (i.e., violation of CVP assumption 4)— sensitivity analysis and decision models that explicitly incorporate uncertainty via probability distributions (i.e., expected value analysis presented in the Appendix). The sensitivity analysis presented here estimates outcomes under various combinations of USP, UVC, FC, and TOI. This approach can be viewed as estimating payoffs (TOI) under a variety of actions (UVC and FC) and states (revenue $). The Appendix explains how to employ payoffs under various action/states of nature in combination with the probabilities of these states occurring in decision models that help mgrs. choose the action that maximizes expected monetary value.

Points to Stress If values of the CVP model's elements aren't known with certainty, they'll have to be estimated. This requires judgment— e.g., reasonable people may disagree in their judgments of expected UVC. Accountants perform sensitivity analyses to find out whether these different UVC estimates significantly affect the results of the CVP analysis.

Reinforcing Problems Exer. 3-24 covers CVP analysis and Margin of Safety.

OBJECTIVE 6
Use CVP analysis to plan costs

- ◆ *Option 1:* $2,000 fixed fee
- ◆ *Option 2:* $800 fixed fee plus 15% of convention revenues
- ◆ *Option 3:* 25% of convention revenues with no fixed fee

Example In this example, all three options have the same indifference point (This would be unusual). Mgrs. can calculate indifference points between pairs of options by setting their profit equations equal to one another. For example for Mary one calculation is:

$$(200 - 120)X - \$2,000$$
$$= [200 - 120 - .015(200)]X$$
$$- 900$$
$$X = 40 \text{ units}$$

Similar indifference points can be calculated for any pair, given the profit equation for each. This information can assist mgrs. in making informed choices.

Mary anticipates selling 40 packages. She is interested in how her choice of a rental agreement will affect the income she earns and the risks she faces. Exhibit 3-5 presents the Profit-Volume (PV) graphs for each option. The graph for option 1 is the same PV graph shown in Exhibit 3-3 (fixed costs of $2,000 and contribution margin per unit of $80). The graph for option 2 uses fixed costs of $800 and a contribution margin per unit of $50 [selling price, $200, minus variable costs per package, $120, minus variable rental fees, $30, (15% × $200)]. The graph for option 3 has fixed costs of $0 and a contribution margin per unit of $30 [$200 − $120 − $50 (25% × $200)].

If Mary sells 40 packages, she should be indifferent across the various options. Each option results in operating income of $1,200. The CVP analysis, however, highlights the different risks and different returns associated with each option if sales vary from 40 units. The downside risk of option 1 comes from its higher fixed costs ($2,000) and hence higher breakeven point (25 units) and lower margin of safety (40 − 25 = 15 units) relative to the other options. The graph of option 1 intersects the x-axis further to the right than the graphs of options 2 and 3.

Consider, for example, operating income under each option if the number of units sold drops to 20. Exhibit 3-5 shows that option 1 leads to an operating loss, whereas options 2 and 3 continue to produce operating incomes. The higher risk in option 1, however, must be evaluated against its potential benefits. Option 1 has the highest contribution margin per unit because of its low variable costs. Once fixed costs are recovered at sales of 25 units, each additional unit adds $80 of contribution margin and operating income per unit. For example, at sales of 60 units, option 1 shows an operating income of $2,800, greater than the operating incomes for sales of 60 units under options 2 and 3. By moving from option 1 toward option 3, Mary faces less risk when demand is low both because of lower fixed costs and be-

EXHIBIT 3-5
Profit-Volume Graph for Alternative Rental Options for Do-All Software

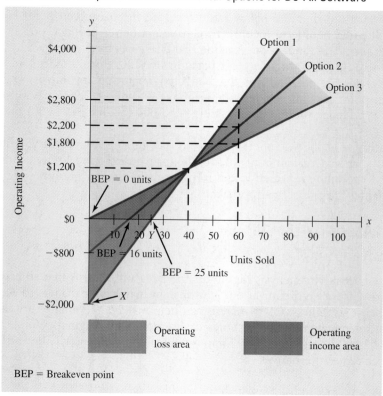

BEP = Breakeven point

cause she loses less contribution margin per unit. She must, however, accept less upside potential when demand is high because of the higher variable costs of option 3. The choice among options 1, 2, and 3 will be influenced by her confidence in the level of demand for Do-All Software and her willingness to risk losses.

The risk-return tradeoff across alternative cost structures is usefully summarized in a measure called *operating leverage*. **Operating leverage** describes the effects that fixed costs have on changes in operating income as changes occur in units sold and hence in contribution margin. Organizations with a high proportion of fixed costs in their cost structures, as is the case under option 1 in our example, have high operating leverage. As a result, small changes in sales lead to large changes in operating incomes. Consequently, if sales increase, operating incomes increase relatively more, yielding higher returns. If sales decrease, however, operating incomes decline relatively more, leading to a greater risk of losses. *At any given level of sales*, the **degree of operating leverage** equals contribution margin divided by operating income.

The following table shows the degree of operating leverage at sales of 40 units for the three alternative rental options.

New in This Edition This edition introduces the idea of operating leverage in a firm's cost structure and its related concept of degree of operating leverage.

Correcting Student Misconceptions Degree of operating leverage (DOL) is specific to a given level of sales as a starting point. The DOL then applies to changes from that starting point. As the starting point changes, the DOL changes. For example, if the starting point was sales of 50 units, the DOL would be:

Option 1: 4,000/2,000 = 2.00
Option 2: 2,500/1,700 = 1.47
Option 3: 1,500/1,500 = 1.00

Note that these are different from the ones calculated in the text for

	Option 1	Option 2	Option 3
1. Contribution margin per unit (p. 70)	$ 80	$ 50	$ 30
2. Contribution margin (Row 1 × 40 units)	$3,200	$2,000	$1,200
3. Operating income (from Exhibit 3-5)	$1,200	$1,200	$1,200
4. Degree of operating leverage (Line 2 ÷ Line 3)	$\frac{\$3,200}{\$1,200} = 2.67$	$\frac{\$2,000}{\$1,200} = 1.67$	$\frac{\$1,200}{\$1,200} = 1.00$

These numbers indicate that, when sales are 40 units, a percentage change in sales and contribution margin will result in 2.67 times that percentage change in operating income for option 1, but the same percentage change in operating income for option 3. Consider, for example, a sales increase of 50% from 40 units to 60 units. Contribution margin will increase by 50% under each option. Operating income, however, will increase by 2.67 × 50% = 133% from $1,200 to $2,800 in option 1 but only by 1.00 × 50% = 50% from $1,200 to $1,800 in option 3 (see Exhibit 3-5). The degree of operating leverage at a given level of sales helps managers calculate the effect of fluctuations in sales on operating incomes.

sales of 40 units (except for Option 3 which will always be 1.0 because it has no fixed costs).

Reinforcing Problems Exer. 3-25 and Prob. 3-39 cover operating leverage.

Effect of Time Horizon

A critical assumption of CVP analysis is that costs can be classified as either variable or fixed. This classification is affected by the time period being considered for a decision. The shorter the time horizon we consider, the higher the percentage of total costs we may view as fixed. Consider United Airlines. Suppose a United Airlines plane will depart from its gate in 60 minutes and there are 20 empty seats. A potential passenger arrives bearing a transferable ticket from a competing airline. What are the variable costs to United of placing one more passenger in an otherwise empty seat? Variable costs (such as one more meal) would be negligible. Virtually all the costs in this decision situation are fixed. In contrast, suppose United must decide whether to include another city in its routes. This decision may have a one-year planning horizon. Many more costs would be regarded as variable and fewer as fixed in this decision. This example underscores that the ability to label costs as really fixed depends heavily on the relevant range, the length of the time horizon in question, and the specific decision situation.

Example In the United example, the crew's salaries and the cost of the airport gate are fixed with respect to the decision whether to accept more passengers on a plane that is about to depart, but variable with respect to the decision to add another city to its routes. Also, note that a seemingly short-term decision can have long-term consequences. If United accepts last-minute passengers at reduced fares (because the CM associated with these passengers is positive), this could have long-term consequences if future passengers expect reduced fares at the last minute.

OBJECTIVE 7

Apply CVP analysis to a multiproduct company

EFFECTS OF SALES MIX ON INCOME

Sales mix is the relative combination of quantities of products (or services) that constitutes total unit sales. If the mix changes, the overall unit sales target may still be achieved. However, the effect on operating income depends on how the original proportions of lower or higher contribution margin products have shifted.

Influencing Cost Structures to Manage the Risk-Return Tradeoff

Building up too many fixed costs can be hazardous to a company's health. Because fixed costs, unlike variable costs, do not automatically decrease as volumes decline, companies with too many fixed costs can lose a considerable amount of money during lean times. The managers at Emery Air Freight understand this concept well. They prefer to buy cargo space from existing airlines on an as-needed basis (a variable-cost structure) rather than purchase their own airplanes (which would produce a fixed cost). As a result, Emery avoids being stuck with costs when business is slow. To avoid losses when their volumes declined in the 1990s, many prominent companies—including IBM, AT&T, and General Motors—had to reduce their fixed costs by closing plants and downsizing their workforces.

As you can tell by the Emery example, managers' decisions influence the mix of fixed and variable costs in a company's cost structure. In making these decisions, managers use forecasts of the effect on net income at different volume levels to evaluate the risk-return tradeoffs involved in various cost structures.

Understanding the distinction between fixed and variable costs and its implications for the risk-return tradeoff is also helpful when marketing products. Consider Mueller-Lehmkuhl, a German company that sells snap-on and tack buttons used on blue jeans and other clothing. Mueller-Lehmkuhl also manufactures and sells the machines that attach the buttons to the clothing. Until it was forced by Japanese competitors to change its strategy, Mueller-Lehmkuhl charged very little for the attaching machines and instead recovered its costs (including those of making the attaching machines) by charging a higher price for buttons. From its customers' standpoint, this strategy converts the fixed costs of the attaching machine into variable costs of buttons, reducing risk. If output declines, customers are not saddled with the fixed costs of the attaching machines. Of course, if output increases, customers wind up paying more overall than they would have had they purchased the attaching machines and paid a lower price for the buttons. Xerox follows a similar strategy by selling copier machines at lower margins along with maintenance and supplies (for example, paper and toner) contracts at higher margins. Similarly, Gillette sells razors at low margins and counts on high margins from selling blades. Cellular phone service companies, also, "give away" the cellular phone instrument itself in exchange for higher revenues from using the network.

Source: Mueller-Lehmkuhl GmbH, Harvard Business School Case Number 9-187-048 and conversations with executives.

New in This Edition The Concepts in Action box is new. It emphasizes the importance of cost structure and the operating risks it imposes.

Suppose Mary is now budgeting for the next convention. She plans to sell two software products—Do-All and Superword—and budgets the following:

	Do-All	Superword	Total
Units sold	60	40	100
Revenues, $200 and $100 per unit	$12,000	$4,000	$16,000
Variable costs, $120 and $70 per unit	7,200	2,800	10,000
Unit contribution margin (UCM), $80 and $30	$ 4,800	$1,200	6,000
Fixed costs			4,500
Operating income			$ 1,500

What is the breakeven point? Unlike in the single product (or service) situation, there is no unique breakeven number of units for a multiple-product situation. The breakeven quantity depends on the sales mix. One possible assumption is that the budgeted sales mix (3 units of Do-All sold for every 2 units of Superword sold) will not change at different levels of total unit sales. With this assumption, we can calculate the breakeven point as follows:

$$\text{Let} \quad 3S = \text{Number of units of Do-All to break even}$$

$$\text{Then} \quad 2S = \text{Number of units of Superword to break even}$$

$$\text{Revenues} - \text{Variable costs} - \text{Fixed costs} = \text{Operating income}$$

$$[\$200(3S) + \$100(2S)] - [\$120(3S) + \$70(2S)] - \$4,500 = 0$$

$$\$800S - \$500S = \$4,500$$

$$\$300S = \$4,500$$

$$S = 15$$

$$\text{Number of units of Do-All to break even} = 3S = 3 \times 15 = 45 \text{ units}$$

$$\text{Number of units of Superword to break even} = 2S = 2 \times 15 = 30 \text{ units}$$

The breakeven point is 75 units when the sales mix is 45 units of Do-All and 30 units of Superword, which maintains the ratio of 3 units of Do-All for 2 units of Superword. At this mix, the total contribution margin of $4,500 (Do-All $80 × 45 = $3,600 + Superword $30 × 30 = $900) equals the fixed costs of $4,500.

An alternative approach to computing the breakeven point is to calculate the weighted-average contribution margin per unit for the two products taken together.

$$\frac{\text{Weighted-average contribution margin per unit}}{} = \frac{(\text{Do-All's UCM} \times \text{No. of units of Do-All sold}) + (\text{Superword's UCM} \times \text{No. of units of Superword sold})}{\text{No. of units of Do-All sold} + \text{No. of units of Superword sold}}$$

$$= \frac{(\$80 \times 60) + (\$30 \times 40)}{60 + 40} = \frac{\$6,000}{100} = \$60$$

We then have

$$\text{Breakeven point} = \frac{\text{Fixed costs}}{\text{Weighted-average contribution margin per unit}} = \frac{\$4,500}{\$60} = 75 \text{ units}$$

Because the ratio of Do-All sales to Superword sales is 60:40 or 3:2, the breakeven point is 45 (60% × 75) units of Do-All and 30 (40% × 75) units of Superword.

We can also calculate the breakeven point in revenues for the multiple product situation using the weighted-average contribution margin percentage.

$$\frac{\text{Weighted-average contribution margin percentage}}{} = \frac{\text{Total contribution margin}}{\text{Total revenues}} = \frac{\$6,000}{\$16,000} = 0.375 \text{ or } 37.5\%$$

$$\frac{\text{Total revenues required to break even}}{} = \frac{\text{Fixed costs}}{\text{Weighted-average contribution margin percentage}} = \frac{\$4,500}{0.375} = \$12,000$$

The $16,000 of revenues are in the ratio of 3:1 ($12,000:$4,000) or 75%:25%. Hence the breakeven revenues of $12,000 should be apportioned in the ratio of 75%:25%. This amounts to breakeven revenue dollars of $9,000 (75% × $12,000) of Do-All and $3,000 (25% × $12,000) of Superword. At a selling price of $200 for Do-All and $100 for Superword, this equals 45 units ($9,000 ÷ $200) of Do-All and 30 units ($3,000 ÷ $100) of Superword.

Alternative sales mixes (in units) that have a contribution margin of $4,500 and thus result in breakeven operations include the following:

					Units					
Do-All	54	48	42	36	30	24	18	12	6	0
Superword	6	22	38	54	70	86	102	118	134	150
Total	60	70	80	90	100	110	120	130	140	150

Points to Stress This section relaxes CVP assumption 5—that there is a single product or that the mix of products is constant. The example illustrates the effects of changing product mix.

Teaching Tip/Reinforcing Problems To help students internalize the mix concept, suggest that they visualize the software being sold only in bundles of 5 units: 3 Do-Alls plus 2 Superword. Explain that "bundling" is a good way to think of the problem, even though it need not be literally true. Exer. 3-28 and Probs. 3-40 through 3-42 reinforce the product mix material. Chap. 16 further examines revenue issues with bundled products.

Points to Stress/Curriculum Linkage This example illustrates how the CM helps firms decide which products to "push." In the absence of production constraints, shifting marketing efforts to high CM products—if successful—can increase profits dramatically. This is 1 reason why car dealers push loaded (high-CM) rather than stripped-down cars. If, however, the firm faces production constraints, such as limited MH or DLH, then mgt. should push products that have the highest CM/unit of the constraint. This idea, explored in more detail in Chap. 11, is also the notion behind the theory of constraints, which students may have discussed in their production courses (Also see Chap. 19).

None of these sales mixes, however, describes the breakeven point in our example. Why? Because they do not match the budgeted sales mix of 3 units of Do-All for every 2 units of Superword. If the sales mix changes to 3 units of Do-All for every 7 units of Superword, the preceding table indicates that the breakeven point will change to 100 units (30 units of Do-All and 70 units of Superword). The breakeven quantity will increase because the sales mix has shifted toward the lower contribution margin product, Superword, thereby decreasing the weighted-average contribution margin per unit.

In general, other things being equal, for any given total quantity of units sold, if the sales mix shifts toward units with higher contribution margins, operating income will be higher. Thus, if the mix shifts toward Do-All (say to 70% Do-All from 60% Do-All), with a contribution margin of more than twice that of Superword, Mary's operating income will increase.

CVP ANALYSIS IN SERVICE AND NONPROFIT ORGANIZATIONS

Thus far our examination of CVP analysis has focused on merchandising companies seeking to make a profit. CVP can also be applied readily to decisions by manufacturing, service, and nonprofit organizations. The key to applying CVP analysis in service and nonprofit organizations is measuring their output. Examples of output measures in various service and nonprofit industries follow.

Industry	Measure of Output
Airlines	Passenger-miles
Hotels/motels	Room-nights occupied
Hospitals	Patient-days
Universities	Student credit-hours

Example A similar illustration can also apply in the service sector. For example, a public acct. firm might project the expected revenue from billable audit intern hours in order to decide how many interns they should hire.

Consider a social welfare agency of the government with a budget appropriation (revenue) for year 2000 of $900,000. This nonprofit agency's major purpose is to assist handicapped people who are seeking employment. On average, the agency supplements each person's income by $5,000 annually. The agency's fixed costs are $270,000. It has no other costs. The agency manager wants to know how many people could be assisted in 2000. We can use CVP analysis here by setting operating income to zero. Let Q be the number of handicapped people to be assisted:

$$\text{Revenues} - \text{Variable costs} - \text{Fixed costs} = \$0$$

$$\$900,000 - \$5,000Q - \$270,000 = \$0$$

$$\$5,000Q = \$900,000 - \$270,000 = \$630,000$$

$$Q = \$630,000 \div \$5,000 \text{ per person} = 126 \text{ people}$$

Suppose the manager is concerned that the total budget appropriation for 2001 will be reduced by 15% to a new amount of $900,000 \times (1 - 0.15) = $765,000. The manager wants to know how many handicapped people could now be assisted. Assume the same amount of monetary assistance per person:

$$\$765,000 - \$5,000Q - \$270,000 = \$0$$

$$\$5,000Q = \$765,000 - \$270,000$$

$$Q = \$495,000 \div \$5,000 \text{ per person} = 99 \text{ people}$$

Note the following two characteristics of the CVP relationships in this nonprofit situation:

Points to Stress This application of CVP in a nonprofit setting is particularly interesting for 2 reasons. First, the effect on gov't. agencies of budget cuts is topical given a political climate that emphasizes reducing spending on social programs. Second, the nonprofit sector constitutes an increasing proportion of the economy.

1. The percentage drop in service, $(126 - 99) \div 126$, or 21.4%, is more than the 15% reduction in the budget appropriation. Why? Because the existence of $270,000 in fixed costs means that the percentage drop in service exceeds the percentage drop in budget appropriation.

2. If the relationships were graphed, the budget appropriation (revenues) amount would be a straight horizontal line of $765,000. The manager could adjust operations to stay within this reduced appropriation in one or more of three basic ways: (a) Reduce the number of people assisted, (b) reduce the variable costs (the assistance per person), or (c) reduce the total fixed costs.

MULTIPLE COST DRIVERS

Throughout the chapter we have assumed that the number of output units is the only revenue and cost driver. In this section we relax this important assumption and describe how some aspects of CVP analysis can be adapted to the more general case of multiple cost drivers.

OBJECTIVE 8

Adapt CVP analysis to multiple cost driver situations

Consider again the single-product Do-All Software example. Suppose that Mary will incur a variable cost of $10 for preparing documents and invoices associated with the sale of Do-All Software. These documents and invoices will need to be prepared for each customer that buys Do-All Software. That is, the cost driver of document-and-invoice-preparation costs is the number of different customers that buy Do-All Software. Mary's operating income can then be expressed as:

New in This Edition This edition discusses the issue of CVP analysis with multiple cost drivers. The analysis is similar to the sales mix

$$\text{Operating income} = \text{Revenues} - \left(\begin{array}{c} \text{Costs of each} \\ \text{Do-All Software} \\ \text{package} \end{array} \times \begin{array}{c} \text{Number of} \\ \text{packages sold} \end{array} \right) - \left(\begin{array}{c} \text{Cost of preparing} \\ \text{each document} \\ \text{and invoice} \end{array} \times \begin{array}{c} \text{Number of} \\ \text{documents} \\ \text{and invoices} \end{array} \right) - \begin{array}{c} \text{Fixed} \\ \text{costs} \end{array}$$

Assuming that Mary sells 40 packages to 15 customers, then:

$$\text{Operating income} = (\$200 \times 40) - (\$120 \times 40) - (\$10 \times 15) - \$2,000$$

$$= \$8,000 - \$4,800 - \$150 - \$2,000 = \$1,050$$

scenario. There is no unique BEP with either multiple cost drivers or multiple products.

If instead Mary sells 40 packages to 40 customers, then:

$$\text{Operating income} = (\$200 \times 40) - (\$120 \times 40) - (\$10 \times 40) - \$2,000$$

$$= \$8,000 - \$4,800 - \$400 - \$2,000 = \$800$$

Reinforcing Problems Exer. 3-31 covers CVP analysis and multiple cost drivers.

Note that the number of packages sold is not the only determinant of Mary's operating income. For a given number of packages sold, Mary's operating income will be lower if Mary sells Do-All Software to more customers. Mary's cost structure depends on two cost drivers—the number of packages sold and the number of customers.

Just as in the case of multiple products, there is no unique breakeven point when there are multiple cost drivers. For example, Mary will break even if she sells 26 packages to 8 customers or 27 packages to 16 customers:

$$(\$200 \times 26) - (\$120 \times 26) - (\$10 \times 8) - \$2,000 = \$5,200 - \$3,120 - \$80 - \$2,000 = \$0$$

$$(\$200 \times 27) - (\$120 \times 27) - (\$10 \times 16) - \$2,000 = \$5,400 - \$3,240 - \$160 - \$2,000 = \$0$$

This example illustrates that CVP-type analysis can be adapted to multiple cost driver situations. However, in cases involving multiple cost drivers the various simple formulas described earlier in the chapter can no longer be used.

CONTRIBUTION MARGIN VERSUS GROSS MARGIN

Contribution margin is a key concept in this chapter. We now contrast contribution margin with the gross margin concept discussed in Chapter 2.

OBJECTIVE 9

Distinguish between contribution margin and gross margin

$$\text{Gross margin} = \text{Revenues} - \text{Cost of goods sold}$$

$$\text{Contribution margin} = \text{Revenues} - \text{All variable costs}$$

Cost of goods sold in the merchandising sector is made up of goods purchased that are then sold. Cost of goods sold in the manufacturing sector consists entirely

Points to Stress This section spells out the difference between CM and GM in merchandising and mfg. companies. The distinction doesn't apply to service companies because they have no CGS and hence no GM.

of manufacturing costs (including fixed manufacturing costs). The phrase "all costs that vary" refers to variable costs in each of the business functions of the value chain.

Service-sector companies can compute a contribution margin figure but not a gross margin figure. Service-sector companies do not have a cost of goods sold line item in their income statement.

Merchandising Sector

Correcting Student Misconceptions There are 2 distinctions between CM and GM. Variable non-mfg. expenses are subtracted to get CM (but not GM), and fixed mfg. costs are subtracted to get GM (but not CM); e.g.,

Selling price/case	$15
Var. mfg./case	2
Var. mkt. & admin. cost/case	4
Fixed mfg./case	5
Fixed mkt. & admin. cost/case	3

CM = $15 − 2 − 4 = $9
GM = $15 − 2 − 5 = $8

The most common difference between contribution margin and gross margin for companies in the merchandising sector is variable items not in cost of goods sold (such as salesperson commissions that are a percentage of revenues). Contribution margin is computed by deducting all variable costs from revenues, whereas gross margin is computed by deducting only cost of goods sold from revenues. The following example (figures assumed and in thousands) illustrates this difference:

Contribution Income Statement Emphasizing Contribution Margin			Financial Accounting Income Statement Emphasizing Gross Margin	
Revenues		$200	Revenues	$200
Variable cost of goods sold	$120		Cost of goods sold	120
Variable operating costs	43	163	Gross margin	80
Contribution margin		37	Operating costs ($43 + $19)	62
Fixed operating costs		19	Operating income	$ 18
Operating income		$ 18		

Manufacturing Sector

The two areas of difference between contribution margin and gross margin for companies in the manufacturing sector are fixed manufacturing costs and variable nonmanufacturing costs. The following example (figures assumed and in thousands) illustrates this difference:

Revenues		$1,000	Revenues	$1,000
Variable manufacturing costs	$250		Cost of goods sold ($250 + $160)	410
Variable nonmanufacturing costs	270	520		
Contribution margin		480	Gross margin	590
Fixed manufacturing costs	160		Nonmanufacturing costs ($270 + $138)	408
Fixed nonmanufacturing costs	138	298		
Operating income		$ 182	Operating income	$ 182

Fixed manufacturing costs are not deducted from revenues when computing contribution margin but are deducted when computing gross margin. Cost of goods sold in a manufacturing company includes all manufacturing costs. Variable nonmanufacturing costs are deducted from revenues when computing contribution margin but are not deducted when computing gross margin.

Like contribution margin, *gross margin* can be expressed as a total, as an amount per unit, or as a percentage. For example, the **gross margin percentage** is the gross margin divided by revenues—59% ($590 ÷ $1,000) in our manufacturing-sector example.

PROBLEM

Wembley Travel is a travel agency specializing in flights between Los Angeles and London. It books passengers on United Airlines. United charges passengers $900 per round-trip ticket. Until last month, United paid Wembley a commission of 10% of the ticket price paid by each passenger. This commission was Wembley's only source of revenues. Wembley's fixed costs are $14,000 per month (for salaries, rent, and so on), and its variable costs are $20 per ticket purchased for a passenger. This $20 includes a $15 per ticket delivery fee paid to Federal Express. (To keep the analysis simple, we assume each round-trip ticket purchased is delivered in a separate package. Thus, the $15 delivery fee applies to each ticket.)

United Airlines has just announced a revised payment schedule for travel agents. It will now pay travel agents a 10% commission per ticket up to a maximum of $50. Any ticket costing more than $500 generates only a $50 commission, regardless of the ticket price.

Required

1. Under the old 10% commission structure, how many round-trip tickets must Wembley sell each month to (a) break even, and (b) earn an operating income of $7,000 per month?
2. How does United's revised payment schedule affect your answers to (a) and (b) in requirement 1?

SOLUTION

1. Wembley receives a 10% commission on each ticket: 10% × $900 = $90. Thus,

$$USP = \$90$$

$$UVC = \$20$$

$$UCM = \$90 - \$20 = \$70$$

$$FC = \$14{,}000 \text{ per month}$$

   a. $Q = \dfrac{FC}{UCM} = \dfrac{\$14{,}000}{\$70} = 200$ tickets per month

   b. When target operating income (TOI) = $7,000 per month:

$$Q = \frac{FC + TOI}{UCM}$$

$$= \frac{\$14{,}000 + \$7{,}000}{\$70} = \frac{\$21{,}000}{\$70}$$

$$= 300 \text{ tickets per month}$$

2. Under the new system, Wembley would receive only $50 on the $900 ticket. Thus,

$$USP = \$50$$

$$UVC = \$20$$

$$UCM = \$50 - \$20 = \$30$$

$$FC = \$14{,}000 \text{ per month}$$

   a. $Q = \dfrac{\$14{,}000}{\$30} = 467$ tickets (rounded up)

   b. $Q = \dfrac{\$21{,}000}{\$30} = 700$ tickets

The $50 cap on the commission paid per ticket causes the breakeven point to more than double (from 200 to 467) and the tickets sold to earn $7,000 per month to also more than double (from 300 to 700). Not surprisingly, travel agents reacted very negatively to the United Airlines announcement to change commission payments.

SUMMARY

The following points are linked to the chapter's learning objectives:

1. Using CVP analysis requires simplifying assumptions, including the assumption that costs are either fixed or variable with respect to the number of output units (units produced and sold) and that total revenue and total cost relationships are linear.

2. CVP analysis assists managers in understanding the behavior of total costs, total revenues, and operating income as changes occur in the output level, selling price, variable costs, or fixed costs.

3. The three methods outlined for computing the breakeven point (the quantity of output where total revenues equal total costs) and the quantity of output to achieve target operating income are the equation method, the contribution margin method, and the graph method. Each method is merely a restatement of the other. Managers often select the method they find easiest to use in their specific situation.

4. Income taxes can be incorporated into CVP analysis by using target net income rather than target operating income. The breakeven point is unaffected by the presence of income taxes because no income taxes are paid if there is no operating income.

5. When making decisions, managers use CVP analysis to compare contribution margins and fixed costs of the different alternatives. Sensitivity analysis, a "what-if" technique, systematically examines how a result will change if the original predicted data are not achieved or if an underlying assumption changes.

6. CVP analysis highlights the downside risk and upside return of alternatives that differ in the structure of their fixed costs and variable costs.

7. When CVP analysis is applied to a multiple-product company, it is assumed that there is a constant sales mix of products as the total quantity of units sold changes.

8. Contribution margin is revenues minus all variable costs (throughout the value chain), while gross margin is revenues minus cost of goods sold.

9. The basic concepts of CVP analysis can be adapted to multiple cost driver situations but the simple formulae of the single cost driver case can no longer be used.

APPENDIX: DECISION MODELS AND UNCERTAINTY

Managers make predictions and decisions in a world of uncertainty. This appendix explores the characteristics of uncertainty and describes an approach managers can use to cope with it. We also illustrate the additional insights gained when uncertainty is recognized in CVP analysis using data from the Do-All Software example on p. 61.

Coping with Uncertainty[5]

Role of a decision model *Uncertainty* is the possibility that an actual amount will deviate from an expected amount. For example, Mary might forecast sales at 40 units, but actual sales may turn out to be 30 units or 60 units. A *decision model* helps managers deal with uncertainty. It is a formal method for making a choice, frequently involving both quantitative and qualitative analyses. The quantitative analysis usually includes the following steps:

Step 1: Identify a choice criterion A **choice criterion** is an objective that can be quantified. This objective can take many forms. Most often the choice criterion is expressed as maximize income or minimize costs. The choice criterion provides a basis for choosing the best alternative action. For example, Mary's choice criterion is to maximize expected operating income at the convention.

[5]The presentation here draws (in part) from teaching notes prepared by R. Williamson.

Step 2: Identify the set of alternative actions to be considered Denoting actions by a, Mary has three possible actions.

a_1 = Pay $2,000 fixed fee

a_2 = Pay $800 fixed fee plus 15% of convention revenues

a_3 = Pay 25% of convention revenues with no fixed fee

Step 3: Identify the set of events that can occur An **event** is a possible occurrence. The set of events should be mutually exclusive and collectively exhaustive. Events are mutually exclusive if they cannot occur at the same time. Events are collectively exhaustive if, taken together, they make up the entire set of possible occurrences (and no other event can occur). Examples are growth or no growth in industry demand and increase, decrease, or no change in interest rates. Only one event in a set of mutually exclusive and collectively exhaustive events will actually occur. Suppose Mary's only uncertainty is the number of units of Do-All Software that she can sell. For simplicity, suppose Mary estimates that sales will be either 30 units or 60 units. Then using x as the notation for an event,

x_1 = 30 units

x_2 = 60 units

Step 4: Assign a probability to each event that can occur A **probability** is the likelihood or chance of occurrence of an event. Assigning probabilities is a key aspect of the decision model approach to coping with uncertainty. A **probability distribution** describes the likelihood (or probability) of each of the mutually exclusive and collectively exhaustive set of events. The probabilities of these events will add to 1.00 because they are collectively exhaustive. In some cases, there will be much evidence to guide the assignment of probabilities. For example, the probability of obtaining a head in the toss of a fair coin is $\frac{1}{2}$, and that of drawing a particular playing card from a standard, well-shuffled deck is $\frac{1}{52}$. In business, the probability of having a specified percentage of defective units may be assigned with great confidence, on the basis of production experience with thousands of units. In other cases, there will be little evidence supporting estimated probabilities—for example, how many units of a new pharmaceutical product will be sold next year. Suppose, on the basis of past experience, Mary assesses a 60% chance that she will sell 30 units and a 40% chance that she will sell 60 units. Using $P(x)$ as the notation for the probability of an event, the probabilities are:

$P(x_1)$ = .60

$P(x_2)$ = .40

Step 5: Identify the set of possible outcomes **Outcomes** measure, in terms of the choice criterion, the predicted economic results of the various possible combinations of actions and events. The outcomes in the Do-All Software example take the form of six possible operating incomes that are displayed in a *decision table* in Exhibit 3-6. A **decision table** is a summary of the contemplated actions, events, outcomes, and probabilities of events.

It is important to distinguish actions from events. Actions are choices available to managers—for example, the particular rental alternative that Mary should choose. Events are the set of all relevant occurrences that can happen—for example, the possible sales of Do-All Software at the convention. The outcome is the operating income the company makes, which depends both on the action the manager selects (rental alternative chosen) and the event that occurs (the actual sales level).

Exhibit 3-7 presents an overview of a decision model, the implementation of the chosen action, its outcome, and subsequent performance evaluation.

Expected value An **expected value** is the weighted average of the outcomes with the probability of each outcome serving as the weight. Where the outcomes are measured in monetary terms, *expected value* is often called **expected monetary**

EXHIBIT 3-6
Decision Table for Do-All Software

		Probability of Events	
		$x_1 = 30$ units sold $P(x_1) = .60$	$x_2 = 60$ units sold $P(x_2) = .40$
Actions			
a_1:	Pay $2,000 fixed fee	$400[l]	$2,800[m]
a_2:	Pay $800 fixed fee plus 15% of convention revenues	$700[n]	$2,200[p]
a_3:	Pay 25% of convention revenues with no fixed fee	$900[q]	$1,800[r]

[l] Operating income = ($200 − $120)(30) − $2,000 = $400
[m] Operating income = ($200 − $120)(60) − $2,000 = $2,800
[n] Operating income = ($200 − $120 − $30*)(30) − $800 = $700
[p] Operating income = ($200 − $120 − $30*)(60) − $800 = $2,200
[q] Operating income = ($200 − $120 − $50**)(30) = $900
[r] Operating income = ($200 − $120 − $50**)(60) = $1,800
*$30 = 15% of selling price of $200
**$50 = 25% of selling price of $200

EXHIBIT 3-7
A Decision Model and Its Link to Performance Evaluation

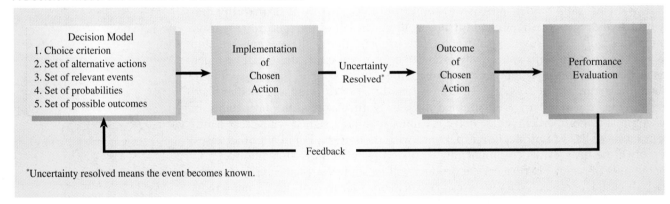

Decision Model
1. Choice criterion
2. Set of alternative actions
3. Set of relevant events
4. Set of probabilities
5. Set of possible outcomes

Implementation of Chosen Action → Uncertainty Resolved* → Outcome of Chosen Action → Performance Evaluation

Feedback

*Uncertainty resolved means the event becomes known.

Example/Curriculum Linkage If students have had a course in decision models, they should be able to calculate the expected value of perfect information (EVPI) in the Do-All example. If demand is certain to be 30 units, a_3 would be the optimal choice. If demand is 60 units, a_1 would be optimal. What's the maximum amount Mary should pay to find out whether demand will be 30 or 60 units?

EVPI
  = ($900)(0.6) + ($2,800)(0.4) − $1,360
  = $300

It would be worth up to $300 to find out whether demand will be 30 units or 60 units.

value. Using information in Exhibit 3-6, the expected monetary value of each booth rental alternative denoted by $E(a_1)$, $E(a_2)$ and $E(a_3)$ is as follows:

Pay $2,000 fixed fee:	$E(a_1) = 0.60(\$400) + 0.40(\$2,800) = \$1,360$
Pay $800 fixed fee plus 15% of revenues:	$E(a_2) = 0.60(\$700) + 0.40(\$2,200) = \$1,300$
Pay 25% of revenues with no fixed fee:	$E(a_3) = 0.60(\$900) + 0.40(\$1,800) = \$1,260$

To maximize expected operating income, Mary should select action a_1—that is, contract to pay Computer Conventions a $2,000 fixed fee.

To interpret the expected value of selecting action a_1, imagine that Mary attends many conventions, each with the probability distribution of operating incomes given in Exhibit 3-6. The expected value of $1,360 is the operating income per convention that Mary will receive when averaged across all conventions. For a specific convention, the operating income will be either $400 or $2,800. But if Mary attends 100 conventions, she will expect to earn $136,000 in total operating income, for an average of $1,360 per convention.

Consider the effect of uncertainty on the preferred action choice. If Mary were certain that she would sell only 30 units of Do-All Software [that is, $P(x_1) = 1$], she would prefer alternative a_3—pay 25% of convention revenues with no fixed fee. To follow this reasoning, examine Exhibit 3-6. When 30 units are sold, alternative a_3 yields the maximum operating income of $900. Because fixed costs are zero, booth rental costs are low when sales are low.

However, if Mary were certain that she would sell 60 units of Do-All Software [that is, $P(x_2) = 1$], she would prefer alternative a_1—pay a \$2,000 fixed fee. Exhibit 3-6 indicates that when 60 units are sold, alternative a_1 yields the maximum operating income of \$2,800. Rental payments under a_2 and a_3 increase with units sold but are fixed under a_1.

Despite the high probability of selling only 30 units, Mary still prefers to take action a_1, that is, pay a fixed fee of \$2,000. Why? Because the high risk of low operating income (the 60% probability of selling only 30 units) is more than offset by the high return from selling 60 units. If however, Mary were more averse to risk (measured in our example by the spread in operating incomes when 30 units are sold versus when 60 units are sold), she may have preferred action a_2 or a_3. For example, action a_2 ensures an operating income of at least \$700, greater than the operating income of \$400 that she would earn under action a_1 if only 30 units are sold. Of course, choosing a_2 limits the upside potential to \$2,200 relative to \$2,800 under a_1 if 60 units are sold. If Mary is very concerned about downside risk, however, she may be willing to forgo some upside benefits to protect against a \$400 outcome by choosing a_2.[6]

Good decisions and good outcomes Always distinguish between a good decision and a good outcome. One can exist without the other. By definition, uncertainty rules out guaranteeing, after the fact, that the best outcome will always be obtained. It is possible that bad luck will produce unfavorable consequences even when good decisions have been made.

Suppose you are offered a one-time-only gamble tossing a fair coin. You will win \$20 if the event is heads, but you will lose \$1 if the event is tails. As a decision maker, you proceed through the logical phases: gathering information, assessing outcomes, and making a choice. You accept the bet. Why? Because the expected value is \$9.50 [0.5(\$20) + 0.5(− \$1)]. The coin is tossed and the event is tails. You lose. From your viewpoint, this was a good decision but a bad outcome.

A decision can be made only on the basis of information available at the time of the decision. Hindsight is flawless, but a bad outcome does not necessarily mean that a bad decision was made. Making a good decision is our best protection against a bad outcome.

TERMS TO LEARN

This chapter and the Glossary at the end of the book contain definitions of the following important terms:

breakeven point (p. 62)
choice criterion (78)
contribution income statement (62)
contribution margin (61)
contribution margin per unit (61)
contribution margin percentage (62)
contribution margin ratio (62)
cost-volume-profit (CVP) analysis (60)
decision table (79)
degree of operating leverage (71)
event (79)
expected monetary value (79)
expected value (79)

gross margin percentage (76)
margin of safety (69)
net income (61)
operating leverage (71)
outcomes (79)
probability (79)
probability distribution (79)
PV graph (66)
revenue driver (60)
sales mix (71)
sensitivity analysis (68)
uncertainty (69)

[6]For more formal approaches, refer to G. Eppen, F. Gould, C. Schmidt, J. Moore, and L. Weatherford *Introductory Management Science: Decision Modeling with Spreadsheets*, 4th ed. (Upper Saddle River, NJ.: Prentice Hall, 1998).

QUESTIONS

Note: To underscore the basic CVP relationships, the assignment material ignores income taxes unless stated otherwise.

3-1 Define cost-volume-profit analysis.

3-2 Describe the assumptions underlying CVP analysis.

3-3 Distinguish between operating income and net income.

3-4 Define contribution margin, contribution margin per unit, and contribution margin percentage.

3-5 Describe three methods that can be used to calculate the breakeven point.

3-6 Why is it more accurate to describe the subject matter of this chapter as CVP analysis rather than as breakeven analysis?

3-7 "CVP analysis is both simple and simplistic. If you want realistic analysis to underpin your decisions, look beyond CVP analysis." Do you agree? Explain.

3-8 How does an increase in the income tax rate affect the breakeven point?

3-9 Describe *sensitivity analysis.* How has the advent of spreadsheet software affected its use?

3-10 Give an example of how a manager can decrease variable costs while increasing fixed costs.

3-11 Give an example of how a manager can increase variable costs while decreasing fixed costs.

3-12 What is operating leverage? How is knowing the degree of operating leverage helpful to managers?

3-13 "There is no such thing as a fixed cost. All costs can be 'unfixed' given sufficient time." Do you agree? What is the implication of your answer for CVP analysis?

3-14 How can a company with multiple products compute its breakeven point?

3-15 "In CVP analysis, gross margin is a less useful concept than contribution margin." Do you agree? Explain briefly.

EXERCISES

3-16 CVP computations. Fill in the blanks for each of the following independent cases.

Case	Revenues	Variable Costs	Fixed Costs	Total Costs	Operating Income	Contribution Margin Percentage
a.	$ —	$500	$ —	$ 800	$1,200	—
b.	2,000	—	300	—	200	—
c.	1,000	700	—	1,000	—	—
d.	1,500	—	300	—	—	40%

3-17 CVP computations. Fill in the blanks for each of the following independent cases.

Case	Selling Price	Variable Costs Per Unit	Total Units Sold	Total Contribution Margin	Total Fixed Costs	Operating Income
a.	$30	$20	70,000	$ —	$ —	− $15,000
b.	25	—	180,000	900,000	800,000	—
c.	—	10	150,000	300,000	220,000	—
d.	20	14	—	120,000	—	12,000

3-18 CVP analysis, changing revenues and costs. Sunshine Tours is a travel agency specializing in flights between Toronto and Jamaica. It books passengers on Canadian Air. Canadian Air charges passengers $1,000 per round-trip ticket. Sunshine receives a commission of 8% of the ticket price paid by the passenger. Sunshine's fixed costs are $22,000 per month. Its variable costs are $35 per ticket, including an $18 delivery fee by Emory Express. (Assume each ticket purchased is delivered in a separate package. Thus, the delivery fee applies to each ticket.)

  1. What is the number of tickets Sunshine must sell each month to (a) break even, and (b) make a target operating income of $10,000?
  2. Assume another company, TNT Express, offers to charge Sunshine only $12 per ticket delivered. How would accepting this offer affect your answers to (a) and (b) in requirement 1?

3-19 CVP analysis, changing revenues and costs (continuation of 3-18). Canadian Air changes its commission structure to travel agents. Up to a ticket price of $600, the 8% commission applies. For tickets costing $600 or more, there is a fixed commission of $48. Assume Sunshine Tours has fixed costs of $22,000 per month and variable costs of $29 per ticket (including a $12 delivery fee by TNT).

Required
  1. What is the number of Toronto-to-Jamaica round-trip tickets Sunshine must sell each month to (a) break even, and (b) make a target operating income of $10,000? Comment on the results.
  2. Sunshine tours decides to charge its customers a delivery fee of $5 per ticket. How would this change affect your answers to (a) and (b) in requirement 1? Comment on the results.

3-20 CVP exercises. The Super Donut owns and operates six donut outlets in and around Kansas City. You are given the following corporate budget data for next year:

Revenues	$10,000,000
Fixed costs	1,700,000
Variable costs	8,200,000

Variable costs change with respect to the number of donuts sold.

Required
Compute the budgeted operating income for each of the following deviations from the original budget data. (Consider each case independently.)

  1. A 10% increase in contribution margin, holding revenues constant
  2. A 10% decrease in contribution margin, holding revenues constant
  3. A 5% increase in fixed costs
  4. A 5% decrease in fixed costs
  5. An 8% increase in units sold
  6. An 8% decrease in units sold
  7. A 10% increase in fixed costs and 10% increase in units sold
  8. A 5% increase in fixed costs and 5% decrease in variable costs

3-21 CVP exercises. The Doral Company manufactures and sells pens. Currently, 5,000,000 units are sold per year at a selling price of $0.50 per unit. Fixed costs are $900,000 per year. Variable costs are $0.30 per unit.

Required
(Consider each case separately.)

  1. a. What is the present operating income for a year?
     b. What is the present breakeven point in revenues?
  Compute the new operating income for each of the following changes:
  2. A $0.04 per unit increase in variable costs
  3. A 10% increase in fixed costs and a 10% increase in units sold
  4. A 20% decrease in fixed costs, a 20% decrease in selling price, a 10% decrease in variable costs per unit, and a 40% increase in units sold
  Compute the new breakeven point in units for each of the following changes:
  5. A 10% increase in fixed costs
  6. A 10% increase in selling price and a $20,000 increase in fixed costs

3-22 CVP analysis, income taxes. The Bratz Company has fixed costs of $300,000 and a variable-cost percentage of 80 percent. The company earns net income of $84,000 in 1999. The income tax rate is 40 percent.

Required
Compute (1) operating income, (2) contribution margin, (3) total revenues, and (4) breakeven revenues.

3-23 CVP analysis, income taxes. The Rapid Meal has two restaurants that are open 24 hours a day. Fixed costs for the two restaurants together total $450,000 per year. Service varies from a cup of coffee to full meals. The average sales check per customer is $8.00. The average cost of food and other variable costs for each customer is $3.20. The income tax rate is 30 percent. Target net income is $105,000.

Required
1. Compute the revenues needed to obtain the target net income.
2. How many sales checks are needed to break even? To earn net income of $105,000?
3. Compute net income if the number of sales checks is 150,000.

3-24 CVP analysis, margin of safety. Suppose Lattin Corp's breakeven point is revenues of $1,000,000. Fixed costs are $400,000.

Required
1. Compute the contribution margin percentage.
2. Compute the selling price if variable costs are $12 per unit.
3. Suppose 80,000 units are sold. Compute the margin of safety.

3-25 Operating leverage. Color Rugs is holding a 2-week carpet sale at Jerry's Club, a local warehouse store. Color Rugs plans to sell carpets for $500 each. The company will purchase the carpets from a local distributor for $350 each with the privilege of returning any unsold units for a full refund. Jerry's Club has offered Color Rugs two payment alternatives for the use of space.

| Option 1: | A fixed payment of $5,000 for the sale period. |
| Option 2: | 10% of total revenues earned during the sale period. |

Assume Color Rugs will incur no other costs.

Required
1. Calculate the breakeven point in units for (a) option 1, and (b) option 2.
2. At what level of revenues will Color Rugs earn the same operating income under either option?
3. a. For what range of unit sales will Color Rugs prefer option 1?
   b. For what range of unit sales will Color Rugs prefer option 2?
4. Calculate the degree of operating leverage at sales of 100 units for the two alternative rental options.
5. Briefly explain and interpret your answer to requirement 4.

3-26 CVP analysis, sensitivity analysis. Hoot Washington is the newly elected charismatic leader of the Republican Party. He is the darling of the right-wing media. His "take no prisoners" attitude has left many an opponent on a talk show feeling run over by a Mack truck.

Media Publishers is negotiating to publish *Hoot's Manifesto*, a new book that promises to be an instant best-seller. The fixed costs of producing and marketing the book will be $500,000. The variable costs of producing and marketing will be $4.00 per copy sold. These costs are before any payments to Hoot. Hoot negotiates an up-front payment of $3 million plus a 15% royalty rate on the net sales price of each book. The net sales price is the listed bookstore price of $30 minus the margin paid to the bookstore to sell the book. The normal bookstore margin of 30% of the listed bookstore price is expected to apply.

Required
1. Prepare a PV graph for Media Publishers.
2. How many copies must Media Publishers sell to (a) break even, and (b) earn a target operating income of $2 million?
3. Examine the sensitivity of the breakeven point to the following changes:
   a. Decreasing the normal bookstore margin to 20% of the listed bookstore price of $30.
   b. Increasing the listed bookstore price to $40 while keeping the bookstore margin at 30 percent.
   c. Comment on the results.

3-27 CVP analysis, international cost structure differences. Knitwear, Inc., is considering three countries for the sole manufacturing site of its new sweater—Singapore, Thailand, and the United States. All sweaters are to be sold to retail outlets in the United States at $32 per unit. These retail outlets add their own markup when selling to final customers. The three countries differ in their fixed costs and variable costs per sweater.

	Annual Fixed Costs	Variable Manufacturing Costs Per Sweater	Variable Marketing & Distribution Costs Per Sweater
Singapore	$ 6.5 million	$ 8.00	$11.00
Thailand	4.5 million	5.50	11.50
United States	12.0 million	13.00	9.00

Required

1. Compute the breakeven point of Knitwear, Inc., in both (a) units sold, and (b) revenues for each of the three countries considered for manufacturing the sweaters.
2. If Knitwear, Inc., sells 800,000 sweaters in 1999, what is the budgeted operating income for each of the three countries considered for manufacturing the sweaters? Comment on the results.

3-28 Sales mix, new and upgrade customers. Zapo 1-2-3 is a top-selling electronic spreadsheet product. Zapo is about to release version 5.0. It divides its customers into two groups—new customers and upgrade customers (those who previously purchased Zapo 1-2-3 4.0 or earlier versions). Although the same physical product is provided to each customer group, sizable differences exist in their selling prices and variable marketing costs:

		New Customers		Upgrade Customers
Selling price		$210		$120
Variable costs				
Manufacturing	$25		$25	
Marketing	65	90	15	40
Contribution margin		$120		$ 80

The fixed costs of Zapo 5.0 are $14,000,000. The planned sales mix in units is 60% new customers and 40% upgrade customers.

Required

1. What is the Zapo 1-2-3 5.0 breakeven point in units, assuming that the planned 60%/40% sales mix is maintained?
2. If the sales mix is maintained, what is the operating income when 200,000 units are sold?
3. Show how the breakeven point in units changes with the following customer mixes:
   a. New 50%/Upgrade 50%
   b. New 90%/Upgrade 10%
   c. Comment on the results.

3-29 Athletic scholarships, CVP analysis. Midwest University has an annual budget of $5,000,000 for athletic scholarships. Students who receive athletic scholarships do not have to pay tuition of $20,000 per year. Fixed costs of the athletic scholarship program is $1,000,000.

Required

1. How many athletic scholarships can Midwest University offer each year?
2. Suppose the total budget for next year is reduced by 20 percent. Fixed costs are to remain the same. Calculate the number of athletic scholarships that Midwest can offer next year.
3. As in requirement 2, assume a budget reduction of 20 percent. Fixed costs are to remain the same. If Midwest wanted to offer the same number of athletic scholarships as it did in requirement 1, how much reduction in tuition would it be able to offer to each student who receives a scholarship?

3-30 Gross margin and contribution margin. (R. Lambert, adapted) Foreman Fork Inc.'s income statement for the year 2000 on production and sales of 200,000 units is as follows:

Revenues	$2,600,000
Cost of goods sold	1,600,000
Gross margin	1,000,000
Marketing and distribution costs	1,150,000
Operating income (loss)	$ (150,000)

Foreman's fixed manufacturing costs were $500,000, and variable marketing and distribution costs were $4 per unit.

Required

1. **a.** Calculate Foreman's variable manufacturing costs per unit in 2000.
   b. Calculate Foreman's fixed marketing and distribution costs in 2000.
2. Foreman's gross margin per unit is $5 ($1,000,000 ÷ 200,000 units). Sam Hogan, Foreman's president, believes that if production and sales had been 230,000 units, it would have covered the $1,150,000 of marketing and distribution costs ($1,150,000 ÷ 5 = 230,000) and enabled Foreman to break even for the year. Calculate Foreman's operating income if production and sales equal 230,000 units. Explain briefly why Sam Hogan is wrong.
3. Calculate the breakeven point for the year 2000 in units and in revenues.

3-31 CVP analysis, multiple cost drivers. Susan Wong is a distributor of brass picture frames. For 1999, she plans to purchase frames for $30 each and sell them for $45 each. Susan's fixed costs for 1999 are expected to be $240,000. Susan's only other costs will be variable costs of $60 per shipment for preparing the invoice and delivery documents, organizing the delivery, and following up for collecting accounts receivable. The $60 cost will be incurred each time Susan ships an order of picture frames, regardless of the number of picture frames in the order.

Required

1. **a.** Suppose Susan sells 40,000 picture frames in 1,000 shipments in 1999. Calculate Susan's 1999 operating income.
   b. Suppose Susan sells 40,000 picture frames in 800 shipments in 1999. Calculate Susan's 1999 operating income.
2. Suppose Susan anticipates making 500 shipments in 1999. How many picture frames must Susan sell to break even in 1999?
3. Calculate another breakeven point for 1999, different from the one described in requirement 2. Explain briefly why Susan has multiple breakeven points.

3-32 Uncertainty, CVP analysis. (Chapter Appendix) Angela King is the Las Vegas promoter for boxer Mike Foreman. King is promoting a new world championship fight for Foreman. The key area of uncertainty is the size of the cable pay-per-view TV market. King will pay Foreman a fixed fee of $2 million and 25% of net cable pay-per-view revenues. Every cable TV home receiving the event pays $29.95, of which King receives $16. King pays Foreman 25% of the $16.

King estimates the following probability distribution for homes purchasing the pay-per-view event:

Demand	Probability
100,000	0.05
200,000	0.10
300,000	0.30
400,000	0.35
500,000	0.15
1,000,000	0.05

Required

1. What is the expected value of the payment King will make to Foreman?
2. Assume the only uncertainty is over cable TV demand for the fight. King wants to know the breakeven point given her own fixed costs of $1 million and her own variable costs of $2 per home. (Also include King's payments to Foreman in calculating your answer.)

PROBLEMS

3-33 CVP analysis, movie production. Royal Rumble Productions has just finished production of *Feature Creatures*, the latest action film directed by Tony Savage and starring Ralph Michaels and Sally Martel. The total production cost to Royal Rumble was $5 million. All the production personnel and actors for *Feature Creatures* received a fixed salary (included in the $5 million) and will have no "residual" (equity interest) in the revenues or operating income from the movie. Media Productions will handle the marketing of *Feature*

Creatures. Media agrees to invest a minimum $3 million to market the movie and will be paid 20% of the revenues Royal Rumble itself receives from the box-office receipts. Royal Rumble receives 62.5% of the total box-office receipts (out of which comes the 20% payment to Media Productions).

Required

1. What is the breakeven point to Royal Rumble for *Feature Creatures* expressed in terms of (a) revenues received by Royal Rumble, and (b) total box-office receipts?
2. Assume in its first year of release, the box-office receipts for Feature Creatures total $300 million. What is the operating income to Royal Rumble from the movie in its first year?

3-34 CVP analysis, cost structure differences, movie production (continuation of 3-33). Royal Rumble is negotiating for *Feature Creatures 2*, a sequel to its mega-blockbuster success *Feature Creatures*. This negotiation is proving more difficult than for the original movie. The budgeted production cost (excluding payments to the director Savage and the stars Michaels and Martel) for *Feature Creatures 2* is $21 million. The agent negotiating for Savage, Michaels, and Martel proposes either of two contracts:

◆ **Contract A:** Fixed-salary component of $15 million for Savage, Michaels, and Martel (combined) with no residual interest in the revenues from *Feature Creatures 2*.

◆ **Contract B:** Fixed-salary component of $3 million for Savage, Michaels, and Martel (combined) plus a residual of 15% of the revenues Royal Rumble receives from *Feature Creatures 2*.

Media Productions will market *Feature Creatures 2*. It agrees to invest a minimum of $10 million. Because of its major role in the success of *Feature Creatures*, Media Productions will now be paid 25% of the revenues Royal Rumble receives from the total box-office receipts from *Feature Creatures 2*. Royal Rumble receives 62.5% of these total box-office receipts (out of which comes the 25% payment to Media Productions).

Required

1. For contracts A and B, what is the breakeven point for Royal Rumble expressed in terms of
   a. revenues received by that company
   b. total box-office receipts for *Feature Creatures 2*?
   Explain the difference between the breakeven points for contracts A and B.
2. Assume in its first year of release *Feature Creatures 2* achieves the same $300 million in box-office receipts as was the case for *Feature Creatures*. What is the operating income to Royal Rumble from *Feature Creatures 2* if it accepts contract B? Comment on the difference in operating income between the two films.

3-35 CVP analysis, shoe stores. The Walk Rite Shoe Company operates a chain of shoe stores. The stores sell ten different styles of inexpensive men's shoes with identical unit costs and selling prices. A unit is defined as a pair of shoes. Each store has a store manager who is paid a fixed salary. Individual salespeople receive a fixed salary and a sales commission. Walk Rite is trying to determine the desirability of opening another store, which is expected to have the following revenue and cost relationships:

Unit variable data (per pair of shoes)	
Selling price	$ 30.00
Cost of shoes	$ 19.50
Sales commissions	1.50
Total variable costs	$ 21.00
Annual fixed costs	
Rent	$ 60,000
Salaries	200,000
Advertising	80,000
Other fixed costs	20,000
Total fixed costs	$360,000

Required

Consider each question independently.

1. What is the annual breakeven point in (a) units sold, and (b) revenues?
2. If 35,000 units are sold, what will be the store's operating income (loss)?

3. If sales commissions were discontinued for individual salespeople in favor of an $81,000 increase in fixed salaries, what would be the annual breakeven point in (a) units sold, and (b) revenues?
4. Refer to the original data. If the store manager were paid $0.30 per unit sold in addition to his current fixed salary, what would be the annual breakeven point in (a) units sold, and (b) revenues?
5. Refer to the original data. If the store manager were paid $0.30 per unit commission on each unit sold in excess of the breakeven point, what would be the store's operating income if 50,000 units were sold? (This $0.30 is in addition to both the commission paid to the sales staff and the store manager's fixed salary.)

3-36 CVP analysis, shoe stores (continuation of 3-35). Refer to requirement 3 of 3-35.

Required
1. Calculate the number of units sold where the operating income under the fixed-salary plan and the lower fixed-salary and commission plan (for salespeople only) would be equal. Above that number of units sold, one plan would be more profitable than the other; below that number of units sold, the reverse would occur.
2. Compute the operating income or loss under each plan in requirement 1 at sales levels of (a) 50,000 units, and (b) 60,000 units.
3. Suppose the target operating income is $168,000. How many units must be sold to reach the target under (a) the fixed-salary plan, and (b) the lower fixed-salary and commission plan?

3-37 Sensitivity and inflation (continuation of 3-36). As president of Walk Rite, you are concerned that inflation may squeeze your profitability. Specifically, you feel committed to the $30 selling price and fear that diluting the quality of the shoes in the face of rising costs would be an unwise move. You expect the cost of shoes to rise by 10% during the coming year. You are tempted to avoid the cost increase by placing a noncancelable order with a large supplier that would provide 50,000 units of the specified quality for each store at $19.50 per unit. (To simplify this analysis, assume that all stores will face identical demands.) These shoes could be acquired and paid for as delivered throughout the year. However, all shoes must be delivered to the stores by the end of the year.

As a shrewd merchandiser, you foresee some risks. If sales were less than 50,000 units, you feel that markdowns of the unsold merchandise would be necessary to sell the goods. You predict that the average selling price of the leftover units would be $18.00. The regular commission of 5% of revenues would be paid to salespeople.

Required
1. Suppose that actual sales for the year is 48,000 units at $30 per unit and that you contracted for 50,000 units. What is the operating income for the store?
2. If you had perfect forecasting ability, you would have contracted for 48,000 units rather than 50,000 units. What would the operating income have been if you had ordered 48,000 units?
3. Given actual sales of 48,000 units, by how much would the average cost per unit have had to rise before you would have been indifferent between having the contract for 50,000 units and not having the contract?

3-38 CVP analysis, income taxes, sensitivity. (CMA, adapted) Almo Company manufactures and sells adjustable canopies that attach to motor homes and trailers. For its year 2001 budget, Almo estimated the following:

Selling price	$400
Variable cost per canopy	$200
Annual fixed costs	$100,000
Net income	$240,000
Income tax rate	40%

The May financial statements reported that sales were not meeting expectations. For the first five months of the year, only 350 units had been sold at the established price, with variable costs as planned, and it was clear that the net income projection for 2001 would not be reached unless some actions were taken. A management committee presented the following mutually exclusive alternatives to the president.

1. Reduce the selling price by $40. The sales organization forecasts that at this signifi-cantly reduced price, 2,700 units can be sold during the remainder of the year. Total fixed costs and variable costs per unit will stay as budgeted.
2. Lower variable costs per unit by $10 through the use of less expensive direct materials and slightly modified manufacturing techniques. The selling price will also be reduced by $30, and sales of 2,200 units are expected for the remainder of the year.
3. Reduce fixed costs by $10,000 and lower the selling price by 5 percent. Variable costs per unit will be unchanged. Sales of 2,000 units are expected for the remainder of the year.

Required
1. If no changes are made to the selling price or cost structure, determine the number of units that Almo Company must sell (a) to break even, and (b) to achieve its net income objective.
2. Determine which alternative Almo should select to achieve its net income objective. Show your calculations.

3-39 Choosing between compensation plans, operating leverage. (CMA, adapted) Marston Corporation manufactures pharmaceutical products that are sold through a net-work of sales agents. The agents are paid a commission of 18% of revenues. The income statement for the year ending December 31, 1999, is as follows:

Marston Corporation
Income Statement
For the Year Ended December 31, 1999

Revenues		$26,000,000
Cost of goods sold		
Variable	$11,700,000	
Fixed	2,870,000	14,570,000
Gross margin		11,430,000
Marketing costs		
Commissions	$ 4,680,000	
Fixed costs	3,420,000	8,100,000
Operating income		$ 3,330,000

Marston is considering hiring its own sales staff to replace the network of sales agents. Marston would pay its sales people a commission of 10% of revenues and incur fixed costs of $2,080,000.

Required
1. Calculate Marston Corporation's breakeven point in revenues for the year 1999.
2. Calculate Marston Corporation's breakeven point in revenues for the year 1999 if the company had hired its own sales force in 1999 to replace the network of sales agents.
3. Calculate the degree of operating leverage at revenues of $26,000,000 if (a) Marston uses sales agents, and (b) Marston employs its own sales staff. Describe the advantages and disadvantages of each alternative.
4. If Marston had hired its own sales staff and increased the commission paid to them to 15%, keeping all other costs the same, how much revenue would Marston have to generate to earn the same operating income it did in 1999?

3-40 Sales mix, three products. The Ronowski Company has three product lines of belts—A, B, and C with contribution margins of $3, $2, and $1, respectively. The president foresees sales of 200,000 units in the coming period, consisting of 20,000 units of A, 100,000 units of B, and 80,000 units of C. The company's fixed costs for the period are $255,000.

Required
1. What is the company's breakeven point in units, assuming that the given sales mix is maintained?
2. If the sales mix is maintained, what is the total contribution margin when 200,000 units are sold? What is the operating income?
3. What would operating income become if 20,000 units of A, 80,000 units of B, and 100,000 units of C were sold? What is the new breakeven point in units if these rela-tionships persist in the next period?

3-41 Multiproduct breakeven, decision making. Evenkeel Corporation manufactures and sells one product—an infant car seat called Plumar—at a price of $50. Variable costs equal $20 per car seat. Fixed costs are $495,000. Evenkeel manufactures Plumar upon the receipt of orders from its customers. In 2000, it sold 30,000 units of Plumar. One of Evenkeel's customers, Glaston Corporation, has asked if in 2001 Evenkeel will manufacture a different style of car seat called Ridex. Glaston will pay $25 for each unit of Ridex. The variable costs for Ridex are estimated to be $15 per seat. Evenkeel has enough capacity to manufacture all the units of Plumar it can sell as well as the units of Ridex that Glaston wants, and will thus incur no additional fixed costs. Evenkeel estimates that, in 2001, it will sell 30,000 units of Plumar (assuming the same price and variable costs in 2000) and 20,000 units of Ridex.

Andy Minton, the president of Evenkeel, checked the effect of accepting Glaston's offer on the breakeven revenues for 2001. Using the planned sales mix for 2001, he was surprised to find that the revenues required to break even appeared to increase. He was not sure that his numbers were correct, but if they were, Andy felt inclined to reject Glaston's offer. He asks for your advice.

Required
1. Calculate the breakeven point in units and in revenues for 2000.
2. Calculate the breakeven point in units and in revenues for 2001 at the planned sales mix.
3. Explain why the breakeven point in revenues calculated in requirements 1 and 2 are different.
4. What would you advise Andy Minton to do? Provide Andy with the support underlying your reasoning.

3-42 Sales mix, two products. The Goldman Company retails two products, a standard and a deluxe version of a luggage carrier. The budgeted income statement for next period is as follows:

	Standard Carrier	Deluxe Carrier	Total
Units sold	150,000	50,000	200,000
Revenues at $20 and $30 per unit	$3,000,000	$1,500,000	$4,500,000
Variable costs at $14 and $18 per unit	2,100,000	900,000	3,000,000
Contribution margins at $6 and $12 per unit	$ 900,000	$ 600,000	1,500,000
Fixed costs			1,200,000
Operating income			$ 300,000

Required
1. Compute the breakeven point in units, assuming that the planned sales mix is maintained.
2. Compute the breakeven point in units (a) if only standard carriers are sold, and (b) if only deluxe carriers are sold.
3. Suppose 200,000 units are sold, but only 20,000 of them are deluxe. Compute the operating income. Compute the breakeven point in units. Compare your answer with the answer to requirement 1. What is the major lesson of this problem?

3-43 CVP analysis, decision making. (M. Rajan, adapted) Tocchet Company manufactures CB1, a citizens' band radio that is sold mainly to truck drivers. The company's plant in Camden, New Jersey, has an annual capacity of 50,000 units. Tocchet currently sells 40,000 units at a selling price of $105. It has the following cost structure:

Variable manufacturing costs per unit	$45
Fixed manufacturing costs	$800,000
Variable marketing and distribution costs per unit	$10
Fixed marketing and distribution costs	$600,000

Required
Consider each question independently. There is no connection between the requirements.

1. Calculate the breakeven point in units and in revenues.
2. The Marketing Department indicates that decreasing the selling price to $99 would increase sales to 50,000 units. This strategy will require Tocchet to increase its fixed marketing and distribution costs. Variable costs per unit will remain the same as before. What is the *maximum* increase in fixed marketing and distribution costs for which Tocchet will prefer to reduce the selling price?

3. The Manufacturing Department proposes changes in the manufacturing process to add new features to the CB1 product. These changes will increase fixed manufacturing costs by $100,000 and variable manufacturing costs per unit by $2. At its current sales quantity of 40,000 units, what is the *minimum* selling price above which Tocchet will prefer to add these new features?

3-44 CVP analysis, income taxes. (CMA) R. A. Ro and Company, a manufacturer of quality handmade walnut bowls, has experienced a steady growth in sales for the past five years. However, increased competition has led Mr. Ro, the president, to believe that an aggressive marketing campaign will be necessary next year to maintain the company's present growth.

To prepare for next year's marketing campaign, the company's controller has prepared and presented Mr. Ro with the following data for the current year, 2000:

Variable costs (per bowl)		
Direct materials	$3.25	
Direct manufacturing labor	8.00	
Variable overhead (Manufacturing, marketing, distribution, and customer service)	2.50	
Total variable costs	$13.75	
Fixed costs		
Manufacturing	$ 25,000	
Marketing, distribution, and customer service	110,000	
Total fixed costs	$135,000	
Selling price	$25.00	
Expected sales, 20,000 units	$500,000	
Income tax rate	40%	

Required

1. What is the projected net income for 2000?
2. What is the breakeven point in units for 2000?
3. Mr. Ro has set the revenue target for 2001 at a level of $550,000 (or 22,000 bowls). He believes an additional marketing cost of $11,250 for advertising in 2001, with all other costs remaining constant, will be necessary to attain the revenue target. What is the net income for 2001 if the additional $11,250 is spent and the revenue target is met?
4. What is the breakeven point in revenues for 2001 if the additional $11,250 is spent for advertising?
5. If the additional $11,250 is spent for advertising in 2001, what is the required 2001 revenues for 2001's net income to equal 2000's net income?
6. At a sales level of 22,000 units, what maximum amount can be spent on advertising if a 2001 net income of $60,000 is desired?

3-45 Review of Chapters 2 and 3. For each of the following independent cases, find the unknowns designated by the capital letters.

	Case 1	Case 2
Direct materials used	$ H	$40,000
Direct manufacturing labor	30,000	15,000
Variable marketing, distribution, and customer-service costs	K	T
Fixed manufacturing overhead	I	20,000
Fixed marketing, distribution, and customer-service costs	J	10,000
Gross Margin	25,000	20,000
Finished goods inventory, January 1, 1999	0	5,000
Finished goods inventory, December 31, 1999	0	5,000
Contribution margin (dollars)	30,000	V
Revenues	100,000	100,000

	Case 1	Case 2
Direct materials inventory, January 1, 1999	12,000	20,000
Direct materials inventory, December 31, 1999	5,000	W
Variable manufacturing overhead	5,000	X
Work in process, January 1, 1999	0	9,000
Work in process, December 31, 1999	0	9,000
Purchases of direct materials	15,000	50,000
Breakeven point (in revenues)	66,667	Y
Cost of goods manufactured	G	U
Operating income (loss)	L	(5,000)

3-46 CVP analysis under uncertainty. (Chapter Appendix, J. Patell) In your new position as supervisor of product introduction, you have to decide on a pricing strategy for a talking-doll specialty product with the following cost structure:

Variable costs per unit	$50
Fixed costs	$200,000

The dolls are manufactured upon receipt of orders, so the inventory levels are insignificant. Your market research assistant is very enthusiastic about probability models and presents the results of his price analysis as follows:

a. If you set the selling price at $100 per unit, the probability distribution of revenues is uniform between $300,000 and $600,000. Under this distribution, there is a .50 probability of equaling or exceeding revenues of $450,000.

b. If you lower the selling price to $70 per unit, the distribution remains uniform, but it shifts up to the $600,000–$900,000 range. Under this distribution, there is a .50 probability of equaling or exceeding revenues of $750,000.

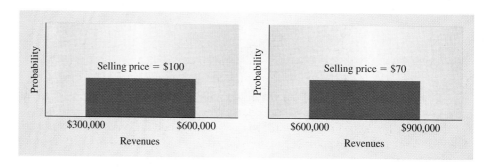

Required

1. This is your first big contract, and, above all, you want to show an operating income. You decide to select the strategy that maximizes the probability of at least breaking even.
   a. What is the probability of at least breaking even with a selling price of $100 per unit?
   b. What is the probability of at least breaking even with a selling price of $70 per unit?
2. Your assistant suggests that maximum expected operating income might be a better objective to pursue. Which pricing strategy would result in the higher expected operating income? (Use the expected revenues under each pricing strategy when making expected operating income computations.)

3-47 CVP analysis under uncertainty. (Chapter Appendix, R. Jaedicke and A. Robichek, adapted) The Jaro Company is considering two new colors for their umbrella products—emerald green and shocking pink. Either can be produced using present facilities. Each product requires an increase in annual fixed costs of $400,000. The products have the same selling price ($10) and the same variable costs per unit ($8).

Management, after studying past experience with similar products, has prepared the following probability distribution:

Event (Units Demanded)	Probability for	
	Emerald Green Umbrella	Shocking Pink Umbrella
50,000	0.0	0.1
100,000	0.1	0.1
200,000	0.2	0.1
300,000	0.4	0.2
400,000	0.2	0.4
500,000	0.1	0.1
	1.0	1.0

Required

1. What is the breakeven point in units for each product?
2. Which product should be chosen, assuming the objective is to maximize expected operating income? Why? Show your computations.
3. Suppose management is absolutely certain that 300,000 units of shocking pink will be sold, but it still faces the same uncertainty about the demand for emerald green as outlined in the problem. Which product should be chosen? Why? What benefits are available to management from having the complete probability distribution instead of just an expected value?

3-48 Ethics, CVP analysis. Allen Corporation produces a molded plastic casing, LX201, for desktop computers. Summary data from its year 2000 income statement are as follows:

Revenues	$5,000,000
Variable costs	3,000,000
Fixed costs	2,160,000
Operating income	$ (160,000)

Jane Woodall, Allen's president, is very concerned about Allen's poor profitability. She asks Max Lemond, production manager, and Lester Bush, controller, to see if there are ways to reduce costs.

After two weeks, Max returns with a proposal to reduce variable costs to 52% of revenues by reducing the costs Allen currently incurs for safe disposal of wasted plastic. Lester is concerned that this would expose the company to potential environmental liabilities. He tells Max, "We would need to estimate some of these potential environmental costs and include them in our analysis." "You can't do that," Max replies. "We are not violating any laws. There is some possibility that we may have to incur environmental costs in the future but if we bring it up now, this proposal will not go through because our senior management always assumes these costs to be larger than they are. The market is very tough and we are in danger of shutting down the company. We don't want all our colleagues to lose their jobs. The only reason our competitors are making money is because they are doing exactly what I am proposing."

Required

1. Calculate Allen's breakeven revenues for the year 2000.
2. Calculate Allen's breakeven revenues if variable costs are 52% of revenues.
3. Calculate Allen's operating income in 2000 if variable costs had been 52% of revenues.
4. Given Max Lemond's comments, what should Lester Bush do?

COLLABORATIVE LEARNING PROBLEM

3-49 Deciding where to produce. (CMA, adapted) The PTO Division of the Galva Manufacturing Company produces the same power take-off units for the farm equipment business in two plants, a newly renovated, automated plant in Peoria, and an older, less automated plant in Moline. The PTO Division expected to produce and sell 192,000 power take-off units during the coming year. The following data are available for the two plants.

	Peoria		Moline	
Selling price		$150.00		$150.00
Variable manufacturing cost per unit	$72.00		$88.00	
Fixed manufacturing cost per unit	30.00		15.00	
Sales commission (5% of revenues)	7.50		7.50	
Variable marketing and distribution cost per unit	6.50		6.50	
Fixed marketing and distribution cost per unit	19.00		14.50	
Total cost per unit		135.00		131.50
Operating income per unit		$ 15.00		$ 18.50
Production rate per day	400 units		320 units	

All fixed costs per unit are calculated based on a normal year of 240 working days. When the number of working days exceeds 240, variable manufacturing costs increase by $3.00 per unit in Peoria and $8.00 per unit in Moline. Capacity for each plant is 300 working days per year.

Wishing to take advantage of the higher operating income per unit at Moline, PTO's production manager has decided to manufacture 96,000 units at each plant. This production plan results in Moline operating at capacity (320 units per day × 300 days) and Peoria operating at its normal volume (400 units per day × 240 days). Galva's corporate controller is not happy with this plan because he does not believe it represents optimal usage of PTO's plants.

Required

Form groups of two or more students to complete the following requirements.

1. Determine the breakeven point in units for the Peoria and Moline plants.
2. Calculate the operating income that would result from the production manager's plan to produce 96,000 units at each plant.
3. Determine how the production of the 192,000 units should be allocated between the Peoria and Moline plants to maximize operating income for the PTO Division. What is the maximum operating income that the PTO Division can earn? Show your calculations.

Job Costing

After studying this chapter, you should be able to

1. Describe the building block concepts of costing systems
2. Distinguish between job costing and process costing
3. Outline a seven-step approach to job costing
4. Distinguish actual costing from normal costing
5. Track the flow of costs in a job-costing system
6. Prorate end-of-period under- or overallocated indirect costs using alternative methods
7. Apply variations of normal costing

John Deere manufactures many different models of tractors with distinct product features to meet the diverse needs of its customers. Different models use different amounts of manufacturing resources. John Deere uses a job-costing system to determine the cost of manufacturing the different models.

How much does it cost Ford Motor Company to manufacture a Ford Bronco and sell it to a dealer? How much does it cost Arthur Andersen to audit Federal Express? How much does it cost Safeway to sell a six-pack of Pepsi? Managers ask such questions for many purposes, including formulating strategies, making pricing and cost management decisions, and meeting external reporting requirements. Chapters 4 and 5 present concepts and techniques that guide the responses to such questions. Chapter 4 presents basic concepts of job costing. Chapter 5 describes applications of activity-based costing.

Before we explore the details of costing systems, four points are worth noting.

1. The cost-benefit approach we discussed in Chapter 1 is essential in designing and choosing costing systems. The costs of elaborate systems, including the costs of educating managers and other personnel to use them, can be quite high. Managers should install a more sophisticated system only if they believe that its additional benefits will outweigh its additional costs.

2. Costing systems should be tailored to the underlying operations, and not vice versa. Any significant change in operations is likely to justify a corresponding change in the costing system. Designing the best system begins with a careful study of how operations are conducted and a resulting determination of what information to gather and report. The worst systems are those that operating managers perceive as misleading or useless.

3. Costing systems accumulate costs to facilitate decisions. Because specific decisions that might need to be made cannot always be foreseen, costing systems are designed to fulfill several general needs that are common among managers. In this chapter, we will focus on decisions regarding product costing. Therefore, we pay most attention to the part of the costing system that aims to report cost numbers that indicate the manner in which particular cost objects—such as products or services—use the resources of an organization. Managers use product costing information for cost management, planning and control, and inventory valuation.

4. Costing systems are only one source of information for managers. When making decisions, managers combine information on costs with other noncost information, including personal observation of operations and nonfinancial performance measures such as setup times, absentee rates, and number of customer complaints.

BUILDING BLOCK CONCEPTS OF COSTING SYSTEMS

We now review some terms introduced in Chapter 2 that we use to discuss costing systems:

◆ *Cost object*—anything for which a separate measurement of costs is desired; an example is a product or service.

◆ *Direct costs of a cost object*—costs that are related to the particular cost object and can be traced to it in an economically feasible (cost-effective) way.

◆ *Indirect costs of a cost object*—costs that are related to the particular cost object but cannot be traced to it in an economically feasible (cost-effective) way. Indirect costs are allocated to the cost object using a cost-allocation method.

The relationship among these three concepts is as follows:

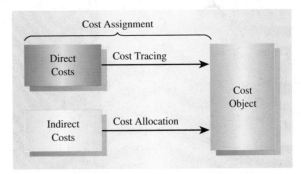

Two terms not previously defined are also important when discussing costing systems:

- **Cost pool**—a grouping of individual cost items. Cost pools can range from the very broad (such as a companywide total-cost pool for operating costs of all cars owned by a company) to the very narrow (such as the costs of operating one particular car used by a salesperson).

- **Cost-allocation base**—a factor that is the common denominator for systematically linking an indirect cost or group of indirect costs to a cost object. If the cost object is a job, product, or customer, the cost-allocation base can also be called a **cost-application base**. A cost-allocation base can be financial (such as direct labor costs) or nonfinancial (such as the number of miles traveled). Companies often seek to use the cost driver of the indirect costs as the cost-allocation base. For example, the number of miles traveled may be used as the base for allocating automobile operating costs among different sales districts.

These five terms constitute the building blocks that we will use to design the costing systems described in this chapter.

JOB-COSTING AND PROCESS-COSTING SYSTEMS

Two basic types of costing systems are used to assign costs to products or services:

- **Job-costing system**. In this system, the cost object is an individual unit, batch, or lot of a *distinct* product or service called a **job**. The product or service is often custom-made, such as specialized machinery made at Hitachi, construction projects managed by Bechtel Corporation, repair jobs done at Sears Automotive Stores, and advertisements produced by Saatchi and Saatchi. Each special machine made by Hitachi is unique and distinct. Similarly, an advertising campaign for one client at Saatchi and Saatchi differs greatly from advertising campaigns for other clients. Because the products and services are distinct, job-costing systems can accumulate costs by each individual product, service, or job.

- **Process-costing system**. In this system, the cost object is masses of *identical* or *similar* units of a product or service. For example, Citibank provides the same service to all its customers when processing customer deposits. Time-Warner provides the same product (say, a weekly issue of *Time*) to each of its customers. Customers of General Chemicals all receive the same product (say, soda ash). In each period, process-costing systems divide the total costs of producing an identical or similar product or service by the total number of units produced to obtain a per unit cost. This average unit cost applies to all the identical or similar units produced.

Exhibit 4-1 presents examples of job and process costing in the service, merchandising, and manufacturing sectors.

These two types of costing systems are best viewed as opposite ends of a continuum:

Many companies have costing systems that are neither pure job costing nor pure process costing. Rather, they combine elements of both job costing and process costing. In this chapter, we focus on job-costing systems. Chapters 17 and 18 discuss process-costing systems.

Teaching Tip/Curriculum Linkage To focus on the "big picture," emphasize that mgt. acctg. provides information for:

1. *planning and control*—mgt. acctg. systems accumulate costs by dept. to compare with budgeted costs for performance evaluation (see Chaps. 6–8 and 23).
2. *product/service costing*—just as financial acctg. requires many choices in determining income, cost acctg. requires many choices to determine the costs of services and products (see Chaps. 2, 4, 5, 14, 15, and 17–19).

EXHIBIT 4-1

Examples of Job Costing and Process Costing in the Service, Merchandising, and Manufacturing Sectors

	Service Sector	Merchandising Sector	Manufacturing Sector
Job Costing Used	◆ Auditing engagements ◆ Consulting firm engagements ◆ Advertising agency campaigns ◆ Law cases ◆ Auto repair shops	◆ Sending special-order items by mail order ◆ Special promotion of new store products	◆ Aircraft assembly ◆ House construction
Process Costing Used	◆ Bank check clearing ◆ Postal delivery (standard items)	◆ Grain dealing ◆ Magazine subscription receipts ◆ Shelving products	◆ Oil refining ◆ Beverage production

Points to Stress Service sector firms and merchandising firms also need to determine the costs of individual jobs. Why? They need job costing info. for cost mgt., profitability analysis, and pricing. Accurate cost info. is particularly important in instances where competition is fierce (e.g., public accounting or internet book stores).

JOB COSTING IN MANUFACTURING

We illustrate job costing using the example of Robinson Company, which operates at capacity to manufacture and install specialized machinery for the paper-making industry at its Green Bay, Wisconsin, plant. In its job-costing system, Robinson accumulates costs incurred on a job in all parts of the value chain—R&D, design, manufacturing, marketing, distribution, and customer service. For simplicity, we focus on Robinson's manufacturing area. To make a machine, Robinson procures some of the components from outside suppliers and makes others itself. A key part of each of Robinson's jobs is assembling and installing the machine at customer sites, integrating it with the customer's other machines and processes, and ensuring its effective functioning.

The specific job we will focus on is the manufacture and installation of a small pulp machine for Western Pulp and Paper Company in the year 2000, for a price of $15,000. A key issue for Robinson in determining this price is the cost of doing the job. Knowledge about its own costs helps Robinson price jobs to make a profit and to make informed estimates of the costs of future jobs.

Consider Robinson's *actual costing* system, a job-costing system that uses *actual costs* to determine the cost of individual jobs. **Actual costing** is a method of job costing that traces direct costs to a cost object by using the actual direct-cost rate(s) times the actual quantity of the direct-cost input(s) and allocates indirect costs based on the actual indirect-cost rate(s) times the actual quantity of the cost-allocation base(s).

General Approach to Job Costing

OBJECTIVE 3

Outline a seven-step approach to job costing

We present a seven-step procedure to assign actual costs to individual jobs. This procedure applies equally to job costing in the manufacturing, merchandising, and service sectors.

Step 1: Identify the Chosen Cost Object(s) The cost object in the Robinson Company example is Job Number WPP 298, manufacturing a pulp machine for the Western Pulp and Paper Company in the year 2000.

Step 2: Identify the Direct Costs of the Job Robinson identifies two direct manufacturing cost categories—direct materials and direct manufacturing labor. Direct materials costs for the Western Pulp and Paper Company job are $4,606, while direct manufacturing labor costs are $1,579.

Step 3: Select the Cost-Allocation Base(s) to Use for Allocating Indirect Costs to the Job Indirect manufacturing costs are costs that cannot be traced to specific jobs. Yet completing various jobs would be impossible without incurring indirect costs such as supervision, manufacturing engineering, utilities, and repairs. These costs must be allocated to jobs. Different jobs require different quantities of indirect resources. The objective of allocating indirect costs is to measure the underlying usage of indirect resources by individual jobs.

Robinson chooses direct manufacturing labor-hours as the only allocation base for linking all indirect manufacturing costs to jobs. Why? Because Robinson believes that direct manufacturing labor-hours measures how individual jobs use manufacturing overhead resources, such as salaries paid to supervisors, engineers, production support staff, and quality management staff. There is a strong cause-and-effect relationship between the indirect manufacturing resources demanded and the direct manufacturing labor-hours required by individual jobs. In the year 2000, Robinson records 27,000 actual direct manufacturing labor-hours.

Step 4: Identify the Indirect Costs Associated with Each Cost-Allocation Base Because Robinson believes that a single cost-allocation base, direct manufacturing labor-hours, can be used to allocate indirect manufacturing costs to products, it creates a single cost pool called *manufacturing overhead costs*. This pool represents the indirect costs of the Green Bay Manufacturing Department that are difficult to trace directly to individual jobs. In 2000, actual indirect manufacturing costs total $1,215,000.

Step 5: Compute the Rate Per Unit of Each Cost-Allocation Base Used to Allocate Indirect Costs to the Job For each cost pool, the **indirect-cost rate** is calculated by dividing total overhead costs in the pool (determined in step 4) by the total quantity of the cost-allocation base (determined in step 3). Robinson calculates the allocation rate for its single manufacturing overhead cost pool as follows:

$$\text{Actual indirect-cost rate} = \frac{\text{Actual total costs in indirect-cost pool}}{\text{Actual total quantity of cost-allocation base}}$$

$$= \frac{\$1,215,000}{27,000 \text{ direct manufacturing labor-hours}}$$

$$= \$45 \text{ per direct manufacturing labor-hour}$$

Step 6: Compute the Indirect Costs Allocated to the Job The indirect costs of a job are computed by multiplying the actual quantities of the different allocation bases (one for each cost pool) used to complete a job by their respective indirect-cost rates (computed in step 5). To make the pulp machine, Robinson uses 88 direct manufacturing labor-hours, the cost-allocation base for its only indirect-cost pool (out of the 27,000 total direct manufacturing labor-hours for the year 2000). Indirect costs allocated to the pulp machine job equal $3,960 ($45 per direct manufacturing labor-hour × 88 hours).

Step 7: Compute the Total Cost of the Job by Adding All Direct and Indirect Costs Assigned to It The cost of the pulp machine job for Western Pulp is $10,145.

Direct manufacturing costs		
Direct materials	$4,606	
Direct manufacturing labor	1,579	$ 6,185
Indirect manufacturing costs ($45 × 88 direct manufacturing labor-hours)		3,960
Total manufacturing costs of job		$10,145

Recall that Robinson was paid $15,000 for the job. Thus, the actual costing system shows a gross margin of $4,855 ($15,000 − $10,145) and a gross margin percentage of 32.37% ($4,855 ÷ $15,000).

Robinson can use the gross margin and gross margin percentage calculations to compare profitability across various jobs and identify the most profitable types of jobs for its sales force to target. At the same time, Robinson can examine the reasons

EXHIBIT 4-2
Job-Costing Overview for Determining Manufacturing Costs of Jobs at Robinson Company

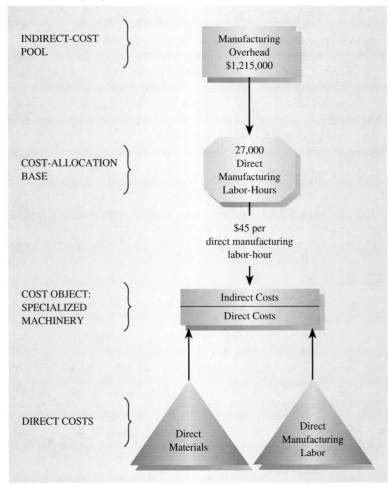

why some jobs show low profitability. Have direct materials been wasted? Is direct manufacturing labor too high? Are there ways to improve the efficiency with which these jobs are done? Or were these jobs simply underpriced? Job cost analysis provides crucial information for judging performance and making future improvements.

Exhibit 4-2 presents an overview of the Robinson Company job-costing system. This exhibit includes the five building block concepts—*cost object, direct costs of a cost object, indirect costs of a cost object, cost pool,* and *cost-allocation base.* Costing-system overviews like Exhibit 4-2 are important learning tools. We urge you to sketch one when you need to understand a costing system in manufacturing, service, or merchandising companies. (The symbols in Exhibit 4-2 are used consistently in the costing-system overviews presented in this book. For example, a triangle always identifies a direct cost.) Note the correspondence between the exhibit diagram and the cost of the pulp machine job described in step 7. Exhibit 4-2 shows two direct-cost categories (direct materials and direct manufacturing labor) and one indirect-cost pool (manufacturing overhead) used to allocate indirect costs. The costs in step 7 also have three dollar amounts that correspond to the two direct- and one indirect-cost categories.

Two Major Cost Objects: Products and Departments

As this book emphasizes, all costs are recorded to help individuals make decisions. Cost objects are chosen to aid decision making. The Exhibit 4-2 overview focuses on one major cost object of an accounting system: *products.* Managers also focus on a second major cost object: *responsibility centers,* which are parts, segments, or subunits of an organization whose managers are accountable for specified sets of activi-

Cost-Allocation Bases Used for Manufacturing Overhead

How do companies around the world allocate manufacturing overhead costs to products? The percentages in the following table indicate how frequently particular cost-allocation bases are used in costing systems in five countries. The reported percentages exceed 100% because many companies surveyed use more than one cost-allocation base.

	United States[a]	Australia[b]	Ireland[c]	Japan[b]	United Kingdom[b]
Direct labor-hours	31%	36%	38%	50%	31%
Direct labor dollars	31	21	13	7	29
Machine-hours	12	19	22	12	27
Direct materials dollars	4	12	7	11	17
Units of production	5	20	28	16	22
Prime costs (%)	—	1	—	21	10
Other	17	—	21	—	—

[a]Adapted from Cohen and Paquette, "Management Accounting."
[b]Blayney and Yokoyama, "Comparative Analysis."
[c]Clarke, "A Survey of"
Full citations are given in Appendix A.

ties. Examples are departments, groups of departments, divisions, or geographic territories. Manufacturing job-costing systems assign costs first to responsibility centers and then to jobs.

The most commonly encountered responsibility center is a department. Identifying department costs helps managers to control costs for which they are responsible. It also enables senior management to evaluate the performance of subordinates and the performance of subunits of the organization as economic investments. For example, Robinson identifies manufacturing as a critical activity and the Manufacturing Department as an important cost object. The costs of the Manufacturing Department include all costs of materials; manufacturing labor; and other manufacturing costs such as supervision, engineering, and production and quality control.

Note especially that costs such as supervision, engineering, and production and quality control that were considered indirect or overhead costs when costing individual jobs are direct costs of the Manufacturing Department. Why? Because although these costs are difficult to trace to individual jobs within the Manufacturing Department in an economically feasible way, they are easily identified with and traced to the Manufacturing Department itself.

Source Documents

Robinson's managers and accountants gather information that goes into their costing systems through **source documents**, which are the original records that support journal entries in an accounting system. The key source document in a job-costing system is a **job cost record** (also called a **job cost sheet**), a document that records and accumulates all the costs assigned to a specific job. The job cost record is started as soon as work begins on a particular job. Exhibit 4-3, Panel A, shows the job cost record for the pulp machine ordered by Western Pulp and Paper Company.

Source documents also exist for individual items in a job cost record. Consider direct materials. On the basis of the engineering specifications and drawings provided by Western Pulp, a manufacturing engineer orders materials from the storeroom. This is done using a basic source document called a **materials requisition record**, which is a form used to charge job cost records and departments for the cost of direct materials used on a specific job. Exhibit 4-3, Panel B, shows a materials requisition record for the Robinson Company. Note how the record specifies

Points to Stress Two cost objects (depts. and products) reflect the 2 major purposes of mgt. acctg.—providing information for (1) planning and control (accumulating costs by dept. helps mgrs. control costs), and (2) determining the costs of products/services (e.g., for external reporting, pricing, and product emphasis decisions). For example, when mfg. custom furniture, the cost of lumber used and workers' wages are allocated to (1) Cutting or Machining and Assembly Dept. for control and performance evaluation (e.g., did workers efficiently cut the lumber or assemble the chair?), and (2) the finished chairs for product costing purposes.

EXHIBIT 4-3
Source Documents at Robinson Company: Job Cost Record, Materials Requisition Record, and
Labor-Time Record

PANEL A

JOB COST RECORD

JOB NO: WPP 298   CUSTOMER: Western Pulp and Paper
Date   Feb. 7, 2000   Date Completed: March 1, 2000
Started:

DIRECT MATERIALS

Date Received	Materials Requisition No.	Part No.	Quantity Used	Unit Cost	Total Costs
Feb. 7, 2000	2000: 198	MB 468-A	8	$14	$ 112
Feb. 7, 2000	2000: 199	TB 267-F	12	63	756
					•
					•
Total					$ 4,606

DIRECT MANUFACTURING LABOR

Period Covered	Labor Time Record No.	Employee No.	Hours Used	Hourly Rate	Total Costs
Feb. 7–13, 2000	LT 232	551-87-3076	25	$18	$ 450
Feb. 7–13, 2000	LT 247	287-31-4671	5	19	95
					•
					•
Total					$ 1,579

MANUFACTURING OVERHEAD*

Date	Cost Pool Category	Allocation Base	Allocation-Base Units Used	Allocation-Base Rate	Total Costs
Dec. 31, 2000	Manufacturing	Direct Manufacturing Labor-Hours	88 hours	$45	$ 3,960
Total					$ 3,960
TOTAL JOB COST					$10,145

PANEL B

MATERIALS REQUISITION RECORD

Materials Requisition Record No.   2000: 198
Job No.: WPP 298   Date: Feb. 7, 2000

Part No.	Part Description	Quantity	Unit Cost	Total Cost
MB 468-A	Metal Brackets	8	$14	$112

Issued By: B. Clyde   Date: Feb. 7, 2000
Received By: L. Daley   Date: Feb. 7, 2000

PANEL C

LABOR-TIME RECORD

Labor-Time Record No.:   LT 232
Employee Name: G. L. Cook   Employee No.: 551-87-3076
Employee Classification Code: Grade 3 Machinist
Hourly Rate: $18
Week Start: Feb. 7, 2000   Week End: Feb. 13, 2000

Job. No.	M	T	W	Th	F	S	Su	Total
WPP 298	4	8	3	6	4	0	0	25
JL 256	3	0	4	2	3	0	0	12
Maintenance	1	0	1	0	1	0	0	3
Total	8	8	8	8	8	0	0	40

Supervisor: R. Stuart   Date: Feb. 14, 2000

*Robinson Company uses a single manufacturing overhead cost pool. The use of multiple overhead cost pools would mean multiple entries in the "Manufacturing Overhead" section of the job cost record.

Points to Stress Exh. 4-3 shows how Robinson's job-cost record uses information from materials requisition and labor time source records.

the job for which the material is requested (WPP 298), description of the material (Part Number MB 468-A, Metal brackets), the actual quantity (8), the actual price ($14), and the actual total cost ($112). The $112 also appears on the job cost record. Adding the cost of all the material requisitions for the pulp machine job gives the actual direct materials costs of $4,606 shown on the job cost record.

The accounting for direct manufacturing labor is similar to that described for direct materials. The basic source document for direct manufacturing labor is a **labor-time record**, which is used to charge job cost records and departments for labor time used on a specific job. Exhibit 4-3, Panel C, shows a typical weekly labor-time record for a particular employee (G. L. Cook). Each day G. L. Cook records the time spent on individual jobs (in this case WPP 298 and JL 256) as well as the time spent on other tasks such as maintenance of machines or cleaning that are not related to a specific job.

The 25 hours that G. L. Cook spends on Job WPP 298 appears on the job cost record in Panel A at a cost of $450 (25 hours × hourly rate of $18 per hour). Similarly the job cost record for job JL256 will carry a cost of $216 (12 hours × $18 per hour). The 3 hours of time spent on maintenance and cleaning at $18 per hour equal $54; this cost is part of indirect manufacturing costs because it is not traceable to any particular job. This indirect cost is included as part of the manufacturing overhead cost pool that is allocated to jobs using direct manufacturing labor-hours. The total direct manufacturing labor costs of $1,579 for the pulp machine that appears on the job cost record in Panel A is the sum of all the direct manufacturing labor costs charged to this job by different employees.

Companies pay special attention to the accuracy of source documents because the reliability of job cost records depends on the reliability of the inputs. Problems occurring in this area include materials recorded on one job being "borrowed" and used on other jobs and erroneous job numbers being assigned to materials or labor inputs.

In many costing systems, the source documents exist only in the form of computer records. Bar coding and other forms of online information recording enable the materials and labor time used on jobs to be recorded without human intervention.

TIME PERIOD USED TO COMPUTE INDIRECT-COST RATES

Robinson Company computes indirect-cost rates in step 5 (p. 99) on the basis of an annual period. Why does Robinson wait until the end of the year to calculate indirect-cost rates? Why can't Robinson calculate indirect-cost rates each week or each month? If it used weekly or monthly rates, Robinson would be able to calculate actual costs of jobs much earlier and not have to wait until the end of the year. There are two important reasons for using longer time periods to calculate indirect-cost rates.

1. The *numerator reason* (indirect cost pool). The shorter the period, the greater the influence of seasonal patterns on the level of costs. For example, if indirect-cost rates were calculated each month, costs of heating (included in the numerator) would be charged only to winter production. The use of an annual period incorporates the effect of all four seasons into a single indirect-cost rate.

Levels of total indirect costs are also affected by nonseasonal erratic costs. Examples include costs incurred in a particular month that benefit operations during future months: repairs and maintenance of equipment, and vacation and holiday pay. If monthly indirect-cost rates were calculated, jobs done in a month with high nonseasonal erratic costs would be loaded with these costs. Pooling all indirect costs together over the course of a full year and calculating a single annual indirect-cost rate helps to smooth out some of the erratic and period-specific bumps.

2. *The denominator reason* (quantity of the allocation base). Another rationale for longer periods is the need to spread monthly fixed indirect costs over fluctuating levels of output. Some indirect costs (for example, supplies) may be variable with respect to the cost-allocation base, whereas other indirect costs are fixed (for example, property taxes and rent).

Suppose a company schedules its production to correspond with a highly seasonal sales pattern. Assume the following mix of variable indirect costs (such as supplies, repairs, and indirect manufacturing labor) and fixed indirect costs (plant depreciation and engineering support):

| | Indirect Costs | | | Direct Manufacturing Labor-Hours | Allocation Rate Per Direct Manufacturing Labor-Hour |
	Variable (1)	Fixed (2)	Total (3)	(4)	(5) = (3) ÷ (4)
High-output month	$40,000	$60,000	$100,000	3,200	$31.25
Low-output month	10,000	60,000	70,000	800	87.50

Note that variable indirect costs change in proportion to changes in direct manufacturing labor-hours. Therefore, the variable indirect-cost rate is the same in both the high-output and low-output months $40,000 ÷ 3,200 = $12.50; $10,000 ÷ 800 = $12.50). Because of the fixed costs of $60,000, monthly total indirect-cost rates vary sizably—from $31.25 per hour to $87.50 per hour. Few managers believe that identical jobs done in different months should be allocated indirect-cost charges per hour that differ so significantly $87.50 ÷ $31.25 = 280%). In our example, management has committed itself to a specific level of capacity far beyond a mere 30 days per month. An average, annualized rate based on the relationship of total annual indirect costs to the total annual level of output will smooth out the effect of monthly variations in output levels.

The nonuniform design of the calendar also affects the calculation of monthly indirect-cost rates. The number of Monday-to-Friday workdays in a month varies from 20 to 23 during a year. If separate rates are computed each month, jobs undertaken in February, the shortest month, would bear a greater share of indirect costs (such as depreciation and property taxes) than would jobs undertaken in March. Many managers believe such results to be unrepresentative and unreasonable. Use of an annual period reduces the effect that the number of working days per month has on unit costs.

NORMAL COSTING

The difficulty of calculating actual indirect-cost rates on a weekly or monthly basis means that managers cannot calculate the actual costs of jobs as they are completed. Managers often want a close approximation of the manufacturing costs of various jobs on a timely basis, not just at the end of the year. Managers want these costs (often together with other costs such as marketing costs) for various ongoing uses, including choosing which job to emphasize or deemphasize, pricing jobs, managing costs, and preparing interim financial statements. Because management benefits from having immediate access to the costs of jobs, few companies wait until the *actual* manufacturing overhead is finally known (at year-end) before allocating overhead costs in computing the costs of jobs. Instead, a *predetermined* or *budgeted* indirect-cost rate is calculated for each cost pool at the beginning of a fiscal year, and overhead costs are allocated to jobs as work progresses. For the numerator and denominator reasons described in the preceding section, the **budgeted indirect-cost rate** is computed for each cost pool using the budgeted *annual* indirect cost and the budgeted *annual* quantity of the cost-allocation base. The use of budgeted indirect-cost rates gives rise to *normal costing*.

Normal costing is a costing method that traces direct costs to a cost object by using the actual direct-cost rate(s) times the actual quantity of the direct-cost input(s) and allocates indirect costs based on the budgeted indirect-cost rate(s) times the actual quantity of the cost-allocation base(s). Note that both actual costing and normal costing trace direct costs to jobs in the same way. The actual quantities and actual rates of direct materials and direct manufacturing labor used on a job are known from the source documents as the work is done. The only difference between actual costing and normal costing is that actual costing uses an *actual* indirect-cost rate(s), whereas normal costing uses a *budgeted* indirect-cost rate(s) to cost jobs. Exhibit 4-4 summarizes the differences between the actual costing and normal costing methods.

We illustrate normal costing for the Robinson Company example using the seven-step procedure described earlier in the chapter. The following budgeted data for the year 2000 pertain to the manufacturing operations of Robinson Company:

	Budget
Total manufacturing overhead costs	$1,280,000
Total direct manufacturing labor-hours	32,000

Steps 1 and 2 are exactly as before. Actual direct materials costs total $4,606, and actual direct manufacturing labor costs equal $1,579. Recall from step 3 that Robin-

EXHIBIT 4-4
Actual Costing and Normal Costing Methods

	Actual Costing	Normal Costing
Direct Costs	◆ Actual direct-cost rate(s) × Actual quantity of direct-cost input(s)	◆ Actual direct-cost rate(s) × Actual quantity of direct-cost input(s)
Indirect Costs	◆ Actual indirect-cost rate(s) × Actual quantity of cost-allocation base(s)	◆ Budgeted indirect-cost rate(s) × Actual quantity of cost-allocation base(s)

son uses a single cost-allocation base, direct manufacturing labor-hours, to allocate all manufacturing overhead costs to jobs. The budgeted quantity of direct manufacturing labor-hours for the year 2000 is 32,000 hours. In step 4, Robinson groups all the indirect manufacturing costs into a single manufacturing overhead cost pool. The budgeted amount of manufacturing overhead costs in the year 2000 is $1,280,000. The budgeted indirect-cost rate for 2000 (step 5) is $40 per direct manufacturing labor-hour:

$$\text{Budgeted indirect-cost rate} = \frac{\text{Budgeted total costs in indirect-cost pool}}{\text{Budgeted total quantity of cost-allocation base}}$$

$$= \frac{\$1,280,000}{32,000 \text{ direct manufacturing labor-hours}}$$

$$= \$40 \text{ per direct manufacturing labor-hour}$$

Indirect costs allocated to the Western Pulp and Paper Company (WPP)'s pulp machine order (step 6) are calculated as the *actual* quantity of direct manufacturing labor-hours used on the job, times the budgeted indirect-cost rate, 88 × $40 = $3,520. The cost of the job under normal costing (step 7) is $9,705, calculated as follows:

Direct manufacturing costs		
Direct materials	$4,606	
Direct manufacturing labor	1,579	$6,185
Indirect manufacturing costs ($40 × 88 actual direct manufacturing labor-hours)		3,520
Total manufacturing costs of job		$9,705

The manufacturing cost of the Western Pulp job is lower by $440 under normal costing ($9,705) than it is under actual costing ($10,145) because the budgeted indirect-cost rate is $40 per hour, whereas the actual indirect-cost rate is $45 per hour.

A JOB-COSTING SYSTEM IN MANUFACTURING

We continue the Robinson Company example to illustrate how a normal job-costing system operates in manufacturing. The following example considers events that occurred in February 2000.

General Ledger and Subsidiary Ledgers

As we have noted, a job-costing system has a separate job cost record for each job. A summary of the job cost record is typically found in a subsidiary ledger. The general ledger account, Work-in-Process Control, presents the totals of these separate job cost records pertaining to all unfinished jobs. The job cost records and Work-in-Process Control account track job costs from the time jobs are started until they are completed.

Teaching Tip When confronted with (1) actual $, (2) budgeted $, (3) actual qty. of base, and (4) budgeted qty. of base, students often become confused about how to calculate budgeted and actual cost rates. Emphasize that all data used to calculate *budgeted* rates *must* be available *before* the period starts. In contrast, actual rates cannot be calculated until the *end* of the period, after all the actual costs and qty. of the base are known. If students have trouble remembering whether costs go in the numerator or denominator, simply remind them that the rate is usually expressed as $ per hr. (or other base) and the "per" means "divided by." Thus, the rate is $ divided by the base qty.

Reinforcing Problems Exer. 4-16, 4-17, and 4-26 and Prob. 4-31 cover normal and actual job costing. Exer. 4-18, 4-20, and 4-24 cover mfg. overhead rate issues.

OBJECTIVE 5

Track the flow of costs in a job-costing system

EXHIBIT 4-5

Manufacturing Job-Costing System Using Normal Costing: Diagram of Ledger Relationships for February 2000

PANEL A: GENERAL LEDGER

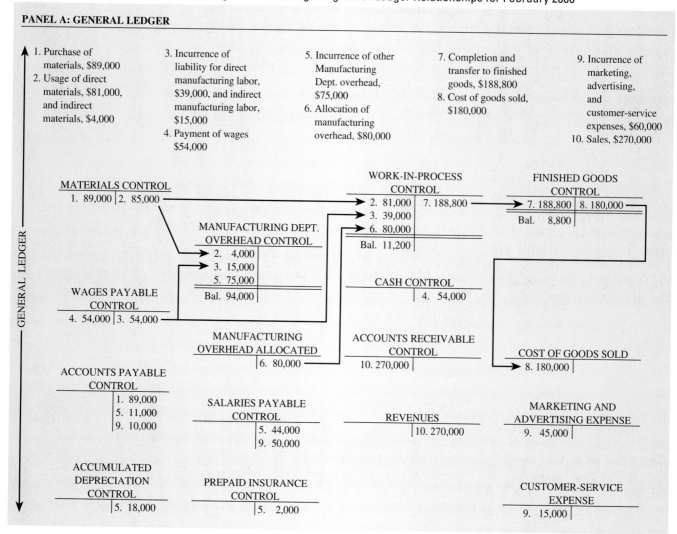

1. Purchase of materials, $89,000
2. Usage of direct materials, $81,000, and indirect materials, $4,000

3. Incurrence of liability for direct manufacturing labor, $39,000, and indirect manufacturing labor, $15,000
4. Payment of wages $54,000

5. Incurrence of other Manufacturing Dept. overhead, $75,000
6. Allocation of manufacturing overhead, $80,000

7. Completion and transfer to finished goods, $188,800
8. Cost of goods sold, $180,000

9. Incurrence of marketing, advertising, and customer-service expenses, $60,000
10. Sales, $270,000

GENERAL LEDGER

MATERIALS CONTROL
1. 89,000 | 2. 85,000

MANUFACTURING DEPT. OVERHEAD CONTROL
2. 4,000 |
3. 15,000 |
5. 75,000 |
Bal. 94,000 |

WAGES PAYABLE CONTROL
4. 54,000 | 3. 54,000

MANUFACTURING OVERHEAD ALLOCATED
| 6. 80,000

ACCOUNTS PAYABLE CONTROL
| 1. 89,000
| 5. 11,000
| 9. 10,000

SALARIES PAYABLE CONTROL
| 5. 44,000
| 9. 50,000

ACCUMULATED DEPRECIATION CONTROL
| 5. 18,000

PREPAID INSURANCE CONTROL
5. 2,000 |

WORK-IN-PROCESS CONTROL
2. 81,000 | 7. 188,800
3. 39,000 |
6. 80,000 |
Bal. 11,200 |

CASH CONTROL
| 4. 54,000

ACCOUNTS RECEIVABLE CONTROL
10. 270,000 |

REVENUES
| 10. 270,000

FINISHED GOODS CONTROL
7. 188,800 | 8. 180,000
Bal. 8,800 |

COST OF GOODS SOLD
8. 180,000 |

MARKETING AND ADVERTISING EXPENSE
9. 45,000 |

CUSTOMER-SERVICE EXPENSE
9. 15,000 |

Continued

Exhibit 4-5 shows T-account relationships for the Robinson Company's general ledger and illustrative records in the subsidiary ledgers. Panel A shows the general ledger section that gives a "bird's-eye view" of the costing system—the amounts are based on the illustration that follows. Panel B shows the subsidiary ledgers and the basic source documents that contain the underlying details—the "worm's-eye view." General ledger accounts with the word *control* in their titles (such as Materials Control and Accounts Payable Control) are supported by underlying subsidiary ledgers that contain additional details, such as each type of material in inventory and individual suppliers that Robinson must pay.

Software programs guide the processing of transactions in most accounting systems. Some programs make general ledger entries simultaneously with entries in the subsidiary ledger accounts. Other software programs make general ledger entries at, say, weekly or monthly intervals, with entries made in the subsidiary ledger accounts on a more frequent basis. The Robinson Company makes entries in its subsidiary ledger when transactions occur and then makes entries in its general ledger on a monthly basis.

A general ledger should be viewed as only one of many tools that assist management in planning and control. To control operations, managers use not only the source documents used to record amounts in the subsidiary ledgers, but also nonfinancial variables such as the percentage of jobs requiring rework.

EXHIBIT 4-5 *(Continued)*

Manufacturing Job-Costing System Using Normal Costing: Diagram of Ledger Relationships for February 2000

PANEL B: SUBSIDIARY LEDGERS

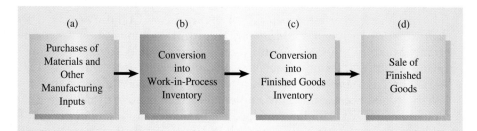

MATERIALS RECORDS BY TYPE OF MATERIALS

Metal Brackets Part No. MB 468-A

Received	Issued					Balance
(1)						
		Reqn				
	Date	No.	Qty	Rate	Amt.	
	2-7	2000:	8	$14	$112	
		198				
		(2)				

Copies of invoices or receiving reports

Copies of materials requisition records

WORK-IN-PROCESS RECORDS BY JOBS

Job No. WPP 298

	In-Process				Completed		Balance	
	Direct	Direct Manuf.	Allocated Manuf.	Total		Total		Total
Date	Materials	Labor	Overhead	Cost	Date	Cost	Date	Cost
2-7	$ 112			$ 112				
2-13		$ 450		$ 450				
	•	•	•	•				
2-28	$4,606	$1,579	$3,520	$9,705	2-28	$9,705	2-28	$0
	(2)	(3)	(6)			(7)		

Copies of materials requisition records

Copies of labor time records

Budgeted rate based on direct manuf. labor-hours

Completed job cost record

FINISHED GOODS RECORDS BY JOB

Job No. WPP 298

Received		Issued		Balance	
Date	Amnt	Date	Amnt	Date	Amnt
2-28	$9,705	2-28	$9,705	2-28	$0
(7)		(8)			

Completed job cost record

Costed sales invoice

LABOR RECORDS BY EMPLOYEE

G. L. Cook Empl. No. 551-87-3076

Week Endg.	Job No.	Hours Worked	Rate	Amnt
2-13	WPP			
	298	25	$18	$450
	JL 256	12	18	216
	Mntnce	3	18	54
				$720
2-20		(3)		

Copies of labor-time record

MANUFACTURING DEPT. OVERHEAD RECORDS BY MONTH

February 2000

Indr. Matr Issued	Indr. Manuf. Labor	Supervn & Engg.	Utilities	Deprn.	Ins.
(2)	(3)	(5)	(5)	(5)	(5)
$4,000	$15,000	$44,000	$11,000	$18,000	$2,000

Manuf. labor-time record or payroll analysis

Payroll analysis invoices, special authorizations

Copies of materials requisitions

Explanations of Transactions

The following transaction-by-transaction summary analysis explains how a job-costing system serves the twin goals of (1) product costing, and (2) department responsibility and control. These transactions track stages (a) through (d):

marized for all jobs and posted, so that transactions appearing in the WIP-Control account summarize the transactions across the individual subsidiary ledger accounts.

(a)	(b)	(c)	(d)
Purchases of Materials and Other Manufacturing Inputs	→ Conversion into Work-in-Process Inventory	→ Conversion into Finished Goods Inventory	→ Sale of Finished Goods

Pricing and Efficiency Gains from Job Costing at Colorscope

Colorscope, Inc., is a special-effects photography laboratory that designs printed advertisements for companies such as Saatchi & Saatchi, J. Walter Thompson, Walt Disney, and R. H. Macy. Competitive pressures and thin profit margins make understanding costs critical in pricing decisions. Each job must be estimated individually because the unique end products demand different amounts of Colorscope's resources.

Previously, Colorscope charged a standard price for all its jobs. Why? Because, regardless of the end result, every customer job goes through five stages—job preparation, scanning, assembly, film developing, and quality control. In the *job preparation* stage the template of the job is created by physically cutting and pasting text, graphics, and photographs and by specifying the layout, font, color, and shading. The job template is then *scanned* into a computer where the job is *assembled* using archives of scanned images adjusted for color and shades. The assembled job is then transferred and *developed* on a large sheet of four-color film. *Quality control* ensures that the job fully satisfies the customer's specifications. If not, or if the customer's requirements have changed, quality control initiates rework.

Andrew Cha, Colorscope's founder and chief executive, observed large differences in the amount of image-scanning and processing activity required by different jobs as well as varying amounts of rework across jobs. Because the jobs used different amounts of resources, by charging roughly the same standard price for all jobs, Colorscope lost money on certain jobs. Cha concluded that a job-costing system measuring costs based on the labor-hours spent at each operation would give him better information about costs incurred on various jobs. Colorscope's job-costing system now traces direct materials to jobs and allocates all other costs (wages, rent, depreciation, and so on) to jobs using an overhead rate per labor-hour for each operation.

Besides better tracing costs to specific jobs, Colorscope's new job-costing system has provided the additional benefit of improving efficiency through process changes. For example, the job-costing system highlighted the significant resources Colorscope had been spending on rework. Colorscope's management discovered that most rework was caused by faulty scanning. These defects were not detected until the job was completed, by which time significant additional resources had also been incurred on the job. Colorscope implemented process changes to reduce faulty scanning and to test for quality immediately after the scanning stage. Thus, Colorscope's job-costing system improves its profitability by pricing jobs better and by increasing efficiency and quality.

Source: Colorscope, Inc., Harvard Business School Case Number 9-197-040.

Teaching Tip The graphic on the previous page (which shows the *physical* flow of product through a mfg. process) clarifies the economic transactions occurring in a mfg. process. Students find the ensuing journal entries easier to understand if you link the discussion of each journal entry to this graphic.

1. *Transaction:* Purchases of materials (direct and indirect), on credit $89,000.

   Analysis: The asset Materials Control and the liability Accounts Payable Control are increased. Both accounts have the word *control* in their title in the general ledger because they are supported by records in the subsidiary ledger. The subsidiary records for materials at the Robinson Company—called *Materials Records*—maintain a continuous record of additions to, and deductions from, inventory. At a minimum, these records would contain columns for quantity received, quantity issued to jobs, and balance (see Panel B of Exhibit 4-5). There is a separate materials record for each type of material in the subsidiary ledger. For example, the subsidiary records contain details of the Metal Brackets (Part No. MB 468-A) issued for the Western Pulp machine job. The following journal entry summarizes all the February 2000 entries in the materials subsidiary ledgers:

Journal Entry: Materials Control   89,000

           Accounts Payable Control   89,000

Post to General Ledger:

Materials Control		Accounts Payable Control	
① 89,000			① 89,000

Materials Control includes all material purchases, whether the items are classified as direct or indirect costs of products.

2. *Transaction:* Materials sent to manufacturing plant floor: direct materials, $81,000, and indirect materials, $4,000.

Analysis: The accounts Work-in-Process Control and Manufacturing Overhead Control are increased. The account Materials Control is decreased. The assumption is that costs incurred on the work in process "attach" to the work in process, thereby making it a more valuable asset. Responsibility is fixed by using *materials requisitions records* as a basis for charging departments for the materials issued to them. Requisitions are accumulated and posted monthly to the general ledger at Robinson Company. As direct materials are used, they are charged to individual job records, which are the subsidiary ledger accounts for the Work-in-Process Control account in the general ledger account. For example, the metal brackets used in the Western Pulp machine job appear as direct materials costs of $112 in the subsidiary ledger under the job cost record for WPP 298. Indirect materials (for example, lubricants) are charged to the Manufacturing Department's overhead cost records, which comprise the subsidiary ledger for Manufacturing Overhead Control at Robinson Company. Note that indirect materials are not added to Work-in-Process Control. Instead, they are added to the Manufacturing Overhead Control account, which accumulates the *actual costs* in all the individual overhead categories. The cost of these indirect materials is allocated to individual jobs as a part of manufacturing overhead.

Each indirect-cost pool in a job-costing system will have its own account in the general ledger. Robinson has only one indirect-cost pool—manufacturing overhead.

Journal Entry: Work-in-Process Control   81,000

           Manufacturing Overhead Control   4,000

                Materials Control   85,000

Post to General Ledger:

Materials Control		Work-in-Process Control	
① 89,000	② 85,000	② 81,000	

Manufacturing Overhead Control	
② 4,000	

3. *Transaction:* Total manufacturing payroll for February: direct, $39,000 and indirect, $15,000.

Analysis: Work-in-Process Control is increased by the direct manufacturing labor amount of $39,000 and Manufacturing Department Overhead Control is increased by the $15,000 of indirect manufacturing labor. Wages Payable Control is increased by $54,000. Direct manufacturing labor costs increase Work-in-Process Control because these costs increase the cost of the work-in-process asset. Direct manufacturing labor helps to transform one asset, namely direct materials, into another, work in process, and eventually into finished goods. Labor-time records are used to trace direct manufacturing labor to Work-in-Process Control (see Panel B of Exhibit 4-5) and to accumulate the indirect manufacturing labor in Manufacturing Department Overhead

Teaching Tip Provide specific examples that distinguish between direct and indirect materials and labor. When producing custom chairs, lumber is a DM, but cleaning supplies are indirect materials. It is cost-effective to trace the cost of the lumber directly to specific job orders for chairs, but it is not worthwhile to trace cleaning supplies to a particular order for chairs. Similarly, carpenters' wages are directly traced to the chairs and hence are direct labor (debited to WIP), but janitors' wages are indirect labor (debited to MOH Control).

Control. The subsidiary ledger employee labor records show the $750 of wages owed to G. L. Cook, Employee No. 551-87-3076 for the week ending February 13. The job cost record for WPP 298 shows direct manufacturing labor costs of $450 for the time G. L. Cook spent on the Western Pulp machine job. The indirect manufacturing labor is, by definition, not traced to an individual job. It is instead allocated to individual jobs as a part of manufacturing overhead.

Journal Entry: Work-in-Process Control   39,000
                 Manufacturing Overhead Control   15,000
                   Wages Payable Control   54,000

Post to General Ledger:

Wages Payable Control		
	③	54,000

Work-in-Process Control		
②	81,000	
③	39,000	

Manufacturing Overhead Control		
②	4,000	
③	15,000	

4. *Transaction:* Payment of total manufacturing payroll for February, $54,000. (For simplicity, payroll withholdings from employees are ignored in this example.)

Analysis: The liability Wages Payable Control and the asset Cash Control are decreased.

Journal Entry: Wages Payable Control   54,000
                    Cash Control   54,000

Post to General Ledger:

Wages Payable Control			
④	54,000	③	54,000

Cash Control		
	④	54,000

For convenience here, wages payable for the month is assumed to be completely paid at month-end.

Points to Stress Students often fail to recognize that utilities, depr., and insurance are debited to MOH Control only if they are related to *producing the product* (these inventoriable costs are assets). In contrast, utilities for a sales office or depr. on executives' autos would not be part of MOH, but would be operating expenses (period cost) instead.

5. *Transaction:* Additional manufacturing overhead costs incurred during February, $75,000. These costs consist of engineering and supervisory salaries, $44,000; utilities and repairs, $11,000; depreciation, $18,000; and insurance, $2,000.

Analysis: The indirect-cost account, Manufacturing Overhead Control, is increased. The liability, Salaries Payable Control, is increased, the liability, Accounts Payable Control, is increased, the asset Equipment Control is decreased by means of a related contra asset account Accumulated Depreciation Control, and the asset Prepaid Insurance Control is decreased. The detail of these costs is entered in the appropriate columns of the individual manufacturing overhead cost records that make up the subsidiary ledger for Manufacturing Overhead Control. The source documents for these distributions include invoices (for example, a utility bill) and special schedules (for example, a depreciation schedule) from the responsible accounting officer.

Journal Entry: Manufacturing Overhead Control   75,000
                 Salaries Payable Control   44,000
                 Accounts Payable Control   11,000
                 Accumulated Depreciation Control   18,000
                 Prepaid Insurance Control   2,000

Post to General Ledger:

Accounts Payable Control		
	①	89,000
	⑤	11,000

Manufacturing Overhead Control		
②	4,000	
③	15,000	
⑤	75,000	

Accumulated Depreciation Control		
	⑤	18,000

Prepaid Insurance Control		
	⑤	2,000

Salaries Payable Control		
	⑤	44,000

Points to Stress Indirect materials, indirect labor, utilities, etc. are classified as MOH because it is not cost-effective to trace them directly to products. The costs of these items are pooled together in a single indirect cost pool system, but they could remain in separate pools in a multiple indirect cost pool system, such as an ABC system (see Chap. 5). Each indirect cost pool is allocated to WIP via an overhead allocation base, preferably a cost driver (e.g., machine hrs. or throughput time). These MOH costs are included in WIP (i.e., they are inventoriable costs for external reporting) because the products cannot be manufactured without them.

6. *Transaction:* Allocation of manufacturing overhead to jobs, $80,000.

Analysis: The asset Work-in-Process Control is increased. The indirect-cost account of Manufacturing Overhead Control is, in effect, decreased by means of its contra account, called Manufacturing Overhead Allocated. **Manufacturing overhead allocated** (also called **manufacturing overhead applied**) is the amount of indirect manufacturing costs allocated to individual jobs based on the budgeted rate multiplied by actual quantity used of the allocation base. Manufacturing overhead allocated comprises all manufacturing costs that are assigned to a product (or service) using a cost-allocation base because they cannot be traced specifically to it in an economically feasible way. Under Robinson's normal costing system, the budgeted manufacturing overhead rate for the year 2000 is $40 per direct manufacturing labor-hour. The job cost record for each individual job in the subsidiary ledger will include a debit item for manufacturing overhead allocated for the actual direct manufacturing labor-hours used on that job. For example, the job cost record for Job WPP 298 shows Manufacturing Overhead Allocated of $3,520 (88 actual direct manufacturing labor-hours used × budgeted rate of $40). It is assumed that 2,000 actual direct manufacturing labor-hours were used for all jobs in February 2000, resulting in a total manufacturing overhead allocation of 2,000 × $40 = $80,000.

Journal Entry:	Work-in-Process Control	80,000	
	Manufacturing Overhead Allocated		80,000

Post to General Ledger:

Manufacturing Overhead Allocated		
	⑥	80,000

Work-in-Process Control		
②	81,000	
③	39,000	
⑥	80,000	

Keep in mind that transactions 5 and 6 are distinct and different. In transaction 5, actual overhead costs incurred throughout the month are debited to Manufacturing Overhead Control account and the subsidiary manufacturing overhead records and *not* to Work-in-Process Control or the individual job cost records. Manufacturing overhead costs are added (debited) to Work-in-Process Control and individual job cost records *only when* manufacturing overhead costs are allocated in transaction 6. At that time, Manufacturing Overhead Control is, *in effect*, decreased (credited). Under the normal-costing system described in our illustration, the budgeted indirect-cost rate of $40 per direct manufacturing labor-hour is calculated at the beginning of the year on the basis of predictions of annual manufacturing overhead costs and predictions of the annual quantity of the cost-allocation base. Almost certainly, the actual amounts will differ from the predictions.

Points to Stress Emphasize that debits to subsidiary MOH records occur at the time actual MOH costs are incurred (e.g., when the utility bill is received or at the end of the period for depr.). In contrast, credits to MOH Allocated occur as the allocation base is consumed (usually the end of the job or at the end of the period). The *incurrence* of the MOH costs is independent of the *allocation* of those costs.

7. *Transaction:* Completion and transfer to finished goods of 12 individual jobs, $188,800.

Analysis: The asset Finished Goods Control is increased, and the asset Work-in-Process Control is decreased to recognize the completion of jobs. The Work-in-Process records in the subsidiary ledger indicate that the costs of the 12 individual jobs completed in February 2000 equal $188,800. Exhibit 4-5, Panel B, shows that Job WPP 298 was one of the jobs completed at a cost of $9,705. Given Robinson's use of normal costing, cost of goods completed consists of *actual* direct materials, *actual* direct manufacturing labor, and the *budgeted* manufacturing overhead allocated to each job. Note that Job WPP 298 also simultaneously appears in the finished goods records of the subsidiary ledger.

Journal Entry:	Finished Goods Control	188,800	
	Work-in-Process Control		188,800

Post to General Ledger:

	Work-in-Process Control					Finished Goods Control	
②	81,000	⑦	188,800	⑦	188,800		
③	39,000						
⑥	80,000						
Bal.	11,200						

The debit balance of $11,200 in the Work-in-Process Control account represents the total costs of all job cost records (in the subsidiary ledger) that have not been completed as of the end of February 2000.

8. *Transaction:* Cost of Goods Sold, $180,000.

Analysis: The $180,000 amount represents the cost of goods sold during February 2000. The account Cost of Goods Sold is increased. The asset Finished Goods Control is decreased. Exhibit 4-5, Panel B, indicates that Job WPP 298 was sold and delivered to the customer in February 2000.

Journal Entry:	Cost of Goods Sold	180,000	
	Finished Goods Control		188,000

Post to General Ledger:

	Finished Goods Control					Cost of Goods Sold	
⑦	188,800	⑧	180,000	⑧	180,000		
Bal.	8,800						

The debit balance of $8,800 in Finished Goods Control account represents the costs of all jobs that have been completed and are part of the Finished Goods records but that have not been sold as of the end of February 2000.

9. *Transaction:* Marketing and customer-service payroll and advertising costs accrued for February:

Marketing Department salaries	$35,000
Advertising costs	10,000
Customer-Service Department salaries	15,000

Analysis: As described in Chapter 2, for financial accounting purposes, Marketing Costs of $45,000 ($35,000 + $10,000) and Customer-Service Costs of $15,000 are noninventoriable costs. These costs are charged directly as period costs for February 2000 to be matched against revenues. Unlike manufacturing costs, these costs are not added to work-in-process assets because they do not transform or change a physical product. Robinson would record the following entries.

Reinforcing Problems Exer. 4-21 through 4-23 and Probs. 4-32 through 4-34 cover job costing journal entries and T-accounts.

Journal Entry:	Marketing and Advertising Costs	45,000	
	Customer-Service Costs	15,000	
	Salaries Payable Control		50,000
	Accounts Payable Control		10,000

Post to General Ledger:

Marketing and Advertising Costs			Salaries Payable Control	
⑨	45,000		⑨	50,000

Customer-Service Costs			Accounts Payable Control	
⑨	15,000		⑨	10,000

10. *Transaction:* Sales revenues, all on credit, $270,000.

Analysis: The $270,000 represents amounts due from customers for sales made in February 2000.

Journal Entry:	Accounts Receivable Control	270,000	
	Revenues		270,000

Post to General Ledger:

Accounts Receivable Control			Revenues	
⑩	270,000		⑩	270,000

At this point, please pause and review all ten entries in the illustration. Be sure to trace each journal entry, step by step, to the general ledger accounts in the general ledger section in Panel A of Exhibit 4-5.

Nonmanufacturing Costs and Job Costing

New in This Edition This edition stresses the importance (for internal management decision making) of allocating nonmanufacturing costs to products which use those activities both upstream and downstream in the value chain from production.

Chapter 2 (p. 43) pointed out that companies use product costs for different purposes. The product costs reported as inventoriable costs to shareholders may differ from those reported to tax authorities and may also differ from those reported to managers for guiding pricing and product-mix decisions. We emphasize that even though, as described previously, marketing and customer-service costs are expensed for financial accounting purposes, companies often trace or allocate these costs to individual jobs for pricing, product mix, and cost management decisions.

To identify marketing and customer-service costs of individual jobs, Robinson can use the same basic approach to job costing described earlier in the chapter in the context of manufacturing. Robinson can trace the direct marketing and customer-service costs to jobs. Robinson can then calculate a budgeted indirect-cost rate by dividing budgeted indirect marketing and customer-service costs by the budgeted quantity of the cost-allocation base, say, revenues. Robinson can use this rate to allocate indirect costs to jobs. For example, if this rate were 15% of revenues, Robinson would allocate $2,250 to Job WPP 298 (0.15 × $15,000, the revenue from the job). By assigning both manufacturing and nonmanufacturing costs to jobs, Robinson can compare all the resources demanded by different jobs against the revenues earned from them.

BUDGETED INDIRECT COSTS AND END-OF-PERIOD ADJUSTMENTS

OBJECTIVE 6

Prorate end-of-period under- or overallocated indirect costs using alternative methods

The advantage of using budgeted indirect-cost rates and normal costing instead of actual costing is that indirect costs can be assigned to individual jobs on an ongoing and timely basis, rather than only at the end of the accounting period when actual costs are known. However, budgeted rates are likely to be inaccurate, because they are based on estimates made up to 12 months before actual costs are incurred. We now consider adjustments that need to be made if, by the year-end, indirect costs allocated differ from the actual indirect costs incurred. Recall that for the numerator and denominator reasons discussed earlier in the chapter, we do not expect actual overhead costs incurred each month to equal overhead costs allocated each month.

Underallocated indirect costs occur when the allocated amount of indirect costs in an accounting period is less than the actual (incurred) amount in that period. **Overallocated indirect costs** occur when the allocated amount of indirect costs in an accounting period is greater than the actual (incurred) amount in that period.

Under- or overallocated indirect costs = Indirect costs incurred − Indirect costs allocated

Equivalent terms are **underapplied** (or **overapplied**) **indirect costs** and **underabsorbed** (or **overabsorbed**) **indirect costs**.

Consider the manufacturing overhead indirect-cost pool. There are two indirect-cost accounts in Robinson's general ledger that pertain to manufacturing overhead:

◆ Manufacturing Overhead Control, which is the record of the *actual* costs in all the individual overhead categories (such as indirect materials, indirect manufacturing labor, supervision, engineering, power, and rent).

◆ Manufacturing Overhead Allocated, which is the record of the manufacturing overhead allocated to individual jobs on the basis of the budgeted rate multiplied by actual direct manufacturing labor-hours.

Assume the following annual data for the Robinson Company:

Manufacturing Overhead Control		Manufacturing Overhead Allocated	
Bal. Dec. 31, 2000. 1,215,000			Bal. Dec. 31, 2000. 1,080,000

The $1,080,000 credit balance in Manufacturing Overhead Allocated results from multiplying the 27,000 actual direct manufacturing labor-hours worked on all the jobs in year 2000 by the budgeted rate of $40 per hour.

The $135,000 difference (a net debit) is an underallocated amount because actual manufacturing overhead costs are greater than the allocated amount. This difference arises from two reasons related to the computation of the $40 budgeted hourly rate:

1. *Numerator reason (indirect cost pool).* Actual manufacturing overhead costs of $1,215,000 are less than the budgeted amount of $1,280,000.

2. *Denominator reason (quantity of allocation base).* Actual direct manufacturing labor-hours of 27,000 are less than the budgeted amount of 32,000 hours.

There are three main approaches to disposing of this $135,000 underallocation of manufacturing overhead caused by Robinson overestimating indirect costs and the quantity of the cost-allocation base. These approaches are (1) the adjusted allocation-rate approach, (2) the proration approach, and (3) the write-off to cost of goods sold approach.

Adjusted Allocation-Rate Approach

The adjusted allocation-rate approach, in effect, restates all entries in the general and subsidiary ledgers by using actual cost rates rather than budgeted cost rates. First, the actual indirect-cost rate is computed at the end of the year. Then, every job to which indirect costs were allocated during the year has its amount recomputed using the actual indirect-cost rate (rather than the budgeted indirect-cost rate). Finally, end-of-year closing entries are made. The result is that every job cost record—as well as the ending Work-in-Process Control, Finished Goods Control, and Cost of Goods Sold accounts—accurately represents actual indirect costs incurred.

The widespread adoption of computerized accounting systems has greatly reduced the cost of using the adjusted allocation-rate approach. Consider the Robinson Company example. The actual manufacturing overhead ($1,215,000) exceeds the manufacturing overhead allocated ($1,080,000) by 12.5% [($1,215,000 − $1,080,000) ÷ $1,080,000]. The actual 2000 manufacturing overhead rate is $45 per direct manufacturing labor-hour ($1,215,000 ÷ 27,000) rather than the budgeted $40 per direct manufacturing labor-hour. At year-end, Robinson could increase the year 2000 manufacturing overhead allocated to each job in that year by 12.5% using a single software directive. The directive would affect both the subsidiary ledger and the general ledger.

For example, consider the Western Pulp Machine Job WPP 298. Under normal costing, the manufacturing overhead allocated to the job is $3,520 (the budgeted rate of $40 per hour × 88 direct manufacturing labor-hours). Increasing the manufacturing overhead allocated by 12.5% or $440 ($3,520 × 12.5%) means that the adjusted amount of manufacturing overhead allocated to Job WPP 298 equals $3,960 ($3,520 + $440). Note from p. 99 that under actual costing, manufacturing overhead allocated is also $3,960 (the actual rate of $45 per hour × 88 manufacturing labor-hours). Making this adjustment for each job in the subsidiary ledger ensures that all $1,215,000 of manufacturing overhead is allocated to jobs.

This approach yields the benefits of both the timeliness and convenience of normal costing during the year and the accuracy of actual costing at the end of the year. Each individual job cost amount and the end-of-year account balances for inventories and cost of goods sold are at actual costs. After-the-fact analysis of actual individual job profitability provides managers with useful insights for future decisions about job pricing and about which jobs to emphasize. These decisions are improved by having the more accurate actual job-profitability numbers on prior jobs.

Points to Stress The adjusted allocation rate approach to under/over allocated MOH "corrects" account balances to what they would have been had accountants had a crystal ball and forecasted MOH cost and qty. of the allocation base perfectly. The feasibility of implementing the adjusted rate approach increases as information processing costs decline.

Reinforcing Problems Exer. 4-24 and 4-25 and Probs. 4-33, 4-35, and 4-36 cover the disposal of under- and overallocated indirect costs.

Proration Approach

Proration is the spreading of under- or overallocated overhead among ending work in process, finished goods and cost of goods sold. Materials inventories are not allocated any manufacturing overhead costs, so they are not included in this proration. Hence, in our Robinson example, it is only the ending balances in Work-in-Process Control, Finished Goods Control, and Cost of Goods Sold for which end-of-period proration is involved. Assume the following actual results for Robinson Company in 2000:

	End-of-Year Balances (Before Proration)	Manufacturing Overhead Allocated Component of Year-End Balances (Before Proration)
Work in process	$ 50,000	$ 16,200
Finished goods	75,000	31,320
Costs of goods sold	2,375,000	1,032,480
	$2,500,000	$1,080,000

How should Robinson prorate the underallocated $135,000 of manufacturing overhead at the end of year 2000?

Robinson should prorate under- or overallocated amounts from each cost pool on the basis of the total amount of manufacturing overhead allocated (before proration) in the ending balances of Work-in-Process Control, Finished Goods Control, and Cost of Goods Sold. In our Robinson Company example, the $135,000 underallocated overhead is prorated over the three pertinent accounts in proportion to their total amount of manufacturing overhead allocated (before proration) in column 3 of the following table, resulting in the ending balances (after proration) in column 5 at actual costs.

Teaching Tip Explain the intuition behind acctg. for under/over allocated MOH. MOH Control is $135,000 greater than MOH-Allocated. MOH-Allocated is too small—we are *underallocated*. This understated MOH-Allocated flowed into WIP, which flowed into FG and CGS. WIP, FG, and CGS are all understated and should be increased (debited). Ideally, we should increase the cost of each job to reflect the actual indirect mfg. cost rate— whether that job is now in WIP, FG, or CGS. However, many firms use simpler proration methods or write-off UAO/OAO directly to CGS (Except in the case of procurement OH, no MOH is allocated to Materials Control, so this account typically needs no adjustment).

Account (1)	Account Balance (Before Proration) (2)	Indirect Costs Allocated Component in the Balance in Column (2) (3)		Proration of $135,000 Underallocated Manufacturing Overhead (4)	Account Balance (After Proration) (5) = (2) + (4)
Work in process	$ 50,000	$ 16,200	(1.5%)	0.015 × $135,000 = $ 2,025	$ 52,025
Finished goods	75,000	31,320	(2.9%)	0.029 × 135,000 = 3,915	78,915
Cost of goods sold	2,375,000	1,032,480	(95.6%)	0.956 × 135,000 = 129,060	2,504,060
	$2,500,000	$1,080,000	100.0%	$135,000	$2,635,000

Recall that the actual manufacturing overhead ($1,215,000) exceeds the manufacturing overhead allocated ($1,080,000) by 12.5 percent. The proration amounts in column 4 can also be derived by multiplying the balances in column 3 by 12.5 percent. For example, the $3,915 proration to Finished Goods is 12.5% × $31,320.

The journal entry to record this proration is:

Work-in-Process Control	2,025	
Finished Goods Control	3,915	
Cost of Goods Sold	129,060	
Manufacturing Overhead Allocated	1,080,000	
Manufacturing Overhead Control		1,215,000

Note that if manufacturing overhead had been overallocated, the Work-in-Process, Finished Goods, and Cost of Goods Sold accounts would be decreased (credited) instead of increased (debited).

This journal entry restates the year 2000 ending balances for Work in Process, Finished Goods, and Cost of Goods Sold to what they would have been had actual cost rates been used rather than budgeted cost rates. This method reports the same 2000 ending balances in the general ledger as does the adjusted allocation-rate approach.

Some companies use the proration approach but base it on the column 2 amounts of the preceding table—that is, the ending balances of Work in Process, Finished Goods, and Cost of Goods Sold before proration. It gives the same results as the previous method only if the proportions of direct costs to manufacturing overhead costs are constant in the Work-in-Process, Finished Goods, and Cost of Goods Sold accounts. Why? Because, if this were the case, prorating based on total costs is the same as prorating based on allocated overhead costs. It is very likely, however, that prorations based on column 2 amounts will *not* be the same as the more accurate prorations based on column 3. This is the case in our example as the following table shows.

Account (1)	Account Balance (2)		Proration of $135,000 Underallocated Manufacturing Overhead (3)	Account Balance (after Proration) (4) = (2) + (3)
Work in process	$ 50,000	(2%)	0.02 × $135,000 = $ 2,700	$ 52,700
Finished goods	75,000	(3%)	0.03 × 135,000 = 4,050	79,050
Cost of goods sold	2,375,000	(95%)	0.95 × 135,000 = 128,250	2,503,250
	$2,500,000	100%	$135,000	$2,635,000

However, proration based on ending balances is frequently justified as being a lower-cost way of approximating the more accurate results based on indirect costs allocated.

Write-Off to Cost of Goods Sold Approach

In this case, the total under- or overallocated overhead is included in this year's Cost of Goods Sold. In our Robinson Company example, the journal entry would be:

Cost of Goods Sold	135,000	
Manufacturing Overhead Allocated	1,080,000	
Manufacturing Overhead Control		1,215,000

Robinson's two Manufacturing Overhead accounts are closed with the difference between them now included in cost of goods sold. The Cost of Goods Sold account after proration equals $2,510,000, the balance before proration of $2,375,000 plus the underallocated overhead amount of $135,000.

No matter which approach is used, the underallocated overhead is not carried in the overhead accounts beyond the end of the year. That is, the ending balances in Manufacturing Overhead Control and Manufacturing Overhead Allocated are closed to Work-in-Process Control, Finished Goods Control, or Cost of Goods Sold, and consequently become zero at the end of each year.

Choice Among Approaches

In choosing among the three approaches, managers should be guided by how the resulting information will be used. If managers desire to develop the most accurate record of individual job costs for profitability analysis purposes, the adjusted allocation-rate approach is preferred. If the purpose is confined to reporting the most accurate inventory and cost of goods sold figures, proration based on the manufacturing overhead-allocated component in the ending balances should be used because it adjusts the balances to what they would have been under actual costing. Note that this approach does not adjust individual job cost records.

The write-off to Cost of Goods Sold is the simplest approach for dealing with under- or overallocated overhead. If the amount of underallocated (or overallocated) overhead is small—in comparison to total operating income, or some other measure of materiality—this approach yields a good approximation to more accurate but more complex approaches. Modern companies are also becoming increasingly conscious of inventory control. Thus, quantities of inventories are lower than they were in earlier years, and Cost of Goods Sold tends to be higher in relation to the dollar amount of work-in-process and finished goods inventories. Also, the inventory balances of job-costing companies are usually relatively small because goods are often made in response to customer orders. Consequently, as is true in our Robinson example, writing off under- or overallocated overhead instead of prorating it is unlikely to cause significant distortions in financial statements. For all these reasons, the cost-benefit test would favor the simplest approach—write-off to Cost of Goods Sold—because the more costly attempts at accuracy represented by the other approaches do not appear to provide sufficient additional useful information.

MULTIPLE OVERHEAD COST POOLS

The Robinson Company illustration assumed that a single manufacturing overhead cost pool with direct manufacturing labor-hours as the cost-allocation base was appropriate for allocating indirect manufacturing costs to jobs. Robinson could have used multiple cost-allocation bases, say, direct manufacturing labor-hours and machine-hours, to allocate indirect costs to jobs. It would do so if Robinson's managers believed that the benefits of the information generated by adding more pools (more accurate costing and pricing of jobs and better ability to manage costs) exceeded the costs of implementing a more complex system. We discuss these issues in more detail in Chapter 5.

To implement a normal-costing system with multiple overhead cost pools, Robinson would determine the budgeted total direct manufacturing labor-hours and the budgeted total machine-hours for the year 2000, and identify the associated budgeted indirect total costs for each cost pool. It would then calculate two indirect-cost rates, one based on direct manufacturing labor-hours and the other based on machine-hours. Indirect costs would be allocated to jobs using these indirect-cost rates and the direct manufacturing labor-hours and machine-hours used by various jobs. The general ledger would contain Manufacturing Overhead Control and Manufacturing Overhead Allocated amounts for each cost pool. End-of-period adjustments for under- or overallocated indirect costs would then need to be made separately for each cost pool.

VARIATIONS OF NORMAL COSTING: A SERVICE-SECTOR EXAMPLE

As we discussed at the start of this chapter, job costing is very useful in service industries such as accounting and consulting firms, advertising agencies, auto repair shops, and hospitals. In an accounting firm, each audit is a job. The costs of the audit are accumulated on a job cost record, much like the document used by Robinson Company, following the seven-step approach described earlier in the chapter. On the basis of labor-time records, direct labor costs of audit partners, audit managers, and audit staff are traced to individual jobs. Other direct costs such as travel, out-of-town meals and lodging, phone, fax, and copying are also traced to jobs. The costs of secretarial support, office staff, rent, and depreciation of furniture and equipment are indirect costs because these costs cannot be traced to jobs in an economically feasible way. Indirect costs are allocated to jobs, for example, using a cost-allocation base such as professional labor-hours.

In some service, merchandising, and manufacturing organizations, a variation of normal costing is helpful because actual direct labor costs (the largest component of total costs) are difficult to trace to jobs when they are completed. For example, in our audit illustration, the actual direct labor costs may include bonuses that are known only at the end of the year (a numerator reason). Also, the hours worked each period might vary significantly depending on the number of working days each month and the demand from clients (a denominator reason). In these situations, to obtain timely information as a job is completed rather than wait until the end of the year, an organization may choose to use budgeted rates for some direct costs in addition to using budgeted rates for indirect costs. All budgeted rates used are calculated at the start of the budget period. Recall that normal costing uses actual cost rates for all direct costs and budgeted cost rates only for indirect costs.

The mechanics of using budgeted rates for direct costs are similar to the methods employed when using budgeted rates for indirect costs in normal costing. We illustrate using Lindsay and Associates, a public accounting firm. At the start of the year 2000, Lindsay budgets total direct labor costs of $14,400,000, total indirect costs of $12,960,000, and total direct (professional) labor-hours of 288,000 for the year. In this case,

$$\text{Budgeted direct labor cost rate} = \frac{\text{Budgeted total direct labor costs}}{\text{Budgeted total direct labor-hours}}$$

$$= \frac{\$14,400,000}{288,000 \text{ hours}} = \$50 \text{ per direct labor-hour}$$

Assuming only one indirect-cost pool and total direct labor costs as the cost-allocation base,

$$\text{Budgeted indirect cost rate} = \frac{\text{Budgeted total costs in indirect-cost pool}}{\text{Budgeted total quantity of cost-allocation base}}$$

$$= \frac{\$12,960,000}{\$14,400,000} = 90\% \text{ of direct labor costs}$$

Suppose an audit of Tracy Transport, a client of Lindsay, completed in March 2000, uses 800 direct labor-hours. Lindsay calculates the direct costs of the Tracy Transport audit by multiplying the budgeted direct-cost rate by the actual quantity of the direct-cost input. It allocates indirect costs to the Tracy Transport audit by multiplying the budgeted indirect-cost rate by the actual quantity of the cost-allocation base. Assuming no other direct costs for travel, outsourcing, computer work and the like, the cost of the Tracy Transport audit is:

Direct labor costs, $50 × 800 =	$40,000
Indirect costs allocated, 90% × $40,000	36,000
Total	$76,000

At the end of the year, the direct costs traced to jobs using budgeted rates will generally not equal the actual direct costs because the actual and budgeted rates are developed at different points in time using different information. End-of-period adjustments for under- or overallocated direct costs would need to be made in the same way that adjustments are made for under- or overallocated indirect costs.

The Lindsay and Associates example illustrates that all costing systems do not neatly match either the actual costing or normal costing system described earlier in the chapter. As another example, engineering consulting firms often have some actual direct costs (cost of making blue prints or fees paid to outside experts), other direct costs traced to jobs using a budgeted rate (professional labor costs), and indirect costs allocated to jobs using a budgeted rate (engineering and office support costs).

MANAGEMENT CONTROL AND TECHNOLOGY

Managers use product-costing information to improve the efficiency of their operations by managing and controlling the materials, labor, and overhead costs used to complete jobs. Modern technology provides managers with quick and accurate product-cost information that facilitates the management and control of jobs.

Consider, for example, direct materials that are charged directly to jobs for product-costing purposes. Managers exercise control of these costs well before materials are used on jobs. Through innovative management processes and modern technologies such as Electronic Data Interchange (EDI), companies like Robinson can order materials from their suppliers by pushing a few keys on a computer terminal. EDI, an electronic computer link between a company and its suppliers, ensures that the order is transmitted quickly and accurately with minimum paper work and costs. A bar code scanner records the receipt of incoming materials. The computer matches the receipt with the order, prints out a check to the supplier, and records the material received in the subsidiary ledger. When a shop floor operator transmits a request for materials from a computer terminal, the computer prepares a materials requisition record, instantly recording the issue of materials in the materials records and job cost records. Each day, the computer sums the materials requisition records charged to a particular job or manufacturing department. A performance report is then prepared comparing budgeted and actual costs of direct materials. If desired, direct materials usage might be reported hourly. Information technology allows managers to obtain quick and frequent feedback about the usage of direct materials by jobs and by departments.

Similarly, information about manufacturing labor is obtained as employees log into shop floor terminals and punch in the job number, employee number, and start and end times for different jobs. Using hourly rates stored for each employee, the computer automatically prints the labor-time record and posts the labor costs to individual jobs. Information technology also provides managers with instantaneous feedback to control manufacturing overhead, jobs in process, jobs completed, and jobs shipped and installed at customer sites.

PROBLEM FOR SELF-STUDY

Reexamine the Exhibit 4-5 (p. 106–107) illustration of a job-costing system. Then try to solve the following problem, which requires consideration of many of this chapter's important points.

PROBLEM
You are asked to bring the following incomplete accounts of Endeavor Printing, Inc., up to date through January 31, 2001. Consider the data that appear in the T-accounts as well as the following information in items (a) through (i).

Endeavor's job-costing system, which uses normal costing, has two direct-cost categories (direct materials and direct manufacturing labor) and one indirect-cost pool (manufacturing overhead, which is allocated using direct manufacturing labor costs).

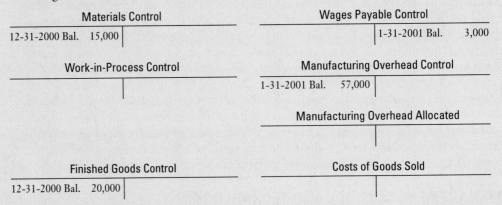

Materials Control		Wages Payable Control	
12-31-2000 Bal. 15,000			1-31-2001 Bal. 3,000

Work-in-Process Control		Manufacturing Overhead Control	
		1-31-2001 Bal. 57,000	

| | | Manufacturing Overhead Allocated | |

Finished Goods Control		Costs of Goods Sold	
12-31-2000 Bal. 20,000			

Additional Information

a. Manufacturing overhead is allocated using a budgeted rate set every December. Management forecasts next year's manufacturing overhead and next year's direct manufacturing labor costs. The budget for 2001 is $600,000 of manufacturing overhead and $400,000 of direct manufacturing labor.

b. The only job unfinished on January 31, 2001, is No. 419, on which direct manufacturing labor costs are $2,000 (125 direct manufacturing labor-hours) and direct materials costs are $8,000.

c. Total materials placed into production during January are $90,000.

d. Cost of goods completed during January is $180,000.

e. Materials inventory as of January 31, 2001 is $20,000.

f. Finished goods inventory as of January 31, 2001 is $15,000.

g. All plant workers earn the same wage rate. Direct manufacturing labor-hours used for January total 2,500. Other labor and supervision labor total $10,000.

h. The gross plant payroll paid in January equals $52,000. Ignore withholdings.

i. All "actual" manufacturing overhead incurred during January has already been posted.

Required

Calculate the following:

1. Materials purchased during January
2. Cost of Goods Sold during January
3. Direct manufacturing labor costs incurred during January
4. Manufacturing Overhead Allocated during January
5. Balance, Wages Payable Control, December 31, 2000
6. Balance, Work-in-Process Control, January 31, 2001
7. Balance, Work-in-Process Control, December 31, 2000
8. Manufacturing Overhead Under- or Overallocated for January 2001

SOLUTION

Amounts from the T-accounts are labeled (T).

1. From Materials Control T-account, Materials purchased: $90,000 (c) + $20,000 (e) − $15,000 (T) = $95,000

2. From Finished Goods Control T-account, Cost of Goods Sold: $20,000 (T) + $180,000 (d) − $15,000 (f) = $185,000

3. Direct manufacturing wage rate: $2,000 (b) ÷ 125 hours (b) = $16 per hour
   Direct manufacturing labor costs: 2,500 hours (g) × $16 = $40,000

4. Manufacturing overhead rate: $600,000 (a) ÷ $400,000 (a) = 150%
   Manufacturing Overhead Allocated: 150% × $40,000 (see 3) = $60,000

5. From Wages Payable Control T-account, Wages Payable Control, December 31, 2000: $52,000 (h) + $3,000 (T) − $40,000 (see 3) − $10,000 (g) = $5,000

6. Work-in-Process Control, January 31, 2001: $8,000 (b) + $2,000 (b) + 150% of $2,000 (b) = $13,000 (This answer is used in item 7.)

7. From Work-in-Process Control T-account, Work-in-Process Control, December 31, 2000: $180,000 (d) + $13,000 (see 6) − $90,000 (c) − $40,000 (see 3) − $60,000 (see 4) = $3,000

8. Manufacturing overhead overallocated: $60,000 (see 4) − $57,000 (T) = $3,000

Entries in T-accounts are lettered in accordance with the preceding additional information and are numbered in accordance with the requirements.

Materials Control

December 31, 2000	Bal. (given)		15,000			
(1)			95,000*	(c)		90,000
January 31, 2001	Bal.	(e)	20,000			

Work-in-Process Control

December 31, 2000	Bal.	(7)	3,000	(d)		180,000
Direct materials		(c)	90,000			
Direct manufacturing labor		(b) (g) (3)	40,000			
Manufacturing overhead allocated		(g) (a) (4)	60,000			
January 31, 2001	Bal.	(b) (6)	13,000			

Finished Goods Control

December 31, 2000	Bal.	(given)	20,000			
		(d)	180,000	(2)		185,000
January 31, 2001	Bal.	(f)	15,000			

Wages Payable Control

(h)		52,000	December 31, 2000	(5)	5,000
				(g)	40,000
					10,000
			January 31, 2001 (given)		3,000

Manufacturing Overhead Control

Total January charges (given)		57,000

Manufacturing Overhead Allocated

		(g) (a) (4)	60,000

Cost of Goods Sold

(f) (2)	185,000	

*Can be computed only after all other postings in the account have been found.

SUMMARY

The following points are linked to the chapter's learning objectives:

1. The building block concepts of a costing system are cost object, direct costs of a cost object, indirect costs of a cost object, cost pool, and cost-allocation base. Costing-system overview diagrams present these concepts in a systematic way. Costing systems aim to report cost numbers that reflect the way that chosen cost objects (such as products or services) use the resources of an organization.

2. Job-costing systems assign costs to distinct units of a product or service. In contrast, process-costing systems assign costs to masses of identical or similar units and compute unit costs on an average basis. These two costing systems are best viewed as opposite ends of a continuum. The costing systems of many companies combine some elements of both job costing and process costing.

3. A general approach to job costing involves identifying (a) the job, (b) the direct-cost categories, (c) the cost-allocation bases, (d) the indirect-cost categories, (e) the cost-allocation rates, (f) the allocated indirect costs of a job, and (g) the total direct and indirect costs of a job.

4. Actual costing and normal costing differ in their use of actual or budgeted indirect-cost rates:

	Actual Costing	Normal Costing
Direct-cost rates	Actual rate(s)	Actual rate(s)
Indirect-cost rates	Actual rate(s)	Budgeted rate(s)

Both methods use actual quantities of inputs for tracing direct costs and actual quantities of the allocation base(s) for allocating indirect costs.

5. The transactions in a job-costing system in manufacturing track (a) the acquisition of materials and other manufacturing inputs, (b) their conversion into work in process, (c) their eventual conversion into finished goods, and (d) the sale of finished goods. Each of the (a) to (d) stages in the manufacture/sale cycle are represented by journal entries in the costing system.

6. The theoretically correct approach to disposing of under- or overallocated manufacturing overhead costs is to adjust the allocation rate or to prorate on the basis of the total amount of the allocated manufacturing overhead cost in the ending balances of inventories and cost of goods sold. Many organizations simply write off immaterial amounts of under- or overallocated manufacturing overhead to cost of goods sold on the basis of simplicity.

7. In some variations of normal costing, organizations use budgeted rates to assign direct costs as well as indirect costs to jobs.

▼ TERMS TO LEARN

This chapter and the Glossary at the end of this book contain definitions of the following important terms:

actual costing (p. 98)
budgeted indirect-cost rate (104)
cost-allocation base (97)
cost-application base (97)
cost pool (97)
indirect-cost rate (99)
job (97)
job cost record (101)
job cost sheet (101)
job-costing system (97)
labor-time record (102)
manufacturing overhead allocated (111)

manufacturing overhead applied (111)
materials requisition record (101)
normal costing (104)
overabsorbed indirect costs (114)
overallocated indirect costs (114)
overapplied indirect costs (114)
process-costing system (97)
proration (115)
source documents (101)
underabsorbed indirect costs (114)
underallocated indirect costs (114)
underapplied indirect costs (114)

▼ ASSIGNMENT MATERIAL

QUESTIONS

4-1 Define cost pool, cost tracing, cost allocation, and cost-allocation base.

4-2 How does a job-costing system differ from a process-costing system?

4-3 Why might an advertising agency use job costing for an advertising campaign by Pepsi while a bank uses process costing for the cost of checking account withdrawals?

4-4 Describe the seven steps in job costing.

4-5 What are the two major cost objects that managers focus on in companies using job costing?

4-6 Describe three major source documents used in job-costing systems.

4-7 What is the main concern about source documents used to prepare job cost records?

4-8 Give two reasons why most organizations use an annual period rather than a weekly or monthly period to compute budgeted indirect-cost rates.

4-9 Distinguish between actual costing and normal costing.

4-10 Describe two ways in which a house construction company may use job cost information.

4-11 Comment on the following statement, "In a normal costing system, the amounts in Manufacturing Overhead Control account will always equal the amounts in Manufacturing Overhead Allocated account."

4-12 Describe three different debit entries to the Work-in-Process Control general ledger T-account.

4-13 Describe three alternative ways to dispose of under- or overallocated indirect costs.

4-14 When might a company use budgeted costs rather than actual costs to compute direct labor rates?

4-15 Describe briefly why modern technology such as Electronic Data Interchange (EDI) is helpful to managers.

EXERCISES

4-16 Actual costing, normal costing, accounting for manufacturing overhead. Destin Products uses a job-costing system with two direct-cost categories (direct materials and direct manufacturing labor) and one manufacturing overhead cost pool. Destin allocates manufacturing overhead costs using direct manufacturing labor costs. Destin provides the following information:

	Budget for Year 2001	**Actual Results for Year 2001**
Direct materials costs	$1,500,000	$1,450,000
Direct manufacturing labor costs	1,000,000	980,000
Manufacturing overhead costs	1,750,000	1,862,000

Required
1. Compute the actual and budgeted manufacturing overhead rates for 2001.
2. During March, the job cost record for Job 626 contained the following information:

Direct materials used	$40,000
Direct manufacturing labor costs	30,000

Compute the cost of Job 626 using (a) actual costing and (b) normal costing.
3. At the end of 2001, compute the under- or overallocated manufacturing overhead under normal costing. Why is there no under- or overallocated overhead under actual costing?

4-17 Job costing, normal and actual costing. Anderson Construction assembles residential houses. It uses a job-costing system with two direct-cost categories (direct materials and direct labor) and one indirect-cost pool (assembly support). Direct labor-hours is the allocation base for assembly support costs. In December 2000, Anderson budgets year 2001 assembly support costs to be $8,000,000 and year 2001 direct labor-hours to be 160,000.

At the end of 2001, Anderson is comparing the costs of several jobs that were started and completed in 2001.

	Laguna Model	**Mission Model**
Construction period	Feb–June 2001	May–Oct 2001
Direct materials	$106,450	$127,604
Direct labor	$ 36,276	$ 41,410
Direct labor-hours	900	1,010

Direct materials and direct labor are paid for on a contract basis. The costs of each are known when direct materials are used or direct labor-hours are worked. The 2001 actual assembly support costs were $6,888,000, and the actual direct labor-hours were 164,000.

Required
1. Compute the (a) budgeted and (b) actual indirect-cost rates. Why do they differ?
2. What is the job cost of the Laguna Model and the Mission Model using (a) normal costing, and (b) actual costing?
3. Why might Anderson Construction prefer normal costing over actual costing?

 4-18 Job costing, accounting for manufacturing overhead, budgeted rates. The Lynn Company uses a job-costing system at its Minneapolis plant. The plant has a Machining Department and an Assembly Department. Its job-costing system has two direct-cost categories (direct materials and direct manufacturing labor) and two manufacturing overhead cost pools (the Machining Department overhead, allocated using actual machine-hours, and the Assembly Department overhead, allocated using actual direct manufacturing labor cost). The 2001 budget for the plant is as follows:

	Machining Department	Assembly Department
Manufacturing overhead	$1,800,000	$3,600,000
Direct manufacturing labor cost	$1,400,000	$2,000,000
Direct manufacturing labor-hours	100,000	200,000
Machine-hours	50,000	200,000

Required
1. Present an overview diagram of Lynn's job-costing system. Compute the budgeted manufacturing overhead rate for each department.
2. During February, the job cost record for Job 494 contained the following:

	Machining Department	Assembly Department
Direct materials used	$45,000	$70,000
Direct manufacturing labor costs	$14,000	$15,000
Direct manufacturing labor-hours	1,000	1,500
Machine-hours	2,000	1,000

Compute the total manufacturing overhead costs of Job 494.
3. At the end of 2001, the actual manufacturing overhead costs were $2,100,000 in Machining and $3,700,000 in Assembly. Assume that 55,000 actual machine-hours were used in Machining and that actual direct manufacturing labor costs in Assembly were $2,200,000. Compute the over- or underallocated manufacturing overhead for each department.

4-19 Job costing, consulting firm. Taylor & Associates, a consulting firm, has the following condensed budget for 2001:

Revenues		$20,000,000
Total costs:		
Direct costs		
Professional labor	$ 5,000,000	
Indirect costs		
Consulting support	13,000,000	18,000,000
Operating income		$ 2,000,000

Taylor has a single direct-cost category (professional labor) and a single indirect-cost pool (client support). Indirect costs are allocated to jobs on the basis of professional labor costs.

Required

1. Present an overview diagram of the job-costing system. Compute the 2001 budgeted indirect-cost rate for Taylor & Associates.
2. The markup rate for pricing jobs is intended to produce operating income equal to 10% of revenues. Compute the markup rate as a percentage of professional labor costs.
3. Taylor is bidding on a consulting job for Red Rooster, a fast-food chain specializing in poultry meats. The budgeted breakdown of professional labor on the job is as follows:

Professional Labor Category	Budgeted Rate Per Hour	Budgeted Hours
Director	$200	3
Partner	100	16
Associate	50	40
Assistant	30	160

Compute the budgeted cost of the Red Rooster job. How much will Taylor bid for the job if it is to earn its target operating income of 10% of revenues?

4-20 Computing indirect-cost rates, job costing. Mike Rotundo, the president of Tax Assist, is examining alternative ways to compute indirect-cost rates. He collects the following information from the budget for 2000:

◆ Budgeted variable indirect costs: $10 per hour of professional labor time

◆ Budgeted fixed indirect costs: $50,000 per quarter

The budgeted billable professional labor-hours per quarter are:

January–March	20,000 hours
April–June	10,000 hours
July–September	4,000 hours
October–December	6,000 hours

Rotundo pays all tax professionals employed by Tax Assist on an hourly basis ($30 per hour, including all fringe benefits).

Tax Assist's job-costing system has a single direct-cost category (professional labor at $30 per hour) and a single indirect-cost pool (office support that is allocated using professional labor-hours).

Tax Assist charges clients $65 per professional labor-hour.

Required

1. Compute the budgeted indirect-cost rate per professional labor-hour using
   a. Quarterly budgeted billable hours as the denominator
   b. Annual budgeted billable hours as the denominator
2. Compute the operating income for the following four customers using
   a. Quarterly indirect-cost rates
   b. An annual indirect-cost rate

   ◆ Stan Hansen: 10 hours in February

   ◆ Lelani Kai: 6 hours in March and 4 hours in April

   ◆ Ken Patera: 4 hours in June and 6 hours in August

   ◆ Evelyn Stevens: 5 hours in January, 2 hours in September, and 3 hours in November

3. Comment on your results in requirement 2.

4-21 Job costing, journal entries. The University of Chicago Press is wholly owned by the university. It performs the bulk of its work for other university departments, which pay as though the Press were an outside business enterprise. The Press also publishes and maintains a stock of books for general sale. A job-costing system is used to cost each job. There are two direct-cost categories (direct materials and direct manufacturing labor) and one indirect-cost pool (manufacturing overhead, allocated on the basis of direct manufacturing labor costs).

The following data (in thousands) pertain to 2001:

Direct materials and supplies purchased on account	$800
Direct materials used	710
Indirect materials issued to various production departments	100
Direct manufacturing labor	1,300
Indirect manufacturing labor incurred by various departments	900
Depreciation on building and manufacturing equipment	400
Miscellaneous manufacturing overhead* incurred by various departments (ordinarily would be detailed as repairs, photocopying, utilities, etc.)	550
Manufacturing overhead allocated at 160% of direct manufacturing labor costs	?
Cost of goods manufactured	4,120
Revenues	8,000
Cost of goods sold	4,020
Inventories, December 31, 2000 (not 2001):	
Materials Control	100
Work-in-Process Control	60
Finished Goods Control	500

*The term *manufacturing overhead* is not used uniformly. Other terms that are often encountered in printing companies include job overhead and shop overhead.

Required
1. Present an overview diagram of the job-costing system at the University of Chicago Press.
2. Prepare journal entries to summarize 2001 transactions. As your final entry, dispose of the year-end under- or overallocated manufacturing overhead as a write-off to Cost of Goods Sold. Number your entries. Explanations for each entry may be omitted.
3. Show posted T-accounts for all inventories, Cost of Goods Sold, Manufacturing Overhead Control, and Manufacturing Overhead Allocated.

4-22 Job costing, journal entries, and source documents (continuation of 4-21). For each journal entry in your answer to Exercise 4-21, (a) indicate the source document that would most likely authorize the entry, and (b) give a description of the entry in the subsidiary ledgers, if any entry needs to be made there.

4-23 Job costing, journal entries. Donnell Transport assembles prestige manufactured homes. Its job-costing system has two direct-cost categories (direct materials and direct manufacturing labor) and one indirect-cost pool (manufacturing overhead allocated at a budgeted $30 per machine-hour in 2001). The following data (in millions) pertain to operations for the year 2001:

Materials Control, December 31, 2000	$ 12
Work-in-Process Control, December 31, 2000	2
Finished Goods Control, December 31, 2000	6
Materials and supplies purchased on account	150
Direct materials used	145
Indirect materials (supplies) issued to various production departments	10
Direct manufacturing labor	90
Indirect manufacturing labor incurred by various departments	30
Depreciation on plant and manufacturing equipment	19
Miscellaneous manufacturing overhead incurred (ordinarily would be detailed as repairs, utilities, etc., with a corresponding credit to various liability accounts)	9
Manufacturing overhead allocated, 2,100,000 actual machine-hours	?
Cost of goods manufactured	294
Revenues	400
Cost of goods sold	292

Required

1. Present an overview diagram of Donnell Transport's job-costing system.
2. Prepare journal entries. Number your entries. Post to T-accounts. What is the ending balance of Work-in-Process Control?
3. Show the journal entry for disposing of under- or overallocated manufacturing overhead directly as a year-end write-off to Cost of Goods Sold. Post the entry to T-accounts.

4-24 Accounting for manufacturing overhead. Consider the following selected cost data for the Pittsburgh Forging Company for 2000.

Budgeted manufacturing overhead	$7,000,000
Budgeted machine-hours	200,000
Actual manufacturing overhead	$6,800,000
Actual machine-hours	195,000

Pittsburgh's job-costing system has a single manufacturing overhead cost pool. Costs are allocated to jobs using a budgeted machine-hour rate and actual machine-hours. Any amount of under- or overallocation is written off to cost of goods sold.

Required

1. Compute the budgeted manufacturing overhead rate.
2. Journalize the allocation of manufacturing overhead.
3. Compute the amount of under- or overallocation of manufacturing overhead. Is the amount significant? Journalize the disposition of this amount on the basis of the ending balances in the appropriate accounts.

4-25 Proration of overhead. (Z. Iqbal, adapted) The Zaf Radiator Company uses a normal-costing system with a single manufacturing overhead cost pool and machine-hours as the cost-allocation base. The following data are for 2001:

Budgeted manufacturing overhead	$4,800,000
Overhead allocation base	Machine-hours
Budgeted machine-hours	80,000
Manufacturing overhead incurred	$4,900,000
Actual machine-hours	75,000

Machine-hours data and the ending balances (before proration of under- or overallocated overhead) are as follows:

	Actual Machine-Hours	End of Year 2001 Balance
Cost of Goods Sold	60,000	$8,000,000
Finished Goods	11,000	1,250,000
Work in Process	4,000	750,000

Required

1. Compute the budgeted manufacturing overhead rate for 2001.
2. Compute the under- or overallocated manufacturing overhead of Zaf Radiator in 2001. Dispose of this amount using
   a. Write-off to Cost of Goods Sold
   b. Proration based on ending balances (before proration) in Work in Process, Finished Goods, and Cost of Goods Sold
   c. Proration based on the allocated overhead amount (before proration) in the ending balances of Work in Process, Finished Goods, and Cost of Goods Sold
3. Which method do you prefer in requirement 2? Explain.

4-26 Job costing; actual, normal, and variation of normal costing. Chirac & Partners is a Quebec-based public accounting partnership specializing in audit services. Its job-costing system has a single direct-cost category (professional labor) and a single indirect-cost pool (audit support, which contains all the costs in the Audit Support Department). Audit support costs are allocated to individual jobs using actual professional labor-hours. Chirac & Partners employs ten professionals who are involved in their auditing services.

Budgeted and actual amounts for 2001 are as follows:

Budget for 2001

Professional labor compensation	$960,000
Audit Support Department costs	$720,000
Professional labor-hours billed to clients	16,000 hours

Actual results for 2001

Audit Support Department costs	$744,000
Professional labor-hours billed to clients	15,500 hours
Actual professional labor cost rate	$58 per hour

Required

1. Compute the direct-cost rate per professional labor-hour and the indirect-cost rate per professional labor-hour for 2001 under (a) actual costing, (b) normal costing, and (c) variation of normal costing that uses budgeted rates for direct costs.
2. The audit of the Montreal Expos done in 2001 was budgeted to take 110 hours of professional labor time. The actual professional labor time on the audit was 120 hours. Compute the 2001 job cost using (a) actual costing, (b) normal costing, and (c) the variation of normal costing that uses budgeted rates for direct costs. Explain any differences in the job cost.

4-27 Job costing; actual, normal, and variation of normal costing. Vista Group provides architectural services for residential and business clients. It employs 25 professionals. Its job-costing system has a single direct-cost category (professional labor) and a single indirect-cost pool (client support, which contains all the costs in the Client Support Department). Client support costs are allocated to individual jobs using actual professional labor-hours. Budgeted and actual amounts for 2001 are as follows:

Budget for 2001

Professional labor compensation	$4,000,000
Client Support Department costs	$2,600,000
Professional labor-hours billed to clients	40,000 hours

Actual results for 2001

Client Support Department costs	$2,436,000
Professional labor-hours billed to clients	42,000 hours
Actual professional labor cost rate	$110 per hour

Required

1. Compute the direct-cost rate per professional labor-hour and the indirect-cost rate per professional labor-hour for 2001 under (a) actual costing, (b) normal costing, and (c) the variation of normal costing that uses budgeted rates for direct costs.
2. In 2001, the Vista Group designed a new retirement village in Tucson, Arizona, for Carefree Years, Inc. Vista budgeted to spend 1,500 professional labor-hours on the project. Actual professional labor-hours spent were 1,720. Compute the job cost of the Carefree Years project using (a) actual costing, (b) normal costing, and (c) the variation of normal costing that uses budgeted rates for direct costs. Explain any differences in the job cost.

PROBLEMS

4-28 Job costing, accounting for manufacturing overhead, budgeted rates. The Solomon Company uses a job-costing system at its Dover, Delaware, plant. The plant has a Machining Department and a Finishing Department. Solomon uses a normal-costing system with two direct-cost categories (direct materials and direct manufacturing labor) and two manufacturing overhead cost pools (the Machining Department, with machine-hours as the allocation base, and the Finishing Department, with direct manufacturing labor costs as the allocation base). The year 2000 budget for the plant is as follows:

	Machining Department	Finishing Department
Manufacturing overhead	$10,000,000	$8,000,000
Direct manufacturing labor costs	$900,000	$4,000,000
Direct manufacturing labor-hours	30,000	160,000
Machine-hours	200,000	33,000

Required

1. Present an overview diagram of Solomon's job-costing system.
2. What is the budgeted overhead rate that should be used in the Machining Department? In the Finishing Department?
3. During the month of January, the job cost record for Job 431 shows the following:

	Machining Department	Finishing Department
Direct materials used	$14,000	$3,000
Direct manufacturing labor costs	$600	$1,250
Direct manufacturing labor-hours	30	50
Machine-hours	130	10

   What is the total manufacturing overhead allocated to Job 431?
4. Assuming that Job 431 consisted of 200 units of product, what is the unit product cost of Job 431?
5. Amounts at the end of 2000 are as follows:

	Machining Department	Finishing Department
Manufacturing overhead incurred	$11,200,000	$7,900,000
Direct manufacturing labor costs	$950,000	$4,100,000
Machine-hours	220,000	32,000

   Compute the under- or overallocated manufacturing overhead for each department and for the Dover plant as a whole.
6. Why might Solomon use two different manufacturing overhead cost pools in its job-costing system?

4-29 Service industry, job costing, law firm. Keating & Associates is a law firm specializing in labor relations and employee-related work. It employs 25 professionals (5 partners and 20 associates) who work directly with its clients. The average budgeted total compensation per professional for 1999 is $104,000. Each professional is budgeted to have 1,600 billable hours to clients in 1999. Keating is a highly respected firm, and all professionals work for clients to their maximum 1,600 billable hours available. All professional labor costs are included in a single direct-cost category and are traced to jobs on a per hour basis.

All costs of Keating & Associates other than professional labor costs are included in a single indirect-cost pool (legal support) and are allocated to jobs using professional labor-hours as the allocation base. The budgeted level of indirect costs in 1999 is $2,200,000.

Required

1. Present an overview diagram of Keating's job-costing system.
2. Compute the 1999 budgeted direct-cost rate per hour of professional labor.
3. Compute the 1999 budgeted indirect-cost rate per hour of professional labor.
4. Keating & Associates is considering bidding on two jobs:
   a. Litigation work for Richardson, Inc., which requires 100 budgeted hours of professional labor
   b. Labor contract work for Punch, Inc., which requires 150 budgeted hours of professional labor
   Prepare a cost estimate for each job.

4-30 Service industry, job costing two direct- and two indirect-cost categories, law firm (continuation of 4-29). Keating has just completed a review of its job-costing system. This review included a detailed analysis of how past jobs used the firm's resources and interviews with personnel about what factors drive the level of indirect costs. Management concluded that a system with two direct-cost categories (professional partner labor and professional associate labor) and two indirect-cost categories (general support and secretarial support) would yield more accurate job costs. Budgeted information for 1999 related to the two direct-cost categories is as follows:

	Professional Partner Labor	Professional Associate Labor
Number of professionals	5	20
Hours of billable time per professional	1,600 per year	1,600 per year
Total compensation (average per professional)	$200,000	$80,000

Budgeted information for 1999 relating to the two indirect-cost categories is:

	General Support	Secretarial Support
Total costs	$1,800,000	$400,000
Cost-allocation base	Professional labor-hours	Partner labor-hours

Required

1. Compute the 1999 budgeted direct-cost rates for (a) professional partners, and (b) professional associates.
2. Compute the 1999 budgeted indirect-cost rates for (a) general support, and (b) secretarial support.
3. Compute the budgeted costs for the Richardson and Punch jobs, given the following information:

	Richardson, Inc.	Punch, Inc.
Professional partners	60 hours	30 hours
Professional associates	40 hours	120 hours

4. Comment on the results in requirement 3. Why are the job costs different from those computed in Problem 4-29?

4-31 Normal costing, overhead allocation, working backwards. (M. Rajan, adapted) Gibson Company uses normal costing. Its job-costing system has two direct-cost categories, direct materials and direct manufacturing labor; and one indirect-cost category, manufacturing overhead. The following information is obtained from the company's records for 2001:

◆ Total manufacturing costs, $8,000,000

◆ Cost of finished goods manufactured, $7,920,000

◆ Manufacturing overhead allocated was 45% of total manufacturing costs

◆ Manufacturing overhead was allocated to production at a rate of 200% of direct manufacturing labor costs

◆ The dollar amount of work-in-process inventory on January 1, 2001 was 80% of the dollar amount of work-in-process inventory on December 31, 2001.

Required

1. What was the total direct manufacturing labor costs in 2001?
2. What was the total cost of direct materials used in 2001?
3. What was the dollar amount of work-in-process inventory on December 31, 2001?

4-32 Overview of general ledger relationships. The Blakely Company is a small machine shop that uses normal costing in its job-costing system. The total debits and credits in certain accounts *just before* year-end are as follows:

	December 30, 1999	
	Total Debits	**Total Credits**
Materials Control	$100,000	$ 70,000
Work-in-Process Control	320,000	305,000
Manufacturing Department Overhead Control	85,000	—
Finished Goods Control	325,000	300,000
Cost of Goods Sold	300,000	—
Manufacturing Overhead Allocated	—	90,000

All materials purchased are for direct materials. Note that "total debits" in the inventory accounts would include beginning inventory balances, if any.

The preceding total debits and total credits above *do not* include the following:

a. The manufacturing labor costs for the December 31 working day: direct manufacturing labor, $5,000, and indirect manufacturing labor, $1,000.
b. Miscellaneous manufacturing overhead incurred on December 31: $1,000.

Additional Information

- Manufacturing overhead has been allocated as a percentage of direct manufacturing labor costs through December 30.
- Direct materials purchased during 1999 were $85,000.
- No direct materials were returned to suppliers.
- Direct manufacturing labor costs during 1999 totaled $150,000, not including the December 31 working day described previously.

Required

1. Compute the inventories (December 31, 1998) of Materials Control, Work-in-Process Control, and Finished Goods Control. Show T-accounts.
2. Prepare all adjusting and closing journal entries for the preceding accounts. Assume that all under- or overallocated manufacturing overhead is closed directly to Cost of Goods Sold.
3. Compute the ending inventories (December 31, 1999), after adjustments and closing, of Materials Control, Work-in-Process Control, and Finished Goods Control.

4-33 **General ledger relationships, under- and overallocation.** (S. Sridhar, adapted) Needham Company uses normal costing in its job-costing system. Partially completed T-accounts and additional information for Needham for the year 2000 are as follows:

Direct Materials Control		Work-in-Process Control		Finished Goods Control	
1-1-2000 30,000	380,000	1-1-2000 20,000		1-1-2000 10,000	900,000
400,000		Dir. manuf.		940,000	
		labor 360,000			

Manufacturing Overhead Control		Manufacturing Overhead Allocated		Cost of Goods Sold	
540,000					

Additional Information

1. Direct manufacturing labor wage rate was $15 per hour.
2. Manufacturing overhead was allocated at $20 per direct manufacturing labor-hour.
3. During the year, sales revenues were $1,090,000, and marketing and distribution costs were $140,000.

Required

1. What was the amount of direct materials issued to manufacturing during 2000?
2. What was the amount of manufacturing overhead allocated to jobs during 2000?
3. What was the cost of jobs completed during 2000?
4. What was the balance of work-in-process inventory on December 31, 2000?
5. What was the cost of goods sold before proration of under- or overallocated overhead?
6. What was the under- or overallocated manufacturing overhead in 2000?
7. Dispose of the under- or overallocated manufacturing overhead using
   a. Write-off to Cost of Goods Sold
   b. Proration based on ending balances (before proration) in Work in Process, Finished Goods, and Cost of Goods Sold
8. Using each of the approaches in requirement 7, calculate Needham's operating income for the year 2000.
9. Which approach in requirement 7 do you recommend Needham use? Explain your answer briefly.

4-34 **General ledger relationships, under- and overallocation, service industry.** John Brody and Co. is an engineering consulting firm. Brody uses a variation of normal costing in its job-costing system. It charges jobs for blueprints made and fees paid to outside experts at actual costs, professional direct labor costs at a budgeted direct labor rate, and engineering support overhead costs (for engineering and office support) at a budgeted indirect-cost rate.

Brody maintains a "Jobs in Process Control" account in its general ledger that accumulates all costs of jobs. As a job is completed, Brody immediately bills the client and transfers the costs of the completed job to a "Cost of Jobs Billed" account to be matched against the revenues billed to the client. Consequently, unlike manufacturing companies, Brody has no accounts that correspond to "Materials Control" and "Finished Goods Control" accounts.

The following data pertain to the year 2001:

Cost of jobs in process on January 1, 2001	$200,000
Direct costs of fees and blueprints (all cash)	$150,000
Actual direct professional labor costs (all cash)	$1,500,000
Direct professional labor allocated at $50 per direct professional labor-hour	?
Actual direct professional labor-hours	29,000
Actual engineering support overhead costs (all cash)	$1,180,000
Engineering support overhead allocated at 80% of direct professional labor costs	?
Cost of jobs billed	$2,500,000
Revenues	$2,800,000

Brody incurs no marketing or business development costs.

Required

1. Summarize the year 2001 transactions by preparing T-accounts for Jobs-in-Process Control, Cost of Jobs Billed, Direct Professional Labor Control, Direct Professional Labor Allocated, Engineering Support Overhead Control, Engineering Support Overhead Allocated, and Cash Control. As your final entry, dispose of the year-end under- or overallocated account balances as direct write-offs to Cost of Jobs Billed.
2. Calculate Brody's operating income for 2001.

4-35 Proration of overhead, two indirect-cost pools. The Glavine Corporation manufactures precision equipment made to order for the semiconductor industry. Glavine uses two manufacturing overhead cost pools—one for the overhead costs incurred in its highly automated Machining Department and another for overhead costs incurred in its labor-paced Assembly Department. Glavine uses normal costing. It allocates Machining Department overhead costs to jobs on the basis of actual machine-hours using a budgeted machine-hour overhead rate. It allocates Assembly Department overhead costs to jobs on the basis of actual direct manufacturing labor-hours using a budgeted direct manufacturing labor-hour rate.

The following data are for the year 2000:

	Machining Department	Assembly Department
Budgeted manufacturing overhead costs	$6,000,000	$5,000,000
Budgeted machine-hours	100,000	
Budgeted direct manufacturing labor-hours		125,000
Actual manufacturing overhead costs	$6,200,000	$4,700,000

Machine-hours and direct manufacturing labor-hours data and the ending balances (before proration of under- or overallocated overhead) are as follows:

	Actual Machine-Hours	Actual Direct Manufacturing Labor-Hours	Balance Before Proration, December 31, 2000
Cost of Goods Sold	67,500	90,000	$16,000,000
Finished Goods Control	4,500	4,800	750,000
Work-in-Process Control	18,000	25,200	3,250,000

Required

1. Compute the budgeted overhead rates for the year 2000 in the Machining and Assembly Departments.
2. Compute the under- or overallocated overhead in *each* department in 2000. Dispose of the under- or overallocated amount in *each* department using:
   a. Write-off to Cost of Goods Sold.
   b. Proration based on ending balances (before proration) in Cost of Goods Sold, Finished Goods Control, and Work-in-Process Control.
   c. Proration based on the allocated overhead amount (before proration) in the ending balances of Cost of Goods Sold, Finished Goods Control, and Work-in-Process Control.
3. Which proration method do you prefer in requirement 2? Explain.

4-36 Allocation and proration of manufacturing overhead. (SMA, heavily adapted) Nicole Limited is a company that produces machinery to customer order. Its job-costing system (using normal costing) has two direct-cost categories (direct materials and direct manufacturing labor) and one indirect-cost pool (manufacturing overhead, allocated using a budgeted rate based on direct manufacturing labor costs). The budget for 2001 was:

Direct manufacturing labor	$420,000
Manufacturing overhead	$252,000

At the end of 2001, two jobs were incomplete: No. 1768B (total direct manufacturing labor costs were $11,000) and No. 1819C (total direct manufacturing labor costs were $39,000). Machine time totaled 287 hours for No. 1768B and 647 hours for No. 1819C. Direct materials issued to No. 1768B amounted to $22,000. Direct materials for No. 1819C were $42,000.

Total charges to the Manufacturing Overhead Control account for the year were $186,840. Direct manufacturing labor costs of all jobs were $400,000, representing 20,000 direct manufacturing labor-hours.

There were no beginning inventories. In addition to the ending work in process, the ending finished goods showed a balance of $156,000 (including direct manufacturing labor costs of $40,000). Revenues for 2001 totaled $2,700,680, cost of goods sold was $1,600,000, and marketing costs were $857,870. Nicole prices on a cost-plus basis. It currently uses a guideline of cost plus 40% of cost.

Required

1. Prepare a detailed schedule showing the ending balances in the inventories and cost of goods sold (before considering any under- or overallocated manufacturing overhead). Show also the manufacturing overhead allocated in these ending balances.
2. Compute the under- or overallocated manufacturing overhead for 2001.
3. Prorate the amount computed in requirement 2 on the basis of
   a. The ending balances (before proration) of Work-in-Process Control, Finished Goods Control, and Cost of Goods Sold.
   b. The allocated overhead amount (before proration) in the ending balances of Work-in-Process Control, Finished Goods Control, and Cost of Goods Sold.
4. Assume that Nicole decides to write off to cost of goods sold any under- or overallocated manufacturing overhead. Will operating income be higher or lower than the operating income that would have resulted from the proration in requirements 3a and 3b?
5. Calculate the cost of job No. 1819C if Nicole Limited had used the adjusted allocation-rate approach to disposing of under- or overallocated manufacturing overhead in 2001.

4-37 Job costing, contracting, ethics. Jack Halpern is the owner and CEO of Aerospace Comfort, a firm specializing in the manufacture of seats for air transport. He has just received a copy of a letter written to the General Audit Section of the U.S. Navy. He believes it is from an ex-employee of Aerospace.

Dear Sir,

Aerospace Comfort manufactured 100 X7 seats for the Navy in 2001. You may be interested to know the following:

1. Direct materials costs billed for the 100 X7 seats were $25,000.

2. Direct manufacturing labor costs billed for 100 X7 seats were $6,000. These costs include 16 hours of setup labor at $25 per hour, an amount included in the manufacturing overhead cost pool as well. The $6,000 also includes 12 hours of design time at $50 an hour. Design time was explicitly identified as a cost the Navy would not reimburse.

3. Manufacturing overhead costs billed for 100 X7 seats were $9,000 (150% of direct manufacturing labor costs). This amount includes the 16 hours of setup labor at $25 per hour that is incorrectly included as part of direct manufacturing labor costs.

   You may also want to know that over 40% of the direct materials is purchased from Frontier Technology, a company that is 51% owned by Jack Halpern's brother.
   For obvious reasons, this letter will not be signed.

c.c: *The Wall Street Journal*
      Jack Halpern, CEO of Aerospace Comfort

Aerospace Comfort's contract states that the Navy reimburses Aerospace at 130% of total manufacturing costs.

Required

Assume that the facts in the letter are correct as you answer the following questions.

1. What is the cost amount per X7 seat that Aerospace Comfort billed the Navy? Assume that the actual direct material costs are $25,000.
2. What is the amount per X7 seat that Aerospace Comfort should have billed the Navy? Assume that the actual direct material costs are $25,000.
3. What should the Navy do to tighten its procurement procedures to reduce the likelihood of such situations recurring in the future?

COLLABORATIVE LEARNING PROBLEM

4-38 **Service industry, job costing, accounting for overhead costs, budgeted rates.** Jefferson Company is a painting contractor for office buildings and manufacturing plants. Jefferson uses normal costing to cost each job. Jefferson's job-costing system has two direct-cost categories (direct materials and direct labor) and one indirect-cost pool called overhead costs. Jefferson uses a budgeted overhead rate for allocating overhead costs to jobs on the basis of direct labor costs.

Jefferson provides the following additional information:

1. Budgeted overhead costs for the year 2001, $1,200,000
   Budgeted direct labor costs for the year 2001, $1,500,000
2. As of January 31, Job A21 was the only job in process, with direct materials costs of $30,000 and direct labor costs of $50,000.
3. Jobs A22, A23, and A24 were started during February.
4. Direct materials used during February, $150,000.
5. Direct-labor costs for February, $120,000.
6. Actual overhead costs for February, $102,000.
7. The only job still in process at February 28, 2001 was job A24, with direct materials costs of $20,000 and direct labor costs of $40,000.

Jefferson maintains a "Jobs-in-Process Control" account in its general ledger. When a job is completed, Jefferson immediately bills the client and transfers the cost of the completed job to "Cost of Jobs Billed" account to be matched against the revenues billed to the client. Consequently, unlike manufacturing companies, Jefferson does not have an account that corresponds to "Finished Goods Control." Each month, Jefferson closes any under- or over-allocated overhead to "Cost of Jobs Billed."

Required

Form groups of two or more students to complete the following requirements.

1. Calculate the budgeted overhead rate for allocating overhead costs in 2001.
2. Calculate the overhead allocated to Job A21 as of January 31, 2001 and the overhead allocated to Job A24 as of February 28, 2001.
3. Calculate the under- or overallocated overhead for February 2001.
4. Calculate the Cost of Jobs Billed for February 2001.

5

Activity-Based Costing and Activity-Based Management

learning objectives

After studying this chapter, you should be able to

1. Explain undercosting and overcosting of products
2. Present three guidelines for refining a costing system
3. Distinguish between the traditional and the ABC approaches to designing a costing system
4. Describe a four-part cost hierarchy
5. Cost products or services using activity-based costing (ABC)
6. Use ABC systems for activity-based management (ABM)
7. Compare ABC and department-costing systems
8. Evaluate the costs and benefits of implementing ABC systems

General Motors uses a variety of rear lamps (taillights) on its different models of cars. These lamps differ in terms of their size, shape, and color. Activity-based costing (ABC) systems measure the cost of the different activities that need to be performed to manufacture different types of lamps. Managers use this information to price products, to modify product designs, and to manage costs.

Example Client A requires 20 partner hrs. and 100 staff hrs., while Client B requires 50 partner hrs. and 70 staff hrs. Client B is located 3 hrs. from the auditor's office and requires a lot of travel, phone calls, and faxes. Client A is 1/2 hr. away and requires less travel and communications. The auditor uses a single direct cost category for DL and budgets labor at $100/DLH. He also uses a single indirect cost pool (allocated based on DLH), and his indirect cost rate is $120/DLH. Ask students which engagement costs the auditor more (Ans: Client B, which requires more partner hrs.,

travel, and communication). Then calculate the costs the current system allocates to each client:

A's allocated cost = [(20 + 100) × $100]
              + (120 × $120)
              = $26,400

B's allocated cost = [(50 + 70) × $100]
              + (120 × $120)
              = $26,400

The single direct cost-single indirect cost pool system doesn't match the costs with the resources consumed. If the auditor sets prices based on these costs, he will likely lose the overcosted Client A and keep the undercosted Client B. More refined multiple direct and indirect cost pool/driver systems help alleviate this problem.

Teaching Tip Ask students, "What jobs tend to be overcosted? Undercosted?" If the cost system uses a single allocation base, then products that consume relatively more of that base will tend to be overcosted, since all indirect costs are loaded on that base. Products that consume proportionally less of the base will tend to be undercosted.

Chapter 4 describes a basic job-costing system. In particular, it uses a single cost pool and a single indirect-cost rate to allocate indirect costs to jobs. An important question is, Does using a single indirect-cost rate provide misleading job cost numbers? The answer depends on whether different jobs, products, and services are relatively alike (identical or at least similar) in the way they consume indirect costs of an organization. If they are alike, as was the case in Chapter 4, then a simple costing system will suffice for job-costing purposes. If they are different, however, a simple costing system will yield inaccurate cost numbers for jobs, products, and services.

As the variety of their products (or services) increases, organizations are finding that different products place varying demands on resources. The need to measure more accurately how different products and services use organization resources has led companies to refine their costing systems. One of the main forms of costing-system refinement that companies around the globe have implemented is activity-based costing (ABC), the focus of this chapter. We describe how ABC systems help companies to make better pricing and product-mix decisions and also how ABC systems assist in cost management decisions by improving processes and product designs.

BROAD AVERAGING VIA PEANUT-BUTTER COSTING APPROACHES

Companies that use a broad average (for example, a single indirect-cost rate) to allocate costs to products often do not produce reliable cost data. The term **cost smoothing** or **peanut-butter costing** describes a costing approach that uses broad averages for assigning (spreading) the cost of resources uniformly to cost objects (such as product or services) when the individual products or services, in fact, use those resources in a nonuniform way.

Undercosting and Overcosting

Cost smoothing can lead to undercosting or overcosting of products:

- **Product undercosting**—a product consumes a relatively high level of resources but is reported to have a relatively low total cost.
- **Product overcosting**—a product consumes a relatively low level of resources but is reported to have a relatively high total cost.

Companies that undercost products may actually make sales that result in losses under the erroneous impression that these sales are profitable. That is, these sales bring in less revenues than the cost of the resources they use. Companies that overcost products may overprice their products and lose market share to existing or new competitors.

Product-Cost Cross-Subsidization

Product-cost cross-subsidization means that at least one undercosted (overcosted) product results in at least one other product being overcosted (undercosted) in the organization. A classic example arises when a cost is uniformly spread (broadly averaged) across multiple users without recognition of their different uses of resources. Consider the costing of a restaurant bill for four colleagues who meet once a month to discuss business developments. Each diner orders separate entrees, desserts, and drinks. The restaurant bill for the most recent meeting is as follows:

	Entree	Dessert	Drinks	Total
Emma	$11	$ 0	$ 4	$ 15
James	20	8	14	42
Jessica	15	4	8	27
Matthew	14	4	6	24
Total	$60	$16	$32	$108
Average	$15	$ 4	$ 8	$ 27

The $108 total restaurant bill produces a $27 average cost per dinner. This cost-smoothing approach treats each diner the same. Emma would probably object to paying $27 because her actual cost is only $15. Indeed, she ordered the lowest-cost entree, had no dessert, and had the lowest-cost drinks. When costs are averaged across all four diners, both Emma and Matthew are overcosted, James is undercosted, and Jessica is accurately costed.

The restaurant example is both simple and intuitive. The amount of cost cross-subsidization of each diner can be readily computed given that all cost items can be *traced* as direct costs to each diner. More complex costing issues arise, however, when there are indirect costs. Then resources are used by two or more individual diners. By definition, indirect costs require allocation—for example, the cost of a bottle of wine shared by two or more diners.

To see the effects of cost smoothing on both direct and indirect costs, we consider the existing costing system at Plastim Corporation.

Points to Stress More refined cost systems are cost-effective when (1) different jobs (customers, services, etc.) consume resources differently, (2) competition in the output market is keen (accurate cost info. helps companies decide what jobs to emphasize and how to price them), and (3) processing costs are lower.

COSTING SYSTEM AT PLASTIM CORPORATION

Reinforcing Problems Exer. 5-16 covers peanut-butter costing.

Plastim Corporation manufactures lenses for the rear lamps (taillights) of automobiles. The lens, made from black, red, orange, or white plastic, is the part of the lamp visible on the automobile's exterior. Lenses are made using injection molding. The molding operation consists of injecting molten plastic into a mold to give the lamp its desired shape. The mold is cooled to allow the molten plastic to solidify, and the part is removed.

Under its contract with Giovanni Motors, a major automobile manufacturer, Plastim makes two types of lenses—a complex lens, CL5, and a simple lens, S3. The complex lens is a large lens with special features such as multicolor molding (where more than one color is injected into the mold) and complex shapes that wrap around the corner of the car. Manufacturing these lenses is more complex because various parts in the mold must align and fit precisely. The simple lens is smaller and has few special features.

Design, Production, and Distribution Processes

The sequence of steps to design, produce, and distribute lenses, whether simple or complex, is as follows:

1. *Design of products and processes.* Each year Giovanni Motors specifies some modifications to the simple and complex lenses. Plastim's Design Department designs the molds from which the lenses will be made and defines the processes needed (details of the manufacturing operations).

2. *Manufacturing operations.* The lenses are molded, as described earlier, finished, cleaned, and inspected.

3. *Shipping and distribution.* Finished lenses are packed and sent to Giovanni Motors.

Points to Stress Note that Plastim performs most of the business functions in the value chain.

Plastim is operating at capacity and incurs very low marketing costs. Because of its high-quality products, Plastim has minimal customer-service costs. Plastim's business environment is very competitive with respect to simple lenses. At a recent meeting, Giovanni's purchasing manager indicated that a new competitor, who makes only simple lenses, was offering to supply the S3 lens to Giovanni at a price of around $53, well below Plastim's price of $63. Unless Plastim lowers its selling price, it will be in jeopardy of losing the Giovanni business for the simple lens, similar to S3, for the upcoming model year. Plastim's management is very concerned about this development. The same competitive pressures do not exist for the complex lens, which Plastim currently sells to Giovanni at a price of $137 per lens.

Plastim's management has various alternatives available to them. Plastim can give up the Giovanni business in simple lenses if it is going to be this unprofitable. They can reduce the price on the simple lens and either accept a lower margin or aggressively seek to reduce costs. But first management needs to understand what it costs to make and sell the S3 and CL5 lenses. To guide their pricing and cost management decisions, Plastim's managers assign all costs, both manufacturing and nonmanufacturing, to the S3 and CL5 lenses. Had the focus been on inventory costing, they would only assign manufacturing costs to the lenses.

Existing Single Indirect-Cost Pool System

To cost products, Plastim currently uses a job-costing system with a single indirect-cost rate, similar to the system described in Chapter 4. The steps are as follows.

Step 1: Identify the Chosen Cost Objects   The cost objects are the 60,000 simple S3 lenses, and the 15,000 complex CL5 lenses that Plastim makes. Plastim's goal is to calculate the *total* costs of manufacturing and distributing these lenses. Plastim then determines unit costs of each lens by dividing total costs of each lens by 60,000 for S3 and 15,000 for CL5.

Step 2: Identify the Direct Costs of the Products   Plastim identifies the direct costs of the lenses—direct materials and direct manufacturing labor—as follows:

	60,000 Simple Lenses (S3)		15,000 Complex Lenses (CL5)		
	Total (1)	Per Unit (2) = (1) ÷ 60,000	Total (3)	Per Unit (4) = (3) ÷ 15,000	Total (5) = (1) + (3)
Direct materials	$1,125,000	$18.75	$675,000	$45.00	$1,800,000
Direct manufacturing labor	600,000	10.00	195,000	13.00	795,000
Total direct costs	$1,725,000	$28.75	$870,000	$58.00	$2,595,000

Step 3: Select the Cost-Allocation Bases to Use for Allocating Indirect Costs to the Products   Most of the indirect costs consist of salaries paid to supervisors, engineers, manufacturing support, and maintenance staff that support direct manufacturing labor. Hence, Plastim uses direct manufacturing labor-hours as the only allocation base to allocate all indirect costs to S3 and CL5. In the current year, 2001, Plastim used 39,750 actual direct manufacturing labor-hours.

Step 4: Identify the Indirect Costs Associated with Each Cost-Allocation Base   Plastim groups all indirect costs totaling $2,385,000 into a single overhead cost pool.

Step 5: Compute the Rate per Unit of Each Cost-Allocation Base Used to Allocate Indirect Costs to the Products

Points to Stress/Curriculum Linkage These are the same 7 steps which were presented in Chap. 4. Note that the $60 rate per direct manufacturing labor hour used to apply indirect costs to both products is the peanut-butter costing approach. It implicitly assumes equal consumption of activities (which use resources) by both products.

$$\text{Actual indirect-cost rate} = \frac{\text{Actual total costs in indirect-cost pool}}{\text{Actual total quantity of cost-allocation base}}$$

$$= \frac{\$2,385,000}{39,750 \text{ hours}} = \$60 \text{ per direct manufacturing labor-hour}$$

Exhibit 5-1, Panel A, shows an overview of Plastim's existing costing system.

Step 6: Compute the Indirect Costs Allocated to the Products   Plastim uses 30,000 total direct manufacturing labor-hours to make the simple S3 lenses and 9,750 direct manufacturing labor-hours to make the complex CL5 lenses. Exhibit 5-1, Panel B, shows indirect costs of $1,800,000 ($60 per direct manufacturing labor-hour × 30,000) allocated to the simple lens and $585,000 ($60 per direct manufacturing labor-hour × 9,750) allocated to the complex lens.

Step 7: Compute the Total Cost of the Products by Adding All Direct and Indirect Costs Assigned to Them   Exhibit 5-1, Panel B, presents the product costs for the simple and complex lenses. The direct costs are calculated in step 2 and the indirect costs in step 6. Note the correspondence between the costing system overview diagram (Exhibit 5-1, Panel A) and the costs calculated in step 7. Panel A shows two direct-cost categories and one indirect-cost pool. Hence the cost of each type of lens in step 7 (Panel B) has three line items: two for direct costs and one for allocated indirect costs.

Plastim's management begins investigating why the S3 lens costs $58.75, well above the $53 price quoted by Plastim's competitor. Are Plastim's technology and

EXHIBIT 5-1
Product Costs at Plastim, Inc., Using Existing Single Overhead Cost Pool

PANEL A: OVERVIEW OF PLASTIM'S EXISTING COSTING SYSTEM

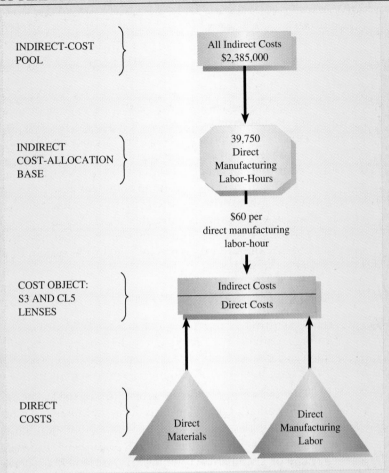

PANEL B: PRODUCT COSTS USING THE EXISTING COSTING SYSTEM

	60,000 Simple Lenses (S3)		15,000 Complex Lenses (CL5)		
	Total (1)	Per Unit (2) = (1) ÷ 60,000	Total (3)	Per Unit (4) = (3) ÷ 15,000	Total (5) = (1) + (3)
Direct materials	$1,125,000	$18.75	$ 675,000	$45.00	$1,800,000
Direct manufacturing labor	600,000	10.00	195,000	13.00	795,000
Total direct costs	$1,725,000	28.75	870,000	58.00	2,595,000
Indirect costs allocated	1,800,000	30.00	585,000	39.00	2,385,000
Total costs	$3,525,000	$58.75	$1,455,000	$97.00	$4,980,000

processes inefficient in manufacturing and distributing the simple S3 lens? Further analysis indicates that such inefficiency is not the reason. Plastim has years of experience in manufacturing and distributing lenses like S3. Because Plastim often makes process improvements, management is confident that their technology and processes for making simple lenses are not inferior to their competitors. However, management is less certain about Plastim's capabilities in manufacturing and distributing complex lenses. Indeed, Plastim has only recently started making this type of lens. Management is pleasantly surprised to learn that Giovanni Motors considers the prices of CL5 lenses to be very competitive. It is puzzling that, even at these prices, Plastim earns very large margins on the CL5 lenses:

	60,000 Simple Lenses (S3)		15,000 Complex Lenses (CL5)		
	Total (1)	Per Unit (2) = (1) ÷ 60,000	Total (3)	Per Unit (4) = (3) ÷ 15,000	Total (5) = (1) + (3)
Revenues	$3,780,000	$63.00	$2,055,000	$137.00	$5,835,000
Costs	3,525,000	$58.75	1,455,000	97.00	4,980,000
Operating income	$ 255,000	$ 4.25	$ 600,000	$ 40.00	$ 855,000
Operating income ÷ Revenues		6.75%		29.20%	

Plastim's managers are surprised that the margins are low on the S3 product where the company has strong capabilities, whereas the margins are quite high on the newer, less-established CL5 product. Since they are not deliberately charging a low price for S3, they wonder whether the costing system overcosts the simple S3 lens (assigning excessive costs to it) and undercosts the complex CL5 lens (assigning too little costs to it).

Plastim's management is quite confident about the direct materials and direct manufacturing labor costs of the lenses. Why? Because these costs can be traced to the lenses in an economically feasible way. They are less certain about the accuracy of the costing system in measuring the overhead resources used by each type of lens. The key question then is, How might the system of allocating overhead costs to lenses be refined?

REFINING A COSTING SYSTEM

OBJECTIVE 2

Present three guidelines for refining a costing system

A **refined costing system** provides better measurement of the nonuniformity in the use of an organization's overhead resources by jobs, products, and services. Increased competition and advances in information technology have accelerated these refinements.

Three guidelines for refining a costing system are:

1. *Direct-cost tracing.* Classify as many of the total costs as direct costs as is economically feasible. This guideline reduces the amount of costs classified as indirect.
2. *Indirect-cost pools.* Expand the number of indirect-cost pools until each of these pools is homogeneous. In a *homogeneous cost pool*, all of the costs have the same or a similar cause-and-effect (or benefits-received) relationship with the cost-allocation base.
3. *Cost-allocation bases.* Identify the preferred cost-allocation base for each indirect-cost pool. In this chapter we focus on the cause-and-effect criterion for choosing allocation bases.

ACTIVITY-BASED COSTING SYSTEMS

OBJECTIVE 3

Distinguish between the traditional and the ABC approaches to designing a costing system

One of the best tools for refining a costing system is *activity-based costing*. **Activity-based costing (ABC)** systems refine costing systems by focusing on individual activities as the fundamental cost objects. An **activity** is an event, task, or unit of work with a specified purpose; for example, designing products, setting up machines, operating machines, and distributing products. ABC systems calculate the costs of individual activities and assign costs to cost objects such as products and services on the basis of the activities undertaken to produce each product or service:[1]

[1]For more details on ABC systems see R. Cooper and R. S. Kaplan, *The Design of Cost Management Systems*, (Upper Saddle River, NJ: Prentice Hall, 1999).

We describe key ideas of an ABC system in the context of our Plastim example. ABC systems focus on indirect costs because direct costs can be traced to products and jobs relatively easily. A key step in implementing ABC at Plastim is to identify activities that help explain why Plastim incurs the costs that it currently classifies as indirect. To define these activities, Plastim organizes a cross-functional team from design, manufacturing, distribution, and accounting and administration. The team identifies key activities using a flowchart of all the steps and processes needed to design, manufacture, and distribute lenses.

Plastim's team identifies seven major activities.

1. Design products and processes.
2. Set up molding machine to ensure the mold is properly held in place and parts are properly aligned before manufacturing starts.
3. Operate machines to manufacture lenses.
4. Maintain and clean the mold after lenses are manufactured.
5. Set up batches of finished lenses for shipment.
6. Distribute lenses to customers.
7. Administer and manage all processes at Plastim.

By defining activities and identifying the costs of performing each activity, ABC systems seek a greater level of detail in understanding how an organization uses its resources. As we describe ABC systems, keep in mind three features:

1. ABC systems create smaller cost pools linked to the different activities. Plastim partitions its original single overhead cost pool into seven activity-related cost pools.

2. For each activity-cost pool, a measure of the activity performed serves as the cost-allocation base. For example, Plastim defines setup hours as a measure of setup activity and cubic feet of packages moved as a measure of distribution activity. Because each activity-cost pool pertains to a narrow and focused set of costs (e.g., setup or distribution), the cost pools are homogeneous—over time, the costs in each cost pool have a cause-and-effect relationship with the cost-allocation base. At Plastim, over the long run, setup hours is a cost driver of setup costs and cubic feet of packages moved is a cost driver of distribution costs.

3. In some cases, costs in a cost pool can be traced directly to products. In the Plastim example, the cleaning and maintenance activity consists of salaries and wages paid to workers responsible for cleaning the mold. Following guideline 1 of refining a costing system, these costs can be traced directly to the specific mold used to produce the lens. Direct tracing of costs improves cost accuracy because it makes no assumptions about the cause-and-effect relationship between the cost pool and the cost-allocation base.

The logic of ABC systems is that more finely structured activity-cost pools with activity-specific cost-allocation bases, which are cost drivers for the cost pool, lead to more accurate costing of activities. Allocating costs to products by measuring the cost-allocation bases of different activities used by different products lead to more accurate product costs. In contrast, consider the case when the cause-and-effect relationship between overhead costs and the cost-allocation base(s) is weak. For example, in its existing costing system, Plastim uses direct manufacturing labor-hours as the cost-allocation base for all overhead costs, whether in setup or distribution. Direct manufacturing labor-hours do not drive the costs in these activity-cost pools. Consequently, measuring the direct manufacturing labor-hours used by various products does not capture the overhead costs demanded by the different products.

By focusing on the setup activity, we illustrate the effect of allocating all overhead costs to products using direct manufacturing labor-hours versus an ABC system with its emphasis on individual activities. Setups frequently entail trial runs, fine-tuning, and adjustments. Improper setups cause quality problems such as scratches on the surface of the lens. The resources needed for each setup depend on the complexity of the manufacturing operation. Complex lenses require more setup resources per setup than do simple lenses. Furthermore, complex lenses can be produced only in small batches because the mold needs to be cleaned more often. Relative to simple lenses, complex lenses not only use more resources per setup, they also need more frequent setups.

Setup data for the simple S3 lens and the complex CL5 lens are as follows:

		Simple S3 Lens	Complex CL5 Lens	Total
1	Quantity of lenses produced	60,000	15,000	
2	Number of lenses produced per batch	240	50	
3 = (1) ÷ (2)	Number of batches	250	300	
4	Setup time per batch	2 hours	5 hours	
5 = (3) × (4)	Total setup-hours	500 hours	1,500 hours	2,000 hours

Plastim identifies the total costs of setups (consisting mainly of allocated costs of process engineers, supervisors, and setup equipment) of $300,000. The following table shows how setup costs are allocated to the simple and complex lenses using direct manufacturing labor-hours and setup-hours, respectively, as the allocation bases. The setup cost per direct manufacturing labor-hour equals $7.54717 ($300,000 ÷ 39,750). The setup cost per setup-hour equals $150 ($300,000 ÷ 2,000 setup-hours).

	Simple S3 Lens	Complex CL5 Lens	Total
Cost allocated using direct manufacturing labor-hours $7.54717 × 30,000; $7.54717 × 9,750	$226,415	$73,585	$300,000
Cost allocated using setup-hours $150 × 500; $150 × 1,500	$75,000	$225,000	$300,000

Teaching Tip Ask students "What are the characteristics of companies that are most likely to find ABC cost-effective?" Give students 2 min. to come up with 2 or 3 characteristics. Divide students into groups to come up with a list of 5 (about 3–4 min.). Call on each group to contribute 1 idea. Most of the ideas will fall into the following categories. ABC is most likely to be cost-effective when a company (1) has many different products/services that make different demands on resources (if there is only 1 product, or if all products make similar demands, a simple system may be sufficient), (2) faces stiff competition where knowledge of costs and cost control are vital for product emphasis and pricing decisions, and (3) has access to the necessary acctg. and information processing expertise to implement and maintain the system. Point out that, over time, the benefits of adopting ABC have been increasing while the costs of implementation have declined, thereby increasing the popularity of ABC.

Which allocation base should Plastim use? Plastim should allocate setup costs on the basis of setup hours. Why? Because, following guidelines 2 and 3, there is a strong cause-and-effect relationship between setup-related overhead costs and setup-hours, but there is almost no relationship between setup-related overhead costs and direct manufacturing labor-hours. Setup costs depend on the number of batches and the complexity of the setups and hence setup-hours drive setup costs. The simple S3 lens attracts more of the setup costs when costs are allocated on the basis of direct manufacturing labor-hours. This occurs because more direct manufacturing labor-hours are needed to produce S3 lenses. However, direct manufacturing labor-hours required by the S3 and CL5 lenses bear no relationship to the setup-hours demanded by the S3 and CL5 lenses.

Note that setup-hours are related to batches (groups) of lenses made, not individual lenses. An important feature of activity-based costing is how it highlights the different levels of activities—for example, individual units of output versus batches of output—when identifying cause-and-effect relationships. As our discussion of setups illustrates, limiting the drivers of costs to only units of output (or cost-allocation bases related to units of output such as direct manufacturing labor-hours) frequently will weaken the cause-and-effect relationship between costs in a cost pool and the cost-allocation base. The *cost hierarchy* distinguishes costs by whether the cost driver is a unit of output (or variables such as machine-hours or direct manufacturing labor-hours that are a function of units of output), or a *group* of units of a product (such as a batch in the case of setup costs), or the *product itself* (such as the complexity of the mold in the case of design costs).

Cost Hierarchies

A **cost hierarchy** categorizes costs into different cost pools on the basis of the different types of cost drivers (or cost-allocation bases) or different degrees of difficulty in determining cause-and-effect (or benefits-received) relationships.

ABC systems commonly use a four-part cost hierarchy—output unit-level costs, batch-level costs, product-sustaining costs, and facility-sustaining costs—to identify cost-allocation bases that are preferably cost drivers of costs in activity cost pools.

Output unit-level costs are resources sacrificed on activities performed on each individual unit of a product or service. Manufacturing operations costs (such as energy, machine depreciation, and repair) that are related to the activity of running the automated molding machines are output unit-level costs. Why? Because the cost of this activity increases with each additional unit of output produced (or machine-hour run).

Suppose that in our Plastim example, each S3 lens requires 0.15 molding machine-hours. Then S3 lenses require a total of 9,000 molding machine-hours (0.15 hour × 60,000 lenses). Similarly, suppose CL5 lenses require 0.25 molding machine-hours. Then the CL5 lens requires 3,750 molding machine-hours (0.25 hour × 15,000 lenses). The *total* molding machine costs allocated to S3 and CL5 depend on the quantity of each type of lens produced, regardless of the number of batches in which the lenses are made. Plastim's ABC system uses machine-hours, an output unit-level cost-allocation base, to allocate manufacturing operations costs to products.

Batch-level costs are resources sacrificed on activities that are related to a group of units of product(s) or service(s) rather than to each individual unit of product or service. In the Plastim example, setup costs are batch-level costs. Setup resources are used each time molding machines are set up to produce a batch of lenses. The S3 lens requires 500 setup-hours (2 hours per setup × 250 batches). The CL5 lens requires 1,500 setup-hours (5 hours per setup × 300 batches). The *total* setup costs allocated to S3 and CL5 depend on the total setup-hours required by each type of lens, not on the number of units of S3 and CL5 produced. Plastim's ABC system uses setup-hours, a batch-level cost-allocation base to allocate setup costs to products.

In companies that purchase many different types of direct materials (Plastim purchases mainly plastic pellets), procurement costs can be significant. Procurement costs include the costs of placing purchase orders, receiving materials, and paying suppliers. These costs are batch-level costs because they are related to the number of purchase orders placed rather than to the quantity or value of materials purchased.

Product-sustaining (or service-sustaining) costs are resources sacrificed on activities undertaken to support individual products or services. In the Plastim example, design costs are product-sustaining costs. Design costs for each type of lens depend largely on the time spent by designers on designing and modifying the product, mold, and process. These costs are a function of the complexity of the mold, measured by the number of parts in the mold multiplied by the area (in square feet) over which the molten plastic must flow (12 parts × 2.5 square feet or 30 parts-square feet for the S3 lens, and 14 parts × 5 square feet or 70 parts-square feet for the CL5 lens). The *total* design costs allocated to S3 and CL5 depend on the complexity of the mold, regardless of the number of units or batches in which the units are produced. Design costs cannot be linked in any cause-and-effect way to individual units of products or to individual batches of products. Plastim's ABC system uses parts-square feet, a product-sustaining cost-allocation base, to allocate design costs to products. Another example of product-sustaining costs is engineering costs incurred to change product designs, although such changes are infrequent at Plastim.

Facility-sustaining costs are resources sacrificed on activities that cannot be traced to individual products or services but support the organization as a whole. In the Plastim example, the general administration costs (including rent and building security) are facility-sustaining costs. It is usually difficult to find good cause-and-effect relationships between these costs and a cost-allocation base. This lack of a cause-and-effect relationship causes some companies not to allocate these costs to products and instead to deduct them from operating income. Other companies, such as Plastim, allocate facility-sustaining costs to products on some basis—for example, direct manufacturing labor-hours—because management believes all costs should be allocated to products. Allocating all costs to products or services becomes particularly important when management wants to set selling prices on the basis of a cost number that includes all costs.

Reinforcing Problems Cost hierarchies are covered in Exer. 5-17 through 5-19 and Prob. 5-40.

Teaching Tip If any students have worked in a mfg. plant (or if you have shown videos of a mfg. process), ask students to illustrate output unit-level, batch-level, product-sustaining, and facility-sustaining costs (and related cost drivers) in that context.

Points to Stress Traditional cost acctg. systems treated all costs as if they were output unit-level costs. It can be difficult to identify drivers of higher-level costs, particularly facility-sustaining costs (e.g., what drives the CEO's salary?). It can be expensive to obtain data on values of higher-level cost drivers, as this information is not generally collected by the cost acctg. system (e.g., batch-level drivers might include # setups, # purchase orders; product-sustaining drivers might include # part numbers, # engineering change orders). Decreasing information processing costs make it less expensive to obtain data on nontraditional cost drivers, and increased competition increases the benefits of accurate cost information. Hence, companies are adopting more complex systems that recognize the hierarchy of costs and cost drivers.

Curriculum Linkage Reducing the # batches by increasing the # units per batch reduces total batch-level costs. However, inventory levels are likely to increase, inconsistent with JIT. JIT emphasizes reducing per batch setup costs to make smaller batch sizes more economical.

Example In a public acctg. firm, developing specialized training in a specific area of tax, such as oil and gas taxation, is a service-sustaining cost (i.e., a cost of the decision to provide oil and gas taxation services). The cost of developing the program depends on the decision to offer the oil and gas tax service and the complexity of the service, not the number of outputs (i.e., billable hrs.), or the number of "batches" (i.e., clients using the service).

IMPLEMENTING ACTIVITY-BASED COSTING AT PLASTIM CORPORATION

Now that we understand the basic concepts of ABC, we use it to refine Plastim's existing costing system. We again follow the seven-step approach to costing presented at the beginning of the chapter and the three guidelines for refining costing systems (increasing direct-cost tracing, creating homogeneous indirect-cost pools, and identifying cost-allocation bases that have a cause-and-effect relationship with costs in the cost pool).

Step 1: Identify the Chosen Cost Objects   The cost objects are the S3 and CL5 lenses. Plastim's goal is to first calculate the *total* costs of manufacturing, and distributing these lenses and then the per-unit costs.

Step 2: Identify the Direct Costs of the Products   Plastim identifies direct materials costs, direct manufacturing labor costs, and mold cleaning and maintenance costs as direct costs of the lenses. In its existing costing system, Plastim classified mold cleaning and maintenance costs as indirect costs and allocated them to products using direct manufacturing labor-hours. However, these costs can be traced directly to a lens because each type of lens can only be produced from a specific mold. Note that because mold cleaning and maintenance costs consist of workers' wages for cleaning molds after each batch of lenses is produced, cleaning and maintenance costs are direct batch-level costs. Complex lenses incur more cleaning and maintenance costs than simple lenses because Plastim produces more batches of complex lenses than simple lenses and because the molds of complex lenses are more difficult to clean. Direct manufacturing labor-hours do not capture the demand that complex and simple lenses place on mold cleaning and maintenance resources.

Plastim's direct costs are as follows:

Description	Cost Hierarchy Category	60,000 Simple Lenses (S3)		15,000 Complex Lenses (CL5)		Total
		Total (1)	Per Unit (2) = (3) ÷ 60,000	Total (3)	Per Unit (4) = (3) ÷ 15,000	Total (5) = (1) + (3)
Direct materials	Output-unit-level	$1,125,000	$18.75	$ 675,000	$45.00	$1,800,000
Direct manuf. labor	Output-unit-level	600,000	10.00	195,000	13.00	795,000
Cleaning & maintenance	Batch-level	120,000	2.00	150,000	10.00	270,000
Total direct costs		$1,845,000	$30.75	$1,020,000	$68.00	$2,865,000

Step 3: Select the Cost-Allocation Bases to Use for Allocating Indirect Costs to the Products   Plastim identifies six activities—design, molding machine setups, manufacturing operations, shipment setup, distribution, and administration—for allocating indirect costs to products. Exhibit 5-2, column 4 shows the cost-allocation base and the quantity of the cost-allocation base for each activity.

The cost-allocation base is pivotal in defining the number of activity pools in an ABC system. For example, rather than define the design activities of product design, process design, and prototyping as separate activities, Plastim defines these activities as part of a combined design activity. Why? Because the complexity of the mold is an appropriate cost driver for costs incurred in all three design subactivities.

A second consideration in choosing a cost-allocation base is the availability of reliable data and measures. Consider, for example, the problem of choosing a cost-allocation base for the design activity. The driver of design cost, a product-sustaining cost, is the complexity of the mold—more complex molds take more time to design. In its ABC system, Plastim measures complexity in terms of the number of parts in the mold and the surface area of the mold. If these data are difficult to obtain, or if measurement errors are large, Plastim may be forced to use some other measure of complexity, such as the amount of material flowing through the mold. The problem then is that the quantity of material flow may not adequately represent the complexity of the design activity.

EXHIBIT 5-2
Activity-Cost Rates for Plastim's Indirect-Cost Pools

Activity (1)	Cost Hierarchy Category (2)	(Step 4) Total Costs (3)	(Step 3) Quantity of Cost-Allocation Base (4)	(Step 5) Overhead Allocation Rate (5) = (3) ÷ (4)	Brief Explanation of the Cause-and-Effect Relationship That Motivates the Choice of the Allocation Base (6)
◆ Design	◆ Product-sustaining	◆ $450,000	◆ 100 parts-square feet	◆ $4,500 per part-square feet	◆ Complex molds (more parts and larger surface area) require greater Design Department resources.
◆ Setups of molding machines	◆ Batch-level	◆ $300,000	◆ 2,000 setup-hours	◆ $150 per setup-hour	◆ Overhead costs of the setup activity increase as setup-hours increase.
◆ Manufacturing operations	◆ Output-unit-level	◆ $637,500	◆ 12,750 molding machine-hours	◆ $50 per molding machine-hour	◆ Plastim has mostly automated molding machines. Manufacturing overhead costs support automated molding machines and hence increase with molding machine usage.
◆ Shipment setup	◆ Batch-level	◆ $ 81,000	◆ 200 shipments	◆ $405 per shipment	◆ Costs incurred to prepare batches for shipment increase with the number of shipments.
◆ Distribution	◆ Output-unit-level	◆ $391,500	◆ 67,500 cubic feet	◆ $5.80 per cubic foot	◆ Overhead costs of the distribution activity increase with cubic feet of packages shipped.
◆ Administration	◆ Facility-sustaining	◆ $255,000	◆ 39,750 direct manufacturing labor-hours	◆ $6.4151 per direct manufacturing labor-hour	◆ Administration Department resources support direct manufacturing labor-hours because the demand for these resources increases with direct manufacturing labor-hours.

Step 4: Identify the Indirect Costs Associated with Each Cost-Allocation Base

In this step, overhead costs incurred by Plastim are assigned to activities, to the extent possible, on the basis of a cause-and-effect relationship between the costs of an activity and the cost-allocation base for the activity. For example, costs in the distribution-cost pool have a cause-and-effect relationship to cubic feet of packages moved. Of course, the strength of the cause-and-effect relationship between costs of an activity and its respective cost-allocation base varies across cost pools. For example, the cause-and-effect relationship between administration activity costs and direct manufacturing labor-hours is not as strong as the relationship between setup activity costs and setup-hours.

Some costs can be directly identified with a particular activity. For example, salaries paid to design engineers are directly identified with the design activity. Other costs need to be allocated across activities. For example, on the basis of interviews or time records, manufacturing engineers and supervisors identify the time spent on design activities, molding machine setup activity, and manufacturing operations. The time spent on these activities serves as a basis for allocating manufacturing engineers' and supervisors' salary costs to various activities. Similarly, other costs are allocated to activity-cost pools using allocation bases that best describe the costs incurred for the different activities. For example, space costs are allocated on the basis of square-feet area used for different activities. However, the allocation base chosen may sometimes be constrained by the availability of reliable data.

The key point here is that all costs do not fit neatly into activity categories. Often, costs may first need to be allocated to activities before the costs of the activities can be allocated to products.

Points to Stress Companies that have successfully implemented ABC usually limit the number of activity/cost pool/allocation bases to 5-10 per dep't., at least in the initial implementation. More activities can be added later if additional complexity is warranted. The danger with identifying too many activities is that the company may get bogged down in a morass of detail and the implementation may fail.

PANEL A: OVERVIEW OF PLASTIM'S ACTIVITY-BASED COSTING SYSTEM

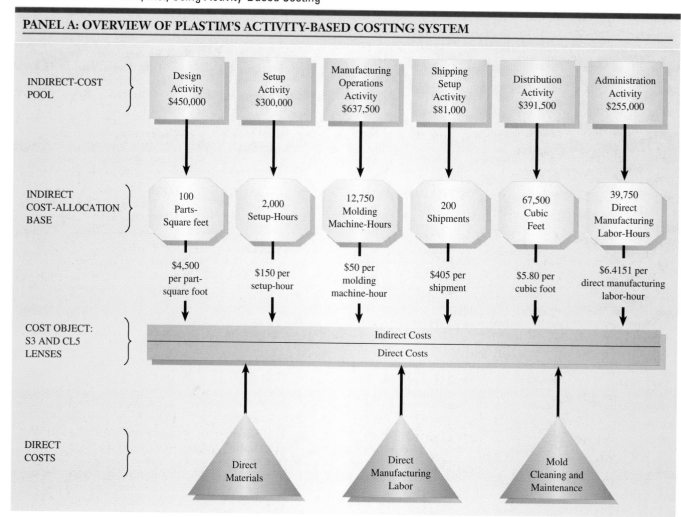

(Continued)

Step 5: Compute the Rate per Unit of Each Cost-Allocation Base Used to Allocate Indirect Costs to the Products Exhibit 5-2 summarizes the calculation of the activity-cost rates using the cost-allocation bases selected in step 3 and the indirect costs of each activity calculated in step 4. Exhibit 5-3, Panel A, presents an overview of the ABC system.

Step 6: Compute the Indirect Costs Allocated to the Products Exhibit 5-3, Panel B, shows indirect costs of $1,153,953 allocated to the simple lens and $961,047 allocated to the complex lens. To calculate indirect costs of each lens, the total quantity of the cost-allocation base used for each activity by each type of lens (using data provided by Plastim's operations personnel) is multiplied by the cost-allocation rate calculated in step 5 (see Exhibit 5-2, column 5). For example, of the 2,000 hours of the setup activity (Exhibit 5-2, column 4), the S3 lens uses 500 setup-hours and the CL5 lens uses 1,500 setup-hours. Hence the total costs of the setup activity allocated to the S3 lens is $75,000 (500 setup-hours × $150, the setup rate calculated in Exhibit 5-2, column 5) and to the CL5 lens is $225,000 (1,500 setup-hours × $150). The setup cost per unit can then be calculated as $1.25 ($75,000 ÷ 60,000 units) for the S3 lens and as $15 ($225,000 ÷ 15,000 units) for the CL5 lens.

PANEL B: PRODUCT COSTS USING THE ACTIVITY-BASED COSTING SYSTEM

Description of Cost and the Quantity of Activity Used by Each Type of Lens	60,000 Simple Lenses (S3)		15,000 Complex Lenses (CL5)		
	Total (1)	Per Unit (2) = (1) ÷ 60,000	Total (3)	Per Unit (4) = (3) ÷ 15,000	Total (5) = (1) + (3)
Direct costs					
Direct materials	$1,125,000	$18.75	$ 675,000	$ 45.00	$1,800,000
Direct manufacturing labor	600,000	10.00	195,000	13.00	795,000
Direct mold cleaning and maintenance costs	120,000	2.00	150,000	10.00	270,000
Total direct costs	1,845,000	30.75	1,020,000	68.00	2,865,000
Indirect costs					
Design activity costs					
S3, 30 parts-square feet × $4,500	135,000	2.25			450,000
CL5, 70 parts-square feet × $4,500			315,000	21.00	
Setup activity costs					
S3, 500 setup-hours × $150	75,000	1.25			300,000
CL5, 1,500 setup-hours × $150			225,000	15.00	
Manufacturing operations activity costs					
S3, 9,000 molding machine-hours × $50	450,000	7.50			637,500
CL5, 3,750 molding machine-hours × $50			187,500	12.50	
Shipping setup activity					
S3, 100 shipments × $405	40,500	0.67			81,000
CL5, 100 shipments × $405			40,500	2.70	
Distribution activity					
S3, 45,000 cubic feet × $5.80	261,000	4.35			391,500
CL5, 22,500 cubic feet × $5.80			130,500	8.70	
Administration activity					
S3, 30,000 direct manufacturing labor-hours × $6.4151	192,453	3.21			255,000
CL5, 9,750 direct manufacturing labor-hours × $6.4151			62,547	4.17	
Total indirect costs	1,153,953	19.23	961,047	64.07	2,115,000
Total costs	$2,998,953	$49.98	$1,981,047	$132.07	$4,980,000

Step 7: Compute the Total Costs of the Products by Adding All Direct and Indirect Costs Assigned to Them Exhibit 5-3, Panel B, presents the product costs for the simple and complex lenses. The direct costs are calculated in step 2 and the indirect costs in step 6. The activity-based costing system overview in Exhibit 5-3, Panel A, shows three direct-cost categories and six indirect-cost pools. Hence the

cost of each lens type in Exhibit 5-3, Panel B, has nine line items, three for direct costs and six for indirect costs. The differences in the ABC product costs of S3 and CL5 calculated in Exhibit 5-3, Panel B, highlight how these products use different amounts of direct costs and different amounts of resources in each activity area.

We emphasize two key features of ABC systems. First, these systems identify all costs used by products, whether the costs are variable or fixed in the short run. Why? Because the focus of ABC systems is on longer-run decisions when more of the costs can be managed and fewer costs are regarded as fixed and given. Hence ABC systems identify all resources used by products regardless of how individual costs behave in the short run. Second, as we have already described, recognizing the hierarchy of costs is critical when allocating costs to products. It is easiest to use the cost hierarchy to calculate *total* costs. For this reason, we recommend calculating total costs first. The per unit costs can then be easily calculated by dividing total costs by the number of units produced.

COMPARING ALTERNATIVE COSTING SYSTEMS

Exhibit 5-4 compares key features of and differences resulting from Plastim's existing single indirect-cost pool system (Exhibit 5-1) and the ABC system (Exhibit 5-3). We emphasize three points in Exhibit 5-4: (1) ABC systems trace more costs as direct costs; (2) ABC systems create more cost pools linked to different activities; and (3) for each activity-cost pool, ABC systems seek a cost-allocation base that has a cause-and-effect relationship with costs in the cost pool.

The homogeneous cost pools and the choice of cost-allocation bases, tied to the cost hierarchy, gives Plastim's managers greater confidence in the activity and product cost numbers from the ABC system. Allocating costs to lenses using only an output unit-level allocation base, direct manufacturing labor-hours, as in the existing single indirect-cost pool system, overcosts the simple S3 lens and undercosts the complex CL5 lens. The CL5 (S3) lens uses a disproportionately larger (smaller) amount of output-unit-level, batch-level, and product-sustaining costs than is represented by the direct manufacturing labor-hour cost-allocation base.

The benefits of ABC systems arise from using ABC information to make better decisions. But these benefits must be traded off against the measurement and implementation costs of these systems. We focus on these issues next.

USING ABC SYSTEMS FOR COST MANAGEMENT AND PROFITABILITY IMPROVEMENT

OBJECTIVE 6

Use ABC systems for activity-based management (ABM)

The emphasis of this chapter so far has been on the role of ABC systems in obtaining better activity and product costs. Companies use ABC information for pricing, product mix, and cost management decisions. **Activity-based management (ABM)** describes management decisions that use activity-based costing information to satisfy customers and improve profitability. Although ABM has many definitions, we define it broadly to include pricing and product-mix decisions, cost reduction and process improvement decisions, and product design decisions.

Pricing and Product-Mix Decisions An ABC system gives management insight into the cost structures for making and selling diverse products. As a result, management can make pricing and product-mix decisions. For example, the ABC system indicates that Plastim can reduce the price of S3 to the $53 range and still make a profit, because the ABC cost of S3 is $49.98. Without this ABC information, Plastim management might erroneously conclude that they would incur an operating loss on the S3 lens at the $53 price. This incorrect conclusion might cause Plastim to reduce its business in simple lenses and focus instead on complex lenses, where its existing single indirect-cost pool system indicates it is very profitable.

Focusing on complex lenses would be a mistake. The ABC system indicates that the cost of making the complex lens is much higher ($132.07 versus $97 under Plastim's existing direct manufacturing labor-based costing system). As Plastim's

EXHIBIT 5-4
Comparing Alternative Costing Systems

	Existing Single Indirect-Cost Pool System (1)	ABC System (2)	Difference (3) = (2) − (1)
◆ Direct-cost categories	2	3	1
	◆ Direct materials	◆ Direct materials	
	◆ Direct manufacturing labor	◆ Direct manufacturing labor	
		◆ Direct cleaning and maintenance labor	
◆ Total direct costs	$2,595,000	$2,865,000	$270,000
◆ Indirect-cost pools	1	6	5
	◆ Single indirect-cost pool allocated using direct manufacturing labor-hours	◆ Design cost pool allocated using parts-square feet	
		◆ Molding machine setup-cost pool allocated using setup-hours	
		◆ Manufacturing operations-cost pool allocated using machine-hours	
		◆ Shipment setup-cost pool allocated using number of shipments	
		◆ Distribution-cost pool allocated using cubic feet of packages shipped	
		◆ Administration-cost pool allocated using direct manufacturing labor-hours	
◆ Total indirect costs	$2,385,000	$2,115,000	($270,000)
◆ Total costs assigned to simple (S3) lens	$3,525,000	$2,998,953	($526,047)
◆ Cost per unit of simple (S3) lens	$58.75	$49.98	($8.77)
◆ Total costs assigned to complex (CL5) lens	$1,455,000	$1,981,047	$526,047
◆ Cost per unit of complex (CL5) lens	$97.00	$132.07	$35.07

operations staff had thought all along, Plastim has no comparative advantage in making CL5 lenses. At a price of $137 per lens for CL5, the margins look very small. As Plastim reduces prices on simple lenses, it will probably have to negotiate a higher price for the complex lenses.

Cost Reduction and Process Improvement Decisions   Manufacturing and distribution personnel use ABC systems to focus cost reduction efforts. Managers set cost reduction targets in terms of reducing the cost per unit of the cost-allocation base in different activity areas. For example, the supervisor of the distribution activity area at Plastim could have a performance target of decreasing the distribution cost per cubic foot of products shipped from $5.80 to $5.40 by reducing distribution labor and warehouse rental costs.

Doing an analysis of the cost of important activities (activity cost pools) and the factors that cause these costs to be incurred (cost drivers and cost-allocation bases) reveals many opportunities for improving efficiency. Management can evaluate whether particular activities can be reduced or eliminated by improving processes. Each of the indirect cost-allocation bases in the ABC system is a nonfinancial variable (number of hours of setup time, cubic feet shipped, and so on). Controlling physical items such as setup-hours or cubic feet shipped is often the most fundamental way that operating

Points to Stress ABC can help mgrs. control costs by assisting them in reducing consumption of the allocation base. Managers control the physical activity which they can see and manage. Remember, the activities consume the resource $, and products consume the resources. The ABC allocation base tells mgrs. which activities need to be managed.

Points to Stress ABC can help mgrs. control costs by providing incentives to reduce the indirect cost allocation rate for each activity (because the cost of each activity is now visible). A mgr. can be rewarded for reducing the indirect cost rate for an activity because the acctg. system

personnel manage costs. For example, Plastim can decrease distribution costs by packing the lenses in a way that reduces the bulkiness of the shipment.

The following table shows the reduction in distribution costs of the S3 and CL5 lenses as a result of process and efficiency improvements that lower the cost per cubic foot (from $5.80 to $5.40) and the total cubic feet of shipments (from 45,000 to 40,000 for S3 and 22,500 to 20,000 for CL5).

	60,000 S3 Lenses		15,000 CL5 Lenses	
	Total (1)	Per Unit (2) = (1) ÷ 60,000	Total (3)	Per Unit (4) = (3) ÷ 15,000
Distribution cost per unit (from Exh. 5-3, Panel B)	$261,000	$4.35	$130,500	$8.70
Distribution costs as a result of process improvements				
S3, 40,000 cubic feet × $5.40	216,000	3.60		
CL5, 20,000 cubic feet × $5.40			108,000	7.20
Savings in distribution cost from process improvements	$ 45,000	$0.75	$ 22,500	$1.50

visibly links the mgr. to this cost reduction. In a single MOH cost pool system, mgrs. have little incentive to reduce MOH. The effects of any reduction are not linked to a particular mgr. if all the MOH is aggregated in 1 pool.

Curriculum Linkage There are often more opportunities for cost reduction in the design stage, before costs are locked in (see Chap. 12). ABC information assists product designers' value engineering efforts to reduce costs while maintaining product characteristics valued by customers.

Design Decisions Management can identify and evaluate new designs to improve performance by evaluating how product and process designs affect activities and costs. Companies can then work with their customers to evaluate the costs and prices of alternative design choices. For example, creative design decisions that decrease the complexity of the mold reduce costs of design, materials, labor, setups, molding machine operations, and mold cleaning and maintenance.

If Plastim uses its existing direct manufacturing labor-hour-based system to choose among alternative designs, which design choices will Plastim favor? Those designs that reduce direct manufacturing labor-hours the most. Why? Because the cost system would erroneously signal that reducing direct manufacturing labor-hours reduces overhead costs. However, as our discussion of ABC systems indicates, direct manufacturing labor-hours has little impact on Plastim's overhead costs.

Planning and Managing Activities As was the case with Plastim, most companies implementing ABC systems for the first time analyze actual costs to identify activity-cost pools and activity-cost rates. Many companies then use ABC systems for planning and managing activities. They specify budgeted costs for activities and use budgeted cost rates to cost products using normal costing. At year-end, budgeted and actual costs are compared to provide feedback on how well activities were managed. Adjustments are also made for under- or overallocated indirect costs for each activity area using the methods described in Chapter 4 (adjusted allocation-rate approach, proration, or write-off to cost of goods sold).

ACTIVITY-BASED COSTING AND DEPARTMENT-COSTING SYSTEMS

OBJECTIVE 7

Compare ABC and department-costing systems

Companies often use costing systems that have features of ABC systems—such as multiple cost pools and multiple cost-allocation bases—but that do not emphasize individual activities. Many companies have evolved their costing systems from using a single indirect-cost rate system, to using separate indirect-cost rates for each department (for example, design, manufacturing, distribution, and so on) or subdepartment (e.g., machining and assembly departments within manufacturing). Why? Because the cost drivers of resources in each department or subdepartment differ from the single, companywide, cost-allocation base. ABC systems are a further refinement of department costing systems. In this section, we compare ABC systems and department costing systems.

Reconsider our Plastim illustration. The indirect-cost rate for the design activity is, in fact, a Design Department indirect-cost rate. Plastim calculates the design activity rate by dividing total Design Department costs by a measure of the

Growing Interest in Activity-Based Costing

Activity-based costing is being implemented by a growing number of companies around the globe. Specific ABC applications vary from organization to organization. A few organizations use ABC as their basic, ongoing cost accounting system. But many ABC applications are selective — special studies within subparts of the organization such as business divisions or particular functions.

One study[a] of 162 U.S.-based companies (including 29 service-sector implementations) reported the following ranking of the primary applications: (1) product/service costing, (2) cost reduction, and (3) process improvement. Areas where ABC-based information produced "significant" or "very significant" changes in decisions ranked as follows: (1) pricing strategy, (2) processes, and (3) product mix.

Among Canadian companies, one survey[b] indicates that 14% of the interviewed businesses have implemented ABC and another 15% are considering using it. What attracts Canadian firms to ABC?

More accurate cost information for product pricing	61%
More accurate profit analysis	61
By product	22
By customer	20
By process	24
By department	43
Improved performance measures	43
Improved insight into cost causation	37

The ABC system has replaced existing systems for 24% of the Canadian respondents, and it is a supplementary (off-line) system for 76 percent.

A United Kingdom survey[c] found that "just under 20% of 251 respondents had used ABC." The ranking of the application areas was (1) cost management, (2) performance measurement, (3) product/service pricing, and (4) cost modeling. A New Zealand survey[d] ranked the benefits of ABC as (1) cost management, (2) product/service pricing, and (3) inventory valuation.

A survey[e] of Irish companies that have implemented ABC reported the following percentages for the actual benefits experienced: (1) more accurate cost information for product costing and pricing (71%), (2) improved cost control and management (66%), (3) improved insight into cost causation (58%), (4) better performance measures (46%), and (5) more accurate customer profitability analysis (25%).

The Canadian survey reported the two most common implementation problems were difficulties in defining activities, and difficulties in selecting cost drivers. Implementation problems in the Irish survey include difficulties in identifying activities and assigning costs to those pools; difficulties in identifying and selecting cost drivers; inadequate computer software; and lack of adequate resources. The two top-ranked problems in the New Zealand survey were difficulties in obtaining reliable data, and lack of middle management acceptance.

---

[a]Adapted from APQC/CAM-I, "*Activity-Based Management*"

[b]Adapted from Armitage, H., and R. Nicholson, "Activity-Based Costing"

[c]Adapted from Innes, J., and F. Mitchell, "A Survey of Activity-Based Costing"

[d]Adapted from Cotton, W., "Activity Based Costing"

[e]Adapted from Clarke, P., "Management Accounting Practices"

Full citations are in Appendix A.

complexity of the mold (the driver of Design Department costs). Plastim does not find it worthwhile to calculate separate activity rates within the design department. Why? Because the complexity of the mold is an appropriate cost-allocation base for costs incurred for all design activities—the Design Department costs are homogeneous.

In contrast, in the Manufacturing (also in the Distribution) Department, Plastim identifies two activity-cost pools—a setup-cost pool and a manufacturing operations-cost pool—instead of using a single Manufacturing Department indirect-cost pool. Why? For two reasons. First, each of these activities within manufacturing incurs significant costs and has a different driver of costs. Second, the S3 and CL5 lenses do not use resources from these two activity areas in the same proportion. For example, CL5 uses 75% (1,500 ÷ 2,000) of the setup-hours but only 29.4% (3,750 ÷ 12,750) of the machine-hours. Using only machine-hours, say, to allocate all Manufacturing Department costs at Plastim would result in CL5 being undercosted because it would not be charged for the significant setup resources it actually uses.

The preceding discussion suggests the following: Using department indirect-cost rates to allocate costs to products results in the same product costs as activity-cost rates if (1) a single activity accounts for a sizable fraction of the department's costs, or (2) significant costs are incurred on different activities within a department but each activity has the same cost-allocation base, or (3) significant costs are incurred on different activities with different cost-allocation bases within a department but different products use resources from the different activity areas in the same proportions.

Where any one of these three conditions holds, using department indirect-cost rates rather than activity rates is often adequate. In companies where none of these conditions hold, department costing systems can be refined using ABC. Emphasizing activities leads to more focused and homogeneous cost pools, and aids in identifying activity-cost-allocation bases that have a better cause-and-effect relationship with the costs in activity-cost pools. But the benefits of an ABC system must be balanced against its costs and limitations.

IMPLEMENTING ABC SYSTEMS

Managers choose the level of detail in their costing systems by evaluating the costs of the system against the benefits that accrue from using these systems to make better decisions. There are "tell-tale" signs that indicate when ABC systems are likely to provide the most benefits. We list some signals here:

1. Significant amounts of indirect costs are allocated using only one or two cost pools.

2. All or most indirect costs are identified as output-unit-level costs (i.e., few indirect costs are described as batch-level, product-sustaining, or facility-sustaining costs).

3. Products make diverse demands on resources because of differences in volume, process steps, batch size, or complexity.

4. Products that a company is well suited to make and sell show small profits, whereas products that a company is less suited to produce and sell show large profits.

5. Complex products appear to be very profitable, and simple products appear to be losing money.

6. Operations staff have significant disagreements with the accounting staff about the costs of manufacturing and marketing products and services.

Even when a company decides to implement ABC, it must make important choices about the level of detail. Should it choose many finely specified activities, cost drivers, and cost pools, or would a few suffice? For example, Plastim could define a different molding machine-hour rate for each different type of molding machine. In making such choices, managers consider the costs and limitations of refining costing systems.

The main costs and limitations of ABC are the measurements necessary to implement the systems. ABC systems require management to estimate costs of activity pools and to identify and measure cost drivers for these pools to serve as cost-allocation bases. Even basic ABC systems require many calculations to determine costs of products and services. These measurements are costly. Activity-cost rates also need to be updated regularly. Very detailed ABC systems are costly to operate and difficult to understand.

In very detailed ABC systems, the allocations necessary to calculate activity costs often result in activity-cost pools being measured with error. At times, companies are also forced to use substitute allocation bases for which data are readily available rather than preferred allocation bases. For example, a company might be forced to use the number of loads moved, instead of the complexity and distance of different loads moved as the allocation base for material handling costs because the former is easier to measure. When measurement errors are large, activity-cost information can be misleading. For example, if the cost per load moved decreases, a company may conclude that it has become more efficient in its materials-handling operations. In fact, the lower cost per load moved may have resulted solely from moving lighter loads over shorter distances.

Managers always trade off the expected benefits of designing a more detailed and accurate ABC system against the expected measurement and implementation costs of the system. Improvements in information technology and accompanying declines in technology costs have enabled ABC to be a practical costing system in many organizations. As such trends continue, ABC systems should be better able to pass the cost-benefit test.

ACTIVITY-BASED COSTING IN SERVICE AND MERCHANDISING COMPANIES

Although many of the early examples of ABC originated in manufacturing, ABC has many applications in the service and merchandising areas. The Plastim example illustrates the application of ABC to a service function, design, and to a merchandising function, distribution. Companies such as the Cooperative Bank in the banking industry, BCTel in the telecommunication industry, Union Pacific in the railroad industry, and Braintree Hospital in the hospital industry, have implemented some form of ABC system to identify profitable product mixes, improve efficiency, and satisfy customers. Similarly, many retail and wholesale companies (for example, Flemings) have worked with ABC systems

The general approach to ABC in the service and merchandising areas is similar to the approach described in this chapter. Costs are divided into homogeneous cost pools and classified as output-unit-level, batch-level, product- or service-sustaining, and facility-sustaining costs. The cost pools correspond to key activities. Costs are allocated to products or customers using activity drivers or cost-allocation bases that have a cause-and-effect relationship with the costs in the cost pool. Service and merchandising sectors also have to confront the problems of measuring activity-cost pools and identifying and measuring allocation bases.

The Cooperative Bank in the United Kingdom followed this approach when it implemented ABC in its retail bank. It calculated the costs of various activities such as performing ATM transactions, opening and closing accounts, administering mortgages, and processing VISA transactions. It then used the activity-cost rates to calculate costs of various products, such as checking account, mortgage, and VISA card. ABC information helped Cooperative Bank to improve its processes and to identify profitable products and customer segments. The Concepts in Action Box presents another application of ABC in the banking industry. The Problem for Self-Study describes an application of ABC in the merchandising sector.

Curriculum Linkage As was pointed out in Chap. 1, the cost-benefit approach is an important criterion for choosing among alternative accounting systems (e.g., ABC versus traditional costing systems).

Example The Concepts in Action box provides an interesting illustration of the results of banks' implementation of ABC. Many students will be aware of (or will have experienced first-hand) banks' increasing charges for services that formerly were not explicitly charged (e.g., charging for face-to-face transactions with a teller, but not charging for ATM transactions). Banks implemented these charges after their new ABC systems revealed how much these services were costing. The ensuing uproar over these new charges has created considerable adverse publicity. Customers who have previously been subsidized are likely to complain (and perhaps take their business elsewhere) whenever they are charged higher rates to cover their consumption of resources as indicated by an ABC system. Customers who are charged higher prices to cover their consumption of resources are likely to consume less of that resource.

Banks End the "Free Lunch" for Many Services

For many years, retail banks provided their customers a wide range of "free" services. A customer who made a $100 minimum deposit received "free" checking, "free" inquiries about past checks written, "free" money orders, "free" drafts in foreign currencies, and so on. But as a famous economist (Milton Friedman) observed, "there is no such thing as a free lunch." What was occurring was cross-subsidization.

A major source of profitability in retail banks is the interest rate spread (the difference between the rate a bank lends or invests money and the rate it pays its depositors). Banks used this interest rate spread to cover the costs of the many "free" services it provided customers. Recently, banks have begun using activity-based costing (ABC) to determine the cost of their numerous individual services. ABC involves examining how each service (such as a checking account) uses the resources of the bank. These ABC studies found banks lose money on customers who hold small balances and make frequent use of the many "free" services. In contrast, customers who hold large balances and make limited use of the "free" services are highly profitable to banks. These customers cross-subsidize those with small balance accounts. This situation did not escape the attention of bank management.

Many banks have responded to increased competition by instituting a detailed set of charges. Consider the following charges by Wells Fargo Bank:

◆ Check deposits	$3 per deposit
◆ Foreign check deposits	$5 per deposit
◆ Special statement requests	$4 per request
◆ Check stop-payment request	$10 per request
◆ 24-hour customer service	
Person-to-person call	$1.50 per call
Automated call	$0.50 per call

These charges are based on an analysis of the activities underlying each service. For example, a customer-service request via a person-to-person call uses more resources than a request that is handled with an automated response. Hence, the person-to-person customer-service cost of $1.50 per call exceeds the $0.50 charge for an automated service call. Customers who hold accounts with large balances have these charges reduced or waived by Wells Fargo.

Not surprisingly, such bank charges have attracted much attention. Consumer advocacy groups typically express outrage. One group argues that the charge "will particularly disadvantage those groups who can least afford it—namely, older persons, kids, and the poor." In contrast, a management consultant calls it "a bold move. They are telling the public what the cost of their interactions will be."

Are there limitations on the extent to which banks are willing to charge for specific services? Yes, for example, ABC studies have documented the costs of having toll-free complaint "hot-lines." Because these calls are the result of quality problems, banks have not instituted (to date) a charge for using these hot-lines. Further, some banks waive customer-service call charges if it is determined that the bank failed to deliver on a promised set of commitments.

Source: Conversations with executives implementing ABC at several banks.

NEW AGE

"Cost Accounting is music to your ears!"

COST ACCOUNTING, *Tenth Edition*
Charles T. Horngren, George Foster, and Srikant M. Datar

New Age musicians don't simply follow the music . . . they create it. They are innovative, inventive, and imaginative and aren't afraid to take their audience up the scale to new heights. Just like New Age musicians, the composers of **Cost Accounting, 10th ed.**, are constantly developing original concepts to bring students to the next level in accounting. For example, with the implementation of activity-based costing (ABC), the authors have crafted their prior melody to blend with the new age of accounting. In other words, they don't simply follow the rules . . . they write them.

◆ Emphasizes the use of **activity-based costing (ABC)** for decision making and activity-based management in a single newly composed Chapter 5.

"I believe setting ABC apart and explaining it has been one of the best parts of the revision of the text. . . . I have found this chapter to be one of the best. The 'whys' are given at the beginning and are followed by an awareness of the role of accounting within the organization."
–Jean Hawkins,
William Jewell College

◆ Discusses **ABC in harmony with the simpler job-costing systems** covered in the previous chapter by using the same seven-step approach and showing how ABC modifies the implementation of these basic steps.

◆ Explains **product costing** using a single cost-pool system, a departmental costing system, and an ABC system.

"This chapter covers activity-based costing in a simple, well-organized, complete manner. . . . It should be especially valuable to nonaccounting majors searching for a simple yet comprehensive explanation of activity-based costing. . . . [The] real-life case study of Plastim, which unifies this chapter, is excellent."
–Russell Taussig,
University of Hawaii

PROBLEM

Family Supermarkets (FS) has decided to increase the size of its Memphis store. It wants information about the profitability of individual product lines: soft drinks, fresh produce, and packaged food.

FS provides the following data for the year 2000 for each product line:

	Soft Drinks	Fresh Produce	Packaged Food
Revenues	$317,400	$840,240	$483,960
Cost of goods sold	240,000	600,000	360,000
Cost of bottles returned	4,800	0	0
Number of purchase orders placed	144	336	144
Number of deliveries received	120	876	264
Hours of shelf-stocking time	216	2,160	1,080
Items sold	50,400	441,600	122,400

FS also provides the following information for the year 2000:

Activity (1)	Description of Activity (2)	Total Costs (3)	Cost-Allocation Base (4)
1. Bottle returns	Returning of empty bottles to store	$ 4,800	Direct tracing to soft-drink line
2. Ordering	Placing of orders for purchases	$ 62,400	624 purchase orders
3. Delivery	Physical delivery and receipt of merchandise	$100,800	1,260 deliveries
4. Shelf-stocking	Stocking of merchandise on store shelves and ongoing restocking	$ 69,120	3,456 hours of stocking time
5. Customer support	Assistance provided to customers, including check out and bagging	$122,880	614,400 items sold

Required

1. Family Supermarkets currently allocates store support costs (all costs other than cost of goods sold) to product lines on the basis of cost of goods sold of each product line. Calculate the operating income and operating income as a percentage of revenues for each product line.
2. If FS allocates store support costs (all costs other than cost of goods sold) to product lines using an ABC system, calculate the operating income and operating income as a percentage of revenues for each product line.
3. Comment on your answers in requirements 1 and 2.

SOLUTION

1. The following table shows the operating income and operating income as a percentage of revenues for each product line. All store support costs (all costs other than cost of goods sold) are allocated to product lines using cost of goods sold of each product line as the cost-allocation base. Total store support costs equal $360,000 (cost of bottles returned, $4,800 + cost of purchase orders, $62,400 + cost of deliveries, $100,800 + cost of shelf-stocking, $69,120 + cost of customer support, $122,880). When cost of goods sold is the cost-allocation base, the allocation rate for store support costs = $360,000 ÷ $1,200,000 = $0.30 per dollar of cost of goods sold. To allocate support costs to each product line, FS multiplies the cost of goods sold of each product line by 0.30.

	Soft Drinks	Fresh Produce	Packaged Food	Total
Revenues	$317,400	$840,240	$483,960	$1,641,600
Cost of goods sold	240,000	600,000	360,000	1,200,000
Store support cost ($240,000; $600,000; $360,000) × 0.30	72,000	180,000	108,000	72,000
Total costs	312,000	780,000	468,000	1,560,000
Operating income	$ 5,400	$ 60,240	$ 15,960	$ 81,600
Operating income ÷ Revenues	1.70%	7.17%	3.30%	4.97%

2. Under an ABC system, FS identifies bottle return costs as a direct cost because these costs can be traced easily to the soft-drink product line. FS then calculates cost-allocation rates for each activity area (as in step 5 described in the chapter, p. 146). The activity rates are as follows:

Activity (1)	Cost Hierarchy (2)	Total Costs (3)	Quantity of Cost-Allocation Base (4)	Overhead Allocation Rate (5) = (3) ÷ (4)
Ordering	Batch-level	$ 62,400	624 purchase orders	$100 per purchase order
Delivery	Batch-level	$100,800	1,260 deliveries	$80 per delivery
Shelf-stocking	Output-unit-level	$ 69,120	3,456 stocking-hours	$20 per stocking-hour
Customer support	Output-unit-level	$122,880	614,400 items sold	$0.20 per item sold

Store support costs for each product line by activity are obtained by multiplying the total quantity of the cost-allocation base for each product line by the activity-cost rate. Operating income and operating income as a percentage of revenues for each product line are as follows:

	Soft Drinks	Fresh Produce	Packaged Food	Total
Revenues	$317,400	$840,240	$483,960	$1,641,600
Cost of goods sold	240,000	600,000	360,000	1,200,000
Bottle return costs	4,800	0	0	4,800
Ordering costs (144; 336; 144) purchase orders × $100	14,400	33,600	14,400	62,400
Delivery costs (120; 876; 264) deliveries × $80	9,600	70,080	21,120	100,800
Shelf-stocking costs (216; 2,160; 1,080) stocking-hours × $20	4,320	43,200	21,600	69,120
Customer support costs (50,400; 441,600; 122,400) items sold × $0.20	10,080	88,320	24,480	122,880
Total costs	283,200	835,200	441,600	1,560,000
Operating income	$ 34,200	$ 5,040	$ 42,360	$ 81,600
Operating income ÷ Revenues	10.77%	0.60%	8.75%	4.97%

3. Managers believe the ABC system is more credible than the previous costing system. The ABC system distinguishes the different types of activities at FS more precisely. It also tracks more accurately how individual product lines use resources. Rankings of relative profitability (the percentage of operating income to revenues) of the three product lines under the previous costing system and under the ABC system are as follows:

Previous Costing System		ABC System	
1. Fresh produce	7.17%	1. Soft drinks	10.77%
2. Packaged food	3.30%	2. Packaged food	8.75%
3. Soft drinks	1.70%	3. Fresh produce	0.60%

The percentage of revenues, cost of goods sold, and activity costs for each product line are as follows:

	Soft Drinks	Fresh Produce	Packaged Food
Revenues	19.34%	51.18%	29.48%
Cost of goods sold	20.00	50.00	30.00
Activity Areas:			
Ordering	23.08	53.84	23.08
Delivery	9.53	69.52	20.95
Shelf-stocking	6.25	62.50	31.25
Customer support	8.20	71.88	19.92
Bottle returns	100.00	0	0

Soft drinks consume fewer resources than either fresh produce or packaged food. Soft drinks have fewer deliveries and require less shelf-stocking than either fresh produce or packaged food. Most major soft-drink suppliers deliver merchandise to the store shelves and stock the shelves themselves. In contrast, the fresh produce area has the most deliveries and consumes a large percentage of shelf-stocking time. It also has the highest number of individual sales items. The previous costing system assumed that each product line used the resources in each activity area in the same ratio as their respective individual cost of goods sold to total cost of goods sold. Clearly, this assumption is inappropriate. The previous costing system is a classic example of broad averaging via cost smoothing.

FS managers can use the ABC information to guide decisions such as how to allocate a planned increase in floor space. An increase in the percentage of space allocated to soft drinks is warranted. Note, however, that ABC information should be but one input into decisions about shelf space allocation. FS may have minimum limits on the shelf space allocated to fresh produce because of shoppers' expectations that supermarkets will carry merchandise from this product line. In many situations, companies cannot make product decisions in isolation, but rather must consider the effect that dropping a product might have on customer demand for other products.

Pricing decisions can also be made in a more informed way with the ABC information. For example, suppose a competitor announces a 5% reduction in soft-drink prices. Given the 10.77% margin FS currently earns on its soft-drink product line, it can reduce prices and still make a profit on this product line. In contrast, the previous costing system erroneously implied that soft drinks only had a 1.70% margin, leaving little room to counter a competitor's pricing initiatives.

SUMMARY

The following points are linked to the chapter's learning objectives:

1. Product undercosting (or overcosting) occurs when a product or service consumes a relatively high (low) level of resource, but is reported to have a relatively low (high) cost. Cost smoothing or peanut-butter costing, a common cause of under- or overcosting, is the result of using broad averages that uniformly assign (spread) the cost of resources to products when the individual products use those resources in a nonuniform way. Product-cost cross-subsidization exists when one undercosted (overcosted) product results in at least one other product being overcosted (undercosted).

2. Refining a costing system means making changes that result in cost numbers that better measure the way cost objects (such as products) differentially use the resources of the organization. These changes can require additional direct-cost tracing, the choice of more indirect-cost pools, or the use of different cost-allocation bases.

3. An activity-based costing (ABC) approach differs from the traditional approach by its fundamental focus on activities. An ABC approach typically results in (a) more indirect-cost pools than the traditional approach, (b) more cost drivers used as cost-allocation bases that are not output unit-level cost drivers, and (c) more frequent use of nonfinancial variables as cost-allocation bases.

4. A cost hierarchy categorizes costs into different cost pools on the basis of the different types of cost-allocation bases or different degrees of difficulty in determining cause-and-effect (or benefits-received) relationships. A four-part cost hierarchy consists of output unit-level costs, batch-level costs, product-sustaining or service-sustaining costs, and facility-sustaining costs.

5. In ABC, costs of activities are used to assign costs to other cost objects such as products or services.

6. Activity-based management (ABM) describes management decisions that use ABC information to satisfy customers and improve profits. ABC systems are used for such management decisions as pricing, product-mix, cost reduction, process improvement, product and process redesign, and planning and managing activities.

7. Department costing systems approximate ABC systems only when each department has a single activity, or a single cost-allocation base for different activities, or when different products use the activities of the department in the same proportions.

8. ABC systems are likely to yield the most benefits when indirect costs are large or products and services make diverse demands on indirect resources. The main costs are the measurements necessary to implement and update the system.

▼ TERMS TO LEARN

This chapter and the Glossary at the end of this book contain definitions of the following important terms:

activity (p. 140)	peanut-butter costing (136)
activity-based costing (ABC) (140)	product-cost cross-subsidization (136)
activity-based management (ABM) (148)	product overcosting (136)
batch-level costs (143)	product-sustaining costs (143)
cost hierarchy (142)	product undercosting (136)
cost smoothing (136)	refined costing system (140)
facility-sustaining costs (143)	service-sustaining costs (143)
output unit-level costs (143)	

▼ ASSIGNMENT MATERIAL

QUESTIONS

5-1 Define cost smoothing, and explain how managers can determine whether it occurs with their costing system.

5-2 Why should managers worry about product over- or undercosting?

5-3 What is costing system refinement? Describe three guidelines for refinement.

5-4 What is an activity-based approach to designing a costing system?

5-5 Describe four levels of a cost hierarchy.

5-6 "The existence of costs other than output unit-level costs means that managers should not compute unit product costs based on total manufacturing costs in all levels of the cost hierarchy." Do you agree? Explain.

5-7 What are the key reasons for product cost differences between traditional costing systems and ABC systems?

5-8 Describe four decisions for which ABC information is useful.

5-9 "Department indirect-cost rates are never activity-cost rates." Do you agree? Explain.

5-10 Describe four signs that help indicate when ABC systems are likely to provide the most benefits.

5-11 What are the main costs and limitations of implementing ABC systems?

5-12 "ABC systems only apply to manufacturing companies." Do you agree? Explain.

5-13 "Activity-based costing is the wave of the present and the future. All companies should adopt it." Do you agree? Explain.

5-14 "Increasing the number of indirect-cost pools is guaranteed to sizably increase the accuracy of product or service costs." Do you agree? Why?

5-15 The controller of a retail company has just had a $50,000 request to implement an ABC system quickly turned down. A senior vice president in rejecting the request noted, "Given a choice, I will always prefer a $50,000 investment in improving things a customer sees or experiences, such as our shelves or our store layout. How does a customer benefit by our spending $50,000 on a supposedly better accounting system?" How should the controller respond?

EXERCISES

5-16 Cost smoothing or peanut-butter costing, cross-subsidization. For many years, five former classmates—Steve Armstrong, Lola Gonzales, Rex King, Elizabeth Poffo, and Gary Young—have had a reunion dinner at the annual meeting of the American Accounting Association. The details of the bill for the most recent dinner at the Seattle Space Needle Restaurant breaks down as follows:

Diner	Entree	Dessert	Drinks	Total
Armstrong	$27	$8	$24	$59
Gonzales	24	3	0	27
King	21	6	13	40
Poffo	31	6	12	49
Young	15	4	6	25

For at least the last ten dinners, King put the total restaurant bill on his American Express card. He then mailed the other four a bill for the average cost. They shared the gratuity at the restaurant by paying cash. King continued this practice for the Seattle dinner. However, just before he sent the bill to the other diners, Young phoned him to complain. He was livid at Poffo for ordering the steak and lobster entree ("She always does that!") and at Armstrong for having three glasses of imported champagne ("What's wrong with domestic beer?").

Required

1. Why is the average-cost approach in the context of the reunion dinner an example of cost smoothing or peanut-butter costing?

2. Compute the average cost to each of the five diners. Who is undercharged and who is overcharged under the average-cost approach? Is Young's complaint justified?

3. Give an example of a dining situation where King would find it more difficult to compute the amount of under- or overcosting. How might the behavior of the diners be affected if each person paid his or her own bill instead of continuing with the average-cost approach?

5-17 Cost hierarchy. Telecom, Inc., manufactures boom boxes (music systems with radio, cassette, and compact disc players) for different well-known companies. The boom boxes differ significantly in their complexity and their manufacturing batch sizes. The following costs were incurred in 1999.

a. Designing processes, drawing process charts, making engineering process changes for products, $800,000.

b. Procurement costs of placing purchase orders, receiving materials, and paying suppliers related to the number of purchase orders placed, $500,000.

c. Direct materials costs, $6,000,000.

d. Costs incurred to set up machines each time a different product needs to be manufactured, $600,000.

e. Direct manufacturing labor costs, $1,000,000.

f. Machine-related overhead costs such as depreciation, maintenance, production engineering, $1,100,000. These resources relate to the activity of running the machines.

g. Plant management, plant rent, and insurance, $900,000.

Required

1. Classify each of the preceding costs as output unit-level, batch-level, product-sustaining, or facility-sustaining. Explain each answer.

2. Consider two types of boom boxes made by Telecom, Inc. One boom box is complex to make and is made in many batches. The other boom box is simple to make and is made in few batches. Suppose that Telecom needs the same number of machine-hours to make each type of boom box and that Telecom allocates all overhead costs using machine-hours as the only allocation base. How, if at all, would the boom boxes be miscosted? Briefly explain why.

3. How is the cost hierarchy helpful to Telecom in managing its business?

5-18 Cost hierarchy, ABC, distribution. (W. Bruns, adapted) Sonoma Winery makes two wines—a regular wine and a specialty wine. Recently, Sonoma has shown small profits on its regular wine and large profits on its specialty wine. As a result, management is considering getting out of the regular wine business and concentrating on specialty wine. This decision is difficult because Sonoma has in the past been very profitable in regular wines, its original business. In fact, the profitability of regular wine dipped substantially only after Sonoma got into the specialty wine business. Before making a decision, Sonoma wants to be sure that it understands what it costs to make and sell the regular and specialty wines. This question focuses on costs in the distribution area.

Sonoma distributes the regular wine and the specialty wine through completely different distribution channels. It distributes 120,000 cases of regular wine through 10 general distributors and 80,000 cases of the specialty wine through 30 specialty distributors. Sonoma incurs $2,130,000 in distribution costs. Under its existing costing system, Sonoma allocates distribution costs to products on the basis of cases shipped.

To understand better the demands on its resources in the distribution area, Sonoma identifies three activities and related activity costs:

1. Promotional activity, including advertising, antique neon signs, and point-of-sales material at each distributor. Sonoma estimates it incurs $8,000 per distributor.

2. Order handling costs, including costs to confirm and input the order into the order-entry system, set aside the correct number of cases, organize shipment and delivery, verify order packing, ensure delivery, send invoices, and follow-up for payments. Sonoma estimates costs of $300 for performing all the activities pertaining to each order. Sonoma's records show that distributors of regular wine place an average of 10 orders per year while distributors of specialty wine place an average of 20 orders per year.

3. Distribution costs, $8 per case for freight.

Required

1. Using Sonoma's existing costing system, calculate the total distribution costs and distribution cost per case for the regular wine and the specialty wine.

2. a. For each activity, classify the cost of the activity as an output unit-level, batch-level, product- (or service-) sustaining, or facility-sustaining cost. Explain each answer.

   b. Using Sonoma's activity-based costing system, calculate the total distribution costs and distribution cost per case for the regular wine and the specialty wine.

3. Explain the cost differences and the accuracy of the product costs calculated using the existing costing system and the ABC system. How might Sonoma's management use the information from the ABC system to manage its business better?

5-19 ABC, cost hierarchy, service. (CMA, adapted) Plymouth Test Laboratories does heat testing (HT) and stress testing (ST) on materials. Under its current costing system, Plymouth aggregates all operating costs of $1,200,000 into a single overhead cost pool. Plymouth calculates a rate per test-hour of $15 ($1,200,000 ÷ 80,000 total test-hours). HT uses 50,000 test-hours and ST uses 30,000 test-hours. Gary Celeste, Plymouth's controller believes that there is enough variation in test procedures and cost structures to establish separate costing and billing rates for HT and ST. The market for test services is becoming competitive. Without this information, any miscosting and mispricing could cause Plymouth to lose business. Celeste divides Plymouth's costs into four activity-cost categories.

1. Direct-labor costs, $240,000. These costs can be directly traced to HT, $180,000 and ST, $60,000.

2. Equipment-related costs (rent, maintenance, energy, and so on), $400,000. These costs are allocated to HT and ST on the basis of test-hours.

3. Setup costs, $350,000. These costs are allocated to HT and ST on the basis of the number of setup-hours required. HT requires 13,500 setup-hours and ST requires 4,000 setup-hours.

4. Costs of designing tests, $210,000. These costs are allocated to HT and ST on the basis of the time required to design the tests. HT requires 2,800 hours and ST requires 1,400 hours.

Required

1. Classify each activity cost as output unit-level, batch-level, product- or service-sustaining, or facility-sustaining. Explain each answer.

2. Calculate the cost per test-hour for HT and ST. Explain briefly the reasons why these numbers differ from the $15 per test-hour that Plymouth calculated using its existing costing system.

3. Explain the accuracy of the product costs calculated using the existing costing system and the ABC system. How might Plymouth's management use the cost hierarchy and ABC information to manage its business better?

5-20 Alternative allocation bases for a professional services firm. The Wolfson Group (WG) provides tax advice to multinational firms. WG charges clients for (a) direct professional time (at an hourly rate), and (b) support services (at 30% of the direct professional costs billed). The three professionals in WG and their rates per professional hour are:

Professional	Billing Rate per Hour
Myron Wolfson	$500
Ann Brown	120
John Anderson	80

WG has just prepared the May 1999 bills for two clients. The hours of professional time spent on each client are as follows:

	Hours per Client	
Professional	Seattle Dominion	Tokyo Enterprises
Wolfson	15	2
Brown	3	8
Anderson	22	30
Total	40	40

Required

1. What amounts did WG bill to Seattle Dominion and Tokyo Enterprises for May 1999?

2. Suppose support services were billed at $50 per professional labor-hour (instead of 30% of professional labor costs). How would this change affect the amounts WG billed to the two clients for May 1999? Comment on the differences between the amounts billed in requirements 1 and 2.

3. How would you determine whether professional labor costs or professional labor-hours is the more appropriate allocation base for WG's support services?

5-21 Plantwide indirect-cost rates. Automotive Products (AP) designs, manufactures, and sells automotive parts. It has three main operating departments: design, engineering, and production.

◆ *Design*—the design of parts, using state of the art, computer-aided design (CAD) equipment

◆ *Engineering*—the prototyping of parts and testing of their specifications

◆ *Production*—the manufacture of parts

For many years, AP had long-term contracts with major automobile assembly companies. These contracts had large production runs. AP's costing system allocates variable manufacturing overhead on the basis of machine-hours. Actual variable manufacturing overhead costs for 2001 were $308,600. AP had three contracts in 2001, and its machine-hours used in 2001 were assigned as follows:

United Motors	120
Holden Motors	2,800
Leland Vehicle	1,080
Total	4,000

Required
1. Compute the plantwide variable manufacturing overhead rate for 2001.
2. Compute the variable manufacturing overhead allocated to each contract in 2001.
3. What conditions must hold for machine-hours to provide an accurate estimate of the variable manufacturing overhead incurred on each individual contract at AP in 2001?

5-22 Department indirect-cost rates as activity rates (continuation of 5-21). The controller of Automotive Parts (AP) decides to interview key managers of the Design, Engineering, and Production Departments. Each manager is to indicate the consensus choice among department personnel as to the cost driver of variable manufacturing overhead costs at his or her department. Summary data are:

	Variable Manufacturing Overhead in 2001	Cost Driver
Design	$ 39,000	CAD design-hours
Engineering	29,600	Engineering-hours
Production	240,000	Machine-hours
	$308,600	

Details pertaining to usage of these cost drivers for each of the three 2001 contracts are:

Activity Area	Cost Driver	United Motors	Holden Motors	Leland Vehicle
Design	CAD design-hours	110	200	80
Engineering	Engineering-hours	70	60	240
Production	Machine-hours	120	2,800	1,080

Required
1. What is the variable manufacturing overhead rate for each department in 2001?
2. What is the variable manufacturing overhead allocated to each contract in 2001 using department variable manufacturing overhead rates?
3. Compare your answer in requirement 2 to that in requirement 2 of Exercise 5-21. Comment on the results.

5-23 ABC, retail product-line profitability. Family Supermarkets (FS) decides to apply ABC analysis to three product lines—baked goods, milk and fruit juice, and frozen foods. It identifies four activities and activity-cost rates for each activity as follows:

Ordering	$100 per purchase order
Delivery and receipt of merchandise	$80 per delivery
Shelf-stocking	$20 per hour
Customer support and assistance	$0.20 per item sold

The revenues, cost of goods sold, store support costs, and activity area usage of the three product lines are as follows:

	Baked Goods	Milk and Fruit Juice	Frozen Products
Financial data			
Revenues	$57,000	$63,000	$52,000
Cost of goods sold	38,000	47,000	35,000
Store support	11,400	14,100	10,500
Activity area usage (cost-allocation base)			
Ordering (purchase orders)	30	25	13
Delivery (deliveries)	98	36	28
Shelf-stocking (hours)	183	166	24
Customer support (items sold)	15,500	20,500	7,900

Under its previous costing system, FS allocated support costs to products at the rate of 30% of cost of goods sold.

Required
1. Use the previous costing system to prepare a product-line profitability report for FS.
2. Use the ABC system to prepare a product-line profitability report for FS.
3. What new insights does the ABC system in requirement 2 provide to FS managers?

5-24 ABC, product-costing at banks, cross-subsidization. First International Bank (FIB) is examining the profitability of its Premier Account, a combined savings and checking account. Depositors receive a 7% annual interest rate on their average deposit. FIB earns an interest rate spread of 3% (the difference between the rate at which it lends money and the rate it pays depositors) by lending money for residential home loan purposes at 10 percent. Thus, FIB would gain $60 on the interest spread if a depositor has an average Premier Account balance of $2,000 in 1999 ($2,000 × 3% = $60).

The Premier Account allows depositors unlimited use of services such as deposits, withdrawals, checking account, and foreign currency drafts. Depositors with Premier Account balances of $1,000 or more receive unlimited free use of services. Depositors with minimum balances of less than $1,000 pay $20 a month service fee for their Premier Account.

FIB recently conducted an activity-based costing study of its services. It assessed the following costs for six individual services. The use of these services in 1999 by three customers is as follows:

	ABC-Based Cost per "Transaction"	Account Usage		
		Robinson	Skerrett	Farrel
Deposit/withdrawal with teller	$2.50	40	50	5
Deposit/withdrawal with automatic teller machine (ATM)	0.80	10	20	16
Deposit/withdrawal on prearranged monthly basis	0.50	0	12	60
Bank checks written	8.00	9	3	2
Foreign currency drafts	12.00	4	1	6
Inquiries about account balance	1.50	10	18	9
Average Premier Account balance for 1999		$1,100	$800	$25,000

Assume Robinson and Farrel always maintain a balance above $1,000 while Skerrett always has a balance below $1,000 in 1999.

Required
1. Compute the 1999 profitability of the Robinson, Skerrett, and Farrel Premier Accounts at FIB.
2. What evidence is there of cross-subsidization among the three Premier Accounts? Why might FIB worry about this cross-subsidization if the Premier Account product offering is profitable as a whole?
3. What changes would you recommend for FIB's Premier Account?

5-25 ABC, activity area cost-driver rates. Idaho Potatoes (IP) processes potatoes into potato cuts at its highly automated Pocatello plant. It sells potatoes to the retail consumer market and, more recently, to the institutional market, which includes hospitals, cafeterias, and university dormitories.

IP's existing costing system has a single direct-cost category (direct materials, which are the raw potatoes) and a single indirect-cost pool (production support). Support costs are allocated on the basis of pounds of potato cuts processed. Support costs include packaging materials. The 1999 total actual costs for producing 1,000,000 pounds of potato cuts (900,000 for the retail market and 100,000 for the institutional market) are:

Direct materials used	$150,000
Production support	$983,000

The existing costing system does not distinguish between potato cuts produced for the retail or the institutional markets.

At the end of 1999, IP unsuccessfully bid for a large institutional contract. Its bid was reported to be 30% above the winning bid. This feedback came as a shock because IP included only a minimum profit margin on its bid. Moreover, the Pocatello plant was widely acknowledged as the most efficient in the industry.

As a result of its review process of the lost contract bid, IP decided to explore ways to refine its costing system. First, it identified that $188,000 of the $983,000 pertain to packaging materials that could be traced to individual jobs ($180,000 for retail and $8,000 for institutional). These costs will now be classified as direct material. The $150,000 of direct materials used were classified as $135,000 for retail and $15,000 for institutional. Second, it used activity-based costing (ABC) to examine how the two products (retail potato cuts and institutional potato cuts) used indirect support resources. The finding was that three activity areas could be distinguished and that different usage occurred in two of these three areas.

- *Cleaning Activity Area*—IP uses 1,200,000 pounds of raw potatoes to yield 1,000,000 pounds of potato cuts. No distinction is made as to the end product when cleaning potatoes. The cost-allocation base is pounds of raw potatoes cleaned. Costs in the cleaning activity area are $120,000.

- *Cutting Activity Area*—IP processes raw potatoes for the retail market independently of those processed for the institutional market. The production line produces (a) 250 pounds of retail potato cuts per cutting-hour, and (b) 400 pounds of institutional potato cuts per cutting-hour. The cost-allocation base is cutting-hours on the production line. Costs in the cutting activity area are $231,000.

- *Packaging Activity Area*—IP packages potato cuts for the retail market independently of those packaged for the institutional market. The packaging line packages (a) 25 pounds of retail potato cuts per packaging-hour, and (b) 100 pounds of institutional potato cuts per packaging-hour. The cost-allocation base is packaging-hours on the production line. Costs in the packaging activity area are $444,000.

Required
1. What is the cost rate per unit of the cost-allocation base in the (a) cleaning, (b) cutting, and (c) packaging activity areas?
2. Present an overview diagram of the ABC system at Idaho Potatoes.
3. How might IP use information about the activity rates computed in requirement 1 to better manage the Pocatello plant?

5-26 ABC, product-cost cross-subsidization (continuation of 5-25). Suppose Idaho Potatoes (IP) uses information from its activity-cost rates to calculate costs incurred on retail market potato cuts and institutional market potato cuts.
Required
1. Using the existing costing system, what is the cost per pound of potato cuts produced by IP?
2. Using the ABC system, what is the cost per pound of (a) retail market potato cuts, and (b) institutional market potato cuts?
3. Comment on the cost differences between the two costing systems in requirements 1 and 2. How might IP use the information in requirement 2 to make better decisions?

5-27 Activity-based job-costing system. The Denver Company manufactures and sells packaging machines. It recently used an activity-based approach to refine the job-costing system at its Colorado plant. The resulting job-costing system has one direct-cost category (direct materials) and four indirect manufacturing cost pools. These four indirect-cost pools and their allocation bases were chosen by a team of product designers, manufacturing personnel, and marketing personnel:

Indirect Manufacturing Cost Pool	Cost-Allocation Base	Budgeted Cost-Allocation Rate
1. Material handling	Component parts	$8 per part
2. Machining	Machine-hours	$68 per hour
3. Assembly	Assembly-hours	$75 per hour
4. Inspection	Inspection-hours	$104 per hour

Cola Supreme recently purchased 50 can-packaging machines from the Denver Company. Each machine has direct materials costs of $3,000, requires 50 component parts, 12 machine-hours, 15 assembly-hours, and 4 inspection-hours.

Denver's previous costing system had one direct-cost category (direct materials) and one indirect-cost category (manufacturing overhead, allocated at the rate of $100 per assembly-hour).

Required

1. **a.** Present overview diagrams of the previous job-costing system and the refined activity-based job-costing system.

   b. Compute the manufacturing cost of each machine and the total manufacturing cost of the Cola Supreme job using the previous system and the ABC system.

2. Denver's activity-based job-costing system has only one manufacturing direct-cost category—direct materials. A competitor of Denver Company has two direct-cost categories at its manufacturing plant—direct materials and direct manufacturing labor. Why might Denver not have a direct manufacturing labor costs category in its job-costing system? Where are the manufacturing labor costs included in the Denver costing system?

3. Explain briefly the cost differences and the accuracy of the job costs calculated using the previous system and the ABC system. What information might members of the team that refined the previous costing system find useful in the activity-based job-costing system?

5-28 Activity-based costing, job-costing system. The Hewlett-Packard (HP) plant in Roseville, California, assembles and tests printed-circuit (PC) boards. The job-costing system at this plant has two direct-cost categories (direct materials and direct manufacturing labor) and seven indirect-cost pools. These indirect-cost pools represent the seven activity areas that operating personnel at the plant determined are sufficiently different (in terms of cost-behavior patterns or in terms of individual products being assembled) to warrant separate cost pools. The cost-allocation base chosen for each activity area is the cost driver at that activity area.

Debbie Berlant, a newly appointed marketing manager at HP, is attending a training session that describes how an activity-based costing approach was used to design the Roseville plant's job-costing system. Berlant is provided with the following incomplete information for a specific job (an order for a single PC board, No. A82):

Direct materials	$75.00	
Direct manufacturing labor	15.00	$90.00
Manufacturing overhead (see below)		?
Total manufacturing cost		$?

Manufacturing Overhead Cost Pool	Cost-Allocation Base	Cost-Allocation Rate	Units of Cost-Allocation Base Used on Job No. A82	Manufacturing Overhead Allocated to Job
1. Axial insertion	Axial insertions	$ 0.08	45	?
2. Dip insertion	Dip insertions	0.25	?	$6.00
3. Manual insertion	Manual insertions	?	11	5.50
4. Wave solder	Boards soldered	3.50	?	3.50
5. Backload	Backload insertions	?	6	4.20
6. Test	Budgeted time board is in test activity	90.00	0.25	?
7. Defect analysis	Budgeted time for defect analysis and repair	?	0.10	8.00

Required

1. Present an overview diagram of the activity-based job-costing system at the Roseville plant.
2. Fill in the blanks (noted by question marks) in the cost information provided to Berlant for Job No. A82.
3. Why might manufacturing managers and marketing managers favor this ABC job-costing system over the previous costing system, which had the same two direct-cost categories but only a single indirect-cost pool (manufacturing overhead allocated using direct manufacturing labor costs)?

PROBLEMS

5-29 Job costing with single direct-cost category, single indirect-cost pool, law firm. Wigan Associates is a recently formed law partnership. Ellery Hanley, the managing partner of Wigan Associates, has just finished a tense phone call with Martin Offiah, president of Widnes Coal. Offiah complained about the price Wigan charged for some conveyancing (drawing up property documents) legal work done for Widnes Coal. He requested a break-down of the charges. He also indicated to Hanley that a competing law firm, Hull & Kingston, is seeking more business with Widnes Coal and that he is going to ask them to submit a bid for a conveyancing job next month. Finally, Offiah noted that if Wigan bids next month's price similar to the one charged last month, Wigan will not get the job.

Hanley is dismayed. He is also puzzled because he believes that conveyancing is an area where Wigan Associates has much expertise and is highly efficient. The Widnes Coal phone call is the bad news of the week. The good news is that yesterday Hanley received a phone call from its only other client (St. Helen's Glass) saying it was very pleased with both the quality of the work (primarily litigation) and the price charged on its most recent job.

Hanley decides to collect data on the Widnes Coal and St. Helen's Glass jobs. Wigan Associates uses a cost-based approach to pricing (billing) each job. Currently it uses a single direct-cost category (for professional labor time) and a single indirect-cost pool (general support). Indirect costs are allocated to cases on the basis of professional labor-hours per case. The job files show the following:

	Widnes Coal	St. Helens Glass
Professional labor time	104 hours	96 hours

Professional labor costs at Wigan Associates are $70 an hour. Indirect costs are allocated to cases at $105 an hour. Total indirect costs in the most recent period were $21,000.

Required

1. Why is it important for Wigan Associates to understand the costs associated with individual jobs?
2. Present an overview diagram of the existing job-costing system.
3. Compute the costs of the Widnes Coal and St. Helen's Glass jobs using Wigan's existing job-costing system.

5-30 Job costing with multiple direct-cost categories, single indirect-cost pool, law firm (continuation of 5-29). Hanley speaks to the other partners about the pricing of the two jobs. Several partners believe that the relative prices charged seem out of line with their intuition. One partner observes that a useful approach to obtaining more accurate job costs is to increase direct-cost tracing.

Hanley asks his assistant to collect details on those costs included in the $21,000 indirect-cost pool that can be traced to each individual job. After further analysis, Wigan is able to reclassify $14,000 of the $21,000 as direct costs:

Other Direct Costs	Widnes Coal	St. Helens Glass
Research support labor	$1,600	$ 3,400
Computer time	500	1,300
Travel and allowances	600	4,400
Telephones/faxes	200	1,000
Photocopying	250	750
Total	$3,150	$10,850

Hanley decides to calculate the costs of each job had Wigan used six direct-cost pools and a single indirect-cost pool. The single indirect-cost pool would have $7,000 of costs and would be allocated to each case using the professional labor-hours base.

Required
1. Present an overview diagram of the refined costing system with multiple direct-cost categories and one indirect-cost pool.
2. What is the revised indirect-cost allocation rate per professional labor-hour for Wigan Associates when total indirect costs are $7,000?
3. Compute the costs of the Widnes and St. Helen's jobs if Wigan Associates had used its refined costing system with multiple direct-cost categories and one indirect-cost pool.
4. Compare the costs of the Widnes and St. Helen's jobs in requirement 3 with those in requirement 3 of Problem 5-29. Comment on the results.

5-31 Job costing with multiple direct-cost categories, multiple indirect-cost pools, law firm (continuation of 5-29 and 5-30). Hanley examines the job-costing approaches in Problems 5-29 and 5-30. He questions the use of a single direct-cost rate and a single indirect-cost rate for all professional labor of Wigan Associates. Wigan has two classifications of professional staff—partners and associates. Hanley asks his assistant to examine the relative use of partners and associates on the recent Widnes Coal and St. Helen's jobs. The Widnes job used 24 partner-hours and 80 associate-hours. The St. Helen's job used 56 partner-hours and 40 associate-hours.

Hanley decides to examine how using separate direct-cost rates for partners and associates and using separate indirect-cost pools for partners and associates would have affected the costs of the Widnes and St. Helen's jobs. Indirect costs in each indirect-cost pool would be allocated on the basis of total hours of that category of professional labor.

The rates per category of professional labor are as follows:

Category of Professional Labor	Direct Cost per Hour	Indirect Cost per Hour
Partner	$100.00	$57.50
Associate	50.00	20.00

The indirect-cost rates are based on a total indirect-cost pool of $7,000; $4,600 of this $7,000 is attributable to the activities of partners, and $2,400 is attributable to the activities of associates. (The indirect cost per hour of $57.50 is calculated by dividing $4,600 by 80 partner-hours; the indirect-cost rate of $20 is calculated by dividing $2,400 by 120 associate-hours.)

Required
1. Present an overview diagram of the refined job-costing system with its multiple direct-cost categories and its multiple indirect-cost pools.
2. Compute the costs of the Widnes and St. Helen's cases with Wigan's further refined system, with multiple direct-cost categories and multiple indirect-cost pools.
3. For what decisions might Wigan Associates find it more useful to use this job-costing approach rather than the approaches in Problems 5-29 or 5-30?

5-32 Activity-based costing, merchandising. Figure Four, Inc., specializes in the distribution of pharmaceutical products. Figure Four buys from pharmaceutical companies and re-sells to each of three different markets:

a. General supermarket chains

b. Drugstore chains

c. Ma and Pa single-store pharmacies

Rick Flair, the new controller of Figure Four, reported the following data for August 1999:

	General Supermarket Chains	Drugstore Chains	Ma and Pa Single Stores
Average revenue per delivery	$30,900	$10,500	$1,980
Average cost of goods sold per delivery	$30,000	$10,000	$1,800
Number of deliveries	120	300	1,000

For many years, Figure Four has used gross margin percentage [(Revenue − Cost of goods sold) ÷ Revenue] to evaluate the relative profitability of its customer groups (distribution outlets).

Flair recently attended a seminar on activity-based costing and decides to consider using it at Figure Four. Flair meets with all the key managers and many staff members. Generally, these individuals agree that there are five key activity areas at Figure Four:

Activity Area	Cost Driver
1. Customer purchase order processing	Purchase orders by customers
2. Line-item ordering	Line items per purchase order
3. Store delivery	Store deliveries
4. Cartons shipped to stores	Cartons shipped
5. Shelf-stocking at customer store	Hours of shelf-stocking

Each customer purchase order consists of one or more line items. A line item represents a single product (such as Extra-Strength Tylenol Tablets). Each store delivery entails the delivery of one or more cartons of products to a customer. Each product is delivered in one or more separate cartons. Figure Four staff stack cartons directly onto display shelves in a store. Currently, there is no charge for this service, and not all customers use Figure Four for this activity.

The August 1999 operating costs (other than cost of goods sold) of Figure Four are $301,080. These operating costs are assigned to the five activity areas. The costs in each area and the quantity of the cost-allocation base used in that area for August 1999 are as follows:

Activity Area	Total Costs in August 1999	Total Units of Cost-Allocation Base Used in August 1999
1. Customer purchase order processing	$ 80,000	2,000 orders
2. Line-item ordering	63,840	21,280 line items
3. Store deliveries	71,000	1,420 store deliveries
4. Cartons shipped to stores	76,000	76,000 cartons
5. Shelf-stocking at customer stores	10,240	640 hours
	$301,080	

Other data for August 1999 include the following:

	General Supermarket Chains	Drugstore Chains	Ma and Pa Single Stores
Total number of orders	140	360	1,500
Average number of line items per order	14	12	10
Total number of store deliveries	120	300	1,000
Average number of cartons shipped per store delivery	300	80	16
Average number of hours of shelf stocking per store delivery	3.0	0.6	0.1

Required

1. Compute the August 1999 gross-margin percentage for each of its three distribution markets. What is the operating income of Figure Four?
2. Compute the August 1999 rate per unit of the cost-allocation base for each of the five activity areas.
3. Compute the operating income of each distribution market in August 1999 using the activity-based costing information. Comment on the results. What new insights are available with the activity-based information?
4. Describe four challenges Flair would face in assigning the total August 1999 operating costs of $301,080 to the five activity areas.

5-33 **Plantwide, department, and activity-cost rates.** (CGA, adapted) The Sayther Company manufactures and sells two products, A and B. The manufacturing activity is organized in two departments. Manufacturing overhead costs at its Portland plant are allocated to each product using a plantwide rate of $17 per direct manufacturing labor-hour. This rate is based on budgeted manufacturing overhead of $340,000 and 20,000 budgeted direct manufacturing labor-hours:

Manufacturing Department	Budgeted Manufacturing Overhead	Budgeted Direct Manufacturing Labor-Hours
1	$240,000	10,000
2	100,000	10,000
Total	$340,000	20,000

The number of direct manufacturing labor-hours required to manufacture each product is:

Manufacturing Department	Product A	Product B
1	4	1
2	1	4
Total	5	5

Per unit costs for the two categories of direct manufacturing costs are:

Direct Manufacturing Costs	Product A	Product B
Direct materials costs	$120	$150
Direct manufacturing labor costs	80	80

At the end of the year, there was no work in process. There were 200 finished units of product A and 600 finished units of product B on hand. Assume that the budgeted production level of the Portland plant was exactly attained.

Sayther sets the selling price of each product by adding 120% to its unit manufacturing costs; that is, if the unit manufacturing costs are $100, the selling price is $220 ($100 + $120). This 120% markup is designed to cover costs upstream to manufacturing (for example, product design) and costs downstream from manufacturing (for example, marketing and customer service) as well as to provide a profit.

Required
1. How much manufacturing overhead cost would be included in the inventory of products A and B if Sayther used (a) a plantwide overhead rate and (b) department overhead rates?
2. By how much would the selling prices of product A and product B differ if Sayther used a plantwide overhead rate instead of department overhead rates?
3. Should Sayther Company prefer plantwide or department overhead rates?
4. Under what conditions should Sayther Company further subdivide the department cost pools into activity-cost pools?

5-34 Plantwide versus department overhead cost rates. (CMA, adapted) The MumsDay Corporation manufactures a complete line of fiberglass attaché cases and suitcases. Mums-Day has three manufacturing departments (molding, component, and assembly) and two support departments (maintenance and power).

The sides of the cases are manufactured in the Molding Department. The frames, hinges, locks, and so on are manufactured in the Component Department. The cases are completed in the Assembly Department. Varying amounts of materials, time, and effort are required for each of the various cases. The Maintenance Department and Power Department provide services to the three manufacturing departments.

MumsDay has always used a plantwide manufacturing overhead rate. Direct manufacturing labor-hours are used to allocate the overhead to each product. The budgeted rate is calculated by dividing the company's total budgeted manufacturing overhead cost by the total budgeted direct manufacturing labor-hours to be worked in the three manufacturing departments.

Whit Portlock, manager of Cost Accounting, has recommended that MumsDay use department overhead rates. Portlock has projected operating costs and production levels for the coming year. They are presented (in thousands) by department in the following table:

	Manufacturing Department		
	Molding	Component	Assembly
Department Operating Data			
Direct manufacturing labor-hours	500	2,000	1,500
Machine-hours	875	125	
Department Costs			
Direct manufacturing materials	$12,400	$30,000	$ 1,250
Direct manufacturing labor	3,500	20,000	12,000
Manufacturing overhead	21,000	16,200	22,600
Total departmental costs	$36,900	$66,200	$35,850
Use of Support Departments			
Estimated usage of maintenance resources in labor-hours for coming year	90	25	10
Estimated usage of power (in kilowatt-hours) for coming year	360	320	120

Estimated costs are $4,000 for the Maintenance Department and $18,400 for the Power Department.

Required

1. Calculate the plantwide overhead rate for the MumsDay Corporation for the coming year using the same method as used in the past.
2. Whit Portlock has been asked to develop department overhead rates for comparison with the plantwide rate. Follow these steps in developing the department rates:
   a. Allocate the Maintenance Department and Power Department costs to the three manufacturing departments.
   b. Calculate department overhead rates for the three manufacturing departments using a machine-hour allocation base for the Molding Department and a direct manufacturing labor-hour allocation base for the Component Department and Assembly Department.
3. Should the MumsDay Corporation use a plantwide rate or department rates to allocate overhead cost to its products? Explain your answer.

5-35 ABC, health care. Uppervale Health Center runs four programs: (1) alcoholic rehabilitation, (2) drug-addict rehabilitation, (3) children's services, and (4) after-care (counseling and support of patients after release from a mental hospital).

The center's budgets for 1999 follow:

Professional salaries:		
6 physicians × $100,000	$600,000	
19 psychologists × $50,000	950,000	
23 nurses × $25,000	575,000	$2,125,000
Medical supplies		300,000
General overhead (administrative salaries, rent, utilities, etc.)		1,275,000
		$3,700,000

Muriel Clayton, the director of the center, is keen on determining the cost of each program. She has limited funds and feels that this information will help her to budget better and allocate resources more effectively. For example, Clayton needs to decide on whether to allocate funds to alcoholic rehabilitation or drug-addict rehabilitation. Her decision rule is that if the cost to treat a drug-addict patient for a year is more than 15% higher than the cost to treat an alcoholic patient for a year, the alcohol program would receive additional funds.

As a first step, Clayton, who has earned uniformly high respect from the professional staff, asked them to fill out a form indicating the time devoted to each of the four programs. She then allocated costs of medical supplies on the basis of physician-hours spent in each program and general overhead on the basis of direct-labor costs (where direct labor is defined to include the time of doctors, psychologists, and nurses multiplied by the salary rate of each).

Clayton compiled the following data describing employee allocations to individual programs:

	Alcohol	Drug	Children	After-care	Total Employees
Physicians		2	4		6
Psychologists	6	4		9	19
Nurses	4	6	4	9	23

Eighty patients are in residence in the alcohol program, each staying about six months. Thus, the clinic provides 40 patient-years of service in the alcohol program. Similarly, 100 patients are involved in the drug program for about six months each. Thus the clinic provides 50 patient-years of service in the drug program.

Clayton has recently become aware of activity-based costing as a method to refine costing systems. She asks her accountant, Huey Deluth, how she should apply this new technique. Deluth obtains the following information:

1. Consumption of medical supplies depends on the number of patients in each department and the length of their stays (that is, patient-years).

2. General overhead costs consists of

Rent and clinic maintenance	$ 200,000
Administrative costs to manage patient charts, food, laundry	800,000
Laboratory services	275,000
Total	$1,275,000

3. Other information about individual departments:

	Alcohol	Drug	Children	After-care	Total
Square feet of space occupied by each program	9,000	9,000	10,000	12,000	40,000
Patient-years of service	40	50	50	60	200
Number of patients	80	100	200	120	500
Number of laboratory tests	400	1,400	3,000	700	5,500

Required

1. a. Compute indirect-cost rates for medical supplies and general overhead under Clayton's existing costing system.
   b. What is the cost of each program and the cost per patient-year of the alcohol and drug programs, using Clayton's existing costing system?
   c. Using the existing costing system, should Clayton allocate additional funds to the drug program or to the alcohol program?

2. a. Selecting cost-allocation bases that you believe are the most appropriate for allocating indirect costs to programs, calculate the indirect-cost rates for medical supplies, rent and clinic maintenance; administrative cost rate for patient charts, food, and laundry; and laboratory services.
   b. Using an activity-based costing approach to cost analysis, calculate the cost of each program and the cost per patient-year of the alcohol and drug programs.
   c. Using the ABC system, should Clayton allocate additional funds to the drug program or to the alcohol program?

3. Explain the cost differences and the accuracy of program costs calculated using the existing system and the ABC system. What other benefits can Uppervale Health Center obtain by implementing the ABC system?

4. What factors, other than cost, do you think Uppervale Health Center should consider in allocating resources to its programs?

5-36 Activity-based costing, product-cost cross-subsidization. Baker's Delight (BD) has been in the food-processing business three years. For its first two years (1999 and 2000), its sole product was raisin cake. All cakes were manufactured and packaged in 1-pound units. BD used a normal costing system. The two direct-cost categories were direct materials and direct manufacturing labor. The sole indirect manufacturing cost category—manufacturing overhead—was allocated to products using units of production as the allocation base.

In its third year, (2001) BD added a second product—layered carrot cake—that was packaged in 1-pound units. This product differs from raisin cake in several ways:

◆ More expensive ingredients are used.
◆ More direct manufacturing labor time is required.
◆ More complex manufacturing is required.

In 2001, BD continued to use its existing costing system where it allocated manufacturing overhead using total units produced of raisin and layered carrot cakes.

Direct materials costs in 2001 were $0.60 per pound of raisin cake and $0.90 per pound of layered carrot cake. Direct manufacturing labor cost in 2001 was $0.14 per pound of raisin cake and $0.20 per pound of layered carrot cake.

During 2001, BD sales staff reported greater-than-expected sales of layered carrot cake and less-than-expected sales of raisin cake. The budgeted and actual sales volume for 2001 is as follows:

	Budgeted	Actual
Raisin cake	160,000 pounds	120,000 pounds
Layered carrot cake	40,000 pounds	80,000 pounds

The budgeted manufacturing overhead for 2001 is $210,800.

At the end of 2001, Jonathan Davis, the controller of BD, decided to investigate how an activity-based costing system would affect the product-cost numbers. After consultation with operating personnel, the single manufacturing overhead cost pool was subdivided into five activity areas. These activity areas, the cost-allocation base, the budgeted 2001 cost-allocation rate, and the quantity of the cost-allocation base used by the raisin and layered carrot cakes are as follows:

Activity	Cost-Allocation Base	Budgeted 2001 Cost per Unit of Cost-Allocation Base	Quantity of Cost-Allocation Base	
			Raisin Cake	Layered Carrot Cake
Mixing	Labor-hours	$0.04	600,000	640,000
Cooking	Oven-hours	$0.14	240,000	240,000
Cooling	Cool room-hours	$0.02	360,000	400,000
Creaming/Icing	Machine-hours	$0.25	0	240,000
Packaging	Machine-hours	$0.08	360,000	560,000

Required

1. Compute the 2001 unit-product cost of raisin cake and layered carrot cake using the original costing system used in the 1999 to 2001 period.
2. Compute the 2001 unit-product cost of raisin cake and layered carrot cake using the activity-based costing system.
3. Explain the differences in unit-product costs computed in requirements 1 and 2.
4. Describe three uses Baker's Delight might make of the activity-based cost numbers.

 5-37 Activity-based job costing. The Schramka Company manufactures a variety of prestige boardroom chairs. Its job-costing system uses an activity-based approach. There are two direct-cost categories (direct materials and direct manufacturing labor) and three indirect-cost pools. The cost pools represent three activity areas at the plant.

Manufacturing Activity Area	Budgeted Costs for 2001	Cost Driver Used as Allocation Base	Cost-Allocation Rate
Materials handling	$ 200,000	Parts	$ 0.25
Cutting	2,000,000	Parts	2.50
Assembly	2,000,000	Direct manufacturing labor-hours	25.00

Two styles of chairs were produced in March, the executive chair and the chairman chair. Their quantities, direct material costs, and other data for March 2001 are as follows:

	Units Produced	Direct Material Costs	Number of Parts	Direct Manufacturing Labor-Hours
Executive chair	5,000	$600,000	100,000	7,500
Chairman chair	100	25,000	3,500	500

The direct manufacturing labor rate is $20 per hour. Assume no beginning or ending inventory.

Required

1. Compute the March 2001 total manufacturing costs and unit costs of the executive chair and the chairman chair.
2. The upstream activities to manufacturing (R&D and design) and the downstream activities (marketing, distribution, and customer service) are analyzed, and the unit costs in 2001 are budgeted to be:

	Upstream Activities	Downstream Activities
Executive chair	$ 60	$110
Chairman chair	146	236

Compute the full costs per unit of each chair. (Full costs of each chair are the sum of the costs in all business function areas.)

5-38 Activity-based job costing, unit-cost comparisons. The Tracy Corporation has a machining facility specializing in jobs for the aircraft components market. The previous job-costing system had two direct-cost categories (direct materials and direct manufacturing labor) and a single indirect-cost pool (manufacturing overhead, allocated using direct manufacturing labor-hours). The indirect cost-allocation rate of the previous system for 2001 would have been $115 per direct manufacturing labor-hour.

Recently a team with members from product design, manufacturing, and accounting used an activity-based costing (ABC) approach to refine its job-costing system. The two direct-cost categories were retained. The team decided to replace the single indirect-cost pool with five indirect-cost pools. The cost pools represent five activity areas at the facility, each with its own supervisor and budget responsibility. Pertinent data are as follows:

Activity Area	Cost-Allocation Base	Cost-Allocation Rate
Material handling	Parts	$ 0.40
Lathe work	Turns	0.20
Milling	Machine-hours	20.00
Grinding	Parts	0.80
Testing	Units tested	15.00

Information-gathering technology has advanced to the point where the data necessary for budgeting in these five activity areas are collected automatically.

Two representative jobs processed under the new system at the facility in the most recent period had the following characteristics:

	Job 410	Job 411
Direct materials costs per job	$ 9,700	$59,900
Direct manufacturing labor costs per job	$ 750	$11,250
Number of direct manufacturing labor-hours per job	25	375
Parts per job	500	2,000
Turns per job	20,000	60,000
Machine-hours per job	150	1,050
Units per job (all units are tested)	10	200

Required

1. Compute the per unit manufacturing costs of each job under the previous job-costing system.
2. Compute the per unit manufacturing costs of each job under the activity-based costing system.
3. Compare the per unit cost figures for Jobs 410 and 411 computed in requirements 1 and 2. Why do the previous and the activity-based costing systems differ in their job cost estimates for each job? Why might these differences be important to Tracy Corporation?
4. How might Tracy Corporation use information from its ABC system to manage its business better?

5-39 ABC, implementation, ethics. (CMA, adapted) Applewood Electronics, a division of Elgin Corporation, manufactures two large-screen television models, the Monarch, which has been produced since 1995 and sells for $900, and the Regal, a new model introduced in early 1998 that sells for $1,140. Based on the following income statement for the year-ended November 30, 1999, senior management at Elgin have decided to concentrate Applewood's marketing resources on the Regal model and to begin to phase out the Monarch model.

Applewood Electronics
Income Statement
for the Fiscal Year Ended November 30, 1999

	Monarch	Regal	Total
Revenues	$19,800,000	$4,560,000	$24,360,000
Cost of goods sold	12,540,000	3,192,000	15,732,000
Gross margin	7,260,000	1,368,000	8,628,000
Selling and administrative costs	5,830,000	978,000	6,808,000
Operating income	$ 1,430,000	$ 390,000	$ 1,820,000
Units produced and sold	22,000	4,000	
Net income per unit sold	$65.00	$97.50	

Unit costs for Monarch and Regal are as follows:

	Monarch	Regal
Direct materials	$208	$584
Direct manufacturing labor		
Monarch (1.5 hours × $12)	18	
Regal (3.5 hours × $12)		42
Machine costs[a]		
Monarch (8 hours × $18)	144	
Regal (4 hours × $18)		72
Manufacturing overhead other than machine costs[b]	200	100
Total costs	$570	$798

[a] Machine costs include lease costs of the machine, repairs, and maintenance.
[b] Manufacturing overhead was allocated to products based on machine-hours at the rate of $25 per hour.

Applewood's controller, Susan Benzo, is advocating the use of activity-based costing and activity-based management and has gathered the following information about the company's manufacturing overhead costs for the year ended November 30, 1999.

Activity Center (Cost-Allocation Base)	Total Activity Costs	Units of the Cost-Allocation Base		
		Monarch	Regal	Total
Soldering (number of solder points)	$ 942,000	1,185,000	385,000	1,570,000
Shipments (number of shipments)	860,000	16,200	3,800	20,000
Quality control (number of inspections)	1,240,000	56,200	21,300	77,500
Purchase orders (number of orders)	950,400	80,100	109,980	190,080
Machine power (machine-hours)	57,600	176,000	16,000	192,000
Machine setups (number of setups)	750,000	16,000	14,000	30,000
Total manufacturing overhead	$4,800,000			

After completing her analysis, Benzo shows the results to Fred Duval, the Applewood Division President. Duval does not like what he sees. "If you show headquarters this analysis, they are going to ask us to phase out the Regal line, which we have just introduced. This whole costing stuff has been a major problem for us. First Monarch was not profitable and now Regal."

"Looking at the ABC analysis, I see two problems. First, we do many more activities than the ones you have listed. If you had included all activities, maybe your conclusions would be different. Second, you used number of setups and number of inspections as allocation bases. The numbers would be different had you used setup-hours and inspection-hours instead. I know that measurement problems precluded you from using these other cost-allocation bases, but I believe you ought to make some adjustments to our current numbers to compensate for these issues. I know you can do better. We can't afford to phase out either product."

Benzo knows her numbers are fairly accurate. On a limited sample, she calculated the profitability of Regal and Monarch using more and different allocation bases. The set of activities and activity rates she chose resulted in numbers that closely approximate those based on more detailed analyses. She is confident that headquarters, knowing that Regal was introduced only recently, will not ask Applewood to phase it out. She is also aware that a sizable portion of Duval's bonus is based on division revenues. Phasing out either product would adversely affect his bonus. Still she feels some pressure from Duval to do something.

Required

1. Using activity-based costing, calculate the profitability of the Regal and Monarch models.
2. Explain briefly why these numbers differ from the profitability of the Regal and Monarch models calculated using Applewood's existing costing system.
3. Comment on Duval's concerns about the accuracy and limitations of ABC.
4. How might Applewood find the ABC information helpful in managing its business?
5. What should Susan Benzo do?

COLLABORATIVE LEARNING PROBLEM

5-40 **Activity-based costing, cost hierarchy.** (CMA adapted) Coffee Bean, Inc. (CBI), is a distributor and processor of a variety of coffee blends. The company buys coffee beans from around the world and roasts, blends, and packages them for resale. CBI currently has 15 different coffees that it offers to gourmet shops in 1-pound bags. The major cost is raw materials; however, there is substantial manufacturing overhead in the predominantly automated roasting and packing process. The company uses relatively little direct labor.

Some of the coffees are very popular and sell in large volumes, whereas a few of the newer blends sell in very low volumes. CBI prices its coffee at budgeted cost, including allocated overhead, plus a markup of 30 percent. If prices for certain coffees are significantly higher than market, the prices are lowered. The company competes primarily on the quality of its products, but customers are price conscious as well.

Data for the 1999 budget include manufacturing overhead of $3,000,000, which has been allocated on the basis of each product's budgeted direct-labor cost. The budgeted direct-labor cost for 1999 totals $600,000. Purchases and use of materials (mostly coffee beans) are budgeted to total $6,000,000.

The budgeted direct costs for 1-pound bags of two of the company's products are:

	Moana Loa	Malaysian
Direct materials	$4.20	$3.20
Direct labor	0.30	0.30

CBI's controller believes the existing costing system may be providing misleading cost information. She has developed an activity-based analysis of the 1999 budgeted manufacturing overhead costs shown in the following table:

Activity	Cost-Allocation Base	Budgeted Activity	Budgeted Cost
Purchasing	Purchase orders	1,158	$ 579,000
Materials handling	Setups	1,800	720,000
Quality control	Batches	600	144,000
Roasting	Roasting-hours	96,100	961,000
Blending	Blending-hours	33,600	336,000
Packaging	Packaging-hours	26,000	260,000
Total manufacturing overhead cost			$3,000,000

Data regarding the 1999 production of the Moana Loa and Malaysian coffee follow. There will be no beginning or ending materials inventory for either of these coffees.

	Moana Loa	Malaysian
Expected sales	100,000 pounds	2,000 pounds
Batch size	10,000 pounds	500 pounds
Setups	3 per batch	3 per batch
Purchase order size	25,000 pounds	500 pounds
Roasting time	1 hour/100 pounds	1 hour/100 pounds
Blending time	0.5 hour/100 pounds	0.5 hour/100 pounds
Packaging time	0.1 hour/100 pounds	0.1 hour/100 pounds

Required

Form groups of two or more students to complete the following requirements.

1. Using CBI's existing costing system:
   a. Determine the company's 1999 budgeted manufacturing overhead rate using direct-labor cost as the single allocation base.
   b. Determine the 1999 budgeted costs and selling prices of 1 pound of Moana Loa coffee and 1 pound of Malaysian coffee.
2. Use the controller's activity-based approach to estimate the 1999 budgeted cost for 1 pound of
   a. Moana Loa coffee
   b. Malaysian coffee
   Allocate all costs to the 100,000 pounds of Moana Loa and the 2,000 pounds of Malaysian. Compare the results with those in requirement 1.
3. Discuss how CBI could use a cost-hierarchy approach to better understand its cost structure.
4. Examine the implications of your answers to requirements 2 and 3 for CBI's pricing and product-emphasis strategy.

CHAPTER 6

Master Budget and Responsibility Accounting

learning objectives

When you have finished studying this chapter, you should be able to

1. Define master budget and explain its major benefits to an organization
2. Describe key advantages of budgets
3. Prepare the operating budget and its supporting schedules
4. Use computer-based financial planning models in sensitivity analysis
5. Explain kaizen budgeting and its importance for cost management
6. Illustrate an activity-based budgeting approach
7. Describe responsibility centers and responsibility accounting
8. Explain how controllability relates to responsibility accounting

Budgeting at airline assembly companies is enhanced by coordinating with companies such as Singapore Airlines and United Airlines about the timing, number, and type of future aircraft purchases.

Budgeting is the most widely used accounting tool for planning and controlling organizations. Budgeting systems turn managers' perspectives forward. By looking to the future and planning, managers are able to anticipate and correct potential problems before they arise. Managers can then focus on exploiting opportunities instead of fighting fires. As one observer said: "Few businesses plan to fail, but many of those that flop failed to plan."

Budgets can financially reflect many of the evolving cost accounting and management themes described in Chapter 1. For example, budgets can quantify the planned financial effects of activities aimed at continuous improvement and cost reduction. In fact, budgets reflect all of the topics we have covered in previous chapters. Understanding cost behavior (Chapters 2 and 3) allows managers to better predict how different projected output levels affect total budgeted costs. Also, understanding cost tracing and cost allocation (covered in Chapters 4 and 5) allows managers to show how different projected revenue and cost amounts will affect the budgeted income statement and budgeted balance sheet. We now discuss the major features of budgets and their role in planning.

BUDGETS AND THE BUDGETING CYCLE

A *budget* is the quantitative expression of a proposed plan of action by management for a future time period and is an aid to the coordination and implementation of the plan. A budget can cover both financial and nonfinancial aspects of these plans and acts as a blueprint for the organization to follow in the upcoming period. Budgets covering financial aspects quantify management's expectations regarding future income, cash flows, and financial position. Just as individual financial statements are prepared covering past periods, so they can be prepared covering future periods—for example, a budgeted income statement, a budgeted statement of cash flows, and a budgeted balance sheet. Underlying these financial budgets can be nonfinancial budgets for, say, units manufactured or sold, head count, and number of new products being introduced to the market.

Well-managed organizations usually have the following budgeting cycle:

1. Planning the performance of the organization as a whole as well as its subunits. The entire management team agrees as to what is expected.

2. Providing a frame of reference, a set of specific expectations against which actual results can be compared.

3. Investigating variations from plans. If necessary, corrective action follows investigation.

4. Planning again, considering feedback and changed conditions.

The **master budget** is a comprehensive expression of management's operating and financial plans for a future time period (usually a year) that is summarized in a set of budgeted financial statements. It embraces the impact of both *operating* decisions and *financing* decisions. Operating decisions center on the use of scarce resources. Financing decisions center on how to obtain the funds to acquire those resources. The focus of this book is on how accounting helps managers make operating decisions. Therefore, this chapter emphasizes operating budgets. Operating managers spend a significant part of their time in budget preparation or analysis. The many advantages of budgeting make this a very wise investment of their energy.

Terminology used to describe budgets varies among organizations. For example, budgeted financial statements are sometimes called **pro forma statements**. The budgeted financial statements of many companies include the budgeted income statement, the budgeted balance sheet, and the budgeted statement of cash flows. Some organizations, such as Hewlett-Packard, refer to budgeting as *targeting*. Indeed, to give a more positive thrust to budgeting, many organizations—for example, Nissan Motor Company and Owens-Corning—describe the budget as a *profit plan*.

ADVANTAGES OF BUDGETS

Budgets are a major feature of most management control systems. When administered wisely, budgets (a) compel planning including the implementation of plans, (b) provide performance criteria, and (c) promote coordination and communication within the organization. However, budgets must be carefully and intelligently administered by management.

Strategy and Plans

Budgeting is most useful when done as an integral part of an organization's strategy analysis. **Strategy** describes how an organization matches its own capabilities with the opportunities in the marketplace to accomplish its overall objectives. It includes consideration of such questions as:

1. What are the overall objectives of the organization?

2. Are the markets for its products local, regional, national, or global? What trends affect its markets? How is the organization affected by the economy, its industry, and its competitors?

3. What forms of organization and financial structures serve the organization best?

4. What are the risks of alternative strategies, and what are the organization's contingency plans if its preferred plan fails?

As shown in Exhibit 6-1, strategy analysis underlies both long-run and short-run planning. In turn, these plans lead to the formulation of budgets. Note the arrowheads in the exhibit are pointing in two directions. Why? Because strategy, plans, and budgets are interrelated and affect one another. Budgets provide feedback to managers about the likely effects of their strategic plans. Managers then use this feedback to revise their strategic plans. Chrysler's decision relating to the pricing of its Dodge Durango illustrates the interrelation between strategy and budgets. The Durango competes in the sports-utility vehicle market with the lower-priced Subaru Forrester and Isuzu Rodeo as well as the comparably priced Chevrolet Blazer. By reducing its price, Chrysler expected to increase the demand for its Durango. The budget, however, indicated that, even at the predicted higher sales quantities, Chrysler would be unable to meet its financial targets. For the strategy to succeed, Chrysler would need to reduce operating costs by streamlining both its manufacturing and marketing activities. It used cross-functional teams with members from different parts of the value chain to seek major cost reductions.

EXHIBIT 6-1
Strategy, Planning, and Budgets

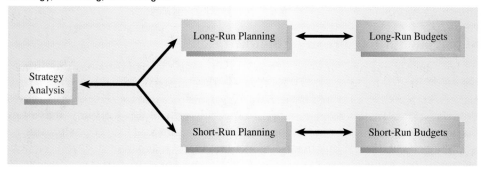

Framework for Judging Performance

Once plans are in place, budgets are also extremely effective as performance measures. Budgeted performance measures can overcome two key limitations of using past performance as a basis for judging actual results. One limitation is that past

OBJECTIVE 2
Describe key advantages of budgets

Curriculum Linkage/New in This Edition Because of its importance, this edition has added a new chapter (13) on strategic profitability analysis. As Exh. 6-1 indicates, strategy, plans, and budgets are interrelated and effect one another.

Points to Stress There are costs (as well as benefits) of budgeting. First, mgrs. often spend much time working on budgets. Studies of large companies suggest that about 5% of staff FTE positions are devoted to budgeting. Second, increasing uncertainty in the rapidly changing business environment makes it difficult to budget. Third, if the budget is rigidly implemented, employees may take actions that will help meet the budget, but will hurt the company in the long run (e.g., deferring maintenance).

Curriculum Linkage The master budget helps coordinate the various business functions. Marketing mgrs. provide the marketing budget and help compile the cornerstone of the master budget—the sales budget. Mfg. personnel usually develop the material, labor, and OH budgets. The finance dept. helps compile the capital budget (discussed in Chap. 21) and the cash budget (see this chapter's appendix). Mgt. accountants usually coordinate this complex budgeting process, which is designed to help all the functions pull together toward top mgt.'s common goals.

results incorporate past miscues and substandard performance. Consider a cellular telephone company (Mobile Communications) examining the year 2001 performance of its sales force. Suppose the past performance in 2000 incorporates the efforts of many salespeople who left because they did not have a good understanding of the marketplace. (As the president of Mobile said, "They could not sell ice cream in a heat wave.") Using the sales record of those departed employees would set the performance bar for new salespeople much too low.

A second limitation of past performance is that the future may be expected to be very different from the past. Consider again our cellular telephone company. Suppose Mobile Communications in 2001 had a 20% revenue increase compared to a 10% revenue increase in 2000. Does this increase indicate stellar sales performance? Before saying yes, consider two additional facts. First, in November 2000 an industry trade association forecast that the 2001 growth rate in industry revenues would be 40 percent. Second, in 2001 the actual growth rate in industry revenues was 50 percent. Mobile's 20% actual revenue gain in 2001 takes on a negative connotation given these two facts, even though it exceeds the 2000 actual growth rate of 10 percent. Use of the 40% figure as the budgeted rate provides a better way to evaluate the 2001 sales performance than does use of the 2000 actual rate of 10 percent.

Coordination and Communication

Coordination is the meshing and balancing of all factors of production or service and of all the departments and business functions so that the company can meet its objectives. *Communication* is getting those objectives understood and accepted by all the employees in the various departments and functions.

Coordination forces executives to think of relationships among individual operations, departments, the company as a whole, and across companies. Consider budgeting at Pace, a United Kingdom–based manufacturer of electronic products. A key product is their decoder boxes for cable television. The Pace production manager for decoder boxes can better budget production schedules by coordinating and communicating with the marketing personnel at Pace. These marketing personnel, in turn, can make better predictions as to future demand for decoder boxes by coordinating and communicating with Pace's customers. Suppose BSKYB, one of Pace's largest customers, is planning to launch a new digital satellite service nine months from now. If Pace's marketing group is able to obtain advance information about the launch date for the digital satellite service, it can share this information with Pace's manufacturing group. This group must then coordinate and communicate with Pace's materials procurement group, and so on. The key point is that Pace is more likely to have a satisfied customer (decoder boxes available for BSKYB in sufficient quantities at the launch date) if Pace coordinates and communicates both within its own business functions and with its suppliers and customers during the budgeting process as well as during the production process.

Management Support and Administration

Budgets help managers, but budgets need help. Top management has the ultimate responsibility for budgets of the organization they manage. *Management at all levels, however, should understand and support the budget and all aspects of the management control system.* Top management support is especially critical for obtaining active line-management participation in the formulation of budgets and for successful administration of the budget. If line managers feel that top management does not "believe" in the budget, these managers are unlikely to be active participants in the budget process. Similarly, a top management that always mechanically institutes "across the board" cost reductions (say, a 10% reduction in all areas) in the face of projected revenue reductions is unlikely to have line managers willing to be "fully honest" in their budget communications.

Budgets should not be administered rigidly. Changing conditions call for changes in plans. A manager may commit to the budget, but a situation might develop in which some unplanned repairs or an unplanned advertising program would

Points to Stress To evaluate current performance, mgt. needs a standard or benchmark for comparison. The text's Mobile Communications cell phone example suggests 2 problems with using historical data as benchmarks for performance evaluation. First, historical data may encompass inefficiencies. Second, mgt. usually expects the future to differ from the past. The advantage of historical data is that they are generally available at low cost. In contrast, budgeted benchmarks may be expensive to develop, but they can reflect anticipated changes and improved efficiency.

Curriculum Linkage To maximize the benefits of budgeting, employees should accept the budget. Acctg. research suggests the following guidelines: (1) visible top mgt. support, (2) provide timely feedback, and (3) be flexible and regard the budget as a means to an end, not the end in itself. Employee participation may also increase acceptance of the budget. The Surveys of Company Practice box (p. 181) suggests that the extent to which mgrs. encourage subordinates to participate in the budget process differs across countries. Participation is less common in Japan than in the U.S.

Curriculum Linkage If students are familiar with JIT (discussed in Chap. 20), point out that JIT requires sophisticated coordination mechanisms. If production is to flow smoothly without inventory buffers, each dept.'s inputs and outputs must precisely coordinate with the "supplier" and "customer" depts.

Points to Stress Both the business environment and human nature induce uncertainty, so the budget will not always be met. The budget should be an adaptable tool to help mgt. achieve its strategic goals. That is, the budget is the means to an end (the strategic goals); the budget is not an end in itself.

Budget Practices Around the Globe[a]

Surveys of financial officers of the largest industrial companies in the United States, Australia, Holland, Japan, and the United Kingdom indicate some interesting similarities and differences in budgeting practices across countries. The use of master budgets is widespread in all countries. Differences arise with respect to other dimensions of budgeting. U.S. controllers and managers prefer more participation and regard return on investment as the most important budget goal. In contrast, Japanese controllers and managers, prefer less participation and regard sales revenues as the most important budget goal. Surveys of Australian[b] and Japanese[c] managers report that budgeting is the management accounting practice that has the single highest benefit to them.

	United States	Japan	Australia	United Kingdom	Holland
1. Percentage of companies that prepare complete master budget	91%	93%	100%	100%	100%

	United States	Japan	Holland
2. Percentage of companies reporting division manager participation in budget committee discussions	78%	67%	82%

	United States	Japan
3. Ranking of the most important budget goals for division managers (1 is most important)		
Return on investment	1	4
Operating income	2	2
Sales revenues	3	1
Production costs	4	3

What reduces the effectiveness of the planning and budgeting processes of companies? A survey of chief financial officers (CFOs) in the United States reported the following four factors in order of importance:[d]

1. Lack of a well-defined strategy
2. Lack of a clear linkage of strategy to operational plans
3. Lack of individual accountability for results
4. Lack of meaningful performance measures

Two planning methodologies viewed as "significant to extremely valuable" by over 60% of CFO's surveyed were "activity-based budgeting" and "rolling budget forecasts."

[a]Adapted from (1) Asada, Bailes, and Amano, "An Empirical Study"; Blayney and Yokoyama, "Comparative Analysis"; and de With and Ijskes "Current Budgeting."
[b]Chenhal and Langfield-Smith, "Adoption and Benefits of Management Accounting Practices."
[c]Inoue, "A Comparative Study of Recent Development of Cost Management Problems In U.S.A., U.K., Canada, and Japan."
[d]Lazere, "All Together Now."
Full citations are in Appendix A.

better serve the interest of the organization. The manager should not defer the repairs or the advertising in order to meet the budget if such actions will hurt the organization in the long run. Attaining the budget should not be an end in itself.

Top managers face the challenge of providing managers at all levels in the organization with incentives to make budget communications truthful and complete. It is unwise to assume that managers will always have adequate incentives or motivation in this regard. One proposed approach is to reward managers based on the subsequent accuracy of their forecasts used in budgets. The more accurate their budget forecasts, the higher their incentive bonuses.

TIME COVERAGE OF BUDGETS

Budgets typically have a set time period (such as a month, quarter, year, and so on). This time period can itself be broken into subperiods. For example, a 12-month cash budget may be broken into 12 monthly periods so that cash inflows and cash outflows can be coordinated better.

The purpose(s) for budgeting should guide the time period chosen for the budget. Consider budgeting for a new Harley-Davidson 500-cc motorcycle. If the purpose is to budget for the total profitability of this new model, a five-year period (or more) may be appropriate (covering design, manufacture, sales, and after-sales support). In contrast, consider budgeting for a Christmas play. If the purpose is to estimate all cash outlays, a six-month period from the planning to staging of the play may be adequate.

The most frequently used budget period is one year. The annual budget is often subdivided by months for the first quarter and by quarters for the remainder of the year. The budgeted data for a year are frequently revised as the year unfolds. For example, at the end of the first quarter, the budget for the next three quarters is changed in light of new information.

Businesses are increasingly using *rolling budgets*. A **rolling budget** is a budget or plan that is always available for a specified future period by adding a month, quarter, or year in the future as the month, quarter, or year just ended is dropped. Consider Electrolux, the global appliance company, which has a 3–5 year strategic plan and a four-quarter rolling budget. A four-quarter rolling budget for the April 2001 to March 2002 period becomes a four-quarter rolling budget for July 2001 to June 2002 the next quarter, and so on. There is thus always a 12-month budget (for the forthcoming year) in place. Rolling budgets constantly force Electrolux's management to think concretely about the forthcoming 12 months, regardless of the quarter at hand.

STEPS IN DEVELOPING AN OPERATING BUDGET

OBJECTIVE 3

Prepare the operating budget and its supporting schedules

The best way to explain the budgeting process is to work through the development of an actual budget. Stylistic Furniture is a manufacturer of prestige coffee tables.[1] Its job-costing system for manufacturing costs has two direct-cost categories (direct materials and direct manufacturing labor) and one indirect-cost category (manufacturing overhead). Manufacturing overhead (both variable and fixed) is allocated to each coffee table using direct manufacturing labor-hours as the allocation base.

Exhibit 6-2 shows a simplified diagram of the various parts of the master budget for Stylistic Furniture. The master budget summarizes the financial projections of all the organization's individual budgets. It then results in a set of related financial statements for a specified time period, usually a year. The bulk of Exhibit 6-2 presents a set of budgets that together is often called the **operating budget**, which is the budgeted income statement and its supporting budget schedules. These schedules cut across the business functions of the value chain from research and development to customer service. The **financial budget** is that part of the master budget that comprises the capital budget, cash budget, budgeted balance sheet, and budgeted statement of cash flows. It focuses on the impact of operations and planned capital outlays on cash. The final master budget is often the result of several iterations. Each of the iterations involves interaction across the various business functions of the value chain.

Points to Stress The length of the budget period also depends on the nature of the business. A firm in a stable industry (e.g., a utility) will have a longer budget horizon than will a small start-up company in a rapidly changing high-tech field.

Teaching Tip Use Exh. 6-2 or a comprehensive prob. such as 6-35 to emphasize the logical flow between the component budgets. Memorization is unnecessary if students understand the intuition. For example, sales + ending inventory = units needed. Subtract the units already on hand (beginning inventory) to get the number of units that must be produced. The DM, DL, and OH budgets then flow from the production budget. With respect to the budgeted statements, the I/S is done first, because income must be added to beginning R/E to get ending R/E for the B/S. In turn, the budgeted B/S is compared to the most recent actual B/S in constructing the Statement of Cash Flows.

[1]For simplicity, we assume Stylistic Furniture makes only one product (coffee tables). In most cases, companies manufacture or sell multiple products. Our master-budget illustration includes manufacturing overhead costs as an indirect-cost category so that the steps we outline for preparing a master budget can be directly extended to multiple-product companies.

EXHIBIT 6-2
Overview of the Master Budget for Stylistic Furniture

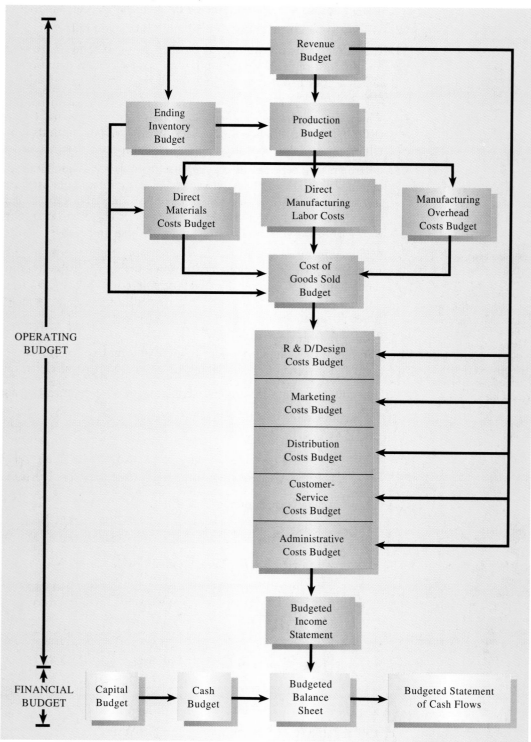

We now present the steps on preparing an operating budget for Stylistic Furniture. The appendix to this chapter presents the cash budget for Stylistic, which is another key component of the master budget.

Stylistic Furniture

We concentrate on Stylistic's operating budget for the year 2001. To highlight key concepts, we make the following assumptions:

1. The only source of revenue is sales of coffee tables. Nonsales-related revenue, such as interest income, is assumed to be zero. Units sold are the sole revenue driver because prices are predicted to be unchanged throughout 2001.

2. Work-in-process inventory is negligible and is ignored.

3. Direct materials inventory and finished goods inventory are costed using the first-in, first-out (FIFO) method. Unit costs of direct materials purchased and finished goods sold remain unchanged throughout each budget year but can change from year to year.

4. There are two types of direct materials—particle board (PB) and red oak (RO). Direct materials costs are variable with respect to units of output (coffee tables) produced.

5. There are two types of direct manufacturing labor—laminating labor and machining labor. Direct manufacturing labor costs are variable with respect to direct manufacturing labor-hours. Direct manufacturing labor rates remain unchanged throughout each budget year but can change from year to year. Direct manufacturing labor workers are hired on an hourly basis and no overtime is worked.

6. Manufacturing overhead has both a variable component and a fixed component. The variable component is variable with respect to direct manufacturing labor-hours. For computing inventoriable costs, Stylistic allocates all manufacturing overhead costs (variable and fixed) using direct manufacturing labor-hours as the allocation base.[2]

7. Nonmanufacturing costs have both a variable component and a fixed component. The variable component (comprising mostly commissions to sales personnel) is assumed to be variable with respect to revenue dollars.[3]

The following data are used by Stylistic in developing its 2001 budget:

a. Each coffee table has the following product specifications:

Direct materials	
Particle board (PB)	9.00 board feet (b.f.) per table
Red oak (RO)	10.00 board feet (b.f.) per table

Direct manufacturing labor	
Laminating labor	0.25 hours per table
Machining labor	3.75 hours per table

b. Inventory information in physical units for 2001 is:

	Beginning Inventory	Target Ending Inventory
Direct materials		
Particle board	20,000 b.f	18,000 b.f
Red oak	25,000 b.f.	22,000 b.f.
Finished goods		
Coffee tables	5,000 units	3,000 units

c. Coffee table revenue assumptions for 2001 are:

Selling price	$392 per table
Units sold	52,000 units

[2]This inventory costing method is termed *absorption costing* and is discussed in Chapter 9.

[3]To keep the Stylistic budget example straightforward, it is assumed that all nonmanufacturing costs are variable with respect to revenue dollars. In practice, some of these costs may be variable with respect to nonrevenue-based factors. For example, some distribution costs may be variable with respect to the weight of the item distributed or the distance required to distribute the product. For case studies, see S. Player and D. Keys (ed.), *Activity-Based Management* (New York: MasterMedia, 1995).

d. Cost assumptions include:

	2000	2001
Particle board (per b.f.)	$ 3.90	$ 4.00
Red oak (per b.f.)	$ 5.80	$ 6.00
Laminating labor (per hour)	$24.00	$25.00
Machining labor (per hour)	$29.00	$30.00

The inventoriable (manufacturing) cost per coffee table in 2000 is $275.00.

e. Other budgeted cost rates and amounts for 2001 are:

- ◆ Variable manufacturing overhead costs—
  $9.50 per direct manufacturing labor-hour
- ◆ Variable nonmanufacturing costs—
  $0.135 per revenue dollar
- ◆ Fixed manufacturing overhead costs—$1,600,000
- ◆ Fixed nonmanufacturing costs—$1,400,000

Most organizations have a budget manual, which contains instructions and relevant information for preparing budgets. Although the details differ among organizations, the following basic steps are common for developing the operating budget for a manufacturing company. Beginning with the revenues budget, each individual budget follows step by step in logical fashion.

Step 1: Prepare the Revenues Budget A revenues budget (Schedule 1) is the usual starting point for budgeting. Why? Because production (and hence costs) and inventory levels generally depend on the forecasted level of unit sales or revenues.

Schedule 1: Revenues Budget
For the Year Ended December 31, 2001

	Selling Price	Units Sold	Total Revenues
Coffee tables	$392.00	52,000	$20,384,000

The $20,384,000 is the amount of revenues in the budgeted income statement. The revenues budget is often the outcome of elaborate information gathering and discussions among sales managers and sales representatives.

Pressures can exist for budgeted revenues to be either overestimates or underestimates of the expected amounts. Some firms set "stretch" or "challenge" targets for revenues. These targets are actually overestimates of expected revenues, intended to motivate employees to put forth extra effort and attain better performance. Conversely, some managers give extremely conservative budget estimates and purposely underestimate expected revenues to ensure that their budgets are met. **Budgetary slack** describes the practice of underestimating budgeted revenues (or overestimating budgeted costs) in order to make budgeted targets more easily achievable. It frequently occurs when budget variances (the differences between actual results and budgeted amounts) are used to evaluate performance. Budgetary slack provides managers with a hedge against unexpected adverse circumstances.

In performing step 1, the usual starting point is to base revenues on expected demand. Occasionally, however, a factor other than budgeted revenue is the starting point. For example, when demand outstrips available productive capacity or a key component is in short supply, the revenues budget would be based on the maximum units that could be produced.

Step 2: Prepare the Production Budget (in Units) After revenues are budgeted, the production budget (Schedule 2) can be prepared. The total finished goods units to be produced depends on budgeted sales and expected changes in inventory levels:

$$
\begin{array}{c}
\text{Budgeted} \\
\text{production} \\
\text{(units)}
\end{array} =
\begin{array}{c}
\text{Budgeted} \\
\text{sales} \\
\text{(units)}
\end{array} +
\begin{array}{c}
\text{Target ending} \\
\text{finished goods} \\
\text{inventory} \\
\text{(units)}
\end{array} -
\begin{array}{c}
\text{Beginning} \\
\text{finished goods} \\
\text{inventory} \\
\text{(units)}
\end{array}
$$

Schedule 2: Production Budget (in Units)
For the Year Ended December 31, 2001

	Coffee Tables
Budgeted unit sales (Schedule 1)	52,000
Add target ending finished goods inventory	3,000
Total requirements	55,000
Deduct beginning finished goods inventory	5,000
Units to be produced	50,000

Step 3: Prepare the Direct Materials Usage Budget and Direct Materials Purchases Budget The decision on the number of units to be produced (Schedule 2) is the key to computing the usage of direct materials in quantities and in dollars.

Schedule 3A: Direct Materials Usage Budget
For the Year Ended December 31, 2001

	Particle Board (PB)	Red Oak (RO)	Total
Physical Units Budget			
PB: 50,000 × 9.00 b.f	450,000		
RO: 50,000 × 10.00 b.f.		500,000	
To be used in production	450,000	500,000	
Cost Budget			
(Available from beginning inventory)			
PB: $3.90 × 20,000 b.f.	$ 78,000		
RO: $5.80 × 25,000 b.f.		$ 145,000	
To be used from purchases of this period:			
PB: $4.00 × (450,000 − 20,000)	1,720,000		
RO: $6.00 × (500,000 − 25,000)		2,850,000	
Direct materials to be used	$1,798,000	$2,995,000	$4,793,000

Schedule 3B computes the budget for direct materials purchases, which depends on the budgeted direct materials to be used, the beginning inventory of direct materials, and the target ending inventory of direct materials:

$$
\begin{array}{c}
\text{Purchases} \\
\text{of direct} \\
\text{materials}
\end{array} =
\begin{array}{c}
\text{Production} \\
\text{usage} \\
\text{of direct} \\
\text{materials}
\end{array} +
\begin{array}{c}
\text{Target ending} \\
\text{inventory} \\
\text{of direct} \\
\text{materials}
\end{array} -
\begin{array}{c}
\text{Beginning} \\
\text{inventory} \\
\text{of direct} \\
\text{materials}
\end{array}
$$

Schedule 3B: Direct Materials Purchases Budget
For the Year Ended December 31, 2001

	Particle Board (PB)	Red Oak (RO)	Total
Physical Units Budget			
Production usage (from Schedule 3A)	450,000	500,000	
Add target ending inventory	18,000	22,000	
Total requirements	468,000	522,000	
Deduct beginning inventory	20,000	25,000	
Purchases	448,000	497,000	
Cost Budget			
PB: 448,000 × $4.00	$1,792,000		
RO: 497,000 × $6.00		$2,982,000	
Purchases	$1,792,000	$2,982,000	$4,774,000

Step 4: Prepare the Direct Manufacturing Labor Budget These costs depend on wage rates, production methods, and hiring plans. The computations of budgeted direct manufacturing labor costs appear in Schedule 4:

Schedule 4: Direct Manufacturing Labor Budget
For the Year Ended December 31, 2001

	Laminating Labor	Machining Labor	Total
Labor-Hours Budget			
LL: 50,000 × 0.25 hours	12,500		
ML: 50,000 × 3.75 hours		187,500	
	12,500	187,500	200,000
Cost Budget			
LL: $25.00 × 12,500	$312,500		
ML: $30.00 × 187,500		$5,625,000	
	$312,500	$5,625,000	$5,937,500

Step 5: Prepare the Manufacturing Overhead Budget The total of these costs depends on how individual overhead costs vary with the assumed cost driver, direct manufacturing labor-hours. The calculations of budgeted manufacturing overhead costs appear in Schedule 5. The individual amounts for variable and fixed manufacturing overhead costs are based on input from Stylistic's operating personnel (See p. 188). The starting point for these amounts is Stylistic's costs in the current and prior years. Management makes adjustments for cost changes expected in the future.

Stylistic treats both variable and fixed manufacturing overhead as inventoriable costs. It inventories manufacturing overhead at the budgeted rate of $17.50 per direct manufacturing labor-hour (total budgeted manufacturing overhead, $3,500,000 ÷ 200,000 budgeted direct manufacturing labor-hours). Stylistic does not use separate variable and fixed manufacturing overhead rates. The budgeted manufacturing overhead cost per coffee table is $70.00 ($3,500,000 ÷ 50,000 coffee tables budgeted to be produced in 2001).

Step 6: Prepare the Ending Inventories Budget Schedule 6A shows the computation of the unit cost of coffee tables started and completed in 2001. This unit cost is used to calculate the cost of target ending inventories of direct materials and finished goods in Schedule 6B.

Schedule 5: Manufacturing Overhead Budget
For the Year Ended December 31, 2001

	At Budgeted Level of 200,000 Direct Manufacturing Labor-Hours	
Variable manufacturing overhead costs		
Supplies	$240,000	
Indirect manufacturing labor	620,000	
Power and energy	460,000	
Maintenance	300,000	
Miscellaneous	280,000	$1,900,000
Fixed manufacturing overhead costs		
Depreciation	$500,000	
Property taxes	350,000	
Property insurance	260,000	
Plant supervision	210,000	
Miscellaneous	280,000	1,600,000
Total manufacturing overhead costs		$3,500,000

Points to Stress Total variable OH costs fluctuate in proportion to the qty. of the cost allocation base (DLH in the Stylistic example), while total fixed OH remains constant across a wide range of output.

Schedule 6A: Computation of Unit Costs of Ending Inventory of Finished Goods
December 31, 2001

	Cost Per Unit of Input	Input		Total
Direct materials				
Particle board	$4.00	9.00	$ 36.00	
Red oak	6.00	10.00	60.00	$ 96.00
Direct manufacturing labor				
Laminating labor	$25.00	0.25	$ 6.25	
Machining labor	30.00	3.75	112.50	118.75
Manufacturing overhead	17.50	4.00		70.00
Total				$284.75

Teaching Tip Walk the students through the computation of the cost/unit of FG. This shows how the DM, DL, and MOH budgets fit together. Students often have trouble with this integration.

This $284.75 unit cost for 2001 compares to $275.00 for 2000.

Correcting Student Misconception The targeted # of units in Ending Inventory is set at the beginning of the master budget process, since it is needed to compute the # of units produced (Schedule 2). The ending inventory budget in Schedule 6B is designed to *cost* the # units of ending inventory decided upon in Schedule 2.

Schedule 6B: Ending Inventories Budget
December 31, 2001

	Cost Per Unit	Units		Total
Direct materials				
Particle board	$4.00	18,000 b.f.	$ 72,000	
Red oak	6.00	22,000 b.f	132,000	$ 204,000
Finished goods				
Coffee tables	$284.75	3,000	$854,250	854,250
Total ending inventory				$1,058,250

Step 7: Prepare the Cost of Goods Sold Budget The information from Schedules 3–6 leads to Schedule 7 (See p. 189).

Step 8: Prepare the Nonmanufacturing Costs Budget. Schedules 2–7 cover budgeting for Stylistic's production function of the value chain. For brevity, other parts of the value chain are combined into a single schedule. Variable costs are variable with respect to revenue dollars at the rate of $0.135 per revenue dollar: $20,384,000 from Schedule 1 × 0.135 = $2,751,840. The individual amounts are

Schedule 7: Cost of Goods Sold Budget
For the Year Ended December 31, 2001

	From Schedule		
Beginning finished goods inventory, January 1, 2001, $275 × 5,000	Given		$ 1,375,000
Direct materials used	3A	$4,793,000	
Direct manufacturing labor	4	5,937,500	
Manufacturing overhead	5	3,500,000	
Cost of goods manufactured			14,230,500
Cost of goods available for sale			15,605,500
Deduct ending finished goods inventory, December 31, 2001	6B		854,250
Cost of goods sold			$14,751,250

Teaching Tip/Curriculum Linkage
Point out that the CGM portion of the CGS budget in Schedule 7 is a summarized version of the analogous CGM Schedule in Exh. 2-6 (Panel B), but with no WIP inventories (The example's basic data assumed that WIP is zero).

based on input for Stylistic's business function managers in different parts of its value chain.

Schedule 8: Nonmanufacturing Costs Budget
For the Year Ended December 31, 2001

Value-Chain Function	Variable Costs	Fixed Costs	Total Costs
R & D/product design	$ 509,600	$ 150,000	$ 659,600
Marketing	1,019,200	690,000	1,709,200
Distribution	509,600	120,000	629,600
Customer service	407,680	140,000	547,680
Administrative	305,760	300,000	605,760
	$2,751,840	$1,400,000	$4,151,840

Step 9: Prepare the Budgeted Income Statement   Schedules 1, 7, and 8 provide the necessary information to complete the budgeted income statement, shown in Exhibit 6-3. Of course, more details could be included in the income statement, and then fewer supporting schedules would be prepared.

Top management's strategies for achieving revenue and operating income goals influence the costs planned for the different business functions of the value chain. As strategies change, the budgeted costs for different elements of the value chain will also change. For example, a shift in strategy toward emphasizing product development and customer service will result in increased costs in these parts of the operating budget.

Reinforcing Problems Probs. 6-28, 6-32, 6-35, and 6-38 are comprehensive budgeting problems. Probs. 6-31 and 6-32 cover budgeted income statements.

EXHIBIT 6-3
Budgeted Income Statement for Stylistic Furniture for the Year Ended December 31, 2001

Revenues	Schedule 1		$20,384,000
Cost of goods sold	Schedule 7		14,751,250
Gross margin			5,632,750
Operating costs			
R & D/product design	Schedule 8	$ 659,600	
Marketing costs	Schedule 8	1,709,200	
Distribution costs	Schedule 8	629,600	
Customer-service costs	Schedule 8	547,680	
Administrative costs	Schedule 8	605,760	4,151,840
Operating income			$ 1,480,910

Using Web Technology to Fast-Track the Budgeting Process

The budgeting process for a large-sized company can be a time-consuming and often frustrating process. Different parts of a company may use different (noncompatible) software packages. Moreover, there can be sizable delays between when a division submits a proposed budget revision and when those revisions are integrated into the master budget of the company.

Advances in information technology are greatly assisting managers improve the budgeting process. For example, CLARUS Corporation has a CLARUS Budget software module that is engineered for use over the World Wide Web. This module enables managers in different divisions and in different locations to log on and have instantaneous access to the proposed budgets of other divisions. Managers can access this module from diverse locations. The budget module is linked to other modules (such as human resource budgeting and capital budgeting) so that a total enterprisewide master budget can be developed online.

Toronto-Dominion Bank proposes to use the CLARUS Budget module in its retail bank and discount brokerage division as part of a comprehensive integration of the World Wide Web into its business processes. Its controller noted that "in the past we have compiled our business plan using hundreds of spreadsheets, and our analysts have spent a disproportionate amount of their time compiling and verifying data from multiple sources. Implementing a web-based enterprisewide budgeting solution will allow our analysts to be proactive in monitoring quarterly results."

CLARUS reports that its web-based budgeting approach frees the finance department to focus on strategy (not spreadsheets) and increased service levels to employees, and it reduces administrative costs.

Source: CLARUS web-site (*www.claruscorp.com*) and Hornyak, *"Budgeting Made Easy," Management Accounting*, Vol. LXXX, No. 4 (October 1998), pp. 18–23.

COMPUTER-BASED FINANCIAL PLANNING MODELS

OBJECTIVE 4

Use computer-based financial planning models in sensitivity analysis

New in This Edition The Concepts in Action box is new and illustrates how web technology is assisting the budgeting process.

Software packages are now readily available to reduce the computational burden and time required to prepare budgets.[4] These packages perform the calculations for **financial planning models,** which are mathematical representations of the interrelationships among operating activities, financial activities, and other factors that affect the master budget. Software packages greatly assist managers with sensitivity analyses in their planning and budgeting activities. *Sensitivity analysis* is a "what-if" technique that examines how a result will change if the original predicted data are not achieved or if an underlying assumption changes.

Consider Stylistic Furniture. Two key parameters in the budget model for 2001 are:

1. Selling price per table is $392.00.

2. Direct materials cost is $4.00 per b.f. for particleboard and $6.00 per b.f. for red oak.

What if the parameters were to change? Exhibit 6-4 presents the budgeted operating income for nine combinations of differing inputs for parameters 1 and 2:

[4]*Accounting Software Comparison* provides comparisons of accounting software packages from numerous vendors—see their website at (www.excelco.com). Many software vendors (such as Hyperion, Great Plains, Solomon Software, and Computer Associates) provide accounting software packages that include budgeting modules. Hyperion's Pillar software is an example of a standalone budgeting package—see their website at (www.hysoft.com).

EXHIBIT 6-4

Effect of Changes in Budget Assumptions on Budgeted Operating Income for Stylistic Furniture

Scenario	Unit Selling Price	Direct Materials Purchase Cost		Budgeted Operating Income	
		Particle Board	Red Oak	Dollars	Change from Master Budget
1	$431.20	$3.80	$5.70	$3,458,226	134% Increase
2	431.20	4.00	6.00	3,244,126	118% Increase
3	431.20	4.20	6.30	3,030,026	105% Increase
4	392.00	3.80	5.70	1,695,010	14% Increase
5[a]	392.00	4.00	6.00	1,480,910	—
6	392.00	4.20	6.30	1,266,810	14% Decrease
7	352.80	3.80	5.70	(68,206)	105% Decrease
8	352.80	4.00	6.00	(282,306)	119% Decrease
9	352.80	4.20	6.30	(496,406)	134% Decrease

[a]Base case from Exhibit 6-3.

a. Selling price per table of (i) $431.20 (10% increase), (ii) $392.00, and (iii) $352.80 (10% decrease).

b. Purchase cost of direct materials of (i) $3.80/$5.70 (5% decrease), (ii) $4.00/$6.00, and (iii) $4.20/$6.30 (5% increase).

The nine combinations in Exhibit 6-4 show how budgeted operating income will change sizably with changes in selling prices and direct material costs. Scenario 5 is the base case from Exhibit 6-3. Scenarios 2 and 8 illustrate the effect of changes in only the selling price. Scenarios 4 and 6 examine the effect of changes in only the direct materials costs. Scenarios 1, 3, 7, and 9 pertain to simultaneous changes in both parameters. Note that a change in Stylistic's selling price per table affects the variable nonmanufacturing costs (such as sales commissions) as well as revenue. Sensitivity analysis is especially useful in incorporating such interrelationships into budgeting decisions by managers. Where the success or viability of a venture is highly dependent on one or more targets being attained, managers should frequently update their budgets as uncertainty is resolved. These updated budgets can assist managers to adjust expenditure levels, change marketing strategies, and so on as circumstances change.

Exhibit 6-4 reports sensitivity analysis for budgeted operating income. Another important use of sensitivity analysis is in cash budgeting. This topic is discussed in the appendix to this chapter.

KAIZEN BUDGETING

Chapter 1 (p. 9) noted how continuous improvement is one of the key issues facing management today. The Japanese use the term *kaizen* for continuous improvement. **Kaizen budgeting** is a budgetary approach that explicitly incorporates continuous improvement during the budget period into the budget numbers.

Consider again our Stylistic Furniture example. Throughout our nine budgeting steps, we assumed that it takes 3.75 hours of machining labor time to manufacture each table. A Kaizen budgeting approach would incorporate continuous improvement (that is, reduction) in these manufacturing labor-hour requirements during 2001. An illustration is:

	Budgeted Machining Hours Per Table
January–March 2001	3.75
April–June 2001	3.70
July–September 2001	3.65
October–December 2001	3.60

Unless Stylistic meets these continuous improvement goals, the actual results will exceed the budgeted amounts in the latter quarters of the year. Note that in Stylistic's budget, the implications of these direct labor-hour reductions would extend to reductions in variable manufacturing overhead costs, because direct manufacturing labor-hours is the driver of these costs.

Kaizen at Citizen Watch

Citizen Watch is the world's largest manufacturer of watches. The assembly areas at its plants are highly automated. Component part costs for each watch are a sizable percentage of the unit cost of each watch. A central part of Citizen's cost management system is kaizen budgeting. All parts of its entire supply chain, including component suppliers, are required to continually seek out cost-reduction opportunities. For example, at its Tokyo plant, Citizen budgets steady cost reductions of 3% per year for purchased materials. Suppliers who exceed this 3% target retain for at least one year any cost reductions above the 3% level. Suppliers who do not attain the 3% target receive the "assistance" of Citizen engineers in the following year.[5]

ACTIVITY-BASED BUDGETING

Most budgeting models to date have used a small number of cost drivers that are predominantly output-based (units produced, units sold, or revenues). Due, in part, to the growing use of activity-based costing (ABC), there is now interest in incorporating a broader set of cost drivers into budgets. The domain of ABC is the reporting and analysis of past and current costs. A natural extension is to use an activity-based approach in the budgeting of future costs. **Activity-based budgeting (ABB)** focuses on the budgeted cost of activities necessary to produce and sell products and services. Adopting an ABB approach to developing the operating budget of Stylistic entails formulating budgets for each activity in its activity management system. As an illustration of ABB, we consider the setup activity of Stylistic. In the Stylistic operating budget outlined in steps 1–9 (pp. 182–191), the costs of the setup activity are included in step 5 (the Manufacturing Overhead Budget). In ABB, the costs of this setup activity (as well as other activities) would be separately predicted. The following information assists in building up the budgeted costs for 2001 in this setup activity:

a. The plant operates 2 shifts a day for 250 working days a year. There are 4 workers in laminating activities per shift and 50 workers in machining activities per shift.

b. Each worker on the production line in both the laminating and machining activities requires 30 minutes of setup each time a new batch of tables is manufactured. The production run of each batch of tables at Stylistic is a shift. In the laminating area, 25 tables per worker are started and completed per shift. Work on 2 tables per worker is started and completed in the machining area per shift.

c. The same hourly rates are paid to workers for setup time as for time spent on laminating or machining—that is, $25.00 per hour for laminating labor and $30.00 per hour for machining labor.

d. Supervisory labor (an indirect cost) for the activity is paid $60 per hour. Stylistic believes there is a cause-and-effect relationship such that 10 hours of worker labor-hours in setup requires 1 hour of supervisory labor time.

This information enables Stylistic to prepare an activity-based budget for the setup activity in its manufacturing plant.

Given that Stylistic budgets to produce 50,000 tables in 2001, the information in **a** and **b** enables the total budgeted setup-hours for 2001 to be determined:

---

[5] See R. Cooper, "Citizen Watch Company, Ltd.: Cost Reduction for Mature Products" (Harvard Business School, 9-194-033).

	Laminating Setup	Machining Setup
Quantity of tables to be produced	50,000	50,000
Number of tables to be produced per batch	25	2
Number of batches (1) ÷ (2)	2,000	25,000
Setup time per batch	0.5 hour	0.5 hour
Total setup-hours (3) × (4)	1,000 hours	12,500 hours

Combining this information with the hourly rates paid per worker from **c** yields the budgeted costs for setup worker time in 2001:

Laminating direct manufacturing labor costs $25 × 1,000 hours	$ 25,000
Machining direct manufacturing labor costs $30 × 12,500 hours	375,000
Total	$400,000

This $400,000 amount is currently included in the indirect manufacturing labor category of the variable manufacturing overhead costs of Stylistic's existing budget (see step 5, pp. 187, 188).

The total costs of the setup activity for Stylistic also includes the costs of supervisory time. Item **d** in the preceding notes that every 10 hours of worker labor-hours requires 1 hour of supervisory labor time at a cost of $60 per hour. For 2001, Stylistic budgets 13,500 hours of setup time (1,000 for laminating + 12,500 for machining) for a production of 50,000 tables. Supervisory labor time for the setup activity in 2001 is budgeted to be 1,350 hours (13,500 × 0.10 = 1,350 hours) at a cost of $60 per hour. Thus, the budgeted cost for supervisory labor in the setup activity in 2001 is:

$$1,350 \text{ supervisory hours} \times \$60 = \$81,000$$

This $81,000 amount is currently included in the plant supervision category of fixed manufacturing overhead costs of Stylistic's existing budget (see step 5, pp. 187, 188).

The total budgeted costs for Stylistic's setup activity in 2001 are thus $481,000, comprising $400,000 for worker-hours and $81,000 for supervisory labor. This activity-cost buildup approach highlights how Stylistic can seek ways to reduce its budgeted setup costs in 2001. These include:

1. Increase the length of the production run per batch. For example, if workers work longer hours per day for fewer days per month, fewer setups at the start of each day would be needed for the budgeted production of 50,000 tables.

2. Decrease the setup time per batch. Shorter setup times means lower total setup hours for the budgeted production of 50,000 tables.

3. Reduce the supervisory time needed per worker setup-hour. Investments in increasing the skill base of laminating or machining workers can result in less supervisory time required per worker-hour.

4. Reduce the hourly labor rates paid to workers and the salaries paid to supervisors.

Activity-based budgeting typically requires more detailed information than does budgeting based purely on output-based cost drivers. The more detailed information, however, can lead to more insight into ways companies can better manage their future costs.[6]

Curriculum Linkage The Survey of Company Practice box (earlier in this chapter) indicated that over 60% of CFO's surveyed viewed ABB as valuable.

Points to Stress Activity-based budgeting (ABB) is helpful for *ex ante* and *ex post* cost control. ABB reveals the costs of different activities so that mgrs. can attempt to reduce consumption of the cost drivers before costs are committed or locked in. After the incurrence of actual costs, comparison of actual costs with ABB can pinpoint activities where (1) the actual cost rate of the activity was higher than budgeted, or (2) the usage of the cost driver was higher than budgeted.

[6]For illustrative purposes, the ABB example uses the setup costs included in Stylistic's variable manufacturing overhead costs budget. ABB implementations in practice may incorporate costs across many parts of the value chain and may include costs that are fixed in the short run but are variable over longer time horizons. For an example, see S. Borjesson, "A Case Study on Activity-Based Budgeting," *Journal of Cost Management*, Vol. 10, No. 4, pp. 7–18.

BUDGETING AND RESPONSIBILITY ACCOUNTING

Organization Structure and Responsibility

To attain the goals described in the master budget, an organization must coordinate the efforts of all its employees—from the top executive through all levels of management to every supervised worker. Coordinating the organization's efforts means assigning responsibility to managers who are accountable for their actions in planning and controlling human and physical resources. Management is essentially a human activity. Budgets exist not for their own sake, but to help managers. How each company structures its own organization significantly shapes how such coordination occurs.

Organization structure is an arrangement of lines of responsibility within the entity. A company such as British Petroleum-Amoco may be organized primarily by business function: exploration, refining, and marketing. Another company, such as Procter & Gamble, the household products giant, may be organized by product or brand line. The managers of the individual divisions (toothpaste, soap, and so on) would each have decision-making authority concerning all the business functions (manufacturing, marketing, and so on) within that division.

Each manager, regardless of level, is in charge of a responsibility center. A **responsibility center** is a part, segment, or subunit of an organization whose manager is accountable for a specified set of activities. The higher the manager's level, the broader the responsibility center, and, generally, the larger the number of his or her subordinates. **Responsibility accounting** is a system that measures the plans (by budgets) and actions (by actual results) of each responsibility center. Four major types of responsibility centers are:

1. **Cost center**—the manager is accountable for costs only
2. **Revenue center**—the manager is accountable for revenues only
3. **Profit center**—the manager is accountable for revenues and costs
4. **Investment center**—the manager is accountable for investments, revenues, and costs

The Maintenance Department of a Marriott hotel would be a cost center because the maintenance manager is responsible only for costs. Hence, the budget would emphasize costs. The Sales Department of the hotel would be a revenue center because the sales manager is responsible only for revenues. Here the budget would emphasize revenues. The hotel manager would be in charge of a profit center because the hotel manager is accountable for both revenues and costs. Here the budget would emphasize both revenues and costs. The regional manager responsible for investments in new hotel projects and for revenues and costs would be in charge of an investment center. Revenue, costs, and the investment base would be emphasized in the budget for this manager.

Judicious choice of a responsibility center can promote a better alignment of individual and organization goals. Until recently, OPD (an office products distributor) operated its Sales Department as a revenue center. Each salesperson received 3% of the revenue per order, regardless of its size, the cost of processing it, or the cost of delivering the office products. An analysis of customer profitability at OPD found many customers were unprofitable. A key reason was numerous orders for which the processing and delivering costs were very high. OPD decided to make the Sales Department a profit center. It changed the incentive system for salespeople to 15% of the monthly profitability per customer. The costs charged to each customer included the ordering and delivery costs for each order. The effect of this change was dramatic. Salespeople at OPD actively encouraged customers to change their ordering behavior to make fewer orders of larger revenue amounts. Customer profitability increased because of a 40% reduction in ordering and delivery costs in one year.[7]

---

[7] Do not assume that in a profit center managers have *control* over all the revenues or costs. Managers in profit centers are sometimes held accountable for revenue or cost items they do not control. For example, a mining company may set up a gold mine as a profit center even though the mine manager does not control the world price of gold.

Feedback and Fixing Blame

Budgets coupled with responsibility accounting provide systematic help for managers, particularly if managers interpret the feedback carefully. Managers, accountants, and students of management accounting repeatedly tend to "play the blame game"—using *variances* appearing in the responsibility accounting system to pinpoint fault for operating problems. In considering variances, initially managers should focus on whom they should ask and not on whom they should blame. Variances only suggest questions or direct attention to persons who should have the relevant information. Thus, variances, properly used, can be helpful in evaluating managers' performance.

RESPONSIBILITY AND CONTROLLABILITY

Definition of Controllability

Controllability is the degree of influence that a specific manager has over costs, revenues, or other items in question. A **controllable cost** is any cost that is primarily subject to the influence of a given *responsibility center manager* for a given *time period*. A responsibility accounting system could either exclude all uncontrollable costs from a manager's performance report or segregate such costs from the controllable costs. For example, a machining supervisor's performance report might be confined to quantities (not costs) of direct materials, direct manufacturing labor, power, and supplies.

In practice, controllability is difficult to pinpoint for at least two reasons:

1. Few costs are clearly under the sole influence of one manager. For example, *costs* of direct materials may be influenced by a purchasing manager, but these costs also depend on market conditions beyond the manager's control. *Quantities* used may be influenced by a production manager, but quantities used also depend on the quality of materials purchased. Moreover, managers often work in teams. How can individual responsibility be evaluated in a team situation?

2. With a long enough time span, all costs will come under somebody's control. However, most performance reports focus on periods of a year or less. A current manager may have inherited problems and inefficiencies from his or her predecessor. For example, present managers may have to work under undesirable contracts with suppliers or labor unions that were negotiated by their predecessors. How can we separate what the current manager actually controls from the results of decisions made by others? Exactly what is the current manager accountable for? Answers to such questions may not be clear-cut.

Senior managers differ in how they embrace the controllability notion when evaluating those reporting to them. For example, a newly appointed president took his management team on a cruise and commented: "I expect everybody to meet their budget targets and those who don't should stand a little closer to the railing." Other presidents believe that a more risk-sharing approach with managers is preferable where noncontrollable factors are taken into account when making judgments about the performance of managers who fail to meet their budget.

Emphasis on Information and Behavior

Managers should avoid overemphasizing controllability. Responsibility accounting is more far-reaching. It focuses on *information and knowledge*, not control. The key question is, Who is the best informed? Put another way, Who is the person who can tell us the most about the specific item in question, regardless of that person's ability to exert personal control? For instance, purchasing managers may be held accountable for total purchase costs, not because of their ability to affect market prices, but because of their ability to predict uncontrollable prices and explain uncontrollable price changes. Similarly, managers at a Pizza Hut unit may be held responsible for operating income of their units, even though they do not fully control selling prices or the costs for many food items, and have minimal flexibility as to items to sell or their ingredients. Why? Because unit managers are in the best position to explain variances between their actual operating income and their budgeted operating income.

Performance reports for responsibility centers also may include uncontrollable items because this approach could change behavior in the direction top management desires. For example, some companies have changed the accountability of a cost center to a profit center. Why? Because the manager will probably behave differently. A cost-center manager may emphasize production efficiency and deemphasize the pleas of sales personnel for faster service and rush orders. In a profit center, the manager is responsible for both costs and revenues. Thus, even though the manager still has no control over sales personnel, the manager will now more likely weigh the impact of his or her decisions on costs and revenues, rather than solely on costs.

Improve Manager's Incentives to Make Honest Budget Forecasts

A major challenge in budgeting is to provide managers with incentives to make honest budget forecasts. Where lower-level managers have superior knowledge about the forecasts used in a budget, top management should be especially alert to the possibilities of budgetary slack. What can top management do in this situation? One approach is to obtain independent insight into the information potentially available to the lower-level managers providing the forecasts. Consider the plant manager of a beverage bottler who is suspected by top management of understating the productivity potential of his bottling lines in his forecasts for the coming year. His presumed motivation is to increase the likelihood of meeting next year's production bonus targets. Suppose top management could purchase a consulting firm's benchmarking study that reports productivity levels (such as the number of bottles filled per hour) at a number of comparable plants owned by other bottling companies. This report shows that their own plant manager's productivity forecasts are well below actual productivity levels already being achieved by other comparable plants. Top management could share this independent information source with their own plant manager and ask him to explain why his productivity differs from that at other comparable plants. They could also base part of the plant manager's compensation on his plant's productivity vis-à-vis other "benchmark" plants rather than on his own productivity compared to earlier forecasts he himself provided. Use of this benchmark performance measure would reduce the plant manager's incentives to understate possible productivity levels in the coming budget period.[8]

HUMAN ASPECTS OF BUDGETING

Why did we cover the two major topics, master budgets and responsibility accounting, in the same chapter? Primarily to emphasize that human factors are crucial parts of budgeting. Too often, students study budgeting as though it were a mechanical tool.

The budgeting techniques themselves are free of emotion. However, their administration requires education, persuasion, and intelligent interpretation. Many managers regard budgets negatively. To them, the word *budget* is about as popular as, say, *downsizing, layoff, or strike*. Top managers must convince their subordinates that the budget is a positive tool designed to help them choose and reach goals. But budgets are not cure-alls. They are not remedies for weak management talent, faulty organization, or a poor accounting system.

The management style of senior managers plays a key role in how budgets are perceived in organizations. For example, the CEO of Campbell Soup argues that "numbers always tell the story." An executive at Campbell noted that "you can miss your plan and not be shot. But you wouldn't want to miss it twice." In contrast, the CEO of General Electric believes that "too much focus on making the numbers in a budget" can lead to dysfunctional decisions being made.

[8]For an excellent discussion of these issues, see Chapter 14 ("Formal Models in Budgeting and Incentive Contracts") of R. S. Kaplan and A. A. Atkinson, *Advanced Management Accounting*, 3rd ed. (Upper Saddle River, N.J.: Simon & Schuster, 1998).

Teaching Tip/Reinforcing Problems
Computers have decreased the importance of technical number-crunching skills, and the focus has shifted to the human side of budgeting. There are many ways to increase employees' acceptance of budgets (e.g., exhibiting top mgt. support, encouraging participation of lower level mgrs., avoiding blame-fixing). This reinforces concepts covered in mgt. courses. Exer. 6-26 covers budgeting and human behavior while Prob. 6-39 covers budgeting and ethics.

(Before trying to solve the homework problems, review the illustration of the operating budget, pp. 182–191.)

PROBLEM

Prepare a budgeted income statement, including all necessary detailed supporting budget schedules. Use the data given in the chapter illustration of an operating budget to prepare your own budget schedules. (See pp. 182–191.)

SUMMARY

The following points are linked to the chapter's learning objectives:

1. The master budget summarizes the financial projections of all the organization's budgets and plans. It expresses management's comprehensive operating and financial plans—the formalized outline of the organization's financial objectives and their means of attainment. Budgets are tools that by themselves are neither good nor bad. How managers administer budgets is the key to their value. When administered wisely, budgets compel management planning, provide definite expectations that are an appropriate framework for judging subsequent performance, and promote communication and coordination among the various subunits of the organization.

2. The advantages of budgets include: (a) they compel planning, (b) they provide performance criteria, and (c) they promote coordination and communication within the organization.

3. The foundation for the operating budget is generally the revenues budget. The following supporting budget schedules are geared to the revenues budget: production budget, direct materials usage budget, direct materials purchases budget, direct manufacturing labor budget, manufacturing overhead costs budget, ending inventory budget, cost of goods sold budget, R&D/design budget, marketing budget, distribution budget, and customer-service budget. The operating budget ends with the budgeted income statement.

4. Computer-based financial planning models are mathematical statements of the relationships among operating activities, financial activities, and other factors that affect the budget. These models allow management to conduct what-if (sensitivity) analyses of the effects on the master budget of changes in the original predicted data or changes in budget assumptions.

5. Kaizen budgeting captures the continuous improvement notion that is a key management concern. Costs in kaizen budgeting are based on future improvements that are yet to be implemented rather than on current practices or methods.

6. Activity-based budgeting focuses on the budgeted costs of activities necessary to produce and sell products and services. It is inherently linked to activity-based costing, but differs in its emphases on future costs and future usage of activity areas.

7. A responsibility center is a part, segment, or subunit of an organization, whose manager is accountable for a specified set of activities. Four major types of responsibility centers are cost centers, revenue centers, profit centers, and investment centers. Responsibility accounting systems measure the plans (by budgets) and actions (by actual results) of each responsibility center.

8. Controllable costs are costs that are primarily subject to the influence of a given manager of a given responsibility center for a given time span. Performance reports of responsibility-center managers, however, often include costs, revenues, and investments that the managers cannot control. Responsibility accounting associates financial items with managers on the basis of which manager has the most knowledge and information about the specific items, regardless of the manager's ability to exercise full control. The important question is whom should be asked, not whom should be blamed.

APPENDIX: THE CASH BUDGET

This chapter features the operating budget. The other major part of the master budget is the *financial budget*, which includes the capital budget, cash budget, budgeted balance sheet, and budgeted statement of cash flows. This Appendix focuses on the cash budget and the budgeted balance sheet. Capital budgeting is discussed in Chapter 21. Coverage of the budgeted statement of cash flows is beyond the scope of this book.

Suppose Stylistic Furniture in our chapter illustration had the balance sheet for the year ended December 31, 2000, shown in Exhibit 6-5. The budgeted cash flows for 2001 are as follows:

	Quarters			
	1	2	3	4
Collections from Customers	$5,331,200	$4,704,000	$4,704,000	$6,272,000
Disbursements				
Direct materials	960,000	1,152,000	1,152,000	1,536,000
Payroll	1,626,300	1,626,300	1,888,600	1,626,300
Other costs	1,580,460	1,580,460	1,580,460	1,580,460
Machinery purchase	0	0	1,800,000	0
Interest expense on long-term debt	60,000	60,000	60,000	60,000
Income taxes	100,000	120,460	100,000	100,000

EXHIBIT 6-5
Balance Sheet for Stylistic Furniture, December 31, 2000

Assets			
Current assets:			
Cash		$ 500,000	
Accounts receivable		1,881,600	
Direct materials		223,000	
Finished goods		1,375,000	$3,979,600
Property, plant, and equipment:			
Land		1,200,000	
Building and equipment	$2,300,000		
Accumulated depreciation	(800,000)	1,500,000	2,700,000
Total			$6,679,600

Liabilities and Stockholders' Equity			
Current liabilities:			
Accounts payable		$ 384,000	
Income taxes payable		20,460	
Total current liabilities		404,460	
Long-term debt (interest at 10% per year)		2,400,000	
Total current and long-term liabilities			$2,804,460
Stockholders' equity			
Common stock, $0.01 par value, 300,000 shares outstanding		$ 3,000	
Retained earnings		3,872,140	3,875,140
Total			$6,679,600

The quarterly data are based on the budgeted cash effects of the operations formulated in Schedules 1–8 in the chapter, but the details of that formulation are not shown here in order to keep the illustration relatively brief and focused.

Long-term debt is $2.4 million at an interest rate of 10%, with $60,000 interest payable every quarter. The company wants to maintain a $100,000 minimum cash balance at the end of each quarter. The company can borrow or repay short-term cash at an interest rate of 12% per year. The minimum borrowing period is six months. Management does not want to borrow any more short-term cash than is necessary. By special arrangement, interest is computed and paid when the principal is repaid. Assume that borrowing takes place (in multiples of $1,000) at the beginning and repayment at the end of the quarters in question. Interest is computed to the nearest dollar.

Suppose an accountant at Stylistic is given the preceding data and the other data contained in the budgets in the chapter (pp. 182–191). He is instructed as follows:

1. Prepare a cash budget for 2001 by quarter. That is, prepare a statement of cash receipts and disbursements by quarter, including details of borrowing, repayment, and interest expense.

2. Prepare a budgeted balance sheet on December 31, 2001.

3. Prepare a budgeted income statement for the year ended December 31, 2001. This statement should include interest expense and income taxes (at a rate of 36% of operating income). In April 2001, Stylistic will pay in cash $120,640 of income taxes. This amount is the remaining payment due on the 2000 income tax year. Stylistic pays in cash $100,000 each quarter of 2001 toward its 2001 income tax bill. Any remaining amount due is paid in April 2002.

Preparation of Budgets

1. The **cash budget** (Exhibit 6-6) is a schedule of expected cash receipts and disbursements. It predicts the effects on the cash position at the given level of operations. Exhibit 6-6 presents the cash budget by quarters to show the impact of cash flow timing on bank loans and their repayment. In practice, monthly—and sometimes weekly—cash budgets are very helpful for cash planning and control. Cash budgets help avoid unnecessary idle cash and unexpected cash deficiencies. They thus keep cash balances in line with needs. Ordinarily, the cash budget has the following main sections:

   a. The beginning cash balance plus cash receipts equals the total cash available before financing. Cash receipts depend on collections of accounts receivable, cash sales, and miscellaneous recurring sources such as rental or royalty receipts. Information on the prospective collectiblity of accounts receivable is needed for accurate predictions. Key factors include bad-debt (uncollectible accounts) experience and average time lag between sales and collections. For simplicity, we assume that Stylistic makes 80% of its sales on credit (payable within one month) and 20% of its sales for cash, and there are no bad debts. There is no discount given for cash payments.

   b. Cash disbursements include the following items:

      (i) *Direct materials purchases.* Suppliers are paid in full two months after the goods are delivered.

      (ii) *Direct labor and other wage and salary outlays.* All payroll-related costs are made in two equal cash installments—on the 5th and the last day of the same month in which the labor effort occurs.

      (iii) *Other costs*–depend on timing and credit terms. *Note that depreciation does not require a cash outlay.*

      (iv) *Other disbursements*—outlays for property, plant, and equipment, and for long-term investments.

      (v) Interest for long-term borrowing.

      (vi) Income tax payments.

EXHIBIT 6-6
Cash Budget for Stylistic Furniture for the Year Ended December 31, 2001

	Quarters				Year as a Whole
	I	II	III	IV	
Cash balance, beginning	$ 500,000	$1,504,440	$1,669,220	$ 100,160	$ 500,000
Add receipts					
Collections from customers	5,331,200	4,704,000	4,704,000	6,272,000	21,011,200
Total cash available for needs (x)	5,831,200	6,208,440	6,373,220	6,372,160	21,511,200
Deduct disbursements					
Direct materials	960,000	1,152,000	1,152,000	1,536,000	4,800,000
Payroll	1,626,300	1,626,300	1,888,600	1,626,300	6,767,500
Other costs	1,580,460	1,580,460	1,580,460	1,580,460	6,321,840
Interest expense (LT debt)	60,000	60,000	60,000	60,000	240,000
Machinery purchase	0	0	1,800,000	0	1,800,000
Income taxes	100,000	120,460	100,000	100,000	420,460
Total disbursements (y)	4,326,760	4,539,220	6,581,060	4,902,760	20,349,800
Minimum cash balance desired	100,000	100,000	100,000	100,000	100,000
Total cash needed	4,426,760	4,639,220	6,681,060	5,002,760	20,449,800
Cash excess (deficiency)[a]	$1,404,440	$1,569,220	$ (307,840)	$1,369,400	$ 1,061,400
Financing					
Borrowing (at beginning)	$ 0	$ 0	$ 308,000	$ 0	$ 308,000
Repayment (at end)	0	0	0	(308,000)	(308,000)
Interest (at 12% per annum)[b]	0	0	0	(18,480)	(18,480)
Total effects of financing	$ 0	$ 0	$ 308,000	$ (326,480)	$ (18,480)
Cash balance, ending[c]	$1,504,440	$1,669,220	$ 100,160	$1,142,920	$ 1,142,920

[a]Excess of total cash available over total cash needed before current financing.
[b]Note that the short-term interest payments pertain only to the amount of principal being repaid at the end of a quarter: $308,000 \times 0.12 \times \frac{1}{2} = \$18,480$.
[c]Ending cash balance is
  Total cash available for needs
  Deduct total disbursements
  Add Total effects of financing

c. Short-term financing requirements depend on how the total cash available for needs, keyed as (x) in Exhibit 6-6, compares with the total cash disbursements, keyed as (y), plus the minimum ending cash balance desired. The financing plans will depend on the relationship between total cash available for needs and total cash needed. If there is excess cash, loans may be repaid or temporary investments made.

d. The ending cash balance.

The cash budget in Exhibit 6-6 shows the pattern of short-term "self-liquidating" cash loans. In quarter III, Stylistic budgets a $307,840 cash deficiency. Hence, it undertakes short-term borrowing of $308,000 for six months. Seasonal peaks of production or sales often result in heavy cash disbursements for purchases, payroll, and other operating outlays as the products are produced and sold. Cash receipts from customers typically lag behind sales. The loan is *self-liquidating* in the sense that the borrowed money is used to acquire resources that are combined for sale, and the proceeds from sales are used to repay the loan. This **self-liquidating cycle** is the movement from cash to inventories to receivables and back to cash.

EXHIBIT 6-7
Budgeted Balance Sheet for Stylistic Furniture, December 31, 2001

Assets

Current assets:			
Cash		$1,142,920	
Accounts receivable		1,254,400	
Direct materials		204,000	
Finished goods		854,250	$3,455,570
Property, plant, and equipment			
Land		1,200,000	
Building and equipment	$4,100,000		
Accumulated depreciation	(1,300,000)	2,800,000	4,000,000
Total			$7,455,570

Liabilities and Stockholders' Equity

Current liabilities:		
Accounts payable	$ 358,000	
Income taxes payable	40,075	
Total current liabilities	398,075	
Long-term debt (interest at 10% per year)	2,400,000	
Total current and long-term liabilities		$2,798,075
Stockholders' equity		
Common stock, $0.01 par value, 300,000 shares outstanding	$ 3,000	
Retained earnings	4,654,495	4,657,495
Total		$7,455,570

Reinforcing Problems Exer. 6-27 and Probs. 6-33, 6-36, and 6-37 cover cash budgets.

2. The budgeted balance sheet is presented in Exhibit 6-7. Each item is projected in light of the details of the business plan as expressed in all the previous budget schedules. For example, the ending balance of accounts receivable of $1,254,400 is computed by adding the budgeted revenues of $20,384,000 (from Schedule 1) to the beginning balance of $1,881,600 (given) and subtracting cash receipts of $21,011,200 (from Exhibit 6-6).

3. The budgeted income statement is presented in Exhibit 6-8. It is merely the budgeted operating income statement in Exhibit 6-3 (p. 189) expanded to include interest expense and income taxes.

For simplicity, the cash receipts and disbursements were given explicitly in this illustration. Frequently, there are lags between the items reported on the accrual basis of accounting in an income statement and their related cash receipts and disbursements. In the Stylistic example, collections from customers are derived under two assumptions: (1) In any month, 20% of sales are cash and 80% of sales are on credit, and (2) the total credit sales are collected in the month after sale.

Sensitivity Analysis and Cash Flows

Exhibit 6-4 (p. 191) shows how differing assumptions about selling prices and direct material costs for Stylistic Furniture led to differing amounts for budgeted operating income. A key use of sensitivity analysis is in cash-flow budgeting. Exhibit 6-9 outlines the short-term borrowing implications of the nine combinations examined in Exhibit 6-4. Scenarios 7–9, with the lower selling price per table ($352.80), require large amounts of short-term borrowing in quarters III and IV. Scenario 9, with the combination of a 10% lower selling price and 5% higher direct materials costs, requires the largest amount of borrowing by Stylistic Furniture. Sensitivity

Teaching Tip If time permits, the study of Exhs. 6-5 to 6-8 is worthwhile because they provide an excellent integrative exercise on budgets and financial statement articulation.

EXHIBIT 6-8
Budgeted Income Statement for Stylistic Furniture for Year Ending December 31, 2001

Revenues	Schedule 1		$20,384,000
Cost of Goods Sold	Schedule 7		14,751,250
Gross Margin			5,632,750
Operating Costs			
R & D/Product			
Design Costs	Schedule 8	$ 659,600	
Marketing Costs	Schedule 8	1,709,200	
Distribution Costs	Schedule 8	629,600	
Customer-Service Costs	Schedule 8	547,680	
Administrative Costs	Schedule 8	605,760	4,151,840
Operating income			1,480,910
Interest Expense			258,480
Income before Income Taxes			1,222,430
Income Taxes			440,075
Net Income			$ 782,355

EXHIBIT 6-9
Sensitivity Analysis—Effects of Key Budget Assumptions in Exhibit 6-4 on Short-Term Borrowing for Stylistic Furniture

	Unit Selling Price	Direct Materials Purchase Cost		Budgeted Operating Income	Short-Term Borrowing by Quarter			
Scenario		Particle Board	Red Oak		Quarter I	Quarter II	Quarter III	Quarter IV
1	$431.20	$3.80	$5.70	$3,458,226	$0	$0	$ 0	$ 0
2	431.20	4.00	6.00	3,244,126	0	0	0	0
3	431.20	4.20	6.30	3,030,026	0	0	0	0
4	392.00	3.80	5.70	1,695,010	0	0	145,000	0
5	392.00	4.00	6.00	1,480,910	0	0	308,000	0
6	392.00	4.20	6.30	1,266,810	0	0	472,000	0
7	352.80	3.80	5.70	(68,206)	0	0	1,413,000	717,000
8	352.80	4.00	6.00	(282,306)	0	0	1,576,000	997,000
9	352.80	4.20	6.30	(496,406)	0	0	1,739,000	1,276,000

analysis helps managers anticipate such outcomes and to take steps to minimize the effects of expected operating cash flow reductions.

TERMS TO LEARN

The chapter and Glossary contain definitions of the following important terms:

activity-based budgeting (ABB) (p. 192)
budgetary slack (185)
cash budget (199)
controllability (195)
controllable cost (195)
cost center (194)
financial budget (182)
financial planning models (190)
investment center (194)
kaizen budgeting (191)
master budget (178)

operating budget (182)
organization structure (194)
pro forma statements (178)
profit center (194)
responsibility accounting (194)
responsibility center (194)
revenue center (194)
rolling budget (182)
self-liquidating cycle (200)
strategy (179)

QUESTIONS

6-1 What are the four elements of the budgeting cycle?

6-2 Define *master budget*.

6-3 "Strategy, plans, and budgets are unrelated to one another." Do you agree? Explain.

6-4 "Budgeted performance is a better criterion than past performance for judging managers." Do you agree? Explain.

6-5 "Production managers and marketing managers are like oil and water. They just don't mix." How can a budget assist in reducing traditional battles between these two areas?

6-6 How might a company benefit by sharing its own internal budget information with other companies?

6-7 "Budgets meet the cost-benefit test. They force managers to act differently." Do you agree? Explain.

6-8 Define *rolling budget*. Give an example.

6-9 Outline the steps in preparing an operating budget.

6-10 "The sales forecast is the cornerstone for budgeting." Why?

6-11 How can use of sensitivity analysis increase the benefits of budgeting?

6-12 What factors reduce the effectiveness of budgeting of companies?

6-13 Define *kaizen budgeting*.

6-14 Describe how nonoutput-based cost drivers can be incorporated into budgeting.

6-15 Explain how the choice of the type of responsibility center (cost, revenue, profit, or investment) affects behavior.

EXERCISES

6-16 Production budget (in units), fill in the missing numbers. The following information is taken from Osage Company's production budget for three models of fax machines in October 2001 (all in units):

	Model 101	Model 201	Model 301
1. Beginning finished goods inventory	11	8	?
2. Target ending finished goods inventory	?	6	33
3. Budgeted production	?	?	855
4. Budgeted sales	180	?	867
5. Total required units (2 + 4)	194	199	?

Required

Fill in the missing numbers.

6-17 Sales and production budget. The Mendez Company expects sales in 2002 of 100,000 units of serving trays. Mendez's beginning inventory for 2002 is 7,000 trays; target ending inventory, 11,000 trays. Compute the number of trays budgeted for production in 2002.

6-18 Direct materials budget. Inglenook Co. produces wine. The company expects to produce 1,500,000 2-liter bottles of Chablis in 2002. Inglenook purchases empty glass bottles from an outside vendor. Its target ending inventory of such bottles is 50,000; its beginning inventory is 20,000. For simplicity, ignore breakage. Compute the number of bottles to be purchased in 2002.

6-19 Budgeting material purchases. The Mahoney Company has prepared a sales budget of 42,000 finished units for a three-month period. The company has an inventory of 22,000 units of finished goods on hand at December 31 and has a target finished goods inventory of 24,000 units at the end of the succeeding quarter.

It takes 3 gallons of direct materials to make one unit of finished product. The company has an inventory of 90,000 gallons of direct materials at December 31 and has a target ending inventory of 110,000 gallons at the end of the succeeding quarter. How many gallons of direct materials should be purchased during the three months ending March 31?

6-20 Sales and production budget. Purity, Inc., bottles and distributes mineral water from the company's natural springs in northern Oregon. Purity markets two products—12-ounce disposable plastic bottles and 4-gallon reusable plastic containers.

Required

1. For the year 2001, Purity marketing managers project monthly sales of 400,000 12-ounce units and 100,000 4-gallon units. Average selling prices are estimated at $0.25 per 12-ounce unit and $1.50 per 4-gallon unit. Prepare a revenues budget for Purity, Inc., for the year ending December 31, 2001.
2. Purity begins 2001 with 900,000 12-ounce units in inventory. The vice president of operations requests that 12-ounce ending inventory on December 31, 2001 be no less than 600,000 units. Based on sales projections as budgeted above, what is the minimum number of 12-ounce units Purity must produce during 2001?
3. The VP of Operations requests that ending inventory of 4-gallon units on December 31, 2001 be 200,000 units. If the production budget calls for Purity to produce 1,300,000 4-gallon units during 2001, what is the beginning inventory of 4-gallon units on January 1, 2001?

6-21 Direct materials usage, unit costs, and gross margins (continuation of 6-20). Purity, Inc., bottles and distributes mineral water from the company's natural springs in northern Oregon. Purity markets two products—12-ounce disposable plastic bottles and 4-gallon reusable plastic containers. The 12-ounce bottles are purchased from Plastico, a plastics manufacturer, at a cost of 6 cents per unit. The 4-gallon containers are sterilized and put back into service at a cost of 30 cents per container. Spring water is extracted at a direct labor cost of 1 cent per 8 ounces (there are 128 ounces in a gallon). Manufacturing overhead is allocated at the rate of 15 cents per unit. (Note: A unit can be a 12-ounce bottle *or* a 4-gallon container). In 2001, the production budget calls for the production of 4,500,000 12-ounce units and 1,300,000 4-gallon units.

Required

1. Assume 4-gallon containers are fully depreciated, so that the only cost incurred is that of sterilization. Beginning and ending inventories for 4-gallon containers are zero. There are 500,000 empty 12-ounce bottles in beginning inventory on January 1, 2001. The vice president of operations would like to end 2001 with 300,000 empty 12-ounce bottles in inventory. Accounting for sterilization as the only cost of the 4-gallon containers, prepare a direct materials usage budget (relating to both bottles and containers) in both units and dollars.
2. The cost of direct manufacturing labor is captured through the extraction cost as detailed above. Based on the data given, prepare a direct manufacturing labor budget for 2001.
3. Calculate the unit cost per manufactured finished good for both products.
4. Assuming average selling prices as above, what are the expected average gross margins per unit?
5. Consider Purity's choice of a cost allocation base for manufacturing overhead. Can you suggest alternative cost allocation bases?

 6-22 Revenues, production, and purchases budgets. The Suzuki Co. in Japan has a division that manufactures two-wheel motorcycles. Its budgeted sales for Model G in 2002 is 800,000 units. Suzuki's target ending inventory is 100,000 units, and its beginning inventory is 120,000 units. The company's budgeted selling price to its distributors and dealers is 400,000 yen (¥) per motorcycle.

Suzuki buys all its wheels from an outside supplier. No defective wheels are accepted. (Suzuki's needs for extra wheels for replacement parts are ordered by a separate division of the company.) The company's target ending inventory is 30,000 wheels, and its beginning inventory is 20,000 wheels. The budgeted purchase price is 16,000 ¥ per wheel.

Required

1. Compute the budgeted revenues in yen.
2. Compute the number of motorcycles to be produced.
3. Compute the budgeted purchases of wheels in units and in yen.

6-23 Budgets for production and direct manufacturing labor. (CMA adapted) Roletter Company makes and sells artistic frames for pictures of weddings, graduations, and other special events. Bob Anderson, the controller, is responsible for preparing Roletter's master budget and has accumulated the following information for 2002:

	2002				
	January	**February**	**March**	**April**	**May**
Estimated sales in units	10,000	12,000	8,000	9,000	9,000
Selling price	$54.00	$51.50	$51.50	$51.50	$51.50
Direct manufacturing labor-hours per unit	2.0	2.0	1.5	1.5	1.5
Wage per direct manufacturing labor-hour	$10.00	$10.00	$10.00	$11.00	$11.00

Besides wages, direct manufacturing labor-related costs include pension contributions of $0.50 per hour, worker's compensation insurance of $0.15 per hour, employee medical insurance of $0.40 per hour, and social security taxes. Assume that as of January 1, 2002, the social security tax rates are 7.5% for employers and 7.5% for employees. The cost of employee benefits paid by Roletter on its employees is treated as a direct manufacturing labor cost.

Roletter has a labor contract that calls for a wage increase to $11.00 per hour on April 1, 2002. New labor-saving machinery has been installed and will be fully operational by March 1, 2002.

Roletter expects to have 16,000 frames on hand at December 31, 2001, and has a policy of carrying an end-of-month inventory of 100% of the following month's sales plus 50% of the second following month's sales.

Required
Prepare a production budget and a direct manufacturing labor budget for Roletter Company by month and for the first quarter of 2002. Both budgets may be combined in one schedule. The direct manufacturing labor budget should include labor-hours and show the details for each labor cost category.

6-24 Activity-based budgeting. Family Supermarkets (FS) is preparing its activity-based budget for January 2002. Its current concern is with its four activities (which are also indirect-cost categories in its product profitability reporting system):

1. Ordering—covers purchasing activities. The cost driver is number of purchase orders.

2. Delivery—covers the physical delivery and receipt of merchandise. The cost driver is number of deliveries.

3. Shelf stocking—covers the stocking of merchandise on store shelves and the ongoing restocking before sale. The cost driver is hours of stocking time.

4. Customer support—covers assistance provided to customers, including checkout and bagging. The cost driver is number of items sold.

Assume FS has only three product types—soft drinks, fresh produce, and packaged food. The budgeted usage of each cost driver in these three types and the January 2002 budgeted cost driver rates are

	Cost-Driver Rates		Jan. 2002 Budgeted Amount of Driver Used		
Activity and Driver	**2001 Actual Rate**	**Jan. 2002 Budgeted Rate**	**Soft Drinks**	**Fresh Produce**	**Packaged Food**
Ordering (per purchase order)	$100	$90	14	24	14
Delivery (per delivery)	$80	$82	12	62	19
Shelf stocking (per hour)	$20	$21	16	172	94
Customer support (per item sold)	$0.20	$0.18	4,600	34,200	10,750

Required
1. What is the total budgeted cost for each activity in January 2002?
2. What advantages might FS gain by using an activity-based budgeting approach over, say, an approach based on a budgeted percentage of the cost of goods sold times the budgeted cost of goods sold?

6-25 Kaizen approach to activity-based budgeting (continuation of 6-24). Family Supermarkets (FS) has a kaizen (continuous improvement) approach to budgeting monthly activity costs for each month of 2002. February's budgeted cost-driver rate is 0.998 times the budgeted January 2002 rate. March's budgeted cost-driver rate is 0.998 times the budgeted February 2002 rate and so on. Assume that March 2002 has the same budgeted amount of cost-driver usage as did January 2002.

Required

1. What is the total budgeted cost for each activity in March 2002?
2. What are the benefits of FS adopting a kaizen budgeting approach? What are the limitations?

6-26 Budgeting and human behavior. (CMA adapted) Many managers claim that budgets are impractical because companies experience so many uncertainties. However, it is very probable that a firm's competitors use budgets as indispensable management tools. A major objective of budgeting is to substitute deliberate, well-conceived business judgment for accidental success or failure in enterprise management. Implicit in this objective is the confidence that a competent management team can plan for, manage, and control in large measure the relevant variables that dominate the life of a business. Managers must grapple with uncertainties, regardless of whether or not they have a budget.

Required

1. Describe at least three benefits, other than improved cost control, that an organization can expect to realize from the implementation of budgeting.
2. Since a reliable prediction of sales is critical to the planning process, describe at least two factors that should be considered when preparing sales forecasts.

6-27 Cash flow analysis, chapter appendix. (CMA adapted) TabComp, Inc., is a retail distributor for MZB-33 computer hardware and related software and support services. TabComp prepares annual sales forecasts of which the first six months for 2002 are presented below.

Cash sales account for 25% of TabComp's total sales, 30% of the total sales are paid by bank credit card, and the remaining 45% are on open account (TabComp's own charge accounts). The cash sales and cash from bank credit-card sales are received in the month of the sale. Bank credit-card sales are subject to a 4% discount deducted at the time of the daily deposit. The cash receipts for sales on open account are 70% in the month following the sale, 28% in the second month following the sale, and the remaining accounts receivable are estimated to be uncollectible.

TabComp's month-end inventory requirements for computer hardware units are 30% of the next month's sales. A one-month lead time is required for delivery from the manufacturer. Thus, orders for computer hardware units are placed on the 25th of each month to assure that they will be in the store by the first day of the month needed. The computer hardware units are purchased under terms of n/45 (payment in full within 45 days of invoice) measured from the time the units are delivered to TabComp. TabComp's purchase price for the computer units is 60% of the selling price.

TabComp Inc.
Sales Forecast
First Six Months of 2002

| | Hardware Sales | | Software | Total |
	Units	Dollars	Sales and Support	Revenues
January	130	$ 390,000	$160,000	$ 550,000
February	120	360,000	140,000	500,000
March	110	330,000	150,000	480,000
April	90	270,000	130,000	400,000
May	100	300,000	125,000	425,000
June	125	375,000	225,000	600,000
Total	675	$2,025,000	$930,000	$2,955,000

Required

1. Calculate the cash that TabComp, Inc., can expect to collect during April 2002. Be sure to show all of your calculations.

2. TabComp, Inc., is determining how many MZB-33 computer hardware units to order on January 25, 2002.

    a. Determine the projected number of computer hardware units that will be ordered.

    b. Calculate the dollar amount of the order that TabComp will place for these computer hardware units.

3. As part of the annual budget process, TabComp prepares a cash budget by month for the entire year. Explain why a company such as TabComp prepares a cash budget by month for the entire year.

PROBLEMS

6-28 Budget schedules for a manufacturer. Sierra Furniture is an elite desk manufacturer. It makes two products:

◆ Executive desks—3' × 5' oak desks

◆ Chairman desks—6' × 4' red oak desks

The budgeted direct-cost inputs for each product in 2002 are:

	Executive Line	Chairman Line
Oak top	16 square feet	0
Red oak top	0	25 square feet
Oak legs	4	0
Red oak legs	0	4
Direct manufacturing labor	3 hours	5 hours

Unit data pertaining to the direct materials for March 2002 are

Actual Beginning Direct Materials Inventory (3/1/2002)

	Executive Line	Chairman Line
Oak top (square feet)	320	0
Red oak top (square feet)	0	150
Oak legs	100	0
Red oak legs	0	40

Target Ending Direct Materials Inventory (3/31/2002)

	Executive Line	Chairman Line
Oak top (square feet)	192	0
Red oak top (square feet)	0	200
Oak legs	80	0
Red oak legs	0	44

Unit cost data for direct-cost inputs pertaining to February 2002 and March 2002 are:

	February 2002 (actual)	March 2002 (budgeted)
Oak top (per square feet)	$18	$20
Red oak top (per square feet)	23	25
Oak legs (per leg)	11	12
Red oak legs (per leg)	17	18
Manufacturing labor cost per hour	30	30

Manufacturing overhead (both variable and fixed) is allocated to each desk on the basis of budgeted direct manufacturing labor-hours per desk. The budgeted variable manufacturing overhead rate for March 2002 is $35 per direct manufacturing labor-hour. The budgeted fixed manufacturing overhead for March 2002 is $42,500. Both variable and fixed manufacturing overhead cost are allocated to each unit of finished goods.

Data relating to finished goods inventory for March 2002 are:

	Executive	Chairman Line
Beginning inventory in units	20	5
Beginning inventory in dollars (cost)	$10,480	$4,850
Target ending inventory in units	30	15

Budgeted sales for March 2002 are 740 units of the executive line and 390 units of the chairman line. The budgeted selling prices per unit in March 2002 are $1,020 for the executive line desk and $1,600 for the chairman line desk. Assume the following in your answer:

1. Work-in-process inventories are negligible and ignored.

2. Direct materials inventory and finished goods inventory are costed using the first-in-first-out method.

3. Unit costs of direct materials purchased and finished goods are constant in March 2002.

Required
1. Prepare the following budgets for March 2002:
   a. Revenues budget
   b. Production budget in units
   c. Direct materials usage budget and direct materials purchases budget
   d. Direct manufacturing labor budget
   e. Manufacturing overhead budget
   f. Ending inventory budget
   g. Cost of goods sold budget
2. Suppose Sierra Furniture decides to incorporate continuous improvement into its budgeting process. Describe two areas where Sierra could incorporate continuous improvement into the budget schedules in requirement 1.

6-29 **Sensitivity analysis and changing budget assumptions.** Choco Chip produces two brands of chocolate chip cookies—Chippo, a cookie rich in chocolate, and Choco, a less sumptuous production for the more weight-conscious. Choco Chip's cookies are produced from two ingredients—chocolate chips and cookie dough. Chippo is 50% chips and 50% dough, while Choco is 25% chips and 75% dough.

Packages of either brand weigh 1 pound (16 ounces). Choco Chips' master budget projects sales of 500,000 packages of Choco and 500,000 packages of Chippo in 2001. According to the master budget for 2001, estimated average selling prices are $3.00 per package (both brands). An industry analyst forecasts 2001 ingredients' costs as follows: 1 pound of chocolate will cost $2.00, and 1 pound of cookie dough will cost $1.00. Assume Choco Chip incurs no other costs in the production of their cookies.

Required
1. Use the preceding information to calculate Choco Chip's budgeted gross margins for 2001.
2. In August 2000, Choco Chips' vice president of marketing is fired after overestimating sales for the first half of 2000 by over 50 percent. Choco Chip's CEO reevaluates the marketing plans for 2001 and believes Chippo cookies can average a selling price of only $2.60 a package. However, he thinks Choco cookies will average a selling price at least $3.20 per package. Based on these new estimates, recalculate budgeted gross margins. Calculate the percentage change in the budgeted gross margin relative to your initial estimate in requirement 1.
3. The original sales quantity estimates allowed for the new production line to begin operations on January 1, 2001. However, engineering reports the new line will only become operational during the second quarter of 2001. Based on this new knowledge, the CEO trims annual sales estimates of Chippo's to 400,000. Choco's sales will be 500,000 units. Using the initial $3.00 price per package, recalculate the budgeted gross margin. Calculate the percentage change from the initial estimate in requirement 1.
4. Bad weather in South America has led to an increase in cocoa prices. As a result, your resident economist reestimates 2001 chocolate prices at $4.00 a pound. Using the initial estimates for quantities and prices (that is, 500,000 packages at $3.00 per package), recalculate the budgeted gross margin and the percentage change from your original estimate in requirement 1.

6-30 Revenue and production budgets. (CPA adapted) The Scarborough Corporation manufactures and sells two products, Thingone and Thingtwo. In July 2002, Scarborough's Budget Department gathered the following data in order to prepare budgets for 2003:

2003 Projected Sales

Product	Units	Price
Thingone	60,000	$165
Thingtwo	40,000	$250

2003 Inventories (in Units)

	Expected	Target
Product	January 1, 2003	December 31, 2003
Thingone	20,000	25,000
Thingtwo	8,000	9,000

The following direct materials are used in the two products:

		Amount Used Per Unit	
Direct Material	Unit	Thingone	Thingtwo
A	pound	4	5
B	pound	2	3
C	each	0	1

Projected data for 2003 with respect to direct materials are as follows:

Direct Material	Anticipated Purchase Price	Expected Inventories January 1, 2003	Target Inventories December 31, 2003
A	$12	32,000 lb.	36,000 lb.
B	$ 5	29,000 lb.	32,000 lb.
C	$ 3	6,000 units	7,000 units

Projected direct manufacturing labor requirements and rates for 2003 are as follows:

Product	Hours Per Unit	Rate Per Hour
Thingone	2	$12
Thingtwo	3	$16

Manufacturing overhead is allocated at the rate of $20 per direct manufacturing labor-hour.

Required

Based on the preceding projections and budget requirements for Thingone and Thingtwo, prepare the following budgets for 2003:

1. Revenues budget (in dollars)
2. Production budget (in units)
3. Direct materials purchases budget (in quantities)
4. Direct materials purchases budget (in dollars)
5. Direct manufacturing labor budget (in dollars)
6. Budgeted finished goods inventory at December 31, 2003 (in dollars)

6-31 Budgeted income statement. (CMA adapted) Easecom Company is a manufacturer of video-conferencing products. Regular units are manufactured to meet marketing projections, and specialized units are made after an order is received. Maintaining the video-conferencing equipment is an important area of customer satisfaction. With the recent downturn in the computer industry, the video-conferencing equipment segment has suffered, leading to a decline in Easecom's financial performance. The following income statement shows results for the year 2001.

Easecom Company
Income Statement
For the Year Ended December 31, 2001
(in thousands)

Revenues:		
Equipment	$6,000	
Maintenance contracts	1,800	
Total revenues		$7,800
Cost of goods sold		4,600
Gross margin		3,200
Operating costs		
Marketing	600	
Distribution	150	
Customer maintenance	1,000	
Administration	900	
Total operating costs		2,650
Operating income		$ 550

Easecom's management team is in the process of preparing the 2002 budget and is studying the following information:

1. Selling prices of equipment are expected to increase by 10% as the economic recovery begins. The selling price of each maintenance contract is unchanged from 2001.

2. Equipment sales in units are expected to increase by 6%, with a corresponding 6% growth in units of maintenance contracts.

3. Cost of each unit sold is expected to increase by 3% to pay for the necessary technology and quality improvements.

4. Marketing costs are expected to increase by $250,000, but administration costs are expected to remain at 2001 levels.

5. Distribution costs vary in proportion to the number of units of equipment sold.

6. Two maintenance technicians are to be added at a total cost of $130,000, which covers wages and related travel costs. The objective is to improve customer service and shorten response time.

7. There is no beginning or ending inventory of equipment.

Required
Prepare a budgeted income statement for 2002.

6-32 Comprehensive operating budget. Slopes, Inc., manufactures and sells snowboards. Slopes manufactures a single model, the Pipex. In the summer of 2000, Slope's accountant gathered the following data in order to prepare budgets for 2001:

Materials and labor requirements

Direct materials	
Wood	5 board feet per snowboard
Fiberglass	6 yards per snowboard
Direct manufacturing labor	5 hours per snowboard

Slopes' CEO expects to sell 1,000 snowboards during 2001 at an estimated retail price of $450 per board. Further, he expects 2001 beginning inventory of 100 boards, and would like to end 2001 with 200 snowboards in stock.

Direct materials inventories

	Beginning Inventory 1/1/2001	Ending Inventory 12/31/2001
Wood	2,000	1,500
Fiberglass	1,000	2,000

Variable manufacturing overhead is allocated at the rate of $7.00 per direct manufacturing labor-hour. There are also $66,000 in fixed manufacturing overhead costs budgeted for 2001. Slopes combines both variable and fixed manufacturing overhead into a single rate based on direct manufacturing labor-hours. Variable marketing costs are allocated at the rate of $250 per sales visit. The marketing plan calls for 30 sales visits during 2001. Finally, there are $30,000 in fixed nonmanufacturing costs budgeted for 2001.

Other data includes:

	2000 Unit Price	2001 Unit Price
Wood	$28.00 per b.f.	$30.00 per b.f.
Fiberglass	$4.80 per yard	$5.00 per yard
Direct manufacturing labor	$24.00 per hour	$25.00 per hour

The inventoriable unit cost for ending finished goods inventory on December 31, 2000 is $374.80. Assume Slopes uses a first-in first-out inventory method for both direct materials and finished goods. Ignore work in process in your calculations.

Required

Use the data and projections supplied by Slopes' managers.

1. Prepare the 2001 revenues budget (in dollars).
2. Prepare the 2001 production budget (in units).
3. Prepare the direct materials usage and purchases budgets.
4. Prepare a direct manufacturing labor budget.
5. Prepare a manufacturing overhead budget.
6. What is the budgeted manufacturing overhead rate?
7. What is the budgeted manufacturing overhead cost per output unit?
8. Calculate the cost of a snowboard manufactured in 2001.
9. Prepare an ending inventory budget for both direct materials and finished goods.
10. Prepare a cost of goods sold budget.
11. Prepare the budgeted income statement for Slopes, Inc., for 2001.

6-33 Cash budgeting, chapter appendix. Retail outlets purchase snowboards from Slopes, Inc., throughout the year. However, in anticipation of late summer and early fall purchases, outlets ramp up inventories from May through August. Outlets are billed when boards are ordered. Invoices are payable within 60 days. From past experience, Slopes' accountant projects 20% of invoices are paid in the month invoiced, 50% are paid in the following month, and 30% of invoices are paid two months after the month of invoice. The average selling price per snowboard is $450.

To meet demand, Slopes increases production from April through July, since the snowboards are produced a month prior to their projected sale. Direct materials are purchased in the month of production, and paid for during the following month (terms are payment in full within 30 days of the invoice date). During this period there is no production for inventory, and no materials are purchased for inventory.

Direct manufacturing labor and manufacturing overhead are paid monthly. Variable manufacturing overhead is incurred at the rate of $7 per direct manufacturing labor-hour. Variable marketing costs are driven by the number of sales visits. However, there are no sales visits during the months studied. Slopes, Inc., also incurs fixed manufacturing overhead costs of $5,500 per month and fixed nonmanufacturing overhead costs of $2,500 per month.

Projected Sales

May	80 units
June	120 units
July	200 units
August	100 units
September	60 units
October	40 units

Direct Materials and Direct Manufacturing Labor Utilization and Cost

	Units Per Board	Price Per Unit	Unit
Wood	5	$30	Board feet
Fiberglass	6	5	Yard
Direct manufacturing labor	5	25	Hour

The beginning cash balance for July 1, 2000 is $10,000. On September 1, 2000, Slopes had a cash crunch and borrowed $30,000 on a 6% 1-year note with interest payable monthly. The note is due October 1, 2001. Using the information provided above, you must determine whether Slopes will be in a position to pay off this short-term debt on October 1, 2001.

Required

1. Prepare a cash budget for the months of July–September, 2001. Show supporting schedules for the calculation of receivables and payables.
2. Will Slopes be in a position to pay off the $30,000 1-year note on October 1, 2001? If not, what actions would you recommend to Slopes' management?
3. Suppose Slopes is interested in maintaining a minimum cash balance of $10,000. Will the company be able to maintain such a balance during all three months analyzed? If not, suggest a suitable cash management strategy.

6-34 Responsibility of purchasing agent. (Adapted from a description by R. Villers) Mark Richards is the purchasing agent for the Hart Manufacturing Company. Kent Sampson is head of the Production Planning and Control Department. Every six months, Sampson gives Richards a general purchasing program. Richards gets specifications from the Engineering Department. He then selects suppliers and negotiates prices. When he took this job, Richards was informed very clearly that he bore responsibility for meeting the general purchasing program once he accepted it from Sampson.

During week 24, Richards is advised that Part No. 1234—a critical part—would be needed for assembly on Tuesday morning of week 32. He found that the regular supplier could not deliver. He called everywhere and finally found a supplier in the Midwest, and accepted the commitment.

He followed up by e-mail. Yes, the supplier assured him, the part would be ready. The matter was so important that on Thursday of week 31, Richards checked by phone. Yes, the shipment had left in time. Richards was reassured and did not check further. But on Tuesday of week 32, the part had not arrived. Inquiry revealed that the shipment had been misdirected by the railroad and was still in Chicago.

Required

What department should bear the costs of time lost in the plant due to the delayed shipment? Why? As purchasing agent, do you think it fair that such costs be charged to your department?

6-35 Comprehensive review of budgeting. British Beverages bottles two soft drinks under license to Cadbury Schweppes at its Manchester plant. Bottling at this plant is a highly repetitive, automated process. Empty bottles are removed from their carton, placed on a conveyor, and cleaned, rinsed, dried, filled, capped, and heated (to reduce condensation). All inventory is in direct materials and finished goods at the end of each working day. There is no work-in-process inventory.

The two soft drinks bottled by British Beverages are lemonade and diet lemonade. The syrup for both soft drinks is purchased from Cadbury Schweppes. Syrup for the regular brand contains a higher sugar content than the syrup for the diet brand.

British Beverages uses a lot size of 1,000 cases as the unit of analysis in its budgeting. (Each case contains 24 bottles.) Direct materials are expressed in terms of lots, where one lot of direct materials is the input necessary to yield one lot (1,000 cases) of beverage. The following purchase prices are forecast for direct materials in 2002:

	Lemonade	Diet Lemonade
Syrup	$1,200 per lot	$1,100 per lot
Containers (bottles, caps, etc.)	$1,000 per lot	$1,000 per lot
Packaging	$ 800 per lot	$ 800 per lot

The two soft drinks are bottled using the same equipment. The equipment is sanitized daily, but it is only rinsed when a switch is made during the day between diet lemonade and lemonade. Diet lemonade is always bottled first each day to reduce the risk of sugar contamination. The only difference in the bottling process for the two soft drinks is the syrup.

Summary data used in developing budgets for 2002 are:

1. Sales

   ◆ Lemonade, 1,080 lots at $9,000 selling price per lot
   ◆ Diet lemonade, 540 lots at $8,500 selling price per lot

2. Beginning (January 1, 2002) inventory of direct materials

   ◆ Syrup for lemonade, 80 lots at $1,100 purchase price per lot

   ◆ Syrup for diet lemonade, 70 lots at $1,000 purchase price per lot

   ◆ Containers, 200 lots at $950 purchase price per lot

   ◆ Packaging, 400 lots at $900 purchase price per lot

3. Beginning (January 1, 2002) inventory of finished goods

   ◆ Lemonade, 100 lots at $5,300 per lot

   ◆ Diet lemonade, 50 lots at $5,200 per lot

4. Target ending (December 31, 2002) inventory of direct materials

   ◆ Syrup for lemonade, 30 lots

   ◆ Syrup for diet lemonade, 20 lots

   ◆ Containers, 100 lots

   ◆ Packaging, 200 lots

5. Target ending (December 31, 2002) inventory of finished goods

   ◆ Lemonade, 20 lots

   ◆ Diet lemonade, 10 lots

6. Each lot requires 20 direct manufacturing labor-hours at the 2002 budgeted rate of $25 per hour. Indirect manufacturing labor costs are included in the manufacturing overhead forecast.

7. Variable manufacturing overhead is forecast to be $600 per hour of bottling time; bottling time is the time the filling equipment is in operation. It takes two hours to bottle one lot of lemonade and two hours to bottle one lot of diet lemonade.

   Fixed manufacturing overhead is forecast to be $1,200,000 for 2002.

8. Hours of budgeted bottling time is the sole cost-allocation base for all fixed manufacturing overhead.

9. Administration costs are forecast to be 10% of the cost of goods manufactured for 2002. Marketing costs are forecast to be 12% of revenues for 2002. Distribution costs are forecast to be 8% of revenues for 2002.

Required
Assume British Beverages uses the first-in, first-out method for costing all inventories. On the basis of the preceding data, prepare the following budgets for 2002:

   a. Revenues budget (in dollars)
   b. Production budget (in units)
   c. Direct materials usage budget (in units and dollars)
   d. Direct materials purchases budget (in units and dollars)
   e. Direct manufacturing labor budget
   f. Manufacturing overhead costs budget
   g. Ending finished goods inventory budget
   h. Cost of goods sold budget
   i. Marketing costs budget
   j. Distribution costs budget
   k. Administration costs budget
   l. Budgeted income statement

6-36 **Cash budget, fill in the blanks, chapter appendix.** Starport manufactures and launches space stations. Use the following information to complete Starport's cash budget in Problem Exhibit 6-36 for the year ending December 31, 2001.

   ◆ Starport's CEO insists that Starport maintain a minimum monthly cash balance of $15 million.

   ◆ In the event of a cash deficiency, you are instructed to borrow exactly as much as is needed to return Starport to the minimum cash balance required. Short-term loans carry an interest rate of 12% per year, calculated from the beginning of the quarter in which the loan is initiated and through the end of the fourth quarter.

   ◆ In the second quarter Starport makes a major long-term investment, investing $85 million in a nuclear-powered lunar launch station.

Cash Budget for Starport (in thousands) for the Year Ended December 31, 2001

	I	II	III	IV	Year as a Whole
			Quarters		
Cash balance, beginning	$ 15,000	?	?	?	?
Add receipts					
Collections from customers	385,000	?	?	$365,000	$1,360,000
Total cash available for needs	?	$347,000	$310,000	?	?
Deduct disbursements					
Direct materials	175,000	125,000	?	155,000	?
Payroll	?	110,000	95,000	118,000	448,000
Other costs	50,000	45,000	40,000	49,000	?
Interest expense (LT debt)	?	?	?	?	?
Machinery purchase	0	?	0	0	85,000
Income taxes	15,000	14,000	12,000	?	61,000
Total disbursements	368,000	?	260,000	345,000	?
Minimum cash balance desired	?	?	?	?	15,000
Total cash needed	?	?	?	?	1,370,000
Cash excess (deficiency)	?	$ (50,000)	?	?	$ 5,000
Financing					
Borrowing (at beginning)	$ 0	?	$ 0	$ 0	
Repayment (at end)	0	0	0	(50,000)	(50,000)
Interest (at 12% per annum)	0	0	0	(4,500)	(4,500)
Total effects of financing	$ 0	?	$ 0	$ (54,500)	$ (4,500)
Cash balance, ending	$ 32,000	?	?	$ 15,500	?

◆ On January 1, 1999, Starport raised $100 million through the issue of a 5-year 12% bond. Interest on this long-term debt is payable quarterly.

Required
There is enough information available for you to complete Starport's cash budget. If you are unable to calculate any of the missing numbers, make an assumption and continue.

 6-37 **Cash budgeting, chapter appendix.** On December 1, 2001, the Itami Wholesale Co. is attempting to project cash receipts and disbursements through January 31, 2002. On this latter date, a note will be payable in the amount of $100,000. This amount was borrowed in September to carry the company through the seasonal peak in November and December.

Selected general ledger balances on December 1 are:

Cash	$ 10,000	
Accounts receivable	280,000	
Allowance for bad debts		$15,800
Inventory	87,500	
Accounts payable		92,000

Sales terms call for a 2% discount if payment is made within the first ten days of the month after purchase, with the balance due by the end of the month after purchase. Experience has shown that 70% of the billings will be collected within the discount period, 20% by the end of the month after purchase, 8% in the following month, and that 2% will be uncollectable. There are no cash sales.

The average selling price of the company's products is $100 per unit. Actual and projected sales are:

October actual	$ 180,000
November actual	250,000
December estimated	300,000
January estimated	150,000
February estimated	120,000
Total estimated for year ended June 30, 2002	1,500,000

All purchases are payable within 15 days. Thus, approximately 50% of the purchases in a month are due and payable in the next month. The average unit purchase cost is $70. Target ending inventories are 500 units plus 25% of the next month's unit sales.

Total budgeted marketing, distribution, and customer-service costs for the year are $400,000. Of this amount, $150,000 is considered fixed (and includes depreciation of $30,000). The remainder varies with sales. Both fixed and variable marketing, distribution and customer-service costs are paid as incurred.

Required

Prepare a cash budget for December and January. Supply supporting schedules for collections of receivables; payments for merchandise; and marketing, distribution, and customer-service costs.

6-38 Comprehensive budget; fill in schedules. The following information is for Newport Stationery Store:

1. Balance sheet information as of September 30, 2001:

Current assets	
Cash	$ 12,000
Accounts receivable	10,000
Inventory	63,600
Equipment—net	100,000
Liabilities as of September 30	None

2. Recent and anticipated sales:

September	$40,000
October	48,000
November	60,000
December	80,000
January	36,000

3. Credit sales: Sales are 75% for cash and 25% on credit. Assume that credit accounts are all collected within 30 days from sale. The accounts receivable on September 30 are the result of the credit sales for September (25% of $40,000).

4. Gross margin averages 30% of revenues. Newport treats cash discounts on purchases in the income statement as "other income."

5. Operating costs: Salaries and wages average 15% of monthly revenues; rent, 5%; other operating costs, excluding depreciation, 4 percent. Assume that these costs are disbursed each month. Depreciation is $1,000 per month.

6. Purchases: Newport keeps a minimum inventory of $30,000. The policy is to purchase each month additional inventory in the amount necessary to provide for the following month's sales. Terms on purchases are 2/10, n/30. (Payments on purchases are to be made in 30 days; a 2% discount is available if the payment is made within ten days after purchase.) Assume that payments are made in the month of purchase and that all discounts are taken.

7. Light fixtures: In October, $600 is spent for light fixtures, and in November, $400 is to be expended for this purpose. These amounts are to be capitalized.

Assume that a minimum cash balance of $8,000 must be maintained. Assume also that all borrowing is effective at the beginning of the month and all repayments are made at the end of the month of repayment. Loans are repaid when sufficient cash is available. Interest is paid only at the time of repaying principal. The interest rate is 18% per year. Management does not want to borrow any more cash than is necessary and wants to repay as soon as cash is available.

Required

On the basis of the facts as given above:

1. Complete Schedule A.

Schedule A
Budgeted Monthly Cash Receipts

Item	September	October	November	December
Total sales	$40,000	$48,000	$60,000	$80,000
Credit sales	10,000	12,000		
Cash sales				
Receipts:				
Cash sales		$36,000		
Collections on accounts receivable		10,000		
Total		$46,000		

2. Complete Schedule B. Note that purchases are 70% of next month's sales.

Schedule B
Budgeted Monthly Cash Disbursements for Purchases

Item	October	November	December	4th Quarter
Purchases	$42,000			
Deduct 2% cash discount	840			
Disbursements	$41,160			

3. Complete Schedule C.

Schedule C
Budgeted Monthly Cash Disbursements for Operating Costs

Item	October	November	December	4th Quarter
Salaries and wages	$ 7,200			
Rent	2,400			
Other cash operating costs	1,920			
Total	$11,520			

4. Complete Schedule D.

Schedule D
Budgeted Total Monthly Cash Disbursements

Item	October	November	December	4th Quarter
Purchases	$41,160			
Cash operating costs	11,520			
Light fixtures	600			
Total	$53,280			

5. Complete Schedule E.

Schedule E
Budgeted Cash Receipts and Disbursements

Item	October	November	December	4th Quarter
Receipts	$46,000			
Disbursement	53,280	_____	_____	_____
Net cash increase				
Net cash decrease	$ 7,280	══════	══════	══════

6. Complete Schedule F (assume that borrowings must be made in multiples of $1,000).

Schedule F
Financing Required

Item	October	November	December	Total
Beginning cash balance	$12,000			
Net cash increase				
Net cash decrease	7,280	_____	_____	_____
Cash position before borrowing	4,720			
Minimum cash balance required	8,000	_____	_____	_____
Excess/Deficiency	(3,280)			
Borrowing required	4,000			
Interest payments				
Borrowing repaid	_____	_____	_____	_____
Ending cash balance	$ 8,720	══════	══════	══════

7. What do you think is the most logical type of loan needed by Newport? Explain your reasoning.

8. Prepare a budgeted income statement for the fourth quarter and a budgeted balance sheet as of December 31. Ignore income taxes.

9. Some simplifications have been included in this problem. What complicating factors might arise in a typical business situation?

6-39 Budgetary slack and ethics. (CMA) Marge Atkins, the budget manager at Norton Company, a manufacturer of infant furniture and carriages, is working on the budget for 2001. In discussions with Scott Ford, the sales manager, Atkins discovers that Ford's sales projections are lower than what Ford actually believes are achievable. When Atkins asks Ford about this, Ford says: "Well, we don't want to fall short of the sales projections, so we generally give ourselves a little breathing room by lowering the sales projections anywhere from 5 to 10 percent." Atkins also finds that Pete Granger, the production manager, makes similar adjustments. He pads budgeted costs, adding 10% to estimated costs.

Required

As a management accountant, should Marge Atkins take the position that the behavior described by Scott Ford and Pete Granger is unethical? Refer to the Standards of Ethical Conduct for Management Accountants described in Chapter 1 (p. 16).

COLLABORATIVE LEARNING PROBLEM

6-40 Athletic Department of a university, budget revision options. Gary Connolly is the athletic director of Pacific University (PU). PU is a men's football and basketball power-house. The women's athletic program, however, has had less success. Last year, the women's basketball team finally had more wins than losses.

Connolly has just had a meeting with Laura Reddy, the newly appointed president of PU. It did not go well. In fact, it went terribly. They discussed what Reddy called "Draft I" of the 2002 Athletic Department budget. Connolly believed it was the final draft. Reddy expresses four grave concerns about "Draft I" in particular and about the PU Athletic Program in general:

Concern 1: The Athletic Department is budgeting a loss of over $3 million. Given the tight fiscal position of the university, this outcome is unacceptable. A budgeted loss of $1 million is the most she will tolerate for 2002. Draft II of the 2002 budget is due in two weeks time. By 2003, the Athletic Department has to operate with a balanced budget. She tells Connolly this is nonnegotiable.

Concern 2: The low allocation of money to the women's athletic program. Frontline, a tabloid television show, recently ran a program titled "Its a Man's World at the Pacific University Athletics' Program." Reddy said Connolly is treating woman athletes as "third-class citizens."

Concern 3: The low academic performance of the men's football athletes, many of whom have full scholarships. She notes that the local TV news recently ran an interview with three football-team students, none of which "exemplified the high academic credentials she wants Pacific to showcase to the world." She calls one student "incoherent" and another "incapable of stringing sentences together."

Concern 4: The outrageous salary paid to Bill Madden, the football coach. She notes it is twice that of the highest paid academic person on campus, a Nobel Prize winner. Moreover, Madden receives other payments from his "Football the Pacific Way" summer program for high school students.

Problem Exhibit 6-40 has a summary of the Draft I Athletic Department budget for 2002.

Required

Form groups of two or more students. Your group is to prepare Draft II of the Athletic Department's 2002 budget. This Draft II will form the basis of a half-day meeting Connolly will have with key officials of the Athletic Department.

PROBLEM EXHIBIT 6-40
Pacific University 2002 Athletic Department Budget ($ millions)

Revenues		
Men's athletic programs	$10.350	
Women's' athletic programs	0.780	
Other (endowment income, gifts)	3.400	$14.530
Costs		
Men's athletic programs	$11.040	
Women's athletic programs	2.800	
Other (not-assigned to programs)	3.700	17.540
Operating income		$ (3.010)

Men's Athletic Programs

	Football	Basketball	Swimming	Other	Total
Revenues	$8.600	$1.500	$0.100	$0.150	$10.350
Costs	7.400	2.700	0.300	0.640	11.040
Full scholarships	37	21	6	4	68

Womens' Athletic Programs

	Basketball	Swimming	Other	Total
Revenues	$0.600	$0.080	$0.100	$0.780
Costs	1.800	0.200	0.800	2.800
Full scholarships	11	4	2	17

7

Flexible Budgets, Variances, and Management Control: I

learning objectives

When you have finished studying this chapter, you should be able to

1. Describe the difference between a static budget and a flexible budget
2. Develop a flexible budget and compute flexible-budget variances and sales-volume variances
3. Compute the price and efficiency variances for direct-cost categories
4. Explain why standard costs are often used in variance analysis
5. Explain why purchasing performance measures should focus on more factors than just price variances
6. Integrate continuous improvement into variance analysis
7. Perform variance analysis in activity-based costing systems
8. Describe benchmarking and how it can be used in cost management

The management of labor costs is facilitated by understanding the causes of direct manufacturing labor price and efficiency cost variances.

In the previous chapter we saw how budgets assist managers in their planning function. We now turn our attention to how budgets—specifically flexible budgets—can be used to evaluate feedback on variances and aid managers in their control function. Recall from Chapter 1 that feedback enables managers to compare actual results with planned performance. Flexible budgets and variances help managers gain insights into why the actual results differ from the planned performance. The "why" makes the topics covered in this chapter and the next especially important.

THE USE OF VARIANCES

Teaching Tip Emphasize that it's important for students to master Chap. 7 material before attempting Chap. 8, since Chap. 8 builds on concepts introduced here.

Each **variance** we compute is the difference between an actual result and a budgeted amount. The budgeted amount is a benchmark, a point of reference from which comparisons may be made. Consider a Goodrich plant in Detroit that manufactures car tires. The budgeted amount could be the cost per tire in the most recent period at that plant, or the cost per tire in the most efficient plant owned by Goodrich, or the cost per tire at the most efficient plant of any company in the industry, or the expected cost at Goodrich's Detroit plant given the new production line at that plant. Organizations differ widely in how they compute and label their budgeted amounts. Some organizations rely heavily on past results when developing budgeted amounts; others rely on detailed engineering studies.

Variances assist managers in their planning and control decisions. **Management by exception** is the practice of concentrating on areas not operating as anticipated (such as a cost overrun on a defense project) and giving less attention to areas operating as anticipated. Managers use information from variances when planning how to allocate their efforts. Areas with sizable variances receive more attention by managers on an ongoing basis than do areas with minimal variances. For example, assume the costs associated with scrap and rework at a Goodrich plant are well above the budgeted amount. These variances will guide managers to seek explanations for this situation and (hopefully) make decisions to ensure that future operations have less scrap and rework. Variances are also used in performance evaluation. For example, production-line managers at Goodrich may have quarterly efficiency incentives linked to achieving a budgeted operating cost amount.

STATIC BUDGETS AND FLEXIBLE BUDGETS

OBJECTIVE 1

Describe the difference between a static budget and a flexible budget

So far, the budgets we have seen in this text have been static budgets. A **static budget** is based on the level of output planned at the start of the budget period. The master budget for Stylistic Furniture in Chapter 6 (pp. 182–191) is an example of a static budget. When variances are computed from a static budget at the end of the period, no adjustment is made to the budgeted amounts irrespective of the actual level of output in the budget period. In this chapter we emphasize flexible budgets. A **flexible budget** is developed using budgeted revenues or cost amounts based on the level of output actually achieved in the budget period. The key difference between a *flexible budget* and a *static budget* is the use of the actual output level in the flexible budget, whereas the static budget uses the output level planned at the start of the budget period. As we will see, a flexible budget enables managers to compute a more informative set of variances than does a static budget.

Points to Stress Distinguish between the static budget discussed in Chap. 6 (very detailed, made at the beginning of the period, for 1 output level) and the FB discussed here (highly summarized, can be made at the beginning or end of the period, can be made for several output levels).

Budgets, both static and flexible, can differ in the level of detail they report. Increasingly, organizations present budgets with broad summary figures that can then be broken down into progressively more detailed figures via computer software programs. This increasing level of detail pertains to both the number of line items examined in the income statement and the number of variances computed. In this book, the term "level" followed by a number denotes the amount of detail shown by a variance analysis. Level 0 reports the least detail, Level 1 provides more information, and so on. We will use the example of Webb Company to illustrate static budgets and flexible budgets and their related variances.

Accounting System at Webb

Webb manufactures and sells a single product, a distinctive jacket that requires tailoring and many hand operations. Sales are made to distributors who sell to independent clothing stores and retail chains. We assume that all units manufactured in April 2000 are sold in April 2000. There are no beginning or ending inventories. Webb has three variable-cost categories. The budgeted variable costs per jacket for each category are:

Cost Category	Variable Cost Per Jacket
Direct materials costs	$60
Direct manufacturing labor costs	16
Variable manufacturing overhead	12
Total variable costs	$88

The cost driver for direct materials, direct manufacturing labor, and variable manufacturing overhead is the *number of units manufactured*. The relevant range for the cost driver is from 8,000 to 16,000 units. The budgeted fixed manufacturing costs are $276,000. The budget selling price is $120 per jacket. This selling price is the same for all distributors. The static budget for April 2000 is based on selling 12,000 jackets. Actual sales in April 2000 were 10,000 jackets.

STATIC BUDGET VARIANCES

A **static-budget variance** is the difference between an actual result and a budgeted amount in the static budget. Exhibit 7-1 presents the Level 0 and Level 1 variance analyses for April 2000. Level 0 gives the least detailed comparison of the actual and

EXHIBIT 7-1
Static-Budget-Based Variance Analysis for Webb Company for April 2000[a]

LEVEL 0 ANALYSIS

Actual operating income	$ 14,900
Budgeted operating income	108,000
Static-budget variance of operating income	$ 93,100 U

LEVEL 1 ANALYSIS

	Actual Results (1)	Static- Budget Variances (2) = (1) − (3)	Static Budget (3)
Units sold	10,000	2,000 U	12,000
Revenues	$1,250,000	$190,000 U	$1,440,000
Variable costs			
Direct materials	621,600	98,400 F	720,000
Direct manufacturing labor	198,000	6,000 U	192,000
Variable manuf. overhead	130,500	13,500 F	144,000
Total variable costs	950,100	105,900 F	1,056,000
Contribution margin	299,900[b]	84,100 U	384,000[c]
Fixed costs	285,000	9,000 U	276,000
Operating income	$ 14,900	$ 93,100 U	$ 108,000

$93,100 U
Total static-budget variance

[a]F = favorable effect on operating income; U = unfavorable effect on operating income.
[b]Contribution margin percentage = $299,900 ÷ $1,250,000 = 24.0%
[c]Contribution margin percentage = $384,000 ÷ $1,440,000 = 26.7%

Points to Stress Variable costs are variable in total and fixed costs are fixed in total (i.e., costs are linear with respect to output) only *within the relevant range*. This is important for Chap. 7. Outside the relevant range, the variable cost per unit and total fixed cost elements of FB (and var. analysis) may change, as illustrated by the "economist's" TR and TC functions drawn in the annotation on p. 64 of Chap. 3.

Correcting Student Misconceptions Companies prepare FBs for two reasons. The first is *ex ante* planning. The FB is a highly summarized model of revenues and costs, so it facilitates planning-oriented sensitivity analyses that predict costs at different output levels. FBs are also prepared *ex post* to facilitate control. Here, the FB is prepared at the end of the period to estimate what costs and revenues should have been at that output (or revenue/cost driver) level. The FB developed for control purposes provides a benchmark against which to compare actual results, as in Exh. 7-2. In this case, the FB can't be prepared until the end of the period because actual output levels (or revenue/cost driver levels) aren't known until the end of the period. In sum, the FB can be used as either a planning tool or a control tool.

Points to Stress The Level 1 analysis compares apples with oranges. For example, variable costs should be lower if only 10,000 units are sold than if 12,000 are sold (as in the static budget). *But are the variable costs exactly what they should be for 10,000 units?* This is the question addressed by comparing actual results to the FB for 10,000 units in Exh. 7-2's Level 2 analysis.

Reinforcing Problems Exer. 7-16 through 7-18, 7-23, 7-25, and 7-31 and Probs. 7-32 and 7-37 cover flexible budgeting.

budgeted operating income. A **favorable variance**—denoted F in this book—is a variance that increases operating income relative to the budgeted amount. For revenue items, F means actual revenues exceed budgeted revenues. For cost items, F means actual costs are less than budgeted costs. An **unfavorable variance**—denoted U in this book—is a variance that decreases operating income relative to the budgeted amount.

The unfavorable variance of $93,100 in Exhibit 7-1 for Level 0 is simply the result of subtracting the static-budget operating income of $108,000 from the actual operating income of $14,900:

$$\frac{\text{Static-budget}}{\text{variance}} = \frac{\text{Actual}}{\text{results}} - \frac{\text{Static-budget}}{\text{amount}}$$

$$= \$14,900 - \$108,000$$

$$= \$93,100 \text{ U}$$

Level 1 analysis in Exhibit 7-1 provides managers with more detailed information on the operating income static-budget variance of $93,100 U. The additional information added in Level 1 pertains to revenues, individual variable costs, and fixed costs. The budgeted contribution margin percentage of 26.7% decreases to 24.0% for the actual results.

Although Level 1 analysis provides more information than does Level 0 analysis, managers might require still more detail about the causes of variances. A flexible budget enables this more detailed level of analysis.

STEPS IN DEVELOPING A FLEXIBLE BUDGET

Webb uses a four-step approach to develop its flexible budget. It is a relatively straightforward approach in which it is assumed that all costs are either variable or are fixed with respect to output units produced. The four steps are:

Step 1: Determine Budgeted Selling Price, Budgeted Variable Costs Per Unit, and Budgeted Fixed Costs Each output unit (a jacket) has a budgeted selling price of $120. The budgeted variable cost is $88 per jacket. The budgeted fixed costs are $276,000.

Step 2: Determine the Actual Quantity of Output In April 2000, Webb produced and sold 10,000 jackets. The cost driver for variable manufacturing costs is output units manufactured.

Step 3: Determine the Flexible Budget for Revenues Based on Budgeted Selling Price and Actual Quantity of Output

$$\text{Flexible-budget revenues} = \$120 \times 10,000$$

$$= \$1,200,000$$

Example Only variable costs put the "flex" in the FB. We expect to produce 20 lamps per week. Wood costs $50/lamp, and it costs $200/week to rent a lathe. Fixed mfg. OH is allocated based on units of production. *Required:* What is the budgeted fixed mfg. OH rate? [Ans: $200/20 = $10/lamp.] What is the FB for 20 lamps? 10 lamps? Use a cost equation: TC = $200 + ($50)(# of lamps).

At 20 lamps,
  TC = $200 + ($50)(20) = $1,200
At 10 lamps,
  TC = $200 + ($50)(10) = $700
Many students will calculate the fixed cost for 10 lamps as: ($10)(10 lamps) = $100, not the $200. The $100 is the fixed mfg. OH *allocated to WIP* for inventory costing. However, for budgeting, we treat fixed mfg. OH correctly—as a lump sum. This idea is developed further in Chap. 8.

Step 4: Determine the Flexible Budget for Costs Based on Budgeted Variable Costs Per Output Unit, Actual Quantity of Output, and the Budgeted Fixed Costs

Flexible-budget variable costs	
Direct materials, $60 × 10,000	$ 600,000
Direct manufacturing labor, $16 × 10,000	160,000
Variable manufacturing overhead, $12 × 10,000	120,000
Total variable costs	880,000
Flexible-budget fixed costs	276,000
Flexible-budget total costs	$1,156,000

These four steps enable Webb to move to a Level 2 variance analysis that uses the flexible budget to obtain more reasons for the $93,100 unfavorable static-budget variance. The flexible budget is the budget that Webb would have used at the start of the budget period had it forecast an output level of 10,000 units.

EXHIBIT 7-2
Level 2 Flexible-Budget-Based Variance Analysis for Webb Company for April 2000[a]

LEVEL 2 ANALYSIS

	Actual Results (1)	Flexible-Budget Variances (2) = (1) − (3)	Flexible Budget (3)	Sales-Volume Variances (4) = (3) − (5)	Static Budget (5)
Units sold	10,000	0	10,000	2,000 U	12,000
Revenues	$1,250,000	$50,000 F	$1,200,000	$240,000 U	$1,440,000
Variable costs					
Direct materials	621,600	21,600 U	600,000	120,000 F	720,000
Direct manufacturing labor	198,000	38,000 U	160,000	32,000 F	192,000
Variable manuf. overhead	130,500	10,500 U	120,000	24,000 F	144,000
Total variable costs	950,100	70,100 U	880,000	176,000 F	1,056,000
Contribution margin	299,900	20,100 U	320,000	64,000 U	384,000
Fixed costs	285,000	9,000 U	276,000	0	276,000
Operating income	$ 14,900	$29,100 U	$ 44,000	$ 64,000 U	$ 108,000

$29,100 U $64,000 U

Total flexible-budget variance   Total sales-volume variance

$93,100 U

Total static-budget variance

[a]F = favorable effect on operating income; U = unfavorable effect on operating income.

FLEXIBLE-BUDGET VARIANCES AND SALES-VOLUME VARIANCES

Exhibit 7-2 presents the Level 2 flexible-budget-based variance analysis for Webb. The Level 1 $93,100 unfavorable static-budget variance of operating income is split into two parts—a flexible-budget variance of $29,100 U and a sales-volume variance of 64,000 U.

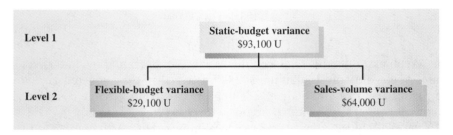

The **flexible-budget variance** is the difference between the actual results and the flexible-budget amount based on the level of output actually achieved in the budget period. The **sales-volume variance** is the difference between the flexible-budget amount and the static-budget amount. These variances help Webb's managers better understand the static-budget variance of $93,100 U.

Flexible-Budget Variances

The first three columns of Exhibit 7-2 compare the actual results with the flexible-budget amounts. Flexible-budget variances are reported in column 2 for each line item in the income statement:

$$\frac{\text{Flexible-budget}}{\text{variance}} = \frac{\text{Actual}}{\text{results}} - \frac{\text{Flexible-budget}}{\text{amount}}$$

Points to Stress Exh. 7-1's Level 1 analysis implies that the variable cost var. is $105,900 F. However, Exh. 7-2's Level 2 analysis shows that variable costs are $70,000 higher than expected for this level of output. The F variable cost static budget var. arises because Webb sold fewer units than expected. Even though the decline in sales is bad for the company, it causes an F variable cost SVV (i.e., lower VC). The more detailed Level 2 analysis portrays a more accurate picture of mgrs.' performance because it reveals that variable costs are higher than they should have been for 10,000 units.

Teaching Tip To calculate an FB for *ex post* control purposes, students should work "backward." First determine the # of actual outputs (or actual units of the revenue/cost driver). Then figure out what costs and revenues should have been for that exact # of outputs. The FBV is the difference between what we actually spent (received) and what we should've spent (received) for the actual # of outputs.

Curriculum Linkage The FBV for revenues is a selling price var. since it arises only because of the difference between budgeted and actual selling prices. This and all revenue variances are covered in more detail in Chap 16.

Correcting Student Misconceptions If the FB is based on *actual outputs* (units of revenue/cost driver), which aren't known until the end of the period, how can it be a *budget*? [Ans.: The FB shows the costs that should have been incurred (i.e., the budgeted costs) to achieve the actual output level. The FB is the budget we would have made at the beginning of the period if we had perfectly predicted the actual # of outputs.]

Points to Stress Can fixed costs have a sales-volume var. (SVV)? If the expected (static budget) and actual (FB) # of outputs are in the same relevant range, then budgeted fixed costs are the same at both levels, and there will be no SVV for fixed costs.

Points to Stress/Reinforcing Problems The SVV arises only because expected qtys. of revenue and cost drivers used to develop the static budget don't equal the actual qtys. of revenue and cost drivers used to develop the FB. Probs. 7-34 and 7-36 through 7-38 cover the SVV.

For the operating income line item, the flexible-budget variance is $29,100 U ($14,900 − $44,000). This $29,100 U arises because the actual selling price, variable costs per unit, input quantities, and fixed costs differ from the budgeted amounts. The actual and budgeted amounts for the selling price and variable costs per unit are:

	Actual Unit Amount	Budgeted Unit Amount
Selling price	$125.00 ($1,250,000 ÷ 10,000)	$120.00 ($1,200,000 ÷ 10,000)
Variable cost	$ 95.01 (950,100 ÷ 10,000)	$ 88.00 ($880,000 ÷ 10,000)

The actual fixed costs of $285,000 are $9,000 more than the budgeted amount of $276,000. Thus, it decreases operating income and this flexible-budget variance is unfavorable.

The flexible-budget variance pertaining to revenues is often called a **selling-price variance** because it arises solely from differences between the actual selling price and the budgeted selling price:

$$\text{Selling-price variance} = \left(\begin{array}{c}\text{Actual} \\ \text{selling price}\end{array} - \begin{array}{c}\text{Budgeted} \\ \text{selling price}\end{array}\right) \times \begin{array}{c}\text{Actual} \\ \text{units sold}\end{array}$$

$$= (\$125 - \$120) \times 10,000$$

$$= \$50,000 \text{ F}$$

Webb has a favorable selling-price variance because the actual selling price exceeds the budgeted amount (by $5). Marketing managers typically are best informed as to why this selling-price difference arose.

Sales-Volume Variances

The flexible-budget amounts in column 3 of Exhibit 7-2 and the static-budget amounts in column 5 are both computed using the budgeted selling prices, budgeted costs, and budgeted input quantities. The only difference is that the flexible-budget amount is calculated using the actual output level whereas the static-budget amount is calculated using the budgeted output level. The variance that arises between these two amounts is labeled the "sales-volume variance" because it represents the difference caused solely by the difference in the quantity of units sold from that in the static budget.

$$\text{Sales-volume variance} = \begin{array}{c}\text{Flexible-budget} \\ \text{amount}\end{array} - \begin{array}{c}\text{Static-budget} \\ \text{amount}\end{array}$$

$$= \$108,000 - \$44,000$$

$$= \$64,000 \text{ U}$$

In our Webb example, this sales-volume variance in operating income arises solely because Webb sold only 10,000 units, 2,000 fewer than the budgeted 12,000 units. Note particularly that any budgeted selling prices or unit variable costs are always held constant when sales-volume variances are computed.

A flexible-budget variance and a sales-volume variance are computed in Exhibit 7-2 for each of the line items in the income statement. We now proceed to a more detailed analysis of the flexible-budget variance for the two direct-cost categories.

PRICE VARIANCES AND EFFICIENCY VARIANCES FOR DIRECT-COST INPUTS

OBJECTIVE 3

Compute the price and efficiency variances for direct-cost categories

Webb's flexible-budget variance (Level 2) captures the difference between the actual results and the flexible budget. The sources of this variance (regarding costs) are individual differences between actual and budgeted *input prices or input quantities*. We can examine this variance further by subdividing it into two more detailed variances—(a) a price variance that reflects the difference between actual and budgeted input prices, and (b) an efficiency variance that reflects the difference between actual and budgeted input quantities. This Level 3 information helps managers better understand past performance and better plan for future performance. The flexible budget used in computing Level 3 variances is based on actual output levels.

Obtaining Budgeted Input Prices and Input Quantities

Webb's two main sources of information about budgeted input prices and budgeted input quantities are:

1. Actual input data from past periods. Most companies have past data on actual input prices and actual input quantities. These past amounts could be used for the budgeted amounts in a flexible budget. Past data are typically available at a relatively low cost. Limitations of using this source include (i) past data can include inefficiencies, and (ii) past data do not incorporate any expected changes for the budget period.

2. Standards developed by Webb. A **standard** is a carefully predetermined price, cost, or quantity amount. It is usually expressed on a per unit basis. Webb uses engineering studies to determine its standard quantity amounts. Webb conducts a detailed breakdown of the steps required to make a jacket. Each step is then assigned a standard time based on work performed by a skilled operator using equipment operating in an efficient manner. The advantages of using standard amounts are as follows: (i) they can exclude past inefficiencies, and (ii) they can take into account changes expected to occur in the budget period. An example of (ii) is the acquisition of new loom machines that operate at a faster speed and enable work to be done with lower reject rates.

Webb has developed standard inputs and standard costs for each of its variable-cost items. A **standard input** is a carefully predetermined quantity of inputs (such as pounds of materials or manufacturing labor-hours) required for one unit of output. A **standard cost** is a carefully predetermined cost. Standard costs can relate to units of inputs or units of outputs. Webb's budgeted cost for each variable direct-cost item is computed as follows:

$$\frac{\text{Standard inputs allowed}}{\text{for one output unit}} \times \frac{\text{Standard cost}}{\text{per input unit}}$$

Direct materials: 2.00 square yards of cloth input allowed per output unit (jacket) manufactured, at $30 standard cost per square yard

Standard cost = $2.00 \times \$30 = \$60.00$ per output unit manufactured

Direct manufacturing labor: 0.80 manufacturing labor-hour of input allowed per output unit manufactured, at $20 standard cost per hour

Standard cost = $0.80 \times \$20 = \$16.00$ per output unit manufactured

These standard-cost computations explain how Webb developed the variable direct-cost numbers presented earlier in this chapter (p. 221).[1]

Data for Webb's Price and Efficiency Variances

Consider Webb's two direct-cost categories. The actual cost for each of these categories in April 2000 is:

Direct materials purchased and used

1. Square yards of cloth input purchased and used	22,200
2. Actual price paid per yard	$28
3. Direct materials cost (1 × 2) [Exhibit 7-2, column 1]	$621,600

Direct manufacturing labor

1. Manufacturing labor-hours	9,000
2. Actual price paid per hour	$22
3. Direct manufacturing labor costs (1 × 2) [Exhibit 7-2, column 1]	$198,000

[1] The variable manufacturing overhead is allocated on the basis of 0.40 machine-hour per output unit manufactured, at $30 standard cost per machine-hour: 0.40 × $30 = $12.00 per output unit manufactured. Chapter 8 contains further discussion of Webb's overhead costs.

The Widespread Use of Standard Costs

Surveys of company practice across the globe report widespread use of standard costs by manufacturers. The following data are representative of surveys conducted in five countries:

	Percentage of Respondents Using Standard Costs in Their Accounting System
United States[a]	86
Ireland[b]	85
United Kingdom[c]	76
Sweden[d]	73
Japan[e]	65

What explains the popularity of standard costs? Companies based in four countries report the following reasons for using standard costs (1 for most important, 4 for least important):[f]

	United States	Canada	Japan	United Kingdom
Cost management	1	1	1	2
Pricing decisions	2	3	2	1
Budgetary planning and control	3	2	3	3
Financial statement preparation	4	4	4	4

The materials price and efficiency variances discussed in this chapter illustrate the use of standard costs in promoting cost management.

[a]Cornick, Cooper, and Wilson, "How Do Companies."

[b]Clarke, "Management Accounting."

[c]Drury, Braund, Osborne, and Tayles, "A Survey."

[d]Ask and Ax, "Trends."

[e]Scarbrough, Nanni, and Sakurai, "Japanese Management."

[f]Inoue, "A Comparative Study." Full citations are in Appendix A.

Teaching Tip Motivate students' interest in std. costing by pointing out that over 85% of responding U.S. companies report that they use std. costs.

For simplicity, we assume here that the quantity of direct materials used is equal to the quantity of direct materials purchased. We now use this Webb Company data to illustrate the price and efficiency variances.

A **price variance** is the difference between the actual price and the budgeted price multiplied by the actual quantity of input in question (such as direct materials purchased or used). Price variances are sometimes called **input-price variances** or **rate variances** (especially when those variances are for direct labor). An **efficiency variance** is the difference between the actual quantity of input used (such as yards of cloth of direct materials) and the budgeted quantity of input that should have been used, multiplied by the budgeted price. Efficiency variances are sometimes called **usage variances**.

Price Variances

The formula for computing the price variance is:

$$\text{Price variance} = \left(\begin{array}{c} \text{Actual price} \\ \text{of input} \end{array} - \begin{array}{c} \text{Budgeted price} \\ \text{of input} \end{array} \right) \times \begin{array}{c} \text{Actual quantity} \\ \text{of input} \end{array}$$

Price variances for each of Webb's two direct-cost categories are:

Direct-Cost Category	$\left(\begin{array}{c}\text{Actual price} - \text{Budgeted price} \\ \text{of input} \quad\quad \text{of input}\end{array}\right) \times$	Actual quantity of input	=	Price Variance
Direct materials	($28 − $30)	× 22,200	=	$44,400 F
Direct manufacturing labor	($22 − $20)	× 9,000	=	18,000 U
				$26,400 F

Always consider a broad range of possible causes for price variances. For example, Webb's favorable direct materials price variance could be due to one or more of the following reasons:

◆ Webb's purchasing manager negotiated more skillfully than was planned in the budget.

◆ Webb's purchasing manager bought in larger lot sizes than budgeted, thus obtaining quantity discounts.

◆ Materials prices decreased unexpectedly due to, say, industry oversupply.

◆ Budgeted purchase prices were set without careful analysis of the market for Webb's materials.

◆ The purchasing manager received unfavorable terms on nonpurchase price factors (such as lower quality materials or minimal inspections by the supplier).

Webb's response to a materials price variance will be vitally affected by the presumed cause of the variance. Assume Webb's managers attribute the favorable variance to the purchasing manager ordering in larger lot sizes than budgeted and thus receiving quantity discounts. Webb could examine if this resulted in higher storage costs. Some companies have dramatically reduced their available storage space for materials to prevent purchasing managers from ordering large lot sizes that result in excessive inventory holding costs.

When interpreting materials price variances, Webb's managers should analyze any change in the relationship with the company's suppliers. For example, assume that midway into a budget period Webb establishes a long-term relationship with a lower-price supplier of material. Webb and the supplier agree to a single purchase price per unit for all material purchases in the next six months. In return for a larger guaranteed purchased quantity, the supplier reduces the purchase price by 10%. The result will be a large favorable price-variance in that budget period.

Efficiency Variance

Computation of an efficiency variance requires measurement of inputs for a given level of output. For any actual level of output, the efficiency variance is the difference between the input that was actually used and the input that should have been used to achieve that actual output, holding input price constant at the budgeted price:

$$\text{Efficiency variance} = \left(\begin{array}{c}\text{Actual} \\ \text{quantity of} - \text{of input allowed} \\ \text{input used} \quad \text{for actual output}\end{array}\right) \times \begin{array}{c}\text{Budgeted price} \\ \text{of input}\end{array}$$

The idea here is that an organization is inefficient if it uses more inputs than budgeted for the actual output units achieved, and it is efficient if it uses fewer inputs than budgeted for the actual output units achieved.

The efficiency variances for each of Webb's direct-cost categories are:

Direct-Cost Category	$\left(\begin{array}{c}\text{Actual} \quad\quad \text{Budgeted quantity} \\ \text{quantity of} - \text{of input allowed} \\ \text{input used} \quad \text{for actual output}\end{array}\right) \times$	Budgeted price of input	=	Efficiency Variance
Direct materials	[22,200 yards − (10,000 units × 2.00 yards)] ×	$30		
	= (22,200 yards − 20,000 yards) ×	$30	=	$66,000 U
Direct manuf. labor	[9,000 hours − (10,000 units × 0.80 hour)] ×	$20		
	= (9,000 hours − 8,000 hours) ×	$20	=	20,000 U
				$86,000 U

The two manufacturing efficiency variances (direct materials and direct manufacturing labor) are both unfavorable because more input was used than was budgeted, resulting in a decrease in operating income.

As with price variances, there is a broad range of possible causes for these efficiency variances. For example, Webb's unfavorable efficiency variance for direct manufacturing labor could be due to one or more of the following reasons:

◆ Webb's personnel manager hired underskilled workers.

◆ Webb's production scheduler inefficiently scheduled work, resulting in more manufacturing labor time being used per jacket.

◆ Webb's Maintenance Department did not properly maintain machines, resulting in more manufacturing labor time being used per jacket.

◆ Budgeted time standards were set without careful analysis of the operating conditions and the employees' skills.

Suppose Webb's managers determine that the unfavorable variance is because of poor machine maintenance. It may have a team consisting of plant machine engineers and machine operators develop a future maintenance schedule so that fewer breakdowns will occur and adversely affect labor time and product quality.

Presentation of Price and Efficiency Variances

Exhibit 7-3 illustrates a convenient way to combine the actual and budgeted input information used to compute the price and efficiency variances. This exhibit assumes that the quantity of materials purchased equals the quantity of materials used.

Exhibit 7-4 is a summary of the Levels 1, 2, and 3 variances for Webb's two direct-cost categories. Note how the individual direct materials, direct manufacturing labor, and the total direct-cost variances in Level 2 aggregate to the static-budget variance in Level 1 while those in Level 3 aggregate to the Level 2 flexible-budget variance.

Impact of Inventories

In order to focus on basic concepts, we make the following assumptions in our Webb Company illustration:

EXHIBIT 7-3
Columnar Presentation of Variance Analysis: Direct Materials Costs for Webb Company for April 2000ᵃ

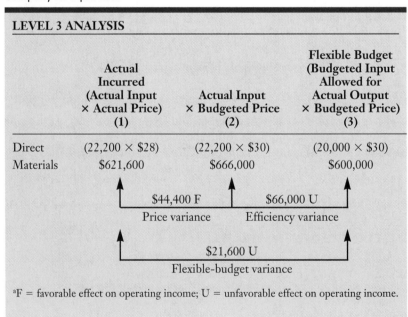

	Actual Incurred (Actual Input × Actual Price) (1)	Actual Input × Budgeted Price (2)	Flexible Budget (Budgeted Input Allowed for Actual Output × Budgeted Price) (3)
Direct Materials	(22,200 × $28) $621,600	(22,200 × $30) $666,000	(20,000 × $30) $600,000

$44,400 F ← Price variance → $66,000 U ← Efficiency variance

$21,600 U ← Flexible-budget variance

ᵃF = favorable effect on operating income; U = unfavorable effect on operating income.

EXHIBIT 7-4
Summary of Level 1, 2 and 3 Variance Analysis for Direct-Cost Categories of Webb Company for April 2000

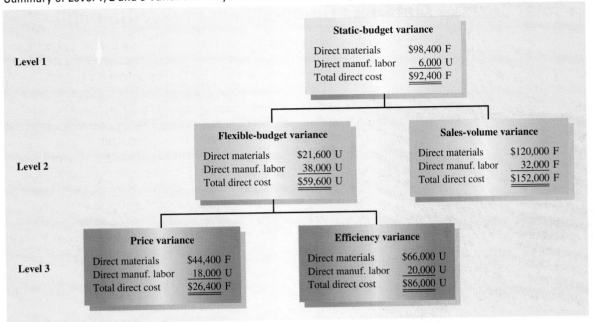

1. All direct materials are purchased and used in the same accounting period. There is no direct materials inventory at either the beginning or the end of the period.

2. All units are manufactured and sold in the same accounting period. There are no work-in-process or finished-goods inventories at either the beginning or the end of the accounting period.

The key concepts introduced in this chapter also apply when these assumptions are relaxed. However, changes in how variances are computed or interpreted may by required in some cases.

A subsequent section of this chapter ("Illustration of Journal Entries Using Standard Costs", pp. 233–234) examines journal entries for Webb in a context where materials purchased differ from materials used. The Problem for Self-Study at the end of the chapter (pp. 237–238) illustrates how to compute direct materials variances when there are differences between the quantity of materials purchased and the quantity of materials used in a period.

PERFORMANCE MEASUREMENT USING VARIANCES

A key use of variance analysis is in performance evaluation. Two attributes of performance are commonly measured:

◆ **Effectiveness**: the degree to which a predetermined objective or target is met

◆ **Efficiency**: the relative amount of inputs used to achieve a given level of output

Be careful to understand the cause(s) of a variance before using it as a performance measure. For example, assume that a Webb purchasing manager has just negotiated a deal that results in a favorable price variance for direct materials. The deal could have achieved a favorable variance for any or all of three reasons:

1. The purchasing manager bargained effectively with suppliers.

2. The purchasing manager secured a discount for buying in bulk with fewer purchase orders. However, she bought higher quantities than necessary for the short run, which resulted in excessive inventory.

3. The purchasing manager accepted a bid from the lowest-priced supplier after only minimal effort to check the supplier's quality-monitoring procedures.

OBJECTIVE 5

Explain why purchasing performance measures should focus on more factors than just price variances

Total Costs of Materials Ownership at Parker-Hannifin

At Parker Hannifin's Compumotor Division, materials costs are over 50% of the total manufacturing costs. P-H has developed a supplier-cost model that recognizes that the total cost of materials includes many items in addition to materials purchase costs. This model is used to guide vendor selection decisions as well as in ongoing cost management of materials-related costs. The supplier-cost ratio is the ratio of nonpurchase costs of materials to total supplier costs. The table below is a hypothetical report for a hypothetical supplier (Acme components).

P-H uses this supplier-cost ratio to examine the performance of each supplier over time. It also uses it to make comparisons across suppliers. P-H uses its model to examine the cause of any change over time in Acme's supplier-cost ratio—for example, if it could be due to an increase in receiving errors. P-H shares this model with its suppliers so that both the purchaser and the supplier can jointly seek cost improvements to make the relationship a more productive one for each party.

Supplier Metric	Output Measure	Number of Output Measures	Cost Per Activity	Total Cost
Ordering				
Automatic Purchase	Flat monthly rate	0	$10	$ 0
Manual Purchase	# of purchase orders	22	$ 2	44
Commodity Complexity	Categories: 1–4 Rating	1	$16	16
Receiving Inspection	Rate per hour	6	$10	60
Receiving Errors	# of vendor errors	2	$25	50
Payment Method				
Automatic Voucher	# of vouchers	0	$ 1	0
Manual	# of vouchers	16	$ 3	48
Inventory Carrying	Av. Balance × Capital Costs			940
1. Total nonpurchase costs				1,158
2. Purchase costs				23,842
3. Total supplier costs (1 + 2)				$25,000
Supplier-cost ratio (1 ÷ 3)				4.632%

Source: Presentation by Parker-Hannifin plus discussion with P-H executives.

If the purchasing manager's performance is evaluated solely on price variances, then the evaluation will be positive. Reason 1 would support this favorable conclusion as the purchasing manager bargained effectively. Reasons 2 and 3 have short-run efficiency gains, from making fewer purchase orders or making less effort to check the supplier's quality-monitoring procedures. However, these short-run efficiency gains could well be offset by higher inventory storage costs or higher inspection costs and reject rates on Webb's production line.

Performance measures increasingly focus on reducing the total costs of the company as a whole. Such a focus is central to the total value-chain-analysis theme discussed in this book. In the purchasing manager example, Webb may ultimately lose more money because of reasons 2 and 3 than it gains from the favorable price variance. Conversely, manufacturing costs may be deliberately increased (for instance, because higher costs are paid for better materials or more manufacturing labor time) in order to obtain better product quality. In turn, the costs of the better product quality may be more than offset by reductions in customer-service costs or higher sales prices.

Example Focusing on labor price vars. may prompt firms to divert mfg. operations to lower wage countries. Although the labor rates may be lower, total costs may not decline if workers have lower levels of training and education.

If any single performance measure (for example, a labor efficiency variance or a consumer rating report) receives excessive emphasis, managers tend to make decisions that maximize their own reported performance in terms of that single performance measure. In turn, managers' actions may conflict with the organization achieving its overall goals. This faulty perspective on performance arises because top management has designed a performance measurement and reward system that does not adequately emphasize total organization objectives.

Multiple Causes of Variances

Often the causes of variances are interrelated. For example, an unfavorable materials efficiency variance can be related to a favorable materials price efficiency variance due to a purchasing manager buying lower-priced, lower-quality materials. It is always best to consider possible interdependencies among variances and not to interpret variances in isolation of each other. In some cases, the causes of variances are in different parts of the value chain in the organization or in other organizations. Consider an unfavorable materials efficiency variance in the production area of Webb. Possible causes of this variance across the value chain of the organization are:

Example Japanese companies have begun helping their suppliers reduce costs, so they can pass along those savings. For example, Toyota requires its suppliers to reduce the prices they charge Toyota for component parts. In turn, Toyota may send their own engineers and other production experts to help the supplier reduce costs by streamlining their production process.

1. poor design of products or processes,
2. poor work in the manufacturing area,
3. inadequate training of the labor force,
4. inappropriate assignment of labor or machines to specific jobs, and
5. congestion due to scheduling a large number of rush orders required by Webb sales representatives.

An even broader perspective is to consider actions taken in the supply chain of organizations. A *supply chain* is the flow of goods, services, and information from cradle to grave (womb to tomb) of a product or service. The supply chain of Webb (the manufacturer) includes:

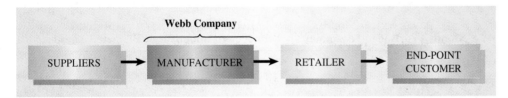

For example, actions taken by Webb's suppliers could cause unfavorable materials efficiency variances at Webb:

6. Webb's suppliers do not manufacture cloth materials of uniformly high quality.

This list of six possible causes is far from exhaustive. However, it does indicate that the cause of a variance in one part of the value chain (production in our example) can be actions taken in other parts of the value chain (for example, product design or marketing) and in other organizations. Note how improvements in the early stages of the supply chain or value chain can sizably reduce the magnitude of variances in subsequent stages.

The most important task in variance analysis is to understand why variances arise and then to use that knowledge to promote learning and continuous improvement. For instance, in our list of examples above, we may seek improvements in product design, in the quality of supplied materials, in the commitment of the manufacturing labor force to do the job right the first time, and so on. Variance analysis should not be a tool to "play the blame game" (that is, for every unfavorable variance a person is sought to blame or even punish). Rather, it should be an essential ingredient that helps promote learning in the organization.

Top management should recognize that this learning/continuous improvement use of variance analysis can be undermined if it places excessive (obsessive) emphasis on meeting individual variance targets. For example, managers may engage in "padding" of the standard input quantities or standard input prices so that their targets are more easily attained. "Padded" numbers in a budget, however, mean that management underperformance potentially is rewarded and less learning and less improvement can occur.

When to Investigate Variances

Points to Stress Investigating var's. entails activities ranging from phone calls to engineering analyses of the production process, and can be expensive. Investigation is warranted only when the expected benefits (e.g., reduced costs, better decisions due to more accurate data) exceed the investigation's expected costs.

When should variances be investigated? Frequently, managers base their answer on subjective judgments, or rules of thumb. For critical items, a small variance may prompt a follow-up. For other items, a minimum dollar variance or a certain percentage of variance from budget may prompt investigations. Of course, a 4% variance in direct materials costs of $1 million may deserve more attention than a 20% variance in repair costs of $10,000. Therefore, rules such as "investigate all variances exceeding $5,000 or 25% of budgeted cost, whichever is lower" are common. Variance analysis is subject to the same cost-benefit test as all other phases of a management control system.

Management accounting systems have traditionally implied that a standard is a single acceptable measure. Practically, however, managers realize that the standard is a range of possible acceptable outcomes. Consequently, they expect variances to vary within some normal limits. A variance within this range is deemed to be from an in-control process and calls for no investigation by managers.

Continuous Improvement

OBJECTIVE 6

Integrate continuous improvement into variance analysis

Variances and flexible budgets can be used to measure specific types of performance goals such as continuous improvement. For example, continuous improvement can be readily incorporated into budgets and thus into variances by the use of a **continuous improvement budgeted cost**. This budgeted cost is progressively reduced over succeeding time periods. The budgeted direct materials cost for each jacket that Webb Company manufactured in April 2000 is $60 per unit. The continuous improvement budgeted cost used in variance analysis for subsequent periods could be based on a targeted 1% reduction each period:

Points to Stress/Reinforcing Problems This section links FB and var. analysis to continuous improvement, one of the mgt. themes highlighted in Chap. 1. However, point out that there's a trade-off between focusing on perfection or continual improvement and the motivational problems associated with judging performance against a goal that workers perceive to be unattainable. Mgt. must recognize that the rate of improvement will likely decrease over time, after "easy" improvements are achieved. Exer. 7-28 and Prob. 7-35 cover continuous improvement issues.

Month	Prior Month's Budgeted Amount	Reduction in Budgeted Amount	Revised Budgeted Amount
April 2000	—	—	$60.00
May 2000	$60.00	$0.600 (0.01 × $60.00)	59.40
June 2000	59.40	0.594 (0.01 × $59.40)	58.81
July 2000	58.81	0.588 (0.01 × $58.81)	58.22

The source of the 1% reduction in budgeted cost could be efficiency improvements or input price reductions. By using continuous improvement budgeted costs, an organization signals the importance of constantly seeking ways to reduce total costs. For example, managers could avoid unfavorable materials efficiency variances by continuously reducing materials waste.

Points to Stress If a production line is malfunctioning, the supervisor cannot wait for an acctg. report with var's. denominated in dollars. The supervisor controls the process by physical observation and timely physical measurements. For example, a Nissan plant compiles data such as % defects, production schedule attainment, etc., and broadcasts it in ticker-tape fashion on screens throughout the plant.

Products in the initial months of their production may have higher budgeted improvement rates than those that have been in production for several years. Improvement opportunities may be much easier to identify when products have just started in production. Once the easy opportunities have been identified ("the low hanging fruit picked"), much more ingenuity may be required to identify successive improvement opportunities.

Financial and Nonfinancial Performance Measures

Almost all organizations use a combination of financial and nonfinancial performance measures rather than relying exclusively on either type. Consider our Webb Company illustration. In its cutting room, fabric is laid out and cut into pieces, which are then matched and assembled. Control is often exercised at the cutting room level by observing workers and by focusing on nonfinancial measures such as the number of square yards of cloth used to produce 1,000 jackets or the percentage of jackets started and completed without requiring any rework. Production managers at Webb also will likely use financial measures to evaluate the overall cost efficiency with which operations are being run and to help guide decisions about, say, changing the mix of inputs used in manufacturing jackets. Financial measures are often critical in an organization because they summarize the economic impact of diverse physical activities in a way managers readily understand. Moreover, these managers are often evaluated on results measured against financial measures.

Illustration of Journal Entries Using Standard Costs

Chapter 4 illustrated journal entries when normal costs are used. We now illustrate journal entries when standard costs are used. We focus on direct materials and direct manufacturing labor.

We will continue with the data in the Webb Company illustration with one exception. Assume that during April 2000 Webb purchases 25,000 square yards of materials. Recall that the actual quantity used is 22,200 yards and that the standard quantity allowed for the actual output manufactured is 20,000 yards. The actual purchase price is $28 per square yard, while the standard price is $30.

Note that in each of the following entries unfavorable variances are always debits and favorable variances are always credits.

Journal Entry 1a: Isolate the direct materials price variance at the time of purchase by debiting Materials Control at standard prices. This is the earliest date possible to isolate this variance.

1a. Materials Control
    (25,000 yards × $30)   750,000
  Direct Materials Price Variance
    (25,000 yards × $2)   50,000
  Accounts Payable Control
    (25,000 yards × $28)   700,000
  To record direct materials purchased.

Journal Entry 1b: Isolate the direct materials efficiency variance at the time of usage by debiting Work-in-Process Control at standard quantities allowed for actual output units manufactured at standard prices.

1b. Work-in-Process Control
    (20,000 yards × $30)   600,000
  Direct Materials Efficiency Variance
    (2,200 yards × $30)   66,000
  Materials Control
    (22,200 yards × $30)   666,000
  To record direct materials used.

Journal Entry 2: Isolate the direct manufacturing labor price and efficiency variances at the time this labor is used by debiting Work-in-Process Control at standard quantities allowed for actual output units manufactured at standard prices. Note that Wages Payable measures the payroll liability and hence is always at actual wage rates.

2. Work-in-Process Control
    (8,000 hours × $20)   160,000
  Direct Manufacturing Labor Price Variance
    (9,000 hours × $2)   18,000
  Direct Manufacturing Labor Efficiency Variance
    (1,000 hours × $20)   20,000
  Wages Payable
    (9,000 hours × $22)   198,000
  To record liability for direct manufacturing labor costs.

A major advantage of this standard costing system is its emphasis on the control feature of standard costs. All variances are isolated at the earliest possible time. For example, by isolating the direct materials price variance at the time of purchase, corrective actions can be taken immediately rather than waiting until the materials are used in production. Suppose top management concludes that a large unfavorable materials price variance is due to the purchasing officer being a poor negotiator. The sooner this situation is observed, the sooner a more effective negotiator can be hired or steps taken to improve the negotiating skills of the current purchasing officer.

FLEXIBLE BUDGETING AND ACTIVITY-BASED COSTING

Activity-based costing (ABC) systems focus on individual activities as the fundamental cost objects. ABC systems classify the costs of various activities into a cost hierarchy—output-unit level, batch level, product sustaining and facility sustaining (see pp. 142–143). The two direct-cost categories in the Webb Company example discussed earlier in this chapter (direct materials costs and direct manufacturing labor costs) are examples of output unit-level costs. In this section, we show how the basic principles and concepts of flexible budgets and variance analysis presented earlier in the chapter can be applied to other levels of the cost hierarchy. We focus on batch-level costs. Batch-level costs are resources sacrificed on activities that are related to a group of units of product(s) or service(s) rather than to each individual unit of product or service.

Relating Batch Costs to Product Output

Consider Lyco Brass Works, a manufacturer of decorative brass faucets. Lyco specializes in manufacturing a faucet called Jacutap used in jacuzzis. Lyco produces Jacutaps in batches. For each product line, Lyco dedicates materials-handling labor to bring materials to the manufacturing area, transport work in process from one work center to the next, and take the finished product to the shipping area. Hence materials-handling labor costs for Jacutaps are direct costs of Jacutaps. Because the materials for a batch are moved together, materials-handling labor costs vary with the number of batches rather than the number of units in a batch. Materials-handling labor costs are direct and variable batch-level costs.

Information regarding Jacutaps for 2001 follows:

	Static-Budget Amounts	Actual Amounts
1. Units of Jacutaps produced and sold	180,000	151,200
2. Batch size (units/batch)	150	140
3. Number of batches (Line 1 ÷ Line 2)	1,200	1,080
4. Materials-handling labor-hours per batch	5	5.25
5. Total materials-handling labor-hours (Line 3 × Line 4)	6,000	5,670
6. Cost per materials-handling labor-hour	$14	$14.50
7. Total materials-handling labor cost (Line 5 × Line 6)	$84,000	$82,215

To prepare the flexible budget for materials-handling labor costs, Lyco starts with the actual units of output produced, 151,200 units, and proceeds in the following steps:

Step 1: Using the Budgeted Batch Size, Calculate the Number of Batches in Which the Actual Output Units Should Have Been Produced At the budgeted batch size of 150 units per batch, Lyco should have produced the 151,200 units of output in 1,008 batches (151,200 ÷ 150).

Step 2: Using the Budgeted Materials-Handling Labor-Hours Per Batch, Calculate the Number of Materials-Handling Labor-Hours That Should Have Been Used At the budgeted quantity of 5 hours per batch, 1,008 batches should have required 5,040 materials-handling labor-hours (1,008 × 5).

Reinforcing Problems Probs. 7-41 and 7-42 cover ABC and variance analysis.

Step 3: Using the Budgeted Cost Per Materials-Handling Labor-Hour, Calculate the Flexible-Budget Amount for Materials-Handling Labor-Hours The flexible-budget amount is 5,040 materials-handling labor-hours × $14, the budgeted cost per materials-handling labor-hour = $70,560.

Note how the flexible-budget calculations for materials-handling costs focus on batch-level quantities (materials-handling labor-hours) rather than on output unit-level amounts (such as materials-handling labor-hours per unit of output). The flexible-budget variance can then be calculated as follows:

$$\frac{\text{Flexible-budget}}{\text{variance}} = \frac{\text{Actual}}{\text{costs}} - \frac{\text{Flexible-budget}}{\text{costs}}$$

$$= 5{,}670 \times \$14.50 - 5{,}040 \times \$14$$

$$= \$82{,}215 - \$70{,}560 = \$11{,}655 \text{ U}$$

The unfavorable variance indicates that materials-handling labor costs were $11,655 higher than the flexible-budget target.

Points to Stress Because materials handling is a batch-level cost, the BQIA is focused at the batch level. The quantity of materials handling labor hours allowed is based on the number of batches it should have taken to produce the actual quantity of output produced.

Price and Efficiency Variances

Insight into the possible reasons for this $11,655 unfavorable variance can be gained by examining the price and efficiency components of the flexible-budget variance.

$$\frac{\text{Price}}{\text{variance}} = \left(\begin{matrix} \text{Actual} \\ \text{price of} \\ \text{input} \end{matrix} - \begin{matrix} \text{Budgeted} \\ \text{price of} \\ \text{input} \end{matrix} \right) \times \begin{matrix} \text{Actual} \\ \text{quantity} \\ \text{of input} \end{matrix}$$

$$= (\$14.50 - \$14) \times 5{,}670 = \$0.50 \times 5{,}670 = \$2{,}835 \text{ U}$$

The unfavorable price variance for materials-handling labor indicates that the actual cost per materials-handling labor-hour ($14.50) exceeds the budgeted cost per materials-handling labor-hour ($14). This variance could be due to (1) Lyco's human resources manager negotiating less skillfully than was planned in the budget, or (2) wage rates increasing unexpectedly due to scarcity of labor.

$$\frac{\text{Efficiency}}{\text{variance}} = \left(\begin{matrix} \text{Actual} \\ \text{quantity of} \\ \text{input used} \end{matrix} - \begin{matrix} \text{Budgeted quantity} \\ \text{of input allowed} \\ \text{for actual output} \end{matrix} \right) \times \begin{matrix} \text{Budgeted} \\ \text{price} \\ \text{of input} \end{matrix}$$

$$= (5{,}670 - 5{,}040) \times \$14 = 630 \times \$14 = \$8{,}820 \text{ U}$$

The unfavorable efficiency variance indicates that the actual number of materials-handling labor-hours (5,670) exceeded the number of materials-handling labor-hours that Lyco should have used (5,040) for the number of units it produced. Two reasons for the unfavorable efficiency variance are (1) smaller actual batch sizes of 140 units instead of the budgeted batch sizes of 150 units; this results in Lyco producing the 151,200 units in 1,080 batches instead of in 1,008 (151,200 ÷ 150) batches; and (2) higher actual materials-handling labor-hours per batch of 5.25 hours instead of budgeted materials-handling labor-hours per batch of 5 hours.

Reasons for smaller than budgeted batch sizes could include (1) quality problems if batch sizes exceed 140 faucets, or (2) high costs of carrying inventory.

Reasons for longer actual materials-handling labor-hours per batch could include (1) inefficient layout of the Jacutap product line relative to the plan, (2) materials-handling labor having to wait at work centers before picking up or delivering materials, (3) unmotivated or inexperienced employees, or (4) inappropriate materials-handling time standards.

Identifying the reasons for the efficiency variance helps Lyco's managers to develop a plan for improving materials-handling labor efficiency.

Focus on Hierarchy

The key idea is to focus the flexible-budget quantity computations at the appropriate level of the cost hierarchy. Because materials handling is a batch-level cost, the flexible-budget quantity calculations focused at the batch level—the quantity of materials-handling labor-hours that Lyco should have used based on the number of batches it should have taken to produce the actual quantity of 151,200 units. If a cost had been a product-sustaining cost, the flexible-budget quantity computations would focus at the product-sustaining level.

BENCHMARKING AND VARIANCE ANALYSIS

The budgeted amounts in the Webb Company and Lyco Brass Works examples in this chapter are based on analysis of operations at those companies. We now turn to the situation where the budgeted amounts are based on operations at other companies. The term **benchmarking** is often used to refer to the continuous process of measuring products, services, and activities against the best levels of performance. These best levels of performance are often found in competing organizations or in other organizations having similar processes.

We will examine United Airlines and eight other U.S. airlines to illustrate the use of benchmarks based on other organizations. Knowledge of cost differences across airlines and of changes over time in these differences are important to both planning and control decisions at United. Consider the unit cost per available seat mile (ASM) for United Airlines. Assume United uses data for eight competing airlines in its benchmark cost comparisons. Summary data are in Exhibit 7-5. The benchmark companies are ranked from lowest unit cost to highest unit cost per ASM—see column 2. Also reported in Exhibit 7-5 are revenue per ASM, gross margin per ASM, labor cost per ASM, fuel cost per ASM, and total ASM (a measure of airline size).

Inferences about United's cost management are highly dependent on the choice of a specific benchmark. United's actual cost of $0.0960 per ASM is $0.0014 higher than the average cost of $0.0946 per ASM of the eight other airlines. The magnitude of this difference is less than 2% of the average cost per ASM of the eight airlines. The implication is that United is similar, in cost competitiveness, to the average of these eight airlines. A very different, and less favorable, picture emerges if United compares itself to Southwest Airlines, the lowest-cost airline at $0.0744 per ASM. United's cost is now $0.0216 higher ($0.0960 − $0.0744). This difference is 29% of Southwest's cost per ASM. Using this benchmark, United appears to have a sizably higher cost structure than the lowest-cost operator of those examined.

EXHIBIT 7-5
Available Seat Mile (ASM) Benchmark Comparison of United Airlines with Eight Other Airlines[a]

Airline (1)	Unit Cost Per ASM (2)	Revenue Per ASM (3)	Gross Margin Per ASM (4) = (3) − (2)	Labor Cost Per ASM (5)	Fuel Cost Per ASM (6)	Total ASM (Millions) (7)
United Airlines	$0.0960	$0.1034	$0.0074	$0.0350	$0.0128	79,250
Airlines Used as Benchmarks						
Southwest Airlines	$0.0744	$0.0858	$0.0114	$0.0255	$0.0117	19,807
Alaska Airlines	0.0860	0.0914	0.0054	0.0282	0.0136	7,309
Delta Airlines	0.0886	0.1020	0.0134	0.0329	0.0123	65,133
Northwest Airlines	0.0953	0.1043	0.0090	0.0318	0.0150	45,656
TWA	0.0960	0.0907	(0.0053)	0.0337	0.0140	19,321
Continental Airlines	0.0961	0.1078	0.0117	0.0261	0.0136	29,703
American Airlines	0.0969	0.1059	0.0090	0.0342	0.0126	78,233
U.S. Airways	0.1232	0.1360	0.0128	0.0497	0.0136	27,716
Average of airlines used as benchmarks	$0.0946	$0.1030	$0.0084	$0.0328	$0.0133	36,610

[a]Data pertain to 1997 as reported by Thomson Financial Networks.

Using benchmarks such as those in Exhibit 7-5 is not without its problems. For example, one problem is ensuring the benchmark numbers are comparable. That is, they need to be "apples to apples" comparisons. Differences can exist across companies in inventory costing methods, depreciation methods, and so on. In our United example, columns 5 and 6 report data for two of the costs included in the unit-cost comparisons—labor cost and fuel cost. On both these cost components, United has a higher cost than Southwest Airlines. For example, United's labor cost per ASM is 37.3% above Southwest ($0.0350 compared to $0.0255). This benchmarking data highlights the potential gains to United of restructuring its labor agreements as a key step in becoming more cost competitive with its lower-cost competitors. The effect on costs of plane size and type, duration of flights, and so on could also be examined. An analyst could also examine whether revenue differences per ASM across airlines are due to, say, differences in perceived quality of service or due to differences in monopoly power at specific airports.

Benchmark-type comparisons across companies illustrate the attention-directing role of the management accountant. Understanding "why" observed cost or revenue differences exist across companies can be a challenging task. An analyst could examine whether fixed-cost/variable-cost differences exist across airlines. Similarly, an analyst could determine whether higher-cost airlines are also able to generate higher revenues per ASM. Management accountants are more valuable to managers when they provide insight into why costs or revenues differ across companies (or plants) as opposed to simply reporting the magnitude of such differences.

Curriculum Linkage This discussion links FB and var. analysis to the dual internal/external focus mgt. theme introduced in Chap. 1. Students are probably familiar with benchmarking from production or mgt. classes. Finding appropriate benchmarks is a major issue in implementing benchmarking. Many companies purchase benchmark data. Consulting divisions of many of the Big 5 are developing benchmarking data bases.

PROBLEM FOR SELF-STUDY

PROBLEM

O'Shea Company manufactures ceramic vases. It uses its standard-costing system when developing its flexible-budget amounts. In April 2001, 2,000 finished units were produced. The following information is related to its two direct manufacturing cost categories of direct materials and direct manufacturing labor.

Direct materials used were 4,400 pounds. The standard direct materials input allowed for one output unit is 2 pounds at $15 per pound. 6,000 pounds of materials were purchased at $16.50 per pound, a total of $99,000.

Actual direct manufacturing labor-hours were 3,250 at a total cost of $66,300. Standard manufacturing labor time allowed is 1.5 hours per output unit, and the standard direct manufacturing labor cost is $20 per hour.

Required
1. Calculate the direct materials price and efficiency variances and the direct manufacturing labor price and efficiency variances. The direct materials price variance will be based on a flexible budget for actual quantities purchased, but the efficiency variance will be based on a flexible budget for actual quantities used.
2. Prepare journal entries for a standard costing system that isolates variances as early as feasible.

SOLUTION

1. Exhibit 7-6 shows how the columnar presentation of variances introduced in Exhibit 7-3 can be adjusted for the difference in timing between the purchase and use of materials. In particular, note the two sets of computations in column 2 for direct materials. The $90,000 pertains to the direct materials purchased; the $66,000 pertains to the direct materials used.

EXHIBIT 7-6
Columnar Presentation of Variance Analysis for O'Shea Company: Direct Materials and
Direct Manufacturing Labor[a]

LEVEL 3 ANALYSIS

	Actual Costs Incurred (Actual Input × Actual Price) (1)		Actual Input × Budgeted Price (2)	Flexible Budget (Budgeted Input Allowed for Actual Output) × Budgeted Price (3)
Direct Materials	(6,000 × $16.50) $99,000	(6,000 × $15.00) $90,000	(4,400 × $15.00) $66,000	(4,000 × $15.00) $60,000

$9,000 U
Price variance

$6,000 U
Efficiency variance

Direct Manufacturing Labor	(3,250 × $20.40) $66,300		(3,250 × $20.00) $65,000	(3,000 × $20.00) $60,000

$1,300 U
Price variance

$5,000 U
Efficiency variance

[a]F = Favorable effect on operating income; U = Unfavorable effect on operating income.

2. Materials Control
   (6,000 pounds × $15)   90,000
   Direct Materials Price Variance
   (6,000 pounds × $1.50)   9,000
        Accounts Payable Control
        (6,000 pounds × $16.50)   99,000

   Work-in-Process Control
   (4,000 pounds × $15)   60,000
   Direct Materials Efficiency Variance
   (400 pounds × $15)   6,000
        Materials Control
        (4,400 pounds × $15)   66,000

   Work-in-Process Control
   (3,000 hours × $20)   60,000
   Direct Manufacturing Labor Price Variance
   (3,250 hours × $0.40)   1,300
   Direct Manufacturing Labor Efficiency Variance
   (250 hours × $20)   5,000
        Wages Payable Control
        (3,250 hours × $20.40)   66,300

SUMMARY

The following points are linked to the chapter's learning objectives:

1. A static budget is based on the level of output planned at the start of the budget period. A flexible budget is adjusted (flexed) to recognize the actual level of output achieved in the budget period. Flexible budgets help managers gain more insight into the causes of variances than do static budgets.

2. A five-step procedure can be used to develop a flexible budget. Where all costs are either variable with respect to output units or fixed, these five steps require only information about budgeted selling price, budgeted variable cost per output unit, budgeted fixed costs, and the actual quantity of output units. The static-budget variance can be broken into a flexible-budget variance (the difference between the actual result and the flexible-budget amount) and a sales-volume variance. The sales-volume variance arises because the actual output units differ from the budgeted output units.

3. The computation of price variances and efficiency variances helps managers gain insight into two different (but not independent) aspects of performance. Price variances focus on the difference between actual and budgeted input prices. Efficiency variances focus on the difference between actual inputs used and the budgeted inputs allowed for the actual output.

4. A standard cost is a carefully predetermined cost that is based on a norm of efficiency. Standard costs can exclude past inefficiencies and they can take into account changes expected to occur in the budget period.

5. Price variances capture only one aspect of a manager's performance. Other aspects include the quality of the inputs the manager purchases and his or her ability to get suppliers to deliver on time.

6. Managers can use continuous improvement budgeted costs in their accounting system to highlight to all employees the importance of continuously seeking ways to reduce total costs.

7. The Level 1, 2, and 3 framework can be applied to variance analysis of activity costs (such as setup costs) to gain insight into why actual activity costs differ from those in the static budget or the flexible budget. Interpreting cost variances for different activities requires an understanding of whether the costs are output-unit-driven, or are of a batch-level, product-sustaining, or facility-sustaining kind.

8. Benchmarking is the continuous process of measuring products, services, and activities against the best levels of performance. Benchmarking facilitates companies using the best levels of performance within their organization, in competitor organizations, or at other noncompetitor organizations to gauge the performance of their own managers.

▼ TERMS TO LEARN

This chapter and the Glossary at the end of the book contain definitions of the following important terms:

QUESTIONS

7-1 What is the relationship between *management by exception* and *variance analysis*?

7-2 What are two possible sources of information a company might use to compute the *budgeted amount* in variance analysis?

7-3 Distinguish between a *favorable variance* and an *unfavorable variance*.

7-4 What is the key difference between a *static budget* and a *flexible budget*?

7-5 Why might managers find a Level 2 flexible-budget analysis more informative than a Level 1 static-budget analysis?

7-6 Describe the steps in developing a flexible budget.

7-7 List four reasons for using standard costs.

7-8 How might a manager gain insight into the causes of a flexible-budget variance for direct materials?

7-9 List three causes of a favorable materials price variance.

7-10 Describe why materials price and materials efficiency variances may be computed with reference to different points in time.

7-11 How might the continuous improvement theme be incorporated into the process of setting budgeted costs?

7-12 Why might an analyst examining variances in the production area look beyond that business function for explanations of those variances?

7-13 Comment on the following statement made by a plant supervisor: "Meetings with my plant accountant are frustrating. All he wants to do is pin the blame on someone for the many variances he reports."

7-14 How can variances be used to analyze costs in individual activity areas?

7-15 "Benchmarking against other companies enables a company to identify the lowest-cost producer. This amount should become the performance measure for next year." Do you agree?

EXERCISES

7-16 Flexible budget. Brabham Enterprises manufactures tires for the Formula I motor racing circuit. For August 2000, it budgeted to manufacture and sell 3,000 tires at a variable cost of $74 per tire and total fixed cost of $54,000. The budgeted selling price was $110 per tire. Actual results in August 2000 were 2,800 tires manufactured and sold at a selling price of $112 per tire. The actual total variable costs were $229,600 and the actual total fixed costs were $50,000.

Required
1. Prepare a performance report (akin to Exhibit 7-2, p. 223) that uses a flexible budget and a static budget.
2. Comment on the results in requirement 1.

7-17 Flexible budget. Connor Company's budgeted prices for direct materials, direct manufacturing labor, and direct marketing (distribution) labor per attaché case are $40, $8, and $12, respectively. The president is pleased with the following performance report:

	Actual Costs	**Static Budget**	**Variance**
Direct materials	$364,000	$400,000	$36,000 F
Direct manufacturing labor	78,000	80,000	2,000 F
Direct marketing (distribution) labor	110,000	120,000	10,000 F

Required
Actual output was 8,800 attaché cases. Is the president's pleasure justified? Prepare a revised performance report that uses a flexible budget and a static budget. Assume all three direct-costs items are variable costs.

7-18 Flexible budget. The Virtual Candy Company sells sweets in bulk over the web. Virtual Candy's budgeted operating income for the year ended December 31, 2001 was $3,150,000. As a result of continued explosive growth on the web, actual operating income totaled $6,556,000.

Required

1. Calculate the total static-budget variance.
2. Flexible-budget operating income was $6,930,000. Calculate the total flexible-budget and total sales-volume variances.
3. Comment on the total flexible-budget variance in the light of the web's explosive growth.

7-19 Price and efficiency variances. Peterson Foods manufactures pumpkin scones. For January 2001, it budgeted to purchase and use 15,000 pounds of pumpkin at $0.89 a pound. Actual purchase and usage for January 2001 was 16,000 pounds at $0.82 a pound. It budgeted for 60,000 pumpkin scones. Actual output was 60,800 pumpkin scones.

Required

1. Compute the flexible-budget variance.
2. Compute the price and efficiency variances.
3. Comment on the results in requirements 1 and 2.

7-20 Materials and manufacturing labor variances. Consider the following data collected for Great Homes, Inc.:

	Direct Materials	Direct Manufacturing Labor
Cost incurred: actual inputs × actual prices	$200,000	$90,000
Actual inputs × standard prices	214,000	86,000
Standard inputs allowed for actual outputs × standard prices	225,000	80,000

Required

Compute the price, efficiency, and flexible-budget variances for direct materials and direct manufacturing labor.

7-21 Price and efficiency variances. CellOne is a cellular phone service reseller. CellOne contracts with major cellular operators for airtime in bulk and then resells service to retail customers. CellOne budgeted to sell 7,800,000 minutes in the month ended March 31, 2001. Actual minutes sold totaled only 7,500,000. Due to fluctuations in hourly usage, CellOne "overbuys" airtime from cellular operators. CellOne plans to buy 10% more airtime than it plans to sell. For example, CellOne's budgets called for the purchase of 8,580,000 minutes based on the plan to sell 7,800,000 minutes. In what follows think of purchased airtime as direct materials.

CellOne's budgets purchased airtime to cost 4.5 cents per minute. Actual purchased airtime in 2001 averaged 5.0 cents per minute. CellOne incurs direct labor costs due to the employment of technicians. One hour of technical support is required for every 5,000 minutes of airtime sold. In practice, 1,600 hours of technical support were used. Technical support was planned at $60 per hour. Actual technical support costs averaged $62 per hour.

Required

1. Calculate the flexible-budget variance for direct materials and direct labor costs. (Use the 8,250,000 (7,500,000 × 1.10) minutes in the flexible budget.)
2. Calculate the price and efficiency variances for direct materials and labor costs.

7-22 Flexible budgets, variance analysis. You have been hired as a consultant by Mary Flanagan, the president of a small manufacturing company that makes automobile parts. Flanagan is an excellent engineer, but she has been frustrated by working with inadequate cost data.

You helped install flexible budgeting and standard costs. Flanagan has asked you to consider the following May data and recommend how variances might be computed and presented in performance reports:

Static budget in output units	20,000
Actual output units produced and sold	23,000
Budgeted selling price per output unit	$40
Budgeted variable costs per output unit	$25
Budgeted total fixed costs per month	$200,000
Actual revenue	$874,000
Actual variable costs	$630,000
Favorable variance in fixed costs	$5,000

Flanagan was disappointed. Although output units sold exceeded expectations, operating income did not. Assume that there was no beginning or ending inventory.

Required

1. You decide to present Flanagan with alternative ways to analyze variances so that she can decide what level of detail she prefers. The reporting system can then be designed accordingly. Prepare an analysis similar to Levels 0, 1, and 2 in Exhibit 7-1 and Level 7-2.
2. What are some likely causes for the variances you report in requirement 1?

7-23 Flexible-budget preparation and analysis. Bank Management Printers, Inc., produces luxury checkbooks with three checks and stubs per page. Each checkbook is designed for an individual customer and is ordered through the customer's bank. The company's operating budget for September 2001 included these data:

Number of checkbooks	15,000
Selling price per book	$20
Variable costs per book	$8
Fixed costs for the month	$145,000

The actual results for September 2001 were:

Number of checkbooks produced and sold	12,000
Average selling price per book	$21
Variable costs per book	$7
Fixed costs for the month	$150,000

The executive vice president of the company observed that the operating income for September was much less than anticipated, despite a higher-than-budgeted selling price and a lower-than-budgeted variable cost per unit. You have been asked to provide explanations for the disappointing September results.

Bank Management develops its flexible budget on the basis of budgeted per-output-unit revenue and per-output unit variable costs without detailed analysis of budgeted inputs.

Required

1. Prepare a Level 1 analysis of the September performance.
2. Prepare a Level 2 analysis of the September performance.
3. Why might Bank Management find the Level 2 analysis more informative than the Level 1 analysis? Explain your answer.

7-24 Flexible budget, working backward. The Specialty Balls Company designs and manufactures ball bearings for extreme performance machinery. Exercise Exhibit 7-24 is a

EXERCISE EXHIBIT 7-24
Schedule 1: Level 2 Variance Analysis for Specialty Balls for 2001 (Incomplete)

	Actual Results (1)	Flexible-Budget Variances (2) = (1) − (3)	Flexible Budget (3)	Sales-Volume Variances (4) = (3) − (5)	Static Budget (5)
Units sold	650,000	_____	_____	_____	600,000
Revenues	$3,575,000	_____	_____	_____	$2,100,000
Variable costs	2,575,000	_____	_____	_____	1,200,000
Contribution margin	1,000,000				900,000
Fixed costs	700,000	_____	_____	_____	600,000
Operating income	$ 300,000	_____	_____	_____	$ 300,000

Total flexible-budget variance

Total sales-volume variance

Total static-budget variance

partially complete Level 2 variance analysis of Specialty Balls' budgeted and actual results from sales of platinum balls for the year ended December 31, 2001.

Required

1. Complete the analysis in Exercise Exhibit 7-24. Calculate all the required variances. If your work is accurate, you will find that the total static-budget variance is $0 (zero).
2. What are the actual and budgeted selling prices per unit? What are the actual and budgeted variable costs per unit?
3. Specialty Balls' CEO is delighted with the lack of a static-budget variance. Is his reaction appropriate? Review the variances you have calculated and discuss possible causes and potential problems.
4. What is the most important lesson one can learn from performing this exercise?

7-25 Flexible-budget variances for finance function activities. Sam Chase is the chief financial officer of Flowers.net, an Internet company that enables customers to order home deliveries of flowers by accessing its website. Flowers.net has a network of florists ("strategic partners") who do the physical delivery of flowers. Flowers.net has a group of representatives that continually visit florists and nurseries. This group monitors product and service quality and explores new products or new partners.

Chase is concerned with the efficiency and effectiveness of the finance function at Flowers.net. He collects the following information for three finance activities in 2001:

Finance Activity	Activity Measure	2001 Budgeted Total Cost of Activity	2001 Budgeted Total Volume of Activity	2001 Actual Cost of Process	2001 Actual Total Volume of Activity
Payables	Number of invoices	$580,000	200,000	$594,020	212,150
Receivables	Number of remittances	639,000	1,000,000	711,000	948,000
Travel and expense	Number of expense reports	15,200	2,000	13,986	1,890

The budgeted amounts are based on an analysis of costs in past periods at Flowers.net. The output measure is the number of deliveries, which is assumed to be the same as the number of remittances. Receivables is an output-unit level driven cost, whereas payables and travel and expense are batch-driven costs.

Required

1. Prepare a flexible-budget based report explaining difference between budgeted and actual costs for each of the three finance activities in 2001. Comment on the results.
2. Why might the variances computed in requirement 1 pertain to efficiency but not effectiveness?
3. How might Chase monitor the effectiveness of the three finance processes in this exercise?

7-26 Finance function activities, benchmarking (continuation of 7-25). Sam Chase, CFO of Flowers.net receives a brochure from The Hackett Group, a consulting firm specializing in benchmarking. He asks the Hackett Group to provide benchmark data from its recent study of the finance function at over 100 retail companies (both traditional retail and Internet-based retail). Hacket's "world-class" cost benchmarks for Flowers.net's three finance activities are:

Finance Activity	World-Class Cost Performance
Payables	$0.71 per invoice
Receivables	$0.10 per remittance
Travel and expense	$1.58 per expense report

Required

1. What new insights might arise with the Hackett benchmark data using the budgeted amounts in Exercise 7-25?
2. Assume you are in charge of travel and expense report processing. What concerns might you have with Sam Chase using the Hackett benchmark of $1.58 per expense report as the key to evaluate your performance next period?

7-27 Price and efficiency variances, journal entries. Chemical, Inc., has set up the following standards per finished unit for direct materials and direct manufacturing labor:

Direct materials: 10 lb. at $3.00 per lb.	$30.00
Direct manufacturing labor: 0.5 hour at $20.00 per hour	10.00

The number of finished units budgeted for March 2001 was 10,000; 9,810 units were actually produced.

Actual results in March 2001 were:

Direct materials: 98,073 lb. used	
Direct manufacturing labor: 4,900 hours	$102,900

Assume that there was no beginning inventory of either direct materials or finished units.

During the month, materials purchases amounted to 100,000 lb., at a total cost of $310,000. Input-price variances are isolated upon purchase. Input-efficiency variances are isolated at the time of usage.

Required
1. Compute the March 2001 price and efficiency variances of direct materials and direct manufacturing labor.
2. Prepare journal entries to record the variances in requirement 1.
3. Comment on the March 2001 price and efficiency variances of Chemical, Inc.
4. Why might Chemical, Inc., calculate materials price variances and materials efficiency variances with reference to different points in time?

7-28 Continuous improvement (continuation of 7-27). Chemical, Inc., adopts a continuous improvement approach to setting monthly standards costs. Assume the direct materials standard costs of $30 per unit and the direct manufacturing labor cost of $10 per unit pertain to January 2001. The standard amounts for February 2001 are 0.997 of the January standard amount. The standard amounts for March 2001 are 0.997 of the February standard amount. Assume the same information for March 2001 as in Exercise 7-26 except for these revised standard amounts.

Required
1. Compute the March 2001 standard amounts for direct materials and direct manufacturing labor.
2. Compute the March 2001 price and efficiency variances for direct materials and direct manufacturing labor.

7-29 Materials and manufacturing labor variances, standard costs. Consider the following selected data regarding the manufacture of a line of upholstered chairs:

	Standards Per Chair
Direct materials	2 square yards of input at $10 per square yard
Direct manufacturing labor	0.5 hour of input at $20 per hour

The following data were compiled regarding actual performance: actual output units (chairs) produced, 20,000; square yards of input purchased and used, 37,000; price per square yard, $10.20; direct manufacturing labor costs, $176,400; actual hours of input, 9,000; labor price per hour, $19.60.

Required
1. Show your computations of price and efficiency variances for direct materials and direct manufacturing labor. Give a plausible explanation of why the variances occurred.
2. Suppose 60,000 square yards of materials were purchased (at $10.20 per square yard) but only 37,000 square yards were used. Suppose further that variances are identified at their most likely control point; accordingly, direct materials price variances are isolated and traced to the Purchasing Department rather than to the Production Department. Compute the price and efficiency variances under this approach.

7-30 Journal entries and T-accounts. Prepare journal entries and post them to T-accounts for all transactions in Exercise 7-29, including requirement 2. Summarize in three sentences how these journal entries differ from the normal costing entries described in Chapter 4, pages 104–113.

7-31 Flexible budget. (Refer to Exercise 7-29.) Suppose the static budget was for 24,000 units of output. The general manager is thrilled about the following report:

	Actual Results	Static Budget	Variance
Direct materials	$377,400	$480,000	$102,600 F
Direct manufacturing labor	$176,400	$240,000	$63,600 F

Required

Is the manager's glee warranted? Prepare a report that provides a more detailed explanation of why the static budget was not achieved. Actual output was 20,000 units.

PROBLEMS

7-32 Flexible-budget preparation, service sector. Meridian Finance helps prospective homeowners of substantial means find low-cost financing and assists existing homeowners in refinancing their current loans at lower interest rates. Meridian works only for customers with excellent borrowing capacity. Hence, Meridian is able to obtain a loan for every customer with whom it decides to work.

Meridian charges clients 1/2% of the loan amount it arranges. In 2001, the average loan amount per customer was $199,000. In 2001, the average loan amount was $200,210. In its 2001 flexible-budgeting system, Meridian assumes the average loan amount will be $200,000. Budgeted cost data per loan application for 2001 are:

◆ Professional labor: 6 hours at a rate of $40 per hour

◆ Fees for filing: $100

◆ Checks on credit worthiness: $120

◆ Courier mailings: $50

Office support (the costs of leases, secretarial workers, and others) is budgeted to be $31,000 per month. Meridian Finance views this amount as a fixed cost.

Required

1. Prepare a static budget for November 2001 assuming 90 loan applications.
2. Actual loan applications in November 2001 were 120. Other actual data for November 2001 were:

◆ Professional labor: 7.2 hours per loan application at $42 per hour

◆ Loan filing fees: $100 per loan application

◆ Credit-worthiness checks: $125 per loan application

◆ Courier mailings: $54 per loan application

Office support costs for November 2001 were $33,500. The average loan amount for November 2001 was $224,000. Meridian received its 1/2% fee on all loans. Prepare a Level 2 variance analysis of Meridian Finance for November 2001.

7-33 Professional labor efficiency and effectiveness (continuation of 7-32). Meridian Finance is analyzing the efficiency and effectiveness of its professional labor staff.

Required

1. Compute professional labor price and efficiency variances for November 2001. (Compute labor price on a per hour basis.)
2. What factors would you consider in evaluating the effectiveness of professional labor in November 2001?

7-34 Comprehensive variance analysis responsibility issues. (CMA adapted) Horizons Unlimited manufactures a full line of well-known sunglasses frames and lenses. Horizons uses a standard costing system to set attainable standards for direct materials, labor, and overhead costs. Standards have been reviewed and revised annually, as necessary. Department managers, whose evaluations and bonuses are affected by their department's performance, are responsible for explaining variances in their department performance reports.

Recently, the manufacturing variances in the Visionaire prestige line of sunglasses have caused some concern. For no apparent reason, unfavorable materials and labor variances have occurred. At the monthly staff meeting, Jim Denton, manager of the Visionaire line, will be expected to explain his variances and suggest ways of improving performance.

Denton will be asked to explain the following performance report for 2001:

	Actual Results	Static-Budget Amounts
Units sold	4,850	5,000
Revenues	$397,700	$400,000
Variable manufacturing costs	234,643	216,000
Fixed manufacturing costs	72,265	75,000
Gross margin	90,792	109,000

Denton collected the following information.

    a. The standard variable manufacturing costs in 2001 comprised three items.

        ◆ Direct materials: Frames. Static budgeted cost of $33,000. The standard input for 2001 is 3.00 ounces per unit.

        ◆ Direct materials: Lenses. Static budgeted costs of $93,000. The standard input for 2001 is 6.00 ounces per unit.

        ◆ Direct manufacturing labor: Static budgeted costs of $90,000. The standard input for 2001 is 1.20 hours per unit.

Assume there are no indirect manufacturing costs.

    b. The actual variable manufacturing costs in 2001 were:

        ◆ Direct materials: Frames. Actual costs of $37,248. Actual ounces used per frame was 3.20 ounces per unit.

        ◆ Direct materials: Lenses. Actual costs of $100,492. Actual ounces used per frame was 7.00 ounces per unit.

        ◆ Direct manufacturing labor. Actual costs of $96,903. The actual labor rate was $14.80 per hour.

Required

1. Prepare a report that includes:
   a. Selling-price variance
   b. Sales-volume variance and flexible-budget variance for

      ◆ revenues

      ◆ variable manufacturing costs

      ◆ fixed manufacturing costs and

      ◆ gross margin

   c. Price and efficiency variances for

      ◆ direct materials: frames

      ◆ direct materials: lenses

      ◆ direct manufacturing labor

2. Give three possible explanations for the direct materials: lenses price and efficiency variances at Horizons in requirement **1c.**

7-35 Continuous improvement (continuation of 7-34). Horizon receives a suggestion that continuous improvement standard costs be used that are updated monthly. Consider monthly revisions in 2002 for the three variable manufacturing cost items.
Required
1. The January 2002 standard is 0.995 times the December 2001 standard. The February 2002 standard is 0.995 times the January 2002 standard. Using the data from Problem 7-34, what is the standard for the direct materials usage for each variable-cost item in January and February 2002?
2. What are the pros and cons of using the approach in requirement 1 as the primary approach to drive the cost competitiveness of Horizon?

7-36 Level 2 variance analysis, solve for unknowns. Homerun Headgear manufactures and distributes baseball caps to ballparks and other sports venues. Homerun's plan for 2002 forecast sales of 600,000 caps. However, only 500,000 caps were sold. Based on the data provided in Problem Exhibit 7-36, calculate the missing numbers and complete the analysis.

PROBLEM EXHIBIT 7-36
Schedule 1: Level 2 Variance Analysis for Homerun Headgear for 2002 (Incomplete)

	Actual Results (1)	Flexible-Budget Variances (2) = (1) − (3)	Flexible Budget (3)	Sales-Volume Variances (4) = (3) − (5)	Static Budget (5)
Units sold	500,000				600,000
Revenues	$5,000,000				$4,800,000
Variable costs	1,400,000				1,800,000
Contribution margin		1,100,000 F		500,000 U	
Fixed costs	1,150,000		1,000,000		1,000,000
Operating income					

Total flexible-budget variance

Total sales-volume variance

Total static-budget variance

Required
1. Calculate the budgeted and actual selling prices.
2. Assuming that the driver for variable costs is units sold, what are the budgeted and actual variable costs per unit?
3. Calculate the flexible-budget operating income.
4. Calculate the total flexible-budget variance.
5. Calculate the total sales-volume variance.
6. Calculate the total static-budget variance.

7-37 Flexible and static budgets, service company. Avanti Transportation Company executives have had trouble interpreting operating performance for a number of years. The company has used a budget based on detailed expectations for the forthcoming quarter. For example, the condensed performance report for a midwestern branch for the most recent quarter is:

	Actual Results	Budget	Variance[a]
Revenues	$9,500,000	$10,000,000	$500,000 U
Variable costs			
Fuel	986,000	1,000,000	14,000 F
Repairs and maintenance	98,000	100,000	2,000 F
Supplies and miscellaneous	196,000	200,000	4,000 F
Variable labor payroll	5,500,000	5,700,000	200,000 F
Total payroll costs[b]	6,780,000	7,000,000	220,000 F
Fixed costs			
Supervision	200,000	200,000	0
Rent	200,000	200,000	0
Depreciation	1,600,000	1,600,000	0
Other fixed costs	200,000	200,000	0
Total fixed costs	2,200,000	2,200,000	0
Total costs	8,980,000	9,200,000	220,000 F
Operating income	$ 520,000	$ 800,000	$280,000 U

[a] U = Unfavorable; F = Favorable.
[b] For purposes of this analysis, assume that all these costs are variable (in relation to revenue dollars). Also assume that the prices and mix of services sold remain unchanged.

Although the branch manager was upset about the unfavorable revenues variance, she was happy that her cost performance was favorable; otherwise her operating income would have been even lower. Her immediate superior, the vice president for operations, was totally unhappy and remarked: "I can see some merit in comparing actual performance with budgeted performance, because we can see whether actual revenue coincided with our best guess for budget purposes. But I can't see how this performance report helps us evaluate the cost control performance of the branch manager."

Required

1. Prepare a columnar flexible budget for Avanti at revenue levels of $9,000,000, $10,000,000, and $11,000,000.
2. Express the flexible budget for costs in formula form.
3. Prepare a condensed contribution income statement showing the static-budget variance, sales-volume variance, and the flexible-budget variance.

7-38 Comprehensive variance analysis review. FlexMem, Inc., manufactures 120-Mbyte diskettes that are compatible with a popular portable storage device. FlexMem sells diskettes wholesale to computer retail chains and direct marketing organizations that resell the diskettes as a house brand. The diskettes retail for an average of $8 per unit, and compete with well-known brands that retail for between $10 and $12 per diskette.

FlexMem's CFO has provided you with the following budgeted standards for the month of February, 2001:

Budgeted average wholesale selling price per diskette	$4.00
Total direct materials standard cost per diskette	0.85
Direct manufacturing labor	
Direct manufacturing standard labor cost per hour	$15.00
Average labor productivity rate (diskettes per hour)	300
Direct marketing cost per unit	$0.30
Fixed overhead	$900,000

The vice-president of marketing forecasts sales of 1,500,000 units for the month.

On March 7th, the vice-president of planning and control meets with the executive committee to discuss February results. He reports as follows:

◆ Unit sales totaled 80% of plan.
◆ Actual average selling price declined to $3.70.
◆ Productivity dropped to 250 diskettes/hour. However, due to favorable market conditions the actual price total direct materials per unit dropped to $0.80.
◆ Actual direct marketing costs were $0.30 per unit.
◆ Fixed costs were $30,000 below plan.

Required

As the senior financial analyst, you are asked to calculate the following:

1. Static-budget and actual operating income
2. Total static-budget variance
3. Flexible-budget operating income
4. Total flexible-budget variance
5. Total sales-volume variance
6. Price and efficiency variances for direct manufacturing labor

7-39 Direct materials and manufacturing labor variances, solving unknowns. (CPA adapted) On May 1, 2001, Bovar Company began the manufacture of a new paging machine known as Dandy. The company installed a standard costing system to account for manufacturing costs. The standard costs for a unit of Dandy follow:

Direct materials (3 lb. at $5 per lb.)	$15.00
Direct manufacturing labor ($\frac{1}{2}$ hour at $20 per hour)	10.00
Manufacturing overhead (75% of direct manufacturing labor costs)	7.50
	$32.50

The following data were obtained from Bovar's records for the month of May:

	Debit	Credit
Revenues		$125,000
Accounts payable control (for May's purchases of direct materials)		68,250
Direct materials price variance	$3,250	
Direct materials efficiency variance	2,500	
Direct manufacturing labor price variance	1,900	
Direct manufacturing labor efficiency variance		2,000

Actual production in May was 4,000 units of Dandy, and actual sales in May was 2,500 units.

The amount shown above for direct materials price variance applies to materials purchased during May. There was no beginning inventory of materials on May 1, 2001.

Required

Compute each of the following items for Bovar for the month of May. Show your computations.

1. Standard direct manufacturing labor-hours allowed for actual output produced.
2. Actual direct manufacturing labor-hours worked.
3. Actual direct manufacturing labor wage rate.
4. Standard quantity of direct materials allowed (in pounds).
5. Actual quantity of direct materials used (in pounds).
6. Actual quantity of direct materials purchased (in pounds).
7. Actual direct materials price per pound.

7-40 Comprehensive variance analysis (CMA). Aunt Molly's Old Fashioned Cookies bakes cookies for retail stores. The company's best-selling cookie is Chocolate Nut Supreme, which is marketed as a gourmet cookie and regularly sells for $8.00 per pound. The standard cost per pound of Chocolate Nut Supreme, based on Aunt Molly's normal monthly production of 400,00 pounds, follows:

Cost Item	Quantity	Standard Unit Costs	Total Standard Cost
Direct materials			
Cookie mix	10 oz.	$ 0.02/oz.	$0.20
Milk chocolate	5 oz.	0.15/oz.	0.75
Almonds	1 oz.	0.50/oz.	0.50
			1.45
Direct manufacturing labor*			
Mixing	1 min.	14.40/hr.	0.24
Baking	2 min.	18.00/hr.	0.60
			0.84
Variable			
Overhead**	3 min.	32.40 hr.	1.62
Total standard cost per pound			$3.91

*Direct manufacturing labor rates include employee benefits.
**Allocated on the basis of direct labor-hours.

Aunt Molly's management accountant, Karen Blair, prepares monthly budget reports based on these standard costs. Presented here is her report for April:

Performance Report
April 2001

	Actual	Budget	Variance
Units (in pounds)	450,000	400,000	50,000 F
Revenues	$3,555,000	$3,200,000	$355,000 F
Direct materials	865,000	580,000	285,000 U
Direct manufacturing labor	348,000	336,000	12,000 U

Justine Molly, president of the company, is disappointed with the results. Despite a sizable increase in the number of cookies sold, the product's expected contribution to the overall profitability of the company decreased. Molly has asked Blair to identify the reasons why the contribution margin decreased. Blair has gathered the following information to help in her analysis of the decrease:

Usage Report
April 2001

Cost Item	Quantity	Actual Cost
Direct materials		
Cookie mix	4,650,000 oz.	$ 93,000
Milk chocolate	2,660,000 oz.	532,000
Almonds	480,000 oz.	240,000
Direct manufacturing labor		
Mixing	450,000 min.	108,000
Baking	800,000 min.	240,000

Required
Compute and discuss the following variances:

1. Selling-price variance
2. Materials-price variance
3. Materials-efficiency variance
4. Labor-efficiency variance

7-41 Activity-based costing, variance analysis. Toymaster, Inc., produces a special kind of plastic toy cars, TGC, for various manufacturers. Toymaster produces TGC in batches. After each batch of TGC is run, the molds are cleaned. The labor costs of cleaning the mold can be traced directly to TGC because TGC can only be produced from a specific mold. Cleaning labor is paid on an hourly basis. The following information pertains to June 2001:

	Static-Budget Amounts	Actual Amounts
Units of TGC produced and sold	30,000	22,500
Batch size (number of units per batch)	250	225
Cleaning labor-hours per batch	3	3.5
Cleaning labor cost per hour	$14	$12.50

Required
1. Calculate the flexible-budget variance for total cleaning labor costs in June 2001.
2. Calculate the price and efficiency variances for total cleaning labor costs in June 2001. Comment on the results.

7-42 Activity-based costing, variance analysis. King Taste is a manufacturer of fruit cakes. One of its plants produces five different cake products. Each cake product differs in terms of material inputs (different fruits, flour, and liquor). They are identical in terms of both the cooking and the setup processes.

King Taste prefers to make long production runs of each cake product. A major benefit is that fewer changeovers are made. A changeover is the process of switching the production line from the manufacture of one product to another product. The costs of a changeover are a batch cost. They comprise the labor cost of the workers who clean the mixing equipment so that the contents of each different product are not mixed together. The following information pertains to March 2000:

	Static-Budget Amounts	Actual Amounts
Units of pound cakes produced and sold	240,000	330,000
Average number of cakes per production run	6,000	10,000
Changeover labor-hours per production run	20 hours	24 hours
Changeover labor cost per hour	$20	$21

ROCK'n'ROLL

"Cost Accounting is music to your ears!"

COST ACCOUNTING, _Tenth Edition_
Charles T. Horngren, George Foster, and Srikant M. Datar

Rock 'n' roll is dynamic, hard-hitting, and gets right to the point...and so does the new, streamlined **Cost Accounting, 10th ed**! Now three chapters shorter, this syncopated and direct revision keeps the beat with today's students of accounting.

◆ Sings a song of clarity, **stream-lined presentations,** and better explanations of concepts, such as cost-volume-profit analysis (Ch.3), job costing methods (Ch. 4), activity-based costing (Ch. 5), variance analysis (Chs. 7 and 8), and process costing (Chs. 17 and 18)

"The treatment is a lot smoother. . . . It is much more readable now and flows evenly."
–Arijit Mukherji,
University of Minnesota

◆ Keeps a short, quick tempo by **combining and consolidating** material from the previous edition

◆ Chapter 14 now contains all material on cost allocation (two separate chapters in the previous edition).

"I like the two chapters combined [Chs. 20 and 21] . . . [and] I appreciate the addition of the "bullwhip" concept. Students should be able to understand and appreciate the concept of JIT better with such explanation."
–Jean Hawkins,
William Jewell College

◆ Chapter 20 contains all material on Just-in-Time.

◆ Chapter 21 consolidates two capital-budgeting chapters into condensed, focused exposition.

"The intuitive graphical depiction of the discounting process embedded in discounting formulas for NPV and IRR impressed me."
–Derrell Moore,
Hardin-Simmons University

Required

1. Compute the flexible-budget variance for total changeover labor costs in March 2000. Comment on the results.
2. Compute the price and efficiency variances for total changeover labor costs in March 2000. Comment on the results.
3. Provide two explanations for each of the price and efficiency variances in requirement 2.

7-43 Procurement costs, variance analysis, ethics. Rick Daley is the manager of the athletic shoe division of Raider Products. Raider is a U.S.-based company that has just purchased Fastfoot, a leading European shoe company. Fastfoot has long-term production contracts with suppliers in two Eastern Europe countries—Hergovia and Tanistan. Daley receives a request from Kevin Neal, President of Raider Products. Daley and his controller, Brooke Mullins, are to make a presentation to the next board of director's meeting on the cost competitiveness of its Fastfoot subsidiary. This report should include budgeted and actual procurement costs for 2001 at its Hergovia and Tanistan supply sources.

Mullins decides to visit the two supply operations. The budgeted average procurement cost for 2001 is $12 per pair of shoes. This cost includes payments to the shoe manufacturer and all other payments to conduct business in each country. Mullin's reports the following to Daley:

◆ *Hergovia.* Total 2001 procurement costs for 250,000 pair of shoes is $3,325,000. Payment to the shoe manufacturer is $2,650,000. Very few receipts exist for the remaining $675,000. Kickback payments are viewed as common in Hergovia.

◆ *Tanistan.* Total 2001 procurement costs for 900,000 pair of shoes is $10,485,000. Payment to the shoe manufacturer is $8,640,000. Receipts exist for $705,000 of the other costs, but Mullins says he is skeptical of their validity. Kickback payments are a "way of business" at Tanistan.

At both the Hergovia and Tanistan plants Mullins is disturbed by the employment of young children (many of them under 15 years). He is told that all major shoe producing companies have similar low-cost employment practices in both countries.

Daley is uncomfortable about the upcoming presentation to the board. He was a leading advocate of the acquisition. A recent business magazine reported that the Fastfoot acquisition would make Raider Products the global low-cost producer in its market lines. The stock price of Raider Products jumped 21% the day the Fastfoot acquisition was announced. Mullins likewise is widely identified as a proponent of the acquisition. He is seen as a "rising star" due for a promotion to a division manager in the near future.

Required

1. What summary procurement cost variances should be reported to the board of directors of Raider Shoes?
2. What ethical issues do (a) Daley and (b) Mullins face when preparing and making a report to the board of directors?
3. How should Mullins address the issues you identify in requirement 2?

COLLABORATIVE LEARNING EXERCISE

7-44 Price and efficiency variances, problems in standard setting, benchmarking. Savannah Fashions manufactures shirts for retail chains. Jorge Andersen, the controller, is becoming increasingly disenchanted with Savannah's six-month-old standard-costing system. The budgeted amounts for both its direct materials and direct manufacturing labor are drawn from its standard-costing system. The budgeted and actual amounts for July 2001 were:

	Budgeted Amounts	Actual Results
Shirts manufactured	4,000	4,488
Direct materials cost	$20,000	$20,196
Direct materials units (rolls of cloth)	400	408
Direct manufacturing labor costs	$18,000	$18,462
Direct manufacturing labor-hours	1,000	1,020

There was no beginning or ending inventory of materials.

Andersen observes that in the last six months he has rarely seen an unfavorable variance of any magnitude. The standard-costing system is based on a study of the operations conducted by an independent consultant. Andersen decides to play detective and observe the plant's workforce unobtrusively. He notes that even at their current output levels, the workers seem to have a lot of time to discuss baseball, sitcoms, and the local hot fishing spots.

At a recent industry conference on "Benchmarking and Competitiveness", Andersen had a discussion with Mary Blanchard, the controller of Winston Fabrics. Blanchard told him that Winston had employed the same independent consultant to design a standard costing system. However, the company dismissed him after two weeks. The Winston employees quickly became aware of the consultant observing their work.

At the industry conference Anderson participated in seminars on "Benchmarking for the Fabric Industry." A consultant for the Benchmarking Clearing House showed how she could develop six-month benchmark reports on the estimated costs of Savannah's major competitors. She indicated that she already was examining the estimated cost of shirts manufactured by the four largest U.S. importers. These importers had taken much business from Savannah in recent years. This information would soon be available by subscribing to the Benchmarking Clearing House monthly service.

Required

Form groups of two or more students to complete the following requirements:

1. Compute the price and efficiency variances of Savannah Fashions for direct materials and direct manufacturing labor in July 2001.
2. Describe the types of actions the employees at Winston Fabrics may have taken to reduce the accuracy of the standards set by the independent consultant. Why would employees take those actions? Is this behavior ethical?
3. Describe how Savannah might use information from the Benchmarking Clearing House when computing the variances in requirement 1.
4. Discuss the pros and cons of Savannah using the Benchmarking Clearing House information to help increase its cost competitiveness.

Flexible Budgets, Variances, and Management Control: II

learning objectives

When you have finished studying this chapter, you should be able to

1. Explain similarities and differences in the planning of variable overhead costs and the planning of fixed overhead costs

2. Identify the key features of a standard costing system

3. Compute variable overhead spending and efficiency variances

4. Explain how the efficiency variance for a variable indirect-cost item differs from the efficiency variance for a direct-cost item

5. Compute the budgeted fixed overhead rate

6. Explain two caveats to consider when interpreting the production-volume variance as a measure of the economic cost of unused capacity

7. Show how the 4-variance analysis approach reconciles the actual overhead incurred with the overhead amounts allocated during the period

8. Illustrate how the flexible-budget variance approach can be used in activity-based costing

Energy and depreciation costs for plant and equipment are major components of the manufacturing overhead costs of paper manufacturing plants.

Overhead costs are a major cost area for many organizations. For example, chemical, paper, and steel companies incur sizable costs to construct and maintain their physical plant and equipment. These costs are part of their overhead costs. Companies like Amazon.com, Netscape, and Yahoo! invest large amounts in software that enable them to provide a broad range of services to their customers in a timely and reliable way. These costs are part of their overhead costs.

Planning and control of overhead costs is an ongoing challenge to managers. This chapter shows how the flexible-budget/variance-analysis approach introduced in Chapter 7 can assist managers in this challenge. Chapter 7 emphasized the direct-cost categories of direct materials and direct manufacturing labor. This chapter emphasizes the overhead categories of variable and fixed manufacturing overhead. We also highlight how managers should carefully interpret variances based on overhead cost concepts developed primarily for financial reporting purposes.

PLANNING OF VARIABLE AND FIXED OVERHEAD COSTS

We continue the Chapter 7 analysis of the Webb Company. Webb manufactures a distinctive jacket that is then sold to distributors. Variable manufacturing overhead costs for Webb include energy, machine maintenance, engineering support, indirect materials, and indirect manufacturing labor. Fixed manufacturing overhead costs include plant-leasing costs, some administrative costs (such as the plant manager's salary), and depreciation.

Planning Variable Overhead Costs

Effective planning of variable overhead costs involves undertaking only those variable overhead activities that add value for customers using the related product or service. Clorox (the bleach-producing company) reported the following in its Annual Report: "Our work simplification initiative is pretty direct—it's about getting the gunk out of our internal systems by eliminating nonvalue-added work so that all of us at Clorox can spend our energy on important value-adding activities that will move the business ahead."

In our example, Webb Company should examine how each of the activities in its variable overhead cost pools is related to delivering a product or service to customers. For example, Webb's customers perceive sewing to be an essential activity at Webb. Hence, maintenance activities for sewing machines—included in Webb's variable overhead costs—are also essential activities. Such maintenance should be done in a cost-effective way. This means, for example, scheduling equipment maintenance in a systematic way rather than waiting for sewing machines to break down.

Planning Fixed Overhead Costs

Effective planning of fixed overhead costs has the same twin set of challenges noted for variable overhead costs—that is, planning to undertake only essential activities and then planning to be efficient in that undertaking. The key added challenge with planning fixed overhead is choosing the appropriate level of capacity or investment that will benefit the company over an extended time period. Consider Webb's leasing of sewing machines, each of which has a fixed cost per year. Failure to lease sufficient machine capacity will result in an inability to meet demand and thus in lost sales of jackets. In contrast, if Webb greatly overestimates demand, it will incur additional fixed leasing costs on machines not fully utilized during the year.

At the start of a budget period, management will have made most of the key decisions that determine the level of fixed overhead costs to be incurred. In contrast, day-to-day, ongoing operating decisions play a larger role in determining the level of variable overhead costs incurred in that period.

STANDARD COSTING AT WEBB COMPANY

Webb Company uses standard costing. Chapter 7 described the development of standards for Webb's direct-cost categories. This chapter discusses Webb's indirect-cost categories. **Standard costing** is a costing method that traces direct costs to a cost object by multiplying the standard price(s) or rate(s) times the standard inputs allowed for actual outputs produced and allocates indirect costs on the basis of the standard indirect rate(s) times the standard inputs allowed for the actual outputs produced.

With a standard costing system, the costs of every product or service planned to be worked on during the period can be computed at the start of that period. This feature enables a simplified recording system to be used. No record need be kept of the actual costs of items used or of the actual quantity of the cost-allocation base used on individual products or services worked on during the period. Once standards have been set, the costs of operating standard costing can be low relative to actual or normal costing. We start by describing the development of budgeted rates for variable overhead costs.

DEVELOPING BUDGETED VARIABLE OVERHEAD COST-ALLOCATION RATES

Variable overhead cost-allocation rates can be developed with a four-step approach.

Step 1: Choose the Time Period Used to Compute the Budget Webb uses a 12-month budget period that includes a full calendar-year cycle spanning different seasonality patterns.

Step 2: Select the Cost-Allocation Bases to Use in Allocating Variable Overhead Costs to the Cost Object(s) Webb's operating managers believe that machine-hours is the cost driver of variable manufacturing overhead. Using the cause-and-effect criterion, Webb selects standard machine-hours as the cost-allocation base. Webb budgets 57,600 machine-hours for a budgeted output of 144,000 jackets in 2000.

Step 3: Identify the Variable Overhead Costs Associated with Each Cost-Allocation Base Webb groups all its variable manufacturing overhead costs in a single cost pool. Costs in this pool include energy, machine maintenance, engineering support, indirect materials, and indirect manufacturing labor. Webb's budgeted variable manufacturing costs for 2000 are $1,728,000.

Step 4: Compute the Rate Per Unit of Each Cost-Allocation Base Used to Allocate Variable Overhead Costs to the Cost Object(s) Dividing the amount in step 3 ($1,728,000) by the amount in step 2 (57,600 hours), Webb estimates a rate of $30 per standard machine-hour for its variable manufacturing overhead costs.

In standard costing, the variable overhead rate per cost-allocation base is often expressed as a standard rate per output unit. This standard rate depends on the number of units of the cost-allocation base (input units) allowed per output unit. Using a time-and-motion study, Webb estimates it will take 0.40 machine-hours per actual output unit. Hence:

$$
\begin{array}{l}
\text{Budgeted variable} \\
\text{overhead cost rate} = \\
\text{per output unit}
\end{array}
\begin{array}{l}
\text{Budgeted inputs} \\
\text{allowed per} \\
\text{output unit}
\end{array}
\times
\begin{array}{l}
\text{Budgeted variable} \\
\text{overhead cost rate} \\
\text{per input unit}
\end{array}
$$

$$= 0.40 \times \$30$$

$$= \$12 \text{ per jacket (output unit)}$$

Webb uses this $12 per output unit rate in both its initial budget for 2000 and in the monthly performance reports it prepares during 2000.

VARIABLE OVERHEAD COST VARIANCES

We now illustrate how the budgeted variable manufacturing overhead rate is used in computing Webb's variable manufacturing overhead cost variances. The following data are for April 2000 when Webb produced and sold 10,000 jackets:

Cost Item/Allocation Base	Actual Results	Flexible-Budget Amount
1. Output units (jackets)	10,000	10,000
2. Machine-hours	4,500	4,000
3. Machine-hours per output unit (2 ÷ 1)	0.45	0.40
4. Variable manufacturing overhead costs	$130,500	$120,000
5. Variable manufacturing overhead costs per machine-hour (4 ÷ 2)	$29.00	$30.00
6. Variable manufacturing overhead costs per output unit (4 ÷ 1)	$13.05	$12.00

The flexible-budget enables Webb to highlight the effect of differences between actual and budgeted costs and quantities for the actual output level of 10,000 jackets in April 2000.

Flexible-Budget Analysis

The **variable overhead flexible-budget variance** measures the difference between the actual variable overhead costs and the flexible-budget variable overhead costs. As Exhibit 8-1 shows,

$$\text{Variable overhead flexible-budget variable} = \text{Actual results} - \text{Flexible-budget amount}$$

$$= \$130,500 - \$120,000$$

$$= \$10,500 \text{ U}$$

This $10,500 unfavorable flexible-budget variance shows that Webb's actual variable manufacturing overhead exceeded its flexible budget amount by $10,500 for the 10,000 jackets actually produced and sold in April 2000.

Just as we did in Chapter 7 with the flexible-budget variance for direct-cost items, we will now extract additional information by subdividing the variable manufacturing overhead flexible-budget variance into its efficiency and spending variances.

Variable Overhead Efficiency Variance

The **variable overhead efficiency variance** measures the efficiency with which the cost-allocation base is used. The formula is:

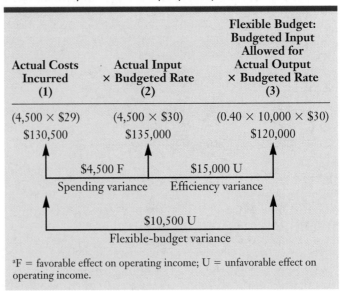

EXHIBIT 8-1
Columnar Presentation of Variable Manufacturing Overhead Variance Analysis: Webb Company for April 2000[a]

[a]F = favorable effect on operating income; U = unfavorable effect on operating income.

$$\begin{array}{l} \text{Variable} \\ \text{overhead} \\ \text{efficiency} \\ \text{variance} \end{array} = \left(\begin{array}{c} \text{Actual units of} \\ \text{variable overhead} \\ \text{cost-allocation base} \\ \text{used for} \\ \text{actual output} \end{array} - \begin{array}{c} \text{Budgeted units of} \\ \text{variable overhead} \\ \text{cost-allocation base} \\ \text{allowed for} \\ \text{actual output} \end{array} \right) \times \begin{array}{c} \text{Budgeted variable} \\ \text{overhead rate} \end{array}$$

$$= [4{,}500 - (0.40 \times 10{,}000)] \times \$30$$

$$= (4{,}500 - 4{,}000) \times \$30 = 500 \times \$30$$

$$= \$15{,}000 \text{ U}$$

Columns 2 and 3 of Exhibit 8-1 present the variable overhead efficiency variance. The variable overhead efficiency variance is computed similarly to the efficiency variance described in Chapter 7 (p. 227–228) for direct-cost items. But the interpretation of the direct-cost efficiency variances differs. In Chapter 7, efficiency variances for direct-cost items are based on differences between actual inputs used and the budgeted inputs allowed for actual output produced. For example, an efficiency variance for direct manufacturing labor for Webb will indicate whether more or less such labor is used per jacket than was budgeted for the actual output produced. In contrast, in Chapter 8 the efficiency variance for variable overhead cost is based on the efficiency with which the cost-allocation base is used. Webb's unfavorable variable overhead efficiency variance of $15,000 means that actual machine-hours (the cost-allocation base) were higher than the budgeted machine-hours allowed to manufacture 10,000 jackets. Possible causes for this higher-than-budgeted machine-hour usage include:

(i) Webb's workers were less skillful in the use of machines than expected.

(ii) Webb's production scheduler inefficiently scheduled jobs, resulting in higher machine usage than budgeted.

(iii) Webb's machines were not maintained in good operating condition.

(iv) Webb promised a distributor a rushed delivery, which resulted in higher machine usage than budgeted.

(v) Budgeted machine time standards were set without careful analysis of the operating conditions.

Management's response to this $15,000 U variance would be guided by which cause(s) best describes the April 2000 results. Cause (i) has implications for employee-hiring practices and training procedures. Causes (ii) and (iii) relate to plant operations and include the possible use of software packages for production scheduling and plant maintenance. Cause (iv) has implications for coordinating production schedules with distributors and sharing information with them. Cause (v) requires managers to commit resources to developing reliable standards.

Variable Overhead Spending Variance

The **variable overhead spending variance** is the difference between the actual amount of variable overhead incurred and the budgeted amount allowed for the actual quantity of the variable overhead allocation base used for the actual output units produced. The formula for the variable overhead spending variance is:

$$\begin{array}{l} \text{Variable} \\ \text{overhead} \\ \text{spending} \\ \text{variance} \end{array} = \left(\begin{array}{c} \text{Actual variable} \\ \text{overhead cost per} \\ \text{unit of cost-} \\ \text{allocation base} \end{array} - \begin{array}{c} \text{Budgeted variable} \\ \text{overhead cost per} \\ \text{unit of cost-} \\ \text{allocation base} \end{array} \right) \times \begin{array}{c} \text{Actual quantity of} \\ \text{variable overhead} \\ \text{cost-allocation base} \\ \text{used for actual output} \end{array}$$

$$= (\$29 - \$30) \times 4{,}500$$

$$= -\$1 \times 4{,}500 = \$4{,}500 \text{ F}$$

Webb operated in April 2000 with a lower-than-budgeted variable overhead cost per machine-hour. Hence, there is a favorable variable overhead spending variance. Columns 1 and 2 in Exhibit 8-1 present this variance.

To understand the variable overhead spending variance, it is important to recognize why the *actual* variable overhead cost per unit of the cost-allocation base is *lower* than the *budgeted* variable overhead cost per unit of the cost-allocation base. The reason is that, relative to the flexible budget, the percentage increase in the actual quantity of the cost-allocation base is *more* than the percentage increase in actual total costs of individual items in the indirect-cost pool. In the Webb example, the 4,500 actual machine-hours are 12.5% greater than the flexible-budget amount of 4,000 machine-hours [(4,500 − 4,000) ÷ 4,000 = 12.5%]. Actual variable overhead costs of $130,500 are only 8.75% greater than the flexible-budget amount of $120,000 [($130,500 − $120,000) ÷ $120,000 = 8.75%]. Because actual variable overhead costs increase relatively less than machine-hours, the actual variable overhead cost per machine-hour is lower than the budgeted rate.

Variable manufacturing overhead costs include costs of energy, machine maintenance, indirect materials, and indirect manufacturing labor. Two main reasons that could explain why actual variable manufacturing overhead costs increase less than machine-hours in the Webb example are:

1. The actual prices of individual items included in variable overhead, such as the purchase price of energy, indirect materials, or indirect manufacturing labor, are lower than the budgeted prices. For example, the actual price of electricity may only be $0.09 per kilowatt-hour compared to a price of $0.10 per kilowatt-hour in the flexible budget.

2. Relative to the flexible budget, the percentage increase in the actual quantity usage of individual items in the variable overhead-cost pool is less than the percentage increase in machine-hours. Suppose, for example, that actual energy usage is 32,400 kilowatt-hours compared to the flexible-budget amount of 30,000 kilowatt-hours. The 8% [(32,400 − 30,000) ÷ 30,000] increase in energy usage compared to the 12.5% increase in machine-hours will lead to a favorable variable overhead spending variance. Thus, the spending variance can be partially or completely traced to the efficient use of energy and other variable overhead.

Price effects have implications for the purchasing area of Webb. Quantity effects have implications for the production area of Webb. Distinguishing between these two effects for a variable overhead spending variance requires detailed information about the budgeted prices and budgeted quantities of the individual line items in the variable overhead cost pool.

To clarify the concepts of variable overhead efficiency and spending variances, consider the following example. Suppose energy is the only item of variable overhead and machine-hours is the cost-allocation base (cost driver). Suppose also that the actual machine-hours used to produce the actual output equals the budgeted machine-hours and that the actual price of energy equals the budgeted price. In this case, there would be no efficiency variance, but there could be a spending variance. The company has been efficient with respect to the number of machine-hours used to produce the actual output. But it could be using too much energy, not because of excessive machine-hours but because of wastage. The cost of this higher energy usage would be measured by the spending variance.

The variable manufacturing overhead variances computed in this section are summarized as follows:

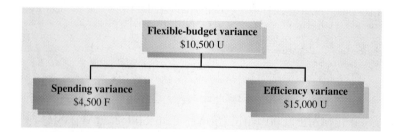

The key cause for Webb's unfavorable flexible-budget variance is the higher-than-budgeted number of machine-hours. Webb subsequently found that the machines in April 2000 operated below budgeted efficiency levels due to the minimal maintenance performed in February and March. A former plant manager delayed maintenance in a presumed attempt to meet monthly budget cost targets. Webb has now strengthened its internal maintenance procedures so that failure to do monthly maintenance raises a "red flag" that must be immediately explained to top management.

From variable overhead costs we now turn our attention to fixed overhead costs.

DEVELOPING BUDGETED FIXED OVERHEAD COST-ALLOCATION RATES

Fixed overhead costs are, by definition, a lump sum that remains unchanged in total for a given time period despite wide changes in the related level of total activity or volume. While total fixed costs are frequently included in flexible budgets, they remain the same total amount within the relevant range regardless of the output level chosen to "flex" the variable costs and revenues. The steps in developing the budgeted fixed overhead rate are:

Step 1: Choose the Time Period Used to Compute the Budget   As with variable overhead costs, the budget period is typically 12 months. Chapter 4 (pp. 103–104) provides three reasons for using annual overhead rates rather than, say, monthly rates: reducing the influence of seasonality, reducing the effect of the varying number of days in a month, and preventing management time from being tied up in setting monthly budget rates.

Step 2: Select the Cost-Allocation Base to Use in Allocating Fixed Overhead Costs to the Cost Object(s)   Webb uses standard machine-hours as the cost-allocation base for fixed manufacturing overhead costs. This is the denominator of the budgeted fixed overhead rate computation and is called the **denominator level**. In manufacturing settings, the denominator level is commonly termed the **production-denominator level**. Standard machine-hours is the same allocation base Webb uses for its variable manufacturing overhead costs. The budgeted machine-hours for 2000 are 57,600 hours for a budgeted output of 144,000 jackets.

Step 3: Identify the Fixed Overhead Costs Associated with Each Cost-Allocation Base   Webb groups all its fixed manufacturing overhead costs in a single cost pool. Costs in this pool include depreciation, plant and equipment leasing costs, the plant manager's salary, and some administrative costs. Webb's fixed manufacturing budget for 2000 is $3,312,000.

Step 4: Compute the Rate Per Unit of Each Cost-Allocation Base Used to Allocate Fixed Overhead Costs to the Cost Object(s)   Dividing the $3,312,000 from step 3 by the 57,600 machine-hours from step 2, Webb estimates a fixed manufacturing overhead cost rate of $57.50 per machine-hour:

$$\text{Budgeted fixed overhead cost rate} = \frac{\text{Budgeted total costs in overhead cost pool}}{\text{Budgeted total quantity of cost-allocation base}}$$

$$= \frac{\$3,312,000}{57,600 \text{ machine-hours}}$$

$$= \$57.50 \text{ per machine-hour}$$

In standard costing, the $57.50 fixed overhead rate per machine-hour is often expressed as a standard rate per output unit:

$$\text{Budgeted fixed overhead cost rate} = \begin{array}{c}\text{Budgeted inputs} \\ \text{allowed per} \\ \text{output unit}\end{array} \times \begin{array}{c}\text{Budgeted fixed} \\ \text{overhead cost rate} \\ \text{per input unit}\end{array}$$

$$= 0.40 \times \$57.50$$

$$= \$23.00 \text{ per output unit}$$

When preparing monthly budgets for 2000, Webb divides the $3,312,000 annual amount into 12 equal monthly amounts of $276,000.

FIXED OVERHEAD COST VARIANCES

The flexible-budget amount for a fixed-cost item is the amount included in the static budget prepared at the start of the period. No adjustment is required for differences between the actual output and the budgeted output for fixed costs. By definition, fixed costs are unaffected by changes in the level of output. At the start of 2000, Webb budgeted fixed manufacturing overhead costs to be $276,000 per month. The actual amount for April 2000 is $285,000. The **fixed overhead flexible-budget variance** is the difference between actual fixed overhead costs and the fixed overhead costs in the flexible-budget:

$$\frac{\text{Fixed overhead}}{\text{flexible-budget variance}} = \frac{\text{Actual costs}}{\text{incurred}} - \frac{\text{Flexible-budget}}{\text{amount}}$$

$$= \$285,000 - \$276,000$$

$$= \$9,000 \text{ U}$$

As Exhibit 8-2 shows, the variance is unfavorable because actual fixed manufacturing overhead costs exceed the $276,000 budgeted for April 2000.

The variable overhead flexible-budget variance described earlier in this chapter has been subdivided into a spending variance and an efficiency variance. Note that there is not an efficiency variance for fixed costs. Why? Because a given lump sum of fixed costs will be unaffected by the degree of operating efficiency in a given budget period. As Exhibit 8-2 shows, the result is that the fixed overhead spending variance is the same amount as the fixed overhead flexible-budget variance:

$$\frac{\text{Fixed overhead}}{\text{flexible-budget variance}} = \frac{\text{Actual costs}}{\text{incurred}} - \frac{\text{Flexible-budget}}{\text{amount}}$$

$$= \$285,000 - \$276,000$$

$$= \$9,000 \text{ U}$$

Webb investigated this variance and found that there was a $9,000 per month unex-

EXHIBIT 8-2
Columnar Presentation of Fixed Manufacturing Overhead Variance Analysis: Webb Company for April 2000[a]

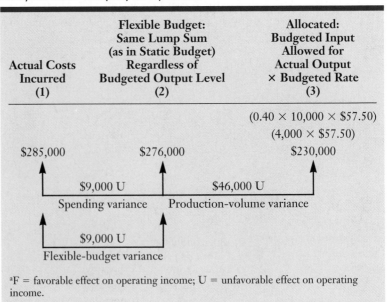

[a]F = favorable effect on operating income; U = unfavorable effect on operating income.

pected increase in its equipment leasing costs. However, management concluded that the new lease rates were still competitive with those available elsewhere.

Webb's budgeted fixed manufacturing overhead is allocated to output units produced during the period at the budgeted $57.50 per standard machine-hour rate. We now consider a variance that arises when the actual level of the denominator for allocating fixed overhead costs differs from the budgeted level assumed at the start of the period. This budgeted level for Webb in 2000 was 57,600 hours (0.40 machine-hour per output unit × 144,000 budgeted output units for 2000).

PRODUCTION-VOLUME VARIANCE

The **production-volume variance** is the difference between budgeted fixed overhead and the fixed overhead allocated on the basis of the budgeted quantity of the fixed overhead allocation base allowed for the actual output produced. Other terms for this variance include **denominator-level variance** and **output-level overhead variance**.

The formula for the production-volume variance, expressed in terms of allocation base units (machine-hours for Webb), is

$$\begin{matrix} \text{Production-} \\ \text{volume} \\ \text{variance} \end{matrix} = \begin{matrix} \text{Budgeted} \\ \text{fixed} \\ \text{overhead} \end{matrix} - \begin{matrix} \text{Fixed overhead allocated using} \\ \text{budgeted input allowed for} \\ \text{actual output units produced} \end{matrix}$$

$$= \$276{,}000 - (0.40 \times 10{,}000 \times \$57.50)$$

$$= \$276{,}000 - \$230{,}000$$

$$= \$46{,}000 \text{ U}$$

The formula can also be expressed in terms of the budgeted fixed costs per output unit:

$$\begin{matrix} \text{Production-} \\ \text{volume} \\ \text{variance} \end{matrix} = \begin{matrix} \text{Budgeted} \\ \text{fixed} \\ \text{overhead} \end{matrix} - \begin{matrix} \text{Fixed overhead allocated using} \\ \text{budgeted amount per output unit} \\ \text{allowed for actual output units produced} \end{matrix}$$

$$= \$276{,}000 - (\$23 \times 10{,}000)$$

$$= \$276{,}000 - \$230{,}000$$

$$= \$46{,}000 \text{ U}$$

As shown in Exhibit 8-2, the amount used for budgeted fixed overhead will be the same lump sum shown in the static budget and also in any flexible budget within the relevant range. Fixed overhead allocated is the sum of the individual fixed overhead costs allocated to each unit of product manufactured during the budget period.

Interpreting the Production-Volume Variance

The production-volume variance arises whenever the actual level of the denominator differs from the level used to calculate the budgeted fixed overhead rate. We compute this rate because inventory costing and some types of contracts require fixed overhead costs to be expressed on a unit-of-output basis. The production-volume variance results from "unitizing" fixed costs. A favorable (unfavorable) variance means we have overallocated (underallocated) the fixed overhead cost to output units produced because the actual denominator units used in this allocation exceeds (is less than) the budgeted denominator level used to compute the fixed overhead allocation rate.

Lump-sum fixed costs represent resources sacrificed in acquiring capacity, such as plant and equipment leases, that cannot be decreased if the resources needed are less than the resources acquired. Sometimes, costs are fixed for contrac-

Correcting Student Misconceptions When we allocate FMOH to WIP for inventory costing, we "unitize" FMOH and treat it as if it were a variable cost. In contrast, FB FMOH is *fixed, fixed, fixed* across output levels, in the relevant range (this is how it's treated for managerial control purposes). FB FMOH equals FMOH allocated to WIP only if the # of output units actually produced equals the denominator level. This creates a variance that's unique to FMOH—the production volume var.

Reinforcing Problems Exer. 8-17, and 8-19 through 8-27, and Probs. 8-29, 8-33, 8-34, and 8-40 cover FMOH spending and production-volume variances.

OBJECTIVE 6

Explain two caveats to consider when interpreting the production-volume variance as a measure of the economic cost of unused capacity

tual reasons such as a lease contract; at other times, as we discussed in Chapter 2, costs are fixed because of lumpiness in acquiring and disposing of capacity.

In our example, Webb leased equipment capacity to produce 12,000 units. Although it produced only 10,000 units, the lease contract prevented Webb from reducing equipment lease costs during 2001. Unitizing and allocating fixed-costs helps Webb to measure the amount of fixed-cost resources it used to produce 10,000 units. The unfavorable production-volume variance of $46,000 measures the amount of extra fixed costs that Webb incurred for manufacturing capacity it planned to use but did not in April 2000. One inference is that the $46,000 U production-volume variance represents inefficient capacity utilization.

Be careful, however, when making inferences about a company's capacity planning and utilization decisions from the sign or magnitude of a production-volume variance. Webb, for example, should consider why it only sold 10,000 jackets in April when interpreting the $46,000 unfavorable variance. Suppose that a new competitor had gained market share by pricing below Webb's selling price. To sell the budgeted 12,000 units, Webb may have had to reduce its own selling price on all 12,000 units. Suppose it decided that selling 10,000 units at a higher price yielded higher operating income than selling 12,000 units at a lower price. The production-volume variance does not take into account such information. Hence, do not interpret the $46,000 U amount as Webb's *total economic cost* of selling 2,000 units below the 12,000-unit denominator level.

Companies plan their plant capacity on the basis of expected usage over some future time horizon. Assume that in 2001 Webb's denominator level is exactly the maximum capacity of the plant for that budget period. Actual demand (and production) in 2001 subsequently turns out to be 5% below the denominator level. Webb would report an unfavorable production-volume variance for 2001. However, it would be incorrect to infer that this means that Webb's management made a bad planning decision regarding the 2001 plant capacity. Demand for Webb's jackets might be highly uncertain. Given this uncertainty and the cost of not having sufficient capacity to meet sudden demand surges (such as lost contribution margins and reduced follow-on business), Webb's management may have made a very judicious choice in planning 2001 plant capacity.

Always explore the *why* of a variance before concluding that the label unfavorable (favorable) necessarily indicates poor (good) management performance. Understanding the reasons for a variance also helps managers decide on courses of future action. Should they try to reduce capacity, increase sales, or do nothing? Chapters 9 and 13 examine these issues in more detail.

INTEGRATED ANALYSIS OF OVERHEAD COST VARIANCES

As our discussion indicates, the variance calculations for variable manufacturing overhead and fixed manufacturing overhead differ. Variable manufacturing overhead has no production-volume variance and fixed manufacturing overhead has no efficiency variance. Exhibit 8-3 presents an integrated summary of variable and fixed overhead variances computed using standard costs at the end of April 2000. The key point of Exhibit 8-3 is highlighting the columns for which no variances are calculated. Panel A shows the variances for variable manufacturing overhead and Panel B shows the variances for fixed manufacturing overhead. As you read Exhibit 8-3, note how the columns in Panels A and B are aligned to measure the different variances. In both Panels A and B,

1. The difference between columns 1 and 2 measures the spending variance.
2. The difference between columns 2 and 3 measures the efficiency variance (where applicable).
3. The difference between columns 3 and 4 measures the production-volume variance (where applicable).

Note that Panel A has an efficiency variance but Panel B does not. A lump-sum amount of fixed costs will be unaffected by the degree of operating efficiency in a

EXHIBIT 8-3
Columnar Presentation of Integrated Variance Analysis: Webb Company for April 2000[a]

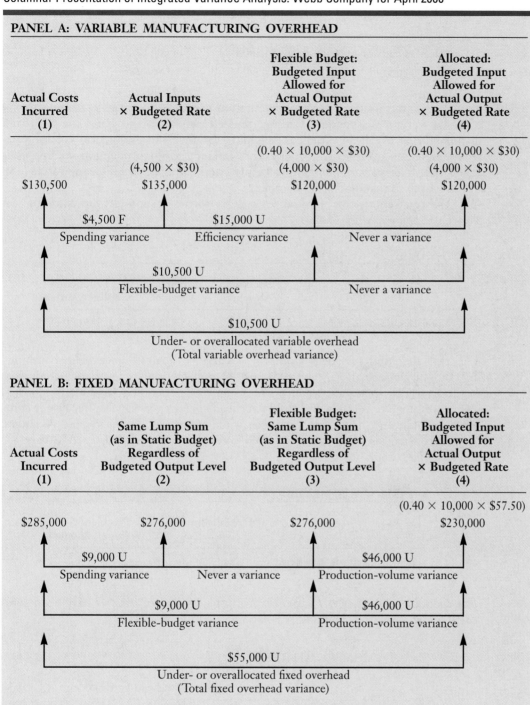

PANEL A: VARIABLE MANUFACTURING OVERHEAD

Actual Costs Incurred (1)	Actual Inputs × Budgeted Rate (2)	Flexible Budget: Budgeted Input Allowed for Actual Output × Budgeted Rate (3)	Allocated: Budgeted Input Allowed for Actual Output × Budgeted Rate (4)
		(0.40 × 10,000 × $30)	(0.40 × 10,000 × $30)
	(4,500 × $30)	(4,000 × $30)	(4,000 × $30)
$130,500	$135,000	$120,000	$120,000

$4,500 F — Spending variance
$15,000 U — Efficiency variance
Never a variance

$10,500 U — Flexible-budget variance
Never a variance

$10,500 U — Under- or overallocated variable overhead
(Total variable overhead variance)

PANEL B: FIXED MANUFACTURING OVERHEAD

Actual Costs Incurred (1)	Same Lump Sum (as in Static Budget) Regardless of Budgeted Output Level (2)	Flexible Budget: Same Lump Sum (as in Static Budget) Regardless of Budgeted Output Level (3)	Allocated: Budgeted Input Allowed for Actual Output × Budgeted Rate (4)
			(0.40 × 10,000 × $57.50)
$285,000	$276,000	$276,000	$230,000

$9,000 U — Spending variance
Never a variance
$46,000 U — Production-volume variance

$9,000 U — Flexible-budget variance
$46,000 U — Production-volume variance

$55,000 U — Under- or overallocated fixed overhead
(Total fixed overhead variance)

[a]F = favorable effect on operating income; U = unfavorable effect on operating income.

Points to Stress The FB var. for VMOH is the difference between the amount spent on all VMOH items compared to the amount allowed (given the cost allocation base and the VMOH rate). The manager needs to analyze each individual overhead item to determine which differences were due to price and/or usage causes.

Points to Stress The FB var. for FMOH really doesn't "flex." It's the difference between the actual FMOH and the budgeted amount. These are real dollars which were spent. The FMOH production-volume var. does *not* indicate that Webb spent too much. It just indicates that the amount allocated to WIP was $46,000 less than budgeted FMOH (and $55,000 less than actual FMOH).

given budget period. Also note that Panel A does not have a production-volume variance. Why? The amount of variable overhead allocated is always the same as the flexible-budget amount.

4, 3, 2 and 1-Variance Analysis

When all four variances in Exhibit 8-3 are presented together, it is called a 4-variance analysis:

4-VARIANCE ANALYSIS

	Spending Variance	Efficiency Variance	Production-Volume Variance
Variable Manufacturing Overhead	$4,500 F	$15,000 U	Never a variance
Fixed Manufacturing Overhead	$9,000 U	Never a variance	$46,000 U

The four variances in this presentation are the two variable manufacturing overhead variances (spending variance and efficiency variance) and the two fixed manufacturing overhead variances (spending variance and production-volume variance). Note the two entries for "Never a variance"—for production-volume variance in the case of variable manufacturing overhead and for efficiency variance in the case of fixed manufacturing overhead.

We can reduce this 4-variance analysis to more summary presentations. A 3-variance analysis would be:

3-VARIANCE ANALYSIS

	Spending Variance	Efficiency Variance	Production-Volume Variance
Total Manufacturing Overhead	$4,500 U	$15,000 U	$46,000 U

The two spending variances from the 4-variance analysis have been combined in the 3-variance analysis. The only loss of information in 3-variance analysis is in the overhead spending variance area—only one spending variance is reported instead of separate variable and fixed overhead spending variances. Because it combines variable and fixed cost variances when reporting overhead cost variances, 3-variance analysis is sometimes called *combined variance analysis*. A 2-variance analysis would be:

2-VARIANCE ANALYSIS

	Flexible-Budget Variance	Production-Volume Variance
Total Manufacturing Overhead	$19,500 U	$46,000 U

The spending and efficiency variances from the 3-variance analysis have been combined under 2-variance analysis. A 1-variance analysis would be:

1-VARIANCE ANALYSIS

	Total Overhead Variance
Total Manufacturing Overhead	$65,500 U

The single variance of $65,500 U in the 1-variance analysis, called total-overhead variance, is the sum of the flexible-budget variance and the production-volume variance under 2-variance analysis. Using figures from Exhibit 8-3, the total-overhead variance ($65,500 U) is the difference between the total actual manufacturing overhead incurred ($130,500 + $285,000 = $415,500) and the manufacturing overhead allocated ($120,000 + $230,000 = $350,000) to the actual output units produced.

The variances in Webb's 4-variance analysis are not necessarily independent of each other. For example, Webb may purchase lower-quality machine fluids (giving rise to a favorable variable overhead spending variance), which results in the machines taking longer to operate than budgeted (giving rise to an unfavorable variable overhead efficiency variance).

Points to Stress Combined OH rates are feasible only when there is a single OH allocation base for all variable and fixed cost categories. This situation is becoming less common as companies adopt multiple cost pool systems such as ABC

Teaching Tip It's helpful to use these charts when discussing related problems in class. Stress that the spending and eff. var's. are subcomponents of the FB var.

Points to Stress The 1-var. analysis is simply the over/under allocated OH introduced in Chap. 4.

Variance Analysis and Control Decisions

There is widespread usage of the variances discussed in Chapters 7 and 8. A survey of United Kingdom companies reported the following percentages:

Variance	Percentage of Companies Computing Variance	Percentage of Companies Viewing the Variance as "Above Average Importance" or "Vitally Important" in Control Decisions
Sales volume	77	70
Selling price	75	69
Materials price	94	69
Materials efficiency	80	66
Labor price	63	36
Labor efficiency	73	65
Overhead spending	89	69
Production volume	41	28

The overhead spending variance reported is from a 3-variance analysis where no distinction is made between variable and fixed costs. The survey did not report details on variable or fixed overhead spending variances. The low percentage use for control decisions of the production-volume variance is consistent with its purpose being predominantly financial reporting.

Source: Drury et. al., "A Survey of Management Accounting Practices in UK Manufacturing Companies." See Appendix A for full citation.

DIFFERENT PURPOSES OF MANUFACTURING OVERHEAD COST ANALYSIS

Different types of cost analysis may be appropriate for different purposes. Consider the planning and control purpose and the inventory costing for financial reporting purpose. Panel A of Exhibit 8-4 depicts variable manufacturing overhead for each purpose, and Panel B depicts fixed manufacturing overhead for each purpose. The horizontal axis in Exhibit 8-4 is output units. For Webb, this horizontal axis could also be scaled in terms of machine-hours, which is the allocation base for both variable and fixed overhead costs.

Variable Manufacturing Overhead Costs

Webb's variable manufacturing overhead is shown in Panel A of Exhibit 8-4 as being variable with respect to output units (jackets) for both the planning and control purpose (graph 1) and the inventory costing purpose (graph 2). The greater the number of output units manufactured, the higher the budgeted total variable manufacturing overhead costs and the higher the total variable manufacturing overhead costs allocated to output units.

Panel A of Exhibit 8-4 presents an overall picture of how total variable overhead might behave. Of course, variable overhead consists of many items, including energy costs, repairs, indirect labor, and so on. Managers help control variable overhead costs by budgeting each line item and then investigating possible causes for any significant variances.

Fixed Manufacturing Overhead Costs

Panel B of Exhibit 8-4 (graph 3) shows that for the planning and control purpose, fixed overhead costs do not change in the 8,000- to 16,000-unit output range.

New in This Edition The Survey of Company Practices box is new to this edition. Note the low percentage use of the production-volume var. for control purposes. This is not surprising since its use is for inventory costing, not control.

Points to Stress VMOH allocated to WIP is always equal to VMOH in the FB. VMOH allocated to WIP is std. cost (BP × BQIA), and this = the FB VMOH (which is BP × BQIA). Hence, the FB var. (FB − Actual VMOH) is always equal to the under/over allocated VMOH.

EXHIBIT 8-4
Behavior of Variable and Fixed Manufacturing Overhead Costs for Planning and Control and for Inventory Costing for Webb Company for April 2000

Reinforcing Problems Prob. 8-31 covers MOH graphs.

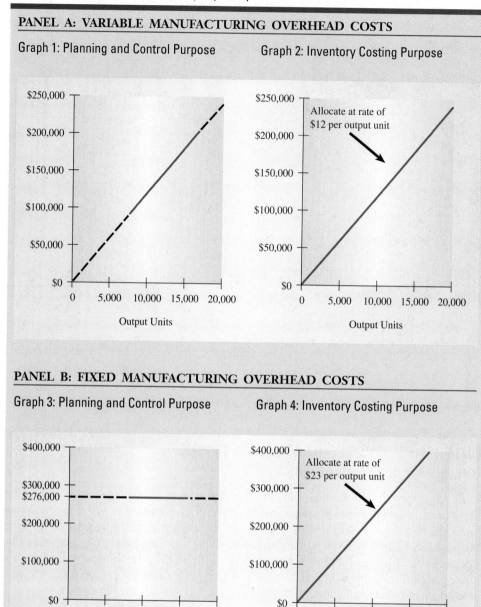

PANEL A: VARIABLE MANUFACTURING OVERHEAD COSTS

Graph 1: Planning and Control Purpose

Graph 2: Inventory Costing Purpose

Allocate at rate of $12 per output unit

PANEL B: FIXED MANUFACTURING OVERHEAD COSTS

Graph 3: Planning and Control Purpose

Graph 4: Inventory Costing Purpose

Allocate at rate of $23 per output unit

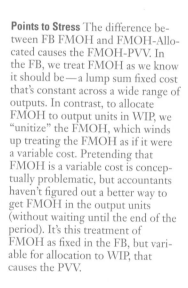

Points to Stress The difference between FB FMOH and FMOH-Allocated causes the FMOH-PVV. In the FB, we treat FMOH as we know it should be—a lump sum fixed cost that's constant across a wide range of outputs. In contrast, to allocate FMOH to output units in WIP, we "unitize" the FMOH, which winds up treating the FMOH as if it were a variable cost. Pretending that FMOH is a variable cost is conceptually problematic, but accountants haven't figured out a better way to get FMOH in the output units (without waiting until the end of the period). It's this treatment of FMOH as fixed in the FB, but variable for allocation to WIP, that causes the PVV.

Webb's budgeted fixed manufacturing overhead cost pool of $276,000 includes a monthly leasing cost of $20,000 for a building under a three-year leasing agreement. Managers control this fixed leasing cost at the time the lease is signed. During any month in the leasing period, management can do little to change this $20,000 lump-sum payment. Contrast this description of fixed overhead with how these costs are depicted for the inventory costing purpose, graph 4 of Panel B. Under generally accepted accounting principles, fixed manufacturing costs are allocated as an inventoriable cost based on the level of output units produced. Every output unit that Webb manufactures will increase the fixed overhead allocated to products by $23. Managers should not use this unitization of fixed manufacturing overhead costs for planning and control.

JOURNAL ENTRIES FOR OVERHEAD COSTS AND VARIANCES

Recording Overhead Costs

The Chapter 4 job-costing example (Robinson Company pp. 98–117) used a single manufacturing overhead control account. This chapter illustrates separate variable and fixed manufacturing overhead control accounts. Each overhead control account requires its own overhead allocated account.

Consider the journal entries for Webb Company. Recall that for April 2000,

	Actual Results	Flexible Budget (10,000 units)	Allocated Amount
Variable manufacturing overhead	$130,500	$120,000[a]	$120,000
Fixed manufacturing overhead	285,000	276,000[b]	230,000[c]

[a]$0.40 \times 10,000 \times \$30 = \$120,000$
[b]$276,000 is the budgeted fixed manufacturing overhead
[c]$0.40 \times 10,000 \times \$57.50 = \$230,000$

The budgeted variable overhead rate is $30 per machine-hour (or $12 per jacket). The denominator level for fixed manufacturing overhead is 57,600 machine-hours with a budgeted rate of $57.50 per machine-hour (or $23 per jacket). Webb uses 4-variance analysis.

During the accounting period, actual variable overhead and actual fixed overhead costs are accumulated in separate control accounts. As each unit is manufactured, the variable and fixed overhead standard cost rates are used to record the amounts in the respective overhead allocated accounts. Webb isolates variances in its accounts on a monthly basis to provide timely feedback to its managers.

Entries for variable manufacturing overhead for April 2000 are:

1 Variable Manufacturing Overhead Control 130,500
    Accounts Payable Control and other accounts 130,500
    To record actual variable manufacturing overhead cost incurred.

2 Work-in-Process Control 120,000
    Variable Manufacturing Overhead Allocated 120,000
    To record variable manufacturing overhead cost allocated:
      (0.40 × 10,000 × $30)

3 Variable Manufacturing Overhead Allocated 120,000
  Variable Manufacturing Overhead Efficiency Variance 15,000
    Variable Manufacturing Overhead Control 130,500
    Variable Manufacturing Overhead Spending Variance 4,500
    To isolate variances for the accounting period. Calculation of
      these variances is in Exhibit 8-1.

Entries for fixed manufacturing overhead for April 2000 are:

1 Fixed Manufacturing Overhead Control 285,000
    Wages Payable, Accumulated Depreciation, etc. 285,000
    To record actual fixed overhead costs incurred.

2 Work-in-Process Control 230,000
    Fixed Manufacturing Overhead Allocated 230,000
    To record fixed manufacturing overhead costs allocated:
      (0.40 × 10,000 × $57.50)

3 Fixed Manufacturing Overhead Allocated 230,000
  Fixed Manufacturing Overhead Spending Variance 9,000
  Fixed Manufacturing Production-Volume Variance 46,000
    Fixed Manufacturing Overhead Control 285,000
    To isolate variances for the accounting period. Calculation of
      these variances is in Exhibit 8-2.

While Webb isolates variances in its accounts on a monthly basis, it waits until the end of each year to make adjustments such that variance accounts end up with zero balances. Chapter 4 (pp. 113–117) explains alternative approaches to making these adjustments.

FINANCIAL AND NONFINANCIAL PERFORMANCE

The overhead variances discussed in this chapter are examples of financial performance measures. Managers also find that nonfinancial measures provide useful information. Examples of such measures that Webb likely would find useful in planning and controlling its overhead costs are:

(i) actual indirect materials usage per machine-hour, relative to budgeted indirect materials usage per machine-hour;

(ii) actual energy usage per machine-hour, relative to budgeted energy usage per machine-hour; and

(iii) actual machine time per jacket, relative to budgeted machine time per jacket.

These performance measures, like the financial variances discussed in this chapter, are best viewed as attention directors, not as problem solvers. These performance measures probably would be reported on the manufacturing floor on a daily or even hourly basis. The manufacturing overhead variances we discussed in this chapter capture the financial effects of items such as (i), (ii), and (iii), which in many cases first appear as nonfinancial performance measures.

Both financial and nonfinancial performance measures are key inputs when evaluating the performance of managers. Exclusive reliance on either is nearly always too simplistic.[1]

OVERHEAD COST VARIANCES IN NONMANUFACTURING SETTINGS

Our Webb Company example examines variable and fixed manufacturing overhead costs. Should the overhead costs of nonmanufacturing areas be examined using the variance analysis framework discussed in this chapter? Variable-cost information pertaining to nonmanufacturing costs as well as manufacturing costs is often used in pricing decisions, and in decisions about which products to push or deemphasize. Variance analysis of all variable overhead costs is important when making such decisions. For example, managers in industries where distribution costs are high may invest in standard-costing systems that give reliable and timely information on variable distribution overhead spending and efficiency variances.

Variance analysis of fixed nonmanufacturing overhead costs is important where a company is doing contract work that is reimbursed on the basis of full actual costs plus a percentage of those costs. Here, information on variances enables more accurate estimates of actual costs to be computed. Variance analysis of fixed nonmanufacturing costs is also useful in capacity planning and utilization decisions and in the management of these costs.

ACTIVITY-BASED COSTING AND VARIANCE ANALYSIS

ABC systems classify costs of various activities into a cost hierarchy—output-unit level, batch level, product sustaining, and facility sustaining (see pp. 142–143). The basic principles and concepts for variable and fixed manufacturing overhead costs presented earlier in the chapter can be extended to ABC systems. In this section, we

---

[1]There is debate over the relative weights to be given to these measures. For example, some writers in the quality literature maintain nonfinancial measures, such as product quality and customer satisfaction, should be given more emphasis than financial measures. Chapter 13 considers this issue in more detail.

Standard Costing and Daily Income Statements at Asia-Pacific Rayon

Asia-Pacific Rayon (APR) manufacturers rayon fiber at its Indonesia plant. Its output is sold on the export market to companies in China, Malaysia, Pakistan, and South Korea as well as to Indonesian spinning mills. APR receives export-market inquiries on a daily basis. Potential customers differ greatly in terms of the size of their orders, prices paid, and related costs of manufacture and distribution. Some customers enter the market unpredictably, buy large quantities, and require large discounts. The owner of APR has developed a daily income reporting system to continually update the profit implications of the everchanging mix of jobs being produced at negotiated terms that can vary dramatically across customers. A standard costing system is a central part of this daily income reporting system. One key use is in negotiations with potential customers on the price and terms of new business.

The daily income statement includes net revenues, cost of goods sold, operating costs, and allocated costs. Net revenues are selling prices less variable selling expenses (such as freight, commissions, and discounts). The materials, manufacturing labor, and plant operating costs are based on a standard costing system. These standards are prepared and updated every month on the basis of new information including that month's actual performance. APR allocates budgeted overhead costs on the basis of budgeted production volume. The overhead costs allocated include fixed selling, general and administrative costs, and interest costs as well as fixed manufacturing overhead costs.

APR's use of a daily income statement is relatively unusual. While many companies track costs for key items on a daily basis, few report a daily income statement. APR believes this statement increases the profit consciousness of the company. The Chief Executive Officer (located away from the production facility) uses the statement to monitor the performance of the top operating managers. For example, the profit implications of equipment breakdowns at the plant are highlighted quickly in a daily income statement. Variances for each of its cost categories are computed monthly. These variances are an integral part of the performance measures the CEO uses to evaluate key operating personnel.

Source: Case by R. Ramanan and L. Lakshmanan, *"Asia-Pacific Rayon Company."*

---

illustrate variance analysis for variable and fixed batch-level setup overhead costs. Batch-level costs are resources sacrificed on activities that are related to a group of units of product(s) or service(s) rather than to each individual unit of product or service.

We continue the Chapter 7 example of Lyco Brass Works, which manufactures Jacutaps, a line of decorative brass faucets for Jacuzzis. Lyco manufactures Jacutaps in batches. To manufacture a batch of Jacutaps, Lyco must set up the machines and molds. Setup costs are batch-level costs because they are associated with batches rather than individual units of products. Doing setups is a skilled activity. Hence, a separate Setup Department is responsible for setting up machines and molds for different types of Jacutaps. Lyco regards setup costs as overhead costs of products.

Setup costs consist of some costs that are variable and some costs that are fixed with respect to the number of setup-hours. Variable costs of setups consist of wages paid to hourly setup labor and indirect support labor, costs of maintenance of setup equipment, and costs of indirect materials and energy used during setups. Fixed setup costs consist of costs of engineers, supervisors, and setup equipment leases.

New in This Edition
The Concepts in Action box is new to this edition. It discusses how the management of APR use standard cost-based daily income statements to manage the business.

Information regarding Jacutaps for 2001 follows:

	Static-Budget Amounts	Actual Amounts
1. Units of Jacutaps produced and sold	180,000	151,200
2. Batch size (units/batch)	150	140
3. Number of batches (Line 1 ÷ Line 2)	1,200	1,080
4. Setup-hours per batch	6	6.25
5 Total setup-hours (Line 3 × Line 4)	7,200	6,750
6. Variable overhead cost per setup-hour	$20	$21
7. Variable setup overhead costs (Line 5 × Line 6)	$144,000	$141,750
8. Total fixed setup overhead costs	$216,000	$220,000

Flexible Budget and Variance Analysis for Variable Setup Overhead Costs

To prepare the flexible budget for variable setup overhead costs, Lyco starts with the actual units of output produced, 151,200 units, and proceeds in the following steps.

Step 1: Using the Budgeted Batch Size, Calculate the Number of Batches That Should Have Been Used to Produce the Actual Output Lyco should have manufactured the 151,200 units of output in 1,008 batches (151,200 ÷ 150).

Step 2: Using Budgeted Setup-Hours Per Batch, Calculate the Number of Setup-Hours That Should Have Been Used At the budgeted quantity of 6 setup-hours per batch, 1,008 batches should have required 6,048 setup-hours (1,008 × 6).

Step 3: Using the Budgeted Variable Cost Per Setup-Hour, Calculate the Flexible Budget for Variable Setup Overhead Costs The flexible-budget amount is 6,048 setup-hours × $20 per setup-hour = $120,960.

$$\begin{matrix} \text{Flexible-budget} \\ \text{variance for} \\ \text{variable setup} \\ \text{overhead costs} \end{matrix} = \begin{matrix} \text{Actual} \\ \text{costs} \end{matrix} - \begin{matrix} \text{Flexible-budget} \\ \text{costs} \end{matrix}$$

$$= 6{,}750 \times \$21 - 6{,}048 \times \$20 = \$141{,}750 - \$120{,}960$$

$$= \$20{,}790 \text{ U}$$

Exhibit 8-5 presents the variances for variable setup overhead costs in columnar form.

The flexible-budget variance for variable setup overhead costs can be subdivided into efficiency and spending variances.

$$\begin{matrix} \text{Variable setup} \\ \text{overhead} \\ \text{efficiency} \\ \text{variance} \end{matrix} = \left(\begin{matrix} \text{Actual units of} \\ \text{variable overhead} \\ \text{cost-allocation base} \\ \text{used for} \\ \text{actual output} \end{matrix} - \begin{matrix} \text{Budgeted units of} \\ \text{variable overhead} \\ \text{cost-allocation base} \\ \text{allowed for} \\ \text{actual output} \end{matrix} \right) \times \begin{matrix} \text{Budgeted} \\ \text{variable} \\ \text{overhead} \\ \text{rate} \end{matrix}$$

$$= (6{,}750 - 6{,}048) \times \$20 = 702 \times \$20 = \$14{,}040 \text{ U}$$

The unfavorable variable setup overhead efficiency variance of $14,040 arises because the actual number of setup-hours (6,750) exceeds the number of setup-hours that Lyco should have used (6,048) for the number of units it produced. Two reasons for the unfavorable efficiency variance are (1) smaller actual batch sizes of 140 units instead of budgeted batch sizes of 150 units, which results in Lyco producing the 151,200 units in 1,080 batches instead of 1,008 batches, and (2) higher actual setup-hours per batch of 6.25 hours instead of the budgeted setup-hours per batch of 6 hours.

New in This Edition This section on ABC and variance analysis builds on the ABC discussions from Chaps. 5 and 7. Since more firms are using ABC, how to calculate variances arising from its use is becoming important.

Reinforcing Problems Prob. 8-35 through 8-37 cover ABC and MOH variance analysis.

EXHIBIT 8-5
Columnar Presentation of Variable Setup Overhead Variance Analysis for Lyco Brass Works for 2001[a]

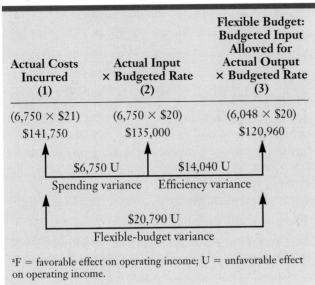

Actual Costs Incurred (1)	Actual Input × Budgeted Rate (2)	Flexible Budget: Budgeted Input Allowed for Actual Output × Budgeted Rate (3)
(6,750 × $21)	(6,750 × $20)	(6,048 × $20)
$141,750	$135,000	$120,960

$6,750 U — Spending variance

$14,040 U — Efficiency variance

$20,790 U — Flexible-budget variance

[a]F = favorable effect on operating income; U = unfavorable effect on operating income.

Points to Stress Because setup costs are at the batch-level, the BQIA is focused at the batch level. The quantity of setup hours allowed is based on the number of batches it should have taken to produce the actual quantity of output. Note that even with ABC, the VMOH costs are still allocated to the product (via a VMOH rate), not traced. The advantage which ABC has is that there is a cause-and-effect link between the costs in the cost pools and the choice of cost driver. The managerial interpretation of the FB var., the SV, and the EV are no different than with non-ABC allocation bases.

Explanations for smaller-than-budgeted batch sizes could include (1) quality problems if batch sizes exceed 140 faucets, or (2) high costs of carrying inventory. Explanations for longer actual setup-hours per batch could include (1) problems with equipment, (2) demotivated or inexperienced employees, or (3) inappropriate setup-time standards.

$$\begin{array}{c}\text{Variable setup}\\\text{overhead}\\\text{spending}\\\text{variance}\end{array} = \left(\begin{array}{c}\text{Actual variable}\\\text{overhead cost per}\\\text{unit of cost-}\\\text{allocation base}\end{array} - \begin{array}{c}\text{Budgeted variable}\\\text{overhead cost per}\\\text{unit of cost-}\\\text{allocation base}\end{array}\right) \times \begin{array}{c}\text{Actual quantity of}\\\text{variable overhead}\\\text{cost-allocation base}\\\text{used for actual output}\end{array}$$

$$= (\$21 - \$20) \times 6{,}750 = \$1 \times 6{,}750 = \$6{,}750\ U$$

The unfavorable spending variance indicates that Lyco operated in 2001 with a higher-than-budgeted variable overhead cost per setup-hour. Two main reasons that could contribute to the unfavorable spending variance are (1) the actual prices of individual items included in variable overhead, such as setup labor, indirect support labor, or energy, are higher than the budgeted prices, and (2) the actual quantity usage of individual items such as indirect support labor and energy increase more than the increase in setup-hours, due perhaps to setups becoming more complex because of equipment problems. Thus, equipment problems could lead to an unfavorable efficiency variance because setup-hours increase, but it could also lead to an unfavorable spending variance because each setup-hour requires more resources from the setup cost pool than the budgeted amounts.

Identifying the reasons for the variances is important because it helps managers plan for corrective action. We now consider fixed setup overhead costs.

Flexible Budget and Variance Analysis for Fixed Setup Overhead Costs

For fixed setup overhead costs, the flexible-budget amount equals the static-budget amount of $216,000. Why? Because there is no "flexing" of fixed costs.

$$\begin{array}{c}\text{Fixed setup}\\\text{overhead}\\\text{flexible-budget}\\\text{variance}\end{array} = \begin{array}{c}\text{Actual}\\\text{costs}\end{array} - \begin{array}{c}\text{Flexible-budget}\\\text{costs}\end{array}$$

$$= \$220{,}000 - \$216{,}000 = \$4{,}000\ U$$

The fixed setup overhead spending variance is the same amount as the fixed overhead flexible-budget variance (because fixed overhead costs have no efficiency variance).

$$\begin{array}{c}\text{Fixed setup}\\\text{overhead}\\\text{spending}\\\text{variance}\end{array} = \begin{array}{c}\text{Actual}\\\text{costs}\end{array} - \begin{array}{c}\text{Flexible-budget}\\\text{costs}\end{array}$$

$$= \$220{,}000 - \$216{,}000 = \$4{,}000 \text{ U}$$

The unfavorable fixed setup overhead spending variance could be due to lease costs of new setup equipment, or higher salaries paid to engineers and supervisors. Lyco may have incurred these costs to alleviate some of the difficulties it was having in setting up machines.

To calculate the production-volume variance, Lyco first computes the budgeted cost-allocation rate for fixed setup overhead costs using the four-step approach described on pp. 259–260.

Step 1: Choose the Time Period Used to Compute the Budget Lyco uses a period of 12 months (the year 2001).

Step 2: Select the Cost-Allocation Base to Use in Allocating Fixed Overhead Costs to the Cost Object(s) Lyco uses budgeted setup-hours as the cost-allocation base for fixed setup overhead costs. Budgeted setup-hours for 2001 per the static budget are 7,200 hours.

Step 3: Identify the Fixed Overhead Costs Associated with the Cost-Allocation Base Lyco's fixed setup overhead cost budget for 2001 is $216,000.

Step 4: Compute the Rate Per Unit of the Cost-Allocation Base Used to Allocate Fixed Overhead Costs to the Cost Object(s) Dividing the $216,000 from step 3 by the 7,200 setup-hours from step 2, Lyco estimates a fixed setup overhead cost rate of $30 per setup-hour:

$$\begin{array}{c}\text{Budgeted fixed}\\\text{setup overhead}\\\text{cost rate}\end{array} = \dfrac{\begin{array}{c}\text{Budgeted total costs}\\\text{in overhead cost pool}\end{array}}{\begin{array}{c}\text{Budgeted total quantity of}\\\text{cost-allocation base}\end{array}} = \dfrac{\$216{,}000}{7{,}200 \text{ setup-hours}}$$

$$= \$30 \text{ per setup-hour}$$

Points to Stress As with VMOH, for FMOH the BQIA is focused at the batch level. The quantity of setup hours allowed is based on the number of batches it should have taken to produce the actual quantity of output. Note that even with ABC, the FMOH costs are still allocated to the product (via a FMOH rate), not traced. The advantage which ABC has is that there is a cause-and-effect link between the costs in the cost pools and the choice of cost driver (although this is *not* nearly as true for FMOH as for VMOH). The managerial interpretation of the FB var. and the PVV is no different than with non-ABC allocation bases.

EXHIBIT 8-6

Columnar Presentation of Fixed Setup Overhead Variance Analysis: Lyco Brass Works for 2001[a]

Actual Costs Incurred (1)	Flexible Budget: Same Lump Sum (as in Static Budget) Regardless of Budgeted Output Level (2)	Allocated: Budgeted Input Allowed for Actual Output × Budgeted Rate (3)
		1008[b] batches × 6 hours/batch × $30)
		(6,048 × $30)
$220,000	$216,000	$181,440

|← $4,000 U →| |← $34,560 U →|
Spending variance   Production-volume variance

|← $4,000 U →|
Flexible-budget variance

[a]F = favorable effect on operating income; U = unfavorable effect on operating income.
[b]1008 batches = 151,200 units ÷ 150 units per batch

$$\begin{array}{ccc}
\text{Production-volume} & \text{Budgeted} & \text{Fixed setup overhead} \\
\text{variance for fixed} & \text{fixed setup} & \text{allocated using budgeted} \\
\text{setup overhead} & = \text{overhead} - & \text{input allowed for} \\
\text{costs} & \text{costs} & \text{actual output units produced}
\end{array}$$

$$= \$216,000 - (1,008 \text{ batches} \times 6 \text{ hours per batch}) \times \$30$$

$$= \$216,000 - (6,048 \times \$30) = \$216,000 - \$181,440$$

$$= \$34,560 \text{ U}$$

Exhibit 8-6 presents the variances for fixed setup overhead costs in columnar form.

During 2001, Lyco planned to produce 180,000 units of Jacutaps but actually produced only 151,200 units. The unfavorable production-volume variance measures the amount of extra fixed setup costs that Lyco incurred for setup capacity it planned to use but did not. One interpretation is that the unfavorable $34,560 production-volume variance represents inefficient utilization of setup capacity. However, Lyco may have earned higher operating income by selling 151,200 units at a higher price than what it would have earned by selling 180,000 units at a lower price. The production-volume variance should be interpreted cautiously because it does not consider such information.

PROBLEM

Maria Lopez is the newly appointed president of Laser Products. She is examining the 2001 results for the Aerospace Products division. This division manufactures wing parts for satellites. Lopez's current concern is with manufacturing overhead costs at the Aerospace Products division. Both variable and fixed manufacturing overhead costs are allocated to the wing parts on the basis of laser-cutting-hours. The budgeted rates are variable manufacturing overhead of $200 per hour and fixed manufacturing overhead of $240 per hour. The budgeted laser-cutting time per wing part is 1.50 hours. Budgeted production and sales for 2001 is 5,000 wing parts. Budgeted fixed manufacturing overhead for 2001 is $1,800,000.

Actual results for 2001 are	
Wing parts produced and sold	4,800 units
Laser cutting hours used	8,400 hours
Variable manufacturing overhead costs	$1,478,400
Fixed manufacturing overhead costs	$1,832,200

Required

1. Compute the spending variance and the efficiency variance for variable manufacturing overhead.
2. Compute the spending variance and the production volume variance for fixed manufacturing overhead.
3. Give two explanations for the variances in requirements 1 and 2.

SOLUTION

1. and 2. See Exhibit 8-7.

3. a. Variable manufacturing overhead spending variance ($201,600 F). One possible reason is that the actual prices of individual items included in variable overhead

EXHIBIT 8-7
Columnar Presentation of Integrated Variance Analysis: Laser Products for 2001[a]

PANEL A: VARIABLE MANUFACTURING OVERHEAD

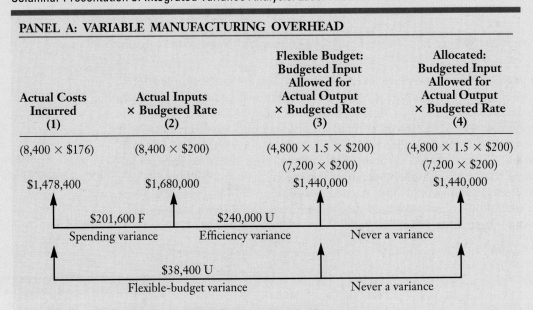

Actual Costs Incurred (1)	Actual Inputs × Budgeted Rate (2)	Flexible Budget: Budgeted Input Allowed for Actual Output × Budgeted Rate (3)	Allocated: Budgeted Input Allowed for Actual Output × Budgeted Rate (4)
(8,400 × $176)	(8,400 × $200)	(4,800 × 1.5 × $200) (7,200 × $200)	(4,800 × 1.5 × $200) (7,200 × $200)
$1,478,400	$1,680,000	$1,440,000	$1,440,000

$201,600 F — Spending variance
$240,000 U — Efficiency variance
Never a variance

$38,400 U — Flexible-budget variance
Never a variance

PANEL B: FIXED MANUFACTURING OVERHEAD

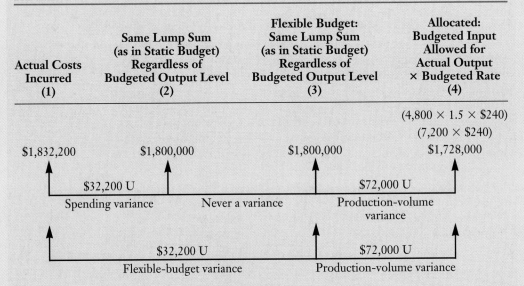

Actual Costs Incurred (1)	Same Lump Sum (as in Static Budget) Regardless of Budgeted Output Level (2)	Flexible Budget: Same Lump Sum (as in Static Budget) Regardless of Budgeted Output Level (3)	Allocated: Budgeted Input Allowed for Actual Output × Budgeted Rate (4)
			(4,800 × 1.5 × $240) (7,200 × $240)
$1,832,200	$1,800,000	$1,800,000	$1,728,000

$32,200 U — Spending variance
Never a variance
$72,000 U — Production-volume variance

$32,200 U — Flexible-budget variance
$72,000 U — Production-volume variance

[a]F = favorable effect on operating income; U = unfavorable effect on operating income.

(such as cutting fluids) are lower than the budgeted prices. A second possible reason is that the percentage increase in the actual quantity usage of individual items in the variable overhead cost pool is less than the percentage increase in machine-hours compared to the flexible budget.

b. Variable manufacturing overhead efficiency variance ($240,000 U). One possible reason is inadequate maintenance of laser machines, causing them to take longer laser time per wing part. A second possible reason is use of lower-trained workers with the laser-cutting machines resulting in longer laser-time per wing part.

c. Fixed manufacturing overheading spending variance ($32,200 U). One possible reason is that the actual prices of individual items in the fixed cost pool unexpectedly increased from those budgeted (such as an unexpected increase in machine leasing costs). A second possible reason is misclassification of items as fixed that are in fact variable.

   d. Production-volume variance ($72,000 U). Actual production of wing parts is 4,800 units compared with the 5,000 units budgeted. One possible reason is demand factors, such as a decline in the aerospace program that led to a decline in the demand for aircraft parts. A second possible reason is supply factors, such as a production stoppage due to labor problems or machine breakdowns.

SUMMARY

The following points are linked to the chapter's learning objectives:

1. Planning of both variable and fixed overhead costs involves planning to undertake only essential activities and then planning to be efficient in that undertaking. The key difference is that for variable-cost planning ongoing decisions during the budget period play a larger role, whereas for fixed-cost planning most key decisions have been made at the start of the period.

2. A standard costing system traces direct costs to a cost object by multiplying the standard price(s) or rate(s) times the standard inputs allowed for actual outputs produced and allocates indirect costs on the basis of the standard indirect rate(s) times the standard inputs allowed for the actual outputs produced.

3. When the flexible budget for variable overhead is developed, a spending overhead variance and an efficiency variance can be computed. The variable overhead spending variance is the difference between the actual amount of variable overhead incurred and the budgeted amount allowed for the actual quantity of the variable overhead allocation base used for the actual output units produced. The variable overhead efficiency variance measures the efficiency with which the cost-allocation base is used. This is a different type of efficiency variance than that calculated in Chapter 7 for direct-cost items, such as direct materials.

4. The efficiency variance for a variable indirect-cost item reflects whether more or less of the cost-allocation base per output unit was used than was assumed in the flexible budget. The efficiency variance for a direct-cost item reflects whether more or less of the physical inputs per output of that direct-cost item were used than was assumed in the flexible budget.

5. The budgeted fixed overhead rate is calculated by dividing the budgeted fixed overhead costs by the denominator level of the allocation base.

6. Caution is appropriate before interpreting the production-volume variance as a measure of the economic cost of unused capacity. One caveat is that management may have maintained some extra capacity to meet uncertain demand surges that are important to satisfy. A second caveat is that the production-volume variance focuses only on costs. It does not take into account any price changes necessary to spur extra demand that would in turn make use of any idle capacity.

7. A 4-variance analysis presents spending and efficiency variances for variable overhead costs and spending and production-volume variances for fixed overhead costs. By analyzing these four variances together, managers can reconcile the actual overhead costs with the overhead amounts allocated during the period.

8. Flexible budgeting in activity-based costing systems enables insight into why actual activity costs differ from those budgeted. With well-defined output and input measures for an activity, a 4-variance analysis can be conducted.

The chapter and the Glossary at the end of the book contain definitions of the following important terms:

denominator level (p. 259)
denominator-level variance (261)
fixed overhead flexible-budget variance (260)
output-level overhead variance (261)
production-denominator level (259)
production-volume variance (261)

standard costing (254)
variable overhead efficiency variance (256)
variable overhead flexible-budget variance (256)
variable overhead spending variance (257)

▼ A S S I G N M E N T   M A T E R I A L

QUESTIONS

8-1 What are the steps in planning variable overhead costs?

8-2 How does the planning of fixed overhead costs differ from the planning of variable overhead costs?

8-3 How does a standard costing system differ from an actual costing system?

8-4 What are the steps in developing a budgeted variable overhead cost-allocation rate?

8-5 The spending variance for variable manufacturing overhead is affected by several factors. Explain.

8-6 Assume variable manufacturing overhead is allocated using machine-hours. Give three possible reasons for a $25,000 favorable variable overhead efficiency variance.

8-7 Describe the difference between a direct materials efficiency variance and a variable manufacturing overhead efficiency variance.

8-8 What are the steps in developing a budgeted fixed overhead rate?

8-9 Why is the flexible-budget variance the same amount as the spending variance for fixed manufacturing overhead?

8-10 Describe one caveat that will affect whether a production-volume variance is a good measure of the economic cost of unused capacity.

8-11 What are the variances in a 4-variance analysis?

8-12 Why is there no efficiency variance for fixed manufacturing overhead costs?

8-13 "Overhead variances should be viewed as interdependent rather than independent." Give an example.

8-14 Explain how the analysis of fixed overhead costs differs for (a) planning and control on the one hand, and (b) inventory costing for financial reporting on the other hand.

8-15 Describe how flexible-budget variance analysis can be used in the control of costs in the activity areas.

EXERCISES

8-16 Variable manufacturing overhead, variance analysis. Esquire Clothing is a manufacturer of designer suits. The cost of each suit is the sum of three variable costs (direct materials costs, direct manufacturing labor costs and manufacturing overhead costs) and one fixed-cost category (manufacturing overhead costs). Variable manufacturing overhead cost is allocated to each suit on the basis of budgeted direct manufacturing labor-hours per suit. For June 2001, each suit is budgeted to take 4 labor-hours. Budgeted variable manufacturing overhead cost per labor-hour is $12. The budgeted number of suits to be manufactured in June 2001 is 1,040.

Actual variable manufacturing costs in June 2001 were $52,164 for 1,080 suits started and completed. There was no beginning or ending inventory of suits. Actual direct manufacturing labor-hours for June were 4,536.

Required

1. Compute the flexible-budget variance, the spending variance, and the efficiency variance for variable manufacturing overhead.
2. Comment on the results.

8-17 Fixed manufacturing overhead, variance analysis (continuation of 8-16). Esquire Clothing allocates fixed manufacturing overhead to each suit using budgeted direct manufacturing labor-hours per suit. Data pertaining to fixed manufacturing overhead costs for June 2001 are budgeted, $62,400, and actual, $63,916.

Required

1. Compute the spending variance for fixed manufacturing overhead. Comment on the results.
2. Compute the production-volume variance for June 2001. What inferences can Esquire Clothing draw from this variance?

8-18 Variable manufacturing overhead variance analysis. The French Bread Company bakes baguettes for distribution to upscale grocery stores. The company has two direct-cost categories, direct materials and direct manufacturing labor. Variable manufacturing overhead is allocated to products on the basis of standard direct manufacturing labor-hours. Following is some pertinent data for the French Bread Company:

Direct manufacturing labor use	0.02 hours per baguette
Variable manufacturing overhead	$10.00 per direct labor-hour

The French Bread Company recorded the following additional data for the year ended December 31, 2001:

Planned (budgeted) output	3,200,000 baguettes
Actual production	2,800,000 baguettes
Direct manufacturing labor	50,400 hours
Actual variable manufacturing overhead	$680,400

Required

1. What is the denominator used for allocating variable manufacturing overhead? (That is, how many direct manufacturing labor-hours is French Bread budgeting for?)
2. Prepare a variance analysis of variable manufacturing overhead. Use Exhibit 8-3 (p. 263) for reference.
3. Discuss the variances you have calculated and give possible explanations for them.

8-19 Fixed manufacturing overhead variance analysis. The French Bread Company bakes baguettes for distribution to upscale grocery stores. The company has two direct-cost categories, direct materials and direct manufacturing labor. Fixed manufacturing overhead is allocated to products on the basis of standard direct manufacturing labor-hours. Following is some pertinent budgeted data for the French Bread Company:

Direct manufacturing labor use	0.02 hours per baguette
Fixed manufacturing overhead	$4.00 per direct labor-hour

The French Bread Company recorded the following additional data for the year ended December 31, 2001:

Planned (budgeted) output	3,200,000 baguettes
Actual production	2,800,000 baguettes
Direct manufacturing labor	50,400 hours
Actual fixed manufacturing overhead	$272,000

Required

1. Prepare a variance analysis of fixed manufacturing overhead cost. Use Exhibit 8-3 (p. 263) as a guide.
2. Is fixed overhead underallocated or overallocated? By what amount?
3. Comment on your results. Discuss the variances and explain what may be driving them.

8-20 Manufacturing overhead, variance analysis. Zyton assembles its CardioX product at its Scottsdale plant. Manufacturing overhead (both variable and fixed) is allocated to each CardioX unit using budgeted assembly-hours. Budgeted assembly time per CardioX product is 2 hours. The budgeted variable manufacturing overhead cost per assembly-hour is $40. The budgeted number of CardioX units to be assembled in March 2001 is 8,000. Budgeted fixed manufacturing overhead costs are $480,000.

Actual variable manufacturing overhead costs for March 2001 were $610,500 for 7,400 units actually assembled. Actual assembly-hours were 16,280. Actual fixed manufacturing overhead costs were $503,420.

Required

1. Prepare a 4-variance analysis for Zyton's Scottsdale plant.
2. Comment on the results in requirement 1.
3. How does the planning and control of variable manufacturing overhead costs differ from that of fixed manufacturing overhead costs?

 8-21 Spending and efficiency overhead variances, service sector. Meals on Wheels (MOW) operates a home meal delivery service. It has agreements with 20 restaurants to pick up and deliver meals to customers who phone or fax orders to MOW. MOW is currently examining its overhead costs for May 2001.

Variable overhead costs for May 2001 were budgeted at $2 per hour of home delivery time. Fixed overhead costs were budgeted at $24,000. The budgeted number of home deliveries (MOW's output measure) in May 2001 was 8,000. Delivery time, the allocation base for variable and fixed overhead costs, is budgeted to be 0.80 hour per delivery.

Actual results for May 2001 were:

Variable overhead	$14,174
Fixed overhead	$27,600
Number of home deliveries	7,460
Hours of delivery time	5,595

Customers are charged $12 per delivery. The delivery driver is paid $7 per delivery.

MOW receives a 10% commission on the meal costs that the restaurants charge the customers who use MOW.

Required

1. Compute spending and efficiency variances for MOW's variable overhead in May 2001. Comment on the results.
2. Compute the spending variance for MOW's fixed overhead in May 2001. Comment on the results.
3. How might MOW manage its variable overhead costs differently from how it manages its fixed overhead costs?

 8-22 Spending and efficiency overhead variances, distribution. Package Postal Service (PPS) operates a parcel delivery service. PPS's costing system has one direct-cost category (delivery driver payments) and two overhead categories—variable delivery overhead and fixed delivery overhead. In 2001, it charged retail companies and mail-order catalog companies $15 per delivery. Delivery drivers in 2001 were contracted at $5 per delivery. Variable delivery overhead for September 2001 was budgeted at $2 per hour of delivery time. Budgeted fixed delivery overhead in September 2001 was $120,000. PPS budgeted 100,000 deliveries for September 2001. Delivery time, the allocation base for variable and fixed overhead costs, is budgeted to be 0.25 hour per delivery.

Actual results for September 2001 were:

Variable delivery overhead	$60,000
Fixed delivery overhead	$128,400
Number of deliveries	96,000
Hours of delivery time	28,800

Required

1. Compute the spending and efficiency variances for PPS's variable delivery overhead costs in September 2001. Compute the spending and production-volume variances for PPS's fixed delivery overhead costs in September 2001. Comment on the results.
2. What problems might PPS face in managing (a) its direct costs, (b) its variable delivery overhead costs, and (c) its fixed delivery overhead costs?

8-23 4-variance analysis, fill in the blanks. Use the following manufacturing overhead data to fill in the blanks below:

	Variable	Fixed
Actual costs incurred	$11,900	$6,000
Costs allocated to products	9,000	4,500
Flexible budget: Budgeted input allowed for actual output produced × budgeted rate	9,000	5,000
Actual input × budgeted rate	10,000	5,000

Use F for favorable and U for unfavorable:

	Variable	Fixed
(1) Spending variance	$	$
(2) Efficiency variance		
(3) Production-volume variance		
(4) Flexible-budget variance		
(5) Underallocated (overallocated) manufacturing overhead		

8-24 Straightforward 4-variance overhead analysis. The Lopez Company uses a standard costing system in its manufacturing plant for auto parts. Its standard cost of an auto part, based on a denominator level of 4,000 output units per year, included 6 machine-hours of variable manufacturing overhead at $8 per hour and 6 machine-hours of fixed manufacturing overhead at $15 per hour. Actual output produced was 4,400 units. Variable manufacturing overhead incurred was $245,000. Fixed manufacturing overhead incurred was $373,000. Actual incurred machine-hours were 28,400.

Required

1. Prepare an analysis of all variable manufacturing overhead and fixed manufacturing overhead variances, using the 4-variance analysis in Exhibit 8-3 (p. 263).
2. Prepare journal entries using the 4-variance analysis.
3. Describe how individual variable manufacturing overhead items are controlled from day to day. Also, describe how individual fixed manufacturing overhead items are controlled.

8-25 Straightforward coverage of manufacturing overhead, standard-costing system. The Singapore division of a Canadian telecommunications company uses a standard costing system for its machine-paced production of telephone equipment. Data regarding production during June are as follows:

- Variable manufacturing overhead costs incurred — $155,100
- Variable manufacturing overhead cost rate — $12 per standard machine-hour
- Fixed manufacturing overhead costs incurred — $401,000
- Fixed manufacturing overhead budgeted — $390,000
- Denominator level in machine-hours — 13,000
- Standard machine-hour allowed per unit of output — 0.30
- Units of output — 41,000
- Actual machine-hours used — 13,300
- Ending work in process inventory — 0

Required

1. Prepare an analysis of all manufacturing overhead variances. Use the 4-variance analysis framework illustrated in pp. 262–264.
2. Prepare journal entries for manufacturing overhead.
3. Describe how individual variable manufacturing overhead items are controlled from day to day. Also, describe how individual fixed manufacturing overhead items are controlled.

8-26 Total overhead, 3-variance analysis. The Wright-Patterson Air Force Base has an extensive repair facility for jet engines. It developed standard costing and flexible budgets to account for this activity. Budgeted variable overhead at a level of 8,000 standard monthly direct labor-hours was $64,000; budgeted total overhead at 10,000 standard direct labor-hours was $197,600. The standard cost allocated to repair output included a total overhead rate of 120% of standard direct labor costs. Total overhead incurred for October was $249,000. Direct labor costs incurred were $202,440. The direct labor price variance was $9,640 unfavorable. The direct labor flexible-budget variance was $14,440 unfavorable. The standard labor price was $16 per hour. The production-volume variance was $14,000, favorable.

Required

1. Compute the direct labor efficiency variance and the spending, efficiency, and production-volume variances for overhead. Also, compute the denominator level.
2. Describe how individual variable manufacturing overhead items are controlled from day to day. Also, describe how individual fixed manufacturing overhead items are controlled.

8-27 4-variance analysis, working backwards. Lookmeup.com is striving to become a web portal. The site allows surfers to find anything they wish to look up—be it a person, a site, a company or news article—through one interactive and easy-to-use interface. Most of Lookmeup.com's operating overhead is due to Internet connection costs. Lookmeup.com faces both fixed as well as variable Internet connection charges. Following is the 4-variance analysis of Lookmeup.com's operating overhead:

	Spending Variance	Efficiency Variance	Production-Volume Variance
Variable Operating Overhead	$37,000 F	$24,000 F	Never a variance
Fixed Operating Overhead	$14,000 U	Never a variance	$17,000 U

Required

1. For total operating overhead, compute the following:
   a. Spending variance
   b. Efficiency variance
   c. Production-volume variance
   d. Flexible-budget variance
   e. Total overhead variance
   Arrange your results in a suitable format for presenting 3-variance, 2-variance, and 1-variance analyses.
2. If Lookmeup.com's total actual operating overhead was $420,000, what was the operating overhead allocated to actual output units provided?
3. Can you say whether fixed operating overhead was underallocated or overallocated? If so, by what amount?
4. Are Lookmeup.com's different variances in the 4-variance analysis above necessarily independent? Explain and provide an example.

8-28 Flexible-budget variances, review of Chapters 7 and 8. *The Monthly Herald* budgets to produce 300,000 copies of its monthly newspaper (the output unit) for August 2001. It is budgeted to have 50 print pages per newspaper. Actual production in August 2001 was 320,000 copies with 17,280,000 print pages run. Each paper was only 50 print pages, but quality problems with paper led to many pages being unusable.

Variable costs are direct materials, direct labor, and variable indirect costs. Variable and fixed indirect costs are allocated to each copy on the basis of good print pages. The driver for all variable costs is the number of print pages.

Data pertaining to August 2001 are:

	Budgeted	Actual
Direct materials	$180,000	$224,640
Direct labor costs	45,000	50,112
Variable indirect costs	60,000	63,936
Fixed indirect costs	90,000	97,000

The actual direct labor rate in August 2001 was $29.00 per hour. Actual and budgeted pages produced per direct labor hour in August 2001 was 10,000 print pages. Data pertaining to revenues for *The Monthly Herald* in August 2001 are:

	Budgeted	Actual
Circulation revenue	$140,000	$154,000
Advertising revenue	360,000	394,600

The Monthly Herald sells for $0.50 per copy. Copies produced but not sold have no value. Advertising revenues covers payments from all advertising sources.

Required

1. Prepare a comprehensive set of flexible-budget variances for the two direct cost items (using Exhibit 7-3, p. 228) and the two indirect cost items (using Exhibit 8-3, p. 263.) for *The Monthly Herald*.
2. Comment on the results in requirement 1.

PROBLEMS

8-29 Comprehensive variance analysis. FlatScreen manufactures flat-panel LCD displays. The displays are sold to major PC manufacturers. Following is some manufacturing overhead data for FlatScreen for the year ended December 31, 2000:

Manufacturing Overhead	Actual	Flexible Budget	Allocated Amount
Variable	$1,532,160	$1,536,000	$1,536,000
Fixed	$7,004,160	$6,961,920	$7,526,400

FlatScreen's budget was based on the assumption that 17,760 units (panels) will be manufactured during 2000. The planned allocation rate was 2 machine-hours per unit. Actual number of machine-hours used during 2000 was 36,480. The static-budget variable manufacturing overhead costs equals $1,420,800.

Required

Compute the following quantities (you should be able to do so in the prescribed order):

a. Budgeted number of machine-hours planned
b. Budgeted fixed manufacturing overhead costs per machine-hour
c. Budgeted variable manufacturing overhead costs per machine-hour
d. Budgeted number of machine-hours allowed for actual output produced
e. Actual number of output units
f. Actual number of machine-hours used per panel
g. Allocated amount for fixed manufacturing overhead

8-30 Journal entries (continuation of 8-29).
Required

1. Prepare journal entries for variable and fixed manufacturing overhead (you will need to calculate the various variances to accomplish this).
2. Overhead variances may be used to adjust the Cost of Goods Sold (COGS) account at the end of the fiscal year. COGS is then entered in the income statement. Show how COGS is adjusted through journal entries.

8-31 Graphs and overhead variances. The Carvelli Company is a manufacturer of housewares. In its job-costing system, manufacturing overhead (both variable and fixed) is allocated to products on the basis of budgeted machine-hours. The budgeted amounts are taken from Carvelli's standard costing system. The budget for 2001 included:

Variable manufacturing overhead	$9 per machine-hour	
Fixed manufacturing overhead	$72,000,000	
Denominator level	4,000,000 machine-hours	

Required

1. Prepare four graphs, two for variable manufacturing overhead and two for fixed manufacturing overhead. Each pair of graphs should display how Carvelli's total manufacturing overhead costs will be depicted for the purposes of (a) planning and control, and (b) inventory costing.

2. Suppose that 3,500,000 machine-hours were allowed for actual output produced in 2001, but 3,800,000 actual machine-hours were used. Actual manufacturing overhead was variable, $36,100,000, and fixed, $72,200,000. Compute (a) variable manufacturing overhead spending and efficiency variances, and (b) the fixed manufacturing overhead spending and production-volume variances. Use the columnar presentation illustrated in Exhibit 8-3 (p. 263).

3. What is the amount of the under- or overallocated variable manufacturing overhead? Of the under- or overallocated fixed manufacturing overhead? Why are the flexible-budget variance and the under- or overallocated overhead amount always the same for variable manufacturing overhead but rarely the same for fixed manufacturing overhead?

4. Suppose the denominator level was 3,000,000 rather than 4,000,000 machine-hours. What variances in requirement 2 would be affected? Recompute them.

8-32 Journal entries. Refer to the preceding problem, requirement 2. Consider variable manufacturing overhead and then fixed manufacturing overhead. Prepare the journal entries for (a) the incurrence of overhead, (b) the allocation of overhead, and (c) the isolation and closing of overhead variances to Cost of Goods Sold for the year.

8-33 4-variance analysis, find the unknowns. Consider each of the following situations—cases A, B, and C—independently. Data refer to operations for April 2001. For each situation, assume a standard costing system. Also assume the use of a flexible budget for control of variable and fixed manufacturing overhead based on machine-hours.

	Cases		
	A	**B**	**C**
(1) Fixed manufacturing overhead incurred	$10,600	—	$12,000
(2) Variable manufacturing overhead incurred	7,000	—	—
(3) Denominator level in machine-hours	500	—	1,100
(4) Standard machine-hours allowed for actual output achieved	—	650	—
Flexible-budget data:			
(5) Fixed manufacturing overhead	—	—	—
(6) Variable manufacturing overhead (per standard machine-hour)	—	8.50	5.00
(7) Budgeted fixed manufacturing overhead	10,000	—	11,000
(8) Budgeted variable manufacturing overhead[a]	—	—	—
(9) Total budgeted manufacturing overhead[a]	—	12,525	—
Additional data:			
(10) Standard variable manufacturing overhead allocated	7,500	—	—
(11) Standard fixed manufacturing overhead allocated	10,000	—	—
(12) Production-volume variance	—	500 U	500 F
(13) Variable manufacturing overhead spending variance	950 F	0	350 U
(14) Variable manufacturing overhead efficiency variance	—	0	100 U
(15) Fixed manufacturing overhead spending variance	—	300 F	—
(16) Actual machine-hours used	—	—	—

[a]For standard machine-hours allowed for actual output produced.

Required

Fill in the blanks under each case. (*Hint:* Prepare a worksheet similar to that in Exhibit 8-3 (p. 263). Fill in the knowns and then solve for the unknowns.)

8-34 Flexible budgets, 4-variance analysis. (CMA, adapted) Nolton Products uses a standard costing system. It allocates manufacturing overhead (both variable and fixed) to products on the basis of standard direct manufacturing labor-hours (DLH). Nolton develops its manufacturing overhead rate from the current annual budget. The manufacturing overhead budget for 2001 is based on budgeted output of 720,000 units requiring 3,600,000 DLH. The company is able to schedule production uniformly throughout the year.

A total of 66,000 output units requiring 315,000 DLH was produced during May 2001. Manufacturing overhead (MOH) costs incurred for May amounted to $375,000. The actual costs as compared with the annual budget and 1/12 of the annual budget are shown below.

Annual Manufacturing Overhead Budget 2001

	Total Amount	Per Output Unit	Per DLH Input Unit	Monthly MOH Budget May 2001	Actual MOH Costs for May 2001
Variable MOH					
Indirect manufacturing labor	$ 900,000	$1.25	$0.25	$ 75,000	$ 75,000
Supplies	1,224,000	1.70	0.34	102,000	111,000
Fixed MOH					
Supervision	648,000	0.90	0.18	54,000	51,000
Utilities	540,000	0.75	0.15	45,000	54,000
Depreciation	1,008,000	1.40	0.28	84,000	84,000
Total	$4,320,000	$6.00	$1.20	$360,000	$375,000

Required

Calculate the following amounts for Nolton Products for May 2001:

1. Total manufacturing overhead costs allocated

2. Variable manufacturing overhead spending variance

3. Fixed manufacturing overhead spending variance

4. Variable manufacturing overhead efficiency variance

5. Production-volume variance

Be sure to identify each variance as favorable (F) or unfavorable (U).

8-35 Variance analysis, service sector. CellOne is a cellular phone service reseller, contracting with major cellular operators for airtime in bulk and then reselling service to retail customers. Having adopted an activity-based costing system last year, CellOne has defined the following activities—contracting, marketing, technical service and customer service.

The technical-service area has one major cost driver, technical-support hours. One hour of technical support is budgeted for every 5,000 minutes of airtime sold (the output measure). For the month ended August 31, 2001, CellOne budgeted to sell 6,850,000 minutes. Actual minutes sold totaled 7,350,000. During the month of August (2001), 1,500 actual technical-support hours were logged. Some additional data for August 2001 are:

Technical-Service Activity Costs	Actual	Budget (on August 1, 2001)
Variable	$31,500	$32,880
Fixed	$67,500	$69,870

Further, you are told that budgeted input allowed for actual output produced totaled 1,470 hours of technical support for August 2001.

Required

1. What is the actual variable technical-service activity cost per technical support hour? Budgeted cost per hour?

2. What is the allocated fixed technical-service activity overhead?
3. Calculate the spending variance, the efficiency variance, and the flexible-budget variance for variable overhead costs. Discuss these variances.
4. Has CellOne management under- or overallocated fixed overhead for August 2001? Show how you calculate the under- or overallocation.

8-36 Activity-based costing, variance analysis. Toymaster, Inc., produces a special line of plastic toy cars, TGC. Toymaster produces TGC in batches. To manufacture a batch of TGC's, Toymaster must set up the machines and molds. Setup costs are batch-level costs because they are associated with batches rather than individual units of products. A separate Setup Department is responsible for setting up machines and molds for different styles of TGC.

Setup overhead costs consist of some costs that are variable and some costs that are fixed with respect to the number of setup-hours. The following information pertains to June 2001.

	Static-Budget Amounts	Actual Amounts
Units of TGC produced and sold	30,000	22,500
Batch size (number of units per batch)	250	225
Setup-hours per batch	5	5.25
Variable overhead cost per setup-hour	$25	$24
Total fixed setup overhead costs	$18,000	$17,535

Required
1. For variable setup overhead costs, compute the flexible-budget, efficiency, and spending variances. Comment on the results.
2. For fixed setup overhead costs, compute the flexible-budget, spending, and the production-volume variances. Comment on the results.

8-37 Variance analysis, flexible-budgeting. Starport manufactures and launches space stations. The stations are custom-made according to specifications furnished by the ordering party. Starport has adopted an ABC system, and has defined these activities: design, prototyping, testing, fabrication, launching, and assembly. In what follows, we focus on the launching activity, which is an output unit-driven cost.

Starport launches space station components into orbit from a base located on a remote island in the Pacific Ocean. Components are assembled in orbit according to the custom designs. Starport sells unused capacity in its launch facilities to launch other companies' products into orbit. The launch activity has both variable and fixed costs. You are presented with the following data for the year ended December 31, 2001:

	Actual	Budget (as of Jan. 1, 2001)
Launches	265	250
Launch-hours	5,300	5,500
Variable launch-activity costs (millions)	$371	$374
Fixed launch-activity costs (millions)	$1,643	$1,694

Required
1. Complete the numbers in Problem Exhibit 8-37. The calculations will assist you in answering requirement 2.
2. Prepare a flexible-budget based variance analysis of Starport's 2001 launch-activity costs.
3. Provide possible explanations for the variances you calculate in requirement 2.

8-38 Comprehensive review of Chapters 7 and 8, working backward from given variances. The Mancusco Company uses a flexible budget and standard costs to aid planning and control of its machining manufacturing operations. Its normal costing system for manufacturing has two direct-cost categories (direct materials and direct manufacturing labor—

	Actual Results	Flexible-Budget Amount
1. Output units (launches)	265	?
2. Launch-hours	5,300	?
3. Launch-hours per test	?	?
4. Variable launch-activity costs	$371,000,000	?
5. Variable launch-activity costs per testing-hour	?	?
6. Variable launch-activity costs per test	?	?
7. Fixed launch-activity costs	$1,643,000,000	?
8. Fixed launch-activity costs per testing-hour	?	?
9. Fixed launch-activity costs per test	?	?

both variable) and two indirect-cost categories (variable manufacturing overhead and fixed manufacturing overhead, both allocated using direct manufacturing labor-hours).

At the 40,000 budgeted direct manufacturing labor-hour level for August, budgeted direct manufacturing labor is $800,000, budgeted variable manufacturing overhead is $480,000, and budgeted fixed manufacturing overhead is $640,000.

The following actual results are for August:

Direct materials price variance (based on purchases)	$176,000 F
Direct materials efficiency variance	69,000 U
Direct manufacturing labor costs incurred	522,750
Variable manufacturing overhead flexible-budget variance	10,350 U
Variable manufacturing overhead efficiency variance	18,000 U
Fixed manufacturing overhead incurred	597,460
Fixed manufacturing overhead spending variance	42,540 F

The standard cost per pound of direct materials is $11.50. The standard allowance is 3 pounds of direct materials for each unit of product. Thirty thousand units of product were produced during August. There was no beginning inventory of direct materials. There was no beginning or ending work in process. In August, the direct materials price variance was $1.10 per pound.

In July, labor unrest caused a major slowdown in the pace of production, resulting in an unfavorable direct manufacturing labor efficiency variance of $45,000. There was no direct manufacturing labor price variance. Labor unrest persisted into August. Some workers quit. Their replacements had to be hired at higher rates, which had to be extended to all workers. The actual average wage rate in August exceeded the standard average wage rate by $0.50 per hour.

Required

1. Compute the following for August:
   a. Total pounds of direct materials purchased
   b. Total number of pounds of excess direct materials used
   c. Variable manufacturing overhead spending variance
   d. Total number of actual direct manufacturing labor-hours used
   e. Total number of standard direct manufacturing labor-hours allowed for the units produced
   f. Production-volume variance

2. Describe how Mancuso's control of variable manufacturing overhead items differs from its control of fixed manufacturing overhead items.

8-39 Review of Chapters 7 and 8, 3-variance analysis. (CPA, adapted) The Beal Manufacturing Company's job-costing system has two direct-cost categories—direct materials and direct manufacturing labor. Manufacturing overhead (both variable and fixed) is allocated to products on the basis of standard direct manufacturing labor-hours (DLH). At the beginning of 2001, Beal adopted the following standards for its manufacturing costs:

	Input	Cost Per Output Unit
Direct materials	3 lb. at $5.00 per lb.	$ 15.00
Direct manufacturing labor	5 hr. at $15.00 per hr.	75.00
Manufacturing overhead:		
Variable	$6.00 per DLH	30.00
Fixed	$8.00 per DLH	40.00
Standard manufacturing cost per output unit		$160.00

The denominator level for total manufacturing overhead per month in 2001 is 40,000 direct manufacturing labor-hours. Beal's flexible budget for January 2001 was based on this denominator level. The records for January indicated the following:

Direct materials purchased	25,000 lb. at $5.20 per lb.
Direct materials used	23,100 lb.
Direct manufacturing labor	40,100 hr. at $14.60 per hr.
Total actual manufacturing overhead (variable and fixed)	$600,000
Actual production	7,800 output units

Required

1. Prepare a schedule of total standard manufacturing costs for the 7,800 output units in January, 2001.
2. For the month of January 2001, compute the following variances, indicating whether each is favorable (F) or unfavorable (U):
    a. Direct materials price variance, based on purchases
    b. Direct materials efficiency variance
    c. Direct manufacturing labor price variance
    d. Direct manufacturing labor efficiency variance
    e. Total manufacturing overhead spending variance
    f. Variable manufacturing overhead efficiency variance
    g. Production-volume variance

COLLABORATIVE LEARNING PROBLEM

8-40 Hospital overhead variances, 4-variance analysis, ethics. Sharon Hospital, a large metropolitan health care complex, has had trouble controlling its accounts receivable. Bills for patients, for various government agencies, and for private insurance companies have frequently been inaccurate and late. This situation has led to intolerable levels of bad debts and investments in receivables.

In conjunction with the Billing Department, a set of standard costs and standard amounts was developed for 2001. These standard costs can be used in a flexible budget with separate variable-cost and fixed-cost categories. The output unit is defined to be a bill.

The accountant to Sharon Hospital provides you with the following for April 2001:

Variable overhead costs, allowance per standard hour	$ 10
Fixed overhead flexible-budget variance, favorable	200
Total budgeted overhead costs for the bills prepared	22,500
Production-volume variance, favorable	900
Variable-cost spending variance, unfavorable	2,000
Variable-cost efficiency variance, favorable	2,000
Standard hours allowed for the bills prepared	1,800

Required

Form groups of two or more students to complete the following requirements.

1. a. Actual hours of input used
    b. Fixed overhead budget
    c. Fixed overhead allocated

d. Budgeted fixed overhead rate per hour

e. Denominator level in hours

2. Ira Stone, the president of Sharon Hospital, has a meeting with the Medical Economics Group (MEG). MEG is a consulting firm in the health services sector. It reports that Sharon's billing operations are grossly inefficient. Its standard cost per bill is above 90% of the 130 hospitals MEG tracks in its Benchmarking Data Base. Stone suspects the billing group deliberately "padded" its standard costs and standard amounts. Despite a large investment in new information systems, the standards for 2001 were not below actual results for 2000. Stone does not want to conduct a witch hunt in the company. However, he wants to "eliminate the fat" in Sharon's cost structure.

a. How might Sharon's billing operations group have "padded" its standard costs and standard amounts? Why might they do this padding?

b. What steps should Stone take to "eliminate the fat" in the overhead costs of the billing operations at Sharon Hospital?

Inventory Costing and Capacity Analysis

Bottling lines can operate at varying degrees of speed. Management considers these different operating speeds, as well as demand factors, when determining the denominator level to use in setting fixed manufacturing overhead cost rates.

The reported income number captures the attention of managers in a way few other numbers do. Consider three examples:

◆ Planning decisions typically include analysis of how the alternatives under consideration would affect future reported income.

◆ Increases in reported income are the object of many decisions related to cost reduction.

◆ Reported income is a key number in the performance evaluation of managers.

This chapter examines two types of cost accounting choices in which the reported income number of manufacturing companies is affected by inventories:

1. *Inventory-costing choices* relate to which manufacturing costs are treated as inventoriable costs. We discuss three choices in Part One of this chapter—absorption costing, variable costing, and throughput costing.[1]

2. *Denominator-level capacity choices* relate to the preselected level of the cost-allocation base used to set budgeted fixed manufacturing cost rates. We discuss four choices in Part Two of this chapter—theoretical capacity, practical capacity, normal capacity utilization, and master-budget capacity utilization.

For both inventory-costing and denominator-level capacity choices, the required alternative for external reporting need not be the preferred alternative for internal routine reporting or internal nonroutine reporting. This chapter further illustrates the different costs for different purposes theme underlying cost accounting.

◆ PART ONE: INVENTORY COSTING FOR MANUFACTURING COMPANIES

The two most commonly encountered methods of costing inventories in manufacturing companies are variable costing and absorption costing. We discuss them first and then explain throughput costing. Absorption costing is the required method for external reporting and tax reporting in many countries.

VARIABLE COSTING AND ABSORPTION COSTING

Variable costing is a method of inventory costing in which all variable manufacturing costs are included as inventoriable costs. All fixed manufacturing costs are excluded from inventoriable costs. They are instead treated as costs of the period in which they are incurred. Recall from Chapter 2 (p. 36) that *inventoriable costs* are all costs of a product that are regarded as an asset when they are incurred and then become cost of goods sold when the product is sold. **Absorption costing** is a method of inventory costing in which all variable manufacturing costs and all fixed manufacturing costs are included as inventoriable costs. That is, inventory "absorbs" all manufacturing costs. Variable costing and absorption costing differ in only one conceptual respect: whether fixed manufacturing costs (both direct and indirect) are inventoriable costs. Under both methods, all nonmanufacturing costs in the value chain (such as research and development and marketing), whether variable or fixed, are recorded as expenses when incurred.

Data for Single-Year Example

To illustrate the difference between variable costing and absorption costing, we will examine Stassen Company, which manufactures and markets optical consumer products. It uses a standard costing system. That is, its direct costs are traced to products using standard prices and standard inputs allowed for actual outputs produced, and indirect (overhead) costs are allocated using standard indirect rate(s) times the standard inputs allowed for the actual outputs produced. The allocation

---

[1] The variable costing versus absorption costing choice is but one of several issues pertaining to inventory costing. For example, a cost flow assumption (FIFO, LIFO, weighted-average, and so on) must also be chosen.

base for all indirect manufacturing costs is budgeted units produced. The allocation base for all indirect marketing costs is budgeted units sold. Stassen's president wants you to prepare an annual income statement for 2000 for the telescope product line. Key operating information for the year is:

	Units
Beginning inventory	0
Production	800
Sales	600
Ending inventory	200

Actual revenue and cost data for 2000 are:

Selling price	$100.00 per unit sold
Variable manufacturing costs	
Direct materials costs	$11.00
Direct manufacturing labor costs	4.00
Indirect manufacturing costs	5.00
Total	$20.00 per unit produced
Variable marketing costs (all indirect)	$19.00 per unit sold
Fixed manufacturing costs (all indirect)	$12,000
Fixed marketing costs (all indirect)	$10,800

The allocation base for variable manufacturing costs is units produced. The allocation base for variable marketing costs is units sold.

We assume the following at Stassen:

1. All variable costs are driven by units produced or sold. Nonoutput-driven costs, such as batch-level and product-sustaining costs, are zero.

2. Work in process is zero.

3. The budgeted denominator level of production in 2000 is 800 units, which is the same as the actual production in 2000.

4. Stassen budgeted for sales of 600 units in 2000, which is the same as the actual sales in 2000.

5. There are no price, efficiency, or spending variances in the examples given. Our first example (2000) has no production-volume variance for manufacturing costs. Later examples (for 2001 and 2002) feature production-volume variances.

6. All variances are written off to cost of goods sold in the period (year) in which they occur.

The heart of the difference between variable costing and absorption costing for financial accounting is the accounting for fixed manufacturing costs. All variable manufacturing costs are inventoriable costs under both methods. That is, they are first recorded as an inventory asset when they are incurred. Under variable costing, fixed manufacturing costs are treated as an expense of the period. Under absorption costing, fixed manufacturing costs are inventoriable costs. They are then deducted as cost of goods sold when sales occur. The standard fixed manufacturing overhead cost rate is $15.00 ($12,000 ÷ 800) per unit produced.

Inventoriable costs in 2000 under the two methods for Stassen are:

	Variable Costing		Absorption Costing	
Variable manufacturing costs				
Direct materials	$11.00		$11.00	
Direct manufacturing labor	4.00		4.00	
Indirect manufacturing costs	5.00	$20.00	5.00	$20.00
Fixed indirect manufacturing costs		—		15.00
Total inventoriable costs		$20.00		$35.00

Example We're producing No. 2 pencils that sell for $8 per box (each box contains 1 gross). DM are $3 per box, DL is $.50 per box, and VMOH is $.25 per box. FMOH is $100,000 per year. Sales commissions are $0.75 per box, and fixed administration expenses are $30,000/year. We expected to and actually produced 50,000 boxes, of which 40,000 were sold. Compute the inventoriable cost per box under VC and AC.
Cost per box for VC:
DM + DL + VMOH =
$3 + 0.50 + 0.25 = $3.75
Note that sales commissions aren't inventoriable.
Cost per box for AC:
DM + DL + VMOH + FMOH =
$3 + 0.50 + 0.25 + 2.00 = $5.75
Note that FMOH is $100,000/50,000 = $2/box.

Correcting Student Misconceptions/Points to Stress Students frequently miss the fact that var. non-mfg. costs often vary with units sold while var. mfg. costs often vary with units produced.

OBJECTIVE 1
Identify the fundamental feature that distinguishes variable costing from absorption costing

Under both methods, all nonmanufacturing costs, whether variable or fixed, are written off in the period (year) in which they are incurred.

Comparing Income Statements

Exhibit 9-1 presents the variable-costing and absorption-costing income statements for the telescope product of Stassen Company for the year 2000. The variable-costing income statement (Panel A) uses the contribution-margin format introduced in Chapter 3. The absorption-costing income statement (Panel B) uses the gross-margin format introduced in Chapter 2. Why these differences in format? The distinction between variable costs and fixed costs is central to variable costing, and is highlighted by the contribution-margin format. Similarly, the distinction between manufacturing and nonmanufacturing costs is central to absorption costing, and is highlighted by the gross-margin format.

EXHIBIT 9-1

Comparison of Variable Costing and Absorption Costing Stassen Company: Telescope Product-Line Income Statements for 2000

PANEL A: VARIABLE COSTING

Revenues: $100 × 600		$60,000
Variable costs		
Beginning inventory	$ 0	
Variable manufacturing costs: $20 × 800	16,000	
Cost of goods available for sale	16,000	
Ending inventory: $20 × 200	4,000	
Variable cost of goods sold	12,000	
Variable marketing costs: $19 × 600	11,400	
Adjustment for variable-cost variances	0	
Total variable costs		23,400
Contribution margin		36,600
Fixed costs		
Fixed manufacturing costs	12,000	
Fixed marketing costs	10,800	
Adjustment for fixed-cost variances	0	
Total fixed costs		22,800
Operating income		$13,800

PANEL B: ABSORPTION COSTING

Revenues: $100 × 600		$60,000
Cost of goods sold		
Beginning inventory	$ 0	
Variable manufacturing costs: $20 × 800	16,000	
Fixed manufacturing costs: $15 × 800	12,000	
Cost of goods available for sale	28,000	
Ending inventory: ($20 + $15) × 200	7,000	
Adjustment for manufacturing variances	0	
Cost of goods sold		21,000
Gross margin		39,000
Operating costs		
Variable marketing costs: $19 × 600	11,400	
Fixed marketing costs	10,800	
Adjustment for operating cost variances	0	
Total operating costs		22,200
Operating income		$16,800

Trace the fixed manufacturing costs of $12,000 in Exhibit 9-1. The income statement under variable costing deducts the $12,000 lump sum as an expense for 2000. In contrast, the income statement under absorption costing regards each finished unit as absorbing $15.00 of fixed manufacturing costs. Under absorption costing the $12,000 ($15.00 × 800) is initially treated as an inventoriable cost in 2000. Given the preceding data for Stassen, $9,000 ($15.00 × 600) subsequently becomes a part of cost of goods sold in 2000, and $3,000 ($15 × 200) remains an asset—part of ending finished goods inventory on December 31, 2000. The variable manufacturing costs of $20.00 per unit are accounted for in the same way in both income statements in Exhibit 9-1. These points can be summarized as follows:

Points to Stress VC I/S use the contribution margin (CM) approach that highlights the distinction between VC and FC that's central to variable costing. The CM approach emphasizes the lump sum FC that's expensed in the period incurred. In contrast, AC I/S use the gross margin approach that distinguishes between mfg. and non-mfg. costs.

	Variable Costing	**Absorption Costing**
Variable manufacturing costs: $20 per telescope produced	Inventoriable	Inventoriable
Fixed manufacturing costs: $12,000 per year	Deducted as an expense of the period	Inventoriable at $15 per telescope produced using budgeted denominator level of 800 units produced per year

Points to Stress The difference between VC and AC operating incomes is a matter of timing. Under VC, FMOH costs are expensed in the period incurred. Under AC, FMOH costs are inventoried, and are not expensed until the related units are sold.

Never overlook the heart of the matter. The difference between variable costing and absorption costing centers on accounting for fixed manufacturing costs. If inventory levels change, operating income will differ between the two methods because of the difference in accounting for fixed manufacturing costs. Compare telescope sales of 600, 700, and 800 units by Stassen in 2000. Fixed manufacturing costs would be included as deductions in the 2000 income statement as follows:

Variable costing, whether

◆ sales are 600, 700 or 800 units $12,000 deduction

Absorption costing, where

◆ sales are 600 units, $3,000 ($15 × 200) is held back in inventory $9,000 deduction

◆ sales are 700 units, $1,500 ($15 × 100) is held back in inventory $10,500 deduction

◆ sales are 800 units, $0 ($15 × 0) is held back in inventory $12,000 deduction

Teaching Tip This chart helps students understand "where the FMOH costs go." You can reinforce this by asking them to figure out where the FMOH costs go (expense vs. inventory) in 1 or 2 homework problems, or by adding this analysis to an in-class example.

Sometimes the term **direct costing** is used to describe the inventory-costing method we call *variable costing*. However, direct costing is an unfortunate choice of terms for two reasons: (1) Variable costing does not include all direct costs as inventoriable costs. Only direct variable manufacturing costs are included. Any direct fixed manufacturing costs, and any direct nonmanufacturing costs, are excluded from inventoriable costs. (2) Variable costing includes as inventoriable costs not only direct manufacturing costs but also some indirect costs (indirect variable manufacturing costs). Note also that *variable costing* is a less than ideal term because not all variable costs are inventoriable costs. Only variable manufacturing costs are inventoriable.

EXPLAINING DIFFERENCES IN OPERATING INCOME

Data for Multiyear Example

The Stassen example in Exhibit 9-1 covered one accounting period (a single year). We now extend the example to cover three years. In both 2001 and 2002, Stassen has a production-volume variance because telescope production differs from the budgeted denominator level of production of 800 units per year.[2] The actual sales levels for 2001 and 2002 are the same as those budgeted for these respective years. Pertinent data in units are as follows:

OBJECTIVE 3

Explain differences in operating income under absorption costing and variable costing

[2]Chapter 8 (pp. 261–262) discusses the computation and interpretation of the production-volume variance.

	2000	2001	2002
Beginning inventory	0	200	50
Production	800	500	1,000
Sales	600	650	750
Ending inventory	200	50	300

All of the other 2000 data we presented in our earlier example still apply for 2001 and 2002.

Comparing Income Statements

Exhibit 9-2 presents comparative income statements under variable costing (Panel A) and absorption costing (Panel B) for Stassen Company in 2000, 2001, and 2002. Keep in mind the following points about absorption costing as you study Panel B of Exhibits 9-1 and 9-2:

1. The inventoriable costs are $35 per unit, not $20, because fixed manufacturing costs ($15) as well as variable manufacturing costs ($20), are assigned to each unit of product.

2. The $15 fixed manufacturing cost rate is based on a budgeted denominator level of 800 telescope units produced per year ($12,000 ÷ 800 = $15). Whenever *production* (not sales) deviates from the denominator level, a production-volume variance arises. The amount of the variance is $15 multiplied by the difference between the actual level of production and the denominator level. In 2001, production was 500 telescope units, 300 lower than the denominator level of 800. The result is an unfavorable production-volume variance of $4,500 ($15.00 × 300). 2002 has a favorable production-volume variance of $3,000 ($15.00 × 200) due to production of 1,000 units exceeding the denominator level of 800.

3. The production-volume variance, which relates to fixed manufacturing overhead, exists under absorption costing but not under variable costing.

4. The absorption-costing income statement classifies costs primarily by *business function*, such as manufacturing and marketing. In contrast, the variable-costing income statement features *cost behavior* (variable or fixed) as the basis of classification. Absorption-costing income statements need not differentiate between the variable and fixed costs. However, Exhibit 9-2 does make this distinction for Stassen Company to highlight how individual line items are classified differently under variable costing and absorption costing.

A summary of the operating income differences for Stassen Company over the 2000–2002 period is as follows:

	2000	2001	2002
1. Absorption-costing operating income	$16,800	$14,600	$26,700
2. Variable-costing operating income	13,800	16,850	22,950
3. Difference: (1) − (2)	3,000	(2,250)	3,750
4. Difference as a % of absorption operating income	17.9%	(15.4%)	14.0%

These percentage differences illustrate why the choice between variable costing and absorption costing is important to managers for whom the reported income number is of much interest.

Why do variable costing and absorption costing usually report different income numbers? In general, if the inventory level increases during an accounting period, less operating income will be reported under variable costing than under absorption costing. Conversely, if the inventory level decreases, more operating income will be reported under variable costing than under absorption costing. Why? Solely because of moving fixed manufacturing costs into inventories as inventories increase and out of inventories as they decrease. The difference between operating

Example It's usually, but not always, true that when # produced > # sold (i.e., EI > BI), AC OI > VC OI. However, if the budgeted FMOH rate falls enough to more than offset the higher # units in EI, there may be less FMOH costs embedded in EI than in BI. For example, assume a company uses FIFO, and has the following data:

BI = 100 units
# Produced = 200 units
# Sold = 180 units
Prior yr. budgeted
  fixed-cost rate = $30/unit
Current yr. budgeted
  fixed-cost rate = $24/unit
AC OI − VC OI
= FMOH in EI − FMOH in BI
= [(100 + 200 − 180 units)($24 per unit)
  − (100 units)($30 per unit)
= −$120

Thus, AC OI is $120 less than VC OI even though # of units in inventory increased from 100 to 120.

Points to Stress The unfavorable PVV arose in 2001 because Stassen produced less than expected. Note that a PVV can also arise under normal (or budgeted) costing if the company's actual production isn't equal to expected production (i.e., denominator volume). Under actual costing, there can be no variances.

Points to Stress The PVV is the difference between lump sum budgeted FMOH costs and the FMOH costs that are allocated to WIP. Since FMOH costs aren't allocated to WIP under VC (FMOH costs are expensed as incurred), there can be no PVV under VC. Also note that all non-mfg. costs are totally expensed under both AC and VC.

EXHIBIT 9-2
Comparison of Variable Costing and Absorption Costing
Stassen Company: Telescope Product-Line Income Statements for 2000, 2001, and 2002

PANEL A: VARIABLE COSTING

	2000		2001		2002	
Revenues: $100 × 600; 650; 750		$60,000		$65,000		$75,000
Variable costs						
Beginning inventory: $20 × 0; 200; 50	$ 0		$ 4,000		$ 1,000	
Variable manufacturing costs: $20 × 800; 500; 1,000	16,000		10,000		20,000	
Cost of goods available for sale	16,000		14,000		21,000	
Ending inventory: $20 × 200; 50; 300	4,000		1,000		6,000	
Variable cost of goods sold	12,000		13,000		15,000	
Variable marketing costs: $19 × 600; 650; 750	11,400		12,350		14,250	
Adjustment for variable cost variances	0		0		0	
Total variable costs		23,400		25,350		29,250
Contribution margin		36,600		39,650		45,750
Fixed costs						
Fixed manufacturing costs	12,000		12,000		12,000	
Fixed marketing costs	10,800		10,800		10,800	
Adjustment for fixed cost variances	0		0		0	
Total fixed costs		22,800		22,800		22,800
Operating income		$13,800		$16,850		$22,950

PANEL B: ABSORPTION COSTING

	2000		2001		2002	
Revenues: $100 × 600; 650; 750		$60,000		$65,000		$75,000
Cost of goods sold						
Beginning inventory: $35 × 0; 200; 50	$ 0		$ 7,000		$ 1,750	
Variable manufacturing costs: $20 × 800; 500; 1,000	16,000		10,000		20,000	
Fixed manufacturing costs: $15 × 800; 500; 1,000	12,000		7,500		15,000	
Cost of goods available for sale	28,000		24,500		36,750	
Ending inventory: $35 × 200; 50; 300	7,000		1,750		10,500	
Adjustment for manufacturing variances[a]	0		4,500 U		3,000 F	
Cost of goods sold		21,000		27,250		23,250
Gross margin		39,000		37,750		51,750
Operating costs						
Variable marketing costs: $19 × 600; 650; 750	11,400		12,350		14,250	
Fixed marketing costs	10,800		10,800		10,800	
Adjustment for operating cost variances	0		0		0	
Total operating costs		22,200		23,150		25,050
Operating income		$16,800		$14,600		$26,700

[a]Production volume variance:
Fixed manufacturing costs per unit × (Denominator volume − Actual volume in units)
2000: $15 × (800 − 800) = $15 × 0 = $0
2001: $15 × (800 − 500) = $15 × 300 = $4,500 U
2002: $15 × (800 − 1,000) = $15 × (200) = $3,000 F

income under absorption costing and variable costing can be computed by Formula 1, which focuses on fixed manufacturing costs in beginning and ending inventory:

FORMULA 1

Absorption-costing operating income	−	Variable-costing operating income	=	Fixed manufacturing costs in ending inventory under absorption costing	−	Fixed manufacturing costs in beginning inventory under absorption costing

2000: $16,800 − $13,800 = ($15 × 200) − ($15 × 0)$

$$\$3,000 = \$3,000$$

2001: $14,600 − $16,850 = ($15 × 50) − ($15 × 200)$

$$-\$2,250 = -\$2,250$$

2002: $26,700 − $22,950 = ($15 × 300) − ($15 × 50)$

$$\$3,750 = \$3,750$$

Fixed manufacturing costs in ending inventory are deferred to a future period under absorption costing. For example, $3,000 of fixed manufacturing overhead is deferred to 2001 at December 31, 2000. Under variable costing, all fixed manufacturing costs are treated as an expense of that period. All $12,000 of fixed manufacturing overhead in 2000 is expensed in that year.

An alternative formula that highlights the movement of costs between inventory and cost of goods sold is:

FORMULA 2

Absorption-costing operating income	−	Variable-costing operating income	=	Fixed manufacturing costs inventoried in units produced under absorption costing	−	Fixed manufacturing costs in cost of goods sold under absorption costing

2000: $16,800 − $13,800 = ($15 × 800) − ($15 × 600)$

$$\$3,000 = \$3,000$$

2001: $14,600 − $16,850 = ($15 × 500) − ($15 × 650)$

$$-\$2,250 = -\$2,250$$

2002: $26,700 − $22,950 = ($15 × 1,000) − ($15 × 750)$

$$\$3,750 = \$3,750$$

There is increasing pressure on managers to reduce inventory levels. Some companies are achieving dramatic reductions in inventory levels using policies such as just-in-time production, and they are also benefiting from better sharing of information between suppliers and manufacturers. One consequence is that operating income differences between absorption costing and variable costing for these companies become less material in amount. If managers hold zero levels of inventory at the start and end of each accounting period, there will be no difference between absorption costing and variable costing.

Effect of Sales and Production on Operating Income

The period-to-period change in operating income under variable costing is driven solely by changes in the unit level of sales, given a constant contribution margin per unit and constant fixed costs. Consider the variable-costing operating income of Stassen in (a) 2001 versus 2000, and (b) 2002 versus 2001:

Change in variable-costing operating income	=	Contribution margin per unit	×	Change in unit level of sales

(a) 2001 vs. 2000: $16,850 − $13,800 = $61 × (650 − 600)$

$$\$3,050 = \$3,050$$

(b) 2002 vs. 2001: $22,950 − $16,850 = $61 × (750 − 650)$

$$\$6,100 = \$6,100$$

Teaching Tip Stress the intuition behind formula 1. VC expenses all FMOH costs in the period incurred. AC allocates FMOH costs to units produced this period and doesn't expense them until the related units are sold. FMOH costs in ending inventory (EI) are current period costs that AC defers to the future (making AC income higher relative to VC income). Conversely, FMOH costs in beginning inventory (BI) are costs deferred from prior periods that AC expenses in the current period, when the related units are sold (making AC lower relative to VC). AC OI exceeds VC OI if there's a net deferral of FMOH costs, and vice versa. For formula 2, AC assigns the FMOH costs of all units produced to WIP/FG (an asset) and takes out from this total, as CGS (an expense), the FMOH costs of all units sold.

Points to Stress The difference between AC and VC is more important for traditional manufacturers with lots of inventory. Under JIT, the distinction becomes less important since FMOH costs in the inventories can be immaterial if inventories are very low.

Question	Variable Costing	Absorption Costing	Comment
Are fixed manufacturing costs inventoried?	No	Yes	Basic theoretical question of when these costs should be expensed.
Is there a production-volume variance?	No	Yes	Choice of denominator level affects measurement of operating income under absorption costing only.
Are classifications between variable and fixed costs routinely made?	Yes	Not always	Absorption costing can be easily modified to obtain subclassifications for variable and fixed costs, if desired (for example, see Exhibit 9-1, Panel B).
How do changes in unit inventory levels affect operating income?[a]			Differences are attributable to the timing of when fixed manufacturing costs are expensed.
Production = sales	Equal	Equal	
Production > sales	Lower[b]	Higher[c]	
Production < sales	Higher	Lower	
What are the effects on cost-volume-profit relationships (for a given level of fixed costs and a given contribution margin per unit)?	Driven by unit level of sales	Driven by (a) unit level of sales, (b) unit level of production, and (c) chosen denominator level	Management control benefit: Effects of changes in production level on operating income are easier to understand under variable costing.

[a]Assuming that all manufacturing variances are written off as period costs, that no change occurs in work-in-process inventory, and no change occurs in the budgeted fixed manufacturing overhead rate between accounting periods.
[b]That is, lower operating income than under absorption costing.
[c]That is, higher operating income than under variable costing.

Note that under variable costing, Stassen managers cannot increase operating income by producing for inventory because the unit level of sales drives operating income. As described later in this chapter, absorption costing enables managers to increase operating income by producing for inventory as well as by increasing the unit level of sales.

Exhibit 9-3 compares key differences between variable costing and absorption costing.

PERFORMANCE MEASURES AND ABSORPTION COSTING

Although absorption costing is the required inventory method for external reporting in most countries, many companies use variable costing for internal reporting. We now discuss why such inventory costing illustrates the different costs for different purposes theme that underlies this text.

Undesirable Buildup of Inventories

Absorption costing enables a manager to increase operating income in a specific period by increasing the production schedule, even if there is no customer demand for the additional production. One motivation could be a manager's bonus plan that is based on reported operating income. Assume that Stassen's managers have such a bonus plan. Exhibit 9-4 shows how Stassen's absorption-costing operating income for 2001 changes as the production level in 2001 changes. This exhibit assumes that all variances (including the production-volume variance) are written off to cost of goods sold at the end of each accounting period. Beginning inventory in 2001 of 200 units and sales in 2001 of 650 units are unchanged from the base case in Exhibit 9-2. Exhibit 9-4 shows that production of only 450 units meets 2001 sales of 650. Operating income at this production level is $13,850. By producing more than 450 units in 2001, Stassen increases absorption-costing operating income. Each unit in 2001 ending inventory will increase operating income by $15. For example,

Reinforcing Problems AC vs. VC and mgt. incentives are covered in Probs. 9-29, 9-30, 9-32, 9-35, 9-37, and 9-38.

OBJECTIVE 4
Understand how absorption costing can provide undesirable incentives for managers

EXHIBIT 9-4

Effect on Absorption-Costing Operating Income of Different Production Levels Holding the Unit Sales Level Constant: Stassen Company Telescope Product-Line Data for 2001 with Sales of 650 Units

Unit Data

Beginning inventory	200	200	200	200	200
Production	450	500	650	800	900
Goods available for sale	650	700	850	1,000	1,100
Sales	650	650	650	650	650
Ending inventory	0	50	200	350	450

Income Statement

Revenues	$65,000	$65,000	$65,000	$65,000	$65,000
Cost of goods sold					
Beginning inventory	7,000	7,000	7,000	7,000	7,000
Variable manufacturing costs	9,000	10,000	13,000	16,000	18,000
Fixed manufacturing costs	6,750	7,500	9,750	12,000	13,500
Cost of goods available for sale	22,750	24,500	29,750	35,000	38,500
Ending inventory	0	1,750	7,000	12,250	15,750
Adjustment for manufacturing variances[a]	5,250 U	4,500 U	2,250 U	0	1,500 F
Cost of goods sold	28,000	27,250	25,000	22,750	21,250
Gross margin	37,000	37,750	40,000	42,250	43,750
Operating costs					
Marketing costs	23,150	23,150	23,150	23,150	23,150
Adj. for marketing variances	0	0	0	0	0
Total operating costs	23,150	23,150	23,150	23,150	23,150
Operating income	$13,850	$14,600	$16,850	$19,100	$20,600

[a]Production-volume variance:
Fixed manufacturing costs per unit × (Denominator volume − Actual volume)
$15 × (800 − 450) = $15 × 350 = $5,250 U
$15 × (800 − 500) = $15 × 300 = $4,500 U
$15 × (800 − 650) = $15 × 150 = $2,250 U
$15 × (800 − 800) = $15 × 0 = $0
$15 × (800 − 900) = $15 × (100) = $1,500 F

if 800 units are produced, ending inventory will be 350 units and operating income $19,100. This amount is $5,250 more than what operating income is with zero ending inventory (350 units × $15 = $5,250) in 2001.

The undesirable effects of producing for inventory may be sizable, and they can arise in several ways. For example,

1. A plant manager may switch production to those orders that absorb the highest amount of fixed manufacturing costs, regardless of the customer demand for these products (called "cherry picking" the production line). Production of items that absorb minimal fixed manufacturing costs may be delayed, resulting in failure to meet promised customer delivery dates (which, in itself, can reduce long-term customer loyalty).

2. A plant manager may accept a particular order to increase production even though another plant in the same company is better suited to handle that order.

3. To meet increased production, a manager may defer maintenance beyond the current accounting period. Although operating income may increase now, future operating income will probably decrease because of increased repairs and less efficient equipment.

The example in Exhibit 9-4 focuses on only one year (2001). A Stassen manager who built up ending inventories of telescopes to 450 in 2001 would have to further increase ending inventories in 2002 in order to increase that year's operating income by producing for inventory. The difficulties of continually increasing inventory levels over time (there may be physical constraints on storage space) may reduce some of the aforementioned undesirable effects of using absorption costing.

Proposals for Revising Performance Evaluation

The dysfunctional aspects associated with absorption costing can be reduced in multiple ways:

1. Careful budgeting and inventory planning to reduce management's latitude for gaming. For example, the budgeted monthly balance sheets have estimates of the dollar amount of inventories. These dollar amounts could be used in a management-by-exception way to highlight unplanned inventory buildups.

2. Change the accounting system. Discontinue the use of absorption costing for internal reporting and instead use variable costing. This change will reduce the incentives of managers to produce for inventory. The next section discusses *throughput costing*, which results in even less incentive to produce for inventory as less costs are inventoried than occur under variable costing. Reducing inventory means less funds are tied up in inventory and typically also means reducing inventory spoilage and obsolescence costs.

3. Incorporate a carrying charge for inventory into the internal accounting system. For example, an inventory carrying charge of 1% per month could be assessed for resources tied up in inventory assets.

4. Change the time period used to evaluate performance. Critics of absorption costing give examples in which managers take actions that maximize quarterly or annual income at the potential expense of long-run income. By evaluating performance over a 3–5 year period, managers will be less tempted to produce for inventory.

5. Include nonfinancial as well as financial variables in the measures used to evaluate performance. Companies are currently using nonfinancial variables, such as the following, to monitor managers' performance in key areas:

a. $\dfrac{\text{Ending inventory in units this period}}{\text{Ending inventory in units last period}}$

b. $\dfrac{\text{Sales in units this period}}{\text{Ending inventory in units this period}}$

Any buildup of inventory at the end of the year would be signaled by tracking the month-to-month behavior of these two nonfinancial inventory measures. Companies that manufacture or sell several products could report the two measures on a product-by-product basis.

THROUGHPUT COSTING

Some critics maintain that even variable costing promotes an excessive amount of costs being inventoried. They argue that only direct materials are "truly variable" and propose throughput costing be used. **Throughput costing** (also called **super-variable costing**) treats all costs except those related to variable direct materials as costs of the period in which they are incurred. Only variable direct material costs are inventoriable costs. This method is a recent proposal and currently has not achieved widespread use by companies.[3]

    Exhibit 9-5 is the throughput-costing income statement for Stassen Company. *Throughput contribution* equals revenues minus all variable direct material costs of

[3]For further discussion of throughput costing, see E. Goldratt, *What Is This Thing Called Theory of Constraints and How Should It Be Implemented?* (Croton-on-Hudson, N.Y.: North River Press, 1990).

EXHIBIT 9-5

Throughput-Costing Telescope Product-Line Income Statement for Stassen Company for 2000, 2001, and 2002

	2000	2001	2002
Revenues: $100 × 600; 650; 750	$60,000	$65,000	$75,000
Variable direct materials cost of goods sold			
Beginning inventory: $11 × 0; 200; 50	0	2,200	550
Direct materials: $11 × 800; 500; 1,000	8,800	5,500	11,000
Cost of goods available for sale	8,800	7,700	11,550
Ending inventory: $11 × 200; 50; 300	2,200	550	3,300
Total variable direct materials cost of goods sold	6,600	7,150	8,250
Adjustment for variances	0	0	0
Total variable direct materials costs	6,600	7,150	8,250
Throughput contribution[a]	53,400	57,850	66,750
Other costs			
Manufacturing[b]	19,200	16,500	21,000
Marketing[c]	22,200	23,150	25,050
Total other costs	41,400	39,650	46,050
Operating income	$12,000	$18,200	$20,700

[a] Throughput contribution equals revenues minus all variable direct material costs of the goods sold.
[b] $12,000 + ($4 + $5) × 800; 500; 1,000
[c] $10,800 + $19 × 600; 650; 750

the goods sold. Compare the operating income amounts reported in Exhibit 9-5 with those for absorption and variable costing:

	2000	2001	2002
Absorption-costing operating income	$16,800	$14,600	$26,700
Variable-costing operating income	13,800	16,850	22,950
Throughput-costing operating income	12,000	18,200	20,700

Only the $11 direct materials cost per unit is inventoriable under throughput costing (compared to $35 for absorption costing and $20 for variable costing). When production exceeds sales (as in 2000 and 2002), throughput costing results in the largest amount of deductions in the current period's income statement. Advocates of throughput costing maintain that it provides less incentive to produce for inventory than do either variable or (especially) absorption costing.

CAPSULE COMPARISON OF INVENTORY-COSTING METHODS

OBJECTIVE 5

Differentiate throughput costing from variable costing and absorption costing

Variable costing, absorption costing, or throughput costing may be combined with actual, normal, or standard costing. Exhibit 9-6 compares product costing under nine alternative inventory-costing systems:

Variable Costing	Absorption Costing	Throughput Costing
1. Actual costing	4. Actual costing	7. Actual costing
2. Normal costing	5. Normal costing	8. Normal costing
3. Standard costing	6. Standard costing	9. Standard costing

Throughput costing is not permitted for the external reporting purpose of accounting systems if it results in materially different numbers than those reported by absorption costing. Advocates of throughput costing emphasize the internal purposes of management accounting data.

EXHIBIT 9-6
Comparison of Alternative Inventory-Costing Systems

		Actual Costing	Normal Costing	Standard Costing
	Variable Direct Materials Costs	◆ Actual prices × Actual inputs used	◆ Actual prices × Actual inputs used	◆ Standard prices × Standard inputs allowed for actual output achieved
	Variable Direct Conversion Costs[a]	◆ Actual prices × Actual inputs used	◆ Actual prices × Actual inputs used	◆ Standard prices × Standard inputs allowed for actual output achieved
	Variable Indirect Manufacturing Costs	◆ Actual variable indirect rates × Actual inputs used	◆ Budgeted variable indirect rates × Actual inputs used	◆ Standard variable indirect rates × Standard inputs allowed for actual output achieved
	Fixed Direct Manufacturing Costs	◆ Actual prices × Actual inputs used	◆ Actual prices × Actual inputs used	◆ Standard prices × Standard inputs allowed for actual output achieved
	Fixed Indirect Manufacturing Costs	◆ Actual fixed indirect rates × Actual inputs used	◆ Budgeted fixed indirect rates × Actual inputs used	◆ Standard fixed indirect rates × Standard inputs allowed for actual output achieved

(Left-margin brackets label the groupings: **Absorption Costing**, **Variable Costing**, **Throughput Costing**.)

[a]Conversion costs are all manufacturing costs minus direct materials costs.

Variable costing has been a controversial subject among accountants—not so much because there is disagreement about the need for delineating between variable and fixed costs for management planning and control, but because there are questions about using variable costing for the external reporting purpose of cost accounting. Those favoring variable costing for external reporting maintain that the fixed portion of manufacturing costs is more closely related to the capacity to produce than to the actual production of specific units. Supporters of absorption costing maintain that inventories should carry a fixed manufacturing cost component. Why? Because both variable and fixed manufacturing cost are necessary to produce goods. Therefore, both types of costs should be inventoriable, regardless of their having different behavior patterns.

Absorption costing (or close variations of it) is the method most commonly used for the external reporting purpose of accounting systems. For example, for reporting to the U.S. Internal Revenue Service, all manufacturing costs plus some product design and administrative costs (such as legal) must be included as inventoriable costs.[4] Legal costs must be allocated between those costs related to manufacturing activities (inventoriable costs) and those not so related. For external reporting to shareholders, companies around the globe tend to follow the generally accepted accounting principle that all manufacturing overhead is inventoriable.

A key issue in absorption costing is the choice of the denominator-level capacity used to compute fixed manufacturing costs per unit. Part Two of this chapter discusses this issue.

Teaching Tip/Curriculum Linkage
Help students integrate Chaps. 2, 4, 7, 8, and 9. As shown in Exh. 9-6, accountants (or managers) must choose among actual (Chap. 2); normal (Chap. 4); and std. costing (Chaps. 7, 8). They also must decide whether to account for FMOH costs using AC (Chaps. 2, and 4); VC (Chap. 9); or throughput costing (Chap. 9). In addition, they must decide whether to accumulate costs by job (Chap. 4) or by process (Chap. 17). Hence, there are a total of 3 (actual, normal, and std.) × 3 (AC, VC, TC) × 2 (job, process) = 18 basic cost-system combinations.

[4]Section 1.471-11 of the Internal Revenue Code (Inventories of Manufacturers) states that "both direct and indirect production costs must be taken into account in the computation of inventoriable costs in accordance with the 'full absorption' method of inventory costing. . . . Costs are considered to be production costs to the extent that they are incident to and necessary for production or manufacturing operations or processes. Production costs include direct production costs and fixed and variable indirect production costs." Case law is useful to examine when determining the precise boundaries between inventoriable and noninventoriable costs.

Usage of Variable Costing by Companies

Surveys of company practice in many countries report that approximately 30–50% of companies use variable costing in their internal accounting system:

	United States[a]	Canada[a]	Australia[b]	Japan[b]	Sweden[c]	United Kingdom[b]
Variable costing used	31%	48%	33%	31%	42%	52%
Absorption costing used	65	52	67	69	58	48
Other	4	0				

Surveys to date have not examined usage of throughput costing.

Many companies using variable costing for internal reporting also use absorption costing for external reporting or tax reporting. How do companies using variable costing treat fixed manufacturing overhead (MOH) in their internal reporting system?

	Australia	Japan	United Kingdom
Prorate fixed MOH to inventory/cost of goods sold at end of period	41%	39%	25%
Use variable costing for monthly costing, and adjust to absorption costing once a year	11	8	4
Use both variable costing and absorption costing as dual systems	23	33	31
Treat fixed MOH as a period cost	25	3	35
Other	0	17	5

The most common problem reported by companies using variable costing is the difficulty of classifying costs into fixed or variable categories.

[a] Adapted from Inoue, "A Comparative Study."

[b] Adapted from Blayney and Yokoyama, "A Comparative Analysis."

[c] Adapted from Ask and Ax, "Trends."

Full citations are given in Appendix A.

PROBLEM

Assume Stassen Company in January 1, 2000 had another company pre-assemble a large percentage of the components of its telescopes. The revised manufacturing cost structure during the 2000 to 2002 period would have been:

Variable manufacturing costs	
Direct materials costs	$30.50
Direct manufacturing labor costs	2.00
Indirect manufacturing costs	1.00
	$33.50 per unit produced

Fixed manufacturing costs (all indirect) $1,200

This revised cost structure meant that a larger percentage of its manufacturing costs would have been variable with respect to units produced. The budgeted denominator level of production in 2000, 2001, and 2002 is 800 units. Assume no other change from the data underlying Exhibits 9-1 and 9-2. Summary information pertaining to absorption costing and variable costing operating income with this revised cost structure is:

	2000	2001	2002
Absorption costing operating income	$16,800	$18,650	$24,000
Variable costing operating income	16,500	18,875	23,625
Difference	$ 300	$ (225)	$ 375

Required
1. Compute the fixed manufacturing overhead cost rate in 2000, 2001, and 2002?
2. Explain the difference between absorption costing and variable costing operating income in 2000, 2001, and 2002, focusing on fixed manufacturing costs in beginning and ending inventory.
3. Why are the differences in requirement 2 smaller than those in Exhibit 9-2?

SOLUTION

1.

$$\text{Budgeted fixed manufacturing overhead rate} = \frac{\text{Budgeted fixed manufacturing overhead costs}}{\text{Budgeted denominator level}}$$

$$= \frac{\$1,200}{800}$$

$$= \$1.50 \text{ per telescope}$$

2.

$$\left(\begin{array}{c}\text{Absorption-}\\\text{costing}\\\text{operating}\\\text{income}\end{array} - \begin{array}{c}\text{Variable-}\\\text{costing}\\\text{operating}\\\text{income}\end{array}\right) = \left(\begin{array}{c}\text{Fixed manufacturing}\\\text{costs in ending inventory}\\\text{under absorption costing}\end{array} - \begin{array}{c}\text{Fixed manufacturing}\\\text{costs in beginning inventory}\\\text{under absorption costing}\end{array}\right)$$

2000: $16,800 - $16,500 = ($1.50 \times 200) - ($1.50 \times 0)$

$$\$300 = \$300$$

2001: $18,650 - $18,875 = ($1.50 \times 50) - ($1.50 \times 200)$

$$-\$225 = -\$225$$

2002: $24,000 - $23,625 = ($1.50 \times 300) - ($1.50 \times 50)$

$$\$375 = \$375$$

3. The subcontracting of a sizable part of manufacturing has greatly reduced the magnitude of fixed manufacturing overhead costs. This reduction, in turn, means differences between absorption costing and variable costing are much lower than in Exhibits 9-1 and 9-2.

◆ **PART TWO: DENOMINATOR-LEVEL CAPACITY CONCEPTS AND FIXED-COST CAPACITY ANALYSIS**

Determining the "right" level of capacity is one of the most challenging tasks facing managers. Having too much capacity relative to demand means incurring sizable costs related to unused capacity. Having too little capacity means that demand from some customers may be unfilled. These customers may go to other sources of supply and never return. We now consider issues that arise with capacity costs. Our analysis first examines a company that uses the absorption-costing inventory method described in Part One of this chapter. Like all manufacturers, this company must choose a denominator-level capacity concept. We then discuss capacity cost issues for companies not holding inventories. As with Part One of this chapter, the different costs for different purposes theme underlying cost accounting is illustrated in Part Two.

ALTERNATIVE DENOMINATOR-LEVEL CAPACITY CONCEPTS FOR ABSORPTION COSTING

Prior chapters of this book (especially Chapters 4, 5 and 8) have highlighted how normal and standard costing systems enable the reporting of costs in an ongoing timely manner throughout an accounting period. The choice of the denominator used to allocate budgeted fixed manufacturing costs to products can greatly affect the numbers a normal or standard costing system will report during the accounting period.

Consider Bushells Company, which produces 12-ounce bottles of iced tea at its Sydney bottling plant. The annual fixed manufacturing costs of the bottling plant are $5,400,000. It currently uses a standard-cost-based absorption costing system for both internal and external reporting purposes. Bushells expresses its denominator in cases (a case is equivalent to 24 12-ounce bottles of iced tea). We will now examine four different denominator-level capacity concepts for computing the fixed manufacturing overhead rate—theoretical capacity, practical capacity, normal capacity, and master-budget capacity utilization.

Theoretical Capacity and Practical Capacity

The term *capacity* means "constraint," an "upper limit." **Theoretical capacity** is the denominator-level concept that is based on producing at full efficiency all the time. Bushells can produce 10,000 cases of iced tea per shift when the bottling lines are operating at maximum speed. Thus, assuming 360 days per year, the theoretical annual capacity for three 8-hour shifts per day is:

$$10,000 \text{ cases per shift} \times 3 \text{ shifts} \times 360 \text{ days} = 10,800,000 \text{ cases}$$

Theoretical capacity is theoretical in the sense that it does not allow for any plant maintenance, any interruptions because of bottle breakages on the filling lines, or a host of other factors. Ideally, it represents a goal or target or benchmark level of capacity usage. Theoretical capacity is unattainable in the real world.

Practical capacity is the denominator-level concept that reduces theoretical capacity by unavoidable operating interruptions such as scheduled maintenance time, shutdowns for holidays, and so on. Assume that the practical production rate is 8,000 cases per shift and that the plant can operate 300 days a year. The practical annual capacity is thus:

$$8,000 \text{ per shift} \times 3 \text{ shifts} \times 300 \text{ days} = 7,200,000 \text{ cases}$$

Engineering and human resource factors are both important when estimating theoretical or practical capacity. Engineers at the Bushells' plant can provide input on the technical capabilities of machines for filling bottles. Human-safety factors, such as increased injury risk when the line operates at faster speeds, are also important to consider in estimating capacity.

Normal Capacity Utilization and Master-Budget Capacity Utilization

Both theoretical capacity and practical capacity measure the denominator level in terms of what a plant can *supply*. In contrast, normal capacity utilization and master-budget capacity utilization measure the denominator level in terms of *demand* for the output of the plant. In many instances, budgeted demand is well below the production capacity available.

Normal capacity utilization is the denominator-level concept based on the level of capacity utilization that satisfies average customer demand over a time period (say, 2–3 years) that includes seasonal, cyclical, and trend factors. **Master-budget capacity utilization** is the denominator-level concept based on the expected level of capacity utilization for the next budget period (typically one year). These two denominator levels can differ—for example, when an industry has cyclical periods of high and low demand or when management believes that the budgeted production for the coming period is not representative of "long-run" demand.

Consider our Bushells example of iced-tea production. The master budget for 2001 is based on production of 4,000,000 cases per year.[5] Hence the master-budget denominator level is 4,000,000 cases. However, senior management believes that over the next three years the normal annual production level will be 5,000,000 cases. They view 2001's budgeted production level of 4,000,000 cases to be "abnormally" low. Why? Because a major competitor (Tea-Mania) has been sharply reducing its selling price and also spending enormous amounts on advertising. Bushells expects that the lower price and advertising blitz will not be a long-run phenomenon and that in 2002 the market share it has lost to this competitor will be regained.

Effect on Budgeted Fixed Manufacturing Overhead Rate

We now illustrate how use of these four denominator levels can affect the budgeted fixed manufacturing overhead rate. Bushells has budgeted annual fixed manufacturing costs of $5,400,000 in 2001. This $5,400,000 is a lump-sum amount incurred to provide the capacity to bottle iced tea. For example, it includes lease costs for bottling equipment and the compensation of the plant manager. The budgeted fixed manufacturing overhead rates in 2001 for the four alternative denominator-level capacity concepts discussed are:

Points to Stress The object is to get FMOH costs into the individual product costs. The only way to do this is to "unitize" the FMOH costs through a FMOH rate. To do so, we need to choose a denominator volume. This choice is the subject of Part 2 of this chapter. Stress that this choice arises in AC but not VC or throughput costing. Neither VC nor throughput costing unitize FMOH costs since they aren't attached to individual products, but are expensed as a lump sum in the period incurred.

Denominator-Level Capacity Concept (1)	Budgeted Fixed Manufacturing Overhead Per Year (2)	Budgeted Denominator Level (in Cases) (3)	Budgeted Fixed Manufacturing Overhead Cost Rate Per Case (4) = (2) ÷ (3)
Theoretical capacity	$5,400,000	10,800,000	$0.50
Practical capacity	5,400,000	7,200,000	0.75
Normal capacity utilization	5,400,000	5,000,000	1.08
Master-budget capacity utilization	5,400,000	4,000,000	1.35

The budgeted fixed manufacturing overhead rate based on master-budget capacity utilization ($1.35) is 170% above the rate based on theoretical capacity ($0.50).

Decision Making and Denominator-Level Capacity Choices

Cost data from a normal or standard-costing system are often used in pricing or product-emphasis decisions. Consider pricing decisions at Bushells. Standard variable manufacturing costs are $5.20 per case. The total standard manufacturing cost per case with alternative denominator-level capacity concepts are:

Denominator-Level Capacity Concept (1)	Variable Manufacturing Cost Per Case (2)	Budgeted Fixed Manufacturing Overhead Cost Rate Per Case (3)	Total Manufacturing Cost Per Case (4) = (2) + (3)
Theoretical capacity	$5.20	$0.50	$5.70
Practical capacity	5.20	0.75	5.95
Normal capacity utilization	5.20	1.08	6.28
Master-budget capacity utilization	5.20	1.35	6.55

[5]Management plans to run one shift for 300 days in 2001 at a speed of 8,000 cases per shift. A second shift will run for 200 days (in the warmer months) at the same speed of 8,000 cases per shift.

Management often wants to keep plants running at full capacity (which really means at practical capacity). Where product costs are used as guides for pricing, some managers say that choosing practical capacity as the denominator induces lower prices and thus maximizes production volume.

The use of normal capacity utilization or master-budget capacity utilization can result in capacity costs being spread over a small number of output units. The danger here is that high, uncompetitive selling prices may be set. The **downward demand spiral** concept is pertinent in this regard. It is the continuing reduction in demand that occurs when the prices of competitors are not met and demand drops, resulting in even higher unit costs and even more reluctance to meet the prices of competitors.

To illustrate the downward demand spiral, assume Bushells uses master-budget utilization of 4,000,000 cases for product costing in 2001. The resulting manufacturing cost is $6.55 per case ($5.20 variable manufacturing cost + $1.35 fixed manufacturing overhead). Hypothetically, assume a competitor (Lipton Iced Tea) in December 2000 offers to supply a major customer of Bushells (budgeted to purchase 1,000,000 cases in 2001) at $6.25 per case. The Bushells manager, not wanting to show a loss on the account, declines to match the competitor and the account is lost. Budgeted fixed manufacturing costs of $5,400,000 would now be spread over the budgeted volume of 3,000,000 cases at a rate of $1.80 per case ($5,400,000 ÷ 3,000,000 cases). Suppose yet another customer of Bushells—also with 1,000,000 budgeted volume—receives a bid from a competitor at $6.60 per case. Assume again the Bushells manager compares this bid with his revised unit cost of $7.00 ($5.20 + $1.80), declines to match the competition, and the account is lost. The planned output would further shrink to 2,000,000 units. The budgeted fixed manufacturing cost per unit for the remaining 2,000,000 cases would now be $2.70 ($5,400,000 ÷ 2,000,000 cases). The effect of spreading fixed manufacturing costs over a shrinking master-budget capacity utilization amount is as follows:

OBJECTIVE 7

Describe how attempts to recover fixed costs of capacity may lead to a downward demand spiral

Example Using a master budget (MB) denominator level (DL) in conjunction with cost-based pricing can lead to unanticipated consequences. When demand is expected to be low, MB DL is low, so the budgeted FMOH cost rate is high. This leads to higher (cost-based) prices. But is it wise to quote higher prices when demand is weak? Conversely, when demand is expected to be high, MB DL is high, leading to lower budgeted FMOH cost rates and lower cost-based prices. Does mgt. want to quote low prices when demand is strong? Mgt. should carefully consider the consequences of using costs based on MB DL as a basis for setting prices.

Reinforcing Problems Probs. 9-34 and 9-36 cover issues related to the downward demand spiral.

Master-Budget Capacity Denominator Level (Cases) (1)	Variable Manufacturing Cost Per Case (2)	Fixed Manufacturing Cost Allocated Per Case ($5,400,000 ÷ (1)) (3)	Total Manufacturing Cost Per Case (4) = (2) + (3)
4,000,000	$5.20	$1.35	$ 6.55
3,000,000	5.20	1.80	7.00
2,000,000	5.20	2.70	7.90
1,000,000	5.20	5.40	10.60

The preceding hypothetical pricing scenario assumes that pricing decisions at Bushells are heavily influenced by reported unit costs. The relevant cost analysis described in Chapter 11 (see pp. 378–383) should guide pricing decisions. However, a product manager making pricing decisions may find it difficult to explain to others why reported unit costs do not provide a minimum pricing base on an ongoing basis.

The use of theoretical capacity or practical capacity as the denominator-level concept would avoid the restatement of unit costs when expected demand levels change. Managers who use reported unit costs in a relatively mechanical way to set prices are less likely to promote a downward demand spiral with use of the theoretical capacity or practical capacity concepts than with use of the normal capacity or master-budget capacity utilization concepts.

OBJECTIVE 8

Explain how the choice of the denominator level affects the production-volume variance

Effect on Financial Statements

The magnitude of the favorable/unfavorable production-volume variance under absorption costing will be affected by the choice of the denominator level. Return to our Bushells example and assume that actual production in 2001 is 4,400,000 cases of iced tea. Actual sales in 2001 are 4,200,000 cases. Also assume no beginning inventory for 2001 and no price, spending, or efficiency variances in manufacturing costs. Budgeted and actual fixed manufacturing overhead costs are $5,400,000. The average selling price per case of iced tea across all customers is $8.00.

Each denominator-level capacity concept will result in a different production-volume variance:

Points to Stress The higher the denominator level, (1) the lower the budgeted fixed cost rate, (2) the lower the amount of FMOH cost deferred in EI (because of the lower budgeted fixed cost rate), and (3) the higher the U PVV (because the higher the denominator level, the more likely actual output will fall far short).

$$\begin{pmatrix} \text{Production-} \\ \text{volume} \\ \text{variance} \end{pmatrix} = \begin{pmatrix} \text{Denominator} \\ \text{level in} \\ \text{output units} - \begin{matrix}\text{Actual} \\ \text{output} \\ \text{units}\end{matrix} \end{pmatrix} \times \begin{pmatrix} \text{Budgeted fixed} \\ \text{manufacturing} \\ \text{overhead cost rate} \\ \text{per output unit} \end{pmatrix}$$

$$\text{Theoretical capacity} = (10,800,000 - 4,400,000) \times \$0.50$$

$$= \$3,200,000 \text{ U}$$

$$\text{Practical capacity} = (7,200,000 - 4,400,000) \times \$0.75$$

$$= \$2,100,000 \text{ U}$$

$$\text{Normal capacity utilization} = (5,000,000 - 4,400,000) \times \$1.08$$

$$= \$648,000 \text{ U}$$

$$\text{Master-budget capacity utilization} = (4,000,000 - 4,400,000) \times \$1.35$$

$$= \$540,000 \text{ F}$$

How Bushells handles its end-of-period variances will determine the effect these production-volume variances have on the company's end-of-period financial statements.

Chapter 4 (pp. 113–117) discussed three alternative approaches:

1. *Adjusted allocation-rate approach*. This approach restates all amounts in the general ledger by using actual cost rates rather than budgeted cost rates. Given that actual fixed manufacturing overhead costs are $5,400,000 and actual production is 4,400,000 units, the restated fixed manufacturing overhead rate is $1.23 (rounded up to nearest cent) per case. This approach results in the choice of the denominator level having no effect on end-of-period financial statements. In effect, an actual costing system is adopted at the end of the period.

Points to Stress FMOH costs are either expensed in the period incurred or else deferred in EI. Hence, the difference in inventory cost arising because of the different denominator levels exactly equals the differences in OI.

2. *Proration approach*. The under- or overallocated overhead is spread among (a) ending work in process, (b) ending finished goods, and (c) cost of goods sold. This approach restates the ending balances of (a), (b), and (c) to what they would have been had actual cost rates rather than budgeted cost rates been used. This approach also results in the choice of the denominator level having no effect on end-of-period financial statements.

3. *Write-off variances to cost of goods sold approach*. Exhibit 9-7 shows how use of this approach affects Bushells' operating income for 2001. Recall that Bushells had no beginning inventory, production of 4,400,000 cases, and sales of 4,200,000 cases. Hence, the ending inventory on December 31, 2001 is 200,000 cases. Using the master-budget capacity utilization as the denominator results in assigning the highest amount of fixed manufacturing overhead costs per case to the 200,000 cases in ending inventory. Accordingly, operating income is highest using the master-budget capacity utilization concept. The differences in operating income for the four denominator-level concepts in Exhibit 9-7 are due to different amounts of fixed manufacturing overhead being inventoried at the end of 2001:

Teaching Tip If students are confused about the effects on income of different denominator levels, walk them through this chart, Exh. 9-7, or a similar example to clarify the effects of different denominator levels on inventory values and AC OI.

	Fixed Manufacturing Overhead in Dec. 31, 2001 Inventory
Theoretical capacity	200,000 × $0.50 = $100,000
Practical capacity	200,000 × 0.75 = 150,000
Normal capacity utilization	200,000 × 1.08 = 216,000
Master-budget capacity utilization	200,000 × 1.35 = 270,000

EXHIBIT 9-7
Income Statement Effects of Using Alternative Denominator-Level Concepts:
Bushells Company for 2001

	Theoretical Capacity	Practical Capacity	Normal Utilization	Master-Budget Utilization
Capacity in cases	10,800,000	7,200,000	5,000,000	4,000,000
Revenues[a]	$33,600,000	$33,600,000	$33,600,000	$33,600,000
Cost of goods sold				
Beginning inventory	0	0	0	0
Variable manufacturing costs[b]	22,880,000	22,880,000	22,880,000	22,880,000
Fixed manufacturing overhead costs[c]	2,200,000	3,300,000	4,752,000	5,940,000
Cost of goods available for sale	25,080,000	26,180,000	27,632,000	28,820,000
Ending inventory[d]	1,140,000	1,190,000	1,256,000	1,310,000
Total COGS (at standard costs)	23,940,000	24,990,000	26,376,000	27,510,000
Adjustment for manuf. variances[e]	3,200,000 U	2,100,000 U	648,000 U	540,000 F
Total COGS	27,140,000	27,090,000	27,024,000	26,970,000
Gross margin	6,460,000	6,510,000	6,576,000	6,630,000
Operating costs	2,810,000	2,810,000	2,810,000	2,810,000
Operating income	$ 3,650,000	$ 3,700,000	$ 3,766,000	$ 3,820,000

[a] $8.00 × 4,200,000 = $33,600,000
[b] $5.20 × 4,400,000 = $22,880,000
[c] Fixed manufacturing overhead costs:
  $0.50 × 4,400,000 = $2,200,000
  $0.75 × 4,400,000 = $3,300,000
  $1.08 × 4,400,000 = $4,752,000
  $1.35 × 4,400,000 = $5,940,000
[d] Ending inventory costs
  ($5.20 + $0.50) × 200,000 = $1,140,000
  ($5.20 + $0.75) × 200,000 = $1,190,000
  ($5.20 + $1.08) × 200,000 = $1,256,000
  ($5.20 + $1.35) × 200,000 = $1,310,000
[e] See text (p. 261) for computation of the production-volume variance.

Thus, in Exhibit 9-7, the $54,000 difference ($3,820,000 − $3,766,000) in operating income between the master-budet capacity utilization concept and the normal capacity utilization concept is due to the difference in fixed manufacturing overhead inventoried ($270,000 − $216,000).

New in This Edition This section on Choosing a Denominator-Level Capacity Concept is new to this edition. It covers the effects of denominator level choice on decision making and IRS requirements.

CHOOSING A DENOMINATOR-LEVEL CAPACITY CONCEPT

There is no requirement that companies use the same denominator-level capacity concept for, say, management planning and control, for external reporting to shareholders, and for income tax purposes. Individual factors management considers in making a choice for a specific purpose include effects on decisions, regulatory requirements, and difficulties in forecasting. The overall guideline is the cost-benefit approach. This approach could include analysis of the costs of record keeping and educating managers, the motivational impact of choices on managers, and the sharing of rewards between managers and other parties.

Effects on Decision Making

A central consideration in the choice of a denominator level is the effect on management planning and control decisions. The effect on pricing decisions has already been discussed in this chapter (pp. 305–306). Consider now performance evaluation and the choice between normal capacity utilization and master-budget capacity

"Stranded Costs" of Electric-Utility Companies and Fixed Manufacturing Overhead Rates

For many years, the U.S. electricity-generating industry was highly regulated. Individual utility companies operated as natural monopolies in designated geographical areas. It was a relatively safe ("cozy") environment in which utilities made very large investments in plant and equipment. State regulators would permit utility companies to include two costs related to the plant and equipment in the cost buildup used to determine the allowable electricity prices:

◆ Depreciation (a return of capital)
◆ Capital charge (a return on capital)

Both the depreciation and the capital charge were based on the historical cost of building the plant and equipment. This cost-buildup approach to setting utility prices encouraged utility companies to construct capacity for the long-run with a high level of certainty their investment would be returned via increased selling prices.

Deregulation of the U.S. electric-utility industry in the late 1990s dramatically changed this "cozy" environment. Enter the cold chilling winds of competition in an industry with much excess capacity! Customers now could purchase electricity from many different utility companies. Economics 101 would predict that the book values of many electric utilities for their plant and equipment were no longer economically justified. Indeed, the phrase *stranded costs* was coined to describe existing investments in plant and equipment that will be unprofitable after electricity markets are deregulated. Industry studies estimate that total stranded costs of U.S. utilities could be $50 billion or more.

Individual utilities are exploring alternative ways to write down the book values of their plant and equipment. For example, Commonwealth Edison (a Chicago-based utility) took several steps. It closed its Zion Nuclear Station and took a $523 million write-off of its book value. It also transferred $6 billion out of its plant book values to a separate company so that the written-down book values better reflected capacity cost charges in the new deregulated era. The net result was a large reduction in the numerator used to compute its fixed capacity cost per kilowat-hour of electricity produced.

An executive of a northeastern U.S. utility commented that utility plant managers would be more motivated toward achieving cost reduction and profitability targets if the depreciation cost component reflected book values in a deregulated environment. He noted that the depreciation charges on plant book values existing in the regulated environment "overwhelmed those costs that were controllable in the current period."

Source: Industry newsletters, analysts reports, and conversations with management.

utilization. Normal capacity is often used as a basis for long-run plans. It depends on the time span selected, the forecasts made for each year, and the weighting of these forecasts. *However, normal volume is an average that has no particular significance with respect to feedback for a particular year.* Attempting to use normal capacity utilization as a reference point for judging current performance is an example of misusing a long-run measure for a short-run purpose. The master-budget capacity utilization, rather than normal capacity utilization or practical capacity, is more germane to the evaluation of current results. The master budget is the principal short-run planning and control tool. Managers feel much more obligated to reach the levels stipulated in the master budget, which should have been carefully set in relation to the maximum opportunities for sales in the current year.

New in This Edition The Concepts in Action box is new to this edition. It discusses the choices deregulated utilities face in choosing both numerator costs and denominator-level capacity for computing FMOH rates.

Where large differences exist between practical capacity and master-budget capacity utilization, several companies (such as Texas Instruments) classify part of this difference as planned unused capacity. A key reason for this approach is performance evaluation. Consider again our Bushells iced-tea example. The manager(s) in charge of capacity planning frequently does not also make pricing decisions. Top management decided to build an iced-tea plant with 7,200,000 cases of practical capacity. Their focus was on demand over the next five years. In contrast, it is Bushells' marketing managers—middle management—who make pricing decisions. These marketing executives believe that they should only be held accountable for manufacturing overhead costs related to their potential customer base in 2001. Assume the maximum potential customer base in 2001 is 5,760,000 cases (80% of the 7,200,000 practical capacity). Using responsibility accounting principles (see Chapter 6, pp. 194–196), only 80% of the numerator ($5,400,000 × 0.80 = $4,320,000) would be attributed to the fixed capacity costs of meeting 2001 demand. The remaining 20% of the numerator ($1,080,000) would be separately charged as the capacity cost of meeting long-run demand increases expected to occur beyond 2001.[6]

Regulatory Requirements and Cost Benefit

For tax reporting purposes in the United States, the IRS requires companies to use the practical capacity concept. At year-end, proration of any variances between inventories and cost of good sold is required (unless the variance is immaterial in amount).[7]

Difficulties in Forecasting Chosen Denominator-Level Concept

The practical capacity concept measures the available supply of capacity. Managers can usually use engineering studies and human resource considerations (such as worker safety) to obtain a reliable estimate of this concept for the budget period.[8] In contrast, it is more difficult to estimate normal utilization reliably. For example, many U.S. steel companies in the 1980s believed they were in the downturn of a demand cycle that would have an upturn within two or three years. After all, steel had been a cyclical business in which upturns followed downturns, making the notion of *normal utilization* appear reasonable. Unfortunately, the steel cycle in the 1980s did not turn up for some companies and numerous plants closed. Some marketing managers are prone to overestimate their ability to regain lost sales (and market share). Their estimate of "normal" demand for their product may be based on an overly optimistic outlook ("anticipating roses where only thorns exist"). Master-budget capacity utilization typically focuses only on the expected capacity utilization for the next year. This concept can be more reliably estimated than can the normal capacity utilization concept.

CAPACITY COSTS AND DENOMINATOR-LEVEL ISSUES

We now consider several additional factors that affect the planning and control of capacity costs.

[6]For further discussion, see T. Klammer, *Capacity Measurement and Improvement* (Chicago: Irwin, 1996). This research was facilitated by CAM-I, an organization promoting innovative cost management practices. CAM-I's research on capacity costs explores ways in which companies can identify types of capacity costs that can be reduced (eliminated) without affecting the required output to meet customer demand. An example is the costs of capacity existing in anticipation of handling difficulties due to imperfect coordination with suppliers and customers.

[7]U.S. tax reporting requires the use of either the adjusted allocation-rate approach or the proration approach. Section 1.471-11 of the Internal Revenue Code states: "The proper use of the standard cost method requires that a taxpayer must reallocate to the goods in ending inventory a pro rata portion of any net negative or net positive overhead variances" (p. 421).

[8]Practical capacity need not be constant over time. For example, improvements in plant layout and increases in worker efficiency both can result in sizable increases in practical capacity for the same plant over time.

1. Costing systems, such as normal costing or standard costing, do not recognize uncertainty in the way managers do. A single amount rather than a range of possible amounts is used as the denominator level in absorption costing. Yet managers face uncertainty about demand (and even their own supply capability). Consider Bushells again. Its plant has estimated practical capacity of 7,200,000 cases. The estimated master-budget capacity utilization for 2001 is 4,000,000 cases. These estimates are uncertain. Managers recognize this uncertainty in their capacity planning decisions. Bushells built its current 7,200,000-case practical capacity in part to provide the capability to meet possible demand surges. Even if these demand surges do not occur in a given period, it is erroneous to conclude all capacity not used in a given period is wasted resources. The gains from being able to meet sudden demand surges may well require having unused capacity in some periods.

2. The fixed manufacturing overhead cost rate is based on a numerator (budgeted fixed manufacturing overhead costs) and a denominator level. Our discussion to date has emphasized issues with the choice of the denominator level. The Concepts in Action box (p. 309) discusses challenging issues in measuring the numerator for electric utility companies. This example also highlights how the capacity cost issues discussed in Part Two of this chapter apply to all companies with manufacturing operations, irrespective of whether they hold inventories.

3. Capacity costs arise in nonmanufacturing parts of the value chain as well as with the manufacturing costs emphasized in this chapter. For example, Bushells may acquire a fleet of vehicles that is capable of distributing the practical capacity of its iced-tea plant. When actual production is below the practical capacity, there will be unused capacity cost issues with the distribution function as well as with the manufacturing function.

Curriculum Linkage/Example The choice of the amount of capacity to build is a decision which "locks-in" costs at the design phase of a product's life cycle (see Chap. 12 for a discussion of locked-in costs). Capacity costs are sometimes referred to as structural cost drivers (i.e., the choice of a cost structure drives these costs for long periods of time).

Example The example of a university adding capacity by building a new building is relevant for students. The new building increases the capacity of the university to offer classes at a given time. But there is a substantial amount of unused capacity in a university building (e.g., between 10:00 p.m. and 6:00 a.m. every day, on weekends, during summer, winter, and spring breaks, etc.).

PROBLEM FOR SELF-STUDY

PROBLEM

Suppose that Bushells Company is computing the operating income for 1999. This year is identical to 2001, the results of which are shown in Exhibit 9-7, except that master-budget capacity utilization for 1999 is 6,000,000 cases instead of 4,000,000 cases. Production in 1999 is 4,400,000 units. There is no beginning inventory on January 1, 1999, and no variances other than the production-volume variance. Bushells writes off this variance to cost of goods sold. Sales in 1999 are 4,200,000 units.

Required

How would the results for Bushells Company in Exhibit 9-7 differ if the year is 1999 rather than 2001? Show your computations.

SOLUTION

The only change in the Exhibit 9-7 results will be for the master-budget capacity utilization level. The budgeted fixed manufacturing overhead cost rate for 1999 is:

$$\frac{\$5,400,000}{6,000,000 \text{ cases}} = \$0.90 \text{ per case}$$

The manufacturing cost per case becomes $6.10 ($5.20 + $0.90). In turn, the production-volume variance for 1999 becomes:

$$(6,000,000 - 4,400,000) \times \$0.90 = \$1,440,000$$

The income statement for 1999 is now

Revenues: $8.00 \times 4,200,000$	$33,600,000
Cost of goods sold	
Beginning inventory	0
Variable manufacturing costs: $5.20 \times 4,400,000$	22,880,000
Fixed manufacturing costs: $0.90 \times 4,400,000$	3,960,000
Cost of goods available for sale	26,840,000
Ending inventory: $6.10 \times 200,000$	1,220,000
Cost of goods sold (at standard costs)	25,620,000
Adjustment for variances	1,440,000 U
Cost of goods sold	27,060,000
Gross margin	6,540,000
Operating costs	2,810,000
Operating income	$ 3,730,000

The higher denominator level in the 1999 master budget means that less fixed manufacturing overhead costs are inventoried in 1999 than in 2001, given identical sales and production levels and assuming all variances are written off to cost of goods sold.

Points to Stress The VC and AC procedures discussed in the text aren't dichotomous choices. They're intermediate points on a continuum that also includes "super-variable" throughput costing (where only DM are inventoried), "super-full-absorption" costing (where mfg.-related administrative costs are attached to products for tax purposes), and full product costs (where costs from all areas of the value chain are attached to products—e.g., for long-term pricing decisions, as in Chap. 12).

SUMMARY

The following points are linked to the chapter's learning objectives:

1. Variable costing and absorption costing differ in only one respect: how to account for fixed manufacturing costs. Under variable costing, fixed manufacturing costs are excluded from inventoriable costs and are a cost of the period in which they are incurred. Under absorption costs, these costs are inventoriable and become a part of cost of goods sold in the period when sales occur.

2. The variable-costing income statement is based on the contribution-margin format. The absorption-costing income statement is based on the gross-margin format.

3. Under variable costing, reported operating income is driven by the unit level of sales. Under absorption costing, reported operating income is driven by the unit level of production as well as by the unit level of sales.

4. Managers can increase operating income when absorption costing is used by producing more units. Critics of absorption costing label this potential outcome as the major negative consequence of treating fixed manufacturing overhead as an inventoriable cost.

5. Throughput costing treats all costs except those related to variable direct materials as costs of the period in which they are incurred. Throughput costing results in a lower amount of manufacturing costs being inventoried than does either variable costing or absorption costing.

6. Denominator levels focusing on the capacity of a plant to *supply* product are theoretical capacity and practical capacity. Denominator levels focusing on the *demand* for the products a plant can manufacture are normal capacity utilization and master-budget capacity utilization.

7. Companies with high fixed costs and unused capacity may encounter ongoing and increasingly greater reductions in demand if they continue to raise selling prices to fully recover variable and fixed costs from a declining sales base. This phenomenon has been termed the downward demand spiral.

8. When the chosen denominator-level concept exceeds (or is less than) the actual production level, there will be an unfavorable (favorable) production-volume variance. Typically, the chosen denominator-level concept exceeds the actual production most when the theoretical capacity concept is used.

APPENDIX: BREAKEVEN POINTS IN VARIABLE COSTING AND ABSORPTION COSTING

Reinforcing Problems Exer. 9-26 and Probs. 9-28 and 9-29 cover AC and BE analysis.

Chapter 3 introduced cost-volume-profit analysis. If variable costing is used, the breakeven point (operating income of $0) is computed in the usual manner. There is only one breakeven point in this case, and it is a function of (1) fixed costs, (2) contribution margin per unit, and (3) unit level of sales. Holding (1) and (2) constant, operating income rises as the unit level of sales rises, and vice versa.

The formula for computing the breakeven point with variable costing is a special case of the more general target operating income formula from Chapter 3 (p. 65):

$$QT = \frac{\text{Total fixed costs} + \text{Target operating income}}{\text{Contribution margin per unit}}$$

$$= \text{Number of units sold to earn the target operating income}$$

Breakeven occurs when the target operating income is $0. In our Stassen illustration for 2001 (see pp. 293–294):

Correcting Student Misconceptions Remind students that when they calculate BEP, all FC (not just FMOH costs) must be covered.

$$QT = \frac{(\$12,000 + \$10,800) + \$0}{\$100 - (\$20 + \$19)} = \frac{\$22,800}{\$61}$$

$$= 374 \text{ units (rounded)}[9]$$

If absorption costing is used, the required number of units sold to achieve a specific target operating income is not unique because of the number of variables involved. The following formula highlights the factors that will affect the target operating income under absorption costing:

Points to Stress The formula shows that under AC, there's a unique (different) BEP for each different # of units produced. Also, there's an inverse relation between the # of units produced and the # sold to break even. The more units produced, the more FMOH costs AC defers in EI, and the fewer sales needed to break even.

$$QT = \frac{\begin{array}{c}\text{Total} \\ \text{fixed} \\ \text{costs}\end{array} + \begin{array}{c}\text{Target} \\ \text{operating} \\ \text{income}\end{array} + \left[\begin{array}{c}\text{Fixed} \\ \text{manufacturing} \\ \text{cost rate}\end{array} \times \left(\begin{array}{c}\text{Breakeven} \\ \text{sales} \\ \text{in units}\end{array} - \begin{array}{c}\text{Units} \\ \text{produced}\end{array}\right)\right]}{\text{Contribution margin per unit}}$$

This formula has three terms in the numerator compared to two terms in the numerator of the QT variable-costing formula stated earlier. The extra term added to the numerator under absorption costing is:

$$\left[\begin{array}{c}\text{Fixed manufacturing} \\ \text{cost rate}\end{array} \times \left(\begin{array}{c}\text{Breakeven sales} \\ \text{in units}\end{array} - \begin{array}{c}\text{Units} \\ \text{produced}\end{array}\right)\right]$$

This term captures the additional amount of target operating income in the numerator due to absorption costing moving fixed manufacturing costs to inventory from

[9]Proof of breakeven point:

Revenues, $100 × 374	$37,400
Variable costs, $39 × 374	14,586
Contribution margin, $61 × 374	22,814
Fixed costs	22,800
Operating income	$ 14

Operating income is not $0 because the breakeven number of units is rounded up to 374 from 373.78.

cost of goods sold under variable costing for all units produced that exceed the breakeven sales quantity. The breakeven point is defined as the quantity for which the target operating income is $0. Consider Stassen Company in 2001. One breakeven point under absorption costing for production of 500 units is:

$$QT = \frac{(\$12{,}000 + \$10{,}800) + \$0 + [\$15(QT - 500)]}{\$100 - (\$20 + \$19)}$$

$$= \frac{\$22{,}800 + \$15QT - \$7{,}500}{\$61}$$

$$\$61QT = \$15{,}300 + \$15QT$$

$$\$46QT = \$15{,}300$$

$$QT = 333 \text{ (rounded)}[10]$$

Example Given the mfg., marketing, and admin. costs in the text's Stassen example, how many units must be produced to break even with zero sales (if all UAO/OAO is written off to CGS)?

$0 = [(\$12{,}000 + \$10{,}800) + \$15(0 - UP)]/[\$100 - (\$20 + \$19)]$
UP = 1,520 units produced
Check:

Revenue	$ 0	
Regular CGS	$ 0	
Overallocated FMOH		
(800 − 1,520)($15)	10,800	10,800
Gross margin		$10,800
Less fixed mkt. exp.		(10,800)
Op. Income		$ 0

The breakeven point under absorption costing depends on (1) fixed costs, (2) contribution margin per unit, (3) unit level of sales, (4) unit level of production, and (5) the denominator-level capacity concept chosen to set the fixed manufacturing overhead cost rate. For Stassen in 2001, a combination of 333 units sold, 500 units produced, and an 800-unit denominator level would result in an operating income of $0. Note, however, that there are many combinations of these five factors that would give an operating income of $0. For example, a combination of 284 units sold, 650 units produced, and an 800-unit denominator level also results in an operating income of $0 under absorption costing.

Suppose in our illustration that actual production in 2001 were equal to the denominator level, 800 units. Also suppose that there were no units sold and no fixed operating costs. All the production would be placed in inventory, and so all the fixed manufacturing overhead would be included in inventory. There would be no production-volume variance. Thus, the company could break even with no sales whatsoever! In contrast, under variable costing the operating loss would be equal to the fixed costs of $12,000.

▼ TERMS TO LEARN

This chapter and the Glossary at the end of the book contain definitions of the following important terms:

absorption costing (p. 290)	practical capacity (304)
direct costing (293)	super-variable costing (299)
downward demand spiral (306)	theoretical capacity (304)
master-budget capacity utilization (304)	throughput costing (299)
normal capacity utilization (304)	variable costing (290)

[10] Proof of breakeven point:

Revenues, $100 × 333		$33,300
Cost of goods sold		
Cost of goods sold, $35 × 333	$11,655	
Production-volume variance, $15 × (800 − 500)	4,500	16,155
Gross margin		17,145
Operating costs		
Variable operating costs, $19 × 333	6,327	
Fixed operating costs	10,800	17,127
Operating income		$ 18

Operating income is not $0 because the breakeven number of units is rounded up to 333 from 332.61.

QUESTIONS

9-1 Differences in operating income between variable costing and absorption costing are due solely to accounting for fixed costs. Do you agree? Explain.

9-2 Why is the term *direct costing* a misnomer?

9-3 Do companies in either the service sector or the merchandising sector make choices about absorption costing versus variable costing?

9-4 Explain the main conceptual issue under variable costing and absorption costing regarding the proper timing for the release of fixed manufacturing overhead as expense.

9-5 "Companies that make no variable-cost/fixed-cost distinctions must use absorption costing and those that do make variable-cost/fixed-cost distinctions must use variable costing." Do you agree? Explain.

9-6 The main trouble with variable costing is that it ignores the increasing importance of fixed costs in manufacturing companies. Do you agree? Why?

9-7 Give an example of how, under absorption costing, operating income could fall even though the unit sales level rises.

9-8 What are the factors that affect the breakeven point under (a) variable costing, and (b) absorption costing?

9-9 Critics of absorption costing have increasingly emphasized its potential for leading to undesirable incentives for managers. Give an example.

9-10 What are two ways of reducing the negative aspects associated with using absorption costing to evaluate the performance of a plant manager?

9-11 What denominator-level capacity concepts emphasize what a plant can supply? What denominator-level capacity concepts emphasize what customers demand for products produced by a plant?

9-12 Describe the downward demand spiral and its implications for pricing decisions.

9-13 Will the financial statements of a company always differ when different choices at the start of the period are made regarding the denominator-level capacity concept?

9-14 What is the IRS's requirement for tax reporting regarding the choice of a denominator-level capacity concept?

9-15 "The difference between practical capacity and master-budget capacity utilization is the best measure of management's ability to balance the costs of having too much capacity and having too little capacity." Do you agree? Explain.

EXERCISES

9-16 Variable and absorption costing, explaining operating income differences. Nascar Motors assembles and sells motor vehicles. Data relating to April and May of 2000 are:

	April	May
Unit data		
Beginning inventory	0	150
Production	500	400
Sales	350	520
Variable costs		
Manufacturing costs per unit produced	$ 10,000	$ 10,000
Operating costs per unit sold	3,000	3,000
Fixed costs		
Manufacturing costs	$2,000,000	$2,000,000
Operating costs	600,000	600,000

The selling price per motor vehicle is $24,000.

Required

1. Present income statements for Nascar Motors in April and May of 2000 under (a) variable costing, and (b) absorption costing.

2. Prepare a numerical reconciliation and explanation of the difference between operating income for each year under absorption costing and variable costing.

9-17 Throughput costing (continuation of Exercise 9-16). The unit variable manufacturing costs of Nascar Motors are:

	April	May
Direct materials	$6,700	$6,700
Direct manufacturing labor	1,500	1,500
Manufacturing overhead	1,800	1,800

Required

1. Present income statements for Nascar Motors in April and May of 2000 under throughput costing.
2. Contrast the results in requirement 1 with those in requirement 1 of Exercise 9-16.
3. Give one motivation for Nascar Motors adopting throughput costing.

9-18 Variable and absorption costing, explaining operating income differences. BigScreen Corporation manufactures and sells 50-inch television sets. Data relating to January, February, and March of 2001 are:

	January	February	March
Unit data			
Beginning inventory	0	300	300
Production	1,000	800	1,250
Sales	700	800	1,500
Variable costs			
Manufacturing costs per unit produced	$ 900	$ 900	$ 900
Operating costs per unit sold	600	600	600
Fixed costs			
Manufacturing costs	$400,000	$400,000	$400,000
Operating costs	140,000	140,000	140,000

The selling price per unit is $2,500.

Required

1. Present income statements for BigScreen in January, February, and March of 2001 under (a) variable costing, and (b) absorption costing.
2. Explain differences between (a) and (b) for January, February, and March.

9-19 Throughput costing (continuation of Exercise 9-18). The unit variable manufacturing costs of BigScreen Corporation are:

	January	February	March
Direct materials	$500	$500	$500
Direct manufacturing labor	100	100	100
Manufacturing overhead	300	300	300
	$900	$900	$900

Required

1. Present income statements for BigScreen in January, February, and March of 2001 under throughput costing.
2. Contrast the results in requirement 1 with those in requirement 1 of Exercise 9-18.
3. Give one motivation for Big Screen adopting throughput costing.

9-20 Variable vs. absorption costing. The Zwatch Company manufactures trendy, high-quality moderately priced watches. As Zwatch's senior financial analyst, you are asked to recommend a method of inventory costing. The CFO will use your recommendation to construct Zwatch's 2001 income statement. The following data are for the year ended December 31, 2001:

Beginning inventory, January 1 2001	85,000 units
Ending inventory, December 31 2001	34,500 units
2001 sales	345,400 units
Selling price (to distributor)	$22.00 per unit
Variable manufacturing cost per unit, including direct materials	$5.10 per unit
Variable operating cost per unit sold	$1.10 per unit sold
Fixed manufacturing overhead	$1,440,000
Denominator-level machine-hours	6,000
Standard production rate	50 units per machine-hour
Fixed operating costs	$1,080,000

Assume standard unit costs are constant. Also, assume no price, spending, or efficiency variances.

Required

1. Prepare income statements under variable and absorption costing for the year ended December 31, 2001.
2. What are Zwatch's operating incomes under each costing method (in percentage terms)?
3. Explain the difference in operating income between the two methods.
4. Which costing method would you recommend to the CFO? Why?

9-21 Absorption and variable costing. (CMA) Osawa, Inc., planned and actually manufactured 200,000 units of its single product in 2001, its first year of operation. Variable manufacturing costs were $20 per unit produced. Variable operating costs were $10 per unit sold. Planned and actual fixed manufacturing costs were $600,000. Planned and actual operating costs totaled $400,000 in 2001. Osawa sold 120,000 units of product in 2001 at a selling price of $40 per unit.

Required

1. Osawa's 2001 operating income using absorption costing is (a) $440,000, (b) $200,000, (c) $600,000, (d) $840,000, (e) none of these.
2. Osawa's 2001 operating income using variable costing is (a) $800,000, (b) $440,000, (c) $200,000, (d) $600,000, (e) none of these.

9-22 Absorption vs. variable costing. Sonnenheim Bamberger is a German pharmaceutical company that produces a single drug—Mimic™—for the treatment of hair loss in men. Sonnenheim began commercial production of Mimic™ on January 1, 2001. Patients use three pills per day (365 days a year). Sonnenheim marketing analysts estimate 50,000 patients will use Mimic™ in 2001. Production in 2001 is 54,750,000 units (pills). However, only 44,800 patients are prescribed Mimic™ during 2001. Each patient used three pills per day for 365 days a year. The average wholesale selling price (the price Sonnenheim receives from distributors) is $1.20 per pill. Sonnenheim's actual costs are as follows:

Variable costs per unit	
Manufacturing costs *per pill produced*	
Direct materials	$0.05
Direct manufacturing labor	0.04
Manufacturing overhead	0.11
Marketing costs *per pill sold*	0.07
Fixed costs	
Manufacturing costs	$ 7,358,400
R&D	4,905,600
Marketing	19,622,400

Required

1. What is the number of Mimic™ pills actually sold in 2001, assuming all patients began using the drug on January 1 and used it through December 31? What is ending inventory on December 31, 2001?

2. Calculate operating income under variable costing and absorption costing for Sonnenheim Bamberger for the year ended December 31, 2001. The allocation base for fixed manufacturing costs under absorption costing is $0.15 per unit (pill) produced. All variances are written off to cost of goods sold.
3. Explain differences in operating income in requirement 2.

9-23 Throughput costing (continuation of Exercise 9-22). Sonnenheim is concerned with the inventory buildup in 2001. It receives advice from a consultant to use throughput costing.

Required
1. Calculate operating income under throughput costing for the year ended December 31, 2001.
2. Why might use of throughput costing reduce inventory buildup?

9-24 Comparison of actual-costing methods. The Rehe Company sells its razors at $3 per unit. The company uses a first-in, first-out actual-costing system. A new fixed manufacturing overhead rate is computed each year by dividing the actual fixed manufacturing overhead cost by the actual production units. The following simplified data are related to its first two years of operation:

	2000	2001
Sales	1,000 units	1,200 units
Production	1,400 units	1,000 units
Costs:		
Variable manufacturing	$ 700	$ 500
Fixed manufacturing	700	700
Variable operating	1,000	1,200
Fixed operating	400	400

Required
1. Prepare income statements based on variable costing for each of the two years.
2. Prepare income statements based on absorption costing for each of the two years.
3. Prepare a numerical reconciliation and explanation of the difference between operating income for each year under absorption costing and variable costing.
4. Critics have claimed that a widely used accounting system has led to undesirable buildups of inventory levels. (a) Is variable costing or absorption costing more likely to lead to such buildups? Why? (b) What can be done to counteract undesirable inventory buildups?

9-25 Denominator-level problem. The Spalding Sails company produces the Spalding 26, a very popular 26-foot recreational yacht. Spalding Sails takes pride in the high quality they build into their affordable yachts. The company has been in business for 35 years. Management has recently adopted absorption costing and is debating which denominator-level concept to use. The Spalding 26 sells for an average price of $15,000. Budgeted fixed manufacturing overhead for 2001 is estimated at $3,800,000. Spalding uses subassembly operators that provide component parts. Assume for simplicity each yacht can be started and completed in a single shift. The following are the denominator-level options that management has been considering:

a. Theoretical capacity—based on 2 shifts, completion of 4 boats per shift, and a 360-day year—2 × 4 × 360 = 2,880.

b. Practical capacity—theoretical capacity adjusted for unavoidable interruptions, breakdowns, etc—2 × 3 × 300 = 1,800.

c. Normal capacity utilization—based on the Marketing Department's estimate of 1,000 units.

d. Master-budget capacity utilization—the booming stock market and a record number of baby boomers retiring over the coming year has prompted the Marketing Department to issue a special estimate for 2001 of 1,200 units.

Required
1. Calculate the budgeted fixed manufacturing overhead cost rates under the four alternative denominator-level concepts.

2. Why compute fixed costs at the individual product level? Why is this only done under absorption costing?
3. Why would Spalding Sails prefer to use either theoretical or practical capacity?
4. Under a cost-based pricing system, what is the negative aspect of a master-budget denominator level? What may be the positive aspect?

9-26 Variable and absorption costing and breakeven points (chapter appendix). Shasta Hills, a winery in northern California, manufactures a premium cabernet and sells primarily to distributors. Wine is sold in cases of one dozen bottles. In the year ended December 31, 2001, Shasta Hills sold 242,400 cases at an average selling price of $94 per case. The following additional data are for Shasta Hills for the year ended December 31, 2001 (assume constant unit costs and no price, spending or efficiency variances):

Beginning inventory, January 1, 2001	32,600 cases
Ending inventory, December 31, 2001	24,800 cases
Fixed manufacturing overhead	$3,753,600
Fixed operating costs	$6,568,800
Variable costs	
Direct materials	
Grapes	$16 per case
Bottles, corks, and crates	$10 per case
Direct labor	
Bottling	$6 per case
Winemaking	$14 per case
Aging	$2 per case

On December 31, 2000 the costs per case for ending inventory are $46 for variable costing and $61 for absorption costing.

Required
1. Calculate cases of production for Shasta Hills in 2001.
2. Find the breakeven point (number of cases) in 2001
   a. under variable costing
   b. under absorption costing
3. Grape prices are expected to increase 25% in 2002. Assuming all other data remain constant, calculate the minimum number of cases Shasta Hills must sell in 2002 to break even:
   a. under variable costing
   b. under absorption costing

PROBLEMS

9-27 Variable costing versus absorption costing. The Mavis Company uses an absorption-costing system based on standard costs. Total variable manufacturing costs, including direct materials costs, are $3 per unit; the standard production rate is 10 units per machine-hour. Total budgeted and actual fixed manufacturing overhead costs are $420,000. Fixed manufacturing overhead is allocated at $7 per machine-hour ($420,000 ÷ 60,000 machine-hours of denominator level). Selling price is $5 per unit. Variable operating costs, which are driven by units sold, are $1 per unit. Fixed operating costs are $120,000. Beginning inventory in 2001 is 30,000 units; ending inventory is 40,000 units. Sales in 2001 are 540,000 units. The same standard unit costs persisted throughout 2000 and 2001. For simplicity, assume that there are no price, spending, or efficiency variances.

Required
1. Prepare an income statement for 2001 assuming that all under- or overallocated overhead is written off at year-end as an adjustment to Cost of Goods Sold.
2. The president has heard about variable costing. She asks you to recast the 2001 statement as it would appear under variable costing.
3. Explain the difference in operating income as calculated in requirements 1 and 2.

4. Graph how fixed manufacturing overhead is accounted for under absorption costing. That is, there will be two lines—one for the budgeted fixed overhead (which is equal to the actual fixed manufacturing overhead in this case) and one for the fixed overhead allocated. Show how the over- or underallocated manufacturing overhead might be indicated on the graph.

5. Critics have claimed that a widely used accounting system has led to undesirable buildups of inventory levels. (a) Is variable costing or absorption costing more likely to lead to such buildups? Why? (b) What can be done to counteract undesirable inventory buildups?

9-28 Breakeven under absorption costing (chapter appendix). Refer to Problem 9-27.

Required
1. Compute the breakeven point (in units) under variable costing.
2. Compute the breakeven point (in units) under absorption costing.
3. Suppose that production is exactly equal to the denominator level, but no units are sold. Fixed manufacturing costs are unaffected. Assume, however, that all operating costs are avoided. Compute operating income under (a) variable costing, and (b) absorption costing. Explain the difference between your answers.

9-29 The All-Fixed Company in 2001. (R. Marple, adapted) It is the end of 2001. The All-Fixed Company began operations in January 2000. The company is so named because it has no variable costs. All its costs are fixed; they do not vary with output.

The All-Fixed Company is located on the bank of a river and has its own hydroelectric plant to supply power, light, and heat. The company manufactures a synthetic fertilizer from air and river water and sells its product at a price that is not expected to change. It has a small staff of employees, all hired on a fixed annual salary. The output of the plant can be increased or decreased by adjusting a few dials on a control panel.

The following data are for the operations of the All-Fixed Company:

	2000	2001*
Sales	10,000 tons	10,000 tons
Production	20,000 tons	—
Selling price	$30 per ton	$30 per ton
Costs (all fixed):		
Manufacturing	$280,000	$280,000
Operating	$40,000	$40,000

*Management adopted the policy, effective January 1, 2001, of producing only as much product as was needed to fill sales orders. During 2001, sales were the same as for 2000 and were filled entirely from inventory at the start of 2001.

Required
1. Prepare income statements with one column for 2000, one column for 2001, and one column for the two years together, using (a) variable costing, and (b) absorption costing.
2. What is the breakeven point under (a) variable costing, and (b) absorption costing?
3. What inventory costs would be carried in the balance sheet on December 31, 2000 and 2001, under each method?
4. Assume that the performance of the top manager of the company is evaluated and rewarded largely on the basis of reported operating income. Which costing method would the manager prefer? Why?

9-30 The Semi-Fixed Company in 2001 (continuation of Problem 9-29). The Semi-Fixed Company began operations in 2000 and differs from the All-Fixed Company (described in Problem 9-29) in only one respect: It has both variable and fixed manufacturing costs. Its variable manufacturing costs are $7 per ton and its fixed manufacturing costs are $140,000 per year. The denominator level is 20,000 tons per year.

Required
1. Using the same data as in Problem 9-29 except for the change in manufacturing cost behavior, prepare income statements with adjacent columns for 2000, 2001, and the two years combined,

a. under variable costing

b. under absorption costing

2. Why did the Semi-Fixed Company have operating income for the two-year period when the All-Fixed Company in Problem 9-29 suffered an operating loss?

3. What inventory costs would be carried in the balance sheet at December 31, 2000 and 2001, under each method?

4. Assume that the performance of the top manager of the company is evaluated and rewarded largely on the basis of reported operating income. Which costing method would the manager prefer? Why?

9-31 Comparison of variable costing and absorption costing. Consider the following data:

Hinkle Company
Income Statements for the Year Ended December 31, 2000

	Variable Costing	Absorption Costing
Revenues	$7,000,000	$7,000,000
Cost of goods sold (at standard)	3,660,000	4,575,000
Fixed manufacturing overhead	1,000,000	—
Manufacturing variances (all unfavorable):		
Direct materials price and efficiency	50,000	50,000
Direct manufacturing labor price and efficiency	60,000	60,000
Variable manufacturing overhead spending and efficiency	30,000	30,000
Fixed manufacturing overhead:		
Spending	100,000	100,000
Production volume	—	400,000
Total marketing costs (all fixed)	1,000,000	1,000,000
Total administrative costs (all fixed)	500,000	500,000
Total costs	6,400,000	6,715,000
Operating income	$ 600,000	$ 285,000

The inventories, carried at standard costs, were:

	Variable Costing	Absorption Costing
December 31, 1999	$1,320,000	$1,650,000
December 31, 2000	60,000	75,000

Required

1. Tim Hinkle, president of Hinkle Company, has asked you to explain why the operating income for 2000 is less than for 1999, even though sales have increased 40% over last year. What will you tell him?

2. At what percentage of denominator level was the plant operating during 2000?

3. Prepare a numerical reconciliation and explanation of the difference between operating income under absorption costing and variable costing.

4. Critics have claimed that a widely used accounting system has led to undesirable buildups of inventory levels. (a) Is variable costing or absorption costing more likely to lead to such buildups? Why? (b) What can be done to counteract undesirable inventory buildups?

9-32 Alternative denominator-level concepts. Lucky Lager recently purchased a brewing plant from a bankrupt company. The brewery is in Austin, Texas. It was constructed only two years ago. The plant has budgeted fixed manufacturing overhead of $42 million ($3.5 million each month) in 2000. Paul Vautin, the controller of the brewery, must decide on the denominator-level concept to use in its absorption costing system for 2000. The options available to him are:

a. Theoretical capacity for 2000: 600 barrels an hour for 24 hours per day × 365 days = 5,256,000 barrels

b. Practical capacity for 2000: 500 barrels an hour for 20 hours per day × 350 days = 3,500,000 barrels

c. Normal capacity utilization for 2000: 400 barrels an hour for 20 hours per day × 350 days = 2,800,000 barrels

d. Master-budget capacity utilization for 2000 (separate rates computed for each half-year)

◆ January–June 2000 budget: 320 barrels an hour for 20 hours a day × 175 days = 1,120,000 barrels

◆ July–December 2000 budget: 480 barrels an hour for 20 hours a day × 175 days = 1,680,000 barrels

Variable standard manufacturing costs per barrel are $45 (variable direct materials, $32; variable manufacturing labor, $6; and variable manufacturing overhead, $7). The Austin brewery "sells" its output to the sales division of Lucky Lager at a budgeted price of $68 per barrel.

Required

1. Compute the budgeted fixed manufacturing overhead rate using each of the four denominator-level concepts for (a) beer produced in March 2000, and (b) beer produced in September 2000. Explain why any differences arise.
2. Explain why the theoretical capacity and practical capacity concepts are different.
3. Which denominator-level concept would the plant manager of the Austin brewery prefer when senior management of Lucky Lager is judging plant manager performance during 2000? Explain.

9-33 Operating income effects of alternative denominator-level concepts (continuation of Problem 9-32). In 2000 the Austin brewery of Lucky Lager showed these results:

Beginning inventory, January 1, 2000	0 barrels
Production	2,600,000 barrels
Ending inventory, December 31, 2000	200,000 barrels

The Austin brewery had actual costs of:

Variable manufacturing costs	$120,380,000
Fixed manufacturing overhead costs	40,632,000

The sales division of Lucky Lager purchased 2,400,000 barrels in 2000 at the $68 per barrel rate.

All manufacturing variances are written off to cost of goods sold in the period in which they are incurred.

Required

1. Compute the operating income of the Austin brewery using the denominator-level concepts of (a) theoretical capacity, (b) practical capacity, and (c) normal capacity utilization. Explain any differences among (a), (b), and (c).
2. What denominator-level concept would Lucky Lager prefer for income tax reporting? Explain.
3. Explain the ways in which the Internal Revenue Service might restrict the flexibility of a company like Lucky Lager, which uses absorption costing, to reduce its taxable income.

9-34 Downward demand spiral and profitability assessment. Iotera, Inc., based in Potatoville, Wyoming, manufactures compact portable storage solutions for the portable personal computer market. Iotera's products are very popular and have attracted an almost cult-like following, especially among laptop warriors and PDA (personal digital assistant) junkies. Iotera's chief competitor, Sybest, is based in Silicon Valley. Iotera is currently engaged in a vicious price war with Sybest. Unfortunately, Iotera must also contend with rapidly dropping prices for high-tech consumer products.

Iotera, Inc., manufactures three products—Duda™, a 1Gb 3.5″ floppy system; Rock™, a 5Gb cartridge-based system; and Funky™, a 1Tb cutting-edge optical mini-disk system. Once the darling of Wall Street, bad times have come to Iotera (and Potatoville. . .). Management is now questioning the profitability of each product. In addition, management would like to discontinue any product whose gross profit margin percentage is less than 10 percent.

Iotera's current cost accounting system is rather simplistic. The single overhead allocation base is direct labor-hours. The allocation rate per hour is calculated by summing variable and fixed overhead costs and dividing by the number of direct labor-hours. Product cost is calculated by multiplying the number of direct labor-hours required to manufacture the product by the overhead rate and adding this amount to the direct labor and direct materials costs.

Total budgeted overhead costs in 2001 are $4,326,408.

Required

1. Complete Problem Exhibit 9-34. What is the overhead allocation rate per labor-hour? Will Iotera discontinue any product? Iotera decides to redirect all available capacity freed up from dropping a product to the most profitable product in total dollar terms that is retained.

2. Consider the products Iotera will produce after any decisions in requirement 1. It now considers average selling prices for 2001 as follows: Duda^{TM}, $43,50, Rock^{TM}, $219.00; and Funky^{TM}, $899.00. Redo Problem Exhibit 9-34 using the new selling prices. Will Iotera discontinue any product?

3. Consider what products Iotera will produce after any decisions in requirements 1 and 2. Assume that anything produced can be sold, and that total overhead is unchanged at $4,326,408. Due to packaging and warehouse constraints, Iotera's capacity is limited to the production of 200,000 units in 2001 (each product produced constitutes a single unit, regardless of product type).

   a. Recalculate costs and gross margins under this scenario.
   b. Will Iotera consider dropping any additional products?
   c. How has the overhead allocation rate changed?
   d. What has happened to the profit margins on the remaining products, and how has this affected Iotera's total gross profits?

4. What recommendations would you make to management regarding the current product-costing system and product decision policies?

PROBLEM EXHIBIT 9-34
Budgeted Cost Data for Iotera, Inc., in 2001

	Total overhead costs	$4,326,408
	Total labor-hours	60,089
	Allocation rate per labor hour	?

	Duda	Rock	Funky	Iotera, Inc.
Product characteristics				
Direct labor-hours per 10 units	1	?	10	
Total units produced	123,190	72,600	?	?
Total labor-hours spent	?	?	4,210	60,089
Product costs				
Direct materials per unit	$16.20	$89.80	$184.60	
Direct labor per unit @ 18.00 per hour	?	?	?	
Allocated overhead per unit	?	?	?	
Total product costs	?	?	?	
Average selling price	$39.80	$159.00	$899.00	
Gross margin per unit	?	?	?	
Total revenues	?	?	?	?
Total costs	?	?	?	?
Operating income	?	?	?	?

9-35 Effects of denominator-level concept choice. The Wong Company installed standard costs and a flexible budget on January 1, 2000. The president has been pondering how fixed manufacturing overhead should be allocated to products. Machine-hours has been chosen as the allocation base. Her remaining uncertainty is the denominator-level concept for machine-hours. She decides to wait for the first month's results before making a final choice of what denominator-level concept should be used from that day forward.

In January 2000, the actual units of output had a standard of 70,000 machine-hours allowed. If the company uses practical capacity as the denominator-level concept, the fixed manufacturing overhead spending variance would be $10,000, unfavorable, and the production-volume variance would be $36,000, unfavorable. If the company uses normal capacity utilization as the denominator-level concept, the production-volume variance would be $20,000, favorable. Budgeted fixed manufacturing overhead was $120,000 for the month.

Required

1. Compute the denominator level, assuming that the normal capacity utilization concept is chosen.
2. Compute the denominator level, assuming that the practical capacity concept is chosen.
3. Suppose you are the executive vice president. You want to maximize your 2000 bonus, which depends on 2000 operating income. Assume that the production-volume variance is added or deducted from operating income at year-end. Which denominator-level concept would you favor? Why?

9-36 **Cost allocation, downward demand spiral.** Western Health Maintenance (WHM) operates a chain of ten hospitals in the Los Angeles area. For many years, it has operated a central food-catering facility in Santa Monica, which delivers meals to the ten hospitals. The Santa Monica facility has the capacity to serve 3,650,000 meals a year (10,000 meals a day). In 2001 it budgeted for 2,920,000 meals (8,000 meals a day), based on demand estimates from each hospital controller. The budgeted variable costs per meal in 2001 are $3.80, which includes delivery to the hospital. Budgeted fixed costs for 2001 are $4,380,000.

In July 2001, the new WHM president announces that each hospital is to be a profit center. In addition, the head of each hospital can purchase services from outside WHM, providing those services meet the WHM quality requirements. The president gives catering as an example. Roy Jenkins, the head of the Santa Monica catering facility, is less than pleased. This facility will also become a profit center (it has been a cost center for many years) under the reorganization.

Jenkins charged each hospital $5.30 per meal in 2001—comprising $3.80 variable cost + $1.50 allocation of budgeted fixed costs. Several hospitals complained about the $5.30 cost as well as the quality of the food. (Jenkins sarcastically labels the quality complaints as "recycled mystery-meat stories.") Indeed, the cost rose from $4.90 in 2000 to $5.30 in 2001. Jenkins defended the increase, claiming he needed to spread the same fixed costs over a smaller number of patient-days in 2001. WHM experienced negative press on a local TV station in 2000 and early 2001, and local doctors are referring fewer patients to the WHM hospitals.

In October 2001, Jenkins started to prepare the 2002 budget, including the new cost to be charged per meal. He estimated that the total annual demand for meals at all ten WHM hospitals will be 2,550,000. Then he learned that three of the ten hospitals will use an outside canteen service, which reduces the 2002 budgeted demand at the Santa Monica facility to 2,000,000 meals. No change in total fixed costs or variable costs per meal is expected in 2002.

Required

1. How did Jenkins compute the budgeted fixed costs per meal in 2001?
2. What alternative cost-per-meal figures might Jenkins compute for meals delivered to WHM hospitals in 2002? Which cost figure should Jenkins use? Why?
3. What factors should Jenkins consider in pricing meals the Santa Monica facility prepares for the WHM hospitals?

9-37 **Cost allocation, budgeted rates, ethics (continuation of Problem 9-36).** The actual meal counts used in 2001 by all of WHM's hospitals were less than the budgeted amounts each hospital controller provided Jenkins at the start of 2001. Jenkins suspects collusion on the part of the hospital controllers. He is concerned that the 2002 budgeted meal counts from the individual hospitals will likewise turn out to be way too optimistic about actual demand.

Required

1. Why might the individual hospital administrators deliberately overestimate the 2001 budgeted meal count demand?
2. Jenkins decides to approach the WHM corporate controller to discuss his concerns about the individual hospital controllers colluding on budgeted meal count demand. What evidence should the corporate controller seek in order to investigate Jenkin's concerns?

3. What steps should the corporate controller take to reduce any incentives individual hospital controllers have to deliberately mis-estimate meal demand for 2002?

COLLABORATIVE LEARNING EXERCISE

9-38 Absorption, variable and throughput costing. The Waterloo, Ontario, plant of Maple Leaf Motors assembles the Icarus motor vehicle. The standard unit manufacturing cost per vehicle in 2000 is:

Direct materials	$6,000
Direct manufacturing labor	1,800
Variable manufacturing overhead	2,000
Fixed manufacturing overhead	?

The Waterloo plant is highly automated. Maximum productive capacity per month is 4,000 vehicles. Variable manufacturing overhead is allocated to vehicles on the basis of assembly time. The standard assembly time per vehicle is 20 hours. Fixed manufacturing overhead in 2000 is allocated on the basis of the standard assembly time for the budgeted normal capacity utilization of the plant. In 2000, the budgeted normal capacity utilization is 3,000 vehicles per month. The budgeted monthly fixed manufacturing overhead is $7,500,000.

On January 1, 2000, there is zero beginning inventory of Icarus vehicles. The actual unit production and sales figures for the first three months of 2000 are:

	January	February	March
Production	3,200	2,400	3,800
Sales	2,000	2,900	3,200

Assume no direct materials variances, no direct manufacturing labor variances, and no manufacturing overhead spending or efficiency variances in the first three months of 2000.

Bret Hart, a vice president of Maple Leaf Motors, is the manager of the Waterloo plant. His compensation includes a bonus that is 0.5% of quarterly operating income. Operating income is calculated using absorption costing. Maple Leaf Motors prepares absorption-costing income statements monthly, which includes an adjustment to cost of goods sold for the total manufacturing variances occurring in that month.

The Waterloo plant "sells" each Icarus to Maple Leaf's marketing subsidiary at $16,000 per vehicle. No marketing costs are incurred by the Waterloo plant.

Required
Form groups of two or more students to complete the following requirements.

1. Compute (a) the fixed manufacturing overhead costs per unit, and (b) the total manufacturing costs per unit.
2. Compute the monthly operating income for January, February, and March under absorption costing. What bonus is paid each month to Bret Hart?
3. How much would use of variable costing change the bonus paid each month to Hart if the same 0.5% figure is applied to variable-costing operating income?
4. Explain the differences in the bonuses paid each month to Hart in requirements 2 and 3.
5. How much would use of throughput costing change the bonus paid each month to Hart if the same 0.5% figure is applied to throughput-costing operating income?
6. Outline different approaches Maple Leaf Motors could use to reduce the possible undesirable behavior associated with the use of absorption costing at its Waterloo plant.

Determining How Costs Behave

Aircraft assembly companies report reductions in unit variable costs as the number of airplanes assembled increases. Managers and workers learn to become more efficient as they produce more units. Boeing has experienced such learning-curve effects when assembling planes at its plant.

Teaching Tip Cost estimation underlies nearly all topics in mgt. acctg. It facilitates planning (CVP analysis in Chap. 3, budgeting in Chaps. 6, 7, and 8); pricing (Chap. 12); and decisions such as make or buy, keep or drop (Chap. 11). It helps separate costs into fixed and variable components. This is useful for identifying cost drivers (Chap. 5); var. analysis (Chaps. 7 and 8); variable costing (Chap. 9), and product costing (e.g., separate fixed and variable OH rates).

K nowing how costs vary by identifying the drivers of costs and by distinguishing fixed from variable costs is frequently the key to making good management decisions. In fact, many management functions, such as planning and control, rely on knowing how costs behave. For example, consider the questions, What price should we charge? Should we make the component part or buy it? What effect will a 20% increase in units sold have on operating income? Why is the variable overhead efficiency variance so large? How should managers choose cost-allocation bases in an activity-based costing system? Knowledge of cost behavior is a key input in answering these questions. This chapter will focus on how to determine cost behavior—that is, on understanding how costs change in relation to changes in activity levels, units of products produced, and so on.

GENERAL ISSUES IN ESTIMATING COST FUNCTIONS

Basic Assumptions and Examples of Cost Functions

Cost behavior is best seen through cost functions. A **cost function** is a mathematical expression describing how a cost changes with changes in the level of an activity. Examples of activities are units of output, direct manufacturing labor-hours, machine-hours, and batches of production. Cost functions can be plotted on a graph by measuring the level of activity on the x-axis and the corresponding amount of total costs on the y-axis.

Estimating cost functions relies on two basic assumptions.

OBJECTIVE 1

Explain the two assumptions frequently used in cost-behavior estimation

1. Variations in the total costs of a cost object are explained by variations in the level of a single activity.

2. Cost behavior is adequately approximated by a linear cost function within the relevant range. A **linear cost function** is a cost function in which the graph of total cost versus the level of a single activity is a straight line within the relevant range.

Reinforcing Problems Exer. 10-17 through 10-19 cover examples of different cost functions.

We use these assumptions throughout most of this chapter. Later sections will discuss cost functions that do not rely on these assumptions.

OBJECTIVE 2

Describe linear cost functions and three common ways in which they behave

To see the role of cost functions in business decisions, consider the negotiations between Cannon Services and World Wide Communications (WWC) for exclusive use of a telephone line between New York and Paris. WWC offers Cannon Services three alternative cost structures.

◆ *Alternative 1*: $5 per minute of phone use. Total costs to Cannon vary with the number of phone-minutes used. That is, the number of phone-minutes used is the only factor whose change causes a change in total costs.

Panel A in Exhibit 10-1 presents this *variable cost* for Cannon Services. Total costs (measured along the vertical y-axis) change in proportion to the number of phone-minutes used (measured along the horizontal x-axis) within the relevant range. (The relevant range, described in Chapter 2, is the range of the activity in which the relationship between total costs and the level of activity is valid.) Under this alternative, there are no fixed costs. Total costs simply increase by $5 for every additional minute. Panel A of Exhibit 10-1 illustrates the $5 **slope coefficient,** the amount by which total costs change when a one-unit change occurs in the level of activity within the relevant range.

We can write the cost function in Panel A of Exhibit 10-1 as

$$y = \$5X$$

Example At what point would Cannon be indifferent between alternatives 1 and 2? When the costs are equal:

Alt. 1 = Alt. 2
$5X = $10,000
X = 2,000 phone-minutes

For high usage (over 2,000 phone-minutes), Cannon would prefer the fixed costs of Alt. 2, and for low usage they would prefer the variable costs in Alt. 1. At what point would they be indifferent between alternatives 1 and 3?

$5X = $3,000 + $2X
X = 1,000 phone-minutes

At less than 1,000 phone-minutes, the purely variable Alt. 1 is preferable, and conversely. The indifference point between Alts. 2 and 3 is 3,500 phone-minutes. To summarize,

< 1,000 phone-minutes
→ Alt. 1 is best

1,000 to 3,499 phone-minutes
→ Alt. 3 is best

> 3,500 phone-minutes
→ Alt. 2 is best

where X measures the actual number of phone-minutes used and y measures the total costs of the phone-minutes used calculated using the cost function. Throughout the chapter, uppercase letters, such as X, refer to the actual observations and lowercase letters, such as y, represent estimates or calculations made using the cost function.

◆ *Alternative 2*: $10,000 per month. The total costs will be $10,000 per month regardless of the phone-minutes used. (Note that we use the same activity

EXHIBIT 10-1
Examples of Linear Cost Functions

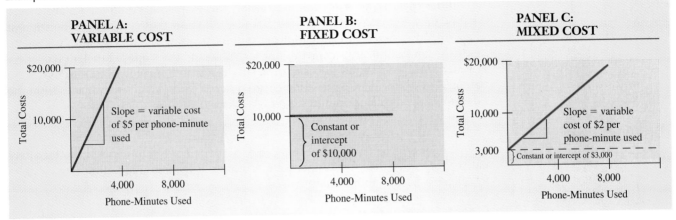

PANEL A: VARIABLE COST — Slope = variable cost of $5 per phone-minute used. PANEL B: FIXED COST — Constant or intercept of $10,000. PANEL C: MIXED COST — Slope = variable cost of $2 per phone-minute used. Constant or intercept of $3,000.

measure, phone-minutes used, to compare cost-behavior patterns under the three alternatives.) The cost is thus fixed, not variable.

Panel B in Exhibit 10-1 presents this *fixed cost* for Cannon Services. Notice that the fixed cost of $10,000 is called a **constant** or **intercept,** which is the component of total costs that, within the relevant range, does not vary with changes in the level of the activity. Under alternative 2, the constant or intercept accounts for all the costs because there are no variable costs. The slope of the cost function is zero. We can write the cost function in Panel B of Exhibit 10-1 as

$$y = \$10,000$$

showing that total costs will be $10,000, regardless of the number of phone-minutes used by Cannon Services.

◆ *Alternative 3*: $3,000 per month plus $2 per minute of phone use. This is an example of a *mixed* cost. A **mixed cost** (or **semivariable cost**) is a cost that has both fixed and variable elements. Under this alternative, the cost has one component that is fixed regardless of the phone-minutes used ($3,000 per month) and another component that is variable with respect to the phone-minutes used ($2 per minute of phone use).

Panel C in Exhibit 10-1 presents this mixed cost for Cannon Services. Unlike the graphs for the previous alternatives, Panel C has both a constant or intercept value ($3,000) and a nonzero slope coefficient ($2). We can write the cost function in Panel C of Exhibit 10-1 as

$$y = \$3,000 + \$2X$$

In the case of mixed costs, the total costs in the relevant range increase as the number of phone-minutes used increases. Note, however, that total costs do not vary strictly in proportion to the number of phone-minutes used within the relevant range. For example, when 4,000 phone-minutes are used, the total costs are [$3,000 + ($2 × 4,000)] = $11,000, but when 8,000 phone-minutes are used, the total costs are [$3,000 + ($2 × 8,000)] = $19,000. Although the number of phone-minutes used has doubled, the total costs have increased to only 1.73 ($19,000 ÷ $11,000) times the original costs.

Cannon's managers must understand the cost-behavior patterns in the three alternatives to choose the best deal with WWC. Suppose Cannon Services expects to use at least 4,000 phone-minutes per month. Its costs for 4,000 phone-minutes under the three alternatives would be as follows: alternative 1, $20,000 ($5 × 4,000); alternative 2, $10,000; alternative 3, $11,000 [$3,000 + ($2 × 4,000)]. Alternative 2 is the least costly. Moreover, if Cannon used more than 4,000 phone-minutes, alternatives 1 and 3 would be even more costly. Cannon's managers should

Curriculum Linkage This linear cost function is consistent with the flexible-budget calculation in Chaps. 7 and 8. Total VC are the only portion of total costs that change at different levels of the cost driver. The total fixed costs do not change because they are fixed in total. This is why it is only the variable costs that put the "flex" in the flexible budget.

Curriculum Linkage For a linear cost function that includes fixed costs, an increase in qty. will cause a less than proportionate increase in total costs, since the fixed costs remain constant despite the increase in qty. As discussed in Chap. 3, this phenomenon is often termed *operating leverage*. The fixed costs act as a lever, magnifying the effect on income of changes in qty.

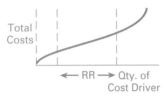
therefore choose alternative 2. Understanding cost behavior helps managers make good decisions.

Note that, as we had assumed earlier, the graphs in Exhibit 10-1 are linear. That is, they appear as straight lines. Because we know these graphs will be straight lines, we do not need to plot multiple points to draw them. We simply need to know the constant or intercept amount (called a) and the slope coefficient (called b). For any linear cost function based on a single activity (our key assumptions), these two pieces of information are sufficient to describe and plot all the values within the relevant range of phone-minutes used. We write the linear cost function as

$$y = a + bX$$

Under alternative 1, $a = \$0$ and $b = \$5$ per phone-minute used; under alternative 2, $a = \$10,000$, $b = \$0$ per phone-minute used; and under alternative 3, $a = \$3,000$, $b = \$2$ per phone-minute used.

Cost Classification and Estimation

Our formula for a linear cost function highlights the variable and fixed components of these functions. Chapter 2 outlined three key ideas when classifying costs into their variable and fixed components. We review them briefly here.

Choice of cost object   A particular cost item could be variable with respect to one cost object and fixed with respect to another. For example, consider Super Shuttle, an airport transportation company. If the fleet of vans owned is the cost object, annual van registration and license costs would be a variable cost with respect to the number of vans owned. But if a particular van is the cost object, registration and license costs for that van is a fixed cost with respect to the miles driven during a year.

Time horizon   Whether a cost is variable or fixed with respect to a particular activity depends on the time horizon considered in the decision situation. The longer the time horizon, other things being equal, the more likely that the cost will be variable. For example, inspection salaries and costs at The Boeing Company are typically fixed in the short run with respect to hours of inspection activity. But in the long run, Boeing's total inspection costs will vary with the inspection time required: More inspectors will be hired if more inspection is needed, while some inspectors will be reassigned to other tasks if less inspection is needed.

Relevant range   Never forget that variable and fixed cost-behavior patterns are valid for linear cost functions only within the given relevant range. Outside the relevant range, variable and fixed cost-behavior patterns change, causing costs to become nonlinear (that is, the graph is not a straight line). For example, Exhibit 10-2 plots the relationship over several years between total direct manufacturing labor costs and the number of valves produced each year by AMC, Inc., at its Cleveland plant. In this case, the nonlinearities outside the relevant range occur because of la-

EXHIBIT 10-2
Linearity within Relevant Range for AMC, Inc.

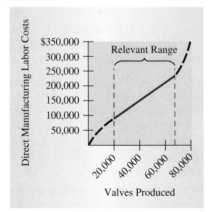

International Comparison of Cost Classification by Companies

Organizations differ in classifying individual costs. A variable-cost item in one organization can be a fixed-cost item in another organization. Consider labor costs. Home construction companies often classify labor cost as a variable cost. These companies rapidly adjust their labor force in response to changes in the demand for housing construction. In contrast, oil-refining companies often classify labor cost as a fixed cost. The labor force is stable even when sizable changes occur in the volume or type of oil products refined.

Surveys indicate significant differences in the percentage of companies in various countries classifying individual cost categories as variable, fixed, or mixed. A lower percentage of U.S. and Australian companies treat labor costs as a fixed cost compared with Japanese companies.

Cost Category	U.S. Companies			Japanese Companies			Australian Companies		
	Variable	Mixed	Fixed	Variable	Mixed	Fixed	Variable	Mixed	Fixed
Production labor	86%	6%	8%	52%	5%	43%	70%	20%	10%
Setup labor	60	25	15	44	6	50	45	33	22
Materials-handling labor	48	34	18	23	16	61	40	30	30
Quality-control labor	34	36	30	13	12	75	21	27	52
Tooling	32	35	33	31	26	43	25	28	47
Energy	26	45	29	42	31	27	—	—	—
Building occupancy	1	6	93	0	0	100	—	—	—
Depreciation	1	7	92	0	0	100	—	—	—

Source: Adapted from the NAA Tokyo Affiliate, "Management Accounting in the Advanced Manufacturing," and Joye and Blayney, "Cost and Management Accounting." Full citations are in Appendix A.

---

bor and other inefficiencies. Knowing the proper relevant range is essential to properly classifying costs.

The Cannon Services/WWC example illustrates variable-, fixed-, and mixed-cost functions using information about future cost structures *proposed* to Cannon by WWC. Often, however, cost functions are *estimated* from past cost data. **Cost estimation** is the attempt to measure a past relationship between costs and the level of an activity. For example, managers could use cost estimation to understand what causes marketing costs to change from year to year (such as the number of cars sold or the number of new car models introduced), and the fixed and variable components of these costs. Managers are interested in estimating past cost-behavior functions primarily because these estimates can help them make more accurate **cost predictions**, or forecasts, about future costs. Better cost predictions help managers make more informed planning and control decisions, such as preparing the marketing costs budget for next year. But better management decisions, cost predictions, and estimation of cost functions depend critically on correctly identifying the factors that affect costs.

THE CAUSE-AND-EFFECT CRITERION IN CHOOSING COST DRIVERS

The most important issue in estimating a cost function is determining whether a cause-and-effect relationship exists between the level of an activity and the costs in question. Without a cause-and-effect relationship, managers will be unable to estimate or predict costs, and hence manage them. The cause-and-effect relationship might arise in several ways:

1. It may be due to a physical relationship between the level of activity and costs. An example of a physical relationship is when units of production is used as the activity that affects direct materials costs. Producing more units requires more direct materials, which results in higher total direct materials costs.

2. It may arise from a contractual arrangement. In alternative 1 of the Cannon Services example described earlier, the phone-minutes used is specified in the contract as the level of activity that affects the telephone line costs.

3. It may be implicitly established by logic and knowledge of operations. An example is when number of parts is used as the activity measure that affects ordering costs. It seems intuitively clear that a product with many parts will incur higher ordering costs than will a simple product with few parts.

Be careful not to interpret a high correlation, or connection, between two variables to mean that either variable causes the other. A high correlation between two variables, u and v, indicates merely that the two variables move together. It is possible that u may cause v, v may cause u, u and v may interact, both may be affected by a third variable z, or the correlation may be due to chance. No conclusions about cause and effect are warranted by high correlations alone. For example, higher production generally results in higher materials costs and higher labor costs. Materials costs and labor costs are highly correlated, but neither causes the other.

Consider another example. Over the past 32 years, the New York Stock Exchange index has almost always increased during the year in which an original National Football League team (such as the San Francisco 49ers) has won the Super Bowl, and almost always decreased in the year in which an original American Football League team (such as the Denver Broncos) has won. There is, however, no plausible cause-and-effect explanation for this high correlation.

Only a true cause-and-effect relationship (based on, say, logic, knowledge, or a contract) not merely correlation, establishes an economically plausible relationship between the level of an activity and costs. Economic plausibility is critical because it gives the analyst confidence that the estimated relationship will appear again and again in other similar sets of data.

Recall from Chapter 2 that when a cause-and-effect relationship exists between the change in the level of an activity and a change in the level of total costs, we refer to the activity measure as a cost driver. Because economic plausibility is essential for cost estimation, we use the terms *level of activity* and *cost driver* interchangeably when estimating cost functions.

COST ESTIMATION APPROACHES

OBJECTIVE 3

Recognize various approaches to cost estimation

Four approaches to cost estimation are

1. Industrial engineering method
2. Conference method
3. Account analysis method
4. Quantitative analysis methods

These approaches differ in how expensive they are to implement, the assumptions they make, and the evidence they provide about the accuracy of the estimated cost function. They are not mutually exclusive. Many organizations use a combination of these approaches.

Industrial Engineering Method

The **industrial engineering method**, also called the **work-measurement method**, estimates cost functions by analyzing the relationship between inputs and outputs in physical terms. This method has its roots in studies and techniques developed by scientific management pioneers Frank and Lillian Gilbreth in the early

20th century. Consider, for example, a carpet manufacturer that uses inputs of cotton, wool, dyes, direct manufacturing labor, machine time, and power. Production output is square yards of carpet. Time-and-motion studies analyze the time and materials required to perform the various operations to produce the carpet. For example, a time-and-motion study may conclude that to produce 10 square yards of carpet requires 1 hour of direct manufacturing labor. Standards and budgets transform these physical input and output measures into costs. The result is an estimated cost function relating direct manufacturing labor costs to the cost driver, square yards of carpet produced.

The industrial engineering method can be very time-consuming. Some government contracts mandate its use. Many organizations, however, find it too costly for analyzing their entire cost structure. For example, physical relationships between inputs and outputs may be difficult to specify for individual cost items, such as R&D and advertising.

Conference Method

The **conference method** estimates cost functions on the basis of analysis and opinions about costs and their drivers gathered from various departments of an organization (purchasing, process engineering, manufacturing, employee relations, and so on). The Cooperative Bank in the United Kingdom has a Cost-Estimating Department that develops cost functions for its retail banking products (checking accounts, VISA cards, mortgages, and so on) on the basis of a consensus of estimates from personnel of the relevant departments.

The conference method encourages interdepartmental cooperation. The pooling of expert knowledge from each value-chain function gives the conference method credibility. Because the method does not require detailed analysis of data, cost functions and cost estimates can be developed quickly. However, the emphasis on opinions rather than systematic estimation means that the accuracy of the cost estimates depends largely on the care and skill of the people providing the inputs.[1]

Account Analysis Method

The **account analysis method** estimates cost functions by classifying cost accounts in the ledger as variable, fixed, or mixed with respect to the identified level of activity. Typically, managers use qualitative rather than quantitative analysis when making these cost-classification decisions. The account analysis approach is widely used.

Consider indirect manufacturing labor costs for a small production area (or cell) at Elegant Rugs, which weaves carpets for homes and offices and uses state-of-the-art automated weaving machines. These costs include wages paid to indirect manufacturing labor for supervision, maintenance, quality control, and setups. During the most recent 12-week period, Elegant Rugs ran the machines in the cell for a total of 862 hours and incurred total indirect manufacturing labor costs of $12,501. Using qualitative analysis, management and the cost analyst determine that indirect manufacturing labor costs are mixed costs. As machine-hours vary, one component of the cost (such as supervision cost) is fixed while another component of the cost (such as routine maintenance cost) is variable. The goal is to use account analysis to estimate a linear cost function for indirect manufacturing labor costs with machine-hours as the cost driver. The cost analyst uses experience and judgment to separate total indirect manufacturing labor costs ($12,501) into costs that are fixed ($2,157) and costs that are variable ($10,344) with respect to the number of machine-hours worked. Variable costs per machine-hour are $10,344 ÷ 862 = $12. The linear cost equation, $y = a + bX$, is

Indirect manufacturing labor costs = $2,157 + ($12 × Number of machine-hours)

The indirect manufacturing labor costs per machine-hour are $12,501 ÷ 862 = $14.50. Management at Elegant Rugs can use the cost function to estimate

[1]The conference method is further described in W. Winchell, *Realistic Cost Estimating for Manufacturing*, 2nd ed. (Dearborn, MI: Society for Manufacturing Engineers, 1989).

Points to Stress The industrial engineering, conference, and account analysis methods require less historical data than do most quantitative analyses. Therefore, cost estimation for a new product will usually begin with one or more of these three methods. Quantitative analysis may be adopted later, after the company gains experience (and the necessary data).

Points to Stress The industrial engineering method is most often used for significant costs that are relatively easy to trace to the products (e.g., DM, DL).

Correcting Student Misconceptions Students often misuse avg. costs. In the Elegant Rugs example, the avg. indirect mfg. labor cost/MH is $12,501/862 MH = $14.50/MH. Stress that the $14.50/MH is valid only at a level of 862 MH. At 800 MH, the costs would be

$2,157 + ($12/MH)(800 MH) = $11,757 And, $11757/800 MH = $14.70/MH

The cost/MH is higher because the $2,157 fixed costs are spread over only 800 MH rather than 862 MH. The $12 VC/MH remains the same at any output level within the RR, but the fixed cost/MH changes at different activity levels (e.g., $2,157/800 MH = $2.70/MH at the 800 MH level; $2,157/862 MH = $2.50/MH at the 862 MH level). Since avg. costs unitize fixed costs, caution students against using avg. costs whenever possible. It's less confusing to keep the fixed costs in total, as in the estimated cost equation in the text.

EXHIBIT 10-3
Weekly Indirect Manufacturing Labor Costs and
Machine-Hours for Elegant Rugs

Week	Indirect Manufacturing Labor Costs (1)	Cost Driver: Machine-Hours (2)
1	$1,190	68
2	1,211	88
3	1,004	62
4	917	72
5	770	60
6	1,456	96
7	1,180	78
8	710	46
9	1,316	82
10	1,032	94
11	752	68
12	963	48

Reinforcing Problems Exer. 10-20 and 10-21 cover account analysis. Exer. 10-20 requires the student to decide whether the costs are variable or fixed.

the indirect manufacturing labor costs of using, say, 950 machine-hours to produce carpet in the next 12-week period. Estimated costs equal $2,157 + (950 × $12) = $13,557. The indirect manufacturing labor costs per machine-hour decrease to $13,557 ÷ 950 = $14.27, as fixed costs are spread over a greater number of machine-hours.

To obtain reliable estimates of the fixed and variable components of cost, organizations must take care to ensure that individuals thoroughly knowledgeable about the operations make the cost-classification decisions. Supplementing the account analysis method by the conference method improves its credibility.

Quantitative Analysis Methods

Quantitative analysis uses a formal mathematical method to fit linear cost functions to past data observations. Columns 1 and 2 of Exhibit 10-3 break down Elegant Rugs's total indirect manufacturing labor costs of $12,501 and the total machine-hours of 862 into weekly data for the most recent 12-week period. Note that the data are paired. For example, week 12 shows indirect manufacturing labor costs of $963 and 48 machine-hours. The next section uses the data in Exhibit 10-3 to illustrate how to use quantitative analysis.

STEPS IN ESTIMATING A COST FUNCTION USING QUANTITATIVE ANALYSIS

OBJECTIVE 4

Outline six steps in estimating a cost function on the basis of current or past cost relationships

There are six steps in estimating a cost function on the basis of a quantitative analysis of current or past cost relationships. A key step is choosing a cost driver and this step is not always straightforward. Frequently, working with a management team, the cost analyst will cycle through the six steps several times trying alternative economically plausible cost drivers to identify a cost driver that best fits the data.

Step 1: Choose the Dependent Variable Choice of the **dependent variable** (the cost to be predicted) will depend on the purpose for estimating a cost function. In the Elegant Rugs example, the dependent variable is indirect manufacturing labor costs. The dependent variable will then include all manufacturing labor costs that are classified as indirect.

Step 2: Identify the Independent Variable(s) or Cost Driver(s) The **independent variable** (level of activity or cost driver) is the factor used to predict the dependent variable (costs). Where the cost is an indirect cost, as in our Elegant Rugs example, the independent variable is also called a cost-allocation base. Although these terms are used interchangeably, usually we use the term *cost driver* to describe the independent variable.

When identifying a cost driver, two aspects are important—the cost driver should have an economically plausible relationship with the dependent variable, and it should be measurable. *Economic plausibility* means that the relationship between the costs and the cost driver makes economic sense and is intuitive to the operating manager and the management accountant. All the individual items included in the dependent variable should have the same cost driver. Some dependent variable-cost categories include more than one item of cost, and sometimes these different items of cost do not have the same cost driver. Where a single relationship does not exist, the cost analyst should investigate the possibility of estimating more than one cost function, one for each cost driver.

Consider several types of fringe benefits paid to employees and their cost drivers:

Fringe Benefit	Cost Driver
Health benefits	Number of employees
Cafeteria meals	Number of employees
Pension benefits	Salaries of employees
Life insurance	Salaries of employees

The costs of health benefits and cafeteria meals can be combined into one cost pool because they both have the same cost driver, number of employees. Pension benefits and life insurance costs have a different cost driver, salaries of employees, and hence should not be combined with health benefits and cafeteria meals. Instead, pension benefits and life insurance should be combined into a separate cost pool and estimated using salaries of employees receiving these benefits as the cost driver.

Step 3: Collect Data on the Dependent Variable and the Cost Driver(s)   This step is usually the most difficult one in cost analysis. Cost analysts obtain data from company documents, from interviews with managers, and through special studies. These data may be time-series data or cross-sectional data. *Time-series data* pertain to the same entity (organization, plant, activity, and so on) over a sequence of past time periods. Weekly observations of indirect manufacturing labor costs and machine-hours in the Elegant Rugs illustration are an example of time-series data. The ideal time-series database would contain numerous observations for a company whose operations have not been affected by economic or technological change. Stable technology ensures that data collected during the estimation period represent the same underlying relationship between the dependent variable and the cost driver(s). Moreover, the time periods (for example, daily, weekly, or monthly) used to measure the dependent variable and the cost driver(s) should be consistent throughout the observations. *Cross-sectional data* pertain to different entities for the same time period. For example, studies of personnel costs and loans processed at 50 individual branches of a bank during March 2000 would produce cross-sectional data for that month. A later section of this chapter describes problems that arise in data collection.

Step 4: Plot the Data   The expression "a picture is worth a thousand words" conveys the benefits of plotting the data. The general relationship between the cost driver and the dependent variable can readily be observed in a plot of the data. Moreover, the plot highlights extreme observations (observations outside the general pattern) that analysts should check. Was there an error in recording the data or an unusual event, such as a labor strike, that makes these observations unrepresentative of the normal relationship between the dependent variable and the cost driver? Plotting the data also provides insight into whether the relationship is approximately linear and what the relevant range of the cost function is.

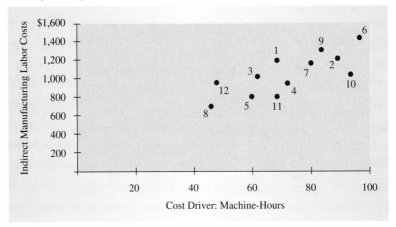

EXHIBIT 10-4
Plot of Weekly Indirect Manufacturing Labor Costs and Machine-Hours for Elegant Rugs

Exhibit 10-4 is a plot of the weekly data from columns 1 and 2 of Exhibit 10-3. There is strong visual evidence of a positive relationship between indirect manufacturing labor costs and machine-hours (that is, when machine-hours go up, so do indirect manufacturing labor costs). There do not appear to be any extreme observations in Exhibit 10-4. The relevant range is from 46 to 96 machine-hours per week.

Step 5: Estimate the Cost Function We show below how to estimate the cost function for our Elegant Rugs data using the high-low method and regression analysis, the two most common forms of quantitative analysis.

Step 6: Evaluate the Cost Driver(s) of the Estimated Cost Function We describe criteria for evaluating the cost driver(s) of the estimated cost function after illustrating the high-low method and regression analysis.

High-Low Method

The simplest method of quantitative analysis is the **high-low method**. It entails using only the highest and lowest observed values of the cost driver within the relevant range and their respective costs. The line connecting these two points becomes the estimated cost function.

We illustrate the high-low method using data from Exhibit 10-3.

	Indirect Manufacturing Labor Costs	**Cost Driver: Machine-Hours**
Highest observation of cost driver (week 6)	$1,456	96
Lowest observation of cost driver (week 8)	710	46
Difference	$ 746	50

$$\text{Slope coefficient } b = \frac{\text{Difference between costs associated with highest and lowest observations of the cost driver}}{\text{Difference between highest and lowest observations of the cost driver}}$$

$$= \$746 \div 50 = \$14.92 \text{ per machine-hour}$$

To compute the constant, we can use either the highest or the lowest observation of the cost driver. Both calculations yield the same answer (because the solution technique solves two linear equations with two unknowns, the slope coefficient and the constant). Since

$$y = a + bX, \qquad a = y - bX$$

therefore at the highest observation of the cost driver,

$$\text{Constant } a = \$1,456 - (\$14.92 \times 96) = \$23.68$$

and at the lowest observation of the cost driver,

$$\text{Constant } a = \$710 - (\$14.92 \times 46) = \$23.68$$

Thus, the high-low estimate of the cost function is

$$y = a + bX$$

$$= \$23.68 + (\$14.92 \times \text{Machine-hours})$$

Teaching Tip Remind students that the high-low method simply calculates the formula for a line, based on 2 data points. The concept is the same as in high school algebra.

The blue line in Exhibit 10-5 shows the estimated cost function using the high-low method. The estimated cost function is a straight line joining the observations with the highest and lowest values of the cost driver (machine-hours). The intercept ($a = \$23.68$), the point where the dashed extension of the blue line meets the y-axis, is the constant component of the equation that provides the best (linear) approximation of how a cost behaves *within the relevant range* of 46 to 96 machine-hours. It should not be interpreted as an estimate of the fixed costs of Elegant Rugs if no machines were run. Why? Because running no machines and shutting down the plant, that is, using zero machine-hours, is outside the relevant range.

Suppose indirect manufacturing labor costs in week 6 were \$1,280 instead of \$1,456 while 96 machine-hours were worked. In this case, the highest observation of the cost driver (machine-hours of 96 in week 6) will not coincide with the newer highest observation of the dependent variable (costs of \$1,316 in week 9). How would this change affect our high-low calculation? Given that causality runs from the cost driver to the dependent variable in a cost function, choosing the highest and lowest observations of the cost driver is appropriate. The high-low method would estimate the new cost function still using data from weeks 6 (high) and 8 (low).

There is an obvious danger of relying on only two observations to estimate a cost function. Suppose that because of provisions in the labor contract that guarantee certain minimum payments in week 8, indirect manufacturing labor costs in week 8 were inflated to \$1,000 instead of \$710 when only 46 machine-hours were worked. The green line in Exhibit 10-5 shows the cost function that would be estimated by the high-low method using this revised value. Other than the two points used to draw the line, all other data lie below the line. In this case, picking the highest and lowest observations for the machine-hours variable would result in an estimated cost function that poorly describes the underlying (linear) cost relationship between indirect manufacturing labor costs and machine-hours.

EXHIBIT 10-5
High-Low Method for Weekly Indirect Manufacturing Labor Costs and Machine-Hours for Elegant Rugs

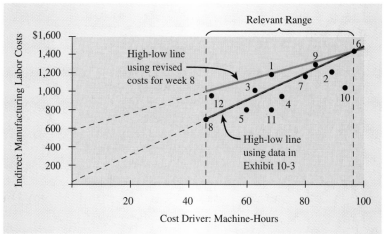

Sometimes the high-low method is modified so that the two observations chosen are a representative high and a representative low. Managers use this modification to avoid having extreme observations, which arise from abnormal events, affect the cost function. Even with such a modification, this method ignores information from all but two observations when estimating the cost function.

Regression Analysis Method

Unlike the high-low method, regression analysis uses all available data to estimate the cost function. **Regression analysis** is a statistical method that measures the average amount of change in the dependent variable that is associated with a unit change in one or more independent variables. In the Elegant Rugs example, the dependent variable is total indirect manufacturing labor costs. The independent variable, or cost driver, is machine-hours. **Simple regression** analysis estimates the relationship between the dependent variable and one independent variable. **Multiple regression** analysis estimates the relationship between the dependent variable and two or more independent variables.

We emphasize the interpretation and use of output from computer software programs for regression analysis and so only present detailed computations for deriving the regression line in the appendix to the chapter. Commonly available programs (for example, SPSS, SAS, and Excel) on mainframes and personal computers calculate almost all the statistics referred to in this chapter.

Exhibit 10-6 shows the line developed using regression analysis that best fits the data in columns 1 and 2 of Exhibit 10-3. The estimated cost function is

$$y = \$300.98 + \$10.31X$$

The regression equation and regression line in Exhibit 10-6 are derived using the least-squares technique. The regression line minimizes the sum of the squared vertical differences from the data points (the various points on the graph) to the regression line. The vertical difference, called **residual term,** measures the distance between actual cost and the estimated cost for each observation. Exhibit 10-6 shows the residual term for the week 1 data. The line from the observation to the regression line is drawn perpendicular to the x-axis. The smaller the residual terms, the better the fit between actual cost observations and estimated costs. Goodness of fit indicates the strength of the relationship between the cost driver and costs. The regression line in Exhibit 10-6 rises reasonably steeply from left to right. The positive slope of this line indicates that, on average, indirect manufacturing labor costs increase as machine-hours increase. The vertical dashed lines in Exhibit 10-6 indicate the relevant range, the range within which the cost function applies.

EXHIBIT 10-6
Regression Model for Weekly Indirect Manufacturing Labor Costs and Machine-Hours for Elegant Rugs

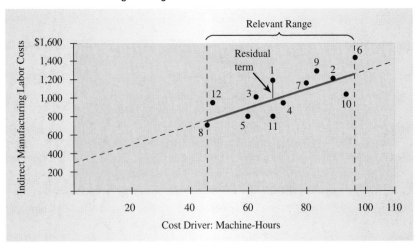

The estimate of the slope coefficient b indicates that the indirect manufacturing labor costs vary at the average amount of $10.31 for every machine-hour within the relevant range. Management can use the regression equation when budgeting for future indirect manufacturing labor costs. For instance, if 90 machine-hours are budgeted for the upcoming week, the predicted indirect manufacturing labor costs would be

$$y = \$300.98 + (\$10.31 \times 90) = \$1,228.88$$

The regression method is more accurate than the high-low method because the regression equation estimates costs using information from all observations while the high-low equation uses information from only two observations. The inaccuracies of the high-low method can mislead managers. Consider the high-low equation in the preceding section, $y = \$23.68 + \$14.92$ per machine-hour. For 90 machine-hours, the predicted weekly cost based on the high-low equation is $23.68 + (\$14.92 \times 90) = \$1,366.48$. Suppose that for 7 weeks over the next 12-week period, Elegant Rugs runs its machines for 90 hours each week. Assume average indirect manufacturing labor costs for those 7 weeks is $1,300. Based on the high-low prediction of $1,366.48, Elegant Rugs would conclude it has performed well. But comparing the $1,300 performance with the more accurate $1,228.88 prediction of the regression model tells a different story, and would probably prompt Elegant Rugs to search for ways to improve its cost performance.

Accurate cost estimation helps managers predict future costs and evaluate the success of cost-reduction initiatives. Suppose the manager at Elegant Rugs is interested in evaluating whether recent changes in the production process that resulted in the data in Exhibit 10-3 have reduced indirect manufacturing labor costs, such as supervision, maintenance and quality control. Using data on machine-hours worked and indirect manufacturing labor costs of the previous process, the manager estimates the regression equation, $y = \$545.26 + (\$15.86 \times \text{machine-hours})$. The constant is somewhat smaller while the slope coefficient is significantly smaller than before. It appears that the new process has decreased indirect manufacturing labor costs.

Reinforcing Problems Exer. 10-24 through 10-26 and Probs. 10-30 and 10-31 reinforce regression analysis, without requiring concepts from the Appendix.

EVALUATING COST DRIVERS OF THE ESTIMATED COST FUNCTION

A key aspect of estimating a cost function is choosing the appropriate cost driver. How does a company go about making this choice? In many cases, the choice of a cost driver is aided substantially by a thorough understanding of both operations (with help and support of operating managers) and cost accounting.

To illustrate, consider the costs to maintain and repair metal cutting machines at Helix Corporation, a manufacturer of filing cabinets. Helix schedules repairs and maintenance when production is at a low level to avoid having to take machines out of service when they are needed most. An analysis of the monthly data will then show high repair costs in months of low production and low repair costs in months of high production. Someone unfamiliar with operations might conclude that there is an inverse relationship between production and repair costs. The engineering link between units of production and repair costs, however, is usually clear-cut. Over time there is a cause-and-effect relationship: The higher the level of production, the higher the repair costs. To estimate the relationship correctly, operating managers and analysts recognize that repair costs will tend to lag behind periods of high production, and hence will use lagged production as the cost driver.

In other cases, choosing a cost driver is more subtle and difficult. Consider again indirect manufacturing labor costs at Elegant Rugs. Management believes that both machine-hours and direct manufacturing labor-hours are plausible cost drivers of indirect manufacturing labor costs. Management is not necessarily sure that machine-hours is the better cost driver. Exhibit 10-7 presents weekly data on indirect manufacturing labor costs and machine-hours for the most recent 12-week period from Exhibit 10-3, together with data on direct manufacturing labor-hours for the same period.

EXHIBIT 10-7
Weekly Indirect Manufacturing Labor Costs, Machine-Hours, and Direct Manufacturing
Labor-Hours for Elegant Rugs

Week	Indirect Manufacturing Labor Costs (1)	Cost Driver: Machine-Hours (2)	Alternative Cost Driver: Direct Manufacturing Labor-Hours (3)
1	$1,190	68	30
2	1,211	88	35
3	1,004	62	36
4	917	72	20
5	770	60	47
6	1,456	96	45
7	1,180	78	44
8	710	46	38
9	1,316	82	70
10	1,032	94	30
11	752	68	29
12	963	48	38

Points to Stress As in most real-world applications, the cost function is not valid at shutdown in the Elegant Rugs example. The intercept does not capture fixed costs at zero machine-hours because at shutdown, some costs can be avoided; e.g., companies can generally cut FC by laying off salaried workers, selling PPE, etc. In sum, zero volume, or shutdown, is typically outside the relevant range, so the intercept should not be interpreted as fixed costs at shutdown. It is simply the constant component of the equation that provides the best (linear) fit.

What guidance do the different cost-estimation methods provide for choosing among cost drivers? The industrial engineering method relies on analyzing physical relationships between costs and cost drivers, which are difficult to specify in this case. The conference method and the account analysis method use subjective assessments to choose a cost driver and to estimate the fixed and variable components of the cost function. In these cases, management must rely on its best judgment. Management cannot use these methods to test and try alternative cost drivers. The major advantages of quantitative methods are that they are objective—a given data set and estimation method results in a unique estimated cost function—and that managers can use these methods to evaluate different cost drivers. We illustrate how, using the regression analysis approach.

First, the cost analyst at Elegant Rugs inputs the data in columns 1 and 3 of Exhibit 10-7 into a computer program and estimates the following regression equation of direct manufacturing labor-hours on indirect manufacturing labor costs:

$$y = \$744.67 + \$7.72X$$

Exhibit 10-8 shows the plots for indirect manufacturing labor costs versus direct manufacturing labor-hours, and the regression line that best fits the data. Exhibit 10-6 shows the corresponding graph when machine-hours is the cost driver. To decide which cost driver Elegant Rugs should choose, the analyst compares the machine-hour and direct manufacturing labor-hour regression equations. There are three important criteria.

OBJECTIVE 5
Describe three criteria to evaluate and choose cost drivers

Points to Stress Cost functions have a good fit either simply by chance, or else because there is an underlying economic relation between the cost and the driver. The cost func-

1. *Economic plausibility.* Both cost drivers are economically plausible. However, in the state-of-the-art, highly automated production environment of Elegant Rugs, managers familiar with the operations believe that costs such as machine maintenance are likely to be more closely related to machine-hours than to direct manufacturing labor-hours.

2. *Goodness of fit.* Compare Exhibits 10-6 and 10-8. The vertical differences between actual and predicted costs are much smaller for machine-hours than they are for direct manufacturing labor-hours. Machine-hours thus has a stronger relationship (or goodness of fit) with indirect manufacturing labor costs.

3. *Slope of regression line.* Again compare Exhibits 10-6 and 10-8. The machine-hours regression line has a relatively steep slope, but the direct manufacturing labor-hours regression line is relatively flat (slight slope). For the same (or

EXHIBIT 10-8

Regression Model for Weekly Indirect Manufacturing Labor Costs and Direct
Manufacturing Labor-Hours for Elegant Rugs

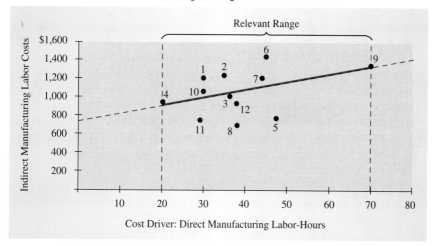

more) scatter of observations about the line (goodness of fit), a relatively flat
regression line indicates a weak relationship between the cost driver and costs.
In our example, changes in direct manufacturing labor-hours appear to have a
minimal effect on indirect manufacturing labor costs.

Elegant Rugs should prefer machine-hours to direct manufacturing labor-
hours as the cost driver and use the cost function $y = \$300.98 + (\$10.31 \times$ machine-hours) to predict future indirect manufacturing labor costs.

Why is choosing the correct cost driver to estimate indirect manufacturing labor costs so important? Consider the following decision that management at Elegant Rugs must make. Elegant Rugs is thinking of introducing a new style of carpet.
Sales of 650 square yards of this carpet are expected each week at a price of $12 per
square yard. Management estimates 72 machine-hours and 21 direct manufacturing
labor-hours would be required each week to produce the square yards of carpet
needed. Using the machine-hour regression equation, Elegant Rugs would predict
costs of $y = \$300.98 + (\$10.31 \times 72) = \$1,043.30$. If it used direct manufacturing
labor-hours as the cost driver, it would have incorrectly predicted costs of
$\$744.67 + (\$7.72 \times 21) = \$906.79$. If Elegant Rugs systematically underestimates
costs and chooses incorrect cost drivers for other indirect costs as well, it would
conclude that the costs of manufacturing the new style of carpet are low and essentially fixed (the regression line is relatively flat). But the actual costs driven by machine-hours and other correct cost drivers would prove to be higher. Without identifying the proper cost drivers, management would be misled into believing the new
style of carpet is more profitable than it actually is.

Incorrectly estimating the cost function will also have repercussions for cost
management and cost control. Suppose direct manufacturing labor-hours is used as
the cost driver, and actual indirect manufacturing labor costs are $970. Actual costs
would then be higher than the predicted costs of $906.79. Management would feel
compelled to find ways to cut costs. In fact, on the basis of the preferred machine-
hour cost driver, the plant has actual costs lower than the predicted amount
($1,043.30)—a performance that management should seek to replicate, not change.

COST DRIVERS AND ACTIVITY-BASED COSTING

In activity-based costing (ABC) systems, operations managers and cost analysts identify key activities, and the cost drivers and costs of each activity at the output unit-
level, batch level or product-sustaining level. The basic approach to evaluating cost
drivers described in the previous section applies to ABC systems as well. An ABC system, however, has a greater number and variety of cost drivers and cost pools.

tion is more likely to predict accurately in the future if that function is
based on an economic relation. It's
important for cost functions to be
economically plausible in addition to
fitting the data well.

Correcting Student Misconceptions
Some students give excessive (sole)
emphasis to the goodness-of-fit criterion. For example, when using simple
regression (where 1 independent variable is used to explain the change in
the dependent variable), students often choose the variable that has the
highest R^2. Stress the need to consider all 3 evaluation criteria.

Activity-Based Costing and Cost Estimation

Cost estimation in activity-based costing and other systems blend the various methods presented in this chapter. To determine the cost of an activity, ABC systems often rely on expert analyses and opinions gathered from operating personnel (the conference method). For example, Loan Department staff at the Cooperative Bank in the United Kingdom subjectively estimates the costs of the loan processing activity and the cost driver of loan processing costs (the number of loans processed, a batch-level cost driver, rather than the value of the loans, an output unit-level cost driver), to derive the cost of processing a loan. ABC systems sometimes use input-output relationships (the industrial engineering method) to identify cost drivers and the cost of an activity. For example, John Deere and Company uses work-measurement methods to identify a batch-level cost driver (the number of standard loads moved) and the cost per load moved within its components plant.

In complex environments, multiple cost drivers are necessary for accurate product costing. Consider how heavy equipment manufacturer Caterpillar identifies the cost driver for receiving costs in its ABC system. Three plausible cost drivers were the weight of parts received, the number of parts received, or the number of shipments received. The weight of parts and number of parts are output unit-level cost drivers, while the number of shipments is a batch-level cost driver. Caterpillar uses the weight of parts as the basis for cost assignment because a regression analysis showed that it is the primary driver of the costs of receiving material. Caterpillar also uses a variety of other cost drivers in assigning costs to its products.

Source: Based on the Co-operative Bank, Harvard Business School Case No. N9-195-196, John Deere Component Works (A), Harvard Business School Case 9-187-107, and discussions with the company managements.

Points to Stress The Concepts in Action box illustrates the use of several cost-estimation approaches (industrial engineering method, conference method, and quantitative analysis method) in developing ABC cost systems. ABC emphasizes interviewing personnel responsible for the activity in order to identify cost drivers. This approach might identify several potential cost drivers that meet the *economic plausibility* criterion. More formal industrial engineering analysis or quantitative analysis could help the cost analyst select the "best" cost driver from the pool of candidate cost drivers identified in the interviews.

Reinforcing Problems Exer. 10-26 and Probs. 10-31, 10-37, and 10-38 cover cost drivers and ABC.

Generally, ABC systems emphasize long-run relationships between the cost driver (level of activity) and cost. The long-run focus means that more costs are variable, which leads to a stronger cause-and-effect relationship between the cost driver and the corresponding cost. Hence, the ideal database to estimate cost driver rates will contain data over a longer time period. If the time period used to estimate the cost relationship is short, the relationship between changes in the cost driver and changes in cost may be weak. Why? Because many costs are acquired in lump-sum amounts and hence are fixed in the short run while the levels of activity vary.

Consider, for example, salaries and fringe benefits of engineers and foremen responsible for supervising the setup activity. In the short run, these costs are fixed and will not vary with changes in the quantity of setup-hours. In the long run, however, there is a clear cause-and-effect relationship between setup-hours and indirect setup costs—increases in setup-hours will cause more engineers and foremen to be hired while decreases will result in engineers and foremen being reassigned to other tasks.

As the Concepts in Action box indicates, managers implementing ABC systems use a variety of methods—conference, industrial engineering, and regression—to estimate cost driver rates. In making these choices, managers trade off level of detail, accuracy, feasibility, and costs of estimating cost functions.

NONLINEARITY AND COST FUNCTIONS

Thus far we have assumed linear cost functions. In practice, cost functions are not always linear. A **nonlinear cost function** is one in which the graph of total costs versus the level of a single activity is not a straight line within the relevant range. Exhibit 10-2 (p. 330) graphs a cost function that is nonlinear if we expand the rele-

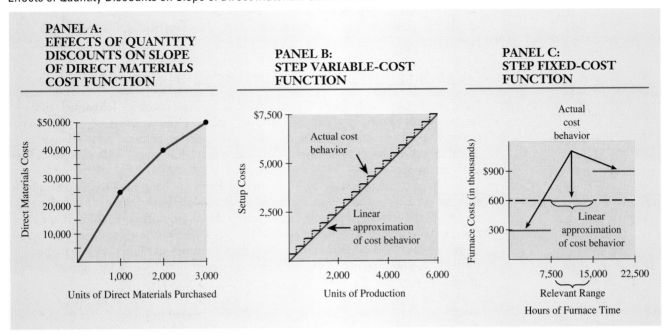

vant range from 0 to 80,000 valves produced beyond the original relevant range of 20,000 to 65,000. Consider another example. Economies of scale in advertising may enable an advertising agency to double the number of advertisements for less than double the costs. Even direct materials costs are not always linear variable costs. Consider quantity discounts on direct materials purchases. As shown in Exhibit 10-9, Panel A, the total direct materials costs rise, but, because of quantity discounts, they rise more slowly as the units of direct materials purchases increase. The cost function in Exhibit 10-9 has $b = \$25$ for 1–1,000 units purchased, $b = \$15$ for 1,001–2,000 units purchased, and $b = \$10$ for 2,000 or more units purchased ($a = \$0$ for all ranges of the units purchased). The cost per unit falls at each price break—that is, the cost per unit decreases with larger orders. Over the entire relevant range from 1 to 3,000 units, the cost function is nonlinear. If, however, the relevant range is defined more narrowly, for example, from 1–1,000 units, the cost function is linear.

Step cost functions are also examples of nonlinear cost functions. A **step cost function** is a cost function in which the cost remains the same over various ranges of the level of activity, but the cost increases by discrete amounts (that is, in steps) as the level of activity changes from one range to the next. Panel B in Exhibit 10-9 shows a *step variable-cost function*, a step cost function in which cost remains the same over *narrow* ranges of the level of activity in each relevant range. Exhibit 10-9, Panel B, presents the relationship between setup costs and units of production. The pattern is a step cost function because, as we described in Chapter 5 on activity-based costing, setup costs are related to each production batch started. Over the entire relevant range from 0 to 6,000 production units, the cost function is nonlinear. However, as shown in Exhibit 10-9, Panel B, management often approximates step variable costs with a variable-cost function. This step-pattern behavior also occurs when inputs such as production scheduling, product design labor, and process engineering labor are acquired in discrete quantities but used in fractional quantities.

Panel C in Exhibit 10-9 shows a *step fixed-cost function* for Crofton Steel, a company that operates large heat-treatment furnaces to harden steel parts. The main difference compared to Exhibit 10-9, Panel B, is that the cost in a step fixed-cost function remains the same over *wide* ranges of the activity in each relevant range. The ranges indicate the number of furnaces being used (each furnace costing $300,000). The cost changes from one range to the next higher range when the

Correcting Student Misconceptions
Students are often confused by the differences between the behavior of total costs vs. unit costs. Exh. 10-9, Panel A illustrates a *cost function that increases at a decreasing rate*. Stress that a declining cost/unit doesn't mean that *total* costs decline (For total costs to decline, unit costs would have to become negative!). With a declining cost/unit, total costs will still increase, but at a decreasing rate, as in Exh. 10-9, Panel A. To illustrate, ask students to think about purchasing personalized business cards. Cards might cost $50 for the first 100, $40 for the next 100, and $30 per 100 thereafter. Even though the cost per 100 declines, students will still pay more for additional cards.

hours of furnace time demanded require the use of another furnace. The relevant range indicates that the company expects to operate with two furnaces at a cost of $600,000. Management considers the cost of operating furnaces as a fixed cost within this relevant range of operation. However, over the range from 0 to 22,500 hours, the cost function is nonlinear.

LEARNING CURVES AND NONLINEAR COST FUNCTIONS

Nonlinear cost functions also result from learning curves. A **learning curve** is a function that shows how labor-hours per unit decline as units of production increase due to workers learning and becoming better at their jobs. Managers use learning curves to predict how labor-hours (or labor costs) will change as more units are produced.

The aircraft-assembly industry first documented the effect that learning has on efficiency. As workers become more familiar with their tasks, their efficiency improves. Managers learn how to improve the scheduling of work shifts. Plant operators learn how best to operate the facility. As a result of improved efficiency, unit costs decrease as productivity increases, and the unit-cost function behaves nonlinearly. These nonlinearities must be explicitly considered when estimating and predicting unit costs.

Managers are now extending the learning-curve notion to other business functions in the value chain, such as marketing, distribution, and customer service. The term *experience curve* describes this broader application of the learning curve. An **experience curve** is a function that shows how the costs per unit in various value-chain functions such as manufacturing, marketing, distribution, and so on, decline as units produced increase.

We now describe two learning-curve models: the cumulative average-time learning model and the incremental unit-time learning model.

Cumulative Average-Time Learning Model

In the **cumulative average-time learning model,** the cumulative average time per unit declines by a constant percentage each time the cumulative quantity of units produced doubles. Exhibit 10-10 illustrates this model with an 80% learning curve. The 80% means that when the quantity of units produced is doubled from X to $2X$, the cumulative average time *per unit* for the $2X$ units is 80% of the cumulative average time *per unit* for the X units. In other words, average time per unit has dropped by 20%. Panel A in Exhibit 10-10 shows the cumulative average time *per unit* as a function of units produced. Panel B in Exhibit 10-10 shows the cumulative *total* labor-hours as a function of units produced. The data points underlying Exhibit 10-10, and the details of their calculation, are presented in Exhibit 10-11. Note that as the number of units produced doubles from 1 to 2, the cumulative average time per unit declines from 100 hours to 80% × 100 = 80 hours. As the number of units doubles from 2 to 4, the cumulative average time per unit declines to 80% × 80 = 64 hours, and so on. To obtain the cumulative total time, multiply the cumulative average time per unit by the cumulative number of units produced. For example, to produce 4 cumulative units would require 256 labor-hours (4 × 64 cumulative average hours).

Incremental Unit-Time Learning Model

In the **incremental unit-time learning model,** the incremental unit time (the time needed to produce the last unit) declines by a constant percentage each time the cumulative quantity of units produced doubles. Exhibit 10-12 illustrates this model with an 80% learning curve. The 80% here means that when the quantity of units produced is doubled from X to $2X$, the time needed to produce the *last unit* at the $2X$ production level is 80% of the time needed to produce the *last unit* at the X production level. Panel A in Exhibit 10-12 shows the cumulative average time *per unit* as a function of cumulative units produced. Panel B in Exhibit 10-12 shows the cumulative *total* labor-hours as a function of units produced. The data points underlying Exhibit 10-12, and the details of their calculation, are presented in

EXHIBIT 10-10
Plots for Cumulative Average-Time Learning Model

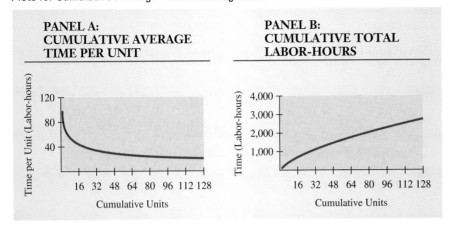

Correcting Student Misconceptions
Students often fail to appreciate the difference between the left-hand (cumulative avg. time/unit) and right-hand (cumulative total time) graphs in Exhs. 10-10 and 10-12. Learning curves generate cumulative total time functions that increase at a decreasing rate. As production increases, *total time (and cost) increases, but the time (and cost) per unit decreases.* Note that the rate of improvement becomes smaller over time as the "easy" gains are realized.

EXHIBIT 10-11
Cumulative Average-Time Learning Model

Cumulative Number of Units (1)	Cumulative Average Time Per Unit (y): Labor Hours (2)	Cumulative Total Time: Labor-Hours (3) = 1 × (2)	Individual Unit Time for Xth Unit: Labor-Hours (4)
1	100.00	100.00	100.00
2	80.00 (100 × 0.8)	160.00	60.00
3	70.21	210.63	50.63
4	64.00 (80 × 0.8)	256.00	45.37
5	59.57	297.85	41.85
6	56.17	337.02	39.17
7	53.45	374.15	37.13
8	51.20 (64 × 0.8)	409.60	35.45
•	•	•	•
•	•	•	•
•	•	•	•
16	40.96 (51.2 × 0.8)	655.36	28.06

NOTE: The mathematical relationship underlying the cumulative average-time learning model is

$$y = aX^b$$

where y = Cumulative average time (labor-hours) per unit
   X = Cumulative number of units produced
   a = Time (labor-hours) required to produce the first unit
   b = Rate of learning

The value of b is calculated as $b = \dfrac{\ln (\% \text{ learning})}{\ln 2}$

For an 80% learning curve, $b = \dfrac{-0.2231}{0.6931} = -0.3219$

As an illustration, when $X = 3$, $a = 100$, and $b = -0.3219$

$$y = 100 \times 3^{-0.3219} = 70.21 \text{ labor-hours}$$

The cumulative total time when $X = 3$ is $70.21 \times 3 = 210.63$ labor-hours.
   The individual unit times in column 4 are calculated using the data in column 3. For example, the individual unit time of 50.63 labor-hours for the third unit is calculated as $210.63 - 160.00$.

EXHIBIT 10-12
Plots for Incremental Unit-Time Learning Model

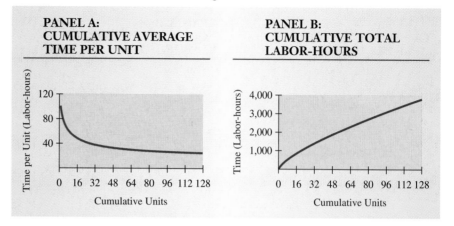

PANEL A:
CUMULATIVE AVERAGE TIME PER UNIT

PANEL B:
CUMULATIVE TOTAL LABOR-HOURS

Correcting Student Misconceptions
Students often confuse the cumulative avg.-time and the incremental unit-time models. In an 80% cumulative avg.-time model, when total (cumulative) production doubles to 2X, the *cumulative avg. time/unit* (*NOT* the time to make the last unit) declines to 80% of what it was at X. The last units were produced faster than this average. In an 80% *incremental* unit-time model, the time to make *the last unit* declines to 80% of what it was at X. Therefore, the cumulative avg.-time model implies learning occurs at a faster rate (compared to the incremental unit-time model). Emphasize these points in the context of an example such as Exhs. 10-11 and 10-13 or Probs. 10-32 and 10-33.

Teaching Tip Results are very sensitive to a change in the learning %, because the effect of the learning % is compounded as production increases. Have students reanalyze a homework problem using a 5% higher learning curve, and compare the results with their original analysis.

EXHIBIT 10-13
Incremental Unit-Time Learning Model

Cumulative Number of Units (1)	Individual Unit Time for Xth Unit (y): Labor Hours (2)	Cumulative Total Time: Labor-Hours (3)	Cumulative Average Time Per Unit: Labor-Hours (4) = (3) ÷ (1)
1	100.00	100.00	100.00
2	80.00 (100 × 0.8)	180.00	90.00
3	70.21	250.21	83.40
4	64.00 (80 × 0.8)	314.21	78.55
5	59.57	373.78	74.76
6	56.17	429.95	71.66
7	53.45	483.40	69.06
8	51.20 (64 × 0.8)	534.60	66.82
•	•	•	•
•	•	•	•
•	•	•	•
16	40.96 (51.2 × 0.8)	892.00	55.75

NOTE: The mathematical relationship underlying the incremental unit-time learning model is

$$y = aX^b$$

where
- y = Time (labor-hours) taken to produce the last single unit
- X = Cumulative number of units produced
- a = Time (labor-hours) required to produce the first unit
- b = Rate of learning

$$b = \frac{\ln (\% \text{ learning})}{\ln 2}$$

For an 80% learning curve, $\quad b = \dfrac{-0.2231}{0.6931} = -0.3219$

As an illustration, when $X = 3$, $a = 100$, and $b = -0.3219$

$$y = 100 \times 3^{-0.3219} = 70.21 \text{ labor-hours}$$

The cumulative total time when $X = 3$ is $100 + 80 + 70.21 = 250.21$ labor-hours.

Reinforcing Problems Exer. 10-27 and 10-28 and Probs. 10-32 and 10-33 cover learning curves.

Exhibit 10-13. We obtain the cumulative total time by summing the individual unit times. For example, to produce 4 cumulative units would require 314.21 labor-hours (100.00 + 80.00 + 70.21 + 64.00).

The incremental unit-time model predicts that a higher cumulative total time is required to produce two or more units than does the cumulative average-time model, assuming the same learning rate for the two models. If we compare the results in Exhibit 10-11 with those in Exhibit 10-13, to produce 4 cumulative units, the 80% incremental unit-time learning model predicts 314.21 labor-hours versus 256.00 labor-hours predicted by the 80% cumulative average-time learning model.

Which of these two models is preferable? The choice can only be made on a case-by-case basis. In each situation, companies choose the model that more accurately approximates the behavior of manufacturing labor-hour usage as production levels increase. Engineers, plant managers, and workers are good sources of information on the amount and type of learning actually occurring as production increases. Plotting this information is helpful in selecting the appropriate model.

Setting Prices, Budgets, and Standards

How do companies use learning curves? Consider the data in Exhibit 10-11 for the cumulative average-time learning model. Suppose the variable costs subject to learning effects consist of direct manufacturing labor ($20 per hour) and related overhead ($30 per hour). Management should predict the costs shown in Exhibit 10-14.

These data show that the effects of the learning curve could have a major influence on decisions. For example, a company might set an extremely low selling price on its product in order to generate high demand. As the company's production increases to meet this growing demand, costs per unit drop. The company rides the product down the learning curve as it establishes a higher market share. Although the company may have earned little operating income on its first unit sold—it may actually have lost money—the company earns more operating income per unit as output increases.

Alternatively, subject to legal and other considerations, the company might set a low price on just the final 8 units. After all, the labor and related overhead costs per unit are predicted to be only $12,288 for these final 8 units ($32,768 − $20,480). The per unit costs of $1,536 on these final 8 units ($12,288 ÷ 8) are much lower than the $5,000 costs per unit of the first unit produced.

Many companies incorporate learning-curve effects when evaluating performance. For example, the Nissan Motor Company expects its workers to learn and improve on the job and evaluates performance accordingly. It sets assembly-labor efficiency standards for new models of cars after taking into account the learning that will occur as more units are produced.

The learning-curve models examined in Exhibits 10-11 to 10-14 assume that learning is driven by a single variable (production output). Other models of learning have been developed by companies such as Analog Devices and Yokogowa Hewlett-Packard, which focus on how quality (rather than manufacturing labor-hours) will change over time (rather than as more units are produced). Some recent studies suggest that factors other than production output—such as job rotation and organizing workers into teams—contribute to learning that improves quality.

Example Pricing down the learning curve helps companies gain market share. Japan dominates the world's FAX machine market because they "priced the machine in the U.S. 2 or 3 years down the learning curve—a good 40% lower (than U.S. manufacturers). They had the market virtually overnight." (Drucker, *WSJ*, 10/21/93.) Another advantage of pricing down the learning curve is that lowering the price of the product can create new markets; e.g., DuPont initially priced nylon well down the learning curve. This stimulated a new market (automobile tires) that became bigger and more profitable than the women's wear market.

EXHIBIT 10-14
Predicting Costs Using Learning Curves

Cumulative Number of Units	Cumulative Average Time Per Unit: Labor-Hours[a]	Cumulative Total Time: Labor-Hours	Cumulative Costs	Additions to Cumulative Costs
1	100.00	100.00	$ 5,000 (100.00 × $50)	$ 5,000
2	80.00	160.00	8,000 (160.00 × $50)	3,000
4	64.00	256.00	12,800 (256.00 × $50)	4,800
8	51.20	409.60	20,480 (409.60 × $50)	7,680
16	40.96	655.36	32,768 (655.36 × $50)	12,288

[a]Based on the cumulative average-time learning model. See Exhibit 10-11 for the computation of these amounts.

DATA COLLECTION AND ADJUSTMENT ISSUES

The ideal database for estimating cost functions quantitatively has two characteristics:

1. It contains numerous reliably measured observations of the cost driver(s) and the cost that is the dependent variable. Errors in measuring the costs and cost driver(s) are particularly serious. They result in inaccurate estimates of the effect of the cost driver(s) on costs.

2. It considers many values for the cost driver that span a wide range. Using only a few values that are grouped closely considers too small a segment of the relevant range and reduces the confidence in the estimates obtained.

Unfortunately, cost analysts typically do not have the advantage of working with a database having both characteristics. This section outlines some frequently encountered data problems and steps the analyst can take to overcome these problems.

Teaching Tip Divide the class into groups of approx. 4 students. Assign each group 1 of the 7 frequently encountered data problems. Ask students to develop an example of the data problem in the context of their experience, and to suggest what *specific* kinds of decisions this problem might affect. Also ask them to suggest a means of dealing with the problem.

1. The time period for measuring the dependent variable (for example, machine-lubricant costs) does not properly match the period for measuring the cost driver(s). This problem often arises when accounting records are not kept on an accrual basis. Consider a cost function with machine-lubricant costs as the dependent variable and machine-hours as the cost driver. Assume that the lubricant is purchased sporadically and stored for later use. Records maintained on a cash basis will indicate no lubricant consumption in many months and sizable lubricant consumption in other months. These records present an obviously inaccurate picture of what is actually taking place. The analyst should use accrual accounting to measure consumption of machine lubricants to better match costs with the cost driver in this example.

2. Fixed costs are allocated as if they are variable. For example, costs such as depreciation, insurance, or rent may be allocated to products to calculate costs per unit of output. *The danger is to regard these costs as variable rather than as fixed. They seem to be variable because of the allocation methods used.* To avoid this problem, the analyst should distinguish carefully between fixed and variable costs, and not treat allocated fixed costs per unit as a variable cost.

Points to Stress Analysts can calculate more accurate product costs by categorizing costs into several smaller (more homogeneous) cost pools, each with its own driver. Such a system is obviously more difficult and expensive to implement and maintain. Deciding what level of decomposition is "best" requires trading off benefits of better decisions from more accurate data, vs. the higher costs of the more detailed system. Reduced cost of information gathering is leading companies to use a larger number of cost pools.

3. Data are either not available for all observations or are not uniformly reliable. Missing cost observations often arise from a failure to record a cost or from classifying a cost incorrectly. Recording data manually rather than electronically tends to result in a higher percentage of missing observations and erroneously entered observations. Errors also arise when data on cost drivers originate outside the internal accounting system. For example, the Accounting Department may obtain data on testing-hours for medical instruments from the company's Manufacturing Department and data on the number of items shipped to customers from the Distribution Department. These departments might not keep accurate enough records. To minimize these problems, the cost analyst should design data collection reports that regularly and routinely obtain the required data, and should follow up immediately whenever data is missing.

4. Extreme values of observations occur from errors in recording costs (for example, a misplaced decimal point); from nonrepresentative time periods (for example, from a period in which a major machine breakdown occurred or from a period in which delay in delivery of materials from an international supplier curtailed production); or from observations being outside the relevant range. Analysts should adjust or eliminate unusual observations before estimating a cost relationship. Otherwise, an incorrect estimate would result.

5. There is no homogeneous relationship between the individual cost items in the dependent variable-cost pool and the cost driver. A homogeneous relationship exists

when each activity whose costs are included in the dependent variable has the same cost driver. In this case, a single cost function can be estimated. As discussed in step 2 for estimating a cost function using quantitative analysis (p. 335), where the cost driver for each activity is different, separate cost functions, each with its own cost driver, should be estimated for each activity.

6. The relationship between the cost driver and the cost is not stationary. That is, the underlying process that generated the observations has not remained stable over time. For example, the relationship between manufacturing overhead costs and machine-hours is unlikely to be stationary if the data cover a period in which new technology was introduced. One way to see if the relationship is stationary is to split the sample into two parts and estimate separate cost relationships for the before- and after-technology change periods. Then, if the estimated coefficients for the two periods are similar, the analyst can pool the data to estimate a single cost relationship. Where feasible, pooling data provides a larger data set for the estimation, which increases the confidence in the cost predictions being made.

7. Inflation has affected the dependent variable, the cost driver, or both. For example, inflation may cause costs to change even when there is no change in the cost driver. To study the underlying cause-and-effect relationship between the cost driver and costs, the analyst should remove purely inflationary price effects from the data.

In many cases, a cost analyst must expend much effort to reduce the effect of these problems before estimating a cost function on the basis of past data.

PROBLEM FOR SELF-STUDY

PROBLEM
The Helicopter Division of Aerospatiale is examining helicopter assembly costs at its plant in Marseilles, France. It has received an initial order for eight of its new land-surveying helicopters. Aerospatiale can adopt one of two methods of assembling the helicopters:

	Labor-Intensive Assembly Method	Machine-Intensive Assembly Method
Direct materials costs per helicopter	$40,000	$36,000
Direct assembly labor time for first helicopter	2,000 labor-hours	800 labor-hours
Learning curve for assembly labor time per helicopter	85% cumulative average time[a]	90% incremental unit time[b]
Direct assembly labor costs	$30 per hour	$30 per hour
Equipment-related indirect manufacturing costs	$12 per direct assembly labor-hour	$45 per direct assembly labor-hour
Materials-handling-related indirect manufacturing costs	50% of direct materials costs	50% of direct materials costs

[a]An 85% learning curve is expressed mathematically as $q = -0.2345$.
[b]A 90% learning curve is expressed mathematically as $q = -0.1520$.

Required
1. How many direct assembly labor-hours are required to assemble the first eight helicopters under (a) the labor-intensive method, and (b) the machine-intensive method?
2. What is the cost of assembling the first eight helicopters under (a) the labor-intensive method, and (b) the machine-intensive method?

SOLUTION

1a. Labor-intensive assembly method based on cumulative average-time learning model (85% learning).

Cumulative Number of Units (1)	Cumulative Average Time Per Unit (y): Labor-Hours (2)	Cumulative Total Time: Labor-Hours (3) = 1 × (2)	Individual Unit Time for Xth Unit: Labor-Hours (4)
1	2,000	2,000	2,000
2	1,700 (2,000 × 0.85)	3,400	1,400
3	1,546	4,638	1,238
4	1,445 (1,700 × 0.85)	5,780	1,142
5	1,371	6,855	1,075
6	1,314	7,884	1,029
7	1,267	8,869	985
8	1,228 (1,445 × 0.85)	9,826	957

The cumulative average time per unit for the Xth unit in column 2 is calculated as $y = aX^b$; see Exhibit 10-11 (p. 345). For example, when $X = 3$, $y = 2,000 \times 3^{-0.2345} = 1,546$ labor-hours.

1b. Machine-intensive assembly method based on incremental unit-time learning model (90% learning).

Cumulative Number of Units (1)	Individual Unit Time for Xth Unit (y): Labor-Hours (2)	Cumulative Total Time: Labor-Hours (3)	Cumulative Average Time Per Unit: Labor-Hours (4) = (3) ÷ (1)
1	800	800	800
2	720 (800 × 0.9)	1,520	760
3	677	2,197	732
4	648 (720 × 0.9)	2,845	711
5	626	3,471	694
6	609	4,080	680
7	595	4,675	668
8	583 (648 × 0.9)	5,258	657

The individual unit time for the Xth unit in column 2 is calculated as $y = ax^b$; see Exhibit 10-13 (p. 346). For example, when $X = 3$, $y = 800 \times 3^{-0.1520} = 677$ labor-hours.

2. Costs of assembling the first eight helicopters are:

	Labor-Intensive Assembly Method	Machine-Intensive Assembly Method
Direct materials: 8 × $40,000; 8 × $36,000	$320,000	$288,000
Direct assembly labor:		
9,826 × $30; 5,258 × $30	294,780	157,740
Indirect manufacturing costs		
Equipment-related:		
9,826 × $12; 5,258 × $45	117,912	236,610
Materials-handling-related:		
.50 × $320,000; .50 × $288,000	160,000	144,000
Total assembly costs	$892,692	$826,350

The machine-intensive method has assembly costs that are $66,342 lower than the labor-intensive method ($892,692 − $826,350).

SUMMARY

The following points are linked to the chapter's learning objectives:

1. Two assumptions frequently made in cost-behavior estimation are (a) that changes in total costs can be explained by changes in the level of a single activity, and (b) that cost behavior can adequately be approximated by a linear function of the activity level within the relevant range.

2. A linear cost function is a cost function where, within the relevant range, the graph of total costs versus the level of a single activity is a straight line. Linear cost functions can be described by a constant (a), which represents the estimate of the total cost component that, within the relevant range, does not vary with changes in the level of the activity, and a slope coefficient (b), which represents the estimate of the amount by which total costs change for each unit change in the level of the activity within the relevant range. Three types of linear cost functions are variable, fixed, and mixed (or semivariable).

3. Four approaches to estimating cost functions are the industrial engineering method, the conference method, the account analysis method, and quantitative analysis methods (the high-low method and the regression analysis method). Regression analysis is a systematic approach to estimating a cost function on the basis of identified cost drivers. Ideally, the cost analyst applies more than one approach. Each approach serves as a check on the others.

4. The six steps in estimating a cost function on the basis of an analysis of current or past cost relationships are (a) choose the dependent variable; (b) identify the cost driver(s); (c) collect data on the dependent variable and the cost driver(s); (d) plot the data; (e) estimate the cost function; and (f) evaluate the estimated cost function. In most situations, working closely with operating management, the cost analyst will cycle through these steps several times before identifying an acceptable cost function.

5. Three criteria for evaluating and choosing cost drivers are (a) economic plausibility, (b) goodness of fit, and (c) slope of the regression line.

6. A nonlinear cost function is a cost function where, within the relevant range, the graph of total costs versus the level of a single activity is not a straight line.

Nonlinear costs can arise due to quantity discounts, step cost functions, and learning-curve effects.

7. The learning curve is an example of a nonlinear cost function. Labor-hours per unit decline as units of production increase. In the cumulative average-time learning model, the cumulative average-time per unit declines by a constant percentage each time the cumulative quantity of units produced doubles. In the incremental unit-time learning model, the incremental unit time (the time needed to produce the last unit) declines by a constant percentage each time the cumulative quantity of units produced doubles.

8. The most difficult task in cost estimation is collecting high-quality, reliably measured data on the dependent variable and the cost driver(s). Common problems include missing data, extreme values of observations, changes in technology, and distortions resulting from inflation.

APPENDIX: REGRESSION ANALYSIS

This Appendix describes the estimation of the regression equation, several commonly used regression statistics, and how to choose among cost functions that have been estimated by regression analysis. We use the data for Elegant Rugs presented in Exhibit 10-3 (p. 334).

Estimating the Regression Line

The least-squares technique for estimating the regression line minimizes the sum of the squares of the vertical deviations (distances) from the data points to the estimated regression line.

The objective is to find the values of a and b in the predicting equation $y = a + bX$, where y is the predicted cost value as distinguished from the observed cost value, which we denote by Y. We wish to find the numerical values of a and b that minimize $\Sigma(Y - y)^2$, the sum of the vertical deviations between Y and y. Generally, these computations are done using software packages such as SPSS, SAS, and Excel. For the data in our example,[2] $a = \$300.98$ and $b = \$10.31$ so that the equation of the least squares line is $y = \$300.98 + \$10.31X$.

---

[2]The formulae for a and b are

$$a = \frac{(\Sigma Y)(\Sigma X^2) - (\Sigma X)(\Sigma XY)}{n(\Sigma X^2) - (\Sigma X)(\Sigma X)} \quad \text{and} \quad b = \frac{n(\Sigma XY) - (\Sigma X)(\Sigma Y)}{n(\Sigma X^2) - (\Sigma X)(\Sigma X)},$$

where for the Elegant Rugs data in Exhibit 10-3,

n = number of data points = 12

ΣX = sum of the given X values = $68 + 88 + \cdots + 48 = 862$

ΣX^2 = sum of squares of the X values

$\qquad = (68)^2 + (88)^2 + \cdots + (48)^2 = 4{,}624 + 7{,}744 + \cdots + 2{,}304 = 64{,}900$

ΣY = sum of given Y values = $1{,}190 + 1{,}211 + \cdots + 963 = 12{,}501$

ΣXY = sum of the amounts obtained by multiplying each of the given X values by the associated observed Y value

$\qquad = (68)(1{,}190) + (88)(1{,}211) + \cdots + (48)(963)$

$\qquad = 80{,}920 + 106{,}568 + \cdots + 46{,}224 = 928{,}716$

$$a = \frac{(12{,}501)(64{,}900) - (862)(928{,}716)}{12(64{,}900) - (862)(862)} = \$300.98$$

$$b = \frac{12(928{,}716) - (862)(12{,}501)}{12(64{,}900) - (862)(862)} = \$10.31$$

Goodness of Fit

Goodness of fit measures how well the predicted values, y, based on the cost driver, X, match actual cost observations, Y. The regression analysis method computes a formal measure of goodness of fit, called the coefficient of determination. The **coefficient of determination, r^2**, measures the percentage of variation in Y explained by X (the independent variable). It also indicates the proportion of the variance of Y, $(Y - \overline{Y})^2 \div n$, that is explained by the independent variable X (where $\overline{Y} = \Sigma Y \div n$). It is more convenient to express the coefficient of determination as 1 minus the proportion of total variance that is *not* explained by the independent variable. The unexplained variance arises because of differences between the actual values of Y and the predicted values of y, which in the Elegant Rugs example is given by[3]

$$r^2 = 1 - \frac{\text{Unexplained variation}}{\text{Total variation}} = 1 - \frac{\Sigma(Y - y)^2}{\Sigma(Y - \overline{Y})^2} = 1 - \frac{290,824}{607,699} = .52$$

The calculations indicate that r^2 increases as the predicted values y more closely approximate the actual observations Y. The range of r^2 is from 0 (implying no explanatory power) to 1 (implying perfect explanatory power). Generally, an r^2 of .30 or higher passes the goodness-of-fit test. Do not rely exclusively on goodness of fit. It can lead to the indiscriminate inclusion of independent variables that increase r^2 but have no economic plausibility as cost driver(s). Goodness of fit has meaning only if the relationship between costs and the drivers is economically plausible.

Significance of Independent Variables

A key question that managers ask is, Do changes in the economically plausible independent variable result in significant changes in the dependent variable, or alternatively, is the slope b of the regression line statistically significant? Recall, for example, that in the regression of machine-hours and indirect manufacturing labor costs in the Elegant Rugs illustration, b is estimated from a sample of 12 observations. The estimate b is subject to random factors, as are all sample statistics. That is, a different sample of 12 data points will give a different estimate of b. The **standard error of the estimated coefficient** indicates how much the estimated value b is likely to be affected by random factors. The t-value of the b coefficient measures how large the value of the estimated coefficient is relative to its standard error. A t-value with an absolute value greater than 2.00 suggests that the b coefficient is significantly different from zero.[4] In other words, a relationship exists between the independent variable and the dependent variable that cannot be attributed to chance alone.

Exhibit 10-15 presents a convenient format for summarizing the regression results for indirect manufacturing labor costs and machine-hours. The t-value for the slope coefficient b is $\$10.31 \div \$3.12 = 3.30$, which exceeds the benchmark of 2.00. Therefore, the coefficient of the machine-hours variable is significantly different from zero—that is, the probability is low (less than 5%) that random factors

Points to Stress Most statistical regression packages can help assess the extent to which the *goodness-of-fit, significance of independent variables, and specification of estimation assumptions* criteria are met. In addition, the packages often provide procedures designed to mitigate the effects of these violations of the regression assumptions. However, in the end it's most important that the cost analyst use judgment to assess whether the independent variable is plausibly a cost driver for the dependent variable costs.

Points to Stress Most statistical packages routinely calculate these t-values, and the resulting statistical significance levels. If the slope of the regression line is not statistically different from zero, the inference is that the cost driver chosen tells the manager very little about the indirect cost.

---

[3]From footnote 2, $\Sigma Y = 12,501$ and $\overline{Y} = 12,501 \div 12 = 1,041.75$.

$$\Sigma(Y - \overline{Y})^2 = (1,190 - 1,041.75)^2 + (1,211 - 1,041.75)^2 + \cdots + (963 - 1,041.75)^2 = 607,699$$

Each value of X generates a predicted value y. For example, in week 1, $y = \$300.98 + (\$10.31 \times 68) = \$1002.06$; in week 2, $y = \$300.98 + (\$10.31 \times 88) = \$1,208.26$; and in week 12, $y = \$300.98 + (\$10.31 \times 48) = \$795.86$.

$$\Sigma(Y - y)^2 = (1,190 - 1,002.06)^2 + (1,211 - 1,208.26)^2 + \cdots + (963 - 795.86)^2 = 290,824$$

[4]The benchmark t-value for inferring that a b coefficient is significantly different from zero is a function of the degrees of freedom in a regression. The benchmark of 2.00 assumes a sample size of 60 observations. The number of degrees of freedom is calculated as the sample size minus the number of a and b parameters estimated in the regression. The smaller the sample size, the greater is the benchmark t-values. For simplicity, we use a cut-off t-value of 2.00 throughout this chapter.

EXHIBIT 10-15

Simple Regression Results with Indirect Manufacturing Labor Costs as Dependent Variable and Machine-Hours as Independent Variable (Cost Driver) for Elegant Rugs

Variable	Coefficient (1)	Standard Error (2)	t-Value (3) = (1) ÷ (2)
Constant	$300.98	$229.75	1.31
Independent variable 1: Machine hours	$10.31	$3.12	3.30
$r^2 = .52$; Durbin-Watson statistic = 2.05			

Points to Stress Putting confidence intervals around the regression coefficients enables mgrs. to assess the range of the likely effect on costs of changes in the independent variable.

could have caused the coefficient b to be positive. Alternatively, we can restate our conclusion in terms of a "confidence interval"—there is less than a 5% chance that the true value of the machine-hours coefficient lies outside the range $10.31 \pm (2.00 \times \$3.12)$ or $10.31 \pm \$6.24$, or from $4.07 and $16.55. Therefore, we can conclude that changes in machine-hours do affect indirect manufacturing labor costs. Similarly, using data from Exhibit 10-15, the t-value for the constant term a is $300.98 \div \$229.76 = 1.31$, which is less than 2.00. This value indicates that, within the relevant range, the constant term is not significantly different from zero.

Specification Analysis of Estimation Assumptions

Teaching Tip Go slowly when presenting specification analysis. Many students find the material "tough to read." Use an example such as Prob. 10-35, 10-36, or 10-37 to illustrate this section.

Specification analysis is the testing of the assumptions of regression analysis. If the assumptions of (1) linearity within the relevant range, (2) constant variance of residuals, (3) independence of residuals, and (4) normality of residuals hold, the simple regression procedures give reliable estimates of unknown coefficient values. This section provides a brief overview of specification analysis. When these assumptions are not satisfied, more complex regression procedures are necessary to obtain the best estimates.[5]

1. *Linearity within the relevant range.* A common assumption and one that appears to be reasonable in many business applications is that a linear relationship exists between the independent variable X and the dependent variable Y within the relevant range. If a linear regression model is used to estimate a fundamentally nonlinear relationship, however, the coefficient estimates obtained will be inaccurate.

Points to Stress Costs are often "sticky" downwards. Once employees become accustomed to a certain level of resources, it can be difficult to reduce those resources, even if the amt. of work to be done has declined. For example, many mgrs. now do their own word processing. However, secretarial costs will not decline unless mgt. consciously reduces the # of secretaries. Thus, the level of control mgt. exerts can affect the linearity of the cost function.

Where there is only one independent variable, the easiest way to check for linearity is to study the data plotted on a scatter diagram, a step that often is unwisely skipped. Exhibit 10-6 (p. 338) presents a scatter diagram for the indirect manufacturing labor costs and machine-hours variables of Elegant Rugs shown in Exhibit 10-3 (p. 334). The scatter diagram reveals that linearity appears to be a reasonable assumption for these data.

The learning-curve models discussed in the chapter (pp. 344–348) are examples of nonlinear cost functions. Costs increase when the level of production increases, but by lesser amounts than would occur with a linear cost function. In this case, the analyst should estimate a nonlinear cost function that explicitly incorporates learning effects.

2. *Constant variance of residuals.* The vertical deviation of the observed value Y from the regression line estimate y is called the *residual term*, *disturbance term*, or *error term*, $u = Y - y$. The assumption of constant variance implies that the residual terms are unaffected by the level of the independent variable. The assumption also implies that there is a uniform scatter, or dispersion, of the data points about the regression line. The scatter diagram is the easiest way to check for *constant variance*. This assumption holds for Panel A of Exhibit 10-16 but not for Panel B. Constant variance is also known as *homoscedasticity*. Violation of this assumption is called *heteroscedasticity*.

[5]For details see, for example, C. J. Watson, P. Billingsley, D. J. Croft and D. V. Huntsberger, *Statistics for Management and Economics*, 5th ed. (Needham Heights, MA: Allyn and Bacon, 1993) and W. H. Greene, *Econometric Analysis*, 3rd ed. (Upper Saddle River, N. J.: Prentice Hall, 1996).

EXHIBIT 10-16
Constant Variance of Residuals Assumption

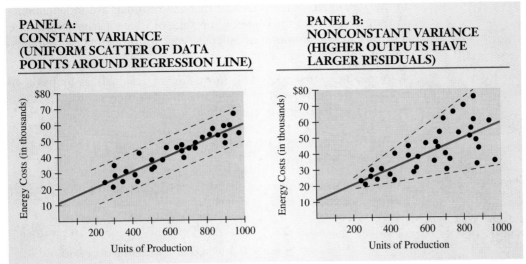

Heteroscedasticity does not affect the accuracy of the regression estimates *a* and *b*. It does, however, reduce the reliability of the estimates of the standard errors, and thus affects the precision with which inferences can be drawn.

3. *Independence of residuals.* The assumption of independence of residuals is that the residual term for any one observation is not related to the residual term for any other observation. The problem of *serial correlation* in the residuals (also called *autocorrelation*) arises when there is a systematic pattern in the sequence of residuals such that the residual in observation *n* conveys information about the residuals in observations *n* + 1, *n* + 2, and so on. The scatter diagram helps in identifying autocorrelation. Autocorrelation does not exist in Panel A of Exhibit 10-17 but does exist in Panel B. Observe the systematic pattern of the residuals in Panel B—positive residuals for extreme quantities of direct materials used and negative residuals for moderate quantities of direct materials used. No such pattern exists in Panel A.

Like nonconstant variance in residuals, serial correlation does not affect the accuracy of the regression estimates *a* and *b*. It does, however, affect the standard errors of the coefficients, which in turn affects the precision with which inferences about the population parameters can be drawn from the regression estimates.

Points to Stress Constant variance of residuals and independence of residuals are relatively technical concepts. The text doesn't pursue these concepts in detail, as the basic concern is with the use of cost data in regression, and not with regression analysis itself. Users of regression analysis may want to consult with technical experts on regression when obtaining a reliable cost function is critical to their decisions.

EXHIBIT 10-17
Independence of Residuals Assumption

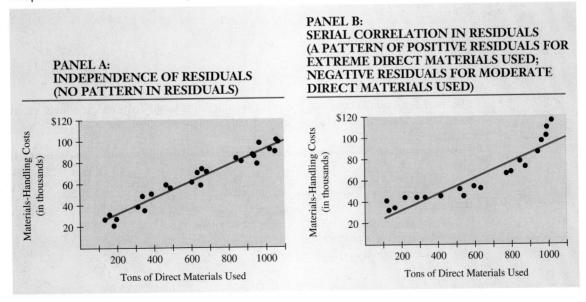

The Durbin-Watson statistic is one measure of serial correlation in the estimated residuals. For samples of 10–20 observations, a Durbin-Watson statistic in the 1.10–2.90 range indicates that the residuals are independent. The Durbin-Watson statistic for the regression results of Elegant Rugs in Exhibit 10-15 is 2.05. Therefore, an assumption of independence in the estimated residuals seems reasonable for this regression model.

4. *Normality of residuals.* The normality of residuals assumption means that the residuals are distributed normally around the regression line. This assumption is necessary for making inferences about *y*, *a*, and *b*.

Using Regression Output to Choose Cost Drivers of Cost Functions

Consider the two choices of cost drivers we described earlier for indirect manufacturing labor costs (*y*):

$$y = a + (b \times \text{Machine-hours})$$

$$y = a + (b \times \text{Direct manufacturing labor-hours})$$

Exhibits 10-6 and 10-8 present plots of the data for the two regressions. Exhibit 10-15 reports regression results for the cost function using machine-hours as the independent variable. Exhibit 10-18 presents comparable regression results for the cost function using direct manufacturing labor-hours as the independent variable.

On the basis of the material in this Appendix, which regression is better? Exhibit 10-19 compares these two cost functions in a systematic way. For several criteria, the cost function based on machine-hours is preferable to the cost function based on direct manufacturing labor-hours. The economic plausibility criterion is especially important.

Do not always assume that any one cost function will perfectly satisfy all the criteria in Exhibit 10-19. A cost analyst must often make a choice among "imperfect" cost functions, in the sense that the data of any particular cost function will not perfectly meet one or more of the assumptions underlying regression analysis.

Multiple Regression and Cost Hierarchies

In some cases, a satisfactory estimation of a cost function may be based on only one independent variable, such as machine-hours. In many cases, however, basing the estimation on more than one independent variable is more economically plausible and improves accuracy. The most widely used equations to express relationships between two or more independent variables and a dependent variable are linear in the form

$$Y = a + b_1 X_1 + b_2 X_2 + \cdots + u$$

EXHIBIT 10-18

Simple Regression Results with Indirect Manufacturing Labor Costs as Dependent Variable and Direct Manufacturing Labor-Hours as Independent Variable (Cost Driver) for Elegant Rugs

Variable	Coefficient (1)	Standard Error (2)	*t*-Value (3) = (1) ÷ (2)
Constant	$744.67	$217.61	3.42
Independent variable 1: Direct manufacturing labor-hours	$7.72	$5.40	1.43
$r^2 = .17$; Durbin-Watson statistic = 2.26			

EXHIBIT 10-19

Comparison of Alternative Cost Functions for Indirect Manufacturing Labor Costs Estimated with Simple Regression for Elegant Rugs

Criterion	Cost Function 1: Machine-Hours as Independent Variable	Cost Function 2: Direct Manufacturing Labor-Hours as Independent Variable
◆ Economic plausibility	◆ A positive relationship between indirect manufacturing labor costs (technical support labor) and machine-hours is economically plausible in a highly automated plant.	◆ A positive relationship between indirect manufacturing labor costs and direct manufacturing labor-hours is economically plausible, but less so than machine-hours in a highly automated plant on a week-to-week basis.
◆ Goodness of fit	◆ $r^2 = .52$ Excellent goodness of fit	◆ $r^2 = .17$ Poor goodness of fit
◆ Significance of independent variable(s)	◆ The t-value of 3.30 is significant.	◆ The t-value of 1.43 is not significant.
◆ Specification analysis of estimation assumptions	◆ Plot of the data indicates that assumptions of linearity, constant variance, independence of residuals (Durbin-Watson statistic = 2.05), and normality of residuals hold, but inferences drawn from only 12 observations are not reliable.	◆ Plot of the data indicates that assumptions of linearity, constant variance, independence of residuals (Durbin-Watson statistic = 2.26), and normality of residuals hold, but inferences drawn from only 12 observations are not reliable.

where

$$Y = \text{cost variable to be predicted}$$

$$X_1, X_2, \cdots = \text{independent variables on which the prediction is to be based}$$

$$a, b_1, b_2, \cdots = \text{estimated coefficients of the regression model}$$

$$u = \text{residual term that includes the net effect of other factors not in the model and measurement errors in the dependent and independent variables}$$

Example Consider the Elegant Rugs data in Exhibit 10-20 (p. 358). The company's ABC analysis indicates that indirect manufacturing labor costs include sizable costs incurred for setup and changeover costs when a new batch of carpets is started. Management believes that in addition to machine-hours (an output unit-level cost driver), indirect manufacturing labor costs are also affected by the number of different batches of carpets produced during each week (a batch-level driver). Elegant Rugs estimates the relationship between two independent variables, machine-hours and number of separate carpet batches worked on during the week, and indirect manufacturing labor costs.

Exhibit 10-21 presents results for the following multiple regression model, using data in columns 1, 2, and 4 of Exhibit 10-20:

$$y = \$42.58 + \$7.60X_1 + \$37.77X_2$$

where X_1 is the number of machine-hours and X_2 is the number of production batches. It is economically plausible that both machine-hours and production batches would help explain variations in indirect manufacturing labor costs at Elegant Rugs. The r^2 of .52 for the simple regression using machine-hours (Exhibit

Curriculum Linkage Multiple regression analysis is useful for estimating TC when there are elements from different levels of the cost hierarchy. The text develops an example using MH (an output unit-level cost driver) and # of batches (a batch-level driver). Both cost drivers are statistically significant in the example. This should not be surprising, given the discussion of batch-level costs in Chap. 5.

EXHIBIT 10-20

Weekly Indirect Manufacturing Labor Costs, Machine-Hours, Direct Manufacturing Labor-Hours, and Number of Production Batches for Elegant Rugs

Week	Indirect Manufacturing Labor Costs (1)	Machine-Hours (2)	Direct Manufacturing Labor-Hours (3)	Number of Production Batches (4)
1	$1,190	68	30	12
2	1,211	88	35	15
3	1,004	62	36	13
4	917	72	20	11
5	770	60	47	10
6	1,456	96	45	12
7	1,180	78	44	17
8	710	46	38	7
9	1,316	82	70	14
10	1,032	94	30	12
11	752	68	29	7
12	963	48	38	14

10-16) increases to .72 with the multiple regression in Exhibit 10-21. The t-values suggest that the independent variable coefficients of both machine-hours and number of production batches are significantly different from zero ($t = 2.74$ is the coefficient for machine-hours, and $t = 2.48$ is the coefficient for number of production batches). The multiple regression model in Exhibit 10-21 satisfies both economic plausibility and statistical criteria, and it explains much greater variation in indirect manufacturing labor costs than does the simple regression model using only machine-hours as the independent variable. Machine-hours and number of production batches are important cost drivers of indirect manufacturing labor costs at Elegant Rugs.

In Exhibit 10-21, the slope coefficients—$7.60 for machine-hours and $37.77 for number of production batches—measure the change in indirect manufacturing labor costs associated with a unit change in an independent variable (assuming that the other independent variable is held constant). For example, indirect manufacturing labor costs increase by $37.77 when one more production batch is added, assuming that the number of machine-hours is held constant.

An alternative approach would create two separate cost pools—one for costs tied to machine-hours and another for costs tied to production batches. Elegant Rugs would then estimate the relationship between the cost driver and overhead costs separately for each cost pool. The difficult task under that approach would be properly dividing overhead costs into the two cost pools.

Points to Stress/Curriculum Linkage-
Compare the results of the multiple regression analysis,

TC = $42.58 + ($7.60/MH)
    (# MH) + ($37.77/batch)
    (# batches)

with the original univariate regression:

TC = $300.98 + ($10.31/MH)
    (# MH)

The original univariate model is misspecified because it omits the effect of the # of batches. The univariate regression's cost/MH is higher than that of the multiple regression. The univariate model will overcost products that use a lot of MH. This is consistent with Chap. 5's explanation that ignoring batch-level, product-sustaining, and facility-sustaining cost drivers generally over-costs high-volume products.

EXHIBIT 10-21

Multiple Regression Results with Indirect Manufacturing Labor Costs and Two Independent Variables or Cost Drivers (Machine-Hours and Production Batches) for Elegant Rugs

Variable	Coefficient (1)	Standard Error (2)	t-Value (3) = (1) ÷ (2)
Constant	$42.58	$213.91	0.20
Independent variable 1: Machine hours	$7.60	$2.77	2.74
Independent variable 2: Number of production batches	$37.77	$15.25	2.48

$r^2 = .72$; Durbin-Watson statistic = 2.49

Multicollinearity

A major concern that arises with multiple regression is multicollinearity. **Multicollinearity** exists when two or more independent variables are highly correlated with each other. Generally, users of regression analysis believe that a coefficient of correlation between independent variables greater than .70 indicates multicollinearity. Multicollinearity increases the standard errors of the coefficients of the individual variables. That is, variables that are economically and statistically significant will appear insignificant.

The coefficients of correlation between the potential independent variables for Elegant Rugs in Exhibit 10-20 are as follows:

Pairwise Combinations	Coefficient of Correlation
Machine-hours and direct manufacturing labor-hours	.12
Machine-hours and production batches	.40
Direct manufacturing labor-hours and production batches	.31

These results indicate that multiple regressions using any pair of the independent variables in Exhibit 10-21 are not likely to encounter multicollinearity problems.

If severe multicollinearity exists, try to obtain new data that do not suffer from multicollinearity problems. Do not drop an independent variable (cost driver) that should be included in a model because it is correlated with another independent variable. Omitting such a variable will cause the estimated coefficient of the independent variable included in the model to be biased away from its true value.

▼ TERMS TO LEARN

This chapter and the Glossary at the end of this book contain definitions of the following important terms:

▼ ASSIGNMENT MATERIAL

QUESTIONS

10-1 What two assumptions are frequently made when estimating a cost function?

10-2 Describe three alternative linear cost functions.

10-3 What is the difference between a linear and a nonlinear cost function? Give an example of each type of cost function.

10-4 "High correlation between two variables means that one is the cause and the other is the effect." Do you agree? Explain.

10-5 Name four approaches to estimating a cost function.

10-6 Describe the conference method for estimating a cost function. What are two advantages of this method?

10-7 Describe the account analysis method for estimating a cost function.

10-8 List the six steps in estimating a cost function on the basis of an analysis of current or past cost relationships. Which step is typically the most difficult for a cost analyst?

10-9 When using the high-low method, should you base the high and low observations on the dependent variable or on the cost driver?

10-10 Describe three criteria for evaluating cost functions and choosing cost drivers.

10-11 Define learning curve. Outline two models that can be used when incorporating learning into the estimation of cost functions.

10-12 Discuss four frequently encountered problems when collecting cost data on variables included in a cost function.

10-13 What are the four key assumptions examined in specification analysis in the case of simple regression?

10-14 "All the independent variables in a cost function estimated with regression analysis are cost drivers." Do you agree? Explain.

10-15 "Multicollinearity exists when the dependent variable and the independent variable are highly correlated." Do you agree? Explain.

EXERCISES

10-16 Estimating a cost function. The controller of the Ijiri Company wants you to estimate a cost function from the following two observations in a general ledger account called Maintenance:

Month	Machine-Hours	Maintenance Costs Incurred
January	4,000	$3,000
February	7,000	3,900

Required
1. Estimate the cost function for maintenance.
2. Can the constant in the cost function be used as an estimate of fixed maintenance cost per month? Explain.

10-17 Identifying variable-, fixed-, and mixed-cost functions. The Pacific Corporation operates car rental agencies at over 20 airports. Customers can choose from one of three contracts for car rentals of one day or less:

◆ Contract 1: $50 for the day

◆ Contract 2: $30 for the day plus $0.20 per mile traveled

◆ Contract 3: $1.00 per mile traveled

Required
1. Plot separate graphs for each of the three contracts, with costs on the vertical axis and miles traveled on the horizontal axis.
2. Express each contract as a linear cost function of the form $y = a + bX$.
3. Identify each contract as a variable-, fixed-, or mixed-cost function.

10-18 Various cost-behavior patterns. (CPA, adapted) Select the graph that matches the numbered manufacturing cost data. Indicate by letter which graph best fits the situation or item described.

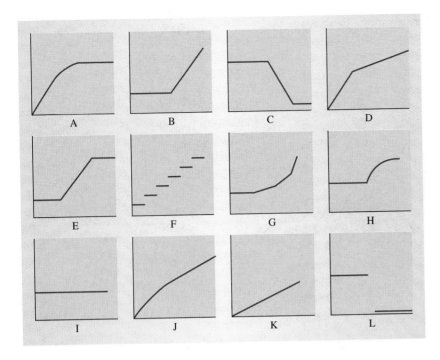

The vertical axes of the graphs represent *total* dollars of cost, and the horizontal axes represent production output during a calendar year. In each case, the zero point of dollars and production is at the intersection of the two axes. The graphs may be used more than once.

1. Annual depreciation of equipment, where the amount of depreciation charged is computed by the machine-hours method.

2. Electricity bill—a flat fixed charge, plus a variable cost after a certain number of kilowatt-hours are used, where the quantity of kilowatt-hours used varies proportionately with quantity of production output.

3. City water bill, which is computed as follows:

First 1,000,000 gallons or less	$1,000 flat fee
Next 10,000 gallons	$0.003 per gallon used
Next 10,000 gallons	$0.006 per gallon used
Next 10,000 gallons	$0.009 per gallon used
and so on	and so on

The gallons of water used vary proportionately with the quantity of production output.

4. Cost of lubricant for machines, where cost per unit decreases with each pound of lubricant used (for example, if 1 pound is used, the cost is $10; if 2 pounds are used, the cost is $19.98; if 3 pounds are used, the cost is $29.94) with a minimum cost per pound of $9.20.

5. Annual depreciation of equipment, where the amount is computed by the straight-line method. When the depreciation schedule was prepared, it was anticipated that the obsolescence factor would be greater than the wear-and-tear factor.

6. Rent on a manufacturing plant donated by the city, where the agreement calls for a fixed-fee payment unless 200,000 labor-hours are worked, in which case no rent is paid.

7. Salaries of repair personnel, where one person is needed for every 1,000 machine-hours or less (that is, 0–1,000 hours requires one person, 1,001–2,000 hours requires two people, and so on).

8. Cost of direct materials used (assume no quantity discounts).

9. Rent on a manufacturing plant donated by the county, where the agreement calls for rent of $100,000 reduced by $1 for each direct manufacturing labor-hour worked in excess of 200,000 hours, but a minimum rental fee of $20,000 must be paid.

10-19 Matching graphs with descriptions of cost behavior. (D. Green) Given below are a number of graphs, each indicating some relationship between the level of an activity and a cost. No attempt has been made to draw these graphs to any particular scale; the absolute numbers on each axis may be closely or widely spaced.

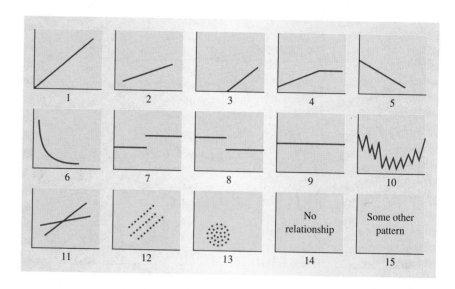

Indicate by number which graph best fits the situation or item described. Each situation or item is independent of all the others; all factors not stated are assumed to be irrelevant. Some graphs will be used more than once; some may not apply to any of the situations. Note that category 14, "No relationship," is not the same as 15, "Some other pattern."

If the horizontal axis represents the production output over the year and the vertical axis represents *total cost* or *revenue*, indicate the one best pattern or relationship for:

1. Direct materials costs

2. Supervisors' salaries

3. A breakeven graph

4. Mixed costs—for example, fixed electrical power demand charge plus variable usage rate

5. Depreciation of plant, computed on a straight-line basis

6. Data supporting the use of a variable-cost rate, such as manufacturing labor cost of $14 per unit produced

7. Incentive bonus plan that pays managers $0.10 for every unit produced above some level of production

8. Interest charges on money borrowed at a fixed rate of interest to finance the acquisition of a plant, before any payments on principal

10-20 Account analysis method. Lorenzo operates a brushless car wash. Incoming cars are put on an automatic, continuously moving conveyor belt. Cars are washed as the conveyor belt carries the car from the start station to the finish station. After the car moves off the conveyor belt, the car is dried manually. Workers then clean and vacuum the inside of the car. Workers are managed by a single supervisor. Lorenzo serviced 80,000 cars in 2001. Lorenzo reports the following costs for 2001.

Account Description	Costs
Car wash labor	$240,000
Soap, cloth, and supplies	32,000
Water	28,000
Power to move conveyor belt	72,000
Depreciation	64,000
Supervision	30,000
Cashier	16,000

Required

1. Classify each account as variable or fixed with respect to the number of cars washed. Explain.

2. Lorenzo expects to wash 90,000 cars in 2002. Use the cost classification you developed in requirement 1 to estimate Lorenzo's total costs in 2002.
3. Calculate the average cost of washing a car in 2001 and 2002. (Use the expected 90,000 car wash level for 2002.)

10-21 Account analysis method. Gower, Inc., a manufacturer of plastic products, reports the following manufacturing costs and account analysis classification for the year ended December 31, 2001.

Account	Classification	Amount
Direct materials	All variable	$300,000
Direct manufacturing labor	All variable	225,000
Power	All variable	37,500
Supervision labor	20% variable	56,250
Materials-handling labor	50% variable	60,000
Maintenance labor	40% variable	75,000
Depreciation	0% variable	95,000
Rent, property taxes, and administration	0% variable	100,000

Gower, Inc., produced 75,000 units of product in 2001. Gower's management is estimating costs for 2002 on the basis of 2001 numbers. The following additional information is available for 2002.

a. Direct materials prices in 2002 are expected to increase by 5% compared with 2001.

b. Under the terms of the labor contract, direct manufacturing labor wage rates are expected to increase by 10% in 2002 compared with 2001.

c. Power rates and wage rates for supervision, materials handling, and maintenance are not expected to change from 2001 to 2002.

d. Depreciation costs are expected to increase by 5%, and rent, property taxes, and administration costs are expected to increase by 7percent.

e. Gower, Inc., expects to manufacture and sell 80,000 units in 2002.

Required
1. Prepare a schedule of variable, fixed, and total manufacturing costs for each account category in 2002. Estimate total manufacturing costs for 2002.
2. Calculate Gower's total manufacturing cost per unit in 2001 and estimate total manufacturing cost per unit in 2002.
3. How can you obtain better estimates of fixed and variable costs? Why would these better estimates be useful to Gower?

10-22 Estimating a cost function, high-low method. Laurie Daley is examining customer-service costs in the Southern Region of Capitol Products. Capitol Products has over 200 separate electrical products that are sold with a 6-month guarantee of full repair or replacement with a new product. When a product is returned by a customer, a service report is prepared. This service report includes details of the problem and the time and cost of resolving the problem. Weekly data for the most recent 10-week period are:

Week	Customer-Service Department Costs	Number of Service Reports
1	$13,845	201
2	20,624	276
3	12,941	122
4	18,452	386
5	14,843	274
6	21,890	436
7	16,831	321
8	21,429	328
9	18,267	243
10	16,832	161

1. Plot the relationship between customer-service costs and number of service reports. Is the relationship economically plausible?
2. Use the high-low method to compute the cost function, relating customer-service costs to the number of service reports.
3. What variables, in addition to number of service reports, might be cost drivers of monthly customer-service costs of Capitol Products?

 10-23 Linear cost approximation. Terry Lawler, managing director of the Memphis Consulting Group, is examining how overhead costs behave with variations in monthly professional labor-hours billed to clients. Assume the following historical data:

Total Overhead Costs	Professional Labor-Hours Billed to Clients
$340,000	3,000
400,000	4,000
435,000	5,000
477,000	6,000
529,000	7,000
587,000	8,000

Required

1. Compute the linear cost function, relating total overhead cost to professional labor-hours, using the representative observations of 4,000 and 7,000 hours. Plot the linear cost function. Does the constant component of the cost function represent the fixed overhead costs of the Memphis Consulting Group? Why?
2. What would be the predicted total overhead costs for (a) 5,000 hours, and (b) 8,000 hours using the cost function estimated in requirement 1? Plot the predicted costs and actual costs for 5,000 and 8,000 hours.
3. Lawler had a chance to accept a special job that would have boosted professional labor-hours from 4,000 to 5,000 hours. Suppose Lawler, guided by the linear cost function, rejected this job because it would have brought a total increase in contribution margin of $38,000, before deducting the predicted increase in total overhead cost, $43,000. What is the total contribution margin actually forgone?

10-24 Cost-volume-profit and regression analysis. Garvin Corporation manufactures a children's bicycle, model CT8. Garvin currently manufactures the bicycle frame. During 1999, Garvin made 30,000 frames at a total cost of $900,000. Ryan Corporation has offered to supply as many frames as Garvin wants at a cost of $28.50 per frame. Garvin anticipates needing 36,000 frames each year for the next few years.

Required

1. **a.** What is the average cost of manufacturing a bicycle frame in 1999? How does it compare to Ryan's offer?
   b. Can Garvin use the answer in requirement 1 to determine the cost of manufacturing 36,000 bicycle frames? Explain.
2. Garvin's cost analyst uses annual data for the past eight years to estimate the following regression equation with total manufacturing costs of the bicycle frame as the dependent variable and bicycle frames produced as the independent variable

$$y = \$432,000 + \$15X$$

During the years used to estimate the regression equation, the production of bicycle frames had varied from 28,000 to 36,000. Using this equation, estimate how much it would cost Garvin to manufacture 36,000 bicycle frames. How much more costly or less costly is it to manufacture the frames rather than to acquire them from Ryan?
3. What other information would you need in order to be confident that the equation in requirement 2 accurately predicts the cost of manufacturing bicycle frames?

10-25 Regression analysis, service company. (CMA, adapted) Bob Jones owns a catering company that prepares banquets and parties for both individual and business functions throughout the year. Jones's business is seasonal, with a heavy schedule during the summer months and the year-end holidays and a light schedule at other times. During peak periods there are extra costs.

One of the major events Jones's customers request is a cocktail party. He offers a standard cocktail party and has developed the following cost structure on a per person basis.

Food and beverages	$15.00
Labor (0.5 hour × $10 per hour)	5.00
Overhead (0.5 hour × $14 per hour)	7.00
Total costs per person	$27.00

Jones is quite certain about his estimates of the food, beverages, and labor costs but is not as comfortable with the overhead estimate. This estimate was based on the actual data for the past 12 months presented below. These data indicate that overhead costs vary with the direct labor-hours used. The $14 estimate was determined by dividing total overhead costs for the 12 months by total labor-hours.

Month	Labor-Hours	Overhead Costs
January	2,500	$ 55,000
February	2,700	59,000
March	3,000	60,000
April	4,200	64,000
May	7,500	77,000
June	5,500	71,000
July	6,500	74,000
August	4,500	67,000
September	7,000	75,000
October	4,500	68,000
November	3,100	62,000
December	6,500	73,000
Total	57,500	$805,000

Jones has recently become aware of regression analysis. He estimated the following regression equation with overhead costs as the dependent variable and labor-hours as the independent variable.

$$y = \$48{,}271 + \$3.93X$$

Required

1. Plot the relationship between overhead costs and labor-hours. Draw the regression line and evaluate it using the criteria of economic plausibility, goodness of fit, and slope of the regression line.
2. Using data from the regression analysis, what is the variable cost per person for a cocktail party?
3. Bob Jones has been asked to prepare a bid for a 200-person cocktail party to be given next month. Determine the minimum bid price that Jones would be willing to submit to earn a positive contribution margin.

10-26 Regression analysis, activity-based costing, choosing cost drivers. Jill Flaherty has been collecting data over the last year in an effort to identify the cost drivers of distribution costs at Saratoga Corporation, a manufacturer of brass door handles. Distribution costs include the costs of organizing different shipments as well as physically handling and moving packaged units. Flaherty believes that because the product is heavy, the number of units moved will affect distribution costs significantly, but she is uncertain. Flaherty collects the following data for the past 12 months.

Month	Distribution Costs	Number of Packaged Units Moved	Number of Shipments Made
January	$ 28,000	51,000	200
February	20,000	43,000	210
March	17,000	28,000	185
April	32,000	67,000	315
May	40,000	73,000	335
June	24,000	54,000	225
July	22,000	37,000	190
August	35,000	72,000	390
September	42,000	71,000	280
October	23,000	56,000	360
November	33,000	52,000	380
December	22,000	45,000	270
Total	$338,000	649,000	3,340

Flaherty estimates the following regression equations:

$$y = \$1,349 + (\$0.496 \times \text{Number of packaged units moved})$$

$$y = \$10,417 + (\$63.77 \times \text{Number of shipments made})$$

Required
1. Prepare plots of the monthly data and the regression lines underlying each of the following cost functions:
   a. Distribution costs $= a + (b \times \text{Number of packaged units moved})$
   b. Distribution costs $= a + (b \times \text{Number of shipments made})$
   Which cost driver for distribution costs would you choose? Explain briefly.
2. Flaherty anticipates moving 40,000 units in 220 shipments next month. Using the cost function you chose in requirement 1, what amount of distribution costs should Flaherty budget?
3. Suppose Flaherty chose the "other" cost function—the cost function you did not choose in requirement 1—and 40,000 units were moved in 220 shipments. Do you think actual costs will be lower than, will be greater than, or will closely approximate the predictions made using the "other" cost driver and cost function. Explain your answer briefly and any other implications of choosing the "other" cost driver and cost function.

10-27 Learning curve, cumulative average-time learning model. Global Defense manufactures radar systems. It has just completed the manufacture of its first newly designed system, RS-32. It took 3,000 direct manufacturing labor-hours (DMLH) to produce this one unit. Global believes that a 90% cumulative average-time learning model for direct manufacturing labor-hours applies to RS-32. (A 90% learning curve implies $q = -0.1520$). The variable costs of producing RS-32 are:

Direct materials costs	$80,000 per unit of RS-32
Direct manufacturing labor costs	$25 per DMLH
Variable manufacturing overhead costs	$15 per DMLH

Required
Calculate the total variable costs of producing 2, 4, and 8 units.

10-28 Learning curve, incremental unit-time learning model. Assume the same information for Global Defense as in Exercise 10-27 except that Global Defense uses a 90% incremental unit-time learning model as a basis for forecasting direct manufacturing labor-hours. (A 90% learning curve implies $q = -0.1520$.)
Required
1. Calculate the total variable costs of producing 2, 3, and 4 units.
2. If you solved Exercise 10-27, compare your cost predictions in the two exercises for 2 and 4 units. Why are the predictions different?

PROBLEMS

10-29 Organizing data, high-low method. Ken Howard, financial analyst at JVR Corporation, a manufacturer of precision parts, is examining the behavior of quarterly maintenance costs for budgeting purposes. Howard collects the following data on machine-hours worked and maintenance costs for the past 13 quarters:

Quarter	Machine-Hours	Maintenance Costs
1	90,000	$235,000
2	110,000	185,000
3	100,000	220,000
4	120,000	200,000
5	85,000	240,000
6	105,000	170,000
7	95,000	215,000
8	115,000	195,000
9	95,000	235,000
10	115,000	190,000
11	105,000	225,000
12	125,000	180,000
13	90,000	250,000

Required
1. **a.** Prepare plots of the quarterly data underlying the cost function: Maintenance costs = $a + (b \times$ Machine-hours$)$.
   b. Estimate the cost function for the data represented by the plots in requirement 1a using the high-low method.
   c. Plot and comment on the estimated cost function.
2. **a.** Construct a table and prepare plots of the quarterly data relating machine-hours in a quarter (t) to maintenance costs in the following quarter $(t + 1)$. That is, plot machine-hours in quarter 1 against maintenance costs in quarter 2, machine-hours in quarter 2 against maintenance costs in quarter 3, and so on.
   b. Estimate the cost function for the data represented by the plots in requirement 2a using the high-low method.
   c. Plot and comment on the estimated cost function.
3. Howard anticipates that JVR will operate machines for 95,000 hours in quarter 14. Calculate the predicted maintenance costs in quarter 14 using the cost functions estimated in requirements 1b and 2b. What maintenance costs should Howard budget for quarter 14? Explain your answer briefly.

10-30 High-low versus regression method. (CIMA, adapted) Anna Martinez, the financial manager at the Casa Real restaurant is working with Jan Brown the marketing manager to determine if there is any relationship between newspaper advertising and sales revenues at the restaurant. They obtain the following monthly data for the past 10 months:

Month	Revenues	Advertising Costs
March	$50,000	$2,000
April	70,000	3,000
May	55,000	1,500
June	65,000	3,500
July	55,000	1,000
August	65,000	2,000
September	45,000	1,500
October	80,000	4,000
November	55,000	2,500
December	60,000	2,500

They estimate the following regression equation:

$$y = \$39,502 + (8.723 \times \text{Advertising costs})$$

where y is the monthly revenues.

Required
1. Plot the relationship between advertising costs and revenues.
2. Draw the regression line and evaluate it using the criteria of economic plausibility, goodness of fit, and slope of the regression line.
3. Use the high-low method to compute the cost function, relating advertising costs and revenues.
4. Using (a) the regression equation and (b) the high-low equation, what is the increase in revenues for each $1,000 spent on advertising within the relevant range?
5. Should Martinez and Brown use the cost function estimated from the regression analysis method or the high-low method to predict the effect of advertising on revenues? Explain briefly.

10-31 Regression analysis, activity-based costing, choosing cost drivers. Larry Chu, the plant controller at Rohan Plastics, has been concerned about correctly identifying cost drivers ever since the plant began implementing activity-based costing a year or so ago. Correctly identifying cost drivers is important for bidding and pricing of jobs and for managing costs within the plant.

The cost drivers for support overhead have been a particular problem. Rohan has eliminated many job categories, so indirect support consists of skilled staff responsible for the efficient functioning of all aspects (setup, production, maintenance, and quality control) of the plastic injection molding facility. In talking to the support staff, Chu has the impression that the staff spends a good portion of their time ensuring that the equipment is set up correctly and checking that the first units of production in each batch are of good quality.

Chu has collected the following data for the past 12 months:

Month	Support Overhead	Machine-Hours	Number of Batches
January	$ 84,000	2,250	309
February	41,000	2,400	128
March	63,000	2,850	249
April	44,000	2,100	159
May	44,000	2,700	216
June	48,000	2,250	174
July	66,000	3,800	264
August	46,000	3,600	162
September	33,000	1,850	147
October	66,000	3,300	219
November	81,000	3,750	303
December	57,000	2,000	106
Total	$673,000	32,850	2,436

Chu estimates the following regression equations:

$$y = \$28,089 + (\$10.23 \times \text{Machine-hours})$$

and

$$y = \$16,031 + (\$197.30 \times \text{Number of batches})$$

where y is the monthly support overhead.

Required
1. Prepare plots of the monthly data and the regression lines underlying each of the following cost functions:
   a. Support overhead costs = $a + (b \times \text{Machine-hours})$
   b. Support overhead costs = $a + (b \times \text{Number of batches})$
   Which cost driver for support overhead costs would you choose? Explain.
2. Chu anticipates 2,600 machine-hours and 300 batches will be run next month. Using the cost driver you chose in requirement 1, what amount of support overhead costs should Chu budget?
3. a. Chu adds 20% to costs as a first attempt for determining target revenues (and hence prices). Costs other than support overhead are expected to equal $125,000

next month. Compare the target revenue numbers obtained if the cost driver is (i) machine-hours, and (ii) number of batches. Discuss what would happen if Chu picked the "other" cost driver—the cost driver you did not choose in requirement 1—to set target revenues and prices.

b. Describe any other implications of choosing the "other" cost driver and cost function.

10-32 Cost estimation, cumulative average-time learning curve. The Nautilus Company, which is under contract to the U.S. Navy, assembles troop deployment boats. As part of its research program, it completes the assembly of the first of a new model (PT109) of deployment boats. The Navy is impressed with the PT109. It requests that Nautilus submit a proposal on the cost of producing another seven PT109s.

The Accounting Department at Nautilus reports the following cost information for the first PT109 assembled by Nautilus:

Direct materials	$100,000
Direct manufacturing labor (10,000 labor-hours $\times$ $30)	300,000
Tooling cost[a]	50,000
Variable manufacturing overhead[b]	200,000
Other manufacturing overhead[c]	75,000
	$725,000

[a] Tooling can be reused at no extra cost, because all of its cost has been assigned to the first deployment boat.
[b] Variable overhead incurred is directly affected by direct manufacturing labor-hours; a rate of $20 per hour is used for purposes of bidding on contracts.
[c] Other overhead is allocated at a flat rate of 25% of direct manufacturing labor costs for purposes of bidding on contracts.

Nautilus uses an 85% cumulative average-time learning model as a basis for forecasting direct manufacturing labor-hours on its assembling operations. (An 85% learning curve implies $q = -0.2345$.)

Required

1. Prepare a prediction of the total costs for producing the seven PT109s for the Navy. (Nautilus will keep the first deployment boat assembled, costed at $725,000, as a demonstration model for other potential customers.)
2. What is the dollar amount of difference between (a) the predicted total costs for producing the seven PT109s in requirement 1, and (b) the predicted total costs for producing the seven PT109s assuming that there is no learning curve for direct manufacturing labor? That is, for (b) assume a linear function for units produced and direct labor-hours.

10-33 Cost estimation, incremental unit-time learning model. Assume the same information for the Nautilus Company as that in Problem 10-32 with one exception. This exception is that Nautilus uses an 85% incremental unit-time learning model as a basis for forecasting direct manufacturing labor-hours on its assembling operations. (An 85% learning curve implies $q = -0.2345$.)

Required

1. Prepare a prediction of the total expected costs for producing the seven PT109s for the Navy.
2. If you solved requirement 1 of Problem 10-32, compare your cost prediction there with the one you made here. Why are the predictions different?

10-34 Promotion of a new product, simple and multiple regression analysis. (Chapter Appendix, J. Patell, adapted) "What does all this mean? All I want to understand are the cost drivers of manufacturing overhead costs," said Mike Moore, the controller of Acro-Cel. Mike has asked for your help in understanding the results of regression analyses that have been prepared by his assistants using monthly data from 1999. Mike continued, "I may not understand 'regression analysis' but I understand this company and I know that when we work more hours and use more material, I get higher bills for overhead costs."

$$y = \text{manufacturing overhead costs}$$

$$X_1 = \text{direct manufacturing labor-hours}$$

$$X_2 = \text{direct materials costs}$$

Standard errors of the coefficients (not t-statistics) are in parentheses.

1. $y = \$4{,}188 + \$3.45\, X_1$ $r^2 = .66$

        ($\$0.78$)

2. $y = \$5{,}951 + \$0.12\, X_2$ $r^2 = .62$

        ($\$0.03$)

3. $y = \$4{,}663 + \$2.24\, X_1 + \$0.05\, X_2$ $r^2 = .68$

        ($\$1.65$)   ($\$0.06$)

Required

1. For each regression, perform a statistical test and indicate whether manufacturing overhead costs are affected by direct manufacturing labor-hours and direct materials costs.

2. Contrast the multiple regression results (equation 3) with the simple regression results (equations 1 and 2) in terms of the statistical tests that you performed in requirement 1. Suggest a possible explanation for any differences in the results of the statistical tests.

3. Given the problem(s) you identified in requirement 2, what would you recommend to Moore?

10-35 Evaluating alternative simple regression models, nonprofit. (Chapter Appendix) Kathy Hanks, executive assistant to the president of Southwestern University is concerned about the overhead costs at her university. Cost pressures are severe, so controlling and reducing overhead costs are very important. Hanks believes overhead costs incurred are generally a function of the number of different academic programs (including different specializations, degrees, and majors) that the university offers and the number of enrolled students. Both have grown significantly over the years. She collects the following data:

Year	Overhead Costs (in thousands)	Number of Academic Programs	Number of Enrolled Students
1	$13,500	29	3,400
2	19,200	36	5,000
3	16,800	49	2,600
4	20,100	53	4,700
5	19,500	54	3,900
6	23,100	58	4,900
7	23,700	88	5,700
8	20,100	72	3,900
9	22,800	83	3,500
10	29,700	73	3,700
11	31,200	101	5,600
12	38,100	103	7,600

She finds the following results for two separate simple regression models:
Regression 1: Overhead costs = $a + (b \times$ Number of academic programs)

Variable	Coefficient	Standard Error	t-Value
Constant	$7,127.75	$3,335.34	2.14
Independent variable 1:			
Number of academic programs	$240.64	$47.33	5.08

$r^2 = .72$; Durbin-Watson statistic $= 1.81$

Regression 2: Overhead costs = $a + (b \times$ Number of enrolled students)

Variable	Coefficient	Standard Error	t-Value
Constant	$5,991.75	$5,067.88	1.18
Independent variable 1:			
Number of enrolled students	$3.78	$1.07	3.53

$r^2 = .55$; Durbin-Watson statistic = 0.77

Required
1. Plot the relationship between overhead costs and each of the following variables: (a) number of academic programs, and (b) number of enrolled students.
2. Compare and evaluate the two simple regression models estimated by Hanks. Use the comparison format employed in Exhibit 10-19 (p. 357).
3. What insights do the analyses provide about controlling and reducing overhead costs at the University?

10-36 Evaluating multiple regression models, nonprofit (continuation of Problem 10-35). (Chapter Appendix)

Required
1. Given your findings in Problem 10-35, should Hanks use multiple regression analysis to better understand the cost drivers of overhead costs? Explain.
2. Hanks decides that the simple regression analysis in Problem 10-35 should be extended to a multiple regression analysis. She finds the following result:
   Regression 3: Overhead costs = $a + (b_1 \times$ Number of academic programs) + $(b_2 \times$ Number of enrolled students)

Variable	Coefficient	Standard Error	t-Value
Constant	$2,779.62	$3,620.05	0.77
Independent variable 1:			
Number of academic programs	$178.37	$51.54	3.46
Independent variable 2:			
Number of enrolled students	$1.87	$0.92	2.03

$r^2 = .81$; Durbin-Watson statistic = 1.84

The coefficient of correlation between number of academic programs and number of students is .60. Use the format in Exhibit 10-19 (p. 357) to evaluate the multiple regression model. (Assume linearity, and constant variance and normality of residuals.) Should Hanks choose the multiple regression model over the two simple regression models of Problem 10-35?
3. How might the president of Southwestern University use these regression results to manage overhead costs?

10-37 Purchasing Department cost drivers, activity-based costing, simple regression analysis. (Chapter Appendix) Fashion Flair operates a chain of 10 retail department stores. Each department store makes its own purchasing decisions. Barry Lee, assistant to the president of Fashion Flair, is interested in better understanding the drivers of Purchasing Department costs. For many years, Fashion Flair has allocated Purchasing Department costs to products on the basis of the dollar value of merchandise purchased. An item costing $100 is allocated 10 times as much overhead costs associated with the Purchasing Department as an item costing $10 is allocated.

Lee recently attended a seminar titled "Cost Drivers in the Retail Industry." In a presentation at the seminar, Couture Fabrics, a leading competitor that has implemented activity-based costing, reported the number of purchase orders and the number of suppliers to be the two most important cost drivers of Purchasing Department costs. The dollar value of merchandise purchased in each purchase order was not found to be a significant cost driver by Couture Fabrics. Lee interviewed several members of the Purchasing Department at the Fashion Flair store in Miami. These people told Lee that they believed that Couture Fabric's conclusions also applied to their Purchasing Department.

Lee collects the following data for the most recent year for the ten retail department stores of Fashion Flair:

Department Store	Purchasing Department Costs (PDC)	Dollar Value of Merchandise Purchased (MP$)	Number of Purchase Orders (No. of PO's)	Number of Suppliers (No. of S's)
Baltimore	$1,523,000	$ 68,315,000	4,357	132
Chicago	1,100,000	33,456,000	2,550	222
Los Angeles	547,000	121,160,000	1,433	11
Miami	2,049,000	119,566,000	5,944	190
New York	1,056,000	33,505,000	2,793	23
Phoenix	529,000	29,854,000	1,327	33
Seattle	1,538,000	102,875,000	7,586	104
St. Louis	1,754,000	38,674,000	3,617	119
Toronto	1,612,000	139,312,000	1,707	208
Vancouver	1,257,000	130,944,000	4,731	201

Lee decides to use simple regression analysis to examine whether one or more of three variables (the last three columns in the table) are cost drivers of Purchasing Department costs. Summary results for these regressions are as follows:

Regression 1: PDC = $a + (b \times$ MP$)$

Variable	Coefficient	Standard Error	t-Value
Constant	$1,039,061	$343,439	3.03
Independent variable 1: MP$	0.0031	0.0037	0.84

$r^2 = .08$; Durbin-Watson statistic = 2.41

Regression 2: PDC = $a + (b \times$ No. of PO's$)$

Variable	Coefficient	Standard Error	t-Value
Constant	$730,716	$265,419	2.75
Independent variable 1: No. of PO's	$156.97	$64.69	2.43

$r^2 = .42$; Durbin-Watson statistic = 1.98

Regression 3: PDC = $a + (b \times$ No. of S's$)$

Variable	Coefficient	Standard Error	t-Value
Constant	$814,862	$247,821	3.29
Independent variable 1: No. of S's	$3,875	$1,697	2.28

$r^2 = .39$; Durbin-Watson statistic = 1.97

Required

1. Compare and evaluate the three simple regression models estimated by Lee. Graph each one. Also, use the format employed in Exhibit 10-19 (p. 357) to evaluate the information.
2. Do the regression results support the Couture Fabrics presentation about Purchasing Department cost drivers? Which of these cost drivers would you recommend in designing an ABC system?
3. How might Lee gain additional evidence on drivers of Purchasing Department costs at each of Fashion Flair's stores?

10-38 Purchasing Department cost drivers, multiple regression analysis (continuation of 10-37). (Chapter Appendix) Barry Lee decides that the simple regression analysis used in Problem 10-37 could be extended to a multiple regression analysis. He finds the following results for several multiple regressions:

Regression 4: PDC = $a + (b_1 \times$ No. of PO's$) + (b_2 \times$ No. of S's$)$

Variable	Coefficient	Standard Error	t-Value
Constant	$485,384	$257,477	1.89
Independent variable 1: No. of PO's	$123.22	$57.69	2.14
Independent variable 2: No. of S's	$2,952	$1,476	2.00

$r^2 = .63$; Durbin-Watson statistic $= 1.90$

Regression 5: PDC $= a + (b_1 \times$ No. of PO's$) + (b_2 \times$ No. of S's$) + (b_3 \times$ MP$\$)$

Variable	Coefficient	Standard Error	t-Value
Constant	$494,684	$310,205	1.59
Independent variable 1: No. of PO's	$124.05	$63.49	1.95
Independent variable 2: No. of S's	$2,984	$1,622	1.84
Independent variable 3: MP$	-0.0002	0.0030	-0.07

$r^2 = .63$; Durbin-Watson statistic $= 1.90$

The coefficients of correlation between pairwise combinations of the variables are:

	PDC	MP$	No. of PO's
MP$	.29		
No. of PO's	.65	.27	
No. of S's	.63	.34	.29

Required

1. Evaluate regression 4 using the economic plausibility, goodness of fit, significance of independent variables, and specification analysis criteria. Compare regression 4 with regressions 2 and 3 in Problem 10-37. Which model would you recommend that Lee use? Why?
2. Compare regression 5 with regression 4. Which model would you recommend that Lee use? Why?
3. Lee estimates the following data for the Baltimore store for next year: dollar value of merchandise purchased, $75,000,000; number of purchase orders, 3,900; number of suppliers, 110. How much should Lee budget for Purchasing Department costs for the Baltimore store for next year?
4. What difficulties do not arise in simple regression analysis that may arise in multiple regression analysis? Is there evidence of such difficulties in either of the multiple regressions presented in this problem? Explain.
5. Give two examples of decisions where the regression results reported here (and in Problem 10-37) could be informative.

10-39 Regression computations, ethics. (Chapter Appendix) Cleveland Engineering manufactures small electric motors. Data on manufacturing labor costs and units produced for the last four quarters follow:

Quarter	Manufacturing Labor Costs	Units Produced
1	$176,000	9,000
2	174,000	10,000
3	165,000	9,000
4	205,000	12,000
Total	$720,000	40,000

The bonus paid to Peter Smith, the manufacturing manager, depends on how manufacturing labor costs in a quarter compare with manufacturing labor costs in the previous four quarters. In the recently concluded quarter 5, Cleveland Engineering produced 12,000 motors and incurred manufacturing labor costs of $208,000. Smith is very happy with the results. Over the previous four quarters, the average manufacturing labor cost per unit is $18 ($720,000 ÷ 40,000 units), resulting in a benchmark for quarter 5 of $18 × 12,000 = $216,000. Just as Smith is thinking about what he might do with the bonus, Allison Hart, the plant controller knocks on Smith's door.

Allison Hart: "I am sorry that we couldn't beat the benchmark over the last four quarters. We certainly gave it our best shot."

Peter Smith: "What do you mean we didn't beat the benchmark? Here are the numbers I just calculated. Against a benchmark of $216,000, we achieved $208,000."

Allison Hart: "No, that's not how the calculations are done. Some of the labor costs are fixed and others vary with production. My analysis here first separates out the fixed from the variable components. My calculations then show that our quarter 5 performance was worse than the previous four quarters.

Peter Smith: "Please review your calculations. You can report a better benchmark than that! Your regression approach is subject to estimation error. You should make some adjustment for that. If we don't show senior management that we are succeeding in reducing labor costs, they might shut us down because they don't believe we can be competitive. I am sure that no one in this plant wants that to happen."

Required

1. Verify, by either using the formulas given in the Appendix or a software program that performs regression analysis, that the regression equation is given by

$$y = \$65,000 + (\$11.5 \times \text{Units produced})$$

with an $r^2 = .88$.

2. What is the benchmark for quarter 5 that Allison Hart had calculated?

3. Why is there a difference between the benchmark calculated by Peter Smith and the benchmark calculated in requirement 2? Which benchmark do you prefer? Explain your answer.

4. Identify the steps that Allison Hart should follow in attempting to resolve the situation created by Peter Smith's comment about adjusting the benchmark.

COLLABORATIVE LEARNING PROBLEM

10-40 High-low method, alternative regression functions, accrual accounting adjustments. Trevor Kennedy, the cost analyst at a can manufacturing plant of United Packaging, is examining the relationship between total engineering support costs reported in the plant records and machine-hours. These costs have two components: (1) labor (which is paid monthly), and (2) materials and parts (which are purchased from an outside vendor every 3 months). After further discussion with the operating manager, Kennedy discovers that the materials and parts numbers reported in the monthly records are on an "as purchased" or cash accounting basis and not on an "as used" or accrual accounting basis. By examining materials and parts usage records, Kennedy is able to restate the materials and parts costs to an "as used" basis. (No restatement of the labor costs was necessary.) The reported and restated costs are as follows:

Month	Labor: Reported Costs (1)	Materials and Parts: Reported Costs (2)	Materials and Parts: Restated Costs (3)	Total Engineering Support: Reported Costs (4) = (1) + (2)	Total Engineering Support: Restated Costs (5) = (1) + (3)	Machine-Hours (6)
March	$347	$847	$182	$1,194	$529	30
April	521	0	411	521	932	63
May	398	0	268	398	666	49
June	355	961	228	1,316	583	38
July	473	0	348	473	821	57
August	617	0	349	617	966	73
September	245	821	125	1,066	370	19
October	487	0	364	487	851	53
November	431	0	290	431	721	42

The regression results, when total engineering support reported costs (column 4) are used as the dependent variable, are

Regression 1: Engineering support reported costs = $a + (b \times$ Machine-hours)

Variable	Coefficient	Standard Error	t-Value
Constant	$1,393.20	$305.68	4.56
Independent variable 1: Machine hours	– $14.23	$6.15	– 2.31

r^2 = .43; Durbin-Watson statistic = 2.26

The regression results, when total engineering support restated costs (column 5) are used as the dependent variable, are

Regression 2: Engineering support restated costs = a + (b × Machine-hours)

Variable	Coefficient	Standard Error	t-Value
Constant	$176.38	$53.99	3.27
Independent variable 1: Machine hours	$11.44	$1.08	10.59

r^2 = .94; Durbin-Watson statistic = 1.31

Required
Form groups of two or more students to complete the following requirements.

1. Prepare a plot of the data for the cost function relating the *reported costs* for total engineering support to machine-hours. Present a plot of the data for the cost function relating the *restated costs* for total engineering support to machine-hours. Comment on the plots.
2. Use the high-low method to compute estimates of the cost functions $y = a + bX$ for (a) reported engineering support costs and machine-hours, and (b) restated engineering support costs and machine-hours.
3. Contrast and evaluate the cost function estimated with regression using restated data for materials and parts with the cost function estimated with regression using the data reported in the plant records. Use the comparison format employed in Exhibit 10-19 (p. 357).
4. Of all the cost functions estimated in requirements 2 and 3, which one would you choose to best represent the relationship between engineering support costs and machine-hours? Why?
5. Kennedy expects 50 machine-hours to be worked in December. What engineering support costs should Kennedy budget for December?
6. What problems might Kennedy encounter when restating the materials and parts costs recorded to an "as used" or accrual accounting basis?
7. Why is it important for Kennedy to pick the correct cost function? That is, illustrate two potential problems Kennedy could encounter, by choosing a cost function other than the one you chose in requirement 4.

Decision Making and Relevant Information

After studying this chapter, you should be able to

1. Use the five-step decision process to make decisions
2. Differentiate relevant costs and revenues from irrelevant costs and revenues in any decision situation
3. Distinguish between quantitative factors and qualitative factors in decisions
4. Identify two potential problems that should be avoided in relevant-cost analysis
5. Describe the opportunity-cost concept and explain why it is used in decision making
6. Describe the key concept in choosing which among multiple products to produce when there are capacity constraints
7. Discuss the key factor managers must consider when adding or dropping customers and segments
8. Explain why the book value of equipment is irrelevant in equipment-replacement decisions
9. Explain how conflicts can arise between the decision model used by a manager and the performance model used to evaluate the manager

Stores, such as GAP, must decide on where to open new stores, which stores to shut down, and how to allocate limited shelf space among different products. Making these decisions requires an analysis of relevant revenues, relevant costs, and contribution margins.

The use of accounting information for decision making is a consistent theme in earlier chapters. Working with managers to make decisions is one of the main functions of the management accountant and an important thrust of this book. In this chapter, we explore the decision-making process and focus on specific decisions such as accepting or rejecting a one-time-only special order, insourcing or outsourcing products or services, and replacing or keeping equipment. We especially stress the importance of distinguishing between *relevant* and *irrelevant* items in making these decisions.

INFORMATION AND THE DECISION PROCESS

Managers frequently follow a method, called a *decision model*, for choosing among different courses of action. A **decision model** is a formal method for making a choice, frequently involving both quantitative and qualitative analyses. Shareholders would like managers to choose those actions that are in the best interest of shareholders. Management accountants work with managers by presenting and analyzing relevant data to guide decisions.

Consider a decision facing Home Appliances, a manufacturer of vacuum cleaners: Should it reorganize its manufacturing process operations to reduce manufacturing labor costs? For simplicity, assume that the only alternatives are "do not reorganize" and "reorganize." The reorganization will eliminate all manual handling of materials. The current manufacturing line uses 20 workers—15 workers operate machines, and 5 workers handle materials. The 5 materials-handling workers have been hired on contracts that permit layoffs without additional payments. Each worker puts in 2,000 hours annually. The cost of reorganization (consisting mostly of equipment leases) is predicted to be $90,000 each year. The predicted production output of 25,000 units will be unaffected by the decision. Also unaffected by the decision are the predicted selling price per unit of $250, direct materials costs per unit of $50, manufacturing overhead of $750,000, and marketing costs of $2,000,000. The cost driver is units of production.

When making decisions such as "do not reorganize" and "reorganize" manufacturing process operations, managers typically use the five-step decision process described in Exhibit 11-1 to choose between the alternatives. In studying this important exhibit, note the sequence of the steps and how step 5, Evaluating Performance, provides feedback about actions taken in the previous steps. The feedback, in turn, might affect future predictions, the prediction method itself, the decision model, or the implementation.

THE MEANING OF RELEVANCE

Relevant Costs and Relevant Revenues

Much of this chapter focuses on step 3 in Exhibit 11-1. In particular, the chapter concentrates on the concepts of relevant costs and relevant revenues when choosing among alternatives. **Relevant costs** and **relevant revenues** are those *expected future costs* and *expected future revenues* that differ among the alternative courses of action being considered. The two key aspects to this definition are that to be relevant, (a) the costs and revenues must occur in the future and (b) that they must differ among the alternative courses of action. We focus on the future because *every decision deals with selecting courses of action for the future. Nothing can be done to alter the past.* Also, the future costs and revenues must differ among the alternatives. Why? Because costs and revenues that do not differ will not matter and hence will have no bearing on the decision being made. The key question is always, What difference will an action make?

Exhibit 11-2 presents the financial data underlying the choice between the "do not reorganize" and the "reorganize" alternatives for Home Appliances. The first two columns present *all data*. The last two columns present only relevant costs or revenues—the $640,000 and $480,000 expected future manufacturing labor costs and the $90,000 expected future reorganization costs that differ between the two al-

EXHIBIT 11-1
Five-Step Decision Process for Home Appliances

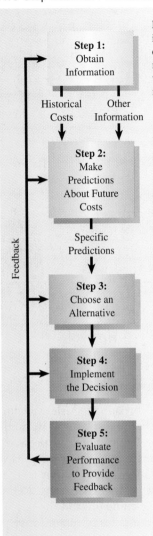

Feedback

Step 1: Obtain Information

Historical Costs   Other Information

Step 2: Make Predictions About Future Costs

Specific Predictions

Step 3: Choose an Alternative

Step 4: Implement the Decision

Step 5: Evaluate Performance to Provide Feedback

Historical labor costs are $14 per hour. A recently negotiated increase in employee benefits of $2 per hour will increase labor costs to $16 per hour in the future. The reorganization of manufacturing operations is expected to reduce the number of workers from 20 to 15 by eliminating all 5 workers who handle materials.

Use the information from step 1 together with an assessment of probability as a basis for predicting the future labor costs. Under the existing "do not reorganize" alternative, costs are predicted to be $640,000 (20 workers × 2,000 hours × $16 per hour) and under the "reorganize" alternative, costs are predicted to be $480,000 (15 workers × 2,000 hours × $16 per hour). The reorganization is predicted to cost $90,000 per year.

The predicted benefits of the different alternatives in step 2 are compared (savings from eliminating materials-handling labor costs, 5 workers × 2,000 hours × $16 per hour = $160,000) and are related to the cost of the reorganization ($90,000) along with other considerations (such as likely effects on employee morale). Management chooses the reorganize alternative.

The manager implements the decision reached in step 3 by reorganizing manufacturing operations.

Evaluation of performance of the decision implemented in step 4 provides the feedback as the five-step sequence is then repeated in whole or in part. Actual results show that the new manufacturing labor costs are $540,000 rather than the predicted $480,000 due to lower-than-expected manufacturing labor productivity. This historical information can help managers in making better subsequent predictions that allow for more learning time. Alternatively, managers may improve implementation through, for example, employee training or better supervision.

ernatives. The revenues, direct materials, manufacturing overhead, and marketing tems can be ignored. Why? Because although they are expected future costs, they lo not differ between the alternatives. They are thus irrelevant.

Note that the past manufacturing labor rate of $14 per hour and total past manufacturing labor costs of $560,000 (2,000 hours × 20 workers × $14 per hour) lo not appear in Exhibit 11-2. *Although they may be a useful basis for making informed predictions of the expected future manufacturing labor costs of $640,000 and $480,000, historical costs themselves are past costs that are irrelevant to decision making.* Past costs that are unavoidable because they cannot be changed no matter what action is taken are called **sunk costs.**

The data in Exhibit 11-2 indicate that reorganizing the production line will increase next year's predicted operating income by $70,000. Note that we reach the same conclusion whether we use "all data" or include only "relevant data" in the analysis. By confining the analysis to only the relevant data, however, managers can clear away the clutter of potentially confusing irrelevant data. Focusing on the relevant data is especially helpful when all the information needed to prepare a detailed income statement is unavailable. Understanding which costs are relevant and which are not helps the decision maker concentrate on obtaining only the pertinent data and saves time.

EXHIBIT 11-2

Determining Relevant Revenues and Relevant Costs for Home Appliances

	All Data		Relevant Data	
	Do Not Reorganize	Reorganize	Do Not Reorganize	Reorganize
Revenues[a]	$6,250,000	$6,250,000	—	—
Costs:				
Direct materials[b]	1,250,000	1,250,000	—	—
Manufacturing labor	640,000[c]	480,000[d]	$ 640,000[c]	$ 480,000[d]
Manufacturing overhead	750,000	750,000	—	—
Marketing	2,000,000	2,000,000	—	—
Reorganization costs	—	90,000	—	90,000
Total costs	4,640,000	4,570,000	640,000	570,000
Operating income	$1,610,000	$1,680,000	$(640,000)	$(570,000)
	$70,000 Difference		$70,000 Difference	

[a] 25,000 × $250 = $6,250,000
[b] 25,000 × $50 = $1,250,000
[c] 20 × 2,000 × $16 = $640,000
[d] 15 × 2,000 × $16 = $480,000

Points to Stress Presenting only relevant data reduces mgrs.' information load. Some mgrs. may prefer the relevant cost focus of the rightmost 2 columns of Exh. 11-2, which reduces the information load by excluding irrelevant data. Research has shown that when inundated with data, people tend to (1) make poorer decisions, (2) take longer to decide, but (3) be more confident in their decisions.

Qualitative and Quantitative Relevant Information

OBJECTIVE 3

Distinguish between quantitative factors and qualitative factors in decisions

We divide the consequences of alternatives into two broad categories: *quantitative and qualitative.* **Quantitative factors** are outcomes that are measured in numerical terms. Some quantitative factors are financial—that is, they can be expressed in financial terms. Examples include the costs of direct materials, direct manufacturing labor, and marketing. Other quantitative factors are nonfinancial—that is, they can be measured numerically, but they are not expressed in financial terms. Reduction in new product-development time for a manufacturing company and the percentage of on-time flight arrivals for an airline company are examples of quantitative nonfinancial factors. **Qualitative factors** are outcomes that cannot be measured in numerical terms. Employee morale is an example.

Relevant cost analysis generally emphasizes quantitative factors that can be expressed in financial terms. But just because qualitative factors and quantitative nonfinancial factors cannot be measured easily in financial terms does not make them unimportant. Managers must at times give more weight to these factors. For example, Home Appliances would want to carefully consider the negative effect on employee morale of laying off materials-handling workers, a qualitative factor, before choosing the "reorganize" alternative. Trading off nonfinancial and financial considerations, however, is seldom easy. Exhibit 11-3 summarizes the key features of relevant information.

Correcting Student Misconceptions Acctg. data are only 1 input for making decisions. Mgt. may choose an alt. for qualitative reasons, even though it's not the "best" alt. per a quantitative analysis. For example, mgt. may decide not to purchase new labor saving equipment because of negative repercussions on employee morale. Quantitative analysis reveals the cost of selecting this alt. for qualitative reasons. If the equipment was estimated to save $50,000 per yr., then mgt. was willing to "pay" $50,000/yr. to maintain employee morale.

New in This Edition Exhibit 11-3 is new to this edition. It summarizes the key features of relevant information.

EXHIBIT 11-3
Key Features of Relevant Information

- ◆ Past (historical) costs may be helpful as a basis for making *predictions.* However, past costs themselves are always irrelevant when making *decisions.*
- ◆ Different alternatives can be compared by examining differences in expected total future revenues and costs.
- ◆ Not all expected future revenues and costs are relevant. Expected future revenues and costs that do not differ across alternatives are irrelevant and hence can be eliminated from the analysis. The key question is always, What difference will it make?
- ◆ Due weight must be given to qualitative factors and quantitative nonfinancial factors.

AN ILLUSTRATION OF RELEVANCE: CHOOSING OUTPUT LEVELS

The concept of relevance applies to numerous decision situations. In this and the following several sections, we present some of these decision situations. We start by considering decisions that affect output levels. For example, managers must choose whether to introduce a new product or sell more units of an existing product. When changes in output levels occur, managers are interested in the effect these changes have on the organization and on operating income.

One-Time-Only Special Orders

One type of decision that affects output levels involves accepting or rejecting special orders when there is idle production capacity and where the order has no long-run implications. We use the term *one-time-only special orders* to describe these conditions.

EXAMPLE 1: Fancy Fabrics manufactures quality bath towels at its highly automated Burlington, North Carolina, plant. The plant has a production capacity of 48,000 towels each month. Current monthly production is 30,000 towels. Retail department stores account for all existing sales. Expected results for the coming month (August) are shown in Exhibit 11-4. (Note that these amounts are predictions.) We assume that all costs can be classified as either variable with respect to a single driver (units of output) or fixed. The manufacturing costs per unit of $12 consist of the following:

	Variable Costs Per Unit	Fixed Costs Per Unit	Total Costs Per Unit
Direct materials	$6.00	$ —	$ 6.00
Direct manufacturing labor	0.50	1.50	2.00
Manufacturing overhead	1.00	3.00	4.00
Manufacturing costs	$7.50	$4.50	$12.00

The marketing costs per unit are $7 ($5 of which is variable). Fancy Fabrics has no R&D costs or product-design costs. Marketing costs include distribution costs and customer-service costs.

As a result of a strike at its existing towel supplier, a luxury hotel chain has offered to buy 5,000 towels from Fancy Fabrics in August at $11 per towel. No subsequent sales to this customer are anticipated. Fixed manufacturing costs are tied to the 48,000-towel production capacity. If Fancy Fabrics accepts the special order, it will use existing idle capacity to produce the 5,000 towels, and hence fixed manufacturing costs will not change. No marketing costs will be necessary for the 5,000-unit one-time-only special order. The acceptance of this special order is not expected to affect the selling price or the quantity of towels sold to regular customers. Should Fancy Fabrics accept the hotel chain's offer?

EXHIBIT 11-4
Budgeted Income Statement for August, Absorption-Costing Format for Fancy Fabrics

	Total	Per Unit
Revenues (30,000 towels × $20)	$600,000	$20
Cost of goods sold (manufacturing costs)	360,000	12
Marketing costs	210,000	7
Full costs of the product	570,000	19
Operating income	$ 30,000	$ 1

Reinforcing Problems Exer. 11-19, 11-23, and 11-24 and Prob. 11-34 cover special orders and CM analysis.

Points to Stress This section emphasizes that the traditional CM approach is appropriate if (1) costs are either totally fixed or purely variable, *and* (2) # of output units is the only cost driver. Current mgt. acctg. thought has restricted the # of situations to which these assumptions apply. A later section relaxes these assumptions and illustrates an approach that can be used in conjunction with ABC and the *hierarchy of costs* described in Chap. 5.

Curriculum Linkage In the Fancy Fabrics example, is it reasonable to expect that the special order won't affect regular business? Marketing concepts suggest that, unless Fancy Fabrics has effectively segmented the market, the special order may well affect regular business. Since a hotel chain is an entirely different class of customer from retail dept. store chains, Fancy Fabrics' market may be sufficiently segmented. The phrase "one-time-only special order" highlights the point that special orders are assumed to be short-term business that don't affect regular business.

EXHIBIT 11-5

One-Time-Only Special-Order Decision for Fancy Fabrics: Comparative Contribution Income Statements

	Without the Special Order, 30,000 Units to Be Sold		With the Special Order, 35,000 Units to Be Sold	Difference: Relevant Amounts for the 5,000-Unit Special Order
	Per Unit	Total	Total	
Revenues	$20.00	$600,000	$655,000	$55,000ᶜ
Variable costs:				
Manufacturing	7.50ᵃ	225,000	262,500	37,500ᵈ
Marketing	5.00	150,000	150,000	— ᵉ
Total variable costs	12.50	375,000	412,500	37,500
Contribution margin	7.50	225,000	242,500	17,500
Fixed Costs:				
Manufacturing	4.50ᵇ	135,000	135,000	— ᶠ
Marketing	2.00	60,000	60,000	— ᶠ
Total fixed costs	6.50	195,000	195,000	—
Operating income	$ 1.00	$ 30,000	$ 47,500	$17,500

ᵃVariable manufacturing costs = Direct materials, $6 + Direct manufacturing labor, $0.50 + Manufacturing overhead, $1 = $7.50.
ᵇFixed manufacturing costs = Direct manufacturing labor, $1.50 + Manufacturing overhead, $3 = $4.50.
ᶜ5,000 × $11.00 = $55,000.
ᵈ5,000 × $7.50 = $37,500.
ᵉNo variable marketing costs would be incurred for the 5,000-unit one-time-only special order.
ᶠFixed manufacturing costs and fixed marketing costs are also unaffected by the special order.

Exhibit 11-4 presents data for this example on an absorption-costing basis. In this presentation, the manufacturing costs of $12 per unit and the marketing costs of $7 per unit include both variable and fixed costs. The sum of *all* costs (variable *and* fixed) in a particular business function in the value chain, such as those in manufacturing or marketing, are called **business function costs. Full costs of the product,** in this case $19 per unit, are the sum of all the variable and fixed costs in all the business functions in the value chain (R&D, design, production, marketing, distribution, and customer service). For Fancy Fabrics, full costs of the product consist of just manufacturing and marketing costs because these are the only business function costs. Because no marketing costs are necessary for the special order, the manager of Fancy Fabrics will focus only on manufacturing costs. Based on the manufacturing cost per unit of $12, which is above the $11 per unit price offered by the hotel chain, the manager might reject the offer.

Exhibit 11-5 separates manufacturing and marketing costs into their variable- and fixed-cost components and presents data in a contribution income statement format. The relevant costs are the expected future costs that differ between the alternatives—the variable manufacturing costs of $37,500 ($7.50 per unit × 5,000 units). The fixed manufacturing costs and all marketing costs (*including variable marketing costs*) are irrelevant in this case. They will not change in total whether or not the special order is accepted. Therefore, the only relevant items here are sales revenues and variable manufacturing costs. Given the $11 relevant revenue per unit (the special-order price) and the $7.50 relevant costs per unit, Fancy Fabrics would gain an additional $17,500 [($11.00 − $7.50) × 5,000] in operating income by accepting the special order. In this example, comparing total amounts for 30,000 units versus 35,000 units or focusing only on the relevant amounts in the difference column (Exhibit 11-5) avoids the misleading implication of the absorption cost per unit (Exhibit 11-4).

The assumption of no long-run or strategic implications is crucial to our analysis of the one-time-only special-order decision. Suppose, for example, that Fancy Fabrics is concerned that the retail department stores (its regular customers) will demand a lower price if it sells towels at $11 a towel to the luxury hotel chain. In this case, revenues from regular customers will become relevant. Why? Because these are future revenues that differ between the alternatives of accepting or rejecting the special offer. The relevant-revenue and relevant-cost analysis of the luxury hotel chain order must be modified to consider both the short-run benefits from accepting the order and the long-run consequences on profitability of possibly lowering prices to its regular customers.

Potential Problems in Relevant-Cost Analysis

Two potential problems should be avoided in relevant-cost analysis. First, watch out for incorrect general assumptions such as all variable costs are relevant and all fixed costs are irrelevant. For instance, in the Fancy Fabrics example, the marketing costs of $5 per unit are variable but not relevant. Why? Because for the special-order decision, Fancy Fabrics incurs no extra marketing costs. Similarly, fixed manufacturing costs could be relevant. Consider again the Fancy Fabrics example. We assumed that the extra production of 5,000 towels per month does not affect fixed manufacturing costs because we assumed that the relevant range is at least from 30,000 to 35,000 towels per month. In some cases, however, producing the extra 5,000 towels might increase fixed manufacturing costs. Suppose Fancy Fabrics would need to run three shifts of 16,000 towels per shift to achieve full capacity of 48,000 towels per month. Increasing the monthly production from 30,000 to 35,000 would require a partial third shift because two shifts alone could produce only 32,000 towels. This extra shift would probably increase fixed manufacturing costs, thereby making any partial additional fixed manufacturing costs relevant for this decision.

Second, unit-cost data can potentially mislead decision makers in two major ways:

1. *When irrelevant costs are included.* Consider the $4.50 amount of fixed direct manufacturing labor and manufacturing overhead costs included in the $12 per unit manufacturing cost in the one-time-only special-order decision for Fancy Fabrics (see Exhibits 11-4 and 11-5). This $4.50 per unit cost is irrelevant given the assumptions of our example and thus should be excluded.

2. *When the same unit costs are used at different output levels.* Generally, use total costs rather than unit costs. Then, if desired, the total costs can be unitized. In the Fancy Fabrics illustration, total fixed manufacturing costs remain at $135,000 even if Fancy Fabrics accepts the special order and produces 35,000 towels. Including the existing fixed manufacturing cost per unit of $4.50 when accepting the special order would lead to the erroneous conclusion that total fixed manufacturing costs would increase to $157,500 ($4.50 × 35,000 towels).

The best way to avoid these potential problems is to keep focusing on total revenues and total costs (rather than unit costs), and on the relevance concept. Always require each item included in the analysis to be expected total future revenues and expected total future costs that differ among the alternatives.

INSOURCING-VERSUS-OUTSOURCING AND MAKE-VERSUS-BUY DECISIONS

We now apply the concept of relevance to another decision, whether a company should make a part or buy it from a supplier. As in the previous section, we retain the assumption of idle capacity.

Outsourcing and Idle Facilities

Outsourcing is the process of purchasing goods and services from outside vendors rather than producing the same goods or providing the same services within the organization, which is called **insourcing**. For example, Kodak prefers to manufacture its own films (insourcing), but has IBM do its data processing (outsourcing). Toyota

OBJECTIVE 4

Identify two potential problems that should be avoided in relevant-cost analysis

Correcting Student Misconceptions Warn students to be very careful with the total cost/unit that includes fixed costs (FC) per unit. Mgrs. often misuse total cost/unit data for decisions where FC aren't relevant (as in the text's Fancy Fabrics example). Mgrs. may also mistakenly multiply the same "total cost/unit" by different numbers of units. They may not realize that the total cost/unit changes as the output level changes because FC are spread over different #s of outputs. Total cost/unit figs. are valid only at the assumed output level. Presenting unit costs at different output levels may help get the point across.

Points to Stress Special orders usually don't incur regular marketing costs because they usually don't go through normal channels. There may be special fixed (marketing) costs of obtaining the order. If there's excess mfg. capacity, a special order may not affect FMOH. However, the special order could increase FMOH if it increases output to a higher relevant range, or if it requires special machinery, etc. FMOH and marketing and distribution costs may or may not be relevant in special order decisions, depending on the specific situation.

Points to Stress In the Fancy Fabrics example, comparing the $12 full mfg. cost (*that includes both relevant and irrelevant costs*) to the $11 relevant revenue leads to an incorrect decision to reject the order.

Points to Stress The term *outsourcing* refers to buying products or services from outside the company instead of within the company.

Reinforcing Problems Exer. 11-20 and Probs. 11-35, 11-36, 11-38, and 11-42 cover make-or-buy decisions.

relies on outside vendors to supply some parts and components but chooses to manufacture other parts internally.

Decisions about whether a producer of goods or services will insource or outsource are also called **make-or-buy decisions.** Sometimes qualitative factors dictate management's make-or-buy decision. For example, Dell Computer buys the Pentium chip for its personal computers from Intel because it does not have the know-how and technology to make the chip itself. Coca Cola does not outsource the manufacture of its concentrate to safeguard its formula and retain control of the product. What are the most important factors in the make-or-buy decision? Surveys of company practice indicate they are quality, dependability of suppliers, and cost.

EXAMPLE 2: The El Cerrito Company manufactures thermostats—consisting of relays, switches, and valves—for home and industrial use. El Cerrito makes its own switches. Columns 1 and 2 of the following table report the current costs for HDS, its heavy-duty switch, based on an analysis of its various manufacturing activities:

	Total Current Costs of Producing 10,000 Units (1)	Current Cost Per Unit (2) = (1) ÷ 10,000	Expected Total Costs of Producing 10,000 Units Next Year (3)	Expected Cost Per Unit (4) = (3) ÷ 10,000
Direct materials	$ 80,000	$ 8.00	$ 80,000	$ 8.00
Direct manufacturing labor	10,000	1.00	10,000	1.00
Variable manufacturing overhead costs for power and utilities	40,000	4.00	40,000	4.00
Mixed (variable and fixed) manufacturing overhead costs of materials handling and setups	17,500	1.75	20,000	2.00
Fixed manufacturing overhead costs of plant lease, insurance, and administration	30,000	3.00	30,000	3.00
Total manufacturing costs	$177,500	$17.75	$180,000	$18.00

Points to Stress Batch-level purchasing, receiving, and setup costs in the El Cerrito outsourcing example don't vary with the # of units, per se. However, they are relevant in the outsourcing decision. If the component is outsourced there will be zero batches, so these batch-level costs will be avoided. Also, even though the number of units remains the same, the total purchasing, receiving, and setup costs increase because the # of batches is doubled. This illustrates why reduction in setup time is key as firms move to small-batch production and delivery JIT systems.

Materials-handling and setup activities occur each time a batch of HDS is made. El Cerrito produces the 10,000 units of HDS in 25 batches of 400 units each. The number of batches is the cost driver for these costs. Total materials handling and setup costs equal fixed costs of $5,000 plus variable costs of $500 per batch [$5,000 + (25 × $500) = $17,500]. El Cerrito commences production only after it receives a customer order. Because they are trying to lower their inventory levels, El Cerrito's customers are pressuring the company to supply thermostats in smaller batch sizes. El Cerrito anticipates that next year, the 10,000 units of HDS expected to be sold will be manufactured in 50 batches of 200 units each. Through continuous improvement, El Cerrito expects to reduce variable costs per batch for materials handling and setup to $300. No other changes in fixed costs or variable costs per unit are anticipated.

Another manufacturer offers to sell El Cerrito 10,000 units of HDS next year for $16 per unit on whatever delivery schedule El Cerrito wants. Assume that financial factors predominate in this make-or-buy decision. Should El Cerrito make or buy HDS?

Columns 3 and 4 of the preceding table indicate the expected total costs and expected cost per unit of producing 10,000 units of HDS next year. Direct materials, direct manufacturing labor, and variable manufacturing overhead costs that vary with units produced are not expected to change because El Cerrito plans to continue to produce 10,000 units next year at the same variable costs per unit as this year. The costs of purchasing, receiving, and setups are expected to increase even though there is no expected change in the total production quantity. Why? Because these costs will vary with the number of batches, not the quantity of production. Expected total materials handling and setup costs = $5,000 + (50 batches × the cost per batch of

EXHIBIT 11-6

Relevant (Incremental) Items for Make-or-Buy Decision for HDS at the El Cerrito Company

Points to Stress The analysis in Exh. 11-6 suggests that unless qualitative benefits of outsourcing are worth $10,000, El Cerrito should make the part itself.

Relevant Items	Total Relevant Costs		Per Unit Relevant Costs	
	Make	Buy	Make	Buy
Outside purchase of parts		$160,000		$16
Direct materials	$ 80,000		$ 8	
Direct manufacturing labor	10,000		1	
Variable manufacturing overhead	40,000		4	
Mixed (variable and fixed) materials-handling and setup overhead[a]	20,000		2	
Total relevant costs	$150,000	$160,000	$15	$16
Difference in favor of making HDS	$10,000		$1	

[a]Alternatively, the $30,000 of depreciation, plant insurance, and plant administration costs could be included under both alternatives. These costs are irrelevant to the decision.

Correcting Student Misconceptions Emphasize that some of the purchasing, receiving, and setup costs in Exh. 11-6 are "fixed" while some vary with batch-level cost drivers.

$300) = $5,000 + $15,000 = $20,000. El Cerrito expects fixed manufacturing overhead costs to remain the same as this year. The expected manufacturing cost per unit for next year equals $18. At this cost, it seems that the company should buy HDS from the outside supplier because the expected cost per unit of making the part appears to be more costly than the $16 per unit it would cost to buy it. A make-or-buy decision, however, is rarely obvious. A key question for management is, What is the difference in relevant costs between the alternatives?

For the moment, suppose the capacity now used to make HDS will become idle next year if HDS is purchased and that the $30,000 of fixed manufacturing overhead will continue to be incurred next year, regardless of the decision made. Assume that the $5,000 in fixed clerical salaries to support setup, receiving, and purchasing will not be incurred if the manufacture of HDS is completely shut down next year.

Exhibit 11-6 presents the relevant-cost computations. El Cerrito will save $10,000 by making HDS rather than buying it from the outside supplier. Alternatively stated, purchasing HDS will cost $160,000 but will save only $150,000 in manufacturing costs. Making HDS is thus the preferred alternative.

Note how the key concepts of relevance presented in Exhibit 11-3 apply here:

1. Current cost data from columns 1 and 2 of the table in Example 2 play no role in the analysis in Exhibit 11-6. Why? Because for next year's make-or-buy decision these costs are past costs and hence irrelevant. Their only role is to help predict what future costs will be.

2. Exhibit 11-6 includes the $20,000 of purchasing, receiving, and setup costs under the make alternative but not under the buy alternative. Why? Because buying HDS and not having to manufacture it will save both the future variable costs per batch and the avoidable fixed costs. The $20,000 represents future costs that differ between the alternatives and hence is relevant to the make-or-buy decision.

3. Exhibit 11-6 excludes the $30,000 of plant lease, insurance, and administration costs under both the make and the buy alternatives. Why? Because although these are future costs, they will not differ between the two alternatives and are hence irrelevant.

A commonly used term in decision making is *incremental costs*. An **incremental cost** is the additional cost incurred for an activity. In Exhibit 11-6, the incremental cost of making HDS is the additional cost of $150,000. Note that the $30,000 of fixed manufacturing overhead is not an incremental cost of making HDS because El

VW Takes Outsourcing to the Limit

Volkswagen's bus and truck plant in Resende, Brazil, is a virtual plant: VW has completely outsourced manufacturing to a team of carefully selected supplier-partners in a radical experiment in production operations. At Resende, VW is transformed from manufacturer to general contractor, overseeing assembly operations performed by seven German, U.S., Brazilian, and Japanese components suppliers, with not one VW employee so much as turning a screw. Only 200 of the total 1,000 Resende workers are actual VW employees.

When designing the Resende plant, VW asked suppliers to bid for the opportunity to own one of seven major modules required to build a car, such as axles and brakes, and engine and transmission. Suppliers have invested $50 million to build, equip, and stock their areas. VW's contract with suppliers is for 10- to 15-year periods with the conditions that suppliers must achieve specified cost and performance targets and maintain cutting-edge technologies.

The plant is divided into seven zones, demarcated by yellow floor stripes. Within the boundaries of its zone, each supplier assembles its component from subcomponents sourced from 400 minor suppliers. In parallel with subcomponent assembly, final assembly occurs as the chassis (the vehicle platform) passes through the zones, and each company adds its respective component-module until the finished VW rolls off the line. Following each vehicle through the line is a single VW employee—a master craftsman assigned to track the vehicle and solve problems on the spot. Suppliers are paid for each completed vehicle that passes final inspection.

Despite representing seven different companies, the suppliers operate as a tightly integrated team, wearing the same uniforms and receiving the same pay. The assembly line is highly cross-functional, with representatives from each supplier meeting each morning to plan the day's production, and each evening to address issues and solve any problems. Each supplier has visibility of the entire production process, which stimulates ideas for simplification, streamlining, and product and process changes.

The specialization and superior component knowledge of each supplier, combined with the close interaction among suppliers, improves quality and efficiency. Co-location of the major component and final assemblies improves production flow and compresses total assembly time. It also simplifies logistics and reduces materials-handling, production control, manufacturing engineering, and coordination costs.

Although the plant remains in startup mode, preliminary results look promising. Resende employs 800 manufacturing workers instead of 2,500 at a comparable older VW plant. The time to assemble a truck has been reduced from 52 hours to 35 hours. These improvements have enabled VW to quickly earn a 19% share in the Brazilian truck market, and a 23% share in the bus market.

Source: D. J. Schemo, "Is VW's New Plant Lean, or Just Mean?" *New York Times* (November 19, 1996); J. Friedland; "VW Puts Suppliers on Production Line," *Wall Street Journal* (February 15, 1996); L. Goering, "Revolution at Plant X," *Chicago Tribune* (April 13, 1997).

New in This Edition This Concepts in Action box is new. VW has taken outsourcing to a new level, creating a virtual plant where most of the work is done by suppliers.

Cerrito will incur these costs whether or not it makes HDS. Similarly, the incremental cost of buying HDS from an outside supplier is the additional cost of $160,000. A **differential cost** is the difference in cost between two alternatives. In Exhibit 11-6, the differential cost between the make-HDS and buy-HDS alternatives is $10,000 ($160,000 − $150,000). Sometimes *incremental cost* and *differential cost* are used interchangeably. When using these terms in practice, always clarify their meaning.

We define *incremental revenue* and *differential revenue* in an analogous manner. **Incremental revenue** is the additional revenue from an activity. **Differential revenue** is the difference in revenue between two alternatives.

The use of otherwise idle resources can often increase profitability or decrease unprofitability. For example, consider the machine-repair plant of Beijing Engineering, where the *China Daily* noted that workers were "busy producing electric plaster-spraying machines" even though the unit cost of 1,230 yuan exceeded the selling price of 985 yuan, resulting in a loss of 245 yuan per sprayer. Still, to meet market demand, the plant continued to produce sprayers. Workers and machines would otherwise be idle, and the plant would still have to pay 759 yuan per sprayer in fixed labor and equipment costs even if no sprayers were made. In the short run, the production of sprayers, even at a loss, actually helped reduce the company's operating loss (from 759 yuan to 245 yuan per sprayer).

Strategic and Qualitative Factors

Several strategic and qualitative factors affect the outsourcing decision. For example, El Cerrito may prefer to manufacture HDS in-house to retain more control over the design, quality, reliability, and delivery schedules of the switches it uses in its thermostats. Conversely, despite the cost advantages documented in Exhibit 11-6, El Cerrito may prefer to outsource, become a smaller and leaner organization, and focus on areas of its core competencies—the manufacture and sale of thermostats. As an example of focus, advertising companies, like J. Walter Thompson, only do the creative and planning aspects of advertising (their core competencies) and outsource production activities such as film, photographs, and illustrations.

Of course, outsourcing is not without its risks. As a company's dependence on its suppliers increases, suppliers could increase prices and let quality and delivery performance slip. To minimize these risks, companies generally enter into long-run contracts with their suppliers that specify costs, quality, and delivery schedules. Intelligent managers will build close partnerships or alliances with a few key suppliers, teaming with suppliers on design and manufacturing decisions, and building a culture and commitment for quality, and timely delivery. Toyota goes so far as to send its own engineers to improve suppliers' processes. Companies (such as Ford, Hyundai, Panasonic, and Sony) have allowed suppliers to gain expertise and grow. These suppliers have researched and developed innovative new products, met demands for increased quantities, maintained quality and on-time delivery, and lowered costs—actions that the companies themselves would not have had the competencies to achieve. The Concepts in Action box describes how Volkswagen has outsourced the entire manufacturing of its trucks and buses at its Resende, Brazil, plant to its suppliers.

OPPORTUNITY COSTS, OUTSOURCING, AND CAPACITY CONSTRAINTS

The calculations in Exhibit 11-6 for the El Cerrito Company assumed that the capacity currently used to make HDS will remain idle if El Cerrito purchases the parts from the outside manufacturer. More generally though, the released facilities can potentially be used for other, more profitable purposes. The choice then is not fundamentally whether to make or buy but how best to use available facilities.

EXAMPLE 3: Suppose that if El Cerrito buys HDS from the outside supplier, El Cerrito's best use of the available capacity is to produce 5,000 units of RS, a regular switch, for Terrence Corporation. John Marquez, the accountant at El Cerrito, estimates the following future revenues and future costs if RS is manufactured and sold:

Additional future revenues		$80,000
Additional future costs		
Direct materials	$30,000	
Direct manufacturing labor	5,000	
Variable overhead (power, utilities)	15,000	
Materials-handling and setup overheads	5,000	
Total additional future costs		55,000
Additional future operating income		$25,000

Example In the Beijing Engineering example, incremental revenue is 985 yuan, but incremental cost is only $1230 - 759 = 471$ yuan. Thus, incremental profit is $985 - 471 = 514$ yuan. The plant should keep producing in the short run (as long as the fixed costs remain fixed). However, fixed costs can be changed in the long run. Workers can be laid off, machines sold, etc. Because the company isn't covering all their costs, they should try to find more profitable uses of their plant, or else consider downsizing—at least in the long run. Chap. 12 discusses these issues in more detail.

OBJECTIVE 5

Describe the opportunity-cost concept and explain why it is used in decision making

Reinforcing Problems Exer. 11-21 and 11-22, and Probs. 11-32, 11-33, and 11-36 cover opportunity cost issues.

Relevant Items	Choices for El Cerrito		
	1. Make HDS and Do Not Make RS	2. Buy HDS and Do Not Make RS	3. Buy HDS and Make RS
PANEL A: TOTAL-ALTERNATIVES APPROACH TO MAKE-OR-BUY DECISIONS			
Total incremental future costs of making/ buying HDS (from Exhibit 11-6)	$150,000	$160,000	$160,000
Excess of future revenues over future costs from RS	0	0	(25,000)
Total relevant costs under total-alternatives approach	$150,000	$160,000	$135,000
PANEL B: OPPORTUNITY-COST APPROACH TO MAKE-OR-BUY DECISIONS			
Total incremental future costs of making/ buying HDS (from Exhibit 11-6)	$150,000	$160,000	$160,000
Opportunity cost: Profit contribution forgone because capacity will not be used to make RS, the next-best alternative	25,000	25,000	0
Total relevant costs under opportunity-cost approach	$175,000	$185,000	$160,000

Note that the differences in costs across the columns in Panels A and B are the same—the cost of alternative 3 is $15,000 less than the cost of alternative 1 and $25,000 less than the cost of alternative 2.

Teaching Tip Most students find the total approach easier to understand. One merely analyzes dollars coming into and going out of the firm. Encourage students to use the total approach until they are sufficiently comfortable with the opportunity cost concept and outsourcing decisions to use the opportunity costs approach.

Correcting Student Misconceptions Students struggle with opportunity costs (OC). For Alt. 1, the OC is the contribution of the *best alternative not chosen* (Alt. 2 = 0 or Alt. 3 = $25,000). For Alt. 2, the OC is the contribution of the *best alternative not chosen* (Alt. 1 = 0 or Alt. 3 = $25,000). For Alt. 3, the OC is the contribution of the best alternative not chosen (Alt. 1 = 0 or Alt. 2 = 0).

El Cerrito can make either HDS or RS, but not both. What should El Cerrito do? The three alternatives available to management are:

1. Make HDS and do not make RS for Terrence.
2. Buy HDS and do not make RS for Terrence.
3. Buy HDS and make RS for Terrence.

Exhibit 11-7, Panel A, summarizes the "total-alternatives" approach—the future costs and future revenues for *all* alternatives. Alternative 3, buying HDS and using the available capacity to make RS and sell it to Terrence, is the preferred alternative. The future incremental costs of buying HDS from an outside supplier are more than the future incremental costs of making HDS in-house ($160,000 to buy versus $150,000 to make). But the capacity that would be freed up by buying HDS from the outside supplier would enable El Cerrito to gain $25,000 in operating income (additional future revenues of $80,000 minus additional future costs of $55,000) by making and selling RS to Terrence. The total relevant costs of buying HDS (and making and selling RS) are $160,000 − $25,000 = $135,000.

Deciding to use a resource in a particular way causes a manager to give up the opportunity to use the resource in alternative ways. The lost opportunity is a cost that the manager must take into consideration when making a decision. **Opportunity cost** is the contribution to income that is forgone (rejected) by not using a limited resource in its next-best alternative use. For example, the (relevant) cost of going to school for an MBA degree is not only the cost of tuition, books, lodging, and boarding, but also the income forgone (opportunity cost) by studying rather than working. Presumably the estimated future benefits of obtaining the degree (for example, the expected future increases in salary) will exceed these costs.

Exhibit 11-7, Panel B, displays the opportunity-cost approach for analyzing the alternatives faced by El Cerrito. Focus on alternative 1, make HDS and do not make RS, and ask, What are all the costs of choosing this alternative? Certainly, El Cerrito will incur $150,000 of incremental costs to make HDS. But is this the entire cost? No, because by deciding to use limited manufacturing resources to make HDS, El Cerrito will give up the opportunity to earn $25,000 from not using these resources to make RS. Therefore, the relevant costs of making HDS are the incremental costs of $150,000 plus the opportunity cost of $25,000. Next consider alternative 2, buy HDS and do not make RS. The incremental costs will be $160,000. But there is also an opportunity cost of $25,000 as a result of deciding not to make RS. Finally consider alternative 3, buy HDS and make RS. The incremental costs will be $160,000. The opportunity cost is zero. Why? Because under this alternative, El Cerrito will not forgo the profit it can earn from making and selling RS. Panel B leads management to the same conclusion as Panel A does—buying HDS and making RS is the preferred alternative.

Panels A and B of Exhibit 11-7 describe two consistent approaches to decision making with capacity constraints. The total-alternatives approach in Panel A includes all future incremental costs and revenues. For example, under alternative 3, the additional future operating income from *using capacity to make and sell RS* is subtracted from the future incremental cost of buying HDS. The opportunity-cost analysis in Panel B takes the opposite approach. *Whenever capacity is not going to be used to make and sell RS*, the future forgone operating income is added as an opportunity cost, as in alternatives 1 and 2. (Note that when RS is made as in alternative 3, there is "no opportunity cost of not making RS.") Thus, whereas Panel A subtracts $25,000 under alternative 3, Panel B adds $25,000 under alternatives 1 and 2. Panel B highlights the idea that when capacity is constrained, the relevant revenues and costs of any alternative equal the incremental future revenues and costs plus the opportunity cost.

Opportunity costs are not often incorporated into formal financial accounting records. Why? Because historical record keeping is limited to transactions involving alternatives actually selected rather than those rejected. Rejected alternatives do not produce transactions and thus are not recorded. For example, if El Cerrito makes HDS, it would not make RS, and it would not record any accounting entries for RS. Yet the opportunity cost of making HDS, which equals the operating income that El Cerrito forgoes by not making RS, is a crucial input into the make-versus-buy decision. Consider again Exhibit 11-7, Panel B. On the basis of incremental costs alone, the costs systematically recorded in the accounting system, it is less costly for El Cerrito to make rather than buy HDS. Recognizing the opportunity cost of $25,000 leads to the different conclusion that it is preferable to buy HDS.

Suppose El Cerrito has sufficient capacity to make RS even if it makes HDS. In this case, El Cerrito has a fourth alternative, Make HDS and Make RS. For this alternative, the opportunity cost of making HDS is zero because El Cerrito does not give up the $25,000 operating income from making RS even if it chooses to manufacture HDS. The relevant costs are $150,000 (incremental costs of $150,000 plus opportunity costs of $0). It follows that, under these conditions, El Cerrito would prefer to make HDS rather than buy it and make RS as well.

Our analysis emphasizes purely quantitative considerations. The final decision, however, should consider strategic and qualitative factors as well. For example, before deciding to buy HDS from an outside supplier, El Cerrito management would consider such qualitative factors as the supplier's reputation for quality and the supplier's dependability for on-time delivery. At the same time, El Cerrito would want to be certain that Terrence does not use RS to produce thermostats that compete with El Cerrito.

As you review this section, note how the key features of the analysis are exactly the same as those presented in Exhibit 11-3, even though the decision setting is different. In particular, note how the different alternatives can be compared using total future revenues and costs as in Panel A or only relevant costs (including opportunity costs) as in Panel B. However, when three or more alternatives are being considered simultaneously, it is generally easier to use the total-alternatives approach.

Carrying Costs of Inventory

We illustrate another example of an opportunity cost in the context of El Cerrito Corporation's decision to purchase HDS. El Cerrito has enough cash to pay for whatever quantity of HDS it buys. The following data are available.

Curriculum Linkage The opportunity cost concept (the benefit foregone by *not* choosing the next best alt.) is borrowed from economics.

Points to Stress One general approach to outsourcing decisions is the following:

Max. we'd pay = Incremental cost
               + Opportunity
               cost of insourcing.

This formula tells us how much we can pay the outside supplier and still make as much profit as if we produced the units ourselves. We're willing to pay at least the *incremental* cost of insourcing (i.e., our outlay cost). If facilities would otherwise be idle, the opportunity cost of insourcing is zero, because there's nothing better to do with the plant. In the El Cerrito example, opportunity costs aren't zero because the plant can be used to produce another product. The incremental cost is $150,000 and opportunity costs are $25,000 (see Panel B of Exh. 11-7). The maximum El Cerrito should pay the outside supplier is $150,000 + $25,000 = $175,000 (or $17.50 per unit). Note that if El Cerrito paid the outside supplier $175,000 for HDS, the total relevant costs would equal those under alt. 1.

Points to Stress Again, emphasize that financial analysis is only 1 consideration in outsourcing decisions. Suppliers' ability to provide high-quality products with timely delivery is also very important, particularly if the firm has adopted JIT.

Curriculum Linkage Chap. 20 explains why inventory carrying costs are inversely related to economic order quantities (EOQ).

Points to Stress At least 2 factors help explain why some companies have had high inventory levels. First, since the cost of capital tied up in inventory isn't reported by the acctg. system, mgt. may never see this information. Second, purchasing managers are frequently rewarded for favorable price var's., so they may be tempted to purchase large qtys. to obtain a qty. discount.

Annual estimated HDS requirements for next year	10,000 units
Cost per unit when each purchase is of 1,000 units	$16.00
Cost per unit when each purchase is equal to or greater than 10,000 units; $16 minus 1% discount	$15.84
Cost of placing each purchase order	$100.00

Alternatives under consideration:

    A. Make 10 purchases of 1,000 units each during next year

    B. Make 1 purchase of 10,000 units at the start of next year

Average investment in inventory:

A. (1,000 units × $16.00) ÷ 2[a]	$8,000
B. (10,000 units × $15.84) ÷ 2[a]	$79,200
Annual interest rate for investment in government bonds	6%

[a]The example assumes that HDS purchased will be used up uniformly throughout the year. The average investment in inventory during the year is the cost of the inventory when a purchase is made plus the cost of inventory just before the next purchase is made (in our example, $0) divided by 2.

What should El Cerrito do? The following table presents El Cerrito's two alternatives.

	Alternative A: Make 10 Purchases of 1,000 Units Each During the Year (1)	Alternative B: Make 1 Purchase of 10,000 Units at Beginning of Year (2)	Difference (3) = (1) − (2)
Annual purchase-order costs (10 × $100; 1 × $100)	$ 1,000	$ 100	$ 900
Annual purchase costs (10,000 × $16.00; 10,000 × $15.84)	160,000	158,400	1,600
Annual interest income that could be earned if investment in inventory were invested in government bonds (opportunity cost) (6% × $8,000; 6% × $79,200)	480	4,752	(4,272)
Relevant costs	$161,480	$163,252	$(1,772)

Points to Stress Compare the example's $4,272 opportunity cost of capital tied up in the excess inventory to the ($16)(1%)(10,000) = $1,600 savings from the qty. discount if 10,000 units are purchased at the beginning of the year. The company would be better off purchasing 1,000 units per order than the 10,000 units at once to get the qty. discount.

The opportunity cost of holding inventory is the income forgone from tying up money in inventory and not investing it elsewhere. The opportunity costs would not be recorded in the accounting system because, once the alternative of investing money elsewhere is rejected, there are no transactions related to this alternative to record. Column 3 indicates that, consistent with the trends toward holding smaller inventories, purchasing smaller quantities of 1,000 units throughout the year is preferred to purchasing all 10,000 units at the beginning of the year. Why? Because the lower opportunity cost of holding smaller inventory exceeds the higher purchase and ordering costs. If the opportunity cost were greater than 6% or if other incremental benefits of holding lower inventory such as lower insurance, materials-handling, storage, obsolescence, and breakage costs were considered, making ten purchases would be even more preferable.

PRODUCT-MIX DECISIONS UNDER CAPACITY CONSTRAINTS

OBJECTIVE 6

Describe the key concept in choosing which among multiple products to produce when there are capacity constraints

In this section, we examine how the concept of relevance applies to **product-mix decisions**, the decisions by companies about how much of each product to sell. These decisions frequently have a short-run focus because the level of capacity can only be expanded in the long run. For example, BMW, the German car manufacturer, must continually adapt the mix of its different models of cars (e.g., 325i, 525i, and 740i) to short-run fluctuations in materials costs, selling prices, and demand. The key to determining product mix is maximizing operating income given the constraints the company faces, such as capacity and demand. Throughout this section, we assume that as short-run changes in product mix occur, the only costs that change are those that are variable with respect to the number of units produced

American Airlines, the Internet, and Opportunity Costs

What are the relevant costs for American Airlines to fly a customer on a round-trip flight from Dallas to San Francisco leaving on Friday, November 12, 1999, and returning on Monday, November 15, 1999? The incremental costs are very small—mainly food costs of, say, $20—because the other costs of the plane, pilots, ticket agents, and baggage handlers are fixed. The important question is, What are the opportunity costs? To determine the opportunity costs, American Airlines must assess what profit it has forgone by selling the seat to a particular customer. The profit forgone depends on whether the flight is full (operating at capacity) or not. American would normally charge $400 for this round-trip ticket. If seats are available, the opportunity cost is zero. If the flight is full, the opportunity cost is $380 ($400 − $20), the profit American would make by selling the same seat to another customer. The relevant cost is $400, the incremental cost of $20 plus the opportunity cost of $380.

If a customer calls to purchase the ticket in early October, 1999, American computes the relevant costs to be $400 because it expects that its flight will be full. But what if on Wednesday November 10, 1999, American finds that the plane will not be full? The relevant cost for each remaining seat on the flight will now be only the $20 incremental cost, and American can lower its prices well below $400—to, say, $100—and still make a profit. Waiting until the last minute and recognizing that opportunity costs are zero enables American to drastically lower its prices in the hopes of attracting more customers while still earning a profit. But how can American tell its potential customers cheaply and quickly about these lowered fares? Welcome to the Internet. Using a technology called "push" technology, American broadcasts information about all flights on which seats are available to subscribers who have registered free of charge on American Airlines' home page http//:www.aa.com. Each Wednesday morning, an electronic mail arrives in each subscriber's e-mail account indicating departure and arrival cities for which cheap fares, often around $100, are available. The requirement? Travel must start on Friday or Saturday and end before the following Monday. By waiting until Wednesday to announce the fares, American can be certain that unfilled seats are available and that the opportunity costs for the fares it offers are thus zero. The Internet allows information to be broadcast to a large audience quickly and at virtually no cost. American Airlines' low-fare subscription service is a good example of how a company that has a good understanding of relevant costs can take advantage of its low variable-cost structure using Internet communications technology.

(and sold). Under these assumptions, the analysis of individual product contribution margins provides insight into the product mix that maximizes operating income.

EXAMPLE 4: Consider Power Recreation, a company that manufactures engines for a broad range of commercial and consumer products. At its Lexington, Kentucky, plant, it assembles two engines—a snowmobile engine and a boat engine. Information on these products is as follows:

	Snowmobile Engine	Boat Engine
Selling price	$800	$1,000
Variable costs per unit	560	625
Contribution margin per unit	$240	$ 375
Contribution margin percentage ($240 ÷ $800; $375 ÷ $1,000)	30%	37.5%

Assume that only 600 machine-hours are available daily for assembling engines. Additional capacity cannot be obtained in the short run. Power Recreation can sell as many engines as it produces. The constraining resource,

New in This Edition This Concepts in Action box is new. American Airlines has used Internet technology to sell airline seats when it determines that its opportunity cost is zero (i.e., it has excess capacity on a particular flight).

then, is machine-hours. It takes 2 machine-hours to produce one snowmobile engine and 5 machine-hours to produce one boat engine. Which product should Power Recreation emphasize?

In terms of contribution margin per unit and contribution margin percentage, boat engines are more profitable than snowmobile engines. The product to be emphasized, however, is not necessarily the product with the higher individual contribution margin per unit or contribution margin percentage. In general, managers should choose the product with *the highest contribution margin per unit of the constraining resource (factor)*—that is, the resource that restricts or limits the production or sale of products. (See also Chapter 19, the theory of constraints, pp. 692–695 for a discussion of methods that companies use to relax the constraining resource.)

	Snowmobile Engine	Boat Engine
Contribution margin per engine	$240	$375
Machine-hours required to produce one engine	2 machine-hours	5 machine-hours
Contribution margin per machine-hour ($240 ÷ 2; $375 ÷ 5)	$120	$75
Total contribution margin for 600 machine-hours ($120 × 600; $75 × 600)	$72,000	$45,000

Producing snowmobile engines contributes more margin per machine-hour, which is the constraining resource in this example. Therefore, choosing to emphasize snowmobile engines is the correct product-mix decision. Other constraints in manufacturing settings can be the availability of direct materials, components, or skilled labor, as well as financial and sales factors. In a retail department store, the constraining resource may be linear feet of display space. Regardless of what the specific constraining resource is, choosing products that give the highest possible contribution margin per unit of the constraining resource yields the maximum operating income. The key is to focus on maximizing *total* contribution margin. Relying on contribution margins per unit and contribution margin percentages can lead to erroneous conclusions.

As you can imagine, in many cases a manufacturer or retailer has the challenge of trying to maximize total operating income for a variety of products, each with more than one constraining resource. Some constraints may require a manufacturer or retailer to stock minimum quantities of products even if these products are not very profitable. For example, supermarkets must stock less profitable products because customers will be willing to shop at a supermarket only if it carries a wide range of products that customers desire. The problem of formulating the most profitable production schedules and the most profitable product mix is essentially that of maximizing the total contribution margin in the face of many constraints. Optimization techniques, such as the linear programming technique discussed in the Appendix to this chapter, help solve these more complex problems.

CUSTOMER PROFITABILITY, ACTIVITY-BASED COSTING, AND RELEVANT COSTS

In addition to making choices among products, companies must often make decisions about adding or discontinuing a product line, a branch, or a business segment. Similarly, if the cost object is a customer, companies must make decisions about adding or dropping customers. We illustrate relevant-revenue and relevant-cost analysis for these decisions using customers rather than products as the cost object.

EXAMPLE 5: Allied West, the West Coast sales office of Allied Furniture, a wholesaler of specialized furniture, supplies furniture to three local retailers, Vogel, Brenner, and Wisk. Exhibit 11-8 presents representative revenues and costs of Allied West by customers for the upcoming year. Additional information on Allied West's costs for different activities at various levels of the cost hierarchy is as follows:

EXHIBIT 11-8
Customer Profitability Analysis for Allied West

	Customer			
	Vogel	**Brenner**	**Wisk**	**Total**
Revenues	$500,000	$300,000	$400,000	$1,200,000
Cost of goods sold	370,000	220,000	330,000	920,000
Materials-handling labor	41,000	18,000	33,000	92,000
Materials-handling equipment cost written off as depreciation	12,000	4,000	9,000	25,000
Rent	14,000	8,000	14,000	36,000
Marketing support	11,000	9,000	10,000	30,000
Purchase orders and delivery processing	13,000	7,000	12,000	32,000
General administration	20,000	12,000	16,000	48,000
Allocated corporate office costs	10,000	6,000	8,000	24,000
Total costs	491,000	284,000	432,000	1,207,000
Operating income	$ 9,000	$ 16,000	$ (32,000)	$ (7,000)

1. Materials-handling labor costs vary with the number of units of furniture shipped to customers.

2. Allied reserves different areas of the warehouse to stock furniture for different customers. Materials-handling equipment in an area and depreciation costs on the equipment are identified with individual customer accounts. Any equipment not used remains idle. The equipment has a zero disposal price.

3. Allied West allocates rent to each customer account on the basis of the amount of warehouse space reserved for that customer.

4. Marketing costs vary with the number of sales visits made to customers.

5. Purchase-order costs vary with the number of purchase orders received; delivery-processing costs vary with the number of shipments made.

6. Allied West allocates fixed general administration costs to customers on the basis of customer revenues.

7. Allied Furniture allocates its fixed corporate office costs to sales offices on the basis of the square feet area of each sales office. Allied West allocates these costs to customers on the basis of customer revenues.

Several questions arise in this situation: Should Allied West drop the Wisk account? Should it add a fourth customer like Wisk? Should Allied Furniture close down Allied West? Should it open another sales office, Allied South, whose revenues and costs are identical to Allied West?

Relevant-Revenue and Relevant-Cost Analysis of Dropping a Customer

Exhibit 11-8 indicates a loss of $32,000 on the Wisk account. Allied West's manager believes the reason for the loss is that Wisk will place many low-volume orders with Allied, resulting in high purchase-order, delivery-processing, materials-handling, and marketing activity. Allied West is considering several possible actions with respect to the Wisk account—reducing its own costs of supporting Wisk by becoming more efficient, cutting back on some of the services it offers Wisk, charging Wisk higher prices, or dropping the Wisk account. The following analysis focuses on the operating income effect of dropping the Wisk account.

The key question is, What are the relevant revenues and relevant costs? The following information about the effect of reducing various activities related to the Wisk account is available.

Curriculum Linkage This example illustrates a keep-or-drop decision, but the object of the decision is a customer rather than a product. This ties in with Chap. 1's customer-focus theme and reinforces Chap. 5's notion that certain customers might be costing the company money. The example also uses ABC information to facilitate the keep-or-drop decision.

Points to Stress The Allied West example relaxes the assumption made earlier in the chapter that all costs are either variable or fixed with respect to a units-of-output cost driver. Here, there are several different types of drivers (e.g., # purchase orders, # sales calls, etc.).

1. Dropping the Wisk account will save cost of goods sold, materials-handling labor, marketing support, purchase-order, and delivery-processing costs incurred on the Wisk account.

2. Dropping the Wisk account will mean that the warehouse space currently occupied by products for Wisk and the materials-handling equipment used to move them will become idle.

3. Dropping the Wisk account will have no effect on fixed general administration costs or corporate office costs.

Points to Stress Exh. 11-8 shows that the Wisk account doesn't generate enough revenue to cover its full costs. Since Exh. 11-9 shows that it does generate enough revenue to more than cover its variable costs, mgt. may keep Wisk in the short term, *if no better alternatives are available*. In the longer run, however, the warehouse rental costs are relevant.

Points to Stress Depreciation expense is NEVER relevant because it is a sunk cost. Allocated costs *which don't change in total* are NEVER relevant. The only thing which changes is which customer (or other cost object) gets allocated those costs, not the total amount of the costs.

Reinforcing Problems Exer. 11-26 covers customer profitability, while Probs. 11-30 and 11-31 cover discontinuing a product line or division.

Exhibit 11-9, column 1, presents the relevant-revenue and relevant-cost computations using data from the Wisk column in Exhibit 11-8. Allied West's operating income will be $15,000 lower if it drops the Wisk account (the cost savings from dropping the Wisk account, $385,000, will not be enough to offset the loss of $400,000 in revenues), so Allied decides to keep the Wisk account.

Note that depreciation is a past cost and hence irrelevant, while rent, general administration, and corporate office costs are irrelevant because they are future costs that will not change if the Wisk account is dropped. Be particularly watchful of allocated overhead costs such as corporate office costs. Always ignore the amounts allocated to the sales office and individual products. The key question to ask in deciding whether corporate office costs are relevant or not is, Will *expected total corporate office costs* decrease as a result of dropping the Wisk account? In our example, they will not, and hence, these costs are irrelevant. If expected total corporate office costs decreased by dropping the Wisk account, the savings would be relevant even if the amount allocated to Allied West did not change.

Now suppose that if Allied drops the Wisk account, it could lease the extra warehouse space to the Sanchez Corporation for $20,000 per year. Then $20,000 would be Allied's opportunity cost of continuing to use the warehouse to service Wisk. Allied would gain $5,000 by dropping the Wisk account ($20,000 from lease revenue minus lost operating income of $15,000). Before reaching a final decision, however, Allied must examine whether Wisk can be made more profitable so that supplying products to Wisk earns more than the $20,000 from leasing to Sanchez. Allied must also consider qualitative factors such as the effect of the decision on Allied's reputation for developing stable, long-run business relationships.

EXHIBIT 11-9
Relevant-Revenue and Relevant-Cost Analysis for Dropping the Wisk Account and Adding the Loral Account

	(Loss in Revenues) and Savings in Costs from Dropping Wisk Account (1)	Incremental Revenues and (Incremental Costs) from Adding Loral Account (2)
Revenues	$(400,000)	$ 400,000
Cost of goods sold	330,000	(330,000)
Materials-handling labor	33,000	(33,000)
Materials-handling equipment cost written off as depreciation	0	(9,000)
Rent	0	0
Marketing support	10,000	(10,000)
Purchase orders and delivery processing	12,000	(12,000)
General administration	0	0
Corporate office costs	0	0
Total costs	385,000	(394,000)
Effect on operating income (loss)	$ (15,000)	$ 6,000

Relevant-Revenue and Relevant-Cost Analysis of Adding a Customer

Suppose that in addition to Vogel, Brenner, and Wisk, Allied West is evaluating the profitability of adding a fourth customer, Loral. Allied is already incurring annual costs of $36,000 for warehouse rent and $48,000 for general administration costs. These costs together with actual total corporate office costs will not change if Loral is added as a customer. Loral is a customer with a profile much like Wisk's. Suppose Allied predicts revenues and costs of doing business with Loral to be the same as those described under the Wisk column of Exhibit 11-8. In particular, Allied would have to acquire materials-handling equipment for Loral costing $9,000 with a 1-year useful life and zero disposal price. Should Allied add Loral as a customer?

Exhibit 11-9, column 2, shows incremental revenues exceed incremental costs by $6,000. Allied would prefer to add Loral as a customer. Note that rent, general administration, and corporate office costs are irrelevant because these costs will not change if Loral is added as a customer. However, the cost of acquiring new equipment to support the Loral order (written off as depreciation of $9,000 in Exhibit 11-9, column 2) is included as a relevant cost. Why? Because this cost can be avoided if Allied decides not to do business with Loral. Note the critical distinction here. Depreciation cost is irrelevant in deciding whether to drop Wisk as a customer (because it is a past cost), but the purchase cost of the new equipment that will then be written off as depreciation in the future is relevant in deciding whether to add Loral as a new customer.

Relevant-Revenue and Relevant-Cost Analysis of Discontinuing or Adding Branches or Segments

Companies periodically confront decisions about discontinuing or adding operations in various branches or business segments. For example, given Allied West's expected loss of $7,000 (see Exhibit 11-8), should it be closed? Suppose that closing Allied West will have no effect on corporate office costs.

Exhibit 11-10, column 1, presents the relevant-cost computations using data from the Total column in Exhibit 11-8. The revenue losses of $1,200,000 will exceed the cost savings of $1,158,000, and will lead to a decrease in operating income of $42,000. Allied West should not be closed down. The key reasons are that

EXHIBIT 11-10
Relevant-Revenue and Relevant-Cost Analysis for Closing Allied West and Opening Allied South

	(Loss in Revenues) and Savings in Costs from Closing Allied West (1)	Incremental Revenues and (Incremental Costs) from Opening Allied South (2)
Revenues	$(1,200,000)	$ 1,200,000
Cost of goods sold	920,000	(920,000)
Materials-handling labor	92,000	(92,000)
Materials-handling equipment cost written off as depreciation	0	(25,000)
Rent	36,000	(36,000)
Marketing support	30,000	(30,000)
Purchase orders and delivery processing	32,000	(32,000)
General administration	48,000	(48,000)
Corporate office costs	0	0
Total costs	1,158,000	(1,183,000)
Effect on operating income (loss)	$ (42,000)	$ 17,000

depreciation of $25,000 is a past (sunk) cost and hence will not be saved, and that no savings in actual total corporate office costs will occur as a result of closing Allied West. Corporate office costs allocated to various sales offices will change. The $24,000 no longer allocated to Allied West will be allocated to some other sales office(s), but no savings in overall corporate office costs will occur. Therefore, the $24,000 of allocated corporate office costs should not be counted as expected cost savings from closing Allied West.

Now suppose Allied Furniture has the opportunity to open another sales office, Allied South, whose revenues and costs are identical to Allied West's (including a cost of $25,000 to acquire materials-handling equipment with a 1-year useful life and zero disposal price). Opening this office will have no effect on corporate office costs. Should Allied Furniture open Allied South? Exhibit 11-10, column 2, indicates that it should do so because it will increase operating income by $17,000. The key point is to ignore allocated corporate office costs and consider only the actual total corporate office costs. Actual total corporate office costs do not differ between the alternatives and hence these costs are irrelevant.

IRRELEVANCE OF PAST COSTS AND EQUIPMENT-REPLACEMENT DECISIONS

OBJECTIVE 8

Explain why the book value of equipment is irrelevant in equipment-replacement decisions

In this section, we apply the concept of relevance to decisions about replacing equipment. We especially emphasize the idea that all past costs and, in particular, **book value** (original cost minus accumulated depreciation) of the existing equipment, are irrelevant.

EXAMPLE 6: Assume that the Toledo Company is considering replacing a metal-cutting machine with a newer model. The new machine is more efficient than is the old machine, but it has a shorter overall life. Revenues from aircraft parts ($1.1 million per year) will be unaffected by the replacement decision. Summary data on the existing (old) machine and the replacement (new) machine follow:

	Old Existing Machine	New Replacement Machine
Original cost	$1,000,000	$600,000
Useful life	5 years	2 years
Current age	3 years	0 years
Remaining useful life	2 years	2 years
Accumulated depreciation	$600,000	Not acquired yet
Book value	$400,000	Not acquired yet
Current disposal price (in cash)	$40,000	Not acquired yet
Terminal disposal price (in cash 2 years from now)	$0	$0
Annual operating costs (maintenance, energy, repairs, coolants, and so on)	$800,000	$460,000

The Toledo Corporation uses straight-line depreciation. To focus on the main concept of relevance, we ignore the time value of money and income taxes.[1] Should Toledo replace its existing machine?

Exhibit 11-11 presents a cost comparison of the two machines. We can apply our definition of relevance to four important items in Toledo's equipment-replacement decisions:

1. *Book value of old machine of $400,000.* Irrelevant, because it is a past (historical) or sunk cost. All past costs are "down the drain." Nothing can change what has already been spent or what has already happened.

---

[1]For a discussion of the time value of money and income tax considerations in such capital investment decisions, see Chapter 21.

EXHIBIT 11-11

Cost Comparison: Replacement of Machinery, Relevant and Irrelevant Items
for the Toledo Company

	Two Years Together		
	Keep (1)	Replace (2)	Difference (3) = (1) − (2)
Revenues	$2,200,000	$2,200,000	—
Operating costs			
Cash-operating costs	1,600,000	920,000	$ 680,000
Book value of old machine			
Periodic write-off as depreciation or	400,000	—	—
Lump-sum write-off	—	400,000[a]	
Current disposal price of old machine	—	(40,000)[a]	40,000
New machine cost, written off periodically as depreciation	—	600,000	(600,000)
Total operating costs	2,000,000	1,880,000	120,000
Operating income	$ 200,000	$ 320,000	$(120,000)

[a]In a formal income statement, these two items would be combined as "loss on disposal of machine" of $360,000.

2. *Current disposal price of old machine of $40,000.* Relevant, because it is an expected future benefit that differs between alternatives.

3. *Gain or loss on disposal of $360,000.* This is the algebraic difference between items 1 and 2. It is a meaningless combination blurring the distinction between the irrelevant book value and the relevant disposal price. Each item should be considered separately.

4. *Cost of new machine of $600,000.* Relevant, because it is an expected future cost that will differ between alternatives.

Exhibit 11-11 should clarify these four assertions. Column 3 in Exhibit 11-11 shows that the book value of the old machine is not an element of difference between alternatives and could be completely ignored for decision-making purposes. No matter what the timing of the charge against revenues, the amount charged is still $400,000 (either as a lump-sum charge in the current year or as depreciation charges over two years) regardless of the alternative chosen because it is a past (historical) cost. In contrast, the $600,000 cost of the new machine is relevant because it can be avoided by deciding not to replace. Note that the operating income from replacing is $120,000 higher for the two years together.

To focus on the key points, Exhibit 11-12 concentrates only on relevant costs and revenues. Note that the same answer (higher operating income of $120,000 by

EXHIBIT 11-12

Cost Comparison: Replacement of Machinery, Relevant Items Only
for the Toledo Company

	Two Years Together		
	Keep	Replace	Difference
Cash-operating costs	$1,600,000	$ 920,000	$ 680,000
Current disposal price of old machine	—	(40,000)	40,000
New machine, written off periodically as depreciation	—	600,000	(600,000)
Total relevant costs	$1,600,000	$1,480,000	$ 120,000

replacing the machine) will be obtained even though the book value is completely omitted from the calculations. The only relevant items are the cash operating costs, the disposal price of the old machine, and the cost of the new machine (represented as depreciation in Exhibit 11-12).[2]

DECISIONS AND PERFORMANCE EVALUATION

Consider our equipment-replacement example in light of the five-step sequence in Exhibit 11-1 (p. 379).

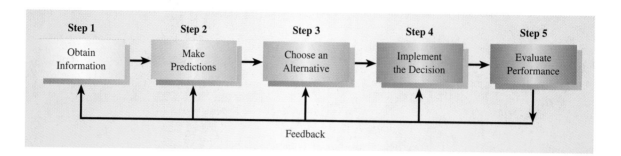

Step 1	Step 2	Step 3	Step 4	Step 5
Obtain Information	Make Predictions	Choose an Alternative	Implement the Decision	Evaluate Performance

Feedback

The decision model analysis (step 3), presented in Exhibits 11-11 and 11-12, dictates replacing rather than keeping. In the real world, however, would the manager replace? An important factor in replacement decisions is the manager's perceptions of whether the decision model is consistent with how the manager's performance is judged (the performance evaluation model in step 5).

Managers tend to favor the alternative that makes their performance look best. If the performance evaluation model conflicts with the decision model, the performance evaluation model often prevails in influencing a manager's behavior. For example, if the promotion or bonus of the manager at Toledo hinges on his or her first year's operating income performance under accrual accounting, the manager's temptation *not* to replace will be overwhelming. Why? Because the accrual accounting model for measuring performance will show a higher first-year operating income if the old machine is kept than if it is replaced (as the following table shows):

First-Year Results: Accrual Accounting

		Keep		Replace
Revenues		$1,100,000		$1,100,000
Operating costs				
Cash-operating costs	$800,000		$460,000	
Depreciation	200,000		300,000	
Loss on disposal	—		360,000	
Total operating costs		1,000,000		1,120,000
Operating income (loss)		$ 100,000		$ (20,000)

Even if top management's goals are over the longer two-year period (consistent with the decision model), the subordinate manager will focus on first-year results if his or her evaluation is based on short-run measures such as first-year operating income.

Resolving the conflict between the decision model and the performance evaluation model is frequently a baffling problem in practice. In theory, resolving the dif-

---

[2]Other applications of relevant revenues and relevant costs appear in Chapter 12, for pricing decisions; Chapter 15, for sell or process further decisions; Chapter 19, for quality management, costs of time, and the theory of constraints decisions; Chapter 20, for just-in-time purchasing and manufacturing, and supplier evaluation decisions; Chapter 21, for capital budgeting decisions; and Chapter 22, for transfer pricing decisions.

ficulty seems obvious—merely design consistent models. Consider our replacement example. Year-by-year effects on operating income of replacement can be budgeted over the planning horizon of two years. The manager would be evaluated on the understanding that the first year would be expected to be poor and the next year much better.

The practical difficulty is that accounting systems rarely track each decision separately. Performance evaluation focuses on responsibility centers for a specific time period, not on projects or individual items of equipment for their entire useful lives. Therefore, the impacts of many different decisions are combined in a single performance report. Top management, through the reporting system, is rarely aware of particular desirable alternatives that were not chosen by subordinate managers.

Consider another conflict between the decision model and the performance evaluation model. Suppose a manager buys a particular machine only to discover shortly thereafter that a better machine could have been purchased in its place. The decision model may suggest replacing the machine that was just bought with the better machine, but the manager may be reluctant to do so. Why? Because replacing the machine so soon after its purchase may reflect badly on the manager's capabilities and performance. If the manager's bosses have no knowledge of the better machine, the manager may prefer to keep the existing machine rather than alert his or her bosses about the better machine.

PROBLEM

Wally Lewis is manager of the engineering development division of Goldcoast Products, Inc. Lewis has just received a proposal signed by all ten of his engineers to replace the workstations with networked personal computers (networked PCs). Lewis is not enthusiastic about the proposal.

Summary data on the workstation and networked PC machines are as follows:

	Workstations	Networked PCs
Original cost	$300,000	$135,000
Useful life	5 years	3 years
Current age	2 years	0 years
Remaining useful life	3 years	3 years
Accumulated depreciation	$120,000	Not acquired yet
Current book value	$180,000	Not acquired yet
Current disposal price (in cash)	$95,000	Not acquired yet
Terminal disposal price (in cash 3 years from now)	$0	$0
Annual computer-related cash-operating costs	$40,000	$10,000
Annual revenues	$1,000,000	$1,000,000
Annual noncomputer-related operating costs	$880,000	$880,000

Lewis's annual bonus includes a component based on division operating income. He has a promotion possibility next year that would make him a group vice-president of Goldcoast Products.

Required
1. Compare the costs of the workstation and networked PC options. Consider the cumulative results for the 3 years together, ignoring income taxes and the time value of money.
2. Why might Lewis be reluctant to purchase the networked PCs?

SOLUTION

1. The following table considers all cost items when comparing future costs of the workstation and networked PC options:

All Items	Three Years Together		
	Workstations (1)	Networked PCs (2)	Difference (3) = (1) − (2)
Revenues	$3,000,000	$3,000,000	$ —
Operating Costs			
Noncomputer-related operating costs	2,640,000	2,640,000	—
Computer-related cash-operating costs	120,000	30,000	90,000
Workstations' book value			
Periodic write-off as depreciation or	180,000	—	—
Lump-sum write-off	—	180,000	
Current disposal price of workstations	—	(95,000)	95,000
Networked PCs, written off periodically as depreciation	—	135,000	(135,000)
Total operating costs	2,940,000	2,890,000	50,000
Operating income	$ 60,000	$ 110,000	$ (50,000)

Alternatively, the analysis could focus on only those items in the preceding table that differ between the alternatives.

Relevant Items	Three Years Together		
	Workstations	Networked PCs	Difference
Computer-related cash-operating costs	$120,000	$ 30,000	$ 90,000
Current disposal price of workstations	—	(95,000)	95,000
Networked PCs, written off periodically as depreciation	—	135,000	(135,000)
Total relevant costs	$120,000	$ 70,000	$ 50,000

The analysis suggests that it is cost effective to replace the workstations with the networked PCs.

2. The accrual accounting operating incomes for the first year under the "keep workstations" versus the "buy networked PCs" alternatives are as follows:

	Keep Workstations	Buy Networked PCs
Revenues	$1,000,000	$1,000,000
Operating costs		
Noncomputer-related operating costs	$880,000	$880,000
Computer-related cash-operating costs	40,000	10,000
Depreciation	60,000	45,000
Loss on disposal of workstations	—	85,000[a]
Total operating costs	980,000	1,020,000
Operating income	$ 20,000	$ (20,000)

[a]$85,000 = Book value of workstations, $180,000 − Current disposal price, $95,000

Lewis would probably be far less happy with the expected operating loss of $20,000 if the networked PCs are purchased than he would be with the expected operating income of $20,000 if the workstations are kept. The decision would eliminate the component of his bonus based on operating income. He might also perceive the $20,000 operating loss as reducing his chances of being promoted to a group vice president.

SUMMARY

The following points are linked to the chapter's learning objectives:

1. The five-step decision process is (a) obtain information, (b) make predictions, (c) choose alternative courses of action, (d) implement decisions, and (e) evaluate performance.

2. To be relevant to a particular decision, a revenue or cost must meet two criteria: (a) It must be an expected future revenue or cost, and (b) it must differ among alternative courses of action.

3. The consequences of alternative actions can be quantitative and qualitative. Quantitative factors are outcomes that are measured in numerical terms. Some quantitative factors can be easily expressed in financial terms, others cannot. Qualitative factors, such as employee morale, cannot be measured in numerical terms. Due consideration must be given to both quantitative and qualitative factors in making decisions.

4. Two potential problems that should be avoided in relevant-cost analysis are (a) making incorrect general assumptions such as all variable costs are relevant and all fixed costs are irrelevant, and (b) losing sight of grand totals and focusing instead on unit costs.

5. Opportunity cost is the contribution to income that is forgone (rejected) by not using a limited resource in its next-best alternative use. The idea of an opportunity cost arises when there are multiple uses for resources and some alternatives are not selected. Opportunity cost is included in decision making because it represents the best alternative way in which an organization may have used its resources if it had not made the decision it did.

6. In choosing among multiple products when resource capacity is constrained, managers should emphasize the product that yields the highest contribution margin per unit of the constraining or limiting resource (factor).

7. Managers should ignore allocated overhead costs when making decisions about dropping and adding customers and segments. They should focus instead on how total costs differ across alternatives.

8. The book value of existing equipment in equipment-replacement decisions represents past (historical) cost and therefore is irrelevant.

9. Top management faces a persistent challenge—that is, making sure that the performance-evaluation model of subordinate managers is consistent with the decision model. A common inconsistency is to tell subordinate managers to take a multiple-year view in their decision making but then judge their performance only on the basis of the current year's operating income.

APPENDIX: LINEAR PROGRAMMING

Linear programming (LP) is an optimization technique used to maximize total contribution margin of a mix of products (the objective function), given multiple constraints. LP models typically assume that all costs can be classified as either variable or fixed with respect to a single driver (units of output). LP models also require certain other linear assumptions to hold. When these assumptions fail, other decision models should be considered.[3]

Consider the Power Recreation example described earlier in the chapter (pp. 391–392). Suppose that both the snowmobile and boat engines must be tested on a very expensive machine before they are shipped to customers. The available machine time for testing is limited. Production data are as follows:

[3]Other decision models are described in G. Eppen, F. Gould, C. Schmidt, J. Moore, and L. Weatherford, *Introductory Management Science: Decision Modeling with Spreadsheets*, 5th ed. (Upper Saddle River, N. J.: Prentice Hall, 1998); and S. Nahmias, *Production and Operations Analysis* 3rd ed. (Homewood, Ill.: Irwin, 1996).

Teaching Tip The LP discussion in this Appendix extends the "maximize CM/unit of scarce resource" notion advanced in the chapter to more complex settings with multiple constraints.

Department	Available Daily Capacity in Hours	Use of Capacity in Hours Per Unit of Product		Daily Maximum Production in Units	
		Snowmobile Engine	Boat Engine	Snowmobile Engine	Boat Engine
Assembly	600 machine-hours	2.0	5.0	300[a]	120
Testing	120 testing-hours	1.0	0.5	120	240

[a]For example, 600 machine-hours ÷ 2.0 machine-hours per snowmobile engine = 300, the maximum number of snowmobile engines that the Assembly Department can make if it works exclusively on snowmobile engines.

Exhibit 11-13 summarizes these and other relevant data. As a result of material shortages for boat engines, Power Recreation cannot produce more than 110 boat engines per day. How many engines of each type should be produced daily to maximize operating income?

Steps in Solving an LP Problem

We use the data in Exhibit 11-13 to illustrate the three steps in solving an LP problem. Throughout this discussion, S equals the number of units of snowmobile engines produced and B equals the number of units of boat engines produced.

Step 1: Determine the Objective The **objective function** of a linear program expresses the objective or goal to be maximized (say, operating income) or minimized (say, operating costs). In our example, the objective is to find the combination of products that maximizes total contribution margin in the short run. Fixed costs remain the same regardless of the product-mix decision and are therefore irrelevant. The linear function expressing the objective for the total contribution margin (TCM) is:

$$TCM = \$240S + \$375B$$

Step 2: Specify the Constraints A **constraint** is a mathematical inequality or equality that must be satisfied by the variables in a mathematical model. The following linear inequalities express the relationships in our example:

Assembly Department constraint	$2S + 5B \leq 600$
Testing Department constraint	$1S + 0.5B \leq 120$
Materials shortage constraint for boat engines	$B \leq 110$
Negative production is impossible	$S \geq 0$ and $B \geq 0$

The three solid lines on the graph in Exhibit 11-14 show the existing constraints for Assembly and Testing and the material shortage constraint.[4] The feasi-

[4]As an example of how the lines are plotted in Exhibit 11-14, use equal signs instead of inequality signs and assume for the Assembly Department that $B = 0$; then $S = 300$ (600 machine-hours ÷ 2 machine-hours per snowmobile engine). Assume that $S = 0$. Then $B = 120$ (600 machine-hours ÷ 5 machine-hours per boat engine). Connect those two points with a straight line.

EXHIBIT 11-13
Operating Data for Power Recreation

	Department Capacity (per Day) in Product Units		Selling Price	Variable Cost Per Unit	Contribution Margin Per Unit
	Assembly	Testing			
Only snowmobile engines	300	120	$ 800	$560	$240
Only boat engines	120	240	$1,000	$625	$375

EXHIBIT 11-14
Linear Programming: Graphic Solution for Power Recreation

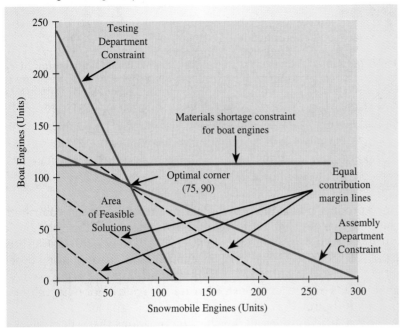

Points to Stress The graphic approach illustrated in Exh. 11-14 is feasible with 2 products; 3 products would require a 3-dimensional graph, etc. Stress that we use the graphic approach to help students develop an intuitive understanding of the basic concepts. In practice, the graphic solution is almost never used since most LP problems involve numerous products and constraints. Companies use computer software packages programmed to solve large LP problems.

ble alternatives are those combinations of quantities of snowmobile engines and boat engines that satisfy all the constraining resources or factors. The shaded "area of feasible solutions" in Exhibit 11-14 shows the boundaries of those product combinations that are feasible, or technically possible.

Step 3: Compute the Optimal Solution We present two approaches for finding the optimal solution: the trial-and-error approach and the graphic approach. These approaches are easy to use in our example because there are only two variables in the objective function and a small number of constraints. An understanding of these two approaches provides insight into LP modeling. In most real-world LP applications, however, managers use computer software packages to calculate the optimal solution.[5]

Trial-and-error approach The optimal solution can be found by trial and error, by working with coordinates of the corners of the area of feasible solutions.

First, select any set of corner points and compute the total contribution margin. Five corner points appear in Exhibit 11-14. It is helpful to use simultaneous equations to obtain the exact coordinates on the graph. To illustrate, the corner point ($S = 75$, $B = 90$) can be derived by solving the two pertinent constraint inequalities as simultaneous equations:

$$2S + 5B = 600 \quad (1)$$
$$1S + 0.5B = 120 \quad (2)$$

Multiplying (2) by 2.0: $\quad 2S + 1B = 240 \quad (3)$

Subtracting (3) from (1): $\quad 4B = 360$

Therefore, $\quad B = 360 \div 4 = 90$

Substituting for B in (2): $\quad 1S + 0.5(90) = 120$

$$S = 120 - 45 = 75$$

Given $S = 75$ and $B = 90$, TCM = $240(75) + $375(90) = $51,750.

---

[5]Although the trial-and-error and graphic approaches can be useful for two or possibly three variables, they are impractical when many variables exist. Standard computer software packages rely on the simplex method. The *simplex method* is an iterative step-by-step procedure for determining the optimal solution to an LP problem. It starts with a specific feasible solution and then tests it by substitution to see whether the result can be improved. These substitutions continue until no further improvement is possible and the optimal solution is obtained.

Second, move from corner point to corner point, computing the total contribution margin at each corner point. The total contribution margin, at each corner point is as follows:

Trial	Corner Point (S, B)	Snowmobile Engines (S)	Boat Engines (B)	Total Contribution Margin
1	(0, 0)	0	0	$240(0) + $375(0) = $0
2	(0, 110)	0	110	$240(0) + $375(110) = $41,250
3	(25, 110)	25	110	$240(25) + $375(110) = $47,250
4	(75, 90)	75	90	$240(75) + $375(90) = $51,750[a]
5	(120, 0)	120	0	$240(120) + $375(0) = $28,800

[a]Indicates the optimal solution.

The optimal product mix is the mix that yields the highest total contribution—75 snowmobile engines and 90 boat engines. To understand the solution, consider what happens when moving from the point (25, 110) to (75, 90). Power Recreation gives up $7,500 [$375 × (110 − 90)] in contribution margin from boat engines while gaining $12,000 [$240 × (75 − 25)] in contribution margin from snowmobile engines. This results in a net increase in contribution margin of $4,500 ($12,000 − $7,500), from $47,250 to $51,750.

Graphic approach Consider all possible combinations that will produce an equal total contribution margin of, say, $12,000. That is,

$$\$240S + \$375B = \$12,000$$

This set of $12,000 contribution margins is a straight dashed line in Exhibit 11-14 through ($S = 50$; $B = 0$) and ($S = 0$, $B = 32$). Other equal total contribution margins can be represented by lines parallel to this one. In Exhibit 11-14, we show three dashed lines. The equal total contribution margin increases as the lines get farther from the origin because lines drawn farther from the origin represent more sales of both products.

The optimal line is the one farthest from the origin but still passing through a point in the area of feasible solutions. This line represents the highest total contribution margin. The optimal solution is the point at the corner ($S = 75$, $B = 90$). This solution will become apparent if you put a ruler on the graph and move it outward from the origin and parallel with the $12,000 line. The idea is to move the ruler as far away from the origin as possible (that is, to increase the total contribution margin) without leaving the area of feasible solutions. In general, the optimal solution in a maximization problem lies at the corner where the dashed line intersects an extreme point of the area of feasible solutions. Moving the ruler out any farther puts it outside the feasible region.

Sensitivity Analysis

What are the implications of uncertainty about the accounting or technical coefficients used in the LP model? Changes in coefficients affect the slope of the objective function (the equal contribution margin lines) or the area of feasible solutions. Consider how a change in the contribution margin of snowmobile engines from $240 to $300 per unit would affect the optimal solution. Assume the contribution margin for boat engines remains unchanged at $375 per unit. The revised objective function will be

$$TCM = \$300S + \$375B$$

Using the trial-and-error approach to calculate the total contribution margin for each of the five corner points described in the table at the top of this page, the optimal solution is still ($S = 75$, $B = 90$). What if the contribution margin of snowmobile engines falls to $160? The optimal solution remains the same ($S = 75$, $B = 90$). Big changes in the contribution margin per unit of snowmobile engines have no effect on the optimal solution in this case.

This chapter and the Glossary at the end of this book contain definitions of the following important terms:

book value (p. 396)
business function costs (382)
constraint (402)
decision model (378)
differential cost (386)
differential revenue (386)
full costs of the product (382)
incremental cost (385)
incremental revenue (386)
insourcing (383)
linear programming (LP) (401)

make-or-buy decisions (384)
objective function (402)
opportunity cost (388)
outsourcing (383)
product-mix decisions (390)
qualitative factors (380)
quantitative factors (380)
relevant costs (378)
relevant revenues (378)
sunk costs (379)

ASSIGNMENT MATERIAL

QUESTIONS

11-1 Outline the five-step sequence in a decision process.

11-2 Define relevant costs. Why are historical costs irrelevant?

11-3 "All future costs are relevant." Do you agree? Why?

11-4 Distinguish between quantitative and qualitative factors in decision making.

11-5 Describe two potential problems that should be avoided in relevant-cost analysis.

11-6 "Variable costs are always relevant, and fixed costs are always irrelevant." Do you agree? Why?

11-7 "A component part should be purchased whenever the purchase price is less than its total manufacturing cost per unit." Do you agree? Why?

11-8 Define opportunity cost.

11-9 "Managers should always buy inventory in quantities that result in the lowest purchase cost per unit." Do you agree? Why?

11-10 "Management should always maximize sales of the product with the highest contribution margin per unit." Do you agree? Why?

11-11 "A branch or business segment that shows negative operating income should be shut down." Do you agree? Explain briefly.

11-12 "Cost written off as depreciation on equipment already purchased is always irrelevant." Do you agree? Why?

11-13 "Managers will always choose the alternative that maximizes operating income or minimizes costs in the decision model." Do you agree? Why?

11-14 Describe the three steps in solving a linear programming problem.

11-15 How might the optimal solution of a linear programming problem be determined?

EXERCISES

11-16 Disposal of assets. Answer the following questions.

1. A company has an inventory of 1,000 assorted parts for a line of missiles that has been discontinued. The inventory cost is $80,000. The parts can be either (a) remachined at total additional costs of $30,000 and then sold for $35,000, or (b) sold as scrap for $2,000. Which action is more profitable? Show your calculations.

2. A truck, costing $100,000 and uninsured, is wrecked its first day in use. It can be either (a) disposed of for $10,000 cash and replaced with a similar truck costing $102,000, or (b) rebuilt for $85,000 and thus be brand new as far as operating characteristics and looks are concerned. Which action is less costly? Show your calculations.

11-17 The careening personal computer. (W. A. Paton) An employee in the Accounting Department of a company was moving a personal computer from one room to another. As he came alongside an open stairway, he slipped and the computer got away from him. It careened down the stairs with a great racket and wound up at the bottom, completely destroyed. Hearing the crash, the office manager came rushing out and turned rather pale when he saw what had happened. "Someone tell me quickly," the manager yelled, "if that is one of our fully depreciated items." A check of the accounting records showed that the smashed computer was, indeed, one of those items that had been written off. "Thank God!" exclaimed the manager.

Required

Explain and comment on the point of this anecdote.

11-18 Multiple choice. (CPA) Choose the best answer.

1. The Woody Company manufactures slippers and sells them at $10 a pair. Variable manufacturing costs are $4.50 a pair, and allocated fixed manufacturing costs are $1.50 a pair. It has enough idle capacity available to accept a one-time-only special order of 20,000 pairs of slippers at $6 a pair. Woody will not incur any marketing costs as a result of the special order. What would the effect on operating income be if the special order could be accepted without affecting normal sales? (a) $0, (b) $30,000 increase, (c) $90,000 increase, (d) $120,000 increase.

2. The Reno Company manufactures Part No. 498 for use in its production line. The manufacturing costs per unit for 20,000 units of Part No. 498 are as follows:

Direct materials	$ 6
Direct manufacturing labor	30
Variable manufacturing overhead	12
Fixed manufacturing overhead allocated	16
Total manufacturing cost per unit	$64

The Tray Company has offered to sell 20,000 units of Part No. 498 to Reno for $60 per unit. Reno will make the decision to buy the part from Tray if there is an overall savings of at least $25,000 for Reno. If Reno accepts Tray's offer, $9 per unit of the fixed overhead allocated would be totally eliminated. Furthermore, Reno has determined that the released facilities could be used to save relevant costs in the manufacture of Part No. 575. For Reno to achieve an overall savings of $25,000, the amount of relevant costs that would have to be saved by using the released facilities in the manufacture of Part No. 575 would be (a) $80,000, (b) $85,000, (c) $125,000, (d) $140,000.

11-19 Special order, activity-based costing. (CMA, adapted) The Award Plus Company manufactures medals for winners of athletic events and other contests. Its manufacturing plant has the capacity to produce 10,000 medals each month. Current production and sales are 7,500 medals per month. The company normally charges $150 per medal. Cost information for the current activity level is as follows:

Variable costs that vary with number of units produced	
Direct materials	$ 262,500
Direct manufacturing labor	300,000
Variable costs (for setups, materials handling, quality control, and so on) that vary with number of batches, 150 batches × $500 per batch	75,000
Fixed manufacturing costs	275,000
Fixed marketing costs	175,000
Total costs	$1,087,500

Award Plus has just received a special one-time-only order for 2,500 medals at $100 per medal. Award Plus makes medals for its existing customers in batch sizes of 50 medals (150 batches × 50 medals per batch = 7,500 medals). The special order requires Award Plus to make the medals in 25 batches of 100 each.

Required

1. Should Award Plus accept this special order? Show your calculations.
2. Suppose plant capacity was only 9,000 medals instead of 10,000 medals each month. The special order must either be taken in full or rejected completely. Should Award Plus accept the special order? Show your calculations.
3. As in requirement 1, assume that monthly capacity is 10,000 medals. Award Plus is concerned that if it accepts the special order, its existing customers will immediately demand a price discount of $10 in the month in which the special order is being filled. They would argue that Award Plus's capacity costs are now being spread over more units, and that existing customers should get the benefit of these lower costs. Should Award Plus accept the special order under these conditions? Show your calculations.

11-20 Make versus buy, activity-based costing. The Svenson Corporation manufactures cellular modems. It manufactures its own cellular modem circuit boards (CMCB), an important part of the cellular modem. It reports the following cost information about the costs of making CMCBs in 2000 and the expected costs in 2001:

	Current Costs in 2000	Expected Costs in 2001
Variable manufacturing costs		
Direct materials costs per CMCB	$ 180	$ 170
Direct manufacturing labor costs per CMCB	50	45
Variable manufacturing costs per batch for setups, materials handling, and quality control	1,600	1,500
Fixed manufacturing costs		
Fixed manufacturing overhead costs that can be avoided if CMCBs are not made	320,000	320,000
Fixed manufacturing overhead costs of plant depreciation, insurance, and administration that cannot be avoided even if CMCBs are not made	800,000	800,000

Svenson manufactured 8,000 CMCBs in 2000 in 40 batches of 200 each. In 2001, Svenson anticipates needing 10,000 CMCBs. The CMCBs would be needed in 80 batches of 125 each.

The Minton Corporation has approached Svenson about supplying CMCBs to Svenson in 2001 at $300 per CMCB on whatever delivery schedule Svenson wants.

Required

1. Calculate the total expected manufacturing (absorption) cost per unit of making CMCBs in 2001.
2. Suppose the capacity currently used to make CMCBs will become idle if Svenson purchases CMCBs from Minton. Should Svenson make CMCBs or buy them from Minton? Show your calculations.
3. Now suppose that if Svenson purchases CMCBs from Minton, its best alternative use of the capacity currently used for CMCBs is to make and sell special circuit boards (CB3s) to the Essex Corporation. Svenson estimates the following incremental revenues and costs from CB3s:

Total expected incremental revenues	$2,000,000
Total expected incremental costs	$2,150,000

Should Svenson make CMCBs or buy them from Minton? Show your calculations.

11-21 Which bases to close, relevant-cost analysis, opportunity costs. The U.S. Defense Department has the difficult decision of deciding which military bases to close down. Military and political factors obviously matter, but cost savings are also an important factor. Consider two naval bases located on the West Coast—one in Alameda, California, and the other in Everett, Washington. The Navy has decided that it needs only one of those two bases permanently, so one must be shut down. The decision regarding which base to shut down will be made on cost considerations alone. The following information is available:

a. The Alameda base was built at a cost of $10 million. The operating costs of the base are $400 million per year. The base is built on land owned by the Navy, so the Navy pays nothing for the use of the property. If the base is closed, the land will be sold to developers for $500 million.

b. The Everett base was built at a cost of $15 million on land leased by the Navy from private citizens. The Navy can choose to lease the land permanently for a lease payment of $3 million per year. If it decides to keep the Everett base open, the Navy plans to invest $60 million in a fixed income note, which at 5% interest will earn the $3 million the government needs for the lease payments. The land and buildings will immediately revert back to the owner if the base is closed. The operating costs of the base, excluding lease payments, are $300 million per year.

c. If the Alameda base is closed down, the Navy will have to transfer some personnel to the Everett facility. As a result, the yearly operating costs at Everett will increase by $100 million per year. If the Everett facility is closed down, no extra costs will be incurred to operate the Alameda facility.

Required
The California delegation in Congress argues that it is cheaper to close down the Everett base for two reasons: (1) It would save $100 million per year in additional costs required to operate the Everett base, and (2) it would save the lease payment of $3 million per year. (Recall that the Alameda base requires no cash payments for use of the land because the land is owned by the Navy.) Do you agree with the California delegation's arguments and conclusions? In your answer, identify and explain all costs that you consider relevant and all costs that you consider irrelevant for the base-closing decision.

11-22 Inventory decision, opportunity costs. Lawnox, a manufacturer of lawn mowers, predicts that 240,000 spark plugs will have to be purchased next year. Lawnox estimates that 20,000 spark plugs will be required each month. A supplier quotes a price of $8 per spark plug. The supplier also offers a special discount option: If all 240,000 spark plugs are purchased at the start of the year, a discount of 5% off the $8 price will be given. Lawnox can invest its cash at 8% per year. It costs Lawnox $200 to place each purchase order.

Required
1. What is the opportunity cost of interest forgone from purchasing all 240,000 units at the start of the year instead of in 12 monthly purchases of 20,000 units per order?
2. Would this opportunity cost ordinarily be recorded in the accounting system? Why?
3. Should Lawnox purchase 240,000 units at the start of the year or 20,000 units each month? Show your calculations.

11-23 Relevant costs, contribution margin, product emphasis. The Beach Comber is a take-out food store at a popular beach resort. Susan Sexton, owner of the Beach Comber, is deciding how much refrigerator space to devote to four different drinks. Pertinent data on these four drinks are as follows:

	Cola	Lemonade	Punch	Natural Orange Juice
Selling price per case	$18.00	$19.20	$26.40	$38.40
Variable costs per case	$13.50	$15.20	$20.10	$30.20
Cases sold per foot of shelf space per day	25	24	4	5

Sexton has a maximum front shelf space of 12 feet to devote to the four drinks. She wants a minimum of 1 foot and a maximum of 6 feet of front shelf space for each drink.

Required
1. What is the contribution margin per case of each type of drink?
2. A co-worker of Sexton's recommends that she maximize the shelf space devoted to those drinks with the highest contribution margin per case. Evaluate this recommendation.
3. What shelf-space allocation for the four drinks would you recommend for the Beach Comber? Show your calculations.

 11-24 Selection of most profitable product. Body-Builders, Inc., produces two basic types of weight-lifting equipment, Model 9 and Model 14. Pertinent data are as follows:

	Per Unit	
	Model 9	**Model 14**
Selling price	$100.00	$70.00
Costs		
Direct materials	28.00	13.00
Direct manufacturing labor	15.00	25.00
Variable manufacturing overhead[a]	25.00	12.50
Fixed manufacturing overhead[a]	10.00	5.00
Marketing costs (all variable)	14.00	10.00
Total costs	92.00	65.50
Operating income	$ 8.00	$ 4.50

[a] Allocated on the basis of machine-hours.

The weight-lifting craze is such that enough of either Model 9 or Model 14 can be sold to keep the plant operating at full capacity. Both products are processed through the same production departments.

Required

Which product should be produced? If both should be produced, indicate the number of each. Briefly explain your answer.

11-25 Closing and opening stores. Sanchez Corporation runs two convenience stores in Connecticut and Rhode Island. Operating income for each store in 2001 is as follows:

	Connecticut Store	Rhode Island Store
Revenues	$1,070,000	$860,000
Operating costs		
Cost of goods sold	750,000	660,000
Lease rent (renewable each year)	90,000	75,000
Labor costs (paid on an hourly basis)	42,000	42,000
Depreciation of equipment	25,000	22,000
Utilities (electricity, heating)	43,000	46,000
Allocated corporate overhead	50,000	40,000
Total operating costs	1,000,000	885,000
Operating income (loss)	$ 70,000	$ (25,000)

The equipment has a zero disposal price. In a senior management meeting, Maria Lopez, the management accountant at Sanchez Corporation, makes the following comment, "Sanchez can increase its profitability by closing down the Rhode Island store or by adding another store like it."

Required

1. By closing down the Rhode Island store, Sanchez can reduce overall corporate overhead costs by $44,000. Calculate Sanchez's operating income if it closes down the Rhode Island store. Is Maria Lopez's statement about the effect of closing down the Rhode Island store correct? Explain.
2. Calculate Sanchez's operating income if it keeps the Rhode Island store open, and opens another store with revenues and costs identical to the Rhode Island store (including a cost of $22,000 to acquire equipment with a 1-year useful life and zero disposal price). Opening this store will increase corporate overhead costs by $4,000. Is Maria Lopez's statement about the effect of adding another store like the Rhode Island store correct? Explain.

11-26 Customer profitability, choosing customers. Broadway Printers operates a printing press with a monthly capacity of 2,000 machine-hours. Broadway has two main customers, Taylor Corporation and Kelly Corporation. Data on each customer for January follows:

	Taylor Corporation	Kelly Corporation	Total
Revenues	$120,000	$80,000	$200,000
Variable costs	42,000	48,000	90,000
Fixed costs (allocated on the basis of revenues)	60,000	40,000	100,000
Total operating costs	102,000	88,000	190,000
Operating income	$ 18,000	$ (8,000)	$ 10,000
Machine-hours required	1,500 hours	500 hours	2,000 hours

Required

The following requirements refer only to the preceding data. There is *no connection* between the requirements.

1. Should Broadway drop the Kelly Corporation business, assuming that dropping Kelly would decrease its total fixed costs by 20 percent? Show all calculations.

2. Kelly Corporation indicates that it wants Broadway to do an *additional* $80,000 worth of printing jobs during February. These jobs are identical to the existing business Broadway did for Kelly in January in terms of variable costs and machine-hours required. Broadway anticipates that the business from Taylor Corporation in February would be the same as that in January. Broadway can choose to accept as much of the Taylor and Kelly business for February as it wants. Assume that total fixed costs for February will be the same as the fixed costs in January. What should Broadway do? What will Broadway's operating income be in February? Show your calculations.

 11-27 Relevance of equipment costs. The Auto Wash Company has just today paid for and installed a special machine for polishing cars at one of its several outlets. It is the first day of the company's fiscal year. The machine cost $20,000. Its annual cash operating costs total $15,000. The machine will have a 4-year useful life and a zero terminal disposal price.

After the machine has been used for only one day, a machine salesperson offers a different machine that promises to do the same job at annual cash operating costs of $9,000. The new machine will cost $24,000 cash, installed. The "old" machine is unique and can be sold outright for only $10,000, minus $2,000 removal cost. The new machine, like the old one, will have a 4-year useful life and zero terminal disposal price.

Revenues, all in cash, will be $150,000 annually, and other cash costs will be $110,000 annually, regardless of this decision.

For simplicity, ignore income taxes and the time value of money considerations.

Required

1. a. Prepare a statement of cash receipts and disbursements for each of the 4 years under both alternatives. What is the cumulative difference in cash flow for the 4 years taken together?

   b. Prepare income statements for each of the 4 years under both alternatives. Assume straight-line depreciation. What is the cumulative difference in operating income for the 4 years taken together?

   c. What are the irrelevant items in your presentations in requirements a and b? Why are they irrelevant?

2. Suppose the cost of the "old" machine was $1 million rather than $20,000. Nevertheless, the old machine can be sold outright for only $10,000, minus $2,000 removal cost. Would the net differences in requirements 1a and 1b change? Explain.

3. Is there any conflict between the decision model and the incentives of the manager who has just purchased the "old" machine and is considering replacing it a day later?

11-28 Equipment upgrade versus replacement. (A. Spero, adapted) The Pacifica Corporation makes steel table lamps. It is considering either upgrading its existing production line or replacing it. The production equipment was purchased 2 years ago for $600,000. It has an expected useful life of 5 years, a terminal disposal price of $0, and is depreciated on a straight-line basis at the rate of $120,000 per year. The equipment has a current book value of $360,000 and a current disposal price of $90,000. The following table presents expected costs under the upgrade and replace alternatives:

	Upgrade	Replace
Expected one-time-only equipment costs	$300,000	$750,000
Variable manufacturing costs per lamp	$12	$9
Expected production and sales of lamps per year	60,000 units	60,000 units
Selling price of lamps	$25	$25

The expected useful life after the machine is upgraded or replaced is 3 years, and the expected terminal disposal price is $0. If the machine is upgraded, the $300,000 would be added to the current book value of $360,000 and depreciated on a straight-line basis. The new equipment, if purchased, will also be depreciated on a straight-line basis.

For simplicity, ignore income taxes and the time value of money considerations.

Required

1. Should Pacifica upgrade its production line or replace it? Show your calculations.
2. **a.** Now suppose the capital expenditure needed to replace the production line is not known. All other data are as given previously. What is the maximum price that Pacifica would be willing to pay for the new line to prefer replacing the existing line over upgrading it?
   b. Assume that the capital expenditure needed to replace the production line is $750,000. Now suppose the expected production and sales quantity is not known. For what production and sales quantity would Pacifica prefer to (i) replace the line, (ii) upgrade the line?
3. Consider again the basic information given in this exercise. Suppose John Azinger, the manager of the Pacifica Corporation, is evaluated on operating income. The coming year's operating income is crucial to Azinger's bonus. What alternative would Azinger choose? Explain.

PROBLEMS

11-29 Product mix, relevant costs. (N. Melumad, adapted) Pendleton Engineering makes cutting tools for metal working operations. It makes two types of tools, R3, a regular cutting tool, and HP6, a high-precision cutting tool. R3 is manufactured on a regular machine, but HP6 must be manufactured on both the regular machine and a high-precision machine. The following information is available.

	R3	HP6
Selling price	$100	$150
Variable manufacturing costs per unit	$60	$100
Variable marketing costs per unit	$15	$35
Budgeted total fixed overhead costs	$350,000	$550,000
Hours required to produce 1 unit on the regular machine	1.0	0.5

Additional information includes:

a. Pendleton faces a capacity constraint on the regular machine of 50,000 hours per year.

b. The capacity of the high-precision machine is not a constraint.

c. Of the $550,000 budgeted fixed overhead costs of HP6, $300,000 are lease payments for the high-precision machine. This cost is charged entirely to HP6 because Pendleton uses the machine exclusively to produce HP6. The lease agreement for the high-precision machine can be canceled at any time without penalties.

d. All other overhead costs are fixed and cannot be changed.

Required

1. What product mix—that is, how many units of R3 and HP6—will maximize Pendleton's operating income?
2. Suppose Pendleton can increase the annual capacity of regular machines by 15,000 machine-hours at a cost of $150,000. Should Pendleton increase the capacity of regular machines by 15,000 machine-hours? By how much will Pendleton's operating income increase? Show your calculations.

3. Suppose that the capacity of the regular machine has been increased to 65,000 hours. Pendleton has been approached by Carter Corporation to supply 20,000 units of another cutting tool S3 for $120 per unit. Pendleton must either accept the order for all 20,000 units or reject it totally. S3 is exactly like R3 except that its variable manufacturing costs are $70 per unit. (It takes 1 hour to produce 1 unit of S3 on the regular machine, and variable marketing costs equal $15 per unit.) What product mix should Pendleton choose to maximize operating income? Show your calculations.

11-30 Discontinuing a product line, selling more units. The Northern Division of Grossman Corporation makes and sells tables and beds. The following estimated revenue and cost information from the division's activity-based costing system is available for 1999.

	4,000 Tables	5,000 Beds	Total
Revenues ($125 × 4,000; $200 × 5,000)	$500,000	$1,000,000	$1,500,000
Variable direct materials and direct manufacturing labor costs ($75 × 4,000; $105 × 5,000)	300,000	525,000	825,000
Depreciation on equipment used exclusively by each product line	42,000	58,000	100,000
Marketing and distribution costs			
$40,000 (fixed) + $750 per shipment × 40 shipments	70,000		205,000
$60,000 (fixed) + $750 per shipment × 100 shipments		135,000	
Fixed general administration costs of the division allocated to product lines on the basis of revenues	110,000	220,000	330,000
Allocated corporate office costs allocated to product lines on the basis of revenues	50,000	100,000	150,000
Total costs	572,000	1,038,000	1,610,000
Operating income (loss)	$ (72,000)	$ (38,000)	$ (110,000)

Additional information includes:

a. On January 1, 1999, the equipment has a book value of $100,000 and zero disposal price. Any equipment not used will remain idle.

b. Fixed marketing and distribution costs of a product line can be avoided if the line is discontinued.

c. Fixed general administration costs of the division and corporate office costs will not change if sales of individual product lines are increased or decreased, or if product lines are added or dropped.

Required
1. Should the Northern Division discontinue the tables product line assuming the released facilities remain idle? Show your calculations.
2. What will be the effect on Northern Division's operating income if it were to sell 4,000 more tables? Assume that to do so, the division would have to acquire additional equipment costing $42,000 with a 1-year useful life. Assume further that the fixed marketing and distribution costs will not change but that the number of shipments will double. Show your calculations.

11-31 Discontinuing or adding another division. Refer to the information presented in Problem 11-30.
Required
1. Given the Northern Division's expected operating loss of $110,000, should Grossman Corporation shut it down? Assume that shutting down the Northern division will have no effect on corporate office costs but will lead to savings of all general administration costs of the division. Show your calculations.
2. Suppose the manager at corporate headquarters responsible for making the decision of whether or not to shut down the Northern Division will be evaluated in 1999 on the Northern Division's operating income after allocating corporate office costs. Will the manager prefer to shut down the division? Show your calculations. Is the decision model consistent with the performance-evaluation model? Explain.
3. Suppose Grossman Corporation has the opportunity to open another division, the Southern Division, whose revenues and costs are expected to be identical to the

Northern Division's revenues and costs (including a cost of $100,000 to acquire equipment with a 1-year useful life and zero disposal price). Opening the new division will have no effect on corporate office costs. Should Grossman open the Southern Division? Show your calculations.

11-32 Relevant costs, opportunity costs. Larry Miller, the general manager of Basil Software, must decide when to release the new version of Basil's spreadsheet package, Easyspread 2.0. Development of the product is complete. If Miller decides to introduce Easyspread right away, it will take a month for the product to be manufactured and packaged. The product can be shipped starting July 1, 2000.

The key problem is that Basil has overstocked the previous version of its spreadsheet package, Easyspread 1.0, because of a threatened strike at its printers. As a result, Basil will still have 60,000 units of Easyspread 1.0 (consisting of diskettes, compact discs, and user manuals) in inventory as of July 1, 2000. Miller knows that once Easyspread 2.0 is introduced, Basil will not be able to sell any more units of Easyspread 1.0. Rather than just throwing away the inventory of Easypread 1.0, Miller is wondering if it might be better to continue to sell Easyspread 1.0 for the next 3 months, and introduce Easyspread 2.0 on October 1, 2000, when the inventory of Easyspread 1.0 will be completely used up.

The following information is available.

	Easyspread 1.0	Easyspread 2.0
Selling price	$150	$185
Cost per unit of diskettes, compact discs, user manuals	20	25
Development costs per unit	65	95
Marketing and administration costs per unit	35	40
Total costs per unit	120	160
Operating income per unit	$ 30	$ 25

a. Basil contracts with outside vendors to print manuals and duplicate compact discs and diskettes.

b. Development costs per unit for each product equal the total costs of developing the software product divided by the anticipated unit sales over the life of the product.

c. Marketing and administration costs are fixed costs in 2000, incurred to support all marketing and administrative activities of Basil Software. Marketing and administration costs are allocated to products on the basis of the budgeted revenues of each product. The preceding units costs assume Easyspread 2.0 will be introduced on October 1, 2000.

Required
1. On the basis of financial considerations alone, should Miller introduce Easyspread 2.0 on July 1, 2000, or wait until October 1, 2000? Show your calculations, clearly identifying relevant and irrelevant revenues and costs.
2. What other factors might Larry Miller consider in making a decision?

11-33 Opportunity costs. (H. Schaefer) The Wolverine Corporation is working at full production capacity producing 10,000 units of a unique product, Rosebo. Manufacturing costs per unit for Rosebo are as follows:

Direct materials	$ 2
Direct manufacturing labor	3
Manufacturing overhead	5
Total manufacturing costs	$10

Manufacturing overhead costs per unit are based on variable costs per unit of $2 and fixed costs of $30,000 (at full capacity of 10,000 units). Selling costs, all variable, are $4 per unit, and the selling price is $20.

A customer, the Miami Company, has asked Wolverine to produce 2,000 units of Orangebo, a modification of Rosebo. Orangebo would require the same manufacturing processes as Rosebo. Miami has offered to pay Wolverine $15 for a unit of Orangebo and half the selling costs per unit.

Required

1. What is the opportunity cost to Wolverine of producing the 2,000 units of Orangebo? (Assume that no overtime is worked.)

2. The Buckeye Corporation has offered to produce 2,000 units of Rosebo for Wolverine so that Wolverine may accept the Orangebo offer. That is, if Wolverine accepts the Buckeye offer, Wolverine would manufacture 8,000 units of Rosebo and 2,000 units of Orangebo and purchase 2,000 units of Rosebo from Buckeye. Buckeye would charge Wolverine $14 per unit to manufacture Rosebo. Should Wolverine accept the Buckeye offer? Show your calculations.

3. Suppose Wolverine had been working at less than full capacity, producing 8,000 units of Rosebo at the time the Orangebo offer was made. Calculate the minimum price Wolverine should accept for Orangebo under these conditions. (Ignore the previous $15 unit price.)

11-34 Contribution approach, relevant costs. Air Frisco owns a single jet aircraft and operates between San Francisco and the Fiji Islands. Flights leave San Francisco on Mondays and Thursdays and depart from Fiji on Wednesdays and Saturdays. Air Frisco cannot offer any more flights between San Francisco and Fiji. Only tourist-class seats are available on its planes. An analyst has collected the following information:

Seating capacity per plane	360 passengers
Average number of passengers per flight	200 passengers
Flights per week	4 flights
Flights per year	208 flights
Average one-way fare	$500
Variable fuel costs	$14,000 per flight
Food and beverage service costs (no charge to passenger)	$20 per passenger
Commission to travel agents paid by Air Frisco (all tickets are booked by travel agents)	8% of fare
Fixed annual lease costs allocated to each flight	$53,000 per flight
Fixed ground services (maintenance, check in, baggage handling) costs allocated to each flight	$7,000 per flight
Fixed flight crew salaries allocated to each flight	$4,000 per flight

For simplicity, assume that fuel costs are unaffected by the actual number of passengers on a flight.

Required

1. Calculate the operating income that Air Frisco earns on each one-way flight between San Francisco and Fiji.

2. The Market Research Department of Air Frisco indicates that lowering the average one-way fare to $480 will increase the average number of passengers per flight to 212. Should Air Frisco lower its fare? Show your calculations.

3. Travel International, a tour operator, approaches Air Frisco on the possibility of chartering (renting out) its jet aircraft twice each month, first to take Travel International's tourists from San Francisco to Fiji and then to bring the tourists back from Fiji to San Francisco. If Air Frisco accepts Travel International's offer, Air Frisco will be able to offer only 184 (208 − 24) of its own flights each year. The terms of the charter are as follows: (a) For each one-way flight, Travel International will pay Air Frisco $75,000 to charter the plane and to use its flight crew and ground service staff; (b) Travel International will pay for fuel costs; and (c) Travel International will pay for all food costs. On purely financial considerations, should Air Frisco accept Travel International's offer? Show your calculations. What other factors should Air Frisco consider in deciding whether or not to charter its plane to Travel International?

11-35 Make or buy, unknown level of volume. (A. Atkinson) Oxford Engineering manufactures small engines. The engines are sold to manufacturers who install them in such products as lawn mowers. The company currently manufactures all the parts used in these engines but is considering a proposal from an external supplier who wishes to supply the starter assembly used in these engines.

The starter assembly is currently manufactured in Division 3 of Oxford Engineering. The costs relating to the starter assembly for the last 12 months were as follows:

Direct materials	$200,000
Direct manufacturing labor	150,000
Manufacturing overhead	400,000
Total	$750,000

Over the last year, Division 3 manufactured 150,000 starter assemblies. The average cost for the starter assembly is computed as $5 ($750,000 ÷ 150,000).

Further analysis of manufacturing overhead revealed the following information. Of the total manufacturing overhead, only 25% is considered variable. Of the fixed portion, $150,000 is an allocation of general overhead that would remain unchanged for the company as a whole if production of the starter assembly is discontinued. A further $100,000 of the fixed overhead is avoidable if production of the starter assembly is discontinued. The balance of the current fixed overhead, $50,000, is the division manager's salary. If production of the starter assembly is discontinued, the manager of Division 3 will be transferred to Division 2 at the same salary. This move will allow the company to save the $40,000 salary that would otherwise be paid to attract an outsider to this position.

Required

1. Tidnish Electronics, a reliable supplier, has offered to supply starter-assembly units at $4 per unit. Since this price is less than the current average cost of $5 per unit, the vice president of manufacturing is eager to accept this offer. Should the outside offer be accepted? Show your calculations. (*Hint:* Production output in the coming year may be different from production output in the last year.)
2. How, if at all, would your response to requirement 1 change if the company could use the vacated plant space for storage and, in so doing, avoid $50,000 of outside storage charges currently incurred? Why is this information relevant or irrelevant?

11-36 Make versus buy, activity-based costing, opportunity costs. (N. Melumad and S. Reichelstein, adapted) The Ace Company produces bicycles. This year's expected production is 10,000 units. Currently, Ace makes the chains for its bicycles. Ace's accountant reports the following costs for making the 10,000 bicycle chains:

	Costs Per Unit	Costs for 10,000 Units
Direct materials	$4.00	$ 40,000
Direct manufacturing labor	2.00	20,000
Variable manufacturing overhead (power and utilities)	1.50	15,000
Inspection, setup, materials handling		2,000
Machine rent		3,000
Allocated fixed costs of plant administration, taxes, and insurance		30,000
Total costs		$110,000

Ace has received an offer from an outside vendor to supply any number of chains Ace requires at $8.20 per chain. The following additional information is available:

a. Inspection, setup, and materials-handling costs vary with the number of batches in which the chains are produced. Ace produces chains in batch sizes of 1,000 units. Ace estimates that it will produce the 10,000 units in ten batches.

b. Ace rents the machine used to make the chains. If Ace buys all its chains from the outside vendor, it does not need to pay rent on this machine.

Required

1. Assume that if Ace purchases the chains from the outside supplier, the facility where the chains are currently made will remain idle. Should Ace accept the outside supplier's offer at the anticipated production (and sales) volume of 10,000 units? Show your calculations.
2. For this question, assume that if the chains are purchased outside, the facilities where the chains are currently made will be used to upgrade the bicycles by adding mud flaps and reflectors. As a consequence, the selling price of bicycles will be raised by $20. The variable costs per unit of the upgrade would be $18, and additional tooling costs of $16,000 would be incurred. Should Ace make or buy the chains, assuming that 10,000 units are produced (and sold)? Show your calculations.

3. The sales manager at Ace is concerned that the estimate of 10,000 units may be high and believes that only 6,200 units will be sold. Production will be cut back, freeing up work space. This space can be used to add the mud flaps and reflectors whether Ace goes outside for the chains or makes them in-house. At this lower output, Ace will produce the chains in eight batches of 775 units each. Should Ace purchase the chains from the outside vendor? Show your calculations.

11-37 Multiple choice, comprehensive problem on relevant costs. The following are the Class Company's *unit* costs of manufacturing and marketing a high-style pen at an output level of 20,000 units per month:

Manufacturing costs	
Direct materials	$1.00
Direct manufacturing labor	1.20
Variable manufacturing indirect costs	0.80
Fixed manufacturing indirect costs	0.50
Marketing costs	
Variable	1.50
Fixed	0.90

Required

The following situations refer only to the preceding data; there is *no connection* between the situations. Unless stated otherwise, assume a regular selling price of $6 per unit. Choose the best answer to each question. Show your calculations.

1. In an inventory of 10,000 units of the high-style pen presented in the balance sheet, the unit cost used should be (a) $3.00, (b) $3.50, (c) $5.00, (d) $2.20, (e) $5.90.
2. The pen is usually produced and sold at the rate of 240,000 units per year (an average of 20,000 per month). The selling price is $6 per unit, which yields total annual revenues of $1,440,000. Total costs are $1,416,000, and operating income is $24,000, or $0.10 per unit. Market research estimates that unit sales could be increased by 10% if prices were cut to $5.80. Assuming the implied cost-behavior patterns continue, this action, if taken, would
   a. Decrease operating income by $7,200.
   b. Decrease operating income by $0.20 per unit ($48,000) but increase operating income by 10% of revenues ($144,000) for a net increase of $96,000.
   c. Decrease unit fixed costs by 10%, or $0.14, per unit, and thus decrease operating income by $0.06 ($0.20 − $0.14) per unit.
   d. Increase unit sales to 264,000 units, which at the $5.80 price would give total revenues of $1,531,200, and lead to costs of $5.90 per unit for 264,000 units, which would equal $1,557,600, and result in an operating loss of $26,400.
   e. None of these.
3. A contract with the government for 5,000 units of the pens calls for the reimbursement of all manufacturing costs plus a fixed fee of $1,000. No variable marketing costs are incurred on the government contract. You are asked to compare the following two alternatives:

Sales Each Month to	Alternative A	Alternative B
Regular customers	15,000 units	15,000 units
Government	0 units	5,000 units

Operating income under alternative B is greater than that under alternative A by (a) $1,000, (b) $2,500, (c) $3,500, (d) $300, (e) none of these.
4. Assume the same data with respect to the government contract as in requirement 3 except that the two alternatives to be compared are:

Sales Each Month to	Alternative A	Alternative B
Regular customers	20,000 units	15,000 units
Government	0 units	5,000 units

Operating income under alternative B relative to that under alternative A is (a) $4,000 less, (b) $3,000 greater, (c) $6,500 less, (d) $500 greater, (e) none of these.

5. The company wants to enter a foreign market in which price competition is keen. The company seeks a one-time-only special order for 10,000 units on a minimum-unit-price basis. It expects that shipping costs for this order will amount to only $0.75 per unit, but the fixed costs of obtaining the contract will be $4,000. The company incurs no variable marketing costs other than shipping costs. Domestic business will be unaffected. The selling price to break even is (a) $3.50, (b) $4.15, (c) $4.25, (d) $3.00, (e) $5.00.

6. The company has an inventory of 1,000 units of pens that must be sold immediately at reduced prices. Otherwise, the inventory will be worthless. The unit cost that is relevant for establishing the minimum selling price is (a) $4.50, (b) $4.00, (c) $3.00, (d) $5.90, (e) $1.50.

7. A proposal is received from an outside supplier who will make and ship these high-style pens directly to the Class Company's customers as sales orders are forwarded from Class's sales staff. Class's fixed marketing costs will be unaffected, but its variable marketing costs will be slashed by 20 percent. Class's plant will be idle, but its fixed manufacturing overhead will continue at 50% of present levels. How much per unit would the company be able to pay the supplier without decreasing operating income? (a) $4.75, (b) $3.95, (c) $2.95, (d) $5.35, (e) none of these.

11-38 Make or buy (continuation of 11-37). Assume that, as in requirement 7 of Problem 11-37, a proposal is received from an outside supplier who will make and ship high-style pens directly to the Class Company's customers as sales orders are forwarded from Class's sales staff. If the supplier's offer is accepted, the present plant facilities will be used to make a new pen whose unit costs will be:

Variable manufacturing costs	$5.00
Fixed manufacturing costs	1.00
Variable marketing costs	2.00
Fixed marketing costs for the new pen	0.50

Total fixed manufacturing overhead will be unchanged from the original level given at the beginning of Problem 11-37. Fixed marketing costs for the new pens are over and above the fixed marketing costs incurred for marketing the high-style pens at the beginning of Problem 11-37. The new pen will sell for $9. The minimum desired operating income on the two pens taken together is $50,000 per year.

Required
What is the maximum purchase cost per unit that the Class Company should be willing to pay for subcontracting the production of the high-style pens?

11-39 Optimal production plan, computer manufacturer. (Chapter Appendix) Information Technology, Inc., assembles and sells two products: printers and desktop computers. Customers can purchase either (a) a computer, or (b) a computer plus a printer. The printers are *not* sold without the computer. The result is that the quantity of printers sold is equal to or less than the quantity of desktop computers sold. The contribution margins are $200 per printer and $100 per computer.

Each printer requires 6 assembly-hours on production line 1 and 10 assembly-hours on production line 2. Each computer requires 4 assembly-hours on production line 1 only. (Many of the components of each computer are preassembled by external vendors.) Production line 1 has 24 assembly-hours available per day. Production line 2 has 20 assembly-hours available per day.

Let X represent units of printers and Y represent units of desktop computers. The production manager must decide on the optimal mix of printers and computers to manufacture.

Required
1. Formulate the production manager's problem in an LP format.
2. Calculate the combination of printers and computers that will maximize the operating income of Information Technology. Use both the trial-and-error and the graphic approaches. Show your work.

11-40 Optimal production mix. (CMA adapted, Chapter Appendix) Della Simpson, Inc., sells two popular brands of cookies, Della's Delight and Cathy's Chocolate Chip. Both cookies go through the Mixing and Baking Departments, but Della's Delight is also dipped in chocolate in the Coating Department.

Michael Sesnowitz, vice president for sales, believes that Della Simpson can sell all of its daily production of Cathy's Chocolate Chips and Della's Delights. Both cookies are made in batches of 300 cookies. The batch times for producing each type of cookie and the minutes available per day are as follows.

	Mixing	Baking	Dipping
Minutes required per batch:			
Della's Delight	30	10	20
Cathy's Chocolate Chip	15	15	0
Minutes available per day	600	300	320

Revenue and cost data for each type of cookie are:

	Della's Delight	Cathy's Chocolate Chip
Revenue per batch	$ 525	$ 335
Variable costs per batch	175	85
Monthly fixed costs (allocated to each product)	20,350	16,650

Required

1. Formulate the decision facing Michael Sesnowitz as an LP model. Use *D* to represent the quantity of Della's Delights made and sold and *C* to represent the quantity of Cathy's Chocolate Chips made and sold.
2. Compute the optimal quantities of Della's Delights and Cathy's Chocolate Chips that Della Simpson should make and sell.

11-41 Make versus buy, ethics. (CMA, adapted) Lynn Hardt, a management accountant with the Paibec Corporation, is evaluating whether a component MTR-2000 should continue to be manufactured by Paibec or purchased from Marley Company, an outside supplier. Marley has submitted a bid to manufacture and supply the 32,000 units of MTR-2000 that Paibec will need for 1999 at a selling price of $17.30 to be delivered according to Paibec's production specifications and needs. While the contract price of $17.30 is only applicable in 1999, Marley is interested in entering into a long-run arrangement beyond 1999.

Hardt has gathered the following information regarding Paibec's costs to manufacture 30,000 units of MTR-2000 in 1998:

Direct materials	$195,000
Direct manufacturing labor	120,000
Plant space rental	84,000
Equipment leasing	36,000
Other manufacturing overhead	225,000
Total manufacturing costs	$660,000

Hardt has also collected the following information related to manufacturing MTR-2000.

◆ Prices of direct materials used in the production of MTR-2000 are expected to increase 8% in 1999.

◆ Paibec's direct manufacturing labor contract calls for a 5% increase in 1999.

◆ Paibec can withdraw from the plant space rental agreement without any penalty. Paibec will have no need for this space if MTR-2000 is not manufactured.

◆ The equipment lease can be terminated by paying $6,000.

◆ 40% of the other manufacturing overhead is considered variable. Variable overhead changes with the number of units produced, but the rate per unit is not expected to change in 1999. The fixed manufacturing overhead costs are expected to remain the same whether or not MTR-2000 is manufactured.

John Porter, plant manager at Paibec Corporation, is concerned that Hardt's analysis may lead to the closing down of the MTR-2000 line. Porter indicates to Hardt that the current performance of the plant can be significantly improved and that the cost increases she is assuming are unlikely to occur. Hence, the analysis should be done assuming costs will be considerably below current levels. Hardt knows that Porter is concerned about outsourcing

MTR-2000 because it will mean that some of his close friends will be laid off. Furthermore, Porter played a key role in convincing management to produce MTR-2000 internally.

Hardt believes that it is unlikely that the plant will achieve the lower costs Porter describes. She is very confident about the accuracy of the information she has collected, but she is unhappy about the possibility of laying off employees.

Required

1. On the basis of the information Hardt has obtained, should Paibec make MTR-2000 or buy it in 1999? Show your calculations.
2. What other factors should Paibec consider before making a decision?
3. What should Lynn Hardt do in response to John Porter's comments?

COLLABORATIVE LEARNING PROBLEM

11-42 Optimal product mix. (CMA, adapted) OmniSport's Plastics Department is currently manufacturing 5,000 pairs of skates annually, making full use of its machine capacity. The selling price and total costs per unit associated with OmniSport's skates are:

Selling price per pair of skates		$98
Costs per pair of skates		
Molded plastic	$ 8	
Other direct materials	12	
Variable machine operating costs ($16 per machine hour)	24	
Manufacturing overhead costs	18	
Marketing and administrative costs	21	83
Operating income per pair of skates		$15

OmniSport believes it can sell 8,000 pairs of skates annually if it had sufficient manufacturing capacity. Colcott Inc., a supplier of quality products, has agreed to provide up to 6,000 pairs of skates per year at a price of $75 per pair delivered to OmniSport's facility.

Jack Petrone, OmniSport's product manager, has suggested that the company can make better use of its Plastics Department by manufacturing snowboard bindings. Petrone believes that OmniSport could expect to sell up to 12,000 snowboard bindings annually at a price of $60 per binding. Petrone's estimate of the selling price and total costs per unit to manufacture 12,000 bindings are:

Selling price per snowboard binding		$60
Costs per snowboard binding		
Molded plastic	$16	
Other direct materials	4	
Variable machine operating costs ($16 per machine hour)	8	
Manufacturing overhead costs	6	
Marketing and administrative costs	10	44
Operating income per snowboard binding		$16

Other information pertinent to OmniSport's operations includes the following:

◆ In the Plastics Department, OmniSport uses machine-hours as the allocation base for manufacturing overhead costs. The fixed manufacturing overhead component of these costs for the current year is the $30,000 of fixed plantwide manufacturing overhead that has been allocated to the Plastics Department. These costs will not be affected by the product-mix decision.

◆ Variable marketing and administrative costs per unit for the various products are as follows:

Manufactured in-line skates	$9
Purchased in-line skates	4
Manufactured snowboard bindings	8

Fixed marketing and administrative costs of $60,000 are not affected by the product-mix decision.

Required

Form groups of two or more students and calculate the quantity of each product that OmniSport should manufacture and/or purchase to maximize operating income in 1999. Show your calculations.

CHAPTER 12

Pricing Decisions and Cost Management

learning objectives

After studying this chapter, you should be able to

1. Discuss the three major influences on pricing decisions
2. Distinguish between short-run and long-run pricing decisions
3. Price products using the target-costing approach
4. Apply the concepts of cost incurrence and locked-in costs
5. Price products using the cost-plus approach
6. Use life-cycle product budgeting and costing when making pricing decisions
7. Describe two pricing practices in which noncost factors are important when setting price
8. Explain the effects of antitrust laws on pricing

Dell Computer sells high-quality products at a competitive price. To achieve its profit goals, Dell sets aggressive target costs. Dell reduces its costs by making innovative product design choices before costs get locked in and by improving its manufacturing and delivery processes.

P ricing decisions are management decisions about what to charge for the products and services that companies deliver. These decisions affect the quantity of product sold and hence product revenues. To maximize operating income, companies produce and sell units so long as the revenue from an additional unit exceeds the cost of producing it. The calculations of product costs, however, are different for different time horizons and different contexts. Understanding cost-behavior patterns, cost drivers, and the concept of relevance introduced in Chapter 11 are key to measuring the costs of a product. This chapter describes how managers evaluate demand at different prices, and manage costs across the value chain and over the product's life cycle to achieve profitability.

MAJOR INFLUENCES ON PRICING DECISIONS

Customers, Competitors and Costs

The price of a product or service is the outcome of the interaction between the demand for the product or service and its supply. Pricing decisions, therefore, must always be based on how demand and supply are expected to be affected. Three major influences on demand and supply are customers, competitors, and costs.

Customers Customers influence prices through their effect on demand. Companies must always examine pricing decisions through the eyes of their customers. Too high a price may cause customers to reject a company's product and choose a competing or substitute product.

Competitors No business operates in a vacuum. Companies must therefore always be mindful of the actions of their competitors. At one extreme, alternative or substitute products of a competitor may affect demand and force a business to lower its prices. A business with knowledge of its rivals' technology, plant capacity, and operating policies is able to estimate its competitors' costs, which is valuable information in setting prices. At the other extreme, a business without a rival in a given situation can set higher prices.

Competition spans international borders. Hence, costs and pricing decisions are also affected by fluctuations in the exchange rates of different countries' currencies. For example, if the yen weakens against the dollar, Japanese products become cheaper in dollar terms and can be priced more competitively in global markets.

Costs Costs influence prices because they affect supply. The lower the cost relative to the price, the greater the quantity of product the company is willing to supply. Understanding the costs of delivering products enables companies to set prices that make products attractive to customers while maximizing companies' operating incomes. In computing the relevant costs for a pricing decision, the manager must consider costs in all value-chain business functions, from R&D to customer service.

Surveys of how managers make pricing decisions reveal that companies weigh customers, competitors, and costs differently. Companies selling similar commodity-type products, such as wheat, rice, and soybeans, in highly competitive markets, have no control over setting prices and must accept the price determined by the market, which consists of many competitors and customers. In these markets, cost information is key, because it helps the company decide on the output level that maximizes operating income. In less competitive markets, such as for cameras and cellular phones, products are differentiated and managers have some discretion in setting prices. All three factors are important when setting prices—the value customers place on the product and the prices competitors charge for competing products affect demand, and the costs of producing and delivering the product influence supply. As competition lessens even more, the key factor affecting pricing decisions is the customers' willingness to pay, not costs or competitors.

Time Horizon of Pricing Decisions

Most pricing decisions are either short run or long run. Short-run decisions typically have a time horizon of less than a year and include decisions such as pricing a one-time-only special order with no long-run implications, and adjusting product mix and output volume in a competitive market. Long-run decisions involve a time horizon of a year or longer and include pricing a product in a major market where there is considerable leeway in price setting. Two key differences affect pricing for the long run relative to the short run: (1) Costs that are often irrelevant for short-run pricing decisions, such as fixed costs that cannot be changed, are generally relevant in the long run, because opportunities exist to alter costs in the long run. (2) Profit margins in long-run pricing decisions are often set to earn a reasonable return on investment. Short-run pricing is more opportunistic—in the short run, prices are decreased when demand is weak and increased when demand is strong. First, consider the easier case of short-run pricing.

COSTING AND PRICING FOR THE SHORT RUN

EXAMPLE: The National Tea Corporation (NTC) operates a plant with a monthly capacity of 1 million cases (each case consisting of 240 cans) of iced tea. Current production and sales are 600,000 cases per month. The selling price is $90 per case. Costs of R&D and product and process design at NTC are negligible. Customer-service costs are also small and are included in marketing costs. All variable costs vary with respect to output units (cases), and production is equal to sales. The variable costs per case and the fixed costs per case (based on a production quantity of 600,000 cases per month) are as follows:

	Variable Costs Per Case	Fixed Costs Per Case	Variable and Fixed Costs Per Case
Manufacturing costs			
Direct material costs	$ 7	$—	$ 7
Packaging costs	18	—	18
Direct manufacturing labor costs	4	—	4
Manufacturing overhead costs	6	13	19
Manufacturing costs	35	13	48
Marketing costs	5	16	21
Distribution costs	9	8	17
Full costs of the product	$49	$37	$86

Calico Tea (CT) has asked NTC and two other companies to bid on supplying 250,000 cases each month for the next four months only. After this period, CT will manufacture and sell its own tea. CT is unlikely to place any future sales orders with NTC. From NTC's standpoint, acceptance or rejection of the order will not affect the revenues (units sold or the selling price) from existing sales outlets.

From a manufacturing-cost viewpoint, the iced tea to be made for CT is identical to that currently made by NTC. If NTC makes the extra 250,000 cases, the existing total fixed manufacturing overhead ($7,800,000 per month) would continue to be incurred. In addition, NTC would incur a further $300,000 in fixed manufacturing overhead (materials procurement costs of $100,000 and process-changeover costs of $200,000) each month. No additional costs will be required for R&D, design, marketing, distribution, or customer service. NTC knows that a price above $45 will probably be noncompetitive because one of its competitors, with a highly efficient plant, has sizable idle capacity and is eager to win the CT contract. What price should NTC bid for the 250,000-case contract?

Exhibit 12-1 presents an analysis of the monthly relevant costs, using concepts developed in Chapter 11. Relevant costs include all manufacturing costs that will change in total if the special order is obtained: all direct and indirect variable manufacturing costs plus materials procurement costs and process-changeover costs related to the special order. *Existing* fixed manufacturing overhead costs are irrelevant. Why? Because these costs will not change if the special order is accepted. But the

Points to Stress Often there is no clear-cut distinction between short-run (SR) and long-run (LR) pricing decisions. The LR is just a series of SRs. Some critics believe that U.S. mgrs. often err by classifying too many decisions as SR. For example, in the SR, accepting a special order for any price above incremental cost will increase profits. Some companies, however, accept a series of special orders that in effect become a LR decision. The text uses the phrase "one-time-only special order" to highlight the limited context in which a focus on only SR incremental costs is appropriate.

Correcting Student Misconceptions Students often erroneously assume that VC are relevant, while FC are irrelevant. However, the text's NTC example shows that some VC are irrelevant (marketing, distribution), while the special order engenders some incremental batch-level costs that are relevant (material procurement, process changeover). Moreover, some, but not all, mfg. costs are relevant (only variable mfg. costs are relevant because the special order doesn't affect regular fixed mfg. costs).

Points to Stress Lowering prices for special orders may adversely affect regular business unless the market is segmented such that (1) regular customers (or *their* customers) can't buy from the special-order customer, (2) the regular customers won't learn about the special order and demand a lower price, and (3) the special-order items are marketed as distinct from the regular items to avoid cheapening the latter's image. In the example, CT appears to be in a different market segment from NTC's regular customers, so it seems reasonable to expect regular demand to be unaffected by the special order.

Reinforcing Problems Exer. 12-16
through 12-18 and Prob. 12-28
cover short-run pricing issues.

Correcting Student Misconceptions
The $48 cost/case yielded by the
absorption costing method is appropriate for external financial reporting, but not for pricing. The $86 full
product cost/case is relevant for
long-term pricing since in the LR
all costs, both fixed and variable,
from all elements of the value chain
must be covered. Exh. 12-1 shows
that for the CT special order, the
relevant cost/case is only $36.20,
since only the incremental costs are
relevant for special orders.

Points to Stress When calculating
relevant costs for a special order, follow the text's example and determine how the order will affect indirect costs such as materials
procurement and process
changeover. Because such costs
aren't usually traced directly to
products, mgrs. may overlook them.
These indirect costs can be sizable
and may be the difference between a
profit and a loss on a special order.

Points to Stress Mgt. could formally
incorporate uncertainty about winning the bid by comparing the expected value of profits at alternative
bid prices: (Profit at bid price) ×
Prob (winning bid at that price).
The appendix to Chap. 3 presents
formal models that incorporate uncertainty into decisions.

Teaching Tip Try this in-class exercise on bidding to demonstrate the
"winner's curse" (the winning bidder
earns less than he thought) in contract bidding. Pass around a sealed
cup with an unknown (to the students) # of paper clips (PC) in it.
The PC represent the unknown
level of a cost driver in constructing
a building (e.g., the amount of granite in the soil). Each student submits
a "sealed" bid of a fixed contract
price based on their estimate of the
# of PC and the firm's profit func-
tion. Set a maximum bid price and
a profit function of: Bid Price −
FC − (VC)(# of PC). The instructor then puts all the bids on the
board and accepts the lowest bid. A
lively discussion follows.

EXHIBIT 12-1
Monthly Relevant Costs for NTC: The 250,000-Case Short-Run Special Order

Direct materials (250,000 cases × $7)		$1,750,000
Packaging (250,000 cases × $18)		4,500,000
Direct manufacturing labor (250,000 cases × $4)		1,000,000
Variable manufacturing overhead (250,000 cases × $6)		1,500,000
Fixed manufacturing overhead		
Materials procurement	$100,000	
Process changeover	200,000	
Total fixed manufacturing overhead		300,000
Total relevant costs		$9,050,000
Relevant costs per case: $9,050,000 ÷ 250,000 cases = $36.20		

additional materials procurement and process-changeover costs of $300,000 per
month for the special order are relevant because they will be incurred only if the
special order is accepted. All nonmanufacturing costs will be unaffected if the special order is accepted, so they are irrelevant.

The total relevant costs for the 250,000-case special order are $9,050,000 (or
$36.20 per case) as shown in Exhibit 12-l. Therefore, $36.20 is the minimum price
per case. Any bid above $36.20 per case will improve NTC's profitability in the
short run. For example, a successful bid of $40 per case will add $950,000 to NTC's
monthly operating income: ($40 − $36.20) × 250,000 = $950,000. Note again
how unit costs can mislead. The table on p. 423 reports total manufacturing costs
to be $48 per case. The $48 cost might erroneously suggest that a bid of $40 per
case for the Calico Tea special order will result in NTC sustaining a $8 per case loss
on the contract. Why is this conclusion erroneous? Because total manufacturing
costs per case include $13 of fixed manufacturing costs per case that will not be in-
curred on the 250,000-case special order. These costs are irrelevant for the special-
order bid.

Cost data, although key information in NTC's decision on the price to bid,
are not the only inputs. NTC must also consider competitors and their likely bids.
For example, if NTC knows that its rival with idle capacity plans to bid $39 per
case, NTC could bid $38 per case instead of $40 per case and still increase operating income by $450,000 [($38 − $36.20) × 250,000] on the special order. NTC's
strategy is to bid as high a price as it can above $36.20, but one that is lower than
competing bids.

Now suppose NTC believes that CT will sell the iced tea in NTC's current
markets but at a lower price than NTC's. Suppose further that customers will not
have a brand or taste preference for either tea (they are, after all, identical) and will
make a purchase based on price alone. If NTC thus has to lower prices in these
markets just to compete with CT, should the relevant costs of the bidding decision
include revenues lost on sales to existing customers? Yes, if supplying tea to CT will
result in NTC having to lower its existing prices and not supplying tea to CT will
allow NTC to maintain existing prices. NTC should bid a price that at least covers
both the incremental cost of $36.20 per case plus the revenues that will be lost on
existing sales when prices are lowered. But what if CT can purchase the tea from
another supplier at the same low price and as a result can force NTC to lower
prices to its current customers? In this case, NTC's potential loss in revenues from
current customers should *not* be considered relevant to the bidding decision. Why?
Because the revenues would be lost whether or not NTC wins the bid, and hence
are irrelevant to the pricing decision.

Our NTC example assumes that NTC has idle capacity and that a competing
bidder with an efficient plant and sizable idle capacity will also bid for the CT order. Hence the focus of our short-run pricing decision is on identifying the minimum price above which NTC will profit from the CT order. In other cases, companies might experience strong demand in the short run and have limited capacity.

In these cases, companies will increase prices in the short run to as much as the market will bear. We observe such high short-run prices in the case of new and innovative products, for example, microprocessors, computer chips, or software.

COSTING AND PRICING FOR THE LONG RUN

Short-run pricing decisions are responses to short-run demand and supply conditions, but they cannot form the basis of a long-run relationship with customers. Buyers—whether a person buying a box of Wheaties, Bechtel Corporation buying a fleet of tractors, or General Foods Corporation buying audit services—typically prefer stable (and predictable) prices over an extended time horizon. A stable price reduces the need for continuous monitoring of suppliers' prices. Greater price stability also improves planning and builds long-run buyer-seller relationships. But to charge a stable price and earn the desired long-run return, a company must know its costs, over the long run, of supplying its product to customers.

Calculating Product Costs

Consider the Astel Computer Corporation. Astel manufactures two brands of personal computers (PCs)—Deskpoint and Provalue. Deskpoint is Astel's top-of-the-line product, a Pentium III chip–based PC. Our analysis focuses on pricing Provalue, a less powerful Pentium chip–based machine.

The manufacturing costs of Provalue are calculated using the activity-based costing (ABC) approach described in Chapter 5. Astel has three direct manufacturing cost categories (direct materials, direct manufacturing labor, and direct machining costs) and three indirect manufacturing cost pools (ordering and receiving, testing and inspection, and rework) in its accounting system. Astel treats machining costs as a direct cost of Provalue because it is manufactured on machines that are dedicated to the production of Provalue.[1] The following table summarizes the activity cost pools, the cost driver for each activity, and the cost per unit of cost driver that Astel uses as an allocation base for each indirect manufacturing cost pool.

Manufacturing Activity	Description of Activity	Cost Driver	Cost Per Unit of Cost Driver
Ordering and receiving	Placing orders and receiving components	Number of orders	$80 per order
Testing and inspection	Testing components and final product	Testing-hours	$2 per testing-hour
Rework	Correcting and fixing errors and defects	Rework-hours	$40 per rework-hour

Astel uses a long-run time horizon to price Provalue. Over this horizon, Astel's management regards direct materials costs as varying with the units of Provalue produced, direct manufacturing labor costs as varying with direct manufacturing labor-hours, and ordering and receiving, testing and inspection, and rework costs as varying with their chosen cost drivers. For example, ordering and receiving costs vary with the number of orders. Staff members responsible for placing orders can be reassigned or laid off (or increased) in the long run if fewer (or more) orders need to be placed. Direct machining costs (rent paid on leased machines) do not vary with changes in machine-hours used over this time horizon, and hence are fixed long-run costs.

Astel has no beginning or ending inventory of Provalue in 2001 and manufactures and sells 150,000 units during the year. How does Astel calculate Provalue's manufacturing costs? It uses the following information, which indicates the resources used to manufacture Provalue in 2001:

[1] If Deskpoint and Provalue had shared the same machines, we could allocate machining costs on the basis of the budgeted machine-hours used to manufacture Deskpoint and Provalue and treat this cost as an indirect fixed cost. The basic analysis would be exactly as described in the chapter except that machining costs would appear as indirect rather than direct fixed costs.

1. Direct materials costs per unit of Provalue are $460.

2. Direct manufacturing labor-hours required to manufacture Provalue equal 480,000 (3.20 direct manufacturing labor-hours per unit of Provalue × 150,000 units) at a cost of $20 per direct manufacturing labor-hour.

3. Direct fixed costs of machines used exclusively for the manufacture of Provalue total $11,400,000 representing a capacity of 300,000 machine-hours at a cost of $38 per hour. Each unit of Provalue requires 2 machine-hours. Hence the entire machining capacity is used to manufacture Provalue (2 machine-hours × 150,000 units = 300,000 machine-hours).

4. Number of orders placed to purchase components required for the manufacture of Provalue is 22,500 at a cost of $80 per order. (We assume for simplicity that Provalue has 450 components supplied by different suppliers, and that 50 orders are placed for each component to match Provalue's production schedule.)

5. Number of testing-hours used for Provalue is 4,500,000 (150,000 Provalue units are tested for 30 hours per unit) at a cost of $2 per testing-hour.

6. Number of units of Provalue reworked during the year is 12,000 (8% of the 150,000 units manufactured). Each unit requires 2.5 hours of rework for a total of 30,000 hours (12,000 × 2.5) at a rate of $40 per rework-hour.

Exhibit 12-2 presents the costs to manufacture Provalue in 2001. The exhibit indicates total manufacturing costs of $102 million and manufacturing cost per unit of $680. Manufacturing, however, is just one business function in the value chain. For setting long-run prices and for managing costs, Astel determines the full costs of producing and selling Provalue.

Astel identifies direct costs, and chooses cost drivers and cost pools in the other value-chain functions to measure the cause-and-effect relationship between the activities and costs within each activity's cost pool. Costs are allocated to Provalue using the quantity of cost driver units that Provalue uses as an allocation base. Exhibit 12-3 summarizes the operating income statement for Provalue for

EXHIBIT 12-2
Manufacturing Costs of Provalue for 2001 Using Activity-Based Costing

	Total Manufacturing Costs for 150,000 Units (1)	Manufacturing Cost Per Unit (2) = (1) ÷ 150,000
Direct manufacturing costs		
Direct materials costs (150,000 units × $460)	$ 69,000,000	$460
Direct manufacturing labor costs (480,000 hours × $20)	9,600,000	64
Direct machining costs (300,000 machine-hours × $38)	11,400,000	76
Direct manufacturing costs	90,000,000	600
Indirect manufacturing costs		
Ordering and receiving costs (22,500 orders × $80)	1,800,000	12
Testing and inspection costs (4,500,000 hours × $2)	9,000,000	60
Rework costs (30,000 hours × $40)	1,200,000	8
Indirect manufacturing costs	12,000,000	80
Total manufacturing costs	$102,000,000	$680

EXHIBIT 12-3
Product Profitability of Provalue for 2001 Using Value-Chain Activity-Based Costing

	Total Costs for 150,000 Units (1)	Cost Per Unit (2) = (1) ÷ 150,000
Revenues	$150,000,000	$1,000
Cost of goods sold[a] (from Exhibit 12-2)		
Direct materials costs	69,000,000	460
Direct manufacturing labor costs	9,600,000	64
Direct machining costs	11,400,000	76
Indirect manufacturing overhead costs	12,000,000	80
Cost of goods sold	102,000,000	680
Operating Costs		
R&D costs	5,400,000	36
Design costs of products and processes	6,000,000	40
Marketing costs	15,000,000	100
Distribution costs	3,600,000	24
Customer-service costs	3,000,000	20
Operating costs	33,000,000	220
Full costs of the product	135,000,000	900
Operating income	$ 15,000,000	$ 100

[a]Cost of goods sold = Total manufacturing costs, because there is no beginning or ending inventory of Provalue in 2001.

the year 2001 based on an activity-based analysis of costs in all value-chain functions (for brevity, supporting calculations for nonmanufacturing value-chain functions are not given). Astel earns $15 million from Provalue, or $100 per unit sold in 2001.

Alternative Long-Run Pricing Approaches

Now that we know how companies calculate their product costs, we can consider how these costs influence long-run pricing decisions. The starting point for pricing decisions can be

1. Market-based
2. Cost-based (also called cost-plus)

The market-based approach to pricing starts by asking, Given what our customers want and how our competitors will react to what we do, what price should we charge? The cost-based approach to pricing starts by asking, What does it cost us to make this product, and hence what price should we charge that will recoup our costs and achieve a desired return on investment?

Companies operating in markets that are competitive (for example, commodities such as oil and gas) use the market-based approach. The items produced or services provided by one company are very similar to those produced or provided by others, so companies have no influence over the prices to charge. In other industries, where there is product differentiation (for example, automobiles, management consulting, and legal services), companies use market-based or cost-based approaches. They choose prices and product and service features on the basis of anticipated customer and competitor reactions and the costs to produce and sell the product. That is, they consider both market and cost aspects.

Some companies first look at costs and then consider customers or competitors (the cost-based approach). Others start by considering customers and competitors and then look at costs (the market-based approach). Both approaches iteratively

Correcting Student Misconceptions For pricing decisions, it's important to assign to products the costs from all the value-chain areas. In the real world, building up these product costs is more complex than students realize. Astel has only 1 mfg. dept., and it has 3 direct cost and 3 indirect cost categories. Most mfg. firms have more categories. If the other 5 elements of the value chain each have 3 direct and 3 indirect costs, then Astel has (3 + 3 = 6 costs/value-chain element) × (6 value chain elements) = 36 cost categories to allocate to products.

Example Companies that fabricate specialized make-to-order industrial equipment typically use cost-plus pricing because there's no established market price for their products. On the other hand, producers of agricultural commodities (e.g., wheat, soybeans) must take the market price as given. They use cost data in deciding what commodities to produce.

consider customers, competitors, and costs. Only their *starting points* differ. Keep in mind that market forces are always important regardless of the specific pricing techniques employed.

In the next two sections, we present details of these two approaches to making long-run pricing decisions. We consider first the market-based approach.

TARGET COSTING FOR TARGET PRICING

An important form of market-based pricing is target pricing. A **target price** is the estimated price for a product (or service) that potential customers will be willing to pay. This estimate is based on an understanding of customers' perceived value for a product and competitors' responses. A company's sales and marketing organization, through close contact and interaction with customers, is often in the best position to identify customers' needs and their perceived value for a product. To gain further insight, companies also conduct market research studies about product features that customers want and the prices they are willing to pay for them. Understanding what customers value is a key aspect of being customer focused, a theme described in Chapter 1.

Unlike its customers, a company has less access to its competitors. To gauge how competitors might react, a company needs to understand competitors' technologies, products, costs, and financial conditions. For example, knowing competitors' technologies and products helps a company to evaluate how distinctive its own products will be in the market, and hence the prices it might be able to charge. Where does a company obtain information about its competitors? Most frequently from competitors' customers, suppliers, and employees. Another important source of information is *reverse engineering*—a process of taking apart and analyzing competitors' products to determine product designs, materials, and technologies used by competitors. Many companies, including Ford, General Motors, and PPG Industries, have departments for competitor analysis.

The target price, calculated using customer and competitor inputs, forms the basis for calculating target costs. The *target cost per unit* is the target price minus *target operating income per unit.* The **target operating income per unit** is the operating income that a company wants to earn per unit of a product (or service) sold. The **target cost per unit** is the estimated long-run cost per unit of a product (or service) that enables the company to achieve its target operating income per unit when selling at the target price.[2]

What relevant costs should we include in the target-cost calculations? *All* future costs, both variable and fixed. Why? Because in the long run, a company's prices and revenues must recover all its costs. If not, the company's best alternative is to shut down, an alternative that results in forgoing all future revenues and saving all future costs, whether fixed or variable.

The target cost per unit is often lower than the existing full cost per unit of the product. The target cost per unit really is a target—something the company must shoot for. To achieve the target cost per unit and the target operating income per unit, the company must reduce the cost of its products and processes. Target costing is widely used among different industries around the world. Examples of companies that use target pricing and target cosing include Daimler-Chrysler, Ford, General Motors, Toyota, and Daihatsu in the automobile industry; Matsushita, Panasonic, and Sharp in the electronics industry; and Compaq and Toshiba in the personal computer industry.

Implementing Target Pricing and Target Costing

There are four main steps in developing target prices and target costs. We illustrate these steps using our Provalue example.

[2]For a more detailed discussion of target costing, see S. Ansari, J. Bell, and The CAM-I Target Cost Core Group, *Target Costing: The Next Frontier in Strategic Cost Management* (Homewood, Ill.: Irwin, 1996).

Step 1: Develop a Product That Satisfies Needs of Potential Customers Astel is in the process of planning design modifications for Provalue. Astel's market research indicates that customers do not value Provalue's extra features such as special audio features and designs that accommodate various upgrades that can make the PC run faster and perform calculations more quickly. They want Astel to redesign Provalue into a no-frills PC and sell it at a much lower price.

Step 2: Choose a Target Price Astel expects its competitors to lower the prices of PCs that compete against Provalue by 15 percent. Astel's management believes that the company must respond aggressively by reducing Provalue's price by 20%, from $1,000 per unit to $800 per unit. At this lower price, Astel's marketing manager forecasts an increase in annual sales from 150,000 to 200,000 units.

Step 3: Derive a Target Cost Per Unit by Subtracting Target Operating Income Per Unit from the Target Price Astel's management wants a 10% target operating income on sales revenues.

Total target sales revenues	$= \$800 \times 200{,}000 \text{ units} = \$160{,}000{,}000$
Total target operating income	$= 10\% \times \$160{,}000{,}000 = \$16{,}000{,}000$
Target operating income per unit	$= \$16{,}000{,}000 \div 200{,}000 \text{ units} = \$80 \text{ per unit}$
Target cost per unit	$=$ Target price $-$ Target operating income per unit
	$= \$800 - \$80 = \$720$
Total current full costs of Provalue	$= \$135{,}000{,}000$ (from Exhibit 12-3)
Current full cost per unit of Provalue	$= \$135{,}000{,}000 \div 150{,}000 \text{ units} = \$900 \text{ per unit}$

Provalue's target cost per unit of $720 is substantially lower than its existing unit cost of $900. Astel's goal is to find ways to reduce its unit cost by $180, from $900 to $720. Cost reduction efforts need to extend to all parts of the value chain—from R&D to customer service—including seeking cost concessions from suppliers. The challenge in step 4 is to achieve the target cost through *value engineering*.

Step 4: Perform Value Engineering to Achieve Target Cost Value engineering is a systematic evaluation of all aspects of the value-chain business functions, with the objective of reducing costs while satisfying customer needs. Value engineering can result in improvements in product designs, changes in materials specifications, or modifications in process methods. We discuss value engineering in the next section.

Value Engineering, Cost Incurrence, and Locked-In Costs

Managers find the distinction between value-added and nonvalue-added activities and costs useful in value engineering. A **value-added cost** is a cost that, if eliminated, would reduce the value or utility (usefulness) customers obtain from using the product or service. Examples are costs of specific product features and attributes desired by customers such as fast response time, adequate memory, preloaded software, clear images on the monitor, easy-to-use keyboards, reliability, and prompt customer service. A **nonvalue-added cost** is a cost that, if eliminated, would not reduce the value or utility customers obtain from using the product or service. It is a cost that the customer is unwilling to pay the company for. Examples of nonvalue-added costs are costs of expediting, rework, and repair.

Activities and the costs of activities do not always fall neatly into value-added or nonvalue-added categories. Some costs, such as materials handling, fall in the gray area in between because they include both value-added and nonvalue-added aspects. Despite these troublesome gray areas, the attempts to distinguish

Example The following example illustrates the benefits of using cross-functional teams to perform value engineering. Hewlett-Packard engineers wanted to design a full-featured printer that was a "mechanical marvel," but marketing suggested that consumers would prefer a simpler machine. "There was near mutiny among the engineers until a product manager . . . forced [the engineers] to do telephone polls of customers . . . People were eager for the [simpler] product the engineers considered a "kludge."" (*WSJ*, 9/8/94).

Points to Stress Traditional cost acctg. systems don't classify costs as value-added (VA) or nonvalue-added (NVA). To obtain this information, mgt. usually orders a special study. Mgt. accountants work closely with production and marketing to classify costs as VA or NVA.

Correcting Student Misconceptions Students usually erroneously believe that employees candidly reveal information. However, employees are unlikely to forthrightly reveal information regarding VA/NVA activities. Employees naturally tend to overestimate the proportion of their time spent on VA tasks, out of concern for job security.

Reinforcing Problems Exer. 12-19 and 12-20 cover issues involved in distinguishing between VA and NVA activities.

value-added from nonvalue-added costs provide a useful overall framework for value engineering.

In the Provalue example, direct materials, direct manufacturing labor, and machining and assembly costs are value-added costs. Ordering and testing costs fall in the gray area (customers perceive some portion but not all of these costs as necessary for adding value). Rework costs (including costs of expediting and delivering reworked products) are nonvalue-added costs.

Value engineering seeks to reduce nonvalue-added activities and hence nonvalue-added costs by reducing the cost drivers of nonvalue-added activities. For example, to reduce rework costs, Astel must reduce rework-hours. Value engineering also attempts to achieve greater efficiency in value-added activities in order to reduce value-added costs. For example, to reduce direct manufacturing labor costs, Astel must reduce the manufacturing labor-hours it takes to make Provalue. But how should Astel reduce rework-hours and direct manufacturing labor-hours?

To manage value-added and nonvalue-added activities and costs, Astel needs to carefully distinguish when costs are incurred and when they are locked in. **Cost incurrence** describes when a resource is sacrificed or forgone to meet a specific objective. We focus on the R&D, design, manufacturing, marketing, distribution and customer-service costs for Provalue. Costing systems emphasize cost incurrence. Astel's costing system, for example, recognizes the direct materials costs of Provalue as each unit of Provalue is assembled and sold. But Provalue's direct materials costs per unit are *locked in* (or *designed in*) much earlier when product designers choose the components that will go into Provalue. **Locked-in costs (designed-in costs)** are those costs that have not yet been incurred but which, based on decisions that have already been made, will be incurred in the future.

OBJECTIVE 4

Apply the concepts of cost incurrence and locked-in costs

Points to Stress A large proportion of costs (often the majority of costs) are *locked in* by the design stage—see Exh. 12-4. Target costing and value engineering help control costs before they are locked in—within the constraints of satisfying customer needs. Traditional cost acctg. hasn't recognized the opportunity for this sort of *ex ante* cost control, and has instead focused on *ex post* comparisons of costs actually incurred with planned or budgeted costs (e.g., var. analysis). Both kinds of cost control are important. However, in many cases there's greater potential for cost reduction in the design stage because (1) a large proportion of the costs are locked in at the design stage, and (2) design has (historically) received less "cost cutting" attention than mfg. (To use an agricultural analogy, "you get the biggest potatoes in the first pass through the field").

Why is it important to distinguish between when costs are locked in and when costs are incurred? Because it is difficult to alter or reduce costs that are already locked in. For example, if Astel experiences quality problems during manufacturing, its ability to improve quality and reduce scrap may be limited by Provalue's design. Scrap and rework costs are incurred during manufacturing, but they may be locked in much earlier in the value chain by a faulty design. Similarly, in the software industry, costs of producing software are often locked in at the design and analysis stage. Costly and difficult-to-fix errors that appear during coding and testing are frequently locked in by bad designs.

Some examples of how Provalue's design decisions affect value-added and nonvalue-added costs in various value-chain functions include the following:

1. Designing Provalue so that various parts snap-fit together (rather than requiring various parts to be soldered together) decreases value-added direct manufacturing labor-hours and costs.

2. Simplifying the Provalue design and using fewer components decreases testing and inspection time and costs, and ordering and materials handling costs.

3. Designing Provalue to reduce repairs and repair costs at customer sites reduces nonvalue-added customer-service costs.

Exhibit 12-4 illustrates how the locked-in cost curve and the cost-incurrence curve might appear in the case of Provalue. The bottom (cost-incurrence) curve uses information from Exhibit 12-3 to plot the cumulative costs per unit incurred in different business functions. The top curve plots the cumulative costs locked in. (The specific numbers underlying this curve are assumed.) Both curves deal with the same total cumulative costs per unit of $900. *The graph emphasizes the wide divergence between the time when costs are locked in and the time when those costs are incurred.* In our example, once the product and processes are designed, more than 86% ($780 ÷ $900) of the unit costs of Provalue are locked in when only about 8% ($76 ÷ $900) of the unit costs are actually incurred. For example, at the end of the design stage, costs such as direct materials, direct manufacturing labor, and many manufacturing, marketing, distribution, and customer-service costs are all locked in.

EXHIBIT 12-4
Pattern of Cost Incurrence and Locked-in Costs for Provalue

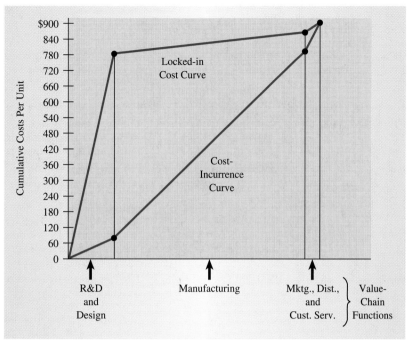

Teaching Tip As mentioned earlier, cost accountants have a long history of providing data for controlling mfg. costs (e.g., var. analysis), but we have less experience in providing info. for controlling costs in the design stage. This is one area where we expect future developments in cost acctg. This is a good opportunity to emphasize that the world is changing so fast that much of what students learn in school will be outdated within 10 yrs. It's imperative that they make a commitment to keep abreast of new techniques and developments if they are to remain competent professionals.

Example To achieve target costs, many companies use *kaizen*, a process of continuous improvement. For example, Hewlett-Packard cut costs on its desktop printers by 50% over a 6-yr period. In some companies, *every* worker makes suggestions for improvement. Much of the cost reduction occurs gradually, via these many small improvements. Also, since DM are often a significant cost, manufacturers often work closely with their suppliers to achieve target DM costs. For example, Toyota has sent its own engineers to help suppliers produce more efficiently—with the proviso that much of the cost savings are passed back to Toyota.

We caution that costs are not always locked in early at the design stage. In some industries, such as legal and consulting, costs are locked in and incurred at about the same time. If costs are not locked in early, cost reduction can be achieved right up to the time when costs are incurred. In these industries, the key to lowering costs is improved operating efficiency and productivity rather than better design.

When a sizable fraction of the costs are locked in at the design stage, as in the Provalue example, the focus of value engineering is on making innovations and modifying designs at the product design stage. The best way to evaluate the effect of alternative design decisions on the target cost per unit is to organize a cross-functional value-engineering team consisting of marketing managers, product designers, manufacturing engineers, production supervisors, purchasing managers, suppliers, and cost accountants. Why a cross-functional team? Because only a cross-functional team can evaluate the impact of design decisions on all value-chain functions.

The cross-functional team generates cost reduction ideas and tests them. The management accountant's challenge is to estimate cost savings and explain cost implications of alternative design decisions. To do so, the management accountant must develop a solid understanding of the technical and business aspects of the entire value chain and interact knowledgeably with other team members. A cross-functional team makes it easier to choose and implement new designs. Why? Because all parts of the organization have "bought into" the new design.

ACHIEVING THE TARGET COST PER UNIT FOR PROVALUE

The value-engineering study leads Astel to discontinue Provalue. In its place, Astel introduces Provalue II. The cross-functional team designs Provalue II as a high-quality, highly reliable machine that has fewer features and that meets customers' price expectations. Provalue II has fewer components and is easier to manufacture and test. The following tables compare the quantities of cost drivers and cost driver rates for Provalue and Provalue II using activity-based costs for different activities. In place of the 150,000 Provalue units manufactured and sold in 2001, Astel expects to make and sell 200,000 Provalue II units in 2002.

Points to Stress To improve product quality, many manufacturers redesign their products to be more tolerant of minor variations in the production process. This is often more cost-effective than striving for perfect-quality mfg. within very tight tolerances.

Cost Category	Cost Driver	Provalue[a]		Provalue II		Explanation of Costs for Provalue II
		Quantity of Cost Driver for 150,000 Units	Cost Per Unit of Cost Driver	Quantity of Cost Driver for 200,000 Units	Cost Per Unit of Cost Driver	

DIRECT COSTS

Cost Category	Cost Driver	Quantity for 150,000	Cost Per Unit	Quantity for 200,000	Cost Per Unit	Explanation
Direct materials	Units produced	150,000	$460	200,000	$385	The Provalue II design will use a simplified main printed circuit board and fewer components.
Direct manufacturing labor	Direct manufacturing labor-hours	480,000	20	530,000	20	Provalue II will require 2.65 direct manufacturing labor-hours per unit compared to 3.20 direct manufacturing labor-hours per unit for Provalue. Total direct manufacturing labor-hours equal 530,000 (2.65 labor-hours × 200,000 units).
Direct machining	Machine-hours capacity	300,000	38	300,000	38	The new design will require 1.5 machine-hours per unit of Provalue II compared to 2 machine-hours required to produce each unit of Provalue. Astel will use the entire 300,000 machine-hours of capacity to produce 200,000 units of Provalue II (1.5 machine-hours × 200,000 units = 300,000 machine-hours).

INDIRECT MANUFACTURING COSTS

Cost Category	Cost Driver	Quantity for 150,000	Cost Per Unit	Quantity for 200,000	Cost Per Unit	Explanation
Ordering	Number of orders	22,500	80	21,250	80	Astel will place 50 orders for each of the 425 components in Provalue II. Total orders for Provalue II will be 21,250 (425 × 50).
Testing	Testing-hours	4,500,000	2	3,000,000	2	Provalue II is easier to test and will require 15 testing-hours per unit. Total testing hours for Provalue II will be 3,000,000 (15 × 200,000 units).
Reworking	Rework-hours	30,000	40	32,500	40	Provalue II will have a lower rework rate of 6.5% because it is easier to manufacture. Total units reworked will be 13,000 (6.5% × 200,000). It will still take 2.5 hours to rework a unit for a total of 32,500 hours (13,000 × 2.5).

[a]From Exhibit 12-2

Note how value engineering reduces both value-added costs (by designing Provalue II to use less costly direct materials and fewer direct manufacturing labor-hours) and nonvalue-added costs (by simplifying the Provalue II design to reduce rework-hours). For simplicity, we assume that value engineering will not reduce the cost per order ($80), the cost per testing-hour ($2), or the cost per rework-hour ($40). By making these activities more efficient, value engineering can also reduce costs by reducing these cost-driver rates (see the Problem for Self Study at the end of this chapter).

The only total costs that value engineering cannot reduce are the total fixed machining costs. Whether or not Astel uses all the 300,000 machine-hours of capacity available to it for manufacturing Provalue II, Astel will incur machining costs

EXHIBIT 12-5
Target Manufacturing Costs of Provalue II for 2002

	Provalue II	Provalue	
	Estimated Manufacturing Costs for 200,000 Units (1)	Estimated Manufacturing Costs Per Unit (2) = (1) ÷ 200,000	Manufacturing Costs Per Unit (Exhibit 12-2, Column 2) (3)
Direct manufacturing costs			
Direct materials costs (200,000 units × $385)	$ 77,000,000	$385.00	$460.00
Direct manufacturing labor costs (530,000 direct manuf. labor-hours × $20)	10,600,000	53.00	64.00
Direct machining costs (300,000 machine-hours × $38)	11,400,000	57.00	76.00
Direct manufacturing costs	99,000,000	495.00	600.00
Indirect manufacturing costs			
Ordering and receiving costs (21,250 orders × $80)	1,700,000	8.50	12.00
Testing and inspection costs (3,000,000 testing-hours × $2)	6,000,000	30.00	60.00
Rework costs (32,500 rework-hours × $40)	1,300,000	6.50	8.00
Indirect manufacturing costs	9,000,000	45.00	80.00
Total manufacturing costs	$108,000,000	$540.00	$680.00

of $11,400,000 (300,000 × $38 per machine-hour). But Astel uses value engineering to reduce the machining-hours required to make Provalue II to 1.5 hours per unit. This reduction allows Astel to use the available machine capacity to make and sell more units of Provalue II (200,000 units versus 150,000 units for Provalue), thereby reducing the machining costs per unit.

Exhibit 12-5 presents the target manufacturing costs of Provalue II, using data about the quantity of the cost driver and the cost per unit of the cost driver from the Provalue II columns on the preceding page. For comparison, Exhibit 12-5 also reproduces the manufacturing costs per unit of Provalue from Exhibit 12-2. As you can see, the new design is expected to reduce the manufacturing cost per unit by $140 (from $680 to $540) at the expected sales quantity of 200,000 units. A similar analysis (not presented) estimates the expected effect of the new design on costs in other value-chain business functions. Exhibit 12-6 shows that the estimated full unit cost of the product equals $720—the target cost per unit for Provalue II. Astel's goal is to sell Provalue II at the target price, achieve target cost, and earn the target operating income.[3]

To attain target costs, many companies combine *kaizen* or *continuous improvement* methods, aimed at improving productivity and eliminating waste, with value engineering and better designs. After actual costs are known, companies compare actual and target costs to gain insights about improvements that can be made in subsequent target costing efforts.

Unless managed properly, value engineering and target costing can have undesired consequences:

◆ The cross-functional team may add too many features in an attempt to accommodate the different wishes of team members.

◆ Long development times may result as alternative designs are evaluated endlessly.

◆ Organizational conflicts may develop as the burden of cutting costs falls unequally on different parts of the organization.

Points to Stress ABC makes explicit how product costs can be reduced by lowering the per unit usage of resources in each activity area. ABC therefore assists in cost mgt., in addition to providing more accurate product cost data for pricing and product emphasis decisions.

Example Compaq used value engineering to redesign its computers—cutting in half the production time for the ProLinea desktop computer (from 20.85 min in 1991 to 10.49 min in 1994) and the number of component parts (from 171 to just 86) (*WSJ*, 8/17/94).

Curriculum Linkage Learning (or experience) curve techniques (see Chap. 10) can be used to estimate the time it will take to produce, test, inspect, etc. the new Provalue II.

[3]For more details, see R. Cooper and R. Slagmulder, *Target Costing and Value Engineering* (Portland, OR: Productivity Press, 1997).

Example Some companies use a matrix approach such as the following to break down the total target cost into target costs for each cost element:

Value-Chain Elements

Costs	R&D	Mfg.	Cust. Serv.	Total
Labor	X	X	X	XX
Materials	X	X	—	XX
.	.	.	.	.
.	.	.	.	.
.	.	.	.	.
Warranty repairs	—	—	X	XX
Total	XX	XX	XX	XXX

EXHIBIT 12-6
Target Product Profitability of Provalue II for 2002

	Estimated Total Costs for 200,000 Units (1)	Estimated Total Cost Per Unit (2) = (1) ÷ 200,000
Revenues	$160,000,000	$800
Cost of goods sold[a] (from Exhibit 12-5)		
Direct materials costs	77,000,000	385
Direct manufacturing labor costs	10,600,000	53
Direct machining costs	11,400,000	57
Indirect manufacturing costs	9,000,000	45
Cost of goods sold	108,000,000	540
Operating Costs		
R&D costs	4,000,000	20
Design of products and processes costs	6,000,000	30
Marketing costs	18,000,000	90
Distribution costs	5,000,000	25
Customer-service costs	3,000,000	15
Operating costs	36,000,000	180
Full costs of the product	144,000,000	720
Operating income	$ 16,000,000	$ 80

[a]Cost of goods sold = Total manufacturing costs, because there is no beginning or ending inventory for Provalue II in 2002.

To avoid these pitfalls, target-costing efforts should always focus on the customer, pay attention to schedules, and build a culture of teamwork and cooperation across business functions.

COST-PLUS PRICING

Instead of using the external market-based approach we have just discussed, managers sometimes use a cost-based approach for their long-run pricing decisions. The general formula for setting a cost-based price adds a markup component to the cost base:

Cost base	$	X
Markup component		Y
Prospective selling price		$X + Y$

Points to Stress Target pricing starts with a desired selling price and subtracts target profit to yield an *allowable target* cost that is usually less than the *currently achievable cost*. Cost-plus pricing usually starts with achievable cost and adds desired profit to yield selling price. When achievable cost exceeds allowable cost, cost-based pricing will yield a higher selling price than target pricing. Of course, each pricing approach is just a starting point. Before setting a final selling price, mgrs. reevaluate both the effect of proposed prices on demand and their ability to cut costs.

As we have emphasized earlier, think of the cost-plus pricing formulas we present in this section only as starting points for pricing decisions. The markup component is rarely a rigid number. Instead, it is flexible, depending on the behavior of customers and competitors. The markup component is ultimately determined by the market.[4]

Cost-Plus Target Rate of Return on Investment

Consider a cost-based pricing formula that Astel could use. Assume that Astel's engineers have redesigned Provalue into Provalue II as described earlier and that Astel uses a 12% markup on the full unit cost of the product in developing the prospective selling price.

[4]Exceptions are pricing of electricity and gas in many countries, where prices are set on the basis of costs plus a return on invested capital. Chapter 14 discusses the use of costs to set prices in the defense-contracting industry. In these situations, where products are not subject to open market forces, cost accounting techniques form the basis for setting prices.

Achieving Target Costs Using Activity-Based Management at Carrier Corporation

Carrier Corporation, a subsidiary of United Technologies' Company, is the largest manufacturer of air-conditioning and heating products in the United States. Although known for the high quality of its products, Carrier operates in a highly competitive market, so it must also keep its prices comparatively low. Because keeping costs low is key to keeping prices low, Carrier establishes target costs for its products. It forms cross-functional teams drawn from the marketing, design, manufacturing, engineering, and accounting functions, and uses activity-based costing to evaluate and monitor its progress in achieving target costs.

Carrier has undertaken multiple initiatives to reach its target-costing goals, focused heavily on reducing the complexity of its operations.

1. *Product design.* Employing value-engineering techniques, Carrier's product design teams work with manufacturing to introduce product designs that use cost-effective manufacturing processes. For example, one new product at Carrier's McMinville plant required three design attempts before meeting its target cost. Designers had to reduce the number of parts required to make the product from 160 to 60, thereby reducing the costs of ordering, materials handling, coordination, and inspection.

2. *Just-in-time (JIT) production.* Carrier has implemented JIT production methods to reduce costs of materials and work-in-process inventories, as well as materials-handling costs.

3. *Parts standardization.* Carrier's parts standardization program aims to reduce the number of components and manufacturing processes. For example, the plant currently maintains 280 different circuit breakers and 580 different fasteners. Carrier's goal—to eliminate over 50% of these components. Carrier uses an activity-based costing system (with its distinctions of output-unit level, batch-level, product-sustaining and facility-sustaining costs) to estimate savings in direct and indirect costs from using a common component in place of three existing components.

4. *Strategic outsourcing.* Using activity-based costing data, Carrier evaluates components it should make internally and those it should outsource. For example, Carrier's decision to purchase prepainted sheet metal rather than paint the sheet metal itself reduced materials-handling, inspection, inventory holding, and environment costs and improved quality.

Source: Adapted from D. W. Swenson, "Managing Costs Through Complexity Reduction at Carrier Corporation," *Management Accounting* (April 1998): 20–28.

Cost base (full unit cost of the product, Exhibit 12-6)	$720.00
Markup component (12% × $720)	86.40
Prospective selling price	$806.40

New in This Edition This Concepts in Action box is new. It discusses how Carrier has reached its target costs using ABC and value engineering techniques.

How is the markup percentage of 12% determined? One approach is to choose a markup to earn a *target rate of return on investment.* The **target rate of return on investment** is the target annual operating income that an organization desires divided by invested capital. Invested capital can be defined in many ways. In this chapter, we define it as total assets (long-term assets plus current assets). Companies usually specify the target rate of return required on investments. Suppose Astel's (pretax) target rate of return on investment is 18 percent. Assume that the capital investment needed for Provalue II is $96 million. The target annual

Teaching Tip The following outline helps students see the big picture:

1. Market-based pricing
   a. Customer-driven external focus
   b. Used by companies facing stiff competition
   c. Target pricing, for example
2. Cost-based pricing
   a. Internal focus
   b. Used by companies facing less competition, or those whose products have no observable market value
   c. Cost-plus pricing, for example

Market-based pricing is becoming more popular as more companies adopt a customer-driven focus.

Curriculum Linkage This section on cost-plus pricing focuses on marking up costs to achieve a target ROI. ROI calculations are defined here, but students who have had a finance course should be familiar with them. Chap. 23 covers ROI in more depth.

Reinforcing Problems Exer. 12-22 and 12-23 and Probs. 12-28 through 12-30 cover cost-plus pricing.

operating income that Astel needs to earn from Provalue II can then be calculated as follows:

Invested capital	$96,000,000
Target rate of return on investment	18%
Target annual operating income (18% × $96,000,000)	$17,280,000
Target operating income per unit of Provalue II ($17,280,000 ÷ 200,000 units)	$86.40

This calculation indicates that Astel needs to earn a target operating income of $86.40 on each unit of Provalue II. What markup does the $86.40 represent? Expressed as a percentage of the full product cost per unit of $720, the markup is equal to 12% ($86.40 ÷ $720).

Do not confuse the 18% target rate of return on investment with the 12% markup percentage. The 18% target rate of return on investment expresses Astel's expected annual operating income as a percentage of investment. The 12% markup expresses operating income per unit as a percentage of the full product cost per unit. Astel first calculates the target rate of return on investment, and then determines the markup percentage.

Alternative Cost-Plus Methods

Companies sometimes find it difficult to determine the capital invested to support a product. Why? Because computing invested capital requires allocations of investments in equipment and buildings (used for design, production, marketing, distribution, and customer service) to individual products—a difficult and somewhat arbitrary task. Some companies therefore prefer to use alternative cost bases and markup percentages that still earn a return on invested capital but do not require explicit calculations of invested capital to set price.

We illustrate these alternatives using the Astel example. Exhibit 12-7 separates the cost per unit for each value-chain business function into its variable and fixed components (without providing details of the calculations). The following table illustrates some alternative cost bases using assumed markup percentages.

Cost Base	Estimated Cost Per Unit of Provalue II (1)	Markup Percentage (2)	Markup Component for Provalue II (3) = (1) × (2)	Prospective Selling Price for Provalue II (4) = (1) + (3)
Variable manufacturing costs	$483.00	65%	$313.95	$796.95
Variable costs of the product	547.00	45	246.15	793.15
Manufacturing function costs	540.00	50	270.00	810.00
Full costs of the product	720.00	12	86.40	806.40

The different cost bases and markup percentages give relatively close prospective selling prices. In practice, a company will choose a cost base that it regards as reliable, and a markup percentage based on its experience in pricing products to recover its costs and earn a desired return on investment. For example, a company may choose the full cost of the product as a base if it is unsure about variable- and fixed-cost distinctions.

The markup percentages in the table vary a great deal, from a high of 65% on variable manufacturing costs to a low of 12% on full costs of the product. Why? Because the cost bases that include less costs have a higher markup percentage to compensate for the costs excluded from the base. The precise markup percentage also depends on the nature of competition in the marketplace. Markups and profit margins tend to be lower in more competitive markets.

Surveys indicate that most managers use full costs of the product for their cost-based pricing decisions (see Surveys of Company Practice on p. 438)—that is, they include both fixed costs and variable costs when calculating the costs per unit.

EXHIBIT 12-7
Estimated Cost Structure of Provalue II for 2002

Business Function	Variable Cost Per Unit	Fixed Cost Per Unit[a]	Business Function Cost Per Unit
R&D	$ 8.00	$ 12.00	$ 20.00
Design of product/process	10.00	20.00	30.00
Manufacturing	483.00	57.00	540.00
Marketing	25.00	65.00	90.00
Distribution	15.00	10.00	25.00
Customer service	6.00	9.00	15.00
Full cost of the product	$547.00	$173.00	$720.00
	↑ Per unit variable cost of the product	↑ Per unit fixed cost of the product	↑ Per unit full cost of the product

[a]Based on budgeted annual production of 200,000 units.

Managers cite the following advantages for including fixed costs per unit in the cost base for pricing decisions:

1. *Full recovery of all costs of the product.* For long-run pricing decisions, full costs of the product inform managers of the minimum costs they need to recover to continue in business rather than shut down. Using variable costs as a base does not give managers this information. There is then a temptation to engage in excessive long-run price cutting as long as prices provide a positive contribution margin. Long-run price cutting, however, may result in losses if long-run revenues are less than long-run full costs of the product.

2. *Price stability.* Managers believe that basing prices on full costs of the product promotes price stability, because it limits the ability of salespersons to cut prices. Managers prefer price stability because it facilitates planning.

3. *Simplicity.* A full-cost formula for pricing does not require a detailed analysis of cost-behavior patterns to separate costs into fixed and variable components for each product. Calculating variable costs for each product is often expensive and prone to errors. Hence, many managers believe that full-cost plus pricing meets the cost-benefit test.

Including fixed costs per unit in the cost base for pricing is not without its problems. Allocating fixed costs to products can be somewhat arbitrary. Also, calculating fixed costs per unit requires a denominator that is often an estimate of capacity or expected units of future sales. Errors in these estimates will cause actual full costs per unit of the product to differ from the estimated amount.

Cost-Plus Pricing and Target Pricing

The selling prices computed under cost-plus pricing are *prospective* prices. For example, suppose Astel's initial product design results in a $750 cost for Provalue II. Assuming a 12% markup, Astel sets a prospective price of $840 [$750 + (12% × $750)]. Because the personal computer market is reasonably competitive, customer and competitor reactions to this price may force Astel to reduce the markup percentage and lower the price to, say, $800. Astel may then want to redesign Provalue II to reduce cost to $720 per unit, as in our example, thus achieving a reasonable markup while keeping the price at $800. The eventual design and cost-plus price chosen must balance the conflicting tensions among costs, markup, and customer reactions.

Differences in Pricing Practices and Cost Management Methods in Various Countries

Surveys of financial officers of the largest industrial companies in several countries indicate similarities and differences in pricing practices around the globe. The use of cost-based pricing appears to be more prevalent in the United States than in Ireland, Japan, and the United Kingdom. Some Japanese survey data indicate that market-based target pricing practices vary considerably among industries. While a majority of Japanese companies in assembly-type operations (for example, electronics and automobiles) use target costing for pricing, it is far less prevalent in Japanese process-type industries (for example, chemicals, oil, and steel).

Ranking of factors primarily used as a starting point to price products (1 is most important):

	United States	Japan	Ireland	United Kingdom
Market based	2	1	1	1
Cost based	1	2	2	2

Japanese companies use value engineering more frequently and involve designers more often when estimating costs.

Use of value engineering and designers in cost management:

	Australia	Japan	United Kingdom
Percentage of companies that use value engineering or analysis for cost reduction	24	58	29
Percentage of companies in which designers are involved in estimating costs	25	46	32

When costs are used for pricing decisions, the pattern is consistent—overwhelmingly, companies around the globe use full costs of the product rather than variable costs.

Ranking of cost methods used in pricing decisions (1 is most important):

	United States	United Kingdom	Ireland
Based on full cost of the product	1	1	1
Based on variable cost of the product	2	2	2

Source: Adapted from Management Accounting Research Group, "Investigation"; Blayney and Yokoyama, "Comparative Analysis"; Grant Thornton, "Survey"; Cornick, Cooper, and Wilson, "How Do Companies"; Mills and Sweeting, "Pricing Decisions"; and Drury, Braund, Osborne, and Tayles, "A Survey." Full citations are in Appendix A.

The target pricing approach reduces the need to go back and forth among prospective cost-plus prices, customer reactions, and design modifications. Instead, the target-pricing approach first determines product characteristics and target price on the basis of customer preferences and expected competitor responses. Market considerations and the target price then serve to focus and motivate managers to reduce costs ("cost down") and achieve the target cost and the target operating income. Sometimes the target cost is not achieved. Managers must then redesign the product, or work with a smaller profit margin.

Suppliers who provide relatively unique products and services—accountants and management consultants, for example—frequently use cost-plus pricing. Professional service firms set prices based on hourly cost-plus billing rates of partners, managers, and associates. These prices are, however, reduced in competitive situations. Professional service firms also consider a multiyear client perspective when deciding on prices. Certified public accountants, for example, sometimes charge a client a low price initially and a higher price later.

LIFE-CYCLE PRODUCT BUDGETING AND COSTING

As we have seen, companies sometimes need to consider how to cost and price a product over a multiyear product life cycle. The **product life cycle** spans the time from initial R&D on a product to when customer servicing and support is no longer offered for that product. For motor vehicles, this time span may range from 5 to 7 years. For some pharmaceutical products, the time span may be 7 to 10 years.

Using **life-cycle budgeting**, managers estimate the revenues and costs attributable to each product from its initial R&D to its final customer servicing and support. **Life-cycle costing** tracks and accumulates the individual value-chain costs attributable to each product from its initial R&D to its final customer servicing and support. The terms "cradle-to-grave costing" and "womb-to-tomb costing" convey the sense of fully capturing all costs associated with the product.

Life-Cycle Budgeting and Pricing Decisions

Budgeted life-cycle costs can provide important information for pricing decisions. Consider Insight, Inc., a computer software company, developing a new accounting package, "General Ledger." Assume the following budgeted amounts for General Ledger over a six-year product life cycle:

YEARS 1 AND 2

R&D costs	$240,000
Design costs	160,000

YEARS 3 TO 6

	One-Time Setup Costs	Costs Per Package
Production costs	$100,000	$25
Marketing costs	70,000	24
Distribution costs	50,000	16
Customer-service costs	80,000	30

To be profitable, Insight must generate revenues to cover costs of all six business functions taken together and, in particular, its high nonproduction costs. Exhibit 12-8 presents the life-cycle budget for General Ledger.

Several features make life-cycle budgeting particularly important:

1. Nonproduction costs are large. Production costs are often visible by product in most accounting systems. However, costs associated with R&D, design, marketing, distribution and customer service are less visible on a product-by-product basis. When nonproduction costs are significant, as in the General Ledger example, identifying these costs by product is essential for target pricing, target costing, value engineering, and cost management.

2. The development period for R&D and design is long and costly. In the General Ledger example, R&D and design span two years, and constitute over 30% of total costs for each of the three combinations of selling price and predicted sales quantity. When a high percentage of total life-cycle costs are incurred before any production begins and before any revenues are received, it is crucial for the company to have as accurate a set of revenue and cost predictions for the product as possible. This is important information for deciding whether the company should commence costly R&D and design activities.

3. Many of the costs predicted to be incurred over several years in production, marketing, distribution, and customer service are locked in at the R&D and design stages (even if the R&D and design costs themselves are small). In our

EXHIBIT 12-8
Budgeted Life-Cycle Revenues and Costs for "General Ledger" Software Package of Insight, Inc.[a]

	Alternative Selling Price/ Sales-Quantity Combinations		
	1	**2**	**3**
Selling price per package	$400	$480	$600
Sales quantity in units	5,000	4,000	2,500
Life-cycle revenues ($400 × 5,000; $480 × 4,000; $600 × 2,500)	$2,000,000	$1,920,000	$1,500,000
Life-cycle costs			
R&D costs	240,000	240,000	240,000
Design costs of product/process	160,000	160,000	160,000
Production costs $100,000 + ($25 × 5,000); $100,000 + ($25 × 4,000); $100,000 + ($25 × 2,500)	225,000	200,000	162,500
Marketing costs $70,000 + ($24 × 5,000); $70,000 + ($24 × 4,000); $70,000 + ($24 × 2,500)	190,000	166,000	130,000
Distribution costs $50,000 + ($16 × 5,000); $50,000 + ($16 × 4,000); $50,000 + ($16 × 2,500)	130,000	114,000	90,000
Customer-service costs $80,000 + ($30 × 5,000); $80,000 + ($30 × 4,000); $80,000 + ($30 × 2,500)	230,000	200,000	155,000
Total life-cycle costs	1,175,000	1,080,000	937,500
Life-cycle operating income	$ 825,000	$ 840,000	$ 562,500

[a]This exhibit does not take into consideration the time value of money when computing life-cycle revenues or life-cycle costs. Chapter 21 outlines how this important factor can be incorporated into such calculations.

Points to Stress Emphasize that GAAP stipulates that pre- and post-production costs must be expensed in the period incurred. If a company uses life-cycle costing, it must therefore do so in addition to regular GAAP reporting.

Points to Stress At the beginning of the life cycle, it's difficult to determine how successful a product will be. Hence, the earlier in a product's life cycle that costs are locked in (i.e., before there is much info. on the probability that the product will succeed), the riskier the product.

General Ledger example, a poorly designed package that is difficult to install and use would result in higher marketing, distribution, and customer-service costs. If the product fails to meet promised quality-performance levels, the costs of marketing, distribution, and customer service would be even higher. A life-cycle revenue and cost budget prevents these causal relationships among business function costs from being overlooked in decision-making. Life-cycle budgeting facilitates value engineering at the design stage before costs are locked in. In fact, the amounts presented in Exhibit 12-8 are the outcome of value engineering.

Insight decides to sell the General Ledger package for $480 because this price maximizes life-cycle operating income. Exhibit 12-8 assumes that the selling price per package is the same over the entire life cycle. For strategic reasons, however, Insight may decide to skim the market—by charging higher prices to customers eager to try General Ledger when it first comes out, and lowering prices later. The life-cycle budget will then incorporate this strategy.

Most accounting systems, including financial statements issued under generally accepted accounting principles (GAAP), emphasize reporting on a calendar basis—monthly, quarterly, and annually. In contrast, product life-cycle reporting does not have this calendar-based focus because products often have life cycles spanning several years. Developing life-cycle reports for each of a company's products requires tracking costs and revenues on a product-by-product basis over several calendar periods. For example, the R&D costs included in a product life-cycle cost report are often incurred in different years. When R&D and other business-function costs are tracked over the entire life cycle, the total magnitude of these costs for each individual product can be computed and analyzed. Comparing actual costs incurred to life-cycle budgets provides feedback and learning that can then be applied to subsequent products.

Uses of Life-Cycle Budgeting and Costing

Life-cycle budgeting is related closely to target pricing and target costing. Consider the automobile industry. Products have long life cycles, and a very large fraction of the total life-cycle costs are actually locked in at the design stage. Design decisions affect costs over several years. Companies such as Daimler-Chrysler, Ford, General Motors, Nissan, and Toyota determine target prices and target costs for their car models using life-cycle budgets that estimate costs and revenues over a multiyear horizon.

Management of environmental costs provides another example of life-cycle costing and value engineering. The enactment of strict environmental laws (for example, the U.S. Clean Air Act and the U.S. Superfund Amendment and Reauthorization Act) has introduced tougher environmental standards and has increased the penalties and fines for polluting the air and contaminating subsurface soil and groundwater. Environmental costs are often locked in at the product and process design stage. To avoid these environmental liabilities, companies do value engineering and design products and processes to prevent and reduce pollution over the product's life cycle. Laptop computer manufacturers (for example, Compaq and Apple) have introduced costly recycling programs to ensure that nickel-cadmium batteries are disposed of in an environmentally safe way at the end of the product's life.

A different notion of life-cycle costs is customer life-cycle costs. **Customer life-cycle costs** focus on the total costs incurred by a customer to acquire and use a product or service until it is replaced. Customer life-cycle costs for a car, for example, include the cost of the car itself plus the costs of operating and maintaining the car minus the disposal price of the car. Customer life-cycle costs can be an important consideration in the pricing decision. For example, Ford's goal is to design cars that require minimal maintenance for 100,000 miles. Ford expects to charge a higher price and/or gain greater market share by selling these cars. Similarly, manufacturers of washing machines, dryers, and dishwashers charge higher prices for models that save electricity and have low maintenance costs.

CONSIDERATIONS OTHER THAN COSTS IN PRICING DECISIONS

In some cases, cost is not a major factor in setting prices. Consider the prices airlines charge for a round-trip flight from San Francisco to Chicago. A coach-class ticket for the flight with a 21-day advance purchase is $350 if the passenger stays in Chicago over a Saturday night. It is $1,600 if the passenger returns without staying over a Saturday night. Can this price difference be explained by the difference in the cost to the airline of these round-trip flights? No, it costs the airline the same amount to transport the passenger from San Francisco to Chicago and back regardless of whether the passenger stays in Chicago over a Saturday night. How then can we explain this difference in price? We must recognize the potential for price discrimination.

Price discrimination is the practice of charging some customers a higher price for the same product or service than is charged other customers. How does price discrimination work in our airline example? The demand for airline tickets comes from two main sources: business travelers and pleasure travelers. Business travelers must travel to conduct business for their companies. Consequently, business travelers' demand for air travel is relatively insensitive to price. The insensitivity of demand to price changes is called *demand inelasticity*. Airlines can earn higher operating income by charging business travelers higher prices because the higher prices have little effect on demand. Also, business travelers generally travel to their destinations and return home within the same week immediately after completing their work.

Pleasure travelers have a less pressing need to return home during the week — in fact, they generally prefer to spend weekends at their destinations. Because they pay for their tickets themselves, they are much more sensitive to price than are

Example Hewlett-Packard has a substantial share of the computer printer market. To maintain their market share, they "cut short" a printer's product life by bringing a newer version to market while the "old" version still has substantial market share. Why do they "cannibalize" their own products? Because, in the computer industry, being first to market is so important in gaining market share that they are willing to cannibalize a good product so that their next generation printer can be first to market.

OBJECTIVE 7

Describe two pricing practices in which non-cost factors are important when setting price

Reinforcing Problems Exer. 12-25 and Probs. 12-27 and 12-31 cover peak time pricing.

Example Another consideration beyond cost for pricing decisions is *low-balling*. In order to attract new clients, public acctg. firms often deliberately bid less than their expected full cost on initial audits (i.e., low-balling). They do this in anticipation that profits from future audits will more than make up for the shortfall.

Example For the 1996 Olympics in Atlanta, hotels initially charged very high rates and required multiday stays. Airlines also charged high fares for flights into or out of many cities in the Southeast for roughly a month around the Games. Given that demand was expected to far exceed capacity, the hospitality industry and airlines employed peak-load pricing to increase their profits.

Curriculum Linkage Have the students go back to Chap. 11 and review the Concepts in Action box which discussed American Airlines' Internet pricing of seats on flights with excess capacity. This is a good example of price discrimination and non-peak-load pricing.

business travelers (demand is more price-elastic). It is profitable for the airlines to keep fares low to stimulate demand among pleasure travelers.

How can airlines keep fares high for business travelers while, at the same time, keeping fares low for pleasure travelers? Requiring a Saturday night stay distinguishes between the two customer segments. The airline company price-discriminates to take advantage of the different sensitivities to prices exhibited by the business and pleasure travelers. Price differences exist even though there is no cost difference in serving the two segments.

In addition to price discrimination, pricing decisions also consider other non-cost considerations such as capacity constraints. **Peak-load pricing** is the practice of charging a higher price for the same product or service when demand approaches physical capacity limits. That is, prices charged during busy periods (when loads on the system are high) represent what competing customers are willing to pay. These prices are greater than the prices charged when slack or excess capacity is available. Peak-load pricing occurs in the telephone, telecommunications, hotel, car rental, and electric utility industries. The following are the daily rental rates charged by the Avis Corporation in April 1999 for mid-sized cars rented at the Detroit Metropolitan Airport:

Weekdays (Monday through Thursday)	$69 per day
Weekends (Friday through Sunday)	$22 per day

Avis's incremental costs of renting a car are the same whether the car is rented on a weekday or a weekend. Why the difference in prices? One explanation is that there is a greater demand for cars on weekdays because of business activity. Faced with capacity limits, Avis charges peak-load prices at levels that the market will bear.

A second explanation is that the rental rates are a form of price discrimination. On weekdays, the demand for cars comes largely from business travelers who need to rent cars to conduct their business and who are relatively insensitive to prices. Charging higher rental rates on weekdays is profitable because it has little effect on demand. In contrast, the demand for weekend rentals comes largely from pleasure travelers who are more price-sensitive. Lower rates stimulate demand from these individuals and increase Avis's operating income. Under either explanation, the pricing decision is not driven by cost considerations.

Another example of when considerations other than costs affect prices significantly is when the same product is sold in different countries. Consider, for example, products such as software, books, and medicines that are produced in one country and sold globally. The price charged in each country varies much more than the costs of delivering the product to each country. These price differences arise because of differences in the purchasing power of consumers in different countries and government restrictions that may limit the prices that can be charged. Within the regulations that different governments impose, companies price products to the maximum levels that buyers in different countries are willing to pay.

EFFECTS OF ANTITRUST LAWS ON PRICING

OBJECTIVE 8

Explain the effects of antitrust laws on pricing

Legal considerations are important in pricing decisions. Companies are not always free to charge whatever they like. For example, under the U.S. Robinson-Patman Act, a manufacturer cannot price-discriminate between two customers if the intent is to lessen or prevent competition for customers. Three key features of the price discrimination laws are (1) they apply to manufacturers, not service providers; (2) price discrimination is permissible if differences in prices can be justified by differences in costs; and (3) price discrimination is illegal only if the intent is to destroy competition. The price discrimination by airlines and car rental companies described earlier is legal both because these companies are service companies and because their practices do not hinder competition.

To comply with U.S. antitrust laws, such as the Sherman Act, the Clayton Act, the Federal Trade Commission Act, and the Robinson-Patman Act, pricing must not be predatory.[5] A company engages in **predatory pricing** when it deliberately prices below its costs in an effort to drive out competitors and restrict supply, and then raises prices rather than enlarge demand.[6]

The U.S. Supreme Court has established the following conditions to prove that predatory pricing has occurred: (1) The predator company charges a price that is below an appropriate measure of its costs, and (2) the predator company has a reasonable prospect of recovering in the future (through larger market share or higher prices) the money it lost by pricing below cost. The Supreme Court has not specified the "appropriate measure of costs."[7]

Most courts in the United States have defined the "appropriate measure of costs" as the short-run marginal and average variable costs.[8] In *Adjustor's Replace-a-Car v. Agency Rent-a-Car*,[9] Adjuster's (the plaintiff) claimed that it was forced to withdraw from the Austin and San Antonio, Texas, markets because Agency had engaged in predatory pricing. To prove predatory pricing, Adjuster pointed to "the net loss from operations" in Agency's income statement, calculated after allocating Agency's headquarters overhead. The judge, however, ruled that Agency had not engaged in predatory pricing because the price it charged for a rental car never dropped below its average variable costs.

It would be wise for companies that have concerns about their conformance to antitrust laws to have an accounting system that incorporates the following procedures:

1. Collect data and keep detailed records of variable costs for all value-chain business functions.

2. Review all proposed prices below variable costs in advance, with a presumption that claims of predatory intent will occur.

The Supreme Court decision in *Brooke Group v. Brown & Williamson Tobacco* (BWT) increased the difficulty of proving predatory pricing. The Court ruled that pricing below average variable costs is not predatory if the company does not have a reasonable chance of later increasing prices or market share to recover its losses.[10] The defendant, BWT, a cigarette manufacturer, sold "brand name" cigarettes and had 12% of the cigarette market. The introduction of generic cigarettes threatened BWT's market share. BWT responded by introducing its own version of generics priced below average variable cost, thereby making it difficult for generic manufacturers to continue in business. The Supreme Court ruled that BWT's action was a competitive response and not predatory pricing. Why? Because, given BWT's current small (12%) market share and the existing competition within the industry, it would be unable to later charge a monopoly price to recoup its losses.

Closely related to predatory pricing is dumping. Under U.S. laws, **dumping** occurs when a non-U.S. company sells a product in the United States at a price below the market value in the country of its creation, and this action materially injures

Points to Stress This section on predatory pricing covers recent Supreme Court rulings. To be proven guilty of predatory pricing, the predator company must (1) charge a price that's below an "appropriate measure of its costs," and (2) have a reasonable prospect of recovering in the future the money it lost when it priced below cost. This second condition represents a recent change that makes it harder to prove predatory pricing claims.

Teaching Tip Accusing foreign producers of dumping product in domestic markets are a way for domestic manufacturers to restrict access by foreign producers to domestic markets and not violate trade agreements. Accountants need to understand and be ready to supply the data needed for a company to defend itself against dumping charges. An interesting case is "Cemex and Antidumping," Graduate School of Business, Stanford University case, S-P-4, 1994.

---

[5]Discussion of the Sherman Act and the Clayton Act is in A. Barkman and J. Jolley, "Cost Defenses for Antitrust Cases," *Management Accounting* 67 (no. 10): 37–40.

[6]For more details, see W. Viscusi, J. Vernon, and J. Harrington, *Economics of Regulation and Antitrust*, 2nd ed. (Cambridge, Mass: MIT Press, 1995); and J. L. Goldstein, "Single Firm Predatory Pricing in Antitrust Law: The Rose Acre Recoupment Test and the Search for an Appropriate Judicial Standard," *Columbia Law Review* 91 (1991): 1557–1592.

[7]*Brooke Group v. Brown & Williamson Tobacco*, 113 S. Ct. (1993); T. J. Trujillo, "Predatory Pricing Standards Under Recent Supreme Court Decisions and Their Failure to Recognize Strategic Behavior as a Barrier to Entry," *Iowa Journal of Corporation Law* (Summer 1994): 809–831.

[8]An exception is *McGahee v. Northern Propane Gas Co.* [858 F, 2d 1487 (1988)] where the Eleventh Circuit Court held that prices below average total cost constitute evidence of predatory intent. For more discussion, see P. Areeda and D. Turner, "Predatory Pricing and Related Practices under Section 2 of Sherman Act", *Harvard Law Review* 88 (1975): 697–733. For an overview of case law, see W. Viscusi, J. Vernon, and J. Harrington, *Economics of Regulation and Antitrust*. 2nd ed. (Cambridge, Mass: MIT Press, 1995). See also the "Legal Developments" section of the *Journal of Marketing* for summaries of court cases.

[9]*Adjustor's Replace-a-Car, Inc. v. Agency Rent-a-Car*, 735 2d 884 (1984).

[10]*Brooke Group v. Brown & Williamson Tobacco*, 113 S. Ct. (1993).

or threatens to materially injure an industry in the United States. If dumping is proven, an antidumping duty can be imposed under U.S. tariff laws equal to the amount by which the foreign price exceeds the U.S. price. Cases related to dumping have occurred in the cement, computer, steel, semiconductor, and sweater industries. For example, in 1998, in response to charges filed by Micron Technology, the U.S. International Trade Commission ruled that several Taiwan companies had dumped static random access memory (SRAM) computer chips in the U.S. market. The Commission levied antidumping tariffs ranging from 7.59% to 113.85% on the prices charged by these companies.[11]

Another violation of antitrust laws is collusive pricing. **Collusive pricing** occurs when companies in an industry conspire in their pricing and output decisions to achieve a price above the competitive price. Collusive pricing violates the antitrust laws of the United States because it restrains trade. In 1990, for example, the Justice Department charged that the use of a common computer reservation system enabled airlines to collude on maintaining noncompetitive prices. The airlines involved—American, Continental, Delta, Midway, Northwest, PanAm, TWA, United, and USAir—have reimbursed customers under the terms of the settlement. In 1996, the Justice Department settled a suit with 35 securities firms, including Kidder Peabody and Herzog, Heine & Geduld, charged with inflating prices and profits from trading shares on the Nasdaq stock market.

PROBLEM FOR SELF-STUDY

PROBLEM

Reconsider the Astel Computer example described earlier (pp. 431–434). Astel's marketing manager realizes that a further reduction in price is necessary to sell 200,000 units of Provalue II. To maintain a target profitability of $16 million, or $80 per unit on Provalue II (the same amounts shown in Exhibit 12-6), Astel will need to reduce costs of Provalue II by $6 million or $30 per unit. The new version is called Modified Provalue II. Astel targets a reduction of $4 million or $20 per unit in manufacturing costs, and the other $2 million or $10 per unit in marketing, distribution, and customer-service costs. The cross-functional team assigned to this task proposes the following changes to manufacture Modified Provalue II:

1. Purchase more subassembled components that combine the functions performed by individual components. This change will not affect Modified Provalue II's quality or performance but will reduce direct materials costs from $385 to $375 per unit.

2. Reengineer processes to reduce ordering and receiving costs per order from $80 to $60. Using component subassemblies will reduce the number of purchased components in Modified Provalue II from 425 to 400. As in the chapter example, Astel will place 50 orders per year for each component.

3. Reduce the labor and power required per hour of testing. This will decrease testing and inspection costs for Modified Provalue II from $2 to $1.70 per testing-hour. Under the new proposal, each Modified Provalue II will be tested for 14 hours rather than 15 hours.

4. Develop new rework procedures that will reduce the rework costs from $40 per hour to $32 per hour. It is expected that 13,000 units (6.5% of 200,000) of Modified Provalue II will be reworked and that it will take 2.5 hours to rework each unit.

No changes are proposed in direct manufacturing labor costs per unit and in total machining costs.

Required

Will the proposed changes achieve Astel's targeted reduction of $4 million (or $20 per unit) in manufacturing costs? Show your computations.

[11]"Duties Placed on Taiwan Chips," *The Washington Post* (April 2, 1998): C2.

SOLUTION

Exhibit 12-9 presents the manufacturing costs for Modified Provalue II. The proposed changes will reduce manufacturing costs from $108 million or $540 per unit (Exhibit 12-5) to $104 million or $520 per unit (Exhibit 12-9), and will thus achieve the target reduction of $4 million or $20 per unit.

EXHIBIT 12-9
Target Manufacturing Costs of Modified Provalue II for 2002

	Estimated Manufacturing Costs for 200,000 Units (1)	Estimated Manufacturing Cost Per Unit (2) = (1) ÷ 200,000
Direct manufacturing costs		
Direct materials costs (200,000 units × $375)	$ 75,000,000	$375.00
Direct manufacturing labor costs (530,000 labor-hours × $20)	10,600,000	53.00
Direct machining costs (300,000 machine-hours × $38)	11,400,000	57.00
Direct manufacturing costs	97,000,000	485.00
Indirect manufacturing costs		
Ordering and receiving costs (20,000[a] orders × $60)	1,200,000	6.00
Testing and inspection costs (2,800,000[b] hours × $1.70)	4,760,000	23.80
Rework costs (32,500[c] hours × $32)	1,040,000	5.20
Indirect manufacturing costs	7,000,000	35.00
Total manufacturing costs	$104,000,000	$520.00

[a]400 components × 50 orders per component = 20,000 orders.
[b]200,000 units × 14 testing-hours per unit = 2,800,000 testing-hours.
[c]13,000 units × 2.5 rework-hours per unit = 32,500 rework-hours.

SUMMARY

The following points are linked to the chapter's learning objectives:

1. Three major influences on pricing decisions are customers, competitors, and costs.

2. Short-run pricing decisions focus on a period of less than a year and have no long-run implications. Long-run pricing decisions focus on a product with a time horizon of a year or longer. The time horizon appropriate to a decision on pricing dictates which costs are relevant, how costs can be managed, and the profits that need to be earned.

3. One approach to long-run pricing is to use a target price. Target price is the estimated price that potential customers are willing to pay for a product (or service). A target operating income per unit is subtracted from the target price to determine the target cost per unit. The target cost per unit is the estimated long-run cost of a product (or service) that when sold enables the company to achieve the target operating income per unit. The challenge for the organization is to make the cost improvements necessary through value-engineering methods to achieve the target cost.

4. Cost incurrence arises when resources are actually sacrificed or used up. Locked-in costs are those costs that have not yet been incurred but which, based on decisions that have already been made, will be incurred in the future. Value engineering is only effective in reducing costs if it is focused on the design stage before costs are locked in.

5. The cost-plus approach to pricing uses a general formula that adds a markup component to a cost base as the starting point for pricing decisions. Many different costs (such as full costs of the product or manufacturing costs) can serve as the cost base in applying the cost-plus formula. Prices are then modified on the basis of customers' reactions and competitors' responses. Therefore, the size of the "plus" is determined by the market.

6. Life-cycle budgeting and life-cycle costing estimate, track, and accumulate the costs (and revenues) attributable to each product from its initial R&D to its final customer servicing and support. Life-cycle budgeting and costing are particularly important when (a) nonproduction costs are large; (b) a high percentage of total life-cycle costs are incurred before production begins and before any revenues are received; and (c) many of the life-cycle costs are locked in at the R&D and design stages. Companies choose prices to maximize the operating incomes earned over a product's life cycle.

7. Price discrimination is the practice of charging some customers a higher price for a given product or service than is charged to other customers. Peak-load pricing is the practice of charging a higher price for the same product or service when demand approaches physical capacity limits. Under price discrimination and peak-load pricing, prices differ among market segments even though the costs of providing the product or service are approximately the same.

8. To comply with antitrust laws, a company must not engage in predatory pricing, dumping, or collusive pricing, which lessens competition or puts another company at a competitive disadvantage.

TERMS TO LEARN

This chapter and the Glossary at the end of the book contain definitions of the following important terms:

collusive pricing (p. 444)	predatory pricing (443)
cost incurrence (430)	price discrimination (441)
customer life-cycle costs (441)	product life cycle (439)
designed-in costs (430)	target cost per unit (428)
dumping (443)	target operating income per unit (428)
life-cycle budgeting (439)	target price (428)
life-cycle costing (439)	target rate of return on investment (435)
locked-in costs (430)	value-added cost (429)
nonvalue-added cost (429)	value engineering (429)
peak-load pricing (442)	

ASSIGNMENT MATERIAL

QUESTIONS

12-1 What are the three major influences on pricing decisions?

12-2 "The relevant costs for pricing decisions are the full costs of the product." Do you agree? Explain.

12-3 Give two examples of pricing decisions with a short-run focus.

12-4 How is activity-based costing useful for pricing decisions?

12-5 Describe two alternative approaches to long-run pricing decisions.

12-6 What is a target cost per unit?

12-7 Describe value engineering and its role in target costing.

12-8 Give two examples each of a value-added cost and a nonvalue-added cost.

12-9 "It is not important for a company to distinguish between cost incurrence and locked-in costs." Do you agree? Explain.

12-10 What is cost-plus pricing?

12-11 Describe three alternative cost-plus pricing methods.

12-12 Give two examples where the difference in the costs of two products or services is much smaller than the difference in their prices.

12-13 What is life-cycle budgeting?

12-14 What are three benefits of using a product life-cycle reporting format?

12-15 Define predatory pricing, dumping, and collusive pricing.

EXERCISES

12-16 Relevant-cost approach to pricing decisions, special order. The following financial data apply to the videotape production plant of the Dill Company for October 2000:

	Budgeted Manufacturing Costs Per Video Tape
Direct materials	$1.50
Direct manufacturing labor	0.80
Variable manufacturing overhead	0.70
Fixed manufacturing overhead	1.00
Total manufacturing costs	$4.00

Variable manufacturing overhead varies with the number of units produced. Fixed manufacturing overhead of $1 per tape is based on budgeted fixed manufacturing overhead of $150,000 per month and budgeted production of 150,000 tapes per month. The Dill Company sells each tape for $5.

Marketing costs have two components:

◆ Variable marketing costs (sales commissions) of 5% of revenues
◆ Fixed monthly costs of $65,000

During October 2000, Lyn Randell, a Dill Company salesperson, asked the president for permission to sell 1,000 tapes at $3.80 per tape to a customer not in its normal marketing channels. The president refused this special order on the grounds that the order would show a loss because the selling price was below the total budgeted manufacturing cost.

Required
1. What would have been the effect on monthly operating income of accepting the special order?
2. Comment on the president's "below manufacturing costs" reasoning for rejecting the special order.
3. What factors do you recommend that the president consider when deciding whether to accept or reject the special order?

12-17 Relevant-cost approach to short-run pricing decisions. The San Carlos Company is an electronics business with eight product lines. Income data for one of the products (XT-107) for the month just ended (June 2001) are as follows:

Revenues, 200,000 units at an average price of $100		$20,000,000
Variable costs		
Direct materials at $35 per unit	$7,000,000	
Direct manufacturing labor at $10 per unit	2,000,000	
Variable manufacturing overhead at $5 per unit	1,000,000	
Sales commissions at 15% of revenues	3,000,000	
Other variable costs at $5 per unit	1,000,000	
Total variable costs		14,000,000
Contribution margin		6,000,000
Fixed costs		5,000,000
Operating income		$ 1,000,000

Abrams, Inc., an instruments company, has a problem with its preferred supplier of XT-107 components. This supplier has had a three-week labor strike and will not be able to supply Abrams 3,000 units next month. Abrams approaches the sales representative, Sarah Holtz, of the San Carlos Company about providing 3,000 units of XT-107 at a price of $80 per unit. Holtz informs the XT-107 product manager, Jim McMahon, that she would accept a flat commission of $6,000 rather than the usual 15% of revenues if this special order were accepted. San Carlos has the capacity to produce 300,000 units of XT-107 each month, but demand has not exceeded 200,000 units in any month in the last year.

Required

1. If the 3,000-unit order from Abrams is accepted, how much will operating income increase or decrease? (Assume the same cost structure that existed in June 2001.)
2. McMahon ponders whether to accept the 3,000-unit special order. He is afraid of the precedent that might be set by cutting the price. He says, "The price is below our full cost of $95 per unit. I think we should quote a full price, or Abrams will expect favored treatment again and again if we continue to do business with them." Do you agree with McMahon? Explain.

12-18 Short-run pricing, capacity constraints. Boutique Chemicals makes a specialized chemical product, Bolzene, from a specially imported material, Pyrone. To make 1 kilogram of Bolzene requires 1.5 kilograms of Pyrone. Bolzene has a contribution margin of $6 per kilogram. Boutique has just received a request to manufacture 3,000 kilograms of Seltium that also requires Pyrone as the material input. An analyst at Boutique calculates the following costs of making 1 kilogram of Seltium:

Pyrone (2 kilograms × $4 per kilogram)	$ 8
Direct manufacturing labor	4
Variable manufacturing overhead costs	3
Fixed manufacturing overhead costs allocated	5
Total manufacturing costs	$20

Boutique has adequate unused plant capacity to make Seltium.

Required

1. Suppose Boutique has adequate Pyrone available to make Seltium. What is the minimum price per kilogram that Boutique should charge to manufacture Seltium?
2. Now suppose Pyrone is in short supply. The Pyrone used to make Seltium will reduce the Bolzene that Boutique can make and sell. What is the minimum price per kilogram that Boutique should charge to manufacture Seltium?

12-19 Value-added, nonvalue-added costs. The Marino Repair Shop repairs and services machine tools. A summary of its costs (by activity) for 2001 is as follows:

a. Materials and labor for servicing machine tools $800,000
b. Rework costs   75,000
c. Expediting costs caused by work delays   60,000
d. Materials-handling costs   50,000
e. Materials procurement and inspection costs   35,000
f. Preventive maintenance of equipment 15,000
g. Breakdown maintenance of equipment 55,000

Required

1. Classify each cost as value-added, nonvalue-added, or in the gray area in between.
2. For any cost classified in the gray area, assume 65% of it is value-added and 35% is nonvalue-added. How much of the total of all seven costs is value-added and how much is nonvalue-added?
3. Marino is considering the following changes at the shop: (a) introducing quality improvement programs whose net effect will be to reduce rework and expediting costs by 75% and materials and labor costs for servicing machine tools by 5%; (b) working with suppliers to reduce materials procurement and inspection costs by 20% and materials-handling costs by 25%; and (c) increasing preventive maintenance costs by 50%

to reduce breakdown maintenance costs by 40 percent. What effect would each of the programs (a), (b), and (c) have on value-added costs, nonvalue-added costs, and total costs? Comment briefly.

12-20 Target operating income, value-added costs, service company. Carasco Associates, a small structural design firm, prepares architectural drawings for various clients to ensure the structural safety of buildings. The architectural plans are then submitted to local government departments for approval. Carasco's income statement for 2001 follows:

Revenues	$680,000
Salaries of professional staff (8,000 hours × $50 per hour)	400,000
Travel	18,000
Administration and support	160,000
Total costs	578,000
Operating income	$102,000

An analysis of the percentage of time spent by professional staff on various activities gives this data:

Doing calculations and preparing drawings for clients	75%
Checking calculations and drawings	4
Correcting errors found in drawings (not billed to clients)	7
Making changes in response to client requests (billed to clients)	6
Correcting errors to meet government building code requirements (not billed to clients)	8
Total	100%

Assume administration and support costs vary with professional labor costs.

Required

Consider each requirement independently. There is no connection between the requirements.

1. How much of the total costs in 2001 are value-added, nonvalue-added, or in the gray area in between? Explain your answers briefly. What actions can Carasco take to reduce its costs?

2. Suppose Carasco continued to check all calculations and drawings but could eliminate all errors so that it did not need to spend any time making corrections and, as a result, could proportionately reduce professional labor costs. Calculate Carasco's operating income.

3. Now suppose Carasco could take on as much business as it could get done, but it could not add more professional staff. Assume, as in requirement 2, that Carasco could eliminate all errors so that it does not need to spend any time making corrections. Suppose Carasco could use the time saved to increase revenues proportionately. Assume travel costs will remain at $18,000. Calculate Carasco's operating income.

12-21 Target prices, target costs, activity-based costing. Snappy Tiles is a small distributor of marble tiles. Snappy identifies its three major activities and cost pools as ordering, receiving and storage, and shipping, and reports the following details for 2000:

Activity	Cost Driver	Quantity of Cost Driver	Cost Per Unit of Cost Driver
1. Placing and paying for orders of marble tiles	Number of orders	500	$50 per order
2. Receiving and storage	Loads moved	4,000	$30 per load
3. Shipping of marble tiles to retailers	Number of shipments	1,500	$40 per shipment

Snappy buys 250,000 marble tiles at an average cost of $3 per tile and sells them to retailers at an average price of $4 per tile. Assume Snappy has no fixed costs.

Required

1. Calculate Snappy's operating income for 2000.
2. For 2001, retailers are demanding a 5% discount off the 2000 price. Snappy's suppliers are only willing to give a 4% discount. Snappy expects to sell the same quantity of marble tiles in 2001 as it did in 2000. If all other costs and cost driver information remain the same, calculate Snappy's operating income for 2001.
3. Suppose further that Snappy decides to make changes in its ordering, and receiving and storing practices. By placing long-run orders with its key suppliers, Snappy expects to reduce the number of orders to 200 and the cost per order to $25 per order. By redesigning the layout of the warehouse and reconfiguring the crates in which the marble tiles are moved, Snappy expects to reduce the number of loads moved to 3,125 and the cost per load moved to $28. Will Snappy achieve its target operating income of $0.30 per tile in 2001? Show your calculations.

 12-22 Cost-plus target return on investment pricing. John Beck is the managing partner of a business that has just finished building a 60-room motel. Beck anticipates that he will rent these rooms for 16,000 nights next year (or 16,000 room-nights). All rooms are similar and will rent for the same price. Beck estimates the following operating costs for next year:

Variable-operating costs	$3 per room-night
Fixed costs	
Salaries and wages	$175,000
Maintenance of building and pool	37,000
Other operating and administration costs	140,000
Total fixed costs	$352,000

The capital invested in the motel is $960,000. The partnership's target return on investment is 25 percent. Beck expects demand for rooms to be about uniform throughout the year. He plans to price the rooms at cost plus a markup to earn the target return on investment.

Required

1. What price should Beck charge for a room-night? What is the markup as a percentage of the full cost of a room-night?
2. Beck's market research indicates that if the price of a room-night determined in requirement 1 is reduced by 10%, the expected number of room-nights Beck could rent would increase by 10 percent. Should Beck reduce prices by 10 percent? Show your calculations.

12-23 Cost-plus and target pricing. (S. Sridhar, adapted) Waterford, Inc., manufactures and sells 15,000 units of a raft, RF17, in 2001. The full cost per unit is $200. Waterford earns a 20% return on an investment of $1,800,000 in 2001.

Required

1. Calculate the selling price of RF17 in 2001. Calculate the markup percentage on the full cost per unit of RF17 in 2001.
2. If the selling price in requirement 1 represents a markup percentage of 40% on variable costs per unit, calculate the variable cost per unit of RF17 in 2001.
3. Calculate Waterford's operating income if it had increased the selling price to $230. At this price Waterford would have sold 13,500 units of RF17. Assume no change in total fixed costs. Should Waterford have increased the selling price of RF17 to $230?
4. In response to competitive pressures, Waterford must reduce the price of RF17 to $210 in 2002, in order to achieve sales of 15,000 units. Waterford plans to reduce its investment to $1,650,000. If Waterford wants to maintain a 20% return on investment, what is the target cost per unit in 2002?

12-24 Target costs, effect of product-design changes on product costs. Medical Instruments manufactures many products. To compute manufacturing costs, it uses a costing system with one direct-cost category (direct materials) and three indirect-cost categories:

a. Batch-related setup, production order, and materials-handling costs, all of which vary with the number of batches.

b. Manufacturing operations costs that vary with machine-hours.

c. Costs of engineering changes that vary with the number of engineering changes made.

In response to competitive pressures at the end of 2000, product designers at Medical Instruments employed value engineering techniques to reduce manufacturing costs. Actual information for 2000 and 2001 follow:

	Actual Results for 2000	Actual Results for 2001
Total setup, production-order, and materials-handling costs	$7,200,000	$7,500,000
Total number of batches	900	1,000
Total manufacturing operations costs	$12,100,000	$12,500,000
Total number of machine-hours worked	220,000	250,000
Total costs of engineering changes	$2,640,000	$2,000,000
Total number of engineering changes made	220	200

The management of Medical Instruments wants to evaluate whether value engineering has succeeded in reducing the target manufacturing cost per unit of one of its products, HJ6, by 12%. Actual results for 2000 and 2001 for HJ6 are:

	Actual Results for 2000	Actual Results for 2001
Units of HJ6 produced	3,500	4,000
Direct materials costs per unit of HJ6	$1,200	$1,100
Total number of batches required to produce HJ6	70	80
Total machine-hours required to produce HJ6	21,000	22,000
Number of engineering changes made	14	10

Required
1. Calculate the manufacturing cost per unit of HJ6 in 2000.
2. Calculate the manufacturing cost per unit of HJ6 in 2001.
3. Did Medical Instruments achieve the target manufacturing cost per unit for HJ6 in 2001? Show your calculations.
4. Comment briefly on how Medical Instruments was able to reduce the manufacturing cost per unit of HJ6 in 2001.

12-25 Considerations other than cost in pricing. Examples of prices charged per minute by AT&T for long-distance telephone calls within the United States at different times of the day and week are as follows:

	Washington, D.C. to Philadelphia	Washington, D.C. to St. Louis	Washington, D.C. to Los Angeles
Peak period (7 A.M. to 7 P.M., Monday through Friday)	$0.28	$0.28	$0.28
Evenings (7 P.M. to 7 A.M., Monday through Friday)	$0.16	$0.16	$0.16
Weekends	$0.12	$0.12	$0.12

Required
1. Are there differences in incremental costs per minute for AT&T for telephone calls made during peak hours compared to telephone calls made at other times of the day?
2. Why do you think AT&T charges different prices per minute for telephone calls made during peak hours compared to telephone calls made at other times of the day?

12-26 Life-cycle product costing, activity-based costing. Destin Products makes digital watches. Destin is preparing a product life-cycle budget for a new watch, MX3. Development on the new watch is to start shortly. Estimates about MX3 are as follows:

Life-cycle units manufactured and sold	400,000
Selling price per watch	$40
Life-cycle costs	
R&D and design costs	$1,000,000
Manufacturing	
Variable costs per watch	$15
Variable costs per batch	$600
Watches per batch	500
Fixed costs	$1,800,000
Marketing	
Variable costs per watch	$3.20
Fixed costs	$1,000,000
Distribution	
Variable costs per batch	$280
Watches per batch	160
Fixed costs	$720,000
Customer-service costs per watch	$1.50

Ignore the time value of money.

Required

1. Calculate the budgeted life-cycle operating income for the new watch.
2. What percentage of the budgeted total product life-cycle costs will be *incurred* by the end of the R&D and design stages?
3. An analysis reveals that 80% of the budgeted total product life-cycle costs of the new watch will be *locked in* at the end of the R&D and design stages. What implications does this finding have for managing MX3's costs?
4. Destin's Market Research Department estimates that reducing MX3's price by $3 will increase life-cycle unit sales by 10 percent. If unit sales increase by 10%, Destin plans to increase manufacturing and distribution batch sizes by 10% as well. Assume that all variable costs per watch, variable costs per batch, and fixed costs will remain the same. Should Destin reduce MX3's price by $3? Show your calculations.

PROBLEMS

12-27 Pricing of hotel rooms on weekends. Paul Diamond is the owner of the Galaxy chain of four-star prestige hotels located in Chicago, London, Los Angeles, Montreal, New York, Seattle, San Francisco, and Tokyo. Diamond is currently struggling to set weekend rates for the San Francisco hotel (the San Francisco Galaxy). From Sunday through Thursday, the Galaxy has an average occupancy rate of 90 percent. On Friday and Saturday nights, however, average occupancy declines to less than 30 percent. Galaxy's major customers are business travelers who stay mainly Sunday through Thursday.

The current room rate at the Galaxy is $150 a night for single occupancy and $180 a night for double occupancy. These rates apply seven nights a week. For many years, Diamond has resisted having rates for Friday and Saturday nights that are different from those for the remainder of the week. Diamond has long believed that price reductions convey a "nonprestige" impression to his guests. The San Francisco Galaxy highly values its reputation for treating its guests as "royalty."

Most room costs at the Galaxy are fixed on a short-stay (per night) basis. Diamond estimates the variable costs of servicing each room to be $20 a night per single occupancy and $22 a night per double occupancy.

Many prestige hotels in San Francisco offer special weekend rates (Friday and/or Saturday) that are up to 50% lower than their Sunday-through-Thursday rates. These weekend rates also include additional items such as a breakfast for two, a bottle of champagne, and discounted theater tickets.

Required

1. Would you recommend that Diamond reduce room rates at the San Francisco Galaxy on Friday and Saturday nights? Show your calculations. What factors should Diamond consider in his decision?
2. In six months' time, the Super Bowl is to be held in San Francisco. Diamond observes that several four-star prestige hotels have already advertised a Friday-through-Sunday

rate for Super Bowl weekend of $300 a night. Should Diamond charge extra for the Super Bowl weekend? Explain.

12-28 Relevant-cost approach to pricing decisions. Stardom, Inc., cans peaches for sale to food distributors. All costs are classified as either manufacturing or marketing. Stardom prepares monthly budgets. The March 2001 budgeted absorption-costing income statement is as follows:

Revenues (1,000 crates × $100 a crate)	$100,000
Cost of goods sold	60,000
Gross margin	40,000
Marketing costs	30,000
Operating income	$ 10,000

Normal markup percentage:
$40,000 ÷ $60,000 = 66.7\%$ of absorption cost

Monthly costs are classified as fixed or variable (with respect to the number of crates produced for manufacturing costs and with respect to the number of crates sold for marketing costs):

	Fixed	Variable
Manufacturing	$20,000	$40,000
Marketing	16,000	14,000

Stardom has the capacity to can 1,500 crates per month. The relevant range in which monthly fixed manufacturing costs will be "fixed" is from 500 to 1,500 crates per month.

Required
1. Calculate the markup percentage based on total variable costs.
2. Assume that a new customer approaches Stardom to buy 200 crates at $55 per crate. The customer does not require additional marketing effort. Additional manufacturing costs of $2,000 (for special packaging) will be required. Stardom believes that this is a one-time-only special order because the customer is discontinuing business in six weeks' time. Stardom is reluctant to accept this 200-crate special order because the $55 per crate price is below the $60 per crate absorption cost. Do you agree with this reasoning? Explain.
3. Assume that the new customer decides to remain in business. How would this longevity affect your willingness to accept the $55 per crate offer? Explain.

12-29 Cost-plus pricing. (CMA, adapted) Hall Company specializes in packaging bulk drugs. Wyant Memorial Hospital has asked Hall to bid on the packaging of 1 million doses of medication at full cost plus a return on full cost of no more than 9% after income taxes. Wyant defines cost as including all variable costs of performing the service, a reasonable amount of fixed overhead, and incremental administrative costs. The hospital will supply all packaging materials and ingredients. Wyant has indicated that any bid over $0.07 per dose will be rejected.

Don Greenway, Director of Cost Accounting at the Hall Company, has accumulated the following information prior to the preparation of the bid:

Variable direct manufacturing labor costs	$16.00/direct manufacturing labor-hour
Variable overhead costs	$9.00/direct manufacturing labor-hour
Fixed overhead costs	$30.00/direct manufacturing labor-hour
Incremental administrative costs	$5,000 for the order
Production rate	1,000 doses/direct manufacturing labor-hour

Hall Company is subject to an income tax rate of 40 percent.

Required
1. Calculate the minimum price per dose that Hall could bid for the Wyant job without changing Hall's net income.
2. Calculate Hall's bid price per dose using the full cost criterion and the maximum allowable return specified by Wyant.
3. Without considering your answer to requirement 2, assume that the price per dose that Hall calculated using the cost-plus criterion specified by Wyant is greater than the

maximum bid of $0.07 per dose allowed by Wyant. Discuss the factors that Hall should consider before deciding whether or not to submit a bid at the maximum price of $0.07 per dose.

12-30 Cost-plus and market-based pricing. California Temps, a large labor contractor, supplies contract labor to building construction companies. For 2001, California Temps has budgeted to supply 80,000 hours of contract labor. Its variable costs are $12 per hour and its fixed costs are $240,000. Roger Mason, the general manager, has proposed a cost-plus approach for pricing labor at full cost plus 20 percent.

Required

1. Calculate the price per hour that California Temps should charge based on Mason's proposal.
2. Sheila Woods, the marketing manager, has supplied the following information on demand levels at different prices:

Price Per Hour	Demand (Hours)
$16	120,000
17	100,000
18	80,000
19	70,000
20	60,000

California Temps can meet any of these demand levels. Fixed costs will remain unchanged for all the demand levels. On the basis of this additional information, calculate the price per hour that California Temps should charge.

3. Comment on your answers to requirements 1 and 2. Why are they the same or not the same?

12-31 Airline pricing, considerations other than cost in pricing. Air Americo is about to introduce a daily round-trip flight from New York to Los Angeles. Air Americo offers only one class of seats—Comfort Class—and is in the process of determining how it should price its round-trip tickets.

The market research group at Air Americo segments the market into business and pleasure travelers. It provides the following information on the effect of two different prices on the estimated number of seats sold and the variable costs per ticket:

	Price Charged	Variable Costs of Food and Commission on Each Ticket	Number of Seats Expected to Be Sold
Business travelers	$ 500	$ 80	200
	2,000	180	190
Pleasure travelers	500	80	100
	2,000	180	20

Assume these prices are the only choices available to Air Americo. The market research team offers one additional fact. Pleasure travelers start their travel during one week, spend at least one weekend at their destination, and return the following week or thereafter. Business travelers usually start and complete their travel within the same week. They do not stay over weekends.

Assume that round-trip fuel costs are fixed costs of $24,000 regardless of the actual number of passengers on a flight and that fixed costs allocated to the round-trip flight for airplane lease costs, ground services (maintenance, check-in, and baggage handling), and flight crew salaries total $188,000.

Required

1. If you could charge different prices to business travelers and pleasure travelers, would you? Show your computations.
2. Explain the key factor (or factors) that affects your answer in requirement 1.
3. How might Air Americo implement price discrimination? That is, what plan could the airline formulate so that business travelers and pleasure travelers each pay the price desired by the airline?

12-32 Target prices, target costs, value engineering, cost incurrence, locked-in costs, activity-based costing. Cutler Electronics makes a radio-cassette player, CE100, which has 80 components. Cutler sells 7,000 units each month for $70 each. The costs of manufacturing CE100 are $45 per unit, or $315,000 per month. Monthly manufacturing costs incurred are as follows:

Direct materials costs	$182,000
Direct manufacturing labor costs	28,000
Machining costs (fixed)	31,500
Testing costs	35,000
Rework costs	14,000
Ordering costs	3,360
Engineering costs (fixed)	21,140
Total manufacturing costs	$315,000

Cutler's management identifies the activity cost pools, the cost drivers for each activity, and the cost per unit of the cost driver for each overhead cost pool as follows:

Manufacturing Activity	Description of Activity	Cost Driver	Cost Per Unit of Cost Driver
1. Machining costs	Machining components	Machine-hours of capacity	$4.50 per machine-hour
2. Testing costs	Testing components and final product (Each unit of CE100 is tested individually.)	Testing-hours	$2 per testing-hour
3. Rework costs	Correcting and fixing errors and defects	Units of CE100 reworked	$20 per unit
4. Ordering costs	Ordering of components	Number of orders	$21 per order
5. Engineering costs	Designing and managing of products and processes	Capacity of engineering hours	$35 per engineering-hour

Cutler's management views direct materials costs and direct manufacturing labor costs as variable with respect to the units of CE100 manufactured. Over a long-run horizon, each of the overhead costs described in the preceding table varies, as described, with the chosen cost drivers.

The following additional information describes the existing design:

a. Testing and inspection time per unit is 2.5 hours.

b. 10% of the CE100s manufactured are reworked.

c. Cutler places two orders with each component supplier each month. Each component is supplied by a different supplier.

d. It currently takes 1 hour to manufacture each unit of CE100.

In response to competitive pressures, Cutler must reduce its price to $62 per unit and its costs by $8 per unit. No additional sales are anticipated at this lower price. However, Cutler stands to lose significant sales if it does not reduce its price. Manufacturing has been asked to reduce its costs by $6 per unit. Improvements in manufacturing efficiency are expected to yield a net savings of $1.50 per radio-cassette player, but that is not enough. The chief engineer has proposed a new modular design that reduces the number of components to 50 and also simplifies testing. The newly designed radio-cassette player, called "New CE100" will replace CE100.

The expected effects of the new design are as follows:

a. Direct materials costs for the New CE100 are expected to be lower by $2.20 per unit.

b. Direct manufacturing labor costs for the New CE100 are expected to be lower by $0.50 per unit.

c. Machining time required to manufacture the New CE100 is expected to be 20% less but machine-hour capacity will not be reduced.

d. Time required for testing the New CE100 is expected to be lower by 20 percent.

e. Rework is expected to decline to 4% of New CE100s manufactured.

f. Engineering-hours capacity will remain the same.

Assume that the cost per unit of each cost driver for CE100 continues to apply to New CE100.

Required

1. Calculate Cutler's manufacturing cost per unit of New CE100.
2. Will the new design achieve the per unit cost reduction targets that have been set for the manufacturing costs of New CE 100? Show your calculations.
3. The problem describes two strategies to reduce costs: (a) improving manufacturing efficiency, and (b) modifying the design. Which strategy has a bigger impact on Cutler's costs? Why? Explain briefly.

 12-33 Product costs, activity-based costing. Executive Power (EP) manufactures and sells computers and computer peripherals to several nationwide retail chains. John Farnham is the manager of the printer division. Its two best-selling printers are P-41 and P-63.

The manufacturing cost of each printer is calculated using EP's activity-based costing system. EP has one direct manufacturing cost category (direct materials) and the following five indirect manufacturing cost pools:

Indirect Manufacturing Cost Pool	Quantity of Allocation Base	Allocation Rate
1. Materials handling	Number of parts	$1.20 per part
2. Assembly management	Hours of assembly time	$40 per hour of assembly time
3. Machine insertion of parts	Number of machine-inserted parts	$0.70 per machine-inserted part
4. Manual insertion of parts	Number of manually-inserted parts	$2.10 per manually-inserted part
5. Quality testing	Hours of quality testing time	$25 per testing-hour

Product characteristics of P-41 and P-63 are as follows:

	P-41	P-63
Direct materials costs	$407.50	$292.10
Number of parts	85 parts	46 parts
Hours of assembly time	3.2 hours	1.9 hours
Number of machine-inserted parts	49 parts	31 parts
Number of manually-inserted parts	36 parts	15 parts
Hours of quality testing	1.4 hours	1.1 hours

Required

What is the manufacturing cost of P-41? Of P-63?

12-34 Target cost, activity-based costing systems (continuation of 12-33). Assume all the information in Problem 12-33. Farnham has just received some bad news. A foreign competitor has introduced products very similar to P-41 and P-63. Given their announced selling prices, Farnham estimates the P-41 clone to have a manufacturing cost of approximately $680 and the P-63 clone to have a manufacturing cost of approximately $390. He calls a meeting of product designers and manufacturing personnel at the printer division. They all agree to use the $680 and $390 figures as target costs for redesigned versions of EP's P-41 and P-63, respectively. Product designers examine alternative ways of designing printers with comparable performance but lower cost. They come up with the following revised designs for P-41 and P-63 (called P-41 REV and P-63 REV, respectively):

	P-41 REV	P-63 REV
Direct materials costs	$381.20	$263.10
Number of parts	71 parts	39 parts
Hours of assembly time	2.1 hours	1.6 hours
Number of machine-inserted parts	59 parts	29 parts
Number of manually-inserted parts	12 parts	10 parts
Hours of quality testing	1.2 hours	0.9 hours

Required

1. What is a target cost per unit?
2. Using the activity-based costing system outlined in Problem 12-33, compute the manufacturing costs of P-41 REV and P-63 REV. How do these costs compare with the $680 and $390 target costs per unit?
3. Explain the differences between P-41 and P-41 REV and between P-63 and P-63 REV.
4. Assume now that John Farnham has achieved major cost reductions in one activity. As a consequence, the allocation rate in the assembly-management activity will be reduced from $40 to $28 per assembly-hour. How will this activity-cost reduction affect the manufacturing costs of P-41 REV and P-63 REV? Comment on the results.

12-35 Life-cycle product costing, product emphasis. Decision Support Systems (DSS) is examining the profitability and pricing policies of its software division. The DSS software division develops software packages for engineers. DSS has collected data on three of its more recent packages:

◆ EE-46: package for electrical engineers

◆ ME-83: package for mechanical engineers

◆ IE-17: package for industrial engineers

Summary details on each package over their two-year "cradle-to-grave" product lives are as follows:

Package	Selling Price	Number of Units Sold Year 1	Year 2
EE-46	$250	2,000	8,000
ME-83	300	2,000	3,000
IE-17	200	5,000	3,000

Assume that no inventory remains on hand at the end of year 2.

DSS is deciding which product lines to emphasize in its software division. In the past two years, the profitability of this division has been mediocre. DSS is particularly concerned with the increase in R&D costs in several of its divisions. An analyst at the software division pointed out that for one of its most recent packages (IE-17), major efforts had been made to reduce R&D costs.

Last week Nancy Sullivan, the software division manager, attended a seminar on product life-cycle management. The topic of life-cycle reporting was discussed. Sullivan decides to use this approach in her own division. She collects the following life-cycle revenue and cost information for the EE-46, ME-83, and IE-17 packages:

	EE-46 Year 1	Year 2	ME-83 Year 1	Year 2	IE-17 Year 1	Year 2
Revenues	$500,000	$2,000,000	$600,000	$900,000	$1,000,000	$600,000
Costs						
R&D	700,000	0	450,000	0	240,000	0
Design of product	185,000	15,000	110,000	10,000	80,000	16,000
Manufacturing	75,000	225,000	105,000	105,000	143,000	65,000
Marketing	140,000	360,000	120,000	150,000	240,000	208,000
Distribution	15,000	60,000	24,000	36,000	60,000	36,000
Customer service	50,000	325,000	45,000	105,000	220,000	388,000

Required

1. How does a product life-cycle income statement differ from an income statement that is calendar-based? What are the benefits of using a product life-cycle reporting format?
2. Present a product life-cycle income statement for each software package. Which package is the most profitable, and which is the least profitable? Ignore the time value of money.

3. How do the three software packages differ in their cost structure (the percentage of total costs in each cost category)?

12-36 Ethics and pricing. Baker, Inc., manufactures ball bearings. Baker is preparing to submit a bid for a new ball-bearings order. Greg Lazarus, controller of the Bearings Division of Baker, has asked John Decker, the cost analyst, to prepare the bid. To determine price, Baker marks up the full costs of the product by 10 percent. Lazarus tells Decker that he is keen on winning the bid and that the price he calculates should be competitive.

Decker prepares the following costs for the bid:

Direct materials costs	$40,000
Direct manufacturing labor costs	10,000
Design and parts administration overhead costs	4,000
Production-order overhead costs	5,000
Setup overhead costs	5,500
Materials-handling overhead costs	6,500
General and administration overhead costs	9,000

All direct costs and 30% of overhead costs are incremental costs of the order.

Lazarus reviews the numbers and says, "As usual your costs are way too high. You have allocated a lot of overhead costs to this job. You know our fixed overhead is not going to change if we win this order and manufacture the bearings. Ever since we installed this new activity-based costing system, we never seem to be able to come up with reasonable product and job costs. Rework your numbers. You have got to make the costs lower."

On returning to his office, Decker rechecks his numbers. He knows that Lazarus wants this order because the additional revenues from the order would lead to a big bonus for Lazarus and the senior division managers. Decker wonders if he can adjust the costs downward. He knows that if he does not come up with a lower bid, Lazarus will be very upset.

Required
1. Using Baker's pricing policy and based on Decker's estimates, calculate the price Baker should bid for the ball-bearings order.
2. Calculate the incremental costs of the ball-bearings order. Why do you think Baker uses full costs of the product rather than incremental costs in its pricing decisions?
3. Evaluate whether Lazarus' suggestion to Decker to use lower cost numbers is unethical. Would it be unethical for Decker to change his analysis so that a lower price can be bid? What steps should Decker take to resolve this situation?

COLLABORATIVE LEARNING PROBLEM

12-37 Target prices, target costs, value engineering. Avery, Inc., manufactures two component parts for the television industry:

◆ Tvez: Annual production and sales of 50,000 units at a selling price of $40.60 per unit.

◆ Premia: Annual production and sales of 25,000 units at a selling price of $60 per unit.

Avery includes all R&D and design costs in engineering costs. Assume that Avery has no marketing, distribution, or customer-service costs.

The direct and indirect costs incurred by Avery on Tvez and Premia are as follows:

	Tvez	Premia	Total
Direct materials costs (variable)	$850,000	$600,000	$1,450,000
Direct manufacturing labor costs (variable)	300,000	200,000	500,000
Direct machining costs (fixed)	150,000	100,000	250,000
Indirect manufacturing costs			
Machine setup costs			86,250
Testing costs			487,500
Engineering costs			450,000
Indirect manufacturing costs			1,023,750
Total costs			$3,223,750

Avery's management identifies the following activity cost pools, cost drivers for each activity, and the costs per unit of cost driver for each overhead cost pool:

Manufacturing Activity	Description of Activity	Cost Driver	Cost Per Unit of Cost Driver
1. Setup	Preparing machine to manufacture a new batch of products	Setup-hours	$25 per setup-hour
2. Testing	Testing components and final product (Avery tests each unit of Tvez and Premia individually)	Testing-hours	$2 per testing-hour
3. Engineering	Designing products and processes and ensuring their smooth functioning	Complexity of product and process	Costs assigned to products by special study

Over a long-run horizon, Avery's management views direct materials costs and direct manufacturing labor costs as variable with respect to the units of Tvez and Premia produced, and overhead costs as variable with respect to their chosen cost drivers. For example, setup costs vary with the number of setup-hours. Direct machining costs represent the cost of machine capacity dedicated to the production of each product (50,000 hours at $3 per hour for Tvez). These costs are fixed and are not expected to vary over the long-run horizon. Additional information is as follows:

	Tvez	Premia
1. Production batch sizes	500 units	200 units
2. Setup time per batch	12 hours	18 hours
3. Testing and inspection time per unit of product produced	2.5 hours	4.75 hours
4. Engineering costs incurred on each product	$170,000	$280,000

Avery is facing competitive pressure to reduce the price of Tvez and has set a target price of $34.80, well below its current price of $40.60. The challenge for Avery is to reduce the cost of Tvez. Avery's engineers have proposed new product design and process improvements for the "New Tvez" to replace Tvez. The new design would improve product quality, and reduce scrap and waste. The reduction in prices will not enable Avery to increase its current unit sales. (However, if Avery does not reduce prices, it will lose sales.)

The expected effects of the new design relative to Tvez are as follows:

a. Direct materials costs for New Tvez are expected to decrease by $2.00 per unit.

b. Direct manufacturing labor costs for New Tvez are expected to decrease by $0.50 per unit.

c. Machining time required to make New Tvez is expected to decrease by 20 minutes. It currently takes 1 hour to manufacture 1 unit of Tvez. The machines will be dedicated to the production of New Tvez.

d. New Tvez will take 7 setup-hours for each setup.

e. Time required for testing each unit of New Tvez is expected to be reduced by 0.5 hour.

f. Engineering costs will be unchanged.

Assume that the batch sizes are the same for New Tvez as for Tvez. If Avery requires additional resources to implement the new design, it can acquire these additional resources in the quantities needed. Further assume the costs per unit of cost driver for the New Tvez are the same as those for Tvez.

Required
Form groups of two or more students to complete the following requirements.

1. Calculate the full cost per unit for Tvez and Premia using activity-based costing.
2. What is the markup on the full cost per unit for Tvez?
3. What is Avery's target cost per unit for New Tvez if it is to maintain the same markup percentage on the full cost per unit as it had for Tvez?
4. Will the New Tvez design achieve the cost reduction targets that Avery has set? Explain.
5. What price will Avery charge for New Tvez if it uses the same markup percentage on the full cost per unit for New Tvez as it did for Tvez?
6. What price should Avery charge for New Tvez? Specify any other management actions that Avery should take regarding New Tvez.

CHAPTER 13

Strategy, Balanced Scorecard, and Strategic Profitability Analysis

learning objectives

After studying this chapter, you should be able to

1. Recognize which of two generic strategies a company is using
2. Identify key aspects of reengineering
3. Present the four perspectives of the balanced scorecard
4. Analyze changes in operating income to evaluate strategy
5. Distinguish between engineered and discretionary costs
6. Identify and manage unused capacity

Deciding and implementing strategy are at the core of any business. Intel Corporation's strategy is to differentiate its products by developing new and more powerful microprocessors. To implement this strategy, Intel emphasizes product innovation and process improvement. Successful product differentiation has been the key to Intel's sustained growth in operating income.

The focus of much of the earlier chapters is on managing operations. In this chapter, we explore the use of management accounting information in the implementation and evaluation of an organization's strategy. Strategy is at the core of any business. It drives the operations of a company and guides managers' short-run and long-run decisions. In this chapter, we describe the balanced scorecard approach to implementing strategy and present ways to analyze operating income for purposes of evaluating strategy. We also show how management accounting information helps strategic initiatives, such as productivity improvement, reengineering and downsizing. We start, however, by discussing what strategy is.

WHAT IS STRATEGY?

Strategy describes how an organization matches its own capabilities with the opportunities in the marketplace in order to accomplish its overall objectives. In formulating its strategy, an organization must thoroughly understand the industry in which it operates. Industry analysis focuses on five forces: (a) competitors, (b) potential entrants into the market, (c) equivalent products, (d) bargaining power of customers, and (e) bargaining power of input suppliers.[1] The collective effect of these forces shapes an organization's profit potential. In general, profit potential decreases with greater competition, stronger potential entrants, products that are similar, and tougher customers and suppliers.

We illustrate these five forces using the example of Chipset, Inc., a manufacturer of linear integrated circuit devices (LICDs) used in modems and communication networks. Chipset produces a single specialized product, CX1. This standard, high-performance microchip can be used in multiple applications that require instant processing of real-time data. CX1 was designed with extensive inputs from key customers.

Competitors Chipset has many growth opportunities, but it also faces significant competition from many small competitors. Companies in the industry have high fixed costs. There is steady pressure to utilize capacity fully; in turn, there is ceaseless pressure on selling prices. Reducing prices of products is critical for industry growth because it allows LICDs to be incorporated into mass-market modems. CX1 enjoys a reputation of having slightly superior product features relative to competitive products, but competition is severe along the dimensions of price, timely delivery, and quality. Quality is important because LICD failure disrupts the communication network.

Potential entrants into the market This is not an attractive industry for new entrants. Competition keeps profit margins small, and significant capital is needed to set up a new manufacturing facility. Companies that have been making LICDs are farther down the learning curve and hence are likely to have lower costs. Existing companies also have the advantage of close relationships with customers.

Equivalent products Chipset uses a technology that allows its customers to use CX1 flexibly to best meet their needs. The flexible design of CX1, and the fact that it is closely integrated into end-products made by Chipset's customers, reduces the potential for equivalent products or new technologies to replace CX1 during the next few years. This risk is reduced even further if Chipset continuously improves CX1's design and processes to decrease costs.

Bargaining power of customers Customers have bargaining power because each buys large quantities of product. Customers can also obtain microchips from other potential suppliers. Signing a contract to deliver microchips is very important to Chipset. Recognizing this fact, customers negotiate hard to keep prices down.

Bargaining power of input suppliers Chipset purchases high-quality materials such as silicon wafers, pins for connectivity, and plastic or ceramic packaging from its suppliers. Chipset also requires skilled engineers, technicians, and manufacturing labor. Materials suppliers and employees have some bargaining power to demand higher prices and higher wages.

[1]M. Porter, *Competitive Strategy* (Free Press, 1980); M. Porter, *Competitive Advantage* (Free Press, 1985); M. Porter, "What Is Strategy." *Harvard Business Review* (November–December, 1996).

New to This Edition This whole chapter is new. It covers the new topics of strategy, the balanced scorecard, strategic profitability analysis, downsizing, and reengineering.

Curriculum Linkage/Points To Stress Management courses deal with strategy all the time. In today's quick changing business environment the whole management team (including accountants) must have a clear understanding of where the firm is headed so that all of the functional areas (accounting, marketing, production, etc.) of the business and all of the value chain functions can work together.

Teaching Tip Explain to students the importance of being aware of the business environment in which your individual firm operates. Everything a firm does should be linked to their strategy, and their strategy is heavily influenced by their environment.

In summary, strong competition and the bargaining powers of customers and suppliers put significant pressure on prices. Chipset is considering responding to these challenges by adopting one of two basic strategies, differentiating its product or achieving cost leadership.

Product differentiation is an organization's ability to offer products or services that are perceived by its customers to be superior and unique relative to those of its competitors. For example, Hewlett Packard has successfully differentiated its products in the electronics industry, as have Merck in the pharmaceutical industry and Coca-Cola in the soft drinks industry. Through innovative product R&D, and by developing processes that bring products to market rapidly, each of these companies has been able to provide better and differentiated products. This differentiation increases brand loyalty and the prices that customers are willing to pay.

Cost leadership is an organization's ability to achieve lower costs relative to competitors through productivity and efficiency improvements, elimination of waste, and tight cost control. Some cost leaders in their respective industries are Home Depot (building products), Texas Instruments (consumer electronics), and Emerson Electric (electric motors). These companies all provide products and services that are similar to, not differentiated from, those of their competitors, but at a lower cost to the customer. Lower selling prices—rather than unique products or services—provide a competitive advantage for these cost leaders.

What strategy should Chipset follow? CX1 is already somewhat differentiated from competing products. Differentiating CX1 further will be costly but it may allow Chipset to charge a higher price. Conversely, reducing the cost of manufacturing and selling CX1 will allow Chipset to reduce the price of CX1 and spur growth. The CX1 technology allows Chipset's customers to achieve different performance levels by simply altering the number of CX1 units in their products. This solution is more cost effective than designing new customized microchips for different applications. Customers want Chipset to keep the current design of CX1 but to lower its price. Chipset's current engineering staff is also more oriented toward making product and process improvements than in creatively designing brand new products and technologies. Chipset concludes that it should pursue a cost leadership strategy. Of course, successful cost leadership would generally increase Chipset's market share and help the company to grow.

To be successful, a company must both formulate an effective strategy and implement it vigorously. In the next section, we focus on the balanced scorecard as a tool for implementing strategy.

Points to Stress/Example Over time, markets may change from ones where product differentiation is much less important than cost leadership. When the only computers were mainframes, IBM was able to differentiate its product through superior service (which few competitors could meet). When the PC was developed, selling price to the end user (and therefore, cost leadership) became much more important as the product changed to one with many more potential customers (both businesses and individuals).

IMPLEMENTATION OF STRATEGY AND THE BALANCED SCORECARD

Consistent with the scorekeeping function, the management accountant has an important role to play in the implementation of strategy. This role takes the form of designing reports to help managers track progress in implementing strategy. Many organizations have introduced a balanced scorecard approach to manage the implementation of their strategies.

The Balanced Scorecard

The **balanced scorecard** translates an organization's mission and strategy into a comprehensive set of performance measures that provides the framework for implementing its strategy.[2] The balanced scorecard does not focus solely on achieving financial objectives. It also highlights the nonfinancial objectives that an organization must achieve in order to meet its financial objectives. The balanced scorecard measures an organization's performance from four key perspectives: (1) financial, (2) customer, (3) internal business processes, and (4) learning and growth. A company's strategy influences the measures used in each of these perspectives.

Reinforcing Problems Balanced scorecard issues are covered in Exer. 13-16, 13-18, and 13-22, and Probs. 13-26, 13-27, and 13-34.

[2]See R. S. Kaplan and D. P. Norton, *The Balanced Scorecard* (Harvard Business School Press, 1996).

The balanced scorecard gets its name from the attempt to balance financial and nonfinancial performance measures to evaluate both short-run and long-run performance in a single report. Consequently, the balanced scorecard reduces managers' emphasis on short-run financial performance, such as quarterly earnings. Why? Because the nonfinancial and operational indicators measure fundamental changes that a company is making. The financial benefits of these changes may not be captured in short-run earnings, but strong improvements in nonfinancial measures signal the prospect of creating economic value in the future. For example, an increase in customer satisfaction signals higher sales and income in the future. By balancing the mix of financial and nonfinancial measures, the balanced scorecard focuses management's attention on both short-run and long-run performance.

We illustrate the four perspectives of the balanced scorecard using the Chipset example. To understand the measures Chipset uses to monitor progress under each perspective, it is important to recognize key elements of Chipset's cost leadership strategy—improve quality and reengineer processes. As a result of these initiatives, Chipset plans to reduce costs and downsize and eliminate capacity in excess of that needed to support future growth. However, it does not want to make deep cuts in personnel that would adversely affect employee morale and hinder future growth.

Quality Improvement and Reengineering at Chipset

One key element of Chipset's strategy to reduce costs is improving quality (that is, reducing defects and improving yields in its manufacturing process). To improve quality, Chipset needs to obtain real-time data about manufacturing process parameters and to implement advanced process control methods. The goal is to ensure that process parameters such as temperature and pressure are maintained within tight ranges. Chipset must also train its front-line workers in quality management techniques to help them identify and resolve defects and problems. Following this training, Chipset needs to empower its workforce to make timely decisions and continuously improve the process.

Another key element of Chipset's strategy to reduce costs is reengineering its order delivery process. **Reengineering** is the fundamental rethinking and redesign of business processes to achieve improvements in critical measures of performance such as cost, quality, service, speed, and customer satisfaction.[3] To illustrate the concept of reengineering, we examine the order delivery system at Chipset, Inc., in 1999. Chipset's salespersons work with customers to identify and plan customer needs. A copy of each purchase order received from a customer is sent to manufacturing where a production scheduler begins the planning for manufacturing the order. Frequently, there is a long waiting time before production begins. After manufacturing is complete, the CX1 chips are sent to the Shipping Department, which matches the quantities of CX1 to be shipped against customer purchase orders. Often, the completed CX1 chips are held in inventory until a truck is available for shipment to the customer. If the quantity shipped does not match the number of chips requested by the customer, a special shipment is scheduled. The shipping documents are sent to the Billing Department for issuing of invoices. Special staff in the Accounting Department follows up with customers for payments.

Chipset discovered that the many transfers across departments (sales, manufacturing, shipping, billing, and accounting) to satisfy a customer order slowed down the process and created delays. A multifunction team from the various departments has reengineered the order delivery process for 2000. Its goal is to make the entire organization more customer-focused and reduce delays by eliminating the number of interdepartment transfers. Under the new system, a customer relationship manager will be responsible for the entire customer relationship. Chipset will enter into long-term contracts with customers that specify quantities and prices.

---

[3]See M. Hammer and J. Champy, *Reengineering the Corporation: A Manifesto for Business Revolution* (New York: Harper, 1993); E. Rühli, C. Treichler, and S. Schmidt, "From Business Reengineering to Management Reengineering—A European Study," *Management International Review* (1995): 361–371; G. Hall, J. Rosenthal, and J. Wade, "How to Make Reengineering Really Work," *Harvard Business Review* (November–December 1993): 119–131.

The customer relationship manager will work closely with the customer and with manufacturing to specify delivery schedules for CX1 one month in advance. The schedule of customer orders will be sent electronically to manufacturing. Completed chips will be shipped directly from the manufacturing plant to customer sites. Each shipment will automatically trigger an invoice that will be sent electronically to the customer.

The experiences of many companies, such as AT&T, Banca di America e di Italia, Cigna Insurance, Ford Motor, Hewlett Packard, and Siemens Nixdorf, indicate that the benefits from reengineering are most significant when it cuts across functional lines to focus on an entire business process (as in the Chipset example). Reengineering only the shipping or invoicing activity at Chipset rather than the entire order delivery process would not be particularly beneficial. Successful reengineering efforts involve changing roles and responsibilities, eliminating unnecessary activities and tasks, using information technology, and developing employee skills. Chipset's balanced scorecard for 2000 must track Chipset's progress in reengineering the order delivery process from both a nonfinancial and financial perspective.

The Four Perspectives of the Balanced Scorecard

Exhibit 13-1 presents Chipset's balanced scorecard. It highlights the four key perspectives of performance—financial, customer, internal business processes, and learning and growth. At the beginning of the year 2000, Chipset specifies the objectives, measures, initiatives to achieve the objectives, and target performance (the first four columns of Exhibit 13-1). The target performance levels for nonfinancial measures are based on competitor benchmarks. They indicate the performance levels necessary to meet customer needs, compete effectively, and achieve financial goals. The fifth column, which describes actual performance, is completed at the end of the year 2000. This column shows how well Chipset has performed relative to its target performance.

Financial perspective This perspective evaluates the profitability of the strategy. Because cost reduction relative to competitors and growth are Chipset's key strategic initiatives, the financial perspective focuses on how much of operating income and return on capital employed results from reducing costs and selling more units of CX1.

Customer perspective This perspective identifies the targeted market segments and measures the company's success in these segments. To monitor its growth objectives, Chipset uses measures such as market share in the communication networks segment, number of new customers, and customer satisfaction.

Internal business process perspective This perspective focuses on internal operations that further both the customer perspective by creating value for customers and the financial perspective by increasing shareholder wealth. Chipset determines internal business process improvement targets after benchmarking against key competitors. As we discussed in Chapter 12, there are different sources of competitor cost analysis—published financial statements, prevailing prices, customers, suppliers, former employees, industry experts, and financial analysts. Chipset also physically takes apart competitors' products to compare them with its own designs. This activity also helps Chipset estimate competitors' costs. The internal business process perspective comprises three principal subprocesses:

1. *The innovation process*: Creating products, services, and processes that will meet the needs of customers. At Chipset, the key to lowering costs and promoting growth is improving the technology of manufacturing.

2. *The operations process*: Producing and delivering existing products and services to customers. Chipset's key strategic initiatives are (a) improving manufacturing quality, (b) reducing delivery time to customers, and (c) meeting specified delivery dates.

3. *Postsales service*: Providing service and support to the customer after the sale or delivery of a product or service. Chipset's sales staff works closely with customers to monitor and understand how well product features of CX1 match customer needs.

Points to Stress Setting the target performance in a balanced scorecard based on competitor benchmarking is very important. The firm shouldn't just aim to be better than it has been, but it must strive to be among the "best in class" so as to effectively better its worldwide competition.

Teaching Tip Point out to students that performance evaluation measures are powerful. Employees have learned that "what is measured *is important*"; that is, the act of collecting and reporting a number makes it powerful. Employees will behave so as to maximize the performance measure. This means that the firm needs to choose these measures with care and think through their implications for employee behavior.

EXHIBIT 13-1
The Balanced Scorecard for Chipset, Inc., for the Year 2000

Objectives	Measures	Initiatives	Target Performance	Actual Performance
Financial Perspective				
Increase shareholder value	Operating income from productivity gain	Manage costs & unused capacity	$2,000,000	$2,100,000
	Operating income from growth	Build strong customer relationships	$3,000,000	$3,420,000
	Revenue growth	Build strong customer relationships	6%	6.48%[a]
Customer Perspective				
Increase market share	Market share in communication networks segment	Identify future needs of customers	6%	7%
	New customers	Identify new target customer segments	5	6[b]
Increase customer satisfaction	Customer satisfaction survey	Increase customer focus of sales organization	90% of customers give top two ratings	87% of customers give top two ratings
Internal Business Process Perspective				
Improve manufacturing capability	Percentage of processes with advanced controls	Organize R&D/manufacturing teams to implement advanced controls	75%	75%
Improve manufacturing quality and productivity	Yield	Identify root causes of problems and improve quality	78%	79.3%[c]
Reduce delivery time to customers	Order delivery time	Reengineer order delivery process	30 days	30 days
Meet specified delivery dates	On-time delivery	Reengineer order delivery process	92%	90%
Learning and Growth Perspective				
Develop process skill	Percentage of employees trained in process and quality management	Employee training programs	90%	92%
Empower workforce	Percentage of front-line workers empowered to manage processes	Have supervisors act as coaches rather than decision makers	85%	90%
Align employee and organization goals	Employee satisfaction survey	Employee participation and suggestions program to build teamwork	80% of employees give top two ratings	88% of employees give top two ratings
Enhance information system capabilities	Percentage of manufacturing processes with real-time feedback	Improve off-line data gathering	80%	80%
Improve manufacturing processes	Number of major improvements in process controls	Organize R&D/manufacturing teams to modify processes	5	5

[a](Revenues in 2000 − Revenues in 1999) ÷ Revenues in 1999 = ($28,750,000 − $27,000,000) ÷ $27,000,000 = 6.48%.
[b]Customers increased from 40 to 46 in the year 2000.
[c]Yield = Units of CX1 produced ÷ Units of CX1 started × 100 = 1,150,000 ÷ 1,450,000 × 100 = 79.3%.

Learning and growth perspective This perspective identifies the capabilities in which the organization must excel in order to achieve superior internal processes that create value for customers and shareholders. Chipset's learning and growth perspective emphasizes three capabilities: (1) employee capabilities measured using employee education and skill levels, surveys of employee satisfaction, employee turnover (proportion of employees who have left the company annually), and employee productivity; (2) information system capabilities measured by percentage of front-line employees that have on-line access to customer information, and percentage of business processes with real-time feedback; and (3) motivation and empowerment measured by number of suggestions per employee, percentage of suggestions implemented, and percentage of compensation based on individual and team incentives.

The arrows in Exhibit 13-1 indicate how gains in the learning and growth perspective lead to improvements in internal business processes, which in turn lead to higher customer satisfaction and market share, and finally to superior financial performance. Note how key elements of Chipset's strategy implementation—empowering workers, training, information systems, quality and process improvements, reengineering, and customer focus—filter through the scorecard. These initiatives have been successful from a financial perspective in 2000. Chipset has earned significant operating income from its cost leadership strategy that has also translated into growth.

Aligning the Balanced Scorecard to Strategy

Different strategies call for different scorecards. Suppose that Visilog, another company in the microchip industry, follows a product differentiation strategy by designing custom chips for the communication networks business. Visilog designs its balanced scorecard to fit its strategy. For example, in the financial perspective, Visilog evaluates how much of its operating income comes from charging premium prices for its products. In the customer perspective, Visilog measures the percentage of its revenues from new products (and new customers). In the internal business process perspective, Visilog measures the development of advanced manufacturing capabilities to produce custom chips. In the learning and growth perspective, Visilog measures new product development time. Of course, Visilog uses some of the measures described in the balanced scorecard in Exhibit 13-1. For example, revenue growth, customer satisfaction ratings, order delivery time, on-time delivery, percentage of front-line workers empowered to manage processes, and employee satisfaction ratings, are important measures under the new strategy. The key point, though, is to align the balanced scorecard to company strategy.[4]

Exhibit 13-2 presents some common balanced scorecard measures that companies have used.

Features of a Good Balanced Scorecard

A good balanced scorecard design has several features:

1. It tells the story of a company's strategy by articulating a sequence of cause-and-effect relationships. For example, because Chipset's goal is to be a low-cost producer and to emphasize growth, the balanced scorecard describes the specific objectives and measures in the learning and growth perspective that lead to improvements in internal business processes. These, in turn, lead to increased customer satisfaction and market share, as well as higher operating income and share-

Teaching Tip The four perspectives of the balanced scorecard are multiple measures of the company that are linked. In Exh. 13-1, note how each of the four perspectives focuses management on different elements of the business, with different measures, initiatives, and target performance goals. But the key is that all of these are *linked* to the company's strategy and are expected to positively affect financial performance. Note how gains in the learning and growth perspective lead to improvements in internal business processes, which lead to higher customer satisfaction and market share, and finally to superior financial performance.

---

[4]For simplicity, we have presented the balanced scorecard in the context of companies that have followed either a cost leadership or a product differentiation strategy. Of course, a company may have some products for which cost leadership is critical and other products for which product differentiation is important. The company will then develop separate scorecards to implement the different product strategies. In still other contexts, product differentiation may be of primary importance, but some cost leadership must also be achieved. The balanced scorecard measures would then link to this strategy.

EXHIBIT 13-2
EXHIBIT 13-2
Frequently Cited Balanced Scorecard Measures

◆ **Financial Perspective**
◆ Operating income, revenue growth, revenues from new products, gross margin percentage, cost reductions in key areas, economic value added[a] (EVA®), return on investment.[a]

◆ **Customer Perspective**
◆ Market share, customer satisfaction, customer retention percentage, time taken to fulfill customer's requests.

◆ **Internal Business Process Perspective**
◆ *Innovation Process*: Manufacturing capabilities, number of new products or services, new product development times, and number of new patents.
◆ *Operations Process*: Yield, defect rates, time taken to deliver product to customers, percentage of on-time deliveries, average time taken to manufacture orders, setup time, manufacturing downtime.
◆ *Postsales Service*: Time taken to replace or repair defective products, hours of customer training for using the product

◆ **Learning and Growth Perspective**
◆ Employee education and skill levels, employee satisfaction scores, employee turnover rates, information system availability, percentage of processes with advanced controls, percentage of employee suggestions implemented, percentage of compensation based on individual and team incentives.

[a] These measures are described in Chapter 23.

holder wealth. Each measure in the scorecard is part of a cause-and-effect chain, a linkage from strategy formulation to financial outcomes.

2. It helps to communicate the strategy to all members of the organization by translating the strategy into a coherent and linked set of understandable and measurable operational targets. Guided by the scorecard, managers and employees take actions and make decisions that aim to achieve the company's strategy. To focus these actions, some companies, such as Mobil and Citigroup, have pushed down and developed scorecards at the division and department levels.

3. In for-profit companies, the balanced scorecard places strong emphasis on financial objectives and measures.[5] Managers sometimes tend to focus too much on innovation, quality, and customer satisfaction as ends in themselves even if they do not lead to tangible payoffs. A balanced scorecard emphasizes nonfinancial measures as a part of a program to achieve future financial performance. When financial and nonfinancial performance measures are properly linked, many of the nonfinancial measures serve as leading indicators of future financial performance. In the Chipset example, the improvements in nonfinancial factors have, in fact, led to improvements in financial factors.

4. The balanced scorecard limits the number of measures used by identifying only the most critical ones. Avoiding a proliferation of measures focuses management's attention on those that are key to the implementation of strategy.

5. The scorecard highlights suboptimal tradeoffs that managers may make when they fail to consider operational and financial measures together. For example, a company for which innovation is key could achieve superior short-run financial performance by reducing spending on R&D. A good balanced scorecard would signal that the short-run financial performance may have been achieved by taking actions that hurt future financial performance because a leading indicator of that performance, R&D spending and R&D output, has declined.

---

[5]Nonprofit organizations have other primary objectives such as number of people served and development goals reached.

Points to Stress Nonfinancial measures are an important part of a balanced scorecard. Many managers feel uncomfortable with accounting numbers. Measuring the correct item that, if performed well, will result in a better achievement of the company's strategy is the goal; it doesn't matter if the item can be measured in financial terms or whether it has a direct financial effect. If the item is properly linked in the balanced scorecard, it will affect the company's financial performance.

Correcting Student Misconceptions Some students are surprised by the limited number of measures on a balanced scorecard, and if asked, would add many more measures. Individuals' limits on processing information and perceiving trade-offs among various measures translates into "less means more." That is, mgt. needs to specify only the critical measures so as to focus efforts on improving items which will make a difference in achieving the firm's strategic goals.

Widening the Performance Measurement Lens Using the Balanced Scorecard[a]

A survey of 100 large U.S. companies indicates that 60% use some variation of the balanced scorecard. Of these adopters, over 80% are either using or planning to use the scorecard or variations of it for incentive compensation purposes.

As the following table shows, companies adopting the scorecard cite the broadening of the performance measures as the most important reason for adopting it.

Reason	Percentage Citing as Highly Important
Combines operational and financial measures	88%
Minimizes reliance on a single measure	67%
Shows if improvement in one area adversely affects another	35%

Despite the broadening of performance measures, companies continue to assign more weight to financial results in performance evaluation.

Performance Measure Category	Average Relative Weight
Financial perspective	55%
Customer perspective	19%
Internal business process perspective	12%
Learning and growth perspective	14%

The survey results indicate some problems and challenges in implementing the balanced scorecard. These include (1) difficulty in evaluating the relative importance of different measures, (2) problems in measuring and quantifying important qualitative data, (3) lack of clarity resulting from a large number of measures, and (4) the time and expense necessary for designing and maintaining the scorecard. Despite these challenges, the survey indicates that executives find the scorecard effective and useful.

[a]Adapted from "CompScan Report," Towers Perrin. Full citations are in Appendix A.

Pitfalls When Implementing a Balanced Scorecard

Pitfalls to avoid when implementing a balanced scorecard include the following:

1. Don't assume the cause-and-effect linkages to be precise. They are merely hypotheses. A critical challenge is to identify the strength and speed of the causal linkages among the nonfinancial and financial measures. Hence, an organization must gather evidence of these linkages over time. With experience, organizations should alter their scorecards to include those nonfinancial objectives and measures that are the best leading indicators of subsequent financial performance (a lagging indicator). Committing to evolve the scorecard over time avoids the paralysis associated with trying to design the "perfect" scorecard at the outset.

2. Don't seek improvements across all of the measures all of the time. This approach may be inappropriate because trade-offs may need to be made across various strategic goals. For example, emphasizing quality and on-time performance beyond a point may not be worthwhile—further improvement in these objectives may be inconsistent with profit maximization.

3. Don't use only objective measures in the scorecard. Chipset's scorecard includes both objective measures (such as operating income from cost leadership, market share and manufacturing yield), as well as subjective measures (such as customer and employee satisfaction ratings). When using subjective measures, though,

Points to Stress The firm does not have to get the balanced scorecard perfect the first time. Expect it to evolve over time as better measures are found and the firm better understands the linkages between processes and profits. As the environment and strategy change over time, the items on the scorecard also will have to change.

Curriculum Linkage Just as in external financial reporting there is a tradeoff between relevance and reliability of data reported on the financial statements, the same is true for measures included on the balanced scorecard. A subjective measure such as customer or employee satisfaction may be very relevant in achieving the firm's strategy, even though it cannot be as reliably measured as manufacturing yield.

management must be careful to trade off the benefits of the richer information these measures provide against the imprecision and potential for manipulation.

4. Don't fail to consider both costs and benefits of initiatives such as spending on information technology and research and development before including these objectives in the scorecard. Otherwise, management may focus the organization on measures that will not result in overall long-run financial benefits.

5. Don't ignore nonfinancial measures when evaluating managers and employees. Managers tend to focus on what their performance is measured by. Excluding nonfinancial measures when evaluating performance will reduce the significance and importance that managers give to nonfinancial scorecard measures.

EVALUATING THE SUCCESS OF A STRATEGY

OBJECTIVE 4

Analyze changes in operating income to evaluate strategy

To evaluate how successful it has been in implementing its strategy, Chipset compares the target and actual performance columns of its balanced scorecard in Exhibit 13-1. This comparison indicates that Chipset met most of the targets it had set on the basis of competitor benchmarks. Meeting the targets suggests that the strategic initiatives that Chipset had identified and measured for learning and growth resulted in improvements in internal business processes, customer measures, and financial performance. The financial measures show that Chipset achieved targeted cost savings and growth. The key question is, How does Chipset isolate operating income from specific sources such as cost savings and growth instead of emphasizing only the aggregate change in operating income?

Some companies might be tempted to gauge the success of their strategies by measuring the change in their operating incomes from one year to the next, but this approach is inadequate. For example, operating income can increase simply because entire markets are expanding, not because a specific strategy has been successful. Also, changes in operating income might be caused by factors outside the strategy. For example, a company such as Chipset that has chosen a cost leadership strategy may find that operating income increases have instead been caused incidentally by, say, some degree of product differentiation. Managers and accountants need to evaluate the success of a strategy on the basis of whether the sources of operating income increases are the result of implementing the chosen strategy.

To use operating income numbers for evaluating the success of a strategy, a company needs to isolate the operating income due to cost leadership from the operating income due to product differentiation. Of course, successful cost leadership or product differentiation generally increases market share and helps a company to grow. To evaluate the success of a company's strategy, we subdivide changes in operating income into components that can be identified with growth, product differentiation, and cost leadership. Subdividing the change in operating income to evaluate the success of a company's strategy is similar to variance analysis, discussed in Chapters 7 and 8. The focus here, however, is on comparing actual operating performance over two different time periods and explicitly linking it to strategic choices. A company is considered to be successful in implementing its strategy when the amounts of the product differentiation, cost leadership, and growth components align closely with its strategy.

STRATEGIC ANALYSIS OF OPERATING INCOME

Points to Stress/Teaching Tip This is a difficult but important section. This strategic analysis is an example of how the modern accountant can add significant insight and value for the management team in assessing the effectiveness of their implementation of their strategy. You will need to spend some time "walking through" this example (or one of the problems) in class.

The following simplified example illustrates how operating income changes between two years can be divided into components that describe how successful a company has been with regard to cost leadership, product differentiation, and growth.[6]

Chipset presents the following data for the years 1999 and 2000.

[6]For other details, see R. Banker, S. Datar, and R. Kaplan, "Productivity Measurement and Management Accounting," *Journal of Accounting, Auditing, and Finance* (1989): 528–554.

	1999	2000
1. Good units of CX1 produced and sold	1,000,000	1,150,000
2. Defective units of CX1 produced and disposed of at zero net disposal price	500,000	300,000
3. Selling price	$27	$25
4. Direct materials (square centimeters of silicon wafer)	3,000,000	2,900,000
5. Direct materials cost per square centimeter	$1.40	$1.50
6. Manufacturing capacity	1,875,000 units	1,750,000 units
7. Total conversion costs	$11,250,000	$10,850,000
8. Conversion costs per unit of capacity (Row 7 ÷ Row 6)	$6	$6.20
9. Selling and customer-service capacity	60 customers	55 customers
10. Total selling and customer-service costs	$4,800,000	$4,400,000
11. Cost per customer of selling and customer-service capacity (Row 10 ÷ Row 9)	$80,000	$80,000
12. R&D employees	40	39
13. Total R&D costs	$4,000,000	$3,900,000
14. R&D costs per employee (Row 13 ÷ Row 12)	$100,000	$100,000

Chipset provides the following additional information.

1. Each unit of CX1 produced requires 2 square centimeters of silicon wafer.

2. *Conversion costs* are all manufacturing costs other than direct materials. Conversion costs for each year depend on production capacity defined in terms of the number of units of CX1 that can be produced. Such costs do not vary with the actual quantity of CX1 units produced. Because direct manufacturing labor costs are small (and tied to capacity), Chipset includes these costs with other manufacturing costs as part of conversion costs rather than as a separate cost category. To reduce conversion costs, management would have to reduce capacity by selling some of the manufacturing equipment and laying off some manufacturing personnel.

3. Most of Chipset's marketing costs are costs of selling chips to customers. Selling and customer-service costs for each year depend on the number of customers that the selling and customer-service functions are designed to support. They do not vary with the actual number of customers Chipset sells to in each year. Chipset had 40 customers in 1999 and 46 customers in 2000. To reduce selling and customer-service costs, Chipset management would have to lay off selling and customer-service staff.

4. At the start of each year, management uses its discretion to determine the amount of R&D to be done. The amount of R&D is independent of the actual quantity of CX1 produced or the number of customers to whom CX1 is sold.

5. The investment base and asset structure are not materially different in the years 1999 and 2000.

Operating income for each year is as follows.

	1999	2000
Revenues ($27 × 1,000,000; $25 × 1,150,000)	$27,000,000	$28,750,000
Costs		
Direct materials costs ($1.40 × 3,000,000; $1.50 × 2,900,000)	4,200,000	4,350,000
Conversion costs ($6 × 1,875,000; $6.20 × 1,750,000)	11,250,000	10,850,000
Selling and customer-service costs ($80,000 × 60; $80,000 × 55)	4,800,000	4,400,000
R&D costs	4,000,000	3,900,000
Total costs	24,250,000	23,500,000
Operating income	$ 2,750,000	$ 5,250,000
Increase in operating income	$2,500,000	

Reinforcing Problems Various types of strategic analysis issues are covered in Exer. 13-17, 13-19, and 13-23, and Prob. 13-28.

Our goal is to evaluate how much of this $2,500,000 increase in operating income was caused by the successful implementation of the company's strategy. To do so, we analyze three main components: growth, price recovery, and productivity.

The **growth component** measures the change in operating income attributable solely to an increase in the quantity of output sold between 1999 and 2000. That is, it measures the increase in revenues minus the increase in costs from selling more units of CX1. The calculations for the growth component are similar to the sales-volume variance introduced in Chapter 7.

The **price-recovery component** measures the change in operating income attributable solely to changes in Chipset's prices of inputs and outputs between 1999 and 2000. The calculations for the price-recovery component are similar to the selling-price variance and input price and spending variances for materials, labor, and overhead introduced in Chapters 7 and 8. The price-recovery component measures the amount by which output price increases outstrip input price increases. A company that has successfully pursued a strategy of product differentiation will be able to increase its output price faster than the increase in its input prices, boosting profit margins and operating income—it will show a large positive price-recovery component.

The **productivity component** measures the change in costs attributable to a change in the quantity of inputs used in 2000 relative to the quantity of inputs that would have been used in 1999 to produce the year 2000 output. The calculations for the productivity component are similar to the efficiency variances introduced in Chapters 7 and 8. The productivity component measures the amount by which operating income increases by using inputs productively to lower costs even when the prices of the products are not increasing. A company that has successfully pursued a strategy of cost leadership will be able to produce a given quantity of output with fewer inputs—it will show a large positive productivity component. Given Chipset's strategy of cost leadership, we expect the increase in operating income to be attributable to the productivity and growth components but not price recovery.

We now examine the three components in detail.

Growth Component

The growth component measures the increase in revenues minus the increase in costs from selling more units of CX1 in 2000 (1,150,000 units) compared to 1999 (1,000,000 units), assuming nothing else has changed. That is, the output prices, input prices, efficiencies, and capacities of 1999 are assumed to continue into 2000.

Revenue effect of growth

$$\text{Revenue effect of growth component} = \left(\begin{array}{c} \text{Actual units of} \\ \text{output sold} \\ \text{in 2000} \end{array} - \begin{array}{c} \text{Actual units of} \\ \text{output sold} \\ \text{in 1999} \end{array} \right) \times \begin{array}{c} \text{Output} \\ \text{price} \\ \text{in 1999} \end{array}$$

$$= (1,150,000 - 1,000,000) \times \$27 = \$4,050,000 \text{ F}$$

This component is favorable (F) because it increases operating income. Decreases in operating income are unfavorable (U).

Note that we keep the 1999 price of CX1 unchanged and focus only on the increase in output sold between 1999 and 2000. Why? Because the objective of the revenue effect of the growth component is to isolate the increase in revenues between 1999 and 2000 due solely to the change in the quantity sold, *assuming* the 1999 selling price continues into 2000.

Cost effect of growth

Of course, to produce the higher output sold in 2000, more inputs were needed. The cost increase from growth measures the amount by which costs in 2000 would have increased (1) if the 1999 relationship between inputs and outputs continued in 2000, and (2) if prices of inputs in 1999 continued in 2000.

$$\text{Cost effect of growth component} = \left(\begin{array}{c} \text{Actual units of input or} \\ \text{capacity that would} \\ \text{have been used in 1999 to produce} \\ \text{year 2000 output assuming} \\ \text{the same input-output} \\ \text{relationship that existed in 1999} \end{array} - \begin{array}{c} \text{Actual units of} \\ \text{inputs or capacity} \\ \text{to produce} \\ \text{1999 output} \end{array} \right) \times \begin{array}{c} \text{Input} \\ \text{prices} \\ \text{in 1999} \end{array}$$

We use 1999 input-output relationships and 1999 input prices because the goal is to isolate the increase in costs caused solely by the growth in the units of CX1 sold between 1999 and 2000. The actual units of input or capacity to produce 1999 output is given in the basic data for Chipset on p. 471. A brief explanation follows of the individual calculations for the actual units of input or capacity that would have been used to produce year 2000 output, assuming the same 1999 input-output relationship.

Direct materials. To produce 1,150,000 units of CX1 in 2000 compared to the 1,000,000 units produced in 1999 (15% more), Chipset would require a proportionate increase in the 3,000,000 square centimeters of direct materials used in 1999. That is, the quantity of direct materials required equals 3,450,000 square centimeters (3,000,000 × 1,150,000/1,000,000).

Conversion costs. For simplicity, our example assumes conversion costs are fixed costs at any given level of capacity. Chipset has 1,875,000 units of manufacturing capacity in 1999 at a cost of $11,250,000. To produce the higher year 2000 output of 1,150,000 units of CX1 in 1999, assuming the same 1999 input-output relationship, Chipset would need to use 1,725,000 units of this capacity. Therefore, Chipset would not need any additional capacity. The calculation of the 1,725,000 units is as follows: To produce 1,000,000 good units of CX1, Chipset actually processed 1,500,000 units of CX1 in 1999 (of which 500,000 units were defective). To produce 15% more units in 1999, assuming the same 1999 input-output (defect-rate) relationship, Chipset would be required to process 1,500,000 × 1.15 (the growth factor) = 1,725,000 units.

Curriculum Linkage Note that how costs behave makes a difference in how they change as volume changes. Because some of the costs of Chipset are fixed (e.g., selling and customer service costs) and the increase did not go outside the relevant range, these total costs would not change. Cost behavior and relevant range are discussed at length in Chaps. 2 and 10.

Selling and customer-service costs. Selling and customer-service costs are fixed costs at any given level of capacity. These costs would not change in 1999 if Chipset had to produce and sell the higher year 2000 volume of CX1 in 1999. The selling and customer-service capacity of 60 customers in 1999 is large enough to support both the 40 customers in 1999 and the 46 customers in 2000.

R&D costs. R&D costs are fixed costs unless management uses its discretion to change the level of costs. The R&D costs would not change in 1999 if Chipset had to produce and sell the higher year 2000 volume in 1999. R&D costs are adequate to support the higher output of CX1. R&D costs do not depend on either the quantity of CX1 produced or the number of customers to whom CX1 is sold.

The cost effects of growth component are:

Direct materials costs	(3,450,000 − 3,000,000) × $1.40	= $630,000 U
Conversion costs	(1,875,000 − 1,875,000) × $6	= 0
Selling and customer-service costs	(60 − 60) × $80,000	= 0
R&D costs	(40 − 40) × $100,000	= 0
Cost effects of growth component		$630,000 U

In summary, the net increase in operating income as a result of growth equals:

Revenue effect of growth component	$4,050,000 F
Cost effect of growth component	630,000 U
Increase in operating income due to growth component	$3,420,000 F

Price-Recovery Component

The price-recovery component of operating income measures the change in revenues and the change in costs to produce the 1,150,000 units of CX1 manufactured in 2000 caused solely by the change in the price of CX1 and the change in the prices of inputs required to make CX1 between 1999 and 2000, assuming that the 1999 relationship between inputs and outputs continued in 2000.

Revenue effect of price recovery

$$\begin{matrix} \text{Revenue effect of} \\ \text{price-recovery} \\ \text{component} \end{matrix} = \left(\begin{matrix} \text{Output price} \\ \text{in 2000} \end{matrix} - \begin{matrix} \text{Output price} \\ \text{in 1999} \end{matrix} \right) \times \begin{matrix} \text{Actual units} \\ \text{of output} \\ \text{sold in 2000} \end{matrix}$$

$$= (\$25 - \$27) \times 1,150,000 = \$2,300,000 \text{ U}$$

Points to Stress When calculating the price-recovery component (both the revenue effect and the cost effect of selling price and input price changes), the current year's units sold (for the revenue effect) and the actual units of inputs or capacity that would have been used to produce this year's output, assuming last year's input-to-output relationship holds (for the cost effect), are used because the firm is attempting to isolate the change in revenues and costs caused solely by price changes.

Note that the calculation focuses on the decrease in the price of CX1 between 1999 and 2000. Why? Because the objective of the revenue effect of price recovery is to isolate the change in revenues between 1999 and 2000 due solely to the change in selling prices.

Cost effect of price recovery

$$\begin{array}{l}\text{Cost effect of} \\ \text{price-recovery} = \\ \text{component}\end{array} \left(\begin{array}{cc}\text{Input} & \text{Input} \\ \text{prices in} - \text{prices in} \\ 2000 & 1999\end{array}\right) \times \begin{array}{c}\text{Actual units of inputs or capacity} \\ \text{that would have been used} \\ \text{to produce year 2000 output} \\ \text{assuming the same input-output} \\ \text{relationship that} \\ \text{existed in 1999}\end{array}$$

Direct materials costs	($1.50 − $1.40) × 3,450,000 =	$345,000 U
Conversion costs	($6.20 − $6.00) × 1,875,000 =	375,000 U
Selling and customer-service costs	($80,000 − $80,000) × 60 =	0
R&D costs	($100,000 − $100,000) × 40 =	0
Total cost effect of price-recovery component		$720,000 U

Note that the quantity of inputs needed to produce the output in year 2000, (using the 1999 input-output relationship), has already been determined when calculating the cost effects of growth. The calculation focuses on the change in costs caused solely by the change in the input prices between 1999 and 2000.

In summary, the net decrease in operating income attributable to price recovery (measured by the change in output prices relative to the change in input prices) is:

Revenue effect of price-recovery component	$2,300,000 U
Cost effect of price-recovery component	720,000 U
Decrease in operating income due to price-recovery component	$3,020,000 U

The price-recovery analysis indicates that, even as the prices of its inputs increased, Chipset could not pass these increases on to its customers via higher prices of CX1.

Productivity Component

The productivity component of operating income uses year 2000 input prices to measure how costs have decreased as a result of using fewer inputs, a better mix of inputs, and less capacity to produce year 2000 output compared to the inputs and capacity that would have been used based on the input-output relationship that existed in 1999.

$$\begin{array}{l}\text{Productivity} \\ \text{component}\end{array} = \left(\begin{array}{cc}\text{Actual units of} \\ \text{inputs or capacity} \\ \text{to produce} \\ \text{year 2000 output}\end{array} - \begin{array}{c}\text{Actual units of} \\ \text{inputs or capacity that} \\ \text{would have been used} \\ \text{to produce year 2000} \\ \text{output assuming the same} \\ \text{input-output relationship} \\ \text{that existed in 1999}\end{array}\right) \times \begin{array}{c}\text{Input} \\ \text{prices in} \\ 2000\end{array}$$

Note that the calculations use year 2000 prices and year 2000 output. Why? Because the objective of the productivity component is to isolate the change in costs between 1999 and 2000 caused solely by the change in the quantities, mix, and capacities of inputs.

The actual units of capacity that would have been used to produce year 2000 output, assuming the same 1999 input-output relationship, have already been calculated and explained when computing the growth component (pp. 472–473). The actual units of inputs or capacity to produce year 2000 output is given in the basic data for Chipset on p. 471.

The productivity component of cost changes is:

Direct materials costs	(2,900,000 − 3,450,000) × $1.50 =	$ 825,000 F
Conversion costs	(1,750,000 − 1,875,000) × $6.20 =	775,000 F
Selling and customer-service costs	(55 − 60) × $80,000 =	400,000 F
R&D costs	(39 − 40) × $100,000 =	100,000 F
Increase in operating income due to productivity component		$2,100,000 F

JAZZ

"COST ACCOUNTING IS MUSIC TO YOUR EARS!"

COST ACCOUNTING, *Tenth Edition*
Charles T. Horngren, George Foster, and Srikant M. Datar

Jazz begins with a core of music, but changes and builds from moment to moment depending on the moods of the players and the audience. A jazz musician must be able to take a situation as it occurs and adapt to it to plan his next move . . . just like a strategic business decision maker. **Cost Accounting, 10th ed.,** teaches students to use accounting information to feel the groove of any business situation and improvise to formulate strategic business decisions.

◆ Cool **NEW Chapter 13 on strategy and balanced scorecard** discusses the applications of management to strategy, implementation of strategy, and the balanced scorecard to evaluate strategy, reengineering, and downsizing, strategic profitability analysis, and productivity measurement. **No other text has a comprehensive chapter treatment of the applications of management accounting to strategy!**

◆ Composes and arranges concepts in a smooth and simple setting, with sections added to show how those concepts can be applied in companies that implement ABC systems.

"The entire chapter covering organizational strategy, the 'balanced scorecard,' and strategic profitability analysis deals with material not usually (or perhaps ever) treated in the typical cost accounting course. This material represents current/emerging thought in the use of accounting for organizational management and control."
—Gary J. Mann,
University of Texas at ElPaso

"The Chipset example, which flows smoothly through the chapter, is an excellent idea. Too often we have these topics taught in abstract segments with no numbers, and this chapter shows how to do it right."
–Arijit Mukherji,
University of Minnesota

"This is a benefit for today's students. I read so much about accountants being involved in top-level management, yet the text topics do not seem to give concrete information about how an accountant would use the tools of accounting to aid in those top-level decisions. . . . I am so pleased to have this material to use with my students in today's business world."
–Jean Hawkins,
William Jewell College

We comment briefly on the individual items of the productivity component.

Direct materials. As indicated earlier, at the 1999 quality levels, Chipset would have required 3,450,000 (3,000,000 × 1,150,000/1,000,000) square centimeters of silicon wafers to produce 1,150,000 good units of CX1 in 2000. As a result of improvements in quality and yield, Chipset processes 2,900,000 square centimeters of silicon wafers [or the equivalent of 1,450,000 (2,900,000 ÷ 2) units of CX1].

Conversion costs are fixed costs that change only if management takes actions to alter manufacturing capacity. Because of the reengineered processes and quality improvements, Chipset needs to put into process only 1,450,000 units to produce 1,150,000 good units of CX1 in the year 2000. In 1999, Chipset had the capacity to process 1,875,000 units. To reduce costs, Chipset's management decreases capacity to 1,750,000 units of CX1, by selling some old equipment and laying off some workers.

Selling and customer-service costs are fixed costs that change only if management takes actions to alter selling and customer-service capacity. Chipset has 46 customers in the year 2000, but it started 2000 with a selling and customer-service capacity of 60 customers. Although Chipset may add more customers, the goal of reengineering the order-delivery process is to enter into long-term contracts to increase sales to existing customers. To reduce costs, Chipset's management decreases capacity to 55 customers by not replacing marketing personnel that retired or quit.

R&D costs are also fixed costs that change only if management takes actions to reduce the number of R&D employees. Chipset has 39 research engineers in the year 2000, but it started 2000 with 40 engineers. Chipset's management did not replace the engineer who quit in 2000.

The productivity component indicates that Chipset was able to increase operating income by improving quality and productivity, eliminating capacity, and reducing costs. The Appendix to the chapter examines partial and total factor productivity changes between 1999 and 2000 and describes how the management accountant can obtain a deeper understanding of Chipset's cost leadership strategy.

Exhibit 13-3 summarizes the growth, price-recovery, and productivity components of the changes in operating income. At a basic level, companies that have been successful at cost leadership will show large favorable productivity and growth components. Companies that have successfully differentiated their products will show large favorable price-recovery and growth components. In Chipset's case, productivity contributed $2,100,000 to the increase in operating income and growth contributed $3,420,000. Operating income suffered because Chipset was unable to pass along increases in input prices. Had Chipset been able to differentiate its product, the price-recovery effects may have been less unfavorable or perhaps even favorable.

EXHIBIT 13-3
Strategic Analysis of Profitability

	Income Statement Amounts in 1999 (1)	Revenue and Cost Effects of Growth Component in 2000 (2)	Revenue and Cost Effects of Price-Recovery Component in 2000 (3)	Cost Effect of Productivity Component in 2000 (4)	Income Statement Amounts in 2000 (5) = (1) + (2) + (3) + (4)
Revenues	$27,000,000	$4,050,000 F	$2,300,000 U	—	$28,750,000
Costs	24,250,000	630,000 U	720,000 U	$2,100,000 F	23,500,000
Operating income	$ 2,750,000	$3,420,000 F	$3,020,000 U	$2,100,000 F	$ 5,250,000

$2,500,000 F
Change in operating income

Reinforcing Problems Exer. 13-20 and 13-24 and Prob. 13-29 cover various issues related to further analysis of growth, price-recovery, and productivity components.

Points to Stress Notice how further analysis is able to give management more strategic information to evaluate its policies. By parcelling out the effect of the growth in the market in the Chipset example, the firm's managers can separate out what they have accomplished (with either cost leadership and/or product differentiation) vs. what was caused by changes in the firm's environment.

Further Analysis of Growth, Price-Recovery, and Productivity Components

As in all variance and profit analysis, the thoughtful analyst will want to analyze the sources of operating income more closely. For instance, in the Chipset example, growth may have been helped by an increase in industry market size. Therefore, at least a part of the increase in operating income may be attributable to favorable economic conditions in the industry rather than to any successful implementation of strategy. Some of the growth may also have come as a result of a management decision at Chipset to take advantage of its productivity gains by decreasing prices. In this case, the increase in operating income from cost leadership equals the productivity gain plus any increase in operating income from growth in market share attributable to productivity improvements minus any decrease in operating income from a strategic decision to lower prices.

To illustrate these ideas, consider again the Chipset example and the following additional information.

◆ The market growth rate in the industry is 10 percent. That is, of the 150,000 $(1,150,000 - 1,000,000)$ units of increase in sales of CX1 between 1999 and 2000, 100,000 ($10\% \times 1,000,000$) units are due to an increase in industry market size (which Chipset would have benefited from regardless of its productivity gains) and the remaining 50,000 units are due to an increase in market share.

◆ During the year 2000, Chipset experiences a $1.35 or 5% decline in the price of CX1 ($5\% \times \$27 = \$1.35$). Taking advantage of productivity gains, management reduces the price of CX1 by an additional $0.65, which leads to the 50,000 unit increase in market share. [Recall that the total decrease in the price of CX1 is $2 ($1.35 + $0.65).]

The effect on Chipset's operating income from the industry-market size factor rather than any specific strategic actions is:

Increase in operating income due to growth in industry market size

$$\$3{,}420{,}000 \text{ (Exhibit 13-3, column 2)} \times \frac{100{,}000}{150{,}000} \qquad \$2{,}280{,}000 \text{ F}$$

Lacking a differentiated product, Chipset experiences a $1.35 decline in output prices even while the prices of its inputs increase. *The effect of product differentiation on operating income* is:

Decrease in operating income due to a decline in the selling price of CX1 (other than the strategic reduction in price included as part of the cost leadership component) $1.35 \times 1,150,000$	$1,552,500 U
Increase in prices of inputs (cost effect of price recovery)	720,000 U
Decrease in operating income due to product differentiation	$2,272,500 U

The effect on operating income from cost leadership as follows:

Productivity component	$2,100,000 F
Effect of strategic decision to reduce price of CX1 ($0.65 \times 1,150,000$ units)	747,500 U
Growth in market share due to productivity improvement and strategic decision to reduce prices	
$\$3{,}420{,}000 \text{ (Exhibit 13-3, column 2)} \times \dfrac{50{,}000 \text{ units}}{150{,}000 \text{ units}}$	1,140,000 F
Increase in operating income due to cost leadership	$2,492,500 F

The change in operating income between 1999 and 2000 can then be summarized as:

Change due to industry market size	$2,280,000 F
Change due to product differentiation	2,272,500 U
Change due to cost leadership	2,492,500 F
Change in operating income	$2,500,000 F

Linking Performance to Strategy at Chrysler Corporation

Chrysler Corporation's impressive profits in recent years have come despite steep reductions in the selling prices of its products. Chrysler, like many of its competitors in the automotive market, offers "manufacturer rebates" (price discounts) to spur sales. For example, through the third quarter that ended on September 30, 1998 (Chrysler's last quarter as an independent company prior to its merger with Daimler-Benz), Chrysler offered significant price discounts on its vehicles to entice buyers. As news of these high 1998 price discounts reached Wall Street, investors and analysts expected Chrysler's operating income to decrease. But Chrysler easily surpassed Wall Street's expectations. How? Through productivity gains that resulted in lower costs. Chrysler passed on these cost savings to its customers in the form of lower prices in return for higher sales and an increase in its North American market share from 15.1% in 1997 to 16% in 1998.

Chrysler's goal was to cut costs by $1.5 billion in 1998. By September 1998, Chrysler had already cut costs by about $1.1 billion. Improvements in efficiency and productivity reduced engineered costs of direct materials and manufacturing labor, as well as indirect manufacturing costs by hundreds of millions of dollars. Chrysler also cut discretionary costs such as advertising.

Chrysler's strategic analysis of operating income for 1998 indicates that operating income increases were due largely to successful implementation of its cost leadership strategy. Cost leadership, however, is not the key strategy in all of Chrysler's businesses. Chrysler is an innovative product differentiator in the minivan and sports utility vehicle (SUV) market. It "invented" the minivan and has a very strong presence in the SUV market. Its Dodge Caravan and Plymouth Voyager minivans and its Dodge Durango, Jeep, and Jeep Cherokee SUVs enjoy high margins because customers are willing to pay premium prices for these innovative products.

Chrysler emphasizes both financial and nonfinancial measures. For example, the company regularly monitors nonfinancial measures of customer satisfaction, customer preferences, delivery times, quality, defects and yields, new product development time, and employee capability, skills, and satisfaction. These nonfinancial measures span the four perspectives—financial, customer, internal business process, and learning and growth—of the balanced scorecard.

Source: Adapted from B. J. Feder, "Chrysler Posts Strong Second Quarter Earning," *New York Times* (July 14, 1998): D2; K. Bradsher, "Chrysler Net Rises 54%, Beating Forecasts," *New York Times* (October 13, 1998): C2. Chrysler Corp. 3rd Quarter 10Q Report, and conversations with Chrysler executives.

Under different assumptions of how the change in selling price affects the quantity of CX1 sold, the analyst will attribute different amounts to the different strategies. The important point, though, is that, consistent with its cost leadership strategy, the productivity gains of $2,100,000 Chipset made in 2000 were key to the operating income increases in 2000. The Problem for Self-Study describes the analysis of the growth, price-recovery and productivity components for a company following a product differentiation strategy.

DOWNSIZING AND THE MANAGEMENT OF CAPACITY

As we saw in our discussion of the productivity component, fixed costs are tied to capacity. Unlike variable costs, fixed costs do not change automatically with changes in activity level (such as units started into production in the case of manufacturing overhead costs). How then can managers reduce capacity-based fixed costs? The key is in measuring and managing *unused capacity*. **Unused capacity** is the additional amount of productive capacity available over and above the productive capacity

OBJECTIVE 5

Distinguish between engineered and discretionary costs

Reinforcing Problems Prob. 13-35 covers downsizing; Exer. 13-21 and 13-25 cover capacity management issues, and Probs. 13-30 and 13-31 cover engineered and discretionary costs.

Teaching Tip Point out to students that the major difference between engineered and discretionary costs are whether the costs have a clear cause-and-effect relationship between output and the costs of the resources available and/or consumed (i.e., the input/output relationship of the process). Engineered costs have that cause-and-effect relationship of inputs-to-outputs with a low level of uncertainty as to the amount of resources needed for a given level of output. Discretionary costs are those mysterious "black boxes" where input-to-output is not clearly defined or understood, and the level of resources needed to achieve a given level of output is very uncertain.

employed to meet consumer demand in the current period. To understand unused capacity, it is important to distinguish between *engineered* and *discretionary* costs.

Engineered costs result from a cause-and-effect relationship between the cost driver, output, and the (direct or indirect) resources used to produce that output. In the Chipset example, direct material costs are an example of direct engineered costs. Conversion costs are an example of indirect engineered costs. Consider the year 2000. The output of 1,150,000 units of CX1 and the efficiency with which inputs are converted into outputs result in 1,450,000 units of CX1 started into production. Manufacturing conversion resources needed and used to process 1,450,000 units of CX1 equal $8,990,000 ($6.20 × 1,450,000), assuming that the cost of resources used increases proportionately with the number of units started. Of course, total conversion costs are higher ($10,850,000) because they are related to the manufacturing capacity of 1,750,000 units ($6.20 × 1,750,000 = $10,850,000). Although these costs are fixed in the short run, over time there is a cause-and-effect relationship between output and manufacturing capacity required (and conversion costs needed). Thus, engineered costs can be variable or fixed in the short run. Selling and customer-service costs are also an example of engineered costs that are fixed in the short run. There is, however, a cause-and-effect relationship between selling and customer-service resources used and the number of customers served.

Discretionary costs have two important features: (1) They arise from periodic (usually annual) decisions regarding the maximum amount to be incurred, and (2) they have no measurable cause-and-effect relationship between output and resources used. There is often a delay between the acquisition of a resource and its eventual use. Examples of discretionary costs include advertising, executive training, R&D, health care, and corporate staff department costs such as legal, human resources, and public relations. The most noteworthy aspect of discretionary costs is that managers are seldom confident that the "correct" amounts are being spent. The founder of Lever Brothers, an international consumer-products company, once noted, "Half the money I spend on advertising is wasted; the trouble is, I don't know which half." In the Chipset example, R&D costs are discretionary costs because there is no measurable cause-and-effect relationship between output of 1,150,000 units produced and R&D resources needed or used.[7]

Relationships between Inputs and Outputs

Engineered costs differ from discretionary costs along two key dimensions: the type of process and the level of uncertainty. Engineered costs pertain to processes that are detailed, physically observable, and repetitive, such as manufacturing or customer-service activities. In contrast, discretionary costs are associated with processes that are sometimes called *black boxes*, because they are less precise and not well understood.

Uncertainty refers to the possibility that an actual amount will deviate from an expected amount. The higher the level of uncertainty about the relationship between resources used and outputs, the less likely a cause-and-effect relationship will exist, leading the cost to be classified as a discretionary cost. R&D costs have an uncertain effect on output because other factors such as overall market conditions, competitors' R&D investments, and new product introductions also affect the level of output produced. In contrast, there is a low level of uncertainty about the effect of output on manufacturing conversion resources used because other factors do not affect this relationship. Uncertainty is greater in the case of discretionary costs such

---

[7]Managers also describe some costs as **infrastructure costs**, costs that arise from having property, plant and equipment, and a functioning organization. Examples are depreciation, long-run lease rental, and the acquisition of long-run technical capabilities. These costs are generally fixed costs, because they are committed to and acquired before they are used. Infrastructure costs can be engineered or discretionary. For instance, manufacturing overhead costs incurred at Chipset to acquire manufacturing capacity is an infrastructure cost that is an example of an engineered cost. In the long run, there is a cause-and-effect relationship between output and lease rental costs needed to produce that output. R&D costs incurred to acquire technical capability is an infrastructure cost that is an example of a discretionary cost. There is no measurable cause-and-effect relationship between output and R&D costs incurred.

EXHIBIT 13-4
Differences Between Engineered and Discretionary Costs

	Engineered Costs	**Discretionary Costs**
◆ Process or activity	◆ **a.** Detailed and physically observable	◆ **a.** Black box (knowledge of process is sketchy or un-available)
	b. Repetitive	**b.** Nonrepetitive or nonrou-tine
◆ Level of uncertainty	◆ Moderate or small (for example, shipping or manufacturing settings)	◆ Large (for example, R&D or advertising settings)

Source: This exhibit is a modification of one suggested by H. Itami.

as R&D because, in most cases, R&D resources are committed well before any out-put is produced. Exhibit 13-4 summarizes these key distinctions between engi-neered and discretionary costs.

Identifying Unused Capacity for Engineered and Discretionary Overhead Costs

How does the distinction between engineered and discretionary costs help a man-ager to understand and manage unused capacity? Actually, the different types of costs have very different relationships to capacity. Consider first the engineered conversion costs. Chipset management indicates that manufacturing capacity can be added or reduced in increments of 125,000 units. Adding or reducing capacity, however, takes time. Conversion costs are a step function as shown in Exhibit 13-5. Each step represents increments of 125,000 units of capacity at a cost of $775,000. At each step, conversion costs are fixed. For example, conversion costs are fixed at

OBJECTIVE 6

Identify and manage un-used capacity

EXHIBIT 13-5
Engineered Costs and Unused Capacity at Chipset, Inc., in 2000

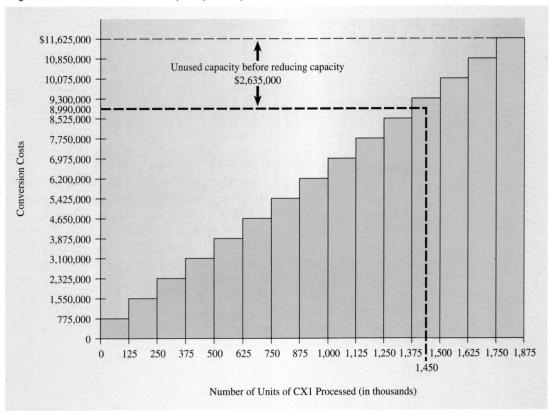

$9,300,000 if Chipset wants enough capacity to process between 1,375,000 and 1,500,000 units.

At the start of the year 2000, Chipset has capacity to process 1,875,000 units. Quality and productivity improvements made during 2000 enable Chipset to produce 1,150,000 units of CX1 by processing 1,450,000 units. Chipset calculates its unused manufacturing capacity as 425,000 (1,875,000 − 1,450,000) units at the beginning of 2000, which corresponds to conversion costs of $2,635,000 ($6.20 × 425,000 units). As shown in Exhibit 13-5, this unused capacity of $2,635,000 can also be calculated as $11,625,000 (manufacturing overhead costs for 1,875,000 units) minus $8,990,000 ($6.20 × 1,450,000, the manufacturing resources used to process 1,450,000 units).

The absence of a cause-and-effect relationship makes identifying unused capacity for discretionary costs much more difficult. Management cannot determine the R&D resources used for the actual output produced to compare R&D capacity against. Consequently, they cannot compute unused capacity as they can in the case of the engineered conversion costs.

Managing Unused Capacity

Points to Stress Notice in the Chipset example how being able to identify the unused capacity for the engineered cost assists management in managing those costs because they know a lot about the input-to-output relationship (in this example a step-fixed cost relationship).

Curriculum Linkage When companies correctly implement downsizing, they do so by eliminating nonvalue-added activities. Nonvalue- and value-added activities and costs are discussed in Chap. 12.

What actions can Chipset management take when it identifies unused capacity? In general, it has two options. It can attempt to eliminate the unused capacity, or it can attempt to grow revenues with the unused capacity.

In recent years, many companies have *downsized* in an attempt to eliminate their unused capacity. **Downsizing** (also called **rightsizing**) is an integrated approach configuring processes, products, and people in order to match costs to the activities that need to be performed for operating effectively and efficiently in the present and future. Companies, such as AT&T, Delta Airlines, General Motors, IBM, and Scott Paper, have downsized to focus on their core businesses and have instituted organization changes to increase efficiency, reduce costs, and improve quality. Downsizing often means eliminating jobs, which can have an adverse effect on employee morale and the culture of the organization. It is important that downsizing be done in the context of the organization's overall strategy, and by retaining individuals with key management, leadership, and technical skills.

Consider Chipset's options with respect to its unused manufacturing capacity. Because it needs to process 1,450,000 units in 2000, it could potentially reduce capacity to 1,500,000 units (recall that manufacturing capacity can be added or reduced only in increments of 125,000 units) resulting in cost savings of $2,325,000 [(1,875,000 − 1,500,000) × $6.20]. Chipset's strategy, however, is not only to reduce costs but also to grow its business. So early in 2000, Chipset reduces its manufacturing capacity by only 125,000 units from 1,875,000 units to 1,750,000 units, saving $775,000 ($6.20 × 125,000). It retains some unused capacity for future growth. By avoiding greater reductions in capacity, it also maintains the morale of its skilled and capable workforce. The success of this strategy will depend on Chipset achieving the future growth it has projected.

Chipset makes similar decisions with respect to the engineered selling and customer-service costs. At the start of 2000, Chipset has the capacity to serve 60 customers. Chipset currently has 46 customers, resulting in unused service capacity of 14 customers, which corresponds to $1,120,000 ($80,000 × 14) in selling and customer-service costs. (Recall that it costs $80,000 to support each customer.) Chipset could potentially reduce selling and customer-service capacity by 10 customers. However, because the company anticipates adding 9 more customers in the near future, it decides to only reduce its selling and customer-service capability from 60 to 55 customers realizing savings of $400,000 ($80,000 × 5). Chipset's goal is to align its selling and customer-service capabilities of 55 customers with its manufacturing capacity of 1,750,000 units.

Because identifying unused capacity for discretionary costs is difficult, downsizing or otherwise managing this unused capacity is also difficult. Chipset's management uses judgment and discretion to reduce R&D costs by $100,000 in 2000. Its rationale is to reduce R&D costs without significantly affecting the output of the

R&D activity. Greater reductions in R&D costs, however, could harm the business by slowing down critically needed product and process improvements. The key is to balance the need for cost reductions without compromising quality, continuous improvement, and future growth. Not balancing these factors led Delta Airlines board of directors to replace the airline's CEO in 1997. Even though aggressive cost cutting had restored Delta Airlines to profitability, the board felt that those cuts had compromised customer satisfaction, a key to the company's future success and growth.

PROBLEM FOR SELF-STUDY

PROBLEM

Following a strategy of product differentiation, Westwood Corporation makes a high-end kitchen range hood, KE8. Westwood presents the following data for the years 1999 and 2000.

	1999	2000
1. Units of KE8 produced and sold	40,000	42,000
2. Selling price	$100	$110
3. Direct materials (square feet)	120,000	123,000
4. Direct materials costs per square foot	$10	$11
5. Manufacturing capacity for KE8	50,000 units	50,000 units
6. Total conversion costs	$1,000,000	$1,100,000
7. Conversion costs per unit of capacity (Row 6 ÷ Row 5)	$20	$22
8. Selling and customer-service capacity	30 customers	29 customers
9. Total selling and customer-service costs	$720,000	$725,000
10. Cost per customer of selling and customer-service capacity (Row 9 ÷ Row 8)	$24,000	$25,000

Westwood produces no defective units, but it reduces direct materials usage per unit of KE8 in 2000. Conversion costs in each year depend on production capacity defined in terms of KE8 units that can be produced. Selling and customer-service costs depend on the number of customers that the selling and service functions are designed to support. Westwood has 23 customers in 1999 and 25 customers in 2000.

Required

1. Describe briefly key elements that you would include in Westwood's balanced scorecard.
2. Calculate the growth, price-recovery, and productivity components that explain the change in operating income from 1999 to 2000.
3. Suppose that during 2000, the market for high-end kitchen range hoods grew at 3%. Suppose further that all increases in market share (that is, sales increases greater than 3%) are due to Westwood's product differentiation strategy. Calculate how much of the change in operating income from 1999 to 2000 is due to the industry-market-size factor, cost leadership, and product differentiation. How successful has Westwood been in implementing its strategy? Explain.

SOLUTION

1. Westwood's scorecard should describe Westwood's product differentation strategy. Key elements that Westwood should include in its balanced scorecard are:

◆ *Financial perspective* Increase in operating income from charging higher margins on KE8.

◆ *Customer perspective* Market share in high-end kitchen range market, and customer satisfaction.

- *Internal business perspective* Manufacturing quality, order delivery time, on-time delivery, and new product features added.
- *Learning and growth perspective* Development time for designing new products and improvments in manufacturing processes.

2. Operating income for each year is as follows:

	1999	2000
Revenues ($100 × 40,000; $110 × 42,000)	$4,000,000	$4,620,000
Costs		
Direct materials costs ($10 × 120,000; $11 × 123,000)	1,200,000	1,353,000
Conversion costs ($20 × 50,000; $22 × 50,000)	1,000,000	1,100,000
Selling & customer service costs ($24,000 × 30; $25,000 × 29)	720,000	725,000
Total costs	2,920,000	3,178,000
Operating income	$1,080,000	$1,442,000

Change in operating income — $362,000 F

Growth Component

$$\begin{array}{c}\text{Revenue effect} \\ \text{of growth} \\ \text{component}\end{array} = \left(\begin{array}{c}\text{Actual units of} \\ \text{output sold} \\ \text{in 2000}\end{array} - \begin{array}{c}\text{Actual units of} \\ \text{output sold} \\ \text{in 1999}\end{array}\right) \times \begin{array}{c}\text{Output} \\ \text{price} \\ \text{in 1999}\end{array}$$

$$= (42,000 - 40,000) \times \$100 = \$200,000 \text{ F}$$

$$\begin{array}{c}\text{Cost effect} \\ \text{of growth} \\ \text{component}\end{array} = \left(\begin{array}{c}\text{Actual units of input or} \\ \text{capacity that would} \\ \text{have been used to produce} \\ \text{year 2000 output assuming} \\ \text{the same input-output} \\ \text{relationship that existed in 1999}\end{array} - \begin{array}{c}\text{Actual units of} \\ \text{inputs or capacity} \\ \text{to produce} \\ \text{1999 output}\end{array}\right) \times \begin{array}{c}\text{Input} \\ \text{prices} \\ \text{in 1999}\end{array}$$

Direct materials costs that would be required in 2000 to produce 42,000 units instead of the 40,000 units produced in 1999, assuming the 1999 input-output relationship continued into 2000, equal 126,000 square feet [(120,000 ÷ 40,000) × 42,000]. Conversion costs and selling and customer-service costs will not change since adequate capacity exists in 1999 to support year 2000 output and customers.

The cost effects of growth component are:

Direct materials costs	(126,000 − 120,000) × $10 =	$60,000 U
Conversion costs	(50,000 − 50,000) × $20 =	0
Selling and customer-service costs	(30 − 30) × $25,000 =	0
Cost effect of growth component		$60,000 U

In summary, the net increase in operating income as a result of the growth component equals:

Revenue effect of growth component	$200,000 F
Cost effect of growth component	60,000 U
Increase in operating income due to growth component	$140,000 F

Price-Recovery Component

$$\begin{array}{c}\text{Revenue effect of} \\ \text{price-recovery} \\ \text{component}\end{array} = \left(\begin{array}{c}\text{Output price} \\ \text{in 2000}\end{array} - \begin{array}{c}\text{Output price} \\ \text{in 1999}\end{array}\right) \times \begin{array}{c}\text{Actual units} \\ \text{of output} \\ \text{sold in 2000}\end{array}$$

$$= (\$110 - \$100) \times 42,000 = \$420,000 \text{ F}$$

$$\begin{array}{c}\text{Cost effect of}\\\text{price-recovery}\\\text{component}\end{array}=\left(\begin{array}{c}\text{Input}\\\text{prices in}\\\text{year}\\2000\end{array}-\begin{array}{c}\text{Input}\\\text{prices in}\\\text{year}\\1999\end{array}\right)\times\begin{array}{c}\text{Actual units of inputs or capacity}\\\text{that would have been used}\\\text{to produce year 2000 output}\\\text{assuming the same input-output}\\\text{relationship that}\\\text{existed in 1999}\end{array}$$

Direct materials costs	($11 − $10) × 126,000 = $126,000 U
Conversion costs	($22 − $20) × 50,000 = 100,000 U
Selling and customer-service costs	($25,000 − $24,000) × 30 = 30,000 U
Total cost effect of price-recovery component	$256,000 U

In summary, the net increase in operating income as a result of the price-recovery component equals

Revenue effect of price-recovery component	$420,000 F
Cost effect of price-recovery component	256,000 U
Increase in operating income due to price-recovery component	$164,000 F

Productivity Component

$$\begin{array}{c}\text{Productivity}\\\text{component}\end{array}=\left(\begin{array}{c}\text{Actual units of}\\\text{inputs or capacity}\\\text{used to produce}\\\text{year 2000 output}\end{array}-\begin{array}{c}\text{Actual units of}\\\text{inputs or capacity that}\\\text{would have been used}\\\text{to produce year 2000}\\\text{output assuming the same}\\\text{input-output relationship}\\\text{that existed in 1999}\end{array}\right)\times\begin{array}{c}\text{Input}\\\text{prices in}\\2000\end{array}$$

The productivity component of cost changes are:

Direct materials costs	(123,000 − 126,000) × $11 = $33,000 F
Conversion costs	(50,000 − 50,000) × $20 = 0
Selling and customer-service costs	(29 − 30) × $25,000 = 25,000 F
Increase in operating income due to productivity component	$58,000 F

The change in operating income between 1999 and 2000 can be analyzed as follows:

	Income Statement Amounts in 1999 (1)	Revenue and Cost Effects of Growth Component in 2000 (2)	Revenue and Cost Effects of Price-Recovery Component in 2000 (3)	Cost Effect of Productivity Component in 2000 (4)	Income Statement Amounts in 2000 (5) = (1) + (2) + (3) + (4)
Revenues	$4,000,000	$200,000 F	$420,000 F	—	$4,620,000
Costs	2,920,000	60,000 U	256,000 U	$58,000 F	3,178,000
Operating income	$1,080,000	$140,000 F	$164,000 F	$58,000 F	$1,442,000

$$\uparrow \qquad \$362,000\ \text{F} \qquad \uparrow$$

Change in operating income

3. *Effect of the industry-market-size factor*
Of the 2,000 unit increase in sales from 40,000 to 42,000 units, 3% or 1,200 units (3% × 40,000) is due to growth in market size and 800 units (2,000 − 1,200) is due to an increase in market share. The increase in Chipset's operating income from the industry-market-size factor rather than specific strategic actions is

$$\$140,000 \text{ (column 2 of preceding table)} \times \frac{1,200}{2,000} \qquad\qquad \$84,000\ \text{F}$$

Effect of product differentiation
The increase in operating income due to:

Increase in the selling price of KE8 (revenue effect of price recovery)	$420,000 F
Increase in prices of inputs (cost effect of price recovery)	256,000 U
Growth in market share due to product differentiation	
$140,000 (column 2 of preceding table) $\times \dfrac{800}{2,000}$	56,000 F
Increase in operating income due to product differentiation	$220,000 F

Effect of cost leadership
The increase in operating income from cost leadership is:

Productivity component	$58,000 F

The change in operating income from 1999 to 2000 can be summarized as follows:

Change due to industry-market-size factor	$ 84,000 F
Change due to product differentiation	220,000 F
Change due to cost leadership	58,000 F
Change in operating income	$362,000 F

The analysis of operating income indicates that a significant amount of the increase in operating income resulted from Westwood's successful implementation of its product differentiation strategy. The company was able to continue to charge a premium price for KE8 and increase market share. Westwood was also able to earn additional operating income from improving its productivity.

Points to Stress Note the differences between the analyses for Chipset (C) and Westwood (W): (1) The items emphasized in their BS are different. Each BS is created based on that company's strategic goals, so we would expect differences as C follows a cost leadership strategy while W emphasizes product differentiation. (2) Some items in the BS are the same. Both focus on mfg. quality, on-time delivery, and improving mfg. processes. (3) W's change in OI was more balanced from the 3 components, while C's was heavily growth and productivity oriented (with a loss from the price component). W's increase in OI vs. C's were: (a) Growth Component W = 39%; C = 137%, (b) Price-recovery Component W = 45%; C = −121%, and (c) Productivity Component W = 16%; C = 84%. The different numerical results are what should be expected from their different strategic focuses.

SUMMARY

The following points are linked to this chapter's learning objectives:

1. Two generic strategies that organizations use are product differentiation and cost leadership. Product differentiation refers to offering products and services that are perceived by customers as being superior and unique. Cost leadership is achieving low costs relative to competitors.

2. Reengineering is the fundamental rethinking of business processes, such as order delivery, to improve critical performance measures such as cost, quality, or customer satisfaction.

3. The balanced scorecard translates an organization's mission and strategy into a comprehensive set of performance measures that provides the framework for a strategic measurement and management system. The scorecard measures performance from four key perspectives: (1) financial, (2) customer, (3) internal business processes, and (4) learning and growth.

4. To evaluate the success of its strategy, a company can subdivide the change in operating income into growth, price-recovery, and productivity components. The growth component measures the change in revenues over costs from selling greater or fewer units, assuming no changes in prices, efficiencies, or capacities. The price-recovery component measures changes in revenues and changes in costs as a result solely of changes in the prices of outputs and inputs. The productivity component measures the decrease in costs from using fewer inputs and from reducing capacity. A company is considered to be successful in implementing its strategy when the changes in operating income align closely with the strategy.

5. Engineered costs result from a cause-and-effect relationship between output and the resources needed to produce that output. Discretionary costs arise from periodic (usually annual) decisions regarding the maximum amount to be incurred. They are not tied to a cause-and-effect relationship between inputs and outputs.

6. Identifying unused capacity is easier for engineered costs than for discretionary costs. Downsizing is an approach to managing unused capacity by matching costs to the activities that need to be performed.

APPENDIX: PRODUCTIVITY MEASUREMENT

Productivity measures the relationship between actual inputs used (both quantities and costs) and actual outputs produced. The lower the inputs for a given quantity of outputs or the higher the outputs for a given quantity of inputs, the higher the level of productivity. Measuring productivity improvements over time highlight the specific input-output relationships that contribute to cost leadership.

Partial Productivity Measures

Partial productivity, the most frequently used productivity measure, compares the quantity of output produced with the quantity of an individual input used. In its most common form, partial productivity is expressed as a ratio:

$$\text{Partial productivity} = \frac{\text{Quantity of output produced}}{\text{Quantity of input used}}$$

The higher the ratio, the greater the productivity.

Consider direct materials productivity at Chipset in the year 2000.

$$\begin{aligned}\text{Direct materials}\\\text{partial productivity}\end{aligned} = \frac{\text{Quantity of CX1 units produced during 2000}}{\text{Direct materials quantity used to produce CX1 in 2000}}$$

$$= \frac{1{,}150{,}000 \text{ units of CX1}}{2{,}900{,}000 \text{ sq. cm. of direct materials}}$$

$$= 0.40 \text{ units of CX1 per sq. cm. of direct materials}$$

Note that the direct materials partial productivity ignores Chipset's other inputs, manufacturing conversion, selling and customer service, and R&D. Partial productivity measures become more meaningful when comparisons are made that examine productivity changes over time, either across several facilities, or relative to a benchmark. Exhibit 13-6 presents partial productivity measures for Chipset's various inputs for 1999 and 2000 using information from the productivity calculations on p. 474. These measures compare the actual inputs used in the year 2000 to produce 1,150,000 units of CX1 with the inputs that would have been used in 2000 had the input-output relationship from 1999 continued in 2000.

Reinforcing Problems Probs. 13-32 and 13-33 cover productivity measures.

Curriculum Linkage/Example Efficiency variances yield insight into productivity of a single factor of production (e.g., professional labor in a public actg. firm). Yield variances address the productivity of a single component of one factor of production (e.g., accountants' labor), while mix variances reveal the effect of substitution within a single factor of production (e.g., substitution of seniors for staff accountants). The productivity measures discussed in this chapter differ from variance analysis in two ways. First, productivity measures are more general in that they capture substitutions between factors of production (e.g., automation of auditing substitutes investment in hardware and software for staff labor) as well as within factors of production. Second, variance analysis compares actual and budgeted prices and quantities. In contrast, productivity measures are based on actual prices and quantities of inputs and outputs that are compared over time or across firms.

Points to Stress Partial productivity (PP) measures are partial in that they measure the # of outputs produced per unit of a single input. If capital (e.g., automation) is substituted for labor, then improved labor productivity is achieved at the expense of reduced capital investment productivity. Thus, increases or decreases in PP measures are not "good" or "bad," per se, unless no substitution is allowed among inputs. Also, PP measures are in terms of physical inputs and outputs and do not use input prices. Changes in input prices thus do not affect PP measures.

EXHIBIT 13-6
Comparing Chipset's Partial Productivities in 1999 and 2000

Input (1)	Partial Productivity in 2000 (2)	Partial Productivity in 1999 (3)	Percentage Change from 1999 to 2000 (4)
Direct materials	$\frac{1{,}150{,}000}{2{,}900{,}000} = 0.40$	$\frac{1{,}150{,}000}{3{,}450{,}000} = 0.33$	$\frac{0.40 - 0.33}{0.33} = 21.2\%$
Manufacturing conversion	$\frac{1{,}150{,}000}{1{,}750{,}000} = 0.66$	$\frac{1{,}150{,}000}{1{,}875{,}000} = 0.61$	$\frac{0.66 - 0.61}{0.61} = 8.2\%$
Selling and customer service	$\frac{1{,}150{,}000}{55} = 20{,}909$	$\frac{1{,}150{,}000}{60} = 19{,}167$	$\frac{20{,}909 - 19{,}167}{19{,}167} = 9.1\%$
R&D	$\frac{1{,}150{,}000}{39} = 29{,}487$	$\frac{1{,}150{,}000}{40} = 28{,}750$	$\frac{29{,}487 - 28{,}750}{28{,}750} = 2.56\%$

Evaluating changes in partial productivities

It is important to distinguish between the partial productivity effects of variable and fixed cost components. Why? Because for variable-cost elements, such as direct materials, productivity improvements automatically result in using fewer input resources. For example, Chipset's improvements in direct materials productivity in 2000 resulted in 2,900,000 square centimeters of direct materials being acquired and used rather than the 3,450,000 square centimeters that would have been required to produce 1,150,000 units of output in 2000 at the 1999 productivity level. On the other hand, for fixed-cost elements such as conversion costs, using less of the available fixed capacity resources will not lead automatically to lowering the cost of these resources. To improve partial productivity in these cases, management must take actions to release workers or reduce capacity. These actions are often more difficult to implement and, as in Exhibit 13-6, result in lower partial productivity gains for fixed-cost categories than for variable-cost categories.

Consider, for example, manufacturing conversion partial productivity. At the 1999 productivity levels, Chipset would need to start 1,725,000 units of CX1 to produce 1,150,000 units. Chipset has manufacturing capacity of 1,875,000 units. Efficiency improvements in 2000 result in Chipset having to start 1,450,000 units in 2000. Reducing the number of units started into production, however, does not automatically lead to a decrease in manufacturing capacity. Partial productivity increases because Chipset's managers take actions to release workers and reduce manufacturing capacity to 1,750,000 units.

A major advantage of partial productivity measures is that they focus on a single input. As a result, they are simple to calculate and easily understood by operations personnel. Managers and operators examine these numbers to understand the reasons underlying productivity changes from one period to the next. For example, Chipset's managers will evaluate whether the lower defect rates (that resulted in management being able to reduce capacity and increase manufacturing conversion partial productivity from 1999 to 2000) was caused by better training of workers, lower absenteeism, lower labor turnover, better incentives, improved methods, or substitution of materials for labor. Isolating the relevant factors is important because it helps Chipset implement and sustain these practices in the future. Chipset can then set targets for gains in manufacturing conversion productivity and monitor planned productivity improvements.

For all their advantages, partial productivity measures also have some serious drawbacks. Because partial productivity focuses on only one input at a time rather than on all inputs simultaneously, it does not allow managers to evaluate the effect of input substitutions on overall productivity. For example, manufacturing conversion partial productivity may increase from one period to the next while direct materials partial productivity may decrease. Partial productivity measures cannot evaluate whether the increase in manufacturing conversion partial productivity offsets the decrease in direct materials partial productivity. Total factor productivity (TFP) or total productivity is a technique for measuring productivity that considers all inputs simultaneously.

Total Factor Productivity

Total factor productivity (TFP) is the ratio of the quantity of output produced to the costs of all inputs used, where the inputs are combined on the basis of current period prices.

$$\text{Total factor productivity} = \frac{\text{Quantity of output produced}}{\text{Costs of all inputs used}}$$

TFP considers all inputs simultaneously and also considers the tradeoffs across inputs based on current input prices. Do not be tempted to think of all productivity measures as physical measures lacking financial content—how many units of output are produced per unit of input. Total factor productivity is intricately tied to minimizing total cost—a financial objective. We next measure changes in TFP at Chipset from 1999 to 2000.

Calculating and comparing total factor productivity

We first calculate Chipset's TFP in 2000, using 2000 prices and 1,150,000 units of output produced (using information from the first column of the productivity component calculations on p. 474).

$$\text{Total factor productivity for 2000 using 2000 prices} = \frac{\text{Quantity of output produced in 2000}}{\text{Costs of inputs used in 2000 based on 2000 prices}}$$

$$= \frac{1,150,000}{(2,900,000 \times \$1.50) + (1,750,000 \times \$6.20) + (55 \times \$80,000) + (39 \times \$100,000)}$$

$$= \frac{1,150,000}{\$23,500,000}$$

$$= 0.048936 \text{ units of output per dollar of input costs}$$

By itself, the 2000 TFP of 0.048936 units of CX1 per dollar of input costs is not particularly helpful. We need something to compare the 2000 TFP against. One alternative is to compare TFPs of other similar companies in 2000. However, finding similar companies and obtaining accurate comparable data are often difficult. Companies therefore usually compare their own TFP over time. In the Chipset example, we use as a benchmark, TFP calculated using the inputs that Chipset would have used in 1999 to produce 1,150,000 units of CX1 at 2000 prices (that is, we use the costs calculated from the second column in the productivity component calculations on p. 474). Why do we use 2000 prices? Because using the current year's (2000) prices in both calculations controls for input price differences and focuses the analysis on the adjustments the manager made in the quantities of inputs in response to changes in prices.

$$\text{Benchmark TFP} = \frac{\text{Quantity of output produced in 2000}}{\begin{array}{c}\text{Costs of inputs that would have been used in 1999}\\ \text{to produce 2000 output}\end{array}}$$

$$= \frac{1,150,000}{(3,450,000 \times \$1.50) + (1,875,000 \times \$6.20) + (60 \times \$80,000) + (40 \times \$100,000)}$$

$$= \frac{1,150,000}{\$25,600,000}$$

$$= 0.044922 \text{ units of output per dollar of input costs}$$

Using year 2000 prices, total factor productivity increased 8.94% [(0.048936 − 0.044922) ÷ 0.044922] from 1999 to 2000. Note that the 8.94% increase in TFP equals the $2,100,000 gain (Exhibit 13-3, column 4) divided by the $23,500,000 of actual costs incurred in 2000 (Exhibit 13-3, column 5). Total factor productivity increased because Chipset produced more output per dollar of input costs in 2000 relative to 1999, measured in both years using 2000 prices. The gain in TFP occurs because Chipset increases the partial productivities of individual inputs and, consistent with its strategy, seeks the least expensive combination of inputs to produce CX1. Note that TFP increases cannot be due to differences in input prices because we used year 2000 prices to evaluate both the inputs that Chipset would have used in 1999 to produce 1,150,000 units of CX1, and the inputs actually used in 2000.

Using Both Partial and Total Factor Productivity Measures

A major advantage of TFP is that it measures the combined productivity of all inputs used to produce output. It therefore explicitly considers gains from using fewer physical inputs as well as substitution among inputs. Managers can analyze these numbers to understand the reasons for changes in TFP. For example, Chipset's managers will try to evaluate whether the increase in TFP from 1999 to 2000 was due to better human resource management practices, higher quality of materials, or improved manufacturing methods. Chipset will adopt the most successful practices

Points to Stress TFP is easy to compute for a single-product firm. A multiproduct firm must make one of 2 adjustments. The first approach is to convert the physical measures to a dollar value common numerator. The second approach is to allocate the input costs to the different outputs. This is most appropriate when the inputs can be reasonably allocated to the different outputs.

Teaching Tip Stress the intuition behind the benchmark TFP calculation. We want to assess whether, to achieve this period's outputs, employees used a combination of inputs that is more cost-effective than simply continuing last period's combination. To see whether employees made appropriate substitutions, we compare current period TFP to a benchmark TFP based on prior period input/output ratios, but using current period prices and current period output levels. Our goal is to see if the current period combination of inputs (at current period prices) is more cost-effective than simply continuing (at current period prices) the input combination used in the prior period.

Points to Stress TFP increases if: (1) The firm uses fewer total inputs per output. This is called technical productivity, because it usually arises due to improvements in production methods, technological advances, and so on, that permit production of more output from less inputs for variable cost efficiency gains; for fixed cost efficiency gains, it means taking actions to reduce fixed costs. (2) The firm uses a less expensive mix of inputs per output. This is called allocative productivity because it arises from changes in the allocation mix.

Curriculum Linkage One problem with TFP is that it measures the ratio of outputs to all inputs. Operations personnel often have control over only some inputs (e.g., their labor, the materials they add to the product). The principle of responsibility accounting introduced in Chap. 6 suggests that workers should be evaluated based on items for which they are responsible. Hence, productivity-based bonuses for workers often are more closely linked with PP measures than with TFP, but we need to make sure that while focusing on PP, expensive capital is not substituted for labor.

Points to Stress Managing labor costs is more difficult than managing costs of inanimate inputs such as DM, energy, or machinery. Mgrs. must consider effects of cost reduction efforts on employees' behavior and morale. The recent wave of productivity initiatives has reduced the number of employees (often through downsizing layoffs) and required remaining employees to work harder and smarter. If carried too far, such initiatives can adversely affect employees' morale, their loyalty to the firm, and their job performance if employees are overworked and anxious about their job security.

and use TFP measures to implement and evaluate strategy by setting targets and monitoring trends.

Many companies such as Monsanto, a manufacturer of fibers, Behlen Manufacturing, a steel fabricator, and Motorola, a microchip manufacturer, use both partial productivity and total factor productivity to evaluate performance. *Partial productivity and TFP measures work best together because the strengths of one offset weaknesses in the other.*

Although TFP measures are comprehensive, operations personnel find financial TFP measures more difficult to understand and less useful than physical partial productivity measures in performing their tasks. Physical measures of manufacturing labor partial productivity, for example, provide direct feedback to workers about output produced per labor-hour worked by focusing on factors within the workers' control. Manufacturing labor partial productivity also has the advantage that it can be easily compared across time periods because it uses physical inputs rather than inputs that are weighted by the prices prevailing in different periods. Workers, therefore, often prefer to tie productivity-based bonuses to gains in manufacturing labor partial productivity. Unfortunately, this situation creates incentives for workers to substitute materials (and capital) for labor, which improves their own productivity measure while possibly decreasing the overall productivity of the company as measured by TFP. To overcome the possible incentive problems of partial productivity measures, some companies—for example, TRW, Eaton, and Whirlpool—explicitly adjust bonuses based on manufacturing labor partial productivity for the effects of other factors such as investments in new equipment and higher levels of scrap. That is, they combine partial productivity with TFP-like measures.

TERMS TO LEARN

This chapter and the Glossary at the end of the book contain definitions of the following important terms:

balanced scorecard (p. 463)	price-recovery component (473)
cost leadership (463)	product differentiation (463)
discretionary costs (478)	productivity (485)
downsizing (480)	productivity component (473)
engineered costs (478)	reengineering (464)
growth component (473)	rightsizing (480)
infrastructure costs (478)	total factor productivity (TFP) (486)
partial productivity (485)	unused capacity (477)

ASSIGNMENT MATERIAL

QUESTIONS

13-1 Define strategy.

13-2 Describe the five key forces when analyzing an industry.

13-3 Describe two generic strategies.

13-4 What are the four key perspectives in the balanced scorecard?

13-5 What is reengineering?

13-6 Describe three features of a good balanced scorecard.

13-7 What are three important pitfalls to avoid when implementing a balanced scorecard?

13-8 Describe three key components in doing a strategic analysis of operating income.

13-9 How can an analyst incorporate the industry-market-size factor and the interrelationships between the growth, price-recovery, and productivity components into a strategic analysis of operating income?

13-10 How does an engineered cost differ from a discretionary cost?

13-11 "The distinction between engineered and discretionary costs is irrelevant when identifying unused capacity." Do you agree? Comment briefly.

13-12 What is downsizing?

13-13 What is a partial productivity measure?

13-14 What is total factor productivity?

13-15 "We are already measuring total factor productivity. Measuring partial productivities would be of no value." Do you agree? Comment briefly.

EXERCISES

13-16 Balanced scorecard. La Quinta Corporation manufactures corrugated cardboard boxes. It competes and plans to grow by producing high-quality boxes at a low cost that are delivered to customers in a timely manner. There are many other manufactures who produce similar boxes. La Quinta believes that continuously improving its manufacturing processes and having satisfied employees are critical to implementing its strategy in 2001.

Required
1. Is La Quinta's 2001 strategy one of product differentiation or cost leadership? Explain briefly.
2. Indicate two measures you would expect to see under each perspective in La Quinta's balanced scorecard for 2001. Explain your answer briefly.

13-17 Analysis of growth, price-recovery, and productivity components (continuation of 13-16). An analysis of La Quinta's operating income changes between 2000 and 2001 shows the following:

Operating income for 2000	$1,600,000
Add growth component	60,000
Deduct price-recovery component	(50,000)
Add productivity component	180,000
Operating income for 2001	$1,790,000

The industry market size for corrugated boxes did not grow in 2001, input prices did not change, and La Quinta reduced the prices of its boxes.

Required
1. Was La Quinta's gain in operating income in 2001 consistent with the strategy you identified in requirement 1 of Exercise 13-16?
2. Explain the productivity component. In general, does it represent savings in only variable costs, only fixed costs, or both variable and fixed costs?

13-18 Strategy, balanced scorecard. Meredith Corporation makes a special-purpose machine D4H used in the textile industry. Meredith has designed the D4H machine for 2000 to be distinct from its competitors. It has been generally regarded as a superior machine. Meredith presents the following data for the years 1999 and 2000.

	1999	2000
1. Units of D4H produced and sold	200	210
2. Selling price	$40,000	$42,000
3. Direct materials (kilograms)	300,000	310,000
4. Direct materials cost per kilogram	$8	$8.50
5. Manufacturing capacity in units of D4H	250	250
6. Total conversion costs	$2,000,000	$2,025,000
7. Conversion costs per unit of capacity	$8,000	$8,100
8. Selling and customer-service capacity	100 customers	95 customers
9. Total selling and customer-service costs	$1,000,000	$940,500
10. Selling and customer-service capacity cost per customer	$10,000	$9,900
11. Design staff	12	12
12. Total design costs	$1,200,000	$1,212,000
13. Design costs per employee	$100,000	$101,000

Meredith produces no defective machines, but it wants to reduce direct materials usage per D4H machine in 2000. Conversion costs in each year depend on production capacity defined in terms of D4H units that can be produced, not the actual units of D4H produced. Selling and customer-service costs depend on the number of customers that Meredith can support, not the actual number of customers Meredith serves. Meredith has 75 customers in 1999 and 80 customers in 2000. At the start of each year, management uses its discretion to determine the number of design staff for the year. The design staff and costs have no direct relationship with the quantity of D4H produced or the number of customers to whom D4H is sold.

Required

1. Is Meredith's strategy one of product differentiation or cost leadership? Explain briefly.
2. Describe briefly key elements that you would include in Meredith's balanced scorecard and the reasons for doing so.

13-19 Strategic analysis of operating income. Refer to the information in Exercise 13-18.

Required

1. Calculate the operating income of Meredith Corporation in 1999 and 2000.
2. Calculate the growth, price-recovery, and productivity components that explain the change in operating income from 1999 to 2000.
3. Comment on your answer in requirement 2. What do these components indicate?

13-20 Analysis of growth, price-recovery, and productivity components (continuation of 13-19). Suppose that during 2000, the market for Meredith's special-purpose machines grew at 3 percent. All increases in market share (that is sales increases greater than 3%) are due to Meredith's product differentiation strategy.

Required

Calculate how much of the change in operating income from 1999 to 2000 is due to the industry-market-size factor, cost leadership, and product differentiation. How successful has Meredith been in implementing its strategy?

13-21 Identifying and managing unused capacity. Refer to the Meredith Corporation information in Exercise 13-18.

Required

1. Where possible, calculate the amount and cost of unused capacity for (a) manufacturing, (b) selling and customer service, and (c) design at the beginning of the year 2000 based on year 2000 production. If you could not calculate the amount and cost of unused capacity, indicate why not.
2. Suppose Meredith can add or reduce its manufacturing capacity in increments of 30 units. What is the maximum amount of costs that Meredith could save in 2000 by downsizing manufacturing capacity?
3. Meredith, in fact, does not eliminate any of its unused manufacturing capacity. Why might Meredith not downsize?

13-22 Strategy, balanced scorecard, service company. Snyder Corporation is a small information systems consulting firm that specializes in helping companies implement sales management software. The market for Snyder's products is very competitive. To compete, Snyder must deliver quality service at a low cost. Snyder bills clients in terms of units of work performed, which depends on the size and complexity of the sales management system. Snyder presents the following data for the year 1999 and 2000.

	1999	2000
1. Units of work performed	60	70
2. Selling price	$50,000	$48,000
3. Software implementation labor-hours	30,000	32,000
4. Cost per software implementation labor-hour	$60	$63
5. Software implementation support capacity (in units of work)	90	90
6. Total cost of software implementation support	$360,000	$369,000
7. Software implementation support capacity cost per unit of work	$4,000	$4,100
8. Number of employees doing software development	3	3
9. Total software development costs	$375,000	$390,000
10. Software development costs per employee	$125,000	$130,000

Software implementation labor-hour costs are variable costs. Software implementation support costs for each year depend on the software implementation support capacity (defined in terms of units of work) that Snyder chooses to maintain each year. It does not vary with the actual units of work performed that year. At the start of each year, management uses its discretion to determine the number of software development employees. The software development staff and costs have no direct relationship with the number of units of work performed.

Required

1. Is Snyder Corporation's strategy, one of product differentiation or cost leadership? Explain briefly.
2. Describe briefly key elements that you would include in Snyder's balanced scorecard and your reasons for doing so.

13-23 Strategic analysis of operating income. Refer to the information in Exercise 13-22.

Required

1. Calculate the operating income of Snyder Corporation in 1999 and 2000.
2. Calculate the growth, price-recovery, and productivity components that explain the change in operating income from 1999 to 2000.
3. Comment on your answer in requirement 2. What do these components indicate?

13-24 Analysis of growth, price-recovery, and productivity components (continuation of 13-23). Suppose that during 2000 the market for implementing sales management software increases by 5% and that Snyder experiences a 1% decline in selling prices. Assume that any further decrease in selling price and increase in market share are strategic choices by Snyder's management to implement their cost leadership strategy.

Required

Calculate how much of the change in operating income from 1999 to 2000 is due to the industry-market-size factor, cost leadership, and product differentiation. How successful has Snyder been in implementing its strategy? Explain.

13-25 Identifying and managing unused capacity. Refer to the Snyder Corporation information in Exercise 13-22.

Required

1. Where possible, calculate the amount and cost of unused capacity for (a) software implementation support, and (b) software development at the beginning of the year 2000 based on units of work performed in 2000. If you could not calculate the amount and cost of unused capacity, indicate why not.
2. Suppose Snyder can add or reduce its software implementation support capacity in increments of 15 units. What is the maximum amount of costs that Snyder could save in 2000 by downsizing software implementation support capacity?
3. Snyder, in fact, does not eliminate any of its unused software implementation support capacity. Why might Snyder not downsize?

PROBLEMS

13-26 Balanced scorecard. R. Kaplan (adapted). Caltex, Inc., refines gasoline and sells it through its own Caltex Gas Stations. On the basis of market research, Caltex determines that 60% of the overall gasoline market consists of "service-oriented customers," medium to high income individuals who are willing to pay a higher price for gas if the gas stations can provide excellent customer service such as a clean facility, a convenience store, friendly employees, a quick turnaround, the ability to pay by credit card, and high-octane premium fuel. The remaining 40% of the overall market are "price shoppers" who look to buy the cheapest gasoline available. Caltex's strategy is to focus on the 60% of service-oriented customers. Caltex's balanced scorecard for the year 2001 follows at the top of the next page. For brevity, the initiatives taken under each objective are omitted.

Required

1. Was Caltex successful in implementing its strategy in 2001? Explain your answer.
2. Would you have included some measure of employee satisfaction and employee training in the learning and growth perspective? Are these objectives critical to Caltex for implementing its strategy? Why or why not? Explain briefly.
3. Explain how Caltex did not achieve its target market share in the total gasoline market but still exceeded its financial targets. Is "market share of overall gasoline market" the correct measure of market share? Explain briefly.

Objectives	Measures	Target Performance	Actual Performance
Financial Perspective			
Increase shareholder value	Operating income changes from price recovery	$90,000,000	$95,000,000
	Operating income changes from growth	$65,000,000	$67,000,000
Customer Perspective			
Increase market share	Market share of overall gasoline market	10%	9.8%
Internal Business Process Perspective			
Improve gasoline quality	Quality index	94 points	95 points
Improve refinery performance	Refinery reliability index (%)	91%	91%
Ensure gasoline availability	Product availability index (%)	99%	100%
Learning and Growth Perspective			
Increase refinery process capability	Percentage of refinery processes with advanced controls	88%	90%

4. Is there a cause-and-effect linkage between improvements in the measures in the internal business process perspective and the measures in the customer perspective? That is, would you add other measures to the internal business process perspective or the customer perspective? Why or why not? Explain briefly.

5. Do you agree with Caltex's decision not to include measures of changes in operating income from productivity improvements under the financial perspective of the balanced scorecard? Explain briefly.

13-27 Balanced scorecard. Lee Corporation manufactures various types of color laser printers in a highly automated facility with high fixed costs. The market for laser printers is competitive. The various color laser printers on the market are comparable in terms of features and price. Lee believes that satisfying customers with products of high quality at low costs is key to achieving its target profitability. For 2001, Lee plans to achieve higher quality and lower costs by improving yields and reducing defects in its manufacturing operations. Lee will train workers and encourage and empower them to take the necessary actions. Currently, a significant amount of Lee's capacity is used to produce products that are defective and cannot be sold. Lee expects that higher yields will reduce the capacity that Lee needs to use to manufacture products. Lee does not anticipate that improving manufacturing will automatically lead to lower costs because Lee has high fixed costs. To reduce fixed costs per unit, Lee could lay off employees and sell equipment or use the capacity to produce and sell more of its current products or improved models of its current products.

Lee's balanced scorecard for the just-completed accounting year 2001 follows at the top of the next page. For brevity, the initiatives taken under each objective are omitted.

Required

1. Was Lee successful in implementing its strategy in 2001? Explain.

2. Is Lee Corporation's balanced scorecard useful in helping Lee understand why it did not reach its target market share in 2001? If it is, explain why. If it is not, explain what other measures you might want to add under the customer perspective and why.

3. Would you have included some measure of employee satisfaction in the learning and growth perspective and new product development in the internal business process perspective? That is, do you think employee satisfaction and development of new products are critical to Lee for implementing its strategy? Why or why not? Explain briefly.

4. What problems, if any, do you see in Lee improving quality and significantly downsizing to eliminate unused capacity?

Objectives	Measures	Target Performance	Actual Performance
Financial Perspective			
Increase shareholder value	Operating income changes from productivity	$1,000,000	$400,000
	Operating income changes from growth	$1,500,000	$600,000
Customer Perspective			
Increase market share	Market share in color laser printers	5%	4.6%
Internal Business Process Perspective			
Improve manufacturing quality	Yield	82%	85%
Reduce delivery time to customers	Order delivery time	25 days	22 days
Learning and Growth Perspective			
Develop process skills	Percentage of employees trained in process and quality management	90%	92%
Enhance information system capabilities	Percentage of manufacturing processes with real-time feedback	85%	87%

13-28 Strategic Analysis of Operating Income. Halsey Company sells women's clothing. Halsey's strategy is to offer a wide selection of clothes and excellent customer service, and to charge a premium price. Halsey presents the following data for the years 2001 and 2002. For simplicity, assume that each customer purchases one piece of clothing.

	2001	2002
1. Pieces of clothing purchased and sold	40,000	40,000
2. Average selling price	$60	$59
3. Average cost per piece of clothing	$40	$41
4. Selling and customer-service capacity	51,000 customers	43,000 customers
5. Selling and customer-service costs	$357,000	$296,700
6. Selling and customer-service capacity cost per customer (Line 5 ÷ Line 4)	$7 per customer	$6.90 per customer
7. Purchasing and administrative capacity measured by the number of distinct clothing designs purchased	980	850
8. Purchasing and administrative costs	$245,000	$204,000
9. Purchasing and administrative capacity cost per distinct design	$250 per design	$240 per design

Total selling and customer-service costs depend on the number of customers that Halsey has created capacity to support, not the actual number of customers that Halsey serves. Total purchasing and administrative costs depend on purchasing and administrative capacity that Halsey has created (defined in terms of the number of distinct clothing designs that Halsey can purchase and administer). Purchasing and administration costs do not depend on the actual number of distinct clothing designs purchased. Halsey purchased 930 distinct designs in 2001 and 820 distinct designs in 2002.

At the start of 2002, Halsey planned to increase operating income by 10% over the operating income in 2001.

Required
1. Is Halsey's strategy one of product differentiation or cost leadership? Explain.
2. Calculate Halsley's operating income in 2001 and 2002.
3. Calculate the growth, price-recovery, and productivity components of changes in operating income between 2001 and 2002.
4. Does the strategic analysis of operating income indicate Halsey was successful in implementing its strategy in 2002? Explain.

13-29 Analysis of growth, price-recovery, and productivity components. Winchester Corporation manufactures special ball bearings. In 2002, it plans to grow and increase operating income by capitalizing on its reputation for manufacturing a product that is superior to its competitors. An analysis of Winchester's operating income changes between 2001 and 2002 shows the following:

Operating income for 2001	$3,450,000
Add growth component	300,000
Add price-recovery component	400,000
Add productivity component	350,000
Operating income for 2002	$4,500,000

Further analysis of these components indicates that had the growth in Winchester's sales kept up with market growth, the growth component in 2002 would have been $750,000. All decreases in market share (that is sales increases less than the market growth) are attributable to Winchester's lack of product differentiation.

Required

1. Is Winchester's 2002 strategy, one of product differentiation or cost leadership? Explain briefly.
2. Provide a brief explanation of why the growth, price-recovery and productivity components are favorable.
3. Was Winchester's gain in operating income in 2002 consistent with the strategy you identified in requirement 1? Explain briefly.

13-30 Engineered and discretionary overhead costs, unused capacity, repairs and maintenance. Rowland Corporation manufactures gears using turning machines. In 2001, Rowland's turning machines operated for 80,000 hours. Rowland employed 4 workers in its repair and maintenance area to repair machines that have broken down or are functioning improperly. In 2001, each repair and maintenance person was paid a fixed annual salary of $40,000 for 250 days of work at 8 hours per day. During 2001, the workers spent 6,000 hours doing repairs and maintenance.

Required

1. Do you think repair and maintenance costs at Rowland Corporation are engineered costs or discretionary costs? Explain your answer.
2. Assume repair and maintenance costs are engineered costs. Calculate the cost of unused repair and maintenance capacity in 2001. Give one reason why Rowland might want to downsize its repair and maintenance capacity and one reason why it might not. Explain your answer briefly.
3. Assume repair and maintenance costs are discretionary costs. What is the cost of unused repair and maintenance capacity in 2001. Explain your answer briefly.

13-31 Engineered and discretionary overhead costs, unused capacity, customer help-desk. Cable Galore, a large cable television operator, had 750,000 subscribers in 1999. Cable Galore employs 5 customer help-desk representatives to respond to customer questions and problems. During 1999, each customer help-desk representative worked 8 hours per day for 250 days at a fixed annual salary of $36,000. Cable Galore received 45,000 telephone calls from its customers in 1999. Each call took an average of 10 minutes.

Required

1. Do you think customer help-desk costs at Cable Galore are engineered costs or discretionary costs? Explain your answer.
2. Where possible, calculate the cost of unused customer help-desk capacity in 1999 under each of the following assumptions: (a) customer help-desk costs are engineered costs, and (b) customer help-desk costs are discretionary costs. If you could not calculate the amount and cost of unused capacity, indicate why not.
3. Assume that Cable Galore had 900,000 subscribers in 2000 and that the 1999 percentage of telephone calls received to total subscribers continued into 2000. Customer help-desk capacity in 2000 was the same as it was in 1999. Where possible, calculate the cost of unused customer help-desk capacity in 2000 under each of the following two assumptions: (a) customer-service costs are engineered costs, and (b) customer-service costs are discretionary costs. If you could not calculate the amount and cost of unused capacity, indicate why not.

13-32 Partial productivity measurement. (Chapter Appendix) Berkshire Corporation makes small steel parts. Berkshire management has some ability to substitute direct materials for direct manufacturing labor. If workers cut the steel carefully, Berkshire can manufacture more parts out of a metal sheet, but this approach will require more direct manufacturing labor-hours. Alternatively, Berkshire can use fewer direct manufacturing labor-hours if it is willing to tolerate a larger quantity of direct materials waste. Berkshire operates in a very competitive market. Its strategy is to produce a quality product at a low cost. Berkshire produces no defective products. It reports the following data for the last two years of operations:

	2001	2002
Output units	375,000	525,000
Direct materials used, in kilograms	450,000	610,000
Direct materials cost per kilogram	$1.20	$1.25
Direct manufacturing labor-hours used	7,500	9,500
Wages per hour	$20	$25
Manufacturing capacity in output units	600,000	582,000
Manufacturing capacity-related fixed costs	$1,038,000	$1,018,500
Fixed manufacturing costs per unit of capacity	$1.73	$1.75

Required
1. Compute the partial productivity ratios for 2002. Compare the partial productivity ratios in 2002 with partial productivity ratios for 2001 calculated based on year 2002 output produced.
2. On the basis of the partial productivity ratios alone, can you conclude whether and by how much productivity improved overall in 2002 relative to 2001? Explain.
3. How might the management of Berkshire Corporation use the partial productivity analysis?

13-33 Total factor productivity (continuation of 13-32). Refer to the information on Berkshire Corporation in Problem 13-32.
Required
1. Compute Berkshire Corporation's total factor productivity in 2002.
2. Compare Berkshire Corporation's total factor productivity performance in 2002 relative to 2001.
3. What does total factor productivity tell you that partial productivity measures do not?

13-34 Balanced scorecard, ethics. John Emburey, Division manager of the Household Products Division, a maker of kitchen dishwashers, had just seen the balanced scorecard for his division for 2001. He immediately calls Patricia Conley, the management accountant for the division into his office for a meeting. "I think the employee satisfaction and customer satisfaction numbers are way too low. These numbers are based on a random sample of subjective assessments made by individual managers and customer representatives. My own experience indicates that we are doing well on both these dimensions. Until we do a formal survey of employees and customers sometime next year, I think we are doing a disservice to ourselves and this company by reporting such low scores for employee and customer satisfaction. These scores will be an embarrassment for us at the division managers' meeting next month. We need to get these numbers up."

Patricia knows that the employee and customer satisfaction scores are subjective, but the procedure she used is identical to the procedures she has used in the past. She knows from the comments she had asked for that the scores represent the unhappiness of employees with the latest work rules and the unhappiness of customers with missed delivery dates. She also knows that these problems will be corrected in time.
Required
1. Do you think that the Household Products Division should include subjective measures of employee satisfaction and customer satisfaction in its balanced scorecard? Explain.
2. What should Patricia Conley do?

COLLABORATIVE LEARNING PROBLEM

13-35 Downsizing. (CMA, adapted) Mayfair Corporation currently subsidizes cafeteria services for its 200 employees. Mayfair is in the process of reviewing the cafeteria services as cost cutting measures are needed throughout the organization to keep the prices of its products competitive. Two alternatives are being evaluated: downsize the cafeteria staff and offer a reduced menu or contract with an outside vendor.

The current cafeteria operation has four employees with a combined base annual salary of $110,000 plus additional employee benefits at 25% of salary. The cafeteria operates 250 days each year, and the costs for utilities and equipment maintenance average $30,000 annually. The daily sales include 100 entrees at $4.00 each, 80 sandwiches or salads at an average price of $3.00 each, plus an additional $200 for beverages and desserts. The cost of all cafeteria supplies is 60% of revenues.

The plan for downsizing the current operation envisions retaining two of the current employees whose combined base annual salaries total $65,000. An entrée would no longer be offered, and prices of the remaining items would be increased slightly. Under this arrangement, Mayfair expects daily sales of 150 sandwiches or salads at a higher average price of $3.60. The additional revenue for beverages and desserts is expected to increase to $230 each day. Because of the elimination of the entrée, the cost of all cafeteria supplies is expected to decline to 50% of revenues. All other conditions of operation would remain the same. Mayfair is willing to continue to subsidize this reduced operation but will not spend more than 20% of the current subsidy.

A proposal has been received from Wilco Foods, an outside vendor who is willing to supply cafeteria services. Wilco has proposed to pay Mayfair $1,000 per month for use of the cafeteria and utilities. Mayfair would be expected to cover equipment repair costs. In addition, Wilco would pay Mayfair 4% of all revenues received above the breakeven point. This payment would be made at the end of the year. All other costs incurred by Wilco to supply the cafeteria services are variable and equal 75% of revenues. Wilco plans to charge $5.00 for an entrée, and the average price for the sandwich or salad would be $4.00. All other daily sales are expected to average $300. Wilco expects daily sales of 66 entrees and 94 sandwiches or salads.

Required

Form groups of two or more students to complete the following requirements.

1. Determine whether the plan for downsizing the current cafeteria operation would be acceptable to Mayfair Corporation. Show your calculations.

2. Is the Wilco Foods proposal more advantageous to Mayfair Corporation than the downsizing plan? Show your calculations.

CHAPTER
14

Cost Allocation

learning objectives

When you have finished studying this chapter, you should be able to

1. Outline four purposes for allocating costs to cost objects
2. Guide cost-allocation decisions using appropriate criteria
3. Discuss key decisions faced when collecting costs in indirect-cost pools
4. Differentiate the single-rate cost-allocation method from the dual-rate cost-allocation method
5. Understand how the risks managers face are affected by the choice between budgeted versus actual cost-allocation rates
6. Distinguish among direct, step-down, and reciprocal methods of allocating support department costs
7. Make decisions that draw on the allocation of common costs using either the stand-alone or incremental methods
8. Explain the importance of explicit agreement between parties when reimbursement is based on costs incurred

The costs of using complex testing equipment can be allocated to products or services using activity-based costing.

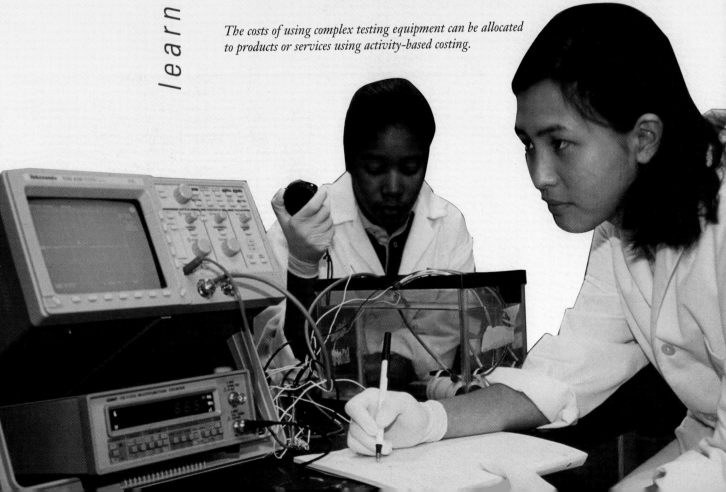

Cost allocation is an inescapable problem in nearly every organization and in nearly every facet of accounting. How should university costs be allocated among undergraduate programs, graduate programs, and research? How should the costs of expensive medical equipment, facilities, and staff be allocated in a hospital? How should manufacturing overhead be allocated to individual products in a multiple-product company such as Heinz?

Television and newspaper stories about questionable cost-charging practices frequently involve questions of cost allocation. In one case, a patient in a hospital was charged $17 for a quart of distilled water—$3.40 of direct costs and $13.60 of cost allocations. Much of this $13.60 was questionably related to the services provided to the patient. Cost-allocation issues inevitably arise in disputes over large cost overruns on construction projects and movies as well.

Chapters 4 and 5 examined topics related to the allocation of indirect costs to individual products or customers. Finding answers to cost-allocation questions is often difficult. The answers are seldom clearly right or clearly wrong. Nevertheless, in this chapter we provide insight into cost allocation and the dimensions of the questions, even if the answers seem elusive. The emphasis in this chapter is primarily on the allocation of costs to divisions, plants, departments, and contracts and secondarily to products and customers.

PURPOSES OF COST ALLOCATION

OBJECTIVE 1
Outline four purposes for allocating costs to cost objects

As discussed in Chapter 2, *indirect costs* of a cost object are costs that are related to the particular cost object but cannot be traced to it in an economically feasible (cost-effective) way. These costs often comprise a sizable percentage of the overall costs assigned to such cost objects as products, customers, and distribution channels. Why do managers allocate indirect costs to these cost objects? Exhibit 14-1 illustrates four essential purposes of cost allocation.

The allocation of a particular cost need not satisfy all four purposes in Exhibit 14-1 simultaneously. Consider the salary of an aerospace scientist in a central research department of Boeing or Airbus. This salary cost

EXHIBIT 14-1
Purposes of Cost Allocation

Purpose	Illustrations
1. To provide information for economic decisions	◆ To decide whether to add a new airline flight ◆ To decide whether to manufacture a component part of a television set or to purchase it from another manufacturer ◆ To decide on the selling price for a customized product or service
2. To motivate managers and other employees	◆ To encourage the design of products that are simpler to manufacture or less costly to service ◆ To encourage sales representatives to push high-margin products or services
3. To justify costs or compute reimbursement	◆ To cost products at a "fair" price, often done with government defense contracts ◆ To compute reimbursement for a consulting firm that is paid a percentage of the cost savings resulting from the implementation of its recommendations
4. To measure income and assets for reporting to external parties	◆ To cost inventories for financial reporting to stockholders, bondholders, and so on (Under generally accepted accounting principles, inventoriable costs include manufacturing costs but exclude research and development, marketing, distribution, and customer-service costs.) ◆ To cost inventories for reporting to tax authorities

- may be allocated as part of central research costs to satisfy purpose 1 (an economic decision such as pricing),
- may or may not be allocated to satisfy purpose 2 (motivation, such as for the assembly plant manager's cost-reduction plan),
- may or may not be allocated to a government contract to satisfy purpose 3 (cost reimbursement, in which the terms of the contract will guide the allocation decision), and
- cannot be allocated to inventory under generally accepted accounting principles to satisfy purpose 4 (income and asset measurement for reporting to external parties).

Different costs are appropriate for different purposes. Consider costs of a product in terms of the business functions in the value chain:

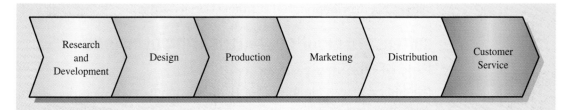

The same set of costs in these six business functions typically will not satisfy each of the four purposes in Exhibit 14-1. For some decisions related to the economic-decision purpose (for example, long-run product pricing), the costs in all six functions

---

SURVEYS OF COMPANY PRACTICE

Why Allocate Corporate and Other Support Costs to Divisions and Departments

Why do managers allocate corporate and other support costs to divisions and departments? A broad set of reasons are given in surveys. One survey of U.S. managers[a] reported the following (ranked by frequency): (1) to remind profit-center managers that indirect costs exist and that profit-center earnings must be adequate to cover some share of corporate as well as their own costs; (2) to encourage use of central services that would otherwise be underutilized; and (3) to stimulate profit-center managers to put pressure on central managers to control service costs.

Canadian executives[b] cited the following objectives, ranked in order of importance, for allocating costs to divisions and departments: (1) to determine costs; (2) to evaluate profit centers; (3) to fix accountability; (4) to allocate costs per unit of usage; (5) to promote more effective resource usage; and (6) to foster cost awareness.

These executives encountered the following difficulties in implementing their cost-allocation programs: the allocations resulting in reported losses, friction among managers, unstable market prices, allocations perceived as arbitrary, usage hard to monitor, agreement on the allocation method difficult to obtain, and time-consuming allocation process.

Similar surveys were conducted among Australian[c] and United Kingdom[d] managers. The two sets of managers gave the same ranking of the following reasons for allocating corporate costs to divisions (in order of importance): (1) to acknowledge that divisions would incur such costs if they were independent units or if the services were not provided centrally; (2) to make division managers aware that central costs exist; (3) to stimulate division managers to put pressure on central support managers to control costs; and (4) to stimulate division managers to economize in usage of central services.

[a]Fremgen and Liao, *The Allocation*; [b]Atkinson, *Intra-firm Cost*; [c]Ramadan, "The Rationale"; [d]Dean, Joye, and Blayney, *Strategic Management*. Full citations are in Appendix A.

should be included. For the motivation purpose, costs from more than one function are often included to emphasize to managers how costs in different functions are related to each other. For example, some Japanese companies require product designers to incorporate costs further down the value chain than design (such as distribution and customer service, as well as production) into their product-cost estimates. The aim is to focus attention on how different product design options affect the total costs of the organization. For the cost-reimbursement purpose, the particular contract will often stipulate whether all six of the business functions or only a subset of them are to be reimbursed. For instance, cost-reimbursement rules governing U.S. government contracts explicitly exclude For the purpose of income and asset measurement for reporting to external parties, inventoriable costs under generally accepted accounting principles include only manufacturing costs (and product design costs in some cases). In the United States, research and development costs in most industries are a period cost when they amarketing costs. re incurred,[1] as are marketing, distribution, and customer-service costs.

CRITERIA TO GUIDE COST-ALLOCATION DECISIONS

Role of Dominant Criteria

Exhibit 14-2 presents four criteria used to guide cost-allocation decisions. These decisions affect both the number of indirect-cost pools and the cost-allocation base for each indirect-cost pool. Managers must first choose the purpose for a particular cost allocation and then select the appropriate criterion to implement the allocation. This book emphasizes the superiority of the cause-and-effect and the benefits-received criteria, especially when the purpose of cost allocation is economic decisions or motivation.[2]

Fairness and ability to bear are less frequently used criteria than cause and effect or benefits received. Fairness is an especially difficult criterion on which to obtain agreement. What one party views as fair, another party may view as unfair.[3] The ability to bear criterion raises issues related to cross-subsidization across users of resources in an organization. Consider a product that consumes a large amount of indirect costs but whose selling price is currently below its direct costs. This product has no ability to bear any of the indirect costs it uses. If the indirect costs it consumes are allocated to other products, these other products are effectively subsidizing the product that is losing money.

The cause-and-effect criterion is the primary one in activity-based costing (ABC) applications. ABC systems use the concept of a cost hierarchy to identify the cost drivers that best demonstrate the cause-and-effect relationship between each activity and the costs in the related cost pool. The cost drivers are then chosen as cost-allocation bases.

Cost-Benefit Approach

Companies place great importance on the cost-benefit approach when designing and implementing their cost-allocation systems. Companies incur costs not only in collecting data but also in taking the time necessary to educate management about

[1] In some industries (such as software), U.S. companies can capitalize research and development costs when certain criterion are met (such as the R&D resulting in a product that is believed to be commercially viable).

[2] The Federal Accounting Standards Advisory Board (which sets standards for management accounting for U.S. government departments and agencies) recommends "Cost assignments should be performed by: (a) directly tracing costs whenever feasible and economically practicable, (b) assigning costs on a cause-and-effect basis, (c) allocating costs on a reasonable and consistent basis." (FASAB, 1995, p. 12).

[3] Kaplow and Shavell, for example, in a review of the legal literature note that "notions of fairness are many and varied. They are analyzed and rationalized by different writers in different ways, and they also typically depend upon the circumstances under consideration. Accordingly, it is not possible to identify a consensus view on these notions. . . ." See L. Kaplow and S. Shavell, *Fairness Versus Welfare Economics in Normative Analysis of Law.* (Working Paper, Harvard University, 1998).

EXHIBIT 14-2
Criteria for Cost-Allocation Decisions

1. **Cause and Effect.** Using this criterion, managers identify the variable or variables that cause resources to be consumed. For example, managers may use hours of testing as the variable when allocating the costs of a quality-testing area to products. Cost allocations based on the cause-and-effect criterion are likely to be the most credible to operating personnel.

2. **Benefits Recieved.** Using this criterion, managers identify the beneficiaries of the outputs of the cost object. The costs of the cost object are allocated among the beneficiaries in proportion to the benefits each receives. For example, consider a corporatewide advertising program that promotes the general image of the corporation rather than any individual product. The costs of this program may be allocated on the basis of division revenues. The higher the revenues, the higher the division's allocated cost of the advertising program. The rationale behind this allocation is the belief that divisions with higher revenues apparently benefit from the advertising more than divisions with lower revenues and therefore ought to be allocated more of the advertising costs.

3. **Fairness or Equity.** This criterion is often cited in government contracts when cost allocations are the basis for establishing a price satisfactory to the government and its supplier. Cost allocation here is viewed as a "reasonable" or "fair" means of establishing a selling price in the minds of the contracting parties. For most allocation decisions, fairness is a lofty objective rather than an operational criterion.

4. **Ability to Bear.** This criterion advocates allocating costs in proportion to the cost object's ability to bear them. An example is the allocation of corporate executive salaries on the basis of division operating income. The presumption is that the more profitable divisions have a greater ability to absorb corporate headquarters' costs.

Points to Stress The benefits received criterion can sometimes be used when cause and effect can't be determined. For example, the cost of renting a plant can be allocated according to benefits received (e.g., sq. ft. of space used), but because the rent is a fixed fee, the cause–effect criterion isn't operational (i.e., won't reduce the rent unless the company moves to a smaller facility).

Teaching Tip The following sequential outline of the cost allocation process helps students see the big picture.
1. Determine the purpose of the allocation, since this determines *what costs* will be allocated.
2. Decide *how* to allocate the costs from step 1. To do so,
   a. Decide *how many indirect cost pools* to develop, and then
   b. Identify an *allocation base* (preferably a cost driver) for each cost pool.

the chosen system. In general, the more sophisticated the system, the higher these education costs.

The costs of designing and implementing a sophisticated cost-allocation system are highly visible, and most companies work to reduce them. In contrast, the benefits from using a well-designed cost-allocation system—managers being able to make better-informed sourcing decisions, pricing decisions, cost-control decisions, and so on—are difficult to measure and are frequently less visible. Still, designers of cost-allocation systems should consider these benefits as well as the costs.

Spurred by rapid reductions in the costs of collecting and processing information, organizations today are moving toward more detailed cost-allocation systems. Many companies have now developed manufacturing or distribution overhead costing systems that use multiple (in some cases more than ten) cost-allocation bases. Also, some businesses have state-of-the-art information technology already in place for operating their plants or distribution networks. Applying this existing technology to the development and operation of a cost-allocation system is less expensive—and thus more inviting—than starting up such a system from scratch.

COST ALLOCATION AND COSTING SYSTEMS

We have seen that cost allocation is used for four essential purposes. In this section, we focus on the first purpose, to provide information for economic decisions such as pricing, by measuring the full costs of manufacturing and delivering products using an ABC system.

Chapter 5 described how ABC systems define activity-cost pools and then use activity-cost drivers as allocation bases to assign costs of the activity-cost pools to products. In this section, we focus on how costs are assigned to the activity-cost pools themselves.

To provide an overview of cost allocation, we will use Consumer Appliances, Inc. (CAI), to illustrate how costs incurred in different parts of an organization can be assigned, and then reassigned, when costing products, services, customers, or contracts. CAI has two divisions, each of which has its own manufacturing plant—the Refrigerator Division with a plant in Minneapolis and the Clothes Dryer Division with a plant in St. Paul. CAI's headquarters is in a separate location in

Minneapolis. In each division, CAI manufactures and sells multiple products that differ in size and complexity.

CAI collects costs at the following levels in its organization:

1. *Corporate costs*—there are three major categories of costs:

   ◆ Treasury costs—interest of $900,000 on debt used to finance the construction of new assembly equipment in the two divisions. Cost of new assembly equipment is $5,200,000 in the Refrigerator Division and $3,800,000 in the Clothes Dryer Division.

   ◆ Human resource management costs—recruitment and ongoing employee training and development, $1,600,000.

   ◆ Corporate administration costs—executive salaries, rent, and general administration costs, $5,400,000.

2. *Division costs*—there are two direct-cost categories (direct materials and direct manufacturing labor) and six indirect-cost categories. Exhibit 14-3 presents the division activity-cost pools and cost-allocation bases. CAI identifies the cost hierarchy category for each cost pool. Output-unit-level costs are resources sacrificed on activities performed on each individual unit of product or service. Batch-level costs are resources sacrificed on activities that are related to a group of units of product(s) or service(s) rather than to each individual unit of product or service. Product-sustaining costs are resources sacrificed on activities undertaken to support individual products or services, regardless of the number of units or batches in which the product is made. Facility-sustaining costs are resources sacrificed on activities that cannot be traced to individual products or services but support the organization as a whole.

Exhibit 14-4 presents an overview diagram of the allocation of corporate and division overhead costs to products for CAI, Inc. Focus first on the lower half of the exhibit beginning with division indirect costs. It is similar to Exhibit 5-3, Panel A (p. 146), which illustrates activity-based costing systems using activity-cost pools and activity drivers. The only additional feature is that CAI has a cost pool called Facility

EXHIBIT 14-3
Division Activity-Cost Pools and Cost-Allocation Bases, CAI, Inc., for Refrigerator Division (R) and Clothes Dryer Division (CD)

Activity	Example of Costs	Amount		Cost Hierarchy Catagory	Cost-Allocation Base	Cause-and-Effect Relationship That Motivates the Choice of Allocation Base
Design	Design engineering salaries	(R)	$6,000,000	Product-sustaining	Parts times cubic feet	Complex products (more parts and larger size) require greater design resources.
		(CD)	4,250,000			
Setups of machines	Setup labor and equipment cost	(R)	$3,000,000	Batch level	Setup-hours	Overhead costs of the setup activity increase as setup-hours increase.
		(CD)	2,400,000			
Manufacturing operations	Plant and equipment, energy	(R)	$25,000,000	Output-unit level	Machine-hours	Manufacturing operations overhead costs support machines and hence increase with machine usage.
		(CD)	18,750,000			
Distribution	Shipping labor and equipment	(R)	$8,000,000	Output-unit level	Cubic feet	Distribution overhead costs increase with cubic feet of product shipped.
		(CD)	5,500,000			
Administration	Division executive salaries	(R)	$1,000,000	Facility-sustaining	Revenues	Weak relationship between division executive salaries and revenues but justified by CAI on a benefits received basis.
		(CD)	800,000			
Facility	Building and space costs	(R)	$4,500,000	All	Square-feet	Facility costs increase with square feet of space.
		(CD)	3,500,000			

EXHIBIT 14-4
Overview Diagram of Allocation of Corporate Overhead and Division Overhead Costs to Products, CAI, Inc.

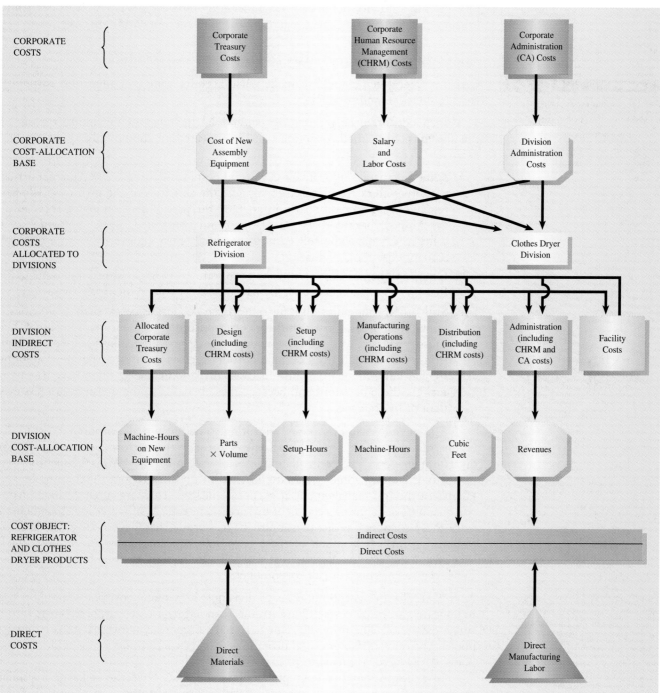

Costs, which accumulates all costs of buildings and space incurred in the division. As the arrows in Exhibit 14-4 indicate, CAI allocates these costs to the other activity-cost pools using the square feet area required for the different activities (design, setup, manufacturing, distribution, and administration). The activity-cost pools then include the costs of the building and facilities needed to perform the various activities.

The activity-cost pools are allocated to products on the basis of activity-cost drivers. As described in Chapter 5, this is done by identifying a cost-allocation base for each activity. The cost-allocation base is chosen so that there is a cause-and-effect relationship between it and the costs in the activity-cost pool. A rate per unit is calculated for each cost-allocation base. Indirect costs are allocated to products on the basis of the total quantity of the cost-allocation base for each activity used by the product.

The key issue that we focus on in this section is the upper half of Exhibit 14-4: How corporate costs are allocated to divisions and then to activity-cost pools. Before getting into the details of the allocations, however, we first consider some broader choices that CAI faces regarding the allocation of corporate costs.

Allocating Corporate Costs to Divisions and Products

OBJECTIVE 3

Discuss key decisions faced when collecting costs in indirect-cost pools

CAI has several key choices to make when accumulating and allocating corporate costs to divisions and products.

1. Which corporate cost categories should be included in the indirect costs of the divisions? Should all corporate costs be allocated, or should only a subset be allocated?

a. Some companies allocate all corporate costs to divisions. They maintain that corporate costs are incurred to support the activities of the divisions. Allocating all corporate costs sparks interest on the part of division managers regarding how corporate costs are planned and controlled. Also, companies that want to calculate the full costs of products must allocate corporate costs to activity-cost pools of divisions.

b. Other companies do not allocate corporate costs to divisions. They maintain that division managers generally have no say or role in incurring these costs.

c. Still other companies allocate only those corporate costs, such as corporate human resources, for which there is widespread agreement that they are either causally related to division activities or they provide explicit benefits to divisions. These companies exclude corporate costs such as corporate donations to charitable foundations both because division managers often have no say in making these decisions and because these benefits to the divisions are less evident or too remote.

For some decision purposes, allocating some but not all corporate costs to divisions may be the preferred alternative. Consider the performance evaluation of division managers. The controllability notion (see pp. 195–196) is frequently used to justify excluding some corporate costs from division reports. For example, the salaries of the top management at corporate headquarters are often excluded from responsibility accounting reports of division managers. While divisions may benefit from these corporate costs, division managers argue they have no say in ("are not responsible for") how much of these corporate resources they use or how much they cost. The contrary argument is that full allocation is justified because the divisions receive benefits from all corporate costs.

Points to Stress The more homogeneous the costs within a cost pool, the more accurate the cost allocation. Ideally, each cost pool has its own allocation base. The more closely the base captures the cause-and-effect relation, the more accurate the cost allocation.

2. If CAI allocates corporate costs to divisions, how many cost pools should it use to allocate corporate costs? One extreme is to aggregate all corporate costs into a single cost pool. The other extreme is to have numerous individual corporate cost pools. A variety of factors may prompt managers to consider using multiple cost pools. A key factor is the concept of homogeneity.

In a **homogeneous cost pool**, all of the costs have the same or a similar cause-and-effect or benefits-received relationship with the cost-allocation base. Why is homogeneity important? Because using homogeneous cost pools enables computing more accurate costs of a given cost object. If a homogeneous cost pool exists, the cost allocations using that pool will be the same as if costs of each individual activity in that pool were allocated separately. The greater the degree of homogeneity, the fewer cost pools are required to explain accurately the differences in how divisions or products use resources of the organization.

For example, when allocating corporate costs to divisions, CAI can combine corporate administration and corporate human resource management costs into a single cost pool if both cost categories have the same or a similar cause-and-effect relationship with the same cost-allocation base. On the other hand, if each cost category has a different cost driver, CAI will prefer to maintain separate cost pools for these costs. Determining cost pool homogeneity requires judgment and should be revisited on a regular basis.

Another factor in deciding on the number of cost pools is the views of affected managers. Do they believe that aggregating corporate costs into a single cost pool ignores important differences in how divisions use corporate resources? A final factor is the costs of implementing a multiple cost pool system. Improvements in information-gathering technology are enhancing the capability of companies and reducing the cost of using multiple cost pools.

3. If CAI allocates corporate costs to divisions, which allocation bases should it use? Generally, they are the ones that have the best cause-and-effect relationship with the costs.

Implementing Corporate Cost Allocations

We illustrate the allocation of corporate costs to divisions in an ABC system using the CAI example. CAI chooses to allocate all corporate costs to divisions. It could have chosen the option of not allocating some corporate costs to divisions and hence products. Not allocating some costs will result in total company profitability being less than the sum of individual product profitabilities.

The demand for corporate resources by the Refrigerator Division and the Clothes Dryer Division depends on the demand that each division's products place on these resources. Exhibit 14-4 diagrams the allocations.

New in This Edition This new subsection, "Implementing Corporate Cost Allocations," links the cost-allocation material in this chapter with the ABC material of Chap. 5. Exh. 14-4 (an ABC diagram used in Chap. 5) leads students through the allocations of corporate costs using the ABC cost hierarchy (i.e., unit level costs, batch-level costs, etc.).

1. CAI allocates treasury costs to each division on the basis of the cost of new assembly equipment installed in each division (the cost driver of treasury costs). That is, the $900,000 of treasury costs are allocated as follows (using information from p. 502):

$$\text{Refrigerator Division:} \quad \$900,000 \times \frac{\$5,200,000}{\$5,200,000 + \$3,800,000} = \$520,000$$

$$\text{Clothes Dryer Division:} \quad \$900,000 \times \frac{\$3,800,000}{\$5,200,000 + \$3,800,000} = \$380,000$$

Each division then creates a separate cost pool consisting of the allocated corporate treasury costs and reallocates these costs to products on the basis of machine-hours used on the new equipment (the cost driver of the allocated treasury cost). Treasury costs are an output unit-level cost because they represent resources sacrificed on activities performed on each individual unit of a product.

2. CAI's analysis indicates that the demand for corporate human resource management (CHRM) costs for recruitment and training varies with salary and labor costs. As a result, these costs are allocated to divisions on the basis of the total salary and labor costs incurred in each division. Suppose salary and labor costs are $44,000,000 in the Refrigerator Division and $36,000,000 in the Clothes Dryer Division. Then CHRM costs are allocated to the divisions as follows:

Teaching Tip Ask students, while referring to Exh. 14-4, to trace the cost allocations in the CHRM example to the product. This also will require them to explain the cost-allocation hierarchy.

$$\text{Refrigerator Division:} \quad \$1,600,000 \times \frac{\$44,000,000}{\$44,000,000 + \$36,000,000} = \$880,000$$

$$\text{Clothes Dryer Division:} \quad \$1,600,000 \times \frac{\$36,000,000}{\$44,000,000 + \$36,000,000} = \$720,000$$

Each division then reallocates the CHRM costs to the indirect-cost pools of product design, manufacturing setup, manufacturing operations, distribution, and division administration on the basis of the salary and labor costs incurred for each of these activities. CHRM costs are thus added to the indirect-cost pools in each division and allocated to products using the cost driver for each cost pool. Thus, CHRM costs are product-sustaining costs (for the portion of CHRM costs allocated as part of the design cost pool), batch-level costs (for the portion of CHRM costs allocated as part of the setup cost pool), output unit-level costs (for the portions of CHRM costs allocated as part of manufacturing operations and distribution cost pools), and facility-sustaining costs (for the portion of CHRM costs allocated as part of the division administration cost pool).

3. CAI allocates corporate administration costs to each division on the basis of division administration costs because corporate administration's main role is to support division management. Corporate administration costs are allocated as follows (using information about division administration costs from Exhibit 14-3):

$$\text{Refrigerator Division:} \quad \$5,400,000 \times \frac{\$1,000,000}{\$1,000,000 + \$800,000} = \$3,000,000$$

$$\text{Clothes Dryer Division:} \quad \$5,400,000 \times \frac{\$800,000}{\$1,000,000 + \$800,000} = \$2,400,000$$

Each division adds the allocated corporate administration costs to the division administration cost pool. The costs in this cost pool are facility-sustaining costs and do not have a cause-and-effect relationship with individual products produced and sold by each division. CAI's policy, however, is to allocate all costs to products. It reallocates the division administration and the allocated corporate administration costs in each division to products on the basis of product revenues (on a benefits-received basis).

Exhibit 14-4 highlights the different ways corporate overhead costs are allocated to divisions and then products.

Reinforcing Problems Prob. 14-29 reinforces the corporate allocation methods.

◆ For corporate treasury costs, CAI uses a separate activity-cost pool at the division level to allocate these costs to products.

◆ For corporate human resource management (CHRM) costs, CAI allocates costs to divisions on the basis of salary and labor costs and then reallocates division costs to individual activity-cost pools on the basis of salary and labor costs in each cost pool. Thus, the activity-cost pools of each division include an allocation of CHRM costs, as shown in Exhibit 14-4.

◆ For corporate administration (CA) costs, CAI allocates costs to divisions on the basis of division administration costs and adds these costs to the division administration cost pool, as shown in Exhibit 14-4.

Thus, corporate overhead costs can be allocated to products by establishing its own activity-cost pool (as was the case for corporate-treasury costs), accumulating these costs in one activity-cost pool (as was the case for corporate administration costs), or accumulating these costs in multiple activity-cost pools (as was the case for corporate human resource management costs).

As we described in Chapter 5, focusing on activities and the hierarchy of costs promotes cost management. The set of activities and hence the actions necessary to manage costs are different if a cost is an output unit-level cost, a batch-level cost, a product-sustaining cost, or a facility-sustaining cost. For example, to manage setup cost, a batch-level cost, CAI must focus on batch-level activities, such as ways to reduce setup-hours and the cost per setup-hour.

Exhibit 14-4 also reinforces the idea that costing systems have multiple cost objects such as corporate headquarters, divisions, departments, and products. An individual cost item can be simultaneously a direct cost of one cost object and an indirect cost of one or more other cost objects. Consider the salary of the head of corporate human resource management at CAI. Her salary is a direct cost of the Corporate Human Resource Management group at CAI's corporate office. It is then allocated as an indirect cost to each of CAI's divisions and then reallocated as an indirect cost of the products in each division.

ALLOCATING COSTS FROM ONE DEPARTMENT TO ANOTHER

Our discussion of cost allocation for CAI in Exhibits 14-3 and 14-4 emphasized two basic issues—choice of cost pools and choice of allocation bases. There are several other issues that arise when allocating costs: (1) Should different methods of allocation be used for fixed costs and for variable costs, (2) should budgeted rates or actual rates be used, and (3) should budgeted quantities or actual quantities be used? We consider these additional choices next.

We illustrate these issues in the context of allocating costs from a corporate department to divisions. The same issues also arise when allocating costs from one cost pool in a division to another cost pool within the division, or when allocating costs from activity-cost pools in a division to products.

Single-Rate and Dual-Rate Methods

The **single-rate cost-allocation method** pools all costs in one cost pool and allocates these costs to cost objects using the same rate per unit of the single allocation base. There is no distinction between costs in the cost pool in terms of cost behavior (such as fixed costs versus variable costs). The **dual-rate cost-allocation method** classifies costs in each cost pool into two subcost pools (a variable-cost subpool and a fixed-cost subpool). Each of these subpools uses a different cost-allocation base.

OBJECTIVE 4

Differentiate the single-rate cost-allocation method from the dual-rate cost-allocation method

Consider Sand Hill Company (SHC), which has a Central Computer Department. This department has only two users—SHC's Microcomputer Division and SHC's Peripheral Equipment Division. The following data apply to the coming budget year:

Reinforcing Problems Exer. 14-17 and 14-18 reinforce the single- and dual-rate methods.

Fixed costs of operating the computer facility in the 6,000- to 18,000-hour relevant range	$3,000,000 per year
Total capacity available	18,000 hours
Budgeted long-run usage	
Microcomputer Division	8,000 hours
Peripheral Equipment Division	4,000 hours
Total	12,000
Budgeted variable costs per hour in the 6,000- to 18,000-hour relevant range	$200 per hour used

Under the single-rate method, the costs of the Central Computer Department would be allocated as follows (assuming budgeted usage is the allocation base and budgeted rates are used):

Total cost pool, $3,000,000 + (12,000 budgeted hours × $200)	$5,400,000 per year
Budgeted usage	12,000 hours
Budgeted total rate per hour, $5,400,000 ÷ 12,000 hours	$450 per hour used
Allocation rate for Microcomputer Division	$450 per hour used
Allocation rate for Peripheral Equipment Division	$450 per hour used

The rate of $450 per hour differs sizably from the $200 budgeted variable costs per hour. The $450 rate includes an allocated amount of $250 per hour ($3,000,000 ÷ 12,000 hours) for the fixed costs of operating the facility. These fixed costs will be incurred whether the computer runs at its 18,000-hour capacity, or (say) at its 12,000-hour budgeted usage.

Using the single-rate method (combined with the budgeted usage allocation base) transforms what is a fixed cost to the Central Computer Department (and to SHC) into a variable cost of $450 per hour to users of that facility. This approach could lead internal users to purchase computer time outside the company. Consider an external vendor that charges less than $450 per hour but more than $200 per hour. A division of SHC that uses this vendor rather than the Central Computer Department will decrease its own division costs, but the overall costs to SHC will increase. For example, suppose the Microcomputer Division uses an external vendor that charges $360 per hour when the Central Computer Department has unused capacity. In the short run, SHC incurs an extra $160 per hour ($360 external purchase price per hour minus the savings of $200 in internal variable costs per hour from not using the in-house facility).

When the dual-rate method is used, allocation bases must be chosen for each cost pool. Assume that the budgeted rates are used. The allocation quantities chosen are *budgeted usage for fixed costs* and *actual usage for variable costs*. The total budgeted usage of 12,000 hours comprises 8,000 hours for the Microcomputer Division

Teaching Tip Ask students whether the dual-rate method will induce optimal (1) short-run and (2) long-run decisions in the SHC example. As explained in the text, the dual-rate method will help users of SHC's Central Computer Dept. make decisions (about purchasing computer time) that are in the short-run best interest of the company. Users will insource as long as the internal VC component is less than the cost of outsourcing. What is in the *long-term* best interests of SHC? SHC's average full cost is $450/hr., but a vendor offers computer time at $360/hr. In the long term, SHC should consider outsourcing this function if there is no quality differential and if they can't cut costs.

and 4,000 hours for the Peripheral Equipment Division. The costs allocated to the Microcomputer Division would be:

Fixed costs, (8,000 hours ÷ 12,000 hours) × $3,000,000	$2,000,000 per year
Variable costs	$200 per hour used

The costs allocated to the Peripheral Equipment Division would be:

Fixed costs, (4,000 hours ÷ 12,000 hours) × $3,000,000	$1,000,000 per year
Variable costs	$200 per hour used

Assume now that during the coming year the Microcomputer Division actually uses 9,000 hours and the Peripheral Equipment Division actually uses 3,000 hours. The costs allocated to these two divisions would be computed as follows:

UNDER THE SINGLE-RATE METHOD

◆ Microcomputer Division: $9,000 × \$450 = \$4,050,000$

◆ Peripheral Equipment Division: $3,000 × \$450 = \$1,350,000$

UNDER THE DUAL-RATE METHOD

◆ Microcomputer Division: $\$2,000,000 + (9,000 × \$200) = \$3,800,000$

◆ Peripheral Equipment Division: $\$1,000,000 + (3,000 × \$200) = \$1,600,000$

One obvious benefit of the single-rate method is the low cost of implementation. It avoids the often expensive analysis necessary to classify the individual cost items of a department into fixed and variable categories. However, the single-rate method may lead division managers to make outsourcing decisions that appear to be in their own best interest but are not in the best interest of the organization as a whole.

An important benefit of the dual-rate method is that it signals to division managers how variable costs and fixed costs behave differently. This important information could guide division managers to make decisions that benefit the organization as a whole as well as each division. For example, it would signal that using a third-party computer provider who charges more than $200 per hour results in SHC being worse-off than using its own Central Computer Department, which has a variable cost of $200 per hour. Why? Because the fixed costs would be charged to each division buying the service separately from the charge for the variable-cost component. These separate charges alert the user to how costs behave at SHC.

Budgeted Versus Actual Rates

The decision whether to use budgeted cost rates or actual cost rates affects the level of uncertainty user divisions face. Budgeted rates let the user departments know in advance the cost rates they will be charged. Users are then better equipped to determine the amount of the service to request and—if the option exists—whether to use the internal department source or an external vendor. In contrast, when actual rates are used, the user departments will not know the rates charged until the end of the period.

Budgeted rates also help motivate the manager of the supplier department (for example, the Central Computer Department) to improve efficiency. During the budget period, the supplier (support) department, not the user departments, bears the risk of any unfavorable cost variances. Why? Because the user departments do not pay for any costs that exceed the budgeted rates. The manager of the support department likely would view the budgeted rates negatively, especially when unfavorable cost variances occur due to price increases outside of his or her control.

Some organizations recognize that it may not always be best to impose the risks of variances from budgeted amounts completely on the supplier department (as when costs are allocated using budgeted rates) or completely on the user departments (as when costs are allocated using actual rates). For example, the two departments may agree to share the risk (through an explicit formula) of a large uncontrollable increase in the price of materials used by the support department.

OBJECTIVE 5

Understand how the risks managers face are affected by the choice between budgeted versus actual cost-allocation rates

Case	Actual Usage		Budgeted Usage As Allocation Base		Actual Usage As Allocation Base	
	Micro. Div.	Perif. Div.	Micro. Div.	Perif. Div.	Micro. Div.	Perif. Div.
1	8,000 hours	4,000 hours	$2,000,000[a]	$1,000,000[b]	$2,000,000[a]	$1,000,000[b]
2	8,000 hours	7,000 hours	$2,000,000[a]	$1,000,000[b]	$1,600,000[c]	$1,400,000[d]
3	8,000 hours	2,000 hours	$2,000,000[a]	$1,000,000[b]	$2,400,000[e]	$ 600,000[f]

$$[a]\frac{8,000}{8,000 + 4,000} \times \$3,000,000 \qquad [c]\frac{8,000}{8,000 + 7,000} \times \$3,000,000 \qquad [e]\frac{8,000}{8,000 + 2,000} \times \$3,000,000$$

$$[b]\frac{4,000}{8,000 + 4,000} \times \$3,000,000 \qquad [d]\frac{7,000}{8,000 + 7,000} \times \$3,000,000 \qquad [f]\frac{2,000}{8,000 + 2,000} \times \$3,000,000$$

Budgeted Versus Actual Usage Allocation Bases

Under the dual-rate method, the choice between actual usage and budgeted usage for allocating fixed costs also can affect a manager's behavior. Consider the budget of $3,000,000 fixed costs at the Central Computer Department of SHC. Assume that actual and budgeted fixed costs are equal. Assume also that the actual usage by the Microcomputer Division is always equal to the budgeted usage. We now look at the effect on allocating the $3,000,000 in total fixed costs based on actual usage, when actual usage by the Peripheral Equipment Division equals (Case 1), is greater than (Case 2), and is less than (Case 3) than the budgeted usage. Recall that the budgeted usage is 8,000 hours for the Microcomputer Division and 4,000 hours for the Peripheral Equipment Division. Exhibit 14-5 presents the allocation of total fixed costs of $3,000,000 to each division for these three cases.

In Case 1, the fixed-cost allocation equals the expected amount. In Case 2, the fixed-cost allocation is $400,000 less to the Microcomputer Division than expected ($1,600,000 vs. $2,000,000). In Case 3, the fixed-cost allocation is $400,000 more than expected ($2,400,000 vs. $2,000,000). Consider Case 3. Why is there an increase of $400,000 to the Microcomputer Division even though this division's actual and budgeted usage are equal? Because the fixed costs are spread over fewer hours of usage. That is, variations in usage in the Peripheral Equipment Division affects the fixed costs allocated to the Microcomputer Division when fixed costs are allocated on the basis of actual usage. When actual usage is the allocation base, user divisions will not know how much cost is allocated to them until the end of the budget period.

When budgeted usage is the allocation base, user divisions will know in advance their allocated costs. This information helps the user divisions with both short-run and long-run planning. The main justification given for the use of budgeted usage to allocate fixed costs relates to long-run planning. Organizations commit to infrastructure costs (such as the fixed costs of a support department) on the basis of a long-run planning horizon; the use of budgeted usage to allocate these fixed costs is consistent with the long-run horizon.

If fixed costs are allocated on the basis of budgeted long-run usage, some managers may be tempted to underestimate their planned usage. In this way, they will bear a lower percentage of the total costs (assuming all other managers do *not* similarly underestimate their usage). Some organizations offer rewards in the form of salary increases and promotions to managers who make accurate forecasts of long-run usage. (This is the carrot approach.) Alternatively, some organizations impose cost penalties for underpredicting long-run usage. For instance, a higher cost rate may be charged after a division exceeds its budgeted usage. (This is the stick approach.)

Correcting Student Misconceptions Why shouldn't fixed costs be allocated according to actual usage? (1) Fixed costs would be "transformed" into variable costs, so (2) the allocation wouldn't capture the cause and effect of cost incurrence (fixed costs are "caused" by long-term expected usage), and (3) changes in one dept's. usage would affect another dept's. allocation (see Exh. 14-5).

Points to Stress Fixed costs provide the *capacity to serve*, so they should be allocated according to the reason the capacity was obtained—long-term expected usage. Variable costs, on the other hand, are directly caused by current usage, so they should be allocated on this basis.

The SHC example highlights generic issues that arise when costs are allocated from one or more departments (divisions) to other departments (divisions). We now examine the special case where two or more of the departments whose costs are being allocated provide reciprocal support to each other as well as to other departments.

ALLOCATING COSTS OF SUPPORT DEPARTMENTS

Operating Departments and Support Departments

Reinforcing Problems Exer. 14-20 and 14-21 reinforce the budgeted vs. actual rate issue.

Reinforcing Problems Exer. 14-25, 14-26, 14-27, and 14-28, and Probs. 14-31, 14-32, and 14-33 cover allocation of support dept. costs via direct, step-down, and reciprocal methods.

Organizations distinguish between operating departments and support departments. An **operating department** (also called a **production department** in manufacturing companies) adds value to a product or service that is observable by a customer. A **support department** (also called a **service department**) provides the services that assist other internal departments (operating departments and other support departments) in the organization. Support departments create special cost-allocation problems when they provide reciprocal support to each other as well as support to operating departments. An example of reciprocal support is a Corporate Human Resource (HR) Department providing services to a Corporate Legal Department (such as advice about hiring of attorneys and secretaries) while the Corporate Legal Department provides services to the HR department (such as advice on compliance with labor laws). This section illustrates alternative ways to recognize these reciprocal relationships in support department cost allocations. More accurate support department cost allocations result in more accurate product, service, and customer costs.

Teaching Tip The following diagram keyed to the text's example illustrates that the 3 methods of allocating support dept. costs differ only in the way they account for the reciprocal services.

Direct method—NO reciprocal services recognized.
Step method—*One-way* reciprocal services recognized:
    Maintenance ⟶ Info. Systems
Reciprocal method—*Two-way* reciprocal services recognized:
    Maintenance ⟷ Info. Systems

Consider Castleford Engineering, which manufactures engines used in electric power generating plants. Castleford has two support departments and two operating departments in its manufacturing facility:

Support Departments	Operating Departments
Plant (and equipment) maintenance	Machining
Information systems	Assembly

The two support departments at Castleford provide reciprocal support to each other as well as to the two operating departments. Costs are accumulated in each department for planning and control purposes. The data for our example are presented in Exhibit 14-6. We illustrate the percentages in this exhibit with the Plant Maintenance Department. This support department provides a total of 8,000 hours

EXHIBIT 14-6
Data for Allocating Support Department Costs at Castleford Engineering for 2001

	Support Departments		Operating Departments		
	Plant Maintenance	Information Systems	Machining	Assembly	Total
Budgeted manufacturing overhead costs before any interdepartment cost allocations	$600,000	$116,000	$400,000	$200,000	$1,316,000
Support work furnished:					
By Plant Maintenance					
Budgeted labor-hours	—	1,600	2,400	4,000	8,000
Percentage	—	20%	30%	50%	100%
By Information Systems					
Budgeted computer-hours	200	—	1,600	200	2,000
Percentage	10%	—	80%	10%	100%

EXHIBIT 14-7
Direct Method of Allocating Support Department Costs for 2001 at Castleford Engineering

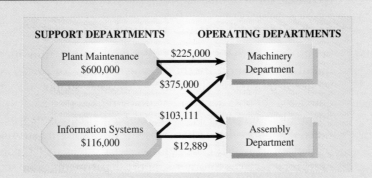

	Support Departments		Operating Departments		
	Plant Maintenance	Information Systems	Machining	Assembly	Total
Budgeted manufacturing overhead costs before any interdepartment cost allocations	$600,000	$116,000	$400,000	$200,000	$1,316,000
Allocation of Plant Maintenance: (3/8, 5/8)[a]	(600,000)		225,000	375,000	
Allocation of Information Systems: (8/9, 1/9)[b]	$ 0	(116,000)	103,111	12,889	
Total budgeted manufacturing overhead of operating departments		$ 0	$728,111	$587,889	$1,316,000

[a]Base is (2,400 + 4,000), or 6,400 hours; 2,400 ÷ 6,400 = 3/8; 4,000 ÷ 6,400 = 5/8.
[b]Base is (1,600 + 200), or 1,800 hours; 1,600 ÷ 1,800 = 8/9; 200 ÷ 1,800 = 1/9.

of support work: 20% (1,600 ÷ 8,000) goes to the Information Systems Department, 30% (2,400 ÷ 8,000) to the Machining Department, and 50% (4,000 ÷ 8,000) to the Assembly Department.

We now examine three methods of allocating the costs of support departments: *direct*, *step-down*, and *reciprocal*. To focus on concepts, we use the single-rate method to allocate the costs of each support department. The Problem for Self-Study at the end of this chapter illustrates the use of the dual-rate method for allocating support department costs.

Direct Allocation Method

The **direct allocation method** (often called the **direct method**) is the most widely used method of allocating support department costs. This method allocates each support department's costs directly to the operating departments. Exhibit 14-7 illustrates this method using the data in Exhibit 14-6. The base used to allocate Plant Maintenance is the budgeted total maintenance labor-hours worked in the operating departments: 2,400 + 4,000 = 6,400 hours. This amount excludes the 1,600 hours of support time provided by Plant Maintenance to Information Systems. Similarly, the base used for allocation of Information Systems costs is 1,600 + 200 = 1,800 hours of computer time, which excludes the 200 hours of support time provided by Information Systems to Plant Maintenance.

The benefit of the direct method is its simplicity. There is no need to predict the usage of support department services by other support departments. A disadvantage of the direct method is its failure to recognize reciprocal services provided among support departments. We now examine a straightforward approach to recognize some of the reciprocal services provided among support departments.

Step-Down Allocation Method

Some organizations use the **step-down allocation method** (also called the **sequential allocation method**), which allows for *partial* recognition of the services rendered by support departments to other support departments. This method requires the support departments to be ranked (sequenced) in the order that the step-down allocation is to proceed. Different sequences will result in different allocations of support department costs to operating departments. A popular step-down sequence begins with the support department that renders the highest percentage of its total services to other support departments. The sequence continues with the department that gives the next-highest percentage of its total services to other support departments, and so on, ending with the support department that renders the lowest percentage of its total services to other support departments.[4]

Exhibit 14-8 shows the step-down method. The Plant Maintenance costs of $600,000 is allocated first; $120,000 is allocated to Information Systems (20% of $600,000), $180,000 to Machining (30% of $600,000) and $300,000 to Assembly (50% of $600,000). The costs in Information Systems now total $236,000 ($116,000 + $120,000 from the first round allocation). This $236,000 is then allocated between the two operating departments—209,778 (8/9 × $236,000) to Machining and $26,222 (1/9 × $236,000) to Assembly.

Under the step-down method, once a support department's costs have been allocated, no subsequent support department costs are allocated back to it. Thus, once the Plant Maintenance Department costs are allocated, it receives no further allocation from other (lower ranked) support departments. The result is that the step-down method does not recognize the total services that support departments provide to each other. The reciprocal method, which fully recognizes all such services, is now examined.

Reciprocal Allocation Method

The **reciprocal allocation method** allocates costs by explicitly including the mutual services provided among all support departments. Conceptually, the direct method and the step-down method are less accurate than the reciprocal method when support departments provide services to one another reciprocally. For example, the Plant Maintenance Department maintains all the computer equipment in the Information Systems Department. Similarly, Information Systems provides data base support for Plant Maintenance. The reciprocal allocation method enables us to incorporate interdepartmental relationships fully into the support department cost allocations. Implementing the reciprocal allocation method requires three steps.

Step 1: Express Support Department Costs and Support Department Reciprocal Relationships in the Form of Linear Equations   Let PM be the *complete reciprocated costs* of Plant Maintenance and IS be the complete reciprocated costs of Information Systems. We then express the data in Exhibit 14-6 as follows:

$$\text{PM} = \$600,000 + 0.1\text{IS} \tag{1}$$

$$\text{IS} \ = \$116,000 + 0.2\text{PM} \tag{2}$$

The 0.1IS term in equation (1) is the percentage of the Information Systems work *used by* Plant Maintenance. The 0.2PM term in equation (2) is the percentage of the Plant Maintenance work used by Information Systems.

By **complete reciprocated costs** in equations (1) and (2), we mean the support department's own costs plus any interdepartmental cost allocations. This com-

Points to Stress/Reinforcing Problems
When one is using the step-down method, selecting a different sequence of the step-down order (because of using a different criterion) will result in different dollar amounts allocated to the operating depts. Exer. 14-25 and Prob. 14-32 reinforce this concept.

Example In the step-down method, the sequence of steps can be important. A local govt. used a sequence where the dept. that supported the most other depts. (Facilities Mgt.) was allocated first to all the other depts., including the Corrections Dept. However, the Corrections Dept. provided much direct labor to the Facilities Mgt. Dept. Even so, Corrections didn't allocate costs to Facilities Mgt. for the labor (because of the step sequence). The significant costs of providing labor to Facilities Mgt. were allocated to *other* users of Correction's labor. These other depts. complained about the high cost of Corrections labor and wanted to contract out because outside labor was less expensive. Thus, the sequence of allocation in the step-down method can cause problems, particularly if there are a lot of internal support dept. costs. (The reciprocal method would alleviate this problem.)

Correcting Student Misconceptions
Students are often confused about why the step method allocation is only one-way. Emphasize that the goal is to get rid of (i.e., allocate) support dept. costs, and once a dept's. cost is allocated, it's counterproductive to allocate costs back to that dept. Hence, once the Plant Maintenance cost is allocated and zeroed out, Info. Systems cost isn't allocated to Plant Maintenance.

Points to Stress Emphasize that allocating costs of support depts. to operating depts. is a special case of the dept.-to-dept. allocation discussed earlier.

---

[4]An alternative approach to selecting the sequence of allocations is to begin with the department that renders the highest dollar amount of services to other support departments. The sequence ends with the allocation of the costs of the department that renders the lowest dollar amount of services to other support departments.

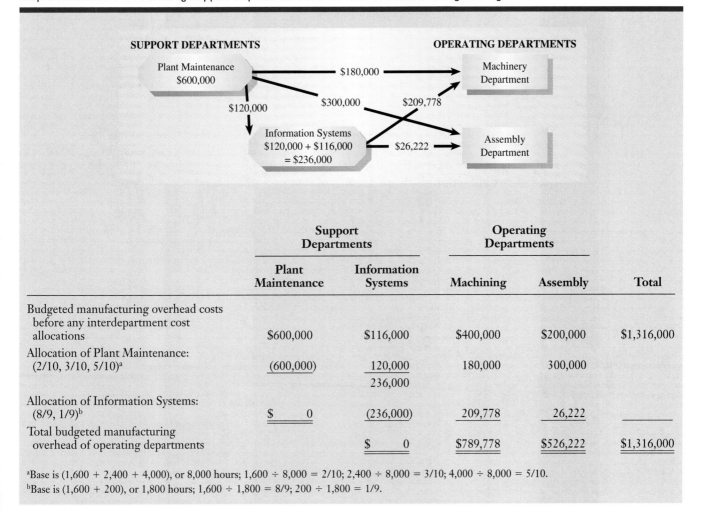

	Support Departments		Operating Departments		
	Plant Maintenance	Information Systems	Machining	Assembly	Total
Budgeted manufacturing overhead costs before any interdepartment cost allocations	$600,000	$116,000	$400,000	$200,000	$1,316,000
Allocation of Plant Maintenance: (2/10, 3/10, 5/10)[a]	(600,000)	120,000	180,000	300,000	
		236,000			
Allocation of Information Systems: (8/9, 1/9)[b]	$ 0	(236,000)	209,778	26,222	
Total budgeted manufacturing overhead of operating departments		$ 0	$789,778	$526,222	$1,316,000

[a]Base is (1,600 + 2,400 + 4,000), or 8,000 hours; 1,600 ÷ 8,000 = 2/10; 2,400 ÷ 8,000 = 3/10; 4,000 ÷ 8,000 = 5/10.
[b]Base is (1,600 + 200), or 1,800 hours; 1,600 ÷ 1,800 = 8/9; 200 ÷ 1,800 = 1/9.

plete reciprocated costs figure is sometimes called the **artificial costs** of the support department.

Step 2: Solve the Set of Linear Equations to Obtain the Complete Reciprocated Costs of Each Support Department   Where there are two support departments, the following substitution approach can be used. Substituting equation (2) into equation (1):

$$PM = \$600,000 + [0.1(\$116,000 + 0.2PM)]$$

$$= \$600,000 + \$11,600 + 0.02PM$$

$$0.98PM = \$611,600$$

$$PM = \$624,082$$

Substituting into equation (2):

$$IS = \$116,000 + 0.2(\$624,082)$$

$$= \$116,000 + \$124,816 = \$240,816$$

Where there are more than two support departments with reciprocal relationships, computer programs such as Excel can be used to calculate the complete reciprocated costs of each support department.

Step 3: Allocate the Complete Reciprocated Costs of Each Support Department to All Other Departments (Both Support Departments and Operating Departments) on the Basis of the Usage Percentages (Based on Total Units

of Service Provided to All Departments)   Consider the Information Systems Department, which has complete reciprocated costs of \$240,816. This amount would be allocated as follows:

$$\text{To Plant Maintenance } (1/10) \times \$240,816 = \$ \ 24,082$$

$$\text{To Machining } (8/10) \times \$240,816 \qquad = \quad 192,652$$

$$\text{To Assembly } (1/10) \times \$240,816 \qquad = \quad \underline{\ \ 24,082}$$

$$\text{Total} \qquad\qquad\qquad\qquad = \underline{\$240,816}$$

Exhibit 14-9 presents summary data pertaining to the reciprocal method.

One source of confusion to some managers using the reciprocal cost-allocation method is why the \$864,898 complete reciprocated costs of the support departments exceeds the budgeted amount of \$716,000.

	Complete Reciprocated Cost of Support Department	Budgeted Cost of Support Department
Plant Maintenance	\$624,082	\$600,000
Information Systems	240,816	116,000
Total	\$864,898	\$716,000

EXHIBIT 14-9
Reciprocal Method of Allocating Support Department Costs for 2001 at Castleford Engineering

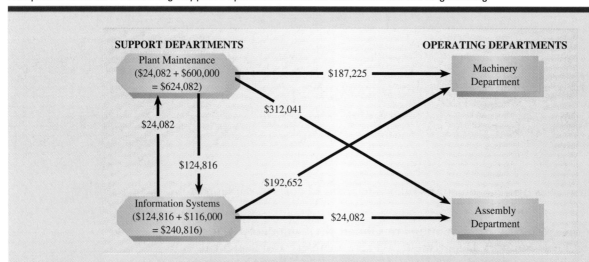

	Support Departments		Operating Departments		
	Plant Maintenance	Information Systems	Machining	Assembly	Total
Budgeted manufacturing overhead costs before any interdepartment cost allocations	\$600,000	\$116,000	\$400,000	\$200,000	\$1,316,000
Allocation of Plant Maintenance: (2/10, 3/10, 5/10)[a]	(624,082)	124,816	187,225	312,041	
Allocation of Information Systems: (1/10, 8/10, 1/10)[b]	24,082	(240,816)	192,652	24,082	
Total budgeted manufacturing overhead of operating departments	\$ 0	\$ 0	\$779,877	\$536,123	\$1,316,000

[a]Base is (1,600 + 2,400 + 4,000), or 8,000 hours; 1,600 ÷ 8,000 = 2/10; 2,400 ÷ 8,000 = 3/10; 4,000 ÷ 8,000 = 5/10.
[b]Base is (200 + 1,600 + 200), or 2,000 hours; 200 ÷ 2,000 = 1/10; 1,600 ÷ 2,000 = 8/10; 200 ÷ 2,000 = 1/10.

Each support department's complete reciprocated cost is greater than the budgeted amount to take into account that the allocation of support costs will be to all departments using its services and not just to operating departments. It is this step that ensures that the reciprocal method fully recognizes all the interrelationships among support departments, as well as relationships between support departments and operating departments. The difference between the complete reciprocated cost and the budgeted cost for each support department ($24,082 for Plant Maintenance and $124,816 for Information Systems) is the total costs that are allocated among support departments. The total costs allocated to the operating departments under the reciprocal allocation method are still only $716,000.

Overview of Methods

Assume that the total budgeted overhead costs of each operating department in the example in Exhibits 14-7 through 14-9 are allocated to individual products on the basis of budgeted machine-hours for the Machining Department (4,000 hours) and budgeted direct labor-hours for the Assembly Department (3,000 hours). The budgeted overhead allocation rates (rounded to the nearest dollar) for each support department allocation method are:

| Support Department Cost-Allocation Method | Total Budgeted Overhead Costs After Allocation of All Support Department Costs | | Budgeted Overhead Rate Per Hour for Product-Costing Purposes | |
	Machining	Assembly	Machining (4,000 machine-hours)	Assembly (3,000 labor-hours)
Direct	$728,111	$587,889	$182	$196
Step-down	789,778	526,222	197	175
Reciprocal	779,877	536,123	195	179

These differences in budgeted overhead rates with alternative support department cost-allocation methods can be important to managers. For example, consider a cost-reimbursement contract that uses 100 hours of Machining Department time and 15 hours of Assembly Department time. The support department costs allocated to this contract would be:

Direct:	$21,140	[($182 × 100) + ($196 × 15)]
Step-down:	22,325	[($197 × 100) + ($175 × 15)]
Reciprocal:	22,185	[($195 × 100) + ($179 × 15)]

Use of the step-down method would result in the highest cost reimbursement to the contractor.

The reciprocal method, while conceptually the most defensible, is not widely used. The advantage of the direct and step-down methods is that they are relatively simple to compute and understand. However, with the ready availability of computer software to solve sets of simultaneous equations, the extra costs of using the reciprocal method will, in most cases, be minimal.

The reciprocal method highlights that the "full costs" of support departments can differ from the budgeted or incurred costs in those departments. Knowing the "full cost" of a support department is a key input for decisions about whether to outsource all the services that the support department provides.

Suppose all of Castleford's support department costs are variable over the period of the possible outsourcing contract. A third party's bid to provide, say, all the information systems services currently provided by Castleford's Information Systems Department may appear to be high relative to the $116,000 costs reported for the Information Systems Department. The fully reciprocated costs of the Information Systems Department, which includes the services the Plant Maintenance Department provides the Information Systems Department, are $240,816 to deliver 2,000 hours of computer time to all other departments at Castleford. The cost for computer time is $120.408 per hour ($240,816 ÷ 2,000 hours) for this department.

Teaching Tip The Problem for Self-Study and Prob. 14-33 illustrate how support dept. allocation methods can be used with dual-rate setting. The difference is that there are two sets of linear equations. Variable costs are allocated according to the *actual* usage equations, and fixed costs are allocated according to the *budgeted* usage equations.

Points to Stress Differences among the 3 methods' allocations increase (1) as the magnitude of the reciprocal services increases and (2) as the differences across operating depts' usage of each support service increase.

Other things being equal, a third party's bid to provide all the same information services as Castleford's internal department at less than $240,816 or $120.408 per hour would improve Castleford's operating income. To see this point, note that the relevant savings from shutting down the Information Systems Department are $116,000 of Information Systems Department costs plus $124,816 of Plant Maintenance Department costs. By closing down the Information Systems Department, Castleford will no longer incur the 20% of Plant Maintenance Department costs (equal to $124,816) that were incurred to support the Information Systems Department. Hence the total relevant-cost savings are $240,816 ($116,000 + $124,816). A third-party bid often can appear much more competitive on cost terms when these other support department costs are recognized when determining the "full" internal costs of a support department.[5]

The reciprocal and step-down methods recognize a challenging context (cost interdependencies among support departments) that other cost-allocation methods (as exemplified by the direct method) do not recognize. We now consider another special class of costs (common costs) for which cost accountants have developed specific allocation methods.

ALLOCATING COMMON COSTS

OBJECTIVE 7

Make decisions that draw on the allocation of common costs using either the stand-alone or incremental methods

A **common cost** is a cost of operating a facility, activity, or like cost object that is shared by two or more users. Consider Jason Stevens, a senior student in Seattle who has been invited to a job interview with an employer in Boston. The round-trip Seattle–Boston airfare costs $1,200. A week prior to leaving Stevens is also invited to an interview with an employer in Chicago. The Seattle–Chicago round-trip airfare costs $800. Stevens decides to combine the two recruiting steps into a Seattle–Boston–Chicago–Seattle trip that will cost $1,500 in airfare. The $1,500 is a common cost that benefits both prospective employers. Two methods of allocating this common cost between the two prospective employers are now discussed—the stand-alone method and the incremental method.

Stand-Alone Cost-Allocation Method

The **stand-alone cost-allocation method** uses information pertaining to each user of a cost object as a separate entity to determine the cost-allocation weights. For the common-cost airfare of $1,500, information about the separate (stand-alone) round-trip airfares ($1,200 and $800) is used to determine the allocation weights:

$$\text{Boston employer:} \quad \frac{\$1,200}{\$1,200 + \$800} \times \$1,500 = 0.60 \times \$1,500 = \$900$$

$$\text{Chicago employer:} \quad \frac{\$800}{\$800 + \$1,200} \times \$1,500 = 0.40 \times \$1,500 = \$600$$

Advocates of this method often emphasize the fairness or equity criterion described in Exhibit 14-2. That is, fairness occurs because each employer bears a proportionate share of total costs in relation to their individual stand-alone costs.

Incremental Cost-Allocation Method

The **incremental cost-allocation method** ranks the individual users of a cost object and then uses this ranking to allocate costs among those users. The first-ranked user of the cost object is termed the primary party and is allocated costs up to the costs of the primary party as a stand-alone user. The second-ranked user is termed the incremental party and is allocated the additional cost that arises from there being two users instead of only the primary user.

Consider again Jason Stevens and his $1,500 airfare cost. Assume the Boston employer is viewed as the primary party. Stevens' rationale is that he had already

Reinforcing Problems Exer. 14-23 and 14-24 reinforce the common cost-allocation issues.

Points to Stress The incremental method creates incentives for parties to avoid being first user. Consider allocating the cost of operating a train. The 1st car is allocated the cost of the locomotive, caboose, their operators, and the necessary fuel. The 2nd car is allocated only the cost of the extra fuel needed to pull that car. Is this a reasonable allocation of the train's cost? If the "incremental" party needs a subsidy, is it better to provide a direct subsidy, or an indirect subsidy that affects the costing system?

[5]Technical issues when using the reciprocal method in outsourcing decisions are discussed in R. S. Kaplan and A. A. Atkinson, *Advanced Management Accounting*, 3rd ed. (Upper Saddle River, N. J.: Prentice-Hall, 1998, pp. 73–81).

committed to go to Boston before accepting the invitation to interview in Chicago. The cost allocations would be:

Party	Costs Allocated	Costs Remaining to Be Allocated to Other Parties
Boston (primary)	$1,200	$300 ($1,500 − $1,200)
Chicago (incremental)	300	0

The Boston employer is allocated the full Seattle–Boston airfare. The nonallocated part of the total airfare is then allocated to the Chicago employer. Had the Chicago employer been chosen as the primary party, the cost allocations would have been Chicago $800 (the stand-alone Seattle–Chicago–Seattle round-trip airfare) and Boston $700 ($1,500 − $800). Where there are more than two parties, this method requires them to be ranked from first to last (say, based on the date on which each employer invited the candidate to interview.)

Under the incremental method, the primary party typically receives the highest allocation of the common costs. Not surprisingly, most users in common-cost situations propose themselves as the incremental party. In some cases, the incremental parties are newly formed organizations or an organization's new subunits such as a new product line or a new sales territory. Chances for their short-run survival may be enhanced if they bear a relatively low allocation of common costs.

Where both parties are viewed as primary users, and there is a large common cost that has to be incurred even if there is only one user, the incremental method both lacks conceptual justification and can cause a sizable dispute among the parties. One approach in such situations is to use the stand-alone cost-allocation method.[6]

A caution is appropriate here regarding Stevens' cost-allocation options. His chosen method must be acceptable to each prospective employer. Indeed, some prospective employers may have guidelines that recruiting candidates must follow. For example, the Boston employer may have a policy that the maximum reimbursable airfare is a seven-day advance booking price in economy class. If this amount is less than the amount that Stevens would receive under, say, the stand-alone method, then the employer's upper-limit guideline would govern how much could be allocated to that employer. Stevens should obtain approval before he purchases his ticket as to what cost-allocation method(s) each prospective employer views as acceptable.

Disputes over how to allocate common costs are often encountered. The final section of this chapter discusses the role of cost data in contracting. This is also an area where disputes about cost allocation frequently arise.

Reinforcing Problems Exer. 14-22 and Prob. 14-34 reinforce the cost-allocation and contracts issues.

COST ALLOCATIONS AND CONTRACTS

Many commercial contracts include clauses that require the use of cost accounting information. Examples include:

OBJECTIVE 8

Explain the importance of explicit agreement between parties when reimbursement is based on costs incurred

1. A contract between the Department of Defense and a company designing and assembling a new fighter plane. The price paid for the plane is based on the contractor's costs plus a preset fixed fee.
2. A research contract between a university and a government agency. The university is reimbursed its direct costs plus an overhead rate that is a percentage of direct costs.
3. A contract between an energy-consulting firm and a hospital. The consulting firm receives a fixed fee plus a share of the energy-cost savings arising from implementing the consulting firm's recommendations.

Contract disputes arise with some regularity, often with respect to cost allocation. The areas of dispute between the contracting parties can be reduced by making the "rules

[6]Further discussion of other alternative approaches, including use of the Shapely value, is in J. Demski, "Cost Allocation Games." S. Moriarity (ed.), *Joint Cost Allocations*. (University of Oklahoma Center for Economic and Management Research, 1981).

of the game" explicit and in writing at the time the contract is signed. Such "rules of the game" include the definition of cost items allowed, the permissible cost-allocation bases, and how differences between budgeted and actual costs are to be handled.

Contracting with the U.S. Government

The U.S. government reimburses most contractors in either one of two main ways:

1. The *contractor is paid a set price without analysis of actual contract cost data*. This approach is used, for example, where there is competitive bidding, where there is adequate price competition, or where there is an established catalog with prices quoted for items sold in substantial quantities to the general public.

2. The *contractor is paid after analysis of actual contract cost data*. In some cases, the contract will explicitly state that reimbursement is based on actual allowable costs plus a set fee.[7] This arrangement is a cost-plus contract. In other cases, the contractor is paid a set price, provided that a government contracting officer views this price as reasonable (that is, close to actual costs).

All contracts with U.S. government agencies must comply with cost accounting standards issued by the **Cost Accounting Standards Board (CASB)**. The CASB has the exclusive authority to make, promulgate, amend, and rescind cost accounting standards and interpretations thereof designed to achieve *uniformity* and *consistency* in regard to measurement, assignment, and allocation of costs to contracts within the United States.[8]

The government contracting environment is one where there is a complex interplay of political and accounting principles. Terms such as "fairness" and "equity," as well as cause and effect and benefits received, are often used in this arena.

Fairness of Pricing

When uncertainty is high, as in many defense contracts involving new weapons and equipment, contracts are rarely subject to competitive bidding. Why? Because no contractor is willing to assume all the risk. Hence, setting a market-based fixed-price fails to attract a contractor, or the resulting price is too outrageously high from the government's standpoint. So the government assumes a major share of the risks. It negotiates contracts by using costs plus a fee as a substitute for selling prices as ordinarily set by suppliers in open markets. In such contracts, a cost allocation may be difficult to defend on the basis of any cause-and-effect reasoning. Nonetheless, the contracting parties may still view it as a "reasonable" or "fair" means to help establish a selling price. Some costs become "allowable," but others are "unallowable." An **allowable cost** is a cost that the contract parties agree to include in the costs to be reimbursed. Some contracts specify how allowable costs are to be determined. For example, only economy-class airfares are allowable for many contracts. Other contracts identify cost categories that are unallowable. For example, the costs of lobbying activities and the costs of alcoholic beverages are not allowable costs on U.S. government contracts.

Example Hughes Aircraft builds standard planes for commercial customers and specialized fighter planes for the armed services. Hughes has fixed-price contracts with commercial customers and cost-plus contracts with the services. What cost-allocation incentives does Hughes face? If Hughes can shift indirect costs away from the (fixed-price) commercial customers and toward the cost-plus armed service contracts, Hughes will increase its revenue. This is one reason why the armed services employ cost accountants—to check the books of defense contractors.

Points to Stress The CASB rank orders selection criteria for allocation bases as follows: (1) measure of input activity consumed (e.g., # of hrs. spent procuring RM); (2) output measure related to inputs, if inputs can't be measured (e.g., # of purchase orders); and (3) surrogate for proportion of services received (e.g., proportion of purchasing personnel assigned to contract).

Points to Stress Cost-based prices are one way of setting prices for products for which no ready market price exists. One problem with a cost-plus contract is that the producer has less incentive to control costs because increases can be passed on to the buyer. Cost-reimbursement contracts must be very specific and, if possible, should include incentives to prevent such abuses.

Contract Disputes Over Reimbursable Cost for U.S. Government Agencies

Allegations about a contractor overcharging a government agency invariably make interesting copy for the media. The following three examples are from cases where contractors "settled with the government" without "admitting liability with respect to the charges." The names of the companies are disguised. The focus of these examples is illustrating several types of cost disputes that arise in practice.

◆ XYZ, Inc., "agreed to pay $4.5 million to settle allegations they illegally overcharged the Navy for labor costs on contracts." It was alleged that managers at XYZ "directed their employees to mischarge labor time to a number of military contracts even though management knew the employees did not devote as much time to the contract as was charged to the government." Note that where labor-hours are used to allocate overhead costs to a contract, overstating labor-hours will result in both direct costs and indirect costs being overcharged. This form of overcharging is sometimes referred to as "double-bilking."

◆ PQR Corp. agreed to "pay the federal government $2.2 million to settle allegations it overcharged the Department of Defense for air filters used in helicopters." It was alleged that "during the negotiations, PQR acquired a machine tool that significantly lowered the cost of producing the filters. PQR failed to disclose that information to the government, as required under federal law. The Army would have shared in those savings through a lower contract price according to the suit."

◆ "STV paid $228,705 in damages to the U.S. government to settle a law suit" alleging "overcharging the Army for tank ammunition." The allegations centered on the price STV "told the government it would pay for two components ($39.89 and $40.95)." It was alleged that STV actually paid lower prices ($39.00 and $39.35) as part of a "multi-year contract with its suppliers."

Source: Articles in *Defense Daily*, *Defense Weekly*, and press releases from the Department of Justice.

PROBLEM

This problem illustrates how support department cost-allocation methods can be used in a setting different from the example examined in the chapter (Exhibits 14-6 through 14-9). In this problem, the costs of central corporate support departments are allocated to operating divisions. The corporate departments provide services to each other as well as to the operating divisions. Also, this problem illustrates the use of the dual-rate method of allocating support department costs. (The dual-rate method can also be used in manufacturing support department cost allocations.)

Computer Horizons budgets the following amounts for its two central corporate support departments (legal and personnel) in supporting each other and the two manufacturing divisions—the Laptop Division (LTD) and the Work Station Division (WSD):

To Be Supplied By	Legal	Personnel	LTD	WSD	Total
		Budgeted Capacity			
Legal (hours)	—	250	1,500	750	2,500
(percentages)	—	10%	60%	30%	100%
Personnel (hours)	2,500	—	22,500	25,000	50,000
(percentages)	5%	—	45%	50%	100%

Details on actual usage are as follows:

To Be Supplied By	Legal	Personnel	LTD	WSD	Total
		Actual Usage By			
Legal (hours)	—	400	400	1,200	2,000
(percentages)	—	20%	20%	60%	100%
Personnel (hours)	2,000	—	26,600	11,400	40,000
(percentages)	5%	—	66.5%	28.5%	100%

The actual costs were

	Legal	Personnel
Fixed	$360,000	$475,000
Variable	$200,000	$600,000

Fixed costs are allocated on the basis of budgeted capacity. Variable costs are allocated on the basis of actual usage.

Required
What amount of support department costs for legal and personnel will be allocated to LTD and WSD using (a) the direct method, (b) the step-down method (allocating the Legal Department costs first), and (c) the reciprocal method?

SOLUTION
Exhibit 14-10 presents the computations for allocating the fixed and variable support department costs. A summary of these costs follows:

	Laptop Division (LTD)	Work Station Division (WSD)
(a) Direct Method		
Fixed costs	$465,000	$370,000
Variable costs	470,000	330,000
	$935,000	$700,000
(b) Step-Down Method		
Fixed costs	$458,053	$376,947
Variable costs	488,000	312,000
	$946,053	$688,947
(c) Reciprocal Method		
Fixed costs	$462,513	$372,487
Variable costs	476,364	323,636
	$938,877	$696,123

Letting L = Legal Department costs and P = Personnel Department costs, the simultaneous equations for the reciprocal method are:

EXHIBIT 14-10
Alternative Methods of Allocating Corporation Support Department Costs to Operating Divisions of Computer Horizons: Dual-Rate Method

Allocation Method	Corporate Support Department		Manufacturing Divisions	
	Legal	Personnel	LTD	WSD
A. Direct Method				
Fixed Costs	$360,000	$475,000		
Legal (1,500 ÷ 2,250; 750 ÷ 2,250)	(360,000)		$240,000	$120,000
Personnel (22,500 ÷ 47,500; 25,000 ÷ 47,500)	$ 0	(475,000)	225,000	250,000
		$ 0	$465,000	$370,000
Variable Costs	$200,000	$600,000		
Legal (400 ÷ 1,600; 1200 ÷ 1,600)	(200,000)		$ 50,000	$150,000
Personnel (26,600 ÷ 38,000; 11,400 ÷ 38,000)	$ 0	(600,000)	420,000	180,000
		$ 0	$470,000	$330,000
B. Step-Down Method				
(Legal Department First)				
Fixed Costs	$360,000	$475,000		
Legal (250 ÷ 2,500; 1,500 ÷ 2,500; 750 ÷ 2,500)	(360,000)	36,000	$216,000	$108,000
Personnel (22,500 ÷ 47,500; 25,000 ÷ 47,500)	$ 0	(511,000)	242,053	268,947
		$ 0	$458,053	$376,947
Variable Costs	$200,000	$600,000		
Legal (400 ÷ 2,000; 400 ÷ 2,000; 1,200 ÷ 2,000)	(200,000)	40,000	40,000	$120,000
Personnel (26,600 ÷ 38,000; 11,400 ÷ 38,000)	$ 0	(640,000)	448,000	192,000
		$ 0	$488,000	$312,000
C. Reciprocal method				
Fixed Costs	$360,000	$475,000		
Legal (250 ÷ 2,500; 1,500 ÷ 2,500; 750 ÷ 2,500)	(385,678)	(38,568)	$231,407	$115,703
Personnel (2,500 ÷ 50,000; 22,500 ÷ 50,000;	25,678	513,568	231,106	256,784
25,000 ÷ 50,000)	$ 0	$ 0	$462,513	$372,487
Variable Costs	$200,000	$600,000		
Legal (400 ÷ 2,000; 400 ÷ 2,000; 1,200 ÷ 2,000)	(232,323)	46,465	$ 46,465	$139,393
Personnel (2,000 ÷ 40,000; 26,600 ÷ 40,000;	32,323	(646,465)	429,899	184,243
11,400 ÷ 40,000)	$ 0	$ 0	$476,364	$323,636

FIXED COSTS

$$L = \$360,000 + 0.05P$$

$$P = \$475,000 + 0.10L$$

$$L = \$360,000 + 0.05(\$475,000 + 0.10L) = \$385,678$$

$$P = \$475,000 + 0.10(\$385,678) = \$513,568$$

VARIABLE COSTS

$$L = \$200,000 + 0.05P$$

$$P = \$600,000 + 0.20L$$

$$L = \$200,000 + 0.05(\$600,000 + 0.20L) = \$232,323$$

$$P = \$600,000 + 0.20(\$232,323) = \$646,465$$

SUMMARY

The following points are linked to the chapter's learning objectives:

1. The four purposes of cost allocation are to provide information for economic decisions, to motivate managers and other employees, to justify costs or compute reimbursement, and to measure income and assets for reporting to external parties. Different cost allocations may be appropriate for different purposes.

2. The cause-and-effect and the benefits-received criteria guide most decisions related to cost allocations. Other criteria found in practice include fairness or equity and ability to bear.

3. A cost pool is a grouping of individual cost items. Two key decisions related to indirect-cost pools are the number of indirect-cost pools that form them and the allowability of individual cost items to be included in those cost pools.

4. The single-rate cost-allocation method pools all costs in one cost pool and allocates them to cost objects using the same rate per unit of the allocation base. In the dual-rate method, costs are grouped in two separate cost pools based on cost-behavior patterns, each of which has a different allocation base.

5. When cost allocations are made using budgeted rates, managers of divisions to which costs are allocated face no uncertainty about the rates to be used in that budget period. In contrast, when actual rates are used for cost allocation, managers do not know the rates to be used until the end of the budget period.

6. The three main methods of allocating support department costs to operating departments are direct, step-down, and reciprocal. The reciprocal method is the most defensible, but the direct and step-down methods are more widely used. The direct method ignores any reciprocal services among support departments. The step-down method allows for partial recognition of services among support departments while the reciprocal method provides full recognition of those services.

7. Common costs are the costs of operating a facility, or an activity or like cost object that are shared by two or more users. The stand-alone cost-allocation method uses information pertaining to each user of a cost object to determine the cost-allocation weights. The incremental cost-allocation method ranks the individual users of a cost object and allocates common costs first to the primary user and then to the other remaining (incremental) users.

8. Contract disputes over amounts to be paid often can be reduced by making the cost assignment rules as explicit as possible (and in writing). These rules should include details such as the allowable cost items, the acceptable cost-allocation bases, and how differences between budgeted and actual costs are to be handled.

▼ **TERMS TO LEARN**

This chapter and the Glossary at the end of the book contain definitions of the following important terms:

QUESTIONS

14-1 "I am going to focus on the customers of my business and leave cost-allocation issues to my accountant." Do you agree with this comment by a division president? Why?

14-2 How can an individual cost item, such as the salary of a plant security guard, be both a direct cost and an indirect cost?

14-3 A given cost may be allocated for one or more purposes. List four purposes.

14-4 What criteria might be used to guide cost-allocation decisions? Which are the dominant criteria?

14-5 What cost-allocation criterion is most frequently used in activity-based costing?

14-6 Cite two benefits of using a cost-hierarchy approach to guide the allocation of corporate costs to divisions and then to products.

14-7 Name three decisions managers face when designing the indirect cost-allocation component of an accounting system.

14-8 Give examples of bases used to allocate corporate cost pools to the operating divisions of an organization.

14-9 Why might a manager prefer budgeted rather than actual indirect cost-allocation rates be used for costs being allocated to her department from another department?

14-10 "To ensure unbiased cost allocations, fixed indirect costs should be allocated on the basis of estimated long-run use by user department managers." Do you agree? Why?

14-11 Distinguish among the three methods of allocating the costs of support departments to operating departments.

14-12 What is conceptually the most defensible method for allocating support department costs? Why?

14-13 Distinguish between two methods of allocating common costs.

14-14 What role does the Cost Accounting Standards Board play when companies contract with the U.S. government?

14-15 What is one key way to reduce cost-allocation disputes arising with government contracts?

EXERCISES

14-16 Cost allocation in hospitals, alternative allocation criteria. Dave Meltzer vacationed at Lake Tahoe last winter. Unfortunately, he broke his ankle while skiing and spent two days at the Sierra University Hospital. Meltzer's insurance company received a $4,800 bill for his two-day stay. One item that caught Meltzer's attention was an $11.52 charge for a roll of cotton. Meltzer is a salesman for Johnson & Johnson and knows that the cost to the hospital of the roll of cotton is in the $2.20–3.00 range. He asked for a breakdown of the $11.52 charge. The accounting office of the hospital sent him the following information:

a. Invoiced cost of cotton roll	$ 2.40	
b. Cost of processing of paperwork for purchase	0.60	
c. Supplies room management fee	0.70	
d. Operating-room and patient-room handling costs	1.60	
e. Administrative hospital costs	1.10	
f. University teaching-related costs	.60	
g. Malpractice insurance costs	1.20	
h. Cost of treating uninsured patients	2.72	
i. Profit component	0.60	
Total	$11.52	

Meltzer believes the overhead charge is obscene. He comments, "There was nothing I could do about it. When they come in and dab your stitches, it's not as if you can say, 'Keep your cotton roll. I brought my own.'"

Required

1. Compute the overhead rate Sierra University Hospital charged on the cotton roll.
2. What criteria might Sierra use to justify allocation of the overhead items b–i in the preceding list? Examine each item separately, and use the allocation criteria listed in Exhibit 14-2 (p. 501) in your answer.
3. What should Meltzer do about the $11.52 charge for the cotton roll?

 14-17 Single-rate vs. dual-rate cost-allocation methods. (W. Crum, adapted) Carolina Company has designed and built a power plant to serve its three factories. Data for 2000 are as follows:

	Usage in Kilowatt-Hours	
Factory	**Budget**	**Actual**
Durham	100,000	80,000
Charlotte	60,000	120,000
Raleigh	40,000	40,000

Actual fixed costs of the power plant were $1 million in 2000; actual variable costs, $2 million.

Required

1. Compute the amount of power costs that would be allocated to Charlotte using the single-rate method.
2. Compute the amount of power costs that would be allocated to Charlotte using the dual-rate method.

14-18 Single-rate vs. dual-rate allocation methods, support department. The Chicago power plant that services all manufacturing departments of MidWest Engineering has a budget for the coming year. This budget has been expressed in the following terms on a monthly basis:

Manufacturing Department	Needed at Practical Capacity Production Level[a] (Kilowatt-Hours)	Average Expected Monthly Usage (Kilowatt-Hours)
Rockford	10,000	8,000
Peoria	20,000	9,000
Hammond	12,000	7,000
Kankakee	8,000	6,000
Totals	50,000	30,000

[a]This factor was the most influential in planning the size of the power plant.

The expected monthly costs for operating the power plant during the budget year are $15,000: $6,000 variable and $9,000 fixed.

Required

1. Assume that a single-cost pool is used for the power plant costs. What amounts will be allocated to each manufacturing department? Use (a) practical capacity, and (b) average expected monthly usage as the allocation bases.
2. Assume the dual-rate method is used with separate cost pools for the variable and fixed costs. Variable costs are allocated on the basis of expected monthly usage. Fixed costs are allocated on the basis of practical capacity. What dollar amounts will be allocated to each manufacturing department? Why might you prefer the dual-rate method?

14-19 Cost allocation to divisions. Rembrandt Hotel & Casino is situated on beautiful Lake Tahoe in Nevada. The complex includes a 300-room hotel, a casino, and a restaurant. As Rembrandt's new controller, you are asked to recommend the basis to be used for allocating fixed overhead costs to the three divisions in 2001. You are presented with the following income statement information for the year 2000:

	Hotel	Restaurant	Casino
Revenue	$16,425,000	$5,256,000	$12,340,000
Direct costs	9,819,260	3,749,172	4,248,768
Segment margin	6,605,740	1,506,828	8,091,232

You are also given the following data on the three segments:

	Hotel	Restaurant	Casino
Floor space (square feet)	80,000	16,000	64,000
Number of employees	200	50	250

You may choose to allocate indirect costs based on direct costs, square feet, or the number of employees. Total fixed overhead for 2000 was $14,550,000.

Required

1. Calculate segment margins in percentage terms prior to allocating fixed overhead costs.
2. Allocate indirect costs to the three divisions using each of the three allocation bases suggested. Calculate segment margins in dollar and percentage terms with each allocation base.
3. Discuss the results. What is your preferred base for allocating indirect costs to the divisions? Why?
4. Would you recommend shutting any of the three divisions (and possibly reallocating resources to other divisions) as a result of your analysis? If so, which division would you close, and why?

14-20 Single-rate cost-allocation method, budgeted vs. actual costs and quantities. Fruit Juice, Inc., processes orange juice at its East Miami plant (part of the Orange Juice Division) and grapefruit juice at its West Miami plant (part of the Grapefruit Juice Division). It purchases oranges and grapefruit from growers' cooperatives in the Orlando area. It owns its own trucking fleet. Each Miami plant is the same distance from Orlando. The trucking fleet is operated as a cost center. Each Miami plant is billed for the direct costs and the indirect costs of each round-trip.

The trucking fleet costs include direct costs (labor costs of drivers, fuel, and toll charges) and indirect costs. Indirect costs include depreciation on tires and the vehicle, insurance, and state registration fees.

At the start of 2001, the Orange Juice Division budgeted for 150 round-trips from Orlando to East Miami while the Grapefruit Juice Division budgeted for 100 round-trips from Orlando to West Miami. Based on these 250 budgeted trips, the budgeted indirect costs of the trucking fleet were $575,000. The following actual results occurred for 2001:

Trucking fleet indirect costs	$645,000
Number of round-trips, Orlando – East Miami plant	200
Number of round-trips Orlando – West Miami plant	100

The trucking fleeting division uses the single-rate method when allocating indirect trucking costs.

Required

1. What is the indirect cost rate per round-trip when (a) budgeted costs and budgeted round-trips are used, and (b) actual costs and actual round-trips are used?
2. From the viewpoint of the Orange Juice Division, what are the effects of using budgeted costs/budgeted round-trips rather than actual costs/actual round-trips?

14-21 Dual-rate cost-allocation method, budgeted vs. actual costs and quantities (continuation of 14-20). Fruit Juice, Inc., decides to examine the effect of using the dual-rate method for allocating indirect trucking costs to each round-trip. At the start of 2001, the budgeted indirect costs were:

Variable indirect costs per round-trip	$ 1,500
Fixed costs	$200,000

The actual results for the 300 round-trips made in 2001 were:

Variable indirect costs	$465,000
Fixed indirect costs	180,000
	$645,000

Assume all other information to be the same as in Exercise 14-20.

Required
1. What is the indirect cost rate per round-trip with the dual-rate method when budgeted costs and budgeted round-trips are used. Total costs are computed using budgeted rate times actual usage (trips) for variable costs and budgeted rate times budgeted usage for fixed costs.
2. Compare the results for requirement 1(a) and (b) above with those in requirement 1(a) and (b) of Exercise 14-20. From the viewpoint of the Orange Juice Division, what are the effects of using the dual-rate method rather than the single-rate method?

14-22 Contracting, cost allocation. Sprout Consulting has been working in 2001 with Gemini Baseballs to improve the baseball production process. In the year ended December 31, 2000, Gemini produced and sold 450,000 baseballs at $5.60 per baseball. Variable costs were $2.80 per baseball, and total fixed manufacturing costs were $1,350,000.

As a result of Sprout's analysis, Gemini has been able to produce and sell 12% more baseballs in 2001. Gemini has also been able to reduce fixed costs by 25% and unit variable costs by 10 percent. The average selling price remained constant from 2000 to 2001.

Sprout's contract was as follows:

◆ a $50,000 fixed fee (not included in $1,350,000 amount)

◆ 10% of the costs saved on production of up to 450,000 baseballs

◆ $0.10 on every baseball produced over and above the year 2000 quantity of 450,000, regardless of any cost savings being achieved

Required
1. What was Gemini's operating income (loss) in 2000?
2. Calculate Gemini's fixed cost per baseball in 2000. What was the total cost per baseball?
3. Repeat requirements 1 and 2 for 2001 (before any payments to Sprout's).
4. What is Sprout's total remuneration for this consulting contract?

14-23 Allocation of common costs. Sam, Sarah, and Tony are members of the New Orleans Fire Brigade. They share a penthouse apartment that has a lounge room with the latest 50" TV. Tony owns the apartment, its furniture, and the TV. He can subscribe to a cable television company that has the following packages available:

	Package	Per Month
A.	Basic news	$32
B.	Premium movies	25
C.	Premium sports	30
D.	Basic news + Premium movies	50
E.	Basic news + Premium sports	54
F.	Premium movies + Premium sports	48
G.	Basic news + Premium movies + Premium sports	70

Sam is a TV news junkie, has average interest in movies, and zero interest in sports ("they are overpaid jocks"). Sarah is a movie buff, likes sports, and avoids the news ("it's all depressing anyway"). Tony is into sports in a big way, has average interest in news, and zero interest in movies ("he always falls asleep before the end"). They all agree that the purchase of the $70 total package is a "win-win-win" situation.

Each of the roommates works on a different eight-hour shift at the fire station, so conflicts in viewing are minimal.

Required
1. What criteria might be used to guide the choice about how to allocate the $70 monthly cable fee among Sam, Sarah, and Tony?
2. Outline two methods of allocating the $70 among Sam, Sarah, and Tony.

14-24 Allocation of travel costs. Joan Ernst, a graduating senior at a university near San Francisco, received an invitation to visit a prospective employer in New York. A few days later she received an invitation from a prospective employer in Chicago. She decided to combine her visits, traveling from San Francisco to New York, New York to Chicago, and Chicago to San Francisco.

Ernst received job offers from both companies. Upon her return, she decided to accept the offer in Chicago. She is puzzled over how to allocate her travel costs between the two employers. She has collected the following data for regular round-trip fares with no stopovers:

San Francisco to New York	$1,400
San Francisco to Chicago	$1,100

Ernst paid $1,800 for her three-leg flight (San Francisco–New York, New York–Chicago, Chicago–San Francisco). In addition, she paid $30 for a limousine from her home to San Francisco Airport and another $30 for a limousine from San Francisco Airport to her home when she returned.

Required

1. How should Ernst allocate the $1,800 airfare between the employers in New York and Chicago? Show the actual amounts you would allocate, and give reasons for your allocations.
2. Repeat requirement 1 for the $60 limousine charges.

14-25 Support department cost allocation; direct and step-down methods. Phoenix Consulting provides outsourcing services and advice to both government and corporate clients. For costing purposes, Phoenix classifies its departments into two support departments (Administrative/Human Resources and Information Systems) and two operating departments (Government Consulting and Corporate Consulting). For the first quarter of 2000, Phoenix incurs the following costs in its four departments:

Administrative/Human Resources (A/H)	$ 600,000
Information Systems (IS)	$ 2,400,000
Government Clients (GOVT)	$ 8,756,000
Corporate Clients (CORP)	$12,452,000

The actual level of support relationships among the four departments for the first quarter of 2000 was:

	Used By			
Supplied By	A/H	IS	GOVT	CORP
A/HR	—	25%	40%	35%
IS	10%	—	30%	60%

The Administrative/Human Resources support percentages are based on headcount. The Information Systems support percentages are based on actual computer time used.

Required

1. Allocate the two support department costs to the two operating departments using the following methods:
   a. Direct method
   b. Step-down method (allocate A/H first)
   c. Step-down method (allocate IS first)
2. Compare and explain differences in the support department costs allocated to each operating department.
3. What approaches might be used to decide the sequence in which to allocate support departments when using the step-down method? What approach would you recommend Phoenix use if, on government consulting jobs, it is required to use the step-down method?

14-26 Support department cost allocation, reciprocal method (continuation of 14-25). Refer to the data given in Exercise 14-25.

Required

1. Allocate the two support department costs to the two operating departments using the reciprocal method.
2. Compare and explain differences in requirement 1 with those in requirement 1 of Exercise 14-25. Which method do you prefer? Why?

14-27 Direct and step-down allocation. *e-books* is an online book retailer. The company has four departments. The two revenue-producing departments are Corporate Sales and Consumer Sales. The two support departments are Administrative (human resources, accounting, and so on), and Information Systems. Each of the sales departments conducts merchandising and marketing operations independently.

The following data are available for the month of September 2001:

Departments	Revenues	Number of Employees	Processing Time Used
Corporate Sales	$1,334,200	42	1920 minutes
Consumer Sales	$ 667,100	28	1600 minutes
Administrative	—	14	320 minutes
Information Systems	—	21	1120 minutes

Costs incurred in the four departments for the month of September 2001 are as follows:

Corporate Sales	$998,270
Consumer Sales	489,860
Administrative	72,700
Information Systems	234,400

Use number of employees to allocate Administrative costs and processing time used to allocate Information Systems costs.

Required
1. Allocate the support department costs to the revenue-producing departments using the direct method.
2. Rank the support departments based on the percentage of its services rendered to other support departments (using September's department costs). Use this ranking to allocate support costs based on the step-down allocation method.
3. How could you have ranked the support departments differently?

14-28 Reciprocal cost allocation (continuation 14-27). Consider *e-books* again. The controller of *e-books* reads a widely used text that states that "the reciprocal method is conceptually the most defensible." He seeks your assistance.

Required
1. Describe the key features of the reciprocal allocation method.
2. Allocate the support department costs (administrative and information systems) to the two revenue-producing departments using the reciprocal allocation method.
3. Under what condition is the reciprocal method more accurate than the direct and step-down methods? In the case presented in this exercise, which method would you recommend? Why?

PROBLEMS

14-29 Allocation of central corporate costs to divisions. Dusty Rhodes, the corporate controller of Richfield Oil Company, is about to make a presentation to the senior corporate executives and the top managers of its four divisions. These divisions are:

Oil & Gas Upstream (the exploration, production, and transportation of oil and gas)
Oil & Gas Downstream (the refining and marketing of oil and gas)
Chemical Products
Copper Mining

Under the existing internal accounting system, costs incurred at central corporate headquarters are collected in a single pool and allocated to each division on the basis of its actual revenues. The central corporate costs (in millions) for the most recent year are:

Interest on debt	$2,000
Corporate salaries	100
Accounting and control	100
General marketing	100
Legal	100
Research and development	200
Public affairs	208
Personnel and payroll	192
	$3,000

Public affairs includes the public relations staff, the lobbyists, and the sizable donations Richfield makes to numerous charities and nonprofit institutions.

Summary data (in millions) related to the four divisions for the most recent year are:

	Oil & Gas Upstream	Oil & Gas Downstream	Chemical Products	Copper Mining	Total
Revenues	$7,000	$16,000	$4,000	$3,000	$30,000
Operating costs	$3,000	$15,000	$3,800	$3,200	$25,000
Operating income	$4,000	$1,000	$200	$(200)	$5,000
Identifiable assets	$14,000	$6,000	$3,000	$2,000	$25,000
Number of employees	9,000	12,000	6,000	3,000	30,000

The top managers of each division share in a divisional income bonus pool. Divisional income is defined as operating income less allocated central corporate costs.

Rhodes is about to propose a change in the method used to allocate central corporate costs. He favors collecting these costs in four separate pools:

◆ *Cost Pool 1—Interest on debt.* Allocated using identifiable assets of divisions
◆ *Cost Pool 2—Corporate salaries, accounting and control, general marketing, legal, and research and development.* Allocated using revenue of divisions
◆ *Cost Pool 3—Public affairs.* Allocated using operating income (if positive) of divisions, with only divisions with positive operating income included in the allocation base
◆ *Cost Pool 4—Personnel and payroll.* Allocated using number of employees in divisions

Required
1. What purposes might be served by the allocation of central corporate costs to each division at Richfield Oil?
2. Compute the operating income of each division when central corporate costs are allocated using revenue of each division.
3. Compute the operating income of each division when central corporate costs are allocated using the four cost pools.
4. What are the strengths and weaknesses of Rhodes' proposal relative to the existing single-cost pool method?

14-30 Cost allocation, monthly reports. (CMA, revised) Bulldog, Inc., is a large manufacturing company that runs its own electrical power plant from the excess steam produced in its manufacturing process. Power is provided to two production departments—Department A and Department B. The capacity of the power plant was originally determined by the expected peak demands of the two production departments. The expected normal usage are, respectively, 60% and 60,000,000 kilowatt-hours (kWh) for Department A, and 40% and 40,000,000 kWh for Department B.

The budgeted monthly costs of producing power, based on normal usage of 100,000,000 kWh, are $30,000,000 in fixed costs and $7,500,000 in variable costs. For the month of November, the actual kilowatt-hours used were 60,000,000 by Department A and 20,000,000 by Department B. Actual fixed costs were $30,000,000 and actual variable costs were $7,500,000.

Terry Lamb, the controller, prepared the following monthly report:

Bulldog Inc.
Monthly Allocation Report
November 2000

Power plant usage	80,000,000 kWh
Actual costs:	
Variable	$ 7,500,000
Fixed	30,000,000
Total	$37,500,000
Rate per kWh, $37,500,000 ÷ 80,000,000 kWh	$0.46875
Allocations:	
To Department A, 60,000,000 kWh × $0.46875	$28,125,000
To Department B, 20,000,000 kWh × $0.46875	9,375,000
Total allocated	$37,500,000

Lamb fully allocated all power plant costs on the basis of actual kilowatt-hours used by each production department. This report will be submitted to the two production department operating managers.

Required

1. Discuss at least two problems with the monthly allocation report prepared by Lamb for November 2000.
2. Prepare a revised monthly allocation report for November 2000 using a flexible-budget approach. Use budgeted rates times actual usage for variable costs and budgeted rates assuming budgeted (normal) usage for fixed costs.
3. Discuss the behavioral implication of Lamb's monthly allocation report for November 2000 on the production manager of Department B.

 14-31 Allocating costs of support departments; step-down and direct methods. The Central Valley Company has prepared department overhead budgets for normal-volume levels before allocations, as follows:

Support departments:		
Building and grounds	$10,000	
Personnel	1,000	
General factory administration	26,090	
Cafeteria: operating loss	1,640	
Storeroom	2,670	
Total		$ 41,400
Operating departments:		
Machining	$34,700	
Assembly	48,900	
Total		83,600
Total for support and operating departments		$125,000

Management has decided that the most appropriate inventory costs are achieved by using individual department overhead rates. These rates are developed after support department costs are allocated to operating departments.

Bases for allocation are to be selected from the following:

Department	Direct Manufacturing Labor-Hours	Number of Employees	Square Feet of Floor Space Occupied	Manufacturing Labor-Hours	Total Number of Requisitions
Building and grounds	0	0	0	0	0
Personnel[a]	0	0	2,000	0	0
General plant administration	0	35	7,000	0	0
Cafeteria: operating loss	0	10	4,000	1,000	0
Storeroom	0	5	7,000	1,000	0
Machining	5,000	50	30,000	8,000	2,000
Assembly	15,000	100	50,000	17,000	1,000
Total	20,000	200	100,000	27,000	3,000

[a]Basis used is number of employees.

Required

1. Using a worksheet, allocate support department costs by the step-down method. Develop overhead rates per direct manufacturing labor-hour for machining and assembly. Allocate the costs of the support departments in the order given in this problem. Use the allocation base for each support department you think is most appropriate.
2. Using the direct method, rework requirement 1.
3. Based on the following information about two jobs, determine the total overhead costs for each job by using rates developed in (a) requirement 1, and (b) requirement 2.

	Direct Manufacturing Labor-Hours	
	Machining	**Assembly**
Job 88	18	2
Job 89	3	17

14-32 Support department cost allocations; single-department cost pools; direct, step-down, and reciprocal methods. The Manes Company has two products. Product 1 is manufactured entirely in Department X. Product 2 is manufactured entirely in Department Y. To produce these two products, the Manes Company has two support departments: A (a materials-handling department) and B (a power-generating department).

An analysis of the work done by Departments A and B in a typical period follows:

		Used By		
Supplied By	**A**	**B**	**X**	**Y**
A		100	250	150
B	500		100	400

The work done in Department A is measured by the direct labor-hours of materials-handling time. The work done in Department B is measured by the kilowatt-hours of power. The budgeted costs of the support departments for the coming year are:

	Department A	**Department B**
Variable indirect labor and indirect materials costs	$ 70,000	$10,000
Supervision	10,000	10,000
Depreciation	20,000	20,000
	$100,000	$40,000
	+ Power costs	+ Materials-handling costs

The budgeted costs of the operating departments for the coming year are $1,500,000 for Department X and $800,000 for Department Y.

Supervisory costs are salary costs. Depreciation in B is the straight-line depreciation of power-generation equipment in its nineteenth year of an estimated 25-year useful life; it is old but well-maintained equipment.

Required
1. What are the allocations of costs of support Departments A and B to operating Departments X and Y using (a) the direct method, (b) the step-down method (allocate Department A first), (c) the step-down method (allocate Department B first), and (d) the reciprocal method?
2. The power company has offered to supply all the power needed by the Manes Company and to provide all the services of the present power department. The cost of this service will be $40 per kilowatt-hour of power. Should Manes accept? Explain.

14-33 Allocating costs of support departments; dual rates; direct, step-down, and reciprocal methods. Magnum T.A., Inc., specializes in the assembly and installation of high-quality security systems for the home and business segments of the market. The four departments at its highly automated state-of-the-art assembly plant are:

Service Departments	**Assembly Departments**
Engineering Support	Home Security Systems
Information Systems Support	Business Security Systems

The budgeted level of service relationships for 2001 is:

		Used By		
Supplied By	**Engineering Support**	**Information Systems Support**	**Home Security Systems**	**Business Security Systems**
Engineering Support	—	0.10	0.40	0.50
Information Systems Support	0.20	—	0.30	0.50

The actual level of service relationships for 2001 is:

	Used By			
Supplied By	Engineering Support	Information Systems Support	Home Security Systems	Business Security Systems
Engineering Support	—	0.15	0.30	0.55
Information Systems Support	0.25	—	0.15	0.60

Magnum collects fixed costs and variable costs for each department in separate cost pools. The actual costs in each pool for 2001 are:

	Fixed-Cost Pool	Variable-Cost Pool
Engineering Support	$2,700,000	$8,500,000
Information Systems Support	8,000,000	3,750,000

Fixed costs are allocated on the basis of the budgeted level of service. Variable costs are allocated on the basis of the actual level of service.

The support department costs allocated to each assembly department are allocated to products on the basis of units assembled. The units assembled in each department during 2001 are:

Home Security Systems	7,950 units
Business Security Systems	3,750 units

Required
1. Allocate the support department costs to the assembly departments using the dual-rate method and (a) the direct method, (b) the step-down method (allocate Information Systems Support first), (c) the step-down method (allocate Engineering Support first), and (d) the reciprocal method. Present results in a format similar to Exhibit 14-10.
2. Compare the support department costs allocated to each Home Security Systems unit assembled and each Business Security Systems unit assembled under (a), (b), (c), and (d) in requirement 1.
3. What factors might explain the limited use of the reciprocal method in practice?

14-34 **Overhead disputes.** (Suggested by Howard Wright) The Azure Ship Company works on U.S. Navy vessels and commercial vessels. General yard overhead (for example, the cost of the Purchasing Department) is allocated to the jobs on the basis of direct labor costs.

In 2001, Azure's total $150 million of direct labor costs consisted of $50 million Navy and $100 million commercial. The general yard overhead was $30 million.

Navy auditors periodically examine the records of defense contractors. The auditors investigated a nuclear submarine contract, which was based on cost-plus-fixed-fee pricing. The auditors claimed that the Navy was entitled to a refund because of double-counting of overhead in 2001.

The government contract included the following provision:

> Par. 15-202. Direct Costs
> (a) A direct cost is any cost which can be identified specifically with a particular cost object. Direct costs are not limited to items which are incorporated in the end product such as material or labor. Costs identified specifically with the contract are direct costs of the contract and are to be charged directly thereto. Cost identified specifically with other work of the contractor are direct costs of that work and are not to be charged to the contract directly or indirectly. When items ordinarily chargeable as indirect costs are charged to the contract as direct costs, the cost of like items applicable to other work must be eliminated from indirect costs allocated to the contract.

Azure formed a special expediting purchasing group, the SE group, to join with the central purchasing group to obtain materials solely for the nuclear submarine. Their direct costs, $5 million, were included as direct labor of the nuclear work. Accordingly, overhead was allocated to the contracts in the usual manner. The SE cost of $5 million was not included in the general yard overhead. The auditors claimed that no overhead should have been allocated to these SE costs.

Required

1. Compute the amount of the refund that the Navy would claim.
2. Suppose the Navy also discovered that $4 million of general yard overhead was devoted exclusively to commercial engine-room purchasing activities. Compute the additional refund that the Navy would claim. (*Note:* This $4 million was never classified as direct labor. Furthermore, the Navy would claim that it should be reclassified as a direct cost but not as direct labor.)

COLLABORATIVE LEARNING EXERCISE

14-35 Cost allocation, pricing decisions. (CMA, adapted) Best Test Laboratories began as a one-man operation 25 years ago to evaluate the reaction of materials to extreme increases in temperature. Much of the company's early growth was attributable to government contracts to test the properties of weapons, transportation equipment, and clothing for use in arid desert regions.

Recent growth has come from diversification and expansion into commercial markets. Environmental testing at Best Test now includes:

Heat testing	(HTT)
Air turbulence testing	(ATT)
Stress testing	(SST)
Arctic condition testing	(ACT)
Aquatic testing	(AQT)

Currently, all of the budgeted operating costs are collected in a single overhead pool. All of the estimated testing hours are also collected in a single pool. One rate per test-hour is used for all five types of testing. This hourly rate is marked up by 45% in order to recover administrative costs, taxes, and profit in the selling price.

Rick Shaw, Best Test's controller, believes that there is enough variation in the test procedures and cost structure to establish separate costing and billing rates. He also believes that the inflexible rate structure currently being used is inadequate in today's competitive environment. After analyzing the following data, he has recommended that new rates be put into effect at the beginning of Best Test's fiscal year.

The budgeted total test laboratory costs for the coming year are as follows:

Test pool labor (10 employees)	$ 420,000
Supervision	72,000
Equipment depreciation	178,460
Heat	170,000
Electricity	124,000
Water	74,000
Set-up	58,000
Indirect materials	104,000
Operating supplies	62,000
Total test lab costs	$1,262,460
Total estimated test-hours	106,000

Shaw has determined the resource usage by test type in the following table:

	HTT	ATT	SST	ACT	AQT
Test pool employees	3	2	2	1	2
Supervision	40%	15%	15%	15%	15%
Depreciation	$48,230	$22,000	$39,230	$32,000	$37,000
Heat	50%	5%	5%	30%	10%
Electricity	30%	10%	10%	40%	10%
Water	—	—	20%	20%	60%
Set-up	20%	15%	30%	15%	20%
Indirect materials	15%	15%	30%	20%	20%
Operating supplies	10%	10%	25%	20%	35%
Test-hours	29,680	12,720	27,560	22,260	13,780
Competitors' hourly billing rates	$17.50	$19.00	$15.50	$16.00	$20.00

Required

Form groups of two or more students to complete the following requirements.

1. Compute the single pool hourly cost and hourly billing rate for Best Test Laboratories.

2. Compute the five separate hourly billing rates for Best Test Laboratories.

3. Discuss what effect the new costing method will have on the pricing structure for each of the five test types, given the competitor's hourly billing rates.

4. In general, identify at least three other internal or external determinants of pricing structure.

Cost Allocation: Joint Products and Byproducts

learning objectives

When you have finished studying this chapter, you should be able to

1. Identify the splitoff point(s) in a joint-cost situation
2. Distinguish between joint products and byproducts
3. Explain why joint costs should be allocated to individual products
4. Allocate joint costs using several different methods
5. Identify the criterion used to support market-based joint-cost-allocation methods
6. Explain why joint costs are irrelevant in a sell-or-process further decision
7. Account for byproducts using two different methods

Computing the costs of individual products (such as milk, cream, and butter) produced in dairies requires the use of joint-cost-allocation methods.

P receding chapters have emphasized costing for companies that produce only single products or companies that produce several products in separate processes. We now consider the more complex case in which companies produce two or more products simultaneously out of the same process(es). For example, a pineapple processing plant produces multiple products (such as rings, juice, and crushed pineapple) out of each pineapple processed. This chapter examines methods for allocating costs to joint products. Some of the topics discussed in this chapter are related to issues covered in Chapter 14. Before reading on, be sure you understand pp. 498–501 of Chapter 14. We also examine how cost numbers appropriate for one purpose (such as external reporting) are not necessarily appropriate for other purposes (such as decisions about the further processing of joint products). This chapter provides yet another illustration of the different costs for different purposes theme that underlies cost accounting.

JOINT-COST BASICS

Joint costs are the costs of a single production process that yields multiple products simultaneously. Consider the distillation of coal, which yields coke, natural gas, and other products. The cost of this distillation is called a joint cost. The splitoff point is the juncture in a joint production process where one or more products become separately identifiable. An example is the point at which coal becomes coke, natural gas, and other products. Separable costs are all costs (manufacturing, marketing, distribution, and so on) incurred beyond the splitoff point that are assignable to one or more individual products. At or beyond the splitoff point, decisions relating to sale or further processing of individual products can be made independently of decisions about other products.

Industries abound in which single production processes simultaneously yield two or more products. Exhibit 15-1 presents examples of joint-cost situations in diverse industries. In each of these examples, no individual product can be produced

EXHIBIT 15-1
Examples of Joint-Cost Situations

Industry	Separable Products at the Splitoff Point
◆ **Agriculture and Food Processing**	
◆ Cocoa beans	◆ Cocoa butter, cocoa powder, cocoa drink mix, tanning cream
◆ Corn	◆ Corn on the cob, whole kernels, cornmeal, grits
◆ Lamb	◆ Lamb cuts, tripe, hides, bones, fat
◆ Hogs	◆ Bacon, ham, spare ribs, pork roast
◆ Raw milk	◆ Cream, liquid skim
◆ Lumber	◆ Lumber of varying grades and shapes
◆ Turkeys	◆ Breast, wings, thighs, drumsticks, digest, feather meal, and poultry meal
◆ **Extractive Industries**	
◆ Coal	◆ Coke, gas, benzol, tar, ammonia
◆ Copper ore	◆ Copper, silver, lead, zinc
◆ Petroleum	◆ Crude oil, gas, raw LPG
◆ Salt	◆ Hydrogen, chlorine, caustic soda
◆ **Chemical Industries**	
◆ Raw LPG (liquefied petroleum gas)	◆ Butane, ethane, propane
◆ **Semiconductor Industry**	
◆ Fabrication of silicon-wafer chips	◆ Memory chips of different quality (as to capacity), speed, life expectancy, and temperature tolerance

EXHIBIT 15-2
Classification of Products of a Joint Production Process

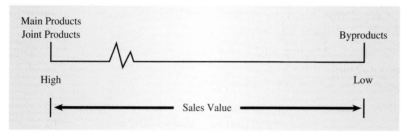

without the accompanying products appearing, although sometimes the proportions can be varied. A poultry farm cannot kill a turkey wing; it has to kill a whole turkey, which yields breasts, thighs, drumsticks, digest, feather meal, and poultry meal in addition to wings. The focus of joint costing is on assigning costs to individual products as disassembly occurs. This focus contrasts with that in preceding chapters, which emphasized assigning costs of individual products as assembly occurs.

The outputs of a joint production process can be classified into two general categories—those with a positive sales value and those with a zero sales value. A **product** is any output that has a positive net sales value (or an output that enables an organization to avoid incurring costs). A **joint product** has relatively high sales value compared to other products yielded by a joint production process. When a joint production process yields only one product with a relatively high sales value, that product is termed a **main product**. A **byproduct** has a relatively low sales value compared with the sales value of a joint or main product. Some outputs of the joint production process have zero sales value. For example, the offshore processing of hydrocarbons to obtain oil and gas also yields water that is recycled back into the ocean. Similarly, the processing of mineral ore to obtain gold and silver also yields dirt that is recycled back into the ground. No journal entries are usually made in the accounting system to record the processing of such outputs with zero sales value. Exhibit 15-2 presents an overview of the key terms introduced in this paragraph.[1]

The distinctions drawn in Exhibit 15-2 are not firm in practice. Moreover, the classification of products (as main, joint, or byproduct) often changes over time, especially for products whose market price can increase or decrease by, say, 30% or more in any one year. As in many areas of accounting, the variety of terminology and accounting practice in the joint-cost area is bewildering. Always gain an understanding of the terms as they are used by the organization you are dealing with.

Why Allocate Joint Costs?

Many contexts require the allocation of joint costs to individual products or services. Examples include:

1. Inventory costing and cost-of-goods-sold computations for financial accounting purposes and reports for income tax authorities.

2. Inventory costing and cost-of-goods-sold computations for internal reporting purposes. Such reports are used in division profitability analysis when compensation is determined for division managers.

3. Cost reimbursement under contracts when only a portion of a business's products or services is sold or delivered to a single customer (such as a government agency).

[1] Some outputs of a joint production process have "negative" revenue when their disposal costs (such as the costs of handling nonsaleable toxic substances that require special disposal procedures) are considered. These disposal costs should be added to the joint production costs that are allocated to joint or main products.

4. Insurance settlement computations when damage claims made by businesses with joint products, main products, or byproducts are based on cost information.

5. Rate regulation when one or more of the jointly produced products or services are subject to price regulation.[2]

6. Litigation in which product cost numbers are key inputs. For example, U.S. dumping litigation can involve joint-cost allocations when one or more joint products are sold in the United States.[3]

These diverse examples are illustrative rather than exhaustive. That the need for joint-cost allocation is so wide-ranging indicates the importance of mastering the allocation methods we present in the next section.

APPROACHES TO ALLOCATING JOINT COSTS

Two basic approaches are used to allocate joint costs.

◆ *Approach 1.* Allocate costs using market-based data such as revenues. This chapter illustrates three methods that use this approach:

- Sales value at splitoff method

- Estimated net realizable value (NRV) method

- Constant gross-margin percentage NRV method

◆ *Approach 2.* Allocate costs using physical-measure-based data such as weight or volume.

In preceding chapters, we emphasized both the cause-and-effect and benefits-received criteria (see Exhibit 14-2, p. 501) for guiding cost-allocation decisions. By definition, joint costs cannot be the subject of cause-and-effect analysis at the individual product level. The benefits-received criterion leads to a preference for methods under approach 1. Revenues, in general, are a better indicator of benefits received than are physical measures such as weight or volume. Mining companies, for example, receive more benefits from one ton of gold than they do from, say, ten tons of coal.

In the simplest joint production process, the joint products are sold at the splitoff point without further processing. We use this case first (Example 1) to illustrate the sales value at splitoff method and the physical-measure method using volume as the metric. Then we consider joint production processes that involve further processing beyond the splitoff point (Example 2). This second example illustrates two additional market-based joint-cost-allocation methods (estimated NRV and constant-gross margin percentage NRV). The numbers used in these two and the remaining examples in this chapter are small to keep the focus on key concepts. In practice, the numbers are typically much larger.

To highlight each joint-cost example, we make extensive use of exhibits. These exhibits use the following notation:

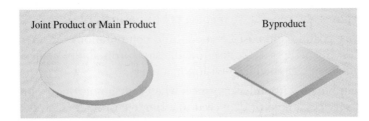

Joint Product or Main Product   Byproduct

[2]See J. Crespi and J. Harris, "Joint Cost Allocation Under the Natural Gas Act: An Historical Review," *Journal of Extractive Industries Accounting* 2 (2): 133–142.
[3]*Dumping* occurs when a non-U.S. company sells a product in the United States at a price below the market value in the country of its creation, and this action materially injures or threatens to materially injure an industry in the United States. U.S. Department of Commerce cases are reported in the *Federal Register*. An example is "Notice of Final Determination of Sales at Less Than Fair Value: Polyvinyl Alcohol From Taiwan" (Friday, March 29, 1996, Vol. 61).

EXHIBIT 15-3
Example 1: Overview of Farmers' Dairy

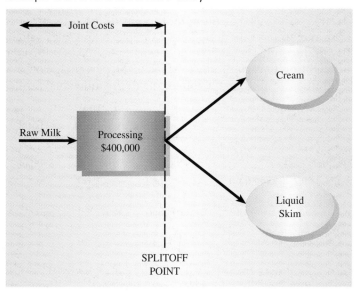

To enable comparisons across the methods, we report for each method gross-margin percentages for individual products.

EXAMPLE 1: Farmers' Dairy purchases raw milk from individual farms and processes it until the splitoff point, where two products (cream and liquid skim) emerge. These two products are sold to an independent company, which markets and distributes them to supermarkets and other retail outlets.

Exhibit 15-3 presents an overview of the basic relationships in this example. Summary data for May 2001 are as follows:

◆ Raw milk processed, 110,000 gallons. Ten thousand gallons of raw milk are lost in the production process due to evaporation, spillage, and the like, yielding 100,000 gallons of good product.

	Production	Sales
◆ Cream	25,000 gallons	20,000 gallons at $8 per gallon
◆ Liquid skim	75,000 gallons	30,000 gallons at $4 per gallon
◆ Inventories		

	Beginning Inventory	Ending Inventory
Raw milk	0 gallons	0 gallons
Cream	0 gallons	5,000 gallons
Liquid skim	0 gallons	45,000 gallons

◆ Cost of purchasing 110,000 gallons of raw milk and processing it until the splitoff point to yield 25,000 gallons of cream and 75,000 gallons of liquid skim, $400,000.

How much of the joint costs of $400,000 should be allocated to the cost of goods sold (20,000 gallons of cream and 30,000 gallons of liquid skim) and to the ending inventory (5,000 gallons of cream and 45,000 gallons of liquid skim)? The joint production costs of $400,000 cannot be uniquely identified with or traced to either product. Why? Because the products themselves were not separated until the splitoff point. The joint-cost-allocation methods we now discuss can be used both for costing the inventories of cream and liquid skim and for determining cost of goods sold.

Points to Stress When there are no beginning inventories and when all products are sold at the splitoff point, the sales value at the splitoff, the estimated NRV, and the constant GM% methods all yield the same results. This is because the 3 methods differ in the way they incorporate post-splitoff costs and revenues in calculating joint cost allocations.

Sales Value at Splitoff Method

Correcting Student Misconceptions
Emphasize that the sales value at splitoff weighting is based on *total sales revenue* (of total production), *not* on sales price per gallon of each product (nor on just the sales revenue for the # of units actually sold).

The **sales value at splitoff method** allocates joint costs to joint products on the basis of the relative sales value at the splitoff point of the total production of these products during the accounting period. In Example 1, the sales value at splitoff of the May 2001 production is $200,000 for cream and $300,000 for liquid skim. We then assign a weighting to each product, which is the percentage of total sales value. Using this weighting, we allocate the joint costs to the individual products:

	Cream	Liquid Skim	Total
1. Sales value at splitoff point (cream, 25,000 gallons × $8; liquid skim, 75,000 gallons × $4)	$200,000	$300,000	$500,000
2. Weighting ($200,000 ÷ $500,000; $300,000 ÷ $500,000)	0.40	0.60	
3. Joint costs allocated (cream, 0.40 × $400,000; liquid skim, 0.60 × $400,000)	$160,000	$240,000	$400,000
4. Joint production costs per gallon (cream, $160,000 ÷ 25,000 gallons; liquid skim, $240,000 ÷ 75,000 gallons)	$6.40	$3.20	

Note that this method uses the sales value of the *entire production* of the accounting period. The reason is that the joint costs were incurred on all units produced, not just those sold in the current period. Exhibit 15-4 presents the product-line income statement, using the sales value at splitoff method of joint-cost allocation. Use of this method enables us to obtain individual product costs and gross margins. As Exhibit 15-4 shows, both cream and liquid skim have gross-margin percentages of 20 percent.[4]

Points to Stress The primary advantage of the sales value at splitoff method is that it's reasonably objective. No assumptions are necessary about actions beyond the splitoff point (e.g., which products will be produced, what separable costs will be incurred). The major disadvantage of the sales value at splitoff method is that there may be no market at splitoff for some products.

As mentioned earlier, this method exemplifies the benefits-received criterion of cost allocation, and you should now see why. Costs are allocated to products in proportion to their potential revenues. This method is both straightforward and intuitive. The cost-allocation base (total sales value at splitoff) is expressed in terms of a common denominator (dollars) that is systematically recorded in the accounting system and well understood by all parties. Key inputs to justify this method are credible market demand and selling prices for all products that emerge at the splitoff point.

[4]The equality of the gross-margin percentages for the two products is the result reached under the sales value at splitoff method when there are no beginning inventories and all products are sold at the splitoff point.

Points to Stress Under the sales value at splitoff method, the gross margin % is identical for all products if there are no separable costs and no beginning inventory. The sales value at splitoff method allocates joint costs on the basis of sales revenue. In the absence of nonjoint costs, this makes all products appear equally profitable.

Reinforcing Problems Exer. 15-16 and Probs. 15-27 through15-29, and 15-32 cover the sales value at splitoff method.

EXHIBIT 15-4

Joint Costs Allocated Using Sales Value at Splitoff Method:
Farmers' Dairy Product-Line Income Statement for May 2001

	Cream	Liquid Skim	Total
Revenues (cream, 20,000 gallons × $8; liquid skim, 30,000 gallons × $4)	$160,000	$120,000	$280,000
Joint costs			
Production costs (cream, 0.4 × $400,000; liquid skim, 0.6 × $400,000)	160,000	240,000	400,000
Deduct ending inventory (cream, 5,000 gallons × $6.40; liquid skim, 45,000 gallons × $3.20)	32,000	144,000	176,000
Cost of goods sold	128,000	96,000	224,000
Gross margin	$ 32,000	$ 24,000	$ 56,000
Gross-margin percentage	20%	20%	20%

Physical-Measure Method

The **physical-measure method** allocates joint costs to joint products on the basis of the relative weight, volume, or other physical measure at the splitoff point of the total production of these products during the accounting period. In Example 1, the $400,000 joint costs produced 25,000 gallons of cream and 75,000 gallons of liquid skim. Using the number of gallons produced as the physical measure, joint costs are allocated as follows:

Reinforcing Problems Exer. 15-16 and Probs. 15-27 through 15-29, and 15-32 (which shows some possible negative consequences) cover the physical measure method.

	Cream	Liquid Skim	Total
1. Physical measure of production (gallons)	25,000	75,000	100,000
2. Weighting (25,000 gallons ÷ 100,000 gallons; 75,000 gallons ÷ 100,000 gallons)	0.25	0.75	
3. Joint costs allocated (cream, 0.25 × $400,000; liquid skim, 0.75 × $400,000)	$100,000	$300,000	$400,000
4. Joint production costs per gallon (cream, $100,000 ÷ 25,000; liquid skim, $300,000 ÷ 75,000 gallons)	$4	$4	

Exhibit 15-5 presents the product-line income statement using this method of joint-cost allocation. The gross-margin percentages are 50% for cream and 0% for liquid skim.

Under the benefits-received criterion, the physical-measure method is less preferred than the sales value at splitoff method. Why? Because it has no relationship to the revenue-producing power of the individual products. Consider a mine that extracts ore containing gold, silver, and lead. Use of a common physical measure (tons) would result in almost all the costs being allocated to the product that weighs the most—lead, which has the lowest revenue-producing power. As a second example, if the joint cost of a hog were assigned to its various products on the basis of weight, center-cut pork chops would have the same cost per pound as pigs feet, lard, bacon, ham, bones, and so forth. In a product-line income statement, the pork products that have a high sales value per pound (for example, center-cut pork chops) would show a fabulous "profit," and products that have a low sales value per pound (for example, bones) would show consistent losses.

Obtaining comparable physical measures for all products is not always straightforward. Consider oil and gas joint-cost settings, where oil is a liquid and gas is a vapor. Use of a physical measure, such as barrels, in this context requires technical assistance from chemical engineers on how to convert the vapor (a gas)

Points to Stress The physical measure method is easy to use but has 2 disadvantages. First, qtys. of the joint products may be measured in different units. For example, natural gas is measured in cu. ft. but oil is measured in barrels. This problem can sometimes be overcome by converting both measures to a common denominator (Btu's in this case). Second, the method doesn't meet any of the cost-allocation criteria: cause and effect, benefits received, fairness, or ability to bear. For example, in meat-packing, the physical measure method would allocate a much larger share of the total joint costs to soup bones and hamburger than to filet. This violates all 4 cost-allocation criteria.

EXHIBIT 15-5
Joint Costs Allocated Using Physical-Measure Method:
Farmers' Dairy Product-Line Income Statement for May 2001

	Cream	Liquid Skim	Total
Revenues (cream, 20,000 gallons × $8; liquid skim, 30,000 gallons × $4)	$160,000	$120,000	$280,000
Joint costs			
Production costs (cream, 0.25 × $400,000; liquid skim, 0.75 × $400,000)	100,000	300,000	400,000
Deduct ending inventory (cream, 5,000 gallons × $4; liquid skim, 45,000 gallons × $4)	20,000	180,000	200,000
Cost of goods sold	80,000	120,000	200,000
Gross margin	$ 80,000	$ 0	$ 80,000
Gross-margin percentage	50%	0%	28.6%

into a measure additive with barrels of oil (the liquid). Technical personnel outside of accounting may be required when using some physical measures in joint-cost-allocation situations.

The choice of products to include in a physical-measure computation can greatly affect the resulting allocations. Outputs with no sales value (such as dirt in gold mining) are invariably excluded. While many more tons of dirt than tons of gold are produced, costs are not incurred to produce outputs that have zero sales value. Outputs with low sales values relative to the joint or main products also are often excluded from the denominator used in the physical-measure method. The general guideline for using the physical-measure method is to include only that subset of outputs termed joint products or main products in the weighting computations.

Estimated Net Realizable Value (NRV) Method

In many cases, products are processed beyond the splitoff point in order to bring them to a marketable form or to increase their value above their selling price at the splitoff point. Our next example examines this production setting. For ease of exposition, the Farmers' Dairy example is extended. The estimated NRV method is typically used in preference to the sales value at splitoff point method only when market selling prices for one or more products at the splitoff point are not available.

EXAMPLE 2: Assume the same situation as in Example 1 except that both cream and liquid skim can be processed further:

◆ Cream → Butter cream: 25,000 gallons of cream are further processed to yield 20,000 gallons of butter cream at additional processing (separable) costs of $280,000. Butter cream, sold for $25 per gallon, is used in the manufacture of butter-based products.

◆ Liquid skim → Condensed milk: 75,000 gallons of liquid skim are further processed to yield 50,000 gallons of condensed milk at additional processing costs of $520,000. Condensed milk is sold for $22 per gallon.

Sales during the accounting period were 12,000 gallons of butter cream and 45,000 gallons of condensed milk. Exhibit 15-6 presents an overview of the basic relationships. Inventory information follows:

EXHIBIT 15-6
Example 2: Overview of Farmers' Dairy

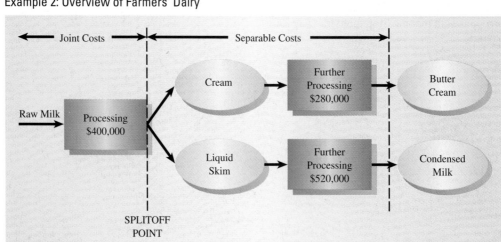

	Beginning Inventory	Ending Inventory
Raw milk	0 gallons	0 gallons
Cream	0 gallons	0 gallons
Liquid skim	0 gallons	0 gallons
Butter cream	0 gallons	8,000 gallons
Condensed milk	0 gallons	5,000 gallons

We use Example 2 to illustrate the estimated net realizable value (NRV) method and the constant gross-margin percentage NRV method.

The **estimated net realizable value (NRV) method** allocates joint costs to joint products on the basis of the relative estimated NRV (expected final sales value in the ordinary course of business minus the expected separable costs) of the total production of these products during the accounting period. Joint costs would be allocated as follows:

Reinforcing Problems Exer. 15-18 through 15-20, 15-22 and 15-23, and Probs. 15-27 through 15-29, and 15-31 cover the estimated NRV method.

	Butter Cream	Condensed Milk	Total
1. Expected final sales value of production (butter cream, 20,000 gallons × $25; condensed milk, 50,000 gallons × $22)	$500,000	$1,100,000	$1,600,000
2. Deduct expected separable costs to complete and sell	280,000	520,000	800,000
3. Estimated net realizable value at splitoff point	$220,000	$ 580,000	$ 800,000
4. Weighting ($220,000 ÷ $800,000; $580,000 ÷ $800,000)	0.275	0.725	
5. Joint costs allocated (butter cream, 0.275 × $400,000; condensed milk, 0.725 × $400,000)	$110,000	$ 290,000	$ 400,000
6. Production costs per gallon (butter cream, [$110,000 + $280,000] ÷ 20,000 gallons; condensed milk, [$290,000 + $520,000] ÷ 50,000 gallons)	$19.50	$16.20	

Exhibit 15-7 presents the product-line income statement using the estimated NRV method. The gross-margin percentages are 22.0% for butter cream and 26.4% for condensed milk.

The estimated NRV method is often implemented using simplifying assumptions. For example, companies that frequently change the number of subsequent steps in further processing, often assume a standard set of subsequent steps. Also, if

EXHIBIT 15-7
Joint Costs Allocated Using Estimated NRV Method:
Farmers' Dairy Product-Line Income Statement for May 2001

	Butter Cream	Condensed Milk	Total
Revenues (butter cream, 12,000 gallons × $25; condensed milk, 45,000 gallons × $22)	$300,000	$990,000	$1,290,000
Cost of goods sold			
Joint costs (butter cream, 0.275 × $400,000; condensed milk, 0.725 × $400,000)	110,000	290,000	400,000
Separable processing costs	280,000	520,000	800,000
Cost of goods available for sale	390,000	810,000	1,200,000
Deduct ending inventory (butter cream, 8,000 gallons × $19.50; condensed milk, 5,000 gallons × $16.20)	156,000	81,000	237,000
Cost of goods sold	234,000	729,000	963,000
Gross margin	$ 66,000	$261,000	$ 327,000
Gross-margin percentage	22.0%	246.4%	25.3%

the selling prices of joint products vary frequently, a standard set of selling prices may be consistently used throughout the accounting period.[5]

Because it does not require knowledge of the subsequent steps in processing, the sales value at splitoff method is less complex than the estimated NRV method. However, using the sales value at splitoff method is not always feasible. Why? Because there may not be market prices at the splitoff point for at least one of the products. Market prices may not first appear until processing occurs beyond the splitoff point.

Constant Gross-Margin Percentage NRV Method

Correcting Student Misconceptions Students are often confused because the constant gross-margin % NRV method seems to work backward. Explain that in fact it does work backward. Expected profits are calculated first, then the joint cost allocation is the "plug" figure. Emphasize that the profit is *expected* GM, based on *expected* sales revenue and *expected* total costs. *The joint cost estimation is based on this expected GM* from step 1. If a company waits until the end of the year to allocate joint costs, they could use actual profits and actual costs in the same "backward" approach.

The **constant gross-margin percentage NRV method** allocates joint costs to joint products in such a way that the overall gross-margin percentage is identical for the individual products. This method entails three steps:

◆ *Step 1*: Compute the overall gross-margin percentage.

◆ *Step 2*: Use the overall gross-margin percentage and deduct the gross margin from the final sales values to obtain the total costs that each product will bear.

◆ *Step 3*: Deduct the expected separable costs from the total costs to obtain the joint-cost allocation.

Exhibit 15-8 presents these three steps for allocating the $400,000 joint costs between butter cream and condensed milk. To determine the joint-cost allocation, Exhibit 15-8 uses the expected final sales value of the *total production* during the accounting period ($1,600,000), *not* the *total sales* of the period. The joint costs allocated to each product need not always be positive under this method. Some products may receive negative allocations of joint costs to bring their gross-margin

Reinforcing Problems Probs. 15-22 and 15-29 cover the constant gross-margin % NRV method.

[5]One extension of the estimated NRV method is to include in the separable costs an imputed interest cost on assets used beyond the splitoff point. This extension raises thorny issues over the valuation of such assets and the interest rate used to determine the imputed interest cost.

EXHIBIT 15-8
Joint Costs Allocated Using Constant Gross-Margin Percentage NRV Method: Farmers' Dairy for May 2001

STEP 1

Expected final sales value of total production during the accounting period: (20,000 gallons × $25) + (50,000 gallons × $22)	$1,600,000
Deduct joint and separable costs ($400,000 + $280,000 + 520,000)	1,200,000
Gross margin	$ 400,000
Gross-margin percentage (400,000 ÷ $1,600,000)	25%

STEP 2

	Butter Cream	Condensed Milk	Total
Expected final sales value of total production during the accounting period: (butter cream, 20,000 gallons × $25; condensed milk, 50,000 gallons × $22)	$500,000	$1,100,000	$1,600,000
Deduct gross margin, using overall gross-margin percentage (25%)	125,000	275,000	400,000
Cost of goods sold	375,000	825,000	1,200,000

STEP 3

	Butter Cream	Condensed Milk	Total
Deduct separable costs to complete and sell	280,000	520,000	800,000
Joint costs allocated	$ 95,000	$ 305,000	$ 400,000

EXHIBIT 15-9

Farmers' Dairy Product-Line Income Statement for May 2001:
Joint Costs Allocated Using Constant Gross-Margin Percentage NRV Method

	Butter Cream	Condensed Milk	Total
Revenues (butter cream, 12,000 gallons × $25; condensed milk, 45,000 gallons × $22)	$300,000	$990,000	$1,290,000
Cost of goods sold			
Joint costs (from Exhibit 15-8)	95,000	305,000	400,000
Separable costs to complete and sell	280,000	520,000	800,000
Cost of goods available for sale	375,000	825,000	1,200,000
Deduct ending inventory (butter cream, 8,000 × $18.75[a]; condensed milk, 5,000 × $16.50[b])	150,000	82,500	232,500
Cost of goods sold	225,000	742,500	967,500
Gross margin	$ 75,000	$247,500	$ 322,500
Gross-margin percentage	25%	25%	25%

[a]$375,000 ÷ 20,000 gallons = $18.75
[b]$825,000 ÷ 50,000 gallons = $16.50

percentages up to the overall company average. In our example, the overall gross-margin percentage is 25 percent. A product-line income statement for the constant gross-margin percentage NRV method is presented in Exhibit 15-9.

The assumption underlying the constant gross-margin percentage NRV method is that all the products have the same ratio of cost to sales value. A constant ratio of cost to sales value across products is rarely seen in companies that produce multiple products but have no joint costs.

The constant gross-margin method is fundamentally different in one key aspect from the two other market-based joint-cost-allocation methods described earlier. The sales value at splitoff point and the estimated NRV methods allocate only the joint costs to the individual products. No account is taken of profits earned either before or after the splitoff point when allocating the joint costs. In contrast, the constant gross-margin percentage NRV method is both a joint-cost and a profit-allocation method. The total difference between the sales value of production of all products and the separable cost of all products includes both (a) the joint costs, and (b) the total gross margin. Both (a) and (b) are allocated to products under the constant gross-margin method so that each product has the same gross-margin percentage.

Comparison of Methods

Which method of allocating joint costs should be chosen? Each one has advantages. The sales value at splitoff method is widely used when selling-price data are available (even if further processing is done). Reasons for this practice, in addition to its objectivity, include the following:

1. *No anticipation of subsequent management decisions.* The sales value at splitoff method does not presuppose an exact number of subsequent steps undertaken for further processing. In contrast, the estimated NRV and constant gross-margin percentage NRV methods require information on (a) the specific sequence of further processing decisions, and (b) the point at which individual products are sold.

2. *Availability of a meaningful common denominator to compute the weighting factors.* Market-based measures, including the sales value at splitoff method, have a meaningful common denominator (revenues). In contrast, the physical-measure method may lack a meaningful common denominator for all of the

Points to Stress The constant GM% method allocates joint costs such that all products have equal GM%. Relative to the NRV method, the constant GM% method "subsidizes" products with relatively high separable costs. The overall GM% is calculated by deducting all products' separable costs and the joint costs from revenue. This GM% is the same for each product, regardless of its separable costs. This effectively "subsidizes" products with high separable costs. This is why the high separable cost product, BC, has 25% GM under the constant GM% method, but only 22% GM under the estimated NRV method, per Exh. 15-7.

Curriculum Linkage It's extremely difficult to set rates in regulated industries where some or all of the products are joint products. Economic factors may play a smaller role than usual in setting these rates. This void will be filled by noneconomic forces, particularly political forces.

Joint-Cost Allocation in the Oil Patch

One of the largest industries in the world, the petroleum industry is a classic example of an industry with joint costs. Petroleum mining and processing starts with hydrocarbons being extracted from either onshore or offshore fields. Oil refineries process (disassemble) hydrocarbons into multiple products such as crude oil, gas, and raw LPG (liquefied petroleum gas). The LPG is often further processed into butane, ethane, and propane. How should the joint refining costs be allocated to the separate marketable products produced at the refinery? These costs include the costs of hydrocarbons put into the refinery and the processing costs at the refinery.

One survey focused on the joint-cost-allocation method chosen by refiners for external reporting purposes:

Market-based measures	
Net realizable value	46%
Other	20
Physical-based measures	
Volume (barrels, gallons, or cubic feet)	27
Mass (weight or molecular mass)	2
Other	5
	100%

Market-based measures are the preferred joint-cost allocation, with the NRV method the predominant choice. The most common other market-based measure reported in the survey was a variation of the NRV method in which the final sales value of each product is used as the allocation base without any deduction for the expected separable costs of production and marketing. This variation illustrates how companies make adjustments to the basic methods described in this chapter, often on the grounds of a perceived cost-benefit basis.

Source: Adapted from Koester and Barnett, "Petroleum Refinery Joint Cost Allocation." See Appendix A for full citation.

individual products (for example, when some products are liquids and other products are solids).

3. *Simplicity.* The sales value at splitoff method is simple. In contrast, the estimated NRV and constant gross-margin percentage NRV methods can be complex in operations with multiple products and multiple splitoff points. This complexity is increased when management makes frequent changes in the specific sequence of further processing decisions or in the point at which individual products are sold.

The purpose of the joint-cost allocation is important in choosing the allocation method. Consider rate regulation. Market-based measures are difficult to use in this context. It is circular reasoning to use selling prices as a basis for setting prices (rates) and at the same time use selling prices to allocate the costs on which prices (rates) are based. To avoid this circular reasoning, the physical-measure method may be used in rate regulation.

Avoiding Joint-Cost Allocation

The preceding methods for allocating joint costs to individual products are all subject to criticism. As a result, some companies refrain from allocation entirely. Instead, they carry their inventories at estimated NRV. Income on each product is recognized when production is completed. Industries that use variations of this approach include meatpacking, canning, and mining.

Curriculum Linkage Financial acctg. theory recognizes revenue when products are sold, not when they are produced (except products such as gold that have a ready market with an established price). Carrying joint product inventories at NRV recognizes profits when the units are produced. Carrying inventories at NRV minus a normal profit margin usually brings the inventory value closer to cost. The market value (replacement cost) in the LCM method for valuing inventories has a "ceiling" value of NRV and a "floor" value of NRV minus a normal profit margin.

Accountants ordinarily criticize carrying inventories at estimated net realizable values. Why? Because when doing so income is recognized *before* sales are made. Partly in response to this criticism, some companies using this no-allocation approach carry their inventories at estimated NRV minus a normal profit margin. The result is that in the year of production, all of the joint costs of that accounting period are matched against the estimated net revenues from the production of that accounting period. When end-of-period inventories are sold the next period, the cost of goods sold will be the revenue amount shown for the ending inventory of the previous accounting period.

IRRELEVANCE OF JOINT COSTS FOR DECISION MAKING

Many manufacturing companies constantly face the decision of whether to further process a joint product. For example, meat products may be sold as cut or may be smoked, cured, frozen, canned, and so forth. In the petroleum refining industry, the refiner must decide whether to sell raw liquefied petroleum gas as a product or process it further into butane, ethane, and propane.

Chapter 11 introduced the key concepts of *relevant revenues* (expected future revenues that differ among alternative courses of action) and *relevant costs* (expected future costs that differ among alternative courses of action). These concepts have important implications for decisions on whether a joint (or main) product should be sold at the splitoff point or processed further. Joint costs incurred up to the splitoff point are past (sunk) costs. None of the methods for allocating joint-product costs discussed earlier in this chapter should guide management decisions on selling a product at the splitoff point or processing it further. When a product is the result of a joint process, the decision to process further should not be influenced either by the total amount of the joint costs or by the portion of the joint costs allocated to individual products.

Sell or Process Further

The decision to incur additional costs for further processing should be based on the incremental operating income attainable beyond the splitoff point. Example 2 assumed that it was profitable for both cream and liquid skim to be further processed, respectively, into butter cream and condensed milk. The incremental analysis for these decisions to process further is as follows:

Further Processing Cream into Butter Cream

Incremental revenues, $500,000 − $200,000	$300,000
Deduct incremental processing costs	280,000
Increase in operating income	$ 20,000

Further Processing Liquid Skim into Condensed Milk

Incremental revenues, $1,100,000 − $300,000	$800,000
Deduct incremental processing costs	520,000
Increase in operating income	$280,000

In this example, the manager should process cream into butter cream and liquid skim into condensed milk. The joint costs incurred up to splitoff ($400,000)—and how they are allocated—are irrelevant in deciding whether to process further. Why? Because the joint costs of $400,000 are the same whether or not further processing occurs.

Incremental costs are those costs that differ between the alternatives being considered (such as sell or process further). Do not assume that all separable costs in joint-cost allocations are always incremental costs. For example, some separable costs may be allocated costs that do not differ between the alternatives being considered.

Joint-Cost Allocation and Performance Evaluation

The potential conflict between the cost concepts used for decision making and those used for evaluating the performance of managers is a key theme of this book. If managers make sell or process further decisions using an incremental revenue/

incremental cost approach, the resulting budgeted product-line income statement using any of the three methods under the market-based approach (sales value at splitoff, estimated NRV, and constant gross-margin percentage NRV) will all show each individual product budgeted to have a positive (or zero) operating income. In contrast, allocating joint costs using a physical measure can show budgeted losses for one or more products that a manager is responsible for even though the company has higher operating income because it produces those products in a joint production process.

Consider again our Example 1 (Farmers' Dairy) with the following change. The selling price per gallon of liquid skim is now $3.80 rather than $4.00. This change does not affect the joint costs allocated and the cost of goods sold computed using the physical-measure method (see Exhibit 15-5, p. 541). However, it does affect the revenues of the liquid skim product. The revised product-line income statement for May 2001 using the physical-measure method is

	Cream	Liquid Skim	Total
Revenues (cream 20,000 × $8; liquid skim 30,000 × $3.80)	$160,000	$114,000	$274,000
Cost of goods sold	80,000	120,000	200,000
Gross margin	$ 80,000	$ (6,000)	$ 74,000

Note that the liquid skim product has a negative gross margin of $6,000. A manager evaluated on the basis of product-by-product gross-margin information may be reluctant to process the raw milk into cream and liquid skim to avoid having to explain why liquid skim is being produced at a negative gross margin. Use of a market-based joint-cost-allocation method will not put a manager in this situation.

ACCOUNTING FOR BYPRODUCTS

Joint production processes may yield not only joint and main products but byproducts as well. Although byproducts have much lower sales value than do joint or main products, the presence of byproducts can affect the allocation of joint costs. We now turn our attention to accounting for byproducts. To simplify the discussion, consider a two-product example consisting of a main product and a byproduct.

EXAMPLE 3: The Meatworks Group processes meat from slaughterhouses. One of its departments cuts lamb shoulders and generates two products:

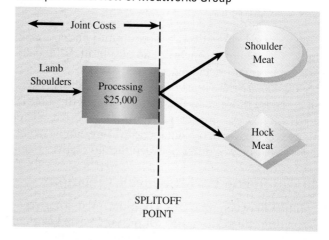

EXHIBIT 15-10
Example 3: Overview of Meatworks Group

- ◆ Shoulder meat (the main product)—sold for $60 per pack
- ◆ Hock meat (the byproduct)—sold for $4 per pack

Both products are sold at the splitoff point without further processing, as Exhibit 15-10 shows. Data (number of packs) for this department in July 2001 are as follows:

	Production	Sales	Beginning Inventory	Ending Inventory
Shoulder meat	500	400	0	100
Hock meat	100	30	0	70

The joint manufacturing costs of these products in July 2001 were $25,000 (comprising $15,000 for direct materials and $10,000 for conversion costs).

Two byproduct accounting methods are presented. Method A (the production method) recognizes byproducts in the financial statements at the time production is completed. Method B (the sale method) delays recognition of byproducts until the time of sale. Recognition of byproducts at the time of production is conceptually correct. Where recognition at the time of sales occurs in practice, it is usually rationalized on the grounds that the dollar amounts of byproducts are immaterial.[6] Exhibit 15-11 presents the income statement of the Meatworks Group under both methods.

Reinforcing Problems Accounting for byproducts is covered in Exer. 15-17, 15-24 through 15-26, and in Probs. 15-31, 15-33, and 15-34.

EXHIBIT 15-11
Income Statement of Meatworks Group for July 2001

New in This Edition The text now focuses on the two basic methods to account for byproducts: (1) recognition at the time of production and (2) recognition at the time of sale. The other alternatives discussed in previous editions are just variants of these two basic methods.

	Byproduct Accounting Method	
	Method A: Recognized at Production	Method B: Recognized at Sale
Revenues		
Main product: shoulder meat (400 × $60)	$24,000	$24,000
Byproduct: Hock meat (30 × $4)	—	120
Total revenues	24,000	24,120
Cost of goods sold		
Total manufacturing costs	25,000	25,000
Deduct byproduct revenue (100 × $4)	400	—
Net manufacturing costs	24,600	25,000
Deduct main product inventory[a]	4,920	5,000
Cost of goods sold	19,680	20,000
Gross margin	$ 4,320	$ 4,120
Gross-margin percentage	18.00%	17.08%
Inventoriable costs (end of period):		
Main product: Shoulder meat	$4,920	$5,000
Byproduct: Hock meat (70 × $4)[b]	280	0

[a](100 ÷ 500) × Net manufacturing cost = (100 ÷ 500) × $24,600 = $4,920.
[b]Recorded at selling prices.

[6]Further discussion on byproduct accounting methods is in C. Cheatham and M. Green, "Teaching Accounting for Byproducts", *Management Accounting News & Views* (Spring, 1988): 14–15; and D. Stout and D. Wygal, "Making Byproducts a Main Product of Discussion: A Challenge to Accounting Educators," *Journal of Accounting Education* (1989): 219–233.

Method A: Byproducts Recognized at Time Production Is Completed

This method recognizes the byproduct in the financial statements—the 100 packs of hock meat—in the month it is produced (July 2001). The estimated net realizable value from the byproduct produced is offset against the costs of the main (or joint) products. The following journal entries illustrate this method:

1.	Work in Process	15,000	
	Accounts Payable		15,000
	To record direct materials purchased and used in production during July.		
2.	Work in Process	10,000	
	Various accounts		10,000
	To record conversion costs in the production process during July; examples include energy, manufacturing supplies, all manufacturing labor, and plant depreciation.		
3.	Byproduct Inventory—Hock Meat (100 × $4)	400	
	Finished Goods—Shoulder Meat ($25,000 − $400)	24,600	
	Work in Process ($15,000 + $10,000)		25,000
	To record cost of goods completed during July.		
4a.	Cost of Goods Sold [(400 ÷ 500) × $24,600]	19,680	
	Finished Goods—Shoulder Meat		19,680
	To record the cost of the main product sold during July.		
b.	Cash or Accounts Receivable (400 × $60)	24,000	
	Revenues—Shoulder Meat		24,000
	To record the sales of the main product during July.		
5.	Cash or Accounts Receivable (30 × $4)	120	
	Byproduct Inventory—Hock Meat		120
	To record the sales of the byproduct during July.		

This method reports the byproduct inventories of hock meat in the balance sheet at their $4 per pack selling price [(100 − 30) × $4 = $280].

One variation of this method would be to report byproduct inventory at its estimated net realizable value reduced by a normal profit margin.[7] When the byproduct inventory is sold in a subsequent period, the income statement would match the selling price with the "net" selling price reported for the byproduct inventory.

Method B: Byproducts Recognized at Time of Sale

This method makes no journal entries until sale of the byproduct occurs. Revenues of the byproduct are reported as a revenue item in the income statement at the time of sale. In the Meatworks Group example, byproduct revenues in July 2001 would be $120 (30 × $4) because only 30 packs of the hock meat are sold in July (of the 100 packs produced). The journal entries would be:

1 and 2.	Same as for method A.		
3.	Finished Goods—Shoulder Meat	25,000	
	Work in Process		25,000
	To record cost of goods completed during July.		

[7]One approach would be to assume all products have the same "normal" profit margin like the constant gross-margin percentage NRV method. Alternatively, the company might allow products to have different profit margins based on an analysis of the margins earned by other companies who sell them as individual products.

Points to Stress Byproducts are distinguished from joint products based on the magnitude of their sales revenue. This is a gray area that requires judgment. Exh. 15-2 illustrates the continuum along which products fall. Stress that, over time, products can change their status as a main product, joint product, byproduct, or scrap. For example, what was once a byproduct can later become a joint product. Once considered byproducts or scrap, changes in culinary tastes have elevated the sales price (and status) of mussels (shellfish) to main or joint-product status. The invention of the gasoline engine elevated gasoline from a scrap product in the production of kerosene to a main product.

Correcting Student Misconceptions Students find acctg. for byproducts confusing, because both methods (technically) violate GAAP concepts. Method A recognizes byproduct *revenues* at the time products are *produced*—a technical violation of GAAP, as revenue shouldn't be recognized until the related products are sold. Method B violates GAAP in that it doesn't recognize inventories as assets. These technical violations are allowed because the dollar amts. are by definition (of byproducts) immaterial.

New in This Edition Journal entries for both byproduct methods have been incorporated into the text. Some students find that comparing and contrasting the two methods via the journal entries assist them in understanding the differences and similarities of the methods.

4a.	Cost of Goods Sold [(400 ÷ 500) × $25,000]	20,000	
	Finished Goods—Shoulder Meat		20,000
	To record the cost of the main product sold during July.		
4b.	Same as for method A.		
5.	Cash or Accounts Receivable	120	
	Revenues—Hock Meat		120
	To record the sales of the byproduct during July.		

Method B is rationalized in practice primarily on grounds that the dollar amounts of byproducts are immaterial. However, this method permits managers to "manage" reported earnings by timing when they sell byproducts. Managers may stockpile byproducts so that they have the flexibility to give revenues a "boost" at opportune times.

Chicken Processing: Costing on the Disassembly Line

Chicken processing operations provide many examples where joint and byproduct costing issues can arise. Each chicken is killed and then "disassembled" into many products. Every effort is made to obtain revenue from each disassembled item.

White breast meat, the highest revenue-generating product, is obtained from the front end of the bird. Dark meat is obtained from the back end of the bird. Other edible products include chicken wings, giblets, and kidneys. There are many nonedible products including feathers and blood, the head, feet, and intestines. The nonedible products have a diverse set of uses. For example, poultry feathers are used in bedding and sporting goods; poultry leftover parts such as bones, beaks, and feet are ground into livestock pellets and fertilizer; and poultry fat is used in animal feed and pet food.

Poultry companies use individual product cost information for several purposes. One purpose is in customer-profitability analysis. Customers (such as supermarkets and fast-food restaurants) differ greatly in the mix of products purchased. Individual product cost data enable companies to determine differences in individual customer profitability. A subset of products is placed into frozen storage, which creates a demand for individual product cost information for inventory valuation.

Companies differ in how they cost individual products. Consider two of the largest U.S. companies—Southern Poultry and Golden State Poultry (disguised names).

Southern Poultry classifies white breast meat as the single main product in its costing system. All other products are classified as byproducts. Selling prices of the many byproducts are used to reduce the chicken processing costs that are allocated to the main product. The white breast meat is often further processed into many individual products (such as trimmed chicken and marinated chicken). The separable cost of this further processing is added to the cost per pound of deboned white breast meat to obtain the cost of further processed products.

Golden State Poultry classifies any product sold to a retail outlet as a joint product. Such products include breast fillets, half breasts, drummettes, thighs, and whole legs. All other products are classified as byproducts. Revenue from byproducts is offset against the chicken processing cost before that cost is allocated among the joint products. The average selling prices of products sold to its retail outlets are used to allocate the net chicken processing cost to the individual joint products. The distribution costs of transporting the chicken products from the processing plants to retail outlets are not taken into account when determining the joint-cost-allocation weights.

Source: Adapted from conversations with executives of Southern Poultry and Golden State Poultry.

PROBLEM

Inorganic Chemicals purchases salt and processes it into products such as caustic soda, chlorine, and PVC (polyvinyl chloride). In July, Inorganic Chemicals purchased salt for $40,000. Conversion costs of $60,000 were incurred up to the splitoff point, at which time two salable products were produced: caustic soda and chlorine. Chlorine can be further processed into PVC.

The July production and sales information are as follows:

	Production	Sales	Selling Price Per Ton
Caustic soda	1,200 tons	1,200 tons	$ 50
Chlorine	800 tons		
PVC	500 tons	500 tons	200

All 800 tons of chlorine were further processed, at incremental costs of $20,000, to yield 500 tons of PVC. There were no byproducts from this further processing of chlorine. There were no beginning or ending inventories of caustic soda, chlorine, or PVC in July.

There is an active market for chlorine. Inorganic Chemicals could have sold all its July production of chlorine at $75 a ton.

Required

1. Calculate how the joint costs of $100,000 would be allocated between caustic soda and chlorine under the following methods: (a) sales value at splitoff, (b) physical measure (tons), and (c) estimated net realizable value.
2. What is the gross-margin percentage of (a) caustic soda, and (b) PVC under the three methods in requirement 1?
3. Lifetime Swimming Pool Products offers to purchase 800 tons of chlorine in August at $75 a ton. This sale of chlorine would mean that no PVC would be produced in August. How would accepting this offer affect Inorganic's August operating income?

SOLUTION

1. **a.** Sales value at splitoff method

	Caustic Soda	Chlorine	Total
1. Sales value at splitoff (caustic soda, 1,200 × $50; chlorine, 800 × $75)	$60,000	$60,000	$120,000
2. Weighting ($60,000 ÷ $120,000; $60,000 ÷ $120,000)	0.5	0.5	
3. Joint costs allocated ($40,000 + $60,000) (caustic soda, 0.5 × $100,000; chlorine, 0.5 × $100,000)	$50,000	$50,000	$100,000

b. Physical-measure method

	Caustic Soda	Chlorine	Total
1. Physical measure (tons)	1,200	800	2,000
2. Weighting (1,200 ÷ 2,000; 800 ÷ 2,000)	0.6	0.4	
3. Joint costs allocated (caustic soda, 0.6 × $100,000; chlorine, 0.4 × $100,000)	$60,000	$40,000	$100,000

c. Estimated net realizable value method

	Caustic Soda	Chlorine	Total
1. Estimated final sales value of production (caustic soda, 1,200 × $50; PVC from chlorine, 500 × $200)	$60,000	$100,000	$160,000
2. Deduct expected separable costs	0	20,000	20,000
3. Estimated net realizable value at splitoff point	$60,000	$ 80,000	$140,000
4. Weighting ($60,000 ÷ $140,000; $80,000 ÷ $140,000)	$\frac{3}{7}$	$\frac{4}{7}$	
5. Joint costs allocated (caustic, $\frac{3}{7}$ × $100,000; chlorine, $\frac{4}{7}$ × $100,000)	$42,857	$ 57,143	$100,000

2. a. Caustic soda

	Sales Value at Splitoff Point	Physical Measure	Estimated Net Realizable Value
Sales	$60,000	$60,000	$60,000
Joint costs	50,000	60,000	42,857
Gross margin	$10,000	$ 0	$17,143
Gross-margin percentage	16.67%	0%	28.57%

b. PVC

	Sales Value at Splitoff Point	Physical Measure	Estimated Net Realizable Value
Sales	$100,000	$100,000	$100,000
Joint costs	50,000	40,000	57,143
Separable costs	20,000	20,000	20,000
Gross margin	$ 30,000	$ 40,000	$ 22,857
Gross-margin percentage	30.00%	40.00%	22.86%

3. Incremental revenues from further processing of chlorine into PVC:

(500 × $200) − (800 × $75)	$40,000
Incremental costs of further processing chlorine into PVC	20,000
Incremental operating income from further processing	$20,000

The operating income of Inorganic Chemicals would be reduced by $20,000 if it sold 800 tons of chlorine to Lifetime Swimming Pool Products instead of further processing the chlorine into PVC.

SUMMARY

The following points are linked to the chapter's learning objectives:

1. A joint cost is the cost of a single production process that yields multiple products. The splitoff point is the juncture in the joint production process where the products become separately identifiable.

2. Joint products have relatively high sales value at the splitoff point. A byproduct has a low sales value at the splitoff point compared with the sales value of a joint or main product. Products can change from byproducts to joint products when their relative sales values increase sizably or change from joint products to byproducts when their relative sales values decrease sizably.

3. The purposes for allocating joint costs to products include inventory costing for financial accounting purposes, internal reporting, cost reimbursement under contracts, insurance settlements, rate regulation, and litigation involving product cost information.

4. Accounting alternatives available to allocate joint costs include a market-based approach (with three methods—sales value at splitoff, estimated NRV, and constant gross-margin percentage NRV) and a physical-measure-based approach. The market-based approach uses selling prices as a key input, while the physical-measure-based approach typically uses weight or volume as a key input when allocating joint costs.

5. The sales value at splitoff method is widely used where market prices exist at splitoff because it is objective and does not anticipate subsequent management decisions on further processing, it uses a meaningful common denominator, and it is simple.

6. The relevant-revenues and relevant-cost analysis introduced in Chapter 11 applies to further processing situations in joint production processes. No techniques for allocating joint-product costs should guide decisions about whether a product should be sold at the splitoff point or processed further because joint costs are irrelevant.

7. Byproduct accounting methods differ on whether byproducts are recognized in the financial statements at the time of production or at the time of sale. Recognition at the time of production is conceptually correct. Recognition at the time of sale is rationalized in practice on the grounds that the dollar amounts of byproducts are immaterial.

▼ TERMS TO LEARN

This chapter and the Glossary at the end of the book contain definitions of the following important terms:

byproduct (p. 537)
constant gross-margin percentage NRV
   method (544)
estimated net realizable value (NRV)
   method (543)
joint cost (536)
joint products (537)

main product (537)
physical-measure method (541)
product (537)
sales value at splitoff method (540)
separable costs (536)
splitoff point (536)

▼ ASSIGNMENT MATERIAL

QUESTIONS

15-1 Give two examples of industries in which joint costs are found. For each example, what are the individual products at the splitoff point?

15-2 What is a joint cost? What is a separable cost?

15-3 Distinguish between a joint product and a byproduct.

15-4 Why might the number of products in a joint-cost situation differ from the number of outputs? Give an example.

15-5 Provide three reasons for allocating joint costs to individual products or services.

15-6 Why does the sales value at splitoff method use the sales value of the total production in the accounting period and not just the sales value of the products sold?

15-7 Describe a situation where the sales value at splitoff method cannot be used but the estimated NRV method can be used for joint-cost allocation.

15-8 Distinguish between the sales value at splitoff method and the estimated NRV method.

15-9 Give two limitations of the physical-measure method of joint-cost allocation.

15-10 How might a company simplify its use of the estimated NRV method when the final selling prices can vary sizably in an accounting period and management makes frequent changes to the point at which it sells individual products?

15-11 Why is the constant gross-margin percentage NRV method sometimes called a "joint-cost and a profit-allocation" method?

15-12 "Managers must decide whether a product should be sold at splitoff or processed further. The sales value at splitoff method of joint-cost allocation is the best method for generating the information managers need." Do you agree? Explain.

15-13 "Managers should consider only additional revenues and separable costs when making decisions about selling at splitoff or processing further." Do you agree? Explain.

15-14 Describe two major methods to account for byproducts.

15-15 Why might managers seeking a monthly bonus based on attaining a target operating income prefer a byproduct accounting method that recognizes byproducts at the time of sale rather than at the time of production?

EXERCISES

15-16 **Joint-cost allocation, insurance settlement.** Chicken Little grows and processes chickens. Each chicken is disassembled into five main parts. Information pertaining to production in July 2001 is:

Parts	Pounds of Product	Wholesale Selling Price Per Pound When Production Is Complete
Breasts	100	$1.10
Wings	20	0.40
Thighs	40	0.70
Bones	80	0.20
Feathers	10	0.10

Joint cost of production in July 2001 was $100.

A special shipment of 20 pounds of breasts and 10 pounds of wings has been destroyed in a fire. Chicken Little's insurance policy provides for reimbursement for the cost of the items destroyed. The insurance company permits Chicken Little to use a joint-cost-allocation method. The splitoff point is assumed to be at the end of the production line.

Required

1. Compute the cost of the special shipment destroyed using:
   a. Sales value at splitoff method, and
   b. Physical-measure method (pounds of finished product).
2. What joint-cost-allocation method would you recommend Chicken Little use? Explain.

15-17 **Joint products and byproducts (continuation of 15-16).** Chicken Little is computing the ending inventory values for its July 31, 2001 balance sheet. Ending inventory amounts on July 31 are 10 pounds of breasts, 4 pounds of wings, 3 pounds of thighs, 5 pounds of bones, and 2 pounds of feathers.

Chicken Little's management wants to use the sales value at splitoff point method. However, they want you to explore the effect on ending inventory values of classifying one or more products as a byproduct rather than a joint product.

Required

1. Assume Chicken Little classifies all five products as joint products. What are the ending inventory values of each product on July 31, 2001?
2. Assume Chicken Little uses a byproduct method that recognizes byproducts in the financial statements at the time production is completed. The total revenues to be received from the sale of byproducts produced that period are offset against the joint cost of production of the joint products. What are the ending inventory values for

each joint product on July 31, 2001, assuming breasts and thighs are the joint products and wings, bones, and feathers are byproducts?

3. Comment on differences in the results in requirements 1 and 2.

 15-18 Estimated net realizable value method. Illawara, Inc., produces two joint products, cooking oil and soap oil, from a single vegetable oil refining process. In July 2001, the joint costs of this process were $24,000,000. Separable processing costs beyond the splitoff point were cooking oil, $30,000,000; soap oil, $7,500,000. Cooking oil sells for $50 per drum. Soap oil sells for $25 per drum. Illawara produced and sold 1,000,000 drums of cooking oil and 500,000 drums of soap oil. There are no beginning or ending inventories of cooking oil or soap oil.

Required

Allocate the $24,000,000 joint costs using the estimated NRV method.

15-19 Alternative joint-cost-allocation methods, further process decision. The Wood Spirits Company produces two products, turpentine and methanol (wood alcohol), by a joint process. Joint costs amount to $120,000 per batch of output. Each batch totals 10,000 gallons: 25% methanol and 75% turpentine. Both products are processed further without gain or loss in volume. Separable processing costs are methanol, $3 per gallon; turpentine, $2 per gallon. Methanol sells for $21 per gallon. Turpentine sells for $14 per gallon.

Required

1. How much joint costs per batch should be allocated to turpentine and to methanol, assuming that joint costs are allocated on a physical-measure (number of gallons at splitoff point) basis?
2. If joint costs are to be assigned on an estimated NRV basis, how much joint cost should be assigned to turpentine and to methanol?
3. Prepare product-line income statements per batch for requirements 1 and 2. Assume no beginning or ending inventories.
4. The company has discovered an additional process by which the methanol (wood alcohol) can be made into a pleasant-tasting alcoholic beverage. The selling price of this beverage would be $60 a gallon. Additional processing would increase separable costs $9 per gallon (in addition to the $3 per gallon separable cost required to yield methanol). The company would have to pay excise taxes of 20% on the selling price of the beverage. Assuming no other changes in cost, what is the joint cost applicable to the wood alcohol (using the estimated NRV method)? Should the company produce the alcoholic beverage? Show your computations.

15-20 Joint-cost allocation, process further. Sinclair Refining Company (SRC) is a 100% owned subsidiary of Sinclair Oil & Gas. SRC operates a refinery that processes hydrocarbons sold to it by Sinclair Production Company, another 100% subsidiary of Sinclair Oil & Gas. SRC's refinery has three outputs from its processing of hydrocarbons—crude oil, natural gas liquids, and gas. The first two outputs are liquids while gas is a vapor. However, gas can be converted into a liquid equivalent using a standard industry conversion factor. For costing purposes, SRC assumes all three outputs are jointly produced until a single splitoff point where each output appears separately and is then further processed individually.

For August, 2000 the following data apply (the numbers are small to keep the focus on key concepts):

◆ Crude oil—150 barrels produced and sold at $18 per barrel. Separable costs beyond the splitoff point are $175.

◆ Natural gas liquids—50 barrels produced and sold at $15 per barrel. Separable costs beyond the splitoff point are $105.

◆ Gas—800 equivalent barrels produced and sold at $1.30 per equivalent barrel. Separable costs beyond the splitoff point are $210.

SRC paid Sinclair Production Company $1,400 for hydrocarbons delivered to it from its offshore platform in August 2000. The cost of operating the refinery in August up to the splitoff point was $400, including $100 of gas charges from Deadhorse Utilities, an independent utility company. Deadhorse signed a long-term contract with SRC several years ago when gas prices were much lower than in 2000.

A new federal law has recently been passed that taxes crude oil at 30% of operating income. No new tax is to be paid on natural gas liquid or natural gas. Starting August 2000, SRC must report a separate product-line income statement for crude oil. One challenge facing SRC is how to allocate the joint cost of producing the three separate salable outputs. Assume no beginning or ending inventory.

Required

1. Draw a diagram showing the joint-cost situation for SRC.
2. Allocate the August 2000 joint cost among the three salable products using:
   a. Physical-measures method, and
   b. Estimated NRV method.
3. Show the operating income for each product using the methods in requirement 2.
4. Discuss the pros and cons of the two methods to Sinclair Oil and Gas for product emphasis decisions.
5. Draft a letter to the taxation authorities on behalf of Sinclair Oil and Gas that justifies the joint-cost-allocation method you recommend Sinclair use.

15-21 Joint-cost allocation, physical-measures method (continuation of 15-20). Assume that SRC is not able to sell its gas output. The refinery is located in a remote area, and a terrorist group has just destroyed major sections of the gas pipeline used to transport the gas to market. The pipeline that carries the crude oil and natural gas liquid is still operational. Sinclair Production Company must now reinject the gas into the offshore field. The costs of the hydrocarbons to SRC will not be reduced, but Sinclair Production (not SRC) will bear the cost of gas reinjection. No separable costs of gas production beyond the splitoff point will now be incurred.

Required

1. Assume the same data for all three outputs for August 2000 apply to the new set of facts. Show the operating income for each salable product using the estimated NRV method of joint-cost allocation.
2. Assume the taxation authorities argue that for crude oil income tax determination the physical-measures method should be used to allocate joint costs and that all outputs (including gas, whether sold or reinjected) should be used in deciding the cost-allocation weights. Draft a letter to the taxation authorities on behalf of Sinclair Oil and Gas. Be specific where possible.

15-22 Alternative methods of joint-cost allocation, ending inventories. The Darl Company operates a simple chemical process to convert a single material into three separate items, referred here to as X, Y, and Z. All three end products are separated simultaneously at a single splitoff point.

Products X and Y are ready for sale immediately upon splitoff without further processing or any other additional costs. Product Z, however, is processed further before being sold. There is no available market price for Z at the splitoff point.

The selling prices quoted below are expected to remain the same in the coming year. During 2001, the selling prices of the items and the total amounts sold were as follows:

◆ X—120 tons sold for $1,500 per ton

◆ Y—340 tons sold for $1,000 per ton

◆ Z—475 tons sold for $700 per ton

The total joint manufacturing costs for the year were $400,000. An additional $200,000 was spent in order to finish product Z.

There were no beginning inventories of X, Y, or Z. At the end of the year, the following inventories of completed units were on hand: X, 180 tons; Y, 60 tons; Z, 25 tons. There was no beginning or ending work in process.

Required

1. Compute the cost of inventories of X, Y, and Z for balance sheet purposes and the cost of goods sold for income statement purposes as of December 31, 2001, using:
   a. Estimated net realizable value method of joint-cost allocation, and
   b. Constant gross-margin percentage NRV method of joint-cost allocation.
2. Compare the gross-margin percentages for X, Y, and Z using the two methods given in requirement 1.

15-23 Process further or sell, joint-cost allocation. (R. Capettini) Henley Company produces three joint products, A, B, and C, from a single joint process with a fixed cost of $5,000 and a variable cost of $2.00 per input unit. Each product can be either processed further or, at the splitoff point, it can be sold or disposed of at a cost. Out of each input unit, Henley Company produces one unit of product A, three units of product B, and two units of product C. Selling and administrative costs are $14,000.

Required

1. Use the following data to decide whether Henley Company should process each product further or dispose of it (or sell it) at the splitoff point if Henley Company inputs 5,000 units. For each product, show how much better off Henley would be if it followed your advice versus making the alternative decision. Assume that if Henley does not further process a product, it does not incur any of the further processing costs.

Product	Selling Price Per Unit at Splitoff Point	Cost Per Unit to Dispose of Product at Splitoff Point	Further Processing Costs		Selling Price Per Unit After Further Processing
			Fixed	Variable Per unit	
A	—	$0.20	$ 6,000	$0.90	$1.50
B	$0.50	—	1,000	1.00	1.50
C	—	0.90	10,000	1.10	5.40

2. What is Henley Company's gross margin at the 5,000-unit input level?

15-24 Process further or sell, byproduct. (CMA adapted) Newcastle Mining Company (NMC) produces and sells bulk raw coal to other coal companies and exporters. NMC mines and stockpiles the coal. The coal is then passed through a one-step crushing process before being loaded onto river barges for shipment to customers. The annual output of 10 million tons, which is expected to remain stable, has an average cost of $20 per ton with an average selling price of $27 per ton.

Management is currently evaluating the possibility of further processing the coal by sizing and cleaning in order to expand markets and enhance product revenues. Management has rejected the possibility of constructing a large sizing and cleaning plant because of the significant long-term capital investment required.

Bill Rolland, controller of NMC, asks Amy Kimbell, mining engineer, to develop cost and revenue projections for further processing the coal using a variety of contractual arrangements. After extensive discussions with vendors and contractors, Kimbell prepares the following projections of incremental costs of sizing and cleaning NMC's annual output:

Newcastle Mining Company
Sizing and Cleaning Processes

	Incremental Costs
Direct labor	$600,000 per year
Supervisory personnel	100,000 per year
Heavy equipment rental, operating, and maintenance costs	25,000 per month
Contract sizing and cleaning	3.50 per ton
Outbound rail freight (per 60-ton rail car)	240 per car

In addition to the preceding cost information, market samples obtained by Kimbell show that electrical utilities enter into contracts for sized and cleaned coal similar to that mined by Newcastle at an expected average price of $36 per ton.

Kimbell has learned that 5% of the raw bulk output that enters the sizing and cleaning process will be lost as a primary product. Normally, 75% of this product loss can be salvaged as coal fines, which are small pieces ranging from dustlike particles up to pieces two inches in diameter. Coal fines are too small for use by electrical utilities but are frequently sold to steel manufacturers for use in blast furnaces.

Unfortunately, the price for coal fines frequently fluctuates between $14 and $24 per ton (F.O.B. shipping point), and the timing of market volume is erratic. While companies generally sell all their coal fines during a year, it is not unusual to stockpile this product for several months before making any significant sales.

Required
1. Prepare an analysis that shows whether it is more profitable for Newcastle Mining Company to continue to sell the raw bulk coal or to process it further through sizing and cleaning. (*Note*: Ignore any value related to the coal fines in your analysis.)
2. Now consider the potential value of the coal fines and prepare an addendum that shows how their value affects the results of your analysis prepared in requirement 1.
3. What other factors should be considered in evaluating a sell-or-process-further decision?

15-25 Accounting for a main product and a byproduct. (Cheatham and Green, adapted) Bill Dundee is the owner and operator of Louisiana Bottling, a bulk soft-drink producer. A single production process yields two bulk soft drinks: Rainbow Dew (the main product) and Resi-Dew (the byproduct). Both products are fully processed at the splitoff point, and there are no separable costs.

For September 2000, the cost of the soft-drink operations is $120,000. Production and sales data are as follows:

	Production (in Gallons)	Sales (in Gallons)	Selling Price Per Gallon
Main product: Rainbow Dew	10,000	8,000	$20.00
Byproduct: Resi-Dew	2,000	1,400	2.00

There were no beginning inventories on September 1, 2000. An overview of operations follows:

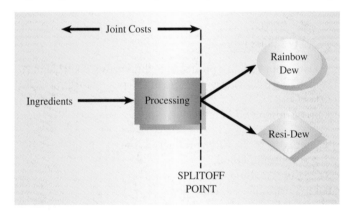

Required
1. What is the gross margin for Louisiana Bottling under methods A and B of byproduct accounting described on p. 549 of this chapter?
2. What are the inventory costs reported in the balance sheet on September 30, 2000, for Rainbow Dew and Resi-Dew under the two methods of byproduct accounting in requirement 1?

15-26 Joint costs and byproducts. (W. Crum) Caldwell Company processes an ore in Department 1, from which comes three products, L, W, and X. Product L is processed further in Department 2. Product W is sold without further processing. Product X is considered a byproduct and is processed further in Department 3. Costs in Department 1 are $800,000, Department 2 costs are $100,000, and Department 3 costs are $50,000. Processing 600,000 pounds in Department 1 results in 50,000 pounds of product L, 300,000 pounds of product W, and 100,000 pounds of product X.

Product L sells for $10 per pound. Product W sells for $2 per pound. Product X sells for $3 per pound. The company wants to make a gross margin of 10% of revenues on product X and needs to allow 25% for marketing costs on product X.

Required
1. Compute unit costs per pound for products L, W, and X, treating X as a byproduct. Use the estimated NRV method for allocating joint costs. Deduct the estimated NRV of the byproduct produced from the joint cost of products L and W.
2. Compute unit costs per pound for products L, W, and X, treating all three as joint products and allocating costs by the estimated NRV method.

PROBLEMS

15-27 Alternative methods of joint-cost allocation, product-mix decision. Pacific Lumber processes lumber products for sale to lumber wholesalers. Its most popular line is oak products. Oak tree growers sell Pacific Lumber whole trees. These trees are jointly processed up to the splitoff point at which raw select oak, raw white oak, and raw knotty oak become separable products. Each raw product is then separately further processed by Pacific Lumber into finished products (select oak, white oak, and knotty oak) that are sold to lumber wholesalers. Data for August 2001 are:

a. Joint processing costs (including cost of oak trees)—$300,000

b. Separable product at splitoff point

- ◆ Raw select oak   30,000 board-feet
- ◆ Raw white oak   50,000 board-feet
- ◆ Raw knotty oak   20,000 board-feet

c. Final product produced and sold

- ◆ Select oak   25,000 board feet at $16 per board-foot
- ◆ White oak   40,000 board feet at $ 9 per board-foot
- ◆ Knotty oak   15,000 board feet at $ 7 per board-foot

d. Separable processing costs

- ◆ For select oak $60,000
- ◆ For white oak $90,000
- ◆ For knotty oak $15,000

There is an active market for raw oak products. Selling prices available in August 2001 were raw select oak ($8 per board-foot), raw white oak ($4 per board-foot), and raw knotty oak ($3 per board-foot).

There were no beginning or ending inventories for August 2001.

Required

1. Allocate the joint costs to the three products using:
   a. Sales value at splitoff method,
   b. Physical-measures method, and
   c. Estimated net realizable value method.
2. Assume that not all final product produced in August 2001 was sold. Ending inventory for August 2001 was select oak (1,000 board-feet), white oak (2,000 board-feet), and knotty oak (500 board-feet). What would be the ending inventory values in the August 30 balance sheet under each product for the three methods in requirement 1?
3. Is Pacific Lumber maximizing its total August 2001 operating income by fully processing each raw oak product into its finished product form? Show your computations.

15-28 Alternative methods of joint-cost allocation, product-mix decisions. The Sunshine Oil Company buys crude vegetable oil. Refining this oil results in four products at the splitoff point: A, B, C, and D. Product C is fully processed at the splitoff point. Products A, B, and D can individually be further refined into Super A, Super B, and Super D. In the most recent month (December), the output at the splitoff point was:

Product A	300,000 gallons
Product B	100,000 gallons
Product C	50,000 gallons
Product D	50,000 gallons

The joint costs of purchasing and processing the crude vegetable oil were $100,000. Sunshine had no beginning or ending inventories. Sales of product C in December were $50,000. Products A, B, and D were further refined and then sold. Data related to December are:

	Separable Processing Costs to Make Super Products	Revenues
Super A	$200,000	$300,000
Super B	80,000	100,000
Super D	90,000	120,000

Sunshine had the option of selling products A, B, and D at the splitoff point. This alternative would have yielded the following revenues for the December production:

Product A	$50,000
Product B	30,000
Product D	70,000

Required
1. Compute the gross-margin percentage for each product sold in December, using the following methods for allocating the $100,000 joint costs:
   a. Sales value at splitoff,
   b. Physical-measure method, and
   c. Estimated net realizable value.
2. Could Sunshine have increased its December operating income by making different decisions about the further processing of products A, B, or D? Show the effect on operating income of any changes you recommend.

15-29 **Comparison of alternative joint-cost-allocation methods, further processing decision, chocolate products.** Roundtree Chocolates manufactures and distributes chocolate products. It purchases cocoa beans and processes them into two intermediate products:

◆ Chocolate-powder liquor base
◆ Milk-chocolate liquor base

These two intermediate products become separately identifiable at a single splitoff point. Every 500 pounds of cocoa beans yields 20 gallons of chocolate-powder liquor base and 30 gallons of milk-chocolate liquor base.

The chocolate-powder liquor base is further processed into chocolate powder. Every 20 gallons of chocolate-powder liquor base yields 200 pounds of chocolate powder. The milk-chocolate liquor base is further processed into milk chocolate. Every 30 gallons of milk-chocolate liquor base yields 340 pounds of milk chocolate.

An overview of the manufacturing operations at Roundtree Chocolates follows:

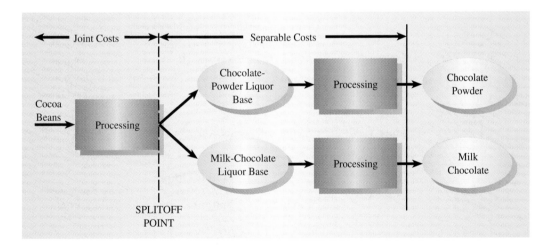

Production and sales data for August 2000 are:

◆ Cocoa beans processed, 5,000 pounds
◆ Costs of processing cocoa beans to splitoff point (including purchase of beans) = $10,000

	Production	Sales	Selling Price
Chocolate powder	2,000 pounds	2,000 pounds	$4 per pound
Milk chocolate	3,400 pounds	3,400 pounds	$5 per pound

The August 2000 separable costs of processing chocolate-powder liquor base into chocolate powder are $4,250. The August 2000 separable costs of processing milk-chocolate liquor base into milk chocolate are $8,750.

Roundtree fully processes both of its intermediate products into chocolate powder or milk chocolate. There is an active market for these intermediate products. In August 2000, Roundtree could have sold the chocolate-powder liquor base for $21 a gallon and the milk-chocolate liquor base for $26 a gallon.

Required

1. Calculate how the joint costs of $10,000 would be allocated between the chocolate-powder and milk-chocolate liquor bases under the following methods:
   a. Sales value at splitoff,
   b. Physical measure (gallons),
   c. Estimated net realizable value, and
   d. Constant gross-margin percentage NRV.
2. What is the gross-margin percentage of the chocolate-powder and milk-chocolate liquor bases under each of the methods in requirement 1?
3. Could Roundtree Chocolates have increased its operating income by a change in its decision to fully process both of its intermediate products? Show your computations.

15-30 Joint-cost allocation, process further or sell. (CMA, adapted) Sonimad Sawmill, Inc. (SSI), purchases logs from independent timber contractors and processes the logs into three types of lumber products:

◆ Studs for residential building (walls, ceilings),

◆ Decorative pieces (fireplace mantels, beams for cathedral ceilings), and

◆ Posts used as support braces (mine support braces, braces for exterior fences around ranch properties).

These products are the result of a joint sawmill process that involves removal of bark from the logs, cutting the logs into a workable size (ranging from 8 to 16 feet in length), and then cutting the individual products from the logs, depending upon the type of wood (pine, oak, walnut, or maple) and the size (diameter) of the log.

The joint process results in the following costs and output of products for a typical month:

Direct materials (rough timber logs)	$ 500,000
Debarking (labor and overhead)	50,000
Sizing (labor and overhead)	200,000
Product cutting (labor and overhead)	250,000
Total joint costs	$1,000,000

Product yield and average sales value on a per unit basis from the joint process are as follows:

Product	Monthly Output of Materials at Splitoff Point	Fully Processed Selling Price
Studs	75,000 units	$ 8
Decorative pieces	5,000 units	100
Posts	20,000 units	20

The studs are sold as rough-cut lumber after emerging from the sawmill operation without further processing by SSI. Also, the posts require no further processing beyond the splitoff point. The decorative pieces must be planed and further sized after emerging from the sawmill. This additional processing costs $100,000 per month and normally results in a loss of 10% of the units entering the process. Without this planing and sizing process, there is still an active intermediate market for the unfinished decorative pieces where the selling price averages $60 per unit.

Required

1. Based on the information given for Sonimad Sawmill, Inc., allocate the joint processing costs of $1,000,000 to each of the three product lines using:

a. Sales value at splitoff method,

b. Physical-measures method (volume in units), and

c. Estimated NRV method.

2. Prepare an analysis for Sonimad Sawmill, Inc., that compares processing the decorative pieces further, as they presently do, with selling them as a rough-cut product immediately at split-off.

3. Assume Sonimad Sawmill announced that in six months it will sell the rough-cut product at splitoff due to increasing competitive pressure. Identify at least three types of likely behavior that will be demonstrated by the skilled labor in the planing and sizing process as a result of this announcement. Include in your discussion how this behavior could be improved by management.

15-31 Joint and byproducts, estimated NRV method. (CPA) The Harrison Corporation produces three products—Alpha, Beta, and Gamma. Alpha and Gamma are joint products, and Beta is a byproduct of Alpha. No joint costs are to be allocated to the byproduct. The production processes for a given year are as follows:

a. In Department 1, 110,000 pounds of direct material, Rho, are processed at a total cost of $120,000. After processing in Department 1, 60% of the units are transferred to Department 2, and 40% of the units (now Gamma) are transferred to Department 3.

b. In Department 2, the material is further processed at a total additional cost of $38,000. Then 70% of the units (now Alpha) are transferred to Department 4, and 30% emerge as Beta, the byproduct, to be sold at $1.20 per pound. Separable marketing costs for Beta are $8,100.

c. In Department 4, Alpha is processed at a total additional cost of $23,660. After this processing, Alpha is ready for sale at $5 per pound.

d. In Department 3, Gamma is processed at a total additional cost of $165,000. In this department, a normal loss of units of Gamma occurs, which equals 10% of the good units of output of Gamma. The remaining good units of output of Gamma are then sold for $12 per pound.

Required

1. Prepare a schedule showing the allocation of the joint costs between Alpha and Gamma using the estimated NRV method. The estimated NRV of Beta should be treated as a reduction of the $120,000 joint cost of Department 1.

2. Independent of your answer to requirement 1, assume that $102,000 of total joint costs were appropriately allocated to Alpha. Assume also that there were 48,000 pounds of Alpha and 20,000 pounds of Beta available to sell. Prepare an income statement through the gross margin line item for Alpha using the following facts:

   a. During the year, sales of Alpha were 80% of the pounds available for sale. There was no beginning inventory.

   b. The estimated NRV of Beta available for sale is to be deducted from the cost of producing Alpha. The ending inventory of Alpha is to be based on the net costs of production.

   c. All other cost and selling price data are listed in A–D above.

15-32 Joint-cost allocation, relevant costs. (R. Capettini) Consider the following scenario. Each day a butcher buys a 200-pound pig for $300. The pig can be processed to yield the following five products:

	Selling Price Per Pound	Weight
Pork chops	$ 4.00	30
Ham	$ 3.00	50
Bacon	$ 1.60	100
Pig's feet	$ 1.00	15
Hide	$10.00	5
		200

Day 1 The butcher buys a pig. The $300 joint cost of the pig is allocated to individual products based on the relative weights of the products.

	Selling Price	Weight (Pounds)	Revenues	−	Joint Costs Allocated	=	Operating Income
Pork chops	$ 4.00	30	$120	−	$ 45.00	=	$ 75.00
Ham	3.00	50	150	−	75.00	=	75.00
Bacon	1.60	100	160	−	150.00	=	10.00
Pig's feet	1.00	15	15	−	22.50	=	(7.50)
Hide	10.00	5	50	−	7.50	=	42.50
			$495	−	$300.00	=	$195.00

Day 2 The butcher buys an identical pig and throws out the pig's feet because they have been shown to lose money. She now has 185 pounds of "good output."

	Selling Price	Weight (Pounds)	Revenues	−	Joint Costs Allocated	=	Operating Income
Pork chops	$ 4.00	30	$120	−	$ 48.65	=	$ 71.35
Ham	3.00	50	150	−	81.08	=	68.92
Bacon	1.60	100	160	−	162.16	=	(2.16)
Hide	10.00	5	50	−	8.11	=	41.89
			$480	−	$300.00	=	$180.00

Day 3 The butcher buys an identical pig and throws out the pig's feet and the bacon because they have been shown to lose money. She now has 85 pounds of "good output."

	Selling Price	Weight (Pounds)	Revenues	−	Joint Costs Allocated	=	Operating Income
Pork chops	$ 4.00	30	$120	−	$105.88	=	$ 14.12
Ham	3.00	50	150	−	176.47	=	(26.47)
Hide	10.00	5	50	−	17.65	=	32.35
			$320	−	$300.00	=	$ 20.00

Day 4 The butcher buys an identical pig and throws out the pig's feet, the bacon, and the ham because they have been shown to lose money. She now has 35 pounds of "good output."

	Selling Price	Weight (Pounds)	Revenues	−	Joint Costs Allocated	=	Operating Income
Pork chops	$ 4.00	30	$120	−	$257.14	=	$(137.14)
Hide	10.00	5	50	−	42.86	=	7.14
			$170	−	$300.00	=	$(130.00)

Day 5 The butcher buys an identical pig and throws out the pig's feet, the bacon, the ham, and the pork chops because they have been shown to lose money. She now has 5 pounds of "good output."

	Selling Price	Weight (Pounds)	Revenues	−	Joint Costs Allocated	=	Operating Income
Hide	$10.00	5	50	−	$300	=	$(250)

Day 6 The butcher buys an identical pig and throws out the whole pig because each product has been shown to lose money. Therefore, she loses $300.

Required

1. Comment on the preceding series of decisions.
2. How would the joint costs be allocated to all five products using the sales value at splitoff method?
3. Should the operating income numbers from requirement 2 be used to determine if the butcher is better off by selling or not selling individual products?

15-33 Estimated NRV method, byproducts. (CMA, adapted) Princess Corporation grows, processes, packages, and sells three joint apple products: (a) sliced apples that are used in frozen pies, (b) applesauce, and (c) apple juice. The outside skin of the apple, processed as animal feed, is treated as a byproduct. Princess uses the estimated NRV method to allocate costs of the joint process to its joint products. The byproduct is inventoried at its estimated selling price when produced. The NRV of the byproduct is used to reduce the joint production costs before the splitoff point. The following details of Princess production process are available:

♦ The apples are washed and the outside skin is removed in the Cutting Department. The apples are then cored and trimmed for slicing. The three joint products and the byproduct are recognizable after processing in the Cutting Department. Each product is then transferred to a separate department for final processing.

♦ The trimmed apples are moved to the Slicing Department, where they are sliced and frozen. Any juice generated during the slicing operation is frozen with the slices.

♦ The pieces of apple trimmed from the fruit are processed into applesauce in the Crushing Department. The juice generated during this operation is used in the applesauce.

♦ The core and any surplus apple pieces generated from the Cutting Department are pulverized into a liquid in the Juicing Department. There is a loss equal to 8% of the weight of the good output produced in this department.

♦ The outside skin is chopped into animal feed and packaged in the Feed Department. It can be kept in cold storage until needed.

A total of 270,000 pounds of apples were processed in the Cutting Department during November. The following schedule shows the costs incurred in each department, the proportion by weight transferred to the four final processing departments, and the selling price of each end product:

Processing Data and Costs
November 2000

Department	Costs Incurred	Proportion of Product by Weight Transferred to Departments	Selling Price Per Pound of Final Product
Cutting	$60,000		
Slicing	11,280	33%	$0.80
Crushing	8,550	30	0.55
Juicing	3,000	27	0.40
Feed	700	10	0.10
Total	$83,530	100%	

Required
1. For the month of November 2000, calculate:
   a. The output of apple slices, applesauce, apple juice, and animal feed, in pounds,
   b. The estimated net realizable value at the splitoff point of each joint product,
   c. The amount of Cutting Department costs assigned to each joint product and the amount assigned to the byproduct following Princess' cost allocation method described above, and
   d. The gross margin in dollars for each joint product.
2. Comment on the significance to management of the gross-margin dollar information by joint product for planning and control purposes, as distinguished from inventory costing purposes.

15-34 Joint product/byproduct distinctions, ethics (continuation of 15-33). Princess Corporation classifies animal feed as a byproduct. The byproduct is inventoried at its selling price when produced. The net realizable value of the product is used to reduce the joint production costs before the splitoff point. Prior to 2000, Princess classified both apple juice and animal feed as byproducts. These byproducts were not recognized in the accounting system until sold. Revenues from their sale were treated as a revenue item in the income statement.

Princess Corporation uses a "management by objectives" basis to compensate its managers. Every six months managers are given "stretch" targets for the operating income to revenue ratio. They receive no bonus if the target is not met and a fixed amount of bonus if the target is met or exceeded.

1. If Princess's managers aim to maximize their bonuses over time, what byproduct method (the pre-2000 method or the 2000 method) would a product manager prefer?
2. How might a controller gain insight into whether the manager of apple products is "abusing" the accounting system in an effort to maximize his bonus?

COLLABORATIVE LEARNING EXERCISE

15-35 **Joint-cost allocation, process further or sell byproducts.** Goodson Pharmaceutical Company manufactures three joint products from a joint process: Altox, Lorex, and Hycol. Data regarding these products for the fiscal year ended May 31, 2000 are as follows:

	Altox	Lorex	Hycol
Units produced	170,000	500,000	330,000
Selling price per unit at splitoff	$3.50	—	$2.00
Separable costs	—	$1,400,000	—
Final selling price per unit	—	$5.00	—

The joint production cost up to the splitoff point where Altox, Lorex, and Hycol become separable products is $1,800,000 (which includes the $17,500 disposal costs for Dorzine as described below).

The president of Goodson, Arlene Franklin is reviewing an opportunity to change the way in which these three products are processed and sold. Proposed changes for each product are as follows:

◆ Altox is currently sold at the splitoff point to a manufacturer of vitamins. Altox can also be processed into a blood pressure medication. However, this additional processing causes a loss of 20,000 units of Altox. The separable costs to further process Altox are estimated to be $250,000 annually. The blood pressure medication sells for $5.50 per unit.

◆ Lorex is currently processed further after the splitoff point and is sold by Goodson as a cold remedy. The company has received an offer from another pharmaceutical company to purchase Lorex at the splitoff point for $2.25 per unit.

◆ Hycol is an oil produced from the joint process and is currently sold at the splitoff point to a cosmetics manufacturer. Goodson's Research Department has suggested that the company process this product further and sell it as an ointment to relieve muscle pain. The additional processing would cost $75,000 annually and would result in 25% more units of product. The ointment sells for $1.80 per unit.

The joint process currently used by Goodson also produces 50,000 units of Dorzine, a hazardous chemical waste product. The company pays $0.35 per unit to properly dispose of the Dorzine. Dietriech Mills, Inc., is interested in using the Dorzine as a solvent. However, Goodson would have to refine the Dorzine at an additional annual cost of $43,000. Dietriech would purchase all the refined Dorzine produced by Goodson and is willing to pay $0.75 for each unit.

Required

Form groups of two or more students to complete the following requirements.

1. Allocate the $1,800,000 joint production cost to Altox, Lorex, and Hycol using the estimated NRV method.
2. Identify which of the three joint products Goodson Pharmaceutical Company should sell at the splitoff point in the future and which of the three joint products the company should process further in order to maximize operating income. Support your decisions with appropriate computations.
3. Assume the Goodson Pharmaceutical Company has decided to refine the waste product Dorzine for sale to Dietriech Mills, Inc., and will treat Dorzine as a byproduct of the joint process in the future.
   a. Evaluate whether or not Goodson made the correct decision regarding Dorzine, supporting your answer with appropriate computations.
   b. Explain whether the decision to treat Dorzine as a byproduct will affect the decisions reached in requirement 2.

16

Revenues, Sales Variances, and Customer-Profitability Analysis

learning objectives

When you have finished studying this chapter, you should be able to

1. Give examples of the bundling of products that gives rise to revenue-allocation issues

2. Allocate the revenues of a bundled package to the individual products in that package

3. Provide additional information about the sales-volume variance by calculating the sales-mix and sales-quantity variances

4. Provide additional information about the sales-quantity variance by calculating the market-share and market-size variances

5. Explain what information is pivotal to the reliability of market-share and market-size variances

6. Discuss why revenues can differ across customers purchasing the same product

7. Apply the concept of cost hierarchy to customer costing

8. Prepare a customer-profitability report

Super market chains increasingly are offering loyalty programs to entice customers to make a high percentage of their lifetime purchases with the chain.

In preceding chapters, we have highlighted how a detailed understanding of costs is essential when making decisions related to products, services, customers, and departments. We have also highlighted the importance of costs in managing company operations. The other half of the profit equation—revenues—is equally important. Companies that prosper make revenue planning and revenue analysis top priorities for their managers.

This chapter covers three revenue-related topics. Part One on Revenue Allocation examines how challenging revenue-allocation issues arise with the now commonly used practice of selling multiple products or services as a single bundle for a single price. Part Two on Sales Variances highlights how the tools introduced in Chapter 7 can be used to analyze the variances of companies with revenues from multiple products. The Appendix shows how the framework explained in Part Two of this chapter helps analyze cost variances for a manufacturing company with substitutable inputs. Part Three on Customer-Profitability Analysis explores topics related to customer revenues and customer costs. Having a customer focus is a key theme underlying many planning and control decisions of managers. Part Three highlights several ways management accountants can help managers better focus on their customers.

◆ PART ONE: REVENUE ALLOCATION

REVENUES AND BUNDLED PRODUCTS

Revenues are inflows of assets (almost always cash or accounts receivable) received for products or services provided to customers. Just as costs can be allocated to specific products, so can revenues. **Revenue allocation** occurs when revenues are related to a particular revenue object, but cannot be traced to it in an economically feasible (cost-effective) way. A *revenue object* is anything for which a separate measurement of revenue is desired. Examples of revenue objects include products, customers, and divisions. We will illustrate revenue-allocation issues using the Software Division of the Superhighway Group. This division develops, sells, and supports three software packages:

1. WordMaster—current version is WordMaster 5.0, which was released 36 months ago. Wordmaster was the company's initial product and is a word-processing program.

2. SpreadMaster—current version is SpreadMaster 3.0, which was released 18 months ago. It is a spreadsheet program.

3. FinanceMaster—current version is FinanceMaster 1.0. This product, the company's most recent, has attracted a lot of favorable media attention. It assists in budgeting and cash management. The 1.0 version was released 6 months ago (July 2000).

Superhighway sells these three products individually and also sells them as bundled products.

A **bundled product** is a package of two or more products (or services), sold for a single price, where the individual components of the bundle also may be sold as separate items at their own "stand-alone" prices. The price for a bundled product is typically less than the sum of the prices of the individual products sold separately. For example, banks often provide individual customers with a bundle of services from different departments (checking, safety deposit box, and investment advisory) for a single fee. A resort hotel may offer, for a single amount per customer, a weekend package that includes services from its Lodging (the room), Food (the restaurant), and Recreational (golf) Departments. Where department or division managers have revenue or profit responsibilities for individual products, the issue arises of how to allocate the bundled revenue amount among the individual products in that bundle.[1]

The Superhighway Group encounters revenue-allocation decisions with its bundled product sales (termed "suite sales"). Here, two or more of its software products are sold as a single package. Managers at Superhighway are keenly interested in individual product-profitability figures because product managers are responsible for the operating income of each product. Moreover, its Software Department engineers are organized on a product-by-product basis and receive a percentage of product profitability as part of their annual bonus. In addition, the WordMaster and SpreadMaster products include components developed by outside (non-Superhighway) developers, and these developers receive a percentage of product revenues as part of their compensation.

REVENUE-ALLOCATION METHODS

How should Superhighway allocate suite revenues to individual products? Information pertaining to the three "stand-alone" and "suite" selling prices of its products in 2000 is as follows:

	Selling Price
Stand-alone	
WordMaster	$125
SpreadMaster	150
FinanceMaster	225
Suite	
Word + Spread	$220
Word + Finance	280
Word + Spread + Finance	380

The manufacturing cost per unit of each software product are WordMaster, $18; SpreadMaster, $20; and FinanceMaster, $25.

The two main revenue-allocation methods are the stand-alone method and the incremental method. We now discuss each method in turn.[2]

Stand-Alone Revenue-Allocation Method

The **stand-alone revenue-allocation method** uses product-specific information on the products in the bundle as weights for allocating the bundled revenues to the individual products. The term "stand-alone" refers to the product as a separate (nonsuite) item. Consider the Word + Finance suite, which sells for $280. Four types of weights for the stand-alone method are as follows:

1. *Selling prices.* The individual selling prices are $125 for WordMaster and $225 for FinanceMaster. The weights for allocating the $280 between the two products are as follows:

$$\text{Word:} \quad \frac{\$125}{\$125 + \$225} \times \$280 = 0.36 \times \$280 = \$101$$

$$\text{Finance:} \quad \frac{\$225}{\$125 + \$225} \times \$280 = 0.64 \times \$280 = \$179$$

The selling prices used in this example are the list prices charged by Superhighway in its direct sales distribution channel. A variation of this approach is to use the

Curriculum Linkage Allocation of rev. to bundled products raises issues similar to those involved in allocation of common costs (Chap. 14). The 2 most common methods of allocating bundled revs. parallel the methods of allocating common costs, as described in Chap. 14: (1) the stand-alone method, and (2) the incremental method.

Points to Stress The stand-alone method allocates common *costs* in proportion to the individ. users' costs (see Chap. 14). However, when allocating bundled *revenues*, the proportion of revs. allocated to each product can be calculated on 4 alternative bases: (1) individual product unit selling prices (*revenues*), (2) individual product unit costs, (3) # of *units*, and (4) stand-alone product *revenues*. Conceptually, it is preferable to allocate common revs. based on unit revs. or stand-alone revs., since they best reflect customers' willingness to pay for the different products. However, if the products are never sold separately, individual selling prices and revs. are unavailable, so revs. are allocated based on unit costs (which should be available in the firm's acctg. records), or simply on the # of units.

---

[1]Revenue-allocation issues also arise in external reporting. Statement of Position 97-2 (Software Revenue Recognition) states that with bundled products, revenue allocation "based on vendor-specific objective evidence of fair value" is required. The "price charged when the element is sold separately" is said to be "objective evidence of fair value." See *Journal of Accountancy* (January 1998, p. 106).

[2]These two methods have their counterparts in cost allocation. See Chapter 14 (pp. 516–517) for discussion.

Points to Stress Allocating common revs. based on unit mfg. costs will make the different products appear equally profitable. In the text's Superhighway example:

	Word	Finance
Revenues	$118	$162
Mfg. cost	(18)	(25)
Gross margin	100	137
Gross margin %	84.7%	84.6%

Points to Stress/Example The physical units-based method of rev. allocation is most appropriate when the values of the diff. products in the bundle are approx. equal. For example, the physical units method would clearly be inappropriate for a bundle that includes a washing machine and a box of detergent. It would be nonsensical to allocate half the rev. to the box of detergent. Similar issues arise with a joint airfare/airport transfer package.

New to This Edition A 4th stand-alone revenue-allocation method has been added: using stand-alone product revenues as the allocation base. This new method weights the allocation based on both quantities and selling prices.

actual average selling prices of the products. This weighting would recognize any price discounting that may occur.

2. *Unit costs.* This method uses the costs of the individual products to determine the weights for the revenue allocations. In this case, we use manufacturing cost per unit.

$$\text{Word:} \quad \frac{\$18}{\$18 + \$25} \times \$280 = 0.42 \times \$280 = \$118$$

$$\text{Finance:} \quad \frac{\$25}{\$18 + \$25} \times \$280 = 0.58 \times \$280 = \$162$$

3. *Physical units.* This method gives each product unit in the suite the same weight when allocating suite revenue to individual products. Thus, with two products in the Word + Finance suite, each product is allocated 50% of the suite revenues.

$$\text{Word:} \quad \frac{1}{1 + 1} \times \$280 = 0.50 \times \$280 = \$140$$

$$\text{Finance:} \quad \frac{1}{1 + 1} \times \$280 = 0.50 \times \$280 = \$140$$

In the special case where all products in the bundle have the same stand-alone selling prices, weighting by physical units and weighting by selling prices will yield identical revenue allocations.

4. *Stand-alone product revenues.* Stand-alone product revenues will capture the quantity of each product sold as well as their selling prices. Assume that the stand-alone revenues in 2000 are WordMaster, $28 milllion; SpreadMaster, $15 million; and FinanceMaster, $7 million. The weights for the Word + Finance suite would be:

$$\text{Word:} \quad \frac{\$28 \text{ million}}{\$28 \text{ million} + \$7 \text{ million}} \times \$280 = 0.80 \times \$280 = \$224$$

$$\text{Finance:} \quad \frac{\$7 \text{ million}}{\$28 \text{ million} + \$7 \text{ million}} \times \$280 = 0.20 \times \$280 = \$56$$

The lower revenue-allocation to FinanceMaster is, in part, due to it only being released partway through 2000 (July 2000).

These four approaches to determining weights for the stand-alone method yield the following revenue allocations to the individual products:

Revenue-Allocation Weights	WordMaster	FinanceMaster
Selling prices	$101	$179
Unit costs	118	162
Physical units	140	140
Stand-alone product revenues	224	56

The selling price and stand-alone product revenue weights have the advantage that they frequently are good indicators of the minimum benefits customers receive from those products. Companies receive revenues because customers exchange cash in return for the benefits from the companies' products. Weighting schemes that use revenue information better capture "benefits received" by customers than do unit costs or physical units. Allocating on the basis of stand-alone product revenues also has the advantage of giving more weight to the product that generates more revenues and that probably drives the sales of the bundled product. The physical units revenue allocation is typically rationalized on ease of use or the limitations of alternative methods (such as when selling prices are unstable or unit costs are difficult to calculate at the individual product level).

Incremental Revenue-Allocation Method

The **incremental revenue-allocation method** ranks the individual products in a bundle according to criteria determined by management, and then uses this ranking to allocate the bundled revenues to the individual products. The first-ranked product is termed the *primary product* in the bundle. The second-ranked product is termed the *first incremental product*, the third-ranked product is the *second incremental product*, and so on.

Who decides on product ranking in the incremental revenue-allocation method? One approach is to survey customers on the relative importance of individual products in their decision to purchase the bundled products. A second approach is to use data on recent stand-alone performance of the individual products in the bundle. A third approach is for top management to decide the rankings based on their knowledge or intuition.

Consider again the Word + Finance suite of Superhighway. Assume Finance-Master is designated as the primary product. If the suite selling price exceeds the stand-alone price of the primary product, the primary product is allocated 100% of its stand-alone revenue. This is the case for the Word and Finance suite. The suite price of $280 exceeds the stand-alone price of $225 for Finance. Thus, Finance is allocated revenues of $225, and the $55 ($280 – $225) remaining revenue is allocated to Word:

Curriculum Linkage The incremental rev.-allocation method parallels the incremental method for allocation of common costs. However, in the common cost situation, nobody wants their product to be identified as the primary user, since the primary user is charged the bulk of the cost. In contrast, for rev. allocation, everyone wants their product to be identified as the primary user, since the primary product will be allocated the bulk of the rev.

Product	Revenue Allocated	Revenue Remaining to Be Allocated to Other Products
Finance	$225	$55 ($280 – $225)
Word	55	0
Total revenue allocated	$280	

If the suite price is less than or equal to the stand-alone price of the primary product, the primary product is allocated 100% of the suite revenue. All other products in the suite would receive zero allocation of revenue.

Where there are more than two products in the suite, the suite revenue is allocated sequentially. Assume Finance is the primary product in SAG's three-product suite (Finance + Spread + Word). This suite sells for $380. Spread is the first incremental product while Word is the second incremental product. The allocation of the $380 suite revenues proceeds as follows:

Points to Stress The incremental method of rev. allocation effectively discounts incremental products, to the benefit of the primary product. Consequently, this method is likely to lead to acrimonious disputes among mgrs.

Product	Revenue Allocated	Revenue Remaining to Be Allocated to Other Products
Finance	$225	$155 ($380 – $225)
Spread	150	5 ($155 – $150)
Word	5	0 ($5 – $5)
Total revenue allocated	$380	

Now suppose Finance is the primary product, Word is the first incremental product, and Spread is the second incremental product:

Product	Revenue Allocated	Revenue Remaining to Be Allocated to Other Products
Finance	$225	$155 ($380 – $225)
Word	125	30 ($155 – $125)
Spread	30	0 ($30 – $30)
Total revenue allocated	$380	

Clearly, the ranking of the individual products in the suite is a key factor in determining the revenues allocated to them.

Product managers at Superhighway likely would differ on how they believe their individual products contribute to sales of the suite products. It is possible that each product manager would claim to be responsible for the primary product in the Word + Spread + Finance suite! Since the stand-alone revenue-allocation method does not require rankings of individual products in the suite, it is less likely to place product managers in highly acrimonious debates.

Other Revenue-Allocation Methods

Management judgment not explicitly based on a specific formula is an alternative method of revenue-allocation. In one case, the president of a software company decided to issue a set of revenue-allocation weights after the managers of the three products in a bundled suite could not themselves agree on a set of weights. The weights chosen by the president for the three products were 45% for product A, 45% for product B, and 10% for product C. The factors the president considered included stand-alone selling prices (all three were very similar), stand-alone unit sales (A and B were over 10 times more than C), product ratings by independent experts, and consumer awareness. The product C manager complained that his 10% weighting dramatically short-changed the contribution of product C to suite revenues. The president responded that its inclusion in the suite greatly increased consumer exposure to product C with the result that product C's total revenues would be far larger (even with only 10% of suite revenues) than had it not been included in the suite.

Part One of this chapter has discussed revenue-allocation. Part Two dicusses sales variances.

PROBLEM FOR SELF-STUDY

PROBLEM

Business Horizons (BH) produces and markets videos for sale to the business community. It hires well-known business speakers to present new developments in their area of expertise in video format. The compensation paid to each speaker is individually negotiated. It always has a component based on the percentage of revenues from the sale of the video, but that percentage is not uniform across speakers. Moreover, some speakers negotiate separate fixed-dollar payments or multiple-video deals.

BH sells most videos as separate items. However, there is a growing trend for videos also to be sold as part of bundled packages. BH offered bundled packages of its three best-selling videos in 2000. Individual and bundled sales of these three videos for 2000 are:

INDIVIDUAL SALES

Speaker	Title	Units Sold	Selling Price	Speaker Royalty
Jeannett Smith	Negotiating for Win-Win	25,000	$150	24%
Mark Coyne	Marketing for the Internet	17,000	$120	16%
Laurie Daley	Electronic Commerce	8,000	$130	19%

BUNDLED PRODUCT SALES

Titles in Bundle	Units Sold	Selling Price
Negotiating for Win-Win + Marketing for the Internet	12,000	$210
Negotiating for Win-Win + Electronic Commerce	5,000	$220
Marketing for the Internet + Electronic Commerce	4,000	$190
Negotiating + Marketing + Electronic	11,000	$280

Required

1. Allocate the bundled product revenues to the individual videos using the stand-alone revenue-allocation method (using selling prices as the weights).
2. Describe (without computations) an alternative method of allocating the bundled product revenues to that in requirement 1.

SOLUTION

1. The weights in the stand-alone method are based on the stand-alone selling prices of the videos in the bundled package. The following table details these weights,

which are then used to allocate the revenues of the bundled package to the three individual videos:

Allocation Formula	Negotiating	Marketing	Electronic
N + M: ($150 ÷ $270) × $210 × 12,000	$1,400,000		
N + E: ($150 ÷ $280) × $220 × 5,000	589,286		
N + M + E: ($150 ÷ $400) × $280 × 11,000	1,155,000		
Total	$3,144,286		
M + N: ($120 ÷ $270) × $210 × 12,000		$1,120,000	
M + E: ($120 ÷ $250) × $190 × 4,000		364,800	
M + N + E: ($120 ÷ $400) × $280 × 11,000		924,000	
Total		$2,408,800	
E + N: ($130 ÷ $280) × $220 × 5,000			$ 510,714
E + M: ($130 ÷ $250) × $190 × 4,000			395,200
E + N + M: ($130 ÷ $400) × $280 × 11,000			1,001,000
Total			$1,906,914

2. An alternative method to allocating the bundled product revenues is the incremental revenue-allocation method. Here the individual videos in the bundle are ranked in order of importance, and the revenues are allocated to each product using stand-alone selling prices until all the bundled revenue has been fully allocated. Use of this approach would likely create some friction among the three business speakers. It would be in each speaker's interest to claim to be the primary speaker driving sales of the bundle. The actual 2000 units sold figures would enable Business Horizons to give a market-success-based ranking of individual business speakers if it used the incremental revenue-allocation method.

◆ PART TWO: SALES VARIANCES

SALES-VOLUME VARIANCE COMPONENTS

The levels of detail approach introduced in Chapter 7 included discussion of the static-budget variance (Level 1), the flexible-budget variance, and the sales-volume variance (Level 2). We extend this detail to the Level 3 and Level 4 variances shown here.[3]

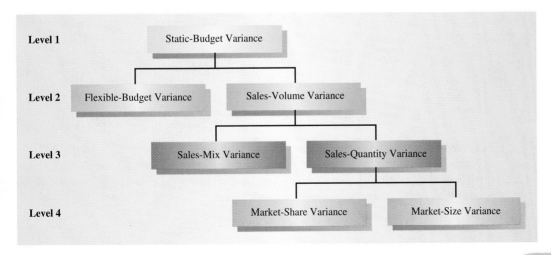

Curriculum Linkage Part Two of this chapter extends the variance analysis discussed in Chap. 7. Chapter 7's sales-volume var. is decomposed here into the sales-mix var. and the sales-quantity var. The SQV is then further decomposed into mkt. size and mkt. share vars. These vars. provide info on why sales differed from expectations, which helps mkt. mgrs. plan and control their activities. A later section explains an analogous decomposition of the flexible-budget var. (for costs) into yield and mix vars.

[3]The presentation of the variances in Part Two and the Appendix to this chapter draws on teaching notes prepared by J. K. Harris.

Reinforcing Problems Revenue and sales variances are covered in Exer. 16-19 through 16-22 and Probs. 16-28 through 16-31.

We continue to use the Superhighway Group in our analysis. This time we examine Superhighway's Computer Division, which manufactures and sells three related products:

1. Plum—is sold mostly to college students and for the home market.
2. Portable Plum—is a portable version of the Plum, with an organizer and Internet capabilities.
3. Super Plum—has a larger memory and more capabilities than the Plum and is targeted at the business market.

Budgeted and actual operating data for 2000 follow:

BUDGET FOR 2000

	Selling Price Per Unit	Variable Costs Per Unit	Contribution Margin Per Unit	Sales Volume in Units	Sales Mix (Based on Units)	Contribution Margin
Plum	$1,200	$ 700	$ 500	700	70%[a]	$350,000
Portable Plum	800	500	300	100	10	30,000
Super Plum	5,000	3,000	2,000	200	20	400,000
Total				1,000	100%	$780,000

[a]For example, percentage of Plum in sales mix = 700 ÷ 1,000 total units = 70 percent.

ACTUAL RESULTS FOR 2000

	Selling Price Per Unit	Variable Costs Per Unit	Contribution Margin Per Unit	Sales Volume in Units	Sales Mix (Based on Units)	Contribution Margin
Plum	$1,100	$ 500	$ 600	825	75%	$495,000
Portable Plum	650	400	250	165	15	41,250
Super Plum	3,500	2,500	1,000	110	10	110,000
Total				1,100	100%	$646,250

The analysis in Part Two emphasizes variance analysis of Superhighway's contribution margin. The basic framework we present can also be used to analyze revenues or individual variable costs.

Static-Budget Variance

Teaching Tip Ask students to distinguish between static budgets and flexible budgets. A flexible budget is adjusted to *actual* outputs achieved, while a static budget is for the *expected* level of outputs.

The *static-budget variance* is the difference between an actual result and a budgeted amount in the static budget. Using the figures for Superhighway's contribution margin:

	Actual Results	−	Static-Budget Amount	=	Static-Budget Variance
Plum	$495,000	−	$350,000	=	$145,000 F
Portable Plum	41,250	−	30,000	=	11,250 F
Super Plum	110,000	−	400,000	=	290,000 U
Total static-budget variance	$646,250	−	$780,000	=	$133,750 U

Superhighway has favorable static-budget variances for Plum and Portable Plum and an unfavorable one for Super Plum. More information about the $133,750 unfavorable total static-budget variance can be gained by subdividing it into the flexible-budget variance and the sales-volume variance.

Flexible-Budget and Sales-Volume Variances

Correcting Student Misconceptions Chapter 7 explained how the flexible-budget variance is decomposed into price and eff. vars. Point out to students that for revenues the entire variance is all a price var. (i.e., we don't measure the efficiency of unit sales).

The *flexible-budget variance* is the difference between an actual result and the flexible-budget amount based on the level of output actually sold in the budget period. The actual result is equal to the actual contribution margin per unit times the actual unit volume. The flexible-budget amount is equal to the budgeted contribution margin times the actual unit volume.

	Actual Results	−	Flexible-Budget Amount	=	Flexible-Budget Variance
Plum	($600 × 825)	−	($500 × 825)	=	$ 82,500 F
Portable Plum	($250 × 165)	−	($300 × 165)	=	8,250 U
Super Plum	($1,000 × 110)	−	($2,000 × 110)	=	110,000 U
Total flexible-budget variance				=	$ 35,750 U

Correcting Student Misconceptions
Students often confuse the decomposition of sales-volume var. (SVV) with Chap. 7's decomposition of the flexible-budget var. (FBV) for costs. They are different. The FBV is based on *inputs*, while the SVV is based on *outputs*. The SVV is decomposed into a sales-mix var. and a sales-quan. var. (SQV). The SQV is further decomposed into a mkt-sh. var. and a mkt-size var.

The $35,750 unfavorable total flexible-budget variance is heavily influenced by the actual contribution margin on Super Plum being only $1,000 per unit compared to the budgeted $2,000 per unit.

The *sales-volume variance* shows the effect of the difference between the actual and budgeted quantity of the variable used to "flex" the flexible budget. For the contribution margin of Superhighway, this variable is units sold. This variance can be computed for each computer product as follows:

	(Actual Sales Quantity in Units	−	Static-Budget Sales Quantity in Units)	×	Budgeted Contribution Margin Per Unit	=	Sales-Volume Variance
Plum	(825	−	700)	×	$500	=	$ 62,500 F
Portable Plum	(165	−	100)	×	$300	=	19,500 F
Super Plum	(110	−	200)	×	$2,000	=	180,000 U
Total sales-volume variance							$ 98,000 U

Note that the total sales-volume variance ($98,000 U) plus the total flexible-budget variance ($35,750 U) is equal to the total static-budget variance ($133,750 U). While the total sales-volume variance is $98,000 unfavorable, there is a combination of favorable variances for Plum and Portable Plum and an unfavorable variance for Super Plum. Managers can gain additional insight into sales-volume changes by separating the sales-volume variance into a sales-mix variance and a sales-quantity variance.

SALES-MIX AND SALES-QUANTITY VARIANCES

Exhibit 16-1 shows how both the sales-mix and sales-quantity variances can be computed using the columnar approach introduced in Chapter 7. Refer to this exhibit when reading the following discussion of these two variances.

OBJECTIVE 3
Provide additional information about the sales-volume variance by calculating the sales-mix and sales-quantity variances

Sales-Mix Variance

The **sales-mix variance** is the difference between two amounts: (1) the budgeted amount for the actual sales mix, and (2) the budgeted amount for the budgeted sales mix. The formula and computations (using data from p. 574) of the sales-mix variance in terms of the contribution margin for SuperHighway are:

Teaching Tip Students find sales-mix and qty. vars. difficult. They tend to get lost in the detailed calculations, so it is important to go slowly. Stress the intuition. For example, the SQV arises because the total qty. of units actually sold differs from the static budget. The SMV arises because the mix of individual products actually sold differs from the budgeted mix. To capture the SQV, we hold the sales mix constant; and to capture the SMV, we hold the sales qty. constant. Add perspective by emphasizing the big picture (e.g., Exh. 16-3).

	Actual Units of All Products Sold	×	(Actual Sales-Mix Percentage	−	Budgeted Sales-Mix Percentage)	×	Budgeted Contribution Margin Per Unit	=	Sales-Mix Variance
Plum	1,100 ×		(0.75	−	0.70)	×	$500	=	$ 27,500 F
Portable Plum	1,100 ×		(0.15	−	0.10)	×	$300	=	16,500 F
Super Plum	1,100 ×		(0.10	−	0.20)	×	$2,000	=	220,000 U
Total sales-mix variance									$176,000 U

A favorable sales-mix variance arises for individual products when the actual sales-mix percentage exceeds the budgeted sales-mix percentage. A favorable sales-mix variance arises for both Plum (75% actual versus 70% budgeted) and Portable Plum (15% actual versus 10% budgeted). In contrast, Super Plum has an unfavorable

EXHIBIT 16-1

Sales-Mix and Sales-Quantity Variance Analysis of the Contribution Margin of Superhighway Group Computer Division for 2000

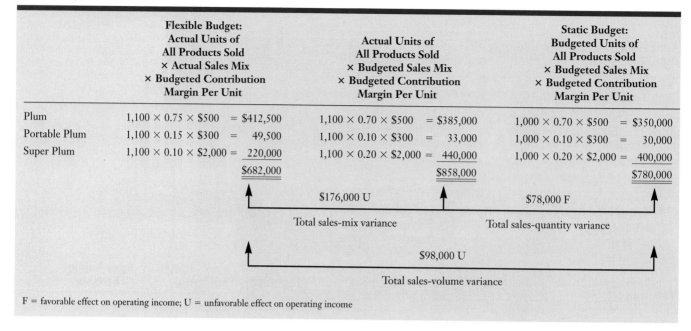

	Flexible Budget: Actual Units of All Products Sold × Actual Sales Mix × Budgeted Contribution Margin Per Unit		Actual Units of All Products Sold × Budgeted Sales Mix × Budgeted Contribution Margin Per Unit		Static Budget: Budgeted Units of All Products Sold × Budgeted Sales Mix × Budgeted Contribution Margin Per Unit	
Plum	1,100 × 0.75 × $500 =	$412,500	1,100 × 0.70 × $500 =	$385,000	1,000 × 0.70 × $500 =	$350,000
Portable Plum	1,100 × 0.15 × $300 =	49,500	1,100 × 0.10 × $300 =	33,000	1,000 × 0.10 × $300 =	30,000
Super Plum	1,100 × 0.10 × $2,000 =	220,000	1,100 × 0.20 × $2,000 =	440,000	1,000 × 0.20 × $2,000 =	400,000
		$682,000		$858,000		$780,000

$176,000 U → Total sales-mix variance

$78,000 F → Total sales-quantity variance

$98,000 U → Total sales-volume variance

F = favorable effect on operating income; U = unfavorable effect on operating income

variance because the actual sales-mix percentage (10%) is less than the budgeted sales-mix percentage (20%).

The concept underlying the sales-mix variance is best explained in terms of the budgeted contribution margin per composite unit of the sales mix. A **composite product unit** is a hypothetical unit with weights based on the mix of individual products. In the following analysis, the composite product unit is computed in column 3 for the actual mix and column 5 for the budgeted mix:

	Budgeted Contribution Margin Per Unit (1)	Actual Sales-Mix Percentage (2)	Budgeted Contribution Margin Per Composite Unit for Actual Mix (3) = (1) × (2)	Budgeted Sales-Mix Percentage (4)	Budgeted Contribution Margin Per Composite Unit for Budgeted Mix (5) = (1) × (4)
Plum	$ 500	0.75	$375	0.70	$350
Portable Plum	300	0.15	45	0.10	30
Super Plum	2,000	0.10	200	0.20	400
			$620		$780

The actual sales mix has a budgeted contribution margin per composite unit of $620. The budgeted sales mix has a budgeted contribution margin per composite unit of $780 (which can alternatively be computed by dividing the total budgeted contribution margin of $780,000 by the total budgeted units of 1,000 (p. 574): $780,000 ÷ 1,000 = $780 per unit). Thus, the effect of the sales-mix shift for Superhighway is to decrease the budgeted contribution margin per composite unit by $160 ($780 − $620). For the 1,100 units actually sold, this decrease translates to an unfavorable sales-mix variance of $176,000 (1,100 × $160).

Managers should probe why the unfavorable sales-mix variance of $176,000 occurred in 2000. Is the major shift in Superhighway's sales-mix due to Plum and Portable Plum having better product performance vis-à-vis Super Plum? Is it due to a major competitor in Super Plum's segment of the market launching a technologically superior product that is lower priced? Is this sales-mix shift due to the initial sales-volume estimates being made without adequate analysis of the potential market in 2000? These and other possible explanations should be examined.

Sales-Quantity Variance

The **sales-quantity variance** is the difference between two amounts: (1) the budgeted amount based on actual units sold of all products and the budgeted mix, and (2) the amount in the static budget (which is based on the budgeted units to be sold of all products and the budgeted mix). The formula and computations for the sales-quantity variance in terms of contribution margin for Superhighway are:

$\left(\begin{array}{c}\text{Actual Units} \\ \text{of All} \\ \text{Products Sold}\end{array}\right.$	$\left.\begin{array}{c}\text{Budgeted} \\ \text{Units of All} \\ \text{Products Sold}\end{array}\right)$	×	Budgeted Sales-Mix Percentage	×	Budgeted Contribution Margin Per Unit	=	Sales-Quantity Variance
Plum	(1,100 − 1,000)	×	0.70	×	$ 500	=	$35,000 F
Portable Plum	(1,100 − 1,000)	×	0.10	×	$ 300	=	3,000 F
Super Plum	(1,100 − 1,000)	×	0.20	×	$2,000	=	40,000 F
Total sales-quantity variance							$78,000 F

This variance is favorable when the actual units of all products sold exceed the budgeted units of all products sold. Superhighway sold 100 more computer units than was budgeted, resulting in a favorable sales-quantity variance in contribution margin terms of $78,000. Managers would want to probe the reasons for the increase in sales. For example, did the higher sales come as a result of a competitor's production problems, the popularity of a particular model, or growth in the overall market?

The favorable sales-quantity variance of $78,000 is the algebraic sum of the sales-quantity variances for the individual products. The total variance can also be computed by using the budgeted contribution margin per composite unit amount: $(1,100 − 1,000) \times \$780 = \$78,000$ F.

Exhibit 16-1 highlights the contribution margin effect of the shift towards a mix with lower contribution-margin units (Plum and Portable Plum) and the effect of the 10% increase in total units sold (actual of 1,100 versus 1,000 budgeted). Further insight into the causes of the sales-quantity variance (the 10% increase in total units sold) can be gained from analyzing changes in Superhighway's share of the total market and in the size of the total market.

MARKET-SHARE AND MARKET-SIZE VARIANCES

Sales depend on overall demand for the industry's products as well as the company's share of the market. Assume that Superhighway derived its total unit sales budget for 2000 from a management estimate of a 20% market share and a total industry sales forecast by Micro-Information Services of 5,000 units. For 2000, Micro-Information reported actual industry sales of 6,875 units, so the actual market share is 16% (1,100 ÷ 6,875). Exhibit 16-2 shows the columnar presentation of the market-share and market-size variances of Superhighway.

Market-Share Variance

The **market-share variance** is the difference between two amounts: (1) the budgeted amount based on actual market size in units, *actual market share*, and budgeted contribution margin per composite unit for the budgeted mix, and (2) the budgeted amount based on actual market size in units, *budgeted market share*, and budgeted contribution margin per composite unit for the budgeted mix. The formula for computing the market-share variance for Superhighway is:

$$\begin{array}{c}\text{Market-share} \\ \text{variance}\end{array} = \begin{array}{c}\text{Actual} \\ \text{market size} \\ \text{in units}\end{array} \times \left(\begin{array}{c}\text{Actual} \\ \text{market} \\ \text{share}\end{array} - \begin{array}{c}\text{Budgeted} \\ \text{market} \\ \text{share}\end{array}\right) \times \begin{array}{c}\text{Budgeted} \\ \text{contribution margin} \\ \text{per composite unit} \\ \text{for budgeted mix}\end{array}$$

$$= 6{,}875 \times (0.16 - 0.20) \times \$780$$

$$= \$214{,}500 \text{ U}$$

OBJECTIVE 4

Provide additional information about the sales-quantity variance by calculating the market-share and market-size variances

Points to Stress Most mktg. mgrs. want to know why actual sales differ from budgeted sales. If the SQV is primarily due to uncontrollable changes in mkt. size, the firm may need to expand, downsize, or shift to new product mkts. In contrast, mkt. share is more controllable, since traditional mktg. activities such as pricing and promotion are more likely to affect mkt. share than total mkt. size. The SMV tells mgrs. whether the mix is shifting in favor of high or low rev. (margin) items when vars. are based on rev. (margins).

Points to Stress Vars. are often interrelated. A fav. sales rev. price var. (caused by a price increase) may reduce mkt. share (U mkt.-share var.) leading to reduced sales volume (U SQV and SVV).

EXHIBIT 16-2

Market-Share and Market-Size Variance Analysis of the Contribution Margin of Superhighway Group Computer Division for 2000

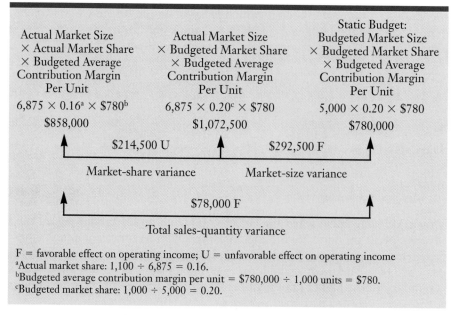

F = favorable effect on operating income; U = unfavorable effect on operating income
[a]Actual market share: 1,100 ÷ 6,875 = 0.16.
[b]Budgeted average contribution margin per unit = $780,000 ÷ 1,000 units = $780.
[c]Budgeted market share: 1,000 ÷ 5,000 = 0.20.

The budgeted contribution margin per composite unit for the budgeted mix is computed using the approach outlined earlier in this chapter (p. 576).

Superhighway lost four market-share percentage points—from the 20% budgeted share to the actual share of 16 percent. The $214,500 unfavorable variance highlights the impact of the contribution margin in this decline.

Market-Size Variance

The **market-size variance** is the difference between two amounts: (1) the budgeted amount based on *actual market size in units*, budgeted market share, and budgeted contribution margin per composite unit for budgeted mix, and (2) the static budget amount based on the *budgeted market size in units*, budgeted market share, and budgeted contribution margin per composite unit for budgeted mix. The formula for computing the market-size variance in terms of contribution margin for Superhighway is:

$$\begin{matrix} \text{Market-size} \\ \text{variance} \end{matrix} = \left(\begin{matrix} \text{Actual} \\ \text{market size} \\ \text{in units} \end{matrix} - \begin{matrix} \text{Budgeted} \\ \text{market size} \\ \text{in units} \end{matrix} \right) \times \begin{matrix} \text{Budgeted} \\ \text{market} \\ \text{share} \end{matrix} \times \begin{matrix} \text{Budgeted} \\ \text{contribution margin} \\ \text{per composite unit} \\ \text{for budgeted mix} \end{matrix}$$

$$= (6,875 - 5,000) \times 0.20 \times \$780$$

$$= \$292,500 \text{ F}$$

The market-size variance is favorable because the market size increased 37.5% [(6,875 − 5,000) ÷ 5,000].

Managers should probe why the market-share and market-size variances occurred in 2000. Was the $214,500 unfavorable market-share variance due to competitors introducing superior products during 2000? Did Superhighway's products experience quality-control problems that were the subject of negative media coverage? Companies that suffer continued large declines in market share often do not maintain the extensive exposure in the trade press that is often key to success in the computer industry. Is the favorable market-size variance of $292,500 due to an increase in market size that can be expected to continue in 2001, 2002, and beyond? If yes, the benefit to Superhighway of regaining or exceeding its budgeted 20% market share is very high. Some companies place more emphasis on the market-share

EXHIBIT 16-3
Overview of Contribution Margin Variances for Superhighway Group Computer Division
for 2000

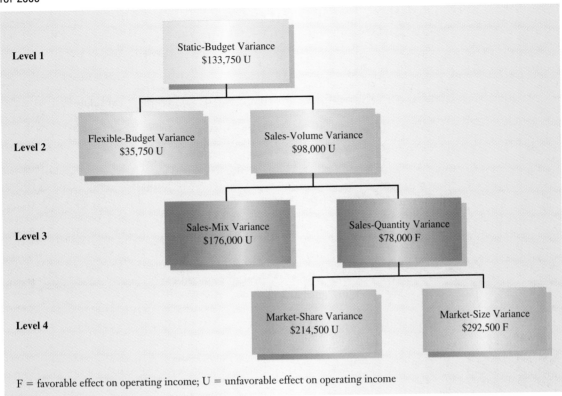

Level 1 — Static-Budget Variance $133,750 U

Level 2 — Flexible-Budget Variance $35,750 U | Sales-Volume Variance $98,000 U

Level 3 — Sales-Mix Variance $176,000 U | Sales-Quantity Variance $78,000 F

Level 4 — Market-Share Variance $214,500 U | Market-Size Variance $292,500 F

F = favorable effect on operating income; U = unfavorable effect on operating income

variance than the market-size variance when evaluating their managers. Why? Because they believe the market-size variance is influenced by growth and interest rates in the economy that are outside the manager's control, whereas the market-share variance measures how well managers performed relative to their peers.

A caution when computing market-size and market-share variances is appropriate. Reliable information on market size and market share is available for some but not all industries. For example, the soft-drink and television industries are cases where market-size and market-share statistics are widely available. In other industries, such as management consulting and personal financial planning, information about market size and market share is far less reliable and not published on a regular basis. Superhighway believes that the market-share and market-size data from Micro-Information Services is reliable and useful in its decision making.

Exhibit 16-3 presents an overview of the Level 1 to Level 4 variances. The appendix to this chapter applies the sales-mix and sales-quantity framework to the analysis of substitutable production inputs.

Parts One and Two of this chapter have discussed revenue allocation and sales variances. Part Three discusses customer-profitability analysis.

PROBLEM

The Payne Company manufactures two types of vinyl flooring. Budgeted and actual operating data for 2000 are:

	Static Budget			Actual Results		
	Commercial	Residential	Total	Commercial	Residential	Total
Units sales in rolls	20,000	60,000	80,000	25,200	58,800	84,000
Contribution margin	$10,000,000	$24,000,000	$34,000,000	$11,970,000	$24,696,000	$36,666,000

In late 1999, a marketing research firm estimated the industry volume for commercial and residential vinyl flooring in 2000 at 800,000 rolls. Actual industry volume for 2000 was 700,000 rolls.

Required

1. Compute the sales-mix variance and sales-quantity variance by type of vinyl flooring and in total.
2. Compute the market-share variance and market-size variance.
3. What insights do the variances in requirements 1 and 2 provide about Payne Company's performance in 2000?

SOLUTION

1. Actual sales-mix percentage:

$$\text{Commercial} = 25{,}200 \div 84{,}000 = 30\%$$

$$\text{Residential} = 58{,}800 \div 84{,}000 = 70\%$$

Budgeted sales-mix percentage:

$$\text{Commercial} = 20{,}000 \div 80{,}000 = 25\%$$

$$\text{Residential} = 60{,}000 \div 80{,}000 = 75\%$$

Budgeted contribution margin per unit:

$$\text{Commercial} = 10{,}000{,}000 \div 20{,}000 = \$500$$

$$\text{Residential} = 24{,}000{,}000 \div 60{,}000 = \$400$$

Actual Units of All Products Sold	×	(Actual Sales-Mix Percentage	−	Budgeted Sales-Mix Percentage)	×	Budgeted Contribution Margin Per Unit	=	Sales-Mix Variance
Commercial 84,000 ×		(0.30	−	0.25)	×	$500	=	$2,100,000 F
Residential 84,000 ×		(0.70	−	0.75)	×	$400	=	1,680,000 U
Total sales-mix variance								$ 420,000 F

(Actual Units of All Products Sold	−	Budgeted Units of All Products Sold)	×	Budgeted Sales-Mix Percentage	×	Budgeted Contribution Margin Per Unit	=	Sales-Quantity Variance
Commercial (84,000 −		80,000)	×	0.25	×	$500	=	$500,000 F
Residential (84,000 −		80,000)	×	0.75	×	$400	=	1,200,000 F
Total sales-quantity variance								$1,700,000 F

2. Actual market $= 84,000 \div 700,000 = 12\%$

Budgeted market share $= 80,000 \div 800,000 = 10\%$

Budgeted contribution margin per composite unit of budgeted mix:

$$\$34,000,000 \div 80,000 = \underline{\$425}$$

or   Commercial $\$500 \times 0.25 = \$125$

plus Residential $\$400 \times 0.75 = \underline{300}$

                                         $\underline{\$425}$

$$\begin{array}{l} \text{Market-share} \\ \text{variance} \end{array} = \begin{array}{c}\text{Actual} \\ \text{market size} \\ \text{in units}\end{array} \times \left(\begin{array}{c}\text{Actual} \\ \text{market} \\ \text{share}\end{array} - \begin{array}{c}\text{Budgeted} \\ \text{market} \\ \text{share}\end{array}\right) \times \begin{array}{c}\text{Budgeted} \\ \text{contribution margin} \\ \text{per composite unit} \\ \text{for budgeted mix}\end{array}$$

$$= 700,000 \times (0.12 - 0.10) \times \$425 = \$5,950,000 \text{ F}$$

$$\begin{array}{l} \text{Market-size} \\ \text{variance} \end{array} = \left(\begin{array}{c}\text{Actual} \\ \text{market size} \\ \text{in units}\end{array} - \begin{array}{c}\text{Budgeted} \\ \text{market size} \\ \text{in units}\end{array}\right) \times \begin{array}{c}\text{Budgeted} \\ \text{market} \\ \text{share}\end{array} \times \begin{array}{c}\text{Budgeted} \\ \text{contribution margin} \\ \text{per composite unit} \\ \text{for budgeted mix}\end{array}$$

$$= (700,000 - 800,000) \times 0.10 \times \$425 = \$4,250,000 \text{ U}$$

Note that the algebraic sum of the market-share variance and market-size variance is equal to the sales-quantity variance: $\$5,950,000$ F $+ \$4,250,000$ U $= \$1,700,000$ F.

3. Both the total sales-mix variance and the total sales-quantity variance are favorable. The favorable sales-mix variance occurs because the actual mix comprises more of the higher margin commercial vinyl flooring. The favorable sales-quantity variance occurs because the actual total quantity of rolls sold exceeds the budgeted amount.

    The company's large favorable market-share variance is due to achieving a 12% market share when a 10% market share was budgeted. The market-size variance is unfavorable because the total rolls actually sold were 100,000 less than the budgeted amount. Payne's performance in 2000 appears to be very good. Payne sold more units than budgeted and relatively more of the higher contribution margin commercial vinyl flooring by gaining market share, despite a decline in the overall market size. The net effect of the market-share and market-size variances is a favorable $1,700,000.

◆ PART THREE: CUSTOMER-PROFITABILITY ANALYSIS

Companies that prosper have a strong customer focus in their decisions. Management accountants are giving increased attention to **customer-profitability analysis**, which is the reporting and analysis of customer revenues and customer costs. Armed with this information, managers can ensure that customers contributing sizably to the profitability of an organization receive a comparable level of attention from the organization.

New to This Edition Part Three, Customer-Profitability Analysis, now integrates both customer revenue and customer cost analysis (using the ABC cost hierarchy of unit-level, batch-level, etc.) into a single example.

CUSTOMER REVENUES AND CUSTOMER COSTS

An analysis of customer differences on both revenues and costs can provide important insight into why differences in customer profitability exist. Consider Spring Distribution Company, which sells bottled water. It has two distribution channels: (1) a wholesale distribution channel that covers sales to supermarkets, drugstores, and other stores, and (2) a retail distribution channel for a few select business

Curriculum Linkage Customer-profitability analysis is mgt. acctg.'s response to the "customer is priority one" philosophy from mgt. and mktg. This section is of special interest to MBA students who are concentrating in mktg., as it clearly shows how acctg. can provide mktg. personnel with useful information.

customers. We will focus mainly on customer-profitability analysis in Spring's retail distribution channel. The list selling price in this channel is $0.60 per bottle while the purchase cost to Spring is $0.50 per bottle. If every bottle is sold at its list price in this distribution channel, Spring would earn a gross margin of $0.10 per bottle.

Customer Revenue Analysis

Let us first consider customer revenues. Data for four of Spring's ten customers in June 2001 are:

	Customer			
	A	**B**	**G**	**J**
1. Bottles sold	1,000,000	800,000	70,000	60,000
2. List selling price	$0.60	$0.60	$0.60	$0.60
3. Invoice price	$0.56	$0.59	$0.55	$0.60
4. Revenues (1 × 3)	$560,000	$472,000	$38,500	$36,000

OBJECTIVE 6

Discuss why revenues can differ across customers purchasing the same product

Customer revenue analysis is enhanced by tracking as much detail as possible about why customer revenues differ. Two variables explain revenue differences across these four customers: (1) the volume of bottles purchased, and (2) the magnitude of price discounting. **Price discounting** is the reduction of selling prices below listed levels in order to encourage increases in customer purchases. Companies that record only the invoice price in their information system cannot readily track the magnitude of their price discounting.[4]

Limiting the amounts of price discounting can be essential to maintaining customer profitability. Price discounts may be due to multiple factors, including the volume of product purchased (higher-volume customers receive higher discounts) and whether having the customer brings marketing benefits (name recognition) that helps promote other sales. Discounts could also be due to poor negotiating by a salesperson or the dysfunctional effect of an incentive plan that is based only on revenues.

Points to Stress Basing sales commissions on unit sales (or even sales rev.) or basing bonuses on achievement of sales targets gives sales people incentives to increase sales even if they must resort to excessive price discounting to close the sale. Basing commissions or bonuses on CM or profits from the sale can help mitigate this problem.

Reinforcing Problems Customer-profitability analysis is covered in Exer. 16-23 and 16-24, and Probs. 16-32 through 16-34, 16-36, and 16-37.

Tracking discounts by customer, and by salesperson, can provide valuable information about ways to improve customer profitability. For example, Spring Distribution may want to ensure that its volume-based price discounting policy is strictly enforced. It may also require its salespeople to obtain approval before giving large discounts to customers not normally qualifying for them. In addition, it could track the future sales of customers that its salespeople argue warrant a sizable price discount due to their predicted "high growth potential." For example, Spring should track future sales to customer G to see if the 5 cent per bottle discount translates into higher future sales. Salespeople who have a poor track record in predicting the future growth of customers may be given additional training in sales forecasting (or may even be encouraged to seek employment elsewhere).

Customer revenues are one element of customer profitability. We now consider the other element, customer costs.

Customer Cost Analysis

Curriculum Linkage Chaps. 11 and 12 suggest that when the firm has excess capacity, accepting special orders at any selling price that covers incremental costs will increase the firm's profits. However, that discussion assumed the special order would not affect regular business (i.e., the mkt. is effectively segmented). As this chap. notes, this assumption is not always valid. If customers learn that someone else has received a lower price, they are likely to press for larger discounts.

Chapters 5 and 14 discussed the *cost hierarchy* concept. Here we apply this concept to customers. A **customer cost hierarchy** categorizes costs related to customers into different cost pools on the basis of different types of cost drivers (or cost-allocation bases) or different degrees of difficulty in determining cause-and-effect (or benefits received) relationships. Spring Distribution has an activity-based costing system that focuses on customers rather than products.

---

[4]Further analysis of customer revenues could distinguish between gross revenues and net revenues. This approach highlights differences across customers in sales returns. Additional discussion of ways to analyze revenue differences across customers is in R. S. Kaplan and R. Cooper, *Cost and Effect.* (Boston, MA: Harvard Business School Press, 1998, Chap. 10).

Spring's ABC system has one direct cost, the cost of bottles, and multiple indirect-cost pools. The indirect costs belong to different categories of the customer cost hierarchy. Spring identifies five categories in its customer cost hierarchy:

OBJECTIVE 7

Apply the concept of cost hierarchy to customer costing

◆ *Customer output-unit-level costs*—resources sacrificed on activities performed to sell each unit (bottle) to a customer. An example is product-handling costs of each bottle sold.

◆ *Customer batch-level costs*—resources sacrificed on activities that are related to a group of units (bottles) sold to a customer. Examples are costs incurred to process orders or to make deliveries.

◆ *Customer-sustaining costs*—resources sacrificed on activities undertaken to support individual customers, regardless of the number of units or each batch of product delivered to customers. Examples are costs of customer visits or costs of displays at customer sites.

◆ *Distribution-channel costs*—resources sacrificed on activities that are related to a particular distribution channel rather than to each unit of product, batches of product, or specific customers. An example is the salary of the manager of Spring's retail distribution channel.

◆ *Corporate-sustaining costs*—resources sacrificed on activities that cannot be traced to individual customers or distribution channels. Examples are top management and general administration costs.

Note from these descriptions that four of the five levels of Spring's cost hierarchy closely parallel the cost hierarchy described in Chapter 5, except that Spring focuses on customers whereas the cost hierarchy in Chapter 5 emphasized products.

Spring has one additional cost hierarchy category, distribution channel costs, for the costs it incurs to support each of its distribution channels. We now consider decisions made at the individual customer level.

Customer-Level Costs

Customer-level costs include cost of goods sold and costs incurred in the first three categories of the customer cost hierarchy—customer output unit-level costs, customer batch-level costs, and customer-sustaining costs. The following table shows five activities (in addition to cost of goods sold) that Spring identifies as resulting in customer-level costs. The table indicates the cost drivers and cost driver rates for each activity as well as the cost-hierarchy category for each activity.

Activity	Cost Driver and Rate	Cost Hierarchy Category
Order taking	$100 per purchase order	Customer batch-level costs
Customer visits	$80 per customer visit	Customer-sustaining costs
Delivery vehicles	$2 per delivery mile traveled	Customer batch-level costs
Product handling	$0.02 per bottle sold	Customer output unit-level costs
Expedited deliveries	$300 per expedited delivery	Customer batch-level costs

Information on the quantity of cost drivers used by each customer follows:

	Customer			
	A	B	G	J
Number of purchase orders	30	25	15	10
Number of customer visits	6	5	4	3
Number of deliveries	60	30	20	15
Miles traveled per delivery	5	12	20	6
Number of expedited deliveries	1	0	2	0

OBJECTIVE 8

Prepare a customer-profitability report

Exhibit 16-4 on the next page shows a customer-profitability analysis for four customers using information on customer revenues previously presented (p. 582) and customer-level costs from its ABC system.

EXHIBIT 16-4
Customer-Profitability Analysis for Four Retail Channel Customers of Spring Distribution for June 2001

	Customer			
	A	B	G	J
Revenues at list prices $0.60 × 1,000,000; 800,000; 70,000; 60,000	$600,000	$480,000	$ 42,000	$ 36,000
Discount $0.04 × 1,000,000; $0.01 × 800,000; $0.05 × 70,000; $0 × 60,000	40,000	8,000	3,500	0
Revenues (at actual prices)	560,000	472,000	38,500	36,000
Cost of goods sold $0.50 × 1,000,000; 800,000; 70,000; 60,000	500,000	400,000	35,000	30,000
Gross margin	60,000	72,000	3,500	6,000
Customer-level operating costs				
Order taking $100 × 30; 25; 15; 10	3,000	2,500	1,500	1,000
Customer visits $80 × 6; 5; 4; 3	480	400	320	240
Delivery vehicles $2 × (5 × 60); (12 × 30); (20 × 20); (6 × 15)	600	720	800	180
Product handling $0.02 × 1,000,000; 800,000; 70,000; 60,000	20,000	16,000	1,400	1,200
Expedited deliveries $300 × 1; 0; 2; 0	300	0	600	0
Total	24,380	19,620	4,620	2,620
Customer-level operating income	$ 35,620	$ 52,380	$(1,120)	$ 3,380

Spring Distribution can use the information underlying Exhibit 16-4 to persuade its customers to reduce usage of the cost drivers. For example, consider customer G, which is only 7% the size of customer A (in terms of bottles purchased—G purchased 70,000 while A purchased 1,000,000). Yet, G uses 50% of purchase orders, $66\frac{2}{3}$% of sales visits, $33\frac{1}{3}$% of deliveries, and twice the number of expedited deliveries in comparison to Customer A. Spring Distribution could seek to have customer G make fewer purchase orders, require fewer customer visits, have fewer deliveries, and reduce expedited deliveries, while preserving opportunities for higher sales to customer G in the future.

The ABC system underlying Exhibit 16-4 provides a road map that facilitates less use of cost drivers by individual customers in order to promote cost reduction. Another advantage of ABC is that it highlights a second way cost reduction can be promoted by Spring Distribution. Spring can take actions to reduce the costs in

EXHIBIT 16-5
Income Statement of Spring Distribution for June 2001

		Customer Distribution Channels									
		Wholesale Customers					Retail Customers				
	Total (1)	Total (2)	A1 (3)	A2 (4)	. . . (5)	. . . (6)	Total (7)	Aª (8)	Bª (9)	. . . (10)	. . . (11)
Revenues	$12,470,000	$10,470,000	$1,946,000	$1,476,000			$2,000,000	$560,000	$472,000		
Customer-level costs	11,939,000	10,073,000	1,868,000	1,416,000			1,866,000	524,380	419,620		
Customer-level operating income	531,000	397,000	$ 78,000	$ 60,000			134,000	$ 35,620	$ 52,380		
Distribution-channel costs	190,000	132,000					58,000				
Distribution-channel-level operating income	341,000	$ 265,000					$ 76,000				
Corporate-sustaining costs	263,000										
Operating income	$ 78,000										

ªFull details are presented in Exhibit 16-4.

Customer-Profitability Analysis Attracts Increasing Attention

A survey of U.S. and Australian managers[a] asked respondents about "the three most important general management priorities that your organization faces today." The top ranked priorities were:

1. Customer profitability/satisfaction
2. Cost management/cost control
3. Quality
4. Growth

A growing number of companies are now developing customer-profitability systems to reinforce this strategic focus on customers. A survey of United Kingdom companies[b] found that 50% had "embarked on customer-profitability analysis. . . . A further 12% planned to pursue it in future." The uses of customer-profitability analysis were ranked as follows (most important = 1):

1. Guidance for pricing policies
2. Renegotiation of customer contracts
3. Guidance for customer relations policies
4. Influence cost control in respect of customers

"The 80/20 rule applied (that is, 20% of their customers were generating 80% of the profits)" to 60% of those who had examined cumulative contributions of customers to total

[a]Foster and Young, Frontiers of Management Accounting Research."

[b]J. Innes and F. Mitchell, "A Survey of Activity-Based Costing in the U.K.'s Largest Companies."

See Appendix A for full citations.

each of its own activities. For example, order taking currently is estimated to cost $100 per purchase order. By making its own ordering process more efficient (such as having its customers order electronically), Spring can reduce its costs even if its customers place the same number of orders.

Exhibit 16-5 shows the monthly operating income for Spring Distribution. The customer-level operating income of customers A and B in Exhibit 16-4 are shown in columns 8 and 9 of Exhibit 16-5. The format of Exhibit 16-5 is structured on Spring Distribution's cost hierarchy. This format dovetails with the different levels at which Spring Distribution makes decisions.

CUSTOMER-PROFITABILITY PROFILES

Managers find customer-profitability analysis useful for several reasons. First, it frequently highlights how vital a small set of customers is to total profitability. Managers need to ensure that the interests of these customers receive high priority. Microsoft uses the phrase "not all revenue dollars are endowed equally in profitability" to stress this key point. Second, when a customer is ranked in the "loss category," managers can focus on ways to make this customer more profitable in the future.

Exhibit 16-6 shows two approaches to presenting customer-profitability profiles for the ten customers in Spring's retail distribution channel. (Four of these customers are already analyzed in Exhibit 16-4.) Panel A ranks customers on customer-level operating income. Column 3 shows the cumulative customer-level operating income for these customers. This column is computed by adding the individual amounts in column 1. For example, row 3 for customer C has a cumulative income of $108,650 in column 3. This is the sum of $52,380 for customer B, $35,620 for customer A, and $20,650 for customer C. Column 4 shows what percentage this

Points to Stress Exh. 16-6 illustrates the importance of customer costing. The all purpose 80–20 rule often applies to customers: 80% of a firm's profits often come from 20% of its customers. Customer-profitability information can help mkt. and customer-service personnel (1) focus on maintaining excellent relations with those 20% of customers, and (2) transform the other 80% into more profitable customers. The idea that companies often lose money on some customers surprises students (particularly mkt. students). Emphasize that the company's first preference is to shift these customers toward a more profitable mix of products/services. Other alternatives include changing prices (if a company loses money on a customer, then prices on some of those products/services must not be covering their full costs), reducing services to the customer, or as a last resort, "firing" the customer. The latter alternative is anathema to mkt. personnel.

PANEL A: CUSTOMERS RANKED ON CUSTOMER-LEVEL OPERATING INCOME

Customer Code	Customer-Level Operating Income (1)	Customer Revenue (2)	Cumulative Customer-Level Operating Income (3)	Customer-Level Operating Income as a % of Total Customer-Level Operating Income (4) = (3) ÷ $134,000
B	$ 52,380	$ 472,000	$ 52,380	39%
A	35,620	560,000	88,000	66
C	20,650	255,000	108,650	81
D	16,840	247,000	125,490	94
F	6,994	123,500	132,484	99
J	3,380	36,000	135,864	101
E	3,176	193,000	139,040	104
G	−1,120	38,500	137,920	103
H	−1,760	38,000	136,160	102
I	−2,160	37,000	134,000	100%
	$134,000	$2,000,000		

PANEL B: CUSTOMERS RANKED ON REVENUES

Customer Code	Customer Revenue (1)	Customer-Level Operating Income (2)	Customer-Level Operating Income as a % of Revenue (3) = (2) ÷ (1)	Cumulative Customer Revenue (4)	Cumulative Customer Revenue as a % of Total Revenues (5) = (4) ÷ $2,000,000
A	$ 560,000	$ 35,620	0.064	$ 560,000	28%
B	472,000	52,380	0.111	1,032,000	52
C	255,000	20,650	0.081	1,287,000	64
D	247,000	16,840	0.068	1,534,000	77
E	193,000	3,176	0.016	1,727,000	86
F	123,500	6,994	0.057	1,850,500	93
G	38,500	−1,120	(0.029)	1,889,000	94
H	38,000	−1,760	(0.046)	1,927,000	96
I	37,000	−2,160	(0.058)	1,964,000	98
J	36,000	3,380	0.094	2,000,000	100%
	$2,000,000	$134,000			

Example After allocating both mfg. and nonmfg. costs, a manufacturer of electronics components (High-Voltage Engineering) found that 30% of their customers generated 70% of their sales and 100% of their profits (WSJ, 1/7/91).

$108,650 amount is of the total customer-level operating income of $134,000 earned in the retail distribution channel. Thus, the three most profitable customers contribute 81% of total customer-level operating income. This high percentage of operating income contributed by a small number of customers is a common finding in many studies. It highlights the importance of Spring Distribution maintaining good relations with this pivotal set of customers.

Exhibit 16-6, Panel B, ranks customers on revenue (after price discounts). Three of the four smallest customers (based on revenue) are unprofitable. Moreover, customer E, with revenues of $193,000, is only marginally profitable. Further analysis revealed that a former sales representative gave customer E excessively high price discounts in an attempt to meet a monthly sales-volume target.

Managers often find the bar chart presentation in Exhibit 16-7 to be the most intuitive way to analyze customer profitability. The highly profitable customers

EXHIBIT 16-7

Bar Chart of Customer-Level Operating Income for Spring Distribution's Retail Channel
Customers in June 2001

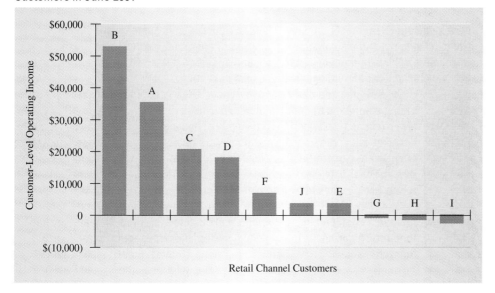

Points to Stress Much of this text focuses on info. mgrs. use for decision making. The format in which this info. is presented can be important. Research results support the old adage that a "picture is worth a thousand words." Humans have limited info. processing ability, and presenting info. in a way that highlights interrelationships (such as graphs and charts) can help mgrs. make faster and better decisions. The increased availability of PC-based graphics software makes it easier for mgt. accountants to provide info. in pictorial form.

clearly stand out. Moreover, the number of loss-customers and the magnitude of their losses are apparent.

Assessing Customer Value

The information in Exhibits 16-4 to 16-7 relates to customer profitability in a monthly accounting period. This is one of several factors that managers should consider in deciding how to allocate resources across customers. Other factors include:

1. *Short-run and long-run customer profitability*. This factor will be influenced by factors 2 and 3 below as well as by the level of resources likely to be required to retain the accounts.

2. *Likelihood of customer retention*. The more likely a customer is to continue doing business with a company, the more valuable the customer. Customers can differ in their loyalty and their willingness to "shop their business" on a frequent basis.

3. *Potential for customer growth*. This factor will be influenced by the likely growth of the customer's industry and the likely growth of the customer (due to, say, its ability to develop new products). This factor will also be influenced by cross-selling opportunities, that is, when a customer of one of the company's products becomes a customer of one or more of the company's other products.

4. *Increases in overall demand from having well-known customers*. Some customers with established reputations are often worth mentioning during customer visits to drive sales. Other customers are valuable because of their willingness to provide product endorsements.

5. *Ability to learn from customers*. Customers can be an important source of ideas about new products or ways to improve existing products. Customers willing to provide such input can be especially valuable.

Managers should be particularly cautious when deciding to drop customers. Long-run profitability reports may provide misleading signals about their short-run profitability. Not all costs assigned to a customer are variable in the short run. Dropping a currently unprofitable customer will not necessarily eliminate in the short run all the costs assigned to that customer.

Customer Profitability Analysis at PHH

PHH is a vehicle management company. It leases vehicles to its customers (both corporations and individuals) and also offers them a broad range of related services. These services include a vehicle maintenance program and accident-related support. PHH has over 750,000 vehicles under contract with its 5,200 plus customers.

PHH has adopted an activity-based costing approach to assist in cost management and the pricing of new business. One key part of its ABC system examines customer profitability. PHH has a menu of the activities it undertakes with respect to its customers. Some activities, such as account maintenance occur for every customer (but often with varying degrees of detail). Other activities, such as vehicle maintenance and accident assistance, are purchased by a subset of its customers.

When its ABC-based customer-profitability system was first implemented, PHH found higher variability in customer profitability than they had thought. The previous price bidding system did not adequately recognize differences in the complexity of different customers. For example, some customers wanted quick vehicle deliveries, whereas others gave PHH relatively long lead times. Orders with short delivery times were more likely to be purchased at a higher cost from a dealer rather than a manufacturer. Customers differed sizably in their accident rates, and in the extent to which vehicle repairs and maintenance were done by PHH or at the customer-site. Customers also differed in the level of detail requested in their vehicle reports from PHH. While PHH had a standardized set of reports, some customers wanted their own customized reports. Fleet vehicle diversity per customer was sizable. Several large customers had a small range of vehicles under lease, whereas some smaller customers had a far more diverse set of vehicles being leased. The ABC system highlighted the extra costs of this fleet vehicle diversity and many other types of diversity when determining customer profitability.

PHH's price quoting group now uses the ABC information to price different vehicle/service combinations for existing and new customers. It has also established a pricing committee that must review new contracts that are below profitability thresholds. The committee was charged with creating a "more consistent and disciplined approach to pricing."

Source: Conversations with PHH management and with D. Swenson of the University of Idaho.

PROBLEM

Spring Distribution is concerned with the level of its profitability. Its June 2001 operating income of $78,000 is less than 1% of revenues ($78,000 ÷ $12,470,000 = 0.63%). Suppose that July 2001 is identical to June 2001 with one exception. In July 2001, Spring conducts an extensive efficiency analysis of its activities and is able to reduce their costs to the following amounts:

Activity	Cost Driver Rate
Order taking	$60 per purchase order
Customer visits	$50 per visit
Delivery vehicles	$1.50 per delivery-mile traveled
Product handling	$0.015 per bottle sold
Expedited deliveries	$200 per expedited delivery

Required

1. What is the effect of these activity-cost reductions on the July 2001 profitability (customer-level operating income) of customers A, B, G, and J in Exhibit 16-4?
2. What are additional ways Spring could seek to improve the profitability of customers A, B, G, and J?

SOLUTION

1. The July 2001 cost driver rate reductions affect only the customer-level operating costs in Exhibit 16-4. The revised customer-level operating incomes are:

	Customer			
	A	B	G	J
Gross margin (from Exhibit 16-4)	$60,000	$72,000	$3,500	$6,000
Customer-level operating costs				
Operating costs				
Order taking				
$60 × 30; 25; 15; 10	1,800	1,500	900	600
Customer visits				
$50 × 6; 5; 4; 3	300	250	200	150
Delivery vehicles				
$1.50 × (5 × 60); (12 × 30); (20 × 20); (6 × 15)	450	540	600	135
Product handling				
$0.015 × 1,000,000; 800,000; 70,000; 60,000	15,000	12,000	1,050	900
Expedited deliveries				
$200 × 1; 0; 2; 0	200	0	400	0
Total	17,750	14,290	3,150	1,785
Customer-level operating income	$42,250	$57,710	$ 350	$4,215

The customer-level operating income has increased for each customer. The total for all four customers is $104,525 in July 2001 compared to $90,260 in June 2001 (calculated from Exhibit 16-4), an increase of 15.8 percent.

2. Spring could also seek to improve customer profitability by reducing cost of goods sold as a result of negotiating lower prices with its supplier. It could also explore the effect of a list price increase, a reduction in price discounts, or encouraging customers to use fewer resources from its five activities. The challenge here is to retain, or possibly increase, the customer's willingness to purchase from Spring given the new pricing and cost parameters.

SUMMARY

The following points are linked to the chapter's learning objectives:

1. Bundling occurs when a package of two or more products (or services) is sold for a single price. Where product managers of the individual components in the bundle seek information on product revenues, revenue-allocation of the bundled price is required.

2. Revenue allocation for a bundled product can be done using the stand-alone method, the incremental method, or by management judgement.

3. Further information on the sales-volume variance can be gained by examining the effect of (a) a change in the actual sales mix from the budgeted sales mix (a sales-mix variance), and (b) a change in the actual unit sales from the budgeted unit sales (a sales-quantity variance).

4. Two key explanations for a sales-quantity variance are (a) a change in the actual share of the market attained compared to its budgeted share (the market-share variance), and (b) a change in the actual market size in units compared to the budgeted market size (the market-size variance).

5. Obtaining reliable information on the total market size and the relative market shares of products is essential to the reliability of the market-share and market-size variances.

6. The revenues of customers purchasing the same product can differ due to differences in the quantity of units purchased and in discounts given from the list price.

7. Customer cost hierarchies are used by companies to highlight how some costs can be reliably assigned to individual customers while other costs can be reliably assigned only to distribution channels or to corporatewide efforts.

8. Customer-profitability reports, shown in a cumulative form, often highlight that a small percentage of customers contribute a large percentage of operating income. It is important that companies devote sufficient resources to maintaining and expanding relationships with these key contributors to profitability.

APPENDIX: MIX AND YIELD VARIANCES FOR SUBSTITUTABLE INPUTS

Reinforcing Problems Mix and yield variances are covered in Exer. 16-25 and 16-26, and Prob. 16-35.

Points to Stress Mix vars. arise only when inputs are substitutable. If there can be no substitutions, the mix of inputs is constant, the mix variance is zero, and the entire efficiency variance is attributable to the yield variance.

Part Two of this chapter analyzed sales-mix and sales-quantity variances for a company with multiple products. This analysis extended the Chapter 7 coverage of the sales-volume variance. The framework for sales-mix and sales-quantity variances explained in Part Two can also be applied to the analysis of production-input variances. The prior discussion of these variances in Chapter 7 (pp. 223–229) is easiest to interpret when the inputs into a production process are *nonsubstitutable*, which is often the case. Consider a company assembling *Voyager* satellites for NASA's space program. Once a product design for a satellite is approved, there is a mandate that it be adhered to. The contractor cannot substitute a different combination of doors and door locks, irrespective of price movements of alternative doors and locks. In other cases, however, managers have some leeway in combining inputs. For example, Del Monte can combine material inputs (such as pineapples, cherries, and grapes) in varying proportions for its cans of fruit salad. Within limits, these individual fruits are *substitutable* inputs in making a fruit salad.

This Appendix presents mix and yield variances that highlight the financial implications of mix and yield decisions by managers. These variances divide the efficiency variance that was discussed in Chapter 7 (pp. 227–228). To illustrate mix and yield variances, we examine Delpino Corporation, which makes tomato ketchup. Our example focuses on direct materials inputs and substitution among three of these inputs. The same approach can also be used to examine substitutable direct labor inputs.

To produce ketchup of the desired consistency, color, and taste, Delpino mixes three types of tomatoes grown in three different regions—Latin American tomatoes (Latoms), California tomatoes (Caltoms), and Florida tomatoes (Flotoms). Delpino's production standards require 1.60 tons of tomatoes to produce 1 ton of ketchup, with 50% of the tomatoes being Latoms, 30% Caltoms, and 20% Flotoms. The direct materials input standards to produce 1 ton of ketchup are:

0.80 (50% of 1.6) ton of Latoms at $70 per ton	$ 56.00
0.48 (30% of 1.6) ton of Caltoms at $80 per ton	38.40
0.32 (20% of 1.6) ton of Flotoms at $90 per ton	28.80
Total standard cost of 1.6 tons of tomatoes	$123.20

Budgeted average cost per ton of tomatoes is $123.20 ÷ 1.60 tons = $77.

Because Delpino uses fresh tomatoes to make ketchup, no inventories of tomatoes are kept. Purchases are made as needed, so all price variances relate to

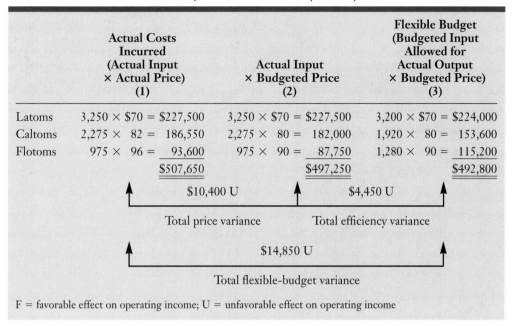

	Actual Costs Incurred (Actual Input × Actual Price) (1)	Actual Input × Budgeted Price (2)	Flexible Budget (Budgeted Input Allowed for Actual Output × Budgeted Price) (3)
Latoms	3,250 × $70 = $227,500	3,250 × $70 = $227,500	3,200 × $70 = $224,000
Caltoms	2,275 × 82 = 186,550	2,275 × 80 = 182,000	1,920 × 80 = 153,600
Flotoms	975 × 96 = 93,600	975 × 90 = 87,750	1,280 × 90 = 115,200
	$507,650	$497,250	$492,800

$10,400 U ← Total price variance → $4,450 U ← Total efficiency variance

$14,850 U

Total flexible-budget variance

F = favorable effect on operating income; U = unfavorable effect on operating income

tomatoes purchased and used. Actual results for June 2000 show that a total of 6,500 tons of tomatoes were used to produce 4,000 tons of ketchup:

3,250 tons of Latoms at actual cost of $70 per ton	$227,500
2,275 tons of Caltoms at actual cost of $82 per ton	186,550
975 tons of Flotoms at actual cost of $96 per ton	93,600
6,500 tons of tomatoes	507,650
Standard cost of 4,000 tons of ketchup at $123.20 per ton	492,800
Total variance to be explained	$ 14,850 U

Given the standard ratio of 1.60 tons of tomatoes to 1 ton of ketchup, 6,400 tons of tomatoes should be used to produce 4,000 tons of ketchup. At the standard mix, the quantities of each type of tomato required are:

Latoms	0.50 × 6,400 = 3,200 tons
Caltoms	0.30 × 6,400 = 1,920 tons
Flotoms	0.20 × 6,400 = 1,280 tons

Direct Materials Price and Efficiency Variances

Exhibit 16-8 presents the columnar analysis of the flexible-budget variance for direct materials discussed in Chapter 7. The direct materials price and efficiency variances are calculated separately for each input material and then added together. The variance analysis prompts Delpino to investigate the unfavorable price and efficiency variances—why did they pay more for the tomatoes and use greater quantities than they should have? Were the market prices of tomatoes higher, in general, or could the Purchasing Department have negotiated lower prices? Did the inefficiencies result from inferior tomatoes or from problems in processing?

Direct Materials Mix and Direct Materials Yield Variances

Managers sometimes have discretion to substitute one material for another. For example, the manager of Delpino's ketchup plant has some leeway in combining Latoms, Caltoms, and Flotoms without affecting quality. We will assume that to maintain quality, the mix percentages of each type of tomato can only vary up to 5% from the standard mix. For example, the percentage of Caltoms in the mix can

Points to Stress The text emphasizes the total mix and yield variances rather than the mix and yield variances of the individual inputs. Focusing on total effects recognizes the joint and interrelated effects of the individual inputs in mix and yield variance calculations.

Correcting Student Misconceptions The mix and yield exhibits (16-8 and 16-9) each have 3 columns, and students often fail to realize that it is *not* the same 3 columns in each exhibit. Emphasize that the 3 columns in Exh. 16-9 are a decomposition of the efficiency variance from Exh. 16-8. Column 1 of Exh. 16-9 corresponds to column 2 in Exh. 16-8, and column 3 in Exh. 16-9 corresponds to column 3 in Exh. 16-8.

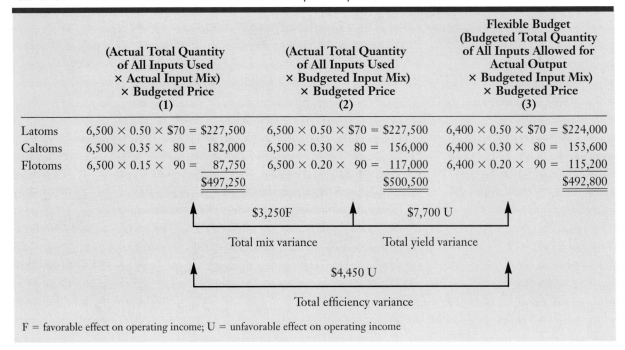

	(Actual Total Quantity of All Inputs Used × Actual Input Mix) × Budgeted Price (1)	(Actual Total Quantity of All Inputs Used × Budgeted Input Mix) × Budgeted Price (2)	Flexible Budget (Budgeted Total Quantity of All Inputs Allowed for Actual Output × Budgeted Input Mix) × Budgeted Price (3)
Latoms	6,500 × 0.50 × $70 = $227,500	6,500 × 0.50 × $70 = $227,500	6,400 × 0.50 × $70 = $224,000
Caltoms	6,500 × 0.35 × 80 = 182,000	6,500 × 0.30 × 80 = 156,000	6,400 × 0.30 × 80 = 153,600
Flotoms	6,500 × 0.15 × 90 = 87,750	6,500 × 0.20 × 90 = 117,000	6,400 × 0.20 × 90 = 115,200
	$497,250	$500,500	$492,800

$3,250F ← Total mix variance → $7,700 U ← Total yield variance

$4,450 U ← Total efficiency variance

F = favorable effect on operating income; U = unfavorable effect on operating income

Curriculum Linkage The intuition behind the materials mix and yield variances is analogous to the intuition behind the sales mix and qty. vars. introduced earlier in this chapter. The yield var. tells us whether we used more or less *total* materials *inputs* than budgeted, given the actual # of outputs. It is the difference between the actual and budgeted quantities of inputs, at the budgeted mix (i.e., holding the mix constant). The materials mix var. arises because the mix of materials differs from the budget. It is the difference between the actual and budgeted mix for the actual total qty. of inputs (i.e., holding total qty. of inputs constant).

vary between 25% and 35% (30% ± 5%). When inputs are substitutable, direct materials efficiency improvement relative to budgeted costs can come from two sources: (1) using a cheaper mix to produce a given quantity of output, and (2) using less input to achieve a given quantity of output. The direct materials yield and mix variances divide the efficiency variance into two variances: The mix variance focuses on how the multiple types of substitutable materials or labor are combined, and the yield variance focuses on how much of those inputs are used.

Holding the actual total quantity of all direct materials inputs used constant, the total **direct materials mix variance** is the difference between two amounts: (1) the budgeted cost for the actual mix of the total quantity of direct materials used, and (2) the budgeted cost of the budgeted mix of the actual total quantity of direct materials used. Holding the budgeted input mix constant, the **direct materials yield variance** is the difference between two amounts: (1) the budgeted cost of direct materials based on the actual total quantity of all direct materials inputs used, and (2) the flexible-budget cost of direct materials based on the budgeted total quantity of direct materials inputs for the actual output produced.

Exhibit 16-9 presents the total direct materials mix and yield variances for the Delpino Corporation.

Direct materials mix variance Compare columns 1 and 2 in Exhibit 16-9. Both columns calculate cost using the actual total quantity of all inputs used (6,500 tons) and budgeted input prices (Latoms, $70; Caltoms, $80; and Flotoms, $90). The *only* difference is that column 1 uses *actual input mix* (Latoms, 50%; Caltoms, 35%; Flotoms, 15%), and column 2 uses *budgeted input mix* (Latoms, 50%; Caltoms, 30%; and Flotoms, 20%). The difference in costs between the two columns is the total direct materials mix variance, attributable solely to differences in the mix of inputs used. The total direct materials mix variance is the sum of the direct materials mix variances for each input:

$$\begin{matrix} \text{Direct} \\ \text{materials} \\ \text{mix variance} \\ \text{for each} \\ \text{input} \end{matrix} = \begin{matrix} \text{Actual total} \\ \text{quantity of all} \\ \text{direct materials} \\ \text{inputs used} \end{matrix} \times \left(\begin{matrix} \text{Actual} \\ \text{direct materials} \\ \text{input mix} \\ \text{percentage} \end{matrix} - \begin{matrix} \text{Budgeted} \\ \text{direct materials} \\ \text{input mix} \\ \text{percentage} \end{matrix} \right) \times \begin{matrix} \text{Budgeted} \\ \text{price of} \\ \text{direct materials} \\ \text{input} \end{matrix}$$

The direct materials mix variances are:

Latoms	$6{,}500 \times (0.50 - 0.50) \times \$70 = 6{,}500 \times 0.00 \times \$70 = \$0$
Caltoms	$6{,}500 \times (0.35 - 0.30) \times \$80 = 6{,}500 \times 0.05 \times \$80 = 26{,}000\text{ U}$
Flotoms	$6{,}500 \times (0.15 - 0.20) \times \$90 = 6{,}500 \times -0.05 \times \$90 = \underline{29{,}250\text{ F}}$
Total direct materials mix variance	$\$3{,}250\text{ F}$

Total direct materials yield variance   Compare columns 2 and 3 of Exhibit 16-9. Column 2 calculates costs using the budgeted input mix and the budgeted prices. Column 3 calculates the flexible-budget cost based on the budgeted cost of the budgeted total quantity of all inputs used (6,400 tons of tomatoes) for the actual output achieved (4,000 tons of ketchup) times the budgeted input mix (Latoms, 50%; Caltoms, 30%; Flotoms, 20%). The only difference in the two columns is that column 2 uses the actual total quantity of all inputs used (6,500 tons), while column 3 uses the budgeted total quantity of all inputs used (6,400 tons). Hence, the difference in costs between the two columns is the total direct materials yield variance, due solely to differences in actual and budgeted total input quantity used. The total direct materials yield variance is the sum of the direct materials yield variances for each input:

$$
\begin{pmatrix}\text{Direct} \\ \text{materials} \\ \text{yield variance} \\ \text{for each input}\end{pmatrix} = \begin{pmatrix}\text{Actual total} \\ \text{quantity of} \\ \text{all direct} \\ \text{materials} \\ \text{inputs used}\end{pmatrix} - \begin{pmatrix}\text{Budgeted total} \\ \text{quantity of all} \\ \text{direct materials} \\ \text{inputs allowed} \\ \text{for actual output}\end{pmatrix} \times \begin{pmatrix}\text{Budgeted} \\ \text{direct materials} \\ \text{input mix} \\ \text{percentage}\end{pmatrix} \times \begin{pmatrix}\text{Budgeted} \\ \text{price of} \\ \text{direct materials} \\ \text{input}\end{pmatrix}
$$

The direct materials yield variances are:

Latoms	$(6{,}500 - 6{,}400) \times 0.50 \times \$70 = 100 \times 0.50 \times \$70 = \$3{,}500\text{ U}$
Caltoms	$(6{,}500 - 6{,}400) \times 0.30 \times \$80 = 100 \times 0.30 \times \$80 = 2{,}400\text{ U}$
Flotoms	$(6{,}500 - 6{,}400) \times 0.20 \times \$90 = 100 \times 0.20 \times \$90 = \underline{1{,}800\text{ U}}$
Total direct materials yield variance	$\underline{\$7{,}700\text{ U}}$

The total direct materials yield variance is unfavorable because Delpino used 6,500 tons of tomatoes rather than the 6,400 tons that it should have used to produce 4,000 tons of ketchup. Holding the budgeted mix and budgeted prices of tomatoes constant, the budgeted cost per ton of tomatoes in the budgeted mix is $77 per ton. The unfavorable yield variance represents the budgeted cost of using 100 more tons of tomatoes, $(6{,}500 - 6{,}400) \times \$77 = \$7{,}700\text{ U}$.

The direct materials variances computed in Exhibits 16-8 and 16-9 can be summarized as follows:

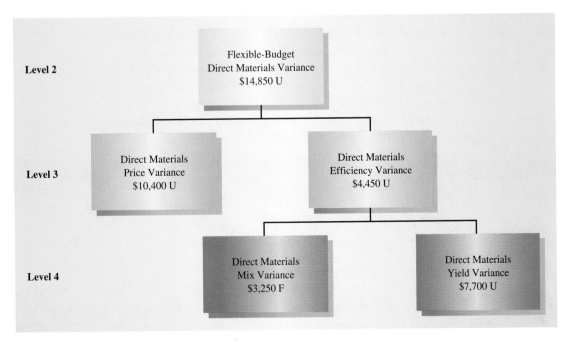

This chapter and the glossary at the end of the book contain definitions of the following important terms:

bundled product (p. 568)
composite product unit (576)
customer cost hierarchy (582)
customer-profitability analysis (581)
direct materials mix variance (592)
direct materials yield variance (592)
incremental revenue-allocation
    method (570)

market-share variance (577)
market-size variance (578)
price discounting (582)
revenue allocation (568)
sales-mix variance (575)
sales-quantity variance (577)
stand-alone revenue-allocation
    method (569)

▼ A S S I G N M E N T   M A T E R I A L

QUESTIONS

16-1 Describe how companies are increasingly facing revenue-allocation decisions.

16-2 Distinguish between the stand-alone revenue-allocation method and the incremental revenue-allocation method.

16-3 Identify and discuss arguments individual product managers may put forward to support their preferred revenue-allocation method.

16-4 How might a dispute over the allocation of revenues of a bundled product be resolved?

16-5 Show how managers can gain insight into the causes of a sales-volume variance by drilling down into the components of this variance.

16-6 How can the concept of a composite unit be used to explain why an unfavorable total sales-mix variance of contribution margin occurs?

16-7 Explain why a favorable sales-quantity variance occurs.

16-8 Distinguish between a market-share variance and a market-size variance.

16-9 Why might some companies not compute market-size and market-share variances?

16-10 Why is customer-profitability analysis a vitally important topic to managers?

16-11 How can the extent of price discounting be tracked on a customer-by-customer basis?

16-12 "A customer-profitability profile highlights those customers that should be dropped to improve profitability." Do you agree? Explain.

16-13 Give an example of three different levels of costs in a customer cost hierarchy.

16-14 Distinguish between processes where the inputs are nonsubstitutable and where they are substitutable.

16-15 Explain how the direct materials mix and yield variances provide additional information about the direct materials efficiency variance.

EXERCISES

16-16 Revenue-allocation, speaking fees. Geoff Carr is a leading public relations expert. He recently convinced three well-known sports personalities to make separate presentations at the same one-day seminar.

◆ Linda Young is a leading soccer coach. She gave six speeches last year, each at $10,000 per appearance. Young refuses most invitations, preferring to focus on ways to win matches or relax at home.

◆ Vince Rock is an Olympic gold medalist. Rock gave 50 speeches last year, each at $4,000 per appearance. He loves publicity and rarely says no to invitations.

◆ Juan Malvido is a television sports commentator. Malvido charged $2,000 for each of the 40 appearances he made last year. His television network actively solicits venues at which Malvido talks.

In the past, each speaker has been the only presenter at events at which they appear. Young, Rock, and Malvido will each speak for two hours at Carr's one-day seminar.

The first three-speaker seminar draws 500 people at $200 per person. Carr promised his three speakers he would give them in aggregate 30% of the total revenues. Without discussing it with each speaker, Carr assumes this 30% would be split equally: 10% of total revenues to Young, 10% to Rock, and 10% to Malvido.

Required

1. Describe two alternative ways (other than equal splitting) to allocate the 30% of total revenues among the three speakers.
2. Discuss possible reactions of each speaker to Carr's proposed equal splitting of the 30% of revenues alloted for speaking fees.

16-17 Revenue-allocation, bundled products. Pebble Resorts operates a five-star hotel with a world-recognized championship golf course. It has a decentralized management structure. There are three divisions:

◆ Lodging (rooms, conference facilities)
◆ Food (restaurants and in-room service)
◆ Recreation (the golf course, tennis courts, and so on)

Starting next month, Pebble will offer a two-day, two-person "getaway package" deal for $700. This deal includes:

◆ Two nights' stay for two in an ocean-view room—separately priced at $640 ($320 per night for two).
◆ Two rounds of golf separately priced at $300 ($150 per round). One person can do two rounds, or two people can do one round each.
◆ Candlelite dinner for two at the exclusive Pebble Pacific Restaurant—separately priced at $80 per person.

Samantha Lee, president of the Recreation Division, recently asked the CEO of Pebble Resorts how her division would share in the $700 revenue from the package. The golf course was operating at 100% capacity (and then some). Under the "getaway package" rules, participants who booked one week in advance were guaranteed access to the golf course. Lee noted that every "getaway" booking would displace a $150 booking. She stressed that the high demand reflected the devotion of her team to keeping the golf course rated in the "Best 10 Courses in the World" listings in *Golf Monthly*. As an aside she also noted that the Lodging and Food Divisions only had to turn away customers on "peak season events such as the New Year's period."

Required

1. Allocate the $700 "getaway package" revenue to the three divisions using:
   a. The stand-alone revenue-allocation method,
   b. The incremental revenue-allocation method (with recreation first, then lodging, and then food), and
      Use selling prices as the weights in a and b.
2. What are the pros and cons of a and b in requirement 1?

16-18 Revenue allocation, bundled products, additional complexities (continuation of 16-17). The individual items in the "getaway package" deal at Pebble Resorts are not fully used by each guest. Assume that 10% of the "getaway package" users in its first month do not use the golfing option, while 5% do not use the food option. The lodging option has a 100% usage rate.

Required

How should Pebble Resorts recognize this nonuse factor in its revenue sharing of the $700 package across the Lodging, Food, and Recreation Divisions? Explain.

16-19 Variance analysis, multiple products. The Detroit Penguins play in the American Ice Hockey League. The Penguins play in the Downtown Arena (owned and managed by the City of Detroit), which has a capacity of 15,000 seats (5,000 lower-tier seats and

10,000 upper-tier seats). The Downtown Arena charges the Penguins a per ticket charge for use of their facility. All tickets are sold by the Reservation Network, which charges the Penguins' a reservation fee per ticket. The Penguins' budgeted contribution margin for each type of ticket in 2001 is computed as follows:

	Lower-Tier Tickets	Upper-Tier Tickets
Selling price	$35	$14
Downtown Arena fee	10	6
Reservation Network fee	5	3
Contribution margin per ticket	$20	$ 5

The budgeted and actual average attendance figures per game in the 2001 season are:

	Budgeted Seats Sold	Actual Seats Sold
Lower-tier	4,000	3,300
Upper-tier	6,000	7,700
Total	10,000	11,000

There was no difference between the budgeted and actual contribution margin for lower-tier or upper-tier seats.

The manager of the Penguins was delighted that actual attendance was 10% above budgeted attendance per game, especially given the depressed state of the local economy in the past six months.

Required

1. Compute the sales-volume variance for individual "product" contribution margin and total contribution margin for the Detroit Penguins in 2001.
2. Compute the sales-quantity and sales-mix variances for individual "product" contribution margin and total contribution margin in 2001.
3. Present a summary of the variances in requirements 1 and 2. Comment on the results.

16-20 7 Up using variances to read the market. The following is an excerpt from an article that appeared in a recent issue of a trade magazine (*Fortune*, Dec. 7, 1998):

> Remember about 30 years back, when 7 Up began describing itself as the Uncola and ran those great commercials celebrating the "uncola nut"? And remember those cool upside-down 7 Up glasses?
>
> Most likely you do remember—and that, paradoxically, is part of 7 Up's problem. As John Sicher, editor of Beverage Digest explains, "7 Up is perceived today as something that appeals to an older generation, not as a hip, with-it brand." Indeed, 7 Up's own research shows that while the soft drink continues to be popular with boomers who grew up on the Uncola campaign, its brand identity is barely a blip on the cultural radar of today's 12- to 24-year-olds, the demographic segment that consumes the most soda. As a result, 7 Up's market share has deteriorated throughout the 90s, even though the share of the citrus-flavored soda category—which includes 7 Up's primary competitor, Sprite—has increased during the same period.

In the ten years prior to the article, 7 Up's market share of the soft-drink market had declined from 3.2% to 2.4 percent. Five years prior to the article, 7 Up held a 2.8% market share compared to Sprite's 4.9% (Sprite is the category leader in the lemon-lime segment of the soft-drink market). 7 Up's slide has been steady and consistent over the last ten years.

Required

1. In light of these comments, what variances should 7 Up management have been tracking over the past decade? What story would those variances have told?
2. What factors should you consider in evaluating 7 Up's strategy in the last decade?

16-21 Variance analysis, working backward. The Jinwa Corporation sells two brands of wine glasses—Plain and Chic. Jinwa provides the following information for sales in the month of June 2000:

Static-budget total contribution margin	$5,600	
Budgeted units to be sold of all glasses in June 2000	2,000 units	
Budgeted contribution margin per unit of Plain	$2 per unit	
Budgeted contribution margin per unit of Chic	$6 per unit	
Total sales-quantity variance	$1,400 U	
Actual sales-mix percentage of Plain	60%	

All variances are to be computed in contribution-margin terms.

Required

1. Calculate the sales-quantity variances for each product for June 2000.
2. Calculate the individual product and total sales-mix variances for June 2000. Calculate the individual product and total sales-volume variances for June 2000.
3. Briefly describe the conclusions you would draw from the variances.

16-22 Variance analysis, multiple countries. Cola-King manufactures and sells cola soft drinks in three countries—Canada, Mexico, and the United States. The same product is sold in each market. Budgeted and actual results for 2000 (all in U.S. dollars) are as follows:

	Budget for 2000			Actual for 2000		
Country	Selling Price Per Carton	Variable Cost Per Carton	Units Sold (Cartons in Thousands)	Selling Price Per Carton	Variable Cost Per Carton	Units Sold (Cartons in Thousands)
Canada	$6.00	$4.00	400,000	$6.20	$4.50	480,000
Mexico	$4.00	$2.80	600,000	$4.25	$2.75	900,000
United States	$7.00	$4.50	1,500,000	$6.80	$4.60	1,620,000

Required

1. Compute the flexible-budget variance, the sales-volume variance, sales-mix variance, and sales-quantity variance of contribution margin. Show results for each country in your computations.
2. What inferences can you make from the variances computed in requirement 1?

16-23 Customer profitability, service company. Instant Service (IS) is a repair-service company specializing in the rapid repair of photocopying machines. Each of its ten clients pays a fixed monthly service fee (based on the type of photocopying machines owned by that client and the number of employees at that site). IS keeps records of the time technicians spend at each client's location as well as the cost of the equipment used to repair each photocopying machine. IS recently decided to compute the profitability of each customer. The following data (in thousands) pertain to May 2000:

	Customer Revenues	Customer Costs
Avery Group	$260	$182
Duran Systems	180	184
Retail Systems	163	178
Wizard Partners	322	225
Santa Clara College	235	308
Grainger Services	80	74
Software Partners	174	100
Problem Solvers	76	108
Business Systems	137	110
Okie Enterprises	373	231

Required

1. Compute the operating income of each customer. Prepare exhibits for Instant Service that are patterned after Exhibits 16-6 and 16-7. Comment on the results.
2. What options regarding individual customers should Instant Service consider in light of your customer-profitability analysis in requirement 1?
3. What problems might Instant Service encounter in accurately estimating the operating costs of each customer?

16-24 Customer profitability, distribution. Figure Four is a distributor of pharmaceutical products. Its activity-based costing system has five activities:

Activity	Cost Driver Rate in 2000
Order processing	$40 per order
Line-item ordering	$3 per line item
Store deliveries	$50 per store delivery
Carton deliveries	$1 per carton
Shelf-stocking	$16 per stocking-hour

Rick Flair, the controller of Figure Four, wants to use this activity-based costing system to examine individual customer profitability within each distribution market. He focuses first on the Ma and Pa single-store distribution market. Two customers are used to exemplify the insights available with the activity-based costing approach. Data pertaining to these two customers in August 2000 are as follows:

	Charleston Pharmacy	Chapel Hill Pharmacy
Total orders	12	10
Average line items per order	10	18
Total store deliveries	6	10
Average cartons shipped per store delivery	24	20
Average hours of shelf-stocking per store delivery	0	0.5
Average revenue per delivery	$2,400	$1,800
Average cost of goods sold per delivery	$2,100	$1,650

Required
1. Use the activity-based costing information to compute the operating income of each customer in August 2000. Comment on the results.
2. Flair ranks the individual customers in the Ma and Pa single-store distribution market on the basis of operating income. The cumulative operating income of the top 20% of customers is $55,680. Figure Four reports negative operating income of $21,247 for the bottom 40% of its customers. Make four recommendations that you think Figure Four should consider in light of this new customer-profitability information.

16-25 Direct materials efficiency, mix, and yield variances. (Chapter Appendix, CMA adapted) The Energy Products Company produces a gasoline additive, Gas Gain, that increases engine efficiency and improves gasoline mileage. The actual and budgeted quantities (in gallons) of materials required to produce Gas Gain and the budgeted prices of materials in August 2000 are as follows:

Chemical	Actual Quantity	Budgeted Quantity	Budgeted Price
Echol	24,080	25,200	$0.20
Protex	15,480	16,800	0.45
Benz	36,120	33,600	0.15
CT-40	10,320	8,400	0.30

Required
1. Calculate the total direct materials efficiency variance for August 2000.
2. Calculate the total direct materials mix and yield variances for August 2000.
3. What conclusions would you draw from the variance analysis?

16-26 Direct materials price, efficiency, mix and yield variances. (Chapter Appendix) Greenwood, Inc., manufactures apple products such as apple jelly and applesauce. It makes applesauce by blending Tolman, Golden Delicious, and Ribston apples. Budgeted costs to produce 100,000 pounds of applesauce in November 2000 are as follows:

45,000 pounds of Tolman apples at $0.30 per pound	$13,500
180,000 pounds of Golden Delicious apples at $0.26 per pound	46,800
75,000 pounds of Ribston apples at $0.22 per pound	16,500

Actual costs in November 2000 are:

62,000 pounds of Tolman apples at $0.28 per pound	$17,360
155,000 pounds of Golden Delicious apples at $0.26 per pound	40,300
93,000 pounds of Ribston apples at $0.20 per pound	18,600

Required
1. Calculate the total direct materials price and efficiency variances for November 2000.
2. Calculate the total direct materials mix and yield variances for November 2000.
3. Comment on your results in requirements 1 and 2.

PROBLEMS

16-27 Revenue allocation, bundled products. Athletic Programs (AP) sells exercise videos through television infomercials. It uses a well-known sports celebrity in each video. Each celebrity receives a share (typically varying between 10% and 25%) of the revenues from sale of that video.

In recent months, AP has started selling their exercise videos in bundled form as well as in individual form. Typically, the bundled products are offered to people who telephone for a specific video after watching an infomercial. Each infomercial is for a specific exercise tape. As a marketing experiment, AP has begun advertising the bundled product at the end of some infomercials in a select set of markets.

Sales in 2000 of three products that have been sold individually, as well as in bundled form, are as follows:

	Average Retail Price	Net Units Sold	Royalty Paid to Celebrity
Individual Sales			
SuperAbs	$40	27,000	15%
SuperArm	$35	53,000	25%
SuperLegs	$25	20,000	18%
Bundled Product Sales			
SuperAbs + SuperArms	$60	18,000	?
SuperAbs + SuperLegs	$52	6,000	?
SuperArms + SuperLegs	$42	11,000	?
SuperAbs + SuperArms + SuperLegs	$65	22,000	?

The AP infomercials have received widespread recognition.

Required
1. What royalty would be paid to the celebrity on each tape for the individual sales in 2000? Show your calculations.
2. Compute the royalty paid to each celebrity for the bundled product sales in 2000 using:
   a. The stand-alone revenue-allocation method (with average retail price as the weight), and
   b. The incremental revenue-allocation method (with SuperArms ranked 1, SuperAbs 2, and SuperLegs 3).
3. Discuss the relative merits of the two revenue-allocation methods in requirement 2.
4. Assume the incremental revenue-allocation method is used. What alternative approaches could be used to determine the sequence in which the bundled revenue could be allocated to individual products?

16-28 Variance analysis, sales-mix and sales-quantity variances. Aussie Infonautics, Inc., produces handheld Windows CE™ compatible organizers. Aussie Infonautics markets three different handheld models. PalmPro is a souped-up version for the executive on the go, PalmCE is a consumer-oriented version, and PalmKid is a stripped-down version for the young adult market. You are Aussie Infonautics Senior Vice President of Marketing. The CEO has discovered that the total contribution margin came in lower than budget, and it is your responsibility to explain to him why actual results are different than the budget. Budgeted and actual operating data for the company's third quarter (2001) are as follows:

BUDGETED OPERATING DATA, THIRD QUARTER 2001

	Selling Price	Variable Costs Per Unit	Contribution Margin Per Unit	Sales Volume in Units
PalmPro	$379	$182	$197	12,500
PalmCE	269	98	171	37,500
PalmKid	149	65	84	50,000
				100,000

ACTUAL OPERATING DATA, THIRD QUARTER 2001

	Selling Price	Variable Costs Per Unit	Contribution Margin Per Unit	Sales Volume in Units
PalmPro	$349	$178	$171	11,000
PalmCE	285	92	193	44,000
PalmKid	102	73	29	55,000
				110,000

Required
1. Compute the actual and budgeted contribution margins in dollars and in percentage terms.
2. Calculate the actual and budgeted sales mix for the three products.
3. Calculate the individual product flexible-budget, sales-volume, sales-mix, and sales-quantity variances of contribution margin for the third quarter of 2001.
4. Calculate total sales-volume, sales-mix, and sales-quantity variances for the third quarter of 2001.
5. Given that your CEO is known to have temper tantrums, you want to be well prepared for this meeting. In order to prepare, write a paragraph or two explaining why actual results were not as good as the budgeted amounts.

16-29 Market-share and market-size variances (continuation of 16-28). Aussie Infonautics' Senior Vice-President of Marketing prepared his budget at the beginning of the third quarter assuming a 25% market share. The total handheld organizer market was estimated by Foolinstead Research to reach sales of 400,000 units worldwide in the third quarter. However, actual sales were 500,000 units.

Required
1. Calculate the market-share and market-size variances for Aussie Infonautics in the third quarter of 2001 (report all variances in terms of contribution margins).
2. Explain what happened based on the market-share and market-size variances.
3. Calculate the actual market-size, in units, that would have led to no market-size variance (again using budgeted contribution margin per unit). Use this market-size figure to find the actual market share that would have led to a zero market-share variance.

16-30 Variance analysis, multiple products. Debbie's Delight, Inc., operates a chain of cookie stores. Budgeted and actual operating data of its three Chicago stores for August 2000 are as follows:

BUDGET FOR AUGUST

	Selling Price Per Pound	Variable Costs Per Pound	Contribution Margin Per Pound	Sales Volume in Pounds
Chocolate chip	$4.50	$2.50	$2.00	45,000
Oatmeal raisin	5.00	2.70	2.30	25,000
Coconut	5.50	2.90	2.60	10,000
White chocolate	6.00	3.00	3.00	5,000
Macadamia nut	6.50	3.40	3.10	15,000
				100,000

ACTUAL FOR AUGUST

	Selling Price Per Pound	Variable Costs Per Pound	Contribution Margin Per Pound	Sales Volume in Pounds
Chocolate chip	$4.50	$2.60	$1.90	57,600
Oatmeal raisin	5.20	2.90	2.30	18,000
Coconut	5.50	2.80	2.70	9,600
White chocolate	6.00	3.40	2.60	13,200
Macadamia nut	7.00	4.00	3.00	21,600
				120,000

Debbie's Delight focuses on contribution margin in its variance analysis.

Required

1. Compute the individual product and total sales-volume variances for August 2000.
2. Compute the individual product and total sales-mix variances for August 2000.
3. Compute the individual product and total sales-quantity variances for August 2000.
4. Comment on your results in requirements 1, 2, and 3.

16-31 Market-share and market-size variances (continuation of 16-30). Debbie's Delight attains a 10% market share of the Chicago market. The total Chicago market is expected to be 1,000,000 pounds in sales volume for August 2000. The actual total Chicago market for August 2000 was 960,000 pounds in sales volume.

Required

Compute the market-share and market-size variances for Debbie's Delight in August 2000. Report all variances in contribution-margin terms. Comment on the results.

16-32 Customer-profitability analysis. Zoot's Suits is a ready-to-wear suit manufacturer with headquarters on Seventh Avenue in New York City. Zoot's has three customers:

◆ April Department Stores, a large department store chain that uses Zoot's to manufacture its own private-label brand

◆ Madison Brothers Stores, a chain of mall-based men's clothing stores

◆ Suitors, a company that sells suits to students on campus through a network of salespersons who travel across the country visiting college campuses

Zoot's owner and CEO, Al Sims, has developed the following activity-based costing system:

Activity	Cost Driver	Rate in 2001
Order Processing	Purchase Order	$ 245 per order
Customer Visits	Customer Visits	$ 1,430 per visit
Delivery—Regular	Regular Delivery	$ 300 per delivery
Delivery—Rushed	Rushed Delivery	$ 850 per delivery
Returns Processing	Return	$185 per return

Each suit returned also incurs a $5 stocking fee. In addition, Zoot's credits the customer's account for the full purchase price of all suits returned. Return suits are inventoried at the average cost per suit. Sims wants to evaluate the profitability of each of the three customers in 2000 in order to explore opportunities for increasing the profitability of his company in 2001. The following data is available:

Item	April	Madison	Suitors
Total number of orders	44	62	212
Total number of customer visits	8	12	22
Regular deliveries	41	48	166
Rush deliveries	3	14	46
Number of return shipments	4	6	16
Average number of suits per order	400	200	30
List selling price per suit	$200	$200	$200
Average selling price per suit	$140	$160	$170
Average cost per suit	$110	$110	$110
Total number of suits returned	880	960	1,280

Required

1. Calculate the operating income per customer. Who is the most profitable customer? Who is the least profitable customer? What contributes to each customer's profitability (or lack thereof)?
2. Provide some recommendations for Al Sims to ponder as he considers his options for increasing the company's profitability in 2001.

16-33 Customer profitability, distribution. Spring Distribution has decided to analyze the profitability of five new customers (see pp. 581–587). It buys bottled water at $0.50 per bottle and sells to retail customers at a list price of $0.60 per bottle. Data pertaining to five customers are:

	Customer				
	P	**Q**	**R**	**S**	**T**
Bottles sold	50,000	210,000	1,460,000	764,000	94,000
List selling price	$0.60	$0.60	$0.60	$0.60	$0.60
Actual selling price	$0.60	$0.59	$0.55	$0.58	$0.54
Number of purchase orders	15	25	30	25	30
Number of customer visits	2	3	6	2	3
Number of deliveries	10	30	60	40	20
Miles traveled per delivery	14	4	3	8	40
Number of expedited deliveries	0	0	0	0	1

Its five activities and their cost drivers are:

Activity	Cost Driver Rate
Order taking	$100 per purchase order
Customer visits	$80 per customer visit
Delivery vehicles	$2 per delivery mile traveled
Product handling	$0.02 per bottle sold
Expedited deliveries	$300 per hot-hot run

Required

1. Compute the customer-level operating income of each of the five retail customers now being examined (P, Q, R, S, and T). Comment on the results.
2. What insights are gained by reporting both the list selling price and the actual selling price for each customer?
3. What factors should Spring Distribution consider in deciding whether to drop one or more of the five customers?

16-34 Customer loyalty clubs and profitability analysis. The Sherriton Hotels chain embarked on a new customer loyalty program in 2000. The 2000 year-end data have been collected, and it is now time for you to determine whether the loyalty program should be continued, discontinued, or perhaps altered to improve loyalty and profitability levels at Sherriton.

Sherriton's loyalty program consists of three different customer loyalty levels. All new customers can sign up for the Sherriton Bronze Card—this card provides guests with a complimentary bottle of wine (cost to the chain is $5 per bottle) and $20 in restaurant coupons each night (cost to the chain is $10). Bronze customers also receive a 10% discount off the nightly rate. The program enables the chain to track a member's stays and activities. Once a customer has stayed and paid for 20 nights at any of the chain's locations worldwide, they are upgraded to Silver Customer status. Silver benefits include the bottle of wine (cost to the chain is $5 per bottle per night), $30 in restaurant coupons per night (cost to the chain is $15), and a 20% off every night from the 21st night on. A customer that reaches the 50-night level is upgraded to Gold Customer status. Gold status increases the nightly discount to 30% and replaces the $5 bottle of wine with a bottle of champagne per night (cost to the chain is $20 per bottle). As well, $40 in restaurant coupons per night are granted (cost to the chain is $20). Assume all bottles and coupons offered are used.

The average full price for one night's stay is $200. The chain incurs variable costs of $65 per night, exclusive of loyalty program costs. Total fixed costs for the chain are $140,580,000. Sherriton operates ten hotels, with, on average, 500 rooms each. All hotels

602 CHAPTER 16

are open for business 365 days a year, and approximate average occupancy rates are around 80%. Following are some loyalty program characteristics:

Loyalty Program	Number of Customers	Average Number of Nights Per Customer
Gold	2,430	60
Silver	8,340	35
Bronze	80,300	10
No program	219,000	1

Note that a Gold Customer would have received the 10% discount for his or her first 20 stays, received the 20% discount for the next 30 stays, and the 30% discount only for the last ten nights. Assume that all program members signed on to the program the first time they stayed with one of the chain's hotels. Also, assume the restaurants are managed by a 100% owned subsidiary of Sherriton.

Required
1. Calculate the program contribution margin for each of the three programs, as well as for the group of customers not subscribing to the loyalty program. Which of the programs is the most profitable? Which is the least profitable? Do not allocate fixed costs to individual rooms or specific loyalty programs.
2. Prepare an income statement for Sherriton for the year ended December 31, 2000.
3. What is the average room rate per night? What are average variable costs per night inclusive of the loyalty program?
4. Explain what drives the profitability (or lack thereof) of Sherriton's loyalty program.

16-35 Direct materials price and efficiency variances, direct materials mix and yield variances. (Chapter Appendix) Tropical Fruits, Inc., processes tropical fruit into fruit salad mix, which it sells to a food-service company. Tropical Fruits has in its budget the following standards for the direct materials inputs to produce a batch of 80 pounds of tropical fruit salad:

50 pounds of pineapple at $1.00 per pound	$50
30 pounds of watermelon at $0.50 per pound	15
20 pounds of strawberries at $0.75 per pound	15
100	$80

Note that 100 pounds of input quantities are required to produce 80 pounds of fruit salad. No inventories of direct materials are kept. Purchases are made as needed, so all price variances are related to direct materials used. The actual direct materials inputs used to produce 54,000 pounds of tropical fruit salad for the month of October were:

36,400 pounds of pineapple at $0.90 per pound	$32,760
18,200 pounds of watermelon at $0.60 per pound	10,920
15,400 pounds of strawberries at $0.70 per pound	10,780
70,000	$54,460

Required
1. Compute the total direct materials price and efficiency variances in October.
2. Compute the total direct materials mix and yield variances for October.
3. Comment on your results in requirements 1 and 2.
4. How might the management of Tropical Fruits, Inc., use information about the direct materials mix and yield variances?

16-36 Customer profitability, responsibility for environmental clean-up, ethics. Industrial Fluids, Inc. (IF), manufactures and sells fluids used by metal-cutting plants. These fluids enable metal cutting to be done more accurately and more safely.

IF has over 1,000 customers. It is currently undertaking a customer-profitability analysis. Ariana Papandopolis, a newly hired MBA, is put in charge of the project. One issue in this analysis is IF's liability for its customers' fluid disposal.

Papandopolis discovers that IF may have a responsibility under U.S. environmental legislation for the disposal of toxic waste by its customers. Moreover, she visits ten customer sites and finds dramatic differences in their toxic-waste-handling procedures. She describes one site owned by Acme Metal as an "environmental nightmare about to become a reality."

She tells the IF Controller that even if they have only one-half of the responsibility for the cleanup at Acme's site, they will still be facing very high damages. He is displeased that Acme Metal has not paid its account to IF for the last three months and has formally announced bankruptcy. He cautions Papandopolis to be careful in her written report. He notes that, "IF does not want any smoking guns in its files in the case of subsequent litigation."

Required

1. As Papandopolis prepares IF's customer-profitability analysis, how should she handle any estimates of litigation and cleanup costs that IF may be held responsible for?

2. How should Papandopolis handle the Acme Metal situation when she prepares a profitability report for that customer?

COLLABORATIVE LEARNING PROBLEM

16-37 Customer profitability, credit-card operations. The Freedom Card is a credit card that competes with national credit cards such as Visa and Master Card. Freedom Card is marketed by the Bay Bank. Mario Verdolini is manager of the Freedom Card division. He is seeking to develop a customer-profitability reporting system. He collects the following information on four users of the Freedom Card:

	Customer			
	A	**B**	**C**	**D**
Annual purchases at retail merchants	80,000	$26,000	$34,000	$8,000
Customer transactions at retail merchant	800	520	272	200
Membership fee paid	$50	$0	$50	$0
Average annual outstanding balance on credit card on which interest is paid to Bay Bank	$6,000	0	$2,000	$100
Inquiries to Bay Bank	6	12	8	2
Credit-card replacement due to loss or theft	0	2	1	0

Customer B pays no membership fee because his card was issued under a special "lifetime promotion program" in which annual fees are waived as long as the card is used at least once a year. Customer D is a student. Bay Bank does not charge a membership fee to student credit-card holders at select universities.

Bay Bank has an activity-based costing system that Verdolini can use in his analysis. The following data apply to 2000:

a. Each customer transaction with a retail merchant costs Bay Bank $0.50 to process.

b. Each customer inquiry to Bay Bank costs $5.

c. Replacing a lost card costs $120.

d. Annual cost to Bay Bank of maintaining a credit-card account is $108 (includes sending out monthly statements).

Bay Bank receives 2.0% of the purchase amount from retail merchants when the Freedom Card is used. Bad debts of the Freedom Card in 2000 were 0.5% of the total purchases at retail merchants. Thus, Bay Bank nets 1.5% of the total purchases made using the Freedom Card.

Bay Bank had an interest spread of 9% in 2000 on the average outstanding balances on which interest is paid by its credit card holders. An interest spread is the difference between what Bay Bank receives from card holders on outstanding balances and what it pays to obtain the funds so used. Thus, on a $500 average annual outstanding balance in 2000, Bay Bank would receive $45 in interest revenues (9% × $500).

Required

Form groups of two or more students to complete the following requirements.

1. Compute the customer profitability of the four representative credit-card users of the Freedom Card for 2000.

2. Develop profiles of (a) profitable card holders, and (b) unprofitable card holders for Bay Bank.

3. Should Bay Bank charge its card holders for making inquiries (such as outstanding balances or disputed charges) or for replacing lost or stolen cards?

4. Verdolini has an internal proposal that Bay Bank discontinue a sizable number of the low-volume credit-card customers. What factors should he consider in evaluating and responding to this proposal?

5. Verdolini seeks your group's advice on an ethical issue he is facing. A chain of gambling casinos (Lucky Roller) has offered to provide Freedom Card holders with money advances of up to $500 at its casinos. Verdolini observes that from a strict financial perspective, providing money advances to its customers would be highly profitable. Should Freedom Card holders be able to obtain money advances at Lucky Roller gambling casinos? Explain.

Process Costing

learning objectives

After studying this chapter, you should be able to

1. Determine when process-costing systems are appropriate
2. Describe five key steps in process costing
3. Calculate and use equivalent units
4. Prepare journal entries for process-costing systems
5. Demonstrate the weighted-average method of process costing
6. Demonstrate the first-in, first-out (FIFO) method of process costing
7. Incorporate standard costs into a process-costing system
8. Apply process-costing methods to cases with transferred-in costs

Tabasco Company mass produces identical bottles of Tabasco sauce in a series of standard production steps. To calculate the cost per bottle of sauce, Tabasco Company uses process-costing systems at its various production plants.

Our study of product costing so far has emphasized job costing. The cost object in a job-costing system is a job that constitutes a distinctly identifiable product or service. However, in many industries—for example, chemical processing, pharmaceutical production, and semiconductor manufacturing—products are mass-produced. In these industries, relatively homogeneous products are processed in a very similar manner. Companies in these industries use process costing, where individual processes form the basis of the costing system.

As we described in Chapters 4 and 5, costing systems serve three principal functions: (1) determining the cost of products or services that aid in planning decisions such as pricing and product mix, (2) valuing inventory and cost of goods sold for external reporting, and (3) controlling and managing costs, and evaluating performance. As we examine process costing in this chapter, we will emphasize the first two functions. We will be concerned only incidentally with the third function—control, cost management and performance evaluation—which is discussed in other chapters (see, for example, Chapters 6, 7, and 8). The ideas described there apply to process-costing systems as well.

ILLUSTRATING PROCESS COSTING

In a *process-costing system*, the unit cost of a product or service is obtained by assigning total costs to many identical or similar units. In a manufacturing process-costing setting, each unit is assumed to receive the same amount of direct materials costs, direct manufacturing labor costs, and indirect manufacturing costs. Unit costs are then computed by dividing total costs by the number of units.

The principal difference between process costing and job costing is the *extent of averaging* used to compute unit costs of products or services. In a job-costing system, individual jobs use different quantities of production resources. Thus, it would be incorrect to cost each job at the same average production cost. In contrast, when identical or similar units of products or services are mass-produced, and not processed as individual jobs, process costing averages production costs over all units produced.

The easiest way to learn process costing is by example. Consider the following illustration.

EXAMPLE: Global Defense, Inc., manufactures thousands of components for missiles and military equipment. These components are assembled in the Assembly Department. Upon completion, the units are immediately transferred to the Testing Department. We will focus on the Assembly Department process for one of these components, DG-19. Every effort is made to ensure that all DG-19 units are identical and meet a set of demanding performance specifications. The process-costing system for DG-19 in the Assembly Department has a single direct-cost category (direct materials) and a single indirect-cost category (conversion costs). *Conversion costs* are all manufacturing costs other than direct materials costs. These include manufacturing labor, indirect materials, energy, plant depreciation, and so on. Direct materials are added at the beginning of the process in Assembly. Conversion costs are added evenly during Assembly.

The following graphic summarizes these facts:

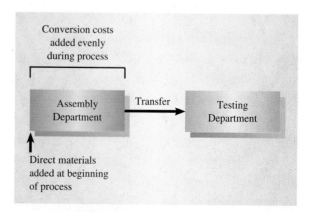

Use of Process Costing in Different Industries

A survey[a] of cost accounting practices in Australian manufacturing companies indicates widespread use of process-costing systems for product costing across a variety of industries. The reported percentages exceed 100% because several companies surveyed use more than one product-costing system.

	Food	Textiles	Primary Metals	Chemicals	Oil Refining	Furniture and Fixtures	Machinery and Computers	Electronics
Process costing	96%	91%	92%	75%	100%	38%	43%	55%
Job costing	4	18	25	25	25	63	65	58
Other	—	—	8	12	—	—	9	10

The survey data indicate that the use of process costing varies considerably among industries. Process costing is widely used in mass production industries that manufacture homogeneous products—food, textiles, primary metals, and refining. In contrast, as we move across the spectrum to industries that produce many distinct and different products, job costing is favored over process costing in industries such as furniture and fixtures, machinery and computers, and electronics.

[a]Adapted from M. Joye and P. Blayney, "Cost and Management Accounting Practices." Full citation is in Appendix A.

Process-costing systems separate costs into cost categories according to the timing of when costs are introduced into the process. Often, as in our Global Defense example, only two cost classifications, direct materials and conversion costs, are necessary to assign costs to products. Why? Because *all* direct materials are added to the process at one time and *all* conversion costs are generally added to the process uniformly through time. If, however, two different direct materials are added to the process at different times, two different direct materials categories would be needed to assign these costs to products. Similarly, if manufacturing labor is added to the process at a time that is different from other conversion costs, an additional cost category (direct manufacturing labor costs) would be needed to separately assign these costs to products.

We will use the production of the DG-19 component in the Assembly Department to illustrate process costing in three cases:

◆ *Case 1*—Process costing with zero beginning and zero ending work-in-process inventory of DG-19—that is, all units are started and fully completed by the end of the accounting period. *This case presents the most basic concepts of process costing and illustrates the key feature of averaging of costs.*

◆ *Case 2*—Process costing with zero beginning work-in-process inventory but some ending work-in-process inventory of DG-19—that is, some units of DG-19 started during the accounting period are incomplete at the end of the period. *This case builds on the basics and introduces the concept of equivalent units.*

◆ *Case 3*—Process costing with both some beginning and some ending work-in-process inventory of DG-19. *This case adds more detail and describes the effect of weighted-average and first-in, first-out (FIFO) cost flow assumptions on cost of units completed and cost of work-in-process inventory.*

We start with the simple case and work toward the more detailed and more complex cases.

Correcting Student Misconceptions
Students often wonder why the Case 3 complexities did not arise in Cases 1 and 2. In Case 1 there are no partially complete units, so EU = physical units and there is no need for a separate EU computation. Cases 1 and 2 avoid the issue of WA versus FIFO since B. WIP is zero. Differences between WA and FIFO arise only when there is B. WIP and costs change from the prior period.

CASE 1: PROCESS COSTING WITH ZERO BEGINNING AND ZERO ENDING WORK-IN-PROCESS INVENTORY

On January 1, 2001, there was no beginning inventory of DG-19 units in the Assembly Department. During January 2001, Global Defense started, completed assembly of, and transferred out to the Testing Department, 400 DG-19 units.

Data for the Assembly Department for January 2001 are:

Physical Units for January 2001

Work in process, beginning inventory (January 1)	0 units
Started during January	400 units
Completed and transferred out during January	400 units
Work in process, ending inventory (January 31)	0 units

Total Costs for January 2001

Direct materials costs added during January	$32,000
Conversion costs added during January	24,000
Total Assembly Department costs added during January	$56,000

Global Defense records direct materials and conversion costs in the Assembly Department as these costs are incurred. By averaging, the assembly costs per unit of DG-19 are $56,000 ÷ 400 units = $140, itemized as follows:

Direct materials costs per unit ($32,000 ÷ 400)	$ 80
Conversion costs per unit ($24,000 ÷ 400)	60
Assembly Department costs per unit	$140

This case shows that in a process-costing system, unit costs can be averaged by dividing total costs in a given accounting period by total units produced in that period. Because each unit is identical, we assume all units receive the same amount of direct materials and conversion costs. This approach can be used by any company that produces a homogeneous product or service but has no incomplete units when each accounting period ends. This situation frequently occurs in service-sector organizations. For example, a bank can adopt this process-costing approach to compute the unit cost of processing 100,000 similar customer deposits made in a month.

CASE 2: PROCESS COSTING WITH ZERO BEGINNING BUT SOME ENDING WORK-IN-PROCESS INVENTORY

In February 2001, Global Defense places another 400 units of DG-19 into production. Because all units placed into production in January 2001 were completely assembled, there is no beginning inventory of partially completed units in the Assembly Department on February 1, 2001. Customer delays in placing orders for DG-19 prevent the complete assembly of all units started in February. Only 175 units are completed and transferred out to the Testing Department.

Data for the Assembly Department for February 2001 are:

Physical Units for February 2001

Work in process, beginning inventory (February 1)	0 units
Started during February	400 units
Completed and transferred out	175 units
Work in process, ending inventory (February 28)	225 units

The 225 partially assembled units as of February 28, 2001, are fully processed with respect to direct materials. Why? Because all direct materials in the Assembly Department are added at the beginning of the assembly process. Conversion costs, however, are added evenly during the assembly process. Based on the work completed relative to the total work required to complete the DG-19

Reinforcing Problems Exer. 17-16 through 17-18 cover situations with no beginning inventory.

units still in the process, an Assembly Department supervisor estimates that the partially assembled units are, on average, 60% complete as to conversion costs.

Total Costs for February 2001

Direct materials costs added during February	$32,000
Conversion costs added during February	18,600
Total Assembly Department costs added during February	$50,600

The accuracy of the completion percentages depends on the care and skill of the estimator and the nature of the process. Estimating the degree of completion is usually easier for direct materials than it is for conversion costs. Why? Because the quantity of direct materials needed for a completed unit and the quantity of direct materials for a partially completed unit can be measured more easily. In contrast, the conversion sequence usually consists of a number of basic operations for a specified number of hours, days, or weeks, for various steps in assembly, testing, and so forth. Thus, the degree of completion for conversion costs depends on what proportion of the total effort needed to complete one unit or one batch of production has been devoted to units still in process. This estimate is more difficult to make accurately. Because of the difficulties in estimating conversion cost completion percentages, department supervisors and line managers—individuals most familiar with the process—often make these estimates. Still, in some industries no exact estimate is possible or, as in the textile industry, vast quantities in process prohibit the making of costly physical estimates. In these cases, all work in process in every department is assumed to be complete to some reasonable degree (for example, one-third, one-half, or two-thirds complete).

The key point to note in Case 2 is that a partially assembled unit is not the same as a fully assembled unit. Faced with some fully assembled and some partially assembled units, how should Global Defense calculate (1) the cost of fully assembled units in February 2001, and (2) the cost of the partially assembled units still in process at the end of February 2001?

Global Defense calculates these costs by using the following five steps:

- ◆ *Step 1*—Summarize the flow of physical units of output.
- ◆ *Step 2*—Compute output in terms of equivalent units.
- ◆ *Step 3*—Compute equivalent unit costs.
- ◆ *Step 4*—Summarize total costs to account for.
- ◆ *Step 5*—Assign total costs to units completed and to units in ending work in process.

Physical Units and Equivalent Units (Steps 1 and 2)

Step 1 tracks the physical units of output. Where did the units come from? Where did the units go? The physical units column of Exhibit 17-1 tracks where the physical units came from—400 units started, and where they went—175 units completed and transferred out, and 225 units in ending inventory.

Step 2 focuses on how the output for February should be measured. The output is 175 fully assembled units plus 225 partially assembled units. Since all 400 physical units are not uniformly completed, output in step 2 is computed in *equivalent units*, not in physical units.

Equivalent units is a derived amount of output units that takes the quantity of each input (factor of production) in units completed or in work in process, and converts it into the amount of completed output units that could be made with that quantity of input. For example, if 50 physical units of a product in ending work-in-process inventory are 70% complete with respect to conversion costs, there are 35 (70% × 50) equivalent units of output for conversion costs. That is, if all the conversion cost input in the 50 units in inventory were used to make completed output

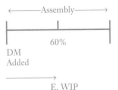
OBJECTIVE 2

Describe five key steps in process costing

OBJECTIVE 3

Calculate and use equivalent units

EXHIBIT 17-1

Steps 1 and 2: Summarize Output in Physical Units and Compute Equivalent Units
Assembly Department of Global Defense, Inc., for February 2001

Flow of Production	(Step 1) Physical Units	(Step 2) Equivalent Units	
		Direct Materials	Conversion Costs
Work in process, beginning	0		
Started during current period	400		
To account for	400		
Completed and transferred out during current period	175	175	175
Work in process, ending[a]	225		
225 × 100%; 225 × 60%		225	135
Accounted for	400		
Work done in current period only		400	310

[a]Degree of completion in this department: direct materials, 100%; conversion costs, 60%.

units, the company would be able to make 35 completed units of output. Equivalent units are calculated separately for each input (cost category). Examples of equivalent-unit concepts are also found in nonmanufacturing settings. For instance, universities often convert their part-time student enrollments into "full-time student equivalents."

When calculating equivalent units in step 2, focus on quantities. Disregard dollar amounts until after equivalent units are computed. In the Global Defense example, all 400 physical units—the 175 fully assembled ones and the 225 partially assembled ones—are complete in terms of equivalent units of direct materials. Why? Because all direct materials are added in the Assembly Department at the initial stage of the process. Exhibit 17-1 shows output as 400 *equivalent* units for direct materials because all 400 units are fully complete with respect to direct materials.

The 175 fully assembled units are completely processed with respect to conversion costs. The partially assembled units in ending work in process are 60% complete (on average). Therefore, the conversion costs in the 225 partially assembled units are *equivalent* to conversion costs in 135 (60% of 225) fully assembled units. Hence, Exhibit 17-1 shows output as 310 *equivalent* units with respect to conversion costs—175 equivalent units assembled and transferred out and 135 equivalent units in ending work-in-process inventory.

Calculation of Product Costs (Steps 3, 4, and 5)

Exhibit 17-2 shows steps 3, 4, and 5. Together, they are called the *production cost worksheet*. Step 3 calculates equivalent-unit costs by dividing direct materials and conversion costs added during February by the related quantity of equivalent units of work done in February (as calculated in Exhibit 17-1).

We can see the importance of using equivalent units in unit-cost calculations by comparing conversion costs for the months of January and February 2001. Observe that the total conversion costs of $18,600 for the 400 units worked on during February are less than the conversion costs of $24,000 for the 400 units worked on in January. However, the conversion costs to fully assemble a unit are $60 in both January and February. Total conversion costs are lower in February because fewer equivalent units of conversion costs work were completed in February (310) than were in January (400). If, however, we had used *physical* units instead of *equivalent* units in the per unit calculation, we would have erroneously concluded that conver-

EXHIBIT 17-2

Steps 3, 4, and 5: Compute Equivalent-Unit Costs, Summarize Total Costs to Account For, and Assign Costs to Units Completed and to Units in Ending Work in Process
Assembly Department of Global Defense, Inc., for February 2001

	Total Production Costs	Direct Materials	Conversion Costs
(Step 3) Costs added during February	$50,600	$32,000	$18,600
Divide by equivalent units of work done in current period (Exhibit 17-1)		÷ 400	÷ 310
Cost per equivalent unit		$ 80	$ 60
(Step 4) Total costs to account for	$50,600		
(Step 5) Assignment of costs:			
Completed and transferred out (175 units)	$24,500	(175[a] × $80) + (175[a] × $60)	
Work in process, ending (225 units):			
Direct materials	18,000	225[b] × $80	
Conversion costs	8,100		135[b] × $60
Total work in process	26,100		
Total costs accounted for	$50,600		

[a]Equivalent units completed and transferred out from Exhibit 17-1, step 2.
[b]Equivalent units in ending work in process from Exhibit 17-1, step 2.

Reinforcing Problems Exer. 17-19, 17-20, and 17-24 and Probs. 17-30, 17-31, 17-35, and 17-36 cover the WA method.

sion costs per unit declined from $60 in January to $46.50 ($18,600 ÷ 400) in February. This incorrect costing might have prompted Global Defense, for example, to lower the price of DG-19 inappropriately.

Step 4 in Exhibit 17-2 summarizes total costs to account for. Because the beginning balance of the work-in-process inventory is zero, total costs to account for (that is, the total charges or debits to Work in Process—Assembly) consist of the costs added during February—direct materials of $32,000, and conversion costs of $18,600, for a total of $50,600.

Step 5 in Exhibit 17-2 assigns these costs to units completed and transferred out and to units still in process at the end of February 2001. *The key idea is to attach dollar amounts to the equivalent output units for direct materials and conversion costs in (a) units completed, and (b) ending work in process calculated in Exhibit 17-1, step 2. To do so, the equivalent output units for each input are multiplied by the cost per equivalent unit calculated in step 3 of Exhibit 17-2.* For example, the 225 physical units in ending work in process are completely processed with respect to direct materials. Therefore, direct materials costs are 225 equivalent units (Exhibit 17-1, step 2) × $80 (cost per equivalent of direct materials calculated in step 3), which equals $18,000. In contrast, the 225 physical units are 60% complete with respect to conversion costs. Therefore, the conversion costs are 135 equivalent units (60% of 225 physical units, Exhibit 17-1, step 2) × $60 (cost per equivalent unit of conversion costs calculated in step 3), which equals $8,100. The total cost of ending work in process equals $26,100 ($18,000 + $8,100).

Teaching Tip It is important to tie the numbers in the production cost report (e.g., Exh. 17-2) to the WIP T-account so students see the big picture. Otherwise, students tend to focus on the mechanics of the production cost report and lose sight of the purpose of process costing.

Journal Entries

Journal entries in process-costing systems are basically like those made in job-costing systems with respect to direct materials and conversion costs. The main difference is that, in process costing, there is often more than one Work-in-Process account, one for each process—in our example, Work in Process—Assembly and Work in Process—Testing. Global Defense purchases direct materials as needed. These materials are delivered directly to the Assembly Department. Using dollar amounts from Exhibit 17-2, summary journal entries for the month of February at Global Defense, Inc., are:

OBJECTIVE 4

Prepare journal entries for process-costing systems

Reinforcing Problems Exer. 17-17 and Probs. 17-31, 17-33, 17-34, 17-36, 17-38, and 17-39 deal with journal entries for all of the methods.

1.	Work in Process—Assembly	32,000	
	Accounts Payable Control		32,000

To record direct materials purchased and used in production during February.

2.	Work in Process—Assembly	18,600	
	Various accounts		18,600

To record Assembly Department conversion costs for February; examples include energy, manufacturing supplies, all manufacturing labor, and plant depreciation.

3.	Work in Process—Testing	24,500	
	Work in Process—Assembly		24,500

To record cost of goods completed and transferred from Assembly to Testing during February.

Exhibit 17-3 shows a general framework for the flow of costs through the T-accounts. Notice how entry 3 for $24,500 follows the physical transfer of goods from the Assembly to the Testing Department. The key T-account, Work in Process—Assembly, shows an ending balance of $26,100, which is the beginning balance of Work in Process—Assembly in March 2001.

EXHIBIT 17-3
Flow of Costs in a Process-Costing System
Assembly Department of Global Defense, Inc., for February 2001

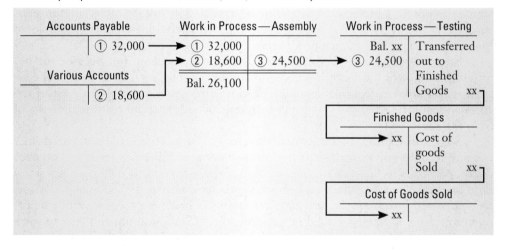

CASE 3: PROCESS COSTING WITH BOTH SOME BEGINNING AND SOME ENDING WORK-IN-PROCESS INVENTORY

At the beginning of March 2001, Global Defense had 225 partially assembled DG-19 units in the Assembly Department. During March 2001, Global Defense placed another 275 units into production. Data for the Assembly Department for March 2001 are:

Correcting Student Misconceptions
The % completion is the % complete *at that point in time*. If B. WIP was 40% complete, 40% of the work was completed by the *beginning* of this period (40% was completed *last* period). The remaining 60% will be done in the current period to complete the units. Conversely, if E. WIP is 50% complete, then 50% of the work has been done *this* period. The 50% to complete the E. WIP will be done *next* period.

Physical Units for March 2001

Work in process, beginning inventory (March 1)	225 units
Direct materials (100% complete)	
Conversion costs (60% complete)	
Started during March	275 units
Completed and transferred out during March	400 units
Work in process, ending inventory (March 31)	100 units
Direct materials (100% complete)	
Conversion costs (50% complete)	

Total Costs for March 2001

Work in process, beginning inventory		
Direct materials (225 equivalent units × $80 per unit)	$18,000	
Conversion costs (135 equivalent units × $60 per unit)	8,100	$26,100
Direct materials costs added during March		19,800
Conversion costs added during March		16,380
Total costs to account for		$62,280

We now have incomplete units in both beginning and ending work-in-process inventory to account for. Our goal is to use the five steps we described earlier to calculate (1) the cost of units completed and transferred out, and (2) the cost of ending work in process. To assign costs to each of these categories, however, we need to choose an inventory cost-flow method. We next describe the five-step approach to process costing using two alternative inventory cost-flow methods—the weighted-average method and the first-in, first-out method. The different assumptions will produce different numbers for cost of units completed and for ending work in process.

WEIGHTED-AVERAGE METHOD

The **weighted-average process-costing method** calculates the equivalent-unit cost of the *work done to date* (regardless of the period in which it was done) and assigns this cost to equivalent units completed and transferred out of the process and to equivalent units in ending work-in-process inventory. The weighted-average cost is the total of all costs entering the Work in Process account (regardless of whether it is from beginning work in process or from work started during the period) divided by total equivalent units of work done to date. We now describe the five-step procedure introduced in Case 2 using the weighted-average method.

Step 1: Summarize the Flow of Physical Units The physical units column of Exhibit 17-4 shows where the units came from—225 units from beginning inventory and 275 units started during the current period—and where they went—400 units completed and transferred out and 100 units in ending inventory. These data for March were given on page 614.

Step 2: Compute Output in Terms of Equivalent Units As we saw in Case 2, even partially assembled units are complete in terms of direct materials because direct materials are introduced at the beginning of the process. For conversion costs, the fully assembled physical units transferred out are, of course, fully completed. The Assembly Department supervisor estimates the partially assembled physical units in March 31 work in process to be 50% complete (on average).

The equivalent-units columns in Exhibit 17-4 show the equivalent units of work done to date—equivalent units completed and transferred out and equivalent units in ending work in process (500 equivalent units of direct materials and 450 equivalent units of conversion costs). Notice that the equivalent units of work done to date *also* equal the sum of the equivalent units in beginning inventory (work done in the previous period) and the equivalent units of work done in the current period, because:

$$\begin{matrix} \text{Equivalent units} \\ \text{in beginning} \\ \text{work in process} \end{matrix} + \begin{matrix} \text{Equivalent units} \\ \text{of work done in} \\ \text{current period} \end{matrix} = \begin{matrix} \text{Equivalent units} \\ \text{completed and} \\ \text{transferred out} \\ \text{in current period} \end{matrix} + \begin{matrix} \text{Equivalent units} \\ \text{in ending} \\ \text{work in process} \end{matrix}$$

The equivalent-unit calculation in the weighted-average method is only concerned with total equivalent units of *work done to date* regardless of (1) whether the work was done during the previous period and is part of beginning work in process, or (2) whether it was done during the current period. That is, the weighted-average method *merges* equivalent units in beginning inventory (work done before March) with equivalent units of work done in the current period. Thus, the stage of

Teaching Tip As the problems become more complex, time lines become more helpful. Consider the following time line for the Global Defense illustration's March data:

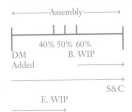

The time line shows that during March, Global Defense finished the B. WIP by adding the remaining 40% of the CC (all DM were added to the B. WIP during February). They started and completed units, adding 100% of both DM and CC. Finally, they started E. WIP by getting these units 50% of the way through the Assembly process. These E. WIP units have all their DM and 50% of their CC. In April, Global will finish these units by adding the remaining 50% of the CC.

EXHIBIT 17-4

Steps 1 and 2: Summarize Output in Physical Units and Compute Equivalent Units
Weighted-Average Method of Process Costing
Assembly Department of Global Defense, Inc., for March 2001

Flow of Production	(Step 1) Physical Units (given p. 614)	(Step 2) Equivalent Units	
		Direct Materials	Conversion Costs
Work in process, beginning	225		
Started during current period	275		
To account for	500		
Completed and transferred out during current period	400	400	400
Work in process, ending[a]	100		
100 × 100%; 100 × 50%		100	50
Accounted for	500		
Work done to date		500	450

[a]Degree of completion in this department: direct materials, 100%; conversion costs, 50%.

completion of the current-period beginning work in process per se is *irrelevant* and *not* used in the computation.

Step 3: Compute Equivalent-Unit Costs Exhibit 17-5, step 3, shows the computation of equivalent-unit costs separately for direct materials and conversion costs. The weighted-average cost per equivalent unit is obtained by dividing the sum of costs for beginning work in process and costs for work done in the current period by total equivalent units of work done to date. When calculating the weighted-average conversion cost per equivalent unit in Exhibit 17-5, for example, we divide total conversion costs, $24,480 (beginning work in process, $8,100, plus work done in current period, $16,380) by total equivalent units, 450 (equivalent units of conversion costs in beginning work in process and in work done in current period), to get a weighted-average cost per equivalent unit of $54.40.

Step 4: Summarize Total Costs to Account For The total costs to account for in March 2001 are described in the example data on page 615—beginning work in process, $26,100 (direct materials, $18,000 and conversion costs, $8,100) plus $36,180 (direct materials costs added during March, $19,800, and conversion costs, $16,380). The total of these costs is $62,280.

Step 5: Assign Costs to Units Completed and to Units in Ending Work in Process The key point in this step is to cost all work done to date: (1) the cost of units completed and transferred out of the process, and (2) the cost of ending work in process. Step 5 in Exhibit 17-5 takes the equivalent units completed and transferred out and equivalent units in ending work in process calculated in Exhibit 17-4, step 2, and attaches dollar amounts to them. These dollar amounts are the weighted-average costs per equivalent unit for direct materials and conversion costs calculated in step 3. For example, note that the total cost of the 100 physical units in ending work in process consists of:

Direct materials:

100 equivalent units × weighted-average cost per equivalent unit of $75.60	$ 7,560

Conversion costs:

50 equivalent units × weighted-average cost per equivalent unit of $54.40	2,720
Total costs of ending work in process	$10,280

The following table summarizes the total costs to account for and the $62,280 accounted for in Exhibit 17-5. The arrows indicate that costs of units completed

EXHIBIT 17-5
Steps 3, 4, and 5: Compute Equivalent-Unit Costs, Summarize Total Costs to Account For, and Assign Costs to Units Completed and to Units in Ending Work in Process
Weighted-Average Method of Process Costing
Assembly Department of Global Defense, Inc., for March 2001

	Total Production Costs	Direct Materials	Conversion Costs
(Step 3) Work in process, beginning (given, p. 615)	$26,100	$18,000	$ 8,100
Costs added in current period (given, p. 615)	36,180	19,800	16,380
Costs incurred to date		$37,800	$24,480
Divide by equivalent units of work done to date (Exhibit 17-4)		÷ 500	÷ 450
Cost per equivalent unit of work done to date		$ 75.60	$ 54.40
(Step 4) Total costs to account for	$62,280		
(Step 5) Assignment of costs:			
Completed and transferred out (400 units)	52,000	$(400^a \times \$75.60) + (400^a \times \$54.40)$	
Work in process, ending (100 units):			
Direct materials	7,560	$100^b \times \$75.60$	
Conversion costs	2,720		$50^b \times \$54.40$
Total work in process	10,280		
Total costs accounted for	$62,280		

^{a}Equivalent units completed and transferred out from Exhibit 17-4, step 2.
^{b}Equivalent units in ending work in process from Exhibit 17-4, step 2.

and transferred out and in ending work in process are calculated using average total costs obtained after merging costs of beginning work in process and costs added in the current period.

Costs to Account For		Costs Accounted For Calculated at Weighted-Average Cost	
Beginning work in process	$26,100	Completed and transferred out	$52,000
Costs added in current period	36,180	Ending work in process	10,280
Total costs to account for	$62,280	Total costs accounted for	$62,280

Before proceeding, please pause and review Exhibits 17-4 and 17-5 carefully to check your understanding of the weighted-average method. Note that Exhibit 17-4 deals only with physical and equivalent units but not costs. Exhibit 17-5 shows the cost amounts.

Using dollar amounts from Exhibit 17-5, summary journal entries under the weighted-average method for the month of March at Global Defense, Inc., are:

1. Work in Process—Assembly   19,800
        Accounts Payable Control   19,800

    To record direct materials purchased and used in production during March.

2. Work in Process—Assembly   16,380
        Various accounts   16,380

    To record Assembly Department conversion costs for March; examples include energy, manufacturing supplies, all manufacturing labor, and plant depreciation.

3. Work in Process—Testing   52,000
        Work in Process—Assembly   52,000

    To record cost of goods completed and transferred from Assembly to Testing during March.

Points to Stress Emphasize that the purpose of Exh. 17-4 and 17-5 for WA, Exh. 17-6 and 17-7 for FIFO, and Exh. 17-8 and 17-9 for standard costing is primarily to obtain the dollar value for the journal entry which debits WIP-Testing and credits WIP-Assembly for the cost of the completed units transferred during March from Assembly to Testing.

The key T-account, Work in Process—Assembly, under the weighted-average method would show the following:

Work in Process—Assembly

Beginning inventory, March 1	26,100		③ Completed and transferred out	
① Direct materials	19,800		to Work in Process—Testing	52,000
② Conversion costs	16,380			
Ending inventory, March 31	10,280			

FIRST-IN, FIRST-OUT METHOD

OBJECTIVE 6

Demonstrate the first-in, first-out (FIFO) method of process costing

Reinforcing Problems Exer. 17-21, 17-22, and 17-25 and Probs. 17-32 and 17-37 cover the FIFO method.

In contrast to the weighted-average method, the **first-in, first-out (FIFO) process-costing method** assigns the cost of the previous period's equivalent units in beginning work-in-process inventory to the first units completed and transferred out of the process, and assigns the cost of equivalent units worked on during the current period first to complete beginning inventory, then to start and complete new units, and finally to units in ending work-in-process inventory. This method assumes that the earliest equivalent units in the Work in Process—Assembly account are completed first.

A distinctive feature of the FIFO process-costing method is that work done on beginning inventory before the current period is kept separate from work done in the current period. Costs incurred in the current period and units produced in the current period are used to calculate costs per equivalent unit of work done in the current period. In contrast, equivalent-unit and cost-per-equivalent-unit calculations in the weighted-average method merge the units and costs in beginning inventory with units and costs of work done in the current period.

We now describe the five-step procedure introduced in Case 2 using the FIFO method.

EXHIBIT 17-6

Steps 1 and 2: Summarize Output in Physical Units and Compute Equivalent Units
FIFO Method of Process Costing
Assembly Department of Global Defense, Inc., for March 2001

Flow of Production	(Step 1) Physical Units	(Step 2) Equivalent Units	
		Direct Materials	Conversion Costs
Work in process, beginning (given p. 614)	225	(work done before current period)	
Started during current period (given p. 614)	275		
To account for	500		
Completed and transferred out during current period:			
From beginning work in process[a]	225		
$225 \times (100\% - 100\%); 225 \times (100\% - 60\%)$		0	90
Started and completed	175[b]		
$175 \times 100\%, 175 \times 100\%$		175	175
Work in process, ending[c] (given p. 614)	100		
$100 \times 100\%; 100 \times 50\%$		100	50
Accounted for	500		
Work done in current period only		275	315

[a]Degree of completion in this department: direct materials, 100%; conversion costs, 60%.
[b]400 physical units completed and transferred out minus 225 physical units completed and transferred out from beginning work-in-process inventory.
[c]Degree of completion in this department: direct materials, 100%; conversion costs, 50%.

Step 1: Summarize the Flow of Physical Units Exhibit 17-6, step 1, traces the flow of physical units of production. The following observations help explain the physical units calculations.

◆ The first physical units assumed to be completed and transferred out during the period are the 225 units from the beginning work-in-process inventory.

◆ Of the 275 physical units started, 175 are assumed to be completed. Recall from the March data given on page 614 that 400 physical units were completed during March. The FIFO method assumes that the first 225 of these units were from beginning inventory; thus 175 (400 − 225) physical units must have been started and completed during March.

◆ Ending work-in-process inventory consists of 100 physical units—the 275 physical units started minus the 175 of these physical units completed.

◆ Note that the physical units "to account for" equal the physical units "accounted for" (500 units).

Step 2: Compute Output in Terms of Equivalent Units Exhibit 17-6 also presents the computations for step 2 under the FIFO method. *The equivalent-unit calculations for each cost category focus on the equivalent units of work done in the current period (March) only.*

Under the FIFO method, the work done in the current period is assumed to first complete the 225 units in beginning work in process. The equivalent units of

EXHIBIT 17-7
Steps 3, 4, and 5: Compute Equivalent-Unit Costs, Summarize Total Costs to Account For, and Assign Costs to Units Completed and to Units in Ending Work in Process
FIFO Method of Process Costing
Assembly Department of Global Defense, Inc., for March 2001

	Total Production Costs	Direct Materials	Conversion Costs
Work in process, beginning (given, p. 615)	$26,100	(costs of work done before current period)	
(Step 3) Costs added in current period (given, p. 615)	36,180	$19,800	$16,380
Divide by equivalent units of work done in current period (Exhibit 17-6)		÷275	÷315
Cost per equivalent unit of work done in current period		$ 72	$ 52
(Step 4) Total costs to account for	$62,280		
(Step 5) Assignment of costs:			
Completed and transferred out (400 units):			
Work in process, beginning (225 units)	$26,100		
Direct materials added in current period	0	0[a] × $72	
Conversion costs added in current period	4,680		90[a] × $52
Total from beginning inventory	30,780		
Started and completed (175 units)	21,700	(175[b] × $72) + (175[b] × $52)	
Total costs of units completed & transferred out	52,480		
Work in process, ending (100 units):			
Direct materials	7,200	100[c] × $72	
Conversion costs	2,600		50[c] × $52
Total work in process, ending	9,800		
Total costs accounted for	$62,280		

[a]Equivalent units used to complete beginning work in process from Exhibit 17-6, step 2.
[b]Equivalent units started and completed from Exhibit 17-6, step 2.
[c]Equivalent units in ending work in process from Exhibit 17-6, step 2.

work done in March on the beginning work-in-process inventory are computed by multiplying the 225 physical units *by the percentage of work remaining to be done to complete these units*: 0% for direct materials, because the beginning work in process is 100% complete with respect to direct materials, and 40% for conversion costs, because the beginning work in process is 60% complete with respect to conversion costs. The results are 0 (0% × 225) equivalent units of work for direct materials and 90 (40% × 225) equivalent units of work for conversion costs.

Next, the work done in the current period is assumed to start and complete the next 175 units. The equivalent units of work done on the 175 physical units started and completed are computed by multiplying 175 units by 100% for both direct materials and conversion costs, because all work on these units is done in the current period.

Finally, the work done in the current period is assumed to start but leave incomplete the final 100 units as ending work in process. The equivalent units of work done on the 100 units of ending work in process are calculated by multiplying 100 physical units by 100% for direct materials (because all direct materials have been added for these units in the current period) and 50% for conversion costs (because 50% of conversion costs work has been done on these units in the current period).

Step 3: Compute Equivalent-Unit Costs   Exhibit 17-7 shows the step 3 computation of equivalent-unit costs *for work done in the current period only* for direct materials and conversion costs. For example, we divide current-period conversion costs of $16,380 by current-period equivalent units for conversion costs of 315 to obtain cost per equivalent unit of $52.

Step 4: Summarize Total Costs to Account For   The total production costs column in Exhibit 17-7 presents step 4 and summarizes the total costs to account for in March 2001 (beginning work in process and costs added in the current period) of $62,280, as described in the example data (p. 615).

Step 5: Assign Costs to Units Completed and to Units in Ending Work in Process   Finally, Exhibit 17-7 shows the step 5 assignment of costs under the FIFO method. The costs of work done in the current period are first assigned to the additional work done to complete the beginning work in process, then to the work done on units started and completed during the current period, and finally to the ending work in process. *The easiest way to follow step 5 is to take each of the equivalent units calculated in Exhibit 17-6, step 2, and attach dollar amounts to them (using the cost-per-equivalent-unit calculations in step 3).* The goal is to determine the total cost of all units completed from beginning inventory and from work started and completed in the current period, and the costs of ending work in process done in the current period.

Notice that the 400 completed units are of two types: 225 units come from beginning inventory, and 175 units are started and completed during March. The FIFO method starts by assigning the costs of the beginning work-in-process inventory of $26,100 to the first units completed and transferred out. This $26,100 is the cost of the 225 equivalent units of direct materials and 135 equivalent units of conversion costs that comprise beginning inventory. The work that generated these costs was done in February, so these units are costed (see data on p. 615) at the February prices of $80 for direct materials and $60 for conversion costs [(225 × $80) + (135 × $60) = $26,100]. As we saw in step 2, an additional 90 equivalent units of conversion costs are needed to complete these units in the current period. The current-period conversion costs per equivalent unit is $52, so $4,680 (90 × $52) of additional costs are needed to complete the beginning inventory. The total production costs for the units in beginning inventory are $26,100 + $4,680 = $30,780. The 175 units started and completed in the current period consist of 175 equivalent units of direct materials and 175 equivalent units of conversion costs. These units are costed at the cost per equivalent unit in the current period (direct materials, $72 and conversion costs, $52) for a total production cost of $21,700.

Under FIFO, the ending work-in-process inventory comes from units that were started but not fully completed during the current period. The total cost of the 100 partially assembled physical units in ending work in process consists of:

Direct materials:
100 equivalent units × cost per equivalent unit in March of $72 $7,200

Conversion costs:
50 equivalent units × cost per equivalent unit in March of $52   2,600

Total costs of work in process on March 31 $9,800

The following table summarizes the total costs to account for and the costs accounted for of $62,280 in Exhibit 17-7. Notice how under the FIFO method, the layers of beginning work in process and costs added in the current period are kept separate. The arrows indicate where the costs in each layer go (that is, to units completed and transferred out or to ending work in process). Be sure to include the costs of beginning work in process ($26,100) when calculating the costs of units completed from beginning inventory.

Costs to Account For		Costs Accounted For Calculated on a FIFO Basis	
		Completed and transferred out:	
Beginning work in process	$26,100 →	Beginning work in process	$26,100
Costs added in current period	36,180 →	Used to complete beginning work in process	4,680
		Started and completed	21,700
		Completed and transferred out	52,480
		Ending work in process	9,800
Total costs to account for	$62,280	Total costs accounted for	$62,280

Before proceeding, please pause and review Exhibits 17-6 and 17-7 carefully to check your understanding of the FIFO method. Note that Exhibit 17-6 deals only with physical and equivalent units but no costs. Exhibit 17-7 shows the cost amounts.

The journal entries under the FIFO method parallel the journal entries under the weighted-average method. The only difference is that the entry to record the cost of goods completed and transferred out would be for $52,480 under the FIFO method instead of for $52,000 under the weighted-average method.

Only rarely is an application of pure FIFO ever encountered in process costing. As a result, it should really be called a *modified* or *departmental* FIFO method. Why? Because FIFO is applied within a department to compile the cost of units transferred *out*, but the units transferred *in* during a given period usually are carried at a single average unit cost as a matter of convenience. For example, the average cost of units transferred out of the Assembly Department is $52,480 ÷ 400 units = $131.20 per DG-19 unit. The Assembly Department uses FIFO to distinguish between monthly batches of production. The succeeding department, Testing, however, costs these units (that consist of costs incurred in February and March) at one average unit cost ($131.20 in this illustration). If this averaging were not done, the attempt to track costs on a pure FIFO basis throughout a series of processes would be unduly cumbersome.

COMPARISON OF WEIGHTED-AVERAGE AND FIFO METHODS

The following table summarizes the costs assigned to units completed and to units still in process under the weighted-average and FIFO process-costing methods for our example:

	Weighted Average (from Exhibit 17-5)	FIFO (from Exhibit 17-7)	Difference
Cost of units completed and transferred out	$52,000	$52,480	+$480
Work in process, ending	10,280	9,800	−$480
Total costs accounted for	$62,280	$62,280	

The weighted-average ending inventory is higher than the FIFO ending inventory by $480, or 4.9% ($480 ÷ $9,800). This is a significant difference when aggregated over the many thousands of products that Global Defense makes. The weighted-average method in our example also results in lower cost of goods sold and hence higher operating income and higher income taxes than does the FIFO method. Differences in equivalent-unit costs of beginning inventory and work done during the current period account for the differences in weighted-average and FIFO costs. Recall from the data on page 615 that direct materials costs per equivalent unit in beginning work-in-process inventory is $80, and conversion costs per equivalent unit in beginning work-in-process inventory is $60. These costs are greater than the $72 direct materials and $52 conversion costs per equivalent unit of work done during the current period. This reduction could be due to a decline in the prices of direct materials and conversion cost inputs or could be a result of Global Defense becoming more efficient.

For the Assembly Department, FIFO assumes that all the higher-cost units from the previous period in beginning work in process are the first to be completed and transferred out of the process, and ending work in process consists of only the lower-cost current-period units. The weighted-average method, however, smoothes out cost per equivalent unit by assuming that more of the lower-cost units are completed and transferred out, and some of the higher-cost units are placed in ending work in process. Hence, in this example, the weighted-average method results in a lower cost of units completed and transferred out and a higher ending work-in-process inventory relative to FIFO.

Cost of units completed and hence operating income can differ materially between the weighted-average and FIFO methods when (1) the direct materials or conversion costs per unit vary significantly from period to period, and (2) the physical inventory levels of work in process are large in relation to the total number of units transferred out of the process. Thus, as companies move toward long-term procurement contracts that reduce differences in unit costs from period to period, and reduce inventory levels, the difference in cost of units completed under the weighted-average and FIFO methods will decrease.[1]

Managers need information from process-costing systems to aid them in pricing and product-mix decisions and to provide them with feedback about their performance. The major advantage of FIFO is that it provides managers with information about changes in the costs per unit from one period to the next. Managers can use this information to evaluate their performance in the current period compared to a benchmark or compared to their performance in the previous period. By focusing on work done and the costs of work done during the current period, the FIFO method provides useful information for these planning and control purposes. The weighted-average method merges unit costs from different periods and so obscures period-to-period comparisons. The major advantages of the weighted-average method, however, are its computational simplicity and its reporting of a more representative average unit cost when input prices fluctuate markedly from month to month.

Note that unlike in job-costing systems, activity-based costing has less applicability in process-costing environments. Why? Because products are homogeneous and hence use resources in a similar way. Furthermore, each process—assembly, testing, and so on—corresponds to the different (production) activities. Managers reduce the costs of activities by controlling the costs of individual processes.

Curriculum Linkage Students need to be reminded how ABC affects process costing. Since there are homogeneous products that use resources in a similar way, there is much less value added by an ABC system to products that use process costing than for the heterogeneous products produced under a job-order costing system.

[1]For example, suppose beginning work-in-process inventory for March is 125 physical units (instead of 225) and suppose cost per equivalent unit of work done in the current period (March) is direct materials, $75, and conversion costs, $55. Assume all other data for March are the same as in our example. In this case, the cost of units completed and transferred out would be $52,833 under the weighted-average method and $53,000 under the FIFO method, and the work-in-process ending inventory would be $10,417 under the weighted-average method and $10,250 under the FIFO method (calculations not shown). These differences are much smaller than in the chapter example. The weighted-average ending inventory is higher than the FIFO ending inventory by only $167 or 1.63% ($167 ÷ $10,250) compared to 4.9% higher in the chapter example.

STANDARD-COSTING METHOD OF PROCESS COSTING

This section assumes that you have already studied Chapters 7 and 8. If you have not, skip to the next major section, Transferred-in Costs in Process Costing, page 626.

As we have mentioned, companies that use process-costing systems produce masses of identical or similar units of output. Setting standards for quantities of inputs needed to produce output is often relatively straightforward in such companies. Standard costs per input unit may then be assigned to these physical standards to develop standard costs per output unit.

The weighted-average and FIFO methods become very complicated when used in process industries that produce a wide variety of similar products. For example, a steel-rolling mill uses various steel alloys and produces sheets of various sizes and of various finishes. Both the items of direct materials and the operations performed are relatively few. But used in various combinations, they yield such a *wide variety* of products that inaccurate costs for each product result if the *broad* averaging procedure of actual process costing is used. Similarly, complex conditions are frequently found, for example, in plants that manufacture rubber products, textiles, ceramics, paints, and packaged food products. The standard-costing method of process costing is especially useful in these situations.

Under the standard-costing method, teams of design and process engineers, operations personnel, and management accountants determine *separate* standard or equivalent-unit costs on the basis of the different technical processing specifications for each product. Identifying standard costs for each product overcomes the disadvantage of costing all products at a single average amount, as under actual costing.

Computations under Standard Costing

We again use the Assembly Department of Global Defense, Inc., as an example, except this time we assign standard costs to the process. The same standard costs apply in February and March of 2001:

Direct materials	$ 74 per unit
Conversion costs	54 per unit
Total standard manufacturing costs	$128 per unit

Data for the Assembly Department are:

Physical Units for March 2001

Work in process, beginning inventory (March 1)	225 units
Direct materials (100% complete)	
Conversion costs (60% complete)	
Started during March	275 units
Completed and transferred out during March	400 units
Work in process, ending inventory (March 31)	100 units
Direct materials (100% complete)	
Conversion costs (50% complete)	

Total Costs for March 2001

Work in process, beginning inventory at standard costs		
Direct materials: 225 equivalent units × $74 per unit	$16,650	
Conversion costs: 135 equivalent units × $54 per unit	7,290	$23,940
Actual direct materials costs added during March		19,800
Actual conversion costs added during March		16,380

We illustrate the standard-costing method of process costing using the five-step procedure introduced earlier in the chapter. Exhibit 17-8 presents steps 1 and 2. These steps are identical to the steps described for the FIFO method in Exhibit 17-6. Work done in the current period equals direct materials (275 equivalent units) and conversion costs (315 equivalent units).

Exhibit 17-9 shows the step 3 computation of equivalent-unit costs. Step 3 is easier under the standard-costing method than it is under the weighted-average and FIFO methods. Why? Because the cost per equivalent unit does not have to be computed, as was done for the weighted-average and FIFO methods. Instead, the costs per equivalent unit *are* the standard costs: direct materials, $74, and conversion costs, $54. Using

EXHIBIT 17-8
Steps 1 and 2: Summarize Output in Physical Units and Compute Equivalent Units
Use of Standard Costs in Process Costing
Assembly Department of Global Defense, Inc., for March 2001

	(Step 1) Physical Units	(Step 2) Equivalent Units	
Flow of Production		**Direct Materials**	**Conversion Costs**
Work in process, beginning (given p. 623)	225		
Started during current period (given p. 623)	275		
To account for	500		
Completed and transferred out during current period:			
From beginning work in process[a]			
225 × (100% − 100%); 225 × (100% − 60%)	225	0	90
Started and completed	175[b]		
175 × 100%, 175 × 100%		175	175
Work in process, ending[c] (given p. 623)	100		
100 × 100%; 100 × 50%		100	50
Accounted for	500		
Work done in current period only		275	315

[a]Degree of completion in this department: direct materials, 100%; conversion costs, 60%.
[b]400 physical units completed and transferred out minus 225 physical units completed and transferred out from beginning work-in-process inventory.
[c]Degree of completion in this department: direct materials, 100%; conversion costs, 50%.

standard costs also simplifies the computations for assigning the total costs to account for to units completed and transferred out and to units in ending work-in-process inventory.

The total costs to account for in Exhibit 17-9, step 4, that is, the total debits to Work in Process—Assembly, differ from the total debits to Work in Process—Assembly under the actual cost-based weighted-average and FIFO methods explained earlier in the chapter. Why? Because, *as in all standard-costing systems*, the debits to the Work-in-Process account are at standard costs rather than actual costs. These standard costs total $61,300.

Exhibit 17-9, step 5, assigns total costs to units completed and transferred out and to units in ending work-in-process inventory, as in the FIFO method. Step 5 attaches dollar amounts, using standard costs, to the equivalent units calculated in Exhibit 17-8. These costs are assigned first to complete beginning work-in-process inventory, then to start and complete new units, and finally to start new units that are in ending work-in-process inventory. Note how the total costs accounted for in step 5 of Exhibit 17-9 ($61,300) equal the total costs to account for.

Accounting for Variances

Process-costing systems using standard costs usually accumulate actual costs incurred separately from the inventory accounts. The following is an example. The actual costs are recorded in the first two entries. Recall that Global Defense purchases direct materials as needed and that these materials are delivered directly to the Assembly Department. The total variances are recorded in the next two entries. The final entry transfers out the completed goods at standard costs.

1. Assembly Department Direct Materials Control (at actual)   19,800
        Accounts Payable Control   19,800

    To record direct materials purchased and used in
    production during March. This cost control
    account is debited with actual costs and immediately credited
    with standard costs assigned to the units worked on (entry 3 below).

EXHIBIT 17-9
Steps 3, 4, and 5: Compute Equivalent-Unit Costs, Summarize Total Costs to Account For, and
Assign Costs to Units Completed and to Units in Ending Work in Process
Use of Standard Costs in Process Costing
Assembly Department of Global Defense, Inc., for March 2001

	Total Production Costs	Direct Materials	Conversion Costs
(Step 3) Standard cost per equivalent unit (given, p. 623)		$ 74	$ 54
Work in process, beginning (given, p. 623)			
Direct materials, $225 \times \$74$; Conversion costs, $135 \times \$54$	$23,940		
Costs added in current period at standard costs			
Direct materials, $275 \times \$74$; Conversion costs, $315 \times \$54$	37,360	20,350	17,010
(Step 4) Costs to account for	$61,300		
(Step 5) Assignment of costs at standard costs:			
Completed and transferred out (400 units):			
Work in process, beginning (225 units)	$23,940		
Direct materials added in current period	0	$0^a \times \$74$	
Conversion costs added in current period	4,860		$90^a \times \$54$
Total from beginning inventory	28,800		
Started and completed (175 units)	22,400	$(175^b \times \$74) + (175^b \times \$54)$	
Total costs of units transferred out	51,200		
Work in process, ending (100 units):			
Direct materials	7,400	$100^c \times \$74$	
Conversion costs	2,700		$50^c \times \$54$
Total work in process, ending	10,100		
Total costs accounted for	$61,300		
Summary of variances for current performance			
Costs added in current period at standard prices (see step 3 above)		$20,350	$17,010
Actual costs incurred (given p. 623)		19,800	16,380
Variance		$ 550 F	$ 630 F

[a]Equivalent units to complete beginning work in process from Exhibit 17-8, step 2.
[b]Equivalent units started and completed from Exhibit 17-8, step 2.
[c]Equivalent units in ending work in process from Exhibit 17-8, step 2.

2.	Assembly Department Conversion Costs Control (at actual)	16,380	
	Various accounts		16,380

To record Assembly Department conversion costs for March.

Entries 3, 4, and 5 use standard cost dollar amounts from Exhibit 17-9.

3.	Work in Process—Assembly (at standard costs)	20,350	
	Direct Materials Variances		550
	Assembly Department Direct Materials Control		19,800

To record actual direct materials used and total direct materials variances.

4.	Work in Process—Assembly (at standard costs)	17,010	
	Conversion Costs Variances		630
	Assembly Department Conversion Costs Control		16,380

To record actual conversion costs and total conversion costs variances.

5.	Work in Process—Testing (at standard costs)	51,200	
	Work in Process—Assembly (at standard costs)		51,200

To record costs of units completed and transferred out
at standard cost from Assembly to Testing.

EXHIBIT 17-10
Flow of Standard Costs in a Process-Costing System
Assembly Department of Global Defense, Inc., for March 2001

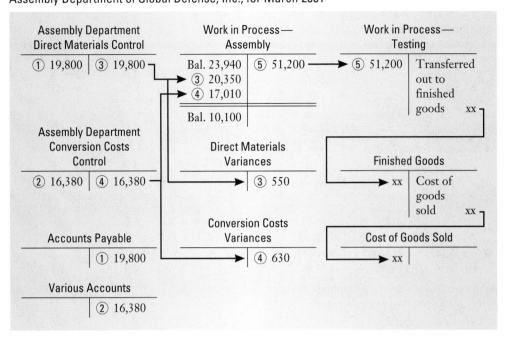

Teaching Tip Students have trouble with transfers-in. In the Global Defense example, units cannot begin Testing until they are completely assembled. These transferred-in (TI) Assembly Dept. costs act like DM that are added at the very beginning of the Testing process. A time line helps students to understand the process.

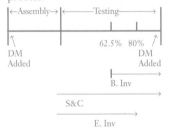

During the current period, the Testing process at Global Defense will (1) finish the B. WIP (0% TI, 37.5% CC, 100% DM), (2) S&C (100% of TI, CC, and DM), and (3) start the E. WIP (100% TI, 80% CC, and 0% DM).

Variances arise under the standard-costing method, as in entries 3 and 4 above. Why? Because the standard costs assigned to products on the basis of work done in the current period do not equal the actual costs incurred in the current period. Variances can be measured and analyzed in little or great detail for planning and control purposes, as described in Chapters 7 and 8. Exhibit 17-10 shows how the standard costs flow through the accounts.

TRANSFERRED-IN COSTS IN PROCESS COSTING

Many process-costing systems have two or more departments or processes in the production cycle. As units move from department to department, the related costs are also transferred by monthly journal entries. If standard costs are used, the accounting for such transfers is relatively simple. However, if the weighted-average or FIFO method is used, the accounting can become more complex. We now extend our Global Defense, Inc., example to the Testing Department. As the assembly process is completed, the Assembly Department of Global Defense immediately transfers DG-19 units to its Testing Department. Here the units receive additional direct materials, such as crating and other packing materials to prepare the units for shipment, at the *end* of the process. Conversion costs are added evenly during the Testing Department's process. As units are completed in Testing, they are immediately transferred to Finished Goods.

The following graphic summarizes these facts:

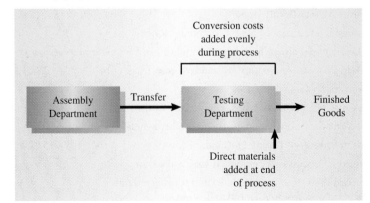

OBJECTIVE 8

Apply process-costing methods to cases with transferred-in costs

Process Costing in the Ceramics Industry

Ceramics, Inc., produces ceramic products (such as multilayer packages for integrated circuits) in a batch-flow manufacturing process. Forming and finishing are the two major production stages.

♦ *Forming.* Ceramic material is mixed, forced through an extruder, and sent to a dryer.

♦ *Finishing.* The products are fired in a kiln, cut, ground, and packaged.

For many years Ceramics, Inc., has manufactured like or similar products in large production runs for industrial customers (termed "original equipment manufacturers," or OEMs) such as computer companies and defense companies.

Ceramic, Inc., costs individual products using standard costs in a process-costing system. Cost data are accumulated and tracked for the forming and finishing operations. Conversion costs are allocated using standard (scheduled) hours of production time in each department. Depreciation on plant and equipment is included in this conversion cost. The controller at Ceramics believes that this system "accurately measures the cost of manufacturing OEM products." These products are manufactured in large batches in a highly standardized way.

Ceramics, Inc., recently added a "custom production line" at its plant. This line manufactures ceramic products that vary greatly in production volume and frequently are tailored to each individual customer's needs. For example, custom-designed nozzles used for pollution control are being manufactured for one customer who needs to rid its flue gas of sulfur.

The controller is skeptical about the accuracy of product costs for these custom products based on the existing process-costing system. She believes that the costs of these products are driven by more variables than standard hours in production at each department. For example, many custom jobs require specialized finishing steps that are undertaken in a job shop adjoining the main production area. Currently she is keeping a separate, largely manual job-costing system that uses some data from the main system and some separately maintained cost data.

The controller is now exploring ways to adapt the formal process-costing system to incorporate some elements of a job-costing system. Her point is that custom jobs put different demands on the resources of Ceramics, Inc., than does the average large production run job. For these custom jobs, a hybrid-costing system with elements of both process costing and job costing may be appropriate.

Source: Adapted from U. Karmarkar, P. Lederer, and J. Zimmerman, "Choosing Manufacturing Production Control and Cost Accounting Systems." In R. Kaplan, *Measures for Manufacturing Excellence* (Boston, MA: Harvard Business School Press, 1990). Ceramics, Inc., is a fictitious name for the actual company.

Data for the Testing Department for the month of March 2001 are:

Physical Units for March 2001

Work in process, beginning inventory (March 1)	240 units
Transferred-in costs (100% complete)	
Direct materials (0% complete)	
Conversion costs (5/8 or 62.5% complete)	
Transferred in during March	400 units
Completed during March	440 units
Work in process, ending inventory (March 31)	200 units
Transferred-in costs (100% complete)	
Direct materials (0% complete)	
Conversion costs (80% complete)	

Reinforcing Problems Transferred-in costs with WA are covered in Exer. 17-27 and Probs. 17-33, 17-38, and 17-40. Transferred-in costs with FIFO are covered in Exer. 17-28 and Probs. 17-34, 17-39, and 17-40.

Costs of Testing Department for March 2001

Work in process, beginning inventory[2]		
Transferred-in costs (240 equivalent units × $140 per equivalent unit)	$33,600	
Direct materials	0	
Conversion costs (150 equivalent units × $120 per equivalent unit)	18,000	$51,600
Transferred-in costs during March		
Weighted-average (from Exhibit 17-5)		52,000
FIFO (from Exhibit 17-7)		52,480
Direct materials costs added during March		13,200
Conversion costs added during March		48,600

Transferred-in costs (also called **previous department costs**) are the costs incurred in a previous department that are carried forward as the product's cost when it moves to a subsequent process in the production cycle. That is, as the units move from one department to the next, their costs are transferred with them. Thus, computations of Testing Department costs consist of transferred-in costs, as well as the direct materials and conversion costs added in Testing.

Transferred-in costs are treated as if they are a separate type of direct material added at the beginning of the process. In other words, when successive departments are involved, transferred units from one department become all or a part of the direct materials of the next department; however, they are called transferred-in costs, not direct materials costs.

Transferred-In Costs and the Weighted-Average Method

To examine the weighted-average process-costing method with transferred-in costs, we use the five-step procedure described earlier (p. 611) to assign costs of the Testing Department to units completed and transferred out and to units in ending work

EXHIBIT 17-11
Steps 1 and 2: Summarize Output in Physical Units and Compute Equivalent Units
Weighted-Average Method of Process Costing
Testing Department of Global Defense, Inc., for March 2001

Flow of Production	(Step 1) Physical Units (given p. 627)	(Step 2) Equivalent Units		
		Transferred-In Costs	Direct Materials	Conversion Costs
Work in process, beginning	240			
Transferred in during current period	400			
To account for	640			
Completed and transferred out during current period	440	440	440	440
Work in process, ending[a]	200			
200 × 100%; 200 × 0%; 200 × 80%		200	0	160
Accounted for	640			
Work done to date		640	440	600

[a]Degree of completion in this department: transferred-in costs, 100%; direct materials, 0%; conversion costs, 80%.

[2]The beginning work-in-process inventory is the same under both the weighted-average and FIFO inventory methods because we assume costs per equivalent unit to be the same in both January and February. If the cost per equivalent unit had been different in the two months, the work-in-process inventory at the end of February (beginning of March) would be costed differently under the weighted-average and FIFO methods. If this were the case, the basic approach to process costing with transferred-in costs would still be the same as what we describe in this section. Only the beginning balances of work in process would be different.

EXHIBIT 17-12
Steps 3, 4, and 5: Compute Equivalent-Unit Costs, Summarize Total Costs to Account For, and Assign Costs to Units Completed and to Units in Ending Work in Process
Weighted-Average Method of Process Costing
Testing Department of Global Defense, Inc., for March 2001

	Total Production Costs	Transferred-In Costs	Direct Materials	Conversion Costs
(Step 3) Work in process, beginning (given, p. 629)	$ 51,600	$33,600	$ 0	$18,000
Costs added in current period (given, p. 629)	113,800	52,000	13,200	48,600
Costs incurred to date		$85,600	$13,200	$66,600
Divide by equivalent units of work done to date (Exhibit 17-11)		÷ 640	÷ 440	÷ 600
Equipment-unit costs of work done to date		$133.75	$ 30	$ 111
(Step 4) Total costs to account for	$165,400			
(Step 5) Assignment of costs:				
Completed and transferred out (440 units)	$120,890	(440^a × $133.75) + (440^a × $30) + (440^a × $111)		
Work in process, ending (200 units):				
Transferred-in costs	26,750	200^b × $133.75		
Direct materials	0		0^b × $30	
Conversion costs	17,760			160^b × $111
Total work in process, ending	44,510			
Total costs accounted for	$165,400			

^{a}Equivalent units completed and transferred out from Exhibit 17-11, step 2.
^{b}Equivalent units in ending work in process from Exhibit 17-11, step 2.

in process. Exhibit 17-11 shows steps 1 and 2. The computations are basically the same as the calculations of equivalent units under the weighted-average method for the Assembly Department in Exhibit 17-4, except for the addition of transferred-in costs. The units are fully completed as to transferred-in costs because these costs are simply carried forward from the previous process. Note, however, that direct materials costs have a zero degree of completion in both the beginning and ending work-in-process inventories because, in Testing, direct materials are introduced at the *end* of the process.

Exhibit 17-12 describes steps 3, 4, and 5 for the weighted-average method. Note that beginning work in process and work done in the current period are combined for purposes of computing equivalent-unit costs for transferred-in costs, direct materials, and conversion costs.

Using the dollar amount from Exhibit 17-12, the journal entry for the transfer out from Testing to finished goods inventory is:

Finished Goods Control	120,890	
Work in Process—Testing		120,890

To record cost of goods completed and transferred from Testing to finished goods.

Entries to the key T-account, Work in Process—Testing, follow (from Exhibit 17-12).

Work in Process—Testing			
Beginning inventory, March 1,	51,600	Transferred out	120,890
Transferred-in costs	52,000		
Direct materials	13,200		
Conversion costs	48,600		
Ending inventory, March 31	44,510		

EXHIBIT 17-13
Steps 1 and 2: Summarize Output in Physical Units and Compute Equivalent Units
FIFO Method of Process Costing
Testing Department of Global Defense, Inc., for March 2001

Flow of Production	(Step 1) Physical Units	(Step 2) Equivalent Units		
		Transferred-In Costs	Direct Materials	Conversion Costs
Work in process, beginning (given, p. 627)	240	(work done before current period)		
Transferred-in during current period (given, p. 627)	400			
To account for	640			
Completed and transferred out during current period:				
From beginning work in process[a]	240			
240 × (100% − 100%); 240 × (100% − 0%);				
240 × (100% − 62.5%)		0	240	90
Started and completed	200[b]			
200 × 100%; 200 × 100%; 200 × 100%		200	200	200
Work in process, ending[c] (given, p. 627)	200			
200 × 100%; 200 × 0%; 200 × 80%		200	0	160
Accounted for	640			
Work done in current period only		400	440	450

[a]Degree of completion in this department: Transferred-in costs, 100%; direct materials, 0%; conversion costs, 62.5%.
[b]440 physical units completed and transferred out minus 240 physical units completed and transferred out from beginning work-in-process inventory.
[c]Degree of completion in this department: transferred-in costs, 100%; direct materials, 0%; conversion costs, 80%.

Transferred-In Costs and the FIFO Method

To examine the FIFO process-costing method with transferred-in costs, we again use the five-step procedure. Exhibit 17-13 shows steps 1 and 2. Other than considering transferred-in costs, the computations of equivalent units are basically the same as those under the FIFO method for the Assembly Department shown in Exhibit 17-6.

Exhibit 17-14 describes steps 3, 4, and 5. Note that the costs per equivalent unit for the current period in step 3 are only calculated on the basis of costs transferred in and work done in the current period. In steps 4 and 5, the total costs to account for and accounted for of $165,880 under the FIFO method differ from the corresponding amounts under the weighted-average method of $165,400. Why? Because of the different costs of completed units transferred-in from the Assembly Department under the two methods ($52,480 under FIFO and $52,000 under weighted average).

Using the dollar amount from Exhibit 17-14, the journal entry for the transfer of completed units to finished goods inventory is:

Finished Goods Control	122,360	
Work in Process—Testing		122,360

To record cost of goods completed and transferred from Testing to finished goods.

Entries to the key T-account, Work in Process—Testing, follow using information from Exhibit 17-14.

Work in Process—Testing			
Beginning inventory, March 1,	51,600	Transferred out	122,360
Transferred-in costs	52,480		
Direct materials	13,200		
Conversion costs	48,600		
Ending inventory, March 31	43,520		

EXHIBIT 17-14

Steps 3, 4, and 5: Compute Equivalent-Unit Costs, Summarize Total Costs to Account For, and Assign Costs to Units Completed and to Units in Ending Work in Process
FIFO Method of Process Costing
Testing Department of Global Defense, Inc., for March 2001

	Total Production Costs	Transferred-In Costs	Direct Materials	Conversion Costs
Work in process, beginning (given, p. 628)	$ 51,600	(costs of work done before current period)		
(Step 3) Costs added in current period (given, p. 628)	114,280	$52,480	$13,200	$48,600
Divide by equivalent units of work done in current period (Exhibit 17-13)		÷400	÷440	÷450
Cost per equivalent unit of work done in current period		$131.20	$ 30	$ 108
(Step 4) Total costs to account for	$165,880			
(Step 5) Assignment of costs:				
Completed and transferred out (440 units):				
Work in process, beginning (240 units)	$ 51,600			
Transferred-in costs added in current period	0	0[a] × $131.20		
Direct materials added in current period	7,200		240[a] × $30	
Conversion costs added in current period	9,720			90[a] × $108
Total from beginning inventory	68,520			
Started and completed (200 units)	53,840	(200[b] × $131.20) + (200[b] × $30) + (200[b] × $108)		
Total costs of units completed and transferred out	122,360			
Work in process, ending (200 units):				
Transferred-in costs	26,240	200[c] × $131.20		
Direct materials	0		0[c] × $30	
Conversion costs	17,280			160[c] × $108
Total work in process, ending	43,520			
Total costs accounted for	$165,880			

[a]Equivalent units used to complete beginning work in process from Exhibit 17-13, step 2.
[b]Equivalent units started and completed from Exhibit 17-13, step 2.
[c]Equivalent units in ending work in process from Exhibit 17-13, step 2.

Remember that in a series of interdepartmental transfers, each department is regarded as being separate and distinct for accounting purposes. All costs transferred in during a given accounting period are carried at one unit-cost figure, as described when discussing modified FIFO on page 621, regardless of whether previous departments used the weighted-average method or the FIFO method.

Common Mistakes with Transferred-In Costs

Here are some common pitfalls to avoid when accounting for transferred-in costs:

1. Remember to include transferred-in costs from previous departments in your calculations.

2. In calculating costs to be transferred on a FIFO basis, do not overlook the costs assigned at the beginning of the period to units that were in process but are now included in the units transferred. For example, do not overlook the $51,600 in Exhibit 17-14.

3. Unit costs may fluctuate between periods. Therefore, transferred units may contain batches accumulated at different unit costs. For example, the 400 units transferred in at $52,480 in Exhibit 17-14 using the FIFO method consist of units that have different unit costs of direct materials and conversion costs

Teaching Tip Students often lose sight of the big picture because of the myriad detailed process-costing computations. At the end of the discussion of process costing, it helps to reemphasize that the goal is to calculate the costs of the units completed. To do so we need cost/unit, which are normally calculated as TC/units. Complications arise from two sources. First, when costs change from period to period, we need to decide which cost flow assumption to use in the total cost computation—WA, FIFO, or standard. Second, when there are incomplete units, we adjust from units to EU.

Teaching Tip Emphasize that students *must* understand this chapter before attempting Chap. 18, which considers spoilage.

when these units were worked on in the Assembly Department (see Exhibit 17-7). Remember, however, that when these units are transferred to the Testing Department, they are costed at *one* average unit cost of $131.20 ($52,480 ÷ 400) as in Exhibit 17-14.

4. Units may be measured in different terms in different departments. Consider each department separately. For example, unit costs could be based on kilograms in the first department and liters in the second department. Accordingly, as units are received in the second department, their measurements must be converted to liters.

HYBRID-COSTING SYSTEMS

Product-costing systems do not always fall neatly into the categories of job costing or process costing. A **hybrid-costing system** blends characteristics from both job-costing systems and process-costing systems. Job-costing and process-costing systems are best viewed as the ends of a continuum:

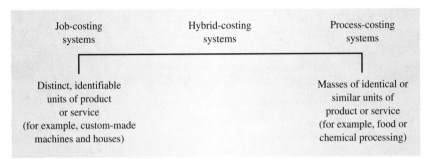

Product-costing systems must often be designed to fit the particular characteristics of different production systems. Many production systems are a hybrid—they have some features of custom-order manufacturing and other features of mass-production manufacturing. Manufacturers of a relatively wide variety of closely related standardized products tend to use a hybrid-costing system. Consider Ford Motor Company. Automobiles may be manufactured in a continuous flow, but individual units may be customized with a special combination of engine size, transmission, music system, and so on. Companies develop hybrid-costing systems in such situations. The Concepts in Action feature describes the evolution of a hybrid-costing system. The Appendix to this chapter explains *operation costing*, a common type of hybrid-costing system.

PROBLEM FOR SELF-STUDY

PROBLEM

Allied Chemicals operates a thermo-assembly process as the second of three processes at its plastics plant. Direct materials in thermo-assembly are added at the end of the process. The following data pertain to the Thermo-Assembly Department for June 2001:

Work in process, beginning inventory	50,000 units
Transferred-in costs (100% complete)	
Direct materials (0% complete)	
Conversion costs (80% complete)	
Transferred in during current period	200,000 units
Completed and transferred out during current period	210,000 units
Work in process, ending inventory	? units
Transferred-in costs (100% complete)	
Direct materials (0% complete)	
Conversion costs (40% complete)	

Required
Compute the equivalent units under (1) the weighted-average method, and (2) the FIFO method.

SOLUTION

1. The weighted-average method uses equivalent units of work done to date to compute equivalent-unit costs. The calculations follow:

Flow of Production	(Step 1) Physical Units (given)	(Step 2) Equivalent Units		
		Transferred-In Costs	Direct Materials	Conversion Costs
Work in process, beginning	50,000			
Transferred in during current period	200,000			
To account for	250,000			
Completed and transferred out during current period	210,000	210,000	210,000	210,000
Work in process, ending[a]	40,000			
40,000 × 100%; 40,000 × 0%; 40,000 × 40%		40,000	0	16,000
Accounted for	250,000			
Work done to date		250,000	210,000	226,000

[a]Degree of completion in this department: transferred-in costs, 100%; direct materials, 0%; conversion costs, 40%.

2. The FIFO method uses equivalent units of work done in current period only when computing equivalent-unit costs. The calculations follow:

Flow of Production	(Step 1) Physical Units	(Step 2) Equivalent Units		
		Transferred-In Costs	Direct Materials	Conversion Costs
Work in process, beginning (given)	50,000			
Transferred in during current period (given)	200,000			
To account for	250,000			
Completed and transferred out during current period				
From beginning work in process[a]	50,000			
50,000 × (100% − 100%); 50,000 × (100% − 0%); 50,000 × (100% − 80%)		0	50,000	10,000
Started and completed	160,000[b]			
160,000 × 100%; 160,000 × 100%; 160,000 × 100%		160,000	160,000	160,000
Work in process, ending[c] (given)	40,000			
40,000 × 100%; 40,000 × 0%; 40,000 × 40%		40,000	0	16,000
Accounted for	250,000			
Work done in current period only		200,000	210,000	186,000

[a]Degree of completion in this department: transferred-in costs, 100%; direct materials, 0%; conversion costs, 80%.
[b]210,000 physical units completed and transferred out minus 50,000 physical units completed and transferred out from beginning work-in-process inventory.
[c]Degree of completion in this department: transferred-in costs, 100%; direct materials, 0%; conversion costs, 40%.

SUMMARY

The following points are linked to the chapter's learning objectives:

1. A process-costing system is used to determine the cost of a product or service when masses of identical or similar units are produced. Unit costs are computed by

first assigning costs to these similar units and then dividing by the number of these units. Industries using process-costing systems include food, textiles, and oil refining.

2. The five key steps in a process-costing system using equivalent units are (a) summarize the flow of physical units of output, (b) compute output in terms of equivalent units, (c) compute equivalent-unit costs, (d) summarize total costs to account for, and (e) assign total costs to units completed and to units in ending work in process.

3. Equivalent units is a derived amount of output units that takes the quantity of each input in units completed or in work in process, and converts it into the amount of completed output units that could be made with that quantity of input. Equivalent-unit calculations are necessary when all physical units of output are not uniformly completed during an accounting period.

4. Journal entries in a process-costing system are similar to entries in a job-costing system. The main difference is that in a process-costing system, there is a separate Work-in-Process account for each department.

5. The weighted-average method of process costing computes unit costs by focusing on the total costs and the total equivalent units completed to date and assigns this average cost to units completed and to units in ending work-in-process inventory.

6. The first-in, first-out (FIFO) method of process costing assigns the costs of the beginning work-in-process inventory to the first units completed, and assigns the costs of the equivalent units worked on during the current period first to complete beginning inventory, then to start and complete new units, and finally to units in ending work-in-process inventory.

7. The standard-costing method simplifies process costing because standard costs serve as the costs per equivalent unit when assigning costs to units completed and to units in ending work-in-process inventory.

8. The weighted-average process-costing method computes transferred-in costs per unit by focusing on total transferred-in costs and total equivalent transferred-in units completed to date, and assigns this average cost to units completed and to units in ending work-in-process inventory. The FIFO process-costing method assigns transferred-in costs in beginning work in process to units completed, and the costs transferred in during the current period first to complete beginning work-in-process units, then to start and complete new units, and finally to units in ending work-in-process inventory.

APPENDIX: OPERATION COSTING

This appendix presents key ideas of operation costing and uses an example to illustrate key calculations and journal entries.

Overview of Operation-Costing Systems

An **operation** is a standardized method or technique that is performed repetitively regardless of the distinguishing features of the finished goods. Operations are usually conducted within departments. For instance, a suit maker may have a cutting operation and a hemming operation within a single department. The term operation, however, is often used loosely. It may be a synonym for a department or process. For example, some companies may call their finishing department a finishing process or a finishing operation.

An **operation-costing system** is a hybrid-costing system applied to batches of similar products. Each batch of products is often a variation of a single design and proceeds through a sequence of selected, though not necessarily the same, activities or operations. Within each operation, all product units are treated exactly alike, using identical amounts of the operation's resources. Batches are also termed production runs.

Consider a company that makes suits. Management may select a single basic design for every suit that the company manufactures. Depending on specifications, batches of suits vary from each other. One batch may use wool; another batch, cotton. One batch may require special hand stitching; another batch, machine stitch-

ENCORE, ENCORE! or PLAY IT AGAIN, SAM!
"Cost Accounting is music to your ears!"

COST ACCOUNTING, *Tenth Edition*
Charles T. Horngren, George Foster, and Srikant M. Datar

"I am pleased to see the 5-step method returned. . . .[This] method works so very well for explaining process costing."
–Jean Hawkins, *William Jewell College*

Horngren, Foster, and Datar are in tune with market feedback. This tenth edition offers a variety of new features but includes refinements to satisfy the audience's requests— such as reinstating the five-step approach in the chapter on **process costing (17).**

◆ Includes a more detailed explanation of equivalent units and the steps in the various methods of process costing.

◆ Features a new appendix to this chapter that discusses hybrid and operation costing

◆ Places a greater emphasis on cost management issues

ing. Other products that are likewise often manufactured in batches are semiconductors, textiles, and shoes.

An operation-costing system uses work orders that specify the needed direct materials and step-by-step operations. Product costs are compiled for each work order. Direct materials that are unique to different work orders are specifically identified with the appropriate work order as in job-costing systems. The conversion costs for each unit passing through a given operation are the same regardless of work order. Why? Because each unit passing through an operation uses identical amounts of that operation's resources. A single average conversion costs per unit is calculated as in process costing. For each operation, this amount is computed by dividing total conversion costs by all units passing through that operation. Our examples assume only two cost categories, direct materials and conversion costs. Of course, operation costing can have more than two cost categories. The costs in each category are identified with work orders using job-costing or process-costing methods as appropriate.

Managers often find operation costing useful in cost management. Why? Because operation costing focuses on the physical processes, or operations, of a given production system. For example, in the manufacturing of clothing, managers are concerned with fabric waste, the number of fabric layers that can be cut at one time, and so on. Operation costing captures the financial impact of the control of physical processes. Feedback from an operation-costing system can therefore provide essential insight into the control of physical processes and the management of operation costs.

Reinforcing Problems Exer. 17-29 and Prob. 17-42 cover operations costing.

Illustration of Operation-Costing System

Baltimore Company, a clothing manufacturer, produces two lines of blazers for department stores. Wool blazers use better-quality materials and undergo more operations than do polyester blazers. Consider the following operations in 2000:

	Work Order 423	Work Order 424
Direct materials	Wool	Polyester
	Satin full lining	Rayon partial lining
	Bone Buttons	Plastic buttons
Operations		
1. Cutting cloth	Use	Use
2. Checking edges	Use	Do not use
3. Sewing body	Use	Use
4. Checking seams	Use	Do not use
5. Machine sewing of collars and lapels	Do not use	Use
6. Hand sewing of collars and lapels	Use	Do not use

Suppose work order 423 is for 50 wool blazers and work order 424 is for 100 polyester blazers. The following costs are assumed for these two work orders, which were started and completed in March 2000:

	Work Order 423	Work Order 424
Number of blazers	50	100
Direct materials costs	$ 6,000	$3,000
Conversion costs allocated:		
Operation 1	580	1,160
Operation 2	400	—
Operation 3	1,900	3,800
Operation 4	500	—
Operation 5	—	875
Operation 6	700	—
Total manufacturing costs	$10,080	$8,835

Points to Stress Calculation of the budgeted CC rate is analogous to calculation of the std. cost/EU in standard process costing. In the text's example, all the units are completed so EU = physical units. If some units were incomplete, the denominator would be the total number of EU (from all product) expected to pass through the production process. In the text's example, the 20,000 unit denominator is the *sum* of wool jackets and polyester jackets (i.e., "apples and oranges"). How can we add wool jackets to polyester jackets? Because each jacket requires the same amount of CC; the two products are identical from the standpoint of consumption of CC.

As in process costing, all product units in any work order are assumed to consume identical amounts of conversion costs of a particular operation. Baltimore Company's operation-costing system uses a budgeted rate to calculate the conversion costs of each operation. For example, the costs of Operation 1 might be budgeted as follows (amounts assumed):

$$\text{Operation 1 budgeted conversion-cost rate in 2000} = \frac{\text{Operation 1 budgeted conversion costs in 2000}}{\text{Operation 1 budgeted product units in 2000}}$$

$$= \frac{\$232,000}{20,000 \text{ units}}$$

$$= \$11.60 \text{ per unit}$$

The budgeted conversion costs of Operation 1 include labor, power, repairs, supplies, depreciation, and other overhead of this operation. If some units have not been completed, so that all units in Operation 1 have not received the same amounts of conversion costs, the conversion-cost rate is computed by dividing budgeted conversion costs by the *equivalent units* of conversion costs, as in process costing.

As goods are manufactured, conversion costs are allocated to the work orders processed in Operation 1 by multiplying the $11.60 conversion costs per unit by the number of product units processed. The conversion costs of Operation 1 for 50 wool blazers (work order 423) are $11.60 × 50 = $580, and for 100 polyester blazers (work order 424) are $11.60 × 100 = $1,160. If work order 424 had contained 75 units, its total costs in Operation 1 would be $870 ($11.60 × 75). If equivalent units are used to calculate the conversion-cost rate, costs are allocated to work orders by multiplying the conversion cost per equivalent unit by the number of equivalent units in the work order. Direct materials costs of $6,000 for the 50 wool blazers (work order 423) and $3,000 for the 100 polyester blazers (work order 424) are specifically identified with each order as in a job-costing system. Note that operation unit costs are assumed to be the same regardless of the work order but direct materials costs vary across orders as the materials themselves vary.

Journal Entries

Actual conversion costs for Operation 1 in March 2000 (assumed to be $24,400, of which $580 are on work order 423 and $1,160 are on work order 424) are entered into a Conversion Costs Control account:

1.

Conversion Costs Control	24,400	
Various accounts (such as Wages Payable and Accumulated Depreciation)		24,400

Summary journal entries for assigning costs to the polyester blazers (work order 424) follow. Entries for the wool blazers would be similar. Of the $3,000 of direct materials for work order 424, $2,975 are used in Operation 1. The journal entry for the use of direct materials, which are traced directly to particular batches, for the 100 polyester blazers is:

2.

Work in Process, Operation 1	2,975	
Materials Inventory Control		2,975

The allocation of conversion costs to products in operation costing uses the budgeted rate $11.60 times the 100 units processed, or $1,160.

3.

Work in Process, Operation 1	1,160	
Conversion Costs Allocated		1,160

The transfer of the polyester blazers from Operation 1 to Operation 3 (recall that the polyester blazers do not go through Operation 2) would be journalized as follows:

4. 　　Work in Process, Operation 3　　　　　　　　　　4,135
　　　　Work in Process, Operation 1　　　　　　　　　　　　4,135

After posting, Work in Process, Operation 1 account, appears as follows:

Work in Process, Operation 1			
② Direct materials	2,975	④ Transferred to Operation 3	4,135
③ Conversion costs allocated	1,160		

The costs of the blazers are transferred through the pertinent operations and then to finished goods in the usual manner. Costs are added throughout the year in the accounts, Conversion Costs Control and Conversion Costs Allocated. Any over- or underallocation of conversion costs is disposed of in the same way as over- or underallocated manufacturing overhead in a job-costing system. (See pp. 113–117 for more discussion.)

▼ TERMS TO LEARN

This chapter and the Glossary at the end of the book contain definitions of the following important terms:

equivalent units (p. 611)
first-in, first out (FIFO) process-costing
　method (618)
hybrid-costing system (632)
operation (634)

operation-costing system (634)
previous department costs (628)
transferred-in costs (628)
weighted-average process-costing
　method (615)

▼ ASSIGNMENT MATERIAL

QUESTIONS

17-1 Give three examples of industries that often use process-costing systems.

17-2 In process costing, why are costs often divided into two main classifications?

17-3 Explain equivalent units. Why are equivalent-unit calculations necessary for process costing?

17-4 What problems might arise in estimating the degree of completion of an aircraft blade in a machine shop?

17-5 Name the five key steps in process costing when equivalent units are computed.

17-6 Name the three inventory methods commonly associated with process costing.

17-7 Describe the distinctive characteristic of weighted-average computations in assigning costs to units completed and to units in ending work in process.

17-8 Describe the distinctive characteristic of FIFO computations in assigning costs to units completed and to units in ending work in process.

17-9 Why should the FIFO method be called a modified or departmental FIFO method?

17-10 Identify a major advantage of the FIFO method for purposes of planning and control.

17-11 Identify the main difference between journal entries in process costing and the ones in job costing.

17-12 "Standard-costing methods are particularly applicable to process-costing situations." Do you agree? Why?

17-13 Why should the accountant distinguish between transferred-in costs and additional direct materials costs for a particular department?

17-14 "Transferred-in costs are those incurred in the preceding accounting period." Do you agree? Explain.

17-15 "There's no reason for me to get excited about the choice between the weighted-average and FIFO methods in my process-costing system. I have long-term contracts with my materials suppliers at fixed prices." State the conditions under which you would (a) agree, and (b) disagree with this statement made by a plant controller. Explain.

EXERCISES

17-16 Equivalent units, zero beginning inventory. International Electronics manufactures microchips in large quantities. Each microchip undergoes assembly and testing. The total assembly costs during January 2001 were:

Direct materials used	$ 720,000
Conversion costs	760,000
Total manufacturing costs	$1,480,000

Required

1. Assume there was no beginning inventory on January 1, 2001. During January, 10,000 microchips were placed into production and all 10,000 microchips were fully completed at the end of January. What is the unit cost of an assembled microchip in January 2001?
2. Assume that during February 10,000 microchips are placed into production. Further assume the same total assembly costs for January are also incurred in February 2001 but only 9,000 microchips are fully completed at the end of February. All direct materials have been added to the remaining 1,000 microchips. However, on average, these remaining 1,000 microchips are only 50% complete as to conversion costs. (a) What are the equivalent units for direct materials and conversion costs and their respective equivalent-unit costs for February? (b) What is the unit cost of an assembled microchip in February 2001?
3. Explain the difference in your answers to requirements 1 and 2.

17-17 Journal entries (continuation of 17-16). Refer to requirement 2 of Exercise 17-16.
Required
Prepare summary journal entries for the use of direct materials and incurrence of conversion costs. Also prepare a journal entry to transfer out the cost of goods completed. Show the postings to the Work-in-Process account.

17-18 Zero beginning inventory, materials introduced in middle of process. Vaasa Chemicals has a Mixing Department and a Refining Department. Its process-costing system in the Mixing Department has two direct materials cost categories (Chemical P and Chemical Q) and one conversion costs pool. The following data pertain to the Mixing Department for July 2001:

Units	
Work in process, July 1	0
Units started	50,000
Completed and transferred to Refining Department	35,000
Costs	
Chemical P	$250,000
Chemical Q	70,000
Conversion costs	135,000

Chemical P is introduced at the start of operations in the Mixing Department, and chemical Q is added when the product is three-fourths completed in the Mixing Department. Conversion costs are added evenly during the process. The ending work in process in the Mixing Department is two-thirds complete.
Required

1. Compute the equivalent units in the Mixing Department for July 2001 for each cost category.
2. Compute (a) the cost of goods completed and transferred to the Refining Department during July, and (b) the cost of work in process as of July 31, 2001.

17-19 Weighted-average method, equivalent units. Consider the following data for the Satellite Assembly Division of Aerospatiale:

	Physical Units (Satellites)	Direct Materials	Conversion Costs
Beginning work in process, (May 1)ᵃ	8	$ 4,933,600	$ 910,400
Started in May 2001	50		
Completed during May 2001	46		
Ending work in process (May 31)ᵇ	12		
Costs added during May 2001		$32,200,000	$13,920,000

ᵃDegree of completion: direct materials, 90%; conversion costs, 40%.
ᵇDegree of completion: direct materials, 60%; conversion costs, 30%.

The Satellite Assembly Division uses the weighted-average method of process costing.

Required

Compute equivalent units for direct materials and conversion costs. Show physical units in the first column of your schedule.

17-20 Weighted-average method, assigning costs (continuation of 17-19).

Required

For the data in Exercise 17-19, calculate cost per equivalent unit for direct materials and conversion costs, summarize total costs to account for, and assign these costs to units completed and transferred out and to units in ending work in process.

17-21 FIFO method, equivalent units. Refer to the information in Exercise 17-19. Suppose the Satellite Assembly Division uses the FIFO method of process costing instead of the weighted-average method.

Required

Compute equivalent units for direct materials and conversion costs. Show physical units in the first column of your schedule.

17-22 FIFO method, assigning costs (continuation of 17-21).

Required

For the data in Exercise 17-19, use the FIFO method to calculate cost per equivalent unit for direct materials and conversion costs, summarize total costs to account for, and assign these costs to units completed and transferred out and to units in ending work in process.

17-23 Standard-costing method, assigning costs. Refer to the information in Exercise 17-19. Suppose the Satellite Assembly Division uses the standard-costing method of process costing. Suppose further that the Satellite Assembly Division determines standard costs of $695,000 per (equivalent) unit for direct materials and $295,000 per (equivalent) unit for conversion costs for both beginning work in process and work done in the current period.

Required

1. Compute equivalent units for direct materials and conversion costs. Show physical units in the first column of your schedule.
2. Summarize total costs to account for, and assign these costs to units completed and transferred out and to units in ending work in process.
3. Compute the total direct materials and conversion costs variances for May 2001.

17-24 Weighted-average method, assigning costs. The Chatham Company makes a water-treatment chemical in a single processing department. Direct materials are added at the start of the process. Conversion costs are added evenly during the process. Chatham uses the weighted-average method of process costing. The following information for July 2001 is available.

		Equivalent Units	
	Physical Units	Direct Materials	Conversion Costs
Work in process, July 1	10,000ᵃ	10,000	7,000
Started during July	40,000		
Completed and transferred out during July	34,000	34,000	34,000
Work in process, July 31	16,000ᵇ	16,000	8,000

ᵃDegree of completion: direct materials, 100%; conversion costs, 70%.
ᵇDegree of completion: direct materials, 100%; conversion costs, 50%.

Total Costs for July 2001

Work in process, beginning		
Direct materials	$60,000	
Conversion costs	70,000	$130,000
Direct materials added during July		280,000
Conversion costs added during July		371,000
Total costs to account for		$781,000

Required
1. Calculate cost per equivalent unit for direct materials and conversion costs.
2. Summarize total costs to account for, and assign these costs to units completed (and transferred out) and to units in ending work in process.

17-25 FIFO method, assigning costs.
Required
Do Exercise 17-24 using the FIFO method. Note that you first need to calculate the equivalent units of work done in the current period (for direct materials and conversion costs) to complete beginning work in process, to start and complete new units, and to produce ending work in process.

17-26 Standard-costing method, assigning costs. Refer to the information in Exercise 17-24. Suppose Chatham determines standard costs of $6.50 per (equivalent) unit for direct materials and $10.30 per (equivalent) unit for conversion costs for both beginning work in process and work done in the current period.
Required
1. Do Exercise 17-24 using the standard-costing method. Note that you first need to calculate the equivalent units of work done in the current period (for direct materials and conversion costs) to complete beginning work in process, to start and complete new units, and to produce ending work in process.
2. Compute the total direct materials and conversion costs variances for July 2001.

17-27 Transferred-in costs, weighted-average method. Hideo Chemicals manufactures an industrial solvent in two departments—mixing and cooking. This question focuses on the Cooking Department. During June 2001, 90 tons of solvent were completed and transferred out from the Cooking Department. Direct materials are added at the end of the process. Conversion costs are added evenly during the process. Hideo Chemicals uses the weighted-average method of process costing. The following information for June 2001 is available.

	Physical Units (Tons)	Equivalent Units (Tons)		
		Transferred-In Costs	Direct Materials	Conversion Costs
Work in process, June 1[a]	40	40	0	30
Transferred in during June	80			
Completed and transferred out during June	90	90	90	90
Work in process, June 30[b]	30	30	0	15

[a]Degree of completion: transferred-in costs, 100%; direct materials, 0%; conversion costs, 75%.
[b]Degree of completion: transferred-in costs, 100%; direct materials, 0%; conversion costs, 50%.

Total Costs for June, 2001

Work in process, beginning		
Transferred-in costs	$40,000	
Direct materials	0	
Conversion costs	18,000	$ 58,000
Transferred-in costs added during June		87,200
Direct materials added during June		36,000
Conversion costs added during June		49,725
Total costs to account for		$230,925

Required

1. Calculate cost per equivalent unit for transferred-in costs, direct materials, and conversion costs.
2. Summarize total costs to account for, and assign these costs to units completed (and transferred out) and to units in ending work in process.

17-28 Transferred-in costs, FIFO method. Refer to the information in Exercise 17-27. Suppose that Hideo uses the FIFO method instead of the weighted-average method in all its departments. The only changes under the FIFO method are that the total transferred-in costs of beginning work in process is $39,200 and that the transferred-in costs added during June is $85,600.

Required

Do Exercise 17-27 using the FIFO method. Note that you first need to calculate equivalent units of work done in the current period (for transferred-in costs, direct materials, and conversion costs) to complete beginning work in process, to start and complete new units, and to produce ending work in process.

17-29 Operation costing. (Chapter Appendix) The Gabriel Corporation produces a standard-sized window in four operations — framing, assembly, staining, and painting. The windows differ in the type of wood (pine, oak) and glass (regular, tempered) used. The framing and assembly operations are common to all windows, but thereafter they are either stained or painted but not both. The total conversion costs for the month of June are

	Framing	Assembly	Staining	Painting
Total conversion costs	$75,000	$105,000	$36,000	$54,000

There is no beginning or ending inventory of windows in the month of June. A total of 3,000 windows are produced in June, half of which are stained and half of which are painted. The conversion cost for each unit passing through a given operation is the same.

Details of two work orders processed in June are as follows:

	Work Order 626	Work Order 750
Number of windows	50	100
Direct materials costs	$5,500	$9,800
Finishing operation	Painting	Staining

Required

1. Calculate the conversion costs of each operation, the total units produced, and the conversion costs per unit.
2. Calculate the total costs and the total costs per window of work order 626 and work order 750.

PROBLEMS

17-30 Weighted-average method. Global Defense, Inc., is a manufacturer of military equipment. Its Santa Fe plant manufactures the Interceptor Missile under contract to the U.S. government and friendly countries. All Interceptors go through an identical manufacturing process. Every effort is made to ensure that all Interceptors are identical and meet many demanding performance specifications. The product-costing system at the Santa Fe plant has a single direct-cost category (direct materials) and a single indirect-cost category (conversion costs). Each Interceptor passes through two departments—the Assembly Department and the Testing Department. Direct materials are added at the beginning of the process in Assembly. Conversion costs are added evenly during the Assembly Department's process. When the Assembly Department finishes work on each Interceptor, it is immediately transferred to Testing.

Global Defense uses the weighted-average method of process costing. Data for the Assembly Department for October 2001 are:

	Physical Units (Missiles)	Direct Materials	Conversion Costs
Work in process, October 1[a]	20	$ 460,000	$120,000
Started during October 2001	80		
Completed during October 2001	90		
Work in process, October 31[b]	10		
Costs added during October 2001		$2,000,000	$935,000

[a]Degree of completion: direct materials, ?%; conversion costs, 60%.
[b]Degree of completion: direct materials, ?%; conversion costs, 70%.

Required

1. For each cost element, compute equivalent units in the Assembly Department. Show physical units in the first column of your schedule.
2. For each cost element, calculate costs per equivalent unit.
3. Summarize total Assembly Department costs for October 2001, and assign these costs to units completed (and transferred out) and to units in ending work in process.

17-31 Journal entries (continuation of 17-30).

Required

Prepare a set of summarized journal entries for all October 2001 transactions affecting Work in Process—Assembly. Set up a T-account for Work in Process—Assembly, and post your entries to it.

 17-32 FIFO method (continuation of 17-30 and 17-31).

Required

Do Problem 17-30 using the FIFO method of process costing. Explain any difference between the costs per equivalent unit in the Assembly Department under the weighted-average method and the FIFO method.

17-33 Transferred-in costs, weighted average (related to 17-30 to 17-32). Global Defense, Inc., as you know, manufactures the Interceptor Missile at its Santa Fe plant. It has two departments—Assembly Department and Testing Department. This problem focuses on the Testing Department. (Problems 17-30 to 17-32 focused on the Assembly Department.) Direct materials are added when the Testing Department process is 90% complete. Conversion costs are added evenly during the Testing Department's process. As work in Assembly is completed, each unit is immediately transferred to Testing. As each unit is completed in Testing, it is immediately transferred to Finished Goods.

Global Defense uses the weighted-average method of process costing. Data for the Testing Department for October 2001 are:

	Physical Units (Missiles)	Transferred-In Costs	Direct Materials	Conversion Costs
Work in process, October 1[a]	30	$ 985,800	$ 0	$ 331,800
Transferred-in during October 2001	?			
Completed during October 2001	105			
Work in process October 31[b]	15			
Costs added during October 2001		$3,192,866	$3,885,000	$1,581,000

[a]Degree of completion: transferred-in costs, ?%; direct materials, ?%; conversion costs, 70%.
[b]Degree of completion: transferred-in costs, ?%; direct materials, ?%; conversion costs, 60%.

Required

1. What is the percentage of completion for (a) transferred-in costs and direct materials in beginning work-in-process inventory, and (b) transferred-in costs and direct materials in ending work-in-process inventory?
2. For each cost category, compute equivalent units in the Testing Department. Show physical units in the first column of your schedule.
3. For each cost category, calculate the cost per equivalent unit, summarize total Testing Department costs for October 2001, and assign these costs to units completed (and transferred out) and to units in ending work in process.
4. Prepare journal entries for October transfers from the Assembly Department to the Testing Department and from the Testing Department to Finished Goods.

17-34 Transferred-in costs, FIFO method (continuation of 17-33).

Required

Using the FIFO process-costing method, do the requirements of Problem 17-33. Under the FIFO method, the transferred-in costs for the beginning work in process in the Testing Department on October 1 are $980,060 and costs transferred in during October to the Testing Department are $3,188,000. All other data are unchanged.

 17-35 Weighted-average method. Star Toys manufactures one type of wooden toy figure. It buys wood as its direct material for the Forming Department of its Madison plant. The toys are transferred to the Finishing Department, where they are hand-shaped and metal is added to them. The product-costing system at Star Toys has a single direct-cost category (direct materials) and a single indirect-cost category (conversion costs). Direct materials are added when the Forming Department process is 10% complete. Conversion costs are added evenly during the Forming Department's process.

Star Toys uses the weighted-average method of process costing. Consider the following data for the Forming Department in April 2001:

	Physical Units (Toys)	Direct Materials	Conversion Costs
Work in process, April 1[a]	300	$ 7,500	$ 2,125
Started during April 2001	2,200		
Completed during April 2001	2,000		
Work in process, April 30[b]	500		
Costs added during April 2001		$70,000	$42,500

[a]Degree of completion: direct materials, 100%; conversion costs, 40%.
[b]Degree of completion: direct materials, 100%; conversion costs, 25%.

Required
Summarize total Forming Department costs for April 2001, and assign these costs to units completed (and transferred out) and to units in ending work in process.

17-36 Journal entries (continuation of 17-35).
Required
Prepare a set of summarized journal entries for all April transactions affecting Work in Process—Forming. Set up a T-account for Work in Process—Forming, and post your entries to it.

17-37 FIFO method (continuation of 17-35).
Required
Do Problem 17-35, using FIFO and three decimal places for unit costs. If you did Problem 17-35, explain any difference between the cost of work completed and transferred out and cost of ending work in process in the Forming Department under the weighted-average method and the FIFO method.

17-38 Transferred-in costs, weighted-average (related to 17-35 through 17-37). Star Toys, as you know, manufactures one type of wooden toy figure at its Madison plant. It has two departments—a Forming Department and a Finishing Department. (Problems 17-35 through 17-37 focused on the Forming Department.) Consider now the Finishing Department, which processes the formed toys through hand shaping and the addition of metal. All additional direct materials are added when the Finishing Department process is 80% complete. Conversion costs are added evenly during finishing operations. When the Finishing Department completes work on each toy, it is immediately transferred to finished goods.

Star Toys uses the weighted-average method of process costing. The following is a summary of the April 2001 operations in the Finishing Department:

	Physical Units (Toys)	Transferred-In Costs	Direct Materials	Conversion Costs
Work in process, April 1[a]	500	$ 17,750	$ 0	$ 7,250
Transferred in during April 2001	2,000			
Completed during April 2001	2,100			
Work in process, April 30[b]	400			
Costs added during April 2001		$104,000	$23,100	$38,400

[a]Degree of completion: transferred-in costs, 100%; direct materials, 0%; conversion costs, 60%.
[b]Degree of completion: transferred-in costs, 100%; direct materials, 0%; conversion costs, 30%.

Required
1. Summarize total Finishing Department costs for April 2001, and assign these costs to units completed (and transferred out) and to units in ending work in process.
2. Prepare journal entries for April transfers from the Forming Department to the Finishing Department and from the Finishing Department to Finished Goods.

17-39 Transferred-in costs, FIFO method (continuation of 17-38).
Required
1. Using the FIFO process-costing method, do the requirements of Problem 17-38. Under FIFO, the transferred-in costs for the beginning work in process in the Finishing

Department on April 1 are $17,520, and the costs transferred in during April were $103,566. All other data are unchanged.

2. If you did Problem 17-38, explain any difference between the cost of work completed and transferred out and cost of ending work in process in the Finishing Department under the weighted-average method and the FIFO method.

17-40 Transferred-in costs, weighted-average and FIFO. Frito-Lay, Inc., manufactures convenience foods, including potato chips and corn chips. Production of corn chips occurs in four departments: cleaning, mixing, cooking, and drying and packaging. Consider the Drying and Packaging Department, where direct materials (packaging) are added at the end of the process. Conversion costs are added evenly during the process. Suppose the accounting records of a Frito-Lay plant provided the following information for corn chips in its Drying and Packaging Department during a weekly period (week 37):

	Physical Units (Cases)	Transferred-In Costs	Direct Materials	Conversion Costs
Beginning work in process[a]	1,250	$29,000	$ 0	$ 9,060
Transferred-in during week 37 from Cooking Department	5,000			
Completed during week 37	5,250			
Ending work in process, week 37[b]	1,000			
Costs added during week 37		$96,000	$25,200	$38,400

[a]Degree of completion: transferred-in costs, 100%; direct materials, ?%; conversion costs, 80%.
[b]Degree of completion: transferred-in costs, 100%; direct materials, ?%; conversion costs, 40%.

Required

1. Using the weighted-average method, summarize the total Drying and Packaging Department costs for week 37, and assign these costs to units completed (and transferred out) and to units in ending work in process.

2. Assume that the FIFO method is used for the Drying and Packaging Department. Under FIFO, the transferred-in costs for work-in-process beginning inventory in week 37 are $28,920 and the transferred-in costs during week 37 from the Cooking Department are $94,000. All other data are unchanged. Summarize the total Drying and Packaging Department costs for week 37, and assign these costs to units completed (and transferred out) and to units in ending work in process using the FIFO method.

17-41 Standard costing with beginning and ending work in process. The Victoria Corporation uses a standard-costing system for its manufacturing operations. Standard costs for the cooking process are $6 per (equivalent) unit for direct materials and $3 per (equivalent) unit for conversion costs. All direct materials are introduced at the beginning of the process, and conversion costs are added evenly during the process. The operating summary for May 2001 include the following data for the cooking process.

Work-in-process inventories:
    May 1, 3,000 units[a]
    (direct materials $18,000; conversion costs $5,400)
    May 31, 5,000 units[b]
    Units started in May, 20,000
Units completed and transferred out of cooking in May: 18,000
Additional actual costs incurred for cooking during May:
    Direct materials, $125,000
    Conversion cost, $57,000

[a]Degree of completion: direct materials, 100%; conversion costs, 60%.
[b]Degree of completion: direct materials, 100%; conversion costs, 50%.

Required

1. Compute the total standard costs of units transferred out in May and the total standard costs of the May 31 inventory of work in process.

2. Compute the total May variances for direct materials and conversion costs.

17-42 Operation costing, equivalent units. (Chapter Appendix, CMA, adapted) Gregg Industries manufactures a variety of plastic products, including a series of molded chairs. The three models of molded chairs, which are all variations of the same design, are Standard (can be stacked), Deluxe (with arms), and Executive (with arms and padding). The company uses batch manufacturing and has an operation-costing system.

Gregg has an extrusion operation and subsequent operations to form, trim, and finish the chairs. Plastic sheets are produced by the extrusion operation, some of which are sold directly to other manufacturers. During the forming operation, the remaining plastic sheets are molded into chair seats and the legs are added. The Standard model is sold after this operation. During the trim operation, the arms are added to the Deluxe and Executive models and the chair edges are smoothed. Only the Executive model enters the finish operation, where the padding is added. All of the units produced receive the same steps within each operation.

The May production run had a total manufacturing cost of $898,000. The units of production and direct materials costs incurred are as follows:

	Units Produced	Extrusion Materials	Form Materials	Trim Materials	Finish Materials
Plastic sheets	5,000	$ 60,000	$ 0	$ 0	$ 0
Standard model	6,000	72,000	24,000	0	0
Deluxe model	3,000	36,000	12,000	9,000	0
Executive model	2,000	24,000	8,000	6,000	12,000
	16,000	$192,000	$44,000	$15,000	$12,000

Manufacturing costs of production assigned during the month of May were:

	Extrusion Operation	Form Operation	Trim Operation	Finish Operation
Direct manufacturing labor	$152,000	$60,000	$30,000	$18,000
Manufacturing overhead	240,000	72,000	39,000	24,000

Required
1. For each product produced by Gregg Industries during the month of May, determine (a) the unit cost, and (b) the total cost. Be sure to account for all costs incurred during the month, and support your answer with appropriate calculations.
2. Without considering your answer in requirement 1, assume that 1,000 units of the Deluxe model produced during May remained in work in process at the end of the month. These units were 100% complete as to materials costs and 60% complete in the trim operation. Determine the cost of the 1,000 units of the Deluxe model in the work-in-process inventory at the end of May.

17-43 Equivalent-unit computations, benchmarking, ethics. Margaret Major is the Corporate Controller of Leisure Suits. Leisure Suits has 20 plants worldwide that manufacture basic suits for retail stores. Each plant uses a process-costing system. At the end of each month, each plant manager submits a production report and a production-cost report. The production report includes the plant manager's estimate of the percentage of completion of the ending work in process as to direct materials and conversion costs. Major uses these estimates to compute the equivalent units of work done in each plant and the cost per equivalent unit of work done for both direct materials and conversion costs in each month. Plants are ranked from 1 to 20 in terms of (a) cost per equivalent unit of direct materials, and (b) cost per equivalent unit of conversion costs. Each month Major publishes a report that she calls "Benchmarking for Efficiency Gains at Leisure Suits." The three top-ranked plants on each category receive a bonus and are written up as the best in their class in the company newsletter.

Major has been pleased with the success of her benchmarking program. However, she has heard some disturbing news. She has received some unsigned letters stating that two plant managers have been manipulating their monthly estimates of percentage of completion in an attempt to obtain best in class status.

Required
1. How and why might plant managers "manipulate" their monthly estimates of percentage of completion?

2. Major's first reaction is to contact each plant controller and discuss the problem raised by the unsigned letters. Is that a good idea?

3. Assume that the plant controller's primary reporting responsibility is to the plant manager and that each plant controller receives the phone call from Major mentioned in requirement 2. What is the ethical responsibility of each plant controller (a) to Margaret Major, and (b) to Leisure Suits in relation to the equivalent-unit information each plant provides for the "Benchmarking for Efficiency" report?

4. How might Major gain some insight into whether the equivalent-unit figures provided by particular plants are being manipulated?

COLLABORATIVE LEARNING PROBLEM

17-44 Transferred-in costs, equivalent-unit costs, working backwards. Lennox Plastics has two processes—extrusion and thermo-assembly. Consider the June 2001 data for physical units in the thermo-assembly process: beginning work in process, 15,000 units; transferred in from the Extruding Department during September, 9,000; ending work in process, 5,000. Direct materials are added when the process in the Thermo-assembly Department is 80% complete. Conversion costs are added evenly during the process. Lennox Plastics uses the FIFO method of process costing. The following information is available.

	Transferred-In Costs	Direct Materials	Conversion Costs
Beginning work in process	$90,000	—	$45,000
Percentage completion of beginning work in process	100%	—	60%
Costs added in current period	$58,500	$57,000	$57,200
Cost per equivalent unit of work done in current period	$6.50	$3	$5.20

Required

Form groups of two or more students to complete the following requirements.

1. For each cost category, compute equivalent units of work done in the current period.

2. For each cost category, compute separately the equivalent units of work done to complete beginning work-in-process inventory, to start and complete new units, and to produce ending work in process.

3. For each cost category, calculate the percentage of completion of ending work-in-process inventory.

4. Summarize total costs to account for, and assign these costs to units completed (and transferred out) and to units in ending work in process.

Spoilage, Rework, and Scrap

Reducing spoilage, reworked units, and scrap are important aspects of managing costs and improving quality. To achieve these goals, companies use sophisticated equiptment and systems to monitor and control their processes. Carefully controlling processes is of particular importance at nuclear power plants such as Duke Power's Catawba nuclear station.

Managers are focusing increasingly on improving quality and reducing defects. They have learned that a rate of defects regarded as normal in the past is no longer tolerable. Many managers believe that reducing defects reduces costs and makes their company more competitive. Consider these words from a speech by George Fisher when he was chief executive officer of Motorola, an electronics manufacturer:

> We want to improve our quality in everything we do by ten times in two years, by a hundred times in four years, and in six years . . . three and a half defects for every million operations, whether typing, manufacturing, or serving a customer.

Recording and highlighting the costs of defects in a timely way helps managers make more informed decisions about managing these costs. Using this information, managers at companies such as AT&T, IBM, and Milliken Corporation, for example, have taken steps to reduce defects and costs by designing better products and processes, investing in production systems such as just-in-time (JIT) and computer-integrated manufacturing (CIM), training and motivating workers, and properly maintaining machines.

This chapter concentrates on three types of costs that arise as a result of defects—spoilage, rework, and scrap—and ways to account for them. The focus is on determining the cost of products and on valuing inventory and cost of goods sold. Chapter 19 discusses other aspects of quality with greater emphasis on cost management and control.

TERMINOLOGY

We start by defining key terms used in the chapter.

Spoilage is unacceptable units of production that are discarded or are sold for reduced prices. Partially completed or fully completed units of output can be spoiled. Examples are defective shirts, jeans, shoes, and carpeting sold as "seconds," and defective aluminum cans sold to aluminum manufacturers for remelting and production of aluminum foils. **Rework** is unacceptable units of production that are subsequently repaired and sold as acceptable finished goods. For example, defective units of products (such as pagers, computer disk drives, computers, and telephones) detected during production or immediately after production but before units are shipped to customers can sometimes be reworked and sold as good products. **Scrap** is material left over when making a product(s). It has low sales value compared with the sales value of the product(s). Examples are shavings and short lengths from woodworking operations, edges left over from plastic molding operations, and frayed cloth and end cuts from suit-making operations.

Some amount of spoilage, rework, or scrap appears to be an inherent part of many production processes. One example is semiconductor manufacturing, where the products produced are so complex and delicate that some spoiled units are invariably produced. In this case, the spoiled units cannot be reworked. An example involving spoilage and rework occurs in the manufacture of high-precision machine tools that must be built to very exacting tolerances. In this case, spoiled units can be reworked to meet standards but only at a considerable cost. And in the mining industry, companies process ore that contains varying amounts of valuable metals and rock. Some amount of rock, which is scrap, is inevitable, but its volume can often be decreased. Managers in all industries must strive to reduce costly spoilage, rework, and scrap. We focus first on spoilage.

DIFFERENT TYPES OF SPOILAGE

The key objectives in accounting for spoilage are determining the magnitude of the costs of spoilage and distinguishing between the costs of normal and abnormal spoilage.[1] To manage spoilage costs, companies need to highlight these costs and

---

[1] The helpful suggestions of Samuel Laimon, University of Saskatchewan, are gratefully acknowledged.

not bury them as an unidentified part of the costs of good units manufactured. Managers can then use this information to cost products and to control and reduce costs by improving the quality of the products and processes.

Normal Spoilage

Normal spoilage is spoilage that is an inherent result of the particular production process and arises even under efficient operating conditions. For a given production process, management must decide the rate of spoilage it is willing to accept as normal. Costs of normal spoilage are typically treated as a component of the costs of good units manufactured because good units cannot be made without the simultaneous appearance of spoiled units.

Normal spoilage rates should be computed using total *good units completed* as the base, not total *actual units started* in production. Why? Because total actual units started also include any abnormal spoilage in addition to normal spoilage. Moreover, normal spoilage is the amount of expected spoilage associated with or related to the good units produced.

Abnormal Spoilage

Abnormal spoilage is spoilage that should not arise under efficient operating conditions. It is not an inherent result of the particular production process. Abnormal spoilage is usually regarded as avoidable and controllable. Line operators and other plant personnel can generally decrease abnormal spoilage by minimizing machine breakdowns, accidents, and the like. Abnormal spoilage costs are written off as losses of the accounting period in which detection of the spoiled units occurs. To gain the most information from abnormal spoilage costs, companies record the units of abnormal spoilage and keep a separate Loss from Abnormal Spoilage account, which appears as a separate line item in the period's income statement.

Many companies, such as the Toyota Motor Corporation, adhere to a perfection standard as a part of their emphasis on total quality control. Their ideal goal is zero defects. Hence, all spoilage would be treated as abnormal.

Issues about accounting for spoilage arise in both process-costing and job-costing systems. We first present the accounting for spoilage in process-costing systems because it is an extension of the discussion of process costing introduced in Chapter 17.

PROCESS COSTING AND SPOILAGE

A key issue in accounting for spoilage in process-costing systems is how to count spoiled units. As we have already discussed, units of abnormal spoilage should be counted and recorded separately. But what about units of normal spoilage? These units can either be counted (approach A) or not counted (approach B) when computing output units—actual or equivalent—in a process-costing system. Approach A leads to more accurate product costs because it makes visible the costs associated with normal spoilage and spreads it over good units. Approach B is less accurate because it spreads the costs of normal spoilage over all units. The following example and discussion illustrates the superiority of approach A over approach B.

Count All Spoilage

EXAMPLE 1: Chipmakers, Inc., manufactures computer chips for television sets. All direct materials are added at the beginning of the production process. To highlight issues that arise with normal spoilage, we assume no beginning inventory and focus only on direct materials costs. In May 2000, $270,000 in direct materials were introduced into production. Production data for May indicate that 10,000 units were started, 5,000 good units were completed, and 1,000 units were spoiled (all normal spoilage).[2] Ending work in process was

OBJECTIVE 2

Describe the general accounting procedures for normal and abnormal spoilage

Teaching Tip This chapter is technically demanding. Discuss recent attention to improving quality, then overview concepts behind accounting for normal and abnormal spoilage in process and job costing:

	Job Costing	Process Costing
Abnormal spoilage	Expense	Expense
Normal spoilage		
1. Due to *this* job	Add to the cost of this job	N/A*
2. Common to all jobs	Add to the cost of all jobs via MOH	Allocate equal cost/unit to all units passing inspection point in that process

*There are no "jobs" in a process-costing system, so spoilage cannot be due to a particular job.

Teaching Tip The question "Should *any* spoilage be considered normal or acceptable?" generates much discussion. Achieving zero defects requires better design of products and processes as well as tighter control in production. But some spoilage is inherent in certain industries, for example, semiconductors. The text's approach highlights the cost of spoilage, whether normal or abnormal.

Teaching Tip Before discussing the technical details of spoilage in a process-costing system, present four assumptions commonly used to simplify calculations.

1. All spoilage occurs at the inspection point. Although spoilage may occur earlier, we don't know that the units are spoiled. So we continue adding resources to the spoiled units until they reach the inspection point.
2. Normal spoilage (NS) is a % of *good units* passing the inspection point.
3. NS is allocated to E. WIP *only if* E. WIP has passed the inspection point.
4. Under FIFO, all spoiled units are treated as if they came from units started this period. This practice avoids separate calculations for spoiled units started last period and spoiled units started in the current period.

[2]For simplicity, we assume that all spoilage (normal and abnormal) has zero net disposal value. If spoiled units could be disposed of at positive value, the costs of normal and abnormal spoilage would be reduced by this value. The section on "Job Costing and Spoilage" presents the accounting for this case.

EXHIBIT 18-1
Effect of Recognizing Equivalent Units in Spoilage for Direct Materials Costs,
Chipmakers, Inc., for May 2000

	Approach A: Recognizing Spoiled Units When Computing Output in Equivalent Units	Approach B: Not Counting Spoiled Units When Computing Output in Equivalent Units
Costs to account for	$270,000	$270,000
Divide by equivalent units	÷ 10,000	÷ 9,000
Cost per equivalent unit	$ 27	$ 30
Assigned to		
Good units completed: 5,000 × $27; 5,000 × $30	$135,000	$150,000
Add normal spoilage: 1,000 × $27	27,000	0
Costs of good units transferred out	$162,000	$150,000
Work in process, ending:		
4,000 × $27; 4,000 × $30	108,000	120,000
Costs accounted for	$270,000	$270,000

Points to Stress There are two advantages of approach A over approach B. In A, the cost of spoiled units appears separately (1,000 spoiled units @ $27). This provides information on spoilage-related production costs. Second, as indicated in the text, units are costed more accurately in approach A. The inspection point is at the *end* of the process, so NS should be allocated to only units that are 100% complete—the units CTO. No spoilage is allocated to E. WIP because it is not complete (and has not yet been inspected).

New to This Edition To be consistent with Chapter 17, this chapter has been rewritten using the five-step approach of the 8th edition in place of the four-step approach used in the 9th edition.

4,000 units (each 100% complete as to direct material costs). Spoilage is detected upon completion of the process.

Spoilage is typically assumed to occur at the stage of completion where inspection takes place. Why? Because spoilage is not detected until this point. In our example, spoilage is assumed to occur at the end of the process.

The direct materials unit costs are computed and assigned using approaches A and B in Exhibit 18-1. Not counting the equivalent units for normal spoilage decreases equivalent units, resulting in a higher cost of each good unit. A $30 equivalent-unit cost (instead of a $27 equivalent-unit cost) is assigned to work in process that has not reached the inspection point. Simultaneously, the direct materials costs assigned to good units completed, which include the cost of normal spoilage, are understated ($150,000 instead of $162,000). Consequently, the 4,000 units in ending work in process contain costs of spoilage of $12,000 ($120,000−$108,000) that do not pertain to those units and that, in fact, belong with the good units completed and transferred out. The 4,000 units in ending work in process undoubtedly include some units that will be detected as spoiled in the subsequent accounting period. The ending work in process is being charged for spoilage in the current period, and it will be charged again in the next period when inspection occurs as the units are completed. In effect, under approach B, these units will bear two charges for spoilage. Such cost distortions do not occur when spoiled units are recognized in the computation of equivalent units. Approach A has a further advantage. It highlights the cost of normal spoilage to management and thereby focuses management's attention on reducing spoilage. Therefore, we will use approach A to present process costing with spoilage.

The Five-Step Procedure for Process Costing with Spoilage

We illustrate process costing with spoilage using the following example.

EXAMPLE 2: Anzio Company manufactures a wooden recycling container in its Forming Department. Direct materials for this product are introduced at the beginning of the production cycle. At the start of production, all direct materials required to make one output unit are bundled in a single kit. Conversion costs are added evenly during the cycle. Some units of this product are spoiled as a result of defects only detectable at inspection of finished units. Normally the spoiled units are 10% of the good output. Summary data for July 2000 are:

Physical Units for July 2000

Work in process, beginning inventory (July 1)	1,500 units
Direct materials (100% complete)	
Conversion costs (60% complete)	
Started during July	8,500 units
Completed and transferred out in July	7,000 good units
Work in process, ending inventory (July 31)	2,000 units
Direct materials (100% complete)	
Conversion costs (50% complete)	

Total Costs for July 2000

Work in process, beginning inventory		
Direct materials (1,500 equivalent units × $8)	$12,000	
Conversion costs (900 equivalent units × $10)	9,000	$ 21,000
Direct materials costs added during July		76,500
Conversion costs added during July		89,100
Total costs to account for		$186,600

The five-step procedure for process costing used in Chapter 17 needs only slight modification to accommodate spoilage. The key change is in calculating the number of spoiled units in step 1.

Step 1: Summarize the Flow of Physical Units of Output Identify units of both normal and abnormal spoilage. In our example, the number of spoiled units is computed as follows:

$$\text{Spoiled units} = \left(\begin{array}{c}\text{Beginning} \\ \text{units}\end{array} + \begin{array}{c}\text{Units} \\ \text{started}\end{array}\right) - \left(\begin{array}{c}\text{Good units} \\ \text{transferred out}\end{array} + \begin{array}{c}\text{Ending} \\ \text{units}\end{array}\right)$$

$$= (1{,}500 + 8{,}500) - (7{,}000 + 2{,}000)$$

$$= 10{,}000 - 9{,}000$$

$$= 1{,}000 \text{ units}$$

Normal spoilage at Anzio's Forming Department is 10% of the 7,000 units of *good* output, or 700 units. Thus,

$$\text{Abnormal spoilage} = \text{Total spoilage} - \text{Normal spoilage}$$

$$= 1{,}000 - 700$$

$$= 300 \text{ units}$$

Step 2: Compute Output in Terms of Equivalent Units Compute equivalent units for spoilage in the same way as for good units. Following approach A, all spoiled units are included in the computation of output units. Because Anzio inspects at the completion point, the same amount of work will be done on each spoiled unit and each completed good unit.

Step 3: Compute Equivalent-Unit Costs The details of this step are similar to those in Chapter 17.

Step 4: Summarize Total Costs to Account For These are all the costs debited to Work in Process. The details of this step are similar to those in Chapter 17.

Step 5: Assign Total Costs to Units Completed, to Spoiled Units, and to Units in Ending Work in Process This step now includes computation of the cost of spoiled units and the cost of good units.

To proceed through the five steps, we first need to specify the inventory costing method—weighted-average, FIFO, or standard costing. We illustrate process costing under each of these inventory methods and show how the computations incorporate normal and abnormal spoilage.

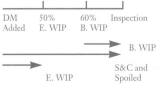

EXHIBIT 18-2
Weighted-Average Method of Process Costing with Spoilage
Forming Department of the Anzio Company for July 2000

PANEL A: STEPS 1 AND 2—SUMMARIZE OUTPUT IN PHYSICAL UNITS AND COMPUTE EQUIVALENT UNITS

Flow of Production	(Step 1) Physical Units (given, p. 651)	(Step 2) Equivalent Units Direct Materials	(Step 2) Equivalent Units Conversion Costs
Work in process, beginning	1,500		
Started during current period	8,500		
To account for	10,000		
Good units completed and transferred out during current period:	7,000	7,000	7,000
Normal spoilage[a]	700		
700 × 100%; 700 × 100%		700	700
Abnormal spoilage[b]	300		
300 × 100%; 300 × 100%		300	300
Work in process, ending[c]	2,000		
2,000 × 100%; 2,000 × 50%		2,000	1,000
Accounted for	10,000		
Work done to date		10,000	9,000

[a]Normal spoilage is 10% of good units transferred out: 10% × 7,000 = 700 units. Degree of completion of normal spoilage in this department: direct materials, 100%; conversion costs, 100%.
[b]Abnormal spoilage = Actual spoilage − Normal spoilage = 1,000 − 700 = 300 units. Degree of completion of abnormal spoilage in this department: direct materials, 100%; conversion costs, 100%.
[c]Degree of completion in this department: direct materials, 100%; conversion costs, 50%.

PANEL B: STEPS 3, 4, AND 5—COMPUTE EQUIVALENT-UNIT COSTS, SUMMARIZE TOTAL COSTS TO ACCOUNT FOR, AND ASSIGN COSTS TO UNITS COMPLETED, TO SPOILAGE UNITS, AND TO UNITS IN ENDING WORK IN PROCESS

		Total Production Costs	Direct Materials	Conversion Costs
(Step 3)	Work in process, beginning (given, p. 651)	$ 21,000	$12,000	$ 9,000
	Costs added in current period (given, p. 651)	165,600	76,500	89,100
			88,500	98,100
	Divide by equivalent units of work done to date		÷ 10,000	÷ 9,000
	Equivalent-unit costs of work done to date		$8.85	$10.90
(Step 4)	Total costs to account for	$186,600		
(Step 5)	Assignment of costs			
	Good units completed and transferred out (7,000 units)			
	Costs before adding normal spoilage	$138,250	(7,000[d] × $8.85) + (7,000[d] × $10.90)	
	Normal spoilage (700 units)	13,825	(700[d] × $8.85) + (700[d] × $10.90)	
(A)	Total cost of good units completed & transferred out	152,075		
(B)	Abnormal spoilage (300 units)	5,925	(300[d] × $8.85) + (300[d] × $10.90)	
	Work in process, ending (2,000 units)			
	Direct materials	17,700	2,000[d] × $8.85	
	Conversion costs	10,900		1,000[d] × $10.90
(C)	Total work in process, ending	28,600		
(A) + (B) + (C)	Total costs accounted for	$186,600		

[d]Equivalent units of direct materials and conversion costs calculated in step 2 in Panel A above.

Weighted-Average Method and Spoilage

O B J E C T I V E   3

Account for spoilage in process costing using the weighted-average method

Exhibit 18-2, Panel A, presents steps 1 and 2 to calculate equivalent units of work done to date and includes calculations of equivalent units of normal and abnormal spoilage. Exhibit 18-2, Panel B, presents steps 3, 4, and 5 (together called the production cost worksheet). Step 3 presents the equivalent-unit cost calculations using the weighted-average method. Note how, for each cost category, the costs of beginning work in process and costs of work done in the current period are totaled and divided by the equivalent units of all work done to date to calculate the weighted-average cost. Step 4 summarizes the total costs to account for. Step 5 assigns costs to completed units, spoiled units, and ending inventory by multiplying the equivalent units calculated in step 2 by the cost per equivalent unit calculated in step 3. Note how the costs of normal spoilage, $13,825, are added to the costs of their related good units. Hence, the cost per good unit completed and transferred out of the process equals the total costs transferred out (including the costs of normal spoilage) divided by the number of good units produced, $152,075 \div 7,000 = 21.725. It is not equal to $19.75, which is the sum of the costs per equivalent unit of direct materials ($8.85) and conversion costs ($10.90). Instead, the cost per good unit is equal to the total cost of direct materials and conversion costs per equivalent unit, $19.75, *plus* a share of the normal spoilage $1.975 ($13,825 \div 7,000$) = 21.725. The $5,925 costs of abnormal spoilage are assigned to the Loss from Abnormal Spoilage account and do not appear in the good-unit costs.[3]

Reinforcing Problems Exer. 18-17, 18-18, 18-21, and 18-24 and Probs. 18-30 and 18-32 cover spoilage and WA process costing.

FIFO Method and Spoilage

Reinforcing Problems Exer. 18-19, 18-20, 18-22, and 18-25 and Probs. 18-31, 18-33, and 18-40 cover spoilage and FIFO process costing. Standard costing and spoilage is covered in Exer. 18-23 and 18-26.

Exhibit 18-3, Panel A, presents steps 1 and 2 using the FIFO method that focuses on equivalent units of work done in the current period. Exhibit 18-3, Panel B, presents steps 3, 4, and 5. Note how the FIFO method keeps the costs of the beginning work-in-process inventory separate and distinct from the costs of work done in the current period when assigning costs. All spoilage costs are assumed to be related to units completed during this period, using the unit costs of the current period.[4] With the exception of accounting for spoilage, the FIFO method here is the same as that presented in Chapter 17.

O B J E C T I V E   4

Account for spoilage in process costing using the first-in, first-out method

Standard-Costing Method and Spoilage

O B J E C T I V E   5

Account for spoilage in process costing using the standard-costing method

This section assumes you have studied Chapters 7 and 8 and the standard-costing method in Chapter 17 (pp. 623–626). If not, skip to the next section. The standard-costing method can also be used to account for normal and abnormal spoilage. We illustrate how much simpler the calculations become by continuing our Anzio Company example.

Suppose Anzio Company develops standard costs for the Forming Department. Assume the same standard costs per unit apply to the beginning inventory (1,500 equivalent units of direct materials and 900 equivalent units of conversion costs) and to work done in July 2000:

Direct materials	$ 8.50
Conversion costs	10.50
Total manufacturing costs	$19.00

Points to Stress Under FIFO, spoiled units are accounted for *as if* they were started this period. While some of the B. WIP units probably did spoil, all spoilage is treated *as if* it came from current production, so as to simplify computations. This avoids separate computations for spoiled units from (1) B. WIP and (2) units started this period.

---

[3]The actual costs of spoilage (and rework) are often greater than the costs recorded in the accounting system because opportunity costs of disruption of the production line, storage, and lost contribution margins are not recorded in accounting systems. Chapter 19 discusses these opportunity costs from a cost management viewpoint.

[4]If the FIFO method were used in its purest form, normal spoilage costs would be split between the goods started and completed during the current period and those completed from beginning work in process—using the appropriate unit costs of the period in which the units were worked on. The simpler, modified FIFO method, as illustrated in Exhibit 18-3, in effect uses the unit costs of the current period for assigning normal spoilage costs to the goods completed from beginning work in process. This modified FIFO method assumes that all normal spoilage traceable to the beginning work in process was started and completed during the current period.

EXHIBIT 18-3
First-in, First-out (FIFO) Method of Process Costing with Spoilage
Forming Department of the Anzio Company for July 2000

PANEL A: STEPS 1 AND 2—SUMMARIZE OUTPUT IN PHYSICAL UNITS AND COMPUTE EQUIVALENT UNITS

Flow of Production	(Step 1) Physical Units	(Step 2) Equivalent Units Direct Materials	(Step 2) Equivalent Units Conversion Costs
Work in process, beginning (given, p. 651)	1,500		
Started during current period (given, p. 651)	8,500		
To account for	10,000		
Good units completed and transferred out during current period:			
From beginning work in process[a]	1,500		
$\quad$ 1,500 × (100% − 100%); 1,500 × (100% − 60%)		0	600
Started and completed	5,500[b]		
$\quad$ 5,500 × 100%; 5,500 × 100%		5,500	5,500
Normal spoilage[c]	700		
$\quad$ 700 × 100%; 700 × 100%		700	700
Abnormal spoilage[d]	300		
$\quad$ 300 × 100%; 300 × 100%		300	300
Work in process, ending[e]	2,000		
$\quad$ 2,000 × 100%; 2,000 × 50%		2,000	1,000
Accounted for	10,000		
Work done in current period only		8,500	8,100

[a]Degree of completion in this department: direct materials, 100%; conversion costs, 60%.
[b]7,000 physical units completed and transferred out minus 1,500 physical units completed and transferred out from beginning work-in-process inventory.
[c]Normal spoilage is 10% of good units transferred out: 10% × 7,000 = 700 units. Degree of completion of normal spoilage in this department: direct materials, 100%; conversion costs, 100%.
[d]Abnormal spoilage = Actual spoilage − Normal spoilage = 1,000 − 700 = 300 units. Degree of completion of abnormal spoilage in this department: direct materials, 100%; conversion costs, 100%.
[e]Degree of completion in this department: direct materials, 100%; conversion costs, 50%.

PANEL B: STEPS 3, 4, AND 5—COMPUTE EQUIVALENT-UNIT COSTS, SUMMARIZE TOTAL COSTS TO ACCOUNT FOR, AND ASSIGN COSTS TO UNITS COMPLETED, TO SPOILAGE UNITS, AND TO UNITS IN ENDING WORK IN PROCESS

		Total Production Costs	Direct Materials	Conversion Costs
(Step 3)	Work in process, beginning (given, p. 651)	$ 21,000		
	Costs added in current period (given, p. 651)	165,600	$76,500	$89,100
	Divide by equivalent units of work done in current period		÷ 8,500	÷ 8,100
	Equivalent-unit costs of work done in current period		$ 9	$ 11
(Step 4)	Total costs to account for	$186,600		
(Step 5)	Assignment of costs:			
	Good units completed and transferred out (7,000 units)			
	$\quad$ Work in process, beginning (1,500 units)	$ 21,000		
	$\quad\quad$ Direct materials added in current period	0	0[f] × $9	
	$\quad\quad$ Conversion costs added in current period	6,600		600[f] × $11
	$\quad\quad$ Total from beginning inventory before normal spoilage	27,600		
	$\quad$ Started and completed before normal spoilage (5,500 units)	110,000	(5,500[f] × $9) +	(5,500[f] × $11)
	$\quad$ Normal spoilage (700 units)	14,000	(700[f] × $9) +	(700[f] × $11)
(A)	$\quad\quad$ Total cost of good units transferred out	151,600		
(B)	Abnormal spoilage (300 units)	6,000	(300[f] × $9) +	(300[f] × $11)
	Work in process, ending (2,000 units)			
	$\quad$ Direct materials	18,000	2,000[f] × $9	
	$\quad$ Conversion costs	11,000		1,000[f] × $11
(C)	$\quad\quad$ Total work in process, ending	29,000		
(A) + (B) + (C)	Total costs accounted for	$186,600		

[f]Equivalent units of direct materials and conversion costs calculated in step 2 in Panel A above.

EXHIBIT 18-4
Use of Standard Costs in Process Costing with Spoilage
Forming Department of the Anzio Company for July 2000

PANEL A: STEPS 1 AND 2—SUMMARIZE OUTPUT IN PHYSICAL UNITS AND COMPUTE EQUIVALENT UNITS

	(Step 1) Physical Units	(Step 2) Equivalent Units Direct Materials	(Step 2) Equivalent Units Conversion Costs
Flow of Production			
Work in process, beginning (given, p. 651)	1,500		
Started during current period (given, p. 651)	8,500		
To account for	10,000		
Good units completed and transferred out during current period:			
From beginning work in process[a]	1,500		
$1,500 \times (100\% - 100\%)$; $1,500 \times (100\% - 60\%)$		0	600
Started and completed	5,500[b]		
$5,500 \times 100\%$; $5,500 \times 100\%$		5,500	5,500
Normal spoilage[c]	700		
$700 \times 100\%$; $700 \times 100\%$		700	700
Abnormal spoilage[d]	300		
$300 \times 100\%$; $300 \times 100\%$		300	300
Work in process, ending[e]	2,000		
$2,000 \times 100\%$; $2,000 \times 50\%$		2,000	1,000
Accounted for	10,000		
Work done in current period only		8,500	8,100

[a]Degree of completion in this department: direct materials, 100%; conversion costs, 60%
[b]7,000 physical units completed and transferred out minus 1,500 physical units completed and transferred out from beginning work-in-process inventory.
[c]Normal spoilage is 10% of good units transferred out: 10% × 7,000 = 700 units. Degree of completion of normal spoilage in this department: direct materials, 100%; conversion costs, 100%.
[d]Abnormal spoilage = Actual spoilage − Normal spoilage = 1,000 − 700 = 300 units. Degree of completion of abnormal spoilage in this department: direct materials, 100%; conversion costs, 100%.
[e]Degree of completion in this department: direct materials, 100%; conversion costs, 50%.

PANEL B: STEPS 3, 4, AND 5—COMPUTE EQUIVALENT-UNIT COSTS, SUMMARIZE TOTAL COSTS TO ACCOUNT FOR, AND ASSIGN COSTS TO UNITS COMPLETED, TO SPOILAGE UNITS, AND TO UNITS IN ENDING WORK IN PROCESS

		Total Production Costs	Direct Materials	Conversion Costs
(Step 3)	Standard cost per equivalent unit (given, p. 653)	$ 19.00	$ 8.50	$ 10.50
	Work in process, beginning (given, p. 656)	$ 22,200		
	Costs added in current period at standard prices			
	Direct materials, 8,500 × $8.50; conversion costs, 8,100 × $10.50	157,300	72,250	85,050
(Step 4)	Costs to account for	$179,500		
(Step 5)	Assignment of costs at standard costs:			
	Good units completed and transferred out (7,000 units)			
	Work in process, beginning (1,500 units)	$ 22,200		
	Direct materials added in current period	0	0[f] × $8.50	
	Conversion costs added in current period	6,300		600[f] × $10.50
	Total from beginning inventory before normal spoilage	28,500		
	Started and completed before normal spoilage (5,500 units)	$104,500	(5,500[f] × $8.50) +	(5,500[f] × $10.50)
	Normal spoilage (700 units)	13,300	(700[f] × $8.50) +	(700[f] × $10.50)
(A)	Total cost of good units transferred out	146,300		
(B)	Abnormal spoilage (300 units)	5,700	(300[f] × $8.50) +	(300[f] × $10.50)
	Work in process, ending (2,000 units)			
	Direct materials	17,000	2,000[f] × $8.50	
	Conversion costs	10,500		1,000[f] × $10.50
(C)	Total work in process, ending	27,500		
(A) + (B) + (C)	Total costs accounted for	$179,500		

[f]Equivalent units of direct materials and conversion costs calculated in step 2 in Panel A above.

Hence, the beginning inventory at standard costs is:

Direct materials 1,500 × $8.50	$12,750	
Conversion costs 900 × $10.50	9,450	
Total costs	$22,200	

Exhibit 18-4, Panel A, presents steps 1 and 2 for calculating physical and equivalent units. These steps are the same as for the FIFO method described in Exhibit 18-3. Exhibit 18-4, Panel B, presents steps 3, 4, and 5. Step 3, the cost per equivalent unit is simply the standard cost: direct materials, $8.50, and conversion costs, $10.50. The standard-costing method makes calculating equivalent-unit costs unnecessary and so simplifies process costing. The costs to account for in step 4 are at *standard* costs and hence differ from the costs to account for under the weighted-average and FIFO methods, which are at *actual* costs. Step 5 assigns costs to units completed (including normal spoilage), to abnormal spoilage, and to ending work-in-process inventory by multiplying the equivalent units calculated in step 2 by the standard cost per equivalent unit presented in step 3. Variances can be measured and analyzed in the manner described in Chapters 7 and 8.[5]

Correcting Student Misconceptions Remind students that AS is a loss that should not have occurred. Debit loss from AS and credit WIP for all types of costing systems.

Journal Entries

The information from Panel B in Exhibits 18-2, 18-3, and 18-4 supports the following journal entries for the transfer to finished goods and to recognize the loss from abnormal spoilage.

	Weighted Average		FIFO		Standard Costs	
Finished Goods	152,075		151,600		146,300	
Work in Process—Forming		152,075		151,600		146,300
To transfer good units completed in July.						
Loss from Abnormal Spoilage	5,925		6,000		5,700	
Work in Process—Forming		5,925		6,000		5,700
To recognize abnormal spoilage detected in July.						

Inspection Points and Allocating Costs of Normal Spoilage

Our Anzio Company illustration assumes inspection upon completion. Spoilage might actually occur at various stages of the production cycle, but it is typically detected only at one or more specific inspection points. An **inspection point** is the stage of the production cycle where products are checked to determine whether they are acceptable or unacceptable units. The cost of spoiled units is assumed to be all costs incurred by spoiled units prior to inspection. When spoiled goods have a disposal value, the net cost of spoilage is computed by deducting disposal value from the costs of the spoiled goods accumulated to the inspection point. The unit costs of normal and abnormal spoilage are the same when the two are detected simultaneously. However, situations might arise when abnormal spoilage is detected at a different point than normal spoilage. In such cases, the unit cost of abnormal spoilage would differ from the unit cost of normal spoilage.

Costs of abnormal spoilage are separately accounted for as losses of the period. Recall, however, that normal spoilage costs are added to costs of good units. Accounting for normal spoilage, therefore, raises an additional issue: Should normal spoilage costs be allocated between completed units and ending work-in-process inventory? *The common approach is to presume that normal spoilage occurs at the inspection point in the production cycle and to allocate its cost over all units that have passed*

Example AS may occur at points other than the inspection point. For example, if a glass factory supervisor discovers that a furnace has been contaminated with foreign matter, AS is known and recorded at that time—well before completed glass products would be inspected.

---

[5]For example, from Exhibit 18-4, Panel B, the standard costs for July are direct materials used, $72,250; conversion costs, $85,050. From p. 651, the actual costs added during July are direct materials, $76,500, and conversion costs, $89,100, yielding a direct materials variance of $72,250 − $76,500 = $4,250 U and a conversion costs variance of $85,050 − $89,100 = $4,050 U. These variances could then be subdivided further as in Chapters 7 and 8. The abnormal spoilage will be part of the efficiency variance.

that point. In the Anzio Company example, spoilage is assumed to occur when units are inspected at the end of the production cycle, so no costs of normal spoilage is allocated to ending work in process.

The costs of normal spoilage are allocated to the units in ending work-in-process inventory, in addition to completed units, if the units in ending work-in-process inventory have passed the inspection point. For example, if the inspection point is at the halfway stage of the production cycle, work in process that is at least 50% completed would be allocated a full measure of normal spoilage costs, calculated on the basis of all costs incurred prior to the inspection point. But work in process that is less than 50% completed would not be allocated any normal spoilage costs. The Appendix to this chapter contains additional discussion concerning different inspection points and spoilage.

Having early and frequent inspections in production processes reduces the amount of material and conversion costs wasted on units that are already spoiled. Thus, in the Anzio Company example, if inspection can occur when units are 80% complete as to conversion costs and 100% complete as to direct materials, and spoilage occurs before this point, the company would avoid incurring the final 20% of conversion costs on the spoiled units.

JOB COSTING AND SPOILAGE

The concepts of normal and abnormal spoilage also apply to job-costing systems. Abnormal spoilage is usually regarded as controllable by the manager. It is separately identified with the goal of eliminating it altogether. Costs of abnormal spoilage are not considered as inventoriable costs and are written off as costs of the period in which detection occurs. Normal spoilage costs in job-costing systems (just as in process-costing systems) are inventoriable costs, although increasingly managements are tolerating only small amounts of spoilage as normal. When assigning costs, job-costing systems generally distinguish between *normal spoilage attributable to a specific job* and *normal spoilage common to all jobs*. Normal spoilage attributable to a specific job is assigned to that job, a step unnecessary in process costing since masses of identical or similar units are manufactured.

We illustrate the accounting for spoilage in job costing using the following example.

> EXAMPLE 3: In the Hull Machine Shop, 5 aircraft parts out of a job lot of 50 aircraft parts are spoiled. Costs assigned prior to the inspection point are $2,000 per part. Hull calculates these costs on the basis of its inventory costing assumptions—weighted-average, FIFO, or standard costs. We do not, however, emphasize cost-flow assumptions in our presentation here or in subsequent sections. The current disposal price of the spoiled parts is estimated to be $600 per part. When the spoilage is detected, the spoiled goods are inventoried at $600 per part.

Normal spoilage attributable to a specific job When normal spoilage occurs because of the specifications of a particular job, that job bears the cost of the spoilage reduced by the current disposal value of that spoilage. The journal entry to recognize the disposal value of the normal spoilage (items in parentheses indicate subsidiary ledger postings) is:

Materials Control (spoiled goods at current disposal value): 5 × $600	3,000	
Work-in-Process Control (specific job): 5 × $600		3,000

Note that the Work-in-Process Control (specific job) has already been debited (charged) $10,000 for the spoiled parts (5 spoiled parts × $2,000 per part). The effect of the $3,000 entry is that the net cost of the normal spoilage, $7,000 ($10,000 − $3,000) becomes an additional cost of the 45 (50 − 5) good units produced. The total cost of the 45 good units is $97,000, $90,000 (45 units × $2,000 per unit) incurred to produce the good units plus the $7,000 net cost of normal spoilage.

Normal spoilage common to all jobs In some cases, spoilage may be considered a normal characteristic of a given production cycle. The spoilage inherent in production only coincidentally occurs when a specific job is being worked on. The spoilage then is not attributable, and hence is not charged, to the specific job. Instead, it is costed as manufacturing overhead. The journal entry is:

Materials Control (spoiled goods at current disposal value): 5 × $600	3,000	
Manufacturing Overhead Control (normal spoilage): ($10,000 − $3,000)	7,000	
Work-in-Process Control (specific job): 5 × $2,000		10,000

When normal spoilage is common to all jobs, the budgeted manufacturing overhead rate includes a provision for normal spoilage cost. Therefore, normal spoilage cost is spread, through overhead allocation, over all jobs rather than loaded on particular jobs only.[6] The total cost of the 45 good units is $90,000 (45 units × $2,000 per unit) incurred to produce the good units plus a prorated share of the $7,000 of normal spoilage overhead costs.

Abnormal spoilage If the spoilage is abnormal, the net loss is highlighted and always charged to an abnormal loss account. Unlike normal spoilage costs, abnormal spoilage costs are not included as a part of the cost of good units produced. The total cost of the 45 good units is $90,000 (45 units × $2,000 per unit).

Materials Control (spoiled goods at current disposal value): 5 × $600	3,000	
Loss from Abnormal Spoilage: ($ 10,000 − $3,000)	7,000	
Work-in-Process Control (specific job): 5 × $2,000		10,000

Even though, for external reporting purposes, abnormal spoilage costs are written off in the period and are not linked to specific jobs or units, companies often identify the specific reasons for abnormal spoilage, and, where appropriate, link abnormal spoilage with specific jobs or units for cost management purposes.

REWORK

Rework is unacceptable units of production that are subsequently repaired and sold as acceptable finished goods. For rework, we again distinguish (1) normal rework attributable to a specific job, (2) normal rework common to all jobs, and (3) abnormal rework.

Consider the Hull Machine Shop data (Example 3). Assume that the five spoiled parts used in our illustration are reworked. The journal entry for the $10,000 of total costs (details of costs assumed) assigned to the five spoiled units before considering rework costs are as follows:

Work-in-Process Control (specific job)	10,000	
Materials Control		4,000
Wages Payable Control		4,000
Manufacturing Overhead Allocated		2,000

Assume that rework costs equal $3,800 (direct materials, $800; direct manufacturing labor, $2,000; manufacturing overhead, $1,000).

Normal rework attributable to a specific job If the rework is normal but occurs because of the requirements of a specific job, the rework costs are charged to that job. The journal entry is as follows:

Work-in-Process Control (specific job)	3,800	
Materials Control		800
Wages Payable Control		2,000
Manufacturing Overhead Allocated		1,000

[6]Note that costs *already assigned to products* are being charged back to Manufacturing Overhead Control, which generally accumulates only *costs incurred*, not both costs incurred and costs already assigned.

Normal rework common to all jobs   When rework is normal and not attributable to any specific job, the costs of rework are charged to manufacturing overhead and spread, through overhead allocation, over all jobs.

Manufacturing Overhead Control (rework costs)	3,800	
Materials Control		800
Wages Payable Control		2,000
Manufacturing Overhead Allocated		1,000

Abnormal rework   If the rework is abnormal, it is recorded by charging abnormal rework to a separate loss account.

Loss from Abnormal Rework	3,800	
Materials Control		800
Wages Payable Control		2,000
Manufacturing Overhead Allocated		1,000

Accounting for rework in a process-costing system also requires abnormal rework to be distinguished from normal rework. A process-costing system accounts for abnormal rework in the same way as a job-costing system. Accounting for normal rework follows the accounting described for normal rework common to all jobs (units) because masses of identical or similar units are manufactured in process-costing systems.

Costing rework highlights to managers the resources wasted on activities that would not have to be undertaken if the product were made correctly. It prompts managers to seek ways to reduce rework, for example, by designing new products or processes, training workers, or investing in new machines. Calculating rework costs helps managers perform cost-benefit analyses for various alternative ways to reduce or eliminate rework. To emphasize the importance of eliminating rework and to simplify the accounting, some companies set a standard of zero rework. All rework is then treated as abnormal and written off as a cost of the current period.

ACCOUNTING FOR SCRAP

Scrap is material left over when making a product(s); it has low sales value compared with the sales value of the product(s). There are no distinctions of normal and abnormal scrap, but scrap attributable to a specific job is distinguished from scrap common to all jobs.

There are two major aspects of accounting for scrap:

1. Planning and control, including physical tracking
2. Inventory costing, including when and how to affect operating income

Initial entries to scrap records are most often in physical terms. In various industries, items such as stamped-out metal sheets or edges of molded plastic parts are quantified by weighing, counting, or some other expedient means. Scrap records not only help measure efficiency, but also control what is often a tempting source for theft. Scrap reports are prepared as source documents for periodic summaries of the amount of actual scrap compared with the budgeted or standard amounts. Scrap is either sold or disposed of quickly, or stored for later sale, disposal, or reuse.

Careful tracking of scrap often extends into the accounting records. For example, in one survey, 60% of the companies maintained a distinct account for scrap costs somewhere in their accounting system.[7] The issues here are similar to those discussed in Chapter 15 regarding the accounting for byproducts:

1. When should the value of scrap be recognized in the accounting records—at the time scrap is produced or at the time scrap is sold?
2. How should revenue from scrap be accounted for?

[7]Price Waterhouse, *Survey of the Cost Management Practices of Selected Midwest Manufacturers.* (Cleveland: Price Waterhouse, 1989, p. 10).

Points to Stress Managers may rework too many spoiled units if AS Expense is penalized more heavily than the unfavorable DM, DL, and VMOH efficiency variances arising from rework.

OBJECTIVE 8

Account for scrap

Reinforcing Problems Scrap issues are covered in Exer. 18-29 and Prob. 18-36.

Rejection in the Electronics Industry

From country to country and from industry to industry, the rates of rejected and reworked units vary tremendously. The data in the following table focus on different segments of the U.S. electronics industry. The data reported are median numbers drawn from companies that are members of the American Electronics Association.[a] The reject rate is the rejects as a percentage of total items checked by quality control. The rework rate is reworked items as a percentage of rejects. The scrap rate reports scrap as a percentage of all materials purchased. Also reported is the operating income to net sales percentage for each segment of the electronics industry.

Segment of Electronics Industry	Reject Rate (% rejects)	Rework Rate (% rework)	Scrap Rate (% scrap)	Operating Income ÷ Net Sales
1. Computers and office equipment—includes mainframes minicomputers, microcomputers, printers, and point-of-sale equipment	2.55%	6.50%	0.62%	5.33%
2. Electronic components and accessories—includes printed circuit boards and semiconductors	1.55	2.00	1.63	4.53
3. Specialized production equipment—includes semiconductor production equipment	7.50	10.00	0.43	5.67
4. Telecommunications equipment—includes telephone, radio and TV apparatus	1.00	2.00	1.29	4.73
5. Aerospace, nautical, and military equipment—includes aircraft manufacture and guided missiles	—	1.50	0.52	6.52
6. Laboratory and measurement devices—includes optical instruments and process control equipment	4.90	3.30	0.66	3.89
7. Prepackaged software	1.00	0.80	0.06	4.02
8. Computer-related services—includes data processing and computer systems design	5.00	N/A	N/A	7.78

The reject rate for specialized production equipment is five times as great as that for electronic components and semiconductors. Electronic components and semiconductors show a low percentage of rework (in part because rework is not always possible when defects arise). Scrap rates are reasonably small across all industry segments. The operating income to net sales percentage ranges from 3.89% for laboratory and measurement devices to 7.78% for computer-related services. Given these profitability percentages, reductions in reject and rework rates can markedly increase the profitability of many companies in the electronics industry.

[a]Adapted from American Electronics Association, *Operating Ratios Survey*. Full citation is in Appendix A.

To illustrate, we extend our Hull example assuming that the manufacture of aircraft parts generates scrap. We further assume that the scrap from a job has a total sales value of $900.

Recognizing Scrap at the Time of Its Sale

When the dollar amount of scrap is immaterial, the simplest accounting is to make a memo of the quantity of scrap returned to the storeroom and to regard scrap sales as a separate line item of other revenues. The only journal entry is:

Sale of scrap:	Cash or Accounts Receivable	900	
	Sales of Scrap		900

When the dollar amount of scrap is material and the scrap is sold quickly after it is produced, the accounting depends on whether the scrap is attributable to a specific job or common to all jobs.

Scrap attributable to a specific job   Job-costing systems sometimes trace the sales of scrap to the jobs that yielded the scrap. This method is used only when the tracing can be done in an economically feasible way. For example, the Hull Machine Shop and particular customers, such as the U.S. Department of Defense, may reach an agreement that provides for charging specific jobs with all rework or spoilage costs and for crediting these jobs with all scrap sales that arise from them. The journal entry is:

Scrap returned to storeroom:	No journal entry.		
	[Memo of quantity received and related job is entered in the inventory record]		
Sale of scrap:	Cash or Accounts Receivable	900	
	Work-in-Process Control		900
	Posting made to specific job cost record.		

Unlike spoilage and rework, there is no cost attached to the scrap, and hence no distinction is made between normal and abnormal scrap. All scrap sales, whatever the amount, are credited to the specific job. Scrap sales reduce the costs of the job.

Scrap common to all jobs   The journal entry in this case is:

Scrap returned to storeroom:	No journal entry.		
	[Memo of quantity received and related job is entered in the inventory record]		
Sale of scrap:	Cash or Accounts Receivable	900	
	Manufacturing Overhead Control		900
	Posting made to subsidiary ledger—"Sales of Scrap" column on department cost record.		

This method does not link scrap with any particular job or product. Instead, all products bear regular production costs without any credit for scrap sales except in an indirect manner: The expected sales of scrap are considered when setting the budgeted manufacturing overhead rate. Thus, the budgeted overhead rate is lower than it would be if the overhead budget had not been reduced by the expected sales of scrap. This accounting for scrap is used in both process-costing and job-costing systems.

Recognizing Scrap at the Time of Its Production

Our preceding illustrations assume that scrap returned to the storeroom is sold quickly and hence not assigned an inventory cost figure. Sometimes, however, as is the case with edges of molded plastic parts, the value of scrap is not immaterial, and the time between storing it and selling or reusing it can be quite long. Under these conditions, the company is justified in inventorying scrap at a conservative estimate of net realizable value so that production costs and related scrap recovery are recognized in the same accounting period. Some companies tend to delay sales of scrap until the market price is most attractive. Volatile price fluctuations are typical for scrap metal. If scrap is inventoried, it should be recorded at some "reasonable value"—a challenging task in the face of volatile market prices.

Scrap attributable to a specific job   The journal entry in the Hull Machine Shop example is:

Scrap returned to storeroom:	Materials Control	900	
	Work-in-Process Control		900

Scrap common to all jobs   The journal entry in this case is:

Scrap returned to storeroom:	Materials Control	900	
	Manufacturing Overhead Control		900

Observe that Materials Control account is debited in place of Cash or Accounts Receivable. When this scrap is sold, the journal entry is:

Points to Stress Rework is recognized at the point of production, as it is often material in value. In contrast, when scrap is insignificant in value, it may not be recognized until the time of sale, rather than the time of production.

Points to Stress In job costing, the cost of scrap is already in the WIP T-account of the job generating the scrap. If the scrap is attributable to that job, the costs are where we want them and no journal entry is necessary (unless the scrap is sold, in which case that particular job's WIP T-account is credited to relieve the job of the recovered scrap costs).

Points to Stress In sum, costs of NS and rework, and revenue from scrap are either

1. Charged to the specific job, if that job caused the spoilage, rework, or scrap (under job costing only) or
2. Spread across all jobs or products (via the budgeted MOH rate) if the rework, spoilage, or scrap is due to the general production process.

Note that revenue from scrap can also be treated as miscellaneous revenue, and that AS and abnormal rework are *expensed* when incurred.

| Sale of scrap: | Cash or Accounts Receivable | 900 | |
| | Materials Control | | 900 |

Scrap is sometimes reused as direct materials rather than sold as scrap. In this case, it should be debited to Materials Control as a type of direct materials and carried at its estimated net realizable value. For example, the entries when the scrap generated is common to all jobs are:

Scrap returned to storeroom:	Materials Control	900	
	Manufacturing Overhead Control		900
Reuse of scrap:	Work-in-Process Control	900	
	Materials Control		900

The accounting for scrap under process costing is like the accounting under job costing when scrap is common to all jobs because process costing applies to the manufacture of masses of identical or similar units.

The high cost of scrap focuses managers' attention on ways to reduce scrap and to use it more profitably. For example, General Motors Corporation has redesigned its plastic injection molding processes to reduce the scrap plastic that must be broken away from its molded products. General Motors also regrinds and reuses the plastic scrap as direct material, saving substantial input costs.

Curriculum Linkage The DuPont example illustrates why manufacturing or production costs are just the tip of the proverbial cost-of-quality iceberg. The next chapter considers other quality-related costs incurred in other elements of the value chain.

CONCEPTS IN ACTION

Managing Waste and Environmental Costs at DuPont Corporation[a]

DuPont Corporation manufactures a wide range of chemicals and chemical products. DuPont uses the term waste to describe the spoilage and scrap it generates. Besides the cost of lost materials, chemical waste is a particular problem because of its impact on the environment. Strict environmental laws require that chemical waste be disposed of in an environmentally safe way, further adding to the cost of generating waste.

DuPont calculates the full costs of waste to include (1) the costs of materials lost in the chemical process minus their scrap value, (2) the full costs of semifinished and finished products spoiled, (3) the full costs of disposing of or treating the waste, such as site charges for hazardous waste, or costs of scrubbers and biotreatment plants to treat the waste, and (4) the costs of any solvents used to clean plant and equipment as a result of generating waste.

DuPont believes that business profits do not have to be gained at the expense of the environment. Consistent with the Environmental Protection Agency's (EPA's) recommendations, DuPont focuses on source reduction (the avoidance of waste altogether, rather than disposal or treatment of waste) as the best way to achieve profitability and environmental performance. DuPont calculates the total costs of waste to highlight to managers the operational and environmental costs of waste. This approach motivates individual plants to take actions, such as redesigning products, reconfiguring processes, or investing in capital equipment to reduce waste altogether.

The company's new process for Terathane®—developed by a DuPont team with members from LaPorte, Texas; Niagara Falls, New York; Deepwater, New Jersey; and Wilmington, Delaware—is a good example of how DuPont reduces waste costs. The new process significantly reduces environmental emissions and energy use. Relative to the old technology, the new technology reduced air emissions by 200,000 pounds, solid waste by 25 million pounds, aqueous waste by 500 million pounds, and steam use by more than 150 million pounds, while generating cost savings of more than $5 million a year.

[a]Adapted from 1998 Safety, Health, and Environmental Excellence Awards, DuPont Corporation, and based on discussions with Dale Martin, Manager, Environmental Effectiveness.

PROBLEM

Burlington Textiles has some spoiled goods that had an assigned cost of $40,000 and zero net disposal value.

Required

Prepare a journal entry for each of the following conditions under (a) process costing (Department A), and (b) job costing:

1. Abnormal spoilage of $40,000.
2. Normal spoilage of $40,000 related to general plant operations.
3. Normal spoilage of $40,000 related to specifications of a particular job.

SOLUTION

	(a) Process Costing			(b) Job Costing		
1.	Loss from Abnormal Spoilage	40,000		Loss from Abnormal Spoilage	40,000	
	Work-in-Process—Dept. A		40,000	Work-in-Process Control (specific job)		40,000
2.	No entry until units are completed and transferred out. Then the normal spoilage costs are transferred as part of the cost of good units.			Manufacturing Overhead Control	40,000	
				Work-in-Process Control (specific job)		40,000
	Work-in-Process—Dept. B	40,000				
	Work-in-Process—Dept. A.		40,000			
3.	Not applicable			No entry. Spoilage cost remains in Work-in-Process Control (specific job).		

SUMMARY

The following points are linked to the chapter's learning objectives:

1. Spoilage is unacceptable units of production that are discarded or sold for reduced prices. Rework is unacceptable units that are subsequently repaired and sold as acceptable finished goods. Scrap is material left over when making a product(s); it has low sales value compared with the sales value of the product(s).

2. Normal spoilage is spoilage that is an inherent result of the particular production process and arises even under efficient operating conditions. Abnormal spoilage is spoilage that does not arise under efficient operating conditions. Generally, accounting systems explicitly recognize both forms of spoilage when computing output units. Normal spoilage is typically included in the cost of good output units, while abnormal spoilage is recorded as a loss for the period.

3. The weighted-average method of process costing combines costs in beginning inventory with costs in the current period when determining the costs of good units (which includes a normal spoilage amount) and the costs of abnormal spoilage.

4. The FIFO method of process costing keeps costs in beginning inventory separate from the costs in the current period when determining the cost of good units (which includes a normal spoilage amount) and the costs of abnormal spoilage.

5. The standard-costing method of process costing uses standard costs to determine the cost of good units (which includes a normal spoilage amount) and the costs of abnormal spoilage.

6. With a job-costing system, companies can decide to assign spoilage to specific jobs. Alternatively, they can allocate spoilage that is common to all jobs as part of manufacturing overhead. Loss from abnormal spoilage is recorded as a cost of the period.

Points to Stress It is difficult to motivate managers to reduce spoilage, rework, and scrap unless the costs of these problems are visible. This chapter has discussed accounting methods that make these costs visible.

7. Completed reworked units should be indistinguishable from nonreworked good units. Normal rework can be assigned to a specific job or, if common to all jobs, as part of manufacturing overhead. Abnormal rework is written off as a cost of the period.

8. Scrap is recognized in the accounting records either at the time of its sale or at the time of its production. Sale of scrap, if immaterial, is often recognized as other revenues. If material, the sale of scrap or its value reduces the cost of a specific job or, if common to all jobs, reduces manufacturing overhead.

APPENDIX: INSPECTION AND SPOILAGE AT INTERMEDIATE STAGES OF COMPLETION IN PROCESS COSTING

Reinforcing Problems Probs. 18-37 and 18-38 cover inspection and spoilage at intermediate stages.

Consider how the timing of inspection at various stages of completion affects the amount of normal and abnormal spoilage. Assume that normal spoilage is 10% of the good units passing inspection in the Forging Department of Dana Corporation, a manufacturer of automobile parts. Direct materials are added at the start of production in the Forging Department. Conversion costs are added evenly during the process.

Consider three cases: Inspection occurs at the 20%, the 50%, or the 100% completion stage. A total of 8,000 units are spoiled in all cases. Note how the number of units of normal spoilage and abnormal spoilage change. Normal spoilage is computed on the basis of the number of *good units* that pass the inspection point *during the current period*. The following data are for October.

	Physical Units: Inspection at Stage of Completion		
Flow of Production	**At 20%**	**At 50%**	**At 100%**
Work in process, beginning (25%)[a]	11,000	11,000	11,000
Started during October	74,000	74,000	74,000
To account for	85,000	85,000	85,000
Good units completed and transferred out (85,000 − 8,000 spoiled − 16,000 ending)	61,000	61,000	61,000
Normal spoilage	6,600[b]	7,700[c]	6,100[d]
Abnormal spoilage (8,000 − normal spoilage)	1,400	300	1,900
Work in process, ending (75%)[a]	16,000	16,000	16,000
Accounted for	85,000	85,000	85,000

[a]Degree of completion for conversion costs of this department at the dates of the work-in-process inventories.
[b]10% × (74,000 units started − 8,000 units spoiled), since only the units started passed the 20% completion inspection point in the current period. Beginning work in process is excluded from this calculation since it is 25% complete.
[c]10% × (85,000 units − 8,000 units spoiled), since *all* units passed the 50% completion inspection point in the current period.
[d]10% × 61,000, since 61,000 units are fully completed and inspected in the current period.

Teaching Tip Students need to be "walked through" the Dana Corp. table of physical units with inspection options at 20%, 50%, and 100% points. The time line in the text is a great way for students to calculate the amount of NS produced this period.

The following diagram shows the flow of physical units for January and illustrates the preceding normal spoilage numbers. Note that 61,000 good units are completed and transferred out (11,000 from beginning work in process and 50,000 started and completed during the period), and 16,000 units are in ending work in process.

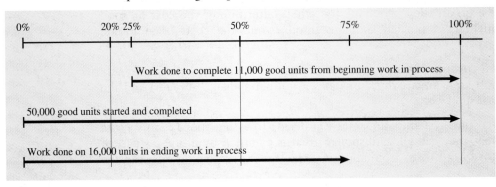

To see the number of units passing each inspection point, consider the vertical lines at the 20%, 50%, and 100% inspection points. Note that the vertical line at 20% cuts two horizontal lines, 50,000 good units started and completed and 16,000 units in ending work in process for a total of 66,000 good units. (It does not cut the line representing work done on the 11,000 good units completed from beginning work in process because these units are already 25% complete at the start of the period and hence are not inspected this period.) Normal spoilage equals $10\% \times 66,000 = 6,600$ units. Similarly, the vertical line at the 50% point cuts all three horizontal lines indicating that $11,000 + 50,000 + 16,000 = 77,000$ good units pass this point. Normal spoilage in this case is $10\% \times 77,000 = 7,700$ units. At the 100% point, normal spoilage $= 10\% \times (11,000 + 50,000) = 6,100$ units.

Exhibit 18-5 shows the computation of equivalent units under the weighted-average method, assuming inspection at the 50% completion stage. The calculations depend on how much direct materials and conversion costs are incurred to get the units to the inspection point. In Exhibit 18-5, the spoiled units have a full measure of direct materials and a 50% measure of conversion costs. The computations of equivalent-unit costs and the assignment of total costs to units completed and to ending work in process would be similar to those in previous illustrations. Because ending work in process has passed the inspection point in this example, these units bear normal spoilage costs, just like the units that have been completed and transferred out. For example, conversion costs for units completed and transferred out include conversion costs for 61,000 good units produced plus $50\% \times (10\% \times 61,000) = 50\% \times 6,100 = 3,050$ equivalent units of normal spoilage. We multiply by 50% to obtain equivalent units of normal spoilage because conversion costs are only 50% complete at the inspection point. Conversion costs of equivalent units in ending work in process include conversion costs of $75\% \times 16,000 = 12,000$ equivalent good units plus $50\% \times (10\% \times 16,000) = 50\% \times 1,600 = 800$ equivalent units of normal spoilage. Note that we take 10% of 16,000 because 16,000 good units currently in ending work in process pass the inspection point. Thus, the equivalent units of normal spoilage accounted for are 3,050 equivalent units identified with units completed and transferred out plus 800 equivalent units identified

EXHIBIT 18-5
Steps 1 and 2: Computing Equivalent Units with Spoilage
Weighted-Average Method of Process Costing
Forging Department of the Dana Corporation for October

| | (Step 1) Physical Units | (Step 2) Equivalent Units | |
Flow of Production		Direct Materials	Conversion Costs
Work in process, beginning[a]	11,000		
Started during current period	74,000		
To account for	85,000		
Good units completed and transferred out	61,000	61,000	61,000
Normal spoilage	7,700		
7,700 × 100%; 7,700 × 50%		7,700	3,850
Abnormal spoilage	300		
300 × 100%; 300 × 50%		300	150
Work in process, ending[b]	16,000		
16,000 × 100%; 16,000 × 75%		16,000	12,000
Accounted for	85,000		
Total work done to date		85,000	77,000

[a]Degree of completion: direct materials, 100%; conversion costs, 25%.
[b]Degree of completion: direct materials, 100%; conversion costs, 75%.

with units in ending work in process for a total of 3,850 equivalent units shown in Exhibit 18-5.

▼ TERMS TO LEARN

This chapter and the Glossary at the end of the book contain definitions of the following important terms:

abnormal spoilage (p. 649)　　　　　　　　　　　rework (648)
inspection point (656)　　　　　　　　　　　　　scrap (648)
normal spoilage (649)　　　　　　　　　　　　　spoilage (648)

▼ ASSIGNMENT MATERIAL

QUESTIONS

18-1 Why is there an unmistakable trend in manufacturing to improve quality?

18-2 Distinguish among spoilage, rework, and scrap.

18-3 "Normal spoilage is planned spoilage." Discuss.

18-4 "Costs of abnormal spoilage are losses." Explain.

18-5 "What has been regarded as normal spoilage in the past is not necessarily acceptable as normal in the present or future." Explain.

18-6 "Units of abnormal spoilage are inferred rather than identified." Explain.

18-7 "In accounting for spoiled goods, we are dealing with cost assignment rather than cost incurrence." Explain.

18-8 "Total input includes abnormal as well as normal spoilage and is therefore irrational as a basis for computing normal spoilage." Do you agree? Explain.

18-9 "The inspection point is the key to the allocation of spoilage costs." Do you agree? Explain.

18-10 "The unit cost of normal spoilage is the same as the unit cost of abnormal spoilage." Do you agree? Explain.

18-11 "In job costing, the costs of normal spoilage that occurs while a specific job is being done is charged to the specific job." Do you agree? Explain.

18-12 "The costs of reworking defective units are always charged to the specific jobs where the defects were originally discovered." Do you agree? Explain.

18-13 "Abnormal rework costs should be charged to a loss account, not to manufacturing overhead." Do you agree? Explain.

18-14 When is a company justified in inventorying scrap?

18-15 How do managers use information about scrap.

EXERCISES

 18-16 Normal and abnormal spoilage in units. The following data, in physical units, describe a grinding process for January:

Work in process, beginning	19,000
Started during current period	150,000
To account for	169,000
Spoiled units	12,000
Good units completed and transferred out	132,000
Work in process, ending	25,000
Accounted for	169,000

Inspection occurs at the 100% completion stage. Normal spoilage is 5% of the good units passing inspection.

Required

1. Compute the normal and abnormal spoilage in units.
2. Assume that the equivalent-unit cost of a spoiled unit is $10. Compute the amount of potential savings if all spoilage were eliminated, assuming that all other costs would be unaffected. Comment on your answer.

18-17 Weighted-average method, spoilage, equivalent units. (CMA, adapted) Consider the following data for November 2000 from Gray Manufacturing Company, which makes silk pennants and operates a process-costing system. All direct materials are added at the beginning of the process and conversion costs are added evenly during the process. Spoilage is detected upon inspection at the completion of the process. Spoiled units are disposed of at zero net disposal price. Gray Manufacturing Company uses the weighted-average method of process costing.

	Physical Units (Pennants)	Direct Materials	Conversion Costs
Work in process, November 1[a]	1,000	$ 1,423	$ 1,110
Started in November 2000	?		
Good units completed and transferred out during November 2000	9,000		
Normal spoilage	100		
Abnormal spoilage	50		
Work in process, November 30[b]	2,000		
Costs added during November 2000		$12,180	$27,750

[a]Degree of completion: direct materials, 100%; conversion costs, 50%.
[b]Degree of completion: direct materials, 100%; conversion costs, 30%.

Required

Compute equivalent units for direct materials and conversion costs. Show physical units in the first column of your schedule.

18-18 Weighted-average method, assigning costs (continuation of 18-17).

Required

For the data in Exercise 18-17, calculate the cost per equivalent unit for direct materials and conversion costs, summarize total costs to account for, and assign these costs to units completed and transferred out (including normal spoilage) to abnormal spoilage, and to units in ending work in process.

18-19 FIFO method, spoilage, equivalent units. Refer to the information in Exercise 18-17. Suppose Gray Manufacturing Company uses the FIFO method of process costing instead of the weighted-average method.

Required

Compute equivalent units for direct materials and conversion costs. Show physical units in the first column of your schedule.

18-20 FIFO method, assigning costs (continuation of 18-19).

Required

For the data in Exercise 18-17, use the FIFO method to calculate the cost per equivalent unit for direct materials and conversion costs, summarize total costs to account for, and assign these costs to units completed and transferred out (including normal spoilage) to abnormal spoilage, and to units in ending work in process.

18-21 Weighted-average method, spoilage. Anderson Plastics makes complex plastic rear lamps for cars using an injection molding process. Direct materials are added at the start of the process. Conversion costs are added evenly during the process. Spoiled units are detected upon inspection at the end of the process and are disposed of at zero net disposal price. Assume normal spoilage is 15% of the good output produced. Anderson Plastics uses the weighted-average method of process costing. The following information about actual costs for April 2001 is available.

| | Physical Units | Equivalent Units | |
		Direct Materials	Conversion Costs
Work in process, April 1[a]	15,000	15,000	9,000
Started during April 2001	25,000		
Good units completed and transferred out during April 2001	20,000	20,000	20,000
Normal and abnormal spoilage	4,000	4,000	4,000
Work in process, April 30[b]	16,000	16,000	12,000

[a]Degree of completion: direct materials, 100%; conversion costs, 60%.
[b]Degree of completion: direct materials, 100%; conversion costs, 75%.

Total Costs for April 2001

Work in process, beginning		
Direct materials	$120,000	
Conversion costs	90,000	$210,000
Direct materials added during April 2001		210,000
Conversion costs added during April 2001		291,600
Total costs to account for		$711,600

Required

1. Calculate the cost per equivalent unit for direct materials and conversion costs.
2. Summarize total costs to account for, and assign these costs to units completed and transferred out (including normal spoilage) to abnormal spoilage, and to units in ending work in process.
3. What is the cost of a good unit completed and transferred out?

18-22 FIFO method, spoilage. Refer to the information in Exercise 18-21.

Required

Do Exercise 18-21 using the FIFO method. Note that you first need to calculate the equivalent units of work done in the current period (for direct materials and conversion costs) to complete beginning work in process, to start and complete new units, for normal and abnormal spoilage units, and to produce ending work in process.

18-23 Standard-costing method, spoilage. Refer to the information in Exercise 18-21. Suppose Anderson determines standard costs of $8.20 per (equivalent) unit for direct materials and $10.50 per (equivalent) unit for conversion costs for both beginning work in process and work done in the current period.

Required

Do Exercise 18-21 using the standard-costing method. Note that you first need to calculate the equivalent units of work done in the current period (for direct materials and conversion costs) to complete beginning work in process, to start and complete new units, for normal and abnormal spoilage units, and to produce ending work in process.

18-24 Weighted-average method, spoilage. Superchip specializes in the manufacture of microchips for aircraft. Direct materials are added at the start of the production process. Conversion costs are added evenly during the process. Some units of this product are spoiled as a result of defects not detectable before inspection of finished goods. Normally the spoiled units are 15% of the good units transferred out. Spoiled units are disposed of at zero net disposal price. Superchip uses the weighted-average method of process costing.

Summary data for September 2000 are:

	Physical Units (Microchips)	Direct Materials	Conversion Costs
Work in process, September 1[a]	400	$ 64,000	$ 10,200
Started in September 2000	1,700		
Good units completed and transferred out during September 2000	1,400		
Work in process, September 30[b]	300		
Costs added during September 2000		$378,000	$153,600

[a]Degree of completion: direct materials, 100%; conversion costs, 30%.
[b]Degree of completion: direct materials, 100%; conversion costs, 40%.

Required

1. For each cost category, compute equivalent units. Show physical units in the first column of your schedule.

2. For each cost category, calculate costs per equivalent unit.

3. Summarize total costs to account for, and assign these costs to units completed and transferred out (including normal spoilage), to abnormal spoilage, and to units in ending work in process.

18-25 FIFO method, spoilage. Refer to the information in Exercise 18-24.

Required

Do Exercise 18-24 using the FIFO method of process costing.

18-26 Standard-costing method, spoilage. Refer to the information in Exercise 18-24. Suppose Superchip determines standard costs of $205 per (equivalent) unit for direct materials and $80 per (equivalent) unit for conversion costs for both beginning work in process and work done in the current period.

Required

Do Exercise 18-24 using the standard-costing method.

18-27 Spoilage and job costing. (L. Bamber) Bamber Kitchens produces a variety of items in accordance with special job orders from hospitals, plant cafeterias, and university dormitories. An order for 2,500 cases of mixed vegetables costs $6 per case: direct materials, $3; direct manufacturing labor, $2; and manufacturing overhead allocated, $1. The manufacturing overhead rate includes a provision for normal spoilage. Consider each requirement independently.

Required

1. Assume that a laborer dropped 200 cases. Suppose part of the 200 cases could be sold to a nearby prison for $200 cash. Prepare a journal entry to record this event. Calculate and explain briefly the unit cost of the remaining 2,300 cases.

2. Refer to the original data. Tasters at the company reject 200 of the 2,500 cases. The 200 cases are disposed of for $400. Assume that this rejection rate is considered normal. Prepare a journal entry to record this event, and calculate the unit cost if
   a. The rejection is attributable to exacting specifications of this particular job.
   b. The rejection is characteristic of the production process and is not attributable to this specific job.
   c. Are unit costs the same in requirements 2a and 2b? Explain your reasoning briefly.

3. Refer to the original data. Tasters rejected 200 cases that had insufficient salt. The product can be placed in a vat, salt added, and reprocessed into jars. This operation, which is considered normal, will cost $200. Prepare a journal entry to record this event and calculate the unit cost of all the cases if
   a. This additional cost was incurred because of the exacting specifications of this particular job.
   b. This additional cost occurs regularly because of difficulty in seasoning.
   c. Are unit costs the same in requirements 3a and 3b? Explain your reasoning briefly.

18-28 Reworked units, costs of rework. White Goods assembles washing machines at its Auburn plant. In February 2001, 60 tumbler units that cost $44 each from a new supplier who subsequently went bankrupt, were defective and had to be disposed of at zero disposal price. White Goods was able to rework all 60 washing machines by substituting new tumbler units purchased from one of its existing suppliers. Each replacement tumbler cost $50.

Required

1. What alternative approaches are there to account for the material costs of reworked units?

2. Should White Goods use the $44 or $50 tumbler to calculate the costs of materials reworked? Explain.

3. What other costs might White Goods include in its analysis of the total costs of rework due to the tumbler units purchased from the (now) bankrupt supplier?

18-29 Scrap, job costing. The Mendoza Company has an extensive job-costing facility that uses a variety of metals. Consider each requirement independently.

Required

1. Job 372 uses a particular metal alloy that is not used for any other job. Assume that scrap is material and sold quickly after it is produced. The scrap is sold for $490. Prepare the journal entry.

2. The scrap from Job 372 consists of a metal used by many other jobs. No record is maintained of the scrap generated by individual jobs. Assume that scrap is accounted for at the time of sale of scrap. Scrap totaling $4,000 is sold. Prepare two journal entries that could be used to account for the sale of scrap.

3. Suppose the scrap generated in requirement 2 is returned to the storeroom for future use and a journal entry is made to record the scrap. A month later, the scrap is reused as direct material on a subsequent job. Prepare the journal entries to record these transactions.

PROBLEMS

18-30 Weighted-average method, spoilage. The Alston Company operates under a weighted-average method of process costing. It has two departments, Cleaning and Milling. For both departments, conversion costs are added evenly during the processes. However, direct materials are added at the beginning of the process in the Cleaning Department, and additional direct materials are added at the end of the milling process. The costs and unit production statistics for May follow. All unfinished work at the end of May is 25% complete as to conversion costs. The beginning inventory (May 1) was 80% complete as to conversion costs as of May 1. All completed work is transferred to the next department.

	Cleaning	Milling
Beginning Inventories		
Cleaning: $1,000 direct materials, $800 conversion costs	$1,800	
Milling: $6,450 transferred-in cost and $2,450 conversion costs		$8,900
Costs Added During Current Period		
Direct materials	$9,000	$640
Conversion costs	$8,000	$4,950
Physical Units		
Units in beginning inventory	1,000	3,000
Units started this month	9,000	7,400
Good units completed and transferred out	7,400	6,000
Normal spoilage	740[a]	300[b]
Abnormal spoilage	260	100

[a]Normal spoilage in Cleaning Department is 10% of good units completed and transferred out.
[b]Normal spoilage in Milling Department is 5% of good units completed and transferred out.

Additional Information

1. Spoilage is assumed to occur at the end of each of the two processes when the units are inspected. Spoiled units are disposed of at zero net disposal price.

2. Assume that there is no shrinkage, evaporation, or abnormal spoilage other than that indicated in the information given.

3. Carry unit-cost calculations to four decimal places where necessary. Calculate final totals to the nearest dollar.

Required

For the Cleaning Department, summarize total costs to account for, and assign these costs to units completed and transferred out (including normal spoilage), to abnormal spoilage, and to units in ending work in process. (Problem 18-32 explores additional facets of this problem.)

18-31 FIFO method, spoilage. Refer to the information in Problem 18-30.
Required
Do Problem 18-30, using the FIFO method of process costing. (Problem 18-33 explores additional facets of this problem.)

18-32 Weighted-average method, Milling Department (continuation of 18-30). Refer to the information in Problem 18-30.
Required
For the Milling Department, summarize total costs to account for, and assign these costs to units completed and transferred out (including normal spoilage), to abnormal spoilage, and to units in ending work in process.

18-33 FIFO method, Milling Department (continuation of 18-31). Refer to the information in Problem 18-30.

Required

For the Milling Department, use the FIFO method to summarize total costs to account for, and assign these costs to units completed and transferred out (including normal spoilage), to abnormal spoilage, and to units in ending work in process.

18-34 Job-costing spoilage and scrap. (F. Mayne) Santa Cruz Metal Fabricators, Inc., has a large job, No. 2734, that calls for producing various ore bins, chutes, and metal boxes for enlarging a copper concentrator. The following charges were made to the job in November 2001:

Direct materials	$26,951
Direct manufacturing labor	15,076
Manufacturing overhead	7,538

The contract with the customer called for the total price to be based on a cost-plus approach. The contract defined cost to include direct materials, direct manufacturing labor costs, and manufacturing overhead to be allocated at 50% of direct manufacturing labor costs. The contract also provided that the total costs of all work spoiled were to be removed from the billable cost of the job and that the benefits from scrap sales were to reduce the billable cost of the job.

Required

1. In accordance with the stated terms of the contract, prepare journal entries for the following two items:
   a. A cutting error was made in production. The up-to-date job cost record for the batch of work involved showed materials of $650, direct manufacturing labor of $500, and allocated overhead of $250. Because fairly large pieces of metal were recoverable, the company believed that the scrap value was $600 and that the materials recovered could be used on other jobs. The spoiled work was sent to the warehouse.
   b. Small pieces of metal cuttings and scrap in November 2001 amounted to $1,250, which was the price quoted by a scrap dealer. No journal entries have been made with regard to the scrap until the price was quoted by the scrap dealer. The scrap dealer's offer was immediately accepted.

2. Consider normal and abnormal spoilage. Suppose the contract described above had contained the clause "a normal spoilage allowance of 1% of the job costs will be included in the billable costs of the job."
   a. Is this clause specific enough to define exactly how much spoilage is normal and how much is abnormal? Explain.
   b. Repeat requirement 1a with this "normal spoilage of 1%" clause in mind. You should be able to provide two slightly different journal entries.

18-35 Job costing, rework. Bristol Corporation manufactures two brands of motors, SM-5 and RW-8. The costs of manufacturing each SM-5 motor, excluding rework costs, are direct materials, $300; direct manufacturing labor, $60; and manufacturing overhead, $190. Defective units are sent to a separate rework area. Rework costs per SM-5 motor are direct materials, $60; direct manufacturing labor, $45; and manufacturing overhead, $75.

In February 2001, Bristol manufactured 1,000 SM-5 and 500 RW-8 motors. Eighty of the SM-5 motors and none of the RW-8 motors required rework. Bristol classifies 50 of the SM-5 motors reworked as normal rework caused by inherent problems in its production process that only coincidentally occurred during the production of SM-5. Hence the rework costs for these 50 SM-5 motors are normal rework costs not specifically attributable to the SM-5 product. Bristol classifies the remaining 30 units of SM-5 motors reworked as abnormal rework. Bristol allocates manufacturing overhead on the basis of machine-hours required to manufacture SM-5 and RW-8. Each SM-5 and RW-8 motor requires the same number of machine-hours.

Required

1. Prepare journal entries to record the accounting for the cost of the spoiled motors and for rework.
2. What were the total rework costs charged to SM-5 motors in February 2001?

18-36 Job costing, scrap. Wong Corporation makes two different types of hubcaps for cars—models HM3 and JB4. Circular pieces of metal are stamped out of steel sheets (leaving the edges as scrap), formed, and finished. The stamping operation is identical for both types of hubcaps. During March, Wong manufactured 20,000 units of HM3 and 10,000 units of JB4. In March, manufacturing costs per unit of HM3 and JB4 before accounting for the scrap are as follows:

	HM3	JB4
Direct materials	$10	$15
Direct manufacturing labor	3	4
Materials-related manufacturing overhead (materials handling, storage, etc.)	2	3
Other manufacturing overhead	6	8
Unit manufacturing costs	$21	$30

Materials-related manufacturing costs are allocated to products at 20% of direct materials costs. Other manufacturing overhead is allocated to products at 200% of direct manufacturing labor costs. Since the same metal sheets are used to make both types of hubcaps, Wong maintains no records of the scrap generated by individual products. Scrap generated during manufacturing is accounted for at the time it is returned to the storeroom as an offset to materials-related manufacturing overhead. The value of scrap generated during March and returned to the storeroom was $7,000.

Required
1. Prepare a journal entry to summarize the accounting for scrap during March.
2. Suppose the scrap generated in March is sold in April for $7,000. Prepare a journal entry to account for this transaction.
3. Do you agree with the manufacturing costs per unit of $21 for HM3 and $30 for JB4? What adjustments, if any, would you make? Explain your answer briefly.

18-37 Physical units, inspection at various stages of completion. (Chapter Appendix) Normal spoilage is 6% of the good units passing inspection in a forging process. In March, a total of 10,000 units were spoiled. Other data include units started during March, 120,000; work in process, beginning, 14,000 units (20% completed for conversion costs); work in process, ending, 11,000 units (70% completed for conversion costs).

Required
In columnar form, compute the normal and abnormal spoilage in units, assuming the inspection point is at 15%, 40%, and 100% stages of completion.

18-38 Weighted-average, inspection at 80% completion. (A. Atkinson) (Chapter Appendix) Ottawa Manufacturing produces a plastic toy in a two-stage molding and finishing operation. The company uses a weighted-average process-costing system. During the month of June, the following data were recorded for the Finishing Department:

Units of beginning inventory	10,000
Percentage completion of beginning units	25%
Cost of direct materials in beginning work in process	$0
Units started	70,000
Units completed	50,000
Units in ending inventory	20,000
Percentage completion of ending units	95%
Spoiled units	10,000
Costs added during current period:	
Direct materials	$655,200
Direct manufacturing labor	$635,600
Manufacturing overhead	$616,000
Work in process, beginning:	
Transferred-in costs	$82,900
Conversion costs	$42,000
Cost of units transferred in during current period	$647,500

Conversion costs are incurred evenly during the process. Direct materials costs are incurred when production is 90% complete. The inspection point is at the 80% stage of production. Normal spoilage is 10% of all good units that pass inspection. Spoiled units are disposed of at zero net disposal price.

Required

For the month of June, summarize total costs to account for, and assign these costs to units completed and transferred out (including normal spoilage), to abnormal spoilage, and to units in ending work in process.

18-39 Job costing, spoilage, ethics. (CMA, adapted) Richport Company manufactures products that often require specification changes or modifications to meet its customers' needs. Still, Richport has been able to establish a normal spoilage rate of 2.5% of *normal input*. Normal spoilage is recognized during the budgeting process and classified as a component of manufacturing overhead when determining the overhead rate.

Rose Duncan, one of Richport's inspection managers, obtains the following information for Job No. N1192-122 that had been recently completed just before the end of Richport's current accounting year. The units will be delivered early in the next accounting year. A total of 122,000 units had been started, and 5,000 spoiled units were rejected at final inspection yielding 117,000 good units. Rejected units were sold at $7 per unit. Duncan indicates that all rejects were related to this specific job.

The total costs for all 122,000 units of Job No. N1192-122 follow. The job has been completed, but the costs are yet to be transferred to finished goods.

Direct materials	$2,196,000
Direct manufacturing labor	1,830,000
Manufacturing overhead	2,928,000
Total manufacturing costs	$6,954,000

Required

1. Calculate the unit quantities of normal and abnormal spoilage.
2. Prepare the appropriate journal entry (or entries) to properly account for Job No. N1192-122 including spoilage, disposal of spoiled units, and transfer of costs to the Finished Goods account.
3. Richport Company has small profit margins and is anticipating very low operating income for the year. The controller, Thomas Rutherford, tells Martha Gonzales, the management accountant responsible for Job No. N1192-122, the following, "This was an unusual job. I think all 5,000 spoiled units should be considered normal." Gonzales knows that Richport's normal spoilage rate has been a good measure of normal spoilage levels on similar jobs in the past and that the spoilage levels for Job N1192-122 were much greater. She feels Rutherford made these comments because he wants to show higher operating income for the year.
   a. Prepare the journal entry (or entries), similar to the journal entry (or entries) prepared in requirement 2, to account for Job No. N1192-l22 if all spoilage were considered normal. By how much will Richport's operating income be affected if all spoilage is considered normal?
   b. What should Martha Gonzales do?

COLLABORATIVE LEARNING PROBLEM

18-40 FIFO method, spoilage, working backwards. The Cooking Department of Spicer, Inc., uses a process-costing system. Direct materials are added at the beginning of the cooking process. Conversion costs are added evenly during the cooking process. Consider the following data for the Cooking Department of Spicer, Inc., for the month of January:

	Physical Units	Direct Materials	Conversion Costs
Work in process, January 1[a]	10,000	$ 220,000	$ 30,000
Started in January	74,000		
Good units completed and transferred out during January	61,000		
Spoiled units	8,000		
Work in process, January 31	15,000		
Costs added during January		$1,480,000	$942,000
Cost per equivalent unit of work done in January		$20	$12

[a]Degree of completion: direct materials, 100%; conversion costs, 25%.

Spicer uses the FIFO method of process costing. Inspection occurs when production is 100% complete. Normal spoilage is 11% of good units completed and transferred out during the current period.

Required

Form groups of two or more students to complete the following requirements.

1. For each cost category, compute equivalent units of work done in the current period (January).
2. For each cost category, compute separately the equivalent units of work done to complete beginning work-in-process inventory, to start and complete new units, for normal and abnormal spoilage, and to produce ending work-in-process inventory.
3. For each cost category, calculate the percentage of completion of ending work-in-process inventory.
4. Summarize total costs to account for, and assign these costs to units completed and transferred out (including normal spoilage), to abnormal spoilage, and to units in ending work in process.

Quality, Time, and the Theory of Constraints

learning objectives

After studying this chapter, you should be able to

1. Explain four cost categories in a costs of quality program
2. Use three methods to identify quality problems
3. Identify the relevant costs and benefits of quality improvements
4. Provide examples of nonfinancial quality measures of customer satisfaction and internal performance
5. Use both financial and nonfinancial measures of quality
6. Describe customer-response time and on-time performance, and explain the reasons for and the cost of delays
7. Implement three main measures in the theory of constraints
8. Manage bottlenecks

Customers are requiring companies to meet demanding quality levels and delivery schedules while maintaining competitive prices. To achieve these goals, Xerox Corporation trains and motivates its workers to improve quality and increase throughput. To monitor performance and to make improvements in quality and timeliness, Xerox uses both financial and nonfinancial measures.

I ncreasingly, customers are becoming intolerant of poor quality and long delivery times. Companies that fail to achieve quality and timeliness bear high costs and put their businesses at significant risk. To satisfy their customers and to be competitive, managers need to find cost-effective ways to continuously improve the quality of their products and to shorten delivery times. This chapter describes how managers identify and overcome a variety of organization constraints and streamline processes to improve quality and reduce delays. In particular, we emphasize the important role that management accountants play in assisting managers to take initiatives in the quality and time areas, and to make decisions when faced with multiple constraints.

QUALITY AS A COMPETITIVE WEAPON

Many companies throughout the world—for example, Hewlett-Packard and Ford Motor Company in the United States and Canada; British Telecom in the United Kingdom; Fujitsu and Toyota in Japan; Crysel in Mexico; and Samsung in Korea—view total quality management as providing an important competitive edge. Why? Because a quality focus reduces costs and increases customer satisfaction. Several prestigious, high-profile awards—for example, the Malcolm Baldridge Quality Award in the United States, the Deming Prize in Japan, and the Premio Nacional de Calidad in Mexico—have been instituted to recognize exceptional quality.

International quality standards have emerged. For example, ISO 9000, developed by the International Organization for Standardization, is a set of five international standards for quality management adopted by more than 85 countries. ISO 9000 was created to enable companies to effectively document and certify their quality system elements. To ensure that their suppliers deliver high-quality products at competitive costs, some companies, such as DuPont and General Electric, are requiring their suppliers to obtain ISO 9000 certification. Thus, certification and an emphasis on quality are rapidly becoming conditions for competing in the global marketplace.

Quality-improvement programs often result in substantial savings and higher revenues in the short run. Quality improvement also benefits a company's long-run performance. For example, a quality focus creates expertise about products and processes that frequently leads to lower future costs, increased customer satisfaction, and higher future revenues. At Dell Computer, quality initiatives, which have increased customer satisfaction, have also fueled its 3,077% increase in revenues, 18,780% increase in profits, and 29,600% increase in stock price over the last eight years. (For details, see Concepts in Action box, p. 686.) Sometimes, the benefit of better quality is preserving revenues, not generating higher revenues. If competitors are improving quality, then a company that does not invest in quality improvement will likely suffer a decline in its market share, revenues, and profits.

As corporations' responsibilities toward the environment grow, managers are applying the ideas of quality management to find cost-effective ways to improve environmental quality and reduce the costs of air pollution, waste water, oil and chemical spills, and hazardous waste disposal. The U.S. costs of environmental damage can be extremely high to corporations under the 1990 amendments to the Clean Air Act. For example, Exxon paid $125 million in fines and restitution on top of $1 billion in civil payments for the 1989 Exxon Valdez oil spill, which harmed the Alaskan coast. In 1994, the International Organization for Standardization announced ISO 14000, an environmental management standard. The standard's goal is to encourage organizations to pursue environmental goals vigorously by developing (1) environmental management systems to reduce environmental costs, and (2) environmental auditing and performance evaluation systems to review and provide feedback on how well an organization has achieved its environmental goals.

Although *quality* refers to a wide variety of factors—such as fitness for use, customer satisfaction, and the degree to which a product conforms to design specifications and engineering requirements—we focus on two basic aspects of quality: *quality of design* and *conformance quality*.[1]

Quality of design refers to how closely the characteristics of a product or service meets the needs and wants of customers. Suppose customers of photocopying machines want copiers that combine copying, faxing, scanning, and electronic printing. Photocopying machines that fail to meet these customer needs fail in the quality of their design. Similarly, if customers of a bank want an online banking system, not providing this service would be a quality-of-design failure.

Conformance quality refers to the performance of a product or service relative to its design and product specifications. For example, if a photocopying machine mishandles paper or breaks down, it fails to satisfy conformance quality. Products not conforming to specifications must be repaired, reworked, or scrapped at an additional cost to the organization. If nonconformance errors remain after the product is shipped and the product breaks down at the customer site, even greater repair costs as well as the loss of customer goodwill—often the highest quality cost of all—may result. In the banking industry, depositing a customer's check into the wrong bank account is an example of conformance quality failure.

To ensure that actual performance achieves customer satisfaction, companies must first design products to satisfy customers through quality of design, and they must then meet design specifications through conformance quality. The following diagram illustrates that actual performance can fall short of customer satisfaction either because of quality of design failure or because of conformance quality failure.

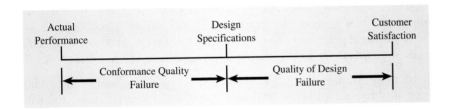

An important question is how to measure the costs of quality. We consider first the easier case of conformance quality.

COSTS OF QUALITY

The **costs of quality (COQ)** refer to costs incurred to prevent, or costs arising as a result of, the production of a low-quality product. These costs focus on conformance quality and are incurred in all business functions of the value chain. Costs of quality are classified into four categories:

OBJECTIVE 1

Explain four cost categories in a costs of quality program

1. **Prevention costs**—costs incurred to preclude the production of products that do not conform to specifications.

2. **Appraisal costs**—costs incurred to detect which of the individual units of products do not conform to specifications.

3. **Internal failure costs**—costs incurred by a nonconforming product *before* it is shipped to customers.

4. **External failure costs**—costs incurred by a nonconforming product *after* it is shipped to customers.

Exhibit 19-1 presents examples of individual cost of quality items, in each of these four categories, reported on COQ reports. Note that the items included in Exhibit 19-1

[1]The American Society for Quality Control defines *quality* as the totality of features and characteristics of a product made or a service performed according to specifications, to satisfy customers at the time of purchase and during use. ANSI/ASQC A3-1978, *Quality Systems Terminology* (Milwaukee, WI: American Society for Quality Control, 1978). See also R. DeVor, T. Chang, and J. Sutherland, *Statistical Quality Design and Control* (New York: Macmillan, 1992); and J. Evans and W. Lindsay, *The Management and Control of Quality* (St. Paul: West, 1993).

EXHIBIT 19-1
Items Pertaining to Costs of Quality Reports

Prevention Costs	Appraisal Costs	Internal Failure Costs	External Failure Costs
Design engineering	Inspection	Spoilage	Customer support
Process engineering	Online product manufacturing and process inspection	Rework	Transportation costs
Quality engineering		Scrap	Manufacturing/process engineering
Supplier evaluations	Product testing	Breakdown maintenance	Warranty repair costs
Preventive equipment maintenance		Manufacturing/process engineering on internal failure	Liability claims
Quality training			
New materials used to manufacture products			

Reinforcing Problems Exer. 19-16 through 19-18 and Prob. 19-37 cover cost of quality issues.

come from all value-chain business functions and are broader than the internal failure costs of spoilage, rework, and scrap in manufacturing considered in Chapter 18.

We illustrate the various issues in managing quality—from computing the costs of quality, to identifying quality problems, to taking actions to improve quality—using the Photon Corporation as an example. Photon makes many products. Our discussion focuses on Photon's photocopying machines, which earned an operating income of $24 million on revenues of $300 million (20,000 copiers) in the year 2000. Photon determines the costs of quality of its photocopying machines using the seven-step activity-based costing approach described in Chapter 5.

Step 1: Identify the Chosen Cost Object(s)   The cost object is the 20,000 photocopying machines that Photon makes. Photon's goal is to calculate the total costs of quality of these machines.

Curriculum Linkage Point out that Chapter 18's consideration of spoilage and rework encompasses only appraisal and internal failure costs. This is just the tip of the iceberg or 38% (19.60/52.02) of Photon's total COQ (including estimated opportunity costs), per Panel A of Exh. 19-2.

Step 2: Identify the Product's Direct Costs of Quality   The photocopying machines have no direct costs of quality.

Step 3: Select the Cost-Allocation Bases to Use for Allocating Indirect Costs of Quality to the Product   Column 1 of Exhibit 19-2, Panel A, classifies activities that result in prevention, appraisal, internal failure, and external failure costs and indicates the value-chain business functions in which the costs occur. For example, the inspection activity results in appraisal costs and occurs in the manufacturing function. Photon chooses the number of inspection-hours rather than the number of inspections as the cost-allocation base for the inspection activity because inspection-hours has a better cause-and-effect relationship with inspection costs. To avoid details, we do not provide information on the total quantities of each of these cost-allocation bases used in all of Photon's operations and businesses.

Step 4: Identify the Indirect Costs of Quality Associated with Each Cost-Allocation Base   These are the total costs (fixed and variable) incurred on each of the costs of quality activities, such as inspections, in all of Photon's operations. To avoid details, we do not provide information about these total costs.

Points to Stress Although quality costs occur in all value-chain functions, most prevention costs occur in R&D/design, and most appraisal and internal failure costs occur in mfg. External failure costs occur primarily in downstream functions: marketing, distribution, customer service.

Step 5: Compute the Rate Per Unit of Each Cost-Allocation Base Used to Allocate Indirect Costs of Quality to the Product   For each activity, the total costs calculated in step 4 are divided by the total quantity of the cost-allocation base (calculated in step 3) to compute the rate per unit for each cost-allocation base. Column 2 of Exhibit 19-2, Panel A, shows these rates (without supporting calculations). For example, Photon calculates the rate of $40 per hour for the inspection activity by dividing the total costs of inspection incurred in all of Photon's operations by the total quantity of inspection-hours for all of Photon's operations.

Step 6: Compute the Indirect Costs of Quality Allocated to the Product
Photon first determines the quantities of each of the cost-allocation bases used by

EXHIBIT 19-2
Analysis of Activity-Based Costs of Quality for Photocopying Machines at Photon Corporation

PANEL A: COQ REPORT

Costs of Quality and Value-Chain Category (1)	Allocation Base or Cost Driver		Total Costs (4) = (2) × (3)	Percentage of Revenues (5) = (4) ÷ $300,000,000
	Rate[a] (2)	Quantity (3)		
Prevention costs				
Design engineering (R&D/Design)	$80 per hour	40,000 hours	$ 3,200,000	1.07%
Process engineering (R&D)/Design)	$60 per hour	45,000 hours	2,700,000	0.90
Total prevention costs			5,900,000	1.97
Appraisal costs				
Inspection (Manufacturing)	$40 per hour	240,000 hours	9,600,000	3.20
Total appraisal costs			9,600,000	3.20
Internal failure costs				
Rework (Manufacturing)	$100 per hour	100,000 hours	10,000,000	3.33
Total internal failure costs			10,000,000	3.33
External failure costs				
Customer support (Marketing)	$50 per hour	12,000 hours	600,000	0.20
Transportation (Distribution)	$240 per load	3,000 loads	720,000	0.24
Warranty repair (Customer service)	$110 per hour	120,000 hours	13,200,000	4.40
Total external failure costs			14,520,000	4.84
Total costs of quality			$40,020,000	13.34%

[a]Amounts assumed.

PANEL B: OPPORTUNITY COST ANALYSIS

Costs of Quality Category (1)	Total Estimated Contribution Margin Lost (2)	Percentage of Sales (3) = (2) ÷ $300,000,000
External failure costs		
Estimated forgone contribution margin and income on lost sales	$12,000,000[b]	4.00%
Total costs of quality	$12,000,000	4.00%

[b]Calculated as total revenues minus all variable costs (whether output-unit, batch, product-sustaining, or facility sustaining) on lost sales.

the photocopying machines. These quantities are shown in column 3 of Exhibit 19-2, Panel A. For example, Photon determines that photocopying machines use 240,000 inspection-hours. Column 4 of Exhibit 19-2, Panel A, shows the indirect costs of quality of the photocopying machines. To calculate these costs, the total quantity of the cost-allocation base used by the photocopying machines for each activity is multiplied by the cost-allocation rate calculated in step 5 (Exhibit 19-2, Panel A, column 2). For example, quality-related inspection costs for the photocopying machines are $9,600,000 ($40 per hour × 240,000 inspection-hours).

Step 7: Compute the Total Costs of Quality by Adding All Direct and Indirect Costs of Quality Assigned to the Product Exhibit 19-2, Panel A, shows Photon's total costs of quality in the COQ report for photocopying machines to be $40.02 million, of which the largest categories are $14.52 million in total external failure costs and $10 million in total internal failure costs—a sum of $24.52 million. Total reported costs of quality for photocopying machines are 13.34% of current revenues.

The total costs of quality typically *shown in COQ reports* exclude some important costs of quality items. COQ reports typically do not consider opportunity costs, such as forgone contribution margin and income from lost sales, lost production, or lower prices, that result from poor quality. Why are opportunity costs excluded? Because they are difficult to estimate and generally are not recorded in accounting systems. Nevertheless, opportunity costs can be substantial and important driving forces in quality-improvement programs. Exhibit 19-2, Panel B, presents the analysis of the opportunity costs of poor quality at Photon. The company's Market Research Department estimates lost sales of 2,000 photocopying machines because of external failures. The forgone contribution margin and operating income of $12 million measures the financial costs from dissatisfied customers who have returned machines to Photon and from sales lost because of quality problems. Total costs of quality (including opportunity costs) equal $52.02 million (Panel A, $40.02 million + Panel B, $12 million), or 17.34% of current revenues. Opportunity costs account for 23% ($12 million ÷ $52.02 million) of Photon's total costs of quality.

The COQ report and the opportunity cost analysis highlight Photon's high internal and external failure costs. To reduce costs of quality, Photon must identify and reduce failures caused by quality problems.

TECHNIQUES USED TO ANALYZE QUALITY PROBLEMS

Three common techniques to identify and analyze quality problems are control charts, Pareto diagrams, and cause-and-effect diagrams.

Control Charts

Statistical quality control (SQC), or statistical process control (SPC), is a formal means of distinguishing between random variation and nonrandom variation in an operating process. A key tool in SQC is a control chart. A **control chart** is a graph of a series of successive observations of a particular step, procedure, or operation taken at regular intervals of time. Each observation is plotted relative to specified ranges that represent the expected statistical distribution. Only those observations outside the control limits are ordinarily regarded as nonrandom and worth investigating.

Exhibit 19-3 presents control charts for the daily defect rates observed at Photon's three photocopying machine production lines. Defect rates in the prior 60 days for each plant were assumed to provide a good basis from which to calculate the distribution of daily defect rates. The arithmetic mean (μ, read mu) and standard deviation (σ, read sigma) are the two parameters of the distribution that are used in the control charts in Exhibit 19-3. On the basis of experience, the company decides that any observation outside the $\mu \pm 2\sigma$ range should be investigated.

EXHIBIT 19-3
Statistical Quality Control Charts: Daily Defect Rate for Photocopying Machines at the Photon Corporation

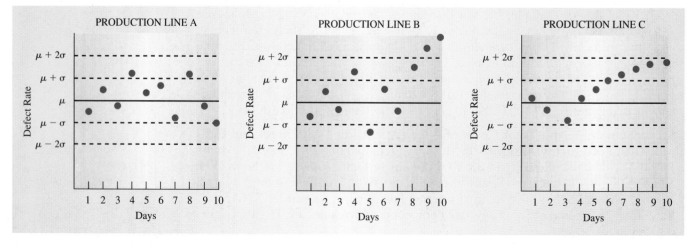

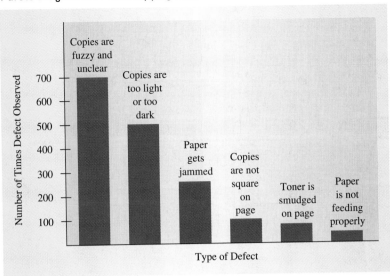

For production line A in Exhibit 19-3, all observations are within the range of $\pm 2\sigma$ from the mean, and management thus believes no investigation is necessary. For production line B, the last two observations signal that an out-of-control occurrence is highly likely. Given the $\pm 2\sigma$ rule, both observations would lead to an investigation. Production line C illustrates a process that would not prompt an investigation under the $\pm 2\sigma$ rule but may well be out of control. Why? Because the last eight observations show a clear direction and the last six are away from the mean. Statistical procedures have been developed using the trend as well as the variation to evaluate whether a process is out of control.

Pareto Diagrams

Observations outside control limits serve as inputs for *Pareto diagrams*. A **Pareto diagram** indicates how frequently each type of failure (defect) occurs. Exhibit 19-4 presents a Pareto diagram of quality problems with respect to photocopying machines. Fuzzy and unclear copies are the most frequently recurring problem.

The problem of fuzzy and unclear copies results in high rework costs because, in many cases, Photon discovers this problem only after the copier has been built. Sometimes fuzzy and unclear copies occur at customer sites, resulting in high warranty and repair costs.

Cause-and-Effect Diagrams

The most frequently recurring and costly problems identified by the Pareto diagram are analyzed using *cause-and-effect diagrams*. A **cause-and-effect diagram** identifies potential causes of failures or defects. As a first step, Photon analyzes the causes of the most frequently occurring failure, fuzzy and unclear copies. Exhibit 19-5 presents the cause-and-effect diagram for this problem. The exhibit identifies four major categories of potential causes of failure—human factors, methods and design factors, machine-related factors, and materials and components factors. As additional arrows are added for each cause, the general appearance of the diagram begins to resemble the bone structure of a fish (hence, cause-and-effect diagrams are also called *fishbone diagrams*).[2] Automated equipment and computers facilitate

Curriculum Linkage Students may be familiar with statistical quality control, Pareto diagrams, and cause-and-effect diagrams from operations mgt. or production courses. Students who have taken statistics should also understand the meaning of the 2-sigma rule. If the defect rates are normally distributed and the production process is truly *in control*, then we would observe a defect rate more than 2 sigma from the mean only about 5% of the time (when the process is truly in control). Mgt. sets the investigation rule (e.g., 1, 2, 3 sigma, etc.) to minimize the total cost of (1) false positives (hypothesizing that the process is out of control when it's actually in control), and (2) false negatives (hypothesizing that the process is in control when it's actually out of control).

Points to Stress Mgt. can use combinations of methods to identify quality problems. In the Photon example, mgt. first used the Pareto diagram to identify the most frequently encountered defect (fuzzy and unclear copies) and then applied the cause-and-effect diagram to identify root causes of the defect.

[2]Managers in U.S. electronics companies consider the following factors (ranked in order of importance with 1 = most important) as contributing to improvements in quality: (1) Better product design, (2) improved process design, (3) improved training of operators, (4) improved products from suppliers, (5) investments in technology and equipment. See G. Foster and L. Sjoblom, "Survey of Quality Practices in the U.S. Electronics Industry," *Journal of Management Accounting Research* 8 (1996), 55–86.

EXHIBIT 19-5
Cause-and-Effect Diagram for Fuzzy and Unclear Photocopies at Photon Corporation

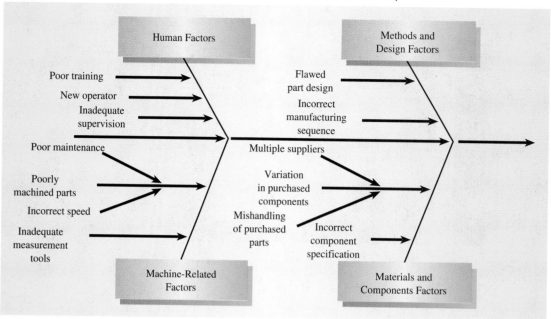

the analysis of quality problems because they maintain a record of both the number and types of defects and the operating conditions that existed at the time the defects occurred. Using these inputs, computer programs simultaneously prepare the related control charts, Pareto diagrams and fishbone diagrams.

RELEVANT COSTS AND BENEFITS OF QUALITY IMPROVEMENT

OBJECTIVE 3

Identify the relevant costs and benefits of quality improvements

Curriculum Linkage/Reinforcing Problems The relevant cost analysis is analogous to the approach introduced in Chap. 11. Exer. 19-20 and Probs. 19-27 and 19-28 reinforce relevant costs and benefits in quality improvement decisions.

Careful analysis of Photon's cause-and-effect diagram reveals that the steel frame (or chassis) of the copier is often mishandled as it travels from the suppliers' warehouses to Photon's plant. The frame must satisfy very precise specifications and tolerances. Otherwise, various copier components (such as drums, mirrors, and lenses) attached to the frame will be aligned improperly. Mishandling causes the dimensions of the frame to vary from specifications, resulting in fuzzy and unclear copies.

The team of engineers working to solve this problem offers two alternative solutions: (1) to improve the inspection of the frames immediately upon delivery, or (2) to redesign and strengthen the frames and the containers used to transport them to better withstand mishandling during transportation.

To evaluate each alternative versus the status quo, management must measure the total relevant costs and total relevant revenues for each alternative. As we described in Chapter 11, relevant-cost and relevant-revenue analysis ignores allocated amounts. The key question is how *total costs and total revenues will change under each alternative*.

Management estimates that additional inspection will cost $400,000. Redesign will cost an additional $460,000. The incremental costs of redesign exceed the incremental costs of inspection, but before making a decision, management must compare the incremental costs of each alternative against the corresponding incremental benefits. These incremental benefits are lower internal and external failure costs and greater contribution margin from higher future sales.

Photon considers only a 1-year time horizon for analyzing this decision because it plans to introduce a completely new line of copiers at the end of the year. Photon believes that the new line of copiers are so different that the choice of either the inspection or the redesign alternative will have no effect on the sales of copiers in future years.

EXHIBIT 19-6

Estimated Effect of Quality Improvement Actions on Costs of Quality for Photocopying Machines at Photon Corporation

Relevant Items	Relevant Costs and Benefits of	
	Further Inspecting Incoming Frames (1)	Redesigning Frames (2)
Additional design engineering costs	—	$ 160,000
Additional process engineering costs	—	300,000
Additional inspection and testing costs	$ 400,000	—
Saving in rework costs		
$40 × 24,000 fewer rework-hours	(960,000)	—
$40 × 32,000 fewer rework-hours		(1,280,000)
Savings in customer-support costs		
$20 × 2,000 fewer customer-support hours	(40,000)	
$20 × 2,800 fewer customer-support hours		(56,000)
Savings in transportation costs for repair parts		
$180 × 500 fewer loads moved	(90,000)	
$180 × 700 fewer loads moved		(126,000)
Savings in warranty repair costs		
$45 × 20,000 fewer repair-hours	(900,000)	
$45 × 28,000 fewer repair-hours		(1,260,000)
Total contribution margin from sales of		
250 additional copiers	(1,500,000)	
300 additional copier		(1,800,000)
Net cost savings and additional contribution margin	$(3,090,000)	$(4,062,000)
Difference in favor of redesigning frame	↑——— $972,000 ———↑	

Photon recognizes that even as it improves quality, it will only be able to save the variable costs of internal and external failure and none of the fixed costs. To identify the cost savings, Photon divides each item of failure costs into costs that are fixed and variable with respect to the cost driver for that item. Exhibit 19-6 shows the relevant costs and benefits for each alternative.

Consider, for example, the internal failure costs of rework of $100 per hour (Exhibit 19-2, Panel A, column 2). Photon determines fixed and variable costs per rework-hour as follows:

Variable costs	$ 40
Allocated fixed costs (equipment, space, and allocated fixed overhead)	60
Total costs	$100

If Photon chooses to inspect the frames more carefully, it expects to rework fewer copiers and eliminate 24,000 rework-hours and to save variable costs of $960,000 ($40 × 24,000) but none of the fixed rework costs. See Exhibit 19-6, column 1. If Photon chooses the redesign alternative, it expects to eliminate 32,000 rework-hours and to save variable costs of $1,280,000 ($40 × 32,000). See Exhibit 19-6, column 2. Fixed costs per rework-hour of $60 are excluded from the Exhibit 19-6 calculations because they are irrelevant—they will not change whether Photon continues its current practices, inspects the frame more carefully, or redesigns the frame. These costs are, however, included in the costs of quality calculations in Exhibit 19-2 because activity-based costs include both the fixed and the variable costs of activities.

Curriculum Linkage Photon is considering designing-in quality by redesigning the frame and transport containers to better withstand mishandling during transportation. This example illustrates how costs locked in during the design stage affect costs incurred in subsequent value-chain elements: mfg., marketing, and customer service, as well as revenues incurred subsequently (higher sales due to better quality). Locked-in costs were discussed in Chap. 12.

Exhibit 19-6 also shows the expected savings in external failure costs that will result from better quality. The expected savings in customer-support hours, loads moved, and repair-hours under each alternative are multiplied by the variable cost per customer-support hour ($20), variable cost per load moved ($180), and variable cost per repair-hour ($45) to obtain total expected savings in external failure costs. Fixed costs of customer-support, transportation, and warranty repair will not be saved whether Photon continues its current practices, inspects the frames more carefully, or redesigns them, and hence are irrelevant and excluded from the analysis.

Reducing internal and external failures by inspecting the frames or redesigning them will enhance Photon's reputation for quality and performance. Photon estimates that its enhanced reputation will lead to additional sales of 250 copiers if it improves quality through inspection and 300 copiers if it improves quality through redesign. Exhibit 19-6 includes as a benefit, the total increase in contribution margin from the estimated increases in sales—$1,500,000 for 250 copiers and $1,800,000 for 300 copiers. This benefit is important. Quality improvements cannot always be translated into lower costs. For example, laying off workers to reduce costs would adversely affect the morale of employees and hurt future quality initiatives. Management should always look for opportunities to leverage quality improvements into higher revenues.

Exhibit 19-6 shows that both the inspection and the redesign alternatives yield net benefits relative to the status quo. However, the net estimated benefits from the redesign alternative are $972,000 greater than the net estimated benefits from the alternative of inspecting the frame. Hence, Photon's management chooses to redesign the frame. The costs of a poorly designed frame appear in the form of higher manufacturing, marketing, distribution, and customer-service costs, as internal and external failures increase. But these costs are locked in when the frame is designed. Thus, it is not surprising that redesign will yield significant savings.

Points to Stress The acceptable proportion of defects depends on a cost–benefit analysis. High internal and external failure costs, relative to prevention and appraisal costs, shift the emphasis toward fewer defects. Historically, many companies have underestimated failure costs, partly because they haven't considered lost CM from lost sales due to customer "bad will," or production capacity squandered on spoiled or reworked units.

Curriculum Linkage Poor quality can reduce CM in 2 ways: (1) lost sales due to customer bad will, and (2) lost sales from wasted production output when the company has a mfg. constraint. Coverage of the theory of constraints later in this chapter continues Chap. 11's explanation that companies with mfg. constraints should maximize the CM/unit of the constraining factor. One way to do this is to reduce the amt. of the constrained resource consumed by spoiled and reworked units that reduce the time and resources otherwise available to produce good units.

In our example, Photon forgoes contribution margin because its repeated external failures damage its reputation for quality and result in lost sales. Photon can also lose contribution margin as a result of internal failures. Suppose Photon's manufacturing capacity is fully used. In this case, reworking defective copiers uses up valuable manufacturing capacity and causes the company to forgo contribution margin from producing and selling additional copiers. Suppose Photon could produce and subsequently sell an additional 600 copiers if it improved quality and reduced rework. The costs of internal failure would then include lost contribution margin of say, $3,600,000 on 600 copiers. This $3,600,000 is an opportunity cost of poor quality.

Photon can use its COQ report to examine interdependencies among the four categories of quality-related costs. In our example, redesigning the frame increases prevention costs (design and process engineering), decreases internal failure costs (rework), and decreases external failure costs (warranty repairs). COQ reports give more insight if managers compare trends over time. In successful quality programs, the costs of quality as a percentage of revenues and the sum of internal and external failure costs as a percentage of total costs of quality decrease over time. Many companies, for example, Compaq and Toyota, believe they should eliminate all failure costs and have zero defects.

COSTS OF DESIGN QUALITY

Our discussion so far has focused on measuring the cost of conformance quality and the methods that companies use to reduce these costs. In addition to conformance quality, companies must also pay attention to quality of design by designing products that satisfy customer needs. The *costs of design quality* refer to costs incurred to prevent, or costs arising as a result of, poor quality of design. These costs include the costs of designing a product, and the production, marketing, distribution, and customer-service costs wasted on supporting a poorly designed product. A significant component of these costs is the opportunity cost of sales lost from not producing a product that customers want. Many of these costs are very difficult to measure precisely. For this reason, most companies do not measure the financial costs of design quality.

NONFINANCIAL MEASURES OF QUALITY AND CUSTOMER SATISFACTION

To evaluate how well their actual performance satisfies customer needs (see diagram on p. 677), companies supplement the available financial measures with nonfinancial measures of quality of design and conformance quality. Nonfinancial measures are helpful in revealing the future needs and preferences of customers and in indicating the specific areas that need improvement. Hence nonfinancial quality measures are useful indicators of future long-run performance, unlike financial measures of quality that have a short-run quality focus. Management accountants are often responsible for maintaining and presenting these nonfinancial measures. We focus first on nonfinancial measures of customer satisfaction (that include nonfinancial measures of quality of design and external failure) and then on internal performances measures (that include nonfinancial measures of prevention, appraisal, and internal failure).

Nonfinancial Measures of Customer Satisfaction

To evaluate how well they are doing, companies such as Compaq, Dell, Federal Express, General Electric, and Motorola track customer-satisfaction measures over time. Some of these measures are:

◆ Market research information on customer preferences and customer satisfaction with specific product features

◆ The number of defective units shipped to customers as a percentage of total units shipped

◆ The number of customer complaints (Companies estimate that for every customer who actually complains, there are 10–20 others who have had bad experiences with the product but did not complain.)

◆ Percentage of products that experience early or excessive failure

◆ Delivery delays (the difference between scheduled delivery date and date requested by the customer)

◆ On-time delivery rate (percentage of shipments made on or before the scheduled delivery date)

Management investigates if these numbers deteriorate over time. If these numbers improve over time, management can be more confident about operating income being strong in future years.

In addition to these routine nonfinancial measures, many companies such as Xerox conduct surveys to measure customer satisfaction. Surveys serve two objectives. First, they provide a deeper perspective into customer experiences and preferences. Second, they provide a glimpse of features that customers would like future products to have.

Nonfinancial Measures of Internal Performance

To satisfy their customers, companies need to constantly improve the quality of work done inside the firm. Companies can use prevention costs, appraisal costs, and internal failure costs to measure quality performance inside the company in financial terms. But most companies supplement these financial measures with nonfinancial measures of internal quality. For example, Analog Devices, a semiconductor manufacturer, follows trends in these gauges of quality:

◆ The number of defects for each product line

◆ Process yield (ratio of good output to total output)

◆ Employee turnover (ratio of the number of employees who leave the company to the total number of employees)

Many companies go further and try to understand the factors that lead to better internal quality (see also, Chapter 13, p. 463–470, on the balanced scorecard). For

Curriculum Linkage The Jenkins Committee advocates expansion of acctg. to "business reporting." Mgt. accountants can help by providing nonfinancial info (e.g., customer response time, % on time deliveries) as well as financial info.

Curriculum Linkage Companies gain insight into customer needs and wants from marketing personnel. Market research staffs assess customer satisfaction and attributes customers desire in future products. Market research may be part of the product mgr's. job, as well. Companies also acquire such information from their sales force.

Example To gain insight into customer needs, textbook publishers conduct focus groups, mail surveys to faculty adopters and to faculty who adopt a competitor's text, and encourage sales reps. to obtain feedback from both customers and noncustomers.

Curriculum Linkage/Reinforcing Problems If mgrs.' performance is based on 1 or 2 criteria (e.g., quarterly profits), they will act to make their performance look better on these criteria, even though such actions may hurt the company's long-run profitability (e.g., delaying maintenance). This is why many companies have revised their performance evaluation schemes to include evaluation on several dimensions (e.g., the balanced scorecard approach discussed in Chap. 13). Prob. 19-30 covers mgt. incentives and compensation.

Dell Computer's QUEST

What has been behind Dell Computer's phenomenal 29,600% increase in stock price, 3,077% growth in revenues and 18,780% increase in profits over the last eight years? Certainly not a high gross margin—Dell's is a modest 22% of revenues. In a word, it is QUEST—Quality Underlies Every Single Task—an employee-oriented initiative of total quality management. QUEST is the bedrock of Dell's execution and innovation, leading to superb product quality, speedy manufacturing, and responsive postsales customer service.

Under the QUEST approach, workers are organized into teams of salespersons, assemblers, testers, technicians, shippers, and maintenance personnel. The QUEST team starts to work on manufacturing a computer only after a salesperson has received a firm order. Only one person, the assembler, builds the system from start to finish. Testers rigorously test the product for reliability and performance, often for over 24 hours. Technicians then install customized and proprietary software, and shippers ship the product directly to customers. Dell does not sell its computers through retailers.

Dell's success is built around customer satisfaction. *Fortune* magazine ranked Dell as one of the top two computer manufacturers in customer satisfaction in 1998. Customers cited hardware quality and reliability, performance and speed, and service and support as the reasons for their satisfaction. How does Dell achieve such high customer satisfaction ratings?

- ◆ *By helping customers to configure their products to meet customers' own requirements and specifications.* As a result, all hardware and software are designed to be compatible with and seamlessly integrated into existing systems.

- ◆ *By manufacturing a high-quality product.* During the manufacturing process, operators receive immediate feedback about the product. If the product fails a test, operators troubleshoot to correct the problem. Dell takes no chances with respect to performance in its testing procedures. Its notebooks, for example, must survive intense shaking on a vibrating table, exposure to extreme temperatures, and a series of drop tests. In 1997, Dell won the top spot in *PC Computing* magazine's "notebook torture test."

- ◆ *By providing excellent technical support after delivering products to its customers.* When customers call with questions, the technical support staff responds promptly with high-quality advice.

Source: Adapted from K. Chambers, "Inside the Cell," *Dell Insider* (May–June 1997); *Dell Computer Annual Report*, 1997. For more information visit the Dell Computer website at http:///www.dell.com.

example, some companies measure employee empowerment and employee satisfaction because managers at these companies believe that these measures are important determinants of quality.

- ◆ A measure of employee empowerment is the ratio of the number of processes where employees have the right to make decisions without consulting supervisors to the total number of processes.

- ◆ A measure of employee satisfaction is the ratio of employees indicating high satisfaction ratings on employee surveys to the total number of employees surveyed.

For a single reporting period, nonfinancial measures of quality have limited meaning. They are more informative when managers examine trends over time. To provide this information clearly, the management accountant must review the nonfinancial measures for accuracy and consistency. Thus, management accountants help companies improve quality in multiple ways—they compute the costs of quality, assist in developing cost-effective solutions to quality problems, and provide feedback about quality improvement.

EVALUATING QUALITY PERFORMANCE

Measuring the financial costs of quality and the nonfinancial aspects of quality have distinctly different advantages.

OBJECTIVE 5

Use both financial and nonfinancial measures of quality

Advantages of COQ Measures

1. Consistent with the attention-directing role of management accounting, COQ focuses attention on how costly poor quality can be.
2. Financial COQ measures assist in problem solving by comparing different quality-improvement programs and setting priorities for achieving maximum cost reduction.
3. Financial COQ measures serve as a common denominator for evaluating trade-offs among prevention costs and failure costs. COQ provides a single, summary measure of quality performance.

Advantages of Nonfinancial Measures of Quality

1. Nonfinancial measures of quality are often easy to quantify and understand.
2. Nonfinancial measures direct attention to physical processes and hence focus attention on the precise problem areas that need improvement.
3. Nonfinancial measures provide immediate short-run feedback on whether quality-improvement efforts have, in fact, succeeded in improving quality.
4. Nonfinancial measures are useful indicators of future long-run performance.

COQ measures and nonfinancial measures supplement each other. Most organizations use both financial and nonfinancial measures to gauge quality performance. Some corporations, for example, McDonald's, evaluate employees and individual franchisees on multiple measures of quality and customer satisfaction. A mystery shopper—an outside party contracted by McDonald's to visit its restaurants—scores each restaurant on quality, cleanliness and service. The performance of the restaurants is then evaluated over time and against other restaurants.

TIME AS A COMPETITIVE WEAPON

Companies increasingly view time as a key success factor.[3] Doing things faster helps to increase revenues and decrease costs. For example, a moving company such as United Van Lines will be able to generate more revenues if it can move goods from one place to another faster and on time. In addition to higher revenues, companies such as AT&T, General Electric, and Wal-Mart also report lower costs because of their emphasis on time. They cite, for example, the need to carry less inventory because of their ability to respond rapidly to customer demands.

Reinforcing Problems Issues related to time as a competitive weapon are covered in Exer. 19-19, 19-21, and 19-22 and Probs. 19-30 and 19-31.

Companies need to measure time in order to manage it properly. In this chapter, we focus on *operational measures of time*, which reveal how quickly companies respond to customers' demands for their products and services and the reliability with which these companies meet scheduled delivery dates. Two common operational measures of time are customer-response time and on-time performance.

Customer-Response Time

Customer-response time is the amount of time from when a customer places an order for a product or requests a service to when the product or service is delivered to the customer. A timely response to customer requests is a key competitive factor in many industries, especially service industries such as construction, banking, car-rental, and fast-food. Some companies, such as Boeing, have to pay penalties to

OBJECTIVE 6

Describe customer-response time and on-time performance, and explain the reasons for and the cost of delays

[3]See G. Stalk and T. Hout, *Competing Against Time* (New York: Free Press, 1990).

EXHIBIT 19-7
Components of Customer-Response Time

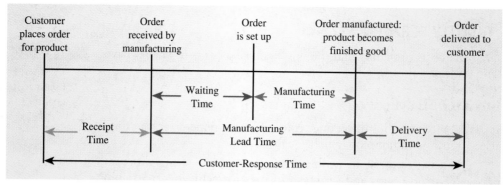

Example Customer response time is particularly important to mail-order catalog companies. To compete more effectively with stores (as well as with other mail-order companies), many companies promise delivery of their products in a week or less. The same is true for e-commerce companies. Amazon.com promises prompt delivery, and, for a fee, customers can obtain express delivery. Note that both catalog and e-commerce companies eliminate the necessity of customers having to leave their homes to shop (which reduces wait time). Second-day express delivery is std. for companies such as Neiman Marcus. Many companies believe their customers are willing to pay a higher price for faster delivery.

Curriculum Linkage Companies that apply JIT reduce mfg. lead time (wait time + mfg. time) by streamlining processes and focusing on value-added activities. Applying JIT in mktg. and distribution as well as mfg. enables companies to reduce customer response time by reducing order receipt time and delivery time, as well as mfg. lead time. On-time delivery is esp. important if the company and/or its customers follow a JIT philosophy (see Chap. 20) where there are no inventory buffers.

Example After on-time arrival statistics began to be publicized, many airlines improved their apparent on-time arrival performance by simply increasing scheduled flight time. For example, "rush hour" flights formerly scheduled to take 1 hr. might now be scheduled for 1 hr. and 15 min.

compensate their airline customers for lost revenues and profits (from being unable to schedule flights) as a result of delays in delivering airplanes to them on time.

Exhibit 19-7 describes the different components of customer-response time. In the case of Boeing, *receipt time* is the time it takes the Marketing Department to specify to Manufacturing the exact requirements in the customer's order. **Manufacturing lead time** (also called **manufacturing cycle time**) is the amount of time from when an order is received by Manufacturing to when it becomes a finished good. Manufacturing lead time is the sum of waiting time and manufacturing time for an order. An aircraft order received by Boeing may need to wait because the equipment the order requires is busy processing orders that arrived earlier. *Delivery time* is the time it takes to deliver a completed order to the customer.

Several companies have adopted manufacturing lead time as the base for allocating indirect manufacturing costs to products. The Zytec Corporation, a manufacturer of computer equipment, believes that using manufacturing lead time motivates managers to reduce the time taken to manufacture products. In turn, over time, total overhead costs decrease and operating income rises.

On-Time Performance

On-time performance refers to situations in which the product or service is actually delivered by the time it is scheduled to be delivered. Consider Federal Express, which specifies a price per package and a next-day delivery time of 10:30 A.M. for its overnight courier service. Federal Express measures on-time performance by how often it meets its stated delivery time of 10:30 A.M. On-time performance is an important element of customer satisfaction because customers want and expect on-time deliveries. Commercial airlines, for example, gain loyal passengers from consistent on-time service. Note that there is a trade-off between customer-response time and on-time performance. Simply scheduling longer customer-response times, such as Federal Express scheduling deliveries at 1 P.M. instead of 10:30 A.M., or airlines lengthening scheduled arrival times, makes achieving on-time performance easier (although this tactic could displease customers).

TIME DRIVERS AND COSTS OF TIME

Managing customer-response time and on-time performance in manufacturing, merchandising, and service companies requires an understanding of the causes of delays and the resulting costs. Delays can occur, for example, in front of a machine in a manufacturing operation, in front of a teller at a bank, or in front of a checkout counter in a store. We focus first on the reasons for delays.

Uncertainty and Bottlenecks as Drivers of Time

A **time driver** is any factor where a change in the factor causes a change in the speed with which an activity is undertaken. Two important drivers of time are:

- Uncertainty about when customers will order products or services. For example, the more randomly Boeing receives orders for its airplanes, the more likely that queues will form and delays will occur.

- Limited capacity and bottlenecks. A **bottleneck** is an operation where the work required to be performed approaches or exceeds the available capacity. For example, a bottleneck is created and delays occur when products that need to be processed at a particular machine arrive while the machine is being used to process other products.

Consider Falcon Works (FW), which uses one turning machine to convert steel bars into one specialty component, a special gear for pumps. FW makes this component only after FW's customers order the gear. To focus on manufacturing lead time, we assume that FW's receipt time and delivery time for orders are minimal.

FW expects it will receive 30 orders, but it could actually receive 10, 30, or 50 orders for gears. Each order is for 1,000 units and will take 100 hours of manufacturing time (8 hours of setup time to clean and prepare the machine, and 92 hours of processing time). The annual capacity of the machine is 4,000 hours. If FW receives the number of orders it expects, the total amount of manufacturing time required on the machine will be 3,000 (100 × 30) hours, which is within the available machine capacity of 4,000 hours. Even though expected capacity utilization is not strained, queues and delays can still occur. Why? Because uncertainty about when FW's customers will place orders can cause an order to be received while the machine is processing another order.

In the single-product case, under certain assumptions about the pattern of customer orders and how orders will be processed,[4] the **average waiting time**, the average amount of time that an order will wait in line before it is set up and processed, equals:

$$
\frac{\text{Average number of orders for gears} \times \left(\text{Manufacturing time for gears}\right)^2}{2 \times \left[\text{Annual machine capacity} - \left(\text{Average number of orders for gears} \times \text{Manufacturing time for gears}\right)\right]}
$$

$$
= \frac{30 \times (100)^2}{2 \times [4,000 - (30 \times 100)]} = \frac{30 \times 10,000}{2 \times (4,000 - 3,000)} = \frac{300,000}{2 \times 1,000} = \frac{300,000}{2,000} = 150 \text{ hours}
$$

Manufacturing time enters the numerator in the formula as a squared term. The longer the manufacturing time, the greater the chance that the machine will be in use when an order arrives, and the longer the delays. The denominator in this formula measures the unused capacity or cushion. The smaller the unused capacity, the greater the delays.

Our formula describes only the *average* waiting time. A particular order may happen to arrive when the machine is free, in which case manufacturing will start immediately. In other situations, FW may receive an order while two other orders are waiting to be processed. In this case, the delay will be longer than 150 hours. The average manufacturing lead time for an order is 250 hours (150 hours of average waiting time + 100 hours of manufacturing time).

Now suppose that FW is considering whether to introduce a new product, a special type of piston (or shaft) for pumps. FW expects to receive ten orders for pistons (each order for 800 units) in the coming year. Each order will take 50 hours of manufacturing time (3 hours of setup time and 47 hours of processing time). The expected demand for gears will be unaffected by whether or not FW introduces pistons.

Curriculum Linkage Students who have taken a quantitative methods course may be familiar with queuing theory, a statistical approach to determining the optimal # of service points (e.g., # of open grocery registers or bank tellers) based on the pattern of customer arrivals and the costs and benefits of adding another service point. This section uses queuing theory to estimate the avg. wait time.

Teaching Tip/Example Focus on the intuition of the avg. wait time calculation. The numerator is an increasing function of the avg. # of orders and the *square* of mfg. time. Thus, mfg. time has a bigger effect on avg. wait time than does the avg. # of orders. This is because the longer the mfg. time, the less flexible the process. Intuitively, when setup time is minimal, avg. wait time is less for processes that have many short jobs than for processes that have fewer, but longer jobs. When jobs are short, even if one is already in process, wait time will be short. In contrast, if a long job is in process, a recently arrived job may have a long wait. For example, avg. wait time is less at grocery express checkouts (many short jobs) than at the regular checkouts (fewer, but longer jobs). The denominator of avg. wait time is the unused capacity cushion (capacity less expected usage). Avg. wait time is inversely related to the amt. of unused capacity in the system. The more unused capacity, the greater the chance that an order will arrive when the process is not "busy."

[4]The technical assumptions are (a) that customer orders for the product follow a Poisson distribution with a mean equal to the expected number of orders (30 in our example), and (b) that orders are processed on a first-in, first-out (FIFO) basis. The Poisson arrival pattern for customer orders has been found to be reasonable in many real-world settings. The FIFO assumption can be modified. Under the modified assumptions, the basic queuing and delay effects will still occur, but the precise formulas will be different.

The average waiting time *before* an order is set up and processed is given by the following formula, which is an extension of the formula described earlier for the single-product case.

$$\frac{\left[\text{Average number of orders of gears} \times \left(\text{Manufacturing time for gears}\right)^2\right] + \left[\text{Average number of orders for pistons} \times \left(\text{Manufacturing time for pistons}\right)^2\right]}{2 \times \left[\text{Annual machine capacity} - \left(\text{Average number of orders for gears} \times \text{Manufacturing time for gears}\right) - \left(\text{Average number of orders for pistons} \times \text{Manufacturing time for pistons}\right)\right]}$$

$$= \frac{[30 \times (100)^2] + [10 \times (50)^2]}{2 \times [4,000 - (30 \times 100) - (10 \times 50)]} = \frac{(30 \times 10,000) + (10 \times 2,500)}{2 \times (4,000 - 3,000 - 500)}$$

$$= \frac{300,000 + 25,000}{2 \times 500} = \frac{325,000}{1,000} = 325 \text{ hours}$$

Points to Stress The introduction of pistons (1) cuts the unused capacity cushion in half (from 1,000 to 500 hrs.), which doubles the avg. wait time by halving the denominator; and (2) increases the demands on the process (i.e., numerator) by 25,000 hrs., which further increases avg. wait time. The total effect is that introducing pistons would increase avg. wait time by $(325 - 150)/150 = 117\%$.

Introducing pistons causes average waiting time to more than double from 150 hours to 325 hours. The reason is that introducing pistons causes unused capacity to shrink, increasing the probability that, at any point in time, new orders will arrive while existing orders are being manufactured or are waiting to be manufactured. Average waiting time is very sensitive to the shrinking of unused capacity.

Average manufacturing lead time for a gear order is 425 hours (325 hours of average waiting time + 100 hours of manufacturing time), and for a piston order it is 375 hours (325 hours of average waiting time + 50 hours of manufacturing time). Note that a piston order spends 86.67% (325 ÷ 375) of its manufacturing lead time just waiting for manufacturing to start!

Given the anticipated effects on manufacturing lead time of adding pistons, should FW introduce pistons? The management accountant is frequently called upon to evaluate the profitability of a new product given capacity constraints (Chapter 11, p. 390–392). To make this decision, FW's management accountant needs to identify and analyze the relevant revenues and relevant costs of adding the piston product and, in particular, evaluate the costs on all products of the resulting delays.

Relevant Revenues and Relevant Costs of Time

To determine the relevant revenues and relevant costs of adding pistons, consider the following additional information:

Product	Average Number of Orders	Average Selling Price Per Order If Average Manufacturing Lead Time Is		Direct Material Costs Per Order	Inventory Carrying Costs Per Order Per Hour
		Less Than 300 Hours	More Than 300 Hours		
Gears	30	$22,000	$21,500	$16,000	$1.00
Pistons	10	10,000	9,600	8,000	0.50

Reinforcing Problems Exer. 19-23 and Probs. 19-32 and 19-33 cover the relevant revenues and relevant costs of time.

Points to Stress This example assumes that the amount of wait time *before* mfg. increases carrying costs. This is reasonable when most or all of the raw material inputs are ready at the beginning of the wait time.

Note that manufacturing lead times affect both revenues and costs in our example. Revenues are affected because, in our example, customers are willing to pay a slightly higher price for faster delivery. On the cost side, direct materials costs and inventory carrying costs are the only costs affected by the decision to introduce pistons. Direct materials inventory carrying costs usually consist of the opportunity costs of investment tied up in inventory (see Chapter 11, p. 389–390) and the relevant costs of storage, such as space rental, spoilage, deterioration, and materials handling. Companies usually calculate inventory carrying costs on a per unit per year basis. To simplify computations, we express inventory carrying costs on a per order per hour basis. As in most companies, FW acquires direct materials by the time the order is set up and hence incurs inventory carrying costs for the duration of the waiting time and manufacturing time.

Exhibit 19-8 presents relevant revenues and relevant costs for each alternative. The preferred alternative is not to introduce pistons. Note that this is the case despite pistons having a positive contribution margin of $1,600 ($9,600 − $8,000) per

EXHIBIT 19-8
Determining Expected Relevant Revenues and Expected Relevant Costs for Falcon Works' Decision to Introduce Pistons

Relevant Items	Alternative 1: Introduce Pistons (1)	Alternative 2: Do Not Introduce Pistons (2)	Difference (3) = (1) − (2)
Expected revenues	$741,000[a]	$660,000[b]	$81,000
Expected variable costs	560,000[c]	480,000[d]	(80,000)
Expected inventory carrying costs	14,625[e]	7,500[f]	(7,125)
Expected total costs	574,625	487,500	(87,125)
Expected revenues minus expected costs	$166,375	$172,500	$(6,125)

[a]($21,500 × 30) + ($9,600 × 10) = $741,000; average manufacturing lead time will be more than 300 hours.
[b]($22,000 × 30) = $660,000; average manufacturing lead time will be less than 300 hours.
[c]($16,000 × 30) + ($8,000 × 10) = $560,000.
[d]$16,000 × 30 = $480,000.
[e](Average manufacturing lead time for gears × Unit carrying costs per order for gears × Expected number of orders for gears) + (Average manufacturing lead time for pistons × Unit carrying costs per order for pistons × Expected number of orders for pistons) = 425 × $1.00 × 30 + 375 × $0.50 × 10 = $12,750 + $1,875 = $14,625.
[f]Average manufacturing lead time for gears × Unit carrying costs per order for gears × Expected number of orders for gears = 250 × $1.00 × 30 = $7,500.

order. Also note that FW's machine has the capacity to process pistons. Even if it produces pistons, FW will, on average, use the machine for only 3,500 of the available 4,000 hours. Why is FW better off by not producing and selling pistons? *The key is to recognize the negative effects that producing pistons will have on the existing product, gears.* The following table presents the *costs of time*—that is, the expected loss in revenues and expected increase in costs as a result of delays caused by using more capacity on the turning machine to manufacture pistons.

Product	Effect of Increasing Average Manufacturing Lead Time — Expected Loss in Revenues for Gears (1)	Effect of Increasing Average Manufacturing Lead Time — Expected Increase in Carrying Costs for All Products (2)	Expected Loss in Revenues plus Expected Increase in Costs of Introducing Pistons (3) = (1) + (2)
Gears	$15,000[a]	$5,250[b]	$20,250
Pistons	—	1,875[c]	1,875
Total	$15,000	$7,125	$22,125

[a]($22,000 − $21,500) × 30 expected orders = $15,000.
[b](425 hours − 250 hours) × $1.00 × 30 expected orders = $5,250.
[c](375 hours − 0) × $0.50 × 10 expected orders = $1,875.

Introducing pistons causes the average manufacturing lead time of gears to increase from 250 hours to 425 hours. The cost of longer manufacturing lead times is an increase in inventory carrying costs and a decrease in gear revenues (caused by average manufacturing lead time for gears exceeding 300 hours). The expected costs of longer lead times from introducing pistons, $22,125, exceeds the expected contribution margin of $16,000 ($1,600 per order × 10 expected orders) from selling pistons, by $6,125 (the difference calculated in Exhibit 19-8).

Our simple setting[5] illustrates that when demand uncertainty is high, *some* unused capacity is desirable. Increasing the capacity of the bottleneck resource reduces lead times and delays. One way to increase capacity is to reduce the time required

---

[5]Other complexities, such as analyzing a network of machines, priority scheduling, and allowing for uncertainty in processing times, are beyond the scope of this book. In these cases, the basic queuing and delay effects persist, but the precise formulas are more complex.

Curriculum Linkage Chap. 11 advocated, in the short run, producing products with positive CM. However, Chap. 11 always assumed that production (and sales) of the new product *had no effect* on revenues and costs of existing products. This section shows how uncertainty about the timing of customer orders can materially affect such analysis.

Example One way to reduce avg. wait time is to reduce batch sizes. What happens to avg. wait time if Falcon Works cuts its batch size from 1,000 units to 500 units? The # of batches doubles from 30 to 60. Each order still requires 8 hrs. of setup but only 46 (92/2) hrs. of processing, so total manufacturing time is 54 hrs./batch. The smaller lot size increases the system's flexibility by reducing the chance the machine will be busy when the order is received. This reduces the avg. wait time from 150 hrs. to 115 hrs.

$$\frac{60 \times 54^2}{2[4,000 - (60 \times 54)]} = 115 \text{ hrs.}$$

for setups and processing by doing these activities more efficiently. Another way to increase capacity is to invest in new equipment such as flexible manufacturing systems that can be programmed to switch quickly from producing one product to producing another. Delays can also be reduced through careful scheduling of orders on machines—for example, by batching similar jobs together for processing.

To monitor performance on lead times and delays, many companies use nonfinancial measures. Some measures such as customer-response time and on-time performance focus on customer satisfaction. Other measures such as order manufacturing time and order waiting time emphasize internal performance. Nonfinancial measures of time help companies identify specific areas for improvement.

THEORY OF CONSTRAINTS AND THROUGHPUT CONTRIBUTION ANALYSIS

In this section, we consider products that are made from multiple parts and processed on many machines. With multiple parts and multiple machines, dependencies arise among operations—some operations cannot be started until parts from a previous operation are available. Furthermore, some operations are bottlenecks and others are not.

The **theory of constraints (TOC)** describes methods to maximize operating income when faced with some bottleneck and some nonbottleneck operations.[6] It defines three measurements:

1. **Throughput contribution** equal to revenues minus direct materials costs of the goods sold.

2. *Investments* equal to the sum of materials costs in direct materials, work-in-process, and finished goods inventories; R&D costs; and costs of equipment and buildings.

3. *Operating costs* equal to all operating costs (other than direct materials) incurred to earn throughput contribution. Operating costs include salaries and wages, rent, utilities, and depreciation.

The objective of TOC is to increase throughput contribution while decreasing investments and operating costs. *TOC considers a short-run time horizon and assumes that operating costs are fixed costs.* The steps in managing bottleneck operations are:

Step 1: Recognize that the bottleneck operation determines throughput contribution of the system as a whole.

Step 2: Find the bottleneck operation by identifying operations with large quantities of inventory waiting to be worked on.

Step 3: Keep the bottleneck operation busy and subordinate all nonbottleneck operations to the bottleneck operation. That is, the needs of the bottleneck operation determine the production schedule of nonbottleneck operations.

Step 3 represents a key concept described in Chapter 11: To maximize operating income, the plant must maximize contribution margin (in this case, throughput contribution) of the constrained or bottleneck resource (see pp. 390–392). For this reason, step 3 suggests that the bottleneck machine must always be kept running. It should not be waiting for jobs. To achieve this objective, companies often maintain a small buffer inventory of jobs waiting for the bottleneck machine. The bottleneck machine sets the pace for all nonbottleneck machines. For example, workers at nonbottleneck machines are instructed to not produce more output than can be processed by the bottleneck machine. Producing more nonbottleneck output only creates excess inventory; it does not increase throughput contribution.

---

[6]See E. Goldratt and J. Cox, *The Goal* (New York: North River Press, 1986); E. Goldratt, *The Theory of Constraints* (New York: North River Press, 1990); E. Noreen, D. Smith, and J. Mackey, *The Theory of Constraints and Its Implications for Management Accounting* (New York: North River Press, 1995).

Step 4: Take actions to increase the efficiency and capacity of the bottleneck operation—the objective is to increase throughput contribution minus the incremental costs of taking such actions. The management accountant plays a key role in step 4 by calculating throughput contribution, identifying relevant and irrelevant costs, and doing cost-benefit analyses of alternative actions.

We illustrate step 4 using the example of Cardinal Industries (CI). CI manufactures car doors in two operations—stamping and pressing. Information about CI follows:

	Stamping	Pressing
Capacity per hour	20 units	15 units
Annual capacity (6,000 hours of capacity available in each of stamping and pressing)	120,000 units	90,000 units
Annual production and sales	90,000 units	90,000 units
Other fixed operating costs (excluding direct materials)	$720,000	$1,080,000
Other fixed operating costs per unit produced ($720,000 ÷ 90,000; $1,080,000 ÷ 90,000)	$8 per unit	$12 per unit

Each door sells for $100 and has direct materials costs of $40. Variable costs in other functions of the value chain—R&D, design of products and processes, marketing, distribution, and customer service—are negligible. CI's output is constrained by the capacity of 90,000 units in the pressing operation. What can CI do to relieve the bottleneck constraint of the pressing operation? Desirable actions include

a. *Eliminate idle time (time when the pressing machine is neither being set up to process products nor actually processing products) at the bottleneck operation.* CI is considering permanently positioning two workers at the pressing operation to unload finished units as soon as one batch of units is processed and to set up the machine to process the next batch. Suppose the annual cost of this action is $48,000 and the effect of this action is to increase bottleneck output by 1,000 units per year. Should CI incur the additional costs? Yes, because CI's relevant throughput contribution increases by $60,000 [1,000 units × (selling price, $100 − direct materials costs, $40)], which exceeds the additional cost of $48,000. All other costs are irrelevant.

b. *Process only those parts or products that increase throughput contribution, not parts or products that remain in finished goods or spare parts inventories.* Manufacturing products that sit in inventory do not increase throughput contribution.

c. *Shift products that do not have to be made on the bottleneck machine to nonbottleneck machines or to outside facilities.* Suppose the Spartan Corporation, an outside contractor, offers to press 1,500 doors at $15 per door from stamped parts that CI supplies. Spartan's quoted price is greater than CI's own operating costs in the Pressing Department of $12 per door. Should CI accept the offer? Yes, because pressing is the bottleneck operation. Getting additional doors pressed by Spartan increases throughput contribution by $90,000 [($100 − $40) × 1,500 doors], while relevant costs increase by $22,500 ($15 × 1,500). The fact that CI's unit cost is less than Spartan's quoted price is irrelevant.

Suppose Gemini Industries, another outside contractor, offers to stamp 2,000 doors from direct materials that CI supplies at $6 per door. Gemini's price is lower than CI's operating cost of $8 per door in the Stamping Department. Should CI accept the offer? Because other operating costs are fixed costs, CI will not save any costs by subcontracting the stamping operations. Total costs will be greater by $12,000 ($6 × 2,000) under the subcontracting alternative. Stamping more doors will not increase throughput contribution, which is constrained by pressing capacity. CI should not accept Gemini's offer.

d. *Reduce setup time and processing time at bottleneck operations (for example, by simplifying the design or reducing the number of parts in the product).* Suppose CI can reduce setup time at the pressing operation by incurring additional costs of $55,000 a year. Suppose further that reducing setup time enables CI to press 2,500 more

Points to Stress The object is to keep the bottleneck working at capacity. Mgt. should consider (1) giving the bottleneck full-time attendants, and (2) running the bottleneck 24 hrs a day. TOC suggests that the only place in the plant that should have inventory is immediately before the bottleneck, to ensure that the bottleneck stays busy.

Reinforcing Problems TOC is covered in Exer. 19-24 through 19-26 and Probs. 19-34, 19-35, and 19-38.

Curriculum Linkage The extreme form of backflush costing illustrated in Chap. 20 (where only DM are capitalized and all other mfg. costs are written off as period expenses) is roughly equivalent to TOC-type acctg.

Curriculum Linkage The opportunity cost of lost throughput contribution arising from quality problems at the bottleneck is an element of internal failure cost. This type of opportunity cost arises only around the bottleneck, or constrained resource.

Throughput Accounting at Allied-Signal, Skelmersdale, United Kingdom

Allied-Signal in Skelmersdale, United Kingdom, manufactures turbochargers for the automotive industry. In the 1990s, the Skelmersdale plant was forced to change from producing few products in large quantities to producing many products in small quantities in a very competitive market. The plant also had to cope with frequent changes in its sales mix. The plant often missed delivery dates and incurred high transportation costs to ship via air those parts urgently needed by its automotive customers. John Darlington, the controller of the Skelmersdale plant, recognized the important role finance and accounting could play in this environment, but "we were just not supporting, communicating with, and complementing shop-floor management—not until we began emphasizing throughput contributions."

Allied-Signal's accountants designed the following format for the throughput contribution-based operating income statement:

Throughput Operating Income Statement (in thousands)

Revenues	£50,000
Direct material costs	28,500
Throughput contribution	21,500
Operating costs (direct manufacturing labor, engineering, marketing, and so on.)	19,500
Operating income	£ 2,000

To maximize throughput contribution, management optimized the size and ordering of batches, reduced the load on the bottleneck machines by shifting operations performed there onto other machines, and made additional investments to increase bottleneck capacity. To motivate workers to improve throughput, Allied-Signal managers introduced "adherence to schedule" in place of efficiency as the key performance measure. Workers at nonbottleneck operations were asked not to produce more than what was required according to the bottleneck schedule. In the surplus time available to these workers, they received training in total quality management practices and in improving operator skills.

The Skelmersdale plant also introduced four other performance measures—costs of quality, customer due-date delivery, days inventory on hand, and manufacturing lead time—all with the objective of satisfying customers and maximizing throughput contribution. The Skelmersdale plant showed dramatic increases in each of these measures, as well as in profitability, cash flow, and return on investment.

Source: Adapted from J. Darlington, J. Innes, F. Mitchell, and J. Woodward, "Throughput Accounting: The Garrett Automotive Experience," *Management Accounting* (April 1992); P. Coughlan, and J. Darlington, "As Fast as the Slowest Operation: The Theory of Constraints," *Management Accounting* (June 1993); J. Darlington, "Throughput Accounting in Practice," *Bristol Center for Management Accounting Research Conference: Contemporary Cost Management in Manufacturing Industry* (May 1997); and discussions with Allied-Signal, Skelmersdale management.

doors a year. Should CI incur the costs to reduce setup time? Yes, because throughput contribution increases by $150,000 [($100 − $40) × 2,500], which exceeds the additional costs incurred of $55,000. Will CI find it worthwhile to incur costs to reduce machining time at the nonbottleneck stamping operation? No. Other operating costs will increase, but throughput contribution will remain unchanged because the bottleneck has not been relieved.

e. *Improve the quality of parts or products manufactured at the bottleneck operation.* Poor quality is often more costly at a bottleneck operation than it is at a nonbottleneck operation. The cost of poor quality at a nonbottleneck operation is the cost of materials wasted. If CI produces 1,000 defective doors at the stamping operation, the cost of poor quality is $40,000 (direct materials costs per unit, $40 × 1,000 doors). No throughput contribution is forgone because stamping has unused capacity. Despite the defective production, stamping can produce and transfer 90,000 good-quality doors to the pressing operation. At a bottleneck operation, the cost of poor quality is the cost of materials wasted *plus* the opportunity cost of lost throughput contribution. Bottleneck capacity not wasted in producing defective units could be used to generate additional throughput contribution. If CI produces 1,000 defective units at the pressing operation, the cost of poor quality is $100,000: direct materials cost of $40,000 (direct materials cost per unit, $40 × 1,000 units) plus forgone throughput contribution of $60,000 [($100 − $40) × 1,000 doors].

The high costs of poor quality at the bottleneck operation mean that bottleneck time should not be wasted processing units that are defective. That is, inspection should be done before processing parts at the bottleneck operation to ensure that only good-quality units are transferred to the bottleneck operation. Also, quality-improvement programs should focus on ensuring that bottlenecks produce minimal defects.

If the actions in step 4 are successful, the capacity of the pressing operation will increase and eventually exceed the capacity of the stamping operation. The bottleneck will then shift to the stamping operation. CI should then focus continuous-improvement actions on increasing stamping efficiency and capacity. For example, the contract with Gemini Industries to stamp 2,000 doors at $6 per door from direct materials supplied by CI becomes attractive now. Why? Because throughput contribution increases by ($100 − $40) × 2,000 = $120,000, while costs increase by $12,000 ($6 × 2,000).

The theory of constraints emphasizes the management of bottleneck operations as the key to improving the performance of the production system as a whole. It focuses on the short-run maximization of throughput contribution—revenues minus materials costs. Because TOC regards operating costs as difficult to change in the short run, it does not identify individual activities and drivers of costs. TOC is therefore less useful for the long-run management of costs. Activity-based costing (ABC) systems, on the other hand, have a longer-run perspective focused on improving processes by eliminating nonvalue-added activities and reducing the costs of performing value-added activities. ABC systems are therefore more useful for long-run pricing, long-run cost control and profit planning, and capacity management. The short-run TOC emphasis on maximizing throughput contribution by managing bottlenecks complements the long-run strategic cost management focus of ABC.

New in This Edition This new discussion describes how TOC and ABC complement one another.

PROBLEM FOR SELF-STUDY

PROBLEM

The Sloan Corporation is a moving company that transports household goods from one city to another within the continental United States. It measures quality of service in terms of (a) time required to transport goods, (b) on-time delivery (within two days of agreed-upon delivery date), and (c) number of lost or damaged shipments. Sloan is considering investing in a new scheduling and tracking system costing $160,000 per year, which should help it improve performance with respect to items (b) and (c). The following information describes Sloan's current performance and the expected performance if the new system is implemented:

	Current Performance	Expected Future Performance
On-time delivery performance	85%	95%
Variable costs per carton lost or damaged	$60	$60
Fixed cost per carton lost or damaged	$40	$40
Number of cartons lost or damaged per year	3,000 cartons	1,000 cartons

Sloan expects that each percentage point increase in on-time performance will result in revenue increases of $20,000 per year. Sloan's contribution margin percentage is 45 percent.

Required

1. Should Sloan acquire the new system?
2. What is the minimum amount of revenue increase that needs to occur for the benefits from the new system to equal the costs?

SOLUTION

1. Additional costs of the new scheduling and tracking system are $160,000 per year. Additional annual benefits of the new scheduling and tracking system are:

Additional annual revenues from 10% improvement in on-time performance $20,000 × (95 − 85)	$200,000
Contribution margin from additional annual revenues 45% × $200,000	$ 90,000
Decrease in costs per year from fewer cartons lost or damaged (only variable costs are relevant) $60 × (3,000 − 1,000)	120,000
Total additional benefits	$210,000

Because the expected benefits of $210,000 exceed the costs of $160,000, Sloan should invest in the new system.

2. As long as Sloan earns a contribution margin of $40,000 (to cover incremental costs of $160,000 minus relevant variable-cost savings of $120,000) from additional annual sales, investing in the new system is beneficial. This contribution margin corresponds to additional sales of $40,000 ÷ 0.45 = $88,889.

SUMMARY

The following points are linked to the chapter's learning objectives:

1. Four cost categories in a costs of quality program are prevention costs (costs incurred to preclude the production of products that do not conform to specifications), appraisal costs (costs incurred to detect which of the individual units of products do not conform to specifications), internal failure costs (costs incurred by a nonconforming product before it is shipped to customers), and external failure costs (costs incurred by a nonconforming product after it is shipped to customers).

2. Three methods that companies use to identify quality problems and to improve quality are control charts, to distinguish random variations from other sources of variation in an operating process; Pareto diagrams, which indicate how frequently each type of failure occurs; and cause-and-effect diagrams, which identify potential factors or causes of failure.

3. The relevant costs of quality improvement are the incremental costs incurred to implement the quality program. The relevant benefits are the cost savings and the estimated increase in contribution margin from the higher sales attributable to the quality improvements.

4. Nonfinancial measures of customer satisfaction include number of customer complaints, defective units as a percentage of total units shipped to customers, and on-time delivery rate. Nonfinancial measures of internal quality performance include product defect levels and process yields.

5. Financial measures are helpful to evaluate trade-offs among prevention costs, appraisal costs, and failure costs. They focus attention on the costs of poor quality.

Nonfinancial measures help focus attention on the precise problem areas that need improvement and also serve as indicators of future long-run performance.

6. Customer-response time is the amount of time from when a customer places an order for a product or requests a service to when the product or service is delivered to the customer. Delays occur because of (a) uncertainty about when customers will order products or services, and (b) limited capacity and bottlenecks. Bottlenecks are operations at which the work to be performed approaches or exceeds the available capacity. The costs of delays include lower revenues and increased inventory carrying costs.

7. The three main measurements in the theory of constraints are throughput contribution (equal to revenues minus direct materials costs of the goods sold); investments (equal to the sum of materials costs in direct materials, work-in-process, and finished goods inventories, R&D costs, and costs of equipment and buildings); and operating costs (equal to all operating costs, other than direct materials costs, incurred to earn throughput contribution).

8. The four steps in managing bottlenecks are (a) recognize that the bottleneck operation determines throughput contribution, (b) find the bottleneck, (c) keep the bottleneck busy and subordinate all nonbottleneck operations to the bottleneck operation, and (d) increase bottleneck efficiency and capacity.

▼ TERMS TO LEARN

This chapter and the Glossary at the end of this book contain definitions of the following important terms:

appraisal costs (p. 677)	manufacturing cycle time (688)
average waiting time (689)	manufacturing lead time (688)
bottleneck (689)	on-time performance (688)
cause-and-effect diagram (681)	Pareto diagram (681)
conformance quality (677)	prevention costs (677)
control chart (680)	quality of design (677)
costs of quality (COQ) (677)	theory of constraints (TOC) (692)
customer-response time (687)	throughput contribution (692)
external failure costs (677)	time driver (688)
internal failure costs (677)	

▼ ASSIGNMENT MATERIAL

QUESTIONS

19-1 Describe two benefits of improving quality.

19-2 How does conformance quality differ from quality of design? Explain.

19-3 Name two items classified as prevention costs.

19-4 Distinguish between internal failure costs and external failure costs.

19-5 Describe three methods that companies use to identify quality problems.

19-6 "Companies should focus on financial measures of quality because these are the only measures of quality that can be linked to bottom-line performance." Do you agree? Explain.

19-7 Give two examples of nonfinancial measures of customer satisfaction.

19-8 Give two examples of nonfinancial measures of internal performance.

19-9 Distinguish between customer-response time and manufacturing lead time.

19-10 "There is no trade-off between customer-response time and on-time performance." Do you agree? Explain.

19-11 Give two reasons why delays occur.

19-12 "Companies should always make and sell all products whose selling prices exceed variable costs." Assuming fixed costs are irrelevant, do you agree? Explain.

19-13 Describe the three main measures used in the theory of constraints.

19-14 Describe the four key steps in managing bottleneck operations.

19-15 Describe three ways to improve the performance of a bottleneck operation.

EXERCISES

19-16 Costs of quality. (CMA, adapted) Bergen, Inc., produces telephone equipment at its Georgia plant. In recent years, the company's market share has been eroded by stiff competition from Asian and European competitors. Price and product quality are the two key areas in which companies compete in this market.

Jerry Holman, Bergen's president, decided to devote more resources to the improvement of product quality after learning that his company's products had been ranked fourth in product quality in a 1999 survey of telephone equipment users. He believed that Bergen could no longer afford to ignore the importance of product quality.

Bergen's quality improvement program has now been in operation for two years, and the cost report shown below has recently been issued. As they were reviewing the report, Sheila Haynes, manager of sales, asked Tony Reese, production manager, what he thought of the quality program. "The work is really moving through the Production Department," replied Reese. "We used to spend time helping the Customer Service Department solve their problems, but they are leaving us alone these days."

Semi-Annual Costs of Quality Report, Bergen, Inc.
(in thousands)

	6/30/2000	12/31/2000	6/30/2001	12/31/2001
Prevention costs				
Machine maintenance	$ 215	$ 215	$ 190	$ 160
Training suppliers	5	45	20	15
Design reviews	20	102	100	95
Total prevention costs	240	362	310	270
Appraisal costs				
Incoming inspection	45	53	36	22
Final testing	160	160	140	94
Total appraisal costs	205	213	176	116
Internal failure costs				
Rework	120	106	88	62
Scrap	68	64	42	40
Total internal failure costs	188	170	130	102
External failure costs				
Warranty repairs	69	31	25	23
Customer returns	262	251	116	80
Total external failure costs	331	282	141	103
Total quality costs	$ 964	$1,027	$ 757	$ 591
Total production and revenues	$4,120	$4,540	$4,650	$4,510

Required
1. Calculate the ratio of each COQ category to revenues for each period. Has Bergen's quality-improvement program been successful? Explain.
2. Jerry Holman believed that a quality-improvement program was essential and that Bergen, Inc., could no longer afford to ignore the importance of product quality. Discuss how Bergen could measure the opportunity cost of not implementing the quality-improvement program.

 19-17 Costs of quality analysis, nonfinancial quality measures. The Hartono Corporation manufactures and sells industrial grinders. The following table presents financial information pertaining to quality in 2000 and 2001 (in thousands):

	2001	2000
Revenues	$12,500	$10,000
Line inspection	85	110
Scrap	200	250
Design engineering	240	100
Cost of returned goods	145	60
Product-testing equipment	50	50
Customer support	30	40
Rework costs	135	160
Preventive equipment maintenance	90	35
Product liability claims	100	200
Incoming materials inspection	40	20
Breakdown maintenance	40	90
Product-testing labor	75	220
Training	120	45
Warranty repair	200	300
Supplier evaluation	50	20

Required

1. Classify the cost items in the table into prevention, appraisal, internal failure, or external failure categories.
2. Calculate the ratio of each COQ category to revenues in 2000 and 2001. Comment on the trends in costs of quality between 2000 and 2001.
3. Give two examples of nonfinancial quality measures that Hartono Corporation could monitor as part of a total quality-control effort.

19-18 Costs of quality analysis, nonfinancial quality measures. Ontario Industries manufactures two types of refrigerators, Olivia and Solta. Information on each refrigerator is as follows:

	Olivia	Solta
Units manufactured and sold	10,000 units	5,000 units
Selling price	$2,000	$1,500
Variable costs per unit	$1,200	$800
Hours spent on design	6,000	1,000
Testing and inspection hours per unit	1	0.5
Percentage of units reworked in plant	5%	10%
Rework costs per refrigerator	$500	$400
Percentage of units repaired at customer site	4%	8%
Repair costs per refrigerator	$600	$450
Estimated lost sales from poor quality	—	300 units

The labor rates per hour for various activities are as follows:

Design	$75 per hour
Testing and inspection	$40 per hour

Required

1. Calculate the costs of quality for Olivia and Solta, classified into prevention, appraisal, internal failure, and external failure categories.
2. For each type of refrigerator, calculate the ratio of each COQ category as a percentage of revenues. Compare and comment on the costs of quality for Olivia and Solta.
3. Give two examples of nonfinancial quality measures that Ontario Industries could monitor as part of a total quality-control effort.

19-19 Nonfinancial measures of quality and time. (CMA, adapted) Eastern Switching Co. (ESC) produces telecommunications equipment. Charles Laurant, ESC's president believes that product quality is the key to gaining competitive advantage. Laurant implemented a total quality management (TQM) program with an emphasis on customer satisfaction. The following information is available for the first year (2001) of the TQM program compared to the previous year.

	2000	2001
Total number of units produced and sold	10,000	11,000
Units delivered before scheduled delivery date	8,500	9,900
Number of defective units shipped	400	330
Number of customer complaints other than for defective units	500	517
Average time from when customer places order for a unit to when unit is delivered to the customer	30 days	25 days
Number of units reworked during production	600	627
Manufacturing lead time	20 days	16 days
Direct and indirect manufacturing labor-hours	90,000	110,000

Required

1. For each of the years 2000 and 2001, calculate
   a. Percentage of defective units shipped
   b. Customer complaints as a percentage of units shipped
   c. On-time delivery rate
   d. Percentage of units reworked during production
2. On the basis of your calculations in requirement 1, has ESC's performance on quality and timeliness improved?
3. Philip Larkin, a member of ESC's Board of Directors, comments that regardless of the effect that the program has had on quality, the output per labor-hour has declined between 2000 and 2001. Larkin believes that lower output per labor-hour will lead to an increase in costs and lower operating income.
   a. How did Larkin conclude that output per labor-hour declined in 2001 relative to 2000?
   b. Why might output per labor-hour decline in 2001?
   c. Do you think that a lower output per labor-hour will decrease operating income in 2001? Explain briefly.

19-20 Quality improvement, relevant costs, and relevant revenues. The Photon Corporation manufactures and sells 20,000 copiers each year. The variable and fixed costs of rework and repair are as follows:

	Variable Costs	**Fixed Costs**	**Total Costs**
Rework costs per hour	$ 40	$60	$100
Repair costs			
Customer-support costs per hour	20	30	50
Transportation costs per load	180	60	240
Warranty repair costs per hour	45	65	110

Photon's engineers are currently working to solve the problem of copies being too light or too dark. They propose changing the lens of the copier. The new lens will cost $50 more than the old lens. Each copier uses one lens. Photon uses a 1-year time horizon for this decision, because it plans to introduce a new copier at the end of the year. Photon believes that even as it improves quality, it will not be able to save any of the fixed costs of rework or repair.

By changing the lens, Photon expects that it will (1) save 12,000 hours of rework, (2) save 800 hours of customer support, (3) move 200 fewer loads, (4) save 8,000 hours of repair, and (5) sell 100 additional copiers for a total contribution margin of $600,000.

Required

Should Photon change to the new lens? Show your calculations.

19-21 Customer-response time, on-time delivery. Pizzafest, Inc., makes and delivers pizzas to homes and offices in the Boston area. Fast, on-time delivery is one of Pizzafest's key strategies. Pizzafest provides the following information for the year 2001 about its customer-response time—the amount of time from when a customer calls to place an order to when the pizza is delivered to the customer.

	January–June	July–December
Pizzas delivered in 30 minutes or less	100,000	150,000
Pizzas delivered in between 31 and 45 minutes	200,000	260,000
Pizzas delivered in between 46 and 60 minutes	80,000	70,000
Pizzas delivered in between 61 and 75 minutes	20,000	20,000
Total pizzas delivered	400,000	500,000

Required

1. For January–June 2001, and July–December 2001, calculate the percentage of pizzas delivered in each of the four time intervals (30 minutes or less, 31–45 minutes, 46–60 minutes, and 61–75 minutes). On the basis of these calculations, has customer-response time improved in July–December 2001 compared to January–June 2001?

2. When customers call Pizzafest, they often ask how long it will take for the pizza to be delivered to their homes or offices. If Pizzafest quotes a long time interval, customers will often not place the order. If Pizzafest quotes too short a time interval and the pizza is not delivered on time, customers get upset and Pizzafest will lose repeat business. Based on the January–June 2001 data, what customer-response time should Pizzafest quote to its customers if
   a. It wants to have an on-time delivery performance of 75 percent?
   b. It wants to have an on-time delivery performance of 95 percent?

3. If Pizzafest had quoted the customer-response times you calculated in requirements 2a and 2b, would it have met its on-time delivery performance targets of 75% and 95%, respectively, for the period July–December 2001? Explain.

4. Pizzafest is considering giving an on-time guarantee for January–June 2002. If the pizza is not delivered within 60 minutes of placing the order, the customer gets the pizza free. Pizzafest estimates that it will make additional sales of 20,000 pizzas as a result of giving this guarantee. It estimates that it will fail to deliver a total of 15,000 pizzas on time. The average price of a pizza is $13, and the variable cost of a pizza is $7.
   a. What is the effect on Pizzafest's operating income of making this offer?
   b. What nonfinancial and qualitative factors should Pizzafest consider before making this offer?
   c. What actions can Pizzafest take to reduce customer-response time?

19-22 Waiting time, banks. Regal Bank has a small branch in Orillia, Canada. The counter is staffed by one teller. The counter is open for 5 hours (300 minutes) each day (the operational capacity). It takes 5 minutes to serve a customer (service time). The Orillia branch expects to serve 40 customers each day. (Note that the number of customers corresponds to the number of orders in the chapter discussion.)

Required

1. Using the formula on p. 689, calculate how long, on average, a customer will wait in line before being served.

2. How long, on average, will a customer wait in line if the branch expects to serve 50 customers each day?

3. The bank is considering ways to reduce waiting time. How long will customers have to wait on average, if the time to serve a customer is reduced to 4 minutes and the bank expects to serve 50 customers each day?

19-23 Waiting time, relevant costs, and relevant revenues. The Orillia branch of Regal Bank is thinking of offering additional services to its customers. Its counter is open for 5 hours (300 minutes) each day (the operational capacity). If it introduces the new services, the bank expects to serve an average of 60 customers each day instead of the 40 customers it currently averages. It will take 4 minutes to serve each customer (service time) regardless of whether or not the new services are offered. (Note that the number of customers corresponds to the number of orders in the chapter discussion.)

Required

1. Using the formula on p. 689, calculate how long, on average, a customer will wait in line before being served.

2. Regal Bank's policy is that the average waiting time in the line should not exceed 5 minutes. The bank cannot reduce the time to serve a customer below 4 minutes without negatively affecting quality. To reduce average waiting time for the 60

customers it expects to serve each day, the bank decides to keep the counter open for 336 minutes each day. Verify that by keeping the counter open for a longer time, the bank will be able to achieve its goal of an average waiting time of 5 minutes or less.

3. The bank expects to generate, on average, $30 in additional operating income each day as a result of offering the new services. The teller is paid $10 per hour and is employed in increments of an hour (that is, the teller can be employed for 5, 6, 7 hours, and so on, but not for a fraction of an hour). If the bank wants average waiting time to be no more than 5 minutes, should the bank offer the new services?

19-24 Theory of constraints, throughput contribution, relevant costs. The Mayfield Corporation manufactures filing cabinets in two operations—machining and finishing. It provides the following information.

	Machining	Finishing
Annual capacity	100,000 units	80,000 units
Annual production	80,000 units	80,000 units
Fixed operating costs (excluding direct materials)	$640,000	$400,000
Fixed operating costs per unit produced ($640,000 ÷ 80,000; $400,000 ÷ 80,000)	$8 per unit	$5 per unit

Each cabinet sells for $72 and has direct materials costs of $32 incurred at the start of the machining operation. Mayfield has no other variable costs. Mayfield can sell whatever output it produces. The following requirements refer only to the preceding data. There is no connection between the requirements.

Required

1. Mayfield is considering using some modern jigs and tools in the finishing operation that would increase annual finishing output by 1,000 units. The annual cost of these jigs and tools is $30,000. Should Mayfield acquire these tools? Show your calculations.

2. The production manager of the Machining Department has submitted a proposal to do faster setups that would increase the annual capacity of the Machining Department by 10,000 units and cost $5,000 per year. Should Mayfield implement the change? Show your calculations.

19-25 Theory of constraints, throughput contribution, relevant costs. Refer to the information in Exercise 19-24 in answering the following requirements. There is no connection between the requirements.

Required

1. An outside contractor offers to do the finishing operation for 12,000 units at $10 per unit, double the $5 per unit that it costs Mayfield to do the finishing in-house. Should Mayfield accept the subcontractor's offer? Show your calculations.

2. The Hunt Corporation offers to machine 4,000 units at $4 per unit, half the $8 per unit that it costs Mayfield to do the machining in-house. Should Mayfield accept the subcontractor's offer? Show your calculations.

19-26 Theory of constraints, throughput contribution, quality. Refer to the information in Exercise 19-24 in answering the following requirements. There is no connection between the requirements.

Required

1. Mayfield produces 2,000 defective units at the machining operation. What is the cost to Mayfield of the defective items produced? Explain your answer briefly.

2. Mayfield produces 2,000 defective units at the finishing operation. What is the cost to Mayfield of the defective items produced? Explain your answer briefly.

PROBLEMS

19-27 Quality improvement, relevant costs, and relevant revenues. The Thomas Corporation sells 300,000 V262 valves to the automobile and truck industry. Thomas has a capacity of 110,000 machine-hours and can produce 3 valves per machine-hour. V262's contribution margin per unit is $8. Thomas sells only 300,000 valves because 30,000 valves (10%

of the good valves) need to be reworked. It takes 1 machine-hour to rework 3 valves so that 10,000 hours of capacity are used in the rework process. Thomas's rework costs are $210,000. Rework costs consist of:

Direct materials and direct rework labor (variable costs)	$3 per unit
Fixed costs of equipment, rent, and overhead allocation	$4 per unit

Thomas's process designers have developed a modification that would maintain the speed of the process and would ensure 100% quality and no rework. The new process would cost $315,000 per year. The following additional information is available:

◆ The demand for Thomas's V262 valves is 370,000 per year.

◆ The Jackson Corporation has asked Thomas to supply 22,000 T971 valves if Thomas implements the new design. The contribution margin per T971 valve is $10. Thomas can make two T971 valves per machine-hour with 100% quality and no rework.

Required
1. Suppose Thomas's designers implemented the new design. Should Thomas accept Jackson's order for 22,000 T971 valves? Show your calculations.
2. Should Thomas implement the new design? Show your calculations.
3. What nonfinancial and qualitative factors should Thomas consider in deciding whether to implement the new design?

19-28 Quality improvement, relevant costs, and relevant revenues. The Tan Corporation uses multicolor molding to make plastic lamps. The molding operation has a capacity of 200,000 units per year. The demand for lamps is very strong. Tan will be able to sell whatever output quantities it can produce at $40 per lamp.

Tan can start only 200,000 units into production in the Molding Department because of capacity constraints on the molding machines. If a defective unit is produced at the molding operation, it must be scrapped, and the scrap yields no revenue. Of the 200,000 units started at the molding operation, 30,000 units (15%) are scrapped. Scrap costs, based on total (fixed and variable) manufacturing costs incurred up to the molding operation equal $25 per unit as follows:

Direct materials (variable)	$16 per unit
Direct manufacturing labor, setup labor, and materials-handling labor (variable)	3 per unit
Equipment, rent, and other allocated overhead including inspection and testing costs on scrapped parts (fixed)	6 per unit
Total	$25 per unit

Tan's designers have determined that adding a different type of material to the existing direct materials would reduce scrap to zero, but it would increase the variable costs by $4 per lamp in the Molding Department.

Required
1. Should Tan use the new material? Show your calculations.
2. What nonfinancial and qualitative factors should Tan consider in making the decision?

19-29 Statistical quality control, airline operations. Peoples Skyway operates daily round-trip flights on the London–New York route using a fleet of three 747s, the *Spirit of Birmingham*, the *Spirit of Glasgow*, and the *Spirit of Manchester*. The budgeted quantity of fuel for each round-trip flight is the mean (average) fuel usage. Over the last 12 months, the average fuel usage per round-trip is 100 gallon-units with a standard deviation of 10 gallon-units. A gallon-unit is 1,000 gallons.

Cilla Black, the operations manager of Peoples Skyway, uses a statistical quality-control (SQC) approach in deciding whether to investigate fuel usage per round-trip flight. She investigates those flights with fuel usage greater than two standard deviations from the mean.

In October, Black receives the following report for round-trip fuel usage by the three planes operating on the London–New York route:

Flight	Spirit of Birmingham (gallon-units)	Spirit of Glasgow (gallon-units)	Spirit of Manchester (gallon-units)
1	104	103	97
2	94	94	104
3	97	96	111
4	101	107	104
5	105	92	122
6	107	113	118
7	111	99	126
8	112	106	114
9	115	101	117
10	119	93	123

Required

1. Using the $\pm 2\sigma$ rule, what variance investigation decisions would be made?
2. Present SQC charts for round-trip fuel usage for each of the three 747s in October. What inferences can you draw from the charts?
3. Some managers propose that Peoples Skyway present its SQC charts in monetary terms rather than in physical quantity terms (gallon-units). What are the advantages and disadvantages of using monetary fuel costs rather than gallon-units in the SQC charts?

19-30 Compensation linked with profitability, on-time delivery, and external quality performance measures. Pacific-Dunlop supplies tires to major automotive companies. It has two tire plants in North America, in Detroit and Los Angeles. The quarterly bonus plan for each plant manager has three components:

a. *Profitability performance.* Add 2% of operating income.
b. *On-time delivery performance.* Add $10,000 if on-time delivery performance to the ten most important customers is 98% or better. If on-time performance to these customers is below 98%, add nothing.
c. *Product quality performance.* Deduct 50% of cost of sales returns from the ten most important customers.

Quarterly data for 2001 for the Detroit and Los Angeles plants are as follows:

	January–March	April–June	July–September	October–December
Detroit				
Operating income	$800,000	$850,000	$700,000	$900,000
On-time delivery rate[a]	98.4%	98.6%	97.1%	97.9%
Cost of sales returns[a]	$18,000	$26,000	$10,000	$25,000
Los Angeles				
Operating income	$1,600,000	$1,500,000	$1,800,000	$1,900,000
On-time delivery rate[a]	95.6%	97.1%	97.9%	98.4%
Cost of sales returns[a]	$35,000	$34,000	$28,000	$22,000

[a]For the ten most important customers.

Required

1. Compute the bonuses paid in each quarter of 2001 to the plant managers of the Detroit and Los Angeles plants.
2. Discuss the three components of the bonus plan as measures of profitability, on-time delivery, and product quality.
3. Why would you want to evaluate plant managers on the basis of both operating income and on-time delivery rate?
4. Give one example of what might happen if on-time delivery rate were dropped as a performance evaluation measure.

19-31 Waiting times, manufacturing lead times. The SRG Corporation uses an injection molding machine to make a plastic product, Z39. SRG makes products only after receiving firm orders from its customers. SRG estimates that it will receive 50 orders for Z39 (each order is for 1,000 units) during the coming year. Each order of Z39 will take 80 hours of machine time (4 hours to clean and prepare the machine, called setup, and 76 hours to process the order). The annual capacity of the machine is 5,000 hours.

Required

1. Calculate the percentage of the total available machine capacity that SRG expects to use during the coming year.
2. Calculate the average amount of time that an order for Z39 will wait in line before it is processed and the average manufacturing lead time per order for Z39.
3. SRG is considering introducing a new product, Y28. SRG estimates that, on average, it will receive 25 orders of Y28 (each order for 200 units) in the coming year. Each order of Y28 will take 20 hours of machine time (2 hours to clean and prepare the machine, and 18 hours to process the order). The average demand for Z39 will be unaffected by the introduction of Y28. Calculate the average waiting time for an order received and the average manufacturing lead time per order for each product, if SRG introduces Y28.
4. If SRG introduces Y28, what fraction of the total manufacturing lead time will each order of Y28 spend, on average, waiting to be processed?
5. Briefly describe why delays occur in the processing of Z39 and Y28.

19-32 Waiting times, relevant revenues, and relevant costs (continuation of 19-31). SRG is still deciding whether or not it should introduce and sell Y28. The following table provides information on selling prices, variable costs, and inventory carrying costs for Z39 and Y28. SRG will incur additional variable costs and inventory carrying costs for Y28 only if it introduces Y28. Fixed costs equal to 40% of variable costs are allocated to all products produced and sold during the year.

Product	Average Number of Orders	Average Selling Price Per Order If Average Manufacturing Lead Time Is		Variable Costs Per Order	Inventory Carrying Costs Per Order Per Hour
		Less Than 320 Hours	More Than 320 Hours		
Z39	50	$27,000	$26,500	$15,000	$0.75
Y28	25	8,400	8,000	5,000	0.25

Required

1. Should SRG manufacture and sell Y28? Show your calculations.
2. Calculate the cutoff price per order above which SRG should manufacture and sell Y28 and below which SRG should choose not to manufacture and sell Y28.

19-33 Manufacturing lead times, relevant revenues, and relevant costs. The Brandt Corporation makes wire harnesses for the aircraft industry. Brandt is uncertain about when and how many customer orders will be received. The company makes harnesses only after receiving firm orders from its customers. Brandt has recently purchased a new machine to make two types of wire harnesses, one for Boeing airplanes (B7) and the other for Airbus Industries airplanes (A3). The annual capacity of the new machine is 6,000 hours. The following information is available for next year:

Customer	Average Number of Orders	Manufacturing Time Required	Average Selling Price Per Order If Average Manufacturing Lead Time Is		Variable Costs Per Order	Inventory Carrying Costs Per Order Per Hour
			Less Than 200 Hours	More Than 200 Hours		
B7	125	40 hours	$15,000	$14,400	$10,000	$0.50
A3	10	50 hours	13,500	12,960	9,000	0.45

Required

1. Calculate the average manufacturing lead times per order (a) if Brandt manufactures only B7, and (b) if Brandt manufactures both B7 and A3.
2. Even though A3 has a positive contribution margin, Brandt's managers are evaluating whether Brandt should (a) make and sell only B7, or (b) make and sell both B7 and A3. Which alternative will maximize Brandt's operating income? Show your calculations.

3. What other factors should Brandt consider in choosing between the alternatives in requirement 2?

19-34 Theory of constraints, throughput contribution, relevant costs. Colorado Industries manufactures electronic testing equipment. Colorado also installs the equipment at the customers' sites and ensures that it functions smoothly. Additional information on the Manufacturing and Installation Departments is as follows (capacities are expressed in terms of the number of units of electronic testing equipment):

	Equipment Manufactured	Equipment Installed
Annual capacity	400 units per year	300 units per year
Equipment manufactured and installed	300 units per year	300 units per year

Colorado manufactures only 300 units per year because the Installation Department has only enough capacity to install 300 units. The equipment sells for $40,000 per unit (installed) and has direct materials costs of $15,000. All costs other than direct materials costs are fixed. The following requirements refer only to the preceding data. There is no connection between the requirements.

Required

1. Colorado's engineers have found a way to reduce equipment manufacturing time. The new method would cost an additional $50 per unit and would allow Colorado to manufacture 20 additional units a year. Should Colorado implement the new method? Show your calculations.

2. Colorado's designers have proposed a change in direct materials that would increase direct materials costs by $2,000 per unit. This change would enable Colorado to install 320 units of equipment each year. If Colorado makes the change, it will implement the new design on all equipment sold. Should Colorado use the new design? Show your calculations.

3. A new installation technique has been developed that will enable Colorado's engineers to install 10 additional units of equipment a year. The new method will increase installation costs by $50,000 each year. Should Colorado implement the new technique? Show your calculations.

4. Colorado is considering how to motivate workers to improve their productivity (output per hour). One proposal is to evaluate and compensate workers in the Manufacturing and Installation Departments on the basis of their productivities. Do you think the new proposal is a good idea? Explain briefly.

19-35 Theory of constraints, throughput contribution, quality, relevant costs. Aardee Industries manufactures pharmaceutical products in two departments—Mixing and Tablet-Making. Additional information on the two departments follows. Each tablet contains 0.5 gram of direct materials.

	Mixing	Tablet Making
Capacity per hour	150 grams	200 tablets
Monthly capacity (2,000 hours available in each of mixing and tablet making)	300,000 grams	400,000 tablets
Monthly production	200,000 grams	390,000 tablets
Fixed operating costs (excluding direct materials)	$16,000	$39,000
Fixed operating costs per tablet ($16,000 ÷ 200,000; $39,000 ÷ 390,000)	$0.08 per gram	$0.10 per tablet

The Mixing Department makes 200,000 grams of direct materials mixture (enough to make 400,000 tablets) because the Tablet-Making Department has only enough capacity to process 400,000 tablets. All direct materials costs are incurred in the Mixing Department. Aardee incurs $156,000 in direct materials costs. The Tablet-Making Department manufactures only 390,000 tablets from the 200,000 grams of mixture processed; 2.5% of the direct materials mixture is lost in the tablet-making process. Each tablet sells for $1. All costs other than direct materials costs are fixed costs. The following requirements refer only to the preceding data. There is no connection between the requirements.

Required

1. An outside contractor makes the following offer: If Aardee will supply the contractor with 10,000 grams of mixture, the contractor will manufacture 19,500 tablets for Aardee (allowing for the normal 2.5% loss during the tablet-making process) at $0.12 per tablet. Should Aardee accept the contractor's offer? Show your calculations.
2. Another firm offers to prepare 20,000 grams of mixture a month from direct materials Aardee supplies. The company will charge $0.07 per gram of mixture. Should Aardee accept the company's offer? Show your calculations.
3. Aardee's engineers have devised a method that would improve quality in the tablet-making operation. They estimate that the 10,000 tablets currently being lost would be saved. The modification would cost $7,000 a month. Should Aardee implement the new method? Show your calculations.
4. Suppose that Aardee also loses 10,000 grams of mixture in its mixing operation. These losses can be reduced to zero if the company is willing to spend $9,000 per month in quality-improvement methods. Should Aardee adopt the quality-improvement method? Show your calculations.
5. What are the benefits of improving quality at the mixing operation compared with the benefits of improving quality at the tablet-making operation?

19-36 Quality improvement, Pareto charts, fishbone diagrams. The Murray Corporation manufactures, sells, and installs photocopying machines. Murray has placed heavy emphasis on reducing defects and failures in its production operations. Murray wants to apply the same total quality management principles to manage its accounts receivable.

Required

1. On the basis of your knowledge and experience, what would you classify as failures in accounts receivable?
2. Give examples of prevention activities that could reduce failures in accounts receivable.
3. Draw a Pareto diagram of the types of failures in accounts receivable and a fishbone diagram of possible causes of one type of failure in accounts receivable.

19-37 Ethics and quality. Information from a quality report for 2001 prepared by Lindsey Williams, assistant controller of Citocell, a manufacturer of electric motors is as follows:

Revenues	$10,000,000
On-line inspection	90,000
Warranty liability	260,000
Product testing	210,000
Scrap	230,000
Design engineering	200,000
Percentage of customer complaints	5%
On-time delivery rate	93%

Davey Evans, the plant manager of Citocell, is eligible for a bonus if the total costs of quality as a percentage of revenues is less than 10%, percentage of customer complaints is less than 4%, and the on-time delivery rate exceeds 92 percent. Evans is unhappy about the 5% number for customer complaints because, when preparing her report, Williams actually surveyed customers regarding customer satisfaction. Evans expected Williams to be less proactive and wait for customers to complain. Evans's concern with Williams's approach is that it introduces subjectivity into the numbers and also fails to capture the seriousness of customers' concerns. "When you wait for a customer to complain, you know they are complaining because it is something important. When you do customer surveys, customers mention whatever is on their mind, even if it is not terribly important."

John Roche, the controller, asks Williams to see him. He tells her about Evans's concerns. "I think Davey has a point. See what you can do." Williams is confident that the customer complaints are genuine and that customers are concerned about quality and service. She believes it is important for Citocell to be proactive and obtain systematic and quick customer feedback, and then to use this information to make future improvements. She is also well aware that Citocell has not done customer surveys in the past, and except for her surveys, Evans would probably be eligible for the bonus. She is confused about how to handle Roche's request.

1. Calculate the ratio of each cost of quality category (prevention, appraisal, internal failure, and external failure) to revenues in 2001. Are the total costs of quality as a percentage of revenues less than 10 percent?
2. Would it be unethical for Williams to modify her analysis? What steps should Williams take to resolve this situation?

COLLABORATIVE LEARNING PROBLEM

19-38 Quality improvement, theory of constraints. The Wellesley Corporation makes printed cloth in two operations, weaving and printing. Direct materials costs are Wellesley's only variable costs. The demand for Wellesley's cloth is very strong. Wellesley can sell whatever output quantities it produces at $1,250 per roll to a distributor who markets, distributes, and provides customer service for the product.

	Weaving	Printing
Monthly capacity	10,000 rolls	15,000 rolls
Monthly production	9,500 rolls	8,550 rolls
Direct materials costs per roll of cloth processed at each operation	$500	$100
Fixed operating costs	$2,850,000	$427,500
Fixed operating costs per roll ($2,850,000 ÷ 9,500; $427,500 ÷ 8,550)	$300 per roll	$50 per roll

Wellesley can start only 10,000 rolls of cloth in the Weaving Department because of capacity constraints of the weaving machines. If the weaving operation produces defective cloth, the cloth must be scrapped and yields zero net revenue. Of the 10,000 rolls of cloth started at the weaving operation, 500 rolls (5%) are scrapped. Scrap costs per roll, based on total (fixed and variable) manufacturing costs per roll incurred up to the end of the weaving operation, equal $785 per roll as follows:

Direct materials costs per roll (variable)	$500
Fixed operating costs per roll ($2,850,000 ÷ 10,000 rolls)	285
Total manufacturing costs per roll in Weaving Department	$785

The good rolls from the Weaving Department (called grey cloth) are sent to the Printing Department. Of the 9,500 good rolls started at the printing operation, 950 rolls (10%) are scrapped and yield zero net revenue. Scrap costs, based on total (fixed and variable) manufacturing costs per unit incurred up to the end of the printing operation, equal $930 per roll calculated as follows:

Total manufacturing costs per roll in Weaving Department		$785
Printing Department manufacturing costs		
Direct materials costs per roll (variable)	$100	
Fixed operating costs per roll ($427,500 ÷ 9,500 rolls)	45	
Total manufacturing costs per roll in Printing Department		145
Total manufacturing costs per roll		$930

The Wellesley Corporation's total monthly sales of printed cloth equals the Printing Department's output.

Required

Form groups of two or more students to complete the following requirements. Each requirement refers only to the preceding data. There is no connection between the requirements.

1. The Printing Department is considering buying 5,000 additional rolls of grey cloth from an outside supplier at $900 per roll. The Printing Department manager is concerned that the cost of purchasing the grey cloth is much higher than Wellesley's cost of manufacturing the grey cloth. The quality of the grey cloth acquired from outside is very similar to that manufactured in-house. The Printing Department expects that 10% of the rolls obtained from the outside supplier will be scrapped. Should the Printing Department buy the grey cloth from the outside supplier? Show your calculations.

2. Wellesley's engineers have developed a method that would lower the Printing Department's scrap rate to 6% at the printing operation. Implementing the new method would cost $350,000 per month. Should Wellesley implement the change? Show your calculations.

3. The design engineering team has proposed a modification that would lower the Weaving Department's scrap rate to 3 percent. The modification would cost the company $175,000 per month. Should Wellesley implement the change? Show your calculations.

CHAPTER

20

Inventory Management, Just-in-Time, and Backflush Costing

learning objectives

When you have finished studying this chapter, you should be able to

1. Identify five categories of costs associated with goods for sale

2. Balance ordering costs and carrying costs using the economic-order-quantity (EOQ) decision model

3. Identify and reduce conflicts that can arise between the EOQ decision model and models used for performance evaluation

4. Use a supply-chain approach to inventory management

5. Differentiate materials requirements planning (MRP) systems from just-in-time (JIT) systems for manufacturing

6. Identify the major features of a just-in-time production system

7. Use backflush costing

8. Describe different ways blackflush costing can simplify traditional job-costing systems

Manufacturers of electronic products, such as Hewlett-Packard, are simplifying their operations by using (a) a just-in-time production and (b) a backflush costing system.

Inventory management is a pivotal part of profit planning for manufacturing and merchandising companies. Materials costs often account for more than 50% of total costs in manufacturing companies and over 70% of total costs in retail companies. Accounting information can play a key role in inventory management. We first consider retail organizations and then manufacturing companies.

INVENTORY MANAGEMENT IN RETAIL ORGANIZATIONS

Inventory management is the planning, coordinating, and controlling activities related to the flow of inventory into, through, and from the organization. Consider retailers where cost of goods sold constitutes the largest single cost item. The following breakdown of operations for three major retailers is illustrative:

	Kroger	Safeway	Wal-Mart
Revenues	100.0%	100.0%	100.0%
Deduct costs:			
Cost of goods sold	76.8	70.4	78.4
Selling and administration costs	18.3	22.5	16.0
Other costs, interest, and taxes	3.5	4.4	2.7
Total costs	98.6	97.3	97.1
Net income	1.4%	2.7%	2.9%

These low percentages of net income to revenues mean that better decisions regarding the purchasing and managing of goods for sale can cause dramatic percentage increases in net income.

Costs Associated with Goods for Sale

The following cost categories are important when managing inventories of goods for sale:

1. *Purchasing costs*: **Purchasing costs** are the costs of goods acquired from suppliers including incoming freight or transportation costs. These costs usually make up the largest single cost category of goods for sale. Discounts for different purchase-order sizes and supplier credit terms affect purchasing costs.

2. *Ordering costs*: **Ordering costs** are the costs of preparing, issuing, and paying purchase orders, plus receiving and inspecting the items included in the orders. Related to the number of purchase orders processed are purchase approval and special processing costs.

3. *Carrying costs*: **Carrying costs** arise when an organization holds an inventory of goods for sale. These costs include the opportunity cost of the investment tied up in inventory (see Chapter 11, pp. 389–390) and the costs associated with storage, such as space rental, insurance, obsolescence, and spoilage.

4. *Stockout costs*: A **stockout** occurs when an organization runs out of a particular item for which there is customer demand. A company may respond to the shortfall or stockout by expediting an order from a supplier. Expediting costs of a stockout include the additional ordering costs plus any associated transportation costs. Alternatively, the company may lose one or more sales due to the stockout. Here the opportunity cost of the stockout includes the lost contribution margin on the sale not made due to the item being unavailable and any contribution margin lost on future sales hurt by customer ill-will caused by the stockout.

5. *Quality costs*: The *quality* of a product or service is its conformance with a preannounced or prespecified standard. As described in Chapter 19, four categories of costs of quality are often distinguished: (a) prevention costs, (b) appraisal costs, (c) internal failure costs, and (d) external failure costs.

The descriptions of the five cost categories indicate that not all the relevant costs for managing goods for sale are available in existing accounting systems. Opportunity costs, which are not typically recorded in accounting systems, are an important component in several of these cost categories.

Advances in information-gathering technology are increasing the reliability and timelines of inventory information and reducing costs in the five cost categories. For example, barcoding technology allows a scanner to capture purchases and sales of individual units. This information creates an instantaneous record of inventory movements and helps in the management of purchasing, carrying, and stockout costs.

Economic-Order-Quantity Decision Model

The first major decision in managing goods for sale is deciding how much of a given product to order. The **economic order quantity (EOQ)** is a decision model that calculates the optimal quantity of inventory to order under a restrictive set of assumptions. The simplest version of this model incorporates only ordering costs and carrying costs into the calculation. It assumes the following:

1. The same fixed quantity is ordered at each reorder point.
2. Demand, ordering costs, and carrying costs are known with certainty. The **purchase-order lead time**—the time between placing an order and its delivery—is also known with certainty.
3. Purchasing costs per unit are unaffected by the quantity ordered. This assumption makes purchasing costs irrelevant to determining EOQ, because purchasing costs of all units acquired will be the same, regardless of the order size in which the units are ordered.
4. No stockouts occur. One justification for this assumption is that the costs of a stockout can be prohibitively high. We assume that to avoid these potential costs, managers always maintain adequate inventory so that no stockout can occur.
5. In deciding the size of the purchase order, managers consider the costs of quality only to the extent that these costs affect ordering costs or carrying costs.

Given these assumptions, EOQ analysis ignores purchasing costs, stockout costs, and quality costs. To determine EOQ, we minimize the relevant ordering costs and carrying costs (those ordering and carrying costs that are affected by the quantity of inventory ordered):

> Relevant total costs = Relevant ordering costs + Relevant carrying costs

EXAMPLE: Video Galore sells packages of blank video tapes to its customers. It also rents out tapes of movies and sporting events. It purchases packages of video tapes from Sontek at $14 a package. Sontek pays all incoming freight to Video Galore. No incoming inspection is necessary because Sontek has a superb reputation for delivering quality merchandise. Annual demand is 13,000 packages, at a rate of 250 packages per week. Video Galore requires a 15% annual return on investment. The purchase-order lead time is two weeks. The following cost data are available:

Relevant ordering costs per purchase order		$200.00
Relevant carrying costs per package per year:		
Required annual return on investment, 15% × $14	$2.10	
Relevant insurance, materials handling, breakage, and so on, per year	3.10	5.20

What is the economic-order quantity of packages of video tapes?

The formula for the EOQ model is:

$$EOQ = \sqrt{\frac{2DP}{C}}$$

Example Costs associated with goods for resale include opportunity costs that aren't recorded in the acctg. system. Examples include imputed interest on funds tied up in inventory (a carrying cost) and lost CM on lost current or future sales due to poor-quality products.

Points to Stress The advantages of the EOQ model are that it's very simple and it captures important trade-offs between *ordering costs* and *carrying costs*. However, the model is based on the simplifying assumption that the other 3 costs associated with goods for sale are irrelevant. This is valid if the *purchase cost*/unit is unaffected by the # of units ordered (e.g., there are no qty. discounts); if *quality* is unaffected by the # purchased (e.g., perishability isn't an important consideration); and if no *stockouts* occur (e.g., the cost of stockouts is so high that mgt. always maintains sufficient safety stock).

Curriculum Linkage This distinction between relevant and irrelevant costs is another application of the relevance concept introduced in Chap. 11.

Correcting Student Misconceptions Carrying costs are higher than students expect. Many companies believe that annual carrying costs exceed 30% of inventory purchase cost. This is consistent with the Video Galore example where carrying costs are $5.20/$14.00 = 37%/yr.

where

$$D = \text{demand in units for a specified time period}$$
$$P = \text{relevant ordering costs per purchase order}$$
$$C = \text{relevant carrying costs of one unit in stock for the time}$$
$$\text{period used for } D \text{ (one year in this example)}$$

The formula indicates that EOQ increases with demand and ordering costs and decreases with carrying costs.

We can use this formula to determine the EOQ for Video Galore as follows:

$$\text{EOQ} = \sqrt{\frac{2 \times 13{,}000 \times \$200}{\$5.20}} = \sqrt{1{,}000{,}000} = 1{,}000 \text{ packages}$$

Therefore, Video Galore should purchase 1,000 tape packages per order to minimize total ordering and carrying costs.

The annual relevant total costs (RTC) for any order quantity, Q, can be calculated using the following formula:

$$\text{RTC} = \begin{matrix} \text{Annual} \\ \text{relevant ordering} \\ \text{costs} \end{matrix} + \begin{matrix} \text{Annual} \\ \text{relevant carrying} \\ \text{costs} \end{matrix}$$

$$= \left(\begin{matrix} \text{Number of} \\ \text{purchase orders} \times \\ \text{per year} \end{matrix} \begin{matrix} \text{Relevant ordering} \\ \text{costs per} \\ \text{purchase order} \end{matrix} \right) + \left(\text{Average inventory} \times \begin{matrix} \text{Annual} \\ \text{relevant carrying} \\ \text{costs of one unit} \end{matrix} \right)$$

$$\text{RTC} = \left(\frac{D}{Q} \times P \right) + \left(\frac{Q}{2} \times C \right)$$

$$= \frac{DP}{Q} + \frac{QC}{2}$$

(Note that in this formula, Q can be any order quantity, not just the EOQ.)

When $Q = 1{,}000$ units,

$$\text{RTC} = \frac{13{,}000 \times \$200}{1{,}000} + \frac{1{,}000 \times \$5.20}{2}$$

$$= \$2{,}600 + \$2{,}600 = \$5{,}200$$

The number of deliveries each time period (in our example, one year) is:

$$\frac{D}{\text{EOQ}} = \frac{13{,}000}{1{,}000} = 13 \text{ deliveries}$$

Exhibit 20-1 graphs the annual relevant total costs of ordering (DP/Q) and carrying inventory ($QC/2$) under various order sizes (Q), and illustrates the trade-off between the two types of costs. The larger the order quantity, the lower the annual relevant ordering costs, but the higher the annual relevant carrying costs. *Annual relevant total costs are at a minimum where the relevant ordering costs and the relevant carrying costs are equal.*

When to Order, Assuming Certainty

The second major decision in managing goods for sale is when to order a given product. The **reorder point** is the quantity level of the inventory on hand that triggers a new order. The reorder point is simplest to compute when both demand and purchase-order lead time are known with certainty:

$$\text{Reorder point} = \begin{matrix} \text{Number of units sold per} \\ \text{unit of time} \end{matrix} \times \begin{matrix} \text{Purchase-order} \\ \text{lead time} \end{matrix}$$

Consider our Video Galore example. We choose a week as the unit of time:

Economic order quantity	1,000 packages
Number of units sold per week	250 packages
Purchase-order lead time	2 weeks

Reinforcing Problems Exer. 20-16 through 20-21 and Probs. 20-26 through 20-28 cover the EOQ model.

Correcting Student Misconceptions Remind students that RTC can be calculated for any order quantity, not just the EOQ. Also, emphasize the intuition behind the RTC computation: D/Q = # orders, so (D/Q)P = Total ordering costs, and Q/2 = avg. # units in inventory, so (Q/2)C = Total carrying costs.

Curriculum Linkage Students may be familiar with EOQ, safety stock, and reorder points from finance or production courses. However, in those courses, the costs were assumed. Accountants help (1) decide what costs should be included in these calculations as relevant costs, and (2) estimate the amounts of these costs.

Example Particularly for low-value items, companies often use simple signals such as painted lines on a bin to prompt a reorder.

EXHIBIT 20-1
Graphic Analysis of Ordering Costs and Carrying Costs for Video Galore

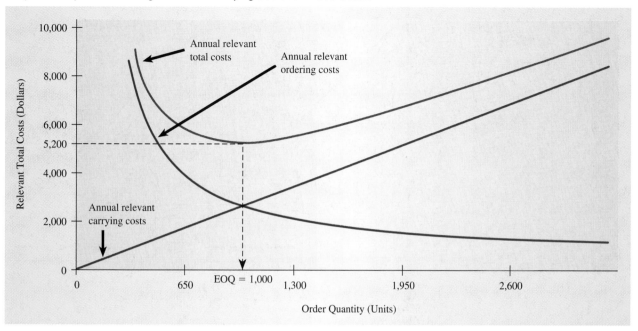

Thus,

$$\text{Reorder point} = \frac{\text{Number of units sold}}{\text{per unit of time}} \times \frac{\text{Purchase-order}}{\text{lead time}}$$

$$= 250 \times 2 = 500 \text{ packages}$$

Video Galore will thus order 1,000 packages of tapes each time its inventory stock falls to 500 packages.

The graph in Exhibit 20-2 presents the behavior of the inventory level of tape packages, assuming demand occurs uniformly throughout each week.[1] If the purchase-order lead time is two weeks, a new order will be placed when the inventory level reaches 500 tape packages, so that the 1,000 packages ordered are received at the time inventory reaches zero.

Safety Stock

So far, we have assumed that demand and purchase-order lead time are known with certainty. When retailers are uncertain about the demand, the lead time, or the quantity that suppliers can provide, they often hold safety stock. **Safety stock** is inventory held at all times regardless of the quantity of inventory ordered using the EOQ model. Safety stock is used as a buffer against unexpected increases in demand or lead time and unavailability of stock from suppliers. In our Video Galore example, expected demand is 250 packages per week, but the company's managers feel that a maximum demand of 400 packages per week may occur. If Video Galore's managers decide that the costs of stockouts are prohibitive, they may decide to hold safety stock of 300 packages. This amount is the maximum excess demand of 150 packages per week for the two weeks of purchase-order lead time. The computation of safety stock hinges on demand forecasts. Managers will have some notion—usually based on experience—of the range of weekly demand.

A frequency distribution based on prior daily or weekly levels of demand provides data for computing the associated costs of maintaining safety stock. Assume

Teaching Tip The intuition behind the reorder point is that we need to reorder when the amt. of inventory on hand just equals that needed to cover sales that will occur during the purchase-order lead time.

Points to Stress The EOQ model trades off order costs vs. carrying costs, assuming that there are no stockouts. One reason for no stockouts is the existence of sufficient *safety stock*. Safety stock computations trade off stockout costs vs. carrying costs.

[1]This handy but special formula does not apply when the receipt of the order fails to increase inventory to the reorder-point quantity (for example, when the lead time is three weeks and the order is a one-week supply). In these cases, orders will overlap.

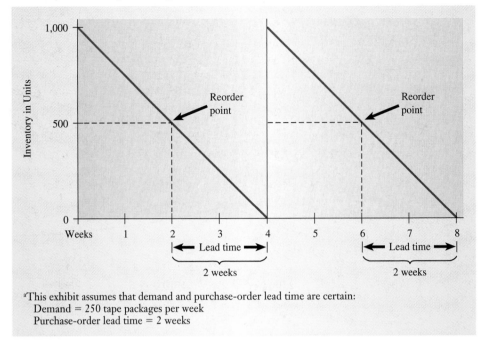

EXHIBIT 20-2
Inventory Level of Tape Packages for Video Galore[a]

[a]This exhibit assumes that demand and purchase-order lead time are certain:
Demand = 250 tape packages per week
Purchase-order lead time = 2 weeks

that one of seven different levels of demand will occur over the two-week purchase-order lead time at Video Galore.

Total Demand for 2 Weeks	200 Units	300 Units	400 Units	500 Units	600 Units	700 Units	800 Units
Probability (sums to 1.00)	.06	.09	.20	.30	.20	.09	.06

We see that 500 is the most likely level of demand for two weeks because it is assigned the highest probability of occurrence. We see also that there is a .35 probability that demand will be 600, 700, or 800 packages (.20 + .09 + .06 = .35).

If a customer contacts Video Galore to buy video tapes, and the store has none in stock, it can "rush" them to the customer at a cost to Video Galore of $4 per package. The relevant stockout costs in this case are $4 per package. The optimal safety stock level is the quantity of safety stock that minimizes the sum of the annual relevant stockout costs and carrying costs. Recall that the relevant carrying costs for Video Galore are $5.20 per unit per year.

Exhibit 20-3 presents the total annual relevant stockout and carrying costs when the reorder point is 500 units. We need only consider safety stock levels of 0, 100, 200, and 300 units, since demand will exceed the 500 units of stock available at reordering by 0 if demand is 500, 100 if demand is 600, 200 if demand is 700, and 300 if demand is 800. The annual relevant total stockout and carrying costs would be minimized at $1,352, when a safety stock of 200 packages is maintained. Think of the 200 units of safety stock as extra stock that Video Galore maintains. For example, Video Galore's total inventory of tapes at the time of reordering its EOQ of 1,000 units would be 700 units (the reorder point of 500 units plus the safety stock of 200 units).

CHALLENGES IN ESTIMATING INVENTORY-RELATED COSTS AND THEIR EFFECTS

As we have seen in earlier chapters, relevance is extremely important in both decision making and the evaluation of those decisions. Determining relevant costs in deciding how much inventory to order and when to order it further illustrates the challenges in these areas.

Points to Stress/Example Marketing personnel favor maintaining enough inventory to avoid stockouts, but financial executives want to minimize $ tied up in inventory. These trade-offs will change in response to economic circumstances. Companies such as Bose (speakers) and K-mart have decided to increase safety stock in times of strong expected demand, in order to avoid stockout costs. Tightened capacity in the electronics industry led to shortages of certain key components in 1994, so some manufacturers increased their safety stocks of these materials (WSJ, 10/25/94).

Points to Stress Quantifying the opportunity-cost component of stockout costs is necessarily subjective. A stockout may cause the loss of a whole series of orders, particularly if the customer uses JIT and ends up switching to another supplier.

EXHIBIT 20-3

Computation of Safety Stock for Video Galore When Reorder Point Is 500 Units

Safety Stock Level in Units (1)	Demand Realizations Resulting in Stockouts (2)	Stockout in Units[a] (3) = (2) − 500 − (1)	Probability of Stockout (4)	Relevant Stockout Costs[b] (5) = (3) × \$4	Number of Orders Per Year[c] (6)	Expected Stockout Costs[d] (7) = (4) × (5) × (6)	Relevant Carrying Costs[e] (8) = (1) × \$5.20	Relevant Total Costs (9) = (7) + (8)
0	600	100	0.20	\$ 400	13	\$1,040		
	700	200	0.09	800	13	936		
	800	300	0.06	1,200	13	936		
						\$2,912	\$ 0	\$2,912
100	700	100	0.09	400	13	\$468		
	800	200	0.06	800	13	624		
						\$1,092	\$ 520	\$1,612
200	800	100	0.06	400	13	\$ 312	\$1,040	\$1,352
300	—	—	—	—	—	\$ 0[f]	\$1,560	\$1,560

[a]Realized demand − Inventory available during lead time (excluding safety stock), 500 units − Safety stock.
[b]Stockout units × Relevant stockout costs of \$4.00 per unit.
[c]Annual demand 13,000 ÷ 1,000 EOQ = 13 orders per year.
[d]Probability of stockout × Relevant stockout costs × Number of orders per year.
[e]Safety stock × Annual relevant carrying costs of \$5.20 per unit (assumes that safety stock is on hand at all times and that there is no overstocking caused by decreases in expected usage).
[f]At a safety stock level of 300 units, no stockouts will occur and hence expected stockout costs = \$0.

Considerations in Obtaining Estimates of Relevant Costs

Obtaining accurate estimates of the cost parameters used in the EOQ decision model is a challenging task. Consider the annual relevant carrying costs of inventory. These costs consist of *relevant incremental costs* plus the *relevant opportunity cost of capital*.

What are the *relevant incremental costs* of carrying inventory? Only those costs of the purchasing company that change with the quantity of inventory held—for example, insurance, property taxes, costs of obsolescence, and costs of breakage. Consider, for example, the salaries paid to clerks, storekeepers, and materials handlers. These costs are irrelevant if they are unaffected by changes in inventory levels. Suppose, however, that as inventories decrease, total salary costs decrease as the clerks, storekeepers, and materials handlers are transferred to other activities or laid off. In this case, the salaries paid to these people are relevant costs of carrying inventory. Similarly, the costs of storage space owned that cannot be used for other profitable purposes when inventories decrease are irrelevant. But if the space has other profitable uses, or if rental cost is tied to the amount of space occupied, storage costs are relevant costs of carrying inventory.

What is the *relevant opportunity cost of capital*? It is the return foregone by investing capital in inventory rather than elsewhere. It is calculated as the required rate of return multiplied by those per-unit costs that vary with the number of units purchased and that are incurred at the time the units are received. (Examples of these per-unit costs are purchase price, incoming freight, and incoming inspection.) Opportunity costs are not computed on investments, say in buildings, if these investments are unaffected by changes in inventory levels.

In the case of stockouts, calculating the relevant opportunity costs requires an estimate of the lost contribution margin on that sale as well as on future sales hurt by customer ill-will resulting from the stockout.

Points to Stress Estimation of EOQ models and safety stock levels require data that most acctg. systems don't routinely provide. In this case, the accountant must do a special analysis to estimate the opportunity cost of capital invested in inventory, and the lost CM from current and future sales lost due to stockouts.

Curriculum Linkage Carrying cost estimates depend on the firm's cost of capital. Finance courses cover the estimation of the cost of capital.

Cost of a Prediction Error

Our discussion suggests that predicting relevant costs requires care and is difficult. Managers understand that their projections will seldom be flawless. This leads to the question, What is the cost of an incorrect prediction when actual relevant costs are different from the predicted relevant cost used for decision making?

Using our Video Galore example, suppose that relevant ordering costs per purchase order are $100 instead of the $200 prediction used. We can calculate the cost of this prediction error using a three-step approach.

Step 1: Compute the Monetary Outcome from the Best Action That Could Have Been Taken, Given the Actual Amount of the Cost Input   The appropriate inputs are $D = 13,000$ units, $P = 100, and $C = 5.20. The EOQ size is:

$$EOQ = \sqrt{\frac{2DP}{C}}$$

$$= \sqrt{\frac{2 \times 13,000 \times \$100}{\$5.20}} = \sqrt{500,000}$$

$$= 707 \text{ packages (rounded)}$$

The annual relevant total costs when EOQ = 707 is:

$$RTC = \frac{DP}{Q} + \frac{QC}{2}$$

$$= \frac{13,000 \times \$100}{707} + \frac{707 \times \$5.20}{2}$$

$$= \$1,838 + \$1,838 = \$3,676$$

Step 2: Compute the Monetary Outcome from the Best Action Based on the Incorrect Amount of the Predicted Cost Input   The planned action when the relevant ordering costs per purchase order are predicted to be $200 is to purchase 1,000 packages in each order (p. 715). The annual relevant total costs using this order quantity when $D = 13,000$ units, $P = 100, and $C = 5.20 are:

$$RTC = \frac{13,000 \times \$100}{1,000} + \frac{1,000 \times \$5.20}{2}$$

$$= \$1,300 + \$2,600 = \$3,900$$

Step 3: Compute the Difference Between the Monetary Outcomes from Step 1 and Step 2

	Monetary Outcome
Step 1	$3,676
Step 2	3,900
Difference	$ (224)

The cost of the prediction error, $224, is less than 7% of relevant total costs. The annual relevant total costs curve in Exhibit 20-1 is relatively flat over the range of order quantities from 650 to 1,300. *The square root in the EOQ model reduces the sensitivity of the decision to errors in predicting its parameters.*

Evaluating Managers and Goal-Congruence Issues

Goal-congruence issues can arise when there is an inconsistency between the EOQ decision model and the model used to evaluate the performance of the manager implementing the inventory management decisions. For example, the absence of recorded opportunity costs in conventional accounting systems raises the possibility of a conflict between the EOQ model's optimal order quantity and the order quantity that the purchasing manager, evaluated on conventional accounting numbers,

Correcting Student Misconceptions Students often find step 2 confusing. Emphasize that the cost of the prediction error is the difference between the costs that would have been incurred had there been no prediction error (if we had a crystal ball) vs. the costs that were actually incurred. The first step is to determine, *ex post*, what would have been the optimal action had there been no prediction error (i.e., if we had known actual costs in advance). Compare the cost of this against the cost of the action actually taken (the action we thought was optimal based on the incorrectly predicted costs).

Points to Stress The small cost of a prediction error (only $224 in total) illustrates that EOQs are seldom sensitive to moderately erroneous predictions. Note that a 100% error in estimating the cost results is only a 6.1% (224/3676) difference in the RTC.

regards as optimal. If the opportunity cost of the investment tied up in inventory is excluded from annual carrying costs when evaluating the managers' performance, they would be inclined to purchase larger quantities of materials. Companies such as Coca Cola and Wal-Mart, resolve this conflict by designing the performance evaluation system so that the carrying costs, including a required return on investment, are charged to the appropriate manager.

The opportunity cost of the investment tied up in inventory can be reduced by reducing inventory levels. We now discuss just-in-time purchasing, an approach that has dramatically reduced inventories for some companies.

Curriculum Linkage Another way to motivate mgrs. to refrain from building up inventories is to evaluate them based on ROI (see Chap. 23, or students may have encountered ROI in finance courses). Higher levels of inventory increase the ROI denominator, thereby reducing ROI. However, ROI has some limitations, as Chap. 23 discusses.

JUST-IN-TIME PURCHASING

Just-in-time (JIT) purchasing is the purchase of goods or materials such that a delivery immediately precedes demand or use. JIT purchasing requires organizations to restructure their relationships with suppliers and place smaller and more frequent purchase orders. JIT purchasing can be implemented in both the retail and manufacturing sectors of the economy. Consider JIT purchasing for Hewlett-Packard's (HP's) manufacture of the Kayak workstation product line. HP has long-term agreements with suppliers who provide the major components for this product line. Each supplier is required to deliver components such that HP's final assembly plants meet their own production schedules and yet have minimal inventories of the various components on hand. Delivery to the production floor rather than to a storeroom is the norm under JIT purchasing. A supplier who does not deliver components on time, or who delivers components that fail to meet agreed-upon quality standards, can cause an HP assembly plant to not meet its own scheduled deliveries for Kayak workstations. Companies adopting JIT purchasing do not have large amounts of materials inventories on hand that enable a production line to continue operating even when some deliveries do not occur on time or where defective materials are delivered. HP shares its planned production schedule with each supplier. JIT purchasing for HP requires a high level of information sharing with suppliers who commit to deliver components in narrow time windows. We now explore the relationship between JIT purchasing and the EOQ decision model discussed earlier.

Reinforcing Problems Prob. 20-29 covers JIT purchasing.

JIT Purchasing and EOQ Model Parameters

Companies moving toward JIT purchasing argue that the cost of carrying inventories (parameter C in the EOQ model) has been dramatically underestimated in the past. This cost includes storage costs, spoilage, obsolescence, and opportunity costs such as investment tied up in inventory. The cost of placing a purchase order (parameter P in the EOQ model) is also being reevaluated. Three factors are causing sizable reductions in P:

◆ Companies increasingly are establishing long-term purchasing arrangements in which price and quality dimensions that apply over an extended period are agreed to by both parties. Individual purchase orders occur without any additional negotiation over price or quality in this period.

◆ Companies are using electronic links, such as the Internet, to place purchase orders. Electronic commerce is one of the fastest growing areas of the Internet. The cost of placing some orders on the Internet is estimated to be less than one-tenth (even less than one-hundredth) the cost of placing orders by telephone or by mail.

◆ Companies are increasing the use of purchase-order cards (similar to consumer credit cards like VISA and MasterCard). Purchasing personnel are given total dollar limits or individual transaction dollar limits. As long as personnel stay within these limits, the traditional labor-intensive procurement approval mechanisms are not required.

Both increases in the carrying cost (C) and decreases in the ordering cost per purchase order (P) result in smaller EOQ amounts.

EXHIBIT 20-4

Sensitivity of EOQ to Variations in Relevant Ordering and Carrying Costs
for Video Galore[a]

Relevant Carrying Costs Per Package Per Year	Relevant Ordering Costs Per Purchase Order			
	$200	$150	$100	$30
$ 5.20	EOQ = 1,000	EOQ = 866	EOQ = 707	EOQ = 387
7.00	862	746	609	334
10.00	721	624	510	279
15.00	589	510	416	228

[a]Assuming annual demand is always 13,000 packages.

Exhibit 20-4 analyzes the sensitivity of Video Galore's EOQ computed earlier (p. 714) to illustrate the economics of smaller and more frequent purchase orders. The analysis presented in Exhibit 20-4 supports JIT purchasing—that is, having a smaller EOQ and placing more frequent orders—as relevant carrying costs increase and relevant ordering costs per purchase order decrease.

Relevant Benefits and Relevant Costs of JIT Purchasing

Curriculum Linkage This section illustrates the use of relevant-cost concepts from Chap. 11 in deciding whether to switch to a JIT purchasing system.

Correcting Student Misconceptions The Video Galore example is simplified in that stockout costs include only the cost of the rush order—there's no lost CM from lost current or future sales because the rush order is assumed to fully satisfy the customer. In many settings, however, stockouts are also likely to incur opportunity costs of lost CM because of lost current and future sales. Such costs usually must be estimated outside the acctg. system.

Curriculum Linkage JIT adopters often strive to minimize global rather than local costs by employing total value-chain analysis (introduced in Chap. 1). Suppliers and customers are considered part of the value chain. In evaluating and choosing suppliers, quality and timely delivery become increasingly important as the emphasis shifts away from minimizing purchase costs and toward minimizing costs across the entire value chain (e.g., minimizing the sum of production costs, warranty costs, opportunity costs from lost current or future sales due to quality or delivery problems, etc.).

JIT purchasing is not guided solely by the EOQ model. As discussed on page 713, the EOQ model is designed to only emphasize the trade-off between carrying costs and ordering costs. Inventory management extends beyond ordering and carrying costs to include purchasing costs, stockout costs, and quality costs. The quality of materials and goods and timely deliveries are important motivations for using JIT purchasing, and stockout costs are an important concern. We add these features as we move from the EOQ decision model to JIT purchasing.

Revisit the Video Galore example, and consider the following information. Video Galore has recently established an Internet business-to-business purchase-order link with Sontek. Video Galore triggers a purchase order for tapes by a single computer entry. Payments are made electronically for batches of deliveries rather than for each individual delivery. These changes reduce ordering costs dramatically to only $2 per purchase order. (It was previously $200 per purchase order.) Video Galore will use the Internet purchase-order link whether or not it shifts to JIT purchasing. Video Galore is negotiating to have Sontek deliver 100 packages of video tapes 130 times per year (5 times every 2 weeks) instead of delivering 1,000 packages 13 times per year as calculated in Exhibit 20-1. Sontek is willing to make these frequent deliveries, but it would add a small additional amount of $0.02 to the price per tape package. Video Galore's required return on investment remains at 15 percent. Assume annual relevant carrying costs of insurance, materials handling, breakage, and so on remain at $3.10 per package per year.

Assume that Video Galore incurs no stockout costs under its current purchasing policy, because demand and purchase-order lead times over each four-week period are known with certainty. Video Galore's major concern is that lower inventory levels from implementing JIT purchasing will lead to more stockouts because demand variations and delays in supplying tapes are more likely to occur in the short time intervals between orders under JIT purchasing. Sontek assures Video Galore that its new manufacturing processes enable it to respond rapidly to changing demand patterns. Consequently, stockouts may not be a serious problem. Suppose Video Galore expects to incur stockout costs on 50 tape packages per year under a JIT purchasing policy. In the event of a stockout, Video Galore will have to rush-order tape packages at a cost of $4 per package. Should Video Galore implement the JIT purchasing option of 130 deliveries per year?

Exhibit 20-5 compares (1) the incremental costs Video Galore incurs when it purchases video tapes from Sontek under its current purchasing policy with (2) the

EXHIBIT 20-5

Annual Relevant Costs of Current Purchasing Policy and JIT Purchasing Policy for Video Galore

	Incremental Costs Under	
Relevant Item	Current Purchasing Policy	JIT Purchasing Policy
Purchasing costs		
$14 per unit × 13,000 units per year	$182,000.00	
$14.02 per unit × 13,000 units per year		$182,260.00
Ordering costs		
$2 per order × 13 orders per year	26.00	
$2 per order × 130 orders per year		260.00
Opportunity carrying costs, required return on investment		
15% per year × $14 cost per unit × 500[a] units of average inventory per year	1,050.00	
15% per year × $14.02 cost per unit × 50[b] units of average inventory per year		105.15
Other carrying costs (insurance, materials handling, breakage, and so on)		
$3.10 per unit per year × 500[a] units of average inventory per year	1,550.00	
$3.10 per unit per year × 50[b] units of average inventory per year		155.00
Stockout costs		
No stockouts	0	
$4 per unit × 50 units per year		200.00
Total annual relevant costs	$184,626.00	$182,980.15
Annual difference in favor of JIT purchasing	$1,645.85	

[a]Order quantity ÷ 2 = 1,000 ÷ 2 = 500
[b]Order quantity ÷ 2 = 100 ÷ 2 = 50

incremental costs Video Galore would incur if Sontek supplied video tapes under a JIT policy. The difference in the two incremental costs is the relevant savings from JIT purchasing. Another way of comparing the two purchasing policies is to include only the relevant costs—those costs that differ between the two alternatives. For example, the relevant purchasing costs in Exhibit 20-5 are $260. Exhibit 20-5 shows net cost savings of $1,645.85 per year by shifting to a JIT purchasing policy.

Supplier Evaluation and Relevant Costs of Quality and Timely Deliveries

The timely delivery of quality product is particularly crucial in JIT purchasing environments. Defective goods and late deliveries often result in contribution margin lost on current and future sales. Companies that implement JIT purchasing choose their suppliers carefully and pay special attention to developing long-run supplier partnerships. Some suppliers are very cooperative with a company's attempt to adopt JIT purchasing. For example, Frito-Lay, which has a large market share in potato chips and other snack foods, makes more frequent deliveries to retail outlets than many of its competitors. The company's corporate strategy emphasizes service to retailers and consistency, freshness, and quality of the delivered product.

What are the relevant costs when choosing suppliers? Consider again our Video Galore example. Denton Corporation also supplies video tapes. It offers to

Curriculum Linkage What role should material price var's. (Chap. 7) play in evaluating a JIT firm's purchasing mgr.? In contrast to traditional firms that minimize Unfav material price var's. (local cost minimization), JIT firms foster minimization of total costs throughout the value chain. While material price var's. may still play some role in the evaluation of purchasing, quality and timely delivery will likely play bigger roles since the costs of poor-quality inputs or delivery failures are likely to be significant. Moreover, the material price var's. of JIT firms are often negligible if they employ long-term fixed price contracts.

Cisco Leads the Way in Streamlining the Purchase-Order Process via the Internet

Cisco Systems, a manufacturer of Internet equipment, is a leading exponent of using Internet-based electronic commerce technology. Cisco is at the forefront of streamlining the procurement process for its customers, who are now experiencing much lower total costs of placing purchase orders for Cisco equipment. Its website (www.cisco.com) plays a central role in this streamlining. Key features of its website include:

- ◆ *Invoice agent*—allows users to view invoice information and print a copy of submitted invoices.
- ◆ *Pricing agent*—provides online access to Cisco's complete price list.
- ◆ *Order-status agent*—provides access to current information about expected shipment dates and electronic proof of delivery with links to FEDEX, UPS, and other couriers.
- ◆ *Lead-time agent*—provides current lead time information on Cisco products.
- ◆ *Contract-status agent*—allows users to view service and support coverage.
- ◆ *Service-Order submit*—allows customers to submit service orders online and receive email or fax confirmation.

All these features are available 7 days a week, 24 hours a day, 365 days a year.

Cisco's website enables the purchaser to view into Cisco's internal information systems in a way that many existing purchase-order systems preclude. Most companies only permit their own employees to view into their own internal data bases.

The new website offers customers many advantages, including a faster and more informed procurement process. It has also reduced customer purchase-order errors. One Cisco manager noted that when customers had much less access to Cisco's internal data bases, errors were occurring "15 to 20% of the time." These errors included wrong prices and inaccurate lead times. Correcting these errors required much manual work and could take "days" to fix. These errors were the source of nonvalue-added costs to both those placing purchase orders and to Cisco itself.

Source: E. Krapf, "Why Cisco Succeeded (and You May Not)," *Business Communications Review* (Nov. 1997).

Example Northrup Aircraft incorporates nonconformance costs of poor quality and delivery failures into their supplier evaluation index:

Supplier Performance index

$$= \frac{\left(\begin{array}{c}\text{Nonconformance costs}\\+ \text{ Purchase costs}\end{array}\right)}{\text{Purchase costs}}$$

The lower the index, the more valued the supplier.

supply all of Video Galore's video tape needs at a price of $13.60 per package (less than Sontek's price of $14.02) under the same JIT delivery terms that Sontek offers. Denton proposes an Internet purchase-order link identical to Sontek's that would make Video Galore's ordering costs $2 per purchase order. Video Galore's relevant carrying costs of insurance, materials handling, breakage, and so on per package per year would be $3.10 if it purchases video tapes from Sontek and $3.00 if it purchases from Denton. Should Video Galore buy from Denton? Not before considering the relevant costs of quality and also the relevant costs of failing to deliver on time.

Video Galore has used Sontek in the past and knows that Sontek fully deserves its reputation for delivering quality merchandise on time. For example, Video Galore does not find it necessary to inspect the tape packages that Sontek supplies. Denton, however, does not enjoy so sterling a reputation for quality. Video Galore anticipates the following negative aspects of using Denton:

- ◆ Video Galore would incur additional inspection costs of $0.05 per package.
- ◆ Average stockouts of 360 tape packages per year would occur, largely resulting from late deliveries. Denton cannot rush-order tape packages to Video Galore

EXHIBIT 20-6
Annual Relevant Costs of Purchasing from Sontek and Denton

Relevant Item	Incremental Costs of Purchasing from	
	Sontek	Denton
Purchasing costs		
$14.02 per unit × 13,000 units per year	$182,260.00	
$13.60 per unit × 13,000 units per year		$176,800.00
Ordering costs		
$2 per order × 130 orders per year	260.00	
$2 per order × 130 orders per year		260.00
Inspection costs		
No inspection necessary	0	
$0.05 per unit × 13,000 units		650.00
Opportunity carrying costs, required return on investment		
15% per year × $14.02 × 50ᵃ units of average inventory per year	105.15	
15% per year × $13.60 × 50ᵃ units of average inventory per year		102.00
Other carrying costs		
(insurance, materials handling, breakage, and so on)		
$3.10 per unit per year × 50ᵃ units of average inventory per year	155.00	
$3.00 per unit per year × 50ᵃ units of average inventory per year		150.00
Stockout costs		
$4 per unit × 50 units per year	200.00	
$8 per unit × 360 units per year		2,880.00
Customer returns costs		
No customer returns	0	
$25 per unit returned × 2% × 13,000 units returned		6,500.00
Total annual relevant costs	$182,980.15	$187,342.00
Annual difference in favor of Sontek	$4,361.85	

ᵃOrder quantity ÷ 2 = 100 ÷ 2 = 50

at short notice. Video Galore anticipates lost contribution margin per unit of $8 from stockouts.

◆ Customers would likely return 2% of all packages sold due to poor quality of the tapes. Video Galore estimates its additional costs to handle each returned package is $25.

Exhibit 20-6 presents the incremental costs of purchasing (1) from Sontek, and (2) from Denton. Even though Denton is offering a lower price per package, there is a net cost savings of $4,361.85 per year by purchasing goods from Sontek. Selling high-quality merchandise also has nonfinancial and qualitative benefits. For example, offering Sontek's high-quality tapes enhances Video Galore's reputation and increases customer goodwill, which may lead to higher future profitability.

OBJECTIVE 4

Use a supply-chain approach to inventory management

INVENTORY MANAGEMENT AND SUPPLY-CHAIN ANALYSIS

The level of inventories held by retailers is influenced by demand patterns of their customers and supply relationships with their distributors, manufacturers, and of suppliers to manufacturers, and so on. The term *supply chain* describes the flow of goods, services, and information from cradle to grave (womb to tomb), regardless of whether those activities occur in the same organization or in other organizations.

Challenges in Obtaining the Benefits from a Supply-Chain Analysis

Supply-chain studies reported in the business press frequently cite a wide range of benefits to both manufacturers and retailers. These benefits include fewer stockouts, reduced manufacture of items not subsequently demanded at the retail level, a reduction in rushed manufacturing orders, and lower inventory levels. A survey of 220 retailers and manufacturers highlights some key issues that companies adopting a supply-chain approach to inventory management must address in order to achieve the full extent of these benefits.

One issue is deciding the information to exchange among companies in the supply chain. Manufacturers gave the following rankings (in terms of importance) of information to receive from retailers stocking their products:

1. Retail sales forecast for the products
2. Sales data on the products (such as daily sales at each retail outlet)
3. Pricing and advertising strategies by the retailer
4. Inventory levels at each retail outlet.

A second issue is reducing the obstacles to manufacturers and retailers achieving the benefits of a supply-chain approach. Respondents cited the following obstacles:

1. Communication obstacles—includes the unwillingness of some parties to share information
2. Trust obstacles—includes the concern that all parties will not meet their agreed-upon commitments.
3. Information system obstacles—includes problems due to the information systems of different parties not being technically compatible.
4. Limited resources—includes problems due to the people and financial resources given to support a supply chain initiative not being adequate.

Adopting a supply-chain approach requires diverse organizations to cooperate and communicate on a broad set of issues. Respondents emphasized this challenge was not always successfully met. Not surprisingly, not all supply-chain initiatives have delivered the initial financial and operating projected benefits.

Source: Research Incorporated, "Synchronizing the Supply Chain Through Collaborative Design." See Appendix A for full citation.

New in This Edition This is a new section on inventory management and supply-chain analysis.

Chapter 1 introduced this concept using the example of a supply chain in the beverage industry (see Exhibit 1-5 p. 10). One point well documented in supply-chain analysis is that there are significant gains to companies in this supply chain from coordinating their activities and sharing information.

Proctor and Gamble's (P&G) experience with their Pampers product illustrates the gains from supply-chain coordination. Retailers selling Pampers encounter some variability in weekly demand, despite babies consuming diapers at a relatively steady rate. However, there was pronounced variability in retailers' orders to the manufacturer (P&G), and even more variability in orders by P&G to its own suppliers. This higher level of variability at suppliers than at manufacturers, and at manufacturers than at retailers, is called the "bullwhip effect" or the "whiplash effect." It is a widely observed phenomenon.[2] One consequence of the bullwhip effect is that high levels of inventory are often held at various stages in the supply chain.

[2]See H. Lee, V. Padmanabhan, and S. Whang, "The Bullwhip Effect in Supply Chains," *Sloan Management Review* (Spring 1997). These authors discuss four major causes of the bullwhip effect: (1) demand forecasting, (2) order batching, (3) price fluctuation, and (4) rationing and shortage gaming.

There are multiple gains to companies in a supply chain by coordinating their activities and sharing information. Suppose all retailers share daily sales information about Pampers with P&G, P&G's distributors, and P&G's suppliers. This updated sales information reduces the level of uncertainty that manufacturers and suppliers to manufacturers have about retail demand for Pampers. This reduction in demand uncertainty can lead to fewer stockouts at the retail level, reduced manufacture of Pampers not subsequently demanded by retailers, a reduction in expedited manufacturing orders, and lower inventories being held by each company in the supply chain.

A supply chain is one way for manufacturers to start managing their own inventory better. Of course, the need to produce high-quality products at competitive cost levels leads managers at manufacturing companies to also seek out additional ways to manage their inventories. Numerous systems have been developed to help managers plan and implement production and inventory activities. We now consider two widely used types of systems—materials requirements planning (MRP) and just-in-time (JIT) production.

Reinforcing Problems Prob. 20-30 covers supply-chain analysis.

INVENTORY MANAGEMENT AND MRP

Materials requirements planning (MRP) is a "push-through" system that manufactures finished goods for inventory on the basis of demand forecasts. MRP uses (1) demand forecasts for the final products; (2) a bill of materials outlining the materials, components, and subassemblies for each final product; and (3) the quantities of materials, components, finished products, and product inventories to predetermine the necessary outputs at each stage of production. Taking into account the lead time required to purchase materials and to manufacture components and finished products, a master production schedule specifies the quantity and timing of each item to be produced. Once scheduled production starts, the output of each department is pushed through the production line whether it is needed or not. The result is often an accumulation of inventory at workstations that receive work they are not yet ready to process.

Inventory management is a key challenge in an MRP system. The management accountant can play several important roles in meeting this challenge. A key role is maintaining accurate and timely information pertaining to materials, work-in-process and finished goods inventories. A major cause of unsuccessful attempts to implement MRP systems has been the problem of collecting and updating inventory records. Calculating the full cost of carrying finished goods inventory motivates other actions. For example, instead of storing product at multiple (and geographically dispersed) warehouses, National Semiconductor contracted with Federal Express to airfreight its microchips from a central location in Singapore to customer sites worldwide. The change enabled National to move products from plant to customer in 4 days rather than 45 days, and to reduce distribution costs from 2.6% to 1.9% of revenues. These benefits subsequently led National to outsource all its logistics to Federal Express, including shipments between its own plants in the United States, Scotland, and Malaysia.

A second role of the management accountant is providing estimates of the setup costs for each production run at a plant, the downtime costs, and carrying costs of inventory. Costs of setting up a production run are analogous to ordering costs in the EOQ model. When the costs of setting up machines or sections of the production line are high (for example, as with a blast furnace in an integrated steel mill), processing larger batches of materials and incurring larger inventory carrying costs is the optimal approach, because it reduces the number of setups that must be made. When setup costs are small, processing smaller batches is optimal because it reduces carrying costs. Similarly, when the costs of downtime are high, there can be sizable benefits from maintaining continuous production.

A key feature of MRP is its push-through approach. We now consider JIT production, which has a demand-pull approach.

OBJECTIVE 5

Differentiate materials requirements planning (MRP) systems from just-in-time (JIT) systems for manufacturing

Curriculum Linkage The EOQ model discussed in relation to purchasing from outside suppliers also can be used to determine optimal batch size by recognizing that mfg. setup costs are analogous to ordering costs.

INVENTORY MANAGEMENT AND JIT PRODUCTION

OBJECTIVE 6

Identify the major features of a just-in-time production system

Reinforcing Problems Exer. 20-22 and 20-23 and Probs. 20-31 and 20-34 cover JIT production.

Just-in-time (JIT) production (also called **lean production**) is a "demand-pull" manufacturing system in which each component in a production line is produced immediately as needed by the next step in the production line. In a JIT production line, manufacturing activity at any particular workstation is prompted by the need for that station's output at the following station. Demand triggers each step of the production process, starting with customer demand for a finished product at the end of the process and working all the way back to the demand for direct materials at the beginning of the process. In this way, demand pulls an order through the production line. The demand-pull feature of JIT production systems achieves close coordination among workstations. It smoothes the flow of goods, despite low quantities of inventory. JIT production systems aim to simultaneously (1) meet customer demand in a timely way, (2) with high-quality products, and (3) at the lowest possible total cost.

Companies implementing JIT production systems manage inventories by eliminating (or at least minimizing) them. There are five main features in a JIT production system:

♦ Organize production in **manufacturing cells**, a grouping of all the different types of equipment used to make a given product. Materials move from one machine to another where various operations are performed in sequence. Materials-handling costs are minimized.

♦ Hire and retain workers who are multiskilled so that they are capable of performing a variety of operations and tasks. These tasks include minor repairs and routine maintenance of equipment. This training adds greatly to the flexibility of the plant.

♦ Aggressively pursue total quality management (TQM) to eliminate defects. Because of the tight links between stages in the production line, and the minimal inventories at each stage, defects arising at one stage quickly affect other stages in the line. JIT creates an urgency for solving problems immediately and eliminating the root causes of defects as quickly as possible. TQM is an essential component of any JIT production system.

♦ Place emphasis on reducing *setup time*, which is the time required to get equipment, tools, and materials ready to start the production of a component or product, and *manufacturing lead time*, which is the amount of time from when an order is ready to start on the production line (ready to be set up) to when it becomes a finished good. Reducing setup time makes production in smaller batches economical, which in turn reduces inventory levels. Reducing manufacturing lead time enables a company to respond faster to changes in customer demand.

♦ Carefully select suppliers who are capable of delivering quality materials in a timely manner. Most companies implementing *JIT production* also implement the *JIT purchasing* methods described earlier in this chapter. JIT plants expect JIT suppliers to provide high-quality goods and make frequent deliveries of the exact quantities specified on a timely basis. Suppliers often deliver materials directly to the shop floor to be immediately placed into production.

Points to Stress When a customer adopts JIT, the supplier's reaction will depend on the supplier's mfg. process. If the supplier has already adopted (or is about to adopt) JIT, then the supplier will likely prefer JIT customers. These customers want frequent small deliveries, which helps smooth the supplier's production. In contrast, if the supplier is a traditional large-batch manufacturer, it will be costly to deliver many small orders, unless the supplier also streamlines production. This explains why large JIT customers often encourage their major suppliers to adopt JIT.

Financial Benefits of JIT and Relevant Costs

Early advocates of JIT production emphasized the benefits of lower carrying costs of inventory. *An important benefit of lower inventories, however, is the heightened emphasis on eliminating the root causes of rework, scrap, and waste and on reducing the manufacturing lead time.* In computing the relevant benefits and relevant costs of reducing inventories in JIT production systems, the cost analyst should take into account all benefits.

Consider Hudson Corporation, a manufacturer of brass fittings. Hudson is considering implementing a JIT production system. Suppose that to implement JIT production, Hudson must incur $100,000 in annual tooling costs to reduce setup times. Suppose further that JIT will reduce average inventory by $500,000. Also, relevant costs of insurance, storage, materials handling, and setup will decline by

$30,000 per year. The company's required rate of return on inventory investments is 10% per year. Should Hudson implement JIT? On the basis of the numbers provided, we would be tempted to say no. Why? Because annual relevant cost savings in carrying costs amount to $80,000 [(10% of $500,000) + $30,000)], which is less than the additional annual tooling costs of $100,000.

Our analysis, however, is incomplete. It has not considered other benefits of lower inventories in JIT production. For example, Hudson estimates that implementing JIT will reduce rework on 500 units each year, resulting in savings of $50 per unit. Also better quality and faster delivery will allow Hudson to charge $2 more per unit on the 20,000 units that it sells each year. The annual relevant quality and delivery benefits from JIT and lower inventory levels equal $65,000 (rework savings, $50 × 500 + additional contribution margin, $2 × 20,000). Total annual relevant benefits and cost savings equal $145,000 ($80,000 + $65,000), which exceeds annual JIT implementation costs of $100,000. Therefore, Hudson should implement a JIT production system.

Performance Measures and Control in JIT Production

To manage and reduce inventories, the management accountant must also design performance measures to control and evaluate JIT production. Examples of information the management accountant may use follow:

◆ Personal observation by production line workers and managers.

◆ Financial performance measures, such as, inventory turnover ratios.

◆ Nonfinancial performance measures of time, inventory, and quality. Examples of such measures are:

● Manufacturing lead time

● Units produced per hour

● Days' inventory on hand

● $\dfrac{\text{Total setup time for machines}}{\text{Total manufacturing time}}$

● $\dfrac{\text{Number of units requiring rework or scrap}}{\text{Total number of units started and completed}}$

Personal observation and nonfinancial performance measures are the dominant methods of control. Why? Because they are the most timely, intuitive, and easy to understand measures of plant performance. Rapid, meaningful feedback is critical because the lack of buffer inventories in a demand-pull system creates added urgency to detect and solve problems quickly.

JIT's Effect on Costing Systems

In reducing the need for materials handling, warehousing, and incoming inspection, JIT systems reduce overhead costs. JIT systems also facilitate the direct tracing of some costs that were formerly classified as overhead. For example, the use of manufacturing cells makes it easy to trace materials handling and machine operating costs to specific products or product families made in specific cells. These costs then become direct costs of those products. Also, the use of multiskilled workers in these cells allows the costs of setup, minor maintenance, and quality inspection to become easily traced direct costs.

The next section discusses *backflush costing*, which is a job-costing system that dovetails with JIT production and is less costly to operate than most traditional costing systems described in Chapters 4, 7, 8, and 9.

BACKFLUSH COSTING

A unique production system such as JIT often leads to its own unique costing system. Organizing manufacturing in cells, reducing defects and manufacturing lead time, and ensuring timely delivery of materials enables purchasing, production, and

Curriculum Linkage Chap. 19 discusses financial and nonfinancial measures of quality and time. In particular, it introduces comprehensive COQ reports and effects of bottlenecks and uncertainty on manufacturing lead-time.

Points to Stress Personal observation is often more effective in JIT plants than in traditional plants. A JIT plant's production process layout is streamlined and logically laid out, and operations aren't obscured by piles of inventory or rework. Such plants are easier to evaluate visually than cluttered plants where the flow of production proceeds haphazardly across the plant.

Points to Stress/Curriculum Linkage Significant changes in the production process mean that mgrs. should consider changing their acctg. systems to dovetail with the new production process. Companies that adopt JIT tend to move toward simpler costing systems. They move away from detailed job costing (Chap. 4), toward process costing (Chap. 17). They also tend to move away from normal costing (Chap. 4) and sequential tracking std. costing (Chaps. 7 and 8), toward backflush std. costing.

sales to occur in quick succession with minimal inventories. The absence of inventories makes choices about cost-flow assumptions (such as weighted-average or first-in, first-out) or inventory costing methods (such as absorption or variable costing) unimportant—all manufacturing costs of the accounting period flow directly into cost of goods sold. The rapid conversion of direct materials to finished goods that are immediately sold simplifies job costing.

Simplified Normal or Standard Job Costing

Traditional normal and standard costing systems (discussed in Chapters 4, 7, and 8) use **sequential tracking**, which is any product-costing method where recording of the journal entries occurs in the same order as actual purchases and progress in production. These traditional systems track costs sequentially as products pass through the following four stages in a cycle going from purchase of direct materials to sale of finished goods:

Correcting Student Misconceptions
Many companies are finding it difficult to successfully maintain low inventories. Some are increasing safety stocks to accommodate customer demands for faster delivery and unforeseen but not unusual events such as strikes and raw material shortages arising due to tightened capacity in many industries. (*WSJ*, 10/20/94.)

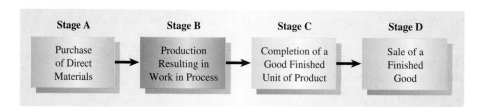

A sequential tracking costing system has four trigger points, corresponding to separate journal entries being made at stages A, B, C, and D. The term **trigger point** refers to a stage in the cycle going from purchase of direct materials (stage A) to sale of finished goods (stage D) at which journal entries are made in the accounting system.

An alternative approach to sequential tracking is backflush costing. **Backflush costing** is a costing system that omits recording some or all of the journal entries relating to the cycle from purchase of direct materials to the sale of finished goods. Where journal entries for one or more stages in the cycle are omitted, the journal entries for a subsequent stage use normal or standard costs to work backward to flush out the costs in the cycle for which journal entries were not made.

The following three examples illustrate backflush costing. To underscore basic concepts, we assume no direct materials variances in any of the examples. The three examples differ in the number and placement of trigger points at which journal entries are made in the accounting system:

Teaching Tip Backflush costing arose as an attempt to streamline and remove nonvalue-added activities from cost acctg. systems. (Sequential tracking is nonvalue-added; sequence—i.e., FIFO or WA—doesn't make much difference provided that inventories are low or stable.)

OBJECTIVE 8

Describe different ways blackflush costing can simplify traditional job-costing systems

Teaching Tip/Reinforcing Problems
Students find backflush costing an interesting innovation in response to JIT. However, they are often confused by the apparent "backward" sequence of the journal entries. Examples 1, 2, and 3 introduce many new concepts, so it's worthwhile to walk the class through a set of homework exercises such as Exer. 20-23 through 20-25, or else Probs. 20-31 through 20-33, or 20-34 through 20-36. Emphasize the logical flow of costs through the T-accounts as in Exh. 20-7 and 20-8. Probs. 20-37 and 20-38 combine backflush costing with ethics and collaborative learning.

	Number of Journal Entry Trigger Points	Location in Cycle Where Journal Entries Made
Example 1	3	Stage A. Purchase of direct materials (called "raw materials")
		Stage C. Completion of good finished units of product
		Stage D. Sale of finished goods
Example 2	2	Stage A. Purchase of direct materials ("raw materials")
		Stage D. Sale of finished goods
Example 3	2	Stage C. Completion of good finished units of product
		Stage D. Sale of finished goods

In all three examples, there are no journal entries in the accounting system for work in process (stage C). These three examples of backflush costing are typically used where the amounts of work in process are small. With JIT production, sizable reductions in work in process have occurred.

Example 1: Trigger points are purchase of direct materials (Stage A), completion of good finished units of product (Stage C), and sale of finished goods (Stage D)

This example uses three trigger points to illustrate how backflushing can eliminate the need for a separate Work-in-Process account. Consider Silicon Valley Computer (SVC), which produces keyboards for personal computers. For April, there were no beginning inventories of raw materials. Moreover, there is zero beginning and ending work in process.

SVC has only one direct manufacturing cost category (raw materials) and one indirect manufacturing cost category (conversion costs). All manufacturing labor costs are included in conversion costs. From its bill of materials (description of the types and quantities of materials) and an operations list (description of operations to be undergone), SVC determines the April standard direct materials costs per keyboard unit of $19 and the standard conversion costs of $12.

SVC has two inventory accounts:

Type	Account Title
Combined materials inventory and materials in work in process	Inventory: Raw and In-Process Control
Finished goods	Finished Goods Control

Trigger point 1 occurs when materials are purchased. These costs are charged to Inventory: Raw and In-Process Control. Actual conversion costs are recorded as incurred under backflush costing, just as in other costing systems, and charged to Conversion Costs Control. Conversion costs are allocated to products at trigger point 2—the transfer of units to Finished Goods Control. Trigger point 3 occurs at the time finished goods are sold. This example assumes that under- or overallocated conversion costs are written off to cost of goods sold monthly.

Points to Stress Note that the actual conversion costs are recorded as incurred throughout the period.

SVC takes the following steps when assigning costs to units sold and to inventories.

Step 1: Record the Direct Materials Purchased During the Accounting Period   Assume April purchases of $1,950,000:

| Entry (a) | Inventory: Raw and In-Process Control | 1,950,000 | |
| | Accounts Payable Control | | 1,950,000 |

Step 2: Record the Incurrence of Conversion Costs During the Accounting Period   Assume conversion costs were $1,260,000:

| Entry (b) | Conversion Costs Control | 1,260,000 | |
| | Various accounts (such as Wages Payable) | | 1,260,000 |

Step 3: Determine the Number of Good Finished Units Manufactured During the Accounting Period   Assume that 100,000 good keyboard units were manufactured in April.

Step 4: Compute the Normal or Standard Costs Per Finished Unit   The standard cost is $31 ($19 direct materials + $12 conversion costs) per unit.

Points to Stress The budgeted or std. cost of each finished unit (step 4) could be obtained from a sophisticated ABC system where there are several pools of conversion costs, each with its own allocation base.

Step 5: Record the Cost of Good Finished Goods Completed During the Accounting Period   100,000 units × $31 = $3,100,000.

Entry (c)	Finished Goods Control	3,100,000	
	Inventory: Raw and In-Process Control		1,900,000
	Conversion Costs Allocated		1,200,000

This step gives backflush costing its name. Note that costs have not been recorded sequentially with the flow of product along its production route through work in process and finished goods. Instead, the output trigger point reaches back and pulls the standard costs of direct materials from Inventory: Raw and In-Process and the standard conversion costs for manufacturing the finished goods.

Points to Stress Because there's no WIP account, the same costs that would normally be allocated to WIP (DM and conversion costs, including DL and MOH) are allocated directly to FG under backflush costing. Explain that this flow of costs is analogous to that in Chap. 4, except here backflush costing bypasses the WIP account.

Step 6: Record the Cost of Goods Sold During the Accounting Period   Assume that 99,000 units were sold in April (99,000 units × $31 = $3,069,000):

| Entry (d) | Cost of Goods Sold | 3,069,000 | |
| | Finished Goods Control | | 3,069,000 |

Step 7: Record Under- or Overallocated Conversion Costs Actual conversion costs may be under- or overallocated in any given accounting period. Chapter 4 (pp. 113–117) discussed various ways to account for under- or overallocated manufacturing overhead costs. Many companies write off underallocations or overallocations to cost of goods sold only at year-end. Other companies, like SVC, do so monthly. Companies that use backflush costing typically have low inventories, so proration of under- or overallocated conversion costs between finished goods and cost of goods sold is less often necessary. The journal entry for the $60,000 difference between actual conversion costs incurred and standard conversion costs allocated would be:

Entry (e)	Conversion Costs Allocated	1,200,000	
	Cost of Goods Sold	60,000	
	Conversion Costs Control		1,260,000

The April ending inventory balances are:

Inventory: Raw and In-Process Control ($1,950,000 − $1,900,000)	$50,000
Finished Goods Control, 1,000 units × $31 ($3,100,000 − $3,069,000)	31,000
Total inventories	$81,000

Exhibit 20-7, Panel A (on p. 732), summarizes the journal entries for this example. Exhibit 20-8, Panel A (on p. 733), provides a general-ledger overview of this version of backflush costing. The elimination of the typical Work-in-Process account reduces the amount of detail in the accounting system. Units on the production line may still be tracked in physical terms, but there is "no attaching of costs" to specific work orders as they flow through the production cycle. In fact, there are no work orders or labor time tickets in the accounting system. Champion International uses a method similar to Example 1 in its specialty papers plant.

The use of three trigger points to make journal entries in Example 1 will result in SVC's backflush costing system reporting costs similar to sequential tracking when SVC has minimal work-in-process inventory. In Example 1, any inventories of raw materials or finished goods are recognized in SVC's backflush costing system when they first appear (as would be done in a costing system using sequential tracking).

Accounting for Variances

The accounting for variances between actual costs incurred and standard costs allowed and the disposition of variances is basically the same under all standard costing systems. The procedures are described in Chapters 7 and 8. In Example 1, suppose the direct materials purchased had an unfavorable price variance of $42,000. Entry (a) would then be:

Inventory: Raw and In-Process Control	1,950,000	
Raw Materials Price Variance	42,000	
Accounts Payable Control		1,992,000

Direct materials are often a large proportion of total manufacturing costs, sometimes over 60 percent. Consequently, many companies will at least measure the direct materials efficiency variance in total by physically comparing what remains in direct materials inventory against what should remain, given the output of finished goods for the accounting period. In our example, suppose that such a comparison showed an unfavorable materials efficiency variance of $90,000. The journal entry would be:

Raw Materials Efficiency Variance	90,000	
Inventory: Raw and In-Process Control		90,000

The under- or overallocated manufacturing overhead costs may be split into various overhead variances (spending variance, efficiency variance, and production-volume variance) as explained in Chapter 8.

Example 2: Trigger points are purchase of direct materials (Stage A) and sale of finished goods (Stage D)

This example, also based on SVC and using the same data, presents a backflush costing system that is a more dramatic departure from a sequential tracking costing system than Example 1. The first trigger point in this example is the same as the first trigger point in Example 1 (purchase of raw materials), but the second trigger point is the sale, not the completion of finished units. Toyota's cost accounting at its Kentucky plant is similar to this type of costing system. There are two justifications for this accounting system:

◆ To remove the incentive for managers to produce for inventory. If the finished goods inventory includes conversion costs, managers can bolster operating income by producing more units than are sold. Having trigger point 2 as the sale instead of the completion of production, however, reduces the attractiveness of producing for inventory by recording conversion costs as period costs instead of capitalizing them as inventoriable costs.

◆ To increase the focus of managers on selling units.

This variation of backflush costing treats all conversion costs as period costs.

The inventory account in this example is confined solely to direct materials (whether they are in storerooms, in process, or in finished goods). There is only one inventory account:

Type	Account Title
Combines direct materials inventory and any direct materials in work-in-process and finished goods inventories	Inventory Control

Exhibit 20-7, Panel B, presents the journal entries in this case. The two trigger points are represented by transactions (a) and (d). Entry (a) is prompted by the same trigger point 1 as in Example 1, the purchase of direct materials. Entry (b) for the conversion costs incurred is recorded in an identical manner as in Example 1. Trigger point 2 is the sale of good finished units (not their production, as in Example 1), so there is no entry corresponding to entry (c) of Example 1. The cost of finished units is computed only when finished units are sold [which corresponds to entry (d) of Example 1]: 99,000 units sold × $31 = $3,069,000, consisting of direct materials (99,000 × $19 = $1,881,000) and conversion costs allocated (99,000 × $12 = $1,188,000).

No conversion costs are inventoried. That is, compared to Example 1, Example 2 does not attach $12,000 ($12 per unit × 1,000 units) of conversion costs to finished goods inventory. Hence, Example 2 allocates $12,000 less in conversion costs to inventory relative to Example 1. Of the $1,260,000 in conversion costs, $1,188,000 is allocated at standard cost to the units sold. The remaining $72,000 ($1,260,000 − $1,188,000) of conversion costs is underallocated. Entry (e) in Exhibit 20-7, Panel B, presents the journal entry if SVC, like many companies, writes off these underallocated costs monthly as additions to cost of goods sold.

The April ending balance of Inventory Control is $69,000 ($50,000 direct materials still on hand + $19,000 direct materials embodied in the 1,000 units manufactured but not sold during the period). Exhibit 20-8, Panel B, provides a general-ledger overview of this version of backflush costing. Entries are keyed to Exhibit 20-7, Panel B. The approach described in Example 2 closely approximates the costs computed using sequential tracking when a company holds minimal work-in-process and minimal finished goods inventories.

Example 3: Trigger points are completion of good finished units of product (Stage C) and sale of finished goods (Stage D)

This example has two trigger points. In contrast to Example 2, the first trigger point is delayed until SVC's completion of good finished units of product. Exhibit 20-7, Panel C, presents the journal entries in this case, using the same data as in

EXHIBIT 20-7
Journal Entries in Backflush Costing

PANEL A, EXAMPLE 1: THREE TRIGGER POINTS—PURCHASE OF RAW MATERIALS, COMPLETION OF FINISHED GOODS, AND SALE OF FINISHED GOODS

Transactions

(a) Purchases of raw materials	Inventory: Raw and In-Process Control	1,950,000	
	Accounts Payable Control		1,950,000
(b) Incur conversion costs	Conversion Costs Control	1,260,000	
	Various Accounts		1,260,000
(c) Completion of finished goods	Finished Goods Control	3,100,000	
	Inventory: Raw and In-Process Control		1,900,000
	Conversion Costs Allocated		1,200,000
(d) Sale of finished goods	Cost of Goods Sold	3,069,000	
	Finished Goods Control		3,069,000
(e) Under- or overallocated conversion costs	Conversion Costs Allocated	1,200,000	
	Cost of Goods Sold	60,000	
	Conversion Costs Control		1,260,000

PANEL B, EXAMPLE 2: TWO TRIGGER POINTS—PURCHASE OF RAW MATERIALS AND SALE OF FINISHED GOODS

Transactions

(a) Purchases of raw materials	Inventory Control	1,950,000	
	Accounts Payable Control		1,950,000
(b) Incur conversion costs	Conversion Costs Control	1,260,000	
	Various Accounts		1,260,000
(c) Completion of finished goods	No entry		
(d) Sale of finished goods	Cost of Goods Sold	3,069,000	
	Inventory Control		1,881,000
	Conversion Costs Allocated		1,188,000
(e) Under- or overallocated conversion costs	Conversion Costs Allocated	1,188,000	
	Cost of Goods Sold	72,000	
	Conversion Costs Control		1,260,000

PANEL C, EXAMPLE 3: TWO TRIGGER POINTS—COMPLETION OF FINISHED GOODS AND SALE OF FINISHED GOODS

Transactions

(a) Purchases of raw materials	No entry		
(b) Incur conversion costs	Conversion Costs Control	1,260,000	
	Various Accounts		1,260,000
(c) Completion of finished goods	Finished Goods Control	3,100,000	
	Accounts Payable Control		1,900,000
	Conversion Costs Allocated		1,200,000
(d) Sale of finished goods	Cost of Goods Sold	3,069,000	
	Finished Goods Control		3,069,000
(e) Under- or overallocated conversion costs	Conversion Costs Allocated	1,200,000	
	Cost of Goods Sold	60,000	
	Conversion Costs Control		1,260,000

EXHIBIT 20-8
General-Ledger Overview of Backflush Costing

PANEL A, EXAMPLE 1: THREE TRIGGER POINTS—PURCHASE OF RAW MATERIALS, COMPLETION OF FINSHED GOODS, AND SALE OF FINISHED GOODS

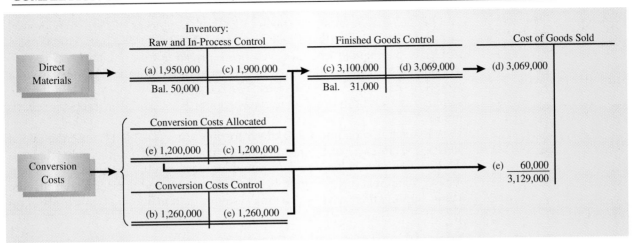

PANEL B, EXAMPLE 2: TWO TRIGGER POINTS—PURCHASE OF RAW MATERIALS AND SALE OF FINISHED GOODS

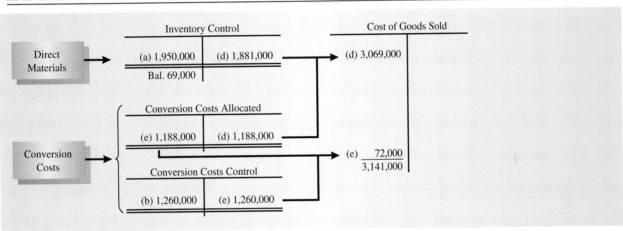

PANEL C, EXAMPLE 3: TWO TRIGGER POINTS—COMPLETION OF FINISHED GOODS AND SALE OF FINISHED GOODS

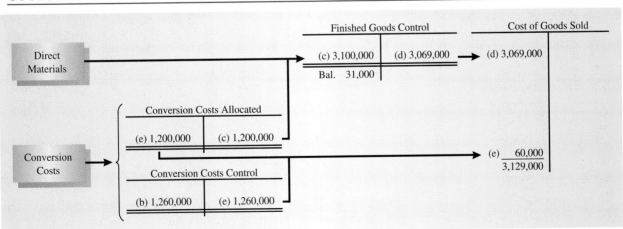

Examples 1 and 2. The first trigger point is represented by transaction (c). Note that since the purchase of direct materials is not a trigger point, there is no entry corresponding to transaction (a)—purchases of direct materials. Exhibit 20-8, Panel C, provides a general-ledger overview of this version of backflush costing. Entries are keyed to Exhibit 20-7, Panel C.

Compare entry (c) in Exhibit 20-7, Panel C, with entries (a) and (c) in Exhibit 20-7, Panel A. The simpler version in Example 3 ignores the $1,950,000 purchases of direct materials [entry (a) of Example 1]. At the end of April, $50,000 of direct materials purchased have not yet been placed into production ($1,950,000 − $1,900,000 = $50,000), nor have they been entered into the inventory costing system. The Example 3 version of backflush costing is suitable for a JIT production system in which both direct materials inventory and work-in-process inventory are minimal.

Extending Example 3, backflush costing systems could also use the sale of finished goods (instead of the production of finished goods) as the only trigger point. This version of backflush costing would be most suitable for a JIT production system with minimal direct materials, work-in-process, and finished goods inventories. Why? Because this backflush costing system would maintain no inventory accounts.

Special Consideration of Backflush Costing

The accounting procedures illustrated in Examples 1, 2, and 3 do not strictly adhere to generally accepted accounting principles. For example, work in process (an asset) exists but is not recognized in the financial statements. Advocates of backflush costing, however, cite the materiality concept in support of these versions of backflushing. As the three backflush examples illustrate, backflush costing can sometimes approximate the costs that would be reported under sequential costing methods by varying the number of trigger points and their location. If material amounts of raw materials inventory or finished goods inventory exist, adjusting entries can be incorporated into backflush costing (as explained below).

Backflush costing is not restricted to companies adopting JIT production methods. Companies that have fast manufacturing lead times, or those that have very stable inventory levels from period to period, may find that a version of backflush costing will report cost numbers similar to what a sequential costing approach would report.

Suppose material differences in operating income and inventories do exist between the results of a backflush costing system and those of a conventional standard costing system. An adjustment can be recorded to make the backflush number satisfy external reporting requirements. For example, the backflush entries in Example 2 would result in expensing all conversion costs as a part of allocated conversion costs in Cost of Goods Sold ($1,188,000 at standard costs + $72,000 write-off of underallocated conversion costs = $1,260,000). But suppose conversion costs were regarded as sufficiently material in amount to be included in Inventory Control. Then entry (e), closing the Conversion Costs accounts, would change as follows:

Original entry (e)	Conversion Costs Allocated	1,188,000	
	Cost of Goods Sold	72,000	
	Conversion Costs Control		1,260,000
Revised entry (e)	Conversion Costs Allocated	1,188,000	
	Inventory Control (1,000 units × $12)	12,000	
	Cost of Goods Sold	60,000	
	Conversion Costs Control		1,260,000

Criticisms of backflush costing focus mainly on the absence of audit trails—the ability of the accounting system to pinpoint the uses of resources at each step of the production process. The absence of large amounts of materials and work-in-process inventory means that managers can keep track of operations by personal observations, computer monitoring, and nonfinancial measures.

What are the implications of JIT and backflush costing systems for activity-based costing (ABC) systems? Simplifying the production process, as in a JIT system, makes more of the costs direct and so reduces the extent of overhead cost allocations. Simplified ABC systems are often adequate for companies implementing JIT. But even these simpler ABC systems can enhance backflush costing. Costs from ABC systems give relatively more accurate budgeted conversion costs per unit for different products, which are then used in the backflush costing system. The activity-based cost data are also useful for product costing, decision making, and cost management.

PROBLEM 1

The Lee Company has a Singapore plant that manufactures transistor radios. One key component is a XT transistor. Expected demand for radio production in March 2000 is 5,200 transistors. Lee purchases the XT transistor from Singapore Electronics. Lee estimates the ordering cost per purchase order to be $250. The carrying cost for one unit of XT in stock is $5.00.

Required
1. Compute the EOQ for the XT transistor.
2. Compute the number of deliveries of XT that Singapore Electronics will make in April 2000.

SOLUTION

1. $\text{EOQ} = \sqrt{\dfrac{2 \times 5,200 \times \$250}{\$5}}$

   $= 721$ transistors (rounded)

2. Number of deliveries $= \dfrac{5,200}{721}$

   $= 7.2$

Singapore will make approximately 8 deliveries (rounded up) in March 2000.

PROBLEM 2

The Lee Company (from Problem 1) seeks to streamline the costing system at its Singapore plant. It will use a backflush costing system with three trigger points:

◆ Purchase of raw materials
◆ Completion of good finished units of product
◆ Sale of finished goods

There are no beginning inventories. The following data pertain to April 2000:

Raw materials purchased	$ 880,000
Raw materials used	850,000
Conversion costs incurred	422,000
Conversion costs allocated	400,000
Costs transferred to finished goods	1,250,000
Costs of goods sold	1,190,000

Required
1. Prepare summary journal entries for April (without disposing of under- or overallocated conversion costs). Assume no direct materials variances.
2. Under an ideal JIT production system, how would the amounts in your journal entries differ from those in requirement 1?

SOLUTION

1. Journal entries for April are as follows:

Entry (a)	Inventory: Raw and In-Process Control	880,000	
	Accounts Payable Control		880,000
	(raw materials purchased)		
Entry (b)	Conversion Costs Control	422,000	
	Various accounts (such as Wages Payable Control)		422,000
	(conversion costs incurred)		
Entry (c)	Finished Goods Control	1,250,000	
	Inventory: Raw and In-Process Control		850,000
	Conversion Costs Allocated		400,000
	(standard cost of finished goods completed)		
Entry (d)	Cost of Goods Sold	1,190,000	
	Finished Goods Control		1,190,000
	(standard costs of finished goods sold)		

2. Under an ideal JIT production system, if the manufacturing lead time per unit is very short, there conceivably would be zero inventories at the end of each day. Entry (c) would be $1,190,000 finished goods production, not $1,250,000. If the Marketing Department could only sell goods costing $1,190,000, the JIT production system would call for direct materials purchases and conversion costs of lower than $880,000 and $422,000, respectively, in entries (a) and (b).

SUMMARY

The following points are linked to the chapter's learning objectives:

1. Five categories of costs associated with goods for sale are purchasing costs, ordering costs (costs of preparing a purchase order and receiving goods), carrying costs (costs of holding inventory of goods for sale), stockout costs (costs arising when a customer demands a unit of product and that unit is not on hand), and quality costs (prevention costs, appraisal costs, internal failure costs, and external failure costs).

2. The economic-order-quantity (EOQ) decision model calculates the optimal quantity of inventory to order by balancing ordering costs and carrying costs. The larger the order quantity, the higher the annual carrying costs and the lower the annual ordering costs. The EOQ model includes both costs routinely recorded in the accounting system and opportunity costs not routinely recorded in the accounting system.

3. The opportunity cost of investment tied up in inventory is a key input in the EOQ decision model. Some companies now include opportunity costs as well as actual costs when evaluating managers so that there is goal congruence between managers and the company.

4. Supply-chain analysis describes the flow of goods, services, and information from cradle to grave (womb to tomb), regardless of whether those activities occur in the same organization or in other organizations.

5. Materials requirements planning (MRP) systems take a "push-through" approach that manufactures finished goods for inventory on the basis of demand forecasts. Just-in-time (JIT) production systems take a "demand-pull" approach in which goods are only manufactured to satisfy customer orders.

6. The five major features of a JIT production system are (a) organizing production in manufacturing cells, (b) hiring and retaining multiskilled workers, (c) emphasizing total quality management, (d) reducing manufacturing lead time and setup time, and (e) building strong supplier relationships.

7. Backflush costing describes a costing system that delays recording some or all of the journal entries relating to the cycle from purchase of direct materials to the sale of finished goods.

8. Traditional job-costing systems use sequential tracking where recording of the journal entries occurs in the same order as actual purchases and progress in production. Most backflush costing systems do not record journal entries for the work-in-process stage of production. Some backflush costing systems also do not record entries for either the purchase of direct materials or the completion of finished goods.

▼ TERMS TO LEARN

This chapter and the Glossary at the end of the book contain definitions of the following important terms:

backflush costing (p. 728)
carrying costs (712)
economic order quantity (EOQ) (713)
inventory management (712)
just-in-time (JIT) production (726)
just-in-time (JIT) purchasing (719)
lean production (726)
manufacturing cells (726)
materials requirements planning (MRP) (725)

ordering costs (712)
purchasing costs (712)
purchase-order lead time (713)
reorder point (714)
safety stock (715)
sequential tracking (728)
stockout (712)
trigger point (728)

▼ ASSIGNMENT MATERIAL

QUESTIONS

20-1 Why do better decisions regarding the purchasing and managing of goods for sale frequently cause dramatic percentage increases in net income?

20-2 Name five cost categories that are important in managing goods for sale in a retail organization.

20-3 What assumptions are made when using the simplest version of the economic-order-quantity (EOQ) decision model?

20-4 Give examples of costs included in annual carrying costs of inventory when using the EOQ decision model.

20-5 Give three examples of opportunity costs that typically are not recorded in accounting systems, although they are relevant to the EOQ model.

20-6 What are the steps in computing the cost of a prediction error when using the EOQ decision model?

20-7 Why might goal-congruence issues arise when an EOQ model is used to guide decisions on how much to order?

20-8 Describe just-in-time (JIT) purchasing and its benefits.

20-9 What are three factors causing reductions in the cost to place purchase orders of materials?

20-10 Describe how the Internet can be used to reduce the costs of placing purchase orders.

20-11 What is supply-chain analysis and how can it benefit manufacturers and retailers?

20-12 What are some obstacles to companies adopting a supply-chain approach?

20-13 What are the main features in a JIT production system?

20-14 Distinguish job-costing systems using sequential tracking from backflush costing.

20-15 Describe three different versions of backflush costing:

EXERCISES

20-16 Economic order quantity for retailer. Football World (FW) operates a mega-store featuring sports merchandise. It uses an EOQ decision model to make inventory decisions. It is now considering inventory decisions for its San Francisco 49er's jerseys product line. This is a highly popular item. Data for 2001 are:

Expected annual demand for 49er's jerseys	10,000
Ordering costs for purchase order	$225
Carrying costs per year	$10 per jersey

Each jersey costs FW $40 and sells for $75. The $10 carrying cost per jersey comprises the required annual return on investment of $3.20 (12% × $40 purchase price) plus $6.80 relevant insurance, handling costs, and theft-related costs. The purchasing lead time is 7 days. FW is open 365 days a year.

Required
1. Calculate the EOQ.
2. Calculate the number of orders that will be placed each year.
3. Calculate the reorder point.

20-17 Economic order quantity, effect of parameter changes (continuation of 20-16). Athletic Products (AP) manufactures the 49er's jerseys that Football World (FW) sells to its customers. AP has recently installed computer software that enables its customers to conduct "one-stop" purchasing using state-of-the-art website technology developed by Cisco Systems. FW's ordering cost per purchase order will be $20 using this new technology.

Required
1. Calculate the EOQ for the 49er's jerseys using the revised ordering cost of $20 per purchase order. Assume all other data from Exercise 20-16 are the same. Comment on the result.
2. Suppose AP proposes to "assist" FW. AP will allow FW's customers to order directly from the AP website. AP would ship directly to these customers. AP would pay $10 to FW for every 49er's jersey purchased by one of FW's customers. How would this offer affect inventory management at FW? Should FW accept AP's proposal? Explain.

 20-18 EOQ for a retailer. The Cloth Center buys and sells fabrics to a wide range of industrial and consumer users. One of the products it carries is denim cloth, used in the manufacture of jeans and carrying bags. The supplier for the denim cloth pays all incoming freight. No incoming inspection of the denim is necessary because the supplier has a track record of delivering high-quality merchandise. The purchasing officer of the Cloth Center has collected the following information:

Annual demand for denim cloth	20,000 yards
Ordering costs per purchase order	$160
Carrying costs per year	20% of purchase costs
Safety stock requirements	None
Cost of denim cloth	$8 per yard

The purchasing lead time is 2 weeks. The Cloth Center is open 250 days a year (50 weeks for 5 days a week).

Required
1. Calculate the EOQ for denim cloth.
2. Calculate the number of orders that will be placed each year.
3. Calculate the reorder point for denim cloth.

 20-19 EOQ for manufacturer. Beaumont Corporation makes air conditioners. It purchases 12,000 units of a particular type of compressor part, CU29, each year at a cost of $50 per unit. Beaumont requires a 12% annual return on investment. In addition, relevant carrying costs (for insurance, materials handling, breakage, and so on) are $2 per unit per year. Relevant costs per purchase order are $120.

Required

1. Calculate Beaumont's EOQ for CU29.
2. Calculate Beaumont's total relevant ordering and carrying costs.
3. Assume that demand is uniform throughout the year and is known with certainty. The purchasing lead time is half a month. Calculate Beaumont's reorder point for CU29.

20-20 Economic order quantity for retailer, ordering and carrying costs. Office Emporium (OE) is deciding the purchase-order quantity for a new modem product. Annual demand is 20,000 units. Ordering costs per purchase order are $120. Carrying costs per modem unit are $10 per year. OE uses an EOQ model in its purchasing decisions. OE is open 360 days a year.

Required

1. Calculate OE's EOQ for modems.
2. Calculate OE's total relevant ordering and carrying costs.
3. Assume that demand is known with certainty and the purchasing lead time is five days. Calculate OE's reorder point for modems.

20-21 Purchase-order size for retailer, EOQ, just-in-time purchasing. The 24 Hour Mart operates a chain of supermarkets. Its best-selling soft drink is Fruitslice. Demand in April for Fruitslice at its Memphis supermarket is estimated to be 6,000 cases (24 cans in each case). In March, the Memphis supermarket estimated the ordering costs per purchase order (P) for Fruitslice to be $30. The carrying costs (C) of each case of Fruitslice in inventory for a month were estimated to be $1. At the end of March, the Memphis 24-Hour Mart reestimated its carrying costs to be $1.50 per case per month to take into account an increase in warehouse-related costs.

During March, 24-Hour Mart restructured its relationship with suppliers. It reduced the number of suppliers from 600 to 180. Long-term contracts were signed only with those suppliers that agreed to make product-quality checks before shipping. Each purchase order would be made by linking into the suppliers' computer network. The Memphis 24-Hour Mart estimated that these changes would reduce the ordering costs per purchase order to $5. The 24-Hour Mart is open 30 days in April.

Required

1. Calculate the EOQ in April for Fruitslice. Assume in turn:
   a. $D = 6,000; P = \$30; C = \$1$
   b. $D = 6,000; P = \$30; C = \$1.50$
   c. $D = 6,000; P = \$5; C = \$1.50$
2. How does your answer to requirement 1 give insight into the retailer's movement toward JIT purchasing policies?

20-22 JIT production, relevant benefits, relevant costs. The Evans Corporation manufactures wireless telephones. Evans is planning to implement a JIT production system, which requires annual tooling costs of $150,000. Evans estimates that the following annual benefits would arise from JIT production.

a. Average inventory will decline by $700,000, from $900,000 to $200,000.
b. Insurance, space, materials-handling, and setup costs, which currently total $200,000, would decline by 30 percent.
c. The emphasis on quality inherent in JIT systems would reduce rework costs by 20%. Evans currently incurs $350,000 on rework.
d. Better quality would enable Evans to raise the selling prices of its products by $3 per unit. Evans sells 30,000 units each year.

Evans's required rate of return on inventory investment is 12% per year.

Required

1. Calculate the net benefit or cost to the Evans Corporation from implementing a JIT production system.
2. What other nonfinancial and qualitative factors should Evans consider before deciding on whether it should implement a JIT system?

20-23 Backflush costing and JIT production. Road Warrior Corp. assembles hand-held computers that have scaled-down capabilities of laptop computers. Each hand-held computer takes 6 hours to assemble. Road Warrior uses a JIT production system and a backflush costing system with three trigger points:

◆ Purchase of direct (raw) materials
◆ Completion of good finished units of product
◆ Sale of finished goods

There are no beginning inventories of materials or finished goods. The following data are for August 2000:

Direct (raw) materials purchased	$2,754,000
Direct (raw) materials used	2,733,600
Conversion cost incurred	723,600
Conversion costs allocated	750,400

Road Warrior records direct materials purchased and conversion costs incurred at actual costs. When finished goods are sold, the backflush costing system "pulls through" standard direct materials costs ($102 per unit) and standard conversion costs ($28 per unit). It produced 26,800 finished goods units in August 2000 and sold 26,400 units. The actual direct materials cost per unit in August 2000 was $102 while the actual conversion cost per unit was $27.

Required

1. Prepare summary journal entries for August 2000 (without disposing of under- or overallocated conversion costs).
2. Post the entries in requirement 1 to T-accounts for applicable Inventory: Raw and In-Process, Conversion Costs Control, Conversion Costs Allocated, and Cost of Goods Sold.
3. Under an ideal JIT production system, how would the amounts in your journal entries differ from those in requirement 1?

20-24 Backflush costing, two trigger points, materials purchase and sale (continuation of 20-23). Assume the same facts in Exercise 20-23, except for the following change. Road Warrior Corp. now uses a backflush costing system with the following two trigger points:

◆ Purchase of direct (raw) materials
◆ Sale of finished goods

The Inventory Control account here will include direct materials purchased but not yet in production, materials in work in process, and materials in finished goods but not sold. No conversion costs are inventoried. Any under- or overallocated conversion costs are written off monthly to Cost of Goods Sold.

Required

1. Prepare summary journal entries for August, including the disposition of under- or overallocated conversion costs.
2. Post the entries in requirement 1 to T-accounts for Inventory Control, Conversion Costs Control, Conversion Costs Allocated, and Cost of Goods Sold.

20-25 Backflush costing, two trigger points, completion of production and sale (continuation of 20-23). Assume the same facts as in Exercise 20-23 except now Road Warrior uses only two trigger points, the completion of a good finished unit of product and the sale of finished goods. Any under- or overallocated conversion costs are written off monthly to cost of goods sold.

Required

1. Prepare summary journal entries for August, including the disposition of under- or overallocated conversion costs.
2. Post the entries in requirement 1 to T-accounts for Finished Goods Control, Conversion Cost Control, Conversion Costs Allocated, and Costs of Goods Sold.

PROBLEMS

20-26 Effect of different order quantities on ordering costs and carrying costs, EOQ. Koala Blue retails a broad line of Australian merchandise at its Santa Monica store. It sells 26,000 Ken Done linen bedroom packages (two sheets and two pillow cases) each year. Koala Blue pays Ken Done Merchandise, Inc., $104 per package. Its ordering costs per purchase order are $72. The carrying costs per package are $10.40 per year.

Liv Carrol, manager of the Santa Monica store, seeks your advice on how ordering costs and carrying costs vary with different order quantities. Ken Done Merchandise, Inc., guarantees the $104 purchase cost per package for the 26,000 units budgeted to be purchased in the coming year.

Required

1. Compute the annual ordering costs, the annual carrying costs, and their sum for purchase-order quantities of 300, 500, 600, 700, and 900. What is the EOQ? Comment on your results.

2. Assume that Ken Done Merchandise, Inc., introduces a computerized ordering network for its customers. Liv Carrol estimates that Koala Blue's ordering costs will be reduced to $40 per purchase order. How will this reduction in ordering costs affect the EOQ for Koala Blue on their linen bedroom packages?

20-27 EOQ, uncertainty, safety stock, reorder point. (CMA adapted) The Starr Company distributes a wide range of electrical products. One of its best-selling items is a standard electric motor. The management of the Starr Company uses the EOQ decision model to determine the optimal number of motors to order. Management now wants to determine how much safety stock to hold.

The Starr Company estimates annual demand (300 working days) to be 30,000 electric motors. Using the EOQ decision model, the company orders 3,000 motors at a time. The lead time for an order is 5 days. The annual carrying costs of one motor in safety stock are $10. Management has also estimated that the stockout costs are $20 for each motor they are short.

The Starr Company has analyzed the demand during 200 past reorder periods. The records indicate the following patterns:

Demand During Lead Time	Number of Times Quantity Was Demanded
440	6
460	12
480	16
500	130
520	20
540	10
560	6
	200

Required

1. Determine the level of safety stock for electric motors that the Starr Company should maintain in order to minimize expected stockout costs and carrying costs. When computing carrying costs, assume that the safety stock is on hand at all times and that there is no overstocking caused by decreases in expected demand. (Consider safety stock levels of 0, 20, 40, and 60 units.)

2. What would be the Starr Company's new reorder point?

3. What factors should the Starr Company have considered in estimating the stockout costs?

20-28 EOQ, cost of prediction error. Ralph Menard is the owner of a truck repair shop. He uses an EOQ model for each of his truck parts. He initially predicts the annual demand for heavy-duty tires to be 2,000. Each tire has a purchase price of $50. The incremental ordering costs per purchase order are $40. The incremental carrying costs per year are $4 per tire plus 10% of the supplier's purchase price per tire.

Required

1. Calculate the EOQ for heavy-duty tires, along with the sum of annual relevant ordering costs and carrying costs.

2. Suppose Menard is correct in all his predictions except the purchase price. (He ignored a new law that abolished tariff duties on imported heavy-duty tires, which led to lower prices from foreign competitors.) If he had been a faultless predictor, he would have foreseen that the purchase price would drop to $30 at the beginning of the year and would be unchanged throughout the year. What is the cost of the prediction error?

20-29 JIT purchasing, relevant benefits, relevant costs. (CMA adapted) The Margro Corporation is an automotive supplier that uses automatic turning machines to manufacture precision parts from steel bars. Margro's inventory of raw steel averages $600,000. John

Oates, president of Margro, and Helen Gorman, Margro's controller, are concerned about the costs of carrying inventory. The steel supplier is willing to supply steel in smaller lots at no additional charge. Helen Gorman identified the following effects of adopting a JIT inventory program to virtually eliminate steel inventory:

◆ Without scheduling any overtime, lost sales due to stockouts would increase by 35,000 units per year. However, by incurring overtime premiums of $40,000 per year, the increase in lost sales could be reduced to 20,000 units. This would be the maximum amount of overtime that would be feasible for Margro.

◆ Two warehouses presently used for steel bar storage would no longer be needed. Margro rents one warehouse from another company under a cancelable leasing arrangement at an annual cost of $60,000. The other warehouse is owned by Margro and contains 12,000 square feet. Three-fourths of the space in the owned warehouse could be rented for $1.50 per square foot per year. Insurance and property tax costs totaling $14,000 per year would be eliminated.

Margro's projected operating results for the 2000 calendar year follow. Long-term capital investments by Margro are expected to produce an annual rate of return of 20 percent. Margro Corporation Budgeted Income Statement for the Year Ending December 31, 2000 (in thousands) is as follows:

Revenues (900,000 units)		$10,800
Cost of goods sold		
Variable costs	$4,050	
Fixed costs	1,450	
Total costs of goods sold		5,500
Gross margin		5,300
Marketing and distribution costs		
Variable costs	$ 900	
Fixed costs	1,500	
Total marketing and distribution costs		2,400
Operating income		$ 2,900

Required

1. Calculate the estimated dollar savings (loss) for the Margro Corporation that would result in 2000 from the adoption of the JIT inventory control method.
2. Identify and explain other factors that Margro should consider before deciding whether or not to install a JIT system.

20-30 Supply-chain analysis, company viewpoints. Manufacturing companies participating in a supply-chain initiative linking manufacturers and retailers recently made the following comments on the benefits of the initiative:

◆ "Receiving better information has allowed us to forecast and reduce inventory levels . . . "

◆ "You only produce what you need and that keeps the product and floor cost down."

◆ "There is more accuracy with the retailer's needs so that we can fine tune our production schedule."

◆ "The inventory levels are lower and we have less waste by not overstocking the warehouses."

Manufacturing companies highlighted the following information from retailers as most valuable to them:

◆ "We would like to see [the retailers] forward-planning expectation of their sales."

◆ "We could use retail store level data on a daily basis and better scanner information."

◆ "Better forecasts and decisions about shelving and shelf allocations by retailers would help."

◆ "I wish we had access to each retailer's sales forecasts and the advertisements that they will be running next."

Required

1. What are the major benefits from adopting a supply-chain approach? Use the preceding comments as a prompt to a more detailed discussion. Explain how these benefits can lead to increased operating income.
2. What are the key obstacles to a manufacturer adopting a supply-chain approach?

20-31 Backflush costing and JIT production. The Action Corporation manufactures electrical meters. For August, there were no beginning inventories of raw materials and no beginning and ending work in process. Acton uses a JIT production system and backflush costing with three trigger points for making entries in the accounting system:

◆ Purchase of raw materials—debited to Inventory: Raw and In-Process Control
◆ Completion of good finished units of product—debited to Finished Goods Control
◆ Sale of finished goods

Action's August standard cost per meter is direct materials, $25; conversion costs, $20. The following data apply to August manufacturing:

Raw materials and components purchased	$550,000
Conversion costs incurred	$440,000
Number of finished units manufactured	21,000
Number of finished units sold	20,000

Required

1. Prepare summary journal entries for August (without disposing of under- or overallocated conversion costs). Assume no direct materials variances.
2. Post the entries in requirement 1 to T-accounts for Inventory: Raw and In-Process Control, Conversion Costs Control, Conversion Costs Allocated, and Cost of Goods Sold.

20-32 Backflush, two trigger points, materials purchase and sale (continuation of 20-31). Assume that the second trigger point for Action Corporation is the sale—rather than the production—of finished goods. Also, the inventory account is confined solely to direct materials, whether these materials are in a storeroom, in work in process, or in finished goods. No conversion costs are inventoried. They are allocated to the units sold at standard costs. Any under- or overallocated conversion costs are written off monthly to Cost of Goods Sold.

Required

1. Prepare summary journal entries for August, including the disposition of under- or overallocated conversion costs. Assume no direct materials variances.
2. Post the entries in requirement 1 to T-accounts for Inventory Control, Conversion Costs Control, Conversion Costs Allocated, and Cost of Goods Sold.

20-33 Backflush, two trigger points, completion of production and sale (continuation of 20-31). Assume the same facts as in Problem 20-31 except now there are only two trigger points, the completion of good finished units of product and the sale of finished goods.

Required

1. Prepare summary journal entries for August, including the disposition of under- or overallocated conversion costs. Assume no direct materials variances.
2. Post the entries in requirement 1 to T-accounts for Finished Goods Control, Conversion Costs Control, Conversion Costs Allocated, and Cost of Goods Sold.

20-34 Backflush costing and JIT production. The Ronowski Company produces telephones. For June, there were no beginning inventory of raw materials and no beginning and ending work in process. Ronowski uses a JIT production system and backflush costing with three trigger points for making entries in its accounting system:

◆ Purchase of direct (raw) materials
◆ Completion of good finished units of product
◆ Sale of finished goods

Ronowski's standard cost per unit of telephone in June is direct materials, $26; conversion costs, $15. There are two inventory accounts:

◆ Inventory: Raw and In-Process Control
◆ Finished Goods Control

The following data apply to June manufacturing:

Raw materials and components purchased	$5,300,000
Conversion costs incurred	$3,080,000
Number of finished units manufactured	200,000
Number of finished units sold	192,000

Required

1. Prepare summary journal entries for June (without disposing of under- or overallocated conversion costs). Assume no direct materials variances.
2. Post the entries in requirement 1 to T-accounts for Inventory: Raw and In-Process Control, Conversion Costs Control, Conversion Costs Allocated, and Cost of Goods Sold.

20-35 Backflush, two trigger points, materials purchase and sale (continuation of 20-34). Assume that the second trigger point for Ronowski Company is the sale—rather than the production—of finished units. Also, the inventory account is confined solely to direct materials, whether they would be in a storeroom, in work in process, or in finished goods.

No conversion costs are inventoried. They are allocated to the units sold at standard. Any under- or overallocated conversion costs are written off monthly to Cost of Goods Sold.

Required

1. Prepare summary journal entries for June, including the disposition of under- or overallocated conversion costs. Assume no direct materials variances.
2. Post the entries in requirement 1 to T-accounts for Inventory Control, Conversion Costs Control, Conversion Costs Allocated, and Cost of Goods Sold. Explain the composition of the ending balance of Inventory Control.
3. Suppose conversion costs were sufficiently material in amount to be included in Inventory Control. Using a backflush system, show how your journal entries would be changed in requirement 1.

20-36 Backflush, two trigger points, completion of production and sale (continuation of 20-34). Assume the same facts as in Problem 20-34 except now there are trigger points at the completion of good finished units of product (which are debited to Finished Goods Control at standard costs) and at the sale of finished goods. Any under- or overallocated conversion costs are written off monthly to Cost of Goods Sold.

Required

1. Prepare summary journal entries for June, including the disposition of under- or overallocated conversion costs. Assume no direct materials variances.
2. Post the entries in requirement 1 or T-accounts for Finished Goods Control, Conversion Cost Control, Conversion Costs Allocated, and Cost of Goods Sold. Explain the composition of the ending balance of Inventory Control.
3. If you did Problem 20-34, compare and explain any differences between the results here and those in Problem 20-34.

20-37 Backflush costing, income manipulation, ethics. Carol Brown, the Chief Financial Officer of Silicon Valley Computer (see pp. 729–735), is an enthusiastic advocate of JIT production. The SVC Keyboard Division that produces keyboards for personal computers has made dramatic improvements in its operations by a highly successful JIT implementation. The Keyboard Division president now wants to adopt backflush costing.

Brown discusses the backflush costing proposal with Ralph Strong, the Controller of SVC. Strong is totally opposed to backflush costing. He argues that it will open up "Pandora's box" by allowing division managers to manipulate reported division operating income. A member of Strong's group outlines the three possible variations of backflush costing shown in Exhibit 20-8 (p. 733) Strong notes that none of these three methods track work in process. He asserts that this omission would allow managers to "artificially change" reported operating income by manipulating work in process levels. He is especially scathing about the backflush costing where no entries are made until a sale occurs. He comments:

> Suppose the Division has already met its target operating income and wants to shift some of this year's income to next year. Under backflush costing with sale of finished goods as the trigger point, the Division will have an incentive to not make sales this year of goods produced this year. This is a bizzare incentive. I rest my case about why we should stay with a job-costing system using sequential tracking.

Strong concludes that as long as reported accounting numbers are central to SVC's performance and bonus reviews, backflush costing should never be adopted.

Required

1. What factors should SVC consider in deciding whether to adopt a version of backflush costing?
2. Are Strong's concerns about income manipulation sufficiently important for SVC to not adopt backflush costing?
3. What other ways has SVC to motivate managers to not "artificially change" reported income?

COLLABORATIVE LEARNING PROBLEM

20-38 Backflushing. The following conversation occurred between Brian Richardson, plant manager at Glendale Engineering, and Charles Cheng, plant controller. Glendale manufactures automotive component parts such as gears and crankshafts for automobile manufacturers. Richardson has been very enthusiastic about implementing JIT and about simplifying and streamlining the production and other business processes.

Richardson: "Charles, I would like to substantially simplify our accounting in the new JIT environment. Can't we just record one accounting entry at the time we ship products to our customers? I don't want to have our staff spending time tracking inventory from one stage to the next, when we have as little inventory as we do."

Cheng: "Brian, I think you are right about simplifying the accounting, but we still have a fair amount of raw materials and finished goods inventory that varies from period to period depending on the demand for specific products. Doing away with all inventory accounting may be a problem."

Richardson: "Well, you know my desire to simplify, simplify, simplify. I know that there are some costs of oversimplifying, but I believe that, in the long run, simplification pays dividends. Why don't you and your staff study the issues involved, and I will put it on the agenda for our next senior plant management meeting."

Required

Form groups of two or more students to complete the following requirements.

1. What version of backflush costing would your recommend that Cheng adopt? Remember Richardson's desire to simplify the accounting as much as possible. Develop support for your recommendation.
2. Think about the three examples of backflush costing shown in Exhibit 20-8 (p. 733). These examples differ with respect to the number and types of trigger points used. Suppose your goal of implementing backflush costing is to simplify the accounting, but only if it closely matches the sequential tracking approach. Which version of backflush costing would you propose if:
   a. Glendale had no raw materials and no work-in-process inventories but did have finished goods inventory?
   b. Glendale had no work-in-process and no finished goods inventories but did have raw material inventory?
   c. Glendale had no raw materials, no work-in-process, and no finished goods inventories?
3. Backflush costing has its critics. In an article in the magazine *Management Accounting*, entitled "Beware of the New Accounting Myths," R. Calvasina, E. Calvasina, and G. Calvasina state:

   The periodic (backflush) system has never been reflective of the reporting needs of a manufacturing system. In the highly standardized operating environments of the present JIT era, the appropriate system to be used is a perpetual accounting system based on an up-to-date, realistic set of standard costs. For management accountants to backflush on an actual cost basis is to return to the days of the outdoor privy (toilet).

   Comment on this statement.

Capital Budgeting
and Cost Analysis

When you have finished studying this chapter, you should be able to

1. Adopt the project-by-project orientation of capital budgeting when evaluating projects spanning multiple years
2. Understand the six stages of capital budgeting for a project
3. Use and evaluate the two main discounted cash flow (DCF) methods—the net present value (NPV) method and the internal rate-of-return (IRR) method
4. Identify relevant cash inflows and outflows for capital budgeting decisions that use DCF methods
5. Use and evaluate the payback method
6. Use and evaluate the accrual accounting rate-of-return (AARR) method
7. Identify and reduce conflicts from using DCF for capital budgeting decisions and accrual accounting for performance evaluation
8. Incorporate depreciation deductions into the computation of after-tax cash flows in capital budgeting

Decisions about the size and location of bridges have a long-term horizon in which both financial and nonfinancial factors are important.

Managers continually face the challenge of balancing long-run and short-run issues. We now consider how managers can systematically incorporate financial and nonfinancial aspects into their long-run planning decisions. The methods of analysis we discuss are called capital budgeting methods because they deal with how to select projects (or programs) that increase rather than decrease the "capital" (value) of an organization. These methods assist managers in analyzing projects that span multiple years.

Prior to describing specific capital budgeting methods, we first highlight how cost analysis for the project-by-project focus of capital budgeting differs from cost analysis for the period-by-period focus found in much of accounting.

TWO FOCUSES OF COST ANALYSIS

Exhibit 21-1 illustrates two different dimensions of cost analysis: (1) a project dimension, and (2) an accounting-period dimension. Each project is represented in Exhibit 21-1 as a distinct horizontal rectangle. The life of each project is longer than one year. Capital budgeting focuses on projects over their entire lives in order to consider *all* the cash flows or cash savings from investing in a project. The vertical rectangle in Exhibit 21-1 illustrates the accounting-period focus on income determination and routine planning and control. This cross section emphasizes the company's performance for the 2001 accounting period. The accounting period is of interest to managers because bonuses are frequently based on reported income. Income reported in an accounting period is also important to a company, because it affects the company's stock price. An excessive focus on short-run accounting income, however, may cause a company to forego long-run profitability.

EXHIBIT 21-1
The Project and Time Dimensions of Capital Budgeting

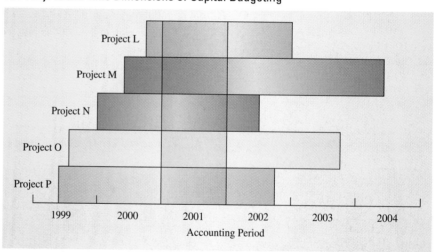

The accounting system that corresponds to the project dimension in Exhibit 21-1 is termed life-cycle costing (also called "cradle to grave" costing). This system, described in Chapter 12, accumulates revenues and costs on a project-by-project basis. For example, a life-cycle costing statement for a new-car project at Ford Motor Company could encompass a seven-year period. It would accumulate costs for all business functions in the value chain, from R&D to customer service expected to be incurred on the project. This accumulation extends the accrual accounting system that measures income on a period-by-period basis to a system that computes cash flow or income over the entire project covering many accounting periods.

STAGES OF CAPITAL BUDGETING

Capital budgeting is the making of long-run planning decisions for investments in projects and programs. It is a decision-making and control tool that focuses primarily on projects or programs that span multiple years. These planning decisions should be guided by the objectives of an organization and its strategies. *Strategy* describes how an organization matches its own capabilities with the opportunities in the marketplace to accomplish its overall objectives. We describe six stages in capital budgeting:

Stage 1: Identification Stage   *To distinguish which types of capital expenditure projects are necessary to accomplish organization objectives.* For example, an objective to increase revenues could be promoted by projects that develop new products, new customers, or new markets. Alternatively, an objective to reduce costs could be promoted by projects that improve productivity and efficiency. Identifying which types of capital projects to invest in is largely the responsibility of line management and should always be linked to the objectives and strategy of the organization.

Stage 2: Search Stage   *To explore alternative capital investments that will achieve organization objectives.* Cross-functional teams from all parts of the value chain evaluate alternative technologies, machines, and project specifications. Some alternatives are rejected early. Others are evaluated more thoroughly in the information-acquisition stage.

Stage 3: Information-Acquisition Stage   *To consider the expected costs and the expected benefits of alternative capital investments.* These costs and benefits can be quantitative or qualitative. Capital budgeting emphasizes quantitative financial factors. But nonfinancial quantitative factors and qualitative factors are also important. Management accountants help identify these factors.

Stage 4: Selection Stage   *To choose projects for implementation.* Organizations choose those projects whose expected benefits exceed expected costs by the greatest amounts. The quantitative analysis includes only expected costs and benefits expressed in financial terms. This chapter outlines alternative decision models that rely on these inputs. Managers reevaluate the conclusions reached on the basis of the formal analysis, using their judgment to take into account nonfinancial considerations.

Stage 5: Financing Stage   *To obtain project funding.* Sources of financing include internally (within the organization) generated cash flow and the capital markets (equity and debt securities). Financing is often the responsibility of the treasury function of an organization.

Stage 6: Implementation and Control Stage   *To get projects underway and monitor their performance.* When the project is implemented, the company must evaluate if capital investments are being made as scheduled and within the budget. As the project generates cash inflows, monitoring and control may include a postinvestment audit in which the projections made at the time the project was selected are compared with the actual results.

We use information from Lifetime Care Hospital to illustrate capital budgeting. We assume first that Lifetime Care is a nonprofit organization and hence not subject to income taxes. Tax considerations in capital budgeting are introduced later in this chapter.

One of Lifetime Care's goals is to improve the productivity of its X-Ray Department. To achieve this goal, the manager of Lifetime Care *identifies* a need to consider the purchase of a new state-of-the-art X-ray machine to replace an existing X-ray machine. The *search* stage yields several alternative models, but the hospital's technical staff focuses on one machine as being particularly suitable—the XCAM8. They next begin to *acquire information* to do a more detailed evaluation. Quantitative financial information for the formal analysis follows:

> Regardless of whether the new X-ray machine is acquired, revenues will not change. Lifetime Care charges a fixed rate for a particular diagnosis, regardless of the number of X-rays taken. The only relevant financial benefit in considering whether to purchase the new X-ray machine is the cash savings in operating costs.
>
> The existing X-ray machine can operate for another five years and will have a terminal disposal price of $0 at the end of five years. The required net initial investment for the new machine is $379,100. The net initial investment

Points to Stress Operating personnel generally perform the *identification* and *search* stages. Accountants help in the *information-acquisition* stage by quantifying, in financial terms, as many consequences of capital expenditures as possible. Accountants also help mgrs. make *selections* by presenting analyses of information (e.g., NPV, IRR, Payback, AARR). The treasurer usually oversees the project's *financing*. Operating personnel *implement* the project. Accountants help in the *control* phase by preparing postinvestment audits. Increasingly, however, there is some blurring of roles as team-based decision making occurs.

Correcting Student Misconceptions/Example Capital budgeting decisions should not be based only on the numbers. Consider a firm deciding on whether to purchase a machine that will replace 10 workers. The project has a positive NPV of $5,000. But is the $5,000 positive NPV sufficient to outweigh potential problems with the union resulting from layoffs?

Correcting Student Misconceptions The reason that income taxes aren't a factor in the text's Lifetime Care illustration is because the organization is a *nonprofit* hospital that, at this stage, we are assuming isn't subject to income taxes.

Correcting Student Misconceptions
Students often fail to appreciate that most capital projects require an increase in working capital (WC) as well as a cash outlay for the fixed assets. This increase in WC consumes cash and so is just as much a part of the investment as is the cost of the fixed assets. The company foregoes interest on this cash until the WC is recovered at the end of the project. It's important that students remember to include additional WC requirements at the beginning of the project and the recovery of WC at the end of the project.

consists of the cost of the new machine—$372,890—plus an additional cash investment in working capital (supplies and spare parts for the new machine) of $10,000 minus cash of $3,790 obtained from the disposal of the existing machine ($372,890 + $10,000 − $3,790 = $379,100).

The manager expects the new machine to have a five-year useful life and a $0 terminal disposal price at the end of five years. The new machine is faster and easier to operate and has the ability to X-ray a larger area. These improvements will decrease labor costs and will reduce the average number of X-rays taken per patient. The manager expects the investment to result in annual cash savings of $100,000 that generally occur uniformly throughout the year. *To simplify computations, all operating cash flows are assumed to occur at the end of the year.* The expected cash savings in operating costs are $100,000 for each of the first four years and $90,000 in year 5. The working capital investment of $10,000 is expected to be recovered in full in year 5.

The manager at Lifetime Care also identifies the following nonfinancial quantitative and qualitative benefits of investing in the new X-ray machine.

1. **Higher quality of X-rays.** The new X-rays will lead to improved diagnoses and better patient treatment.

2. **Safety of technicians and patients.** The greater efficiency of the new machine would mean that X-ray technicians and patients are less exposed to the possibly harmful effects of radiation.

These nonfinancial quantitative and qualitative benefits are not considered in the formal financial analysis.

In the *selection* stage, the manager must decide whether or not Lifetime Care should purchase the new X-ray machine. She starts with financial information. This chapter discusses the following capital budgeting methods:

Points to Stress/Curriculum Linkage
In the *selection* stage (the 4th capital budgeting stage), quantitative analysis can be performed via any or all of the 4 methods: NPV, IRR, payback, or AARR. Finance courses advocate the NPV method because theory suggests that acceptance of all positive NPV projects maximizes firm value.

1. Net present value (NPV)
2. Internal rate of return (IRR)
3. Payback
4. Accrual accounting rate of return (AARR)

Both the NPV and IRR methods use a discounted cash flow approach.

DISCOUNTED CASH FLOW

Discounted cash flow (DCF) methods measure all expected future cash inflows and outflows of a project as if they occurred at a single point in time. DCF methods incorporate the time value of money. The **time value of money** takes into account that a dollar (or any other monetary unit) received today is worth more than a dollar received at any future time. The reason is that $1 received today can be invested to start earning a return of, say, 12% per year so that it grows to $1.12 at the end of the year. The time value of money is the opportunity cost (the return of $0.12 foregone per year) from not having the money today. Because discounted cash flow methods explicitly weight cash flows by the time value of money, they are usually the best (most comprehensive) methods to use for capital budgeting decisions. DCF focuses on *cash* inflows and outflows rather than on *operating income* as determined in conventional accrual accounting. Cash is invested now with the expectation of receiving a greater amount of cash in the future.

The compound interest tables and formulas used in DCF analysis are included in Appendix C, pp. 871–878. If you are unfamiliar with compound interest, do not proceed until you have studied Appendix C. The tables in Appendix C will be used frequently in this chapter.

There are two main DCF methods:

1. Net present value (NPV) method
2. Internal rate of return (IRR) method

OBJECTIVE 3

Use and evaluate the two main discounted cash flow (DCF) methods— the net present value (NPV) method and the internal rate-of-return (IRR) method

Points to Stress Mgt. accountants usually ignore the time value of money in short-term analyses because the interest foregone is unlikely to be material over short time spans.

NPV is calculated using the **required rate of return (RRR)**, which is the minimum acceptable rate of return on an investment. The RRR is the return that the organization could expect to receive elsewhere for an investment of comparable risk. The RRR is also called the **discount rate**, **hurdle rate**, or **(opportunity) cost of capital**. When working with IRR, the RRR is used as a point of comparison.

Assume that the required rate of return for Lifetime Care's X-ray machine project is 8 percent. (This relatively low rate is not unusual for nonprofit organizations, which can borrow funds at low rates because lenders pay no income taxes on interest received from these loans.)

Net Present Value Method

The **net present value (NPV) method** calculates the expected monetary gain or loss from a project by discounting all expected future cash inflows and outflows to the present point in time, using the required rate of return. Only projects with a zero or positive net present value are acceptable. Why? Because the return from these projects equals or exceeds the cost of capital (the return available by investing the capital elsewhere). If all other things are equal, the higher the NPV, the better. Using the NPV method entails the following steps:

Step 1: Draw a Sketch of Relevant Cash Inflows and Outflows   The right side of Exhibit 21-2 shows how these cash flows are sketched. Outflows appear in parentheses. The sketch helps the decision maker organize the data in a systematic way. Note that Exhibit 21-2 includes the outflow for the new machine at the end of *year 0*, the time of the acquisition. The NPV method focuses only on cash flows. NPV analysis is indifferent as to where the cash flows come from (operations, purchase or sale of equipment, or investment or recovery of working capital). Do not inject

EXHIBIT 21-2
Net Present Value Method: Lifetime Care Hospital's New X-Ray Machine

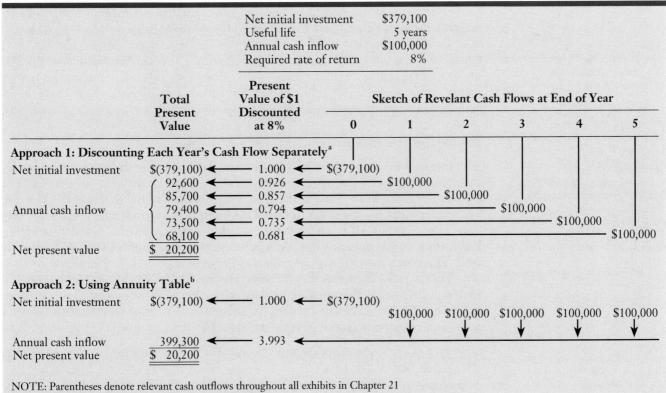

NOTE: Parentheses denote relevant cash outflows throughout all exhibits in Chapter 21
[a]Present values from Table 2, Appendix C at the end of the text.
[b]Annuity present values from Table 4, Appendix C. The annuity table value of 3.993 is the sum of the individual discount rates 0.926 + 0.857 + 0.794 + 0.735 + 0.681, subject to rounding error.

accrual accounting into the determination of cash inflows and outflows. For example, depreciation is deducted as an accrual expense when calculating operating income. Depreciation is not deducted in DCF analysis because depreciation expense entails no cash outflow.

Step 2: Choose the Correct Compound Interest Table from Appendix C   In our example, we can discount each year's cash flow separately using Table 2, or we can compute the present value of an annuity using Table 4, both in Appendix C. If we use Table 2, we find the discount factors for periods 1–5 under the 8% column. Approach 1 in Exhibit 21-2 presents the five discount factors. Because the investment produces an *annuity*, a series of equal cash flows at equal-time intervals, we may use Table 4. We find the discount factor for five periods under the 8% column. Approach 2 in Exhibit 21-2 shows that this discount factor is 3.993 (3.993 is the sum of the five discount factors used in approach 1). To obtain the present value figures, multiply the discount factors by the appropriate cash amounts in the sketch in Exhibit 21-2.

Step 3: Sum the Present Value Figures to Determine the Net Present Value   If the NPV is zero or positive, the project should be accepted. That is, its expected rate of return equals or exceeds the required rate of return. If the NPV is negative, the project should not be accepted. Its expected rate of return is below the required rate of return.

Exhibit 21-2 indicates an NPV of $20,200 at the required rate of return of 8 percent. The expected return from the project exceeds the 8% required rate of return. Therefore, the project is desirable based on quantifiable financial information. The cash flows from the project are adequate to (1) recover the net initial investment in the project, and (2) earn a return greater than 8% on the investment tied up in the project over its useful life.

Of course, the manager of Lifetime Care must also weigh nonfinancial factors. Consider the reduction in the average number of individual X-rays taken per patient with the new machine. This reduction is a qualitative benefit of the new machine, given the health risks to patients and technicians from X-rays. Other qualitative benefits of the new machine are the better diagnoses and treatments that patients receive. If the NPV had been negative, the manager would need to judge whether the nonfinancial benefits outweigh the negative NPV.

Pause here and do not proceed until you thoroughly understand Exhibit 21-2. Compare approach 1 with approach 2 in Exhibit 21-2 to see how Table 4 in Appendix C merely aggregates the present value factors of Table 2. That is, the fundamental table is Table 2. Table 4 merely reduces calculations when there is an annuity—a series of equal cash flows at equal intervals.

Internal Rate-of-Return Method

The **internal rate-of-return (IRR) method** calculates the discount rate at which the present value of expected cash inflows from a project equals the present value of expected cash outflows. That is, the IRR is the discount rate that makes NPV = $0. We illustrate the computation of the IRR using the X-ray machine project of Lifetime Care. Exhibit 21-3 presents the cash flows and shows the calculation of the NPV using a 10% discount rate. At a 10% discount rate, the NPV of the project is zero. Therefore, the IRR for the project is 10 percent.

How do we determine the discount rate that yields NPV = $0? In most cases, analysts solving capital budgeting problems have a calculator or computer program to provide the internal rate of return. Without a calculator or computer program, a trial-and-error approach can provide the answer.

- ◆ *Step 1*: Try a discount rate and calculate the NPV of the project using that discount rate.
- ◆ *Step 2*: If the NPV is less than zero, try a lower discount rate. (A lower discount rate will increase the NPV. Remember that we are trying to find a discount rate for which NPV = $0.) If the NPV is greater than zero, try a higher discount rate

EXHIBIT 21-3
Internal Rate-of-Return Method[a]: Lifetime Care Hospital's New X-Ray Machine

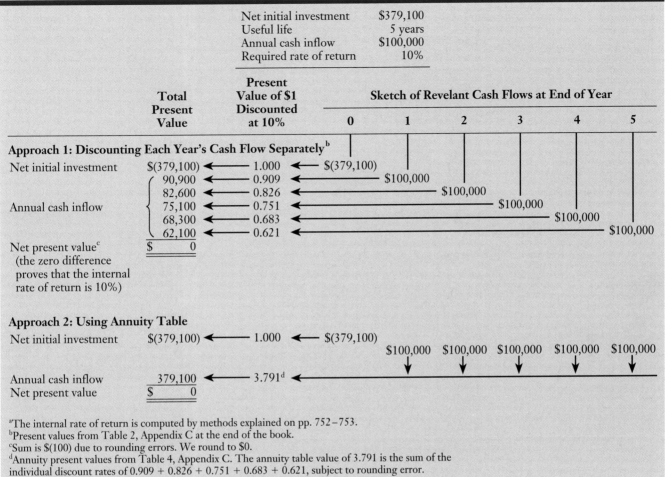

	Net initial investment	$379,100
	Useful life	5 years
	Annual cash inflow	$100,000
	Required rate of return	10%

[a]The internal rate of return is computed by methods explained on pp. 752–753.
[b]Present values from Table 2, Appendix C at the end of the book.
[c]Sum is $(100) due to rounding errors. We round to $0.
[d]Annuity present values from Table 4, Appendix C. The annuity table value of 3.791 is the sum of the individual discount rates of 0.909 + 0.826 + 0.751 + 0.683 + 0.621, subject to rounding error.

to lower the NPV. Keep adjusting the discount rate until NPV = $0. In the Lifetime Care example, a discount rate of 8% yields an NPV of +$20,200 (see Exhibit 21-2). A discount rate of 12% yields an NPV of −$18,600 (3.605, the present value annuity factor from Table 4, × $100,000 minus $379,100). Therefore, the discount rate that makes NPV = $0 must lie between 8% and 12 percent. We try 10% and get NPV = $0. Hence, the IRR is 10 percent.

The step-by-step computations of an internal rate of return are easier when the cash inflows are equal, as in our example. Information from Exhibit 21-3 can be expressed by the following equation:

$$\$379,100 = \text{Present value of annuity of }\$100,000\text{ at }X\%\text{ for 5 years}$$

Or, what factor F in Table 4 (Appendix C) will satisfy the following equation?

$$\$379,100 = \$100,000F$$

$$F = \$379,000 \div \$100,000 = 3.791$$

On the five-period line of Table 4, find the percentage column that is closest to 3.791. It is exactly 10 percent. If the factor (F) falls between the factors in two columns, straight-line interpolation is used to approximate the IRR. This interpolation is illustrated in the Problem for Self-Study.

A project is accepted only if the internal rate of return equals or exceeds the required rate of return. In the Lifetime Care example, the X-ray machine has an IRR of 10%, which is greater than the required rate of return of 8 percent. On the

Points to Stress Although tedious, the trial-and-error method helps students understand present-value calculations. It is also necessary when computer programs or calculators are unavailable and cash flows are unequal. When cash flows are equal each period, students can solve for the discount factor as shown here.

Correcting Student Misconceptions Emphasize that Tables 3 (future value of an annuity) and 4 (present value of an annuity) of App. C are only appropriate when cash flows are equal for all periods. When cash flows are unequal, students must compound (or discount) each period's cash flow separately, using Table 1 (future value) or Table 2 (present value).

Teaching Tip Urge students not to use preprogrammed calculators for the first few problems assigned. Note that some calculators produce different answers from those generated by the tables in the text. The tables in the Appendix assume that all cash flows occur at the end of the period(s) in question, but some calculators assume that cash flows compound continuously. Note also that App. C uses only 3 decimal digits, whereas many calculators use 8 or more decimal digits.

Curriculum Linkage Students who have had finance courses may recognize another advantage of NPV over IRR. Under capital rationing, acceptance of projects with the highest IRR may not maximize profits. Ranking projects based on IRR presumes that mgt. can reinvest cash recovered from these projects at the project's IRR, which isn't always true.

Reinforcing Problems Exer. 21-17 through 21-20, 21-22, and 21-24 and Prob. 21-27 cover basic comparisons among the 4 capital budgeting methods. Exer. 21-16 is a compound-interest exercise, and its solution appears at the end of the assignment material.

Points to Stress Given the rapid pace of technological change, estimating a project's useful life can be one of the most challenging aspects of capital budgeting.

Example Show how the terminal disposal price of equipment with a *long life* may be unimportant. Why? Because the present value is immaterial, especially if the required rate of return is high. For example, 20 yrs. hence a terminal disposal price of $1,000,000 has present values of $215,000 at 8%, $37,000 at 18%, and $5,000 at 30%.

basis of financial factors, Lifetime Care should invest in the new machine. If IRR exceeds RRR, then the project has a positive NPV. If IRR equals RRR, NPV = $0. If IRR is less than RRR, the NPV is negative. Obviously, managers prefer projects with higher IRRs to projects with lower IRRs, if all other things are equal. The IRR of 10% means that the cash inflows from the project are adequate (1) to recover the net initial investment in the project, and (2) to earn a return of exactly 10% on the investment tied up in the project over its useful life.

Comparison of Net Present Value and Internal Rate-of-Return Methods

This text emphasizes the NPV method, which has the important advantage that the end result of the computations is expressed in dollars, and not a percentage. Therefore, we can sum the NPVs of individual projects to see the effect of accepting a combination of projects. In contrast, the IRRs of individual projects cannot be added or averaged to derive the IRR of a combination of projects.

A second important advantage of the NPV method is that we can use it in situations where the required rate of return varies over the life of the project. For example, suppose the X-ray machine being considered by Lifetime Care has a required rate of return of 8% in years 1, 2, and 3 and 12% in years 4 and 5. The total present value of the cash inflows is:

Year	Cash Inflows	Required Rate of Return	Present Value of $1 Discounted at Required Rate	Total Present Value of Cash Inflows
1	$100,000	8%	0.926	$ 92,600
2	100,000	8	0.857	85,700
3	100,000	8	0.794	79,400
4	100,000	12	0.636	63,600
5	100,000	12	0.567	56,700
				$378,000

Given the net initial investment of $379,100, the NPV calculations indicate that the project is undesirable: The NPV is −$1,100 ($378,000 − $379,100). However, it is not possible to use the IRR method in this case to decide that the project should be rejected. The existence of different required rates of return in different years (8% for years 1, 2, and 3 versus 12% for years 4 and 5) means there is not a single RRR that the IRR (a single figure) must exceed for the project to be acceptable.

SENSITIVITY ANALYSIS

To highlight the basic differences between the NPV and IRR methods, we have assumed that the expected values of cash flows will occur for certain. Obviously, such predictions are imperfect. To examine how a result will change if the predicted financial outcomes are not achieved or if an underlying assumption changes, managers can use *sensitivity analysis*, a "what-if" technique introduced in Chapter 3.

Sensitivity analysis can take various forms. For example, suppose the Lifetime Care manager believes forecasted savings are uncertain and difficult to predict. She could then ask, "What is the minimum annual cash savings that will cause us to invest in the new X-ray machine (that is, for NPV = $0)?" For the data in Exhibit 21-2, let A = annual cash flow and let NPV = $0. The net initial investment is $379,100, and the present value factor at the 8% required rate of return for a five-year annuity of $1 is 3.993. Then:

$$\text{NPV} = \$0$$

$$(3.993A) - \$379,100 = \$0$$

$$3.993A = \$379,100$$

$$A = \$94,941$$

EXHIBIT 21-4
Net Present Value Calculations for Lifetime Care Hospital Under Different Assumptions of Annual Cash Inflows and Required Rate of Return[a]

Required Rate of Return	Annual Cash Inflows				
	$80,000	$90,000	$100,000	$110,000	$120,000
6%	$(42,140)	$ (20)	$42,100	$84,220	$126,340
8%	$(59,660)	$(19,730)	$20,200	$60,130	$100,060
10%	$(75,820)	$(37,910)	$ 0	$37,910	$ 75,820

[a]All entries in cells assume a useful project life of five years.

Thus, at the discount rate of 8%, annual cash flow can decrease to $94,941 (a decline of $100,000 − $94,941 = $5,059) before the NPV falls below zero. If the manager believes she can attain annual cash savings of at least $94,941, she could justify investing in the new X-ray machine on financial grounds.

Exhibit 21-4 shows how the NPV of the X-ray machine project is affected by variations in (1) the annual cash inflows, and (2) the required rate of return. NPVs can also vary with different useful lives of a project. Sensitivity analysis helps managers focus on the most sensitive decisions, and it eases their minds about those decisions that are not so sensitive. For the X-ray machine project, Exhibit 21-4 shows that variations in either the annual cash inflows or the required rate of return have sizable effects on NPV.

RELEVANT CASH FLOWS IN DISCOUNTED CASH FLOW ANALYSIS

One of the biggest challenges in DCF analysis is determining which cash flows are relevant to making the investment selection. Relevant cash flows are expected future cash flows that differ among the alternatives. At Lifetime Care, the alternatives are to continue to use the old X-ray machine or to replace it with the new machine. The relevant cash flows are the differences in cash flows between continuing to use the old machine and purchasing the new one. *When reading this section, focus on identifying future expected cash flows of each alternative and the differences in cash flows between alternatives.*

Ignoring for the moment tax factors (discussed later in this chapter), a capital investment project typically has three major categories of cash flows: (1) net initial investment in the project, which includes the acquisition of a new asset, required additions of working capital, minus the cash flow from current disposal of an existing asset, (2) cash flow from operations, and (3) cash flow from terminal disposal of an asset and recovery of working capital. The Lifetime Care example is used to discuss these three categories.

1. Net Initial Investment   Three components of net initial investment cash flows are (a) the cash outflow to purchase the machine, (b) the working-capital cash outflow, and (c) the cash inflow from current disposal of the old machine.

a. *Initial machine investment.* These outflows, made for purchasing plant and equipment, occur at the beginning of the project's life and include cash outflows for transporting and installing the item. In the Lifetime Care example, the $372,890 cost (including transportation and installation) of the X-ray machine is an outflow in year 0. These cash flows are relevant to the capital budgeting decision because they will be incurred only if Lifetime decides to purchase the new machine.

b. *Initial working capital investment.* Investments in plant and equipment are invariably accompanied by incremental investments in working capital. These investments take the form of current assets, such as accounts receivable and inventories

Points to Stress Emphasize that in capital budgeting problems, students should focus on *relevant cash flows: cash flows that differ among alternatives.*

Curriculum Linkage This section covers material that is consistent with Chap. 11 on relevant revenues and costs.

minus current liabilities, such as accounts payable. Working-capital investments are similar to plant and equipment investments in that they require cash.

The Lifetime Care example assumes a $10,000 incremental investment in working capital (supplies and spare parts inventory) if the new machine is acquired. The incremental working-capital investment is the difference between the working capital required to operate the new machine (say, $15,000) and the working-capital investment required to operate the old machine (say, $5,000). The $10,000 *additional* investment in working capital is a cash outflow in year 0.

c. *Current disposal of old machine.* Any cash received from disposal of the old machine is a relevant cash inflow (in year 0) because it is an expected future cash flow that differs between the alternatives of investing and not investing in the new machine. If Lifetime Care invests in the new X-ray machine, it will be able to dispose of its old machine for $3,790. These proceeds are included as cash inflow in year 0. The net initial investment for the new X-ray machine, $379,100, is the initial machine investment plus the additional working-capital investment minus the current disposal price of the old machine: $372,890 + $10,000 − $3,790 = $379,100.

Recall from Chapter 11 (p. 396) that the book value (original cost minus accumulated depreciation) of the old equipment is irrelevant to the decision. It is a past (sunk) cost. Nothing can change what has already been spent or what has already happened.

2. Cash Flow from Operations This category includes the difference between each year's cash flow from operations under the alternatives. Organizations make capital investments to generate cash inflows in the future. These inflows may result from producing and selling additional goods or services, or, as in the Lifetime Care example, from savings in cash operating costs. Annual cash flow from operations can be net outflows in some years. For example, oil production may require large expenditures every, say, five years to improve oil extraction rates. Focus on operating cash flows, not on revenues and expenses under accrual accounting.

To underscore this point, consider the following additional facts about the Lifetime Care example:

◆ Total X-Ray Department overhead costs will not change whether the new machine is purchased or the old machine is kept. The X-Ray Department overhead costs are allocated to individual X-ray machines—Lifetime has several—on the basis of the labor costs for operating each machine. Because the new X-ray machine will have lower labor costs, overhead allocated to it will be $30,000 less than the amount allocated to the machine it would replace.

◆ Depreciation on the new X-ray machine using the straight-line method is $74,578 ([original cost, $372,890 − expected terminal disposal price, $0] ÷ useful life, 5 years).

The savings in operating cash flows (labor and materials) of $100,000 in each of the first four years and $90,000 in the fifth year are clearly relevant because they are expected future cash flows that will differ between the alternatives of investing and not investing in the new machine. But what about the decrease in allocated overhead costs of $30,000? What about the depreciation of $74,578?

a. *Overhead costs.* The key question is, "Do *total* overhead costs of the X-Ray Department decrease as a result of acquiring the new machine?" In our example, they do not. Total X-Ray Department overhead costs remain the same whether or not the new machine is acquired. Only the overhead allocated to individual machines changes. The overhead costs allocated to the new machine are $30,000 less. These $30,000 will be allocated to *other* machines in the department. No cash flow savings in total overhead occur. Therefore, the $30,000 should not be included as part of annual cash savings from operations.

b. *Depreciation.* The depreciation line item is itself irrelevant in DCF analysis. It is a noncash allocation of costs while DCF is based on inflows and outflows of *cash*. In DCF methods, the initial cost of equipment is regarded as a *lump-sum* outflow of cash in year 0. Deducting depreciation expenses from operating cash inflows would result in counting the lump-sum amount twice.

3. Terminal Disposal of Investment   The disposal of the investment generally increases cash inflow when the project terminates. Errors in forecasting the terminal disposal price are seldom critical for long-duration projects because the present value of amounts to be received in the distant future is usually small. Two components of the terminal disposal price of an investment are (a) the terminal disposal price of the machine, and (b) recovery of working capital.

a. *Terminal disposal price of machine.* At the end of the useful life of the project, the machine's terminal disposal price may be zero or an amount considerably less than the net initial investment. The relevant cash inflow is the difference in expected terminal disposal prices at the end of five years under the two alternatives—the terminal disposal price of the new machine (zero in the case of Lifetime Care) minus the terminal disposal price of the old machine (also zero in this example).

b. *Recovery of working capital.* The initial investment in working capital is usually fully recouped when the project is terminated. At that time, inventories and accounts receivable necessary to support the project are no longer needed. The relevant cash inflow is the difference in the expected working capital recovered under the two alternatives. If the new X-ray machine is purchased, Lifetime Care will recover $15,000 of working capital in year 5. If the new machine is not acquired, Lifetime will recover $5,000 of working capital in year 5, at the end of the useful life of the old machine. The relevant cash inflow in year 5 if Lifetime invests in the new machine is $10,000 ($15,000 − $5,000).

Some capital investment projects *reduce* working capital. Assume that a computer-integrated manufacturing (CIM) project with a seven-year life will reduce inventories and hence working capital by $20 million from, say, $50 million to $30 million. This reduction will be represented as a $20 million cash *inflow* for the project in year 0. At the end of seven years, the recovery of working capital will show a relevant incremental cash *outflow* of $20 million. Why? Because the company recovers only $30 million of working capital under CIM rather than the $50 million of working capital it would have recovered had it not implemented CIM.

Exhibit 21-5 presents the relevant cash inflows and outflows for Lifetime Care's decision to purchase the new machine as described in items 1–3 above. The total relevant cash flows for each year are the same as the relevant cash flows used in Exhibits 21-2 and 21-3 to illustrate the NPV and IRR methods.

EXHIBIT 21-5
Relevant Cash Inflows and Outflows for Lifetime Care Hospital's New X-Ray Machine

	Sketch of Relevant Cash Flows at End of Year					
	0	**1**	**2**	**3**	**4**	**5**
1. a. Initial machine investment	$(372,890)					
b. Initial working capital investment	(10,000)					
c. Current disposal price of old machine	3,790					
Net initial investment	(379,100)					
2. Annual cash flow from operations		$100,000	$100,000	$100,000	$100,000	$ 90,000
3. a. Terminal disposal price of machine						0
b. Recovery of working capital						10,000
Total relevant cash flows as shown in Exhibits 21-2 and 21-3	$(379,100)	$100,000	$100,000	$100,000	$100,000	$100,000

Did the Bengals Score a Touchdown on Hamilton County?

Building and financing a new sports stadium is a challenging task. Paul Brown Stadium, "home" of the Cincinnati Bengals football team starting in 2000, illustrates many of the issues that arise. The stadium will be owned by Hamilton County in Ohio. The Bengals have a 26-year lease to use and operate it. The final contract between Hamilton County and the Bengals includes sharing rules covering revenues and costs. These sharing rules can dramatically affect the economics of the stadium project to the owners (Hamilton County and its taxpayers) and the economics of owning the Cincinnati Bengals.

Examples of some of the sharing rules and projected revenues (before present value discounting) over the 26-year lease are

1. *Ticket revenues.* Bengals receive all ticket revenues over the 26-year lease, estimated at $995 million (including a 3% annual price increase.

2. *Luxury seats.* Private-suite revenues from 104 luxury boxes, projected to be $246 million, all go to the Bengals.

3. *Club seats.* The stadium will have 7,600 club seats. All $243 million in projected revenues goes to the Bengals.

4. *County park.* The county can use the facilities for year-round parking. Estimated revenue of $112 million for the 26 years goes to the County.

5. *Advertising, naming rights, and food concessions.* Bengals receive all revenues estimated at $209 million.

The county borrowed $334 million to build the stadium, which had a budgeted cost of $400 million. Operating costs, estimated to be $239 million over the 26-year lease, will be paid mostly by the Bengals. The county can collect a 25 cents per ticket surcharge on every ticket sold, bringing in $4 million in revenue over the entire period.

Critics of such stadium projects note that on a present value basis, they are questionable investments to a county. The county pays for the upfront construction (or much of it) and receives a limited percentage of the ongoing revenues. Supporters of stadium projects (including football team owners) invariably stress the nonfinancial and qualitative benefits of a stadium project. Benefits cited include a greater sense of community from having a NFL team and the ability to retain employment for many businesses that exist because there is a NFL team in town (such as those operating concessions at the stadium).

Source: Street and Smith's *Sports Business Journal* and Paul Brown Stadium website.

OBJECTIVE 5

Use and evaluate the payback method

Example The "ideal" payback time is zero. As an investor said when told by a salesperson that he would get his money back in less than 2 yrs., "I already have my money back." However, in business, one must usually "spend money to make money."

PAYBACK METHOD

We now consider the third method for analyzing the financial aspects of projects. **Payback** measures the time it will take to recoup, in the form of expected future cash flows, the net initial investment in a project. Like NPV and IRR, the payback method does not distinguish between the origins of cash flows (operations, purchase or sale of equipment, or investing in or recovery of working capital). Unlike NPV and IRR, payback ignores profitability. Payback is simplest to calculate when a project has uniform cash flows. We consider this case first.

Uniform Cash Flows

In the Lifetime Care example, the X-ray machine costs $379,100, has a five-year expected useful life, and generates a $100,000 *uniform* cash flow each year. The payback calculations follow:

$$\text{Payback} = \frac{\text{Net initial investment}}{\text{Uniform increase in annual future cash flows}}$$

$$= \frac{\$379,100}{\$100,000} = 3.8 \text{ years}^1$$

The payback method highlights liquidity, which is often an important factor in capital budgeting decisions. Managers prefer projects with shorter paybacks (more liquid) to projects with longer paybacks, if all other things are equal. Projects with shorter paybacks give the organization more flexibility because funds for other projects become available sooner. Also, managers are less confident about cash flow predictions that stretch far into the future.

Under the payback method, organizations often choose a cutoff period for a project. The greater the risks of a project, the shorter the cutoff period. Japanese companies favor the payback method over other methods (see Surveys of Company Practice, p. 761) and often use cutoff periods ranging from 3 to 5 years. Projects with a payback period less than the cutoff period should be accepted, while those with a payback period longer than the cutoff period should be rejected. For example, if Lifetime Care's cutoff period under the payback method is three years, it will reject the new machine.

The major strength of the payback method is that it is easy to understand. Like the DCF methods described previously, the payback method is not affected by accrual accounting conventions such as depreciation. Advocates of the payback method argue that it is a useful measure (1) when preliminary screening of many proposals is necessary, and (2) when the expected cash flows in later years of the project are highly uncertain.

Two major weaknesses of the payback method are (1) it fails to incorporate the time value of money, and (2) it does not consider a project's cash flows after the payback period. Consider an alternative to the $379,100 X-ray machine mentioned earlier. Assume that another X-ray machine, with a three-year useful life and zero terminal disposal price, requires only a $300,000 net initial investment and will also result in cash inflows of $100,000 per year. First, compare the two payback periods:

$$\text{Machine 1} = \frac{\$379,100}{\$100,000} = 3.8 \text{ years}$$

$$\text{Machine 2} = \frac{\$300,000}{\$100,000} = 3.0 \text{ years}$$

The payback criterion would favor buying the $300,000 machine, because it has a shorter payback. In fact, if the cutoff period is three years, then Lifetime Care would not acquire machine 1, because it fails to meet the payback criterion. By itself, payback concentrates on the *time* it takes to recoup the initial investment. It ignores *profitability*.

Consider next the NPV of the two investment options using Lifetime Care's 8% required rate of return for the X-ray machine investment. At a discount rate of 8%, the NPV of machine 2 is − $42,300 (2.577, the present value annuity factor for three years at 8% from Table 4, times $100,000 = $257,700 minus the net initial investment of $300,000). Machine 1, as we know, has a positive NPV of $20,200 (from Exhibit 21-2). The NPV criterion suggests that Lifetime Care should acquire machine 1. Machine 2, with a negative NPV, would fail to meet the NPV criterion.

The payback method gives a different answer than the NPV method gives, because the payback method does not take into account the ultimate objective of most organizations—profitability. It does not discount cash flows, and it does not consider cash flows after the payback period. An added problem with the payback

Points to Stress The text's example shows that the payback method doesn't necessarily maximize profits because it's silent about project profitability. However, companies often use payback in conjunction with DCF analyses and select those positive NPV projects that also have an acceptable payback period. Mgt. is most likely to emphasize payback period when the future is very uncertain (and they don't want to tie up cash for long) and when interest rates are high (making it expensive to tie up cash for long periods of time). The major deficiencies of the payback computation are that (1) it doesn't necessarily lead to profit maximization, and (2) it discourages selection of long-term projects (e.g., major R&D or automation projects may have a long payback period, but nevertheless may be critical to a company's long-term survival). Too much focus on payback can contribute to short-term "myopia".

[1] Cash savings from the new X-ray machine occur uniformly *throughout* the year, but for simplicity in calculating NPV and IRR, we assume they occur at the *end* of each year. A literal interpretation of this assumption would imply a payback of four years because Lifetime Care will only recover its investment when cash inflows occur at the end of the fourth year. The calculations shown in the chapter, however, better approximate Lifetime Care's payback on the basis of uniform cash flows throughout the year.

method is that choosing too short a cutoff period for project acceptance may promote the selection of only short-lived projects. The organization will tend to reject long-run, positive-NPV projects.

Nonuniform Cash Flows

The payback formula (p. 759) is designed for uniform annual cash flows. When cash flows are not uniform, the payback computation takes a cumulative form. The years' cash flows are accumulated until the amount of the net initial investment is recovered. Assume that Venture Law Group is considering the purchase of a $150,000 video conferencing facility that will enable executives to see each other in a conference format without physically traveling. The facility is expected to provide a total cash savings of $380,000 over the next five years—due to a combination of reduced travel costs and more effective use of executive time. The cash savings occur evenly throughout each year, but nonuniformly across years. Payback occurs during the third year:

Year	Cash Savings	Cumulative Cash Savings	Net Initial Investment Yet to Be Recovered at End of Year
0	—	—	$150,000
1	$ 50,000	$ 50,000	100,000
2	60,000	110,000	40,000
3	80,000	190,000	—
4	90,000	280,000	—
5	100,000	380,000	—

Straight-line interpolation within the third year reveals that the final $40,000 needed to recover the $150,000 investment (that is, $150,000 − $110,000 recovered by the end of year 2) will be achieved halfway through year 3 (in which $80,000 of cash savings occur):

$$\text{Payback} = 2 \text{ years} + \left(\frac{\$40,000}{\$80,000} \times 1 \text{ year} \right) = 2.5 \text{ years}$$

The video conferencing example has a single cash outflow of $150,000 in year 0. When a project has multiple cash outflows occurring at different points in time, these outflows are added to derive a total cash outflow figure for the project. No adjustment is made for the time value of money when adding these cash outflows in computing the payback period.

ACCRUAL ACCOUNTING RATE-OF-RETURN METHOD

OBJECTIVE 6

Use and evaluate the accrual accounting rate-of-return (AARR) method

We now consider a fourth method for analyzing the financial aspects of capital budgeting projects. The **accrual accounting rate-of-return (AARR)** method divides an accounting measure of income by an accounting measure of investment. It is also called the **accounting rate of return**. We illustrate AARR for the Lifetime Care example using the project's net initial investment as the denominator:

$$\frac{\text{Accrual accounting}}{\text{rate of return}} = \frac{\text{Increase in expected average annual operating income}}{\text{Net initial investment}}$$

If Lifetime Care purchases the new X-ray machine, the increase in expected average annual savings in operating costs will be $98,000. This amount is the total operating savings of $490,000 ($100,000 for four years and $90,000 in year 5) ÷ 5. Since the new machine has a zero terminal disposal price, straight-line depreciation on the new machine is $74,578 ($372,890 ÷ 5). The net initial investment is $379,100. The accrual accounting rate of return is equal to:

$$\text{AARR} = \frac{\$98,000 - \$74,578}{\$379,100} = \frac{\$23,422}{\$379,100} = 6.2\%$$

The AARR of 6.2% indicates the rate at which a dollar of investment generates

---

Points to Stress The payback formula for uniform cash flows is just a special case of the nonuniform cash flows. Both methods can use the cumulative cash savings approach.

Correcting Student Misconceptions Students are often confused about when to include depreciation expense in evaluating a capital budgeting project. NPV, IRR, and payback methods are all based on cash flows. Depreciation expense isn't a cash flow. In contrast, the AARR is accrual acctg. income divided by investment. Depreciation expense *is* relevant in computing accrual acctg. income.

International Comparison of Capital Budgeting Methods

What methods do companies around the world use for analyzing capital investment decisions? The percentages in the following table indicate how frequently particular capital budgeting methods are used in eight countries. The reported percentages exceed 100% because many companies surveyed use more than one capital budgeting method.

	United States[a]	Australia[b]	Canada[c]	Ireland[d]	Japan[b]	Scotland[e]	South Korea[f]	United Kingdom[g]
Payback	59%	61%	50%	84%	52%	78%	75%	76%
Internal rate of return (IRR)	52%	37%	62% }	84%	4%	58%	75%	39%
Net present value (NPV)	28%	45%	41% }		6%	48%	60%	38%
Accrual accounting rate of return (AARR)	13%	24%	17%	24%	36%	31%	68%	28%
Other	44%	7%	8%	—	5%	—	—	7%

Some observations on these surveys follow.

1. Companies in the United States, Australia, Canada, Ireland, Scotland, South Korea, and the United Kingdom tend to use two methods, on average, to evaluate capital investments. (The sum of the capital budgeting percentages in the columns for each of these countries is approximately 200%.)

2. Japanese companies tend to use only one method. (The sum of the capital budgeting percentages for Japan is approximately 100%.)

3. The payback method is a very popular method among companies in all countries. Japanese companies use the payback method as their primary method of analysis in their capital budgeting decisions. Companies in the United States, Australia, Canada, Ireland, Scotland, South Korea, and the United Kingdom use discounted cash flow (DCF) methods (IRR and NPV) extensively.

4. The accrual accounting rate-of-return (AARR) method lags behind DCF methods in the United States, Australia, Canada, Ireland, Scotland, and the United Kingdom. It is on par with DCF methods in South Korea, and it is very much preferred to DCF methods in Japan.

5. Smaller companies often use DCF methods less than do larger companies. One survey of small U.S. companies (sales less then $5 million) found that the payback method was the primary method for 43% of companies, accounting rate of return for 22%, IRR for 16%, NPV for 11%, and other methods for 8 percent. Reasons given for the preference for payback was its emphasis on liquidity, the difficulty of small companies having access to capital, and simplicity.

[a]Adapted from Smith and Sullivan, "Survey of Cost." [b]Blayney and Yokoyama, "Comparative Analysis." [c]Jog and Srivastava, "Corporate Financial." [d]Clarke, "Management Accounting." [e]Sangster, "Capital Investment." [f]Kim and Song, "Accounting Practices." [g]Block, "Capital Budgeting." Full citations are in Appendix A.

operating income. Projects whose AARR exceeds an accrual accounting required rate of return for the project are considered desirable—the higher, the better.

The AARR method is similar to the IRR method in that both methods calculate a rate-of-return percentage. While the AARR calculates return using operating income numbers after considering accruals, the IRR method calculates return on the basis of cash flows and the time value of money. For capital budgeting decisions, the IRR method is conceptually superior to the AARR method.

The AARR computations are easy to understand, and use numbers reported in the income statement. Unlike the payback method, the AARR method considers profitability. Unlike the NPV and IRR methods, however, the AARR focuses on operating income and hence considers accruals. It does not track cash flows and ignores the time value of money. Critics cite these arguments as major drawbacks of the AARR method.

EVALUATING MANAGERS AND GOAL-CONGRUENCE ISSUES

A manager who uses DCF methods to make capital budgeting decisions can face goal congruence problems if AARR is used for performance evaluation. Consider the manager of the X-Ray Department at Lifetime Care Hospital. The NPV method indicates that the manager should purchase the new X-ray machine since it has a positive NPV of $20,200.

Suppose top management of Lifetime Care uses the AARR for judging performance. The manager of the X-Ray Department may consider not purchasing the new X-ray machine if the AARR of 6.2% on the investment reduces the overall AARR and so negatively affects the department's performance. The AARR on the new X-ray machine is low because the investment increases the denominator and, as a result of depreciation, also reduces the numerator (operating income) in the AARR computation.

Obviously, there is an inconsistency between citing the NPV method as being best for capital budgeting decisions and then using a different method to evaluate performance over short time horizons. In this situation, managers are tempted to make capital budgeting decisions on the basis of short-run accrual accounting results, even though these decisions, in terms of DCF, are not in the best long-run interest of the organization. Such temptations become more pronounced if managers are frequently transferred (or promoted), or if their bonuses are affected by the level of year-to-year accrual income.[2]

Example A firm is considering a new machine investment of $2,500 today with net cash inflows of $500 in year 1 and $3,000 in year 2. The firm uses SL depreciation, the machine has no salvage value, and the required rate of return is 10%.

$$\text{NPV:} = \$434$$

Choice: The firm should invest.

AARR:

	AARR Yr. 1	AARR Yr. 2
Incr. Rev.	$500	$3,000
Deprec. Exp. 2500/2	(1,250)	(1,250)
Op. Inc. (Loss)	(750)	1,750
Investment	2,500	2,500
AARR	(30)%	(70)%

Choice: Mgrs. who are evaluated based on AARR may reject the project because of its yr.-1 AARR, even though it has a positive NPV.

INCOME-TAX CONSIDERATIONS

The Lifetime Care example in Exhibits 21-2 to 21-5 illustrates capital budgeting for an organization that is not subject to income taxes. However, income taxes are a fact-of-life for most corporations and individuals. As Benjamin Franklin said, "Two things in life are certain: death and taxes." We now consider how income taxes can be incorporated into stage 4 (the selection stage) of the six stages of capital budgeting.

Assume now that Lifetime Care Hospital, discussed earlier in this chapter, is a taxable corporation. The following additional assumptions are made:

1. Lifetime Care is a profitable company. The income tax rate is 40% of operating income each year.
2. Lifetime uses the straight-line depreciation method, which means an equal amount of depreciation is taken each year.
3. Gains or losses on the sale of depreciable assets are taxed at the same rate as ordinary income.
4. The tax effects of cash inflows and outflows occur at the same time that the inflows and outflows occur.

[2]Managers are often interested in how the adoption of a project will affect a bonus plan that is based on reported annual accrual accounting numbers. Do not assume that the AARR computed by the formula on p. 760 is the appropriate number to use in examining the effect that adoption of a project will have on a manager's bonus plan. It is necessary to examine on a year-by-year basis how the accounting rate of return is computed when determining bonuses. For example, the numerator in the formula is the "increase in expected average annual operating income." This average increase need not be the same each year during a project. Assume the president of Lifetime Care receives an annual $50,000 lump-sum bonus if the accounting rate of return on assets exceeds 8% in that year. Project A has an AARR over its five-year life of 10% and a net present value of $20,000. Project B has an AARR over its five-year life of 9% and a net present value of $18,000. Project A has cash inflows in years 1 and 5 but zero cash inflows in years 2, 3 and 4. Project B has equal cash inflows in years 1–5. It could well be that the president would receive higher bonuses with project B—the project with a lower NPV.

5. Lifetime Care uses an 8% required rate of return for discounting after-tax cash flows.

Teaching Tip Keep students focused on the big picture. Income tax laws are very detailed and the tax rates, useful lives, depreciation patterns, and tax credits often change. However, the DCF *approach* to measuring the impact of income tax laws on cash flows doesn't change with changes in specific income tax rates, useful lives allowed, etc. (although the specific numbers in the analysis will be affected).

Summary data for the X-ray machines are:

	Old X-Ray Machine	New X-Ray Machine
Current book value	$50,000	$372,890
Current disposal price	3,790	Not applicable
Terminal disposal price 5 years from now	0	0
Annual depreciation	$10,000[a]	74,578[b]
Working capital required	5,000	15,000

[a]$50,000 ÷ 5 years = $10,000 annual depreciation
[b]$372,890 ÷ 5 years = $74,578 annual depreciation

Relevant After-Tax Flows

The earlier analysis of Lifetime Care's decision to purchase the new X-ray machine used the *differential approach* to decision making introduced in Chapter 11. That is, we compared (1) the cash outflows resulting from replacing the old machine with (2) the savings in future cash outflows resulting from using the new machine rather than the old machine. We continue using the differential approach to illustrate how income tax considerations can be incorporated into NPV analysis.

Before we examine the steps in detail, it is important to understand how income tax affects cash flows in each period. Exhibit 21-6 shows how investing in the new machine will affect Lifetime Care's cash flow from operations and its income taxes in year 1. Recall that Lifetime Care will save $100,000 in before-tax cash

Points to Stress This chapter assumes that firms have positive taxable income. If not, the effect of taxes depends on whether the firm can use carrybacks and carryforwards, a tax topic that is beyond the scope of this text. If the firm has no current income and no carrybacks nor likely carryforwards, taxes have no effect, because the effective tax rate is zero. (In this case, however, the firm has bigger problems than the effect of taxes on capital budgeting!)

EXHIBIT 21-6
Effect on Cash Flow from Operations, Net of Income Taxes in Year 1 for Lifetime Care's Investment in the New X-Ray Machine

PANEL A: TWO METHODS BASED ON THE INCOME STATEMENT		
(S)	Savings in cash costs	$100,000
(D)	Additional depreciation deductions	64,578
(OI)	Increase in operating income	35,422
(T)	Income taxes (Income tax rate t × OI) = 40% × $35,422	14,169
(NI)	Net income	$ 21,253

Cash flow from operations, net of income taxes, is
Method 1: $S - T = \$100,000 - \$14,169 = \$85,831$ or
Method 2: $NI + D = \$ 21,253 + \$64,578 = \$85,831$

PANEL B: ITEM-BY-ITEM METHOD		
	Effect of cash operating flows	
(S)	Savings in cash costs	$100,000
($t \times S$)	Deduct income tax cash outflow at 40%	40,000
$\left. \begin{array}{c} S - t \times S \\ = (1 - t) \times S \end{array} \right\}$	After-tax cash flow from operations (excluding depreciation effects)	60,000
	Effect of depreciation	
(D)	Additional depreciation deductions, $64,578	
($t \times D$)	Income tax cash savings from additional depreciation deductions at 40% × $64,578	25,831
$\begin{array}{c} (1 - t) \times S + (t \times D) \\ = S - (t \times S) + (t \times D) \end{array}$	Cash flow from operations, net of income taxes	$ 85,831

operating outflows by investing in the new machine (p. 750), but will record additional depreciation of $64,578 ($74,578 − $10,000, per the table on p. 763). Panel A shows the year 1 cash flow from operations, net of income taxes, equals $85,831, using two methods based on the income statement. The first method focuses on cash items, the $100,000 cash savings minus income taxes of $14,169. The second method starts with $21,253 net income and adds back additional depreciation deductions of $64,578 because depreciation is an operating cost that reduces net income but does not reduce cash outflow.

Panel B of Exhibit 21-6 describes a third method that we will use frequently to compute cash flow from operations, net of income taxes. The easiest way to interpret the third method is to think of the government as a 40% (equal to the tax rate) partner in Lifetime Care. Each time Lifetime Care obtains cost savings, S, (or higher revenues minus cash costs), its income *is higher* by S, and so it will pay 40% of the cash savings (0.40S) in taxes, resulting in after-tax cash operating flows of S − 0.40S [$100,000 − (0.40 × $100,000) = $60,000 in this example].

To achieve the higher cash savings of S, Lifetime Care incurred higher depreciation charges of D from investing in the new machine. Depreciation cost itself does not affect cash flow because depreciation is a noncash cost, but higher depreciation cost *lowers* Lifetime Care's income by D, saving income tax cash outflows of 0.40D (0.40 × $64,578 = $25,831 in this example).

Letting t = tax rate, cash flow from operations, net of income taxes, in this example, equals the cash savings, S, minus the tax payments on these savings, t × S, plus the tax savings on depreciation deductions, t × D [$100,000 − (0.40 × $100,000) + (0.40 × $64,578) = $85,831].

By the same logic, each time Lifetime Care shows a gain on sale of assets, G, it will show tax outflows of t × G, and each time it shows a loss on sale of assets, L, it will show tax benefits or savings of t × L.

We focus on the three categories of cash flows considered earlier, but we now incorporate the associated tax flows for each category.

1a. *Initial machine investment.* The introduction of taxes does not change the $372,890 cost of the new X-ray machine.

1b. *Initial working-capital investment.* The introduction of income taxes also has no effect on the additional $10,000 of working capital required.

1c. *After-tax cash flow from current disposal of old machine.* The first step is to compute the gain or loss on disposal:

Current disposal price of old machine (given, p. 750)	$ 3,790
Deduct current book value of old machine (given, p. 763)	50,000
Loss on disposal of machine	$(46,210)

Recall from our earlier discussion that any loss on sale of assets lowers taxable income and results in tax savings. The after-tax cash flow from disposal of the old machine[3] equals:

Current disposal price of old machine	$ 3,790
Tax savings on loss (0.40 × $46,210)	18,484
After-tax cash flow from current disposal of old machine	$22,274

Items 1a, 1b, and 1c appear in Exhibit 21-7 as the net initial investment of $360,616 ($372,890 + $10,000 − $22,274) for replacing the old X-ray machine with the new X-ray machine.

2a. *Annual after-tax cash flow from operations (excluding depreciation effects).* The 40% tax rate reduces the benefit of the annual $100,000 operating cash flow savings with

---

[3] We are assuming Lifetime Care has sufficient positive taxable income so that the full amount of the loss on disposal of the old machine can be claimed as a deduction in year 1.

EXHIBIT 21-7
Net Present Value Method Incorporating Income Taxes: Lifetime Care Hospital's New X-Ray Machine

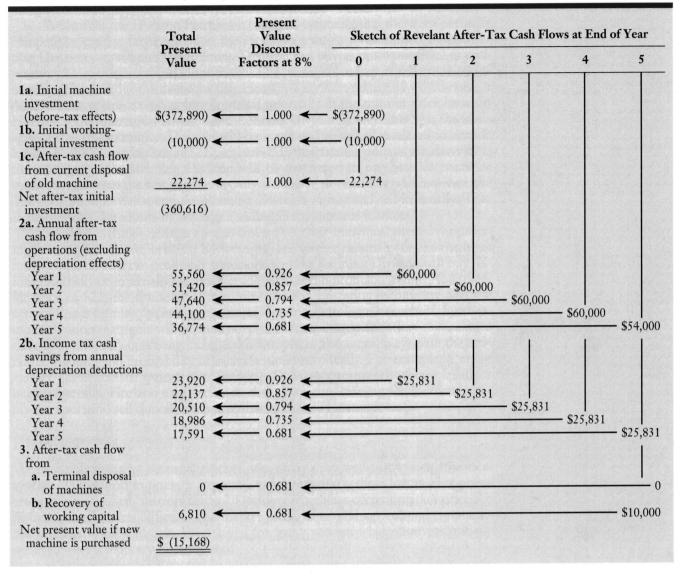

	Total Present Value	Present Value Discount Factors at 8%	Sketch of Revelant After-Tax Cash Flows at End of Year					
			0	1	2	3	4	5
1a. Initial machine investment (before-tax effects)	$(372,890) ←	1.000 ←	$(372,890)					
1b. Initial working-capital investment	(10,000) ←	1.000 ←	(10,000)					
1c. After-tax cash flow from current disposal of old machine	22,274 ←	1.000 ←	22,274					
Net after-tax initial investment	(360,616)							
2a. Annual after-tax cash flow from operations (excluding depreciation effects)								
Year 1	55,560 ←	0.926 ←		$60,000				
Year 2	51,420 ←	0.857 ←			$60,000			
Year 3	47,640 ←	0.794 ←				$60,000		
Year 4	44,100 ←	0.735 ←					$60,000	
Year 5	36,774 ←	0.681 ←						$54,000
2b. Income tax cash savings from annual depreciation deductions								
Year 1	23,920 ←	0.926 ←		$25,831				
Year 2	22,137 ←	0.857 ←			$25,831			
Year 3	20,510 ←	0.794 ←				$25,831		
Year 4	18,986 ←	0.735 ←					$25,831	
Year 5	17,591 ←	0.681 ←						$25,831
3. After-tax cash flow from								
a. Terminal disposal of machines	0 ←	0.681 ←						0
b. Recovery of working capital	6,810 ←	0.681 ←						$10,000
Net present value if new machine is purchased	$ (15,168)							

the new X-ray machine. For years 1–4, the after-tax flow (excluding depreciation effects) is:

Annual cash flow from operations with new machine	$100,000
Deduct income tax payments (0.40 × $100,000)	40,000
Annual after-tax cash flow from operations	$ 60,000

For year 5, the after-tax cash flow (excluding depreciation effects) is:

Annual cash flow from operations with new machine	$90,000
Deduct income tax payments (40% of $90,000)	36,000
Annual after-tax cash flow from operations	$54,000

Exhibit 21-7, item 2a, shows the $60,000 amounts for years 1–4 and $54,000 for year 5.

2b. *Income tax cash savings from annual depreciation deductions.* Depreciation tax deductions result in tax savings that, in effect, partially offset the cost of acquiring the new X-ray machine. The following table calculates the income for cash savings from the additional depreciation deductions each year as a result of acquiring the new machine.

Year	Depreciation Deduction on New X-Ray Machine (p. 763)	Depreciation Deduction on Old X-Ray Machine (p. 763)	Difference in Depreciation Deduction	Income Tax Rate	Increase In Income Tax Cash Savings from Depreciation Deductions with New X-Ray Machine
1	$74,578	$10,000	$64,578	40%	$25,831
2	74,578	10,000	64,578	40%	25,831
3	74,578	10,000	64,578	40%	25,831
4	74,578	10,000	64,578	40%	25,831
5	74,578	10,000	64,578	40%	25,831

Exhibit 21-7, item 2b, shows these $25,831 amounts for years 1–5.

3a. *After-tax cash flow from terminal disposal of machines.* Both the existing X-ray machine and the new X-ray machine have zero terminal disposal prices in year 5. Hence, the difference in after-tax terminal disposal prices is also zero. The general approach for computing the relevant amounts (illustrated for the new machine) is:

Terminal disposal price of new machine at end of year 5	$0
Deduct book value of old machine at end of year 5	0
Gain (or loss) on disposal of old machine	$0
Terminal disposal price of new machine at end of year 5	$0
Deduct taxes on gain (0.40 × $0)	0
After-tax cash inflow from terminal disposal of new machine	$0

3b. *After-tax cash flow from recovery of working capital.* Lifetime Care receives cash equal to the book value of its working capital. Thus, there is no gain or loss on working capital and hence no tax consequences. At the end of year 5, Lifetime recovers $15,000 cash from working capital if it invests in the new X-ray machine versus $5,000 if it continues to use the old X-ray machine—a net cash inflow of $10,000.

Exhibit 21-7 shows a NPV of −$15,168 from Lifetime Care investing in the new X-ray machine when the income tax rate is 40 percent. Recall from Exhibit 21-2 that the NPV was $20,200 when Lifetime Care was not subject to income tax (due to our assuming it was a nonprofit institution). Why the reduction in NPV with the introduction of income taxes? Both Exhibits 21-2 and 21-7 use the same five-year period and the same present value discount factors. The key reason is that the present value of the cash flow from operations is reduced by 40%, whereas the present value of the investment is reduced by less than 40 percent. Had Lifetime Care been able to deduct its initial machine investment of $372,890 as a depreciation deduction in year 0, the present value of its investment would have been reduced by 40% (as a result of the tax savings occurring in year 0). However, the depreciation deductions and the tax savings are spread over five years. As a result, the present value of the tax savings are considerably less than 40% of the investment.

The NPV of −$15,168 shown in Exhibit 21-7 summarizes the quantitative financial aspects of the new X-ray machine project.[4] Both nonfinancial quantitative

Reinforcing Problems Exer. 21-19 and 21-26 and Probs. 21-28, 21-31, and 21-32 cover the NPV method with taxes. Exer. 21-25 covers various methods with taxes.

[4]Exhibit 21-7 uses the same 8% RRR as does Exhibit 21-2. The only difference between these two exhibits is the recognition of income taxes. If this introduction of income taxes also requires a higher RRR (due, say, to Lifetime's investors demanding higher returns in a world with income taxes), the new X-ray machine has an even more negative NPV:

RRR	NPV
8%	$(15,168)
10%	$(32,833)
12%	$(48,927)

and qualitative aspects also should be considered. For example, qualitative considerations (such as the higher quality of X-rays and the safety of technicians and patients) may favor making the investment in the new X-ray machine. Management at Lifetime Care must judge whether or not these considerations more than offset the NPV of −$15,168 in Exhibit 21-7.

There is a general rule in tax planning: Where there is a legal choice, take the depreciation (or any other deduction) sooner rather than later. For economic policy reasons, usually to encourage (or in some cases discourage) investments, a government's tax laws will specify which depreciation methods and which depreciable lives will be allowed. Suppose the government, as under U.S. income tax laws, permitted accelerated depreciation to be used in Exhibit 21-7. This would result in higher depreciation deductions in earlier years. In turn, income tax savings would occur earlier causing an increase in the net present values.

MANAGING THE PROJECT

This section discusses stage 6 of capital budgeting—implementation and control. Two different aspects of management control are discussed—management control of the investment activity itself and management control of the project as a whole.

Management Control of the Investment Activity

Some initial investments, such as purchasing an X-ray machine or a video conferencing facility, are relatively easy to implement. Other initial investments, such as building shopping malls or new manufacturing plants, are more complex and take more time. In the latter case, monitoring and controlling the investment schedules and budgets is critical to the success of the overall project.

Management Control of the Project—Postinvestment Audit

A postinvestment audit compares the actual results for a project to the costs and benefits expected at the time the project was selected. This audit provides management with feedback about performance. Suppose, for example, that actual outcomes (operating cash savings from the new X-ray machine in the Lifetime Care example) are much lower than expected outcomes. Management must then investigate to determine if this result occurred because the original estimates were overly optimistic or because there were problems in implementing the project. Both types of problems are a concern.

Optimistic estimates are a concern because they may result in the acceptance of a project that otherwise should have been rejected. To discourage optimistic estimates, companies such as DuPont maintain records comparing actual results with the estimates made by individual managers when seeking approval for capital investments. DuPont believes that postinvestment audits discourage managers from making unrealistic forecasts. Problems in implementing a project are an obvious concern because the returns from the project will not meet expectations. Postinvestment audits can point to areas of corrective action.

Care should be exercised when performing a postinvestment audit. It should be done only after project outcomes have stabilized. Doing the audit early may give a misleading picture. Obtaining actual results to compare against estimates is often not easy. For example, actual labor cost savings from the new X-ray machine may not be comparable to the estimated savings because the actual number and types of X-rays taken may be different from the quantities assumed during the selection stage. Other benefits, such as the impact on patient treatment, may be difficult to quantify.

INTANGIBLE ASSETS AND CAPITAL BUDGETING

Intangible assets, whether or not they are recognized for external reporting purposes, are critical to most organizations. Examples include brand names, the customer base, and the intellectual capital of employees. These intangible assets have

Correcting Student Misconceptions/Curriculum Linkage Postinvestment audits require information on the costs and benefits actually realized from the project. It can be difficult to disentangle a company's overall cash flows and attribute them to specific projects. One helpful mechanism for doing so is life-cycle costing (see Chap. 12), in which journal entries are coded to specific projects as well as to functional accounts.

New in This Edition This new section on intangible assets and capital budgeting covers a very important and growing area.

the potential to yield net cash inflows for many years in the future. The magnitude or timing of these future net cash inflows can change from year to year. Top management can use a capital budgeting tool, such as NPV, to summarize the difference in the future net cash inflows from an intangible asset at two different points in time.

Consider the customer base as an intangible asset. The phrase "customers are our most important asset" is frequently used by managers. NPV analysis can highlight the importance of long-term considerations when evaluating customers. Consider Potato Supreme, which produces potato products for sale to retail outlets (such as supermarkets) and large institutions (such as hospitals and dormitory canteens). It is currently analyzing two of its customers. Customer A (Shine Stores) is a supermarket chain that has large but rather dated stores that are located in a declining population area. Customer B (Always Open) is a rapidly growing chain of 24-hour convenience stores. Potato Supreme predicts the following net cash inflows (in thousands) from each customer account for the next five years (these net cash inflows incorporate both revenues and costs associated with each customer):

	2001	2002	2003	2004	2005
Shine Stores	$1,450	$1,305	$1,175	$1,058	$ 950
Always Open	690	1,160	1,900	2,950	4,160

Which customer is more valuable to Potato Supreme? Using the current period (2001) only, Shine Stores provides over 200% higher net cash inflows than Always Open ($1,450 versus $690). A different picture emerges, however, with a longer five-year horizon. Using Potato Supreme's 10% required rate of return, the net present value of the Always Open customer is $7,610 compared to $4,591 for Shine Stores.[5] Note how NPV captures the future growth of Always Open in its estimate of customer value. Managers can use this information when allocating resources (such as extra sales persons) to service individual customers.

The preceding estimates of customer value can be refined in at least three ways:

1. *By recognizing an even longer time horizon.* For simplicity, we examined only a five-year horizon. Many companies (such as insurance companies and retail stores) have customers with much longer time horizons.

2. *By recognizing that not all customers will be retained over an extended time period.* The **customer retention rate** measures the percentage of existing customers that will be retained next period. Companies are now using NPV calculations to examine the effect of alternative ways of increasing customer retention. Customer loyalty programs, such as frequent-flyer programs, are an example of customer retention initiatives.

3. *By recognizing that new customers will be attracted.* These new customers can be due to referrals from existing customers, from better marketing, from entering new markets, and so on.

A comparison of year-to-year changes in customer NPV estimates highlights whether managers have been successful in maintaining long-run profitable relationships with their customers. Suppose the NPV of Potato Supreme's customer base declines 15% in one year. This decline could be because of factors controllable by managers. Suppose the salesperson in charge of the Always Open account offered very large price discounts over an extended period so as to attain a special bonus in Potato Supreme's marketing incentive program. Absent any large volume increase, this price discount will reduce the NPV of the customer. Potato Supreme would view this action as conflicting with maintaining long-run profitable relationships with its customers. Alternatively, the price discount could be due to factors less con-

---

[5]These NPV amounts are calculated using the 10% present value discount factor from Appendix C (pp. 871–878). For example, year 1 has a present value of $1,318 ($1,450 × 0.909) for Shine Stores and $627 ($690 × 0.909) for Always Open.

trollable by Potato Supreme's managers. Suppose a major competitor aggressively bids for the Always Open account. Potato Supreme may increase its price discount to meet the competition. The NPV of the account may have been reduced in comparison to the value at the end of the prior year. However, top management may well view a price discount made to meet competition differently from that made by its own salesperson to attain a short-run bonus.

Capital One, a financial services company, uses NPV to estimate the value of different credit-card customers. This approach is also used in the cellular telecommunications industry. Here much effort is made to capture multiple years of service with each customer rather than having a customer sign a short-run mobile phone service contract and then switch to another company at the end of that contract. This switching is called "customer churn." The higher the probability of customer churn, the lower the NPV of the customer to the telecommunications company.

Points to Stress Keeping profitable customers (and generating new ones) is one key to any business staying viable. There are many opportunities in which the management accountant can supply valuable information needed by other members of the management team. "A management accountant should always "look for the possibilities" of where relevant information can be used to add value to the firm."

PROBLEM FOR SELF-STUDY

PROBLEM (PART A)

Revisit the Lifetime Care X-ray machine project. Assume, as before, that Lifetime is a nonprofit organization and the expected annual cash inflows from the operating cost savings are $30,000 higher in each year (that is, $130,000 in years 1–4 and $120,000 in year 5). All other facts are unchanged: a $379,100 net initial investment, a five-year useful life, a zero terminal disposal price, and an 8% required rate of return. Year 5 cash inflows of $130,000 include $10,000 recovery of working capital.

Required
Compute the following:
1. Net present value
2. Internal rate of return
3. Payback period
4. Accrual accounting rate of return on net initial investment

SOLUTION

1. NPV = ($130,000 × 3.993) − $379,100

   = $519,090 − $379,100 = $139,990

2. There are several approaches to computing the IRR. One is to use a calculator with an IRR function: This approach gives an IRR of 21.18 percent. An alternative approach is to use Table 4 in Appendix C at the end of the text:

   $$\$379,100 = \$130,000F$$

   $$F = \frac{\$379,100}{\$130,000} = 2.916$$

On the five-period line of Table 4, the column closest to 2.916 is 22 percent. To obtain a more accurate number, straight-line interpolation can be used:

	Present Value	**Factors**
20%	2.991	2.991
IRR	—	2.916
22%	2.864	—
Difference	0.127	0.075

$$\text{IRR} = 20\% + \frac{0.075}{0.127}(2\%) = 21.18\%$$

3.

$$\text{Payback} = \frac{\text{Net initial investment}}{\text{Uniform increase in expected annual future cash flows}}$$

$$= \$379{,}100 \div \$130{,}000 = 2.9 \text{ years}$$

4.

$$\text{AARR} = \frac{\text{Increase in expected average annual operating income}}{\text{Net initial investment}}$$

$$\text{Increase in expected average annual cash operating savings} = [(\$130{,}000 \times 4) + \$120{,}000] \div 5$$

$$= \$128{,}000$$

$$\text{Average annual depreciation} = \$372{,}890 \div 5 = \$74{,}578$$

$$\text{Increase in expected average annual operating income} = \$128{,}000 - \$74{,}578 = \$53{,}422$$

$$\text{AARR} = \frac{\$53{,}422}{\$379{,}100} = 14.09\%$$

PROBLEM (PART B)

Assume that Lifetime Care is subject to income tax at a 40% rate. All other facts from Part A are unchanged. Compute the NPV of the new X-ray machine project.

SOLUTION

Exhibit 21-8 shows the computations. Item 2a. is where the new $130,000 cash flow assumption affects the NPV analysis (compared to Exhibit 21-7). For years 1–4, the after-tax flow (excluding depreciation effects) is:

Annual cash flow from operations with new machine	$130,000
Deduct income tax payments (40% of $130,000)	52,000
Annual after-tax cash flow from operations	$ 78,000

For year 5, the after-tax flow (excluding depreciation effects) is:

Annual cash flow from operations with new machine	$120,000
Deduct income tax payments (40% of $120,000)	48,000
Annual after-tax cash flow from operations	$ 72,000

The NPV in Exhibit 21-8 is $56,706. As computed in Part A, the NPV when there are no income taxes is $139,990.

SUMMARY

The following points are linked to the chapter's learning objectives:

1. Capital budgeting is a long-term planning process for proposed capital projects. The life of a project is usually longer than one year, so capital budgeting decisions consider revenues and costs over relatively long periods. In contrast, accrual accounting measures income on a year-by-year basis.

2. Capital budgeting is a six-stage process: (a) the identification stage, (b) the search stage, (c) the information-acquisition stage, (d) the selection stage, (e) the financing stage, and (f) the implementation and control stage.

3. Discounted cash flow (DCF) is a conceptually appealing approach to capital budgeting. It explicitly includes all project cash flows and recognizes the time value of money. Two DCF methods are the net present value (NPV) method and the in-

EXHIBIT 21-8

Net Present Value Method Incorporating Income Taxes: Lifetime Care Hospital's New X-Ray Machine with Revised Annual Cash Flow from Operations

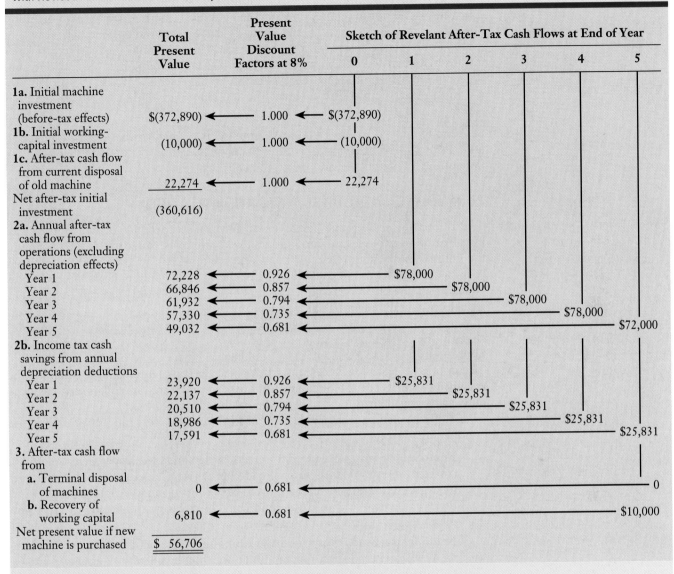

	Total Present Value	Present Value Discount Factors at 8%	Sketch of Revelant After-Tax Cash Flows at End of Year					
			0	1	2	3	4	5
1a. Initial machine investment (before-tax effects)	$(372,890) ←	1.000 ←	$(372,890)					
1b. Initial working-capital investment	(10,000) ←	1.000 ←	(10,000)					
1c. After-tax cash flow from current disposal of old machine	22,274 ←	1.000 ←	22,274					
Net after-tax initial investment	(360,616)							
2a. Annual after-tax cash flow from operations (excluding depreciation effects)								
Year 1	72,228 ←	0.926 ←		$78,000				
Year 2	66,846 ←	0.857 ←			$78,000			
Year 3	61,932 ←	0.794 ←				$78,000		
Year 4	57,330 ←	0.735 ←					$78,000	
Year 5	49,032 ←	0.681 ←						$72,000
2b. Income tax cash savings from annual depreciation deductions								
Year 1	23,920 ←	0.926 ←		$25,831				
Year 2	22,137 ←	0.857 ←			$25,831			
Year 3	20,510 ←	0.794 ←				$25,831		
Year 4	18,986 ←	0.735 ←					$25,831	
Year 5	17,591 ←	0.681 ←						$25,831
3. After-tax cash flow from								
a. Terminal disposal of machines	0 ←	0.681 ←						0
b. Recovery of working capital	6,810 ←	0.681 ←						$10,000
Net present value if new machine is purchased	$ 56,706							

ternal rate-of-return (IRR) method. The NPV method calculates the expected net monetary gain or loss from a project by discounting all expected future cash inflows and outflows to the present point in time, using the required rate of return. A project is desirable if it has a positive NPV. The IRR method computes the rate of return (discount rate) at which the present value of expected cash inflows from a project equals the present value of expected cash outflows from a project. A project is desirable if its IRR exceeds the required rate of return.

4. Relevant cash inflows and outflows are (a) expected future cash flows that (b) differ among the alternatives. Only cash inflows and outflows matter. Accrual accounting concepts such as accrued revenues and accrued expenses are irrelevant for the DCF methods.

5. The payback method measures the time it will take to recoup, in the form of cash inflows, the total cash amount invested in a project in the form of cash inflows. The payback method neglects profitability and the time value of money.

6. The accrual accounting rate of return (AARR) is operating income divided by a measure of investment. The AARR considers profitability but ignores the time value of money.

7. The widespread use of accrual accounting for evaluating the performance of a manager or division impedes the adoption of DCF methods in capital budgeting. Frequently, the optimal decision made using a DCF method will not report good "operating income" results in the project's early years under accrual accounting methods, so managers are tempted to not use DCF methods even though the decisions that stem from them would be optimal for the company over the long run. This conflict can be reduced by evaluating managers on a project-by-project basis, looking at their ability to meet the amounts and timing of forecasted cash flows.

8. Although depreciation is a noncash expense, it is a deductible cost for calculating tax outflows. The taxes saved as a result of depreciation deductions increase cash flows in DCF computations.

APPENDIX: CAPITAL BUDGETING AND INFLATION

Points to Stress It is important to account for inflation in capital budgeting. The capital budgeting specialist needs to understand that because of inflation the cash inflows received in future periods will be measured in dollars that have less value than the dollars invested in the asset today. Failure to account for inflation will make the project appear more attractive than it really is.

The Lifetime Care example (Exhibits 21-2 to 21-6) does not include adjustments for inflation in the relevant revenues and relevant costs. **Inflation** is the decline in the general purchasing power of the monetary unit. An inflation rate of 10% per year means that what you could buy with $100 at the beginning of the year will cost you $110 at the end of the year. We now illustrate how inflation can be incorporated into capital budgeting analysis.

Why is it important to account for inflation in capital budgeting? Because declines in the general purchasing power of the monetary unit (say, dollars) will inflate future cash flows above what they would have been in the absence of inflation. These inflated cash flows will cause the project to look better than it is, unless the analyst recognizes that the inflated cash flows are measured in dollars that have less purchasing power than the dollars that were initially invested.

When analyzing inflation, distinguish between the real rate of return and the nominal rate of return:

Real rate of return is the rate of return demanded to cover investment risk (with no inflation). This rate is made up of two elements: (a) a risk-free element, the pure rate of return on risk-free long-term government bonds when there is no expected inflation, and (b) a business-risk element, the risk premium that is demanded for bearing risks.

Points to Stress The required rate of return in the financial markets is the nominal rate, since investors expect to be compensated for both investment risk and inflation.

Nominal rate of return is made up of three elements: (a) a risk-free element when there is no expected inflation, (b) a business-risk element, and (c) an inflation element. Items (a) and (b) make up the real rate of return to cover investment risk. The inflation element is the premium above the real rate that is demanded for the anticipated decline in the general purchasing power of the monetary unit. The rates of return (or interest) earned in the financial markets are nominal rates, because investors want to be compensated both for the investment risks they take, as well as for the expected decline in the general purchasing power of the money they get back as a result of inflation.

Assume that the real rate of return for investments in high-risk cellular data transmission equipment at Network Communications is 20% and that the expected inflation rate is 10 percent. The nominal rate of return is:

$$\text{Nominal rate} = (1 + \text{Real rate})(1 + \text{Inflation rate}) - 1$$

$$= (1 + 0.20)(1 + 0.10) - 1$$

$$= (1.20 \times 1.10) - 1 = 1.32 - 1 = 0.32$$

The nominal rate of return is related to the real rate of return and the inflation rate:

Real rate of return	0.20
Inflation rate	0.10
Combination (0.20 × 0.10)	0.02
Nominal rate of return	0.32

The combination component captures the joint interaction of the real return and the inflation rate.[6]

Note that the nominal rate is slightly higher than the real rate (0.20) plus the inflation rate (0.10). Why? Because the nominal rate recognizes that inflation also decreases the purchasing power of the real rate of return earned during the year.

Net Present Value Method and Inflation

The watchwords when incorporating inflation into the net present value (NPV) method are *internal consistency*. There are two internally consistent approaches:

◆ *Nominal approach*—predicts cash inflows and outflows in nominal monetary units *and* uses a nominal rate as the required rate of return.

◆ *Real approach*—predicts cash inflows and outflows in real monetary units *and* uses a real rate as the required rate of return.

We will limit our discussion to the nominal approach. Consider an investment that is expected to generate sales of 100 units and a net cash inflow of $1,000 ($10 per unit) each year for two years *absent inflation*. If inflation of 10% is expected each year, net cash inflows from the sale of each unit would be $11 ($10 × 1.10) in year 1 and $12.10 ($11 × 1.10, or $10 × (1.10)^2) in year 2, resulting in net cash inflows of $1,100 in year 1 and $1,210 in year 2. The net cash inflows of $1,100 and $1,210 are nominal cash inflows because they include the impact of inflation. *Nominal cash flows are the cash flows that are recorded in the accounting system.* The cash inflows of $1,000 each year are real cash flows. The accounting system does not record these cash flows. Many managers find the nominal approach easier to understand and use because they observe nominal cash flows in their accounting systems and the nominal rates of return in financial markets.

Assume that Network Communications can purchase equipment to make and sell a cellular data transmission product at a net initial investment of $750,000. It is expected to have a four-year useful life with a zero terminal disposal price. An annual inflation rate of 10% is expected over this four-year period. Network Communications requires an after-tax nominal rate of return of 32% (see p. 772).

The following table presents the predicted amounts of real (assuming no inflation) and nominal (after considering cumulative inflation) net cash inflows from the equipment over the next four years (excluding the $750,000 investment in the equipment and before any income tax payments):

Year (1)	Before-Tax Cash Inflows in Real Dollars (2)	Cumulative Inflation Rate Factor[a] (3)	Before-Tax Cash Inflows in Nominal Dollars (4) = (2) × (3)
1	$500,000	(1.10)^1 = 1.1000	$550,000
2	600,000	(1.10)^2 = 1.2100	726,000
3	600,000	(1.10)^3 = 1.3310	798,600
4	300,000	(1.10)^4 = 1.4641	439,230

[a]1.10 = 1.00 + 0.10 inflation rate.

[6]The real rate of return can be expressed in terms of the nominal rate of return as follows:

$$\text{Real rate} = \frac{1 + \text{Nominal rate}}{1 + \text{Inflation rate}} - 1 = \frac{1 + 0.32}{1 + 0.10} - 1 = 0.20, \text{ or } 20\%$$

EXHIBIT 21-9

Net Present Value Method Using Nominal Approach to Inflation for Network Communication's New Equipment

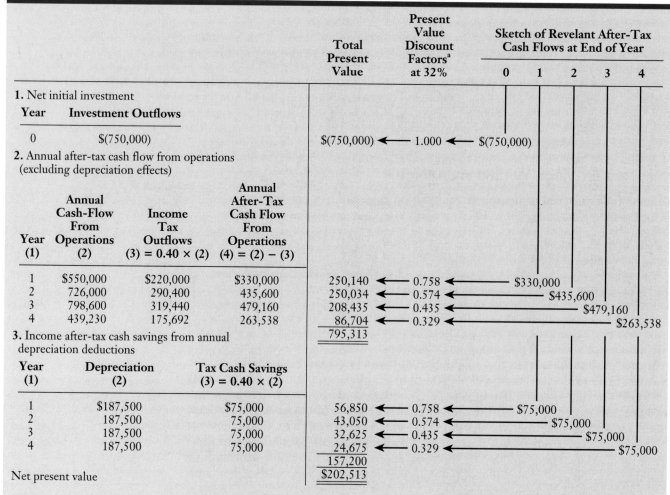

		Total Present Value	Present Value Discount Factors[a] at 32%	Sketch of Relevant After-Tax Cash Flows at End of Year				
				0	**1**	**2**	**3**	**4**

1. Net initial investment

Year	Investment Outflows
0	$(750,000)

$(750,000) ← 1.000 ← $(750,000)

2. Annual after-tax cash flow from operations (excluding depreciation effects)

Year (1)	Annual Cash-Flow From Operations (2)	Income Tax Outflows (3) = 0.40 × (2)	Annual After-Tax Cash Flow From Operations (4) = (2) − (3)
1	$550,000	$220,000	$330,000
2	726,000	290,400	435,600
3	798,600	319,440	479,160
4	439,230	175,692	263,538

250,140 ← 0.758 ← $330,000
250,034 ← 0.574 ← $435,600
208,435 ← 0.435 ← $479,160
86,704 ← 0.329 ← $263,538
795,313

3. Income after-tax cash savings from annual depreciation deductions

Year (1)	Depreciation (2)	Tax Cash Savings (3) = 0.40 × (2)
1	$187,500	$75,000
2	187,500	75,000
3	187,500	75,000
4	187,500	75,000

56,850 ← 0.758 ← $75,000
43,050 ← 0.574 ← $75,000
32,625 ← 0.435 ← $75,000
24,675 ← 0.329 ← $75,000
157,200

Net present value $202,513

[a]The nominal discount rate of 32% is made up of the real rate of interest of 20% and the inflation rate of 10% [(1 + 0.20) (1 + 0.10)] − 1 = 0.32.

As done elsewhere in this chapter, we make the simplifying assumption that cash flows occur at the end of each year. The income tax rate is 40 percent. For tax purposes, the equipment will be depreciated using the straight-line method.

Exhibit 21-9 shows the calculation of NPV with cash flows in nominal dollars and using a nominal discount rate. The calculations in Exhibit 21-9 include the net initial machine investment, annual after-tax cash flow from operations (excluding depreciation effects), and income tax cash savings from depreciation deductions. The project has a net present value of $202,513 and therefore should be accepted.

▼ **T E R M S   T O   L E A R N**

This chapter and the Glossary at the end of the book contain definitions of the following important terms:

accounting rate of return (p. 760)
accrual accounting rate of return (AARR) (760)
capital budgeting (748)
customer retention rate (768)

discounted cash flow (DCF) method (750)
discount rate (751)
hurdle rate (751)
inflation (772)

internal rate-of-return (IRR)
   method (752)
net present value (NPV) method (751)
nominal rate of return (772)
(opportunity) cost of capital (751)

payback (758)
real rate of return (772)
required rate of return (RRR) (751)
time value of money (750)

QUESTIONS

21-1 "Capital budgeting has the same focus as accrual accounting." Do you agree? Explain.

21-2 List and briefly describe each of the six stages in capital budgeting.

21-3 What is the essence of the discounted cash flow method?

21-4 "Only quantitative outcomes are relevant in capital budgeting analyses." Do you agree? Explain.

21-5 How can sensitivity analysis be incorporated in DCF analysis?

21-6 What is the payback method? What are its main strengths and weaknesses?

21-7 Describe the accrual accounting rate-of-return method. What are its main strengths and weaknesses?

21-8 "The trouble with discounted cash flow techniques is that they ignore depreciation costs." Do you agree? Explain.

21-9 "Let's be more practical. DCF is not the gospel. Managers should not become so enchanted with DCF that strategic considerations are overlooked." Do you agree? Explain.

21-10 "All overhead costs are relevant in NPV analysis." Do you agree? Explain.

21-11 Bill Watts, president of Western Publications, accepts a capital budgeting project advocated by Division X. This is the division in which the president spent his first ten years with the company. On the same day, the president rejects a capital budgeting project proposal from Division Y. The manager of Division Y is incensed. She believes that the Division Y project has an internal rate of return at least ten percentage points above the Division X project. She comments, "What is the point of all our detailed DCF analysis? If Watts is panting over a project, he can arrange to have the proponents of that project massage the numbers so that it looks like a winner." What advice would you give the manager of Division Y?

21-12 Distinguish different categories of cash flows that an equipment replacement decision by a tax-paying company should consider?

21-13 Describe three ways income taxes can affect the cash inflows or outflows in a motor vehicle replacement decision by a tax-paying company.

21-14 How can capital budgeting tools assist in evaluating a manager who is responsible for retaining customers of a cellular telephone company?

21-15 Distinguish the nominal rate of return from the real rate of return.

EXERCISES

21-16 **Exercises in compound interest, no income taxes**. To be sure that you understand how to use the tables in Appendix C at the end of this book, solve the following exercises. Ignore income tax considerations. The correct answers, rounded to the nearest dollar, appear on pages 784–785.

Required

1. You have just won $5,000. How much money will you have at the end of ten years if you invest it at 6% compounded annually? At 14 percent?

2. Ten years from now, the unpaid principal of the mortgage on your house will be $89,550. How much do you have to invest today at 6% interest compounded annually to accumulate the $89,550 in ten years?

3. If the unpaid mortgage on your house in ten years will be $89,550, how much money do you have to invest annually at 6% to have exactly this amount on hand at the end of the tenth year?

4. You plan to save $5,000 of your earnings at the end of each year for the next ten years. How much money will you have at the end of the tenth year if you invest your savings compounded at 12% per year?

5. You have just turned 65 and an endowment insurance policy has paid you a lump sum of $200,000. If you invest the sum at 6%, how much money can you withdraw from your account in equal amounts each year so that at the end of ten years (age 75) there will be nothing left?

6. You have estimated that for the first ten years after you retire you will need an annual cash inflow of $50,000. How much money must you invest at 6% at your retirement age to obtain this annual cash inflow? At 20 percent?

7. The following table shows two schedules of prospective operating cash inflows, each of which requires the same net initial investment of $10,000 now:

Annual Cash Inflows

Year	Plan A	Plan B
1	$ 1,000	$ 5,000
2	2,000	4,000
3	3,000	3,000
4	4,000	2,000
5	5,000	1,000
Total	$15,000	$15,000

The required rate of return is 6% compounded annually. All cash inflows occur at the end of each year. In terms of net present value, which plan is more desirable? Show your computations.

 21-17 Comparison of approaches to capital budgeting, no income taxes. The Building Distributors Group is thinking of buying, at a cost of $220,000, some new packaging equipment that is expected to save $50,000 in cash-operating costs per year. Its estimated useful life is ten years, and it will have zero terminal disposal price. The required rate of return is 16%. Ignore income tax issues in your answers.

Required

Compute the following:

1. Net present value
2. Payback period
3. Internal rate of return
4. Accrual accounting rate of return based on net initial investment (Assume straight-line depreciation.)

 21-18 Capital budgeting methods, no income taxes. City Hospital, a not-for-profit organization, estimates that it can save $28,000 a year in cash operating costs for the next ten years if it buys a special-purpose eye-testing machine at a cost of $110,000. A zero terminal disposal price is expected. City Hospital's required rate of return is 14 percent.

Required

1. Compute the following:
   a. Net present value
   b. Payback period
   c. Internal rate of return
   d. Accrual accounting rate of return based on net initial investment (Assume straight-line depreciation.)
2. What factors should City Hospital consider in deciding whether to purchase the special purpose eye-testing machine?

21-19 Capital budgeting, income taxes. Assume the same facts as in Exercise 21-18 except that City Hospital is now a taxpaying entity. The income tax rate is 30% for all transactions that affect income taxes.

Required

1. Re-do your computations in requirement 1 of Exercise 21-18.
2. How would your computations in requirement 1 of this exercise be affected if the special-purpose machine has a $10,000 terminal disposal price at the end of ten years? Assume depreciation deductions are based on the $110,000 purchase cost using a straight-line method. Answer briefly in words without new computations.

21-20 Capital budgeting with uneven cash flows, no income taxes. Southern Cola is considering the purchase of a special-purpose bottling machine for $28,000. It is expected to have a useful life of seven years with a zero terminal disposal price. The plant manager estimates the following savings in cash operating costs:

Year	Amount
1	$10,000
2	8,000
3	6,000
4	5,000
5	4,000
6	3,000
7	3,000
Total	$39,000

Southern Cola uses a required rate of return of 16% in its capital budgeting decisions. Ignore income taxes in your analysis.

Required

Compute the following:

1. Net present value
2. Payback period
3. Internal rate of return
4. Accrual accounting rate of return based on net initial investment (Assume straight-line depreciation. Use the average annual savings in cash operating costs when computing the numerator of the accrual accounting rate of return.)

21-21 Comparison of projects, no income taxes. (CMA, adapted) Fox Valley Healthcare, Inc., is a nonprofit organization that operates eight nursing homes and ten assisted-living facilities. The company has grown considerably over the last three years and expects to continue to expand in the years ahead, particularly in the area of assisted-living facilities for seniors.

Jim Ruffalo, president of Fox Valley, has developed a plan to add a new building for top management and the administrative staff. He has selected a building contractor. Vukacek Construction Co., and has reached agreement on the building and its construction. Vukacek is ready to start as soon as the contract is signed and will complete the work in two years.

The building contractor has offered Fox Valley a choice of three payment plans, as follows:

◆ *Plan I* Payment of $200,000 on the signing of the contract and $3,000,000 at the time of completion.

◆ *Plan II* Payment of $1,000,000 on the signing of the contract and $1,000,000 at the end of each of the two succeeding years. The end of the second year is the completion date.

◆ *Plan III* Payment of $100,000 on the signing of the contract and $1,000,000 at the end of each of the three succeeding years.

Ruffalo is not sure which payment plan he should accept. He has asked the treasurer, Lisa Monroe, for her assessment and advice. Fox Valley will finance the construction with a long-term loan and has a borrowing rate of 12 percent.

Required

1. Using the net present value method, calculate the comparative cost of each of the three payment plans being considered by Fox Valley Heathcare, Inc.
2. Which payment plan should the treasurer recommend? Explain.
3. Discuss the financial factors, other than the cost of the plan, that should be considered in selecting an appropriate payment plan.

21-22 Payback and NPV methods, no income taxes. (CMA, adapted) Cording Manufacturing is a small company that is currently analyzing capital expenditure proposals for the purchase of equipment. The capital budget is limited to $500,000, which Cording believes is the maximum capital it can raise.

Richard King, an outside financial advisor, is preparing an analysis of four projects that Walter Minden, Cording's president, is considering. King has projected the future cash flows for each potential purchase. The information concerning the four projects is as follows:

	Project A	Project B	Project C	Project D
Projected Cash Outflow				
Net initial investment	$200,000	$190,000	$250,000	$210,000
Projected cash inflows				
Year 1	$50,000	$40,000	$75,000	$75,000
Year 2	50,000	50,000	75,000	75,000
Year 3	50,000	70,000	60,000	60,000
Year 4	50,000	75,000	80,000	40,000
Year 5	50,000	75,000	100,000	20,000

Required

1. Since Cording Manufacturing's cash is limited, Walter Minden thinks that the payback method for calculating investments would be the best method for choosing capital budgeting projects.
   a. Explain what the payback method measures and how it is used. Include in your explanation several benefits and limitations of the payback method.
   b. Calculate the payback period for each of the four projects. Ignore income tax considerations.
2. King would like to compare the projects using the net present value method. The required rate of return for Cording is 12 percent. All cash flows occur at the end of the year. Calculate the net present value for each project. Ignore income tax considerations.
3. Which projects, if any, would you recommend funding? Briefly state your reasons.

21-23 NPV, sharing rules and stadium projects, no income taxes. Santa Clara County will soon begin the construction of a brand new football stadium for the San Jose Wafers, a new GFL (Global Football League) expansion team. The stadium will be ready on January 1, 2001. An independent accounting firm has made the following projections for cash inflows and cash outflows over the stadium's expected five-year life (admittedly a simplification). Assume all revenue and operating costs cash flows occur at year end from 2001 to 2005.

Revenues	
Tickets and suites	$52 million per year
Advertising, naming rights, and concessions	$38 million per year
Parking	$12 million per year
Costs	
Operating costs	$35 million per year

The Wafers will receive a five-year lease on the stadium. Construction costs total $120 million, incurred on January 1, 2000.

The law firm representing the Wafers has presented the County with the following two optional sharing rules:

◆ *Sharing rule A*   County pays all construction costs and Wafers pays all operating costs. County receives all parking revenues. Wafers receives all tickets and suite revenues, and all advertising, naming rights, and concession revenues.

◆ *Sharing rule B*   Wafers pays 20% of construction costs and 80% of the operating costs. Everything else is as in sharing rule A above.

Assume the San Jose Wafers do not pay corporate income taxes.

Required

1. Calculate the NPV of the stadium project from the perspective of the Wafers (a) under sharing rule A, and (b) under sharing rule B. Assume a required rate of return of 10 percent.
2. How much of the construction cost can the Wafers bear and still have a positive NPV under (a) sharing rule A, and (b) sharing rule B?
3. Do you think the County should construct the stadium? What qualitative factors may affect your decision?

21-24 DCF, accrual accounting rate of return, working capital, evaluation of performance, no income taxes. Hammerlink Company has been offered a special-purpose metal-cutting machine for $110,000. The machine is expected to have a useful life of eight years with a terminal disposal price of $30,000. Savings in cash operating costs are expected to be $25,000 per year. However, additional working capital is needed to keep the machine running efficiently and without stoppages. Working capital includes such items as filters, lubricants, bearings, abrasives, flexible exhaust pipes, and belts. These items must continually be replaced, so that an investment of $8,000 must be maintained in them at all times, but this investment is fully recoverable (will be "cashed in") at the end of the useful life. Hammerlink's required rate of return is 14 percent. Ignore income taxes in your analysis.

Required

1. Compute the net present value.
2. Compute the internal rate of return.
3. Compute the accrual accounting rate of return based on the net initial investment. Assume straight-line depreciation.
4. You have the authority to make the purchase decision. Why might you be reluctant to base your decision on the DCF methods?

21-25 New equipment purchase, income taxes. Presentation Graphics prepares slides and other aids for individuals making presentations. It estimates it can save $35,000 a year in cash operating costs for the next five years if it buys a special-purpose color-slide workstation at a cost of $75,000. The workstation will have a zero terminal disposal price at the end of year 5. No change in working capital will be required. Presentation Graphics has a 12% after-tax required rate of return. Its income tax rate is 40 percent.

Required

1. Assume that Presentation Graphics uses straight-line depreciation on its tax return. Compute (a) net present value, (b) payback period, and (c) internal rate of return.
2. Compare and contrast the capital budgeting methods in requirement 1.

21-26 Selling a plant, income taxes. (CMA, adapted) Waterford Specialties Corporation, a clothing manufacturer, has a plant that will become idle on December 31, 1999. John Landry, corporate controller, has been asked to look at three options regarding the disposition of the plant.

◆ *Option 1:* The plant, which has been fully depreciated for financial reporting and tax purposes, can be sold immediately for $9,000,000.

◆ *Option 2:* The plant can be leased to Auburn Mills, one of Waterford's suppliers for four years. Under the lease terms, Auburn would pay Waterford $200,000 rent per month (payable at year-end) and would grant Waterford a special 10% discount off the normal price of $2 per yard on 2,370,000 yards of fabric purchased by another Waterford plant (assume discount received at year-end for each of the four years). Auburn would bear all of the plant's ownership costs including property taxes. Waterford expects to sell this plant for $2,000,000 at the end of the four-year lease.

◆ *Option 3:* The plant could be used for four years to make souvenir jackets for the 2004 Olympics. Fixed overhead costs (a cash outflow) before any equipment upgrades, are estimated to be $200,000 annually for the four-year period. The jackets are expected to sell for $42 each. Variable costs per unit are expected to be as follows: direct materials, $20.80; direct manufacturing, marketing and distribution labor, $6.40; variable manufacturing, marketing and distribution overhead, $5.80. The following production and sales of jackets are expected: 2000, 200,0000 units; 2001, 300,000 units; 2002, 400,000 units; 2003, 100,000 units. In order to manufacture the souvenir jackets, some of the plant equipment would need to be upgraded at an immediate cost of $1,500,000 to be depreciated using straight-line depreciation over the four years it will be in use. Because of the modernization of the equipment, Waterford could sell the plant for $3,000,000 at the end of four years. No change in working capital will be required.

Waterford treats all cash flows as if they occur at the end of the year, and uses an after-tax cost of capital of 12 percent. Waterford is subject to a 40% income tax rate.

Required

1. Calculate the net present value of each of the options available to Waterford and determine which option Waterford should select using the net present value criterion.
2. What nonfinancial qualitative factors should Waterford consider before making its choice?

PROBLEMS

21-27 Equipment replacement, no income taxes. Superfast Chips manufactures and delivers prototype chips to customers within 24 hours. The current production facility was set up when the company began operations in Dublin, Ireland, in 1994. It is outdated and constrains future growth. In 2001, Superfast expects to deliver 460 prototype chips at an average price of $80,000 per prototype. Superfast's marketing vice president forecasts growth of 50 prototype chips per year through 2010. That is, demand is 460 in 2001, 510 in 2002, 560 in 2003, and so on.

The current facility cannot produce more than 500 prototypes annually. To meet future demand, Superfast must either modernize the current facility or replace it. The old equipment is fully depreciated and can be sold for $3,000,000. If the current facilities are modernized, such costs are to be capitalized and depreciated over the useful life of the updated facility. The old equipment is retained as part of the modernize alternative. Following is some data on the two options available to Superfast:

	Modernize	Replace
Initial investment in 2001	$28,000,000	$49,000,000
Terminal disposal price in 2007	$ 5,000,000	$12,000,000
Useful life	7 years	7 years
Total annual cash operating costs per prototype	$62,000	$56,000

Superfast uses straight-line depreciation for income reporting, assuming zero terminal disposal price. For simplicity, we assume no change in prices or costs in future years. The investment will be made at the beginning of 2001, and all transactions thereafter occur on the last day of the year. Superfast's required rate of return is 12 percent.

There is no difference between the modernize and replace alternatives in terms of required working capital. Superfast Chips has a special waiver on income taxes until the year 2010.

Required

1. Sketch the cash inflows and cash outflows of the modernize and replace alternatives over the 2001 to 2007 period.
2. Compute the payback period for the modernize and replace alternatives.
3. Compute the NPV of the modernize and replace alternatives.
4. What factors should Superfast Chips consider in choosing between the modernize and replace alternatives?

21-28 Equipment replacement, income taxes (continuation of 21-27). Assume the same facts as in Problem 21-27, except that the plant is located in Austin, Texas. Superfast has no special waiver on income taxes. It pays a 30% tax rate on all income. Proceeds from sale of equipment above book value are taxed at the same 30% rate.

Required

1. Sketch the after-tax cash inflows and cash outflows of the modernize and replace alternatives over the 2001 to 2007 period.
2. Compute the NPV of the modernize and replace alternatives.
3. Suppose Superfast is planning to build several more plants. It wants to have the most advantageous tax position possible. It has been approached by Spain, Malaysia, and Australia to construct a plant in their country. Use the data in Problems 21–27 and this problem to briefly describe the basics of a Superfast proposal to each country as to income tax. You should discuss the magnitude and timing of cost deductions in your description.

21-29 DCF, sensitivity analysis, no income taxes. (CMA, adapted) Bristol Engineering, Inc., manufactures electronic components for the automotive and computer industries, as well as producing a variety of small electronic appliances that are distributed through wholesalers. The company's R&D Department has developed an electronic device that management believes could be modified and marketed as an electronic game.

The following information for the new product was developed from the best estimates for the marketing and production managers:

Annual sales volume	1,000,000 units
Selling price	$10 per unit
Cash variable costs	$4 per unit
Cash fixed costs	$2,000,000 per year
Investment required	$12,000,000
Project life	5 years

At the end of the five-year useful life, there will be a zero terminal disposal price.

Bristol Engineering uses discounted cash flow analysis in its decision making. Its required rate of return on this project is 14 percent.

The toy and game industry is a new market for Bristol Engineering, and management is concerned about the reliability of the estimates. The controller has proposed applying sensitivity analysis to selected factors, and is investigating some alternatives. Ignore income taxes in your computations.

Required

1. What is the net present value of this investment proposal?
2. What is the effect on the net present value of the following three changes in assumptions? (Treat each item independently of the others.)
   a. 10% reduction in the selling price
   b. 10% reduction in annual sales in units
   c. 10% increase in the variable cost per unit
3. Discuss how management would use the data developed in requirements 1 and 2 in its consideration of the proposed capital investment.

21-30 NPV and customer profitability, no income taxes. Christen Granite sells granite countertops to the construction industry. Christen Granite has three customers: Homebuilders, a small construction company that builds private luxury homes; Kitchen Constructors, a company that designs and builds kitchens for hospitals and hotels; and Subdivision Erectors, a construction company that builds large subdivisions in major metropolitan suburbs. Following are Christen Granite's revenue and cost data by customer for the year ended December 31, 2000:

	Homebuilders	Kitchen Constructors	Subdivision Erectors
Revenues	$45,000	$325,000	$860,000
Cost of goods sold	22,000	180,000	550,000
Operating costs	10,000	75,000	235,000

Operating costs include order processing, sales visits, delivery and special-delivery costs. Jay Christen, the owner, estimates that revenue and costs will increase as follows on an annual basis:

	Homebuilders	Kitchen Constructors	Subdivision Erectors
Revenues	5%	15%	8%
Cost of goods sold	4%	4%	4%
Operating costs	4%	4%	4%

Christen Granite's required rate of return is 10 percent. Assume that (a) all transactions occur at year-end, (b) all revenues are cash inflows, and (c) all costs are cash outflows. Ignore income tax considerations in your analysis.

Required

1. Calculate operating income per customer for 2000 and for each year of the 2001–2005 period.
2. Christen estimates the value of each customer by calculating the customer's projected NPV over the next five years (2001–2005). Use the operating incomes calculated above to compute the value of each of its three customers.
3. Recently, Kitchen Constructors (KC) has been threatening to switch suppliers. Lawson Tops, Christen's fiercest competitor, has offered KC a greater discount. KC demands a 20% discount in 2001 (with no price increases in the 2001 to 2005 period) to continue using Christen as a supplier. Should Christen grant KC the 20% discount? What is

the five-year value of KC after incorporating the 20% discount? What other factors should Christen consider before making its final decision?

4. What are possible adverse effects of caving in to KC's pressure?

21-31 NPV of JIT, income taxes. (CMA, adapted) Rosen Manufacturing Corporation produces office furniture equipment and sells it wholesale to furniture distributors. Rosen's management is reviewing a proposal to purchase a just-in-time inventory (JIT) system to better serve its customers. The JIT system will include a computer system and materials-handling equipment. The decision will be based on whether or not the new JIT system is cost effective to the organization for the next five years.

The computer system for both hardware and software, will initially cost $1,250,000. Materials-handling equipment will cost $450,000. Both groups of equipment will have a five-year useful life for tax reporting of depreciation (straight-line). At the end of the five years, the newly acquired materials-handling equipment will be sold for $150,000. The computer system will have a zero terminal disposal price at the end of five years.

Other factors to be considered over the next five years for this proposal include the following:

◆ Due to the service improvement resulting from this new JIT system, Rosen will realize a $800,000 increase in revenues during the first year. Rosen expects this initial $800,000 revenue increase to continue to grow by 10% per year thereafter.

◆ The contribution margin is 60 percent.

◆ Annual materials-ordering cost will increase $50,000 due to a greater level of purchase orders.

◆ There will be a one-time decrease in working-capital investment of $150,000 at the end of the first year.

◆ There will be a 20% savings in warehouse rent due to less space being needed. The current annual rent is $300,000.

Rosen used an after-tax required rate of return of 10% and is subject to an income tax rate of 40%. Assume that all cash flows occur at year end for tax purposes except for any initial purchase amounts.

Required

1. Prepare an analysis of the after-tax effects for the purchase of the just-in-time system at Rosen using the net present value method for evaluating capital expenditures. Be sure to show all of your computations.

2. Determine whether Rosen should purchase the just-in-time inventory system. Explain your answer.

21-32 Replacement of a machine, income taxes, sensitivity. (CMA, adapted) WRL Company operates a snack-food center at the Hartsfield Airport. On January 1, 1997, WRL purchased a special cookie-cutting machine, which has been used for three years. WRL is considering purchasing a newer, more efficient machine. If purchased, the new machine would be acquired today, January 1, 2000. WRL expects to sell 300,000 cookies in each of the next four years. The selling price of each cookie is expected to average $0.50.

WRL has two options: (1) Continue to operate the old machine, or (2) sell the old machine and purchase the new machine. The seller of the new machine offered no trade-in. The following information has been assembled to help management decide which option is more desirable:

	Old Machine	New Machine
Initial purchase costs of machine	$80,000	$120,000
Terminal disposal price at the end of useful life assumed for depreciation purposes	$10,000	$ 20,000
Useful life from date of acquisition	7 years	4 years
Expected annual cash operating costs:		
Variable cost per cookie	$0.20	$0.14
Total fixed costs	$15,000	$ 14,000
Depreciation method used for tax purposes	Straight-line	Straight-line
Estimated disposal prices of machines:		
January 1, 2000	$40,000	$120,000
January 1, 2003	$ 7,000	$ 20,000

WRL is subject to a 40% income tax rate. Assume that any gain or loss on the sale of machines is treated as an ordinary tax item and will affect the taxes paid by WRL in the year in which it occurs. WRL has an after-tax required rate of return of 16 percent.

Required

1. Use the net present value method to determine whether WRL should retain the old machine or acquire the new machine.
2. How much more or less would the recurring after-tax cash operating savings have to be for WRL to exactly earn the 16% after-tax required rate of return? Assume all other data about the investment does not change.
3. Assume that the financial differences between the net present values of the two options are so slight that WRL is indifferent between the two proposals. Identify and discuss the nonfinancial and qualitative factors that WRL should consider.

21-33 Capital budgeting, inflation, income taxes, Appendix. (J. Fellingham, adapted) Abbie Young is manager of the customer-service division of an electrical appliance store. Abbie is considering buying a repair machine that costs $10,000 on December 31, 2000. The machine will last five years. Abbie estimates that the incremental pretax cash savings from using the machine will be $3,000 annually. The $3,000 is measured at current prices and will be received at the end of each year. For tax purposes, she will depreciate the machine using straight-line, assuming zero terminal disposal price. Abbie requires a 10% after-tax real rate of return (that is, the rate of return is 10% when all cash flows are denominated in December 31, 2000 dollars).

Required

Treat each of the following cases independently.

1. Abbie lives in a world without income taxes and without inflation. What is the net present value of the machine in this world?
2. Abbie lives in a world without inflation, but there is an income tax rate of 40 percent. What is the net present value of the machine in this world?
3. There are no income taxes, but the annual inflation rate is 20 percent. What is the net present value of the machine? The cash savings each year will be increased by a factor equal to the cumulative inflation rate. Use the nominal discount rate in your computations.
4. The annual inflation rate is 20 percent, and the income tax rate is 40 percent. What is the net present value of the machine? Use the same nominal discount rate as in requirement 3 in your computations.

21-34 Ethics, capital budgeting. (CMA, adapted) Evans Company must expand its manufacturing capabilities to meet the growing demand for its products. The first alternative is to expand its current manufacturing facility, which is located next to a vacant lot in the heart of the city. The second alternative is to convert a warehouse, already owned by Evans, located 20 miles outside the city. Evans's controller, George Watson, directs Helen Dodge, assistant controller, to use net present value computations to evaluate both proposals. On completing her analysis, Dodge reports to Watson that the proposal to expand the current manufacturing facility has a slightly positive net present value. The proposal to convert the warehouse has a large negative net present value.

Watson is upset over Dodge's conclusions. He returns the proposal to her with the comment, "You must have made an error. The warehouse proposal should look better and have a positive net present value. Work on the projections and estimates."

Dodge suspects that Watson is anxious to have the warehouse proposal selected because this location would eliminate his long commute into the city. Feeling some pressure, she checks her calculations but finds no errors. Dodge reviews her projections and estimates. These too are quite reasonable. Even so, she replaces some of her original estimates with new estimates that are more favorable to the warehouse proposal, although these new estimates are less likely to occur. The revised proposal still has a negative net present value. Dodge is confused about what she should do.

Required

1. Referring to the "Standards of Ethical Conduct for Management Accountants" described in Chapter 1 (p. 16), explain:
    a. whether George Watson's conduct was unethical when he gave Helen Dodge specific instructions on reviewing the proposal.
    b. whether Helen Dodge's revised proposal for the warehouse conversion was unethical.
2. Identify the steps that Helen Dodge should take in attempting to resolve this situation.

COLLABORATIVE LEARNING PROBLEM

21-35 **Relevant costs, outsourcing, capital budgeting, income taxes.** The Strubel Company currently makes as many units of Part No. 789 as it needs. David Lin, general manager of the Strubel Company, has received a bid from the Gabriella Company for making Part No. 789. Current plans call for Gabriella to supply 1,000 units of Part No. 789 per year at $50 a unit. Gabriella can begin supplying on January 1, 2001, and continue for 5 years, after which time Strubel will not need the part. Gabriella can accommodate any change in Strubel's demand for the part and will supply it for $50 a unit, regardless of quantity.

Jack Tyson, the controller of the Strubel Company, reports the following costs for manufacturing 1,000 units of Part No. 789:

Direct materials	$22,000
Direct manufacturing labor	11,000
Variable manufacturing overhead	7,000
Depreciation on machine	10,000
Product and process engineering	4,000
Rent	2,000
Allocation of general plant overhead costs	5,000
Total costs	$61,000

The following additional information is available:
- **a.** Part No. 789 is made on a machine used exclusively for the manufacture of Part No. 789. The machine was acquired on January 1, 2000, at a cost of $60,000. The machine has a useful life of 6 years and zero terminal disposal price. Depreciation is calculated on the straight-line method.
- **b.** The machine could be sold today for $15,000.
- **c.** Product and process engineering costs are incurred to ensure that the manufacturing process for Part No. 789 works smoothly. Although these costs are fixed in the short run, with respect to units of Part No. 789 produced, they can be saved in the long run if this part is no longer produced. If Part No. 789 is outsourced, product and process engineering costs of $4,000 will be incurred for 2001 but not thereafter.
- **d.** Rent costs of $2,000 are allocated to products on the basis of the floor space used for manufacturing the product. If Part No. 789 is discontinued, the space currently used to manufacture it would become available. The company could then use the space for storage purposes and save $1,000 currently paid for outside storage.
- **e.** General plant overhead costs are allocated to each department on the basis of direct manufacturing labor dollars. These costs will not change in total. But no general plant overhead will be allocated to Part No. 789 if the part is outsourced.

Assume that Strubel requires a 12% rate of return for this project.

Required
1. Should David Lin outsource Part No. 789? Prepare a quantitative analysis.
2. Describe any sensitivity analysis that seems advisable, but you need not perform any sensitivity calculations.
3. What other factors should Lin consider in making a decision?
4. Lin is particularly concerned about his bonus for 2001. The bonus is based on Strubel's accounting income. What decision will Lin make if he wants to maximize his bonus in 2001?

Answers to Exercises in Compound Interest (Problem 21-16)
The general approach to these exercises centers on a key question: Which of the four basic tables in Appendix C should be used? No computations should be made until this basic question has been answered with confidence.

1. *From Table 1.* The $5,000 is the present value P of your winnings. Their future value S in 10 years will be:

$$S = P(1 + r)^n$$

The conversion factor, $(1 + r)^n$, is on line 10 of Table 1.

Substituting at 6%: $S = 5,000(1.791) = \$8,955$

Substituting at 14%: $S = 5,000(3.707) = \$18,535$

2. *From Table 2.* The $89,550 is an *amount of future worth*. You want the present value of that amount. $P = S \div (1 + r)^n$. The conversion factor, $1 \div (1 + r)^n$, is on line 10 of Table 2. Substituting,

$$P = \$89,550(0.558) = \$49,969$$

3. *From Table 3.* The $89,550 is *future worth*. You are seeking the uniform amount (annuity) to set aside annually. Note that $1 invested each year for ten years at 6% has a future worth of $13.181 after ten years, from line 10 of Table 3.

$$S_n = \text{Annual deposit } (F)$$

$$\$89,550 = \text{Annual deposit } (13.181)$$

$$\text{Annual deposit} = \frac{\$89,550}{13.181} = \$6,794$$

4. *From Table 3.* You are seeking the *amount of future worth* of an annuity of $5,000 per year. Note that $1 invested each year for ten years at 12% has a future worth of $17.549 after ten years.

$$S_n = \$5,000F, \text{ where } F \text{ is the conversion factor}$$

$$S_n = \$5,000(17.549) = \$87,745$$

5. *From Table 4.* When you reach age 65, you will get $200,000, a present value at that time. You must find the annuity that will exactly exhaust the invested principal in ten years. To pay yourself $1 each year for ten years when the interest rate is 6% requires you to have $7.360 today, from line 10 of Table 4.

$$P_n = \text{Annual withdrawal } (F)$$

$$\$200,000 = \text{Annual withdrawal } (7.360)$$

$$\text{Annual withdrawal} = \frac{\$200,000}{7.360} = \$27,174$$

6. *From Table 4.* You need to find the present value of an annuity for ten years.

$$\text{At 6\%:} \quad \begin{cases} P_n = \text{Annual withdrawal } (F) \\ P_n = \$50,000(7.360) \\ P_n = \$368,000 \end{cases}$$

$$\text{At 20\%:} \quad \begin{cases} P_n = \$50,000(4.192) \\ P_n = \$209,600, \text{ a much lower figure} \end{cases}$$

7. Plan B is preferable. The net present value of plan B exceeds that of plan A by $980 ($3,126 − $2,146):

		Plan A		Plan B	
Year	PV Factor at 6%	Cash Inflows	PV of Cash Inflows	Cash Inflows	PV of Cash Inflows
0	1.000	$(10,000)	$(10,000)	$(10,000)	$(10,000)
1	0.943	1,000	943	5,000	4,715
2	0.890	2,000	1,780	4,000	3,560
3	0.840	3,000	2,520	3,000	2,520
4	0.792	4,000	3,168	2,000	1,584
5	0.747	5,000	3,735	1,000	747
			$ 2,146		$ 3,126

Even though plans B and A have the same total cash inflows over the five years, plan B is preferred to plan A because it has greater cash inflows occurring earlier.

Management Control Systems, Transfer Pricing, and Multinational Considerations

learning objectives

After studying this chapter, you should be able to

1. Describe a management control system and its three key properties
2. Describe the benefits and costs of decentralization
3. Explain transfer prices and four criteria used to evaluate them
4. Calculate transfer prices using three different general methods
5. Illustrate how market-based transfer prices generally promote goal congruence in perfectly competitive markets
6. Avoid making suboptimal decisions when transfer prices are based on full cost plus a markup
7. Understand the range over which two divisions generally negotiate the transfer price when there is excess capacity
8. Construct a general guideline for determining a minimum transfer price
9. Incorporate income tax considerations in multinational transfer pricing

Choosing transfer prices is an important aspect of transactions between internal divisions such as the exploration, pipeline transportation, and refining divisions of integrated oil companies. Companies consider factors such as goal congruence, incentives, and autonomy when determining transfer pricing policy. Transfer prices affect the profits reported in each division and hence affect the taxes companies pay when divisions are located in different countries.

Which company has the better management control system: Ford Motor Company or Toyota Motor Company? Michelin or Pirelli? The answer lies in how well each system achieves its stated goal of guiding and improving decisions for the benefit of the company in a cost-effective way, and whether each system performs as it was technically designed. Beyond the technical aspects, it is essential to consider how the system will influence the behavior of the people who use it. What role can accounting information play in management control systems? For example, how does cost, budget, and pricing information help in planning and coordinating the actions of multiple divisions within these companies? This chapter develops the links between strategy, organization structure, management control systems, and accounting information. It examines the benefits and costs of centralized and decentralized organization structures and looks at the pricing of products or services transferred between subunits of the same organization.

MANAGEMENT CONTROL SYSTEMS

A **management control system** is a means of gathering and using information to aid and coordinate the process of making planning and control decisions throughout the organization and to guide the behavior of its managers and employees. The goal of the management control system is to improve the collective decisions within an organization in an economically feasible way.

Consider General Electric (GE). GE's management control system gathers and reports information for management control at various levels:

1. *Total-organization level*—for example, stock price, net income, return on investment, cash flow from operations, total employment, pollution control, and contributions to the community.

2. *Customer/market level*—for example, customer satisfaction, time taken to respond to customer requests for products, and cost of competitors' products.

3. *Individual-facility level*—for example, materials costs, labor costs, absenteeism rates, and accidents in various divisions or business functions (such as R&D, production, and distribution).

4. *Individual-activity level*—for example, the time taken and costs incurred for receiving, storing, assembling, and dispatching goods in a warehouse; scrap rates, defects, and units reworked on a manufacturing line; the number of sales transactions and revenue dollars per salesperson; and the number of shipments per employee at distribution centers.

As the preceding examples indicate, management control systems collect both financial data (for example, net income, materials costs, and storage costs) and nonfinancial data (for example, the time taken to respond to customer requests for products, absenteeism rates, and accidents). Some of the information is obtained from within the company (such as net income and number of shipments per employee). Other information is obtained from outside the company (such as stock price and costs of competitors' products). Some companies present financial and nonfinancial information in a single report called the *balanced scorecard* (see Chapter 13 for details).

The four levels in GE's management control system indicate the different kinds of information that are needed by managers performing different tasks. For example, stock price information is important for upper management at the total-organization level but less important for line managers managing individual activities in a warehouse. To manage these activities, information about the time taken for receiving and storing is more relevant. At the individual-activity level, management control reports focus on internal financial and nonfinancial data. At upper management levels, management control reports, in addition, also emphasize external financial and nonfinancial data.

The term *management control systems* refers to both formal and informal control systems. The formal management control system of an organization includes those explicit rules, procedures, performance measures, and incentive plans that guide the behavior of its managers and employees. The formal control system itself consists of several systems. The management accounting system is a formal accounting system that provides information regarding costs, revenues, and income. Examples of other formal control systems are human resources systems (providing information on recruiting, training, absenteeism, and accidents), and quality systems (providing information on scrap, defects, rework, and late deliveries to customers).

The informal management control system includes such aspects as shared values, loyalties, and mutual commitments among members of the organization, organization culture, and the unwritten norms about acceptable behavior for managers and employees. Examples of slogans that reinforce values and loyalties are "At Ford, Quality Is Job 1," and "At Home Depot, Low Prices Are Just the Beginning."

EVALUATING MANAGEMENT CONTROL SYSTEMS

To be effective, management control systems should be closely aligned to an organization's strategies and goals. Examples of strategies are developing innovative products to increase market share in key product areas, or maximizing short-run income by forgoing risky long-run investments in R&D. Suppose management decides, wisely or unwisely, to emphasize maximizing short run income as a strategy. The management control system must then reinforce this strategy. It should provide managers with information—such as contribution margins on individual products—that will help them make short-run decisions. It should tie managers' rewards to short-run income numbers.

A second important feature of management control systems is that they should be designed to fit the organization's structure and the decision-making responsibility of individual managers. Consider, for example, the R&D manager at Glaxo Welcome, a pharmaceutical company. The management control system for this manager should focus on the R&D activities required for different drug projects, the number of scientists needed, the scheduled dates for completing different projects, and the preparation of reports comparing actual and budgeted performance.

Now consider another example—a product-line manager responsible for the manufacture, sale, and distribution of ketchup at Heinz, a food products company. The management control system for this manager should focus on information about customer satisfaction, market share, manufacturing costs and product-line profitability that helps the manager plan and control the business better. The manager of the Heinz ketchup product line requires very different information than does the R&D manager at Glaxo Welcome. Note, however, that in both cases, the information provided is designed to aid the actions of managers.

Finally, effective management control systems should motivate managers and employees. **Motivation** is the desire to attain a selected goal (the goal-congruence aspect) combined with the resulting drive or pursuit toward that goal (the effort aspect).

Goal congruence exists when individuals and groups work toward achieving the organization's goals—that is, managers working in their own best interest take actions that align with the overall goals of top management. Goal-congruence issues have arisen in earlier chapters. For example, in capital budgeting, making decisions based on discounting long-run cash flows at the required rate of return best achieves organization goals. But if the management control system evaluates managers on the basis of short-run accrual accounting income, managers will be tempted to make decisions to maximize accrual accounting income, which may not be in the long-run best interest of the organization.

Effort is defined as exertion toward a goal. Effort goes beyond physical exertion, such as a worker producing at a faster rate, to include all conscientious actions (physical and mental).

Management control systems motivate managers and employees to exert effort toward attaining organization goals through a variety of rewards tied to the achievement of those goals. These incentives can be monetary (cash, company shares, use of a company car, or membership in a club) or nonmonetary (power, self-esteem, or pride in working for a successful company).

To summarize, the primary criterion for evaluating a system is how it promotes the collective attainment of top management's goals in a cost-effective manner. Central to applying this criterion is how well the management control system fits the organization's structure and the decision-making responsibility of individual managers, as well as how well it motivates individuals within the organization.

ORGANIZATION STRUCTURE AND DECENTRALIZATION

As we have just seen, management control systems must fit an organization's structure. Many organizations have decentralized structures, which raise an additional set of management control issues.

The essence of **decentralization** is the freedom for managers at lower levels of the organization to make decisions. **Autonomy** refers to the degree of freedom to make decisions. The greater the freedom, the greater the autonomy. As we discuss the issues of decentralization and autonomy, we use the term *subunit* to refer to any part of an organization. In practice, a subunit may be a large division (the Chevrolet Division of General Motors) or a small group (the two-person advertising department of a local clothing chain). Decentralization empowers managers and employees of subunits to take decisive actions.

Total decentralization *means minimum constraints and maximum freedom for managers at the lowest levels of an organization to make decisions.* Total centralization *means maximum constraints and minimum freedom for managers at the lowest levels of an organization to make decisions.* Most companies' structures fall somewhere in between these two extremes because there are both benefits and costs of decentralization.

Benefits of Decentralization

How much decentralization is optimal? Conceptually, managers try to choose the degree of decentralization that maximizes benefits over costs. From a practical standpoint, top management can seldom quantify either the benefits or the costs of decentralization. Still, the cost-benefit approach helps them focus on the central issues.

Advocates of decentralizing decision making and granting responsibilities to managers of subunits stress the following benefits:

1. *Creates greater responsiveness to local needs.* Information is the key to wise decisions. Compared with top managers, subunit managers are better informed about their customers, competitors, suppliers, and employees, as well as about local factors that affect the performance of their jobs such as ways to decrease costs and improve quality. Eastman Kodak reports that two advantages of decentralization are an "increase in the company's knowledge of the marketplace and improved service to customers."

2. *Leads to gains from quicker decision making.* Decentralization speeds decision making, creating a competitive advantage over centralized organizations. Centralization slows decision making as responsibility for decisions creeps upward through layer after layer of management. Interlake, a manufacturer of materials-handling equipment, notes this important benefit of increased decentralization: "We have distributed decision-making powers more broadly to the cutting edge of product and market opportunity." Interlake's materials-handling equipment must often be customized to fit individual customers' needs. Delegating decision making to the salesforce allows Interlake to respond quickly to changing customer requirements.

3. *Increases motivation of subunit managers.* Subunit managers are usually more highly motivated when they can exercise greater individual initiative. Johnson & Johnson, a highly decentralized company, maintains that "Decentralization = Creativity = Productivity."

4. *Aids management development and learning.* Giving managers more responsibility promotes the development of an experienced pool of management talent—a pool to draw from for higher-level management positions. The organization also learns which people are not management material. Tektronix, an electronics instruments company, expressed this benefit as follows: "Decentralized units provide a training ground for general managers, and a visible field of combat where product champions may fight for their ideas."

5. *Sharpens the focus of subunit managers.* In a decentralized setting, the manager of a small subunit has a concentrated focus. A small subunit is more flexible and nimble than a larger subunit and is better able to adapt itself quickly to a fast-opening market opportunity. Also, top management, relieved of the burden of day-to-day operating decisions, can spend more time and energy on strategic planning for the entire organization.

Costs of Decentralization

Advocates of more centralized decision making point out the following costs of decentralizing decision making:

1. *Leads to **suboptimal decision making** (also called **incongruent** or **dysfunctional decision making**), which arises when a decision's benefit to one subunit is more than offset by the costs or loss of benefits to the organization as a whole.* This cost arises because top management has given up control over decision making.

Suboptimal decision making may occur (1) when there is a lack of harmony or congruence among the overall organization goals, the subunit goals, and the individual goals of decision makers, or (2) when no guidance is given to subunit managers concerning the effects of their decisions on other parts of the organization. Suboptimal decision making is most likely to occur when the subunits in the organization are highly interdependent, such as when the end product of one subunit is used or sold by another subunit. For example, a manufacturing manager evaluated on the basis of manufacturing costs may be unresponsive to requests from marketing to schedule a special production order for a customer, if altering production schedules will increase manufacturing costs. From the company's viewpoint, however, supplying the product to the customer may be preferred both because the customer is willing to pay a premium price and because the company expects the customer to place many orders in the future.

2. *Focuses manager's attention on the subunit rather than the organization as a whole.* Individual subunit managers may regard themselves as competing with managers of other subunits in the same organization as if they were external rivals. Consequently, managers may be unwilling to share information or to assist when another subunit faces an emergency. Also, subunit managers may use information they have about local conditions to further their own self-interest rather than the organization's goals. For example, they may ask for more resources than they need from the organization in order to reduce the effort they need to exert.

3. *Increases costs of gathering information.* Managers may spend too much time obtaining information about different subunits of the organization in order to coordinate their actions.

4. *Results in duplication of activities.* Several individual subunits of the organization may undertake the same activity separately. For example, there may be a duplication of staff functions (accounting, human resources, and legal) if an organization is highly decentralized. Centralizing these functions helps to consolidate, streamline, and downsize these activities.

Comparison of Benefits and Costs

To choose an appropriate organization structure, top managers must compare the benefits and costs of decentralization, often on a function-by-function basis. For example, the controller's function may be highly decentralized for many problem-solving and attention-directing purposes (such as preparing operating budgets and performance reports) but highly centralized for other purposes (such as processing accounts receivable and developing income tax strategies). Decentralizing

Curriculum Linkage If participation in budgeting increases employees' commitment to achieve the budget (see Chap. 6), then participation in a wide variety of decisions (i.e., decentralization) should increase employees' commitment to those decisions and to the organization.

Points to Stress Interdivisional transfers (and transfer pricing) are a major source of suboptimal decisions. The selling division wants a high price, but the buying division wants a low price. If both divisions act in their own best interests, their decisions will sometimes hurt the company as a whole, as is illustrated later in the chapter in the Horizon Petroleum example.

budgeting and cost reporting enables the marketing manager of a subunit, for example, to influence the design of product-line profitability reports for the subunit. Tailoring the report to the specific information that the manager needs helps the manager make better decisions and hence increases income. Centralizing income tax strategies, however, allows the organization to trade off income in a subunit with losses in other subunits to evaluate the impact on the organization as a whole.

Surveys of U.S. and European companies report that the decisions made most frequently at the decentralized level and least frequently at the corporate level are related to sources of supplies, products to manufacture, and product advertising. In these areas, local managers have information that is critical to the decision, and must make decisions quickly. Decisions related to the type and source of long-term financing are made least frequently at the decentralized level and most frequently at the corporate level. In these cases, corporate managers have better information about financing terms in different markets and can obtain the best rates.[1] The benefits of decentralization are generally greater when companies are large and unregulated, face great uncertainties in their environments, require detailed local knowledge for performing various jobs, and have few interdependencies among divisions.[2]

Decentralization in Multinational Companies

Points to Stress This subsection highlights benefits and costs of decentralizing multinational corporations. The primary benefit is that business practices and customs vary so greatly across countries that local mgrs. often have the most relevant info. for making decisions. The primary cost is loss of control, as illustrated by the Barings PLC bankruptcy and the Sumitomo Corp. $2.6-billion loss referenced in the text.

Multinational corporations are often decentralized because centralized control of a company with subunits in three or four different continents is often physically and practically impossible. Also, language, customs, cultures, business practices, rules, laws, and regulations vary significantly across countries. Decentralization enables managers in different countries to make decisions that exploit their knowledge of local business and political conditions and to deal with uncertainties in their individual environments. Philips, a global electronics company headquartered in the Netherlands, delegates marketing and pricing decisions for its television business in the Indian and Singaporean markets to the managers in those countries. Multinational corporations often rotate managers between foreign locations and corporate headquarters. Job rotation combined with decentralization helps develop managers' abilities to operate in the global environment.

Of course, there are several drawbacks to decentralizing multinational companies. One of the most important is the lack of control. Barings PLC, a British investment banking firm, went bankrupt and had to be sold when one of its traders in Singapore caused the firm to lose over £1 billion on unauthorized trades. Similarly, a trader at Sumitomo Corporation racked up $2.6 billion in copper-trading losses because of poor controls. Multinational corporations that implement decentralized decision making usually also design their management control systems to measure and monitor division performance. Information and communications technology facilitates the flow of information for reporting and control.

Choices About Responsibility Centers

To measure the performance of subunits in centralized or decentralized organizations, the management control system uses one or a mix of the four types of responsibility centers presented in Chapter 6:

♦ *Cost center*—the manager is accountable for costs only.

♦ *Revenue center*—the manager is accountable for revenues only.

♦ *Profit center*—the manager is accountable for revenues and costs.

♦ *Investment center*—the manager is accountable for investments, revenues, and costs.

---

[1]*Evaluating the Performance of International Operations* (New York: Business International, 1989, p. 4); and *Managing the Global Finance Function* (London: Business International, 1992, p. 31).

[2]See A. Christie, M. Joye, and R. Watts, "Decentralization of the Firm: Theory and Evidence" (Working Paper, University of Rochester, April 1991).

Centralization or decentralization is not mentioned in these descriptions because each of these responsibility units can be found in either centralized or decentralized organizations.

A common misconception is that the term *profit center* (and, in some cases, *investment center*) is a synonym for a decentralized subunit and that *cost center* is a synonym for a centralized subunit. *Profit centers can be coupled with a highly centralized organization, and cost centers can be coupled with a highly decentralized organization.* For example, managers in a division organized as a profit center may have little freedom in making decisions. They may need to obtain approval from corporate headquarters for every expenditure over, say, $10,000 and may be forced to accept central-staff "advice." In another company, divisions may be organized as cost centers, but their managers may have great latitude on capital expenditures and on where to purchase materials and services. In short, the labels "profit center" and "cost center" are independent of the degree of centralization or decentralization in an organization.

TRANSFER PRICING

In decentralized organizations, much of the decision-making power resides in the individual subunits. In these settings, the management control system often uses *transfer prices* to coordinate actions and to evaluate performance of the subunits.

A **transfer price** is the price one subunit (segment, department, division, and so on) charges for a product or service supplied to another subunit of the same organization. The transfer price creates revenues for the selling subunit and purchase costs for the buying subunit, affecting each subunit's operating income. The operating incomes can be used to evaluate subunit performance and to motivate managers. The product transferred between subunits of an organization is called an **intermediate product**. It can either be processed further by the receiving subunit or, if transferred from production to marketing, resold to an external customer.

In one sense, transfer pricing is a curious phenomenon. Activities within an organization are clearly nonmarket in nature—products and services are not bought and sold as they are in market transactions. Yet, establishing prices for transfers among subunits of an organization has a distinctly market flavor. The rationale for transfer prices is that subunit managers, when evaluating decisions, need only focus on how their actions will affect subunit performance without evaluating their impact on companywide performance. In this sense, transfer prices ease the subunit managers' information-processing and decision-making tasks. In a well-functioning transfer-pricing system, optimizing subunit performance leads to optimizing the performance of the organization as a whole.

As in all management control systems, transfer prices should help achieve an organization's strategies and goals and fit its structure. In particular, they should promote *goal congruence* and a sustained high level of *management effort*. Subunits selling a product or service should be motivated to hold down its costs, and subunits buying the product or service should be motivated to acquire and use inputs efficiently. The transfer price should also help top management evaluate the performance of individual subunits and their managers. If top management favors a high degree of decentralization, transfer prices should also promote a high level of subunit *autonomy* in decision making. That is, subunit managers seeking to maximize subunit operating income should have the freedom to transact with other subunits of the organization (on the basis of transfer prices) or, if they so choose, to transact with outside parties.

Transfer-Pricing Methods

There are three general methods for determining transfer prices:

1. *Market-based transfer prices.* Upper management may choose to use the price of a similar product or service publicly listed in, say, a trade association website. Also, upper management may select, for the internal price, the external price that a subunit charges to outside customers.

Curriculum Linkage Ask students what mgt. acctg. tools are used in performance evaluations for each of the 4 responsibility centers:
Cost centers—var. analysis: Chaps. 7, 8
Revenue centers—var. analysis: Chaps. 7, 16
Profit centers—CM I/S by segments: Chap. 14; or customer profitability analysis: Chap. 16
Investment centers—ROI, residual income: Chap. 23

OBJECTIVE 3
Explain transfer prices and four criteria used to evaluate them

Teaching Tip Help students organize the TP concepts by outlining a series of questions mgrs. must address. The 1st is a policy question: Should divisions be permitted to source externally when internal goods are available? The 2nd is an operational question: At what price will the transfer be made? This 2nd question involves deciding (1) which type of TP method will be used (market, cost, or negotiated), (2) how the exact TP is determined once the method is selected, and (3) how disputes are resolved (negotiation, arbitration, or directives).

Teaching Tip Help students visualize the TP situation by putting a diagram on the board (or overhead) similar to Exh. 22-1. Then, walk through an example so they understand the major concepts, including that the TP is both a revenue and an expense for the firm. This will give them a framework to understand the whole concept of TP.

Reinforcing Problems
Exer. 22-19 through 22-22, 22-25, and 22-26 and Probs. 22-27 through 22-30 and 22-33 through 22-35 cover transfer pricing issues.

OBJECTIVE 4
Calculate transfer prices using three different general methods

Teaching Tip Ideally, a transfer price should:

1. Promote goal congruence (mgr.'s and organization's interests are aligned so that selecting an action in a mgr.'s best interest is also in the organization's best interest).

2. Be useful for evaluating divisional performance.

3. Motivate sellers to hold down costs and buyers to use inputs efficiently.

4. Allow subunit mgrs. the autonomy to make their own decisions (if the company is decentralized).

As you cover each transfer-pricing method, ask students how well the method satisfies each of these 4 criteria. It should become apparent that no single method consistently satisfies all 4 criteria.

2. *Cost-based transfer prices.* Upper management may choose a transfer price based on the costs of producing the product in question. Examples include variable production costs, variable and fixed production costs, and full costs of the product. Full costs of the product include all production costs plus costs from the other business functions (R&D, design, marketing, distribution, and customer service). The costs used in cost-based transfer prices can be actual costs or budgeted costs. Sometimes, the cost-based transfer price includes a markup or profit margin that represents a return on subunit investment.

3. *Negotiated transfer prices.* In some cases, the subunits of a company are free to negotiate the transfer price between themselves and then to decide whether to buy and sell internally or deal with outside parties. Subunits may use information about costs and market prices in these negotiations, but there is no requirement that the chosen transfer price bear any specific relationship to either cost or market-price data. Negotiated transfer prices are often employed when market prices are volatile and change occurs constantly. The negotiated transfer price is the outcome of a bargaining process between the selling and the buying subunits.

To see how each of these three methods works, and to see the differences among these methods, we examine transfer pricing at Horizon Petroleum against the criteria described above—goal congruence, management effort, subunit performance evaluation, and subunit autonomy (if desired).

AN ILLUSTRATION OF TRANSFER PRICING

Horizon Petroleum has two divisions. Each operates as a profit center. The Transportation Division purchases crude oil in Matamoros, Mexico. It also operates a pipeline that transports crude oil from Matamoros to Houston, Texas. The Refining Division manages a refinery at Houston that processes crude oil into gasoline. (For simplicity, assume that gasoline is the only salable product the refinery makes and that it takes two barrels of crude oil to yield one barrel of gasoline.)

Variable costs in each division are assumed to be variable with respect to a single cost driver in each division: barrels of crude oil transported by the Transportation Division, and barrels of gasoline produced by the Refining Division. The fixed costs per unit are based on the budgeted annual output of crude oil to be transported and the budgeted annual output of gasoline to be produced. Horizon Petroleum reports all costs and revenues of its non-U.S. operations in U.S. dollars using the prevailing exchange rate.

- The Transportation Division has obtained the rights to certain oil fields in the Matamoros area. It has a long-term contract to purchase crude oil produced from these fields at $12 per barrel. The Division transports the oil to Houston, and then "sells" it to the Refining Division. The pipeline from Matamoros to Houston has the capacity to carry 40,000 barrels of crude oil per day.

- The Refining Division has been operating at capacity, 30,000 barrels of crude oil a day, using oil supplied by Horizon's Transportation Division (an average of 10,000 barrels per day) and oil bought from other producers and delivered to the Houston Refinery (an average of 20,000 barrels per day, at $21 per barrel).

- The Refining Division sells the gasoline it produces at $58 per barrel.

Exhibit 22-1 summarizes Horizon Petroleum's variable and fixed costs per barrel of crude oil in the Transportation Division and per barrel of gasoline in the Refining Division, the external market prices of buying crude oil, and the external market prices of selling gasoline. The only important figure that is missing in the exhibit is the actual transfer price from the Transportation Division to the Refining Division. Of course, this figure will vary depending on the transfer pricing method used. Transfer prices from the Transportation Division to the Refining Division under each of the three methods are:

- Method A: Market-based transfer price of $21 per barrel of crude oil based on the competitive market price in Houston

EXHIBIT 22-1
Operating Data for Horizon Petroleum

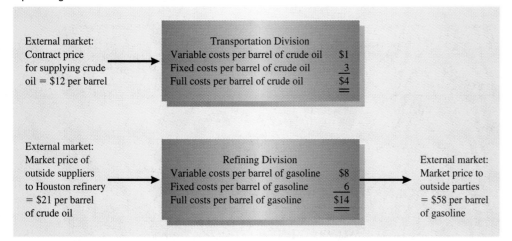

Method B: Cost-based transfer prices at 110% of full costs, where full costs are the costs of the crude oil purchased plus the Transportation Division's own variable and fixed costs = 1.10 ($12 + $1 + $3) = $17.60

Method C: Negotiated transfer price of $19.25 per barrel of crude oil, which is between the market-based and cost-based transfer price

Exhibit 22-2 presents division operating incomes per 100 barrels of crude oil purchased under each transfer-pricing method. Transfer prices create income for the selling division and corresponding costs for the buying division that cancel out when divisional results are consolidated. The exhibit assumes that all three transfer-pricing methods yield transfer prices that are in a range that does not cause division managers to change the business relationships shown in Exhibit 22-1. That is, Horizon Petroleum's total operating income from purchasing, transporting, and refining the 100 barrels of crude oil and selling the 50 barrels of gasoline is the same, $600 (revenues of $2,900 minus costs of crude oil purchases of $1,200, transportation costs of $400, and refining costs of $700), regardless of the internal transfer prices used. Note further that in all three methods, adding the two division operating incomes equals Horizon Petroleum's total operating income of $600. By keeping total operating income the same, we focus attention on the effects different transfer-pricing methods have on operating income of each division. Subsequent sections of this chapter relax this assumption.

Consider first methods A and B in the first two columns of Exhibit 22-2. The operating income of the Transportation Division is $340 more ($500 − $160) if transfer prices are based on market prices (method A) rather than on 110% of full costs (method B). However, the operating income of the Refining Division is $340 more ($440 − $100) if transfer prices are based on 110% of full costs (method B) rather than market prices (method A). If its sole criterion were to maximize its own division operating income, the Transportation Division would favor transfer prices at market prices. Similarly, the Refining Division would prefer transfer prices at 110% of full costs. Little wonder that subunit managers take considerable interest in the setting of transfer prices, especially those managers whose compensation or promotion directly depends on subunit operating income. To reduce the excessive focus of subunit managers on their own subunits, many companies compensate subunit managers on the basis of both subunit and companywide operating incomes.

If market prices of crude oil in the Houston area fluctuated in response to local supply and demand conditions, under market-based method A, the operating incomes of the Transportation and Refining Divisions would fluctuate as well. The Transportation and Refining Divisions may instead prefer to negotiate a more stable, long-run transfer price. Method C assumes a transfer price of $19.25, which is between the full cost and market-based transfer prices. In our example, the negotiated transfer price

Points to Stress The TP allocates profits to subunits for (1) performance evaluation, and (2) motivation. Profits are *not* allocated for product-costing purposes because product costs don't include a profit component.

Points to Stress/Example Although companywide profit is the sum of the divisions' profits, the revenues and costs are *not* because the TP is included as a revenue for one division and an expense for another. For example, Division A sells poultry parts externally and to Division B. B produces canned chicken that sells for $6 per lb. A incurs costs of $0.70/lb, whereas B incurs costs of $3.50/lb. If the TP is set at $1.50/lb, what's the operating income (per lb) for A, B, and the company as a whole?

	Div. A	Div. B	Whole firm
Rev.	$1.50	$6.00	$6.00[a]
Cost	(0.70)	(5.00)[c]	(4.20)[b]
Op. Inc.	$0.80 +	$1.00 =	$1.80

[a]$0 + $6.00 = $6.00
[b]$0.70 + $3.50 = $4.20
[c]$1.50 + $3.50 = $5.00

EXHIBIT 22-2
Division Operating Income of Horizon Petroleum for 100 Barrels of Crude Oil Under Alternative
Transfer-Pricing Methods

	Method A: Internal Transfers at Market Prices	Method B: Internal Transfers at 110% of Full Costs	Method C: Internal Transfers at Negotiated Prices
Transportation Division			
Revenues, $21, $17.60, $19.25 × 100 barrels of crude oil	$2,100	$1,760	$1,925
Deduct:			
Crude-oil purchase costs $12 × 100	1,200	1,200	1,200
Division variable costs, $1 × 100 barrels of crude oil	100	100	100
Division fixed costs, $3 × 100 barrels of crude oil	300	300	300
Division operating income	$ 500	$ 160	$ 325
Refining Division			
Revenues, $58 × 50 barrels of gasoline	$2,900	$2,900	$2,900
Deduct:			
Transferred-in costs, $21, $17.60, $19.25 × 100 barrels of crude oil	2,100	1,760	1,925
Division variable costs, $8 × 50 barrels of gasoline	400	400	400
Division fixed costs, $6 × 50 barrels of gasoline	300	300	300
Division operating income	$ 100	$ 440	$ 275
Operating income of both divisions together	$ 600	$ 600	$ 600

From the companywide perspective, the revenue from external sources is $6 ($0 + $6.00), and costs paid to external parties total $4.20 ($0.70 + $3.50). Although the $1.50 is a cost to B, it's a revenue to A. This $1.50 cost and $1.50 revenue are both irrelevant from the company-wide perspective. Note that the TP allocates the $1.80 companywide profit across the 2 subunits. A TP of $0.70 would have allocated all the profit to B. A TP of $2.50 would have allocated all the profit to A.

splits the $600 of operating income almost equally between the divisions ($325 for the Transportation Division and $275 for the Refining Division). Note that the transfer price under method B also has the effect of shielding both divisions from fluctuations in crude oil prices in Houston. As Exhibit 22-2 shows, the transfer price calculation of $17.60 depends only on the full costs of the Transportation Division. The market price of crude oil in Houston is irrelevant to and does not enter into this calculation.

The example illustrates how the choice of a transfer-pricing method divides the companywide operating income pie among individual divisions. Subsequent sections of this chapter illustrate that the choice of a transfer-pricing method can also affect the decisions that individual division managers make and hence the size of the operating income pie itself. We consider this effect as we expand our discussion of market-based, cost-based, and negotiated transfer prices.

MARKET-BASED TRANSFER PRICES

Perfectly Competitive Market Case

OBJECTIVE 5

Illustrate how market-based transfer prices generally promote goal congruence in perfectly competitive markets

Transferring products or services at market prices generally leads to optimal decisions when three conditions are satisfied: (1) the market for the intermediate product is perfectly competitive, (2) interdependencies of subunits are minimal, and (3) there are no additional costs or benefits to the company as a whole in buying or selling in the external market instead of transacting internally. A **perfectly competitive market** exists when there is a homogeneous product with equivalent buying and selling prices and no individual buyers or sellers can affect those prices by their own actions. By using market-based transfer prices in perfectly competitive markets, a company can achieve (1) goal congruence, (2) management effort, (3) subunit performance evaluation, and (4) subunit autonomy (if desired).

Reconsider the Horizon Petroleum example, assuming that there is a perfectly competitive market for crude oil in the Houston area. As a result, the Transportation Division can sell and the Refining Division can buy as much crude oil as each wants at $21 per barrel. Horizon would like its managers to buy or sell crude oil internally. Think about the decisions that Horizon's division managers would make if each had the option to sell or buy crude oil externally. If the transfer price between Horizon's Transportation Division and Refining Division is set below $21, the manager of the Transportation Division will be motivated to sell all crude oil to outside buyers in the Houston area at $21 per barrel. If the transfer price is set above $21, the manager of the Refining Division will be motivated to purchase all crude oil requirements from outside suppliers. Only a transfer price of $21 will motivate the Transportation Division and the Refining Division to buy and sell internally. That is, neither division profits by buying or selling in the external market.

Suppose division managers are evaluated on their individual division's operating income. The Transportation Division will sell (either internally or externally) as much crude oil as it can profitably transport, and the Refining Division will buy (either internally or externally) as much crude oil as it can profitably refine. At a transfer price of $21, the actions that maximize division operating income are also the actions that maximize operating income of Horizon Petroleum as a whole. Furthermore, division managers will be motivated to exert management effort to maximize their own division's operating income. Market prices also serve to evaluate the economic viability and profitability of each division individually. For example, if under market-based transfer prices, the Refining Division consistently shows small or negative profits, Horizon may decide to shut down the Refining Division and simply transport and sell the oil to other refineries in the Houston area.

Distress Prices

When supply outstrips demand, market prices may drop well below their historical average. If the drop in prices is expected to be temporary, these low market prices are sometimes called "distress prices." Deciding whether a current market price is a distress price is often difficult. The market prices of several agricultural commodities, such as wheat and oats, have stayed for many years at what observers initially believed were temporary distress levels.

Which transfer price should be used for judging performance if distress prices prevail? Some companies use the distress prices themselves, but others use long-run average prices, or "normal" market prices. In the short run, the manager of the selling division should meet the distress price as long as it exceeds the incremental costs of supplying the product or service. If not, the selling division should stop selling the product or service to the buying division, which should buy the product or service from an outside supplier. These actions would increase overall companywide operating income. If the long-run average market price is used, forcing the manager to buy internally at a price above the current market price will hurt the buying division's short-run performance and understate its profitability. Using the long-run average market price, however, provides a better measure of the long-run viability of the supplier division. If price remains low in the long run, though, the company should use the distress price as the transfer price. The manager of the selling division must then decide whether to dispose of some manufacturing facilities or shut down and have the buying division purchase the product from an outside supplier.

COST-BASED TRANSFER PRICES

Cost-based transfer prices are helpful when market prices are unavailable, inappropriate, or too costly to obtain. For example, the product may be specialized or unique, price lists may not be widely available, or the internal product may be different from the products available externally in terms of quality and customer service.

Full-Cost Bases

OBJECTIVE 6

Avoid making subopti-
mal decisions when
transfer prices are based
on full cost plus a
markup

In practice, many companies use transfer prices based on full costs. To approximate
market prices, cost-based transfer prices are sometimes set at full cost plus a margin.
These transfer prices, however, can lead to suboptimal decisions. Assume that Horizon Petroleum makes internal transfers at 110% of full cost. Recall that the Refining Division purchases, on average, 20,000 barrels of crude oil per day from a local
Houston supplier, who delivers the crude oil to the refinery at a price of $21 per
barrel. To reduce crude oil costs, the Refining Division has located an independent
producer in Matamoros, Gulfmex Corporation, that is willing to sell 20,000 barrels
of crude oil per day at $16 per barrel, delivered to Horizon's pipeline in Matamoros.
Given Horizon's organization structure, the Transportation Division would purchase the 20,000 barrels of crude oil in Matamoros from Gulfmex, transport it to
Houston, and then sell it to the Refining Division. The pipeline has unused capacity
and can ship the 20,000 barrels at its variable costs of $1 per barrel without affecting
the shipment of the 10,000 barrels of crude oil per day acquired under its existing
long-term contract arrangement. Will Horizon Petroleum incur lower costs by purchasing crude oil from Gulfmex in Matamoros or by purchasing crude oil from the
Houston supplier? Will the Refining Division show lower crude oil purchasing costs
by using oil from Gulfmex or by using its current Houston supplier?

The following analysis shows that operating income of Horizon Petroleum as
a whole would be maximized by purchasing oil from Gulfmex. The analysis compares the incremental costs in both divisions under the two alternatives. The analysis assumes that the fixed costs of the Transportation Division will be the same regardless of the alternative chosen. That is, the Transportation Division cannot save
any of its fixed costs if it does not transport Gulfmex's 20,000 barrels of crude oil
per day.

- *Alternative 1*: Buy 20,000 barrels from Houston supplier at $21 per barrel. To-
  tal costs to Horizon Petroleum are 20,000 × $21 = $420,000.
- *Alternative 2*: Buy 20,000 barrels in Matamoros at $16 per barrel and trans-
  port it to Houston at a variable cost of $1 per barrel. Total costs to Horizon
  Petroleum are 20,000 × ($16 + $1) = $340,000.

There is a reduction in total costs to Horizon Petroleum of $80,000 ($420,000 −
$340,000) by acquiring oil from Gulfmex.

In turn, suppose the Transportation Division's transfer price to the Refining
Division is 110% of full cost. The Refining Division will see its reported division
costs increase if the crude oil is purchased from Gulfmex:

$$\text{Transfer price} = 1.10 \times \left(\begin{array}{c} \text{Purchase price} \\ \text{from} \\ \text{Gulfmex} \end{array} + \begin{array}{c} \text{Unit variable costs} \\ \text{of Transportation} \\ \text{Division} \end{array} + \begin{array}{c} \text{Unit fixed costs} \\ \text{of Transportation} \\ \text{Division} \end{array} \right)$$

$$= 1.10 \times (\$16 + \$1 + \$3) = 1.10 \times \$20 = \$22$$

- *Alternative 1*: Buy 20,000 barrels from Houston supplier at $21 per barrel. To-
  tal costs to Refining Division are 20,000 × $21 = $420,000.
- *Alternative 2*: Buy 20,000 barrels from the Transportation Division of Horizon
  Petroleum that are purchased from Gulfmex. Total costs to Refining Division
  are 20,000 × $22 = $440,000.

As a profit center, the Refining Division can maximize its short-run division operating income by purchasing from the Houston supplier ($420,000 versus $440,000).

*The transfer-pricing method has led the Refining Division to regard the fixed cost
(and the 10% markup) of the Transportation Division as a variable cost.* Why? Because
the Refining Division looks at each barrel that it obtains from the Transportation
Division as a variable cost of $22—if 10 barrels are transferred, it costs the Refin-
ing Division $220. If 100 barrels are transferred, it costs $2,200. From the viewpoint of Horizon Petroleum as a whole, its variable costs per barrel are $17 ($16 to
purchase the oil from Gulfmex and $1 to transport it to Houston). The remaining
$5 ($22 − $17) per barrel are fixed costs and markups of the Transportation Divi-

sion. Buying crude oil in Houston costs Horizon Petroleum an additional $21 per barrel. For the company, it is cheaper to buy from Gulfmex in Matamoros. But the Refining Division sees the problem differently. From its standpoint, it prefers buying from the Houston supplier at a cost of $420,000 (20,000 barrels × $21 per barrel) because buying from Gulfmex costs the division $440,000 (20,000 barrels × $22). In this example, goal incongruence is induced by the transfer price based on full cost plus a markup.

What transfer price will promote goal congruence for both the Transportation Division and the Refining Division? The minimum transfer price is $17 per barrel. A transfer price below $17 does not provide the Transportation Division with an incentive to purchase crude oil from Gulfmex in Matamoros, whereas a transfer price above $17 generates contribution margin to cover its fixed costs. The maximum transfer price is $21 per barrel. A transfer price above $21 will cause the Refining Division to purchase crude oil from the external market rather than from the Transportation Division. A transfer price between the minimum and maximum transfer prices of $17 and $21 will promote goal congruence—each division will increase its own reported division operating income by purchasing crude oil from Gulfmex in Matamoros while increasing Horizon Petroleum's operating income. For example, a transfer price based on the full costs of $20 without a markup will achieve goal congruence. The Transportation Division will show no operating income and will be evaluated as a cost center.

In the absence of a market-based transfer price, senior management at Horizon Petroleum cannot easily determine the profitability of the investment made in the Transportation Division and hence whether it should keep or sell the pipeline. Furthermore, if the transfer price had been based on the actual costs of the Transportation Division, it would provide the division with no incentive to control costs. Inefficiencies of the Transportation Division will get passed along as part of the full-cost transfer price.[3] However, surveys indicate that, despite their limitations, managers prefer to use full-cost-based transfer prices because they yield relevant costs for long-run decisions, they facilitate external pricing based on variable and fixed costs, and they are the least costly to administer.

Using full-cost-based transfer prices requires an allocation of each subunit's fixed costs to products. Full-cost transfer pricing raises many issues. How are indirect costs allocated to products? Have the correct activities, cost pools, and cost-allocation bases been identified? Are the chosen fixed-cost rates actual or budgeted rates? The issues here are similar to the issues that arise in allocating fixed costs, introduced in Chapter 14. Calculations of full-cost-based transfer prices using activity-based cost drivers can provide more refined allocation of costs to products. Using budgeted costs and budgeted rates lets both divisions know the transfer price in advance. It overcomes the problem of inefficiencies in actual costs getting passed along to the receiving division. Also, variations in the total quantity of units produced by the selling division do not affect the transfer price.

Variable Cost Bases

As the previous section illustrated, transferring 20,000 barrels of crude oil from the Transportation Division to the Refining Division at the variable cost of $17 per barrel achieves goal congruence. The Refining Division would buy from the Transportation Division because the variable costs of the Transportation Division (which are also the relevant incremental costs for Horizon Petroleum as a whole), are less than the $21 price charged by outside suppliers. At this transfer price, the Transportation Division would record an operating loss. Horizon Petroleum would not be able to determine the profitability of the investment made in the division, and the manager would not be motivated to exert effort. At the same time, the Refining Division would show large profits because it would be charged only for the variable costs of the Transportation Division. One approach to addressing this problem is to

1.1 × ($16 + $1 + $3) = $22, and (2) buying externally for $21. For the firm as a whole—assuming no incremental fixed costs are incurred —the relevant cost of buying from Transportation is only $17 ($16 to Matamoros + $1 variable cost). Transportation's $3 fixed costs and 10% markup are irrelevant from the firm-wide perspective. In sum, costs that are relevant to 1 division are not necessarily relevant to the firm as a whole, and this difference can lead to suboptimal decisions.

Points to Stress The text explains how to calculate the min. and max. TP at which the subunits will be willing to trade. The min. TP is the incremental cost to the seller ($16 + 1 = $17 to the Transportation Div.) plus the opportunity cost to the seller ($0 to Transportation, since there's no alternative use of its capacity). This "floor" TP is what the seller gives up to produce the units, since the seller will not willingly sell for less. The max. TP is the price at which the buyer could purchase externally (Refining could purchase at $21). The buyer wouldn't willingly pay more than market, so this establishes a "ceiling" price. The max. TP ($21) allocates all profit to the seller (Transportation) and the min. TP ($17) allocates all profit to the buyer (Refining).

Points to Stress Another rationale for using TP based on full cost is the following: If the selling subunit's full cost exceeds the market price, the buying unit will prefer to outsource. While this may be suboptimal in the short run, it appears more reasonable in the long run. If the seller can't produce at a competitive cost, mgt. should consider reallocating resources elsewhere.

New in This Edition Using VC as the TP is another option. It will result in the selling division (Transportation) recording an operating loss unless other business covers its fixed costs. Having the buying division (Refining) pay the selling division VC plus a lump sum amount to cover FC and profit would solve this problem.

[3]Some recent research examines cost-based transfer prices where margins over cost are not constant but increase as the actual costs decrease. The goal is to create incentives for division managers supplying products to decrease costs.

have the Refining Division make a lump-sum transfer payment to cover fixed costs and generate some operating income for the Transportation Division while the Transportation Division continues to make transfers at variable costs. The fixed payment is the price the Refining Division pays for using the capacity of the Transportation Division. The income earned by each division can then be used to evaluate the performance of each division and its manager.

Prorating the Difference between Maximum and Minimum Transfer Prices

An alternative cost-based approach is for Horizon Petroleum to choose a transfer price that splits, on some equitable basis, the $4 difference between the maximum transfer price the Refining Division is willing to pay ($21) and the minimum transfer price the Transportation Division is willing to charge ($17). Suppose Horizon Petroleum allocates the $4 difference on the basis of the budgeted variable costs of the Transportation Division and the Refining Division for a given quantity of crude oil. Using the data in Exhibit 22-2 (p. 796), the variable costs are as follows:

Transportation Division's variable costs to transport 100 barrels of crude oil	$100
Refining Division's variable costs to refine 100 barrels of crude oil	400
	$500

The Transportation Division gets to keep ($100 ÷ $500) × $4.00 = $0.80, and the Refining Division gets to keep ($400 ÷ $500) × $4.00 = $3.20 of the $4 difference. That is, the transfer price between the Transportation Division and the Refining Division would be $17.80 per barrel of crude oil ($16 purchase cost + $1 variable costs + $0.80 that the Transportation Division gets to keep). Essentially, this approach is a budgeted variable cost plus transfer price. The "plus" indicates the setting of a transfer price above variable costs.

To decide on the $0.80 and $3.20 allocation of the $4.00 contribution to total company operating income per barrel, the divisions must share information about their variable costs. In effect, each division does not operate (at least for this transaction) in a totally decentralized manner. Because most organizations are hybrids of centralization and decentralization anyway, this approach deserves serious consideration when transfers are significant. Note, however, that each division has an incentive to overstate its variable costs in order to receive a more favorable transfer price.

Dual Pricing

There is seldom a *single* cost-based transfer price that simultaneously meets the criteria of goal congruence, management effort, subunit performance evaluation, and subunit autonomy (if desired). As a result, some companies choose **dual pricing**, using two separate transfer-pricing methods to price each interdivision transaction. An example of dual pricing arises when the selling division receives a full cost plus markup-based price and the buying division pays the market price for the internally transferred products. Assume that Horizon Petroleum purchases crude oil from Gulfmex in Matamoros at $16 per barrel. One way of recording the journal entry for the transfer between the Transportation Division and the Refining Division is:

1. Credit the Transportation Division (the selling division) with the 110%-of-full-cost transfer price of $22 per barrel of crude oil.

2. Debit the Refining Division (the buying division) with the market-based transfer price of $21 per barrel of crude oil.

3. Debit a corporate cost account for the $1 ($22 − $21) difference between the two transfer prices for the cost of crude oil borne by corporate rather than the Refining Division.

The dual-pricing system promotes goal congruence because it makes the Refining Division no worse off if it purchases the crude oil from the Transportation Division rather than from the outside supplier. In either case, the Refining Division's cost is

$21 per barrel of crude oil. This dual-pricing system essentially gives the Transportation Division a corporate subsidy. The effect of dual pricing is that the operating income for Horizon Petroleum as a whole is less than the sum of the operating incomes of the divisions.

Dual pricing is not widely used in practice even though it reduces the goal-congruence problem associated with a pure cost-based transfer-pricing method. One concern is that dual pricing leads to some problems when computing the taxable income of divisions when divisions are located in different tax jurisdictions (for example, if the Transportation Division is taxed in Mexico while the Refining Division is taxed in the United States). A second concern of top management is that the manager of the supplying division does not have sufficient incentive to control costs with a dual-pricing system. A third concern is that the dual-pricing system confuses division managers about the level of decentralization sought by top management. Above all, dual pricing tends to insulate managers from the frictions of the marketplace. Managers should know as much as possible about their subunits' buying and selling markets, and dual pricing reduces the incentive to gain this knowledge.

NEGOTIATED TRANSFER PRICES

Negotiated transfer prices result from a bargaining process between selling and buying divisions. Consider again the choice of a transfer price between the Transportation Division and Refining Division of Horizon Petroleum. The Transportation Division has unused capacity that it can use to transport oil from Matamoros to Houston. The Transportation Division will only be willing to purchase oil from Gulfmex and sell oil to the Refining Division if the transfer price equals or exceeds $17 per barrel of crude oil (its variable costs). The Refining Division will only be willing to buy crude oil from the Transportation Division if the price does not exceed $21 per barrel (the price at which the Refining Division can buy crude oil in Houston).

From the viewpoint of Horizon Petroleum as a whole, operating income would be maximized if the Refining Division purchased from the Transportation Division rather than from the Houston market (incremental costs of $17 per barrel versus incremental costs of $21 per barrel). Both divisions would be interested in transacting with each other (thereby achieving goal congruence) if the transfer price is set between $17 and $21. For example, a transfer price of $19.25 per barrel will increase the Transportation Division's operating income by $19.25 − $17 = $2.25 per barrel. It will increase the Refining Division's operating income by $21 − $19.25 = $1.75 per barrel because the Refining Division can now buy the oil for $19.25 internally rather than for $21 in the outside market.

The key question is, Where between $17 and $21 will the transfer price be set? The answer depends on the bargaining strengths of the two divisions, the information the Transportation Division has about the demand for its services from outside refineries, and the information the Refining Division has about its other available sources of oil. Negotiations become particularly sensitive because Horizon Petroleum can now evaluate each division's performance on the basis of division operating income. The price negotiated by the two divisions will, in general, have no specific relationship to either costs or market price. But cost and price information are often useful starting points in the negotiation process. A negotiated transfer price strongly preserves division autonomy because the transfer price is the outcome of direct negotiations between division managers. It also has the advantage that each division manager is motivated to put forth effort to increase division income. Its major disadvantage is the time and energy spent on the negotiations.

A GENERAL GUIDELINE FOR TRANSFER-PRICING SITUATIONS

Exhibit 22-3 summarizes the properties of the different transfer-pricing methods using the criteria described earlier in the chapter. As the exhibit indicates, there is no all-pervasive rule for transfer pricing that leads to optimal decisions for the

Domestic and Multinational Transfer-Pricing Practices

What transfer-pricing practices are used around the world? The following tables indicate how predominantly particular transfer-pricing methods are used in different countries.

A. Domestic Transfer-Pricing Methods

Methods	United States[a]	Australia[b]	Canada[c]	Japan[a]	India[d]	United Kingdom[e]	New Zealand[f]
Market-based	37%	13%	34%	34%	47%	26%	18%
Cost-based:							
Variable costs	4	N.D.	6	2	6	10	10
Absorption or full costs	41	N.D.	37	44	47	38	61
Other	1	N.D.	3	—	—	1	—
Total	46%	65%	46%	46%	53%	49%	71%
Negotiated	16%	11%	18%	19%	—	24%	11%
Other	1%	11%	2%	1%	—	1%	—
	100%	100%	100%	100%	100%	100%	100%

B. Multinational Transfer-Pricing Methods

Methods	United States[a]	Australia[b]	Canada[c]	Japan[a]	India[d]	United Kingdom[g]	New Zealand[f]
Market-based	46%	—	37%	37%	—	31%	—
Cost-based:							
Variable costs	3	—	5	3	—	5	—
Absorption or full costs	37	—	26	38	—	28	—
Other	1	—	2	—	—	5	—
Total	41%	—	33%	41%	—	38%	—
Negotiated	13%	—	26%	22%	—	20%	—
Other	0%	—	4%	—	—	11%	—
	100%	—	100%	100%	—	100%	—

Note: Dashes indicate information was not disclosed in survey.

The surveys indicate that for domestic transfer pricing, managers in all countries use cost-based transfer prices more frequently than market-based transfer prices. For multinational transfer pricing, managers use market-based and cost-based methods equally frequently. Many multinational companies have market-based transfer prices in some divisions and cost-based transfer prices in others.

What factors do executives consider important in decisions on domestic transfer pricing? Survey evidence indicates the following (in order of importance): (1) performance evaluation, (2) management motivation, (3) pricing and product emphasis, and (4) external market recognition.[h]

Factors cited as important in decisions on multinational transfer-pricing policy are (in order of importance) (1) total income of the company, (2) income tax rate and other tax differences among countries, (3) income or dividend repatriation restrictions, and (4) competitive position of subsidiaries in their respective markets.[c,i]

[a]Adapted from Tang, Walter, and Raymond, "Transfer Pricing."
[b]Joye and Blayney, "Cost and Management Accounting."
[c]Tang, "Canadian Transfer."
[d]Govindarajan and Ramamurthy, "Transfer Pricing."
[e]Drury, Braund, Osborne, and Tayles, *A Survey of Management Accounting*.
[f]Hoque and Alam, "Organization Size."
[g]Mostafa, Sharp, and Howard, "Transfer Pricing."
[h]Price Waterhouse, *Transfer Pricing Practices*.
[i]J. Elliott, "International Transfer Pricing." Full citations are in Appendix A.

EXHIBIT 22-3

Comparison of Different Transfer-Pricing Methods

Criteria	Market Price	Cost-Based	Negotiated
◆ Achieves goal congruence	◆ Yes, if markets competitive	◆ Often but not always	◆ Yes
◆ Useful for evaluating subunit performance	◆ Yes, if markets competitive	◆ Difficult unless transfer price exceeds full costs	◆ Yes, but transfer prices are affected by bargaining strengths
◆ Motivates management effort	◆ Yes	◆ Yes, if based on budgeted costs; less incentive to control costs if transfers based on actual costs	◆ Yes
◆ Preserves subunit autonomy	◆ Yes, if markets competitive	◆ No, since it is rule-based	◆ Yes, because it is based on negotiations between subunits
◆ Other factors	◆ No market may exist or markets may be imperfect or in distress	◆ Useful for determining full cost of products and services Easy to implement	◆ Bargaining and negotiations take time and may need to be reviewed repeatedly as conditions change

organization as a whole. Why? Because market conditions, the goal of the transfer-pricing system, and the criteria of goal congruence, management effort, subunit performance evaluation, and subunit autonomy (if desired), must all be considered simultaneously. The "correct" transfer price depends on the economic circumstances and the decision at hand. The following general guideline (formula), however, has proven to be a helpful first step in setting a minimum transfer price in many situations:

$$\text{Minimum transfer price} = \begin{array}{c}\textit{Incremental costs}\\\text{per unit}\\\text{incurred up}\\\text{to the point of transfer}\end{array} + \begin{array}{c}\textit{Opportunity costs}\\\text{per unit}\\\text{to the selling division}\end{array}$$

The term *incremental costs* in this context means the additional costs of producing and transfering the products or services. *Opportunity costs* here are the maximum contribution forgone by the selling division if the products or services are transferred internally. For example, if the selling division is operating at capacity, the opportunity cost of transferring a unit internally rather than selling it externally is equal to the market price minus variable costs. Why? Because by transferring a unit internally, the division forgoes the contribution margin it could have obtained by selling the unit in the outside market. We distinguish incremental costs from opportunity costs because the accounting system typically records incremental costs but not opportunity costs. The guideline measures a *minimum* transfer price because the selling division will be motivated to sell the product to the buying division only if the transfer price covers the incremental costs the selling division incurs to produce the product and the opportunity cost it forgoes by selling the product internally rather than in the external market. We illustrate the general guideline in some specific situations using data from the Transportation and Refining Divisions of Horizon Petroleum.

1. *A perfectly competitive market for the intermediate product exists, and the selling division has no idle capacity.* If the market for crude oil in Houston is perfectly competitive, the Transportation Division can sell all the crude oil it transports to the external market at $21 per barrel, and it will have no idle capacity. The Transportation Division's incremental costs (as shown in Exhibit 22-1, p. 795) are $13 per barrel of crude oil for oil purchased under the long-term contract (purchase cost of $12 per barrel plus variable transportation costs of $1 per barrel) or $17 per barrel for oil purchased at current market prices from Gulfmex in the Matamoros area (purchase

New in This Edition Exh. 22-3 summarizes how the different TP methods meet the four criteria of achieving goal congruence, evaluating subunit performance, motivating management, and subunit autonomy.

Correcting Student Misconceptions The "general guideline" yields the minimum TP the seller can accept and be as well off as under the next best alternative. It's a starting point for negotiations—not a "recommended" TP.

Teaching Tip/Curriculum Linkage The concept of opportunity cost was discussed in Chap. 11 and also is covered in economics courses. In the TP context, opportunity cost is the profit the seller forgoes by selling to the sister subunit, rather than externally. Assume the seller has no idle capacity and can sell all they produce at $4. Incremental cost is $1.00. If the seller sells internally, the profit forgone (opportunity cost) is $3 ($4 revenue − $1 outlay cost). Alternatively, if the seller has excess capacity with no alternative use, no profit is forgone by selling internally (opportunity cost is zero).

Reinforcing Problems Prob 22-34 is a challenging problem that covers capacity utilization issues.

cost of $16 plus variable transportation costs of $1). The Transportation Division's opportunity cost per barrel of transferring the oil internally is the contribution margin per barrel forgone by not selling the crude oil in the external market: $8 for oil purchased under the long-term contract (market price, $21 − variable costs, $13) and $4 for oil purchased from Gulfmex (market price, $21 − variable costs, $17). In either case,

$$\begin{array}{c} \text{Minimum transfer price} \\ \text{per barrel} \end{array} = \begin{array}{c} \text{Incremental costs} \\ \text{per barrel} \end{array} + \begin{array}{c} \text{Opportunity costs} \\ \text{per barrel} \end{array}$$

$$= \$13 + \$8 \text{ or } \$17 + \$4 = \$21 = \text{Market price per barrel}$$

Market-based transfer prices are ideal in perfectly competitive markets when there is no idle capacity in the selling division.

2. *An intermediate market exists that is not perfectly competitive, and the selling division has idle capacity.* In markets that are not perfectly competitive, capacity utilization can only be increased by decreasing prices. Idle capacity exists because decreasing prices is often not worthwhile—it decreases operating income.

If the Transportation Division has idle capacity, its opportunity cost of transferring the oil internally is zero because the division does not forgo any external sales and hence does not forgo any contribution margin from internal transfers. In this case,

$$\begin{array}{c} \text{Minimum transfer price} \\ \text{per barrel} \end{array} = \begin{array}{c} \text{Incremental costs} \\ \text{per barrel} \end{array} = \begin{array}{c} \text{\$13 per barrel for oil purchased under the} \\ \text{long-term contract, or \$17 per barrel for} \\ \text{oil purchased from Gulfmex in Matamoros} \end{array}$$

Note that any transfer price above incremental costs but below $21 (the price at which the Refining Division can buy crude oil in Houston) motivates the Transportation Division to transport crude oil to the Refining Division and the Refining Division to buy crude oil from the Transportation Division. In this situation, the company could either use a cost-based transfer price or allow the two divisions to negotiate a transfer price between themselves.

In general though, in markets that are not perfectly competitive, the potential to influence demand and operating income through prices makes measuring opportunity costs more complicated. The transfer price depends on constantly changing levels of supply and demand. There is not just one transfer price. Rather, a transfer-pricing schedule yields the transfer price for various quantities supplied and demanded, depending on the incremental costs and opportunity costs of the units transferred.

3. *No market exists for the intermediate product.* This situation would occur, for example, in the Horizon Petroleum case if the grade of oil transported by the Transportation Division can be used only by the Houston refinery (due to, say, its tar content) and hence will not be wanted by outside parties. Here, the opportunity cost of supplying crude oil internally is zero because the inability to sell crude oil externally means no contribution margin is forgone. For the Transportation Division of Horizon Petroleum, the minimum transfer price under the general guideline would be the incremental costs per barrel (either $13 or $17). As in the previous case, any transfer price between the incremental costs and $21 will achieve goal congruence.

MULTINATIONAL TRANSFER PRICING AND TAX CONSIDERATIONS

OBJECTIVE 9

Incorporate income tax considerations in multinational transfer pricing

Transfer prices often have tax implications. Tax factors include not only income taxes, but also payroll taxes, customs duties, tariffs, sales taxes, value-added taxes, environment-related taxes, and other government levies on organizations. Full consideration of the tax aspects of transfer-pricing decisions is beyond the scope of this book. Our aim here is to highlight tax factors and, in particular, income taxes as an important consideration in determining transfer prices.

Consider the Horizon Petroleum data in Exhibit 22-2 (p. 796). Assume that the Transportation Division based in Mexico pays Mexican income taxes at 30% of operating income and that the Refining Division based in the United States pays income taxes at 20% of operating income. Horizon Petroleum would minimize its total income tax payments with the 110%-of-full-costs transfer-pricing method, as shown in the following table, because this method minimizes income reported in Mexico that is taxed at a higher rate than U.S. income.

Teaching Tip This section highlights the importance of taxes in setting TP. Emphasize the intuition that companies want to set TP so as to minimize profits reported in the higher-taxed jurisdiction. However, as in the Horizon Petroleum example, the tax minimization method can conflict with the method preferred for goal congru-

| Transfer-Pricing Method | Operating Income for 100 Barrels of Crude Oil | | | Income Tax on 100 Barrels of Crude Oil | | |
	Transportation Division (Mexico) (1)	Refining Division (U.S.) (2)	Total (3) = (1) + (2)	Transportation Division (Mexico) (4) = 0.30 × (1)	Refining Division (U.S.) (5) = 0.20 × (2)	Total (6)= (4) + (5)
Market price	$500	$100	$600	$150.00	$20	$170.00
110% of full costs	160	440	600	48.00	88	136.00
Negotiated price	325	275	600	97.50	55	152.50

Tax considerations raise additional issues. Tax issues, however, may conflict with other objectives of transfer pricing. Suppose that the market for crude oil in Houston is perfectly competitive. In this case, the market-based transfer price achieves goal congruence and provides incentives for management effort. It also helps Horizon to evaluate the economic profitability of the Transportation Division. But it is costly from an income tax standpoint. To minimize taxes, Horizon Petroleum would favor using 110% of full costs for tax reporting. Tax laws in the United States and Mexico, however, constrain this option. In particular, the Mexican tax authorities are fully aware of Horizon Petroleum's incentives to minimize income taxes by reducing the income reported in Mexico. They would challenge any attempts to shift income to the Refining Division through an unreasonably low transfer price.

Section 482 of the U.S. Internal Revenue Code governs taxation of multinational transfer pricing. Section 482 requires that transfer prices for both tangible and intangible property between a company and its foreign division or subsidiary be set to equal the price that would be charged by an unrelated third party in a comparable transaction. Section 482 recognizes that transfer prices can be market-based or cost-plus-based (where the plus represents margins on comparable transactions).[4]

If the market for crude oil in Houston is perfectly competitive, Horizon Petroleum would probably be required to use the market price for transfers from the Transportation Division to the Refining Division. Horizon Petroleum might successfully argue that the transfer price should be set below the market price because the Transportation Division incurs no marketing and distribution costs when selling crude oil to the Refining Division. Under the U.S. Internal Revenue Code, Horizon Petroleum could obtain advanced approval of the transfer-pricing arrangements from the tax authorities.

To meet multiple transfer-pricing objectives, a company may choose to keep one set of accounting records for tax reporting and a second set for internal management reporting. The difficulty here is that tax authorities may interpret two sets of books as suggestive of the company manipulating its reported taxable income to avoid tax payments.

Additional factors that arise in multinational transfer pricing include tariffs and customs duties levied on imports of products into a country. The issues here are similar to the income tax considerations discussed earlier—companies will have

ence and managerial motivation (i.e., market price). While companies may keep 2 sets of books using different transfer prices for mgt. and tax purposes, this can undermine their tax position if audited by taxation authorities. These issues arise in interstate as well as multinational tax contexts.

Reinforcing Problems Exer. 22-18, 22-23, and 22-24 and Probs. 22-31 and 22-32 cover multinational TP and tax issues.

Points to Stress The Surveys of Company Practice box shows that cost-based prices are most popular in domestic TP, whereas market-based and cost-based TP are equally popular in multinational contexts. One explanation is that tax considerations become more important in multinational TP, and companies may find it easier to justify market-based TP to international tax authorities.

Teaching Tip The following 3-step approach is helpful for TP problems. *First*, apply the general guideline to obtain the min. price the seller can accept to be as well off as under the next best alternative. *Second*, determine whether the buyer will buy at that price. (Can the buyer get a better deal elsewhere? Will the buyer still make a profit at the TP? What is the max. price the buyer can pay and still make a profit?) *Third*, verify that the buyer's decision is in the best interest of the company as a whole.

[4]Business International Corporation, *International Transfer Pricing* (New York, 1991); A. King, "The IRS's New Neutron Bomb", *Management Accounting* (December 1992); Coopers and Lybrand, *Tax Topics Advisory* (January 21, 1993); P. Rooney and N. Suit, "IRS Relaxes Transfer Pricing Rules," *International Tax Review* (October 1994); and D. K. Dolan and D. Bower, "Final Transfer Pricing Regulations," *Tax Management International Journal* (July 1994).

U.S. Internal Revenue Service, Japanese National Tax Agency, and Transfer-Pricing Games

Tax authorities and government officials all over the world pay close attention to taxes paid by foreign corporations operating within their boundaries. At the heart of the issue: the transfer prices that companies use to transfer products from one country to another.

For example, in 1993, the U.S. Internal Revenue Service (IRS) investigated and concluded that Nissan Motor Company had minimized U.S. taxes by setting transfer prices on passenger cars and trucks imported from Japan at "unrealistically" high levels. Nissan argued that it had maintained low margins in the United States to increase long-run market share in a very competitive market. Eventually, Nissan agreed to pay the IRS $170 million. But Nissan suffered no loss. The Japanese National Tax Agency (NTA), Japan's tax authority, refunded Nissan the full amount of the IRS payment.

Conversely, in May 1994, Japan's NTA alleged that Coca-Cola Corporation had deliberately underrecorded profits earned in Japan both by charging "excessive" transfer prices to its local subsidiary for materials and concentrate imported from the parent company, and by levying "excessive" royalty payments on its Japanese subsidiary for use of its brand name and for marketing and management services. The NTA imposed taxes and penalties of $150 million. Coca-Cola filed a complaint with the IRS charging that the levying of the Japanese tax resulted in the same income being taxed twice, because Coca-Cola had already paid tax on this income in the United States. This complaint led to negotiations between Japanese and U.S. tax authorities as to which country gets to tax Coke's Japanese income. In a 1998 compromise settlement, Japan's NTA reduced its tax levy against Coke from $150 million to $50 million. For its part, the IRS reduced Coca-Cola's U.S. income tax liability.

The dispute over what is a "fair" transfer price arises because of the absence of an easily observable market price for the transferred product. Multinational transfer-pricing disputes are likely to remain a significant issue given the substantial and increasing amounts of multinational investments.

Source: Adapted from C. Pass, "Transfer Pricing in Multinational Companies," *Management Accounting* (September 1994); and "Coca-Cola Gets 10 Billion Yen Reprieve in Back Taxes," *The Yomiuri Shimbun* (February 24, 1998).

incentives to lower transfer prices for products imported into a country to reduce the tariffs and customs duties charged on those products.

In addition to the various motivations for choosing transfer prices already described, multinational transfer prices are sometimes influenced by restrictions that some countries place on dividend or income-related payments to parties outside their national borders. By increasing the prices of goods or services transferred into divisions in these countries, companies can increase the cash paid out of these countries without appearing to violate dividend or income-related restrictions.

PROBLEM FOR SELF-STUDY

PROBLEM

The Pillercat Corporation is a highly decentralized company. Each division manager has full authority for sourcing decisions and selling decisions. The Machining Division of Pillercat has been the major supplier of the 2,000 crankshafts that the Tractor Division needs each year.

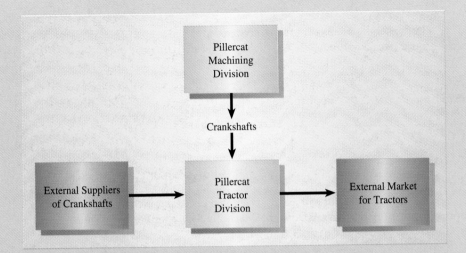

The Tractor Division, however, has just announced that it plans to purchase all its crankshafts in the forthcoming year from two external suppliers at $200 per crankshaft. The Machining Division of Pillercat recently increased its price for the forthcoming year to $220 per unit (from $200 per unit in the current year).

Juan Gomez, manager of the Machining Division, feels that the 10% price increase is fully justified. It results from a higher depreciation charge on some new specialized equipment used to manufacture crankshafts and an increase in labor costs. Gomez wants the president of Pillercat Corporation to direct the Tractor Division to buy all its crankshafts from the Machining Division at the price of $220. The incremental costs per unit that Pillercat incurs to produce each crankshaft are the Machining Division's variable costs of $190. Fixed costs per crankshaft in the Machining Division are $20.

Required

1. Compute the advantage or disadvantage (in terms of annual operating income) to the Pillercat Corporation as a whole if the Tractor Division buys crankshafts internally from the Machining Division under each of the following cases.
   a. The Machining Division has no alternative use for the facilities used to manufacture crankshafts.
   b. The Machining Division can use the facilities for other production operations, which will result in monthly cash operating savings of $29,000.
   c. The Machining Division has no alternative use for its facilities, and the external supplier drops the price to $185 per crankshaft.
2. As the president of Pillercat, how would you respond to Juan Gomez's request to order the Tractor Division to purchase all of its crankshafts from the Machining Division? Would your response differ according to the scenarios described in parts a, b, and c of requirement 1? Why?

SOLUTION

1. Computations for the Tractor Division buying crankshafts internally.

	Case		
	a	b	c
Total purchase costs if buying from an external supplier (2,000 × $200, $200, $185)	$400,000	$400,000	$370,000
Incremental costs if buying from the Machining Division (2,000 × $190)	380,000	380,000	380,000
Total opportunity costs of the Machining Division	—	29,000	—
Total relevant costs	380,000	409,000	380,000
Annual operating income advantage (disadvantage) to Pillercat Corporation of buying from the Machining Division	$ 20,000	$ (9,000)	$ (10,000)

The "general guideline" that was introduced in the chapter (p. 803) as a first step in setting a transfer price can be used to highlight the alternatives:

Case	Incremental Costs Per Unit Incurred to Point of Transfer	+	Opportunity Costs Per Unit to the Supplying Division	=	Transfer Price	External Market Price
a	$190	+	$0	=	$190	$200
b	$190	+	$14.50 ($29,000 ÷ 2,000)	=	$204.50	$200
c	$190	+	$0	=	$190	$185

The Tractor Division will maximize annual operating income of Pillercat Corporation as a whole by purchasing from the Machining Division in case a and by purchasing from the external supplier in cases b and c.

2. Pillercat Corporation is a highly decentralized company. If no forced transfer were made, the Tractor Division would use an external supplier, resulting in an optimal decision for the company as a whole in cases b and c of requirement 1 but not in case a.

Suppose that in case a, the Machining Division refuses to meet the price of $200. This decision means that the company will be $20,000 worse off in the short-run. Should top management interfere and force a transfer at $200? This interference would undercut the philosophy of decentralization. Many top managements would not interfere because they would view the $20,000 as an inevitable cost of a suboptimal decision that can occur under decentralization. But how high must this cost be before the temptation to interfere would be irresistible? $30,000? $40,000?

Any top management interference with lower-level decision making weakens decentralization. Of course, such interference may occasionally be necessary to prevent costly blunders. But recurring interference and constraints simply transform a decentralized organization into a centralized organization.

SUMMARY

The following points are linked to the chapter's learning objectives:

1. A management control system is a means of gathering and using information to aid and coordinate the process of making planning and control decisions throughout the organization, and to guide the behavior of managers and employees. Effective management control systems are (a) closely aligned to the organization's strategy, (b) fit the organization's structure, and (c) motivate managers and employees to give effort to achieve the organization's goals.

2. The benefits of decentralization include (a) greater responsiveness to local needs, (b) gains from quicker decision making, (c) increased motivation of subunit managers, (d) greater management development and learning, and (e) sharpened focus of subunit managers. The costs of decentralization include (a) suboptimal decision making (loss of control), (b) duplication of activities, (c) decreased loyalty toward the organization, and (d) increased costs of information gathering.

3. A transfer price is the price one subunit charges for a product or service supplied to another subunit of the same organization. Transfer prices should achieve (a) goal congruence, (b) management effort, (c) subunit performance evaluation, and (d) subunit autonomy (if desired).

4. Transfer prices can be (a) market-based, (b) cost-based, or (c) negotiated. Different transfer-pricing methods produce different revenues and costs for individual subunits, and hence different operating incomes for them.

5. In perfectly competitive markets, there is no idle capacity, and division managers can buy and sell as much as they want at the market price. Setting the transfer price at the market price motivates division managers to deal internally and to take exactly the same actions as they would if they were dealing in the external market.

6. A transfer price based on full cost plus a markup may lead to suboptimal decisions because it leads the buying division to regard the fixed costs and the markup of the selling division as variable costs.

7. When there is unused capacity, the transfer price range for negotiations generally lies between the minimum price at which the selling division is willing to sell (its variable costs) and the maximum price that the buying division is willing to pay (the price at which the product is available from outside suppliers).

8. The general guideline for transfer pricing states that the minimum transfer price equals the incremental costs per unit incurred up to the point of transfer plus the opportunity costs per unit to the supplying division resulting from transferring products or services internally.

9. Transfer prices can reduce income tax payments by recognizing more income in low-tax-rate countries and less income in high-tax-rate countries. However, tax regulations of different countries restrict the transfer prices that companies can choose.

This chapter and the Glossary at the end of this book contain definitions of the following important terms:

autonomy (p. 790)
decentralization (790)
dual pricing (800)
dysfunctional decision making (791)
effort (789)
goal congruence (789)
incongruent decision making (791)

intermediate product (793)
management control system (788)
motivation (789)
perfectly competitive market (796)
suboptimal decision making (791)
transfer price (793)

▼ **ASSIGNMENT MATERIAL**

QUESTIONS

22-1 What is a management control system?

22-2 Describe three criteria you would use to evaluate whether a management control system is effective.

22-3 What is the relationship among motivation, goal congruence, and effort?

22-4 Name three benefits and two costs of decentralization.

22-5 "Organizations typically adopt a consistent decentralization or centralization philosophy across all their business functions." Do you agree? Explain.

22-6 "Transfer pricing is confined to profit centers." Do you agree? Explain.

22-7 What are the three general methods for determining transfer prices?

22-8 What properties should transfer-pricing systems have?

22-9 "All transfer-pricing methods give the same division operating income." Do you agree? Explain.

22-10 Under what conditions is a market-based transfer price optimal?

22-11 What is one potential limitation of full-cost-based transfer prices?

22-12 Give two reasons why the dual-pricing system of transfer pricing is not widely used.

22-13 "Cost and price information play no role in negotiated transfer prices." Do you agree? Explain.

22-14 "Under the general guideline for transfer pricing, the minimum transfer price will vary depending on whether the supplying division has idle capacity or not." Do you agree? Explain.

22-15 Why should managers consider income tax issues when choosing a transfer-pricing method?

EXERCISES

22-16 Decentralization, responsibility centers. Quinn Corporation manufactures and sells lighting products. Quinn's sales and marketing divisions are organized along product lines—wall sconces, recessed lights, track lights, and so on. The Manufacturing Division produces lighting products for all the sales and marketing divisions.

During the planning process, each sales and marketing division specifies the quantity of each style of light to be manufactured. Senior management then assigns the task of manufacturing the lights to different plants in the Manufacturing Division. Because manufacturing capacity is limited, some of the production is also outsourced. Senior management determines the manufacturing schedule on the basis of detailed studies that have been done to measure the time and cost of manufacturing different types of lighting products. Manufacturing managers are evaluated based on achieving target output within budgeted costs.

Required
1. Are the manufacturing plants in the Manufacturing Division cost centers or profit centers? Explain.
2. Quinn Corporation is considering decentralizing its marketing and manufacturing decisions by letting manufacturing and marketing managers directly negotiate the prices for manufacturing various products.
   a. How should Quinn evaluate manufacturing plant managers under this proposal?
   b. Would you recommend that Quinn Corporation decentralize its marketing and manufacturing decisions? Explain.

22-17 Decentralization, goal congruence, responsibility centers. Hexton Chemicals consists of seven operating divisions that operate independently. The operating divisions are assisted by a number of support groups such as R&D, human resources, and environmental management. The environmental management group consists of 20 environmental engineers. These engineers must seek business from the operating divisions—that is, the projects they work on must be mutually agreed to and paid for by one of the operating divisions. Under Hexton's rules, the environmental group is required to charge the operating divisions for environmental services at cost.

Required
1. Is the environmental management group centralized or decentralized?
2. What type of responsibility center is the environmental management group?
3. What benefits and problems do you see in structuring the environmental management group the way Hexton has? Does it lead to goal congruence and motivation? Explain.

22-18 Multinational transfer pricing, effect of alternative transfer-pricing methods, global income tax minimization. User Friendly Computer, Inc., with headquarters in San Francisco, manufactures and sells desk-top computers. User Friendly has three divisions, each of which is located in a different country:

a. China Division—manufactures memory devices and keyboards.
b. South Korea Division—assembles desk-top computers, using internally manufactured parts and memory devices and keyboards from the China Division.
c. U.S. Division—packages and distributes desk-top computers.

Each division is run as a profit center. The costs for the work done in each division for a single desk-top computer unit are as follows:

China Division:	Variable costs	= 1,000 yuan
	Fixed costs	= 1,800 yuan
South Korea Division:	Variable costs	= 360,000 won
	Fixed costs	= 480,000 won
U.S. Division:	Variable costs	= $100
	Fixed costs	= $200

Chinese income tax rate on China Division's operating income	40%	
South Korean income tax rate on South Korea Division's operating income	20%	
U.S. income tax rate on U.S. Division's operating income	30%	

Each desk-top computer is sold to retail outlets in the United States for $3,200. Assume that the current foreign exchange rates are:

$$8 \text{ yuan} = \$1 \text{ U.S.}$$

$$1{,}200 \text{ won} = \$1 \text{ U.S.}$$

Both the China and the South Korea Divisions sell part of their production under a private label. The China Division sells the comparable memory/keyboard package used in each User Friendly desk-top computer to a Chinese manufacturer for 3,600 yuan. The South Korea Division sells the comparable desk-top computer to a South Korean distributor for 1,560,000 won.

Required

1. Calculate the after-tax operating income per unit earned by each division under the following transfer-pricing methods: (a) market price, (b) 200% of full costs, and (c) 300% of variable costs. (Income taxes are *not* included in the computation of the cost-based transfer prices.)

2. Which transfer-pricing method(s) will maximize the net income per unit of User Friendly Computer?

22-19 Transfer-pricing methods, goal congruence. British Columbia Lumber has a Raw Lumber Division and a Finished Lumber Division. The variable costs are:

◆ Raw Lumber Division: $100 per 100 board-feet of raw lumber
◆ Finished Lumber Division: $125 per 100 board-feet of finished lumber

Assume that there is no board-feet loss in processing raw lumber into finished lumber. Raw lumber can be sold at $200 per 100 board-feet. Finished lumber can be sold at $275 per 100 board-feet.

Required

1. Should British Columbia Lumber process raw lumber into its finished form? Show your computations.

2. Assume that internal transfers are made at 110% of variable costs. Will each division maximize its division operating income contribution by adopting the action that is in the best interest of British Columbia Lumber? Explain.

3. Assume that internal transfers are made at market prices. Will each division maximize its division operating income contribution by adopting the action that is in the best interest of British Columbia Lumber? Explain.

22-20 Effect of alternative transfer-pricing methods on division operating income. (CMA, adapted) Ajax Corporation has two divisions. The Mining Division makes toldine, which is then transferred to the Metals Division. The toldine is further processed by the Metals Division and is sold to customers at a price of $150 per unit. The Mining Division is currently required by Ajax to transfer its total yearly output of 400,000 units of toldine to the Metals Division at 110% of full manufacturing cost. Unlimited quantities of toldine can be purchased and sold on the outside market at $90 per unit.

The following table gives the manufacturing costs per unit in the Mining and Metals Divisions for the year 2001:

	Mining Division	Metals Division
Direct materials	$12	$ 6
Direct manufacturing labor costs	16	20
Manufacturing overhead costs	32[a]	25[b]
Total manufacturing costs per unit	$60	$51

[a]Manufacturing overhead costs in the Mining Division are 25% fixed and 75% variable.
[b]Manufacturing overhead costs in the Metals Division are 60% fixed and 40% variable.

Required

1. Calculate the operating incomes for the Mining and Metals Divisions for the 400,000 units of toldine transferred under the following transfer-pricing methods: (a) market price, and (b) 110% of full manufacturing costs.

2. Suppose Ajax rewards each division manager with a bonus, calculated as 1% of division operating income (if positive). What is the amount of bonus that will be paid to each division manager under the transfer-pricing methods in requirement 1? Which transfer-pricing method will each division manager prefer to use?

3. What arguments would Brian Jones, manager of the Mining Division, make to support the transfer-pricing method that he prefers?

22-21 Transfer pricing, general guideline, goal congruence. (CMA, adapted). Nogo Motors operates as a decentralized multidivision company. The Igo Division of Nogo Motors, Inc., purchases most of its airbags from the Airbag Division. The Airbag Division's incremental costs for manufacturing the airbags are $110 per unit. The Airbag Division is currently working at 80% of capacity. The current market price of the airbags is $140 per unit.

Required

1. Using the general guideline presented in the chapter, what is the minimum price at which the Airbag Division would sell airbags to the Igo Division?

2. Suppose that Nogo Motors, Inc., requires that whenever divisions with idle capacity sell products internally, they must do so at incremental costs. Evaluate this transfer-pricing policy using the criteria of goal congruence, evaluating division performance, motivating management effort, and preserving division autonomy.

3. If the two divisions were to negotiate a transfer price, what is the range of possible transfer prices? Evaluate this negotiated transfer-pricing policy using the criteria of goal congruence, evaluating division performance, motivating management effort, and preserving division autonomy.

4. Do you prefer the transfer-pricing policy in requirement 2 or requirement 3? Explain your answer briefly.

22-22 General guideline, transfer price range. The Shamrock Company manufactures and sells television sets. The Assembly Division assembles the television sets. It buys the screens for the television sets from the Screen Division. The Screen Division is operating at capacity. The incremental cost of manufacturing the screens is $70 per unit. The Screen Division can sell as many screens as it wants in the outside market at a price of $110 per screen. If it sells screens in the outside market, the Screen Division will incur variable marketing and distribution costs of $4 per unit. Similarly, if the Assembly Division purchases screens from outside suppliers, it will incur variable purchasing costs of $2 per screen.

Required

1. Using the general guideline presented in the chapter, what is the minimum transfer price at which the Screen Division will sell screens to the Assembly Division?

2. Suppose division managers act autonomously to maximize their division's operating income either by transacting internally or buying and selling in the market. If the two division managers were to negotiate a transfer price, what is the range of acceptable transfer prices?

22-23 Multinational transfer pricing, global tax minimization. The Mornay Company manufactures telecommunications equipment at its Wisconsin plant in the United States. The company has marketing divisions throughout the world. A Mornay marketing division in Vienna, Austria, imports 1,000 units of Product 4A36 from the United States. The following information is available:

U.S. income tax rate on the U.S. division's operating income	40%
Austrian income tax rate on the Austrian division's operating income	44%
Austrian import duty	10%
Variable manufacturing cost per unit of Product 4A36	$350
Full manufacturing cost per unit of Product 4A36	$500
Selling price (net of marketing and distribution costs) in Austria	$750

Suppose the U.S. and Austrian tax authorities only allow transfer prices that are between the full manufacturing cost per unit and a market price of $650 based on comparable imports into Austria. The Austrian import duty is charged on the price at which the product is transferred into Austria. Any import duty paid to the Austrian authorities is a deductible expense for calculating Austrian income taxes due.

Required

1. Calculate the after-tax operating income earned by the U.S. and Austrian divisions from transferring 1,000 units of Product 4A36 (a) at full manufacturing cost per unit, and (b) at market price of comparable imports. (Income taxes are *not* included in the computation of the cost-based transfer prices.)
2. Which transfer price should the Mornay Company select to minimize the total of company import duties and income taxes? Remember that the transfer price must be between the full manufacturing cost per unit of $500 and the market price of $650 of comparable imports into Austria. Explain your reasoning.

22-24 Multinational transfer pricing, goal congruence (continuation of 22-23). Suppose that the U.S. division could sell as many units of Product 4A36 as it makes at $600 per unit in the U.S. market, net of all marketing and distribution costs.

Required

1. From the viewpoint of the Mornay Company as a whole, would after-tax operating income be maximized if it sold the 1,000 units of Product 4A36 in the United States or in Austria? Show your computations.
2. Suppose division managers act autonomously to maximize their division's after-tax operating income. Will the transfer price calculated in requirement 2 of Exercise 22-23 result in the U.S. division manager taking the actions determined to be optimal in requirement 1 of this exercise? Explain.
3. What is the minimum transfer price that the U.S. division manager would agree to? Does this transfer price result in the Mornay Company as a whole paying more import duty and taxes than the answer to requirement 2 of Exercise 22-23? If so, by how much?

22-25 Transfer-pricing dispute. The Allison-Chambers Corporation, manufacturer of tractors and other heavy farm equipment, is organized along decentralized lines, with each manufacturing division operating as a separate profit center. Each division manager has been delegated full authority on all decisions involving the sale of that division's output both to outsiders and to other divisions of Allison-Chambers. Division C has in the past always purchased its requirement of a particular tractor-engine component from Division A. However, when informed that Division A is increasing its selling price to $150, Division C's manager decides to purchase the engine component from outside suppliers.

Division C can purchase the component for $135 in the open market. Division A insists that, because of the recent installation of some highly specialized equipment and the resulting high depreciation charges, it will not be able to earn an adequate return on its investment unless it raises its price. Division A's manager appeals to top management of Allison-Chambers for support in the dispute with Division C and supplies the following operating data:

C's annual purchases of the tractor-engine component	1,000 units
A's variable costs per unit of the tractor-engine component	$120
A's fixed costs per unit of the tractor-engine component	$20

Required

1. Assume that there are no alternative uses for internal facilities. Determine whether the company as a whole will benefit if Division C purchases the component from outside suppliers for $135 per unit. What should the transfer price for the component be set at so that division managers acting in their own division's interest take actions that are in the best interest of the company as a whole?
2. Assume that internal facilities of Division A would not otherwise be idle. By not producing the 1,000 units for Division C, Division A's equipment and other facilities would be used for other production operations that would result in annual cash-operating savings of $18,000. Should Division C purchase from outside suppliers? Show your computations.
3. Assume that there are no alternative uses for Division A's internal facilities and that the price from outsiders drops $20. Should Division C purchase from outside suppliers? What should the transfer price for the component be set at so that division managers acting in their own division's interest take actions that are in the best interest of the company as a whole?

22-26 Transfer-pricing problem (continuation of 22-25). Refer to Exercise 22-25. Assume that Division A can sell the 1,000 units to other customers at $155 per unit with variable marketing costs of $5 per unit.

Required

Determine whether Allison-Chambers will benefit if Division C purchases the 1,000 components from outside suppliers at $135 per unit. Show your computations.

PROBLEMS

22-27 Pertinent transfer price. Europa, Inc., has two divisions, A and B, which manufacture expensive bicycles. Division A produces the bicycle frame, and Division B assembles the rest of the bicycle onto the frame. There is a market for both the subassembly and the final product. Each division has been designated as a profit center. The transfer price for the subassembly has been set at the long-run average market price. The following data are available for each division:

Estimated selling price for final product	$300
Long-run average selling price for intermediate product	200
Incremental costs for completion in Division B	150
Incremental costs in Division A	120

The manager of Division B has made the following calculation:

Selling price for final product		$300
Transferred-in costs (market)	$200	
Incremental costs for completion	150	350
Contribution (loss) on product		$(50)

Required

1. Should transfers be made to Division B if there is no unused capacity in Division A? Is the market price the correct transfer price? Show your computations.
2. Assume that Division A's maximum capacity for this product is 1,000 units per month and sales to the intermediate market are now 800 units. Should 200 units be transferred to Division B? At what transfer price? Assume that for a variety of reasons, Division A will maintain the $200 selling price indefinitely. That is, Division A is not considering lowering the price to outsiders even if idle capacity exists.
3. Suppose Division A quoted a transfer price of $150 for up to 200 units. What would be the contribution to the company as a whole if the transfer were made? As manager of Division B, would you be inclined to buy at $150? Explain.

22-28 Pricing in imperfect markets (continuation of 22-27). Refer to Problem 22-27.
Required
1. Suppose the manager of Division A has the option of (a) cutting the external price to $195 with the certainty that sales will rise to 1,000 units, or (b) maintaining the outside price of $200 for the 800 units and transferring the 200 units to Division B at some price that would produce the same operating income for Division A. What transfer price would produce the same operating income for Division A? Is that price consistent with that recommended by the general guideline in the chapter so that the desirable decision for the company as a whole would result?
2. Suppose that if the selling price for the intermediate product is dropped to $195, outside sales can be increased to 900 units. Division B wants to acquire as many as 200 units if the transfer price is acceptable. For simplicity, assume that there is no outside market for the final 100 units of Division A's capacity.
   a. Using the general guideline, what is (are) the minimum transfer price(s) that should lead to the correct economic decision? Ignore performance-evaluation considerations.
   b. Compare the total contributions under the alternatives to show why the transfer price(s) recommended lead(s) to the optimal economic decision.

22-29 Effect of alternative transfer-pricing methods on division operating income. Oceanic Products is a tuna fishing company based in San Diego. It has three divisions:

a. Tuna Harvesting—operates a fleet of 20 trawling vessels.
b. Tuna Processing—processes the raw tuna into tuna fillets.
c. Tuna Marketing—packages tuna fillets in 2-pound packets that are sold to wholesale distributors at $12 each.

The Tuna Processing Division has a yield of 500 pounds of processed tuna fillets from 1,000 pounds of raw tuna provided by the Tuna Harvesting Division. The Tuna Marketing Division has a yield of 300 2-pound packets from every 500 pounds of processed tuna fillets provided by the Tuna Processing Division. (The weight of the packaging material is included in the 2-pound weight.) Cost data for each division are as follows:

Tuna Harvesting Division

Variable costs per pound of raw tuna	$0.20
Fixed costs per pound of raw tuna	$0.40

Tuna Processing Division

Variable costs per pound of processed tuna	$0.80
Fixed costs per pound of processed tuna	$0.60

Tuna Marketing Division

Variable costs per 2-pound packet	$0.30
Fixed costs per 2-pound packet	$0.70

Fixed costs per unit are based on the estimated quantity of raw tuna, processed tuna, and 2-pound packets to be produced during the current fishing season.

Oceanic Products has chosen to process internally all raw tuna brought in by the Tuna Harvesting Division. Other tuna processors in San Diego purchase raw tuna from boat operators at $1 per pound. Oceanic Products has also chosen to process internally all tuna fillets into the 2-pound packets sold by the Tuna Marketing Division. Several fish-marketing companies in San Diego purchase tuna fillets at $5 per pound.

Required

1. Compute the overall operating income to Oceanic Products of harvesting 1,000 pounds of raw tuna, processing it into tuna fillets, and then selling it in 2-pound packets.
2. Compute the transfer prices that will be used for internal transfers (i) from the Tuna Harvesting Division to the Tuna Processing Division, and (ii) from the Tuna Processing Division to the Tuna Marketing Division under the following transfer-pricing methods:
   a. *200% of variable costs*. Variable costs are the costs of the transferred-in product (if any) plus the division's own variable costs.
   b. *150% of full costs*. Full costs are the costs of the transferred-in product (if any) plus the division's own variable and fixed costs.
   c. *Market price*.
3. Oceanic rewards the division manager with a bonus, calculated as 10% of division operating income (if positive). What bonus will be paid to each division manager under the three transfer-pricing methods in requirement 2? Which transfer-pricing method will each division manager prefer to use?

22-30 Goal-congruence problems with cost-plus transfer-pricing methods, dual-pricing system (continuation of 22-29). Assume that Oceanic Products uses a transfer price of 150% of full cost. Pat Forgione, the company president, attends a seminar on the virtues of decentralization. Forgione decides to implement decentralization at Oceanic Products. A memorandum is sent to all division managers: "Starting immediately, each division of Oceanic Products is free to make its own decisions regarding the purchase of its direct materials and the sale of its finished product."

Required

1. Give two examples of goal-congruence problems that may arise if Oceanic continues to use the 150%-of-full-costs transfer-pricing method and a policy of decentralization is adopted.
2. Forgione is investigating whether a dual transfer-pricing policy will reduce goal-congruence problems at Oceanic Products. Transfers out of each selling division will be made at 150% of full costs. Transfers into each buying division will be made at market price. Using this dual transfer-pricing policy, compute the operating income of each division for a harvest of 1,000 pounds of raw tuna that is further processed and marketed by Oceanic Products.
3. Compute the sum of the division operating incomes in requirement 2. Why might this sum not equal the overall corporate operating income from the harvesting of 1,000 pounds of raw tuna and its further processing and marketing?

4. What problems may arise if Oceanic Products uses the dual transfer-pricing system described in requirement 2?

22-31 Multinational transfer pricing, global tax minimization. Industrial Diamonds, Inc., based in Los Angeles, has two divisions:

a. *Philippine Mining Division*—operates a mine in the Philippines containing a rich body of raw diamonds.
b. *U.S. Processing Division*—processes the raw diamonds into polished diamonds used in industrial applications.

The costs of the Philippine Mining Division are:

◆ Variable costs, 4,000 pesos per pound of raw industrial diamonds
◆ Fixed costs, 8,000 pesos per pound of raw industrial diamonds

Industrial Diamonds has a corporate policy of further processing diamonds in Los Angeles. Several diamond-polishing companies in the Philippines buy raw diamonds from other local mining companies at 16,000 pesos per pound. Assume that the current foreign exchange rate is 40 pesos = $1 U.S. The costs of the U.S. Processing Division are:

◆ Variable costs, $200 per pound of polished industrial diamonds
◆ Fixed costs, $600 per pound of polished industrial diamonds

Assume that it takes 2 pounds of raw industrial diamonds to yield 1 pound of polished industrial diamonds. Polished diamonds sell for $4,000 per pound.

Required
1. Compute the transfer price (in $U.S.) for 1 pound of raw industrial diamonds transferred from the Philippine Mining Division to the U.S. Processing Division under two methods: (a) 300% of full costs, and (b) market price.
2. Assume a world of no income taxes. Also assume that 1,000 pounds of raw industrial diamonds are mined by the Philippine Division and then processed and sold by the U.S. Processing Division. Compute the operating income (in $U.S.) for each division of Industrial Diamonds, Inc., under the two transfer-pricing methods in requirement 1.
3. Assume that the corporate income tax rate is 20% in the Philippines and 35% in the United States. Compute the after-tax operating income (in $U.S.) for each division under the transfer-pricing methods in requirement 1. (Income taxes are not included in the computation of the cost-based transfer price. Industrial Diamonds does not pay U.S. taxes on income already taxed in the Philippines.)
4. Which transfer-pricing method in requirement 1 will maximize the total after-tax operating income of Industrial Diamonds? Show your computations.
5. What factors, in addition to global tax minimization, might Industrial Diamonds consider in choosing a transfer-pricing method for transfers between its two divisions?

22-32 Multinational transfer pricing and taxation. (Richard Lambert, adapted) Anita Corporation, headquartered in the United States, manufactures state-of-the-art milling machines in the United States. It has two marketing subsidiaries, one in Brazil and one in Switzerland, that sell its products. Anita is building one new machine, at a cost of $500,000. There is no market for the equipment in the United States. The equipment can be sold in Brazil for $1,000,000, but the Brazilian subsidiary would incur transportation and modification costs of $200,000. Alternatively, the equipment can be sold in Switzerland for $950,000, but the Swiss subsidiary would incur transportation and modification costs of $250,000. The U.S. company can sell the equipment to either its Brazilian subsidiary or its Swiss subsidiary but not to both. The Anita Corporation and its subsidiary companies operate in a very decentralized manner. Managers in each company have considerable autonomy, with managers interested in maximizing their own company's income.

Required
1. From the viewpoint of Anita and its subsidiaries taken together, should the Anita Corporation manufacture the equipment? If it does, where should it sell the equipment to maximize total operating income? What would the operating income for Anita and its subsidiaries be from the sale? Ignore any income tax effects.
2. What range of transfer prices will result in achieving the actions determined to be optimal in requirement 1? Explain your answer.
3. The effective income tax rates are as follows: 40% in the United States, 60% in Brazil, and 15% in Switzerland. The tax authorities in the three countries are uncertain about

the cost of the intermediate product and will allow any transfer price between $500,000 and $700,000. If Anita and its subsidiaries want to maximize after-tax operating income, (a) should the equipment be manufactured, and (b) where and at what price should it be transferred and sold? Show your computations.

4. Now suppose managers act autonomously to maximize their own company's after-tax operating income. The tax authorities will allow transfer prices only between $500,000 and $700,000. Which subsidiary will get the product and at what price? Is your answer the same as your answer in requirement 3? Explain why or why not.

22-33 Transfer pricing, goal congruence. The Sather Corporation manufactures and sells 10,000 boom boxes. The Assembly Division assembles the boom boxes. It buys the cassette deck for the boom box from the Cassette Deck Division. The Cassette Deck Division can manufacture at most 12,000 cassette decks. The demand for cassette decks is strong. Any cassette deck not sold to the Assembly Division can be sold in the outside market for $35 per unit. The Cassette Deck Division currently sells 10,000 cassette decks to the Assembly Division and 2,000 cassette decks in the outside market. The incremental cost of manufacturing the cassette deck is $25 per unit.

A crucial component for producing high-quality cassette decks is the (cassette) head mechanism. The Cassette Deck Division manufactures the head mechanism for its cassette decks. Many outside suppliers have offered to supply cassette decks to Sather. To ensure quality, Sather requires that any outside supplier wanting to supply cassette decks to Sather must purchase the head mechanism from the Cassette Deck Division. The Cassette Deck Division will charge $18 per unit for the head mechanism. The incremental cost of manufacturing the head mechanism is $12 per unit out of the total incremental costs of $25 per unit to manufacture the cassette deck. The Cassette Deck Division has unused capacity for manufacturing the head mechanism. That is, even if the Cassette Deck Division manufactures the head mechanism for outside suppliers, it will still be able to manufacture and sell 12,000 cassette decks for sale in the outside market at $35 per unit.

Johnson Corporation, an outside supplier, is currently negotiating to supply 10,000 cassette decks to the Assembly Division for a price in the range of $37 to $43. If Johnson gets the business, it will buy the head mechanism from the Cassette Deck Division for $18 per unit.

Required

Consider each question independently.

1. From the standpoint of Sather Corporation as a whole, should the Assembly Division accept Johnson Corporation's offer (a) at a price of $37 per cassette deck? (b) at a price of $43 per cassette deck? Show your computations.

2. What transfer price for cassette decks will result in the Cassette Deck Division and the Assembly Division taking actions that are optimal for Sather Corporation as a whole? Explain your answer.

22-34 Transfer pricing, utilization of capacity. (J. Patell, adapted) The California Instrument Company (CIC) consists of the Semiconductor Division and the Process-Control Division, each of which operates as an independent profit center. The Semiconductor Division employs craftsmen who produce two different electronic components, the new high-performance Super-chip and an older product called Okay-chip. These two products have the following cost characteristics:

	Super-chip	Okay-chip
Direct materials	$ 2	$1
Direct manufacturing labor		
2 hours × $14; 0.5 hour × $14	28	7

Annual overhead in the Semiconductor Division totals $400,000, all fixed. Owing to the high skill level necessary for the craftsmen, the Semiconductor Division's capacity is set at 50,000 hours per year.

One customer orders a maximum of 15,000 Super-chips per year, at a price of $60 per chip. If CIC cannot meet this entire demand, the customer curtails its own production. The rest of the Semiconductor Division's capacity is devoted to the Okay-chip, for which there is unlimited demand at $12 per chip.

The Process-Control Division produces only one product, a process-control unit, with the following cost structure:

Direct materials (circuit board) $60
Direct manufacturing labor (5 hours × $10)   50

Fixed overhead costs of the Process-Control Division are $80,000 per year. The current market price for the control unit is $132 per unit.

A joint research project has just revealed that a single Super-chip could be substituted for the circuit board currently used to make the process-control unit. Using Super-chip would require an extra 1 hour of labor per control unit for a new total of 6 hours per control unit.

Required

1. Calculate the contribution margin per hour of selling Super-chip and Okay-chip. If no transfers of Super-chip were made to the Process-Control Division, how many Super-chips and Okay-chips should the Semiconductor Division sell? Show your computations.
2. The Process-Control Division expects to sell 5,000 control units this year. From the viewpoint of California Instruments as a whole, should 5,000 Super-chips be transferred to the Process-Control Division to replace circuit boards? Show your computations.
3. If demand for the control unit is certain to be 5,000 units, but its *price is uncertain*, what should the transfer price of Super-chip be to ensure that the division managers' actions maximize operating income for CIC as a whole? (All other data are unchanged.)
4. If demand for the control unit is certain to be 12,000 units, but its *price is uncertain*, what should the transfer price of Super-chip be to ensure that the division managers' actions maximize operating income for CIC as a whole? (All other data are unchanged.)

22-35 Ethics, transfer pricing. The Belmont Division of Durham Industries manufactures component R47, which it transfers to the Alston Division at 200% of variable costs. The variable costs of R47 are $14 per unit. Joe Lasker, the management accountant of the Belmont Division calls Hal Tanner, his assistant, into his office. Lasker says, "I am not sure about the fixed and variable cost distinctions you are making. I think the variable costs are higher than $14 per unit."

Tanner knows that showing higher variable costs will increase the Belmont Division's profits and lead to higher bonuses for the division employees. However, Tanner is uncomfortable about making any changes because he has used the same method to classify costs as either variable or fixed over the last few years. Nevertheless, Tanner recognizes that fixed- and variable-cost distinctions are not always clear-cut.

Required

1. Calculate Belmont Division's contribution margin from transferring 10,000 units of R47 in 2001 (a) if variable costs are $14 per unit, and (b) if variable costs are $16 per unit.
2. Evaluate whether Lasker's suggestion to Tanner regarding variable costs is ethical. Would it be ethical for Tanner to revise the variable costs per unit? What steps should Tanner take to resolve this situation?

COLLABORATIVE LEARNING PROBLEM

22-36 Goal congruence, income taxes, different market conditions. The San Ramon Corporation makes water pumps. The Engine Division makes the engines and supplies them to the Assembly Division where the pumps are assembled. San Ramon is a successful and profitable corporation that attributes much of its success to its decentralized operating style. Each division manager is compensated on the basis of division operating income.

The Assembly Division currently acquires all its engines from the Engine Division. The Assembly Division manager could purchase similar engines in the market for $400 each.

The Engine Division is currently operating at 80% of its capacity of 4,000 units and has the following particulars:

Direct materials ($125 per unit × 3,200 units)	$400,000
Direct manufacturing labor ($50 per unit × 3,200 units)	160,000
Variable manufacturing overhead costs ($25 per unit × 3,200 units)	80,000
Fixed manufacturing overhead costs	520,000

All the Engine Division's 3,200 units are currently transferred to the Assembly Division. No engines are sold in the outside market.

The Engine Division has just received an order for 2,000 units at $375 per engine that would utilize half the capacity of the plant. The order has either to be taken in full or rejected. The order is for a slightly different engine than what the Engine Division currently makes but takes the same amount of manufacturing time. To produce the new engine would require direct materials per unit of $100, direct manufacturing labor per unit of $40, and variable manufacturing overhead costs per unit of $25.

Required

Form groups of two or more students to complete the following requirements.

1. From the viewpoint of the San Ramon Corporation as a whole, should the Engine Division accept the order for the 2,000 units? Show your computations.
2. What range of transfer prices will result in achieving the actions determined to be optimal in requirement 1, if division managers act in a decentralized manner?
3. The manager of the Assembly Division has proposed a transfer price for the engines equal to the full costs of the engines including an allocation of overhead costs. The Engine Division allocates overhead costs to engines on the basis of the total capacity of the plant used to manufacture the engines.
   a. Calculate the transfer price for the engines transferred to the Assembly Division under this arrangement.
   b. Do you think that the transfer price calculated in requirement 3a will result in achieving the actions determined to be optimal in requirement 1, if division managers act in a decentralized manner?
   c. Comment in general on one advantage and one disadvantage of using full costs of the producing division as the basis for setting transfer prices.
4. Now consider the effect of income taxes.
   a. Suppose the Assembly Division is located in a state that imposes a 10% tax on income earned within its boundaries, while the Engine Division is located in a state that imposes no tax on income earned within its boundaries. What transfer price would be chosen by the San Ramon Corporation to minimize income tax payments for the corporation as a whole? Assume that only transfer prices that are greater than or equal to full manufacturing costs and less than or equal to the market price of "substantially similar" engines are acceptable to the tax authorities.
   b. Suppose that the San Ramon Corporation announces the transfer price computed in requirement 4a to price all transfers between the Engine and Assembly Divisions. Each division manager then acts autonomously to maximize division operating income. Will division managers acting in a decentralized manner achieve the actions determined to be optimal in requirement 1? Explain.
5. Consider your responses to requirements 1–4 and assume the Engine Division will continue to have opportunities for outside business as described in requirement 1. What transfer-pricing policy would you recommend San Ramon use, and why? Would you continue to evaluate division performance on the basis of division operating incomes? Explain.

CHAPTER

23

Performance Measurement, Compensation, and Multinational Considerations

learning objectives

After studying this chapter, you should be able to

1. Measure performance from a financial and nonfinancial perspective
2. Design an accounting-based performance measure
3. Analyze profitability using the DuPont method
4. Use the residual-income (RI) measure and recognize its advantages
5. Describe the economic value added (EVA®) method
6. Contrast current-cost and historical-cost asset measurement methods
7. Indicate the difficulties that arise when comparing the performance of divisions operating in different countries
8. Recognize the role of salaries and incentives in compensation arrangements
9. Describe the management accountant's role in helping organizations provide better incentives

Hotels, such as the Carlton, aim to maximize return on investment by increasing the income earned on each dollar of revenue and by increasing revenue per dollar of investment. Hotel managers' performance measures generally include both financial performance measures, such as return on investment, and nonfinancial performance measures, such as occupancy levels.

Teaching Tip Overview *accounting* performance evaluation tools used in different responsibility centers:

Cost centers—flexible budgets and var. analysis (Chaps. 7 and 8)

Revenue centers—flexible budgets and var. analysis (Chaps. 7 and 16)

Profit centers—CM I/S by segments (Chap. 14)

Investment centers—ROI, residual income, and EVA® (Chap. 23)

Remind students that accounting-based performance measures comprise only a subset of the measures mgrs. use to evaluate subordinates (see Balanced Scorecard in Chap. 13).

OBJECTIVE 1

Measure performance from a financial and nonfinancial perspective

Points to Stress This section emphasizes multidimensional performance evaluation. The *balanced scorecard* approach often includes profitability, customer satisfaction, innovation, and productivity/quality/time measures. This encourages companies to move beyond the traditional internal/financial measures (e.g., ROI), to incorporate internal/nonfinancial measures (e.g., new-product–development time), external/financial

OBJECTIVE 2

Design an accounting-based performance measure

measures (e.g., stock price), and external/nonfinancial measures (e.g., market share). The balanced scorecard approach encourages employees to adopt a balanced perspective and to take actions that are in the company's long-run interests.

Reinforcing Problems Exer. 23-20 and Prob. 23-36 cover nonfinancial measures of performance. Also see Chap. 13 problems dealing with the balanced scorecard.

Teaching Tip Emphasize the intuition behind the 5 steps. Mgt. must first *decide what to measure* (e.g., ROI); op-

W e have discussed performance measurement in many of the earlier chapters, each time within a specific accounting context. Chapter 11, for example, described situations in which the correct decision based on a relevant-cost analysis (say, buying new equipment) might not be implemented because the performance measurement system induced the manager to act differently. This chapter discusses the design, implementation, and uses of performance measures more generally.

Performance measures are a central component of management control systems. Making good planning and control decisions requires information about how different subunits of the organization have performed. To be effective, performance measures (both financial and nonfinancial) must also motivate managers and employees at all levels of the organization to strive to achieve organization goals. Performance evaluation and rewards are key elements for motivating individuals in an organization.

FINANCIAL AND NONFINANCIAL PERFORMANCE MEASURES

Chapter 22 noted how the information used in a management control system can be financial or nonfinancial. Many widely used performance measures such as operating income rely on internal financial information. Increasingly, companies are supplementing internal financial measures with measures based on external financial information (for example, stock prices), internal nonfinancial information (such as defect rates, manufacturing lead time, and number of new patents), and external nonfinancial information (such as customer satisfaction ratings and market share), often benchmarked against other subunits within the organization and other organizations.

Some organizations present financial and nonfinancial performance measures for their subunits in a single report called the *balanced scorecard* (see Chapter 13, p. 463). Different organizations stress different elements in their scorecards, but most scorecards include (1) profitability measures; (2) customer-satisfaction measures; (3) internal measures of efficiency, quality, and time; and (4) innovation measures.[1] Companies, for example, Mobil Oil and Ford Motor Company, use such balanced scorecard measures to evaluate the performance of subunit managers and the subunits themselves.

Some performance measures, such as the number of new patents developed, have a long-run time horizon. Other measures, such as direct materials efficiency variances and overhead spending variances, have a short-run time horizon. We focus on the most widely used performance measures for organization subunits covering an intermediate to long-run time horizon. These are internal financial measures based on accounting numbers routinely reported by organizations.

Designing such accounting-based performance measure requires six steps:

Step 1: Choose Performance Measures That Align with Top Management's Financial Goal(s) For example, does operating income, net income, return on assets, or revenues best measure a subunit's financial performance?

Step 2: Choose the Time Horizon of Each Performance Measure in Step 1 For example, should performance measures, such as return on assets, be calculated for one year or for a multiyear time horizon?

Step 3: Choose a Definition of the Components in Each Performance Measure in Step 1 For example, should assets be defined as total assets or net assets (total assets minus total liabilities)?

Step 4: Choose a Measurement Alternative for Each Performance Measure in Step 1 For example, should assets be measured at historical cost or current cost?

Step 5: Choose a Target Level of Performance For example, should all subunits have identical targets such as the same required rate of return on assets?

---

[1]See R. Kaplan and D. Norton, *The Balanced Scorecard* (Boston: Harvard Business School Press, 1996); and S. Hronec, *Vital Signs* (New York: American Management Association, 1993).

Step 6: Choose the Timing of Feedback For example, should manufacturing performance reports be sent to top management daily, weekly, or monthly?

These six steps need not be done sequentially. The issues considered in each step are interdependent, and a decision maker will often proceed through these steps several times before deciding on one or more accounting-based performance measures. The answers to the questions raised at each step depend on top management's beliefs about how well each alternative measure fulfills the behavioral criteria of goal congruence, management effort, subunit performance evaluation, and subunit autonomy discussed in Chapter 22.

CHOOSING AMONG DIFFERENT PERFORMANCE MEASURES

This section considers step 1 of designing an accounting-based performance measure by describing four measures commonly used to evaluate the economic performance of organization subunits. We illustrate these measures using the example of Hospitality Inns.

Hospitality Inns owns and operates three hotels in San Francisco, Chicago, and New Orleans. Exhibit 23-1 summarizes data for each hotel for the most recent year (2000). At present, Hospitality Inns does not allocate the total long-term debt of the company to the three separate hotels. Exhibit 23-1 indicates that the New Orleans hotel generates the highest operating income, $510,000, when compared to Chicago, $300,000, and San Francisco, $240,000. But is this comparison appropriate? Is the New Orleans hotel the most "successful"? A major weakness of comparing operating incomes alone is ignoring differences in the *size of the investment* in each hotel. **Investment** refers to the resources or assets used to generate income. The question then is not how large operating income is per se, but how large it is in relation to the investment made to earn it.

Three approaches include investment in the performance measure: return on investment, residual income, and economic value added. A fourth approach measures return on sales.

erationally define the metric (e.g., OP, Inc./TA); decide *how to attach dollar values* to the measure (e.g., current costs); *choose a benchmark* against which performance is measured (e.g., target ROI of 20%); and *choose the time period* between successive performance evaluations (e.g., quarterly, annually, or biannually).

Curriculum Linkage Chap. 22 explains that TP methods are evaluated on how well they meet 4 behavioral criteria: goal congruence (acting in own self-interest also promotes organizational interest), mgt. effort (to produce efficiently and use resources wisely), evaluating subunit performance, and subunit autonomy. These 4 criteria can also be used to assess alternative performance evaluation methods, as discussed in this chapter.

EXHIBIT 23-1

Annual Financial Data for Hospitality Inns for 2000 (in Thousands)

	San Francisco Hotel (1)	Chicago Hotel (2)	New Orleans Hotel (3)	Total (4) = (1) + (2) + (3)
Hotel revenues	$1,200,000	$1,400,000	$3,185,000	$5,785,000
Hotel variable costs	310,000	375,000	995,000	1,680,000
Hotel fixed costs	650,000	725,000	1,680,000	3,055,000
Hotel operating income	$ 240,000	$ 300,000	$ 510,000	1,050,000
Interest costs on long-term debt at 10%	—	—	—	450,000
Income before income taxes	—	—	—	600,000
Income taxes at 30%	—	—	—	180,000
Net income	—	—	—	$ 420,000
Net book values for 2000:				
Current assets	$ 400,000	$ 500,000	$ 660,000	$1,560,000
Long-term assets	600,000	1,500,000	2,340,000	4,440,000
Total assets	$1,000,000	$2,000,000	$3,000,000	$6,000,000
Current liabilities	$ 50,000	$ 150,000	$ 300,000	$ 500,000
Long-term debt	—	—	—	4,500,000
Stockholders' equity	—	—	—	1,000,000
Total liabilities and stockholders' equity				$6,000,000

Return on Investment

Return on investment (ROI) is an accounting measure of income divided by an accounting measure of investment.

$$\text{Return on investment (ROI)} = \frac{\text{Income}}{\text{Investment}}$$

Return on investment is the most popular approach to incorporating the investment base into a performance measure. ROI has conceptual appeal because it blends all the ingredients of profitability (revenues, costs, and investment) into a single percentage. It can be compared with the rate of return on opportunities elsewhere, inside or outside the company. Like any single performance measure, however, ROI should be used cautiously and in conjunction with other performance measures.

ROI is also called the accounting rate of return or the accrual accounting rate of return (described in Chapter 21, p. 760). Managers usually use the term ROI when evaluating the performance of a division or subunit, and accrual accounting rate of return when evaluating a project. Companies vary in the way they define both the numerator (income) and the denominator (investment) of the ROI calculation. For example, some companies use operating income for the numerator. Other companies use net income. Some companies use total assets in the denominator. Others use total assets minus current liabilities.

Hospitality Inns can increase ROI by increasing revenues or decreasing costs (both of these actions increase the numerator), or by decreasing investment (decreases the denominator). ROI can often provide more insight into performance when it is divided into the following components:

$$\frac{\text{Income}}{\text{Investment}} = \frac{\text{Revenues}}{\text{Investment}} \times \frac{\text{Income}}{\text{Revenues}}$$

also written as $\qquad$ ROI = Investment turnover × Return on sales

Correcting Student Misconceptions
From the DuPont formula, it appears that changing revenues would not affect ROI, since Revenues in the numerator of the investment turnover ratio and the denominator of the return-on-sales ratio cancel out:

$$\frac{\text{Revenues}}{\text{Investment}} \times \frac{\text{Income}}{\text{Revenues}}$$

However, increasing revenues without increasing costs proportionally increases income, which, in turn, increases ROI.

Teaching Tip Explain the intuition behind the two ROI components. Investment turnover tells us how many revenue $'s are generated by each $ of investment. The goal is to make each investment $ "work harder" to generate more sales. The return-on-sales ratio (also called income margin) tells us how much of each revenue $ goes to income. The goal is to get higher income per revenue dollar. The product of these two ratios, ROI, tells us how much income each $ of investment generates.

This approach is widely known as the *DuPont method of profitability analysis*. The DuPont method recognizes that there are two basic ingredients in profit making: using assets to generate more revenues and increasing income per dollar of revenues. An improvement in either ingredient without changing the other increases ROI.

Consider the ROIs of the three Hospitality hotels in Exhibit 23-1. For our calculations, we are using the operating income of each hotel for the numerator and total assets of each hotel for the denominator.

Hotel	Operating Income	÷	Total Assets	=	ROI
San Francisco	$240,000	÷	$1,000,000	=	24%
Chicago	300,000	÷	2,000,000	=	15%
New Orleans	510,000	÷	3,000,000	=	17%

Points to Stress In the Hospitality Inn example, ROI is measured as operating income divided by total assets. This definition matches operating income, which is the entire income "pie" [before it is split up across (1) creditors in the form of interest, (2) the government in the form of taxes, and (3) investors in the form of dividends and increased RE], with total assets, the entire amount of investment available to earn the entire income "pie."

Using these ROI figures, the San Francisco hotel appears to make the best use of its total assets.

Assume that the top management at Hospitality Inns adopts a 30% target ROI for the San Francisco hotel. How can this return be attained? The DuPont method at the top of the next page illustrates the present situation and three alternatives. Other alternatives such as increasing the selling price per room could increase both the revenues per dollar of total assets and the operating income per dollar of revenues.

ROI highlights the benefits that managers can obtain by reducing their investment in current or long-term assets. Some managers are conscious of the need to boost revenues or to control costs but pay less attention to reducing their investment base. Reducing the investment base means decreasing idle cash, managing credit judiciously, determining proper inventory levels, and spending carefully on long-term assets.

	$\dfrac{\text{Revenues}}{\text{Total Assets}}$	$\times$	$\dfrac{\text{Operating Income}}{\text{Revenues}}$			=	$\dfrac{\text{Operating Income}}{\text{Total Assets}}$
Present Situation	$\dfrac{\$1,200,000}{\$1,000,000}$	$\times$	$\dfrac{\$240,000}{\$1,200,000}$	=	1.20×0.20	=	0.24 or 24%
Alternatives							
A. Decrease assets (such as receivables) keeping revenues and operating income per dollar of revenue constant.	$\dfrac{\$1,200,000}{\$800,000}$	$\times$	$\dfrac{\$240,000}{\$1,200,000}$	=	1.50×0.20	=	0.30 or 30%
B. Increase revenues (via a higher occupancy rate) keeping assets and operating income per dollar of revenues constant.	$\dfrac{\$1,500,000}{\$1,000,000}$	$\times$	$\dfrac{\$300,000}{\$1,500,000}$	=	1.50×0.20	=	0.30 or 30%
C. Decrease costs (via, say, efficient maintenance) to increase operating income per dollar of revenues, keeping revenues and assets constant.	$\dfrac{\$1,200,000}{\$1,000,000}$	$\times$	$\dfrac{\$300,000}{\$1,200,000}$	=	1.20×0.25	=	0.30 or 30%

Residual Income

OBJECTIVE 4

Use the residual-income (RI) measure and recognize its advantages

Residual income (RI) is an accounting measure of income minus a required dollar return on an accounting measure of investment.

$$\text{Residual income (RI)} = \text{Income} - (\text{Required rate of return} \times \text{Investment})$$

The required rate of return multiplied by investment is also called the *imputed cost of the investment.* **Imputed costs** are costs recognized in particular situations that are not usually recognized by accrual accounting procedures. The use of imputed costs is an attempt to obtain more accurate accounting measures of economic impacts. When investments are considered in performance measures, the imputed cost of the investment represents the opportunity cost or return forgone as a result of tying up cash in the investment rather than earning returns elsewhere on investments of similar risk. In RI computations, a 12% required rate of return, say, used to calculate the imputed cost of the investment might include an interest outlay of 5%, say, on the amount of investment financed by long-term debt.

Assume that each hotel faces similar risks. Hospitality Inns defines residual income for each hotel as hotel operating income minus a required rate of return of 12% of the total assets of the hotel:[2]

Hotel	Operating Income	$-$	Required Rate of Return	$\times$ Investment	=	Residual Income
San Francisco	$240,000	$-$	$120,000 (12% $\times$ $1,000,000)		=	$120,000
Chicago	$300,000	$-$	$240,000 (12% $\times$ $2,000,000)		=	$ 60,000
New Orleans	$510,000	$-$	$360,000 (12% $\times$ $3,000,000)		=	$150,000

Given the 12% required rate of return, the New Orleans hotel is performing best in terms of RI.

Some companies favor the RI measure because managers will concentrate on maximizing an absolute amount (dollars of RI) rather than a percentage (return on investment). The objective of maximizing RI means that as long as a subunit earns a rate in excess of the required return for investments, that subunit should expand.

Reinforcing Problems Exer. 23-16 through 23-19, 23-21, 23-23, 23-24 and Probs. 23-28 through 23-31, 23-33, 23-34, and 23-36 cover ROI. RI is covered in Exer. 23-18 and 23-21 through 23-24 and Probs. 23-31, 23-33, and 23-36.

Curriculum Linkage What rate of return should mgt. use to compute residual income? Students who have studied finance should realize that the cost of capital is the appropriate rate of return. Conceptually, it should be the cost of capital for that particular business segment, to reflect the segment's risk level. For example, an oil exploration segment might warrant a higher required rate of return than an oil refining segment.

---

[2]Just as in the case of ROI, companies using RI vary in the way they define income (for example, operating income or net income) and investment (for example, total assets or total assets minus current liabilities).

The objective of maximizing ROI may induce managers of highly profitable subunits to reject projects that, from the viewpoint of the organization as a whole, should be accepted. To illustrate, suppose Hospitality Inns is considering upgrading room features and furnishings at the San Francisco hotel. The upgrade will increase operating income of the San Francisco hotel by $70,000 and increase its total assets by $400,000. The ROI for the expansion is 17.5% ($70,000 ÷ $400,000), which is attractive to Hospitality Inns as a whole because this rate exceeds the required rate of return. By making this expansion, however, the San Francisco manager will see the hotel's ROI decrease:

$$\text{Pre-upgrade ROI} = \frac{\$240,000}{\$1,000,000} = 24\%$$

$$\text{Post-upgrade ROI} = \frac{\$240,000 + \$70,000}{\$1,000,000 + \$400,000} = \frac{\$310,000}{\$1,400,000} = 22.1\%$$

The annual bonus paid to the San Francisco manager may decrease if ROI is a key component in the bonus calculation and the upgrading option is selected. In contrast, if the annual bonus is a function of RI, the San Francisco manager will view the expansion favorably:

$$\text{Pre-upgrade RI} = \$240,000 - (12\% \times \$1,000,000) = \$120,000$$

$$\text{Post-upgrade RI} = \$310,000 - (12\% \times \$1,400,000) = \$142,000$$

Goal congruence is more likely to be promoted by using RI rather than ROI as a measure of the subunit manager's performance.

Economic Value Added[3]

Economic value added is a specific type of residual income calculation that has recently attracted considerable attention. **Economic value added (EVA®)** equals after-tax operating income *minus* the (after-tax) weighted-average cost of capital *multiplied* by total assets minus current liabilities.

$$\begin{array}{l}\text{Economic value} \\ \text{added (EVA®)}\end{array} = \begin{array}{l}\text{After-tax} \\ \text{operating income}\end{array} - \left[\begin{array}{l}\text{Weighted-} \\ \text{average} \\ \text{cost of capital}\end{array} \times \left(\begin{array}{l}\text{Total} \\ \text{assets}\end{array} - \begin{array}{l}\text{current} \\ \text{liabilities}\end{array} \right) \right]$$

EVA® substitutes the following numbers in the RI calculations: (1) income equal to after-tax operating income, (2) a required rate of return equal to the weighted-average cost of capital, and (3) investment equal to total assets minus current liabilities.[4]

We use the Hospitality Inns data in Exhibit 23-1 to illustrate the basic EVA® calculations. The key calculation is the weighted-average cost of capital (WACC), which equals *after-tax* average cost of all the long-term funds used by Hospitality Inns. The company has two sources of long-term funds—long-term debt with a market value and book value of $4.5 million issued at an interest rate of 10%, and equity capital that also has a market value of $4.5 million (and a book value of $1 million).[5] Because interest costs are tax-deductible, the after-tax cost of debt financ-

[3]G. B. Stewart, III, "EVA: Fact and Fantasy," *Journal of Applied Corporate Finance* (Summer 1994); B. Birchard, "Mastering the New Metrics," *CFO* (October 1994); M. Topkis, "A New Way to Find Bargains," *Fortune* (December 9, 1996).

[4]When implementing EVA®, companies make several adjustments to the operating income and asset numbers reported under generally accepted accounting principles (GAAP). For example, when calculating EVA®, costs such as R&D, restructuring costs, and leases that have long-run benefits are recorded as assets (which are then amortized), rather than as current operating costs. The goal of these adjustments is to obtain a better representation of the economic assets, particularly intangible assets, used to earn income. Naturally, the specific adjustments applicable to a company will depend on its individual circumstances.

[5]The market value of Hospitality Inns equity exceeds book value because book values, based on historical costs, do not measure the current values of the company's assets and because various intangible assets, such as the company's brand name, are not shown at current value in the balance sheet under GAAP.

ing equals $0.10 \times (1 - \text{Tax rate}) = 0.10 \times (1 - 0.30) = 0.10 \times 0.70 = 0.07$, or 7 percent. The cost of equity capital is the opportunity cost to investors of not investing their capital in another investment that is similar in risk to Hospitality Inns. Suppose that Hospitality's cost of equity capital is 14 percent.[6] The WACC computation, which uses market values of debt and equity, is as follows:

Curriculum Linkage Students who have had finance courses should be familiar with calculating the WACC. EVA® uses the *after-tax* weighted average cost of all funds used (debt plus equity), as explained in the text.

$$\text{WACC} = \frac{(7\% \times \text{Market value of debt}) + (14\% \times \text{Market value of equity})}{\text{Market value of debt} + \text{Market value of equity}}$$

$$= \frac{(0.07 \times \$4,500,000) + (0.14 \times \$4,500,000)}{\$4,500,000 + \$4,500,000}$$

$$= \frac{\$315,000 + \$630,000}{\$9,000,000}$$

$$= \frac{\$945,000}{\$9,000,000} = 0.105 \text{ or } 10.5\%$$

The company applies the same WACC to all its hotels because each hotel faces similar risks.

Total assets minus current liabilities (see Exhibit 23-1) can also be computed as:

Correcting Student Misconceptions EVA® defines investment as TA − CL (rather than as LTL + SE) because it is often easier to allocate TA and CL to individual business segments than to allocate LTL and SE to business segments.

Total assets − Current liabilities = Long-term assets + Current Assets − Current liabilities

= Long-term assets + Working capital

where working capital = current assets − current liabilities. After-tax hotel operating income is:

$$\frac{\text{Hotel operating}}{\text{income}} \times (1 - \text{Tax rate}) = \frac{\text{Hotel operating}}{\text{income}} \times (1 - 0.30) = \frac{\text{Hotel operating}}{\text{income}} \times 0.70$$

EVA® calculations for Hospitality Inns are as follows:

Hotel	After-Tax Operating Income −	[Weighted-Average Cost of Capital × (Total Assets − Current Liabilities)]		= Economic Value Added (EVA®)
San Francisco	$240,000 × 0.7 −	[10.5% × ($1,000,000 − $ 50,000)]	= $168,000 − $ 99,750 =	$68,250
Chicago	$300,000 × 0.7 −	[10.5% × ($2,000,000 − $150,000)]	= $210,000 − $194,250 =	$15,750
New Orleans	$510,000 × 0.7 −	[10.5% × ($3,000,000 − $300,000)]	= $357,000 − $283,500 =	$73,500

The New Orleans hotel has the highest EVA®. Economic value added, like residual income, charges managers for the cost of their investments in long-term assets and working capital. Value is created only if after-tax operating income exceeds the cost of investing the capital. To improve EVA®, managers must earn more after-tax operating income with the same capital, use less capital to earn the same after-tax operating income, or invest capital in high-return projects.

Managers in companies such as Briggs and Stratton, Coca-Cola, CSX, Equifax, and FMC use the estimated impact on EVA® to guide their decisions. Division managers find EVA® particularly helpful because it allows them to incorporate the cost of capital, which is generally only available at the companywide level, into decisions at the division level. Comparing the actual EVA® achieved to the estimated EVA® is useful for evaluating performance and providing feedback. CSX, a railroad company, credits EVA® for decisions such as running trains with three locomotives instead of four and scheduling arrivals just-in-time for unloading rather than having trains arrive at their destination several hours in advance. The result? Higher income because of lower fuel costs and less capital needed for investment in locomotives.

Reinforcing Problems Exer. 23-21 and 23-22 cover EVA® issues.

[6]For details on calculating cost of equity capital adjusted for risk, see J. Van Horne, *Corporate Financial Management and Policy* (Upper Saddle River, NJ: Prentice Hall, 1998).

Equifax, AT&T, and EVA®

A recent *Fortune* magazine article described EVA® as "Today's hottest financial idea and getting hotter." Equifax, the world leader in information services, transaction processing and knowledge-based businesses, agrees.

Equifax believes that EVA® streamlines decision making, enhances accountability, and strengthens incentives. Thus, EVA® analysis is central to Equifax's investment decisions. So far, EVA® has helped Equifax (1) earn more operating income without adding capital, (2) reduce capital investments needed to earn operating income, and (3) invest in and retain only those projects and businesses for which operating income exceeds the cost of capital.

To earn more operating income, Equifax took strategic initiatives to cut operating costs by, for example, centralizing its payables, payroll, and travel management departments. The move reduced equipment and space costs and increased Equifax's bargaining power to lower its costs of supplies, travel, and hotels. Equifax also generated profitable revenue by finding new markets, such as telecommunications and healthcare, for its existing products. To reduce capital invested in its businesses, Equifax outsourced its computer operations and disposed of its data processing equipment. Also, EVA-based analysis led Equifax to sell its National Decision Systems business in 1997.

How does Equifax get its managers to think in terms of EVA®? First, the company carefully explains EVA® concepts to them. Second, Equifax budgets for EVA® and links a significant portion of incentive compensation to achieving the EVA® projections. Equifax's management credits EVA®, in part, for contributing to the almost 200% increase in market capitalization from $1.6 billion in 1992 when it first implemented EVA® to $4.6 billion in 1998.

EVA®, however, has not worked for everyone. AT&T began using EVA® in 1992, but found the measure to be incomplete. Within two years, the company supplemented EVA® with two nonfinancial measures—Customer Value Added and People Value Added. Furthermore, AT&T found that although internal EVA® results from 1992 to 1996 increased, total shareholder return was −6.46%, substantially lower than that of its competitors. In 1997, following AT&T's replacement of CEO Robert Allen with Mike Armstrong, the company dropped EVA® in favor of traditional accounting measures. The company considered EVA® too complex, noting that despite extensive training, employees outside of corporate headquarters had difficulty understanding how their actions affected EVA® results.

Source: Adapted from the Equifax brochure on EVA®, interviews with Equifax management, and C. Ittner and D. Larcker, "Innovations in Performance Measurement: Trends and Research Implications (Working Paper, University of Pennsylvania, June 1998). The website http://www.sternstewart.com contains more information on EVA®.

Return on Sales

The income-to-revenues (sales) ratio—often called *return on sales (ROS)*—is a frequently used financial performance measure. ROS is one component of ROI in the DuPont method of profitability analysis. To calculate the ROS of each of Hospitality's hotels, we use operating income divided by revenues. The ROS for each hotel is

Hotel	Operating Income	÷	Revenues (Sales)	=	Return on Sales (ROS)
San Francisco	$240,000	÷	$1,200,000	=	20.0%
Chicago	$300,000	÷	$1,400,000	=	21.4%
New Orleans	$510,000	÷	$3,185,000	=	16.0%

The Chicago hotel has the highest ROS, whereas its performance is rated worse than the other hotels using performance measures such as ROI, RI, and EVA®. We compare performance measures in the next section.

Comparing Performance Measures

The following table summarizes the performance and ranking of each hotel (given in parentheses) under the four performance measures:

Hotel	ROI	RI	EVA®	ROS
San Francisco	24% (1)	$120,000 (2)	$68,250 (2)	20.0% (2)
Chicago	15% (3)	$ 60,000 (3)	$15,750 (3)	21.4% (1)
New Orleans	17% (2)	$150,000 (1)	$73,500 (1)	16.0% (3)

The RI and EVA® rankings differ from the ROI and ROS rankings. Consider the ROI and RI rankings for the San Francisco and New Orleans hotels. The New Orleans hotel has a smaller ROI. Although its operating income is only slightly more than twice that of the San Francisco hotel ($510,000 versus $240,000), its total assets are three times as large ($3 million versus $1 million). The return on assets invested in the New Orleans hotel is not as high as the return on assets invested in the San Francisco hotel. The New Orleans hotel has a higher RI because it earns a higher income after covering the 12% required return on investment. The Chicago hotel has the highest ROS but the lowest ROI. Why? Because although it earns very high income per dollar of revenues, it generates very low revenues per dollar of assets invested. Is any one method superior to the others? No, because each evaluates a slightly different aspect of performance. For example, in markets where revenue growth is limited and investment levels are fixed, ROS is the most meaningful indicator of a subunit's performance.

To evaluate overall aggregate performance, ROI, RI, or EVA® measures are more appropriate than ROS because they consider both income earned and investments made. ROI indicates which investment yields the highest return. RI and EVA® measures overcome some of the goal-congruence problems that ROI measures might introduce. Some managers favor EVA® because it explicitly considers tax effects while pre-tax RI measures do not. Other managers favor pre-tax RI because it is easier to compute, and because in most cases it leads to the same conclusions as EVA®.

CHOOSING THE TIME HORIZON OF THE PERFORMANCE MEASURES

We now consider step 2 of designing accounting-based performance measures—choosing the time horizon of the performance measures. The ROI, RI, EVA®, and ROS calculations represent the results for a single time period, a year in our example. Managers could take actions that cause short-run increases in these measures but are in conflict with the long-run interest of the organization. For example, managers may curtail R&D and plant maintenance in the last 3 months of a fiscal year to achieve a target level of annual operating income. For this reason, many companies evaluate subunits on the basis of ROI, RI, EVA®, and ROS over multiple years.

Another reason for evaluating subunits over a multiyear time horizon is that the benefits of actions taken in the current period may not show up in short-run performance measures such as the current year's ROI or RI. For example, the investment in a new hotel may adversely affect ROI and RI in the short run but benefit ROIs and RIs in the long-run.

A multiyear analysis highlights another advantage of the RI measure: The net present value of all the cash flows over the life of an investment equals the net

Points to Stress/Example Very low levels of investment lead to very high investment turnover ratios that can dominate the ROI calculation—even if mgt. of the few assets is economically less critical than mgt. of income margin. Consider an accounting firm with $1,000,000 in revenue, $200,000 operating income, and $10,000 in PPE. The partners want to double their investment in PPE. Pre and post expansion ROI's follow:

Pre:
$$\frac{1,000,000}{10,000} \times \frac{200,000}{1,000,000} =$$
$$100 \times 0.2 = 2,000\%$$

Post:
$$\frac{1,000,000}{20,000} \times \frac{200,000}{1,000,000} =$$
$$50 \times 0.2 = 1,000\%$$

Spending 5% of one year's income on PPE would cut ROI by half. But "real" performance has not deteriorated. Hence, ROS (20%) would probably be a more informative measure of the firm's profitability. This example illustrates why firms in service industries often use ROS.

present value of RIs.[7] This characteristic means that if managers use the net present value method to make investment decisions (as prescribed in Chapter 21), using multiyear RI to evaluate managers' performances achieves goal congruence.

Another way that companies motivate managers to take a long-run perspective is by compensating them on the basis of changes in the market price of the company's stock (in addition to using multiyear accounting-based performance measures). Why does this approach help to extend managers' time horizons? Because stock prices more rapidly incorporate the expected future period effects of current decisions.

CHOOSING ALTERNATIVE DEFINITIONS FOR PERFORMANCE MEASURES

Correcting Student Misconceptions
Students often confuse steps 3 and 4. Step 3 requires mgrs. to *define* the constructs in the performance measurement selected in step 1. For example, step 3 requires mgrs. to define "investment" as TA, TAE, TAE − CL, or SE. After selecting the definition in step 3, mgrs. select the basis for assigning *dollar values* to the definition (e.g., historical cost, current cost) in step 4.

To illustrate step 3 of designing accounting-based performance measures, we consider the alternative definitions of investment that companies use:

1. *Total assets available*—includes all assets, regardless of their particular purpose.

2. *Total assets employed*—defined as total assets available minus the sum of idle assets and assets purchased for future expansion. For example, if the New Orleans hotel in Exhibit 23-1 has unused land set aside for potential expansion, the total assets employed by the hotel would exclude the cost of that land.

3. *Total assets employed minus current liabilities*—this definition excludes that portion of total assets employed that are financed by short-term creditors. One negative feature of defining investment in this way is that it may encourage subunit managers to use an excessive amount of short-term debt.

4. *Stockholders' equity*—use of this definition for each individual hotel in Exhibit 23-1 requires allocation of the long-term liabilities of Hospitality Inns to the three hotels, which would then be deducted from the total assets of each hotel. One drawback of this method is that it combines operating decisions made by hotel managers with financing decisions regarding equity made by corporate management.

Companies that employ ROI or RI, generally use total assets available as the definition of investment. When top management directs a subunit manager to carry extra assets, total assets employed can be more informative than total assets available. Companies that adopt EVA® define investment as total assets employed minus current liabilities. The most common rationale for using total assets employed minus current liabilities is that the subunit manager often influences decisions on current liabilities of the subunit.

[7]We are grateful to S. Reichelstein for pointing this out. To see this equivalence, suppose the $400,000 investment in the San Francisco hotel increases operating income by $70,000 per year as follows: Increase in operating cash flows of $150,000 each year for five years minus depreciation of $80,000 ($400,000 ÷ 5) per year, assuming straight-line depreciation and zero terminal disposal price. Depreciation reduces the investment amount by $80,000 each year. Assuming a required rate of return of 12%, net present values of cash flows and residual incomes are as follows:

Year	0	1	2	3	4	5	Net Present Value
(1) Cash flow	− $400,000	$150,000	$150,000	$150,000	$150,000	$150,000	
(2) Present value of $1 discounted at 12%	1	0.89286	0.79719	0.71178	0.63552	0.56743	
(3) Present value: (1) × (2)	− $400,000	$133,929	$119,578	$106,767	$ 95,328	$ 85,114	$140,716
(4) Operating income		$ 70,000	$ 70,000	$ 70,000	$ 70,000	$ 70,000	
(5) Assets at start of year		$400,000	$320,000	$240,000	$160,000	$ 80,000	
(6) Capital charge: (5) × 12%		$ 48,000	$ 38,400	$ 28,800	$ 19,200	$ 9,600	
(7) Residual income: (4) − (6)		$ 22,000	$ 31,600	$ 41,200	$ 50,800	$ 60,400	
(8) Present value of RI: (7) × (2)		$ 19,643	$ 25,191	$ 29,325	$ 32,284	$ 34,273	$140,716

Examples of Key Financial Performance Measures in Different Companies Around the Globe[a]

Surveys indicate extensive use of net income as a performance measure and reliance on multiple measures:

Company	Country Headquarters	Product/Business	Key Financial Performance Measures
Dow Chemical	U.S.	Chemicals	Income
Xerox	U.S.	Photocopiers	ROS and ROI
Ford Motor	U.S.	Automotive	ROS and ROI
Quaker Oats	U.S.	Food products	RI, EVA®
Varity	U.S.	Automotive components	RI, EVA®
Guinness	U.K.	Consumer products	Income and ROS
Krones	Germany	Machinery/equipment	Revenues and income
Mayne Nickless	Australia	Security/transportation	ROI and ROS
Mitsui	Japan	Trading	Revenues and income
Pirelli	Italy	Tires/manufacturing	Income and cash flow
Swedish Match	Sweden	Consumer products	ROI

When comparing U.S. and Japanese companies, it appears that U.S. companies favor ROI (or EVA®) over ROS, whereas Japanese companies use ROS more than ROI. These differences are also consistent with differences in pricing practices in the two countries: Japanese companies emphasize sales margins, whereas U.S. companies emphasize ROI.[b] Some researchers speculate that Japanese managers favor ROS because it is easier to calculate and because achieving a sufficient sales margin is likely to benefit ROI sooner or later. Deemphasizing ROI has other advantages. For example, managers are not induced to delay investment in facilities or equipment because of the negative effects it might have on ROI in the short run.

[a]Adapted from R. Schlank, "Evaluating the Performance"; Business International Corporation, "101 More Checklists"; and G. B. Stewart, "EVA®, Fact and Fantasy."

[b]K. Smith and C. Sullivan, "Survey of Cost Management"; P. Scarbrough, A. Nanni, and M. Sakurai, "Japanese Management Accounting." Full citations are in Appendix A.

CHOOSING MEASUREMENT ALTERNATIVES FOR PERFORMANCE MEASURES

To illustrate step 4 of designing accounting-based performance measures, consider different ways to measure assets included in the investment calculations. For example, should they be measured at historical cost or current cost? Should gross book value (original cost) or net book value (original cost minus accumulated depreciation) be used for depreciable assets? We now examine these issues.

Current Cost

Current cost is the cost of purchasing an asset today identical to the one currently held, or the cost of purchasing the services provided by that asset if an identical one cannot currently be purchased. Of course, measuring assets at current costs will result in different ROIs compared to the ROIs calculated based on historical costs.

We illustrate the current-cost ROI calculations using the Hospitality Inns example (see Exhibit 23-1) and then compare current-cost-based ROIs and historical-cost-based ROIs. Assume the following information about the long-term assets of each hotel:

> **OBJECTIVE 6**
>
> Contrast current-cost and historical-cost asset measurement methods

	San Francisco	Chicago	New Orleans
Age of facility (at end of 2000)	8 years	4 years	2 years
Gross book value (original cost)	$1,400,000	$2,100,000	$2,730,000
Accumulated depreciation	$800,000	$600,000	$390,000
Net book value (at end of 2000)	$600,000	$1,500,000	$2,340,000
Depreciation for 2000	$100,000	$150,000	$195,000

Hospitality Inns assumes a 14-year estimated useful life, assumes no terminal disposal price for the physical facilities, and calculates depreciation on a straight-line basis.

An index of construction costs for the 8-year period that Hospitality Inns has been operating (1992 year-end = 100) is as follows:

Year	1993	1994	1995	1996	1997	1998	1999	2000
Construction cost index	110	122	136	144	152	160	174	180

Curriculum Linkage Students who have had economics should have seen adjustments for changes in purchasing power. The concept is the same here, except that there are different price indices for different assets.

Curriculum Linkage When companies replace assets, they usually purchase new assets with more advanced technology. However, in the 1970s, the SEC's ASR 190 stipulated that mgrs. must approximate the cost to buy replacement assets that have the *old assets' technology*. This is one reason mgrs. complained about ASR 190, which required large companies to disclose replacement cost data. That regulation forced mgrs. to spend considerable resources to approximate the results of an uneconomical (hypothetical) investment strategy.

Curriculum Linkage Financial accounting courses frequently discuss current cost asset valuation methods for reporting to shareholders. The FASB experimented with supplementary current cost disclosures in the 1980s but dropped a mandatory disclosure requirement because of limited evidence that external parties actually used these disclosures.

Teaching Tip/Reinforcing Problem Students have difficulty with these calculations. Walk through Exh. 23-2 or a similar problem, such as 23-29.

Example Students are often confused about the difference between current costs and general price-level adjusted costs. The following example illustrates the distinction. The cost of a calculator that adds, subtracts, multiplies, and divides was $120 in 1972. A *general price-level adjustment* would value this asset in 1999 at about $469:

$$120 \times \frac{1.64 \ (1999 \ CPI)}{.42 \ (1972 \ CPI)}$$

This is very different from the *current cost* to purchase a calculator that performs the same functions for about $7.

Earlier in this chapter, we computed an ROI of 24% for San Francisco, 15% for Chicago, and 17% for New Orleans (see p. 824). One possible explanation of the high ROI for the San Francisco hotel is that this hotel's long-term assets are expressed in terms of 1992 construction price levels (8 years ago) and that the long-term assets for the Chicago and New Orleans hotels are expressed in terms of the higher, more recent construction price levels, which depress ROIs for these hotels.

Exhibit 23-2 illustrates a step-by-step approach for incorporating current-cost estimates of long-term assets and depreciation into the ROI calculation. The aim is to approximate what it would cost today to obtain assets that would produce the same expected operating income that the subunits currently earn. (Similar adjustments to represent current costs of capital employed and depreciation can also be made in the RI and EVA® calculations.) The current-cost adjustment dramatically reduces the ROI of the San Francisco hotel.

	Historical Cost ROI	Current Cost ROI
San Francisco	24%	10.81%
Chicago	15%	11.05%
New Orleans	17%	14.75%

Adjusting assets to recognize current costs negates differences in the investment base that are caused solely by differences in construction price levels. Consequently, compared to historical-cost ROI, current-cost ROI is a better measure of the current economic returns from the investment. If Hospitality Inns were to invest in a new hotel today, investing in one like the New Orleans hotel offers the best ROI.

A drawback of using current cost is that it can be difficult to obtain current-cost estimates for some assets.[8] Why? Because the estimate requires a company to consider technological advances when determining the current cost of assets needed to earn today's operating income. We next consider whether depreciable assets should be measured at gross or net book value.

Long-Term Assets: Gross or Net Book Value?

Because historical-cost investment measures are often used in practice, there has been much discussion about the relative merits of using gross book value or net book value. Using the data in Exhibit 23-1 on page 823, the ROI calculations using net book values and gross book values of plant and equipment are as follows on page 833:

---

[8]When a specific cost index (such as the construction cost index) is not available, companies often use a general index (such as the consumer price index) to approximate current costs.

EXHIBIT 23-2
ROI for Hospitality Inns: Computed Using Current-Cost Estimates as of the End of 2000 for Depreciation and Long-Term Assets

◆ **Step 1:** Restate long-term assets from gross book value at historical cost to gross book value at current cost as of the end of 2000.

	Gross book value of long-term assets at historical cost	×	Construction cost index at 2000	÷	Construction cost index in year of construction	=	Gross book value of long-term assets at current cost at end of 2000
San Francisco:	$1,400,000	×	(180	÷	100)	=	$2,520,000
Chicago:	$2,100,000	×	(180	÷	144)	=	$2,625,000
New Orleans:	$2,730,000	×	(180	÷	160)	=	$3,071,250

◆ **Step 2:** Derive net book value of long-term assets at current cost as of the end of 2000. (Assume estimated useful life of each hotel is 14 years.)

	Gross book value of long-term assets at current cost at end of 2000	×	Estimated useful life remaining	÷	Estimated total useful life	=	Net book value of long-term assets at current cost at end of 2000
San Francisco:	$2,520,000	×	(6	÷	14)	=	$1,080,000
Chicago:	$2,625,000	×	(10	÷	14)	=	$1,875,000
New Orleans:	$3,071,250	×	(12	÷	14)	=	$2,632,500

◆ **Step 3:** Compute current cost of total assets in 2000. (Assume current assets of each hotel is expressed in year 2000 dollars.)

	Current assets at end of 2000 (from Exhibit 23-1)	+	Long-term assets from step 2 above	=	Current cost of total assets at end of 2000
San Francisco:	$400,000	+	$1,080,000	=	$1,480,000
Chicago:	$500,000	+	$1,875,000	=	$2,375,000
New Orleans:	$660,000	+	$2,632,500	=	$3,292,500

◆ **Step 4:** Compute current-cost depreciation expense in 2000 dollars.

	Gross book value of long-term assets at current cost at end of 2000 (from step 1)	×	1	÷	Estimated total useful life	=	Current-cost depreciation expense in 2000 dollars
San Francisco:	$2,520,000	×	(1	÷	14)	=	$180,000
Chicago:	$2,625,000	×	(1	÷	14)	=	$187,500
New Orleans:	$3,071,250	×	(1	÷	14)	=	$219,375

◆ **Step 5:** Compute 2000 operating income using 2000 current-cost depreciation.

	Historical-cost operating income	−	Current-cost depreciation expense in 2000 dollars (from step 4)	−	Historical-cost depreciation	=	Operating income for 2000 using 2000 current-cost depreciation
San Francisco:	$240,000	−	($180,000	−	$100,000)	=	$160,000
Chicago:	$300,000	−	($187,500	−	$150,000)	=	$262,500
New Orleans:	$510,000	−	($219,375	−	$195,000)	=	$485,625

◆ **Step 6:** Compute ROI using current-cost estimates for long-term assets and depreciation.

	Operating income for 2000 using 2000 current-cost depreciation (from step 5)	÷	Current cost of total assets at end of 2000 (from step 3)	=	ROI using current-cost estimate
San Francisco:	$160,000	÷	$1,480,000	=	10.81%
Chicago:	$262,500	÷	$2,375,000	=	11.05%
New Orleans:	$485,625	÷	$3,292,500	=	14.75%

	San Francisco	Chicago	New Orleans
ROI for 2000 using net book value of total assets given in Exhibit 23-1 and calculated earlier	$\dfrac{\$240,000}{\$1,000,000} = 24\%$	$\dfrac{\$300,000}{\$2,000,000} = 15\%$	$\dfrac{\$510,000}{\$3,000,000} = 17\%$
ROI for 2000 using gross book value of total assets obtained by adding accumulated depreciation from p. 832 to net book value of total assets in Exhibit 23-1	$\dfrac{\$240,000}{\$1,800,000} = 13.33\%$	$\dfrac{\$300,000}{\$2,600,000} = 11.54\%$	$\dfrac{\$510,000}{\$3,390,000} = 15.04\%$

Points to Stress The net book value method's declining denominator works to increase ROI as assets age, *ceteris paribus*. Evaluating mgrs. based on net assets rather than gross assets exacerbates incentives for retaining old PPE rather than investing in new PPE.

Using gross book value, the ROI of the older San Francisco hotel (13.33%) is lower than that of the newer New Orleans hotel (15.04%). Those who favor using gross book value claim that it enables more accurate comparisons across subunits. For example, using gross book value calculations, the return on the original plant and equipment investment is higher for the newer New Orleans hotel than for the older San Francisco hotel. This difference probably reflects the decline in earning power of the San Francisco hotel. In contrast, using the net book value masks this decline in earning power because the constantly decreasing investment base results in a higher ROI for the San Francisco hotel (24%). This higher rate may mislead decision makers into thinking that the earning power of the San Francisco hotel has not decreased.

The proponents of using net book value as an investment base maintain that it is less confusing because (1) it is consistent with the amount of total assets shown in the conventional balance sheet, and (2) it is consistent with income computations that include deductions for depreciation. Surveys of company practice report net book value to be the dominant asset measure used by companies in their internal performance evaluations.

CHOOSING TARGET LEVELS OF PERFORMANCE

We next consider step 5 of designing an accounting-based performance measure— setting targets to compare actual performance against. Recall that historical-cost-based accounting measures are often inadequate for evaluating economic returns on new investments and sometimes create disincentives for expansion. Despite these problems, historical-cost ROIs can be used to evaluate current performance by establishing *target ROIs*. Consider our Hospitality Inns example. The key is to recognize that the hotels were built in different years, which in turn means they were built at different levels of the construction-cost index. Top management could adjust the target historical cost ROIs accordingly, say by setting San Francisco's ROI at 26%, Chicago's at 18%, and New Orleans' at 19 percent.

Points to Stress The judicious selection of benchmarks or targets can help offset shortcomings with traditional, historical cost-based ROI, RI, or EVA® measures. For example, since older assets valued at historical cost inflate ROI (particularly if investment is defined as net rather than gross assets), mgt. may set higher target ROIs for divisions with older assets.

The alternative of comparing actual results to target (budgeted) performance is frequently overlooked. The budget should be carefully negotiated with full knowledge of historical-cost accounting pitfalls. *The desirability of tailoring a budget to a particular subunit, a particular accounting system, and any type of performance measure cannot be overemphasized.* For example, many problems of asset valuation and income measurement (whether based on historical cost or current cost) can be satisfactorily solved if top management gets everybody to focus on what is attainable in the forthcoming budget period—regardless of whether ROI, RI, or EVA® is used and regardless of whether the financial measures are based on historical costs or some other measure, such as current costs.

Reinforcing Problems Prob. 23-27 covers performance evaluation issues.

A popular way to establish targets is to set continuous improvement targets. For example, if a company is using EVA® as a performance measure, top management can evaluate operations on year-to-year changes in EVA®, rather than on absolute measures of EVA®. Evaluating performance on the basis of *improvements* in EVA® makes the initial method of calculating EVA® less important.

CHOOSING THE TIMING OF FEEDBACK

Step 6, the final step in designing accounting-based performance measures, is the timing of feedback. Timing of feedback depends largely on how critical the information is for the success of the organization, the specific level of management that is receiving the feedback, and the sophistication of the organization's information technology. For example, hotel managers responsible for room sales want information on the number of rooms sold each day on a daily or weekly basis. Why? Because a large percentage of hotel costs are fixed costs, so that achieving high room sales and taking quick action to reverse any declining sales trends are critical to the financial success of each hotel. Supplying managers with daily information about room sales would be much easier if Hospitality Inns had a computerized room-reservation and check-in system. Senior management, however, in their oversight role may look at information about daily room sales only on a monthly basis. In some instances, for example, because of concern about the low sales to total assets ratio of the Chicago hotel, they may want the information weekly.

PERFORMANCE MEASUREMENT IN MULTINATIONAL COMPANIES

Comparing the performance of divisions of a multinational company, that is, a company operating in different countries, creates additional difficulties.[9]

Points to Stress Lower level mgrs., who are responsible for day-to-day operations, usually require more frequent feedback than senior executives, who primarily exercise oversight over the lower level mgrs.

OBJECTIVE 7

Indicate the difficulties that arise when comparing the performance of divisions operating in different countries

◆ The economic, legal, political, social, and cultural environments differ significantly across countries.

◆ Governments in some countries may impose controls and limit selling prices of a company's products. For example, developing countries in Asia, Latin America, and Eastern Europe impose tariffs and custom duties to restrict the import of certain goods.

◆ Availability of materials and skilled labor, as well as costs of materials, labor, and infrastructure (power, transportation, and communication) may also differ significantly across countries.

◆ Divisions operating in different countries keep score of their performance in different currencies. Issues of inflation and fluctuations in foreign currency exchange rates affect performance measures in important ways.

In the next section, we describe the adjustments necessary to compare performance measures across countries.

Points to Stress/Reinforcing Problems When divisions operate within a single country, it is difficult to compare, say, ROI across divisions if the age of the assets or risk differs across divisions. When divisions are located in different countries, additional complications arise including tariffs, fluctuations in foreign currency exchange rates, and differential availability of input resources (e.g., materials, skilled labor). Exer. 23-24 and 23-25 cover performance evaluation in multinational companies.

Calculating the Foreign Division's ROI in the Foreign Currency

Suppose Hospitality Inns invests in a hotel in Mexico City. The investment consists mainly of the costs of buildings and furnishings. Also assume the following information:

◆ The exchange rate at the time of Hospitality's investment on December 31, 1999 is 10 pesos = $1.

◆ During 2000, the Mexican peso suffers a steady decline in its value.

The exchange rate on December 31, 2000 is 15 pesos = $1.

The average exchange rate during 2000 is [(10 + 15) ÷ 2] = 12.5 pesos = $1.

The investment (total assets) in the Mexico City hotel is 30,000,000 pesos.

The operating income of the Mexico City hotel in 2000 is 6,000,000 pesos.

What is the historical-cost-based ROI for the Mexico City hotel in 2000?

Several questions arise. Should we calculate the ROI in pesos or in dollars? If we calculate the ROI in dollars, what exchange rate should we use? How does the ROI of Hospitality Inns Mexico City (HIMC) compare with the ROI of Hospitality Inns New Orleans (HINO), which is also a relatively new hotel of approximately the same size? Hospitality Inns may be interested in this information for making future investment decisions.

Points to Stress Inflation increases revenues and costs, and therefore income (assuming revenues exceed costs), relative to the historical cost-based value of the investment. ROI is too high because income is measured in dollars (or pesos in the Hospitality Inn example) of low purchasing power, whereas investment is measured in older dollars (or pesos) of higher purchasing power. Calculating ROI based on current cost data would help mitigate this problem.

$$\text{HIMC's ROI (calculated using pesos)} = \frac{\text{Operating income}}{\text{Total assets}} = \frac{6{,}000{,}000 \text{ pesos}}{30{,}000{,}000 \text{ pesos}} = 20\%$$

[9]M. Z. Iqbal, T. Melcher, and A. Elmallah, *International Accounting—A Global Perspective* (Cincinnati: Southwestern ITP, 1996).

HIMC's ROI of 20% is higher than HINO's ROI of 17% (computed on p. 824). Does this mean that HIMC outperformed HINO based on the ROI criterion? Not necessarily. Why? Because HIMC operates in a very different economic environment than does HINO.

The peso has declined in value relative to the dollar in 2000. Research studies show that the peso's decline is correlated with correspondingly higher inflation in Mexico relative to the United States.[10] A consequence of the higher inflation in Mexico is that HIMC will charge higher prices for its hotel rooms, which will increase HIMC's operating income and lead to a higher ROI. Inflation clouds the real economic returns on an asset and makes ROI calculated on historical cost of assets unrealistically high. Why? Because had there been no inflation, HIMC's room rates and hence operating income would have been lower. Differences in inflation rates between the two countries make a direct comparison of HIMC's peso-denominated ROI with HINO's dollar-denominated ROI misleading.

Calculating the Foreign Division's ROI in U.S. Dollars

One way to achieve greater comparability of historical-cost-based ROIs is to restate HIMC's performance in dollars. But what exchange rate(s) should we use to make the comparison meaningful? Assume operating income was earned evenly throughout 2000. We use the average exchange rate of 12.5 pesos = $1 to convert the operating income from pesos to dollars: 6,000,000 pesos ÷ 12.5 = $480,000. The effect of dividing the operating income in pesos by the higher pesos-to-dollar exchange rate is that any increase in operating income in pesos as a result of inflation is eliminated when converting back to dollars.

At what rate should we convert HIMC's total assets of 30,000,000 pesos? At the exchange rate prevailing when the assets were acquired on December 31, 1999, namely, 10 pesos = $1. Why? Because HIMC's assets are recorded at the December 31, 1999 cost, and are not revalued as a result of inflation in Mexico in 2000. Because the cost of assets recorded on HIMC's books is unaffected by subsequent inflation, the exchange rate used to convert it into dollars should reflect this fact. Using exchange rates after December 31, 1999 would be incorrect because these rates incorporate the higher inflation in Mexico in 2000. Total assets would be converted to 30,000,000 pesos ÷ 10 = $3,000,000. Then,

$$\text{HIMC's ROI (calculated using dollars)} = \frac{\text{Operating income}}{\text{Total assets}} = \frac{\$480,000}{\$3,000,000} = 16\%$$

These adjustments make the historical-cost-based ROIs of the Mexico City and New Orleans hotels comparable because they negate the effects of any differences in inflation rates between the two countries. HIMC's ROI of 16% is less than HINO's ROI of 17 percent.

Residual income calculated in pesos suffers from the same problems as ROI calculated using pesos. Instead, calculating HIMC's RI in dollars adjusts for changes in exchange rates and facilitates comparisons with Hospitality's other hotels:

$$\text{HIMC's RI} = \$480,000 - (12\% \times \$3,000,000)$$

$$= \$480,000 - \$360,000 = \$120,000$$

which is also less than HINO's RI of $150,000. In interpreting HIMC's and HINO's ROI and RI, note that they are historical-cost-based calculations. They do, however, pertain to relatively new hotels.

[10]W. Beaver and M. Wolfson, "Foreign Currency Translation Gains and Losses: What Effect Do They Have and What Do They Mean?" *Financial Analysts Journal* (March–April 1984); F. D. S. Choi, "Resolving the Inflation/Currency Translation Dilemma," *Management International Review* (Vol. 34, Special Issue, 1994).

DISTINCTION BETWEEN MANAGERS AND ORGANIZATION UNITS[11]

As noted before in this and several other chapters, the performance evaluation of a *manager* should be distinguished from the performance evaluation of an *organization subunit*, such as a division of a company. Consider the following example. Companies often put the most skillful division manager in charge of the division producing the poorest economic returns in an attempt to change its fortunes. Such an effort may take years to bear fruit. Furthermore, the manager's efforts may result merely in bringing the division up to a minimum acceptable ROI. The division may continue to be a poor profit performer in comparison with other divisions, but it would be a mistake to conclude from the poor performance of the division that the manager is necessarily performing poorly. The division's performance may be adversely affected by economic conditions over which the manager has no control.

This section develops basic principles for evaluating the performance of an individual subunit manager. The concepts we discuss apply, however, to all organization levels. Later sections consider specific examples at the individual-activity level and the total-organization level. For specificity, we use the RI performance measure throughout.

The Basic Trade-Off: Creating Incentives Versus Imposing Risk

Performance evaluation often affects managers' and employees' rewards. Compensation arrangements run the range from a flat salary with no direct performance-based incentive (bonus), as in the case of many government employees, to rewards based only on performance, as in the case of real estate agents. Most often, however, a manager's total compensation includes some combination of salary and a performance-based incentive. An important consideration in designing compensation arrangements is the trade-off between creating incentives and imposing risk. We illustrate this trade-off in the context of our Hospitality Inns example.

Sally Fonda owns the Hospitality Inns chain of hotels. Roger Brett manages the Hospitality Inns San Francisco (HISF) hotel. Assume that Fonda uses RI to measure performance. To achieve good results as measured by RI, Fonda would like Brett to control costs, provide prompt and courteous service, and reduce receivables. But even if Brett did all those things, good results are by no means guaranteed. HISF's RI is affected by many factors outside Fonda's and Brett's control, such as a recession in the San Francisco economy, or an earthquake that might negatively affect HISF. Alternatively, uncontrollable factors might have a positive influence on HISF's RI. Uncontrollable factors make HISF's profitability uncertain and risky.

Fonda is an entrepreneur and does not mind bearing risk, but Brett does not like being subject to risk. One way of "insuring" Brett against risk is to pay Brett a flat salary, regardless of the actual amount of RI attained. All the risk would then be borne by Fonda. This arrangement creates a problem, however, because the effort that Brett exerts is difficult to monitor, and the absence of performance-based compensation will provide Brett with no incentive to work harder or undertake extra physical and mental effort beyond what is necessary to retain his job or to uphold his own personal values.

Moral hazard[12] describes situations in which an employee prefers to exert less effort (or report distorted information) compared to the effort (or information) desired by the owner because the employee's effort (or information) cannot be accurately monitored and enforced. In some repetitive jobs—for example, in electronic

---

[11]The presentations here draw (in part) from teaching notes prepared by S. Huddart, N. Melumad, and S. Reichelstein.

[12]The term *moral hazard* originated in insurance contracts to represent situations where insurance coverage caused insured parties to take less care of their properties than they might otherwise. One response to moral hazard in insurance contracts is the system of deductibles (that is, the insured pays for damages below a specified amount).

Points to Stress Incentive compensation plans are most likely to be cost effective if

1. the owner and mgr. have different goals (e.g., owner wants profits, mgr. is work averse). If goals are identical, owners' and mgrs.' interests are aligned, so incentive compensation is unnecessary.
2. the owner cannot monitor the mgrs.' actions. Otherwise, the owner would compensate the mgr. based on the mgrs.' actions, in order to reduce the risk shifted to the mgr.
3. the mgr. has considerable control over the performance measure outcome (If the mgr. has little control over the outcome, the incentive plan will place undue risk on the risk-averse mgr., and he will demand a premium for bearing this risk).

Reinforcing Problems Exer. 23-26 and Prob. 23-32 cover risk-sharing issues.

OBJECTIVE 9

Describe the management accountant's role in helping organizations provide better incentives

---

Curriculum Linkage When possible, owners use performance evaluation measures that are tightly linked to mgrs.' efforts. This is consistent with the Chap. 6 notion that mgrs. should be evaluated based on factors (e.g., costs, revenues, investment) for which they are *responsible*. Mgrs. are evaluated based on things they can affect, even if these factors are not completely controllable. For example, sales people often earn commissions based on the amount of sales revenue they generate. Sales people obviously can affect the amount of sales they generate by deciding to work harder, but they cannot completely control the level of sales because other factors such as the economy and competitors' products also affect sales.

Points to Stress A recent survey showed that over 70% of respondent companies had recently altered, or else planned to change, their performance evaluation systems. Most are establishing a stronger link between pay and performance.

assembly—a supervisor can monitor the workers' actions, and the moral hazard problem may not arise. However, a manager's job is often to gather information and exercise judgment on the basis of the information obtained, and monitoring a manager's effort is thus considerably more difficult.

Paying no salary and rewarding Brett *only* on the basis of some performance measure—RI in our example—raises different concerns. Brett would now be motivated to strive to increase RI because his rewards would increase with increases in RI. But compensating Brett on RI also subjects Brett to risk. Why? Because HISF's RI depends not only on Brett's effort, but also on factors such as the local economic conditions over which Brett has no control.

To compensate Brett (who does not like being subject to risk) for taking on uncontrollable risk, Fonda must pay Brett some extra compensation within the structure of the RI-based arrangement. Thus, using performance-based bonuses will cost Fonda more money, *on average*, than paying Brett a flat salary. Why "on average"? Because Fonda's compensation payment to Brett will vary with RI outcomes. When averaged over these outcomes, the RI-based compensation will cost Fonda more than would paying Brett a flat salary. The motivation for having some salary and some performance-based bonus in compensation arrangements is to balance the benefit of incentives against the extra cost of imposing uncontrollable risk on the manager.

Intensity of Incentives and Financial and Nonfinancial Measurements

What dictates the intensity of the incentives? That is, how large should the incentive component be relative to salary? The key to answering these questions is understanding how well the performance measure captures the manager's actions.

Preferred performance measures are ones that are sensitive to or change significantly with the manager's performance and do not change much with changes in factors that are beyond the manager's control. Performance measures that are sensitive to the manager's performance motivate the manager as well as limit the manager's exposure to uncontrollable risk, reducing the cost of providing incentives. Performance measures that are less sensitive to the manager's performance fail to capture the manager's performance and fail to induce the manager to improve. When owners have performance measures that are sensitive to the manager's performance available to them, they place greater reliance on incentive compensation.

Suppose Brett has no authority to determine investments. Further suppose revenues are determined largely by external factors such as the local economic conditions. Brett's actions influence only costs. Using RI as a performance measure in these circumstances subjects Brett's bonus to excessive risk because two components of the performance measure (investments and revenues) are largely unrelated to his actions. The management accountant might suggest that, to create stronger incentives, Fonda should consider using a different performance measure for Brett—perhaps HISF's costs—that more closely captures Brett's effort. Note that in this case, RI may be a perfectly good measure of the economic viability of HISF, but it is not a good measure of Brett's performance.

The benefits of tying performance measures more closely to a manager's efforts encourage the use of nonfinancial measures. Consider, for example, two possible measures for evaluating the manager of the Housekeeping Department at one of Hospitality's hotels: (1) the costs of the Housekeeping Department, and (2) the average time taken by the housekeeping staff to properly clean a room. Suppose housekeeping costs are affected by factors such as wage rates, which the housekeeping manager does not set. In this case, the average time taken to properly clean a room may more precisely capture the manager's performance.

The salary component of compensation dominates in the absence of performance measures that are sensitive to managers' actions. This is the case, for example, for some corporate staff and government employees. A high salary component, however, does not mean that incentives are completely absent. Promotions and salary increases do depend on some overall measure of performance, but the incentives are less direct. The incentive component of compensation is higher when performance measures that are sensitive to a manager's performance are available, and when monitoring the employee's effort is difficult (real estate agencies, for example, reward sales agents mainly on commissions for houses sold).

Surveys show that division managers' compensation plans include a mix of salary, bonus, and long-term compensation tied to earnings and stock price of the company. The goal is to balance division and companywide incentives, as well as short-term and long-term incentives. One survey of companies reports average annual contingent compensation as follows: (1) bonuses based on short-run performance equal to 40% of current salary, and (2) average annual cash and stock compensation based on long-run performance equal to 57% of current salary. These percentages, however, vary widely over the sample—some companies use much stronger performance incentives than do others.[13]

Benchmarks and Relative Performance Evaluation

Owners can use benchmarks to evaluate performance. Benchmarks representing best practice may be available inside or outside the organization. In our Hospitality Inns example, benchmarks could be other similar hotels, either within or outside the Hospitality Inns chain. Suppose Brett has responsibility for revenues, costs, and investments. In evaluating Brett's performance, Fonda would want to use as a benchmark, a hotel of a similar size that is influenced by the same uncontrollable factors—for example, location, demographic trends, and economic conditions—that affect HISF. *Differences* in performances of the two hotels occur only because of differences in the two managers' performances, not because of other factors. Thus, benchmarking, also called *relative performance evaluation*, "filters out" the effects of the common uncontrollable factors.

Can the performance of two managers responsible for running similar operations within a company be benchmarked against one another? Yes, but a problem arises: The use of these benchmarks may reduce incentives for these managers to help one another. That is, a manager's performance evaluation measure improves either by doing a better job or by making the other manager look bad. Not cooperating and working together is not in the best interest of the organization as a whole. In this case, using internal benchmarks for performance evaluation can lead to goal incongruence.

PERFORMANCE MEASURES AT THE INDIVIDUAL ACTIVITY LEVEL

Two important issues arise when evaluating performance at the individual activity level: designing performance measures for activities that require multiple tasks and designing performance measures for activities done in teams. We focus on these issues next.

Performing Multiple Tasks

Most employees perform more than one task as part of their jobs. Marketing representatives sell products, provide customer support, and gather market information. Other jobs have multiple aspects to them. Manufacturing workers, for example, are responsible for both the quantity and quality of their output. Employers want employees to allocate their time and effort intelligently among various tasks or aspects of their jobs.

Consider, for example, mechanics at an auto repair shop. Their jobs have at least two distinct and important aspects. The first aspect is the repair work. Performing more repair work would generate more revenues for the shop. The second aspect is customer satisfaction. The higher the quality of the job, the more likely

[13]R. Bushman, R. Indjejikian, and A. Smith, "Aggregate Performance Measures in Business Unit Manager Compensation: The Role of Intrafirm Interdependencies," *Journal of Accounting Research* (Vol. 33 Supplement, 1995).

Teaching Tip To help students understand why incentive compensation is becoming more popular, even if it places more risk on the mgr, ask them to consider experiences they have had with government bureaucrats (e.g., obtaining driver's license, obtaining financial aid at a state university). The problems caused by the relative absence of incentive compensation should be immediately obvious.

Teaching Tip Have students write an essay on the dysfunctional consequences of using accounting numbers in performance evaluation. Encourage students to find real-world examples of dysfunctional consequences, either by interviewing mgrs. or by finding articles in the business press.

the customer will be pleased. If the employer wants an employee to focus on both these aspects, then the employer must measure and compensate performance on both.

Suppose the employer can easily measure the quantity of auto repairs but not their quality. If the employer rewards workers on a by-the-job rate—which pays workers only on the basis of the number of repairs actually performed—mechanics will likely increase the number of repairs they make at the expense of quality. Sears, Roebuck and Co. experienced this problem when they introduced by-the-job rates for its mechanics. Sears' management responded by taking three steps to motivate workers to balance both quantity and quality: (1) They dropped the by-the-job rate system and paid mechanics an hourly salary, a step that deemphasized the quantity of repair. Mechanics' promotions and pay increases were determined on the basis of management's assessment of each mechanic's overall performance regarding quantity and quality of repairs. (2) They began evaluating employees, in part, using data such as customer-satisfaction surveys, the number of dissatisfied customers, or the number of customer complaints. (3) They used independent staff to randomly monitor whether the repairs performed were of high quality.

Note that nonfinancial measures (such as customer-satisfaction measures) play a central role in motivating mechanics to emphasize both quantity and quality. The goal is to measure both aspects of the mechanics' jobs and to balance incentives so that both aspects are properly emphasized.

Team-Based Compensation Arrangements

Many manufacturing, marketing, and design problems require employees with multiple skills, experiences, and judgments to pool their talents. In these situations, a team of employees achieves better results than individuals acting on their own.[14] Companies give incentives to individuals on the basis of team performance. Team incentives encourage individuals to help one another as they strive toward a common goal. The blend of knowledge and skills needed to change methods and improve efficiency puts a team in a better position than a lone individual to respond to incentives.

The specific forms of team-based compensation vary across companies. Colgate Palmolive rewards teams on the basis of each team's performance. Novartis, the Swiss pharmaceutical company, uses a team-based gain-sharing program to focus teams on companywide performance—a certain amount of team-based bonuses are paid only if the company reaches certain goals. To encourage the development of critical skills, Tennessee Eastman's skill-based plan rewards team members using a checklist of team skills. Whether team-based compensation is desirable depends, to a great extent, on the culture and management style of a particular organization. One criticism of teams, especially in the United States, is that individual incentives to excel are dampened, harming overall performance. Another challenge is to manage team members who are not productive contributors to the team's success but who continue to share in the team's rewards.

EXECUTIVE PERFORMANCE MEASURES AND COMPENSATION

The principles of performance evaluation described in the previous sections also apply to executive compensation plans. These plans are based on both financial and nonfinancial performance measures and consist of a mix of (1) base salary; (2) annual incentives (for example, cash bonus based on achieving a target annual RI); (3) long-run incentives [for example, stock options (described later in this section) based on achieving a target return by the end of a 5-year period]; and (4) fringe benefits (for example, life insurance, an office with a view, or a personal assistant). Designers of executive compensation plans emphasize three factors: achievement of

---

[14]J. Katzenbach and D. Smith, *The Wisdom of Teams* (Boston: The Harvard Business School Press, 1993).

organization goals, administrative ease, and the likelihood that affected executives will perceive the plan as fair.

Well-designed plans use a compensation mix that carefully balances risk with short-run and long-run incentives. For example, evaluating performance on the basis of annual ROI would sharpen an executive's short-run focus. And using ROI and stock option plans over, say, 5 years would motivate the executive to take a long-run view as well.

Stock options give executives the right to buy company stock at a specified price (called the exercise price) within a specified period. Suppose on February 16, 1998, Marriott International gave its CEO the option to buy 100,000 shares of Marriott stock at any time before June 30, 2002, at the February 16, 1998, market price of $72 per share. If Marriott's stock price rises to, say, $87 per share on March 24, 2002, and the CEO chooses to exercise his option on all 100,000 shares, he will earn $1.5 million. (The CEO would exercise his right to buy Marriott stock from the company on March 24, 2002, for $72 per share and sell it in the market at $87 per share, earning $15 per share on 100,000 shares.) If Marriott's stock price stays below $72 the entire period, the CEO will simply forgo his right to buy the shares. Hence, by linking CEO compensation to increases in the company's stock price, the stock option plan serves to motivate the CEO to improve the company's long-run performance.

In 1995, the Financial Accounting Standards Board (FASB) issued Statement Number 123 on accounting for stock options. For most stock options granted, the exercise price of the option equals or exceeds the market price of the stock on the day the options are granted. In these cases, Statement 123 encourages, but does not require, a company to record a compensation cost in its income statement. The company can choose not to recognize cost even though the company has sacrificed something of value—the potentially large income the executive will receive if the price of the stock increases. If the company records no cost in its income statement, it must disclose in a footnote to the financial statements the effect on net income and earnings per share had the company recognized cost equal to the estimated fair market value of the options on the date they were granted.[15]

Responding to some concerns about high executive compensation payments despite poor company performance, the Securities and Exchange Commission (SEC), in 1992, issued rules requiring more detailed disclosures of the compensation arrangements of top-level executives. In complying with these rules in 1998, Marriott International, for example, disclosed a summary compensation table showing the salary, bonus, stock options, other stock awards, and other compensation earned by its top five executives during the 1995, 1996, and 1997 fiscal years. Marriott also disclosed how well its stock performed relative to the overall market (S&P 500 Index) and stocks of other motels and hotels (the S&P Lodging Hotel Index). Investors use this information to evaluate the relationship between compensation and performance across companies generally, or across companies of similar sizes, or across companies operating in similar industries.

The SEC rules also require companies to disclose the principles underlying their executive compensation plans and the performance criteria—such as profitability, revenue growth, and market share—used in determining compensation. In its annual report, Marriott International described these principles as "building a strong correlation between stockholder return and executive compensation, offering incentives that encourage attainment of short-run and long-run business goals, and providing a total level of pay that is commensurate with performance." Marriott uses cash flow, earnings per share, and guest satisfaction as performance criteria to determine annual cash incentives for its executives.

---

[15]If the exercise price is less than the market price of the stock on the date the options are granted, the company must recognize compensation cost equal to the difference between the two prices. This amount is less than the fair market value of the options. The company can choose to either recognize the full fair market value as a cost or disclose in a footnote the effect on net income and earnings per share.

ENVIRONMENTAL AND ETHICAL RESPONSIBILITIES

As they strive to achieve the performances goals of their organizations, managers should be keenly aware of their environmental and ethical responsibilities. Environmental violations (such as water and air pollution) and unethical and illegal practices (such as bribery and corruption) carry heavy fines and are prison offenses under the laws of the United States and other countries. But environmental responsibilities and ethical conduct extend beyond legal requirements.

Socially responsible companies set aggressive environmental goals and measure and report their performance against them. German, Swiss, Dutch, and Scandinavian companies report on environmental performance as part of a larger set of social responsibility disclosures (which include employee welfare and community development information). Some companies, such as DuPont, make environmental performance a line item on every employee's salary appraisal report. Duke Power Company appraises employees on reducing solid waste, cutting emissions and discharges, and implementing environmental plans. The result: Duke Power has met all its environmental goals.

Ethical behavior on the part of managers is paramount. In particular, the numbers that subunit managers report should not be tainted by "cooking the books." They should be uncontaminated by, for example, overstated assets, understated liabilities, fictitious revenues, and understated costs.

Codes of business conduct are circulated in some organizations to signal appropriate and inappropriate individual behavior. The following is a quote from Caterpillar Tractor's "Code of Worldwide Business Conduct and Operating Principles":

> The law is a floor. Ethical business conduct should normally exist at a level well above the minimum required by law. Caterpillar employees shall not accept costly entertainment or gifts (excepting mementos and novelties of nominal value) from dealers, suppliers and others with whom we do business. And we won't tolerate circumstances that produce, or reasonably appear to produce, conflict between personal interests of an employee and interests of the company.

Division managers often cite enormous top-management pressures "to make the budget" as excuses or rationalizations for not adhering to ethical accounting policies and procedures. A healthy amount of motivational pressure is not undesirable—as long as the "tone from the top" simultaneously communicates the absolute need for all managers to behave ethically at all times. Management should promptly and severely reprimand unethical conduct irrespective of the benefits that accrue to the company from such actions. Some companies such as Lockheed-Martin emphasize ethical behavior by routinely evaluating employees against a business code of ethics.

PROBLEM FOR SELF-STUDY

PROBLEM
The Baseball Division of Home Run Sports manufactures and sells baseballs. Budgeted data for February 2000 are as follows:

Current assets	$ 400,000
Long-term assets	600,000
Total assets	$1,000,000
Production output	200,000 baseballs per month
Target ROI (Operating income ÷ Total assets)	30%
Fixed costs	$400,000 per month
Variable costs	$4 per baseball

Required

1. Compute the minimum selling price per baseball necessary to achieve the target ROI of 30 percent.
2. Using the selling price from requirement 1, separate the target ROI into its two components using the DuPont method.
3. Compute the RI of the Baseball Division for February 2000, using the selling price from requirement 1. Home Run Sports uses a 12% required rate of return on total division assets when computing division RI.
4. In addition to her salary, Pamela Stephenson, the division manager, receives 3% of the monthly RI of the Baseball Division as a bonus. Compute Stephenson's bonus. Why do you think Stephenson is rewarded using both salary and a performance-based bonus? Stephenson does not like bearing risk.

SOLUTION

1.

$$\text{Target operating income} = 30\% \text{ of } \$1,000,000$$

$$= \$300,000$$

$$\text{Let } P = \text{Selling price}$$

$$\text{Revenues} - \text{Variable costs} - \text{Fixed costs} = \text{Operating income}$$

$$200,000P - (200,000 \times \$4) - \$400,000 = \$300,000$$

$$200,000P = \$300,000 + \$800,000 + \$400,000$$

$$= \$1,500,000$$

$$P = \$7.50$$

Proof:

Revenues, 200,000 × $7.50	$1,500,000
Variable costs, 200,000 × $4	800,000
Contribution margin	700,000
Fixed costs	400,000
Operating income	$ 300,000

2.

$$\frac{\text{Revenues}}{\text{Investment}} \times \frac{\text{Income}}{\text{Revenues}} = \frac{\text{Income}}{\text{Investment}}$$

$$\frac{\$1,500,000}{\$1,000,000} \times \frac{\$300,000}{\$1,500,000} = \frac{\$300,000}{\$1,000,000}$$

$$1.5 \times 0.2 = 0.30, \text{ or } 30\%$$

3.

$$\text{RI} = \text{Operating income} - \text{Required return on investment}$$

$$= \$300,000 - (0.12 \times \$1,000,000)$$

$$= \$300,000 - \$120,000$$

$$= \$180,000$$

4.

$$\text{Stephenson's bonus} = 3\% \times \text{RI}$$

$$= 3\% \times \$180,000 = \$5,400$$

The Baseball Division's RI is affected by many factors outside Stephenson's control such as general economic conditions. These uncontrollable factors make the Baseball Division's profitability uncertain and risky. Because Stephenson does not like bearing risk, paying her a flat salary, regardless of RI would shield Stephenson from this risk. The problem with this compensation arrangement is one of moral hazard. Because Stephenson's effort is difficult to monitor, the absence of performance-based compensation will provide Stephenson with no incentive to undertake extra physical and mental effort beyond what is necessary to retain her job or uphold her personal values.

Paying no salary and rewarding Stephenson only on the basis of RI provides Stephenson with incentives to work hard but also subjects her to excessive risk because of uncontrollable factors that will affect RI and hence Stephenson's compensation. A compensation arrangement based only on RI would be more costly for Home Run Sports because it would have to compensate Stephenson for taking on uncontrollable risk.

A compensation arrangement that consists of both a salary and an RI-based performance bonus balances the benefits of incentives against the extra costs of imposing uncontrollable risk.

SUMMARY

The following points are linked to the chapter's learning objectives:

1. Financial measures such as return on investment and residual income can capture important aspects of both manager performance and organization-subunit performance. In many cases, however, financial measures are supplemented with nonfinancial measures of performance, such as those relating to customer satisfaction ratings, number of defects, and productivity.

2. The steps in designing accounting-based performance measures are (a) choose performance measures that align with top management's financial goal(s), (b) choose the time horizon of each performance measure, (c) choose a definition of the components in each performance measure, (d) choose a measurement alternative for each performance measure, (e) choose a target level of performance, and (f) choose the timing of feedback.

3. The DuPont method describes return on investment (ROI) as the product of two components: income divided by revenues (return on sales) and revenues divided by investment (investment turnover). ROI can be increased in three ways—by increasing revenues by decreasing costs, and by decreasing investment.

4. Residual income (RI) is income minus a required dollar return on the investment. RI is designed to overcome some of the limitations of ROI. For example, RI is more likely than ROI to promote goal congruence. That is, actions that are in the best interests of the organization maximize RI. The objective of maximizing ROI, conversely, may induce managers of highly profitable divisions to reject projects that, from the standpoint of the organization as a whole, should be accepted.

5. Economic value added (EVA®) is a variation of the RI calculation. It equals the after-tax operating income minus the product of after-tax weighted-average cost of capital and total assets minus current liabilities.

6. The current cost of an asset is the cost now of purchasing an identical asset to the one currently held. Historical-cost asset measurement methods generally consider the net book value of the assets, which is the original cost net of accumulated depreciation. Historical-cost measures are often inadequate for measuring economic returns. However, this weakness can be overcome by comparing actual performance against targets. More generally, problems in any performance measure can be overcome by emphasizing budgets and targets that stress steady improvement.

7. Comparing the performance of divisions operating in different countries is difficult because of legal, political, social, economic, and currency differences. ROI calculations for subunits operating in different countries need to be adjusted for differences in inflation between the two countries and changes in exchange rates.

8. Organizations create incentives by rewarding managers on the basis of performance. But managers may face risks because factors beyond their control may also affect performance. Owners choose a mix of salary and incentive compensation to trade off the incentive benefit against the cost of imposing risk.

Correcting Student Misconceptions
Many criticisms of performance measures are directed at how the measures are used, rather than at the measures themselves. If mgrs.' bonuses depend only on quarterly ROI, mgrs. will have a short-run focus. However, this is a shortcoming of the evaluation scheme, not of ROI *per se*. If mgrs.' bonuses depend on (1) 5-year average ROI, (2) current year ROI, and (3) achievement of key strategic objectives (e.g., market share, product quality, reducing solid waste), mgrs. should have a more balanced focus. Performance evaluation should include long-run as well as short-run, nonfinancial as well as financial, and external as well as internal, measures.

9. Obtaining performance measures that are more sensitive to employee performance is critical for implementing strong incentives. Many management accounting practices, such as the design of responsibility centers and the establishment of financial and nonfinancial measures, have as their goal better performance evaluation.

▼ TERMS TO LEARN

This chapter and the Glossary at the end of this book contain definitions of the following important terms:

current cost (p. 831)
economic value added (EVA®) (826)
imputed costs (825)
investment (823)

moral hazard (837)
residual income (RI) (825)
return on investment (ROI) (824)

▼ ASSIGNMENT MATERIAL

QUESTIONS

23-1 Give two examples of financial performance measures and two examples of nonfinancial performance measures.

23-2 What are the six steps in designing accounting-based performance measures?

23-3 What factors affecting ROI does the DuPont method of profitability analysis highlight?

23-4 "RI is not identical to ROI although both measures incorporate income and investment into their computations." Do you agree? Explain.

23-5 Describe EVA®.

23-6 Give three definitions of investment used in practice when computing ROI.

23-7 Distinguish between measuring assets based on current cost and historical cost.

23-8 What special problems arise when evaluating performance in multinational companies?

23-9 Why is it important to distinguish between the performance of a manager and the performance of the organization subunit for which the manager is responsible? Give an example.

23-10 Describe moral hazard.

23-11 "Managers should be rewarded only on the basis of their performance measures. They should be paid no salary." Do you agree? Explain.

23-12 Explain the management accountant's role in helping organizations design stronger incentive systems for their employees.

23-13 Explain the role of benchmarking in evaluating managers.

23-14 Explain the incentive problems that can arise when employees have to perform multiple tasks as part of their jobs.

23-15 Describe two disclosures required by the SEC with respect to executive compensation.

EXERCISES

23-16 ROI, comparisons of three companies. (CMA, adapted) Return on investment (ROI) is often expressed as follows:

$$\frac{\text{Income}}{\text{Investment}} = \frac{\text{Revenue}}{\text{Investment}} \times \frac{\text{Income}}{\text{Revenues}}$$

Required

1. What advantages are there in the breakdown of the computation into two separate components?

2. Fill in the following blanks:

	Companies in Same Industry		
	A	B	C
Revenues	$1,000,000	$500,000	?
Income	$ 100,000	$ 50,000	?
Investment	$ 500,000	?	$5,000,000
Income as a percentage of revenues	?	?	0.5%
Investment turnover	?	?	2
ROI	?	1%	?

After filling in the blanks, comment on the relative performance of these companies as thoroughly as the data permit.

 23-17 Analysis of return on invested assets, comparison of three divisions. Quality Products, Inc., is a soft-drink and food-products company. It has three divisions: soft drinks, snack foods, and family restaurants. Results (in millions) for the past 3 years are as follows:

	Soft-Drink Division	Snack-Foods Division	Restaurant Division	Quality Products, Inc.
Operating Revenues				
2000	$2,800	$2,000	$1,050	$5,850
2001	3,000	2,400	1,250	6,650
2002	3,600	2,600	1,530	7,730
Operating Income				
2000	120	360	105	585
2001	160	400	114	674
2002	240	420	100	760
Total Assets				
2000	1,200	1,240	800	3,240
2001	1,250	1,400	1,000	3,650
2002	1,400	1,430	1,300	4,130

Required
Use the DuPont method of profitability analysis to explain changes in the operating income to total assets ratio over the 2000–2002 period for each division. Comment on the results.

23-18 ROI and RI. (D. Kleespie) The Gaul Company produces and distributes a wide variety of recreational products. One of its divisions, the Goscinny Division, manufactures and sells "menhirs," which are popular with cross-country skiers. The demand for these menhirs is relatively insensitive to price changes. The Goscinny Division is considered to be an investment center and in recent years has averaged a ROI of 20 percent. The following data are available for the Goscinny Division and its product:

Total annual fixed costs	$1,000,000
Variable costs per menhir	$300
Average number of menhirs sold each year	10,000
Average operating assets invested in the division	$1,600,000

Required
1. What is the minimum selling price per unit that the Goscinny Division could charge in order for Mary Obelix, the division manager, to get a favorable performance rating? Management considers an ROI below 20% to be unfavorable.
2. Assume that the Gaul Company judges the performance of its investment center managers on the basis of RI rather than ROI. The company's required rate of return is 15 percent. What is the minimum selling price per unit that the Goscinny Division should charge for Obelix to receive a favorable performance rating?

23-19 Pricing and ROI. Hardy, Inc., assembles motorcycles and uses long-run (defined as 3–5 years) average demand to set the budgeted production level and costs for pricing. Prices are then adjusted only for large changes in assembly wage rates or direct materials prices. You are given the following data:

Direct materials, assembly wages, and other variable costs	$1,320 per unit
Fixed costs	$300,000,000 per year
Target ROI	20%
Normal utilization of capacity (average output)	1,000,000 units
Investment (total assets)	$900,000,000

Required

1. What return on sales is needed to attain the target ROI of 20 percent?
2. What selling price is needed to attain the target ROI of 20 percent?
3. Using the selling price calculated in requirement 2, what ROI will be earned if Hardy assembles and sells 1,500,000 units? 500,000 units?
4. The company has a management bonus plan based on yearly division performance. Assume that Hardy assembled and sold 1,000,000, 1,500,000, and 500,000 units in three successive years. Three people each served as division manager for 1 year before being killed in a motorcycle accident. As the principal heir of the third manager, comment on the bonus plan.

23-20 Financial and nonfinancial performance measures, goal congruence. (CMA, adapted) Summit Equipment specializes in the manufacture of medical equipment, a field that has become increasingly competitive. Approximately 2 years ago, Ben Harrington, president of Summit, decided to revise the bonus plan (based, at the time, entirely on operating income) to encourage division managers to focus on areas that were important to customers and that added value without increasing cost. In addition to a profitability incentive, the revised plan also includes incentives for reduced rework costs, reduced sales returns, and on-time deliveries. Bonuses are calculated and awarded semiannually on the following basis. A base bonus is calculated at 2% of operating income. This amount is then adjusted as follows:

a. (i) Reduced by excess of rework costs over and above 2% of operating income.
   (ii) No adjustment if rework costs are less than or equal to 2% of operating income.

b. (i) Increased by $5,000 if over 98% of deliveries are on time, and by $2,000 if 96–98% of deliveries are on time.
   (ii) No adjustsment if on-time deliveries are below 96 percent.

c. (i) Increased by $3,000 if sales returns are less than or equal to 1.5% of sales.
   (ii) Decreased by 50% of excess of sales returns over 1.5% of sales.

Note: If the calculation of the bonus results in a negative amount for a particular period, the manager simply receives no bonus, and the negative amount is *not* carried forward to the next period.

Results for Summit's Charter Division and Mesa Division for the year 2000, the first year under the new bonus plan, follow. In the previous year, 1999, under the old bonus plan, the Charter Division manager earned a bonus of $27,060 and the Mesa Division manager, a bonus of $22,440.

	Charter Division		Mesa Division	
	January 1, 2000 to June 30, 2000	**July 1, 2000 to December 31, 2000**	**January 1, 2000 to June 30, 2000**	**July 1, 2000 to December 31, 2000**
Revenues	$4,200,000	$4,400,000	$2,850,000	$2,900,000
Operating income	$462,000	$440,000	$342,000	$406,000
On-time delivery	95.4%	97.3%	98.2%	94.6%
Rework costs	$11,500	$11,000	$6,000	$8,000
Sales returns	$84,000	$70,000	$44,750	$42,500

Required

1. Why did Harrington need to introduce these new performance measures? That is, why does Harrington need to use these performance measures in addition to the operating income numbers for the period?

2. Calculate the bonus earned by each manager for each 6-month period and for the year 2000.

3. What effect did the change in the bonus plan have on each manager's behavior? Did the new bonus plan achieve what Harrington desired? What changes, if any, would you make to the new bonus plan?

23-21 ROI, RI, EVA®. (D. Solomons, adapted) Consider the following data for the two geographical divisions of the Potomac Electric Company that operate as profit centers:

	Atlantic Division	Pacific Division
Total assets	$1,000,000	$5,000,000
Current liabilities	250,000	1,500,000
Operating income	200,000	750,000

Required

1. Calculate the ROI for each division using operating income as the measure of income and using total assets as the measure of investment.

2. Potomac Electric has used RI as a measure of management performance, the variable it wants a manager to maximize. Using this criterion, what is the RI for each division using operating income and total assets, if the required rate of return on investment is 12 percent?

3. Potomac Electric has two sources of funds: long-term debt with a market value of $3,500,000 and an interest rate of 10%, and equity capital with a market value of $3,500,000 at a cost of equity of 14 percent. Potomac's income tax rate is 40 percent. Potomac applies the same weighted-average cost of capital to both divisions, since each division faces similar risks. Calculate the EVA® for each division. Which of the measures calculated in requirements 1, 2, and 3 would you recommend Potomac Electric use? Why? Explain briefly.

23-22 RI, EVA®. The Burlingame Transport Company operates two divisions, a Truck Rental Division that rents to individuals, and a Transportation Division that transports goods from one city to another. Results reported for the last year are as follows:

	Truck Rental Division	Transportation Division
Total assets	$650,000	$950,000
Current liabilities	120,000	200,000
Operating income	75,000	160,000

Required

1. Calculate the RI for each division using operating income and investment equal to total assets minus current liabilities. The required rate of return on investment is 12 percent.

2. The company has two sources of funds: long-term debt with a market value of $900,000 at an interest rate of 10% and equity capital with a market value of $600,000 at a cost of equity of 15 percent. Burlingame's income tax rate is 40 percent. Burlingame applies the same weighted-average cost of capital to both divisions, since each division faces similar risks. Calculate the EVA® for each division.

3. Using your answers to requirements 1 and 2, what would you conclude about the performance of each division? Explain briefly.

23-23 ROI, RI, measurement of assets. (CMA, adapted) Ashton Corporation recently announced a bonus plan to be awarded to the manager of the most profitable division. The three division managers are to choose whether ROI or RI will be used to measure profitability. In addition, they must decide whether investment will be measured using gross book value or net book value of assets. Ashton defines income as operating income and investment as total assets. The following information is available for the year just ended:

Division	Gross Book Value of Assets	Accumulated Depreciation	Division Operating Income
Bristol	$800,000	$430,000	$94,700
Darden	760,000	410,000	91,700
Gregory	500,000	280,000	61,400

Ashton uses a required rate of return of 10% on investment to calculate RI.

Required

Each division manager has selected a method of bonus calculation that ranks his or her division Number 1. Identify the method for calculating profitability that each manager selected, supporting your answer with appropriate calculations.

23-24 Multinational performance measurement, ROI, RI. The Sandvik Corporation manufactures electric motors in the United States and Sweden. The U.S. and Swedish operations are organized as decentralized divisions. The following information is available for 2000 where ROI is calculated as operating income divided by total assets:

	U.S. Division	Swedish Division
Operating income	?	9,180,000 kronas
Total assets	$8,000,000	60,000,000 kronas
ROI	15%	?

The exchange rate at the time of Sandvik's investment in Sweden on December 31, 1999 was 8 kronas = $1. During 2000, the Swedish krona declined steadily in value so that the exchange rate on December 31, 2000 is 9 kronas = $1. The average exchange rate during 2000 is $[(8 + 9) \div 2] = 8.5$ kronas = $1.

Required

1. a. Calculate the U.S. division's operating income for 2000.
   b. Calculate the Swedish division's ROI for 2000 in kronas.
2. Senior management wants to know which division earned a better ROI in 2000. What would you tell them? Explain your answer.
3. Which division do you think had the better RI performance? Explain your answer. The required rate of return on investment (calculated in U.S. dollars) is 12 percent.

23-25 Multinational performance measurement, ROI, RI. Loren Press has two printing presses that operate as separate divisions, one located in Durham, North Carolina, and the other in Lyon, France. The following information is available for 2001. The required rate of return on investments is 15 percent.

	Durham Division	Lyon Division
Operating income	$765,000	3,600,000 francs
Total assets	$4,500,000	20,000,000 francs

Both investments were made on December 31, 2000. The exchange rate at the time of Loren's investment in France on December 31, 2000, was 4 francs = $1. During 2001, the French franc declined steadily in value reaching an exchange rate on December 31, 2001, of 5 francs = $1. The average exchange rate during 2001 is $[(4 + 5) \div 2] = 4.5$ francs = $1.

Required

1. (a) Calculate Durham Division's ROI for 2001. (b) Calculate Lyon Division's ROI for 2001 in French francs. (c) Which division earned a better ROI in 2001? Explain.
2. Senior management wants to compare the performance of the two divisions using RI. Which division do you think had the better RI performance? Explain your answer.
3. On the basis of your answers to requirements 1 and 2, which division is performing better? If you had to promote one of the division managers to vice president, which manager would you choose? Explain.

23-26 Risk sharing, incentives, benchmarking, multiple tasks. The Dexter Division of AMCO sells car batteries. AMCO's corporate management gives Dexter management considerable operating and investment autonomy in running the division. AMCO is considering how it should compensate Jim Marks, the general manager of the Dexter Division. Proposal 1 calls for paying Marks a fixed salary. Proposal 2 calls for paying Marks no salary and compensating him only on the basis of the division's ROI, calculated based on operating income before any bonus payments. Proposal 3 calls for paying Marks some salary and some bonus based on ROI. Assume that Marks does not like bearing risk.

Required

1. Evaluate the three proposals, specifying the advantages and disadvantages of each.
2. Suppose that AMCO competes against Tiara Industries in the car battery business. Tiara is approximately the same size and operates in a business environment that is similar to Dexter's. The senior management of AMCO is considering evaluating Marks on the basis of Dexter's ROI minus Tiara's ROI. Marks complains that this approach is unfair because the performance of another company, over which he has no control, is included in his performance evaluation measure. Is Marks's complaint valid? Why or why not?
3. Now suppose that Marks has no authority for making capital investment decisions. Corporate management makes these decisions. Is ROI a good performance measure to use to evaluate Marks? Is ROI a good measure to evaluate the economic viability of the Dexter Division? Explain.
4. Dexter's salespersons are responsible for selling and providing customer service and support. Sales are easy to measure. Although customer service is important to Dexter in the long run, it has not yet implemented customer-service measures. Marks wants to compensate his salesforce only on the basis of sales commissions paid for each unit of product sold. He cites two advantages to this plan: (a) It creates strong incentives for the salesforce to work hard, and (b) the company pays salespersons only when the company itself is earning revenues. Do you like his plan? Why or why not?

PROBLEMS

23-27 Relevant costs, performance evaluation, goal congruence. (N. Melumad, adapted) Pike Enterprises has three operating divisions. The managers of these divisions are evaluated on their division operating income, a figure that includes an allocation of corporate overhead proportional to the revenues of each division. The operating income statement (in thousands) for the first quarter of 2001 is as follows:

	Andorian Division	Orion Division	Tribble Division	Pike Enterprises
Revenues	$2,000	$1,200	$1,600	$4,800
Cost of goods sold	1,050	540	640	2,230
Gross margin	950	660	960	2,570
Division overhead	250	125	160	535
Corporate overhead	400	240	320	960
Division operating income	$ 300	$ 295	$ 480	$1,075

John Moore, the manager of the Andorian Division, is unhappy that his profitability is about the same as the Orion Division's and is much less than the Tribble Division's, even though his revenues are much higher than either of these divisions. Moore also knows that he is carrying one line of products with low profitability. He was going to replace this line of business as soon as more profitable product opportunities became available, but he has kept it because the line is marginally profitable and uses facilities that would otherwise be idle. Moore now realizes, however, that the sales from this product line are attracting a fair amount of corporate overhead because of the allocation procedure in use. This low-margin line of products had the following characteristics (in thousands) for the most recent quarter:

Revenues	$800
Cost of goods sold	600
Avoidable division overhead	100

Required

1. Prepare the income statement for Pike Enterprises for the second quarter of 2001. Assume that revenues and operating results are identical to the first quarter except that Moore has dropped the low-margin product line.
2. Is Pike Enterprises better off from dropping the low-margin product line?
3. Is Moore better off from dropping the low-margin product line?

4. Suggest changes for Pike's system of division reporting and evaluation that will motivate division managers to make decisions that are in the best interest of Pike Enterprises as a whole. Discuss any potential disadvantages of your proposal.

23-28 Historical-cost and current-cost ROI measures. Nobillo Corporation owns and manages convenience stores. The following information on three stores is collected for the year 2000:

	City Plaza	South Station	Central Park
Operating income	$ 90,000	$120,000	$ 60,000
Investment at historical cost	$300,000	$500,000	$240,000
Investment at current cost	$600,000	$700,000	$450,000
Age of store	10 years	5 years	8 years

Required
1. Compute the ROI for each store where investment is measured at (a) historical cost, and (b) current cost.
2. How would you judge the performance of each store?

23-29 ROI performance measures based on historical cost and current cost. Mineral Waters Ltd. operates three divisions that process and bottle sparkling mineral water. The historical-cost accounting system reports the following information for 2001:

	Calistoga Division	Alpine Springs Division	Rocky Mountains Division
Revenues	$500,000	$ 700,000	$1,100,000
Operating costs (excluding depreciation)	300,000	380,000	600,000
Plant depreciation	70,000	100,000	120,000
Operating income	$130,000	$ 220,000	$ 380,000
Current assets	$200,000	$ 250,000	$ 300,000
Long-term assets—plant	140,000	900,000	1,320,000
Total assets	$340,000	$1,150,000	$1,620,000

Mineral Waters estimates the useful life of each plant to be 12 years with a zero terminal disposal price. The straight-line depreciation method is used. At the end of 2001, the Calistoga plant is 10 years old, the Alpine Springs plant is 3 years old, and the Rocky Mountains plant is 1 year old.

An index of construction costs for the 10-year period that Mineral Waters has been operating (1991 year-end = 100) is:

1991	1998	2000	2001
100	136	160	170

Given the high turnover of current assets, management believes that the historical-cost and current-cost measures of current assets are approximately the same.

Required
1. Compute the ROI ratio (operating income to total assets) of each division using historical-cost measures. Comment on the results.
2. Use the approach in Exhibit 23-2 (p. 833) to compute the ROI of each division, incorporating current-cost estimates as of 2001 for depreciation and long-term assets. Comment on the results.
3. What advantages might arise from using current-cost asset measures as compared with historical-cost measures for evaluating the performance of the managers of the three divisions?

23-30 Evaluating managers, ROI, value-chain analysis of cost structure. User Friendly Computer is one of the largest personal computer companies in the world. The board of directors was recently (March 2001) informed that User Friendly's president, Brian Clay, was resigning to "pursue other interests." An executive search firm recommends that the board consider appointing Peter Diamond (current president of Computer Power) or Norma Provan (current president of Peach Computer). You collect the following financial information (in millions) on Computer Power and Peach Computer for 1999 and 2000:

	Computer Power		Peach Computer	
	1999	2000	1999	2000
Revenues	$400.0	$320.0	$200.0	$350.0
Costs				
R&D	36.0	16.8	18.0	43.5
Design	15.0	8.4	3.6	11.6
Production	102.0	112.0	82.8	98.6
Marketing	75.0	92.4	36.0	66.7
Distribution	27.0	22.4	18.0	23.2
Customer service	45.0	28.0	21.6	46.4
Total costs	300.0	280.0	180.0	290.0
Operating income	$100.0	$ 40.0	$ 20.0	$ 60.0
Total assets	$360.0	$340.0	$160.0	$240.0

In early 2001, a computer magazine gave Peach Computer's main product five stars, its highest rating. Computer Power's main product was given three stars, down from five stars a year ago because of customer-service problems. The computer magazine also ran an article on new-product introductions in the personal computer industry. Peach Computer received high marks for new products in 2000. Computer Power's performance was called "mediocre." One "unnamed insider" of Computer Power commented: "Our new-product cupboard is empty."

Required

1. Use the DuPont method of profitability analysis to compute the ROI of Computer Power and Peach Computer in 1999 and 2000. Comment on the results.
2. Compute the percentage of costs in each of the six business-function cost categories for Computer Power and Peach Computer in 1999 and 2000. Comment on the results.
3. Rank Diamond and Provan as potential candidates for president of User Friendly Computer. Explain your ranking.

23-31 ROI, RI, ROS, management incentives. (CMA, adapted) The Jump-Start Division (JSD) of Mason Industries manufactures go-carts and other recreational vehicles. JSD is considering building a new plant in 2001. The investment will cost $2.5 million. The expected revenues and costs for the new plant in 2001 are:

Revenues	$2,400,000
Variable costs	800,000
Fixed costs	1,120,000
Operating income	$ 480,000

JSD's ROI in 2000 is 24% and its return on sales (ROS) is 19 percent. ROI is defined as operating income divided by total assets. The bonus of Maureen Grieco, the division manager of JSD, is based on division ROI.

Required

1. Explain why Grieco would be reluctant to build the new plant. Show your computations.
2. Suppose Mason Industries used RI to determine Grieco's bonus. Suppose further that the required rate of return on investment is 15 percent. Would Grieco be more willing to build the new plant? Explain.
3. Suppose Mason Industries used ROS to determine Grieco's bonus. Would Grieco be more willing to build the new plant? What are the advantages and disadvantages of using ROS to determine Grieco's bonus.

23-32 Division manager's compensation, risk sharing, incentives (continuation of 23-31). The management of Mason Industries is considering the following alternative compensation arrangements for Maureen Grieco, the division manager of JSD:

- Make Grieco's compensation a fixed salary without any bonus. Mason's management believes that one advantage of this arrangement is that Grieco will be less inclined to reject future investments just because of their impact on ROI or RI.

- Make all of Grieco's compensation depend on the division's RI. The benefit of this arrangement is that it creates incentives for Grieco to aggressively seek and accept all proposals that increase JSD's RI.

- Evaluate Grieco's performance using benchmarking by comparing JSD's RI against the RI achieved by managers of other companies that also manufacture and sell go-carts and recreational vehicles and have comparable levels of investment. Mason's management believes that the advantage of benchmarking is that it focuses attention on Grieco's performance relative to peers rather than on the division's absolute performance.

Required
1. Assume Grieco is risk averse and does not like bearing risk. Using concepts of performance evaluation described in this chapter, evaluate the three proposals that Mason's management is considering. Indicate the positive and negative features of each proposal.
2. What compensation arrangement would you recommend? Explain briefly.

23-33 ROI, RI, investment decisions. The Media Group has three major divisions:

a. Newspapers—owns leading newspapers on four continents

b. Television—owns major television networks on three continents

c. Film studios—owns one of the five largest film studios in the world

Summary financial data (in millions) for 1999 and 2000 are as follows:

	Operating Income		Revenues		Total Assets	
	1999	**2000**	**1999**	**2000**	**1999**	**2000**
Newspapers	$900	$1,100	$4,500	$4,600	$4,400	$4,900
Television	130	160	6,000	6,400	2,700	3,000
Film studios	220	200	1,600	1,650	2,500	2,600

Division managers have an annual bonus plan based on division ROI. ROI is defined as operating income divided by total assets. Senior executives from divisions reporting increases in ROI from the prior year are automatically eligible for a bonus. Senior executives of divisions reporting a decline in the division ROI have to provide persuasive explanations for the decline to be eligible for a limited bonus.

Ken Kearney, manager of the Newspapers Division, is considering a proposal to invest $200 million in fast-speed printing presses with color-print options. The estimated increment to 2001 operating income would be $30 million. The Media Group has a 12% required rate of return for investments in all three divisions.

Required
1. Use the DuPont method of profitability analysis to explain differences among the three divisions in their division ROI for 2000. Use total assets in 2000 as the investment base.
2. Why might Kearney be less than enthusiastic about the fast-speed printing press investment proposal?
3. Rupert Prince, chairman of the Media Group, receives a proposal to base senior executive compensation at each division on division RI. Compute the RI of each division in 2000.
4. Would adoption of an RI measure reduce Kearney's reluctance to adopt the fast-speed printing press investment proposal?

23-34 Division managers' compensation (continuation of 23-33). Rupert Prince seeks your advice on revising the existing bonus plan for division managers of the Media Group. Assume division managers do not like bearing risk. He is considering three ideas:

- Make each division manager's compensation depend on division ROI.

- Make each division manager's compensation depend on companywide ROI.

- Use benchmarking, and compensate division managers on the basis of their division's ROI minus the average ROI of the other two divisions.

Required

Evaluate the three ideas Prince has put forth using performance evaluation concepts described in this chapter. Indicate the positive and negative features of each proposal.

23-35 Ethics, manager's performance evaluation. (A. Spero, adapted) Hamilton Semiconductors manufactures specialized chips that sell for $20 each. Hamilton's manufacturing costs consist of variable costs of $2 per chip and fixed costs of $9,000,000. Hamilton also incurs $400,000 in fixed marketing costs each year.

Hamilton calculates operating income using absorption costing—that is, Hamilton calculates manufacturing costs per unit by dividing total manufacturing costs by actual production. Hamilton costs all units in inventory at this rate and expenses the costs in the income statement at the time when the units in inventory are sold. The next year, 2001, appears to be a difficult year for Hamilton. It expects to sell only 500,000 units. The demand for these chips fluctuates considerably so Hamilton usually holds minimal inventory.

Required

1. Calculate Hamilton's operating income in 2001 if Hamilton manufactures (a) 500,000 units, and (b) 600,000 units.
2. Would it be unethical for Randy Jones, the general manager of Hamilton Semiconductors, to produce more units than can be sold in order to show better operating results? Jones's compensation has a bonus component based on operating income. Explain your answer.
3. Would it be unethical for Jones to ask distributors to buy more product than they need? Hamilton follows the industry practice of booking sales when products are shipped to distributors. Explain your answer.

COLLABORATIVE LEARNING PROBLEM

23-36 ROI, RI, division manager's compensation, nonfinancial measures. Key information for the Peoria Division (PD) of Barrington industries for 2000 follows.

Revenues	$15,000,000
Operating income	1,800,000
Total assets	10,000,000

PD's managers are evaluated and rewarded on the basis of ROI defined as operating income divided by total assets. Barrington Industries expects its divisions to increase ROI each year.

The year 2001 appears to be a difficult year for PD. PD had planned new investments to improve quality but, in view of poor economic conditions, has postponed the investment. ROI for 2001 was certain to decrease had PD made the investment.

Management is now considering ways to meet its target ROI of 20% for next year. It anticipates revenues to be steady at $15,000,000 in 2001.

Required

Form groups of two or more students to complete the following requirements.

1. Calculate PD's return on sales (ROS) and ROI for 2000.
2. a By how much would PD need to cut costs in 2001 to achieve its target ROI of 20% in 2001, assuming no change in total assets between 2000 and 2001?
   b. By how much would PD need to decrease total assets in 2001 to achieve its target ROI of 20% in 2001, assuming no change in operating income between 2000 and 2001?
3. Calculate PD's RI in 2000 assuming a required rate of return on investment of 15 percent.
4. PD wants to increase RI by 50% in 2001. Assuming it could cut costs by $45,000 in 2001, by how much would PD have to decrease total assets in 2001?
5. Barrington Industries is concerned that the focus on cost cutting and asset sales will have an adverse long-run effect on PD's customers. Yet Barrington wants PD to meet its financial goals. What other measurements, if any, do you recommend that Barrington use? Explain briefly.

DELL COMPUTER CORPORATION
Cost Accounting Fundamentals and Job Costing

What does it cost to produce a computer for a customer? What are the activity centers for manufacturing, and how well are we managing them? How can we improve corporate performance? These are just a few of the questions managers at Dell Computer Corporation are called upon to answer. In most cases, the source of their replies can be traced back to the company's internal accounting systems, which collect data on the many aspects of Dell's operations and provide information that managers use to answer questions and make decisions.

Dell Computer Corporation, headquartered in Austin, Texas, is a global computer manufacturing company. Dell does not make computer components, such as processor chips or disk drives, but instead focuses on the assembly of the components into computers that are distributed and sold worldwide. Dell produces four categories of personal computers: (1) the Optiplex line of high-end desktop computers, (2) the Dimension line of value-priced computers, (3) notebook computers, and (4) network servers. The company's manufacturing facilities (located in Austin, Texas; Ireland; and Malaysia) serve customers around the globe from these locations. Each computer is built to customer order, so no finished goods inventory exists at Dell. Raw materials inventory is turned over every 30 days.

Dell's goal is to fill each customer's order in an average of five to six days. Each computer in an order is considered a separate job because the total cost of the components that make up each unit will vary, based on the customer's specifications. For example, costs are tracked to the computer unit level and include direct materials, direct labor, and a standard manufacturing overhead rate. The manufacturing overhead rate is developed in conjunction with Dell's Engineering Group, based upon cost levels in its product manufacturing work cells or "mods." The overhead rates are revised every quarter. Product assembly mods are responsible for computer unit assembly, including putting together individual unit direct materials and testing the components in each computer. Fully assembled and tested units pass out of each assembly mod to the shipping mod, where they are packed and prepared for shipment to the customer.

To remain competitive, Dell maintains a Product Group, which is responsible for research and development of new product ideas. This group works in conjunction with its strategic partners, such as Intel Corporation, a major microprocessor chip manufacturer, to create products that can continue to meet the demands of the marketplace for more processing power and speed. New products that have the latest technology command higher margins, so Dell works hard to minimize the time it takes to develop and produce them. Often, new products are announced the same day component manufacturers unveil their new technological advances.

Dell is implementing an activity-based management system throughout its manufacturing operations. Six cost pools have been identified: receiving, preparation and part kitting, assembly, testing, packaging, and shipping. Managers hope that focusing on these cost pools will achieve even tighter control and reduction of product costs. Work is underway to identify indirect costs down to a work cell (mod) level. Currently, indirect facility costs are allocated at the facility level, warehousing costs for raw materials are allocated based on the number of component parts in each computer, and engineering costs are allocated on a units of production basis.

QUESTIONS

1. Using the seven-step approach to job costing, give an overview of manufacturing costs for Dell Computer Corporation.
2. What kinds of journal entries would you expect Dell to make as part of its job-costing system?
3. Identify the events composing Dell's value chain. In which activities would you expect to find Dell adding the most value? Why?
4. Give examples of Dell's costs that would be considered (1) inventoriable costs, and (2) noninventoriable costs.
5. Dell Computer Corporation is implementing an activity-based management system in its manufacturing operations as a step toward activity-based product costing. Cost pools, as described in this case, have been identified. Describe what steps should be taken next by Dell to complete their transition to activity-based costing.

Video Case 2

DELL COMPUTER CORPORATION
Activity-Based Costing

When Dell Computer Corporation embarked on its activity-based costing (ABC) change initiative in 1994, few managers knew quite what to expect. The Austin, Texas-based maker of made-to-order personal computers had "hit a wall", according to Ken Hashman, Director of Service Logistics. Net revenues for 1994 were $2.87 billion, but the year ended with a #35.8 million loss. The company was poised for tremendous growth, yet managers weren't sure which products and markets were going to produce the greatest profitability. Managers needed to know which product lines were driving profits and which ones were not.

So, when management chose to implement an activity-based costing system, few people were resistant to the idea. In fact, Dell managers were quick to recognize the value of better product cost information and wanted to work the details of implementing ABC in dozens of areas. In reflecting on this enthusiasm, Ken Hashman noted that the company actually had to pull back at first to get managers to focus on "the critical few" areas that held the greatest promise for big gains.

To begin the ABC process, cross-functional employee teams identified about ten key activities. The activities mirror the logical flow of production, starting with inbound freight and duty, receiving, parts issuance, assembly, shipping, outbound distribution, and warranty. The assembly activity was further broken down for different product lines.

When it came time to estimate total indirect costs of the activities, the Dell teams went to work gathering data. Cost driver identification followed indirect cost estimation. Some of the cost drivers required rethinking by managers. For example, the Purchasing function supports all product lines, and acquires hundreds of parts for the computer assembly process. The cost of acquiring a part, whether that part costs $1.00 or $100.00 is pretty much the same. So, the number of part numbers for each line of business became relevant. Before ABC, the cost of the Purchasing function was simply part of overhead and not identified with individual product lines.

Total cost driver quantities were collected through Dell's internal computer information system. Initially, spreadsheets were used to create the ABC models and analyze the data collected about the cost drivers. The spreadsheets made it easy to create the formulas to calculate the estimated indirect costs for each activity. The spreadsheets were also used to allocate the cost of activities to cost objects, such as different computer lines, based on the actual quantities used.

Five years later, the effort literally has paid off. Net revenues for fiscal year 1998 were $12.3 billion, an increase of 329% from 1994. Net income for 1998 topped $944 million. Even more significant, managers now say they have a much better understanding of where the company makes money, and where it doesn't. John Jonez, Vice President and Controller Dell Americas Operations says it best. "Activity-based costing has really allowed Dell to go to the next level of understanding the profitability of each product it sells." Through the efforts of Dell's teams, managers can use the resulting ABC information to perform activity-based management to truly affect profitability and decision-making.

QUESTIONS

1. Why did Dell use cross-functional teams to identify company activities?

2. Prior to implementing activity-based costing and activity-based management, Dell used a simple job costing model. How does job costing differ from activity-based costing, and why was it important for Dell to make this change? What did Dell risk by not making such a change?

3. Dell focused its initial ABC efforts on approximately ten key activities. Was this a good decision? Why or why not?

RITZ-CARLTON HOTEL COMPANY
Budgets and Responsibility Accounting

Video Case 3

"Ladies and gentlemen serving ladies and gentlemen." That's the motto of the Ritz-Carlton, based in Atlanta, Georgia, a region known for southern hospitality and old-fashioned elegance. It may seem a bit indiscreet, then, to talk about such mundane topics as costs and budgets when referring to the activities of the hotel. Yet it is precisely the attention given to these items that helps make the company so successful.

Each hotel's performance is the responsibility of the general manager and controller at each of thirty-one worldwide locations. Local forecasts and budgets are prepared annually and are the basis of subsequent performance evaluation. Preparation of the annual budget begins with the sales budget, prepared by the hotel's sales director. Budgeted sources of revenue include hotel rooms; convention, wedding, and meeting facilities; merchandise; and food and beverage. The controller then seeks input from all employees, from maintenance staff to kitchen workers, about anticipated payroll changes, operating expenses, and planned events or promotions that might affect costs. Standard costs, based on cost per occupied room, are used to build the budget for guest room stays. Other standards are used for meeting rooms and food and beverage. After employee input is provided, the completed sales budget and annual operating budget are sent to corporate headquarters. From there, actual monthly performance against plan is monitored. Each property is allowed a five percent variance in profitability goals each month and must provide explanations when targets are not met.

On the twenty-fifth of each month, budgets for the next three months are reviewed to be sure goals are still accurate. Accuracy can be critical for a business whose occupancy can fluctuate significantly from day to day, depending on group or company bookings, special events, or changes in local competition. The changes are communicated to corporate headquarters, with explanations of revisions provided as needed. Local hotel managers also meet daily to review performance to date and have the ability to adjust prices in the reservation system at any time to make sure profitability targets are met. Adjusting prices can be particularly important if a large group cancels at the last minute, or if other unforeseen events cause occupancy to drop suddenly.

Meeting the monthly budgeted goals is primarily the responsibility of each hotel's controller. The controller at each location receives a monthly report from corporate headquarters that shows how all thirty-one hotels performed against their goals. Controllers compare their performance against their own budgets, as well as comparing actual performance against the other hotel properties. Ideas for boosting revenues and reducing costs are regularly shared among the company's controllers, who recognize the value of contributing to the entire organization's success, not just their own.

QUESTIONS

1. How would you expect the Ritz-Carlton to develop its standard costs per occupied room? How would these standards differ among locations?

2. The Ritz-Carlton recently started giving all employees the chance to meet with the controller to review budgets and reports on actual performance, as a form of participatory budgeting. What advantages or disadvantages do you see with this approach?

3. How might the Ritz-Carlton use benchmarking within its own chain to improve efficiency?

4. What factors might affect the Ritz-Carlton's annual sales forecast for room occupancy? For restaurants? For use of meeting rooms and conference facilities?

5. How is uncertainty handled in the budget process?

6. The Ritz-Carlton uses responsibility accounting for its worldwide hotel and resort operations. What levels of responsibility reports would you expect to see throughout the company?

Video Case 4

McDONALD'S CORPORATION
Flexible Budgets, Standards, and Variances

The store manager at the new McDonald's restaurant in north Phoenix, Arizona, doesn't spend much time thinking about cost accounting. But that doesn't mean he's not familiar with the concepts. Instead, he's busy living them, every minute of the workday, at his busy store.

At the core of every McDonald's store manager's training is an in-depth education in store operations that has cost accounting fundamentals at the center. Surprised? Think about it. Why do you suppose a Big Mac is the same every time it's served, whether it is purchased in Detroit, Dallas, or Denver? The simple answer is "standards." Customers have come to expect a certain level of quality, service, cleanliness, and value in every restaurant, every time they visit. McDonald's simply calls it "QSCV." Those expectations can be traced back to the high standards McDonald's sets for its stores, which tie back to cost accounting.

Jerry Calabrese, Vice President of Accounting for McDonald's, says that McDonald's has to differentiate itself in the fast food market through "great execution." To do this, licensees and store managers in each of the company's 24,800 stores compare their actual performance in QSCV against standards and budgeted levels of performance. Any difference between actual and expected levels is a variance. And variances have everything to do with cost accounting.

Let's look at two examples. Materials and labor comprise the two largest costs for McDonald's. Budgets, standards, and variances are used to control both of them at the store level. There are standard costs and quantities for every ingredient used for menu items. The costs and quantities of condiments, french fries, hamburger patties, and buns are monitored. Each store manager receives a report called the "Quality Cost Report" that contains actual food costs versus budgeted food cost standards. Of course, managers don't use the report to figure out why pickle costs are fifty cents too high at the end of the day, although they could. Instead, the Quality Cost Report focuses attention on the bigger areas of opportunity, in which larger dollar amounts are involved, by comparing the cost of the items sold to the cost of items used. One example of its use might be to highlight elevated hamburger patty costs. If the cost is way out of line, the store manager might investigate to see if cases of hamburgers are walking out the back door instead of being sold through the front.

Labor levels are carefully monitored also. For each level of expected sales, the store manager budgets a corresponding level of standard labor hours, spread across the different operational areas of the restaurant. Variances can occur here, too, when there is a difference between the standard hourly wage multiplied by the difference in actual quantity used, and the budgeted quantity of hours for the actual sales levels. So, if sales are significantly different from expected levels, either up or down, adjustments must be made to minimize the effect on both the customer and the store's profitability.

Nonfinancial measures are also monitored by store managers. One of the most challenging measures concerns cleanliness. How often is "often enough" for keeping public areas clean? According to Mr. Calabrese, if the restaurant is not clean when the next customer comes in, their perception of that restaurant and their dining experience will be marred. Store managers get feedback from customer surveys taken by "mystery shoppers," who drop in to company-owned stores without notice and rate their entire dining experience, including cleanliness.

Strict adherence to standards, along with consistent monitoring, are critical to the success of McDonald's. Although they may not call it "cost accounting" in the stores, their daily pursuit of QSCV has its roots in the time-honored and proven techniques used by organizations of all sizes and types the world over.

QUESTIONS

1. The Quality Cost Report used by store managers to monitor food costs contains the basic elements of a particular type of cost accounting report. Which report does it resemble?

2. Labor costs are carefully monitored by every McDonald's store manager. Which type of cost accounting report was described in the case? What decision might a store manager use it to make?

3. Nonfinancial measures are important to the operations of each McDonald's store. Cleanliness of public areas is one such measure. What other nonfinancial measures do you think the company has? Why do nonfinancial measures matter in cost accounting?

GRAND CANYON RAILWAY
Pricing

Video Case 5

In the high mountain country of Arizona, you can travel back to a time when the West was wild and adventure ruled the day. The Grand Canyon Railway, originally established in 1901 and re-established in 1989, offers visitors to Northern Arizona a chance to relive a piece of history aboard its vintage train. Departing once a day from the historic depot in Williams, Arizona, the train transports travelers to the south rim of the Grand Canyon, one of nature's most incredible natural landmarks. At the canyon, visitors are free to explore. They then board the train in the afternoon for the return trip to the depot.

Riders have a choice of three classes of service aboard the Grand Canyon Railway: Coach class—which features travel in fully-restored 1923 Harriman coaches, the Club car—which includes bar service, and the Chief car—offering elegant first class service. The railway also operates a gift shop, a museum, and an upscale hotel located in the historic Williams Depot complex. Because capacity in each railcar is fixed, managers rely on a wide range of information to determine the best mix of prices to charge in filling seats. For instance, data are gathered regularly about operating costs such as fuel costs, labor costs, food and beverage costs, and maintenance costs. Indirect costs, such as those for administration and the reservation center, are also captured. Peak-load pricing is practiced during the summer season (April to September), when demand for travel approaches capacity.

The railway's cost structure is heavily weighted toward fixed costs, such as depreciation on railroad track, engines, physical facilities, and administrative salaries. Pricing must cover variable costs to make a contribution toward covering these fixed costs. Costs can be driven by a number of factors. For example, unit passenger-driven costs would include those for food and beverage; unit trip-driven costs would include those for fuel, engineer, and entertainment; and facility-sustaining costs encompass advertising and railroad track costs. Understanding how costs are affected by different cost drivers is useful for making future cost predictions and setting prices.

In addition to historical costs and sales data, managers rely on monthly reports of future bookings and past travel patterns for predicting expected future behaviors. Managers analyze gross margins and look at demographic data to determine where customers come from. They also analyze data on pricing promotions to

determine which offers are best received in the marketplace and most profitable for the railway. Based on this information, managers at the Grand Canyon Railway recently reduced the number of discounts and packages offered to travelers. Although the number of passengers traveling the railway decreased by 12% from 1994 to 1995, profitability increased 67%, attributable to better management of costs and pricing.

QUESTIONS

1. What environmental and market factors might affect the Grand Canyon Railway's pricing decisions?
2. What are the implications of the Grand Canyon Railway's cost structure?
3. Because capacity on the railway is fixed each trip, what ways might managers try to fill empty seats in the Club and Chief cars on the day of departure?
4. How does offering fewer pricing packages affect Grand Canyon Railway's costs?
5. Why might it make sense for Grand Canyon Railway to attempt to increase revenues through booking tour packages including transportation, hotels, and meals?

Video Case 6

McDONALD'S CORPORATION
The Balanced Scorecard

The challenge for McDonald's Corporation is truly global—to be the world's best quick-service restaurant experience. This vision is supported by five global strategies:

1. Develop the organization's people, beginning in its restaurants

2. Foster innovation in menu, facilities, marketing, operations, and technology

3. Share best practices and leverage best people resources around the world

4. Continue to implement change in the McDonald's organization, and

5. Re-invent the quick-service restaurant category and develop other business and growth opportunities.

Decades ago, McDonald's revolutionized the restaurant business with its emphasis on quality food and fast service in a clean store environment. Founder Ray Kroc had a feeling this type of setting would be a big hit with the American public. He was right. With close to 25,000 stores in over 114 countries, the McDonald's store operating model set the standard in the industry.

Knowing its position is challenged daily, management at McDonald's has placed its stores in convenient locations. When people are hungry, McDonald's wants to be there when the first hunger pangs strike. Once in the restaurant, employee focus is directed at making each customer's experience one of quality, all the way from hassle-free service to the perception of value and store cleanliness.

There are many factors that affect the company's ability to maintain its position in the industry and fulfill its vision. These factors focus on financial performance, customers, employees, and store operational execution. Success in all areas is critical because they are all interrelated. If performance is poor in one area, such as cus-

tomer satisfaction, it could trigger poor performance in another, such as lower sales. Likewise, if employees are not committed or satisfied, it could result in poor customer satisfaction.

Performance results are provided to store managers on a monthly report called the "Store Manager Scorecard." This one-page report focuses on the four areas listed above: finance, customers, employees, and store operations. The contents of these categories are linked to McDonald's vision and strategies and contain only those items that store managers can control. For example, customer and employee satisfaction ratings are linked to developing the organization's people. The reasoning is that employees who are trained and treated well will stay with the job. Those same well-trained employees also will pay closer attention to product preparation standards so that costs are more tightly controlled. When taking customer orders, the well-trained employee could attempt to upsell customers on dessert items or larger portion sizes to boost sales. Every event and customer interaction affects store performance.

From the perspective of McDonald's management, the keys to developing and using its scorecard system have been the following guidelines. First, link performance measures to the key drivers of the business and the corporate vision. Second, create objective measures that cannot be manipulated at the store level so as to make the store's performance look better than it really is. Third, make sure any measurements are within the control of the person being evaluated and that they are attainable. For example, a target of zero turnover for a store that's been historically experiencing 100% turnover is not realistic.

Other important considerations for McDonald's include making sure the information collected and reported on the scorecard is accurate and that any discussions about performance center on actual performance. The number of areas measured also needs to be manageable, so that personnel can focus on being effective in the areas of greatest importance. Finally, McDonald's management has learned that, once the scorecard results are provided, managers must be given time to resolve the problems.

McDonald's managers are confident that the current balanced scorecard approach is appropriate for the business. But they aren't complacent. Because the business is changing, the scorecard also must change. As the vision and strategies are updated, the scorecard's measures are, too.

QUESTIONS

1. Analyze McDonald's using the five forces industry analysis tool. Which force appears strongest? Which one is the weakest? How could McDonald's management use this analysis?

2. What strategy is McDonald's pursuing? Cost leadership or production differentiation?

3. Think about the four areas on the McDonald's scorecard. If you were a store manager, what would you want included in each area and why?

NALLY & GIBSON GEORGETOWN, INC

Cost Allocation and Process Costing

Video Case 7

You drive on it, walk on it, wear it, and even brush your teeth with it. For 3 cents, you can buy 10 pounds of it. What is it? Limestone. It's a versatile natural resource found in asphalt highways, concrete sidewalks, cosmetics, and toothpaste, to name a few. Nally & Gibson Georgetown, Inc., in central Kentucky, has been a primary supplier of quality limestone products since 1955. Over the years, the company has seen many changes as its business and its local economy have matured. Its rock quarry operations are a good example of the role cost accounting can play in a process-based business.

Considered a commodity, limestone rock is extracted from Nally & Gibson's underground mine located 350 feet below the original 200-acre surface of the quarry. Limestone used to be mined on the surface, but the supply of quality surface rock has been exhausted. Engineers estimate that close to 40 million tons of good quality limestone rock still remain to be mined underground. The production process involves three primary stages. First, the rock is blasted with dynamite charges to loosen it. The large limestone rocks are loaded into 35-ton capacity trucks for transport to one of two rock-crushing plants located at the quarry. Next, the rock is dumped into a crusher, which breaks the rocks into smaller pieces. These pieces then travel by conveyer to a second crusher, where the split-off point for various sizes of rock occurs. Finally, the rocks are separated into different sizes. Filtering screens are used to separate the pieces into their respective size groupings. The different sizes of rock are carried by multiple conveyers to various stockpiles, where they can be loaded onto trucks for customers or moved to a storage pile away from the crushing plant. Nally & Gibson uses process costing to determine the cost per ton of limestone rock processed. All rock is processed in a relatively homogeneous way, and all costs are placed into a single cost pool. By this use of a single cost pool, the company can calculate an equivalent cost per ton of limestone rock.

Pricing of the quarry's thirty-six different sizes of rock is largely driven by market conditions and competitive forces. The most popular rock sizes are those with diameters of 1/4 to 3/8 inch, and they command a higher per-ton price. While the rock-crushing process produces varying sizes of rock, nothing goes to waste. Rocks that are too large to be crushed and the fine sand produced in crushing are used to fill in reclaimed surface land at the quarry. Byproducts, such as unpopular rock sizes that are unavoidable in the crushing process, are sold at lower prices as dictated by the market.

Within a 25-mile radius of Nally & Gibson are six other quarries that offer the same products. Because pricing is so competitive, managers at Nally & Gibson keep a close eye on costs to ensure operations remain profitable. Major costs for the business include depreciation on $5 million worth of equipment; labor, repair, and maintenance; fuel; transportation; and safety and environmental protection costs. The results of operations are reviewed weekly by the company's management team. The cost data have been particularly useful for identifying whether certain expenditures are within expected ranges and have given managers better information with which to maximize the quarry's profitability.

QUESTIONS

1. Which costing system would you suggest Nally & Gibson use to determine product costs?

2. Because the mining of limestone rock has an effect on the surrounding environment, what costs would you expect Nally & Gibson to incur related to maintaining and preserving the environment?

3. What quality issues might be associated with the mining and production of different rock sizes? How are costs and prices affected by these issues?

4. If Nally & Gibson called the processing plant a joint cost area, how would it use an estimated net realizable value joint costing method?

5. How might Nally & Gibson use a revenue mix variance analysis to examine profitability changes over time?

Video Case 8

RITZ-CARLTON HOTEL COMPANY
Quality

The Ritz-Carlton. The name alone evokes images of luxury and quality. At least, that's what the managers at their thirty-one hotels and resorts around the world hope. As the first hotel company ever to win the prestigious Malcolm Baldrige National Quality Award, the Ritz treats quality as more than a mere buzzword. Quality is the heartbeat of the company, and it means a daily commitment to meeting customer expectations and making sure each hotel is free of deficiency.

In the hotel industry, quality can be hard to quantify. Guests do not purchase a product when they stay at the Ritz; they buy an experience. So creating the right combination of elements to make the experience stand out is the challenge and goal of every employee, from maintenance to management.

Earning the Baldrige Award represented a major achievement for the company, but while the company was delighted to be selected, managers realized that work still remained to be done. Before applying for consideration, company management undertook a rigorous self-examination of its operations in an attempt to measure and quantify quality. Nineteen processes were studied, including room-service delivery, guest reservation and registration, message delivery, and breakfast service. This period of self-study included statistical measurement of process work flows and cycle times for areas ranging from room service delivery times and reservations, to valet parking and housekeeping efficiency. Each hotel focused on one of the nineteen areas for a year. The results were used to develop benchmarks of performance against which future activity could be measured.

With specific, quantifiable targets in place, managers at the Ritz-Carlton now focus on continuous improvement.

The goal is 100% customer satisfaction. Each hotel and resort property is run as an independent business, so the general manager at each location takes ownership for monitoring quality and taking appropriate action to prevent problems from arising or affecting a guest. Performance is reviewed at both daily and weekly management meetings, and results are communicated back to employees. After all, if a guest's experience does not meet expectations, the Ritz-Carlton risks losing a valued guest to the competition.

One way the company has put more meaning behind its quality efforts is to organize its employees into "self-directed" work teams. The teams are formed within each functional area of the hotel, such as guest services, valet services, food and beverage, housekeeping, and maintenance. Managers no longer operate in command-and-control mode, where orders are dictated and expected to be carried out. Instead, the employee teams determine employee work scheduling, what work needs to be done, and what to do about quality problems in their areas. Managers are expected to become facilitators and resources for helping the teams achieve their quality goals. Employees are also given the opportunity to take additional training about how the hotel is run, so that they can see the relationship of their specific area's efforts to the overall goals of the hotel. Training topics range from budgets and purchasing to payroll and controllable costs. Employees are then tested and compensated for successful completion of training. Ritz-Carlton expects that a more educated and informed employee will be in a better position to make decisions that are in the best interest of the organization.

QUESTIONS

1. In what ways could the Ritz-Carlton monitor its success at achieving quality?
2. Many companies say that their goal is to provide quality products or services. What actions might you expect from a company that intends quality to be more than a slogan or buzzword?
3. How does lack of quality, or missing a quality goal, affect the Ritz-Carlton's contribution margin?
4. Why might it cost the Ritz-Carlton less to "do things right" the first time?
5. How could control charts, pareto diagrams, and cause-and-effect diagrams be used to identify quality problems?
6. What are some nonfinancial measures of customer satisfaction that might be used by the Ritz-Carlton?

DEER VALLEY RESORT
Capital Budgeting Planning

Video Case 9

From the moment you arrive until your departure, you can feel the difference at Deer Valley Resort. Nestled deep in the Wasatch Mountains near Park City, Utah, this world-class ski resort strives for excellence at every turn. Each winter since the resort's opening in 1980, a growing number of skiers have chosen to experience the "Deer Valley Difference"—meticulously groomed slopes, friendly staff, and gourmet cuisine. With owners and managers eager to pamper skiers beyond expectations, a $13 million renovation of the base lodge and facilities was approved for 1995.

The project began in April of 1995 and added close to 50,000 square feet of guest service space. The number of ticket windows doubled to sixteen, child-care space was expanded, and lockers and basket check service were added. The lodge's restaurants were remodeled and expanded, and new retail and ski rental spaces were built. The project was completed in December of 1995, just in time for a full opening to the 1995–96 ski season.

So how did the renovation project come into existence? Deer Valley management follows a structured approach to capital budgeting and planning. First, management maintains a rolling 10-year capital plan. This plan contains the master list of all projects planned for funding in the next 10 years. It is updated each spring, reflecting how well the resort performed during the preceding winter season.

In the identification stage, ideas for capital projects come from each major operating department: ski school, food and beverage, mountain operations, accounting, and more. Each idea submitted must come with a description of the project, its anticipated benefits, and detailed cost estimates, including bids. During the search stage, proposed ideas are reviewed by the ski area's "Futures Committee," composed of senior management and area owners. Proposals are ranked and prioritized for funding. The final decision on how much to spend and which projects to pursue each year rests with the ski resort's general manager and owners.

The base lodge renovation was assigned a high priority in 1995 because the owners saw the direct and immediate benefit to enhancing Deer Valley's image and reputation through expanded restaurant and ski-lift services, as well as through reduced bottlenecks in guest service areas such as ticket sales and rentals.

For the information-acquisition stage in the capital budgeting process, managers considered which areas to renovate and where to add square footage to the lodge. Although preliminary plans and drawings were used to review the project for funding, management worked with architects to finalize the plans. Quantitative measures—such as

return on skier days (increased demand), speed of lift-ticket and ski-school sales, increased child-care revenues, and greater food and beverage sales—were determined. Net present value and payback periods comprised part of the analysis. Qualitative measures—such as increased customer satisfaction and enhanced resort image—were considered as well. Deer Valley regularly ranks at or near the top of ski magazine consumer surveys in these areas. Since the base lodge is such an integral part of each guest's overall impression of their ski experience, the qualitative measures carried significant weight in the final decision to fund the project made in the selection stage of the capital budgeting process.

The financing stage came next. Deer Valley routinely starts and completes its capital projects between April and December of each year, so standing lines of credit at local banks were used for funding. Resort owners expect to pay off the balance owed on the project in two years, based on increases in lift-tickets and restaurant revenues from additional skier days. With the renovation complete, a post-decision audit as part of the implementation and control stage is underway to evaluate project success and contribution to resort profitability and image.

QUESTIONS

1. What other types of capital budgeting projects would you expect Deer Valley to have in its rolling 10-year plan? If you were making the decision to allocate funds for projects, what factors would you consider in your analysis?

2. What influence might competition and the coming 2002 Winter Olympics—to be held in Park City—have on Deer Valley's capital budgeting and planning?

3. What risks do you expect Deer Valley faced with the base lodge renovation project?

4. Deer Valley Resort is a partnership. How does this form of ownership make a difference in whether to consider the tax implications of a capital budgeting project?

5. Based upon the facts in the case, was the decision to pursue this project a good one? Why or why not?

Video Case 10

McDONALD'S CORPORATION
Performance Measurement and Compensation Issues

Not long ago, McDonald's Corporation faced a challenge. Senior management wanted to revise the compensation package for managers in all 1,800 of its U.S.-based, company-owned stores. The revision was considered important to make sure the company continued to offer a competitive compensation package to managers. Senior management also was interested in tightening the linkage between its corporate vision and management incentives. The question facing management was this: how best to structure the new plan?

McDonald's was founded in 1955 upon the vision of Ray Kroc, a milkshake machine salesman of great personal ambition. On a chance visit to a restaurant in Southern California, he noted the long line of customers waiting to buy one of the store's thick shakes. If customers would come and wait at one restaurant for shakes, he reasoned, certainly they would come if there were other locations. The restaurant was owned by the McDonald's brothers. Ray Kroc approached the brothers about expanding to multiple locations, and the rest is history.

Ray Kroc built McDonald's around a new food production system that applied precise procedures that not only helped to streamline operations for efficient service, but also created a pleasant family atmosphere for dining. Standards were established for food portions, and equipment designed to prepare meals quickly. The words "quality, service, cleanliness, and value", or QSCV, stood behind every meal, every customer interaction, every day. Ray Kroc wanted each customer's restaurant experience to be the best.

The vision of being the best is still alive today at McDonald's. Managers are trained in all aspects of McDonald's operations at the company's central training center in Oak Brook, Illinois. Called Hamburger University, the facility provides intensive courses of study to help managers understand how to deliver QSCV. The managers are quite loyal to McDonald's, but the job market is competitive. McDonald's knows that its compensation scheme and incentives had better meet the expectations of its managers, or they risk losing them. So, what should be rewarded and how?

For the managers at company-owned stores in some markets, McDonald's has chosen incentives tied to performance in four areas: Operational excellence, customer satisfaction, people, and profitability. These areas are all linked to the corporate vision of being the best quick service restaurant experience, and are reported to the stores on a monthly report called a "scorecard". Managers are evaluated on the elements of the four areas that are within the direct control of the store managers. For example, McDonald's believes that taking care of its people is key to success. So, managers are given incentives to reduce turnover and increase employee commitment. For profitability, sales are important, but can't always be controlled by store managers. For example, a store located near roadway construction may see a decline in sales due to limited access. Weather also affects business. Instead, the store manager may be compensated more heavily for achieving adjusted "bottom line" targets or cost control targets, or operational excellence as measured by mystery shoppers or store performance grading. The key is linking incentive payouts to actual results. If goals are not achieved, no payouts occur. The amount of the rewards are appropriate for the effort required to achieve the desired result, so managers will feel the effort was worth it. If the rewards are presented frequently and in a timely manner, there is strong reinforcement of the actions that resulted in the performance initially, which increases the likelihood that the actions will be repeated. That's a challenge McDonald's would like all its managers to take!

QUESTIONS

1. Of the 25,000-plus stores that McDonald's operates around the globe, 1,800 of them are company-owned. Does it make sense to devise a single compensation plan for use in all locations? Why or why not?

2. Return on investment (ROI) has been used in the past as part of a store manager's performance evaluation. For company-owned stores, is this a viable measure of performance for store managers? Why or why not?

3. Put yourself in the position of a store manager at McDonald's. Since the stores operate with the same vision, should McDonald's use benchmarking and relative performance evaluation to compensation store managers? What are the benefits? Costs?

Appendix A

SURVEYS OF COMPANY PRACTICE

This appendix provides the full citations to the individual publications cited in the many Surveys of Company Practice boxes included in the text.

American Electronics Association, *Operating Ratios Survey 1993–94*, (Santa Clara, CA: American Electronics Association, 1993)—cited in Chapter 18.

APQC/CAM-I, *Activity Based Management Consortium Study* (American Productivity and Quality Center/CAM-I, 1995)—cited in Chapter 5.

Armitage, H., and R. Nicholson, "Activity-Based Costing: A Survey of Canadian Practice," Supplement to *CMA Magazine* (1993)—cited in Chapter 5.

Asada, T., J. Bailes, and M. Amano, "An Empirical Study of Japanese and American Budget Planning and Control Systems," (Working Paper, Tsukuba University and Oregon State University, 1989)—cited in Chapter 6.

Ask, U., and C. Ax, "Trends in the Development of Product Costing Practices and Techniques—A Survey of the Swedish Manufacturing Industry," (Working Paper, Gothenburg School of Economics, Gothenburg, Sweden, 1992)—cited in Chapters 7 and 9.

Atkinson, A., *Intrafirm Cost and Resource Allocations: Theory and Practice*, (Hamilton, Canada: Society of Management Accountants of Canada and Canadian Academic Accounting Association Research Monograph, 1987)—cited in Chapter 14.

Berry, L. E., and J. Scheumann. "The Controller's Good Intentions," *Financial Executive*, (January/February 1998)—cited in Chapter 1.

Blayney, P., and I. Yokoyama, "Comparative Analysis of Japanese and Australian Cost Accounting and Management Practices," (Working Paper. The University of Sydney, Sydney, Australia, 1991)—cited in chapters 2, 4, 6, 9, 12, 21, and 22.

Block, S., "Capital Budgeting Techniques Used by Small Business in the 1990's," *The Engineering Economist* (Summer 1998)—cited in Chapter 21.

Business International Corporation, 101, *More Checklists for Global Financial Management* (New York, 1992)—cited in Chapter 23.

Chenhall, R. H., and K. Langfield-Smith, "Adoption and Benefits of Management Accounting Practices: An Australian Study," *Management Accounting Research* (March 1998)—cited in Chapter 6.

Clarke, P., "Management Accounting Practices and Techniques in Irish Manufacturing Firms," (Working Paper, Trinity College, Dublin, Ireland, 1995)—cited in Chapters 7 and 22.

Clarke, P., "A Survey of Activity-Based Costing in Large Manufacturing Firms in Ireland," (Working Paper, Trinity College, Dublin, Ireland, 1996)—cited in Chapters 4 and 5.

Clarke, P. and T. ODea, "Management Accounting Systems: Some Field Evidence from Sixteen Multinational Companies in Ireland," (Working Paper, Trinity College, Dublin, Ireland, 1993)—cited in Chapter 21.

865

Cohen, J., and L. Paquette, "Management Accounting Practices: Perceptions of Controllers," *Journal of Cost Management* (Fall 1991)—cited in Chapter 4.

Cornick, M., W. Cooper, and S. Wilson, "How Do Companies Analyze Overhead," *Management Accounting* (June 1988)—cited in Chapters 7 and 12.

Cotton, W., "Activity Based Costing in New Zealand," (Working paper, SUNY Genesco, 1993)—cited in Chapter 5.

Dean, G., M. Joye, and P. Blayney, *Strategic Management Accounting Survey*, (Sydney, Australia: The University of Sydney, 1991)—cited in Chapter 14.

deWith, E., and E. Ijskes, "Current Budgeting Practices in Dutch Companies," (Working Paper, Vrije Universiteit, 1992, Amsterdam, Netherlands)—cited in Chapter 6.

Drury, C., S. Braund, P. Osborne, and M. Tayles, *A Survey of Management Accounting Practices in UK Manufacturing Companies*, (London, U.K., Chartered Association of Certified Accountants, 1993)—cited in chapters 4, 7, 8, 12, and 22.

Elliott, J., "International Transfer Pricing, A Survey of U.K. and Non-U.K. Groups," *Management Accounting*, CIMA, November 1998—cited in Chapter 22.

Foster, G. and S. M. Young, "Frontiers of Management Accounting Research," *Journal of Management Accounting Research* (1997)—cited in Chapter 16.

Fremgen, J., and S. Liao, *The Allocation of Corporate Indirect Costs* (New York: National Association of Accountants, 1981)—cited in Chapter 14.

Goldratt, E., *What Is This Thing Called the Theory of Constraints and How Should It Be Implemented?* (Croton-on-Hudson, NY: North River Press, 1990).

Govindarajan, V., and B. Ramamurthy, "Transfer Pricing Policies in Indian Companies: A Survey," *Chartered Accountant* (November 1983)—cited in Chapter 22.

Grant, Thornton, *Survey of American Manufacturers*, (New York: Grant Thornton, 1992)—cited in Chapter 12.

Hoque, Z., and M. Alam, "Organization Size, Business Objectives, Managerial Antonomy, Industry Conditions, and Management's Choice of Transfer Pricing Methods: A Contextual Analysis of New Zealand Companies," (Working Paper, Victoria University of Wellington, Wellington, New Zealand)—cited in Chapter 22.

Innes, J., and F. Mitchell, "A Survey of Activity-Based Costing in the U.K.'s Largest Companies," *Management Accounting Research* (June 1995)—cited in Chapters 5 and 16.

Inoue, S., "A Comparative Study of Recent Development of Cost Management Problems in U.S.A., U.K., Canada, and Japan," Kagawa University Economic Review (June 1988)—cited in Chapters 6, 7, and 9.

Jog, V., and A. Srivastava, "Corporate Financial Decision Making in Canada, *Canadian Journal of Administrative Sciences* (June 1994)—cited in Chapter 21.

Joye, M., and P. Blayney, "Cost and Management Accounting Practices in Australian Manufacturing Companies: Survey Results." (Accounting Research Centre, The University of Sydney, 1991)—cited in Chapters 10, 17, and 22.

Kim, I., and J. Song, "U.S., Korea, and Japan: Accounting Practices in Three Countries," *Management Accounting* (August 1990)—cited in Chapter 21.

Koester, R. J., and D. J. Barnett, "Petroleum Refinery Joint Cost Allocation" (Working paper, California State University, Dominguez Hills, 1996)—cited in Chapter 15.

Lazere, C., "All Together Now," *CFO* (February 1998)—cited in Chapter 6.

Management Accounting Research Group, "Investigation into the Actual State of Target Costing, Corporate Accounting," (Working Paper, Kobe University, Japan, May 1992)—cited in Chapter 12.

Mills, R., and C. Sweeting, "Pricing Decisions in Practice: How Are They Made in U.K. Manufacturing and Service Companies?" (London, U.K.: Chartered Institute of Management Accountants, Occasional Paper, 1988)—cited in Chapter 12.

Mostafa, A., J. Sharp, and K. Howard, "Transfer Pricing—A Survey Using Discriminant Analysis," Omega, (Vol. 12, No. 5, 1984)—cited in Chapter 22.

Mowen, M., *Accounting for Costs as Fixed and Variable* (National Association of Accountants: Montvale, NJ, 1986)—cited in Chapter 2.

NAA Tokyo Affiliate, "Management Accounting in the Advanced Manufacturing Surrounding: Comparative Study on Survey in Japan and U.S.A.," (Tokyo, Japan, 1988)—cited in Chapter 10.

Price Waterhouse, *Transfer Pricing Practices of American Industry* (New York: Price Waterhouse, 1984)—cited in Chapter 22.

Ramadan, S., "The Rationale for Cost Allocation: A Study of U.K. Divisionalised Companies," *Accounting and Business Research* (Winter 1989)—cited in Chapter 14.

Research Incorporated, "Synchronizing the Supply Chain Through Collaborative Design," (Alpharetta, Georgia, 1998)—cited in Chapter 20.

Sangster, A., "Capital Investment Appraisal Techniques: A Survey of Current Usage," *Journal of Business Finance & Accounting* (April 1993)—cited in Chapter 21.

Scarbrough, P., A. Nanni, and M. Sakurai, "Japanese Management Accounting Practices and the Effects of Assembly and Process Automation," *Management Accounting Research* (March 1991)—cited in Chapters 7 and 23.

Schlank, R., "Evaluating the Performance of International Operations," (New York: Business International Corporation, 1989)—cited in Chapter 23.

Siegel, G. and B. Kulesza, "The Practice Analysis of Management Accounting," *Management Accounting* (March 1996)—cited in Chapter 1.

Smith, K., and C. Sullivan, "Survey of Cost Management Systems in Manufacturing," (Working Paper, Purdue University, West Lafayette, Indiana, 1990)—cited in Chapters 21 and 23.

Stewart, G.B., "Eva®, Fact and Fantasy," *Journal of Applied Corporate Finance* (Summer, 1994)—cited in Chapter 23.

Tang, R., "Canadian Transfer Pricing in the 1990s," *Management Accounting* (February 1992)—cited in Chapter 22.

Tang, R., C. Walter, and R. Raymond, "Transfer Pricing—Japanese vs. American Style," *Management Accounting* (January 1979)—cited in Chapter 22.

Towers, Perrin, "CompScan Report: Inside the Balanced Scorecard," January 1996—cited in Chapter 13.

Appendix B

RECOMMENDED READINGS

The literature on cost accounting and related areas is vast and varied. The following books illustrate recent publications that capture current developments:

Ansari, S., J. Bell, and CAM-I Target Cost Core Group, *Target Costing: The Next Frontier in Strategic Cost Management.* Chicago: Irwin Professional Publishing, 1996.

Brimson, J., *Activity Accounting: An Activity-Based Costing Approach.* New York: John Wiley & Sons, 1997.

Connell, R., *Measuring Customer and Service Profitability in the Finance Sector.* London, U.K.: Chapman & Hall, 1996.

Cooper, R., and R. Kaplan, *The Design of Cost Management Systems.* Englewood Cliffs, NJ: Prentice-Hall, 1998.

Ditz, D., J. Ranganathan, and R. Banks, *Green Ledgers: Case Studies in Corporate Environmental Accounting.* World Resources Institute, 1995.

Hronec, S., *Vital Signs.* New York: American Management Association, 1993.

Johnson, T., *Relevance Regained.* New York: Free Press, 1992.

Miller, J., *Implementing Activity-Based Management in Daily Operation.* New York: John Wiley & Sons, 1996.

Player, S., and D. Keys, *Activity-Based Management.* New York: MasterMedia Limited, 1995.

Schweitzer, M., E. Trossmann, and G. Lawson, *Break-even Analyses: Basic Model, Variants, Extensions.* Chichester, U.K.: Wiley, 1992.

Shank, J., and V. Govindarajan, *Strategic Management Accounting.* New York: The Free Press, 1993.

Books of readings related to cost or management accounting include:
Aly, I., ed., *Readings in Management Accounting.* Dubuque, Iowa: Kendall/Hunt, 1995.

Brinker, B., ed., *Emerging Practices in Cost Management.* Boston, MA: Warren, Gorham, and Lamont, 1995.

Ratnatunga, J., J. Miller, N. Mudalige, and A. Sohalled, eds., *Issues in Strategic Management Accounting.* Sydney, Australia: Harcourt Brace Jovanovich, 1993.

Young, M., ed., *Readings in Management Accounting.* Englewood Cliffs, N.J.: Prentice-Hall, 1997.

The Harvard Business School series in accounting and control offers important contributions to the cost accounting literature, including:
Anthony, R., *The Management Control Function.* Boston: Harvard Business School Press, 1988.

Berliner, C., and J. Brimson, eds., *Cost Management for Todays Advanced Manufacturing: The CAMI Conceptual Design.* Boston: Harvard Business School Press, 1988.

Bruns, W., ed., *Performance Measurement, Evaluation, and Incentives.* Boston: Harvard Business School Press, 1992.

Bruns, W., and R. Kaplan, eds., *Accounting and Management: Field Study Perspectives.* Boston: Harvard Business School Press, 1987.

Cooper, R., *When Lean Enterprises Collide.* Boston: Harvard Business School Press, 1995.

Johnson, H., and R. Kaplan, *Relevance Lost: The Rise and Fall of Management Accounting.* Boston: Harvard Business School Press, 1987.

Kaplan, R., ed., *Measures for Manufacturing Excellence.* Boston: Harvard Business School Press, 1990.

Kaplan, R., and R. Cooper, *Cost and Effect.* Boston: Harvard Business School Press, 1998.

Kaplan, R., and D. P. Norton, *The Balanced Scorecard.* Boston: Harvard Business School Press, 1996.

Merchant, K.A., *Rewarding Results: Motivating Profit Center Managers.* Boston: Harvard Business School Press, 1989.

Simons R., *Levers of Control.* Boston: Harvard Business School Press, 1995.

Productivity Press publishes many books with a global focus on cost and management accounting, including:
Cooper, R., and R. Slagmulder, *Target Costing and Value Engineering.* Portland: Productivity Press, 1997.

Monden, Y., *Cost Management in the New Manufacturing Age: Innovations in the Japanese Automotive Industry.* Cambridge, MA: Productivity Press, 1993.

Sakurai, M., *Integrated Cost Management.* Portland, OR: Productivity Press, 1996.

The Institute of Management Accountants publishes monographs and books covering cost accounting topics, such as:
Atkinson, A., J. Hamburg, and C. Ittner, *Linking Quality to Profits,* Montvale, NJ: Institute of Management Accountants and Milwaukee, WI: ASQC Quality Press, 1994.

Cooper, R., R. Kaplan, L. Maisel, E. Morrissey, and R. Oehm, *Implementing Activity-Based Cost Management: Moving from Analysis to Action.* Montvale, NJ: Institute of Management Accountants, 1993.

Dhavale, D., *Management Accounting Issues in Cellular Manufacturing and Focused-Factory Systems.* Montvale, NJ: Institute of Management Accountants, 1996.

Epstein, M., *Measuring Corporate Environmental Performance.* Montvale, NJ: IMA Foundation of Applied Research, 1995.

Klammer, T., *Managing Strategic and Capital Investment Decisions.* Burr Ridge, IL: Irwin and IMA, 1994.

Martinson, O., *Cost Accounting in the Service Industry.* Montvale, NJ: Institute of Management Accountants, 1994.

Noreen, E., D. Smith, and J.T. Mackey, *The Theory of Constraints and Its Implications for Management Accounting.* Great Barrington, MA: North River Press, 1995.

The Financial Executives Research Foundation publishes monographs and books concerning topics of interest to financial executives, such as:
Howell, R., J. Shank, S. Soucy, and J. Fisher, *Cost Management for Tomorrow: Seeking the Competitive Edge.* Morristown, NJ: Financial Executives Research Foundation, 1992.

Keating, P., and S. Jablonsky, *Changing Roles of Financial Management.* Morristown, NJ: Financial Executives Research Foundation, 1990.

The Chartered Institute of Management Accountants, London, U.K., publishes monographs and books, including:

Drury, C., ed., *Management Accounting Handbook*. London, U.K.: Butterworth Heinemann and Chartered Institute of Management Accountants, 1997.

Ezzamel, M., C. Green, S. Lilley, and H. Willmott, *Changing Managers and Managing Change*. London, UK: Chartered Institute of Management Accountants, 1995.

Friedman, A., and S. Lylne, *Activity-Based Techniques: The Real Life Consequences*. London, UK: Chartered Institute of Management Accountants, 1995.

Murphy, C., J. Currie, M. Fahy, and W. Golden, *Deciding the Future: Management Accountants as Decision Support Personnel*. London, UK: Chartered Institute of Management Accountants, 1995.

Ward, K., *Strategic Management Accounting*. Oxford, U.K.: Butterworth Heinemann and Chartered Institute of Management Accountants, 1992.

Jai Press publishes *Advances in Management Accounting* on an annual basis. It is edited by M. Epstein and K. Poston and includes a broad cross-section of research articles and case studies.

Case books on cost and management accounting include:

Rotch, W., B. Allen, and E. Brownlee, *Cases in Management Accounting and Control Systems*. Englewood Cliffs, NJ: PrenticeHall, 1995.

Shank, J., *Cases in Cost Management: A Strategic Emphasis*. Cincinnati, Ohio: South Western Publishing, 1996.

The following are detailed annotated bibliographies of the cost and management accounting research literatures:

Clancy, D., *Annotated Management Accounting Readings*. Management Accounting Section of the American Accounting Association, 1986.

Deakin, E., M. Maher, and J. Cappel, *Contemporary Literature in Cost Accounting*. Homewood, IL: Richard D. Irwin, 1988.

Klemstine, C., and M. Maher, *Management Accounting Research: 1926–1983*. New York: Garland Publishing, 1984.

The *Journal of Cost Management for the Manufacturing Industry* contains numerous articles on modern management accounting. It is published by Warren, Gorham, and Lamont, 210 South Street, Boston, MA 02111.

Two journals bearing on management accounting are published by sections of the American Accounting Association, 5717 Bessie Drive, Sarasota, FL 34233: *Journal of Management Accounting Research and Behavioral Research in Accounting*.

Professional associations that specialize in serving members with cost and management accounting interests include:

◆ *Institute of Management Accountants*, 10 Paragon Drive, P.O. Box 433, Montvale, NJ 07645. Publishes the *Management Accounting* journal.

◆ *Financial Executives Institute*, 10 Madison Avenue, P.O. Box 1938, Morristown, NJ 07960. Publishes *Financial Executive*.

◆ *Society of Cost Estimating and Analysis*, 101 South Whiting Street, Suite 313, Alexandria, VA 22304. Publishes the *Journal of Cost Analysis* and monographs related to cost estimation and price analysis in government and industry.

◆ *The Institute of Internal Auditors*, 249 Maitland Avenue, Altamonte Springs, FL 32701. Publishes *The Internal Auditor* journal. Also publishes monographs on topics related to internal control.

◆ *Society of Management Accountants of Canada*, 154 Main Street East, MPO Box 176, Hamilton, Ontario, L8N 3C3. Publishes the *CMA Magazine*.

◆ *The Chartered Institute of Management Accountants*, 63 Portland Place, London, WIN 4AB. Publishes the *Management Accounting* journal. Also publishes monographs covering cost and managerial accounting topics.

In many countries, individuals with cost and management accounting interests belong to professional bodies that serve members with financial reporting and taxation, as well as cost and management accounting, interests.

Appendix C

NOTES ON COMPOUND INTEREST AND INTEREST TABLES

Interest is the cost of using money. It is the rental charge for funds, just as renting a building and equipment entails a rental charge. When the funds are used for a period of time, it is necessary to recognize interest as a cost of using the borrowed ("rented") funds. This requirement applies even if the funds represent ownership capital and if interest does not entail an outlay of cash. Why must interest be considered? Because the selection of one alternative automatically commits a given amount of funds that could otherwise be invested in some other alternative.

Interest is generally important, even when short-term projects are under consideration. Interest looms correspondingly larger when long-run plans are studied. The rate of interest has significant enough impact to influence decisions regarding borrowing and investing funds. For example, $100,000 invested now and compounded annually for 10 years at 8% will accumulate to $215,900; at 20%, the $100,000 will accumulate to $619,200.

INTEREST TABLES

Many computer programs and pocket calculators are available that handle computations involving the time value of money. You may also turn to the following four basic tables to compute interest.

Table 1—Future Amount of $1

Table 1 shows how much $1 invested now will accumulate in a given number of periods at a given compounded interest rate per period. Consider investing $1,000 now for three years at 8% compound interest. A tabular presentation of how this $1,000 would accumulate to $1,259.70 follows:

Year	Interest per Year	Cumulative Interest Called Compound Interest	Total at End of Year
0	$ —	$ —	$1,000.00
1	80.00	80.00	1,080.00
2	86.40	166.40	1,166.40
3	93.30	259.70	1,259.70

This tabular presentation is a series of computations that could appear as follows:

$$S_1 = \$1,000(1.08)^1$$

$$S_2 = \$1,000(1.08)^2$$

$$S_3 = \$1,000(1.08)^3$$

The formula for the "amount of 1," often called the "future value of $1" of "future amount of $1," can be written

$$S = P(1 + r)^n$$

$$S = \$1,000(1 + .08)^3 = \$1,259.70$$

S is the future value amount; P is the present value, $1,000 in this case; r is the rate of interest; and n is the number of time periods.

Fortunately, tables make key computations readily available. A facility in selecting the *proper* table will minimize computations. Check the accuracy of the preceding answer using Table 1, p. 875.

Table 2 — Present Value of $1

In the previous example, if $1,000 compounded at 8% per year will accumulate to $1,259.70 in 3 years, then $1,000 must be the present value of $1,259.70 due at the end of 3 years. The formula for the present value can be derived by reversing the process of *accumulation* (finding the future amount) that we just finished.

$$S = P(1 + r)n$$

If

$$P = \frac{S}{(1 + r)^n}$$

then

$$P = \frac{\$1,259.70}{(108)^3} = \$1,000$$

Use Table 2, p. 876, to check this calculation.

When accumulating, we advance or roll forward in time. The difference between our original amount and our accumulated amount is called *compound interest.* When discounting, we retreat or roll back in time. The difference between the future amount and the present value is called *compound discount.* Note the following formulas (where $P = \$1,000$):

$$\text{Compound interest} = P[(1 + r)^n - 1] = \$259.70$$

$$\text{Compound discount} = S\left[1 - \frac{1}{(1 + r)^n}\right] = \$259.70$$

Table 3 — Amount of Annuity of $1

An (ordinary) *annuity* is a series of equal payments (receipts) to be paid (or received) at the end of successive periods of equal length. Assume that $1,000 is invested at the end of each of 3 years at 8%:

End of Year		Amount
1st payment	$1,000.00 ➤ $1,080.00 ➤	$1,166.40, which is $1,000(1.08)^2
2nd payment	$1,000.00 ➤	1,080.00, which is $1,000(1.08)^1
3rd payment		1,000.00
Accumulation (future amount)		$3,246.40

The preceding arithmetic may be expressed algebraically as the amount of an ordinary annuity of $1,000 for 3 years = $1,000(1 + r)^2 + $1,000(1 + r)^1 + $1,000. We can develop the general formula for S_n, the amount of an ordinary annuity of $1, by using the example above as a basis:

1. $S_n = 1 + (1 + r)^1 + (1 + r)^2$
2. Substitute: $S_n = 1 + (1.08)^1 + (1.08)^2$
3. Multiply (2) by (1 + r): $(1.08)S_n = (1.08)^1 + (1.08)^2 + (1.08)^3$

4. Subtract (2) from (3): $\quad 1.08 S_n - S_n = (1.08)^3 - 1$
   Note that all terms on
   the right-hand side are
   removed except $(1.08)^3$
   in equation (3) and 1
   in equation (2).

5. Factor (4): $\quad S_n(1.08 - 1) = (1.08)^3 - 1$

6. Divide (5) by $(1.08 - 1)$: $\quad S_n = \dfrac{(1.08)^3 - 1}{1.08 - 1} = \dfrac{(1.08)^3 - 1}{.08}$

7. The general formula for
   the amount of an ordi-
   nary annuity of $1
   becomes: $\quad S_n = \dfrac{(1 + r)^n - 1}{r} \text{ or } \dfrac{\text{Compound interest}}{\text{Rate}}$

This formula is the basis for Table 3, p. 877. Look at Table 3 or use the formula itself to check the calculations.

Table 4—Present Value of an Ordinary Annuity of $1

Using the same example as for Table 3, we can show how the formula of P_n, *the present value of an ordinary annuity*, is developed.

End of Year		0	1	2	3

1st payment $\quad \dfrac{1,000}{(1.08)^1} = \$ \ 926.14 \longleftarrow \$1,000$

2nd payment $\quad \dfrac{1,000}{(1.08)^2} = \$ \ 857.52 \longleftarrow \$1,000$

3rd payment $\quad \dfrac{1,000}{(1.08)^3} = \$ \ 794.00 \longleftarrow \$1,000$

Total present value $\quad \underline{\$2,577.66}$

For the general case, the present value of an ordinary annuity of $1 may be expressed as:

1. $\quad P_n = \dfrac{1}{1 + r} + \dfrac{1}{(1 + r)^2} + \dfrac{1}{(1 + r)^3}$

2. Substitute $\quad P_n = \dfrac{1}{1.08} + \dfrac{1}{(1.08)^2} + \dfrac{1}{(1.08)^3}$

3. Multiply by $\dfrac{1}{1.08}$: $\quad P_n \dfrac{1}{1.08} + \dfrac{1}{(1.08)^2} + \dfrac{1}{(1.08)^3} + \dfrac{1}{(1.08)^4}$

4. Subtract (3) from (2): $\quad P_n - P_n \dfrac{1}{1.08} = \dfrac{1}{1.08} - \dfrac{1}{(1.08)^4}$

5. Factor: $\quad P_n\left(1 - \dfrac{1}{(1.08)}\right) = \dfrac{1}{1.08}\left[1 - \dfrac{1}{(1.08)^3}\right]$

6. or $\quad P_n\left(\dfrac{.08}{1.08}\right) = \dfrac{1}{1.08}\left[1 - \dfrac{1}{(1.08)^3}\right]$

7. Multiply by $\dfrac{1.08}{.08}$: $\quad P_n = \dfrac{1}{.08}\left[1 - \dfrac{1}{(1.08)^3}\right]$

The general formula for the present value of an annuity of $1.00 is:

$$P_n = \dfrac{1}{r}\left[1 - \dfrac{1}{(1 + r)^n}\right] = \dfrac{\text{Compound discount}}{\text{Rate}}$$

Solving,

$$P_n = \frac{.2062}{.08} = 2.577$$

The formula is the basis for Table 4, p. 878. Check the answer in the table. The present value tables, Tables 2 and 4, are used most frequently in capital budgeting.

The tables for annuities are not essential. With Tables 1 and 2, compound interest and compound discount can readily be computed. It is simply a matter of dividing either of these by the rate to get values equivalent to those shown in Tables 3 and 4.

TABLE 1

Compound Amount of $1.00 (The Future Value of $1.00)

$S = P(1 + r)^n$. In this table $P = \$1.00$

Periods	2%	4%	6%	8%	10%	12%	14%	16%	18%	20%	22%	24%	26%	28%	30%	32%	40%	Periods
1	1.020	1.040	1.060	1.080	1.100	1.120	1.140	1.160	1.180	1.200	1.220	1.240	1.260	1.280	1.300	1.320	1.400	1
2	1.040	1.082	1.124	1.166	1.210	1.254	1.300	1.346	1.392	1.440	1.488	1.538	1.588	1.638	1.690	1.742	1.960	2
3	1.061	1.125	1.191	1.260	1.331	1.405	1.482	1.561	1.643	1.728	1.816	1.907	2.000	2.097	2.197	2.300	2.744	3
4	1.082	1.170	1.262	1.360	1.464	1.574	1.689	1.811	1.939	2.074	2.215	2.364	2.520	2.684	2.856	3.036	3.842	4
5	1.104	1.217	1.338	1.469	1.611	1.762	1.925	2.100	2.288	2.488	2.703	2.932	3.176	3.436	3.713	4.007	5.378	5
6	1.126	1.265	1.419	1.587	1.772	1.974	2.195	2.436	2.700	2.986	3.297	3.635	4.002	4.398	4.827	5.290	7.530	6
7	1.149	1.316	1.504	1.714	1.949	2.211	2.502	2.826	3.185	3.583	4.023	4.508	5.042	5.629	6.275	6.983	10.541	7
8	1.172	1.369	1.594	1.851	2.144	2.476	2.853	3.278	3.759	4.300	4.908	5.590	6.353	7.206	8.157	9.217	14.758	8
9	1.195	1.423	1.689	1.999	2.358	2.773	3.252	3.803	4.435	5.160	5.987	6.931	8.005	9.223	10.604	12.166	20.661	9
10	1.219	1.480	1.791	2.159	2.594	3.106	3.707	4.411	5.234	6.192	7.305	8.594	10.086	11.806	13.786	16.060	28.925	10
11	1.243	1.539	1.898	2.332	2.853	3.479	4.226	5.117	6.176	7.430	8.912	10.657	12.708	15.112	17.922	21.199	40.496	11
12	1.268	1.601	2.012	2.518	3.138	3.896	4.818	5.936	7.288	8.916	10.872	13.215	16.012	19.343	23.298	27.983	56.694	12
13	1.294	1.665	2.133	2.720	3.452	4.363	5.492	6.886	8.599	10.699	13.264	16.386	20.175	24.759	30.288	36.937	79.371	13
14	1.319	1.732	2.261	2.937	3.797	4.887	6.261	7.988	10.147	12.839	16.182	20.319	25.421	31.691	39.374	48.757	111.120	14
15	1.346	1.801	2.397	3.172	4.177	5.474	7.138	9.266	11.974	15.407	19.742	25.196	32.030	40.565	51.186	64.359	155.568	15
16	1.373	1.873	2.540	3.426	4.595	6.130	8.137	10.748	14.129	18.488	24.086	31.243	40.358	51.923	66.542	84.954	217.795	16
17	1.400	1.948	2.693	3.700	5.054	6.866	9.276	12.468	16.672	22.186	29.384	38.741	50.851	66.461	86.504	112.139	304.913	17
18	1.428	2.026	2.854	3.996	5.560	7.690	10.575	14.463	19.673	26.623	35.849	48.039	64.072	85.071	112.455	148.024	426.879	18
19	1.457	2.107	3.026	4.316	6.116	8.613	12.056	16.777	23.214	31.948	43.736	59.568	80.731	108.890	146.192	195.391	597.630	19
20	1.486	2.191	3.207	4.661	6.727	9.646	13.743	19.461	27.393	38.338	53.358	73.864	101.721	139.380	190.050	257.916	836.683	20
21	1.516	2.279	3.400	5.034	7.400	10.804	15.668	22.574	32.324	46.005	65.096	91.592	128.169	178.406	247.065	340.449	1171.356	21
22	1.546	2.370	3.604	5.437	8.140	12.100	17.861	26.186	38.142	55.206	79.418	113.574	161.492	228.360	321.184	449.393	1639.898	22
23	1.577	2.465	3.820	5.871	8.954	13.552	20.362	30.376	45.008	66.247	96.889	140.831	203.480	292.300	417.539	593.199	2295.857	23
24	1.608	2.563	4.049	6.341	9.850	15.179	23.212	35.236	53.109	79.497	118.205	174.631	256.385	374.144	542.801	783.023	3214.200	24
25	1.641	2.666	4.292	6.848	10.835	17.000	26.462	40.874	62.669	95.396	144.210	216.542	323.045	478.905	705.641	1033.590	4499.880	25
26	1.673	2.772	4.549	7.396	11.918	19.040	30.167	47.414	73.949	114.475	175.936	268.512	407.037	612.998	917.333	1364.339	6299.831	26
27	1.707	2.883	4.822	7.988	13.110	21.325	34.390	55.000	87.260	137.371	214.642	332.955	512.867	784.638	1192.533	1800.927	8819.764	27
28	1.741	2.999	5.112	8.627	14.421	23.884	39.204	63.800	102.967	164.845	261.864	412.864	646.212	1004.336	1550.293	2377.224	12347.670	28
29	1.776	3.119	5.418	9.317	15.863	26.750	44.693	74.009	121.501	197.814	319.474	511.952	814.228	1285.550	2015.381	3137.935	17286.737	29
30	1.811	3.243	5.743	10.063	17.449	29.960	50.950	85.850	143.371	237.376	389.758	634.820	1025.927	1645.505	2619.996	4142.075	24201.432	30
35	2.000	3.946	7.686	14.785	28.102	52.800	98.100	180.314	327.997	590.668	1053.402	1861.054	3258.135	5653.911	9727.860	16599.217	130161.112	35
40	2.208	4.801	10.286	21.725	45.259	93.051	188.884	378.721	750.378	1469.772	2847.038	5455.913	10347.175	19426.689	36118.865	66520.767	700037.697	40

APPENDIX C

TABLE 2 *(Place a clip on this page for easy reference.)*
Present Value of $1.00.

$P = \dfrac{S}{(1 + r)^n}$. In this table $S = \$1.00$.

Periods	2%	4%	6%	8%	10%	12%	14%	16%	18%	20%	22%	24%	26%	28%	30%	32%	40%	Periods
1	0.980	0.962	0.943	0.926	0.909	0.893	0.877	0.862	0.847	0.833	0.820	0.806	0.794	0.781	0.769	0.758	0.714	1
2	0.961	0.925	0.890	0.857	0.826	0.797	0.769	0.743	0.718	0.694	0.672	0.650	0.630	0.610	0.592	0.574	0.510	2
3	0.942	0.889	0.840	0.794	0.751	0.712	0.675	0.641	0.609	0.579	0.551	0.524	0.500	0.477	0.455	0.435	0.364	3
4	0.924	0.855	0.792	0.735	0.683	0.636	0.592	0.552	0.516	0.482	0.451	0.423	0.397	0.373	0.350	0.329	0.260	4
5	0.906	0.822	0.747	0.681	0.621	0.567	0.519	0.476	0.437	0.402	0.370	0.341	0.315	0.291	0.269	0.250	0.186	5
6	0.888	0.790	0.705	0.630	0.564	0.507	0.456	0.410	0.370	0.335	0.303	0.275	0.250	0.227	0.207	0.189	0.133	6
7	0.871	0.760	0.665	0.583	0.513	0.452	0.400	0.354	0.314	0.279	0.249	0.222	0.198	0.178	0.159	0.143	0.095	7
8	0.853	0.731	0.627	0.540	0.467	0.404	0.351	0.305	0.266	0.233	0.204	0.179	0.157	0.139	0.123	0.108	0.068	8
9	0.837	0.703	0.592	0.500	0.424	0.361	0.308	0.263	0.225	0.194	0.167	0.144	0.125	0.108	0.094	0.082	0.048	9
10	0.820	0.676	0.558	0.463	0.386	0.322	0.270	0.227	0.191	0.162	0.137	0.116	0.099	0.085	0.073	0.062	0.035	10
11	0.804	0.650	0.527	0.429	0.350	0.287	0.237	0.195	0.162	0.135	0.112	0.094	0.079	0.066	0.056	0.047	0.025	11
12	0.788	0.625	0.497	0.397	0.319	0.257	0.208	0.168	0.137	0.112	0.092	0.076	0.062	0.052	0.043	0.036	0.018	12
13	0.773	0.601	0.469	0.368	0.290	0.229	0.182	0.145	0.116	0.093	0.075	0.061	0.050	0.040	0.033	0.027	0.013	13
14	0.758	0.577	0.442	0.340	0.263	0.205	0.160	0.125	0.099	0.078	0.062	0.049	0.039	0.032	0.025	0.021	0.009	14
15	0.743	0.555	0.417	0.315	0.239	0.183	0.140	0.108	0.084	0.065	0.051	0.040	0.031	0.025	0.020	0.016	0.006	15
16	0.728	0.534	0.394	0.292	0.218	0.163	0.123	0.093	0.071	0.054	0.042	0.032	0.025	0.019	0.015	0.012	0.005	16
17	0.714	0.513	0.371	0.270	0.198	0.146	0.108	0.080	0.060	0.045	0.034	0.026	0.020	0.015	0.012	0.009	0.003	17
18	0.700	0.494	0.350	0.250	0.180	0.130	0.095	0.069	0.051	0.038	0.028	0.021	0.016	0.012	0.009	0.007	0.002	18
19	0.686	0.475	0.331	0.232	0.164	0.116	0.083	0.060	0.043	0.031	0.023	0.017	0.012	0.009	0.007	0.005	0.002	19
20	0.673	0.456	0.312	0.215	0.149	0.104	0.073	0.051	0.037	0.026	0.019	0.014	0.010	0.007	0.005	0.004	0.001	20
21	0.660	0.439	0.294	0.199	0.135	0.093	0.064	0.044	0.031	0.022	0.015	0.011	0.008	0.006	0.004	0.003	0.001	21
22	0.647	0.422	0.278	0.184	0.123	0.083	0.056	0.038	0.026	0.018	0.013	0.009	0.006	0.004	0.003	0.002	0.001	22
23	0.634	0.406	0.262	0.170	0.112	0.074	0.049	0.033	0.022	0.015	0.010	0.007	0.005	0.003	0.002	0.002	0.000	23
24	0.622	0.390	0.247	0.158	0.102	0.066	0.043	0.028	0.019	0.013	0.008	0.006	0.004	0.003	0.002	0.001	0.000	24
25	0.610	0.375	0.233	0.146	0.092	0.059	0.038	0.024	0.016	0.010	0.007	0.005	0.003	0.002	0.001	0.001	0.000	25
26	0.598	0.361	0.220	0.135	0.084	0.053	0.033	0.021	0.014	0.009	0.006	0.004	0.002	0.002	0.001	0.001	0.000	26
27	0.586	0.347	0.207	0.125	0.076	0.047	0.029	0.018	0.011	0.007	0.005	0.003	0.002	0.002	0.001	0.001	0.000	27
28	0.574	0.333	0.196	0.116	0.069	0.042	0.026	0.016	0.010	0.006	0.004	0.002	0.002	0.001	0.001	0.000	0.000	28
29	0.563	0.321	0.185	0.107	0.063	0.037	0.022	0.014	0.008	0.005	0.003	0.002	0.001	0.001	0.000	0.000	0.000	29
30	0.552	0.308	0.174	0.099	0.057	0.033	0.020	0.012	0.007	0.004	0.003	0.002	0.001	0.001	0.000	0.000	0.000	30
35	0.500	0.253	0.130	0.068	0.036	0.019	0.010	0.006	0.003	0.002	0.001	0.001	0.000	0.000	0.000	0.000	0.000	35
40	0.453	0.208	0.097	0.046	0.022	0.011	0.005	0.003	0.001	0.001	0.000	0.000	0.000	0.000	0.000	0.000	0.000	40

TABLE 3
Compound Amount of Annuity of $1.00 in Arrears* (Future Value of Annuity)

$$S_n = \frac{(1+r)^n - 1}{r}$$

Periods	2%	4%	6%	8%	10%	12%	14%	16%	18%	20%	22%	24%	26%	28%	30%	32%	40%	Periods
1	1.000	1.000	1.000	1.000	1.000	1.000	1.000	1.000	1.000	1.000	1.000	1.000	1.000	1.000	1.000	1.000	1.000	1
2	2.020	2.040	2.060	2.080	2.100	2.120	2.140	2.160	2.180	2.200	2.220	2.240	2.260	2.280	2.300	2.320	2.400	2
3	3.060	3.122	3.184	3.246	3.310	3.374	3.440	3.506	3.572	3.640	3.708	3.778	3.848	3.918	3.990	4.062	4.360	3
4	4.122	4.246	4.375	4.506	4.641	4.779	4.921	5.066	5.215	5.368	5.524	5.684	5.848	6.016	6.187	6.362	7.104	4
5	5.204	5.416	5.637	5.867	6.105	6.353	6.610	6.877	7.154	7.442	7.740	8.048	8.368	8.700	9.043	9.398	10.946	5
6	6.308	6.633	6.975	7.336	7.716	8.115	8.536	8.977	9.442	9.930	10.442	10.980	11.544	12.136	12.756	13.406	16.324	6
7	7.434	7.898	8.394	8.923	9.487	10.089	10.730	11.414	12.142	12.916	13.740	14.615	15.546	16.534	17.583	18.696	23.853	7
8	8.583	9.214	9.897	10.637	11.436	12.300	13.233	14.240	15.327	16.499	17.762	19.123	20.588	22.163	23.858	25.678	34.395	8
9	9.755	10.583	11.491	12.488	13.579	14.776	16.085	17.519	19.086	20.799	22.670	24.712	26.940	29.369	32.015	34.895	49.153	9
10	10.950	12.006	13.181	14.487	15.937	17.549	19.337	21.321	23.521	25.959	28.657	31.643	34.945	38.593	42.619	47.062	69.814	10
11	12.169	13.486	14.972	16.645	18.531	20.655	23.045	25.733	28.755	32.150	35.962	40.238	45.031	50.398	56.405	63.122	98.739	11
12	13.412	15.026	16.870	18.977	21.384	24.133	27.271	30.850	34.931	39.581	44.874	50.895	57.739	65.510	74.327	84.320	139.235	12
13	14.680	16.627	18.882	21.495	24.523	28.029	32.089	36.786	42.219	48.497	55.746	64.110	73.751	84.853	97.625	112.303	195.929	13
14	15.974	18.292	21.015	24.215	27.975	32.393	37.581	43.672	50.818	59.196	69.010	80.496	93.926	109.612	127.913	149.240	275.300	14
15	17.293	20.024	23.276	27.152	31.772	37.280	43.842	51.660	60.965	72.035	85.192	100.815	119.347	141.303	167.286	197.997	386.420	15
16	18.639	21.825	25.673	30.324	35.950	42.753	50.980	60.925	72.939	87.442	104.935	126.011	151.377	181.868	218.472	262.356	541.988	16
17	20.012	23.698	28.213	33.750	40.545	48.884	59.118	71.673	87.068	105.931	129.020	157.253	191.735	233.791	285.014	347.309	759.784	17
18	21.412	25.645	30.906	37.450	45.599	55.750	68.394	84.141	103.740	128.117	158.405	195.994	242.585	300.252	371.518	459.449	1064.697	18
19	22.841	27.671	33.760	41.446	51.159	63.440	78.969	98.603	123.414	154.740	194.254	244.033	306.658	385.323	483.973	607.472	1491.576	19
20	24.297	29.778	36.786	45.762	57.275	72.052	91.025	115.380	146.628	186.688	237.989	303.601	387.389	494.213	630.165	802.863	2089.206	20
21	25.783	31.969	39.993	50.423	64.002	81.699	104.768	134.841	174.021	225.026	291.347	377.465	489.110	633.593	820.215	1060.779	2925.889	21
22	27.299	34.248	43.392	55.457	71.403	92.503	120.436	157.415	206.345	271.031	356.443	469.056	617.278	811.999	1067.280	1401.229	4097.245	22
23	28.845	36.618	46.996	60.893	79.543	104.603	138.297	183.601	244.487	326.237	435.861	582.630	778.771	1040.358	1388.464	1850.622	5737.142	23
24	30.422	39.083	50.816	66.765	88.497	118.155	158.659	213.978	289.494	392.484	532.750	723.461	982.251	1332.659	1806.003	2443.821	8032.999	24
25	32.030	41.646	54.865	73.106	98.347	133.334	181.871	249.214	342.603	471.981	650.955	898.092	1238.636	1706.803	2348.803	3226.844	11247.199	25
26	33.671	44.312	59.156	79.954	109.182	150.334	208.333	290.088	405.272	567.377	795.165	1114.634	1561.682	2185.708	3054.444	4260.434	15747.079	26
27	35.344	47.084	63.706	87.351	121.100	169.374	238.499	337.502	479.221	681.853	971.102	1383.146	1968.719	2798.706	3971.778	5624.772	22046.910	27
28	37.051	49.968	68.528	95.339	134.210	190.699	272.889	392.503	566.481	819.223	1185.744	1716.101	2481.586	3583.344	5164.311	7425.699	30866.674	28
29	38.792	52.966	73.640	103.966	148.631	214.583	312.094	456.303	669.447	984.068	1447.608	2128.965	3127.798	4587.680	6714.604	9802.923	43214.343	29
30	40.568	56.085	79.058	113.263	164.494	241.333	356.787	530.312	790.948	1181.882	1767.081	2640.916	3942.026	5873.231	8729.985	12940.859	60501.081	30
35	49.994	73.652	111.435	172.317	271.024	431.663	693.573	1120.713	1816.652	2948.341	4783.645	7750.225	12527.442	20188.966	32422.868	51869.427	325400.279	35
40	60.402	95.026	154.762	259.057	442.593	767.091	1342.025	2360.757	4163.213	7343.858	12936.535	22728.803	39792.982	69377.460	120392.883	207874.272	1750091.741	40

*Payments (or receipts) at the end of each period.

APPENDIX C

TABLE 4 (Place a clip on this page for easy reference.)
Present Value of Annuity $1.00 in Arrears*.

$$P_n = \frac{1}{r}\left[1 - \frac{1}{(1+r)^n}\right]$$

Periods	2%	4%	6%	8%	10%	12%	14%	16%	18%	20%	22%	24%	26%	28%	30%	32%	40%	Periods
1	0.980	0.962	0.943	0.926	0.909	0.893	0.877	0.862	0.847	0.833	0.820	0.806	0.794	0.781	0.769	0.758	0.714	1
2	1.942	1.886	1.833	1.783	1.736	1.690	1.647	1.605	1.566	1.528	1.492	1.457	1.424	1.392	1.361	1.331	1.224	2
3	2.884	2.775	2.673	2.577	2.487	2.402	2.322	2.246	2.174	2.106	2.042	1.981	1.923	1.868	1.816	1.766	1.589	3
4	3.808	3.630	3.465	3.312	3.170	3.037	2.914	2.798	2.690	2.589	2.494	2.404	2.320	2.241	2.166	2.096	1.849	4
5	4.713	4.452	4.212	3.993	3.791	3.605	3.433	3.274	3.127	2.991	2.864	2.745	2.635	2.532	2.436	2.345	2.035	5
6	5.601	5.242	4.917	4.623	4.355	4.111	3.889	3.685	3.498	3.326	3.167	3.020	2.885	2.759	2.643	2.534	2.168	6
7	6.472	6.002	5.582	5.206	4.868	4.564	4.288	4.039	3.812	3.605	3.416	3.242	3.083	2.937	2.802	2.677	2.263	7
8	7.325	6.733	6.210	5.747	5.335	4.968	4.639	4.344	4.078	3.837	3.619	3.421	3.241	3.076	2.925	2.786	2.331	8
9	8.162	7.435	6.802	6.247	5.759	5.328	4.946	4.607	4.303	4.031	3.786	3.566	3.366	3.184	3.019	2.868	2.379	9
10	8.983	8.111	7.360	6.710	6.145	5.650	5.216	4.833	4.494	4.192	3.923	3.682	3.465	3.269	3.092	2.930	2.414	10
11	9.787	8.760	7.887	7.139	6.495	5.938	5.453	5.029	4.656	4.327	4.035	3.776	3.543	3.335	3.147	2.978	2.438	11
12	10.575	9.385	8.384	7.536	6.814	6.194	5.660	5.197	4.793	4.439	4.127	3.851	3.606	3.387	3.190	3.013	2.456	12
13	11.348	9.986	8.853	7.904	7.103	6.424	5.842	5.342	4.910	4.533	4.203	3.912	3.656	3.427	3.223	3.040	2.469	13
14	12.106	10.563	9.295	8.244	7.367	6.628	6.002	5.468	5.008	4.611	4.265	3.962	3.695	3.459	3.249	3.061	2.478	14
15	12.849	11.118	9.712	8.559	7.606	6.811	6.142	5.575	5.092	4.675	4.315	4.001	3.726	3.483	3.268	3.076	2.484	15
16	13.578	11.652	10.106	8.851	7.824	6.974	6.265	5.668	5.162	4.730	4.357	4.033	3.751	3.503	3.283	3.088	2.489	16
17	14.292	12.166	10.477	9.122	8.022	7.120	6.373	5.749	5.222	4.775	4.391	4.059	3.771	3.518	3.295	3.097	2.492	17
18	14.992	12.659	10.828	9.372	8.201	7.250	6.467	5.818	5.273	4.812	4.419	4.080	3.786	3.529	3.304	3.104	2.494	18
19	15.678	13.134	11.158	9.604	8.365	7.366	6.550	5.877	5.316	4.843	4.442	4.097	3.799	3.539	3.311	3.109	2.496	19
20	16.351	13.590	11.470	9.818	8.514	7.469	6.623	5.929	5.353	4.870	4.460	4.110	3.808	3.546	3.316	3.113	2.497	20
21	17.011	14.029	11.764	10.017	8.649	7.562	6.687	5.973	5.384	4.891	4.476	4.121	3.816	3.551	3.320	3.116	2.498	21
22	17.658	14.451	12.042	10.201	8.772	7.645	6.743	6.011	5.410	4.909	4.488	4.130	3.822	3.556	3.323	3.118	2.498	22
23	18.292	14.857	12.303	10.371	8.883	7.718	6.792	6.044	5.432	4.925	4.499	4.137	3.827	3.559	3.325	3.120	2.499	23
24	18.914	15.247	12.550	10.529	8.985	7.784	6.835	6.073	5.451	4.937	4.507	4.143	3.831	3.562	3.327	3.121	2.499	24
25	19.523	15.622	12.783	10.675	9.077	7.843	6.873	6.097	5.467	4.948	4.514	4.147	3.834	3.564	3.329	3.122	2.499	25
26	20.121	15.983	13.003	10.810	9.161	7.896	6.906	6.118	5.480	4.956	4.520	4.151	3.837	3.566	3.330	3.123	2.500	26
27	20.707	16.330	13.211	10.935	9.237	7.943	6.935	6.136	5.492	4.964	4.524	4.154	3.839	3.567	3.331	3.123	2.500	27
28	21.281	16.663	13.406	11.051	9.307	7.984	6.961	6.152	5.502	4.970	4.528	4.157	3.840	3.568	3.331	3.124	2.500	28
29	21.844	16.984	13.591	11.158	9.370	8.022	6.983	6.166	5.510	4.975	4.531	4.159	3.841	3.569	3.332	3.124	2.500	29
30	22.396	17.292	13.765	11.258	9.427	8.055	7.003	6.177	5.517	4.979	4.534	4.160	3.842	3.569	3.332	3.124	2.500	30
35	24.999	18.665	14.498	11.655	9.644	8.176	7.070	6.215	5.539	4.992	4.541	4.164	3.845	3.571	3.333	3.125	2.500	35
40	27.355	19.793	15.046	11.925	9.779	8.244	7.105	6.233	5.548	4.997	4.544	4.166	3.846	3.571	3.333	3.125	2.500	40

*Payments (or receipts) at the end of each period.

Appendix D

COST ACCOUNTING IN PROFESSIONAL EXAMINATIONS

This appendix describes the role of cost accounting in professional examinations. We use professional examinations in the United States, Canada, Australia, Japan, and the United Kingdom to illustrate the role.[1] A conscientious reader who has solved a representative sample of the problems at the end of the chapters will be well prepared for the professional examination questions dealing with cost accounting. This appendix aims to provide perspective, install confidence, and encourage readers to take the examinations.

AMERICAN PROFESSIONAL EXAMINATIONS

CPA and CMA Designations

Many American readers may eventually take the Certified Public Accountant (CPA) examination or the Certified Management Accountant (CMA) examination. Certification is important to professional accountants for many reasons, such as:

1. Recognition of achievement and technical competence by fellow accountants and by users of accounting services
2. Increased self-confidence in one's professional abilities
3. Membership in professional organizations offering programs of career-long education
4. Enhancement of career opportunities
5. Personal satisfaction

The CPA certificate is issued by individual states; it is necessary for obtaining a state's license to practice as a Certified Public Accountant. A prominent feature of public accounting is the use of independent (external) auditors to give assurance about the reliability of the financial statements supplied by managers. These auditors are called Certified Public Accountants in the United States and Chartered Accountants in many other English-speaking nations. The major U.S. professional association in the private sector that regulates the quality of external auditing is the American Institute of Certified Public Accountants (AICPA).

The CMA designation is offered by the Institute of Management Accountants (IMA). The IMA is the largest association of management accountants in the world.[2] The major objective of the CMA certification is to enhance the development of the management accounting profession. In particular, focus is placed on the modern role of the management accountant as an active contributor to and a participant in management. The CMA designation is gaining increased stature in the business community as a credential parallel to the CPA designation.

[1] We appreciate help from Tom Craven (United States), Bill Langdon (Canada), John Goodwin (Australia), Michi Sakurai (Japan), and Louise Drysdale and Andrea Jeffries (U.K.).

[2] The IMA has a wide range of activities driven by many committees. For example, the Management Accounting Practices Committee issues statements on both financial accounting and management accounting. The IMA also has an extensive continuing-education program.

The CMA examination is given in a computer-based format and consists of 4 parts.

- ◆ Part 1: Economics, finance, and management
- ◆ Part 2: Financial accounting and reporting
- ◆ Part 3: Management reporting, analysis, and behavioral issues
- ◆ Part 4: Decision analysis and information systems

Questions regarding ethical issues will appear on any part of the examination. A person who has successfully completed the U.S. CPA examination is exempt from Part 2.

Cost/management accounting questions are prominent in the CMA examination. The CPA examination also includes such questions, although they are less extensive than questions regarding financial accounting, auditing, and business law. On the average, cost/managerial accounting represents 35% to 40% of the CMA examination and 5% of the CPA examination. This book includes many questions and problems used in past CMA and CPA examinations. In addition, a supplement to this book, *Student Guide and Review Manual* [John K. Harris (Englewood Cliffs, NJ: Prentice Hall, 2000)], contains over one hundred CMA and CPA questions and explanatory answers. Careful study of appropriate topics in this book will give candidates sufficient background for succeeding in the cost accounting portions of the professional examinations.

The IMA publishes *Management Accounting* monthly. Each issue includes advertisements for courses that help students prepare for the CMA examination.[3]

CANADIAN PROFESSIONAL EXAMINATIONS

Three professional accounting designations are available in Canada:

Designation	Sponsoring Organization
◆ Certified Management Accountant (CMA)	◆ Society of Management Accountants (SMA)
◆ Certified General Accountant (CGA)	◆ Certified General Accountants' Association (CGA)
◆ Chartered Accountant (CA)	◆ Canadian Institute of Chartered Accountants

The SMA represents over 27,000 certified management accountants employed throughout Canadian business, industry, and government.

The CMA Entrance Examination is a two-day examination, divided into three broad categories:

1. Management accounting area   50%–60%
2. Financial accounting area   20%–30%
3. Management studies   15%–25%

Multiple-choice questions comprise 40% to 50% and cases studies and short-answer questions 50% to 60% of the exam. Topics covered on recent examinations in the management accounting area include relevant costing, transfer pricing, capital budgeting, performance measures, activity-based costing, cost allocation, and productivity.

The Society of Management Accountants publishes *CMA: The Management Accounting Magazine* monthly. This magazine includes details of courses that assist students in preparing for the CMA examination.

---

[3]Other U.S. professional associations also require detailed knowledge of cost accounting. For example, the Certified Cost Estimator/Analyst (CCEA) program is administered by the Society of Cost Estimating and Analysis, 101 South Whiting Street, Suite 313, Alexandria, VA 22304. The society's primary purpose is to improve the effectiveness of cost estimation and price analysis. Special attention is given to contract cost estimation.

AUSTRALIAN PROFESSIONAL EXAMINATIONS

The Australian Society of Certified Practising Accountants is the largest body representing accountants in Australia. Their professional designation is termed a CPA (Certified Practising Accountant). The basic entry requirement for Associate membership of the Society is having an approved Bachelors degree. Associates of the Society can advance to CPA status by passing the CPA program and having the required amount of relevant work experience. There are two compulsory core segments in the program. Core I covers the practical application of the more common accounting standards and ethics, while more technical standards (such as foreign currency translation) are covered in the Core II segment. Candidates are then required to take three segments from eight elective subjects. These subjects are: (1) external reporting, (2) insolvency and reconstruction, (3) management accounting, (4) management of information systems, (5) auditing, (6) treasury, and (7) taxation, and (8) personal financial planning and superannuation.

The management accounting segment topics include:

1. Management accounting in the contemporary business environment
2. Accounting for strategic management
3. Longterm project planning and management
4. Costing for decision making
5. Performance measurement and reward systems.

The Australian CPA, published each month (except January), includes advertisements for courses that help students prepare for the CPA examination.

The Institute of Chartered Accountants in Australia (ICAA) has membership requirements that include passing four core modules (Taxation, Accounting I, Accounting II, and Ethics) and one elective module (one of which is Advanced Management Accounting). Management-accounting-related topics are in both the Accounting II and Advanced Management Accounting modules. These include:

◆ purpose and perspective (including strategic and operational management, organizations, goals, ethics, operational environments, and cost concepts);

◆ strategic management accounting (including strategic applications, project evaluation and capital budgeting);

◆ operational management accounting (including decision analysis, financial planning and management, product and service costing, control and performance evaluation).

JAPANESE PROFESSIONAL EXAMINATIONS

There are two major management accounting organizations—Japanese Industrial Management and Accounting Association and Enterprise Management Association. The JIMAA is the oldest, largest, and most authoritative accounting organization of its kind in Japan. It directs a School of Cost Control and a School of Corporate Tax Accounting. There are two courses in the School of Cost Control—Preparatory Course and Cost Control Course. These courses are taught by university professors and executives from member corporations. The Enterprise Management Association is the Japanese chapter of the U.S.-based Institute of Management Accountants.

UNITED KINGDOM PROFESSIONAL EXAMINATIONS

The Chartered Institute of Management Accountants (CIMA) is the largest professional management accounting body in the United Kingdom. CIMA provides a wide range of services to members in commerce, education, government, and the accounting profession.

The syllabus for the CIMA examination consists of four stages:

1. Preparation for business and accounting (including "cost accounting and quantitative methods")

2. The tools of management accounting (including "operational cost accounting")

3. The rules of a profession (including "management accounting applications")

4. The application of knowledge to business management and finance (including "strategic management accountancy and marketing" and "management accounting control systems")

Management Accounting, published monthly by CIMA, includes details of courses assisting students in preparing for their examinations.

Management accounting topics are also covered by several other professional bodies. The syllabus for the examinations of the Chartered Association of Certified Accountants (ACCA) has three stages: I (Foundation), II (Certificate), and III (Professional). Skills examined in III include information for control and decision making, management and strategy, and financial strategy. Other accounting bodies include the Institute of Chartered Accountants in England and Wales (ICAEW) and the Institute for Chartered Accountants of Scotland (ICAS). Both institutes have requirements that cover proficiency in "general management" topics as well as professional accounting topics.

Glossary

Abnormal spoilage. Spoilage that should not arise under efficient operating conditions; it is not an inherent result of the particular production process. (649)

Absorption costing. Method of inventory costing in which all variable manufacturing costs and all fixed manufacturing costs are included as inventoriable costs. (290)

Account analysis method. Approach to cost estimation that classifies cost accounts in the ledger as variable, fixed, or mixed with respect to the identified activity. Typically, qualitative rather than quantitative analysis is used in making these classification decisions. (333)

Accounting rate of return. See *accrual accounting rate-of-return (AARR)*.

Accrual accounting rate-of-return (AARR). Capital budgeting method that divides an accounting measure of income by an accounting measure of investment. Also called *accounting rate of return* or *return on investment (ROI)*. (760)

Activity. An event, task, or unit of work with a specified purpose. (140)

Activity-based budgeting (ABB). Budgeting approach that focuses on the budgeted cost of activities necessary to produce and sell products and services. (192)

Activity-based costing (ABC). Approach to costing that focuses on individual activities as the fundamental cost objects. It uses the costs of these activities as the basis for assigning costs to other cost objects such as products or services. (140)

Activity-based management (ABM). Management decisions that use activity-based costing information to satisfy customers and improve profits (148)

Actual cost. Cost incurred (a historical cost) as distinguished from budgeted or forecasted costs. (28)

Actual costing. A costing method that traces direct costs to a cost object by using the actual direct-cost rate(s) times the actual quantity of the direct-cost input(s) and allocates indirect costs based on the actual indirect-cost rate(s) times the actual quantity of the cost-allocation base(s). (98)

Allowable costs. Costs that parties to a contract agree to include in the costs to be reimbursed. (518)

Appraisal costs. Costs incurred to detect which of the individual units of products do not conform to specifications. (677)

Artificial cost. See complete reciprocated cost.

Attention directing. Helping managers properly focus their attention role of management accounting. (6)

Autonomy. The degree of freedom to make decisions. (790)

Average costs. See *unit cost*.

Average waiting time. The average amount of time that an order will wait in line before it is set up and processed. (689)

Backflush costing. Costing system that omits recording some or all of the journal entries relating to the cycle from purchase of direct material to the sale of finished goods. (728)

Balanced Scorecard. A framework for implementing strategy by translating an organization's mission and strategy into a comprehensive set of performance measures. (463)

Batch-level costs. The costs of resources sacrificed on activities that are related to a group of units of product(s) or service(s) rather than to each individual unit of product or service. (143)

Benchmarking. The continuous process of measuring products, services, and activities against the best levels of performance. (236)

Book value. The original cost minus accumulated depreciation of an asset. (396)

Bottleneck. An operation where the work required to be performed approaches or exceeds the available capacity. (689)

Breakeven point. Quantity of output where total revenues and total costs are equal; that is where the operating income is zero. (62)

Budget. Quantitative expression of a proposed plan of action by management for a future time period and is an aid to the coordination and implementation of the plan. (4)

Budgetary slack. The practice of underestimating budgeted revenues (or overestimating budgeted costs) in order to make budgeted targets more easily achievable. (185)

Budgeted indirect-cost rate. Budgeted annual indirect cost in a cost pool divided by the budgeted annual quantity of the cost-allocation base. (104)

Bundled product. A package of two or more products (or services), sold for a single price, where the individual components of the bundle also may be sold as separate items at their own "stand-alone" prices. (568)

Business function costs. The sum of all costs (variable and fixed) in a particular business function in the value chain. (382)

Byproduct. Product from a joint production process that has a relatively low sales value compared with the sales value of a joint or main product. (537)

Capital budgeting. The making of long-run planning decisions for investments in projects and programs. (748)

883

Carrying costs. Costs associated with an organization holding an inventory of goods for sale. (712)

Cash budget. Schedule of expected cash receipts and disbursements. (199)

Cause-and-effect diagram. Diagram that identifies the potential causes of failures or defects. Four major categories of potential causes of failure are human factors, methods and design factors, machine-related factors, and materials and components factors. Also called a *fishbone diagram*. (681)

Certificate management accountant (CMA). Certifies that the holder has met the admission criteria and demonstrated the competency of technical knowledge required by the *Institute of Management Accountants*. (15)

Chief financial officer (CFO). Senior officer empowered with overseeing the financial operations of an organization. Also called *finance director*. (12)

Choice criterion. Objective that can be quantified in a decision model. (78)

Coefficient of determination (r^2). Measures the percentage of variation in a dependent variable explained by one or more independent variables. (353)

Collusive pricing. Companies in an industry conspire in their pricing and output decisions to achieve a price above the competitive price. (444)

Common cost. Cost of operating a facility, activity, or like cost object that is shared by two or more users. (516)

Complete reciprocated cost. The support department's own costs plus any interdepartmental cost allocations. Also called the *artificial cost* of the support department. (512)

Composite product unit. Hypothetical unit with weights based on the mix of individual products. (576)

Conference method. Approach to cost estimation that develops cost estimates on the basis of analysis and opinions about costs and their drivers gathered from various departments of an organization (purchasing, process engineering, manufacturing, employee relations, and so on). (333)

Conformance quality. Refers to the performance of a product or service relative to its design and product specifications. (677)

Constant. The component of total costs that, within the relevant range, does not vary with changes in the level of the activity. Also called *intercept*. (329)

Constant gross-margin percentage NRV method. Method that allocates joint costs to joint products in such a way that the overall gross-margin percentage is identical for the individual products. (544)

Constraint. A mathematical inequality or equality that must be satisfied by the variables in a mathematical model. (402)

Continuous improvement budgeted cost. Budgeted cost that is progressively reduced over succeeding time periods. (232)

Contribution income statement. Income statement that groups line items by cost behavior patterns to highlight the contribution margin. (62)

Contribution margin. Total revenues minus total variable costs. (61)

Contribution margin per unit. Difference between selling price and variable cost per unit. (61)

Contribution margin percentage. Contribution margin per unit divided by selling price. Also called *contribution margin ratio*. (62)

Contribution margin ratio. See *contribution margin percentage*. (62)

Control. Deciding on and taking actions that implement the planning decisions, and deciding on performance evaluation and the related feedback that will help future decision making. (4)

Control chart. Graph of a series of successive observations of a particular step, procedure, or operation taken at regular intervals of time. Each observation is plotted relative to specified ranges that represent the expected statistical distribution. (680)

Controllability. Degree of influence that a specific manager has over costs, revenues, or other items in question. (195)

Controllable cost. Any cost that is primarily subject to the influence of a given responsibility center manager for a given time period. (195)

Controller. The financial executive primarily responsible for both management accounting and financial accounting. Also called *chief accounting officer*. (12)

Conversion costs. All manufacturing costs other than direct material costs. (39)

Cost. Resource sacrificed or forgone to achieve a specific objective. (28)

Cost accounting. Measures and reports financial and nonfinancial information that relates to the cost of acquiring or consuming resources by an organization. It provides information for both management accounting and financial accounting. (3)

Cost Accounting Standards Board (CASB). Government agency that has the exclusive authority to make, promulgate, amend, and rescind cost accounting standards and interpretations thereof designed to achieve uniformity and consistency in regard to measurement, assignment, and allocation of costs to contracts within the United States. (518)

Cost accumulation. Collection of cost data in some organized way be means of an accounting system. (28)

Cost allocation. The assignment of indirect costs to the particular cost object. (29)

Cost-allocation base. A factor that is the common denominator for systematically linking an indirect cost or group of indirect costs to a cost object. (97)

Cost application base. Cost-allocation base when the cost object is a job, product or customer. (97)

Cost assignment. General term that encompasses both (1) tracing accumulated costs to a cost object, and (2) allocating accumulated costs to a cost object. (28)

Cost-benefit approach. Approach to decision-making based on a comparison of the expected benefits and the expected costs. (10)

Cost center. Responsibility center where the manager is accountable for costs only. (194)

Cost driver. A factor, such as the level of activity or volume, that causally affects costs (over a given time span). (31)

Cost estimation. The measurement of a past relationship between costs and the level of an activity. (331)

Cost function. Mathematical expression describing how a cost changes with changes in the level of an activity. (328)

Cost hierarchy. Categorization of costs into different cost pools on the basis of different types of cost drivers (or cost-allocation bases), or different degrees of difficulty in determining cause-and-effect (or benefits received) relationships. (142)

Cost incurrence. Occurs when a resource is sacrificed or forgone to meet a specific objective. (430)

Cost leadership. Organization's ability to achieve lower costs relative to competitors through productivity and efficiency improvements, elimination of waste, and tight cost control. (463)

Cost management. The activities of managers in short-run and long-run planning and control of costs. (3)

Cost object. Anything for which a separate measurement of costs is desired. (28)

Cost of goods manufactured. Cost of goods brought to completion, whether they were started before or during the current accounting period. (37)

Cost pool. A grouping of individual cost items. (97)

Cost predictions. Forecast of future costs. (331)

Cost smoothing. A costing approach that uses broad averages for assigning (spreading) the cost of resources uniformly to cost objects (such as products or services) when the individual products or services, in fact use those resources in a nonuniform way. Also called *peanut-butter costing*. (136)

Costs of quality (COQ). Costs incurred to prevent, or costs arising as a result of, the production of a low-quality product. (677)

Cost-volume-profit (CVP) analysis. Examines the behavior of total revenues, total costs, and operating income as changes occur in the output level, selling price, variable costs per unit, or fixed costs; the number of output is the only revenue and cost driver. (60)

Cumulative average-time learning model. Learning curve model in which the cumulative average time per unit declines by a constant percentage each time the cumulative quantity of units produced is doubled. (344)

Current cost. Asset measure based on the cost of purchasing an asset today identical to the one currently

held or the cost of purchasing the services provided by that asset if an identical one cannot currently be purchased. (831)

Customer cost hierarchy. Hierarchy that categorizes costs related to customers into different cost pools on the basis of different types of cost drivers (or cost-allocation bases) or different degrees of difficulty in determining cause-and-effect (or benefits received) relationships. (582)

Customer life-cycle costs. Focuses on the total costs incurred by a customer to acquire and use a product or service until it is replaced. (444)

Customer profitability analysis. The reporting and analysis of customer revenues and customer costs. (581)

Customer-response time. Amount of time from when a customer places an order for a product or requests a service to when the product or service is delivered to the customer. (687)

Customer retention rate. Measures the percentage of existing customers that will be retained next period. (768)

Customer service. The after-sale support activities provided to customers. (7)

Decentralization. The freedom for managers at lower levels (subunits) of the organization to make decisions. (790)

Decision model. Formal method for making a choice, frequently involving both quantitative and qualitative analyses. (378)

Decision table. Summary of the contemplated actions, events, outcomes, and probabilities of events in a decision. (79)

Degree of operating leverage. Contribution margin divided by operating income at any given level of sales. (71)

Denominator level. The denominator of the budgeted fixed overhead rate computation. (259)

Denominator-level variance. See *production-volume variance*.

Dependent variable. The cost to be predicted. (334)

Design of products, services, or processes. The detailed planning and engineering of products, services, or processes. (7)

Designed-in costs. See *locked-in costs*. (430)

Differential cost. Difference in cost between two alternatives. (386)

Differential revenue. Difference in revenue between two alternatives. (386)

Direct allocation method. Cost allocation method that allocates each support department's costs directly to the operating departments. Also called *direct method*. (511)

Direct costing. See *variable costing*.

Direct costs of a cost object. Costs related to the particular cost object and can be traced to it in an economically feasible (cost-effective) way. (28)

Direct manufacturing labor costs. Include the compensation of all manufacturing labor that can be traced to the cost object in an economically feasible way. (36)

Direct materials costs. Acquisition costs of all materials that eventually become part of the cost object ("work in process" or "finished goods"), and that can be traced to the cost object in an economically feasible way. (36)

Direct materials inventory. Direct materials in stock and awaiting use in the manufacturing process. (35)

Direct materials mix variance. The difference between (1) the budgeted cost for the actual mix of the total quantity of direct materials used, and (2) the budgeted costs of the budgeted mix of the actual total quantity of direct materials used. (592)

Direct materials yield variance. The difference between (1) the budgeted cost of direct materials based on the actual total quantity of all direct materials used, and (2) the flexible-budget cost of direct materials based on the budgeted total quantity of direct materials inputs for the actual output produced. (592)

Direct method. See *direct allocation method.*

Discount rate. See *required rate of return (RRR).*

Discounted cash flow (DCF) method. Capital budgeting method that measures all expected future cash inflows and outflows of a project as if they occurred at a single point in time. (750)

Discretionary costs. Arise from periodic (usually yearly) decisions regarding the maximum costs to be incurred. They are not tied to a clear cause-and-effect relationship between output and resources used. (478)

Distribution. The delivery of products or services to the customer. (7)

Downsizing. An integrated approach to configuring processes, products, and people in order to match costs to the activities that need to be performed for operating effectively and efficiently in the present and future. Also called *rightsizing.* (480)

Downward demand spiral. Pricing context where prices are raised to spread capacity costs over a smaller number of output units. Continuing reduction in demand occurs when the prices of competitors are not met and demand drops. This results in even higher unit costs and higher prices. (306).

Dual pricing. Approach to transfer pricing using two separate transfer-pricing methods to price each interdivision transaction. (800)

Dual-rate cost-allocation method. Allocation method with costs classified into two cost subpools (a variable-cost subpool and a fixed-cost subpool). (507)

Dumping. Under U.S. laws, occurs when a non-U.S. company sells a product in the United States at a price below the market value in the country of its creation, and this action materially injures or threatens to materially injure an industry in the United States. (443)

Dysfunctional decision making. See *suboptimal decision making.* (791)

Economic order quantity (EOQ). Decision model that calculates the optimal quantity of inventory to order under a restrictive set of assumptions. (713)

Economic value added (EVA®). After-tax operating income minus the (after-tax) weighted average cost of capital multiplied by total assets minus current liabilities. (826)

Effectiveness. The degree to which a predetermined objective target is met. (229)

Efficiency variance. The difference between the actual quantity of input used and the budgeted quantity of input that should have been used, multiplied by the budgeted price. Also called *usage variance.* (226)

Efficiency. The relative amount of inputs used to achieve a given level of output. (229)

Effort. Exertion toward a goal. (789)

Engineered costs. Costs that result from a cause-and-effect relationship between the cost driver, output, and the (direct or indirect) resources used to produce that output. (478)

Equivalent units. Derived amount of output units that takes the quantity of each input (factor of production) in units completed or work in process, and converts it into the amount of completed output units that could be made with that quantity of input. (611)

Estimated net realizable value (NRV) method. Method that allocates joint costs to joint products on the basis of the relative estimated NRV (expected final sales value in the ordinary course of business minus the expected separable costs) of the total production of these products during the accounting period. (543)

Event. A possible occurrence in a decision model. (79)

Expected monetary value. See *expected value.* (79)

Expected value. Weighted average of the outcomes of a decision with the probability of each outcome serving as the weight. Also called *expected monetary value.* (79)

Experience curve. Function that shows how the costs per unit in various value-chain areas such as manufacturing, marketing, distribution, and so on, decline as units produced increase. (344)

External failure costs. Costs incurred by a nonconforming product after it is shipped to customers. (677)

Facility-sustaining costs. The costs of resources sacrificed on activities that cannot be traced to individual products or services but support the organization as a whole. (143)

Factory overhead costs. See *indirect manufacturing costs.*

Favorable variance. Variance that increases operating income relative to the budgeted amount. Denoted F. (222)

Feedback. Involves managers examining past performance and systematically exploring alternative ways to make better informed decisions in the future. (5)

Finance director. See *chief financial officer (CFO)*.

Financial accounting. Measures and records business transactions and provides financial statements that are based on generally accepted accounting principles. It focuses on reporting to external parties. (3)

Financial budget. Part of the master budget that focuses on the impact of operations and planned capital outlays on cash. It comprises the capital budget, cash budget, budgeted balance sheet, and budgeted statement of cash flows. (182)

Financial planning models. Mathematical representation of the interrelationships among operating activities, financial activities, and other factors that affect the master budget. (190)

Finished goods inventory. Goods fully completed but not yet sold. (35)

First-in, first-out (FIFO) process-costing method. Method of process costing that assigns the cost of the previous period's equivalent units in beginning work-in-process inventory to the first units completed and transferred out, and assigns the cost of the most recent equivalent units worked on during the period first to complete beginning inventory, then to start and complete new units, and finally to units in ending work-in-process inventory. (618)

Fixed cost. Cost that remains unchanged in total for a given time period despite wide changes in the related level of total activity or volume. (30)

Fixed overhead flexible-budget variance. The difference between actual fixed overhead costs and the fixed overhead costs in the flexible budget. (260)

Flexible budget. Budget developed using budgeted revenues or cost amounts based on the level of output actually achieved in the budget period. (220)

Flexible-budget variance. The difference between the actual results and the flexible-budget amount based on the level of output actually achieved in the budget period. (223)

Full costs of the product. The sum of all the variable and fixed costs in all the business functions in the value chain, R&D, design, production, marketing, distribution, and customer service. (382)

Goal congruence. Exists when individuals and groups work toward achieving the organization goals that top management desires. (789)

Gross margin percentage. Gross margin divided by revenues. (76)

Growth component. Change in operating income attributable solely to an increase in the quantity of output sold between one period and the next. (473)

High-low method. Method used to estimate a cost function that entails using only the highest and lowest observed values of the cost driver within the relevant range and their respective costs. (336)

Homogeneous cost pool. Cost pool in which all of the costs have the same or a similar cause-and-effect or benefits-received relationship with the cost-allocation base. (504)

Hurdle rate. See *required rate of return (RRR)*.

Hybrid costing system. Costing system that blends characteristics from both job-costing systems and process-costing systems. (632)

Idle time. Wages paid for unproductive time caused by lack of orders, machine breakdowns, material shortages, poor scheduling, and the like. (42)

Imputed costs. Costs recognized in particular situations that are not usually recognized by accrual accounting procedures. (825)

Incongruent decision making. See *suboptimal decision making*. (791)

Incremental cost. Additional costs incurred for an activity. (385)

Incremental cost-allocation method. Method that ranks the individual users of a cost object and then uses this ranking to allocate costs among those users. (516)

Incremental revenue. Additional revenue from an activity. (386)

Incremental revenue-allocation method. Method that ranks the individual products in a bundle according to criteria determined by management, and then uses this ranking to allocate the bundled revenues to the individual products. (570)

Incremental unit-time learning model. Learning curve model in which the incremental unit time (the time needed to produce the last unit) declines by a constant percentage each time the cumulative quantity of units produced is doubled. (344)

Independent variable. Level of activity or cost driver used to predict the dependent variable (costs) in a cost estimation or prediction model. (334)

Indirect costs of a cost object. Costs related to the particular cost object but cannot be traced to it in an economically feasible (cost-effective) way. (29)

Indirect-cost rate. Total overhead costs in a cost pool divided by the total quantity of the cost-allocation base for that cost pool. (99)

Indirect manufacturing costs. All manufacturing costs that are considered part of the cost object, units finished or in process, but that cannot be traced to that cost object in economically feasible way. Also called *manufacturing overhead costs* and *factory overhead costs*. (36)

Industrial engineering method. Approach to cost estimation that first analyzes the relationship between inputs and outputs in physical terms. Also called *work measurement method*. (332)

Inflation. The decline in the general purchasing power of the monetary unit. (772)

Infrastructure costs. Costs that arise from having property, plant, equipment, and a functioning organization. (478)

Input-price variance. See *price variance*.

Insourcing. Process of producing goods or providing services within the organization rather than purchasing those same goods or services from outside vendors. (383)

Inspection point. Stage of the production cycle where products are checked to determine whether they are acceptable or unacceptable units. (656)

Institute of management accountants (IMA). A profession accounting organization. It is the largest association of management accountants in the United States. (13)

Intercept. See *constant*. (329)

Intermediate product. Product transferred from one subunit to another subunit of the organization. This product may be processed further or simply resold to an external customer. (793)

Internal failure costs. Costs incurred by a nonconforming product before it is shipped to customers. (677)

Internal rate of return (IRR) method. Capital budgeting DCF method that calculates the discount rate at which the present value of expected cash inflows from a project equals the present value of expected cash outflows. (752)

Inventoriable costs. All cost of a product that are regarded as an asset when they are incurred and then become cost of goods sold when the product is sold. (36)

Inventory management. The planning, coordinating, and control activities related to the flow of inventory into, through, and from the organization. (712)

Investment. Resources or assets used to generate income. (823)

Investment center. Responsibility center where the manager is accountable for investments, revenues, and costs. (194)

Job. An individual unit, batch, or lot of a distinct product or service. (97)

Job cost record. Source document that records and accumulates all the costs assigned to a specific job. Also called *job cost sheet*. (101)

Job cost sheet. See *job cost record*. (101)

Job-costing system. Costing system in which the cost of a product or service is obtained by assigning costs to a distinct unit, batch, or lot of a product or service. (97)

Joint cost. Cost of a single production process that yields multiple products simultaneously. (536)

Joint product. Product that has relatively high sales value compared to other products yielded by a joint production process. (537)

Just-in-time (JIP) production. Demand-pull manufacturing system in which each component in a production line is produced immediately as needed by the next step in the production line. Also called *lean production*. (726)

Just-in-time (JIT) purchasing. The purchase of goods or materials such that a delivery immediately precedes demand or use. (719)

Kaizen budgeting. Budgetary approach that explicitly incorporates continuous improvement during the budget period into the budget numbers. (191)

Labor time record. Document used to charge job cost records and departments for labor time used on a specific job. (102)

Lean production. See *just-in-time (JIT) production*.

Learning curve. Function that shows how labor-hours per unit decline as units of production increase. (344)

Life-cycle budgeting. Budget that incorporates the revenues and costs attributable to each product from its initial R&D to its final customer servicing and support. (439)

Life-cycle costing. System that tracks and accumulates the individual value-chain costs attributable to each product from its initial R&D to its final customer servicing and support. (439)

Line management. Mangers who are directly responsible for attaining the objectives of the organization. (12)

Linear cost function. Cost function in which the graph of total costs versus the level of a single activity is a straight line within the relevant range. (328)

Linear programming (LP). Optimization technique used to maximize an objective function (for example, contribution margin of a mix of products), given multiple constraints. (401)

Locked-in costs. Costs that have not yet been incurred but which, based on decisions that have already been made, will be incurred in the future. Also called *designed-in costs*. (430)

Main product. Product from a joint production process in which only one product has a relatively high sales value. (537)

Make-or-buy decisions. Decisions about whether a producer of goods or services will insource (produce goods or services within the firm) or outsource (purchase them from outside vendors). (384)

Management accounting. Measures and reports financial and nonfinancial information that helps managers make decisions to fulfill the goals of an organization. It focuses on internal reporting. (2)

Management by exception. Practice of concentrating on areas not operating as anticipated and giving less attention to areas operating as anticipated. (220)

Management control system. Means of gathering and using information to aid and coordinate the process of making planning and control decisions throughout the organization and to guide the behavior of managers and employees. (788)

Manufacturing cells. Grouping of all the different types of equipment used to make a given product. (726)

Manufacturing cycle time. See *manufacturing lead time*. (688)

Manufacturing lead time. Time from when an order is received by production to when it becomes a finished good. Also called *manufacturing cycle time*. (688)

Manufacturing overhead allocated. Indirect manufacturing costs allocated to a job, product, or service based on the budgeted rate multiplied by the actual quantity used of the cost-allocation base. Also called *manufacturing overhead applied*. (111)

Manufacturing overhead applied. See *manufacturing overhead allocated*. (111)

Manufacturing overhead costs. See *indirect manufacturing costs*.

Manufacturing-sector company. Company that purchases materials and components and converts them into different finished goods. (35)

Margin of safety. Amount of budgeted revenues over and above breakeven revenues. (69)

Marketing. The manner by which companies promote and sell their products or services to customers or prospective customers. (7)

Market-share variance. The difference between (1) the budgeted amount based on actual market size in units, actual market share, and the budgeted contribution margin per composite unit for the budgeted mix, and (2) the budgeted amount based on actual market size in units, budgeted market share, and budgeted contribution margin per composite unit for the budgeted mix. (577)

Market-size variance. The difference between (1) the budgeted amount based on actual market size in units, budgeted market share, and budgeted contribution margin per composite unit for budgeted mix, and (2) the static budget amount based on the budgeted market size in units, budgeted market share, and budgeted contribution margin per composite unit for budgeted mix. (578)

Master budget. Comprehensive expression of management's operating and financial plans for a future time period (usually a year) that is summarized in a set of budgeted financial statements. (178)

Master-budget capacity utilization. The denominator-level concept based on the expected level of capacity utilization for the next budget period (typically one year). (304)

Materials requirements planning (MRP). Push-through system that manufactures finished goods for inventory on the basis of demand forecasts. (725)

Materials requisition record. Document used to charge job cost records and departments for the cost of direct materials used on a specific job. (101)

Merchandising-sector company. Company that purchases and then sells tangible products without changing their basic form. (35)

Mixed cost. A cost that has both fixed and variable elements. Also called a *semivariable cost*. (329)

Moral hazard. Describes situations in which an employee prefers to exert less effort (or report distorted information) than the effort (or information) desired by the owner because the employee's effort (or information) cannot be accurately monitored and enforced. (837)

Motivation. The desire to attain a selected goal (the goal-congruence aspect) combined with the resulting drive or pursuit toward that goal (the effort aspect). (789)

Multicollinearity. Exists when two or more independent variables in a regression model are highly correlated with each other. (359)

Multiple regression. Regression model that estimates the relationship between the dependent variable and multiple independent variables. (338)

Net income. Operating income plus nonoperating revenues (such as interest revenue) minus nonoperating costs (such as interest cost) minus income taxes. (61)

Net present value (NPV) method. Capital budgeting DCF method that calculates the expected monetary gain or loss from a project by discounting all expected future cash inflows and outflows to the present point in time, using the required rate of return. (751)

Nominal rate of return. Made up of three elements: (a) a risk-free element when there is no expected inflation, (b) a business-risk element, and (c) and inflation element. (772)

Nonlinear cost function. Cost function in which the graph of total costs versus the level of a single activity is not a straight line within the relevant range. (342)

Nonvalue-added cost. A cost that, if eliminated, would not reduce the value or utility customers obtain from using the product or service. (429)

Normal capacity utilization. The denominator-level concept based on the level of capacity utilization that satisfies average customer demand over a time period (say, 2-3 years) that includes seasonal, cyclical, and trend factors. (304)

Normal costing. A costing method that traces direct costs to a cost object by using the actual direct cost rate(s) times the actual quantity of the direct cost input(s) and allocates indirect costs based on the budgeted indirect cost rate(s) times the actual quantity of the cost allocation base(s). (104)

Normal spoilage. Spoilage that is an inherent result of the particular production process and arises even under efficient operating conditions. (649)

Objective function. Expresses the objective to be maximized (for example, operating income) or minimized (for example, operating costs) in a decision model (for example, a linear programming model). (402)

On-time performance. Situations in which the product or service is actually delivered by the time it is scheduled to be delivered. (688)

Operating budget. Budgeted income statement and its supporting budget schedules. (182)

Operating department. Department that adds value to a product or service that is observable by a customer. Also called a *production department* in manufacturing companies. (510)

Operating income. Total revenues from operation minus cost of goods sold and operating costs (excluding income taxes). (38)

Operating leverage. Effects that fixed costs have on changes in operating income as changes occur in units sold and hence in contribution margin. (71)

Operation. A standardized method or technique that is performed repetitively regardless of the distinguishing features of the finished goods. (634)

Operation costing system. Hybrid-costing system applied to batches of similar products. Each batch of products is often a variation of a single design and proceeds through a sequence of selected (though not necessarily the same) activities or operations. Within each operation all product units use identical amounts of the operation's resources. (634)

Opportunity cost. The contribution to income that is forgone (rejected) by not using a limited resource in its best alternative use. (388)

Opportunity cost of capital. See *required rate of return (RRR)*.

Ordering costs. Costs of preparing, issuing, and paying purchase orders, plus receiving and inspecting the items included in the orders. (712)

Organization structure. Arrangement of lines of responsibility within the entity. (194)

Outcomes. Predicted economic results of the various possible combinations of actions and events in a decision model. (79)

Output unit-level costs. The costs of resources sacrificed on activities performed on each individual unit of product or service. (143)

Output-level overhead variance. See *production-volume variance*.

Outsourcing. Process of purchasing goods and services from outside vendors rather than producing the same goods or providing the same services within the organization. (383)

Overabsorbed indirect costs. See *overallocated indirect costs*. (114)

Overallocated indirect costs. Allocated amount of indirect costs in an accounting period is greater than the actual (incurred) amount in that period. Also called *overapplied indirect costs* and *overabsorbed indirect costs*. (114)

Overapplied indirect costs. See *overallocated indirect costs*. (114)

Overtime premium. Wage rate paid to all workers (for both direct labor and indirect labor) in *excess* of their straight-time wage rates. (42)

Pareto diagram. Diagram that indicates how frequently each type of failure (defect) occurs. (680)

Partial productivity. Measures the quantity of output produced divided by the quantity of an individual input used. (485)

Payback. Capital budgeting method that measures the time is will take to recoup, in the form of expected future cash flows, the net initial investment in a project. (758)

Peak-load pricing. Practice of charging a higher price for the same product or service when demand approaches physical capacity limits. (442)

Peanut-butter costing. See *cost smoothing*. (136)

Perfectly competitive market. Exists when there is a homogeneous product with equivalent buying and selling prices and no individual buyers or sellers can affect those prices by their own actions. (796)

Period costs. All costs in the income statement other than cost of goods sold. (36)

Physical measure method. Method that allocates joint costs to joint products on the basis of the relative weight, volume, or other physical measure at the splitoff point of the total production of these products during the accounting period. (541)

Planning. Deciding on organization goals, predicting results under various alternative ways of achieving those goals, and then deciding how to attain the desired goals. (3)

Practical capacity. The denominator-level concept that reduces theoretical capacity by unavoidable operating interruptions such as scheduled maintenance time, shutdown for holidays, and so on. (304)

Predatory pricing. Company deliberately prices below its costs in an effort to drive out competitors and restrict supply, and then raises prices rather than enlarge demand. (443)

Prevention costs. Costs incurred to preclude the production of products that do not conform to specifications. (677)

Previous department costs. See *transferred-in costs*. (628)

Price discounting. Reduction of selling prices below listed levels in order to encourage increases in customer purchases. (582)

Price discrimination. Practice of charging some customers a higher price for the same product or service than is charged to other customers. (441)

Price-recovery component. Change in operating income attributable solely to changes in prices of inputs and outputs between one period and the next. (473)

Price variance. The difference between the actual price and the budgeted price multiplied by the actual quantity of input in question. Also called *input-price variance* or *rate variance* (226)

Prime costs. All direct manufacturing costs. (39)

Pro forma statements. Budgeted financial statements. (178)

Probability. Likelihood or chance of occurrence of an event. (79)

Probability distribution. Describes the likelihood (or probability) of each of the mutually exclusive and collectively exhaustive set of events. (79)

Problem solving. Comparative analysis for decision making role of a management accountant. (5)

Process-costing system. Costing system in which the cost of a product or service is obtained by using broad averages to assign costs to masses of identical or similar units. (97)

Product. Any output that has a positive net sales value (or an output that enables an organization to avoid incurring costs). (537)

Product cost. Sum of the costs assigned to a product for a specific purpose. (43)

Product-cost cross-subsidization. Costing outcome where at least one undercosted (overcosted) product results in at least one other product being overcosted (undercosted) in the organization. (136)

Product differentiation. An organization's ability to offer products or services that are perceived by its customers to be superior and unique relative to those of its competitors. (463)

Product life cycle. Spans the time from initial R&D on a product to when customer support is no longer offered for that product. (439)

Product-mix decisions. Decisions about how much of each product to sell. (390)

Product overcosting. A product consumes a relatively low level of resources but is reported to have a relatively high total cost. (136)

Product-sustaining costs. The costs of resources sacrificed on activities undertaken to support individual products. (143)

Product undercosting. A product consumes a relatively high level of resources but is reported to have a relatively low total cost. (136)

Production. The acquisition, coordination, and assembly of resources to produce a product or deliver a service. (7)

Production department. Department that adds value to a product or service that is observable by a customer. Also called an *operating department*. (510)

Production-denominator level. The denominator of the budgeted manufacturing fixed overhead rate computation. (259)

Production-volume variance. The difference between budgeted fixed overhead and the fixed overhead allocated on the basis of the budgeted quantity of the fixed overhead allocation base allowed for the actual output produced. Also called *denominator-level variance* and *output-level overhead variance*. (261)

Productivity. Measures the relationship between actual inputs used (both quantities and costs) and actual outputs produced; the lower the inputs for a given quantity of outputs or the higher the outputs for a given quantity of inputs, the higher the productivity. (485)

Productivity component. Reduction in costs attributable to a reduction in the quantity of inputs used in the current period relative to the prior period to produce the quantity of current period output. (473)

Profit center. Responsibility center where the manager is accountable for revenues and costs. (194)

Proration. The spreading of underallocated or overallocated overhead among ending work in process, finished goods, and cost of goods sold. (115)

Purchase order lead time. The time between placing an order and its delivery. (713)

Purchasing costs. Cost of goods acquired from suppliers including incoming freight or transportation costs. (712)

PV graph. Shows the impact on operating income of changes in the output level. (66)

Qualitative factors. Outcomes that cannot be measured in numerical terms. (380)

Quality of design. Refers to how closely the characteristics of a product or service meets the needs and wants of customers. (677)

Quantitative factors. Outcomes that are measured in numerical terms. (380)

Rate variance. See *price variance*.

Real rate of return. The rate of return demanded to cover investment risk (with no inflation). It has a risk-free element and a business-risk element. (772)

Reciprocal allocation method. Cost allocation method that explicitly includes the mutual services provided among all support departments. (512)

Reengineering. The fundamental rethinking and redesign of business processes to achieve improvements in critical performance measures such as cost, quality, service, speed, and customer satisfaction. (464)

Refined costing system. Costing system that provides better measurement of the nonuniformity in the use of an organization's overhead resources by jobs, products, and services. (140)

Regression analysis. Statistical method that measures the average amount of change in the dependent variable that is associated with a unit change in one or more independent variables. (338)

Relevant costs. Expected future costs that differ among alternative courses of action being considered. (378)

Relevant range. Band of activity or volume in which a specific relationship between the level of activity or volume and the cost in question is valid. (32)

Relevant revenues. Expected future revenues that differ among alternative courses of action being considered. (378)

Reorder point. The quantity level of inventory on hand that triggers a new order. (714)

Required rate of return (RRR). The minimum acceptable rate of return on an investment. Also called the *discount rate*, *hurdle rate*, or *(opportunity) cost of capital*. (751)

Research and development. The generation of, and experimentation with, ideas related to new products, services, or processes. (7)

Residual income (RI). Income minus a required dollar return on an accounting measure of investment. (825)

Residual term. The difference between the actual and predicted amount of a dependent variable (such as a cost) for each observation in a regression model. (338)

Responsibility accounting. System that measures the plans (by budgets) and actions (by actual results) of each responsibility center. (194)

Responsibility center. Part, segment, or subunit of an organization whose manager is accountable for a specified set of activities. (194)

Return on investment (ROI). See *accrual accounting rate of return.* (824)

Revenue. Inflows of assets (almost always cash or accounts receivable) received for products or services provided to customers. (37)

Revenue allocation. The allocation of revenues to a particular revenue object where they cannot be traced to it in an economically feasible (cost-effective) way. (568)

Revenue center. Responsibility center where the manager is accountable for revenues only. (194)

Revenue driver. Any factor that affects revenues. (60)

Rework. Unacceptable units of production that are subsequently repaired and sold as acceptable finished goods. (648)

Righsizing. See *downsizing.* (480)

Rolling budget. Budget or plan that is always available for a specified future period by adding a month, quarter or year in the future as the month, quarter, or year just ended is dropped. (182)

Safety stock. Inventory held as all times regardless of the quantity of inventory ordered using the EOQ model. (715)

Sales mix. Relative combination of quantities of products or services that constitutes total unit sales. (71)

Sales-mix variance. The difference between two amounts: (1) the budgeted amount for the actual sales mix, and (2) the budgeted amount for the budgeted sales mix. (575)

Sales-quantity variance. The difference between (1) the budgeted amount based on actual units sold of all products and the budgeted-mix, and (2) the amount in the static budget (which is based on the budgeted units to be sold of all products and the budgeted mix). (577)

Sales value at splitoff method. Method that allocates joint costs to joint products on the basis of the relative sales value at the splitoff point of the total production of these products during the accounting period. (540)

Sales-volume variance. The difference between the flexible-budget amount and the static-budget amount. (223)

Scorekeeping. Accumulating data and reporting results to all levels of management role of a management accountant. (5)

Scrap. Material leftover when making a product(s). (648)

Self-liquidating cycle. The movement from cash to inventories to receivables and back to cash. (200)

Selling-price variance. The difference between the actual selling price and the budgeted selling price multiplied by the actual units sold. (224)

Semivariable cost. See *mixed cost.* (329)

Sensitivity analysis. A what-if technique that examines how a result will change if the original predicted data are not achieved or if an underlying assumption changes. (68)

Separable costs. All costs (manufacturing, marketing, distribution, and so on) incurred beyond the splitoff point that are assignable to one or more individual products. (536)

Sequential allocation method. See *step-down allocation method.*

Sequential tracking. Approach in a product-costing method where recording of the journal entries occurs in the same order as actual purchases and progress in production. (728)

Service department. See *support department.*

Service-sector company. Company that provides services or intangible products to their customers. (35)

Service-sustaining costs. The costs of resources sacrificed on activities undertaken to support individual services. (143)

Simple regression. Regression model that estimates the relationship between the dependent variable and one independent variable. (338)

Single-rate cost-allocation method. Allocation method in which all costs are in one cost pool. These costs are allocated to cost objects using the same rate per unit of the single allocation base. (507)

Slope coefficient. Coefficient term in a cost estimation model that indicates how much total costs change when a one-unit change occurs in the level of activity within the relevant range. (328)

Source documents. The original records that support journal entries in an accounting system. (101)

Specification analysis. Testing of the assumptions of regression analysis. (354)

Splitoff point. The juncture in a joint-production process where one or more products become separately identifiable. (536)

Spoilage. Unacceptable units of production that are discarded or are sold for reduced prices. (648)

Staff management. Staff who provide advice and assistance to line management. (12)

Stand-alone cost allocation method. Method that uses information pertaining to each user of a cost object as a separate entity to determine the cost-allocation weights. (516)

Stand-alone revenue-allocation method. Method that uses product-specific information on the products in the bundle as weights for allocating the bundled revenues to the individual products. (569)

Standard. A carefully predetermined price, cost, or quantity amount. It is usually expressed on a per unit basis. (225)

Standard cost. A carefully predetermined cost. (225)

Standard costing. Costing method that traces direct costs to a cost object by multiplying the standard price(s) or rate(s) times the standard inputs allowed for actual outputs produced and allocates indirect costs on the basis of the standard indirect rate(s) times the standard inputs allowed for the actual outputs produced. (254)

Standard error of the estimated coefficient. Regression statistic that indicates how much the estimated value is likely to be affected by random factors. (353)

Standard input. A carefully predetermined quantity of inputs required for one unit of output. (225)

Static budget. Budget based on the level of output planned at the start of the budget period. (220)

Static-budget variance. Difference between an actual result and a budgeted amount in the static budget. (221)

Step cost function. A cost function in which the cost remains the same over various ranges of the level of activity, but the cost increases by discrete amounts (that is, in steps) as the level of activity changes from one range to the next. (343)

Step-down allocation method. Cost allocation method that allows for partial recognition of the services rendered by support departments to other support departments. Also called *sequential allocation method.* (512)

Stockout. Occurs when an organization runs out of a particular item for which there is customer demand. (712)

Strategy. Describes how an organization matches its own capabilities with the opportunities in the market place to accomplish its overall objectives. (179)

Suboptimal decision making. Decisions in which the benefit to one subunit is more than offset by the costs or loss of benefits to the organization as a whole. Also called *incongruent decision making* or *dysfunctional decision making.* (791)

Sunk costs. Past costs that are unavoidable because they cannot be changed no matter what action is taken. (379)

Super-variable costing. See *throughput costing.*

Supply chain. Describes the flow of goods, services, and information from cradle to grave, regardless of whether those activities occur in the same organization or other organizations. (10)

Support department. Department that provides the services that assist other internal departments (operating departments and other support departments) in the organization. Also called a *service department.* (510)

Target cost per unit. Estimated long-run cost per unit of a product (or service) that enables the company to achieve its target operating income per unit when

selling at the target price. Target cost per unit is derived by subtracting the target operating income per unit from the target price. (428)

Target operating income per unit. Operating income that a company wants to earn on each unit of a product (or service) sold. (428)

Target price. Estimated price for a product (or service) that potential customers will be willing to pay. (428)

Target rate of return on investment. The target operating income that an organization desires divided by invested capital. (435)

Theoretical capacity. The denominator-level concept based on producing at full efficiency all the time. (304)

Theory of constraints (TOC). Describes methods to maximize operating income when faced with some bottleneck and some nonbottleneck operations. (692)

Throughput contribution. Revenues minus all variable direct materials costs of the goods sold. (692)

Throughput costing. Method of inventory costing in which only variable direct materials costs are included as inventoriable costs. Also called *super-variable costing.* (299)

Time driver. Any factor where a change in the factor causes a change in the speed with which an activity is undertaken. (688)

Time value of money. Takes into account the fact that a dollar (or any other monetary unit) received today is worth more than a dollar received at any future time. (750)

Total factor productivity (TFP). The ratio of the quantity of output produced to the costs of all inputs used, where the inputs are combined on the basis of current period prices. (486)

Transfer price. Price one subunit (segment, department, division, and so on) of an organization charges for a product or service supplied to another subunit of the same organization. (793)

Transferred-in costs. Costs incurred in a previous department that are carried forward as the product's costs when it moves to a subsequent process in the production cycle. Also called *previous department costs.* (628)

Trigger point. Refers to a stage in the cycle going from purchase of direct materials to sale of finished goods at which journal entries are made in the accounting system. (728)

Uncertainty. The possibility that an actual amount will deviate from an expected amount. (69)

Underabsorbed indirect costs. See *underallocated indirect costs.* (114)

Underallocated indirect costs. Allocated amount of indirect costs in an accounting period is less than the actual (incurred) amount in that period. Also called *underapplied indirect costs* or *underabsorbed indirect costs.* (114)

Underapplied indirect costs. See *underallocated indirect costs.* (140)

Unfavorable variance. Variance that decreases operating income relative to the budgeted amount. Denoted U. (222)

Unit cost. Cost computed by dividing some amount of total costs by the related number of units. Also called *average cost*. (33)

Unused capacity. The additional amount of productive capacity available over and above the productive capacity employed to meet consumer demand in the current period. (477)

Usage variance. See *efficiency variance*.

Value-added cost. A cost that, if eliminated, would reduce the value or utility customers obtain from using the product or service. (429)

Value chain. The sequence of business functions in which usefulness is added to the products of services of an organization. (6)

Value engineering. Systematic evaluation of all aspects of the value-chain business functions, with the objective of reducing costs while satisfying customer needs. (429)

Variable cost. Cost that changes in total proportion to changes in the related level of total activity or volume. (30)

Variable costing. Method of inventory costing in which all variable manufacturing costs are included as inventoriable costs. Also called *direct costing*. (290)

Variable overhead efficiency variance. The difference between the actual units of variable overhead cost-allocation base used for actual output and the budgeted units of variable overhead cost-allocation base allowed for actual output times the budgeted variable overhead rate. (256)

Variable overhead flexible-budget variance. The difference between the actual variable overhead costs and the flexible-budget variable overhead costs. (256)

Variable overhead spending variance. The difference between the actual amount of variable overhead incurred and the budgeted amount allowed for the actual quantity of the variable overhead allocation base used for the actual output units produced. (257)

Variance. The difference between an actual result and a budgeted amount. (220)

Weighted-average process-costing method. Method of process costing that assigns the equivalent-unit cost of the work done to date (regardless of when it was done) to equivalent units completed and transferred out, and to equivalent units in ending work-in-process inventory. (615)

Work in progress. See *work-in-process inventory*. (35)

Work-in-process inventory. Goods partially worked on but not yet fully completed. Also called *work in progress*. (35)

Work-measurement method. See *industrial-engineering method*. (332)

Author Index

Company Index

Subject Index

W

COST ACCOUNTING, Tenth Edition, A Managerial Emphasis

HORNGREN, FOSTER, DATAR

Prentice-Hall, Inc.

READ THE FOLLOWING TERMS AND CONDITIONS CAREFULLY BEFORE OPENING THIS DISK PACKAGE. THIS LEGAL DOCUMENT IS AN AGREEMENT BETWEEN YOU AND PRENTICE-HALL, INC. BY OPENING THIS SEALED DISK PACKAGE, YOU ARE AGREEING TO THE TERMS AND CONDITIONS OF THIS AGREEMENT. IF YOU DO NOT AGREE WITH THESE TERMS AND CONDITIONS, DO NOT OPEN THE DISK PACKAGE. PROMPTLY RETURN THE UNOPENED DISK PACKAGE AND ALL ACCOMPANYING ITEMS TO THE PLACE YOU OBTAINED THEM. THESE TERMS APPLY TO ALL LICENSED SOFTWARE ON THE DISK EXCEPT THAT THE TERMS FOR USE OF ANY SHAREWARE OR FREEWARE ON THE DISKETTES ARE AS SET FORTH IN THE ELECTRONIC LICENSE LOCATED ON THE DISK:

GRANT OF LICENSE In consideration of your adoption of textbooks and/or other materials published by the Company, and your agreement to abide by the terms and conditions of this Agreement, the Company grants to you a nonexclusive, nontransferable, permanent license to use and display the copy of the enclosed software program (hereinafter the SOFTWARE) on a single computer (i.e., with a single CPU) at a single location so long as you comply with the terms of this Agreement. The Company reserves all rights not expressly granted to you under this Agreement.

OWNERSHIP OF SOFTWARE You own only the magnetic or physical media (the enclosed disks) on which the SOFTWARE is recorded or fixed, but the Company retains all the rights, title, and ownership to the SOFTWARE recorded on the original disk copy(ies) and all subsequent copies of the SOFTWARE, regardless of the form or media on which the original or other copies may exist. This license is not a sale of the original SOFTWARE or any copy to you.

RESTRICTIONS ON COPYING, USE AND TRANSFER This SOFTWARE and the accompanying printed materials and user manual (the Documentation) are the subject of copyright and is licensed to you only. You may not copy the documentation or the Software except that you may make a single copy of the SOFTWARE for backup or archival purposes only. You may not network the SOFTWARE or otherwise use it on more than one computer or computer terminal at the same time. You may physically transfer the SOFTWARE from one computer to another provided that the SOFTWARE is used on only one computer at a time. You may not distribute copies of the SOFTWARE or Documentation to others. You may not reverse engineer, disassemble, decompile, modify, adapt, translate, or create derivative works based on the SOFTWARE or the Documentation without the prior written consent of the Company. The enclosed SOFTWARE may not be transferred to any one else without the prior written consent of the Company. Any unauthorized transfer of the SOFTWARE shall result in the immediate termination of this Agreement. You may be held legally responsible for any copying or copyright infringement which is caused or encouraged by your failure to abide by the terms of these restrictions.

TERMINATION This license is effective until terminated. This license will terminate automatically without notice from the Company and become null and void if you fail to comply with any provisions or limitations of this license. Upon termination, you shall destroy the Documentation and all copies of the SOFTWARE. All provisions of this Agreement as to warranties, limitation of liability, remedies or damages, and our ownership rights shall survive termination.

MISCELLANEOUS THIS AGREEMENT SHALL BE CONSTRUED IN ACCORDANCE WITH THE LAWS OF THE UNITED STATES OF AMERICA AND THE STATE OF NEW YORK, APPLICABLE TO CONTRACTS MADE IN NEW YORK, AND SHALL BENEFIT THE COMPANY, ITS AFFILIATES AND ASSIGNEES.

LIMITED WARRANTY AND DISCLAIMER OF WARRANTY The Company warrants that the SOFTWARE, when properly used in accordance with the Documentation, will operate in substantial conformity with the description of the SOFTWARE set forth in the Documentation. The Company does not warrant that the SOFTWARE will meet your requirements or that the operation of the SOFTWARE will be uninterrupted or error-free. The Company warrants that the media on which the SOFTWARE is delivered shall be free from defects in materials and workmanship under normal use for a period of thirty (30) days from the date of your purchase. Your only remedy and the Company's only obligation under these limited warranties is, return of the warranted item for replacement of the item. Any replacement of SOFTWARE or media under the warranties shall not extend the original warranty period. The limited warranty set forth above shall not apply to any SOFTWARE which the Company determines in good faith has been subject to misuse, neglect, improper installation, repair, alteration, or damage by you. EXCEPT FOR THE EXPRESSED WARRANTIES SET FORTH ABOVE, THE COMPANY DISCLAIMS ALL WARRANTIES, EXPRESS OR IMPLIED, INCLUDING WITHOUT LIMITATION, THE IMPLIED WARRANTIES OF MERCHANTABILITY AND FITNESS FOR A PARTICULAR PURPOSE. EXCEPT FOR THE EXPRESS WARRANTY SET FORTH ABOVE, THE COMPANY DOES NOT WARRANT, GUARANTEE, OR MAKE ANY REPRESENTATION REGARDING THE USE OR THE RESULTS OF THE USE OF THE SOFTWARE IN TERMS OF ITS CORRECTNESS, ACCURACY, RELIABILITY, CURRENTNESS, OR OTHERWISE. IN NO EVENT, SHALL THE COMPANY OR ITS EMPLOYEES, AGENTS, SUPPLIERS, OR CONTRACTORS BE LIABLE FOR ANY INCIDENTAL, INDIRECT, SPECIAL, OR CONSEQUENTIAL DAMAGES ARISING OUT OF OR IN CONNECTION WITH THE LICENSE GRANTED UNDER THIS AGREEMENT, OR FOR LOSS OF USE, LOSS OF DATA, LOSS OF INCOME OR PROFIT, OR OTHER LOSSES, SUSTAINED AS A RESULT OF INJURY TO ANY PERSON, OR LOSS OF OR DAMAGE TO PROPERTY, OR CLAIMS OF THIRD PARTIES, EVEN IF THE COMPANY OR AN AUTHORIZED REPRESENTATIVE OF THE COMPANY HAS BEEN ADVISED OF THE POSSIBILITY OF SUCH DAMAGES.

SOME JURISDICTIONS DO NOT ALLOW THE LIMITATION OF IMPLIED WARRANTIES OR LIABILITY FOR INCIDENTAL, INDIRECT, SPECIAL, OR CONSEQUENTIAL DAMAGES, SO THE ABOVE LIMITATIONS MAY NOT ALWAYS APPLY. THE WARRANTIES IN THIS AGREEMENT GIVE YOU SPECIFIC LEGAL RIGHTS AND YOU MAY ALSO HAVE OTHER RIGHTS WHICH VARY IN ACCORDANCE WITH LOCAL LAW.

ACKNOWLEDGMENT YOU ACKNOWLEDGE THAT YOU HAVE READ THIS AGREEMENT, UNDERSTAND IT, AND AGREE TO BE BOUND BY ITS TERMS AND CONDITIONS. YOU ALSO AGREE THAT THIS AGREEMENT IS THE COMPLETE AND EXCLUSIVE STATEMENT OF THE AGREEMENT BETWEEN YOU AND THE COMPANY AND SUPERSEDES ALL PROPOSALS OR PRIOR AGREEMENTS, ORAL, OR WRITTEN, AND ANY OTHER COMMUNICATIONS BETWEEN YOU AND THE COMPANY OR ANY REPRESENTATIVE OF THE COMPANY RELATING TO THE SUBJECT MATTER OF THIS AGREEMENT. Should you have any questions concerning this agreement or if you wish to contact the Company for any reason, please contact in writing:

Director of New Media, Higher Education Division
Prentice-Hall, Inc.
1 Lake Street
Upper Saddle River, NJ 07458